P9-DNJ-951

ENCYCLOPEDIA OF AMERICAN HISTORY

Civil War and Reconstruction
1856 to 1869

VOLUME V

ENCYCLOPEDIA OF AMERICAN HISTORY

ENCYCLOPEDIA OF AMERICAN HISTORY

Civil War and Reconstruction
1856 to 1869

VOLUME V

Joan Waugh, Editor
Gary B. Nash, General Editor

Facts On File, Inc.

Encyclopedia of American History:
Civil War and Reconstruction (1856 to 1869)

Editorial Director: Laurie E. Likoff
Editor in Chief: Owen Lancer
Chief Copy Editor: Michael G. Laraque
Associate Editor: Dorothy Cummings
Production Director: Olivia McKean
Production Manager: Rachel L. Berlin
Production Associate: Theresa Montoya
Art Director: Cathy Rincon
Interior Designer: Joan M. Toro
Desktop Designers: Erika K. Arroyo and David C. Strelecky
Maps and Illustrations: Dale E. Williams and Jeremy Eagle

Facts On File, Inc.
132 West 31st Street
New York NY 10001

Library of Congress Cataloging-in-Publication Data

Encyclopedia of American history / Gary B. Nash, general editor.
p.   cm.
Includes bibliographical references and indexes.
Contents: v. 1. Three worlds meet — v. 2. Colonization and settlement —
v. 3. Revolution and new nation — v. 4. Expansion and reform — v. 5. Civil War
and Reconstruction — v. 6. The development of the industrial United States —
v. 7. The emergence of modern America — v. 8. The Great Depression and
World War II — v. 9. Postwar United States — v. 10. Contemporary
United States. — v. 11 Comprehensive index
ISBN 0-8160-4371-X (set)   ISBN 0-8160-4365-5 (v. 5)
1. United States—History—Encyclopedias. I. Nash, Gary B.
E174 .E53 2002
973′.03—dc21   2001051278

Contents

★

List of Entries

★

About the Editors

───

General Editor: Gary B. Nash received a Ph.D from Princeton University. He is currently director of the National Center for History in the Schools at the University of California, Los Angeles, where he teaches American history of the colonial and Revolutionary era. He is a published author of college and precollegiate history texts. Among his best-selling works is *The American People: Creating a Nation and Society* (Addison Wesley, Longman), now in its fifth edition.

Nash is an elected member of the Society of American Historians, American Academy of Arts and Sciences, and the American Philosophical Society. He has served as past president of the Organization of American Historians, 1994–95, and was a founding member of the National Council for History Education, 1990.

Volume Editor: Joan Waugh is a professor of history at the University of California, Los Angeles, where she specializes in the Civil War and Reconstruction periods. She is the author of *Unsentimental Reformer: The Life of Josephine Shaw Lowell* (Harvard University Press, 1998) and the forthcoming *Ulysses S. Grant and the Union Cause* (University of North Carolina Press, 2004).

Foreword

The Encyclopedia of American History series is designed as a handy reference to the most important individuals, events, and topics in U.S. history. In 10 volumes, the encyclopedia covers the period from the 15th century, when European explorers first made their way across the Atlantic Ocean to the Americas, to the present day. The encyclopedia is written for precollegiate as well as college students, for parents of young learners in the schools, and for the general public. The volume editors are distinguished historians of American history. In writing individual entries, each editor has drawn upon the expertise of scores of specialists. This ensures the scholarly quality of the entire series. Articles contributed by the various volume editors are uncredited.

This 10-volume encyclopedia of "American history" is broadly conceived to include the historical experience of the various peoples of North America. Thus, in the first volume, many essays treat the history of a great range of indigenous people before contact with Europeans. In the same vein, readers will find essays in the first several volumes that sketch Spanish, Dutch, and French explorers and colonizers who opened up territories for European settlement that later would become part of the United States. The venues and cast of characters in the American historical drama are thus widened beyond traditional encyclopedias.

In creating the eras of American history that define the chronological limits of each volume, and in addressing major topics in each era, the encyclopedia follows the architecture of *The National Standards for United States History, Revised Edition* (Los Angeles: National Center for History in the Schools, 1996). Mandated by the U.S. Congress, the national standards for U.S. history have been widely used by states and school districts in organizing curricular frameworks and have been followed by many other curriculum-building efforts.

Entries are cross-referenced, when appropriate, with *See also* citations at the end of articles. At the end of most entries, a listing of articles and books allows readers to turn to specialized sources and historical accounts. In each volume, an array of maps provide geographical context, while numerous illustrations help vivify the material covered in the text. A time line is included to provide students with a chronological reference to major events occurring in the given era. The selection of historical documents in the back of each volume gives students experience with the raw documents that historians use when researching history. A comprehensive index to each volume also facilitates the reader's access to particular information.

In each volume, long entries are provided for major categories of American historical experience. These categories may include: African Americans, agriculture, art and architecture, business, economy, education, family life, foreign policy, immigration, labor, Native Americans, politics, population, religion, urbanization, and women. By following these essays from volume to volume, the reader can access what might be called a mini-history of each broad topic, for example, family life, immigration, or religion.

— Gary B. Nash
University of California, Los Angeles

Introduction

Civil War and Reconstruction (1856 to 1869) offers a compelling overview of one of the central events in U.S. history: the "War of the Rebellion." The issues at stake in this era—sovereignty and freedom—reached from the highest levels of the constitutional and political arenas into the lives of ordinary people—rich and poor, black and white, men and women, Northern and Southern. *Civil War and Reconstruction* provides the eager student of the period, roughly covering the last half of the 19th century, with an understanding of the dramatic political and military conflict and an appreciation of the sheer tragedy of the American Civil War. Additionally, Volume V of the Encyclopedia of American History tells the story of the war itself within a framework for analyzing the larger social and economic processes that transformed the United States. Thus, students consulting the entries in *Civil War and Reconstruction* will be able to formulate answers to the three major questions that have fascinated people since the end of the conflict: What were the causes of the war? Why did the North win? Was Reconstruction a success or failure?

The entries in *Civil War and Reconstruction* reflect the wide diversity and richness of the scholarship on the war and its aftermath. No student of the period can be considered well educated without a solid understanding of, for example, Bleeding Kansas, the rise of the Republican Party, the presidency of Abraham Lincoln, the secession of the Southern states, the establishment of the Confederate States of American, the Battle of Gettysburg, the significance of the so-called Reconstruction Amendments, and the impeachment trial of Andrew Johnson. In short, Volume V covers the constitutional, military, political, and economic aspects of the Civil War, with an extensive entry list of people, places, laws, battles, and social movements. Similarly, the student of the 21st century must be aware of the cultural, racial, and gender issues that have cast a new light on traditional assumptions. The experiences of the common soldiers, changing women's roles, the revolutionary nature of enrolling African-American men to fight as Union soldiers, the breakdown of slavery, and bringing the reality of emancipation to bear upon an embittered white Southern population are all important parts of the time that are well covered in *Civil War and Reconstruction*.

The poet and writer Robert Penn Warren once famously assessed the Civil War as the most important event in our history. "It may," he claimed, "in fact, be said to *be* American history." The legacy of the Civil War and Reconstruction continues to shape the current United States in profoundly importantly ways. This volume should be considered both a departure point for those who wish to begin their exploration of the era, as well as for those who want to acquire more knowledge about particular aspects of the United States during a crucial turning point in its history. It is truly a saga of epic proportions.

—Joan Waugh
University of California, Los Angeles

ENTRIES
A TO Z

A

abolition

Abolition refers to the immediate and unconditional end to SLAVERY. In the United States, abolition movements offered varied plans of reform, with conservative, moderate, and radical approaches. Many abolitionists, although not all, believed in racial equality; many also cooperated with international efforts to halt slavery.

Opposition to African slavery in North America dates to the 17th century, when some Protestant denominations, particularly Methodists and the SOCIETY OF FRIENDS (Quakers), condemned the practice. Until the Revolutionary War, abolitionist views were not widespread among Britain's North American colonists. However, calls for liberty and consent provoked some colonists to take abolition arguments more seriously. During the 1780s, antislavery sentiment influenced the wording of the Northwest Ordinance of 1787, which banned carrying slaves into the future states of Ohio, Indiana, Michigan, Illinois, Wisconsin, and Minnesota. By 1800, Pennsylvania and all states north of it had begun to abolish slavery, though largely by gradual rather than immediate EMANCIPATION.

From Maryland south, slavery was far more important to existing economic interests than in the North. The abolition argument did not find a large audience in the tobacco-growing states on Chesapeake Bay (Virginia, Maryland, and Delaware) and in the Carolinas and Georgia, where rice and indigo cultivation flourished.

A few Southern planters did in fact seek to end slavery in the South. Thomas Jefferson, for instance, argued that slave ownership bred habits of arrogance and arbitrary power ill-suited to the needs of a republic based on shared power and popular consent. Jefferson also believed that African-American slaves posed serious threats to all white people: a threat of revolt if kept in servitude, particularly worrisome in wartime, and a threat of resentful hostility of a landless underclass if set free. Slavery was wrong, Jefferson wrote, but slavery could not end without expelling former slaves from North America. "We have the wolf by the ears," Jefferson wrote, "we can neither hold him nor safely let him go."

Jefferson, Madison, and others, both North and South, hoped that slavery would end gradually. While the Constitution granted Congress no power to abolish slavery, it did permit Congress to prohibit the importation of slaves beginning in 1808. Without slaves from Africa and the West Indies, prices for slaves would increase. Two important consequences would occur: the ending of the Southern plantation system and the return to Africa of masses of former slaves. Jefferson's conviction that expulsion from North America would be best for white and black people alike was shared by Henry Clay and other prominent sponsors of the American Colonization Society.

Colonization faced serious opposition, however. As early as the 1790s, there were voices raised against both gradual emancipation and colonization schemes. Philadelphia African Americans such as Richard Allen and Absalom Jones joined Benjamin Franklin and others in the Philadelphia Society for the Abolition of Slavery. In 1790 the organization petitioned Congress under Franklin's name to abolish slavery throughout the country. Ominously, the petition earned a stern rebuke from Southerners, whose views on slavery were less compromising than Jefferson's. Thomas Tucker, a South Carolina representative, declared that such a petition would "never be submitted to by the Southern States without a civil war."

Despite Tucker's warning, calls for immediate abolition became more urgent during the 1820s. A number of factors contributed to the growing unwillingness of some antislavery activists to compromise. The first was the obvious failure of gradual emancipation in the South. With the introduction of Eli Whitney's cotton gin in 1793, slavery profitably expanded well beyond the plantations of the Atlantic coast and into what would soon come to be called the Southern "cotton belt."

1

A group of abolitionists known as the Oberlin Rescuers, outside the Cuyahoga County Jail, Ohio, from which they had rescued a fugitive slave named John Price *(Hulton/Archive)*

As slavery expanded further, fewer Southern planters shared Jefferson's doubts about slavery and more embraced a strong defense of the South's "peculiar institution." The debates over slave-state Missouri's admittance to the Union in 1819–20, though they ended in compromise, demonstrated Southern resolve on the issue while revealing deep divisions within the North. Southern views hardened further in the aftermath of a Virginia slave revolt led by Nat Turner in 1832.

Abolition activists were also deeply influenced by the "Second Great Awakening," a period of evangelical revivalism that peaked between 1810 and 1840. Those who opposed slavery on religious grounds condemned the practice as nothing less than an abomination. These more militant attitudes crystallized in the late 1820s and early 1830s, informing the work of such abolitionists as David Walker (1785–1830), Lydia Maria Child (1802–80), and WILLIAM LLOYD GARRISON (1805–79). Unlike Benjamin Franklin, these activists would not plea or petition for emancipation; rather, they would demand it.

Walker, an African American, was born free in North Carolina. Loathing the South's poisonous atmosphere of slavery and oppression, he left for Massachusetts, establishing a small business there while taking an active role in the city's free black community. In 1829, Walker published a pamphlet entitled "An Appeal to the Colored Citizens of the World." Targeting Thomas Jefferson's

remarks in *Notes on the State of Virginia*, Walker declared that white Americans had proven themselves "unjust, jealous, unmerciful, avaricious, and bloodthirsty . . . always seeking after power and authority." Only abolition of slavery would free white Americans from their own degradation; "what a happy country this will be if whites will listen."

Lydia Maria Child, a self-educated New Englander, came to public attention with *An Appeal in Favor of that Class of Americans Called Africans* (1833). Like Walker, Child's rhetoric burned. The races, she declared, were equal to one another in every way. White people had enslaved black people only because the white people had acted with "treachery, fraud, and violence." Child's commitment to racial equality and her willingness to enter a public arena generally closed to women outraged many Americans, including some who were committed to the antislavery movement.

William Lloyd Garrison was as uncompromising as Walker or Child. Introducing *The Liberator*, his influential abolitionist newspaper, Garrison famously declared, "I am in earnest, I will not equivocate, I will not excuse, I will not retreat a single inch, AND I WILL BE HEARD." For Garrison, not even the Constitution was sacred. Because the Constitution implicitly protected slavery, Garrison thundered, the document was immoral. On July 4, 1852, in a well-publicized demonstration, Garrison publicly burned a copy of the Constitution, while shouting "so perish all compromises with tyranny!"

Abolitionists like Walker, Child, and Garrison asserted that the Constitution and majority opinion both ranked well below a "higher law," God's law. Though the Constitution itself prohibited any state from harboring an escaped slave, abolitionists successfully urged several Northern states to enact "personal liberty" laws that forbade state officials from assisting in the recapture of escapees. Personal liberty laws enraged Southerners, but they were based on the same STATES' RIGHTS argument Southerners themselves embraced in other circumstances.

By the 1830s, Southern planters and their Northern sympathizers came to see abolitionism as a grave threat to their lives and property. Proslave apologists condemned abolitionists as treasonous and violent extremists who sought nothing less than a slave revolt, the murder of white people, and the destruction of the white race. Such fears convinced President Andrew Jackson to forbid the distribution of abolitionist literature through the mails. Congress was persuaded to forbid the reading and debate of all antislavery petitions brought to its attention. This happened despite a First Amendment guarantee of the right to petition for redress of grievances. In the North, mobs often pelted abolitionist speakers with everything from rotten food to rocks, burned abolitionist presses, and vandalized meeting halls. While Garrison was rescued from a violent Boston mob, abolitionist Elijah Lovejoy was not so lucky, and he was murdered by another mob in Alton, Illinois, on November 7, 1837. African-American abolitionist David Walker inspired particular hatred: $1,000 was offered for his dead body.

Though abolitionists did not always face such violence, they remained a distinct minority within the North well into the CIVIL WAR. Most white Northerners simply accepted as a matter of course that black people were an inferior race; many concurred with Southerners that slavery was essential both to protect African Americans from their own passions and to protect white people from black people. Many Northerners also feared that if slavery were ended, free African Americans would compete for jobs, forcing white workers to accept lower wages and worse conditions. For these workers, African-American freedom would mean white slavery.

Abolitionists were also divided among themselves. While black and white abolitionists worked side by side in Garrison's American Anti-Slavery Society, differences of emphasis and organization ensured that African Americans supported their own distinct institutions. Though Garrison's *Liberator* remained the preeminent abolitionist journal among white Americans, FREDERICK DOUGLASS's *North Star* was widely read among free African Americans. Black church and community groups independently organized support for escaped slaves; under activists such as HARRIET TUBMAN, these groups became the foundation for the network of escape routes, "conductors," and safehouses called the UNDERGROUND RAILROAD.

Abolitionists also differed over strategy. In 1840 abolitionist Lewis Tappan split with Garrison's American Antislavery Society and established a rival organization, the American and Foreign Antislavery Society. Tappan and others in the new group were dismayed at Garrison's alleged opposition to RELIGION, support for women's equality, and reliance on "moral suasion" rather than direct political action to end slavery.

Gender also divided abolitionists. Like Lydia Child, abolitionists such as Lucretia Mott, Susan B. Anthony, and ELIZABETH CADY STANTON found a cool and sometimes hostile reception from the men who led abolitionist organizations. To fight against slavery, they concluded, they had to emancipate women as well. Though some male abolitionists voiced contempt for feminism, others, such as Frederick Douglass, provided active support.

Despite these divisions, abolitionism grew stronger, particularly after the Mexican-American War of 1846–48. The conquest of Mexican territory reopened an angry debate over the expansion of slavery last heard during the debates leading to the Missouri Compromise of 1820. In the wake of U.S. victories, Congressman David Wilmot introduced his WILMOT PROVISO to prohibit slavery in any lands seized as a result of the war. Though ultimately defeated, Wilmot's bill spread antislavery sentiment.

Most Americans who opposed slavery in the territories were not abolitionists but Free Soilers. Free Soilers did not oppose slavery in the South but believed that if slavery were permitted in the West, wealthy Southern planters would buy up the best farmland. Northern farmers of more modest means would have nothing. Free Soilers shared with abolitionists a deep disdain for what they both characterized as the South's "slaveocracy."

Abolitionists were divided on the wisdom of working with Free-Soil Democrats and Whigs. William Lloyd Garrison refused to work with anyone who sought less than full and immediate emancipation. Tappan and other abolitionists disagreed. Abolitionists had already experimented with electoral politics in the form of the Liberty Party, whose support had grown from 7,000 presidential votes in 1840 to 60,000 in 1844. In 1848, many abolitionists joined the Free-Soil Party, which garnered more than a quarter million votes for presidential candidate Martin Van Buren. When the KANSAS-NEBRASKA ACT shattered the Whig Party in 1854, most Northern Whigs joined Free Soilers and abolitionists to establish the REPUBLICAN PARTY. Though the Republican Party officially embraced only Free-Soil ideas, abolitionists now had a strong voice in a mainstream political movement.

Even so, Garrisonian "moral suasion" remained vital to the abolitionist cause. HARRIET BEECHER STOWE's popular 1852 novel *Uncle Tom's Cabin* condemned the abuses of slavery in vivid prose. As many as one-third of literate Northerners read Stowe's book. African Americans who had escaped slavery now found large and enthusiastic audiences for their speeches and books.

However, moral suasion was clearly not going to end slavery by itself. During the 1850s, the debate over slavery provoked increasing violence. From Preston Brooks's assault on Senator CHARLES SUMNER in the Senate chambers to BLEEDING KANSAS, and from JOHN BROWN's attack on the federal armory at HARPERS FERRY to Southern calls for SECESSION, slavery had become the most divisive national issue. In 1860, hoping to allay the fears of white Northerners, the Republican Party passed over WILLIAM H. SEWARD, an abolitionist sympathizer, and instead nominated ABRAHAM LINCOLN, a Free Soiler who had condemned John Brown's raid and promised to protect slavery where it already existed.

At the beginning of the Civil War, most white Northerners—and certainly most Union soldiers—still opposed abolition of slavery. Lincoln himself entertained the idea that the United States might gradually end slavery and that former slaves might be returned to Africa. Yet Garrison, Douglass, and other abolitionists urged Lincoln to reject gradualism, reject colonization, and reject anything short of full citizenship. Throughout the Civil War, abolitionists struggled to ensure that African Americans could serve as combat soldiers in the UNION ARMY and that those soldiers would earn the same pay as white soldiers. Abolitionists also lobbied for other causes: that Union commanders end slavery in Southern territories they occupied, that the U.S. government grant captured plantation lands to former slaves, and that Congress declare and protect the civil rights of African Americans.

The THIRTEENTH AMENDMENT brought the end of slavery in 1865, and abolition's mission had been fulfilled. Some former abolitionists, their life's work accomplished, retreated from politics. Others remained active within the Republican Party. Still others joined moral crusades modeled after abolitionism and seeking reform of other elements of American life. However, veteran abolitionists found themselves divided in their approaches to RECONSTRUCTION and an industrializing ECONOMY. As a political movement, abolition was finished. Even so, fundamental issues arising out of race were never fully resolved by the Civil War. In many ways, they remain as vital to American society today as they did when abolitionists first raised them.

Further reading: Edward Magdol, *The Antislavery Rank and File: A Social Profile of the Abolitionist Constituency* (Westport, Conn.: Greenwood Press, 1986); James M. McPherson, *The Struggle for Equality: Abolitionists and the Negro in the Civil War and Reconstruction* (Princeton, N.J.: Princeton University Press, 1995); Ronald G. Walters, *The Antislavery Appeal: American Abolitionism after 1830* (New York: Norton, 1984).

—Tom Laichas

African-American regiments

President ABRAHAM LINCOLN initially opposed the inclusion of African Americans in the Union forces, fearing alienation of the border states, Northern prejudice and public opinion, the possibility of slave rebellion, and even the quality of fight he might get from black soldiers. By the summer of 1862, as the resilience of the Confederacy became more evident, he began to change his mind. He looked the other way as Senator James H. Lane of Kansas, a veteran of clashes with proslavery Missourians during the 1850s, formed black regiments in August. Lincoln determined that one way to weaken the South might be to undermine SLAVERY. The EMANCIPATION PROCLAMATION of January 1, 1863, included a carefully measured endorsement of the armament of African Americans. These forces became known as United States Colored Troops.

The Union's recruitment of black soldiers began in earnest March 1863 and ultimately resulted in raising nearly 180,000 troops, about 7,000 of whom served as noncommissioned officers. Unlike the celebrated Irish Brigade or the many proud German units, regiments comprising only African Americans were not so much the result of choice but of segregation. They were denied promotions and paid on a lower pay scale. They also were most often given white leadership; it was generally believed that white soldiers would never obey African-American officers. Commissions were given to only 110 African Americans, and more than 70 of them resigned due to the persistent harassment. Further, African-American members of the UNION ARMY fought knowing that if the Confederates captured them, they would be considered rebel slaves and might be tortured or executed. Some Confederate generals refused to take African-American prisoners.

White Union officers were offered incentives to raise and command African-American units and had to pass rigorous examinations, so black regiments most often had experienced and able leadership. Because of the great increase in promotions, white military personnel generally began to accept the inclusion of African Americans as a necessary measure of war. When finally allowed to fight, African Americans served with distinction. They led

Flag of the 22nd Regiment U.S. Colored Troops depicting an African-American soldier bayoneting a fallen Confederate soldier *(Library of Congress)*

three charges without white support at Port Hudson, Louisiana. At the BATTLE OF MILLIKEN'S BEND, they participated in some of the war's most brutal hand-to-hand combat. Robert Gould Shaw led the 54TH MASSACHUSETTS REGIMENT on a Union version of Pickett's charge at Fort Wagner. In all, African-American regiments participated in 41 major battles and about 450 smaller actions. By the end of the war, African Americans accounted for 12 percent of the Union army and about two-thirds of the forces in the Mississippi Valley. An additional 20,000 served in the UNION NAVY. Approximately 37,000 African Americans died in service, representing a 35 percent greater loss, proportionately, than Union white troops. Sixteen were awarded the congressional MEDAL OF HONOR.

See also CARNEY, WILLIAM HARVEY.

Further reading: Joseph T. Glatthaar, *Forged in Battle: The Civil War Alliance of Black Soldiers and White Officers* (Baton Rouge: Louisiana State University Press, 2000); Noah Andre Trudeau, *Like Men of War: Black Troops in the Civil War, 1862–1865* (Boston: Little, Brown, 1998).

—Richard J. Roder

African Methodist Episcopal Church

Founded in 1816, the African Methodist Episcopal (AME) Church became one of the leading social, cultural, and religious institutions in African-American life.

The AME Church grew out of tensions within the biracial Methodist Church following the American Revolution. Methodist churches opposed SLAVERY and encouraged the participation of free African Americans in the church, both as congregants and as preachers. At the same time, the white leaders of the Methodist movement believed that African-American styles of worship threatened the church's practices. Increasingly, they advocated the subordination and segregation of African-American congregants.

Over time, naturally, tension between black and white Methodists grew. During the early 1800s, antislavery attitudes in the Methodist organization weakened, as did the willingness of the Methodist leadership to ordain African Americans as ministers or include them in denominational decision making.

In response, a number of African Methodist congregations meeting in Philadelphia in April 1816 organized the African Methodist Episcopal Church, naming Richard Allen its first bishop. Spreading swiftly throughout the North and West before the CIVIL WAR, the church also established a strong presence in the South despite prohibitions against its presence.

Before the Civil War, the AME Church emphasized EDUCATION, ABOLITION, and community self-help. AME churches, including Philadelphia's "Mother Bethel," served as havens for men and women escaping slavery on the UNDERGROUND RAILROAD. Churches offered classes for congregants, stressing literacy, mathematics, and familiarity with the Bible. Church members also founded Ohio's Wilberforce University in 1856, the first college for African Americans in the United States.

By the mid-19th century the AME Church had become one of the most prolific publishers of African-American writing. The church's earliest works included hymnals and other religious literature. In 1841 the church began publishing the AME *Church Magazine* (later the *Christian Recorder*), one of the first African-American newspapers published in North America. Between 1858 and 1864, the church published African-American essays, poetry, and short stories in its *Repository of Religion and Literature*, an effort it revived in 1884 with the *A.M.E. Church Review*.

Politically, the AME was a strong advocate of EMANCIPATION during the Civil War and voting rights for African Americans after the war. As segregation and discrimination hardened in the years after RECONSTRUCTION, AME churches remained centers of African-American cultural and spiritual life, sustaining black communities into the 20th century.

Further reading: Clarence Earl Walker, *A Rock in a Weary Land: The African Methodist Episcopal Church during the Civil War and Reconstruction* (Baton Rouge: Louisiana State University Press, 1982).

—Tom Laichas

agriculture

Agriculture was the mainstay of the American ECONOMY both before and after the CIVIL WAR. The majority of the population of the United States, North and South, was rural, and nearly three-fourths of the nation's exports were agricultural in 1860. The actual type of agriculture and methods of farming varied enormously within the vast country, however. This was a reflection of a number of variables: the topography and quality of the soil, land policy, access to markets, availability of labor to tend crops, and the use of farm technology.

The South was the most agrarian section of the United States. Southern agricultural exports accounted for three-quarters of the total U.S. agricultural exports before the Civil War. The South's staple crop was cotton, and everyone from large planters to yeoman farmers grew the crop. Cotton required a large amount of labor due to the many steps involved in its production, from the sowing of cottonseeds to months of picking, ginning, hauling, and baling the finished product. Planters relied on slave labor as much as possible, according to their financial ability. At one extreme, wealthy planters used gangs of slaves while at the other, yeoman farmers tended to rely on family labor. For this reason, planters could generally focus on growing only cotton, while smaller farmers diversified and also grew the food needed for family sustenance.

Cotton was profitable because owners of England's textile mills provided a market for American cotton. As a result of the soaring demand for the crop, planters grew cotton year after year instead of diversifying their crop. When the soil inevitably became depleted, they often secured new land farther west and started the process over again. The boom in the cotton economy came in Alabama and Mississippi in the 1830s and expanded westward across Louisiana to Texas.

Similar patterns characterized the growing of the second-most-important commercial Southern crop, tobacco. As in cotton production, large slaveholding growers monopolized the land and trade. Commercial tobacco growing depleted the land almost as much as growing cotton, and like cotton growers, tobacco planters would often migrate westward. The old tobacco states of Maryland and

Virginia eventually gave way to Kentucky, Tennessee, and North Carolina.

The Civil War largely destroyed all forms of Southern agriculture. The Northern blockade uprooted the critical cotton trade. Further, invading armies destroyed the Southern TRANSPORTATION system, along with most of the crops and supplies of food in their path. Southern troops also harmed farmers. They confiscated meat, grain, and other produce for their food. At the close of the war, the production of Southern farmers was a fraction of prewar levels.

In the years after the Civil War, agriculture gradually reemerged in the South, with cotton remaining the primary crop. In fact, Southern farmers became even more dependent on a one-crop economy. Large PLANTATIONS continued to dominate agriculture, but now Northern capitalists replaced some of the Southern planters. For the ex-slaves who received neither land nor money, a new system of dependence emerged in the form of SHARECROPPING. Sharecroppers obtained food, farming tools, and a plot of land from merchant planters on credit. In return, sharecroppers agreed to turn over their crop to the merchant to pay their debts with interest. Under the conditions established by the merchants, the sharecroppers never were able to get out of debt from year to year, and they remained permanently tied to their land.

Like the South, the North was a primarily agrarian region. In the North, however, farming more clearly reflected the influence of urbanization and manufacturing, both increasingly important over the course of the 19th century. The price of land increased near cities, while at the same time city dwellers created a demand for agricultural produce. In order to afford the land they needed, farmers specialized in products that were sold to the cities. Many New England and mid-Atlantic farmers turned to the production of butter, milk, cheese, eggs, or vegetables. Other farmers gave up their eastern farms and headed west, where land was cheaper.

The prairie states of Illinois, Indiana, Missouri, Wisconsin, and Iowa became the breadbasket of the nation by the time of the Civil War. Farming on the prairies was very challenging—tall grasses stretching out for miles were supported by a dense, dank root system that defied traditional plows and bred mosquitoes and disease. The lack of timber for housing and fences along with poor access to transportation added to farmers' problems.

The Civil War accelerated trends in the North and Midwest that were already underway. The needs of the army increased demand for farm goods and raised prices. At the same time, enlistments drained farm hands from rural areas and caused a rapid increase in mechanization. Given the high costs of mechanical equipment, farmers were drawn away from subsistence agriculture into the commercial economy, with its complicated relationships to creditors, middlemen, and food processors. Farmers were becoming businessmen. Meanwhile, Northern farming interests shifted increasingly westward, as the states of New England and the Atlantic coast became more and more urbanized.

During the war, several pieces of legislation served to widen farmers' horizons. The Department of Agriculture was established as part of the national government, furnishing farmers with information on crop conditions, weather reports, scientific advances, and agricultural business trends. Land-grant college legislation was passed, establishing new universities geared toward scientific agriculture. A third piece of legislation, the HOMESTEAD ACT of 1862, had a more ambiguous impact. It established a procedure for settlers to acquire 160 acres of free land. While this would seem to be a boon for farmers, by the 1860s the principal tracts of land available were only good for livestock or other types of large-scale agriculture that required more land than 160 acres.

In the postwar years, agricultural settlement of the plains and the West proceeded at a furious pace. In the plains states, family farmers found life difficult economically and socially. Wealthy wheat ranchers with vast acres and expensive machinery were the ones who most prospered. In California and the southwestern states, the ongoing transition from Mexican to American jurisdiction revolutionized land policy and farming techniques. Mexicans in California and New Mexico had been accustomed to raising livestock in a partly subsistence and partly commercial agricultural economy. American farmers brought dramatic changes geared toward commercial agriculture. Some farmers were able to buy up huge chunks of land as they worked to find profitable cash crops that could be transported and sold to distant markets in the East and abroad. Their main successes were in the grain industry and, after the 1870s, in the orchard industry.

After the Civil War, the increased settlement of the plains and the West, along with the reemergence of Southern agriculture, turned the United States into the world's foremost producer of agricultural goods. Despite this, the predominant theme of the postwar era was the rise of manufacturing and big business. Increasing numbers of Americans abandoned farming for jobs in the cities. Those farmers who remained were increasingly forced to mechanize and to involve themselves directly in the national economy. Farmers found themselves subject to economic and human factors beyond their control, often to their great detriment. Ultimately, this would give rise to increasing political militancy among farmers in the 1870s and 1880s. The era of Thomas Jefferson's independent, yeoman farmer ended during the Civil War years.

See also MORRILL LAND-GRANT ACT.

Further reading: David Danbom, *Born in the Country: A History of Rural America* (Baltimore, Md.: Johns Hopkins University Press, 1995); Paul Wallace Gates, *The Farmer's Age: Agriculture 1815–1860* (Armonk, N.Y.: M. E. Sharpe, 1989); Fred A. Shannon, *The Farmer's Last Frontier: Agriculture 1860–1897* (Armonk, N.Y.: M. E. Sharpe, 1989).

—Jaclyn Greenberg

Alexander, Edward P. (1835–1910)

Confederate general and author Edward Porter Alexander was born on May 26, 1835, on the Fairfield plantation in Wilkes County, Georgia. His wealthy parents, Adam and Sarah Alexander, demanded academic excellence from their 10 children and were disappointed that Alexander decided to become a soldier. Graduated from the UNITED STATES MILITARY ACADEMY AT WEST POINT in 1857, he stood third in his class and accepted a coveted commission in the engineer corps. He married Virginian Bettie Mason shortly thereafter.

Following Georgia's SECESSION in 1861, Alexander left the U.S. Army and put his considerable engineering and organizational skills to work for the Confederacy. Commissioned as an artillery captain, he joined Gen. P. G. T. BEAUREGARD's staff before the FIRST BATTLE OF BULL RUN and quickly became chief of ordinance and artillery. Appointed colonel of artillery in Gen. JAMES LONGSTREET's First Corps in 1862, Alexander saw significant action at the BATTLES OF FREDERICKSBURG, CHANCELLORSVILLE, and GETTYSBURG. During the latter, he directed the artillery bombardment that preceded Pickett's Charge. Promoted to brigadier general in 1864, he spent the remainder of the war as Longstreet's chief of artillery. After recovering from a minor wound suffered at Petersburg in June 1864, Alexander rejoined the army for its final retreat and surrender in 1865.

During the 1870s and 1880s, Alexander built a postwar career as a railroad executive, managing several Georgia lines while mostly steering clear of the railroad industry financial scandals that in 1892 forced his retirement. In 1897 President Grover Cleveland appointed Alexander to a lucrative post as the American engineer responsible for settling a border dispute between Costa Rica and Nicaragua.

Alexander published *Military Memoirs of a Confederate* in 1907. Years earlier he had contributed narratives based on his personal experiences to the *Southern Historical Society Papers* and *Century Magazine*'s "Battles and Leaders of the Civil War" series. In his later memoirs, Alexander evaluated the campaigns he had witnessed in strictly military terms, adopting a scholarly approach that former compatriots mistook for arrogance. His harsh analysis of the Gettysburg campaign condemned Gen. ROBERT E. LEE's decision to invade Pennsylvania, criticized Lee's use of offensive battle tactics, and acquitted Longstreet of blame for the Confederate loss.

Alexander died on April 27, 1910, in Savannah, Georgia.

See also TACTICS AND STRATEGY.

Further reading: Edward Porter Alexander, *Military Memoirs of a Confederate: A Critical Narrative* (Dayton, Ohio: Morningside Bookshop, 1977); Edward Porter Alexander, *Fighting for the Confederacy: The Personal Recollections of General Edward Porter Alexander,* ed. Gary W. Gallagher (Chapel Hill: University of North Carolina Press, 1989); Maury Klein, *Edward Porter Alexander* (Athens: University of Georgia Press, 1971).

—Amy J. Kinsel

American Missionary Association

The American Missionary Association (AMA) was a nondenominational Christian organization dedicated to achieving full political and social equality for African Americans. The AMA's members were motivated by their belief that the teachings of Jesus Christ promoted racial harmony.

The AMA was incorporated in 1846 by Lewis Tappan, one of the founders of the American Anti-Slavery Society, and Simeon Jocelyn. Tappan and Jocelyn, along with most of the other early members of the AMA, had been active in the Amistad slave case that had secured the freedom of a number of illegally imported slaves. At first, the AMA focused on establishing overseas missions for freed slaves. By the 1850s, however, the AMA had turned primarily to ABOLITION. For the next decade, AMA members supported a number of abolitionist causes, most prominently the UNDERGROUND RAILROAD.

During the CIVIL WAR, the AMA began working to educate former slaves. Over 500 schools were founded during the Civil War and in the decades thereafter. Most were elementary schools, but a number of institutions of higher learning were also established, including Atlanta University, Fisk University, Hampton Institute, Howard University, Huston-Tillotson College, and Talladega College. The AMA remains in operation to the present day and has continued to focus on EDUCATION and other assistance for the underprivileged, including African Americans, NATIVE AMERICANS, Mexican Americans, Chinese immigrants, and Appalachian people.

See also RELIGION.

Further reading: Joe M. Richardson, *Christian Reconstruction: The American Missionary Association and Southern Blacks, 1861–1890* (Athens: University of Georgia Press, 1986).

—Mark Groen

amnesty, acts of

Amnesty refers to a formal procedure by which a group of people is forgiven for past misdeeds, while a pardon is official forgiveness for a single individual. During the CIVIL WAR and RECONSTRUCTION period, Presidents ABRAHAM LINCOLN and ANDREW JOHNSON, along with the U.S. Congress, issued several proclamations of amnesty and pardon. These proclamations must be placed in the context of the unfolding policy of Reconstruction during and after the war. Two questions dominated: What would be the best way to bring the rebellious states and people back into the Union? and Who should control the process, the president or Congress?

Even as war was being waged on the battlefields, large portions of the South had come under Union military occupation. President Lincoln desired that loyal Southerners regain control of their states as soon as possible. He also sought to demonstrate to the South that returning to the United States could be relatively easy, in hopes of convincing the Confederacy to abandon its rebellion. On December 8, 1863, Lincoln issued the first "Proclamation of Amnesty and Reconstruction," in which he used his constitutional war powers to seize control of the reconciliation process for the executive branch. Known in history as Lincoln's Ten Percent Plan, it offered a full pardon to all "insurgents," or people who had engaged in the rebellion against the United States.

Of course, there were conditions and exemptions. Several classes of Southerners, including high Confederate officials and military officers, were not to be granted amnesty under Lincoln's act. Eligible applicants, a category that included the majority of Southerners, had to take an oath pledging their loyalty to the U.S. Constitution, including all acts and laws passed regarding the ex-slaves. As soon as 10 percent of the voters of 1860 had taken the oath, their rights and privileges as citizens were restored fully. They could then re-form their state governments and hold ELECTIONS for national offices. If these steps were followed, the U.S. government would accept Southern states back into the Union, as well as their national representatives back into the House of Representatives and the Senate.

Lincoln's proclamation, which was put into action in Louisiana, stirred protest by a group of men who would shortly be called the RADICAL REPUBLICANS. Led by Senators CHARLES SUMMER of Massachusetts and BENJAMIN WADE of Ohio, they put forward a different and far harsher plan for Reconstruction that emphasized punishment for Southern white "traitors." Many wanted to reward the newly freed and loyal African Americans with the vote, making them the focus of a reconstructed South. Most importantly, they wanted Congress and not the president to control Reconstruction. The issue was put on the back burner for most of 1864 and into 1865 as the presidential elections, the end of the war, and the ASSASSINA-TION OF ABRAHAM LINCOLN commanded the attention of the country.

With Lincoln's death, Andrew Johnson was left in control of Reconstruction. Acting on the authority given in Article II, Section 2 of the Constitution, which states that the president "shall have power to grant reprieves and pardons for offenses against the United States," Johnson issued the next "Proclamation of Amnesty" on May 29, 1865. Like Lincoln's proclamation, Johnson's offered amnesty to all insurgents who took the oath. Since the war was over, Johnson dispensed with the 10 percent plan and instead appointed provisional GOVERNORS who would preside over the reestablishment of loyal governments. Johnson's plan expanded the list of people who were exempted from amnesty, including those whose taxable income was worth more than $20,000. These individuals could apply to the president for a personal pardon. Despite the many bureaucratic obstacles to obtaining the pardons, Johnson granted thousands of them over the summer of 1865. Johnson would go on to issue two more Proclamations of Amnesty on July 4, 1868, and on December 25, 1868, that clarified the details and enlarged the scope of the earlier ones.

Johnson's proclamations formed the basis of a generous Reconstruction for the South. So generous was it, in fact, that congressional Republicans revived the struggle over control of the timing and nature of reconciliation. From 1866 to 1868, Congress and the president presented competing versions of Reconstruction to the nation during a period of rising Southern white violence against African Americans. Northern voters in the 1866 fall elections rejected decisively Johnson's lenient Reconstruction policy. Congressional Republicans, powerful and united by their desire to remake the South more like Northern society, put the entire defeated region under control of the military with a series of RECONSTRUCTION ACTS. Many citizens in the South were thrown into confusion as Johnson's proclamations of amnesty were rendered null and void. Instead, Congress declared that the more exclusionary FOURTEENTH AMENDMENT was the guideline for citizenship.

As the popular support for a harsh Reconstruction declined, so too did congressional resistance to leniency toward former rebels. In 1872 Congress passed another Amnesty Act that removed office-holding disabilities for everyone except a few of the highest-ranking officials and officers of the former Confederacy. In 1898 Congress issued a universal amnesty for all those who had not been granted it in earlier acts. In the long and bumpy road toward sectional peace, the North in the end had decided on a sectional reconciliation that emphasized harmony and forgiveness over the rights of freedmen.

Further reading: Jonathan Truman Dorris, *Pardon and Amnesty under Lincoln and Johnson: The Restoration of the Confederates to their Rights and Privileges, 1861–1898* (Chapel Hill: University of North Carolina Press, 1953); William C. Harris, *With Charity for All: Lincoln and the Restoration of the Union* (Lexington: University Press of Kentucky, 1997).

Anderson, Robert (1805–1871)

Born in Kentucky, Robert Anderson became a career army officer, veteran of four wars and, in his defense of FORT SUMTER, the first hero of the CIVIL WAR.

Graduating in 1825 at the middle of his West Point class, Anderson joined the army as a second lieutenant. Through service in the Black Hawk War (1832), the Seminole War (1837–38), and the Mexican-American War (1846–48), Anderson rose to the rank of major (1857). In 1845 he married Elizabeth Bayard Clinch from Georgia, with whom he would have four children.

In November 1860, Anderson was appointed commander of Fort Moultrie, an obsolete island post in South Carolina that was easily accessible from the mainland and vulnerable to capture from its rear. One mile away, at the entrance to Charleston Harbor, workers were completing FORT SUMTER, a man-made granite island with brick walls 40 feet high and 8 feet thick. Sumter was designed in such a way that with a full force of 650 soldiers manning 146 large guns, it could halt any craft entering or leaving the harbor.

When South Carolina seceded in December 1860, Anderson was placed in a precarious position. Although a Kentuckian and a slaveholder, he remained loyal to the Union and worked to keep Forts Sumter and Moultrie in Northern hands. He knew that any misstep on his part could lead to war, as Charleston militiamen stood prepared to attack the Federal force. Anderson requested guidance and received ambiguous orders from Washington that he interpreted as allowing him to move from Moultrie to Sumter if he thought it necessary to deter an attack. He did so under the cover of darkness on the evening of December 26. The people of the North were elated, those of the South indignant.

At Sumter, Anderson faced a severe shortage of supplies. Fort Sumter's symbolic value was high, but Anderson could not hope to resist if the North could not resupply him. He made an urgent request for food and other necessities that President ABRAHAM LINCOLN ultimately decided to grant. When Confederate Gen. P. G. T. BEAUREGARD learned of this, he began shelling Fort Sumter. The shelling began before 5 A.M. on April 12 and continued until April 14, when Anderson and his men (127 total, including civilian employees) were forced to surrender.

Anderson's struggle to keep Fort Sumter for the Union made him the North's first war hero. He was rewarded with a promotion to brigadier general and assigned to the Department of the Cumberland. Soon, however, he was forced to give up his command to WILLIAM T. SHERMAN because of ill health. He retired in 1863 but returned to Charleston at the end of the war to replace the American flag that had been torn down in 1861. After the war Anderson and his family relocated to France. He died in Charleston on October 26, 1871.

Further reading: David Detzer, *Allegiance: Fort Sumter, Charleston, and the Beginning of the Civil War* (New York: Harcourt, 2001); W. A. Swanberg, *First Blood: The Story of Fort Sumter* (New York: Scribner, 1957).

—Richard J. Roder

Andersonville Prison, Georgia

Officially named Camp Sumter, the notorious Andersonville Prison was one of the largest prison camps during the American CIVIL WAR.

In the latter part of 1863, Union forces began penetrating deeper into the Southern states. As a result, Confederates captured prisoners of war in greater numbers than ever before. This influx quickly showed that the detention facilities used during the prior two years of war—mainly old forts, warehouses, and jails—were insufficient. The Southern captors feared that the prominent presence of Yankee prisoners would increase the possibility of overrunning the northernmost facilities just as they had threatened RICHMOND, the Confederate capital, in 1862.

In order to rectify the problem, Confederate officials were sent to Georgia in November 1863 to scout a potential prison site in Sumter County near the town of Andersonville. They determined that the area in south-central Georgia was an ideal location for the facility because it was, at the time, far from the reach of the Union forces. Other reasons for selecting the area included the availability of potable water from a nearby creek, the close proximity of the Georgia Southwestern Railway, and the plentiful timber supply. In addition, because the town of Andersonville itself had a population of only about 20 people, little political resistance to the facility developed. Finally, local slaves could be impressed by the army to build the prison.

Andersonville's construction began in December 1863. On February 24, 1864, 600 prisoners from Libby Prison in Richmond, Virginia, arrived. One entire wall of the stockade was still under construction. Confederate artillery pieces were positioned by the opening to deter any attempts to escape until the work was finished. Once completed, the walls of the prison formed a rectangle of rough-hewn pine standing 15–20 feet in height and built on a 16 1/2-acre tract intended to house no more than 10,000 Union prisoners of war.

During the first few months, conditions at Andersonville were fair. But by July the facility was jammed with over 32,000 soldiers, almost all enlisted men. This increase occurred because of renewed Union aggression and the decision of Northern officials to stop the exchange of prisoners. They believed that keeping Southern soldiers in Northern PRISONS would deprive the South of desperately needed manpower and thus hasten the end of the war.

The Northern leadership's decision was a hard blow for Union soldiers in prisons like Andersonville. The open-air stockade was expanded to 26 acres but remained horribly overcrowded, and conditions became more and more intolerable. Nevertheless, thousands of soldiers continued to be shipped to the prison. Running through the middle of the camp was a stagnant stream, sarcastically referred to as "Sweet Water Branch," which served as a sewer as well as a source of water for bathing and drinking. There were no barracks; prisoners were forbidden to construct shelters. Some did erect tents, but most were left fully exposed to the elements. No clothing was distributed to the captives, so most wore ragged remnants of their uniform or sometimes nothing at all. Medical treatment and supplies were virtually nonexistent.

With the South barely able to provide for its own men, the prisoners starved. Their daily diet might consist of only rancid grain and a few tablespoons of beans or peas. The poor food and sanitation, the lack of shelter and health care, the crowding, and the hot Georgia sun took their toll in the form of dysentery, scurvy, and malaria. Capt. Henry Wirz, who assumed command of Andersonville in June 1864, wrote the Confederacy's War Department to ask for additional supplies to sustain the prisoners but received no assistance. Attempts to improve the situation were futile, given the limited supplies available. Beyond that, many embittered Confederates were unwilling to do anything to make conditions better because they believed that all Union soldiers should die.

During the summer months, more than 100 prisoners died of disease on a daily basis. Others fell victim to thieves and marauders among their fellow captives. The desperate situation led a Confederate medical commission to recommend relocating those prisoners who were not too ill to move, and in September 1864, as WILLIAM T. SHERMAN's army approached, most of Andersonville's able-bodied inmates were sent to other camps.

Remaining in operation until the war's conclusion, Andersonville held more captured Union soldiers than any other Confederate camp, a total of over 45,000. Nearly 30 percent of these died in captivity. The North had learned of the camp's appalling conditions well before the emaciated survivors were released in April 1865, and outraged citizens urged retribution on Southern prisoners of war. Of course, the Union had wretched prison camps of its own. Death rates were high in some of these as well, even though the North was far better equipped to cope with captured soldiers. Mismanagement and severe shortages were more to blame for the terrors of Andersonville than any deliberate attempt to mistreat prisoners. Nevertheless, many Northerners insisted that the abuse was deliberate and demanded vengeance. Consequently, after being tried by a U.S. military court and convicted of war crimes, Henry Wirz was hanged. Meanwhile, government workers led by CLARA BARTON compiled a list of 12,912 prisoners who had died at the camp. Andersonville's mass graves were replaced by a national cemetery, which is today still used as a burial ground for American VETERANS.

See also PRISONS.

Further reading: William Best Hesseltine, *Civil War Prisons: A Study in War Psychology* (Columbus: Ohio State University Press, 1998); William Marvel, *Andersonville: The Last Depot* (Chapel Hill: University of North Carolina Press, 1994).

—Emily E. Holst

Andrews's Raid (April 12, 1862)
In the spring of 1862, one of the western UNION ARMY's most trusted spies, James J. Andrews, was given the task of launching a secret commando raid deep into the South. Also known as "The Great Locomotive Chase," Andrews's Raid is a perennial favorite among those who enjoy colorful war tales and has been the subject of paintings, songs, and at least two movies. Andrews had no trouble recruiting 22 volunteers for the daring adventure. Their aim was to cut the rail line that served as the supply link between Marietta, Georgia, and Chattanooga, Tennessee. The plan developed by Andrews was simple. His men would divide up into small groups, out of uniform, and go to Marietta where they would board a northbound train headed for Big Shanty, Georgia (now Kennesaw Mountain). The tiny crossroads town was a meal stop on the railroad, and when the other passengers were eating their breakfast, Andrews and his men would steal a locomotive and race unhindered toward Chattanooga, stopping only to cut TELEGRAPH lines, burn bridges, and render unusable a critical part of the Confederacy's railroad lifeline.

The execution of the plan, however, did not go as planned. One major setback arose when the weather turned very wet, making the roads impassable and bridges unburnable. Another unforeseen complication was that the Confederates had established a military camp at Big Shanty. Now, instead of few or no rebel soldiers, there were hundreds in the area. Nevertheless, Andrews and his men

started their raid on the night of April 12 with high hopes. They did manage to capture a locomotive, called "The General," along with three boxcars, and then took off in a hurry. Their deed immediately discovered, the Confederates grabbed another engine and went in hot pursuit. The wild chase continued for almost 90 miles, until "The General" ran out of fuel near Grayville, about 18 miles south of Chattanooga. At that point, Andrews and his men jumped off the train and hid in the woods, where all were captured.

As the raiders were out of uniform when arrested, they were treated as spies. Two months later, Andrews and seven Union soldiers were court-martialed and executed. Eight other raiders escaped, and the rest were paroled in an exchange organized by Secretary of War EDWIN M. STANTON. Later, the survivors of Andrews's Raid became the first recipients of the MEDAL OF HONOR, the nation's highest award for bravery.

See also RAILROADS.

Further reading: William Pittenger, *Daring and Suffering: A History of the Great Railroad Adventure* (Philadelphia: J. W. Daughaday, 1887).

Anthony, Susan B.   See Volume VI

Antietam/Sharpsburg, Battle of (September 17, 1862)
Antietam was a campaign and battle fought in the eastern theater of operations between Union Maj. Gen. GEORGE B. MCCLELLAN's Army of the Potomac and Confederate general ROBERT E. LEE's Army of Northern Virginia. The failure of Lee's invasion of Maryland ensured enough of a Northern victory to allow President ABRAHAM LINCOLN to issue the preliminary EMANCIPATION PROCLAMATION. Thus, Antietam marked a turning point in the war for the North, as the goal changed from union to union and freedom.

Following his success on the Virginia Peninsula (March–June 1862) and at the SECOND BATTLE OF BULL RUN (August 1862), Lee capitalized on apparent Union demoralization by invading the North. Crossing the Potomac River during the first week of September, he encamped his approximately 40,000 soldiers near Frederick, Maryland, on September 9. Disregarding the UNION ARMY, he divided his forces, sending one corps commanded by THOMAS J. "STONEWALL" JACKSON to capture HARPERS FERRY and the other under JAMES LONGSTREET toward Hagerstown. Together, these two operations would stop east-west Union rail traffic. Ultimately, he intended to unite his army near Hagerstown or Boonsboro.

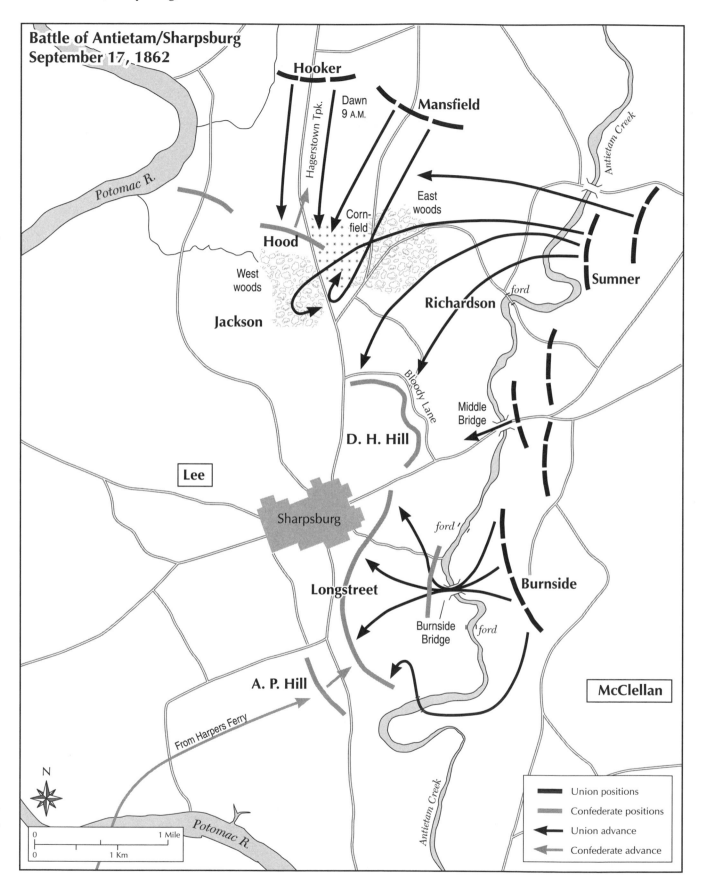

**Battle of Antietam/Sharpsburg
September 17, 1862**

Hooker

Mansfield

Dawn
9 A.M.

Hagerstown Tpk.

Potomac R.

Antietam Creek

East
woods

Corn-
field

Hood

West
woods

Jackson

Richardson

ford

Sumner

Bloody Lane

Middle
Bridge

D. H. Hill

Lee

Sharpsburg

Longstreet

ford

Burnside

Burnside
Bridge

ford

A. P. Hill

McClellan

From Harpers Ferry

N

Antietam Creek

Potomac R.

0   1 Mile
0   1 Km

▬▬▬	Union positions
▬▬▬	Confederate positions
➤	Union advance
➤	Confederate advance

Union general McClellan, a master of military organization and recently appointed to command all forces near WASHINGTON, D.C., soon had roughly 75,000 soldiers searching for the Confederate troops. By September 12 he was in the vicinity of Lee's former campground near Frederick, where his soldiers found a copy of the Confederate operations order. Within 48 hours, the Union troops had crossed Catoctin Mountain and were threatening to break through the passes at South Mountain.

Realizing that the enemy was about to split his army, Lee ordered a concentration near the western Maryland town of Sharpsburg. To buy him the time he needed, he directed Maj. Gens. D. H. Hill and J. E. B. STUART to hold the passes on South Mountain. They resisted the Union advance at Crampton, Fox, and Turner's Gaps, but by noon on September 15 they were withdrawing back to Sharpsburg. With Lee's army pinned against the Potomac, and much of it still on the road from Harpers Ferry, McClellan failed to capitalize on Confederate disorganization and weakness by attacking immediately. Instead, he wasted the entire next day leisurely deploying his troops in sight of Lee's rapidly improving command.

The Union attack progressed from north to south. At 6 A.M. McClellan opened with the I Corps (JOSEPH HOOKER) attacking due south on the Hagerstown-Sharpsburg Turnpike. A little over an hour later his XII Corps (Joseph Mansfield) joined the fight. The heaviest fighting took place in sight of a small white building called Dunkard Church in a recently harvested cornfield. Fighting was intense as brigades from Jackson's, JOHN BELL HOOD's and RICHARD S. EWELL's divisions launched fierce counterattacks throughout the morning. By 9 A.M., Maj. Gen. John Sedgwick's division of II Corps, with the corps commander Edwin V. Sumner in the lead, joined the fight in the cornfield. In response, Lee moved John Walker's division from the southern portion of the line. Then his and Lafayette McLaws's divisions struck Sedgwick's troops, driving them back in disarray. By noon, fighting was all but over on the northern portion of the battlefield, as the Confederates had stood their ground.

Sumner's other two divisions followed the first without guidance or a clear objective. As they crossed Antietam Creek they diverged from the rest of the corps and drifted south. Wandering over a small rise, they ran into the Confederate commands of D. H. Hill and Richard Anderson along a small sunken farm road. The bloody and intense struggle continued as Gen. William French's division took the brunt of the Southern defenses. A little after noon, Gen. Israel Richardson's trailing division penetrated the rebel positions, inflicting a withering fire on the retreating defenders. The way was open to Sharpsburg, and McClellan still had John Porter's V Corps in reserve. However, he did not take advantage of his opportunity.

Gen. AMBROSE E. BURNSIDE began IX Corps's attack on the southern portion of the battle line around 10 A.M. The greatly outnumbered Confederate force, occupying the high ground on the far bank, dominated the Antietam Creek and its stone bridge. Not until 1 P.M. was Samuel Sturgis's division able to cross the creek. Two hours later, Burnside had two divisions (Orlando Wilcox's and Isaac Rodman's) on their way to Sharpsburg. Lee had no more troops at hand, and McClellan appeared to be on the verge of a decisive victory. Burnside, however, failed to secure the rise on his left flank. Just as he was about to enter the town, Maj. Gen. A. P. HILL's small division, returning from the Harpers Ferry operation, arrived on the ridge. Arrayed on the ridge line, the Confederate troops appeared to confirm McClellan's worst fears about being outnumbered. The Union attack stalled and then withdrew back toward Antietam Creek.

McClellan had almost destroyed the CONFEDERATE ARMY. Yet, Lee remained defiant on September 18, and the Union commander did not use his several fresh corps to finish him off. On the next day, the Southerners withdrew across the Potomac, at the only ford available, without an effective Union pursuit. President Abraham Lincoln, disgusted by McClellan's inability to destroy the Army of Northern Virginia, relieved him of command in November.

This battle was the bloodiest single day in the CIVIL WAR with more than 12,000 Union and almost 14,000 Confederate soldiers killed and wounded. It was one of the first photographed battlefields, and its horrific pictures created shock and dismay among civilians.

See also BRADY, MATHEW B.

Further reading: James M. McPherson, *Crossroads of Freedom, Antietam 1862: The Battle that Changed the Course of Civil War History* (New York: Oxford University Press, 2000); Stephen Sears, *Landscape Turned Red: The Battle of Antietam* (New Haven, Conn.: Ticknor & Fields, 1983).

—Stephen A. Bourque

Appomattox Court House, Virginia (April 9, 1865)

Appomattox Court House was the site of the historic surrender of Confederate forces to Lt. Gen. ULYSSES S. GRANT on April 9, 1865. A note from General Grant sums up the feeling of the moment. It was addressed to "General R. E. Lee, Commanding General of the CONFEDERATE STATES OF AMERICA" and was dated April 7, 1865. "Dear General," wrote Grant, "The result of the last week must convince you of the hopelessness of further resistance on the part of the Army of Northern Va. in this struggle. I feel that it is so and regard it as my duty to shift from myself, the responsibility of any further effusion of blood, by asking of you the surrender of that portion of the C.S. Army known as the Army of Northern Va."

Grant's words show that the story of the Appomattox campaign of March 25–April 9, 1865, was a grim one for the Confederates. The BATTLE OF FIVE FORKS on April 1, 1865, destroyed the last supply line for the Army of Northern Virginia. Lee's subsequent evacuation from RICHMOND and Petersburg left his fast-dwindling army hungry and weak. His goal was to escape somehow the clutches of the Federals by going southwest to meet up with Gen. JOSEPH E. JOHNSTON's force in North Carolina. There, the combined Confederate armies could take on Union forces at a spot of their own choosing.

Grant's cavalry and infantry moved quickly to cut off all escape routes. The Confederates were dealt a heavy blow on April 6, when 80,000 Yankee troops chased after 35,000 of Lee's men and stopped them from turning south at Sayler's Creek, near Farmville, where Union forces had captured 7,000 Southern soldiers. The next day, Grant's note went out to Lee asking him to surrender. Lee refused. Worse was yet to come for the Confederates. On April 8, Gen. PHILIP H. SHERIDAN's cavalry troops captured two trainloads of rations meant for Lee's starving troops.

April 9 was Palm Sunday, and early morning found Lee and the remnants of his army in desperate flight across the Appomattox River, headed for the safe harbor of Lynchburg, Virginia. A quick look at the massed Federal army blocking the way revealed the hopelessness of the Confederate position. Lee said: "There is nothing left for me to do but to go and see General Grant, and I would rather die a thousand deaths." Grant was nursing a migraine when Lee's request for an immediate interview to discuss terms of surrender was delivered. Grant wrote later: "I was still suffering with the sick headache; but the instant I saw the contents of the note I was cured." It was agreed that the two generals would meet in Appomattox Court House, a small community deep in the countryside of Virginia, about 20 miles southeast of Lynchburg.

A little after 1:30 P.M., Grant and his staff rode into the village and stopped their horses at the two-story brick farmhouse of Wilmer McLean. In the parlor of McLean's residence sat ROBERT E. LEE and a lone aide, waiting for them. General Lee was dressed in his best uniform, with a beautiful sword by his side, looking every inch the Southern gentleman he was. The commanding general of the Northern armies was much less formal. His dress uniform not available, Grant was in his preferred casual field uniform complete with mud splatters from his journey. The two men exchanged some pleasantries. Grant observed his

This painting depicts the surrender of Robert E. Lee and his army at the Appomattox Court House, Virginia, to General Ulysses S. Grant   *(Library of Congress)*

counterpart's emotionless face closely during the conversation and remarked, "What General Lee's feelings were I do not know. As he was a man of much dignity with an impassible face it was impossible to say whether he felt inwardly glad that the end had finally come. . . ."

ELY S. PARKER, Grant's military secretary, brought over a table for him to begin writing out the terms of surrender. "I only knew what was in my mind," reflected Grant. Characteristically direct and simple, Grant's terms were also magnanimous and reflected his and President ABRAHAM LINCOLN's great desire that the beaten Confederates neither be humiliated nor punished. Total defeat was enough. The rebels were to "lay down arms," return home as paroled prisoners, and promise to obey the laws of the United States. Grant would not require Lee to hand over his sword, and Southern officers would be able to keep their side arms. Both officers and enlisted men could bring their horses and mules back with them. "This will have the best possible effect upon the men," Lee said. "It will be very gratifying, and will do much toward conciliating our people." Copies of the surrender were then made, and Lee wrote out a letter accepting the terms. Lee's request for rations for his men was approved, and at 4:00 P.M. the two men shook hands. Lee then mounted his horse, Traveller, and slowly moved down the road to the Confederate camp.

News of the surrender spread quickly through the Union camps, and soon thousands of soldiers were cheering and throwing their hats into the air. A 100-gun salute was begun, but Grant immediately stopped it, saying, "The war is over. The Rebels are our countrymen again." Perhaps the most common emotion for the weary soldiers of both sides was a great relief that the war, and the killing, was finally over. The great problems of reconstructing the Union and easing the bitterness between North and South lay ahead.

Shortly after Lee's departure, Grant TELEGRAPHed EDWIN M. STANTON, the secretary of war: "General Lee surrendered the Army of Northern Virginia this afternoon on terms proposed by myself." WASHINGTON, D.C., went wild with happiness. Back at Appomattox, on April 12, the formal ceremony of the laying down of arms occurred in an atmosphere of respectful conciliation. Although several more Confederate armies would surrender in the months to come, the meeting between Grant and Lee at Appomattox Court House is considered the end of the American CIVIL WAR.

See also RECONSTRUCTION ACTS.

Further reading: Bruce Catton, *A Stillness at Appomattox* (Garden City, N.Y.: Doubleday, 1953); William Marvel, *A Place Called Appomattox* (Chapel Hill: University of North Carolina Press, 2000).

Armistead, Lewis A. (1817–1863)

Confederate general Lewis Addison Armistead was born on February 18, 1817, in New Bern, North Carolina. His parents were army engineer Walker Keith Armistead and Elizabeth Stanly. Raised on his family's farm near Upperville, Virginia, Armistead entered the UNITED STATES MILITARY ACADEMY AT WEST POINT in 1834 but was expelled in 1836 for rowdy behavior. Through his father's connections, he joined the Sixth U.S. Infantry as a second lieutenant in 1839, serving in Florida and the West. He fought in the Mexican-American War and was promoted for his bravery at the Battle of Churubusco in 1847. After the war, Armistead was assigned to frontier duty.

Armistead's personal life was marked by tragedy. In 1844 he married fellow Virginian Cecelia Lee Love, who bore him a son and a daughter. The daughter and Cecelia both died in 1850. In 1853 Armistead married a Virginia widow, Cornelia Lee Taliaferro Jamison. An infant son died in 1854, and Cornelia succumbed to cholera in 1855. Armistead's surviving son, Walker Keith Armistead, served as his aide-de-camp during the CIVIL WAR.

Stationed in the Far West in 1861, Armistead resigned from the army and returned to Virginia to fight for the Confederacy. Appointed as colonel of the 57th Virginia Infantry in 1861, Armistead was quickly promoted to brigadier general. He saw significant action in the Battles of Seven Pines and Malvern Hill and was wounded at the BATTLE OF ANTIETAM.

Armistead's heroism at the BATTLE OF GETTYSBURG, where his brigade fought in Pickett's division, became legendary. Leading his brigade on foot during JAMES LONGSTREET's assault on July 3, 1863, Armistead held his hat aloft on his sword for his men to follow. As the remnants of Pickett's division reached the Federal position on Cemetery Ridge, Armistead shouted, "Come on boys, give them the cold steel. Who will follow me?" Mortally wounded, his final words were addressed to his close friend, Gen. WINFIELD SCOTT HANCOCK: "Say to General Hancock for me that I have done him and you all a grievous injury for which I shall always regret."

Further reading: Wayne Motts, *Trust in God and Fear Nothing: Lewis A. Armistead, CSA* (Gettysburg, Pa.: Farnsworth House, 1997).

—Amy J. Kinsel

art

All forms of art, from genre painting to landscape tableaux to portraiture, evolved over the course of the 19th century. There was a blending of European artistic styles with uniquely American themes.

One popular art form was genre painting, which depicted scenes of groups of people interacting in everyday life. The scenes were often comical and sometimes moral and sentimental, featuring portrayals of American stereotypes based on region, race, and gender, such as the crafty Yankee peddler or the hayseed Kentuckian. Artists associated with genre painting included Richard Caton Woodville, George Caleb Bingham, William Sidney Mount, and Lilly Martin Spencer. This art form flourished before the CIVIL WAR but died out after the war when the homey stereotypes no longer rang true. After the Civil War came more-entrenched class, racial, and ethnic divisions. They ceased being comical, and Americans craved more universal images.

Landscape painting also changed over time. Before the Civil War, artists associated with the Hudson River school painted romantic pictures of nature that were rich in shadow and drama. In the landscapes, in the distance, there might be a tiny and solitary person or two overwhelmed in scale by the rendering of the landscape. The paintings were emotive, inspiring awe and a view of God's presence in nature. Landscape paintings tended to reflect some major themes about Americans' attitudes toward nature and about the relationship of the individual to God. The landscapes of vast territories also resonated with the ideology of Manifest Destiny. A major artist associated with the first generation of the Hudson River school was Thomas Cole (1801–48).

The second generation of the Hudson River school artists took landscape painting in different directions. Around the time of the Civil War, in a style that is now labeled Luminism, landscape artists tried to present a direct, unmediated portrayal of nature. Some scholars have suggested that Luminism was related to the philosophy of Transcendentalism. Painted on small canvases with shiny surfaces, Luminism emphasized light, horizontal planes and could look almost surreal. Martin Johnson Heade's (1819–1904) work falls in this category.

Other landscape artists painted in a more naturalistic fashion. For example, Frederic Edwin Church (1826–1900) attempted to combine scientific truth with a dramatic portrayal of nature. On another front, landscapes of the American West satisfied transatlantic fascination with the land, NATIVE AMERICANS, cowboys, and the like. Albert Bierstadt (1830–1902) painted monumental grand landscapes, from the minutest detail to grandeur. George Caitlin (1796–1872) concentrated on Native Americans. Frederic Remington (1861–1909) became known for his epic cowboy paintings.

In portraiture, an artist was usually commissioned to paint an individual or a family. The patron might have wanted a portrait to reinforce his or her social standing or to portray a memory. Before the advent of PHOTOGRAPHY, many artists painted portraits. Painters who often traveled from town to town proliferated as part of a growing material culture in the first half of the 19th century. In the second half of the century, portraits tended to become more restricted to upper-class clients. Thomas Sully (1783–1872) was Philadelphia's leading portrait painter in the first half of the century, painting more than 2,000 portraits.

Few individual painters are more worthy of note than Thomas Eakins (1844–1916). He realistically portrayed people either in repose or engaged in an activity. Interested in the scientific study of the human form in motion, Eakins emphasized the use of nude models and took anatomy classes. His paintings were intense revelations of character. Not a painter of high society, Eakins rarely received commissions and was not distinguished in his own time, although now he is considered one of America's great portrait painters.

Perhaps the most famous artist of the 19th century was Winslow Homer (1836–1910), known for his freshness of observation and unsophisticated style. Starting with his early paintings—bucolic scenes of rural life and recreation—he rose to prominence as an illustrator and a painter of Civil War soldiers and Union camp life. Beginning in the 1880s, Homer grew progressively more serious in outlook and somber in color. His dramatic and heroic paintings portrayed a Darwinian contest of man against nature, most often in the form of a stormy sea. His view of nature as a source of elemental danger differed from the attitudes of early landscapists, for whom nature evoked reverence and awe.

As the influence of modernization began to be reflected in the paintings of Winslow Homer and others, so too was the influence of European artistic currents. Throughout the 19th century, many artists made trips abroad to study the old masterpieces and learn contemporary styles. When the Metropolitan Museum of Art and the Philadelphia Museum of Art both opened in 1870, a large portion of the work exhibited was European. Some American artists, such as Mary Cassatt and James McNeill Whistler, worked entirely within a European framework, and John Singer Sargent's work reflected international inclinations.

See also FASHION.

Further reading: Barbara Groseclose, *Nineteenth Century American Art* (New York: Oxford University Press, 2000); David Lubin, *Picturing a Nation: Art and Social Change in Nineteenth Century America* (New Haven, Conn.: Yale University Press, 1994); Barbara Novak, *American Painting in the Nineteenth Century: Realism, and the American Experience* (New York: Harper & Row, 1979).

—Jaclyn Greenberg

assassination of Abraham Lincoln (April 14, 1865) "Sic semper tyrannis!" These words, which translate as "thus always to tyrants," were spoken by Brutus as he assassinated Julius Caesar in the play by William Shakespeare. When the famous actor JOHN WILKES BOOTH shouted the phrase after leaping to the stage during a Ford's Theatre performance of *Our American Cousin* on April 14, 1865, most of the audience assumed he was part of the cast. It was not until he had disappeared into the wings that it became clear that he had just shot President ABRAHAM LINCOLN.

The notion of Booth as an assassin was shocking to those in the audience that night, many of whom had seen him perform on that very stage. Indeed, the idea might even have been shocking to Booth himself in the early years of the CIVIL WAR. A Marylander, Booth was pro-Southern from the outset, describing SLAVERY as "a blessing." In the early years of the war, however, he was not especially devoted in his commitment to the Confederacy. In deference to his mother's wishes, he did not enlist in the army, and his actions on behalf of the cause were largely limited to occasional smuggling of medical supplies from the North to the South.

Over time, Booth's militancy grew, as did his desire to do something dramatic to help the sagging fortunes of the Confederacy. Finally, in the summer of 1864, Booth came up with a plan. During the summer months, WASHINGTON, D.C., was hot, humid, and filled with mosquitoes. To escape the miserable climate, President Lincoln was in the habit of spending his nights at the Soldiers' Home on the outskirts of the city. Booth hoped to capture Lincoln during one of these trips and take him hostage. In addition to creating chaos in the North, Booth's hope was that he could exchange Lincoln for Confederate prisoners of war, who were no longer being exchanged for Union prisoners as a result of an April 1864 order by Gen. ULYSSES S. GRANT.

Booth knew he needed accomplices, so he recruited two childhood friends, Samuel Arnold and Michael O'Laughlin. They readily agreed, and Booth began his scheming in earnest. He also began to scout out escape routes through southern Maryland. In December 1864 he met John Surratt, who would prove to be a valuable ally. Surratt, like Booth, was engaged in smuggling on behalf of the Confederacy, and he was intimately familiar with the terrain between Washington, D.C., and Virginia. He was also in contact with a network of pro-Southern sympathizers, including David E. Herold and George Atzerodt, both of whom quickly agreed to join the conspiracy. The number of participants grew to seven in March 1865, when Booth enlisted escaped prisoner of war Lewis Powell, who preferred to use the alias Lewis Paine. Booth even went so far as to arrange to have his $15,000 theatrical wardrobe transported to the South, making the assumption that he would resume his acting career after the kidnapping.

After more than six months of effort, Booth had made all the necessary arrangements for the kidnapping plot, and he had all the men he needed. By this time, however, summer was long over, and the president no longer traveled back and forth to the Soldiers' Home. Other attempts to catch the president while he was vulnerable came to nothing. And so, toward the end of March 1865, Booth gathered his coconspirators and proposed a new plan, wherein the president would be kidnapped while watching a play at Ford's Theatre in Washington. The idea was not well-received because the odds of all seven men escaping successfully were very low. Booth was unwilling to budge, and Samuel Arnold, Michael O'Laughlin, and John Surratt left the group.

Without enough men to pull off a kidnapping, Booth began to get desperate. On April 3, 1865, the Confederate government fled RICHMOND, which meant that there was nowhere to hold Lincoln hostage even if he were kidnapped. On April 9, the Army of Northern Virginia surrendered, and Booth knew that time was quickly running out for him to put a stop to Lincoln's "lawless tyranny." On the morning of April 14 he heard that the president would be at the THEATER that evening. Booth concluded that this was his last chance and that, since he lacked the resources for a kidnapping, he would have to resort to murder.

Booth still had three coconspirators left, and he found roles for them to play on the evening of April 14, although he did not tell them until 8:00 P.M. that evening, two hours before they were supposed to carry out their assignments. Atzerodt was instructed to kill Vice President ANDREW JOHNSON, while Paine was supposed to take the life of Secretary of State WILLIAM H. SEWARD. Herold, meanwhile, was responsible for helping the mentally retarded Paine find his way out of Washington. In the end, neither Paine nor Atzerodt was successful. Paine inflicted several serious stab wounds on Seward but failed to kill him, while Atzerodt lost his nerve and never made an attempt to kill Johnson.

After giving Atzerodt, Paine, and Herold their assignments, Booth headed over to Ford's Theatre. He had no difficulty gaining access to the president's box, aided by his celebrity as an actor as well as lax security. Though Lincoln had received many threats on his life, there were few precautions taken to ensure his safety. In part, this was because an earlier attempt to protect the president's life—by sneaking him into Washington before his inauguration—had caused a great deal of political embarrassment. And in part it was because Lincoln felt that such protection was impractical.

Lincoln did have a personal bodyguard, Ward Hill Lamon, but at Lincoln's request Lamon traveled to Rich-

Engraving showing the assassination of Abraham Lincoln by John Wilkes Booth at Ford's Theatre *(Hulton/Archive)*

mond on the night of April 14. MARY TODD LINCOLN selected a temporary replacement from the ranks of the Washington, D.C., police department, John H. Parker. Parker had a poor record and had a reputation for laziness. Shortly after the play started, he abandoned his post to watch the performance. Booth proceeded without challenge to the president's box.

Observing Lincoln through a hole he had drilled in the door of the president's box earlier in the day, Booth waited for the big laugh coming at the beginning of the third act that would cover the sound of the gunshot. When the moment came, Booth entered the box and shot Lincoln in the back of the head with a single-shot Derringer pistol. He scuffled briefly with Maj. Henry Reed Rathbone, who had joined the president's party at the last minute when General and Mrs. Grant had decided not to attend the play. Booth then leapt the 12 feet to the stage, breaking his leg in the process, and made his exit.

After being shot, Lincoln was carried across the street to the Peterson house. Dr. Charles Leale, who had been in attendance at the play, attended Lincoln initially and was eventually joined by several other surgeons, including Lin-

coln's personal physician. They all realized there was nothing that could be done. The president faded quickly and died early on the morning of April 15 without regaining consciousness. "Now he belongs to the ages," said Secretary of War EDWIN M. STANTON.

Booth fled Washington, trying to work his way South, where he felt he would be hailed as a hero. He was badly mistaken. Slowed by his broken leg, Booth was eventually trapped in a Maryland farmhouse. After refusing to surrender, he was shot and killed, never to answer for his crime. A military tribunal tried eight of Booth's alleged coconspirators. The hastily conducted trial resulted in death sentences for Herold, Paine, Atzerodt, and Mary Surratt. Four others were sentenced to prison terms. Many people thought the assassination a Confederate plot, funded and supported by JEFFERSON DAVIS's administration. In the years after the trial, some have argued this point of view, with others suggesting that there was a conspiracy within the Union itself. However, no compelling evidence exists linking any person or group to the assassination besides Booth and his three accomplices.

After Lincoln's death, the work of reconstructing the shattered nation was left to Vice President Andrew Johnson, who was sworn in as president by Chief Justice SALMON P. CHASE several hours after the assassination. Johnson proved to be ill-equipped for the task that Lincoln left behind. His mishandling of the situation led to his impeachment and allowed the RADICAL REPUBLICANS to gain control of RECONSTRUCTION policy. The result was a difficult time in the political life of the nation that might have unfolded in a very different fashion if Lincoln had lived.

Further reading: Timothy Good, *We Saw Lincoln Shot: One Hundred Eyewitness Accounts* (Jackson: University Press of Mississippi, 1995); Edward Steers Jr., *Blood on the Moon: John Wilkes Booth, Samuel A. Mudd and the Assassination of Abraham Lincoln* (Lexington: University Press of Kentucky, 2001); James L. Swanson and Daniel R. Weinberg, *Lincoln's Assassins: Their Trial and Execution* (Santa Fe, N.Mex.: Arena Editions, 2001).

—Christopher Bates

Atlanta campaign (May–September 1864)

During the spring and summer of 1864, Union forces under the command of WILLIAM T. SHERMAN battled to take control of Atlanta, Georgia. On September 2, 1864, the mayor of Atlanta surrendered the city to the Union general. "Atlanta is ours, and fairly won," exulted Sherman in a TELEGRAPH to his commander in chief. Sherman's triumph secured the election of 1864 for Lincoln and the REPUBLICAN PARTY.

Plans for the capture of Atlanta, the Confederacy's largest railroad hub, as well as the destruction of JOSEPH E. JOHNSTON's Army of Tennessee, were first formulated in February and March 1864. ULYSSES S. GRANT hoped that the Atlanta campaign, in tandem with Union offensives in Virginia, would ultimately destroy the Confederacy. In Atlanta, the Union planned to tear up Southern railroad lines and cut off all supplies to Confederate troops. Grant left the specifics of each campaign up to the commander assigned to it.

In April, Sherman revealed his plan. He proposed to push Johnston and his soldiers back to Atlanta, cut off all railroad lines, and then force a Confederate retreat and surrender of the city. To achieve these goals, Sherman had by May 1864 assembled a "grand army" of 110,000 men composed of infantry, cavalry, and artillerymen from the Union's Army of the Cumberland, Army of Tennessee, and Army of the Ohio. Sherman held another 93,500 soldiers ready for duty at Union posts in Tennessee, Kentucky, Alabama, and Mississippi. Sherman's "grand army" would outnumber Johnston's nearly two to one. Confident in his numerical advantage, Sherman assured Grant of his army's ability to defeat the Southern troops.

The fight for Atlanta, which would be contested across much of northern Georgia, got underway near Dalton on May 5, when Union skirmishers engaged Confederate pickets. Although some Southern troops successfully held their positions, others had trouble. Johnston's use of reinforcements ultimately forced the enemy to withdraw temporarily, but the Union troops were not to be deterred. By May 9, Northern forces threatened Johnston from two sides—Resaca and Dalton. Johnston took his forces south to Resaca on May 12 to meet the enemy.

From May 13 to May 15, the two sides engaged each other in the Battle of Resaca. Neither side gained an advantage during the first day of fighting, but on the second day, the Confederates managed to drive the enemy back. However, after hearing reports of Union successes in gaining position, Johnston scrapped his plan of a morning attack on May 15 and instead evacuated his forces to Calhoun and then Adairsville. Casualties at Resaca numbered 5,100 Confederates and 6,500 Federals.

After his retreat, Johnston planned to ambush Sherman's forces on the Cassville road. He positioned his forces by early morning May 19, but after Union forces flanked JOHN BELL HOOD's corps, the entire army was forced to retreat and wait for a Union attack. When Johnston's commanders disagreed over the army's position, the Army of Tennessee evacuated on May 20 to Allatoona, near the Etowah River. Union and Confederate armies met again on May 24 at the Battle of New Hope Church near Allatoona and, on May 28, the Battle of Dallas. The Confederates' strong defensive position allowed them to drive back five Union attacks and stop Union advances.

By June 4, Johnston and his troops held a strong position in the hills between the Etowah River and Atlanta. They ultimately withdrew about two miles to Kennesaw Mountain, from where they could survey the surrounding countryside and protect themselves from the enemy. Sherman, not deterred by the strength of the Confederate position, launched a full-scale attack on the Confederate lines on June 27. The resulting Battle of Kennesaw Mountain ended in 3,000 Federal and 552 Confederate casualties.

Sherman continued to force Confederate retreats throughout July—to Smyrna on July 3, the Chattahoochee River on July 6, and south of the river on July 9. The retreats would ultimately lead to the dismissal of Johnston as a commander. Throughout the campaign, Confederate president JEFFERSON DAVIS and military advisor BRAXTON BRAGG had expressed their lack of confidence in Johnston. In mid-July, frustrated with Confederate retreats and fearful that Atlanta would fall, Davis removed Johnston from

Ruins of a train depot, blown up on Sherman's departure from Atlanta, Georgia *(Library of Congress)*

his post, giving John Bell Hood command of the Army of Tennessee on July 18.

Hood pursued an aggressive strategy. On July 20, Southern troops launched an unsuccessful attack on Sherman at Peachtree Creek. The unorganized Confederates suffered a high number of casualties during the offensive. Hood launched a second assault, the Battle of Atlanta, on July 22. Again, Southern forces suffered defeat at the hands of their enemies. Hood led yet another unsuccessful attack on the Union troops at the Battle of Ezra Church on July 28. In his short tenure as commander, Hood had lost 17,500 men. He saw no option but retreat into Atlanta, where he and his troops waited for Sherman's next move.

Union troops laid siege to Atlanta, continually bombarding the city for the next 40 days. The danger scared the city's inhabitants, many of whom fled. The siege also ended municipal government in Atlanta, with the mayor Thomas Calhoun and the city council meeting for the last time on July 18.

Sherman moved his troops to the south side of Atlanta at the end of August, hoping to cut the last rail line and then lure Confederate troops out of the city. Once Sherman and his men had taken their positions, they ceased firing and waited for the Confederate response. Hood ordered an attack at Jonesboro on August 31, but again Union forces easily defeated the Southern offensive. This was Hood's fourth and last attempt to protect and hold Atlanta. The series of defeats had resulted in a loss of 25 percent of Hood's army. The commander evacuated his troops from Atlanta on September 1, 1864.

As they evacuated, Southern troops destroyed any ammunition and military stores that they could not take with them. The next morning, Atlanta's mayor and a group of citizens officially surrendered the city to Sherman. By noon, Sherman and his troops occupied and controlled the city. The Union occupied Atlanta until November 15, 1864, when they torched the city before embarking on SHERMAN'S MARCH THROUGH GEORGIA.

See also REFUGEES.

Further reading: Lee B. Kennett, *Marching through Georgia* (New York: HarperCollins, 1995); James L. McDonough and James Pickett Jones, *"War So Terrible": Sherman and Atlanta* (New York: Norton, 1987); R. McMurry, *Atlanta 1864: Last Chance for the Confederacy* (Lincoln: University of Nebraska Press, 2000).

—Lisa Tendrich Frank

B

Balloon Corps

Lighter-than-air balloons were first developed in France in the 1780s by brothers Joseph and Jacques de Montgolfier. Not long thereafter, French officials started using balloons on a limited basis for military purposes. Despite this precedent, as well as the obvious value of being able to see enemy positions from above, American military leaders were hesitant to use the technology in the years before the CIVIL WAR. In part, this was due to the unpredictability of balloons, whose flight could be difficult to control once they were in the air. The reluctance to use balloons also stemmed from a general unwillingness to try new and different approaches to warfare. Opposition to ballooning finally began to break down during the Civil War, when leaders on both sides experimented with the technology.

Over the course of the 1840s and 1850s, a number of Americans made names for themselves as balloon pilots, or aeronauts. These included John Wise, James Allen, John LaMountain, and Professor Thaddeus Lowe. When the Civil War broke out, several of these men made their way to WASHINGTON, D.C., to suggest the use of balloons to military and political officials. Lowe had the best political connections, and after staging several balloon demonstrations he was able to arrange a meeting with President ABRAHAM LINCOLN on June 11, 1861. Lincoln was impressed with what he heard and was even more impressed a week later, when Lowe sent him a telegram from a balloon using a wire that stretched from the ground into the air. Lowe continued to stage demonstrations, during which he took a number of important military leaders up into the air, including Irwin McDowell, Fitz-John Porter, and GEORGE B. MCCLELLAN. Finally, on August 2, 1861, Lincoln summoned Lowe for a meeting with Union general in chief Winfield Scott, and he was hired to build and pilot balloons for the U.S. military.

Lowe immediately got to work, determined to prove how valuable he and his balloons could be. On September 24, 1861, he used a TELEGRAPH line and signal flags to direct Union artillery fire at Confederate positions around Falls Church. Emboldened by his success, Lowe went to McClellan, commander of the Army of the Potomac. Lowe suggested that an official Balloon Corps be formed, and McClellan agreed. The general named Lowe as chief aeronaut of the Army of the Potomac and instructed him to recruit more pilots and to build six balloons and the 12 generators needed to fill the balloons with hydrogen. A total of 10 men served at one time or another as pilots in the United States Balloon Corps.

Lowe's corps had a number of successes in 1862. He and his staff modified a coal barge, the *George Washington Parke Custis,* so that it could transport balloons and fuel them with hydrogen. The *George Washington Parke Custis* thus became the world's first aircraft carrier. The U.S. Balloon Corps also conducted hundreds of flights that provided valuable intelligence during McClellan's PENINSULAR CAMPAIGN. For example, one of McClellan's adjutants wrote that "it may safely be claimed that the UNION ARMY was saved from destruction at the Battle of Fair Oaks . . . by the frequent and accurate reports of Professor Lowe."

The removal of George B. McClellan from command after the BATTLE OF ANTIETAM began the downfall of Lowe and his corps. McClellan's successor, Gen. JOSEPH HOOKER, insisted on exercising a great deal of oversight over Lowe's operations. The egotistical Lowe was used to operating with virtual autonomy, and his pride was hurt. After several months of bickering, he resigned in May 1862, and the Balloon Corps was dissolved. The generals that followed Hooker saw little value in the technology and did not pursue it. Lowe continued to give demonstrations for naval leaders as late as 1864, but they were also uninterested.

The Confederacy also experimented with balloons, although on a more limited basis. Union soldiers reported sighting a Confederate balloon as early as June 14, 1861. Although these reports were never verified, Confederates certainly had balloons in use during the Peninsular campaign of 1862. EDWARD P. ALEXANDER, who would eventually become commander of artillery in the Army of Northern Virginia, was the Confederacy's most successful aeronaut. In particular, he helped coordinate troop movements from a balloon during the Seven Days' Battle.

Although they never formally organized a ballooning unit, the Confederates continued to use balloons through the rest of the year, particularly in connection with the defense of Charleston. As was the case with the Union, however, Confederate experiments in ballooning largely ended after 1862. The Confederacy lacked the resources to make balloons or to construct the hydrogen generators necessary to fill them. Beyond that, the Confederacy had less use for the intelligence provided by balloons because their superior cavalry was generally able to accurately and quickly discern troop locations and strength.

Ultimately, the Civil War represented a small step toward the era of large-scale aerial warfare. A precedent had been set, and balloons would play a much larger role in the United States's next major conflict, the Spanish-American War of 1898. By the time of World War I, planes would begin to replace balloons, and war in the air would become as important as war on land or at sea.

See also TACTICS AND STRATEGY.

Further reading: Frederick Stansbury Haydon, *Aeronautics in the Union and Confederate Armies* (Baltimore: Johns Hopkins University Press, 2000); Charles Ross, *Trial By Fire: Science, Technology and the Civil War* (Shippensburg, Pa.: White Mane Books, 2000).

—Christopher Bates

Baltimore, Maryland, riots (April 19, 1861)

The Baltimore riots of April 19, 1861, saw some of the first casualties of the CIVIL WAR. For several days after the riots, Northerners worried that Maryland had joined the Confederacy.

Maryland was part of the upper South, a tier of states extending from Delaware to Missouri. The SECESSION issue deeply divided these states, for while they permitted SLAVERY, all had deep commercial links to the North. In addition, all had fewer slaves than their Confederate sisters, and in some ways their societies reflected Northern values. For the Union, Maryland's strategic significance was enormous: If the state seceded, the Confederacy would surround the Union capital of WASHINGTON, D.C.

Any Northern troops bound for Washington, D.C., had to pass through Baltimore. On April 19, 1861, the Sixth Massachusetts Infantry arrived, the first Northern unit to enter the city. Because no direct rail line ran all the way through Baltimore, the soldiers disembarked at the President Street Station and prepared to make their way across town to the Calvert Street Station. To avoid confrontation, troops did not march but instead remained in railway cars, pulled by horses down a connecting line between the two stations.

Fearing that the UNION ARMY would occupy Maryland before the state could even consider joining the Confederacy, angry secessionists attacked the rail cars, injuring a few soldiers. Members of the Sixth Massachusetts opened fire. At the end of the day, four soldiers and 12 civilians had been killed. Soon after, Confederate sympathizers began destroying bridges and TELEGRAPH lines linking Washington to the rest of the country.

Following behind the Sixth Massachusetts with the Eighth Massachusetts, Gen. BENJAMIN F. BUTLER learned of the riots and found an alternative route through Annapolis, reaching Washington on April 25, to ABRAHAM LINCOLN's profound relief. Butler then turned back into Maryland, restored the state's rail lines, and occupied Baltimore.

On May 8, continuing concern over Baltimore's loyalties prompted a declaration of martial law. Over the next several months, the Union army arrested Baltimore's mayor, police marshal, and a number of other leading citizens for their alleged role in the riot or support of secession. In a controversial decision, Lincoln suspended the right of HABEAS CORPUS in these cases. With the leading supporters of secession imprisoned and the Union army in control of the state, Unionists won Maryland's November 1861 election, effectively ensuring Maryland's political loyalty.

See also PEACE MOVEMENT.

Further reading: William Brown, *Baltimore and The Nineteenth of April, 1861* (Baltimore: City of Baltimore, 1887); Mark E. Neely, Jr., *The Fate of Liberty* (New York: Oxford University Press, 1991).

—Tom Laichas

banking and currency

In the years before the CIVIL WAR, the relationship between banks and currency was generally quite simple. The federal government, some state governments, and many private banks issued currency that was backed by either silver or gold held in the vaults of the issuing institution. The currency could be redeemed for the metal that backed it; for example, a $20 note issued by the federal government could be taken to a government depository and exchanged for $20 worth of gold. During the Civil War, the demands of a wartime ECONOMY necessitated the creation of a more complex financial system than the one the nation had known in the antebellum era, with profound effects in both the North and the South.

At the outset of the war, the Confederacy enjoyed one important economic advantage over the Union. Despite its vastly larger economy, the North had a fairly primitive banking system. Northern banks were largely independent of one another, and coordinated action between them was generally difficult. Even simple tasks, such as the transfer of funds, could only be accomplished through a labyrinthine system of informal agreements and personal alliances. The Southern banking system, on the other hand, was structured in a fashion that was decidedly more modern. Most Southern banks had a central office chartered by the government of the state in which it was located. This central office, in turn, was empowered to establish branches in the various townships of the state. Branch banking is a much more efficient way to move money around as it is needed and to transmit information about local financial conditions.

Whatever advantages could be derived from the South's strong banking system, however, were soon outweighed by the weakness of Confederate currency. There are two things upon which a currency is generally based. The first is precious metals such as gold and silver, also known as specie. Specie provided the basis for the vast majority of currency in the antebellum era. The second is the backing of a stable and responsible government. Money of this sort is called fiat currency and is the basis of most modern economies. The South began the war with very little specie in its possession. As such, Confederate treasury Secretary Christopher Memminger had no choice but to utilize fiat currency, with the promise that notes printed by the government would be redeemable in specie two years after the war ended. This arrangement would prove to be disastrous for the financial system of the South.

To start, the South had great difficulty printing the currency it required. Skilled engravers were needed to make the plates to print paper money, and the entire South had only three men who were qualified. The special paper that was needed was also in short supply. The Confederates had even more problems making coins. The government had seized several U.S. mints, but it lacked the materials or expertise to use the equipment. A die for a 50-cent coin was struck, but it broke after only four coins had been minted. No further attempts were made, and so the Confederacy had no coins in circulation during the war.

Once the Confederate government had finally managed to print some paper money, it ran into the much greater problem of keeping its "bluebacks" stable. The government had difficulty raising enough money through taxes and bond issues, so it was compelled to print increasing quantities of fiat currency. State and local governments were forced to do the same. With far too much money in circulation, inflation became rampant. The situation was made worse by the fact that Confederate currency was not

Confederate currency *(Private collection)*

designated by the Congress as legal tender. What this meant was that people and businesses were not required by law to accept Confederate money as payment for goods and services. In part, the withholding of legal status for Confederate currency reflected Southern distrust of a strong central government. In addition, it was meant to inspire confidence in Confederate currency by making a statement that Confederate money was so strong that people would not have to be forced to accept it. In the end, however, the plan backfired. Southerners declined Confederate currency whenever possible, since they were legally able to do so, preferring to utilize specie or barter or even Union currency for their transactions. This tendency contributed to the rapid devaluation of Confederate money. At the end of 1861, the Confederate dollar was worth approximately 80 cents worth of gold. By 1865 a Confederate dollar had fallen to about 1.5 cents worth of gold.

The banking system might have been able to mitigate some of these difficulties, but the Confederate government demanded too much of the banks. In April 1861, the Congress passed a law requiring banks to purchase government bonds in amounts proportional to the banks' resources. This compulsory loan drained the banks of their specie and the currency they had printed, both of which were vastly more stable than the bonds they were receiving in return. Over the next several years, the government made the situation worse through excessive TAXATION on banks, additional forced loans, and its inability to control inflation. The ongoing war also took its toll. Slaves and land comprised a large portion of Southern banks' assets, and as Union armies conquered territory and freed slaves, these assets were lost. The banks also suffered from manpower shortages, as men were compelled to leave their jobs to take up arms. In the face of all these difficulties, the South's banking system had essentially collapsed by the end of the war.

On the Union side, the situation was far less bleak. Despite the North's poorly organized banking system, the strong Northern economy and an abundance of specie kept the economy fairly stable for nearly two years, allowing the government to finance the war effort with relative ease. Eventually, the mounting costs of the war required action on the part of the Union government, and between 1862 and 1864 a series of banking and currency acts were passed by the Congress. In 1862 the Legal Tender Act provided for the printing of $150 million in fiat currency and specified that these GREENBACKS, as they came to be called, would be legal tender for all transactions except the payment of interest on bonds. In 1863 the National Banking Act was passed, which allowed for the charter of national banks that could print currency backed by government bonds. This system, devised largely by Secretary of the Treasury SALMON P. CHASE, had several benefits. First, it greatly strengthened the bonds issued by the U.S. government by creating demand for them. National banks would be required to purchase the bonds, and other investors would be attracted by the payments of interest in specie. Strong bonds made it much easier for the government to raise money to finance the war.

Chase's system also helped stabilize the fiat currency that the government had begun printing in 1862. In part, this was because the currency was now backed by strong bonds issued by a stable government. The Union also benefited by learning from the mistakes of the Confederacy. In choosing to make greenbacks legal tender, the Union government compelled its citizens to utilize its paper money. In 1864 the Congress passed an act establishing a 10 percent tax for currency printed by state banks. This effectively took state banks out of the money-printing business, thus allowing the federal government to maintain tight control of the amount of money in circulation. By giving its currency a strong backing, requiring the use of greenbacks as a medium of exchange, and keeping a lid on the amount of dollars in print, the Union essentially managed to avoid the inflation that crippled the Confederacy. Over the course of the war, inflation was only about 80 percent in the Union, compared with 9,000 percent in the Confederacy.

The changes in America's financial systems during the Civil War had a variety of implications in the postwar era. Although the North emerged from the war with a robust economy, the nation's financial systems ultimately took a step backward in the years after the war ended. The Union and Confederacy had utilized some of the hallmarks of modern finance, such as fiat currency and branch banks, but after the war these were largely abandoned by Northern bankers and government authorities. Instead, the North was left with a banking system that was not well suited to the conservative economic climate of the postbellum years nor to the rapid expansion of the industrial era.

The negative impact of the Civil War on banks and finance was felt even more keenly in the South. Many Southerners lost most or all of their money when the FOUR-

TEENTH AMENDMENT forbade repayment of bonds issued by the Confederate government. Even more devastating was the situation created by the near total absence of banks in the South. Without the credit offered by banks, poor white people and freedmen had virtually no hope of acquiring the land and materials necessary to be independent farmers. Many of the South's poorest citizens, especially the freedmen, were forced into informal borrowing or into SHARECROPPING. The borrower in these situations had few legal protections in terms of how much interest could be charged or how disputes could be resolved. The end result was the creation of a class of permanently indebted citizens. Undoubtedly, the failures of RECONSTRUCTION can be traced in part to the disastrous state of the financial system of the South after the Civil War.

See also FREEDMAN'S SAVING BANK.

Further reading: Douglas D. Ball, *Financial Failure and Confederate Defeat* (Urbana: University of Illinois Press, 1991); Milton Friedman and Anna Jacobson Schwartz, *Monetary History of the United States, 1867–1960* (Princeton, N.J.: Princeton University Press, 1971); Larry Schweikart, ed., *Banking and Finance to 1913: Encyclopedia of American Business History and Biography* (New York: Facts On File, 1990).

—Christopher Bates

Barton, Clara (1821–1912)

CIVIL WAR nurse Clara Barton was the founder of the American Association of the Red Cross and served as its president for 23 years. She was born on Christmas Day in 1821 and spent her youth in North Oxford, Massachusetts. A shy but determined child, she was educated informally at home by her older sisters and brothers and attended local schools. In turn, she taught in neighboring schools when she was 18. After a year of advanced study at the Liberal Institute of Clinton, New York, Barton returned to teaching. She successfully founded the first public school in Bordentown, New Jersey, in 1852. Moving to WASHINGTON, D.C., she was appointed a clerk in the United States Patent Office by a Republican senator. When the administration changed hands in 1857 with a Democratic victory, she lost her post and returned to her hometown.

The needs of soldiers during the Civil War engaged Barton, launching a new direction in her life's work. Her outstanding contribution to the war effort was to gather supplies and provisions for the soldiers, who were in short supply of bandages, medicine, and food. Witnessing the absence of any medical facilities at the FIRST BATTLE OF BULL RUN, she took it upon herself to advertise for supplies in a Massachusetts newspaper and gather the provisions. In 1862 she and a few friends began to distribute the supplies to military hospitals and to the men at the battlefront. Traveling by mule team, they traversed Virginia and Maryland, heading to the battlefields. Barton was amazingly resourceful at giving aid during and immediately after a battle. She provided candles for a doctor treating wounded soldiers at night, for example, and prepared soup and coffee for thousands of men in the midst of the fighting. Barton became less active at the battlefront as the war progressed and the Union established commissions to provide for and nurse the sick.

After the war Barton undertook the daunting task of tracing the identity of the war dead. With President ABRAHAM LINCOLN's approval, she established an office where she and a few assistants published the names of the missing in newspapers, soliciting information from returned soldiers and ex-prisoners of war. She organized the information she received and wrote to the soldiers' families. In addition, with the help of an ex-prisoner, she identified those who died in the infamous ANDERSONVILLE PRISON in Georgia and marked their graves. Between identifying the missing and lecturing around the country about her war experiences, she suffered a nervous collapse and retreated to Europe in 1869.

It was in Switzerland that Barton found a new way to broaden her mission of providing for people in need. At the Geneva Convention, organized to bring humane assistance to war zones throughout the world, the International Committee of the Red Cross was established as a neutral body offering aid to wounded soldiers and medical personnel. Belligerent countries were to yield to the emblem of a red cross on a white background. Barton worked for the International Red Cross during the Franco-Prussian War of 1870–71.

Back in the United States, after convalescing from another breakdown, Barton campaigned tirelessly for the United States to ratify the Geneva Treaty. Finally, in 1882, Barton's campaign succeeded. President Arthur signed the Geneva Treaty. Two weeks later the Senate ratified it.

At the same time, Barton had launched a crusade for the establishment of an American Red Cross. She educated the public about the Red Cross through lectures and a pamphlet she wrote. Barton's conception of an American Red Cross included offering relief in times of natural disasters such as floods, railway accidents, and droughts as well as in battle. In 1881 Barton and prominent associates organized the American Association of the Red Cross. Barton was chosen president, a post she held, with just one short interruption, until 1904. During her tenure the organization provided relief in 21 disasters, including a heavy flood in Johnstown, Pennsylvania, the Russian famine of 1892, and a yellow fever epidemic in Florida.

Barton had specific ideas about the way the American Red Cross should be run. She opposed government subsidies, preferring to appeal to the public in time of crisis. Keeping a tight rein on the organization, she alone judged when the need for relief was genuine. She managed all the finances and went into the field to do the work of relief herself. At the age of 77 she traveled by mule cart in Cuba to provide aid during the Spanish-American War. Barton also broadened the focus of relief to encompass rehabilitation. Assistance included material for building houses and agricultural tools where needed. In the Galveston hurricane disaster, for example, the Red Cross provided strawberry plants to enable farmers to resume AGRICULTURE.

Barton's rigid control of the management of the Red Cross provoked some criticism. One problem was that the relationship between the national Red Cross and local auxiliaries was undefined. Critics felt that Barton should be in the national office administering the organization, not in the field. Further, Barton could not delegate authority. She took offense at anyone questioning her handling of finances. Although Barton had provided an unswerving commitment to the Red Cross, her management was becoming outmoded in the new era at the turn of the century. In 1900 Congress provided a federal charter to bring about reorganization. Under pressure, Barton reluctantly resigned in 1904.

Clara Barton *(National Archives)*

In her final years she pursued various interests and supported the women's rights movement. She died at 91 in her home near Washington, D.C., on April 12, 1912.

See also MEDICINE AND HOSPITALS; WOMEN'S STATUS AND RIGHTS.

Further reading: Stephen Oates, *A Woman of Valor: Clara Barton and the Civil War* (New York: Free Press, 1994); Ishbel Ross, *Angel of the Battlefield: The Life of Clara Barton* (New York: Harper, 1956).

—Jaclyn Greenberg

battle flags

During the CIVIL WAR, battle flags were symbols of bravery, pride, and patriotism. They were also practical markers, identifying the location of battle units during military engagements. The size, shape, and colors of each regimental flag varied greatly and depended on whether the soldiers were part of an infantry, cavalry, or artillery regiment.

In the North, Union regulations required that infantry regiments carry at least two flags. The first was the national flag. Better known as the "Stars and Stripes" of 1861, this flag contained the stars of 34 states. Regiments were also required to carry a flag bearing the arms of the United States and the name of the specific regiment. This flag was blue with the national eagle emblazoned in the center. Additionally, many regiments carried "colors" that identified their state and listed the battles in which they had fought.

Union cavalry regiments were issued a blue flag with the national coat of arms and, just below, a scroll painted with the regimental name and number. Artillery units in the North carried both national and regimental colors. The flags of the artillery, however, were yellow with a crossed cannon in the center.

Shortly after the first seven Southern states seceded, the Confederate states adopted an official flag, better known as the "Stars and Bars." This flag contained three horizontal stripes—red, white, red—with a blue section in the upper left with seven white stars. Because it was hard to distinguish the Stars and Bars from the Stars and Stripes during battle, the flag was replaced in May 1863 by the "stainless banner," a rectangular white flag with a red section displaying a white-bordered blue cross studded with 13 white stars.

The Confederate armies also carried what became known as the "Southern Cross," or the Southern battle flag. This was a square flag that consisted of a red field with a blue cross, bordered in white, with the necessary number of stars aligned on the bars of the cross. The only difference between the flags of the infantry, artillery, and cavalry units

Flag of the Confederate 11th Tennessee Regiment *(Hulton/Archive)*

was size; infantry regiments carried a larger flag than artillery batteries and cavalry units. The Southern battle flag is the one most commonly identified with the Confederacy.

For both the North and South, a color bearer carried the flag into battle. The battle flag created a focal point for the regiment to rally around and to use as a guide in the midst of the fighting. However, they also provided the enemy with a large, visible target. As a result, the mortality rate of color bearers was very high. The fact that a large number of men were willing to step forward and bear the colors demonstrates how each flag not only represented a particular state and region, but also the pride of its unit's soldiers.

Further reading: Devereaux D. Cannon, *The Flags of the Confederacy: An Illustrated History* (Memphis, Tenn.: St. Lukes Press, 1988); C. McKeever, *Civil War Battle Flags of the Union Army and Order of Battle* (New York: Knickerbocker Press, 1997).

—Fiona Galvin

Beauregard, Pierre Gustave Toutant (1818–1893)

The controversial Confederate general P. G. T. Beauregard was born in Louisiana on May 28, 1818, to parents of French descent. Beauregard commanded Confederate armies at many important battles in both the eastern and western theaters of war. He also designed the famous Confederate BATTLE FLAG.

At age 16, Beauregard entered the UNITED STATES MILITARY ACADEMY AT WEST POINT. Four years later, he graduated second in his class. Early in his career, Beauregard distinguished himself both in building coastal fortifications along the Gulf Coast and by his service in the Mexican-American War (1846–48). In 1861, Beauregard returned to West Point to serve as superintendent. His term lasted only five days, however, because President ABRAHAM LINCOLN fired him for his secessionist sympathies.

Upon the SECESSION of Louisiana in January 1861, Beauregard resigned from the Federal army. Soon after this, JEFFERSON DAVIS awarded him a commission as a brigadier general in the CONFEDERATE ARMY. Beauregard assumed command of the forces facing down the Union garrison at FORT SUMTER. The surrender of the Union garrison on April 15, 1861, made Beauregard a hero throughout the Confederacy.

Beauregard commanded the Confederate forces in their early victory at the FIRST BATTLE OF BULL RUN. As the Confederate army chased the UNION ARMY from the field, Beauregard argued unsuccessfully that the Confederates should pursue the enemy all the way back to WASHINGTON, D.C. Beauregard lost his popularity when he chastised President Davis in public for not endorsing his plan.

In 1862, Beauregard became second in command of the Army of the West under Gen. ALBERT SIDNEY JOHNSTON. After Johnston's death during the first day of fighting at the BATTLE OF SHILOH, Beauregard took command of the army and nearly secured a victory. After the battle, Beauregard turned command of the western army over to BRAXTON BRAGG and returned to Charleston in hopes of recovering from chronic throat pain. Soon after, Jefferson Davis entrusted Beauregard with the defense of Charleston. Thanks to his able preparations, Beauregard and his men were able to repulse a massive Union siege launched against the city in 1863. In the last year of the CIVIL WAR, Beauregard worked under the direction of Gen. ROBERT E. LEE to protect RICHMOND, the Confederate capital, from invasion.

Immediately after the Civil War, Beauregard became superintendent of the New Orleans, Jackson, and Great Northern Railroad. From 1879 to 1888, he commanded the Louisiana state militia, after which he served as commissioner of public works in New Orleans. In his later years, Beauregard engaged in frequent and bitter disputes about the Civil War, especially with JOSEPH E. JOHNSTON and Jefferson Davis. He died in New Orleans on February 20, 1893.

Further reading: Alfred Roman, *The Military Operations of General Beauregard* (New York: Da Capo Press, l994); Harry T. Williams, *P. G. T. Beauregard: Napoleon in Gray* (Baton Rouge: Louisiana State University Press, 1995).

—Chad Vanderford

Benjamin, Judah P. (1811–1884)

Born in St. Croix in the West Indies in 1811, Judah Philip Benjamin became a prominent New Orleans attorney, the only Jewish cabinet member in the Confederate government, and a distinguished member of the British bar. Benjamin's parents were Philip Benjamin, a small-scale merchant, and Rebecca de Mendes. Leaving St. Croix while Judah was very young, the Benjamins relocated to Charleston, South Carolina. Benjamin grew up there before going to Connecticut to attend Yale University in 1825. After two years, Benjamin left Yale and relocated to New Orleans, where he held various positions to support his study of law. Admitted to the bar in 1833, Benjamin married Marie St. Martin, a Catholic. Judah and Marie had one daughter, but their marriage was not a success. Marie moved to Paris in 1845, and Benjamin saw her rarely thereafter.

While a New Orleans attorney, Benjamin argued two Supreme Court cases, and copublished a learned legal treatise. Benjamin was fairly successful in New Orleans, but he never earned enough money to enable him to live as a rich man. Instead, the law provided him an opportunity to enter into politics. First winning a state representative seat in 1842, Benjamin went on to be elected to the U.S. Senate in 1852 and reelected in 1859. Initially a Whig, Benjamin became a Democrat in the 1850s.

When Louisiana seceded from the Union, Benjamin resigned his Senate seat and returned to the South. Although his relationship with JEFFERSON DAVIS had not been cordial in WASHINGTON, D.C., the new president of the Confederacy asked Benjamin to assume the attorney generalship of the Confederacy. Over time, Benjamin and Davis built a strong working and personal relationship, overcoming their previous differences. As attorney general, Benjamin founded the Confederate Justice Department, which was responsible for a variety of legal affairs.

When the secretary of war resigned in 1861, Benjamin's efficiency as attorney general led Davis to appoint Benjamin to the vacant post. He ultimately proved to be unsuited to the job. He clashed with Confederate generals, who disdained his lack of military experience. The greatest failure of his tenure was the loss of Roanoke Island in early 1862, for which he was widely blamed. With Benjamin's popularity plummeting and constant conflict between commanders in the field and the War Department, a change was necessary. Davis appointed Benjamin secretary of state, which was a job much better suited both to Benjamin's talents and to his relationship with Davis. The State Department allowed Benjamin to apply his interest in efficiency and organization to a variety of civil issues, including foreign relations. Although Benjamin was not able to convince France or England to recognize the

Confederacy, he did arrange the Erlanger loan in 1863. The loan, which was coordinated by a Parisian bank, provided nearly $10 million for the Confederate war effort.

By 1865 Benjamin was searching for ideas to help avert disaster for the Confederacy. He proposed that Davis offer EMANCIPATION of slaves in exchange for recognition from France and England, but that proposal failed. Recognizing the seriously depleted state of Confederate military units, he pursued Emancipationist policies. This outraged many Confederate politicians, who tried to remove him from office. In the end, Benjamin evacuated RICHMOND with Davis in April 1865. Separated from Davis near Savannah, Georgia, Benjamin narrowly missed capture by Union troops. Instead, he was able to leave the country through Florida and the Caribbean, eventually settling in England.

Benjamin remained in England until his death, working as a barrister. He earned a distinguished reputation in English legal circles and was appointed Queen's Counsel in 1870. Between 1880 and 1882, Benjamin suffered several blows to his health which led to his death in Paris in 1884.

Although Benjamin was not a FIRE-EATER, his commitment to the Confederacy led him to make enormous commitments of time and energy to its cause. Nevertheless, a variety of factors, including anti-Semitism, led to almost constant criticism of his actions by Confederate leaders and newspapers. He was simultaneously one of the Confederacy's best assets and one of its least appreciated ones.

Further reading: William C. Davis, *Jefferson Davis: The Man and His Hour* (New York: HarperCollins, 1991); Eli N. Evans, *Judah P. Benjamin, the Jewish Confederate* (New York: Free Press, 1988); Robert Douthat Meade, *Judah P. Benjamin, Confederate Statesman* (London, New York: Arno Press, 1975).

—Fiona Galvin

Bentonville, Battle of (March 19–21, 1865)

The Battle of Bentonville, fought from March 19 to March 21, 1865, was the last significant confrontation between two major armies in the CIVIL WAR. Confederate forces under Gen. JOSEPH E. JOHNSTON attacked Union forces under Maj. Gen. WILLIAM T. SHERMAN near the small town of Bentonville, North Carolina, about 20 miles west of Goldsboro. The Union XIV and XX Corps, commanded by Maj. Gen. Henry W. Slocum, were in the advance column, and Johnston wanted to attack before Sherman and the rest of his troops could arrive. The UNION ARMY was marching northeast on the Goldsboro Road, while the CONFEDERATE ARMY was positioned on both sides of the road, south of Bentonville.

In the morning on the first day of the battle, March 19, the Confederates under Lt. Gens. Alexander P. Stewart and William J. Hardee and Maj. Gens. Robert F. Hoke and D. H. Hill broke the Union left wing and drove it back about a mile south of the Goldsboro Road. The Confederates then attacked the exposed Union right, but Brig. Gen. William Cogswell of the XX Corps reinforced the beleaguered Union forces under Brigadier General James D. Morgan's division of the XIV Corps. This movement upon the Union right is considered the turning point of the battle, with the Union offensive gaining the advantage. Succeeding Confederate demonstrations against the Union left flank failed, and the fighting came to a stalemate.

On the morning of the second day, March 20, Johnston strengthened his line north of the Goldsboro Road to protect Mill Creek Bridge, the only escape route for the Confederate army. After the arrival of Sherman and the rest of the Union army, the blue troops outnumbered the gray by about 60,000 to 21,000. Sherman deployed the newly arrived troops on his right flank, though the only activity that day was some heavy skirmishing.

On the third day, March 21, Union major general Joseph A. Mower initiated an attack on the Confederate left. While Hardee's troops managed to stall this offensive, Johnston and his army nonetheless withdrew on the night of the 21st across Mill Creek Bridge and toward Smithfield. Sherman's forces pursued Johnston on the 22nd, with little effect.

Further reading: Mark L. Bradley, *Last Stand in the Carolinas: The Battle of Bentonville* (New York: Da Capo Press, 2000); Nathaniel Cheairs Hughes Jr., *Bentonville: The Final Battle of Sherman and Johnston* (Chapel Hill: University of North Carolina Press, 1996).

—Stacey Graham

Bickerdyke, Mary Ann (Mother) (1817–1901)

Mary Ann "Mother" Bickerdyke was a beloved nurse and fundraiser during the CIVIL WAR. She grew up in Ohio as Mary Ann Ball, moving between a number of relatives after her mother died. Married in 1847 to Robert Bickerdyke, Mary Ann migrated with her husband to Illinois a decade later. Widowed in 1859, Bickerdyke supported herself and her three children by nursing.

During a church service in 1861, Bickerdyke learned about the harsh conditions of young volunteer soldiers suffering from typhoid and dysentery. Church members proceeded to organize a relief fund, and Bickerdyke volunteered to deliver it. This mission convinced Bickerdyke to commit herself to caring for Union soldiers for the rest of the war. She threw herself into relief work on her own initiative, doing whatever needed to be done. Ignoring protocol and defying male authority, she cleaned, nursed, and fed thousands of sick and wounded men, both at hospital camps and at the front lines of battle.

Bickerdyke acquired her name of "Mother Bickerdyke" from the wounded soldiers at the BATTLE OF SHILOH in April 1862. She soon became an agent of the UNITED STATES SANITARY COMMISSION, and she gained a measure of fame when the country learned of her extraordinary dedication to the wounded at many battlefields and hospitals.

Along with her nursing duties on the front lines with Grant's and Sherman's armies, Bickerdyke also embarked on speaking tours in the Midwest to raise money and obtain food. Bickerdyke was with Sherman's army in North Carolina when the war was finally won, and she joined in the North's victory parade in 1865 in WASHINGTON, D.C.

After the war, Bickerdyke worked on various benevolent causes. She died in 1901 in Kansas after spending her final years on her son's farm.

See also DISEASE AND EPIDEMICS.

Further reading: Nina Brown Baker, *Cyclone in Calico: The Story of Mary Ann Bickerdyke* (Boston: Little, Brown, 1952).

—Jaclyn Greenberg

Black Codes

Black Codes were laws enacted by Southern state legislatures in late 1865 and in 1866 to restrict the economic activities and control the social behavior of freedmen and freedwomen. In effect for only a short time, the Black Codes reflected Southern unwillingness to accept EMANCIPATION and its consequences after the CIVIL WAR. The laws contributed to the end of Presidential RECONSTRUCTION and to the imposition of a much greater federal role during congressional, or Radical, Reconstruction.

Black Codes had their origins before the end of the Civil War. It was clear that the Southern ECONOMY, based predominantly on AGRICULTURE, would need revitalization. Union generals sometimes pressured ex-slaves to return to PLANTATIONS, hoping that labor contracts would protect the workers from mistreatment by their former masters. This did not prove to be the case. During the summer of 1865, planters organized county associations to set wage scales and prevent competition for black labor. Communities tried to reestablish white control over former slaves through local ordinances that made vagrancy a crime and prohibited African Americans from holding certain jobs and owning real property.

It was only a matter of time until such controls began to be established at the state level. Mississippi was the first state to enact a Black Code in November 1865. Every African-American worker was required to have a written EMPLOYMENT contract during the first ten days of January that covered the remainder of the year. Any worker who violated the terms of the contract lost wages earned under the contract and was subject to arrest. Penalties were imposed on any employer who tried to hire a black worker already under contract. Other restrictions were included that defined the limits of work. African Americans were forbidden to rent land in urban areas and were limited to doing agricultural labor. To ensure that they did indeed work, the Mississippi Black Code included criminal penalties for vagrancy. Insulting gestures or language were also made into criminal offenses.

Many Southern states quickly enacted their own Black Codes. South Carolina, for example, taxed African Americans from $10 to $100 for business activities other than farming or being a servant. In addition to required annual labor contracts, a worker could not leave the plantation without the employer's permission. In Louisiana, a worker who did not comply with his labor contract could be arrested and forced to work on public work projects without pay until willing to return to his contract employer.

The Black Codes were drafted by conservative, respectable judges, lawyers, and law professors, many of whom had not been advocates of SECESSION. The Black Codes reflected a Southern ideology that assumed that African Americans would not work voluntarily and were naturally self-indulgent, unskilled, and illiterate. White Southerners believed that African Americans needed protection from these inclinations. Fearful of insurrections, white Southerners also wanted the protection they believed that the Black Codes could provide.

Southern leaders knew that the rest of the country was watching to see how white Southerners treated the newly emancipated slaves in their reestablished political and legal systems. As such, the Black Codes did grant certain rights to the former slaves, including the right to make contracts, the right to sue and be sued, the right to marry other African Americans, and the right to buy, own, and transfer property. Ultimately, this was not enough to convince Northern leaders that Southerners had changed their ways.

Black Codes proved a good source of propaganda for RADICAL REPUBLICANS. Although few Northerners believed in the inherent equality of black and white people, most did advocate equal access to the legal system, equal application of criminal laws, and equal rights to sell one's labor in a free market. Even Republican moderates were offended that the former Confederate states, so soon after rejoining the Union, rejected the free labor system that existed throughout the rest of the United States.

The perception that white Southerners were unreformed created a hostile climate in Congress. In December 1865, congressional leaders responded by refusing to seat delegations elected to represent the former Confederate states. In early 1866, Congress extended the life of the FREEDMEN'S BUREAU beyond its initial one year and added new powers, including the oversight of labor agreements. Eventually, Congress put the South under military control and tried to impose equality on the South. The Black Codes were forcibly repealed by legislative action or by federal officials overseeing the Reconstruction governments, and virtually none of them remained on the books after 1867.

The disappearance of the Black Codes was a short-lived victory for African Americans. Eventually, Northerners lost interest in the status of the freedmen, and by 1876 Reconstruction had come to an end. SHARECROPPING, the legalization of segregation, and a number of other factors allowed white Southerners to create the racial order they desired. African Americans in the South would remain in a subordinate position for at least another century.

Further reading: Eric Foner, *Reconstruction: America's Unfinished Revolution, 1863–1877* (New York: Harper & Row, 1988); Theodore Brantner Wilson, *The Black Codes of the South* (Tuscaloosa.: University of Alabama Press, 1965).

—Martha Kadue

Blair, Francis Preston, Jr. (1821–1875)

As a Missouri legislator, a member of the House of Representatives (1857–62), a general, a vice presidential candidate (1868), and a U.S. senator (1871–73), Francis P. Blair Jr. was a key political figure of the 1860s and 1870s and an important opponent of Radical RECONSTRUCTION.

Born in Lexington, Kentucky, in 1821, Frank Blair grew up in a family immersed in politics. Blair's grandfather had been among Kentucky's earliest political leaders, building a social and political network that the family maintained for the next 80 years. In the late 1820s, Blair's father became an ally of Andrew Jackson, following Jackson to WASHINGTON, D.C., in 1829. There, Blair's father established the *Washington Globe*, the era's leading DEMOCRATIC PARTY newspaper.

After being educated in Washington, D.C., private schools, Frank Blair went on to college at Princeton and then to legal studies at Kentucky's Transylvania College. After completing his EDUCATION, Blair relocated to Missouri, established a legal practice, and served in the Mexican-American War. After the war, Blair's father successfully lobbied to make him attorney general of the New Mexico Territory. Returning to Missouri, Blair won a seat in the state legislature, where he served for four years. While Frank Blair was building his political career, his father, Francis Blair, was reconsidering his Democratic Party allegiance. The elder Blair was no ABOLITIONist, but he vehe-mently opposed expansion of SLAVERY into the new territories, believing that the nation should reserve them for white settlers. After a brief flirtation with the Free-Soil Party, Francis Blair broke decisively with the Democrats over the KANSAS-NEBRASKA ACT and joined the new REPUBLICAN PARTY.

Frank and his brother Montgomery followed their father into the Republican Party. During the CIVIL WAR, Montgomery joined ABRAHAM LINCOLN's cabinet as postmaster general while Frank served in Congress and in the UNION ARMY. Lincoln's relationship with the Blairs reflected the president's anxiety about Missouri, Kentucky, and the other border states. Though these slave states had remained within the Union, Confederate sympathies ran high in all of them. If the Union lost any of these states, Lincoln believed the North might well lose the entire war. Lincoln carefully cultivated his friends in these states, reaching out to former Democrats like the Blairs.

Frank Blair did a great deal to ensure that Missouri remained in the Union during the tense months following FORT SUMTER. He joined the Federal army in April 1861 as a colonel and was soon promoted to brigadier general and then again to major general. These promotions were given by Lincoln to reward Blair's loyalty to the administration. In contrast to most political generals, Blair performed credibly as a military commander. ULYSSES S. GRANT and WILLIAM T. SHERMAN both spoke favorably about his abilities as a general, and he distinguished himself with his service during the VICKSBURG CAMPAIGN, the BATTLE OF CHATTANOOGA, the ATLANTA CAMPAIGN, and SHERMAN'S MARCH THROUGH GEORGIA.

Frank Blair and his family recognized that the EMANCIPATION PROCLAMATION rang the death knell of slavery throughout the South. However, they expected that former slaves would remain subservient to white men. Once the war ended, Frank Blair, like his father, vigorously opposed the RADICAL REPUBLICANS, who sought full civil rights for African Americans. As former Democrats, the Blairs were natural allies of the new president, Tennessee Democrat ANDREW JOHNSON. While many Republicans counseled Johnson to work with Radicals in the party, the Blairs advised him to build his majority around Democrats in the South, border state Unionists, and conservative Republicans. Johnson's increasingly heated attacks on Republican radicals contributed to Republican gains in the 1866 congressional ELECTIONS, and the poisoned relationship between the president and Congress led to Johnson's impeachment and trial. Most of Lincoln's men turned on Johnson, but the Blairs joined WILLIAM H. SEWARD and a few others to support the president. None of them were again welcome in the Republican Party. Having stood with Johnson, Frank Blair now returned to the Democratic Party after a 10-year absence.

In 1868 Democrats nominated New York governor Horatio Seymour for the presidency and chose Blair as his running mate. Bitter over Johnson's failure to control Reconstruction, Blair used his campaign appearances to revisit the Democratic Party's prewar boast that it was the "white man's party." Blair denounced Southern Reconstruction governments as controlled by "a semi-barbarous race of blacks who are worshippers of fetishes and polygamists" and who "subject the white women to their unbridled lust." Blair's incendiary outbursts alienated many Northerners and made Blair himself a campaign issue. "Seymour was opposed to the late war," said Republican wags, and "Blair is in favor of the next one." Seymour and Blair were soundly defeated in the election by Republican Ulysses S. Grant.

Though the country chose Grant, Missouri stuck by Frank Blair, making him a U.S. senator. Until his death in 1875, Blair energetically but unsuccessfully opposed any concession designed to help African Americans achieve economic or political equality. Blair's vision of a "white man's republic" soon prevailed throughout the South as Americans retreated from Reconstruction-era commitments.

Further reading: William E. Parrish, *Frank Blair: Lincoln's Conservative* (Columbia: University of Missouri Press, 1998); William E. Smith, *The Francis Preston Blair Family in Politics* (New York: Da Capo Press, 1969).

—Tom Laichas

Bleeding Kansas (1854–1865)

"Bleeding Kansas" is the name given to the conflict between Free-Soil supporters and SLAVERY supporters in the Kansas and Nebraska Territories, both before and during the CIVIL WAR. Tensions between proslavery settlers, often called "BUSHWHACKERS," and antislavery settlers, often labeled "JAYHAWKERS," became so strong that newspapers of the day called the pitched battles a "civil war" long before shots had been fired on FORT SUMTER.

The troubles of Bleeding Kansas were rooted in the Missouri Compromise of 1820, which had drawn a line across the unorganized territories west of the Appalachians, dividing them into slave and free territories. For three decades after the adoption of the Missouri Compromise, the South blocked attempts to organize the Kansas Territory into states because it fell on the free-labor side of the Missouri Compromise line. Congress, seeking to defuse tensions between North and South over slavery's expansion into the territories, eventually passed the KANSAS-NEBRASKA ACT in 1854. The act, supported by Illinois senator STEPHEN A. DOUGLAS, divided the Kansas Territory into two areas, Kansas and Nebraska, and left the territo-

ries' disposition as to slavery to the settlers of the respective territories under the new doctrine of popular sovereignty, which dictated that the decision on whether or not to allow slavery within an organizing territory would be left up to a vote of the territory's settlers. The Missouri Compromise was effectively repealed by the popular sovereignty of the Kansas-Nebraska Act, since voters in territories north of the Missouri Compromise line could now decide to adopt slavery where it had once been forbidden. The Kansas-Nebraska Act infuriated Northern free-labor advocates and ABOLITIONists.

In preparation for the election to decide Kansas's legal stand on slavery, both proslavery and antislavery settlers poured into the newly formed territory. In the North, the New England Emigrant Aid Company collected funds in an effort to help promote settlement of Free-Soil, antislavery people in Kansas. Despite the press that the organization garnered, they were generally unsuccessful in their efforts, raising little money and sending few settlers to the territory. Southerners also rallied to support settlement in Kansas. Missouri governor David Rice Atchison claimed that a victory for antislavery forces in Kansas would lead to the end of slavery in the entire nation, advising his fellow Southerners that the "game must be played boldly." The South did play boldly, with Atchison leading the way. Groups of what were termed "border ruffians" were organized to cross from Missouri to Kansas to vote in the territorial ELECTIONS and strike whatever other blows were deemed necessary to guarantee Kansas would be a slave state.

Kansas truly began to bleed in May 1856, with the sack of the antislavery town of Lawrence by a mob of proslavery supporters. The mob burned buildings and destroyed the local Free-Soil press. Lawrence did not go quietly, however. JOHN BROWN, failed businessman and passionate abolitionist, led a retaliatory raid against the proslavery settlement at Pottawatomie Creek, killing five men and boys by hacking them to death with broadswords.

It was not in Kansas alone that tempers flared. In WASHINGTON, D.C., Senator CHARLES SUMNER of Massachusetts denounced the violence in Kansas and claimed it was caused entirely by slave-supporting forces. In his widely publicized "Crime against Kansas" speech, Sumner declared that Kansas had been "raped" and forced into the "hateful embrace of slavery." Sumner called the proslavery forces in Kansas "thugs" and "robbers" and accused Southern politicians of "cavorting" with the "harlot, Slavery." Sumner's speech named several Southern politicians whom he saw as particularly guilty, including Senator Andrew P. Butler of South Carolina. Butler's cousin, Preston Brooks, serving then as a representative from South Carolina, attacked Sumner with a cane in the Senate chamber shortly thereafter, beating him senseless. Throughout the South, Brooks was applauded, while throughout the North his actions were decried as barbaric.

By 1857 Kansas was a pitched battlefield, with Bushwhackers and Jayhawkers arming themselves with whatever weapons they could manage. By that time, the majority of legitimate Kansas settlers were opposed to slavery. However, President FRANKLIN PIERCE, a Northerner who sympathized with Southern interests, chose to recognize the proslavery provisional legislature elected through fraudulent votes cast by thousands of "border ruffians" from Missouri. The provisional legislature proceeded to pass proslavery and antiabolitionist legislation for the territory. President JAMES BUCHANAN succeeded Pierce, and he continued to provide presidential support for the proslavery government by putting his weight behind the Lecompton Constitution, which was ostensibly meant to be the state constitution for Kansas. However, because the Lecompton Constitution had been written by the provisional legislature, it naturally included strong protection for slavery. The citizens of Kansas were supposed to vote whether to accept the Lecompton Constitution or not, but the election was fraudulent and was boycotted by antislavery settlers. A second election was called by Congress, but that was boycotted by proslavery forces. Ultimately, Buchanan's support

for the Lecompton Constitution proved moot, and Kansas did not enter the Union until after the Civil War was under way.

Meanwhile, through all the political fighting, the armed conflicts between bushwhackers and jayhawkers went on unabated, and Kansas continued to "bleed." The attacks on property and people seemed to prove that the North and South were on radically different paths. The "little civil war," as abhorrent and unimaginable to Americans as it was, proved to be only the tip of the iceberg of animosity and hostility that the regions had in store for each other.

Further reading: Thomas Goodrich, *War to the Knife: Bleeding Kansas, 1854–1861* (Mechanicsburg, Pa.: Stackpole Books, 1998); Kenneth Stampp, *America in 1857: A Nation on the Brink* (New York: Oxford University Press, 1990).

—Ruth A. Behling

Booth, John Wilkes (1838–1865)

ABRAHAM LINCOLN's assassin, John Wilkes Booth, was born in Maryland in 1838, the son of famous actor Junius Brutus Booth and his mistress Mary Ann Holmes. Junius, known as "the mad tragedian," was often away on tour, and even when he was home he was often incapacitated by alcoholism and mental disease. Young John was largely raised by his mother. He received some formal EDUCATION, mostly at St. Timothy's Episcopal Military Academy, where he became an Episcopalian and learned how to shoot and ride a horse.

Junius died in 1851, and shortly thereafter John decided to follow his famous brother Edwin into the family business, making his stage debut in Baltimore in August 1855. John was known less for his acting skill and more for his boisterous style and penchant for gymnastic leaps around the stage. Nonetheless, he was very well-received, and by the time he turned 25 he had played the lead in nine different Shakespearean plays and was receiving more than 100 pieces of fan mail every week.

Booth toured the North and the South, enjoying success in both regions of the increasingly divided nation. However, he regarded himself as a primarily Southern actor, and he preferred performing in front of Southern audiences. He also became very outspoken when it came to politics. Junius had disliked SLAVERY, but John defended the institution and denounced Northern ABOLITIONists. After JOHN BROWN's failed insurrection attempt at HARPERS FERRY, Booth temporarily suspended his acting career in order to join a militia unit called the Richmond Grays. In that capacity, he witnessed Brown's hanging on

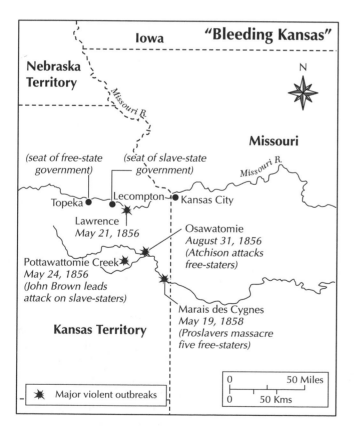

"Bleeding Kansas"

Iowa

Nebraska Territory

Missouri R.

Missouri

Missouri R.

(seat of free-state government)

(seat of slave-state government)

Topeka ● ● Lecompton ● Kansas City

Lawrence
May 21, 1856

Osawatomie
August 31, 1856
(Atchison attacks free-staters)

Pottawattomie Creek ✸
May 24, 1856
(John Brown leads attack on slave-staters)

Marais des Cygnes
May 19, 1858
(Proslavers massacre five free-staters)

Kansas Territory

N

0   50 Miles
0   50 Kms

✸ Major violent outbreaks

December 2, 1859. While in Richmond, Booth also joined the Knights of the Golden Circle, a secret society dedicated to promoting the expansion of slavery and SECESSION.

In early 1860, Booth returned to his stage career. When war finally broke out in April 1861, he declined to take up arms, in deference to his mother's wishes. He continued to speak out against Lincoln and the Union war effort, even though he was still appearing regularly in Northern cities, in front of increasingly hostile audiences. He was even arrested in St. Louis in 1862 for saying that he wished "the whole damn government would go to hell," but he was released shortly thereafter. Booth continued crisscrossing the North and South, and evidence suggests he regularly took advantage of the opportunity to smuggle medicine to the South.

By the fall of 1864 Booth had grown tired of being an armchair rebel. He was despondent over the sagging fortunes of the Confederacy and wanted to do something dramatic to help out the cause. He organized a group of conspirators with the intention of kidnapping Abraham Lincoln. Booth felt this action would end the war or at the very least would allow the Confederacy to negotiate for all of its prisoners of war being held in Union PRISONS. Booth and his coconspirators made several attempts to abduct the president while he was vulnerable, but each time they were foiled by bad luck or bad timing, and eventually several of Booth's accomplices abandoned him.

By April 1865 the Confederacy was collapsing, and Booth was growing increasingly desperate. He was present at Lincoln's second inaugural address, and he found the president's references to limited black suffrage to be intolerable. Booth no longer had the time or the manpower for a kidnapping, and so he settled upon murder. When an announcement was made on the morning of April 14 that the president would be attending a performance at Ford's Theater that evening, Booth decided to strike. He had no difficulty gaining access to the president when he arrived at the THEATER, since security was lax and he was well known to the stagehands. Booth loitered in the hallway behind the president, waiting for a big laugh to cover the sound of the gunshot. When the moment came, he entered the president's box and quickly fired his single-shot Derringer into the back of the Lincoln's head. After briefly scuffling with Lincoln's companion, Maj. Henry Reed Rathbone, Booth leaped to the stage 12 feet below, breaking his leg in the process. With a shout of "sic semper tyrannis!" ("thus always to tyrants") to the confused audience, Booth escaped into the night.

Booth felt he would be hailed as a hero in the South, but he was largely in error. Most individuals on both sides of the conflict cursed his assassin. After meeting up with David Herold, one of his coconspirators, and pausing to

John Wilkes Booth *(Hulton/Archive)*

get his broken leg set by Dr. Samuel Mudd, Booth fled through Maryland into Virginia. He and Herold were sheltered for six days by Samuel Cox and then relocated to the farm of Richard H. Garrett. On April 26, while sleeping in Garrett's barn, Herold and Booth were surrounded by Union cavalry. Herold surrendered, but Booth refused to be taken alive. The barn was set on fire in hopes of smoking Booth out. Booth made a desperate charge and was shot by Sgt. Boston Corbett, who ignored explicit orders to keep Booth alive. After lingering for several hours, Booth died shortly after dawn on April 27, 1865.

See also ASSASSINATION OF ABRAHAM LINCOLN.

Further reading: John Rhodehamel and Louise Taper, eds., *"Right or Wrong, God Judge Me": The Writings of John Wilkes Booth* (Urbana: University of Illinois Press, 1997); Gene Smith, *American Gothic: The Story of America's Legendary Theatrical Family—Junius, Edwin and John Wilkes Booth* (New York: Simon & Schuster, 1992).

—Christopher Bates

bounty system

The bounty system was an important part of the raising of a VOLUNTEER ARMY in the CIVIL WAR, particularly in the North. In the first year of the conflict, states, counties, private organizations, and the federal government all offered modest bounties to recruit soldiers. For example, on July 22, 1861, the U.S. Congress passed a law authorizing each volunteer to receive $100 for volunteering, in addition to the monthly soldier's pay. In this way, patriotism was rewarded with more than parades and cheers. Bounties were also used in the CONFEDERATE STATES OF AMERICA early in the war, but the system was discontinued due to lack of funds.

As the war progressed, mounting Northern casualties dampened the enthusiasm for voluntary military service. In July 1862, President ABRAHAM LINCOLN called for 300,000 more soldiers to be added to the UNION ARMY. When the states could not meet the quotas set for them by the government, bounties were raised, which increased the number of men in the ranks. Still, even more men were desperately needed to replenish the ranks of the Union armies, especially after the losses suffered at Fredericksburg, Virginia, in December 1862. To encourage volunteering, the federal government passed the CONSCRIPTION Act of 1863.

Conscription, also known as "the draft," was never seriously considered as the primary method to provide troops for the Union. Only 6 percent of men in both Union and Confederate armies were raised through the draft. The Conscription Act was intended only as a stimulus for volunteering. Every state was assigned a quota that it had to meet by a given time. If the state did not meet that quota through volunteers, then it had to raise the required number through a draft. Since the draft was unpopular in the North, it was in the interest of states, townships, counties, and cities to encourage volunteer enlistment to meet their quotas, and avoid the draft entirely. They did this by awarding ever-larger bounties. As in 1861, all units of government—local, state, and national—contributed money for bounties. The local government of Cook County, Illinois, spent more than $3 million on bounties. By 1864 some volunteers were receiving $1,000 for their enlistment.

The bounty system played an integral role in mobilizing Northern men for duty from 1863 onward. There were, however, negative repercussions to the late-war bounties. Some men took advantage of the system by enlisting, receiving their bounty, then deserting the army at the first opportunity. Many of these so-called bounty-jumpers not only got away with their crime but also reenlisted several times. Sometimes they were caught and punished, sometimes not. Another issue was that men who enlisted just for the money were often terrible soldiers and were resented by their battle-tested comrades. These negatives were balanced out, however, by the benefits of the bounty system. Most importantly, the bounty system encouraged three-year VETERANS to reenlist in the critical winter, spring, and summer months of 1864, when the Union army needed every experienced soldier it could muster.

See also COMMON SOLDIER.

Further reading: James W. Geary, *We Need Men: The Union Draft in the Civil War* (DeKalb: Northern Illinois University Press, 1991); Emory Thomas, *The Confederate Nation: 1861–1865* (New York: Harper & Row, 1979).

Boyd, Belle (1844–1900)

Born May 9, 1844, in Martinsburg, Virginia (now West Virginia), Belle Boyd became one of the Confederacy's most active and well-known female spies. Boyd's success as a spy resulted, in part, from her ability to use her femininity to escape detection and punishment. Called "La Belle Rebelle" by the French press and "That Secesh Cleopatra" by unfriendly Northern reporters, Boyd was bold, brash, and beautiful.

Boyd's parents, Mary Rebecca Glenn and Reed Boyd, both came from prominent Virginia families. She received her EDUCATION at Mount Washington Female College of Baltimore, Maryland, returning home at the outbreak of the CIVIL WAR to serve as a nurse and to raise money for the Confederacy. She also organized groups of women to visit Southern troops. When a Northern soldier broke into her house and insulted her mother in 1861, Boyd shot and killed him. She escaped punishment because the shooting was seen as self-defense. Approximately a week later, Boyd began her career as a Confederate spy. To gather information, she engaged Federal soldiers in flirtatious conversations. Boyd passed on to Confederate officials any information that they revealed concerning Union movements and plans.

Generals P. G. T. BEAUREGARD and THOMAS J. "STONEWALL" JACKSON used Boyd as a courier in late 1861. She successfully carried information, supplies, and weapons across enemy lines. Her role became vital in the spring of 1862, when Boyd delivered information to Jackson as he launched an offensive in the Shenandoah Valley. For her part in the Confederate successes in this campaign, Union forces arrested Boyd on July 29, 1862, on the order of Secretary of War EDWIN M. STANTON. For the next month, they held her in WASHINGTON, D.C.'s Old Capitol Prison. In June 1863 she was again arrested, this time in her hometown of Martinsburg, and imprisoned in Washington's Carroll Prison. After contracting typhoid, Boyd was released in December 1863 and banished to the South.

Boyd did not wait long to resume her spying activities. In early 1864 she boarded a ship for England, presumably for her health, but in reality, she was on her way to deliver Confederate dispatches. Before the mission could be carried out, however, Union forces captured Boyd's ship, placed her under arrest, and brought her ship back to the United States. Boyd escaped from Federal custody in Boston and fled to Canada and then to England. Union officials held responsible Ens. Samuel Wylde Hardinge Jr., the officer in command of the captured ship. They court-martialed and imprisoned him. Before his case could be heard, Hardinge followed Boyd to England, where they married in 1864 and had a daughter. He died soon after. From England, Boyd published her memoirs, *Belle Boyd in Camp and Prison* (1865), to recruit support for the Confederacy.

After the war, Boyd pursued a stage career, first in Europe and then in the United States. She married two more times and had four more children. In the 1880s, Boyd lectured throughout the United States about her wartime activities. At the end of each speech, she stressed the importance of national unity and reunion. Boyd's speeches proved particularly popular with Union VETERANS.

Belle Boyd died of a heart attack on June 11, 1900, while in Kilbourne, Wisconsin.

See also GREENHOW, ROSE O'NEAL; ESPIONAGE.

Further reading: Belle Boyd, *Belle Boyd in Camp and Prison* (1865; reprint, Baton Rouge: Louisiana State University Press, 1998); Ruth Scarborough, *Belle Boyd: Siren of the South* (Macon, Ga.: Mercer University Press, 1983).

—Lisa Tendrich Frank

Brady, Mathew B. (1823–1896)

Photographer and businessman Mathew Brady's magnificent pictorial record of the CIVIL WAR has provided generations of Americans with an enduring legacy of that conflict. Born in 1823 in upstate New York, Brady began his studies with portrait artist William Page. In 1839 Page took Brady to NEW YORK CITY to study with Samuel F. B. Morse. Recently returned from Paris, where he had met Louis Daguerre, Morse's enthusiasm for the new "daguerreotype" process of PHOTOGRAPHY inspired Brady to learn the craft. Fascinated, Brady absorbed what he could from Morse, and soon he opened his own studio in 1844. Using aesthetic enhancements, such as makeup, lighting, costuming, and camera positions, Brady's innovations refined the medium, and he quickly gained renown as a portrait artist. Working in a lavishly appointed gallery, Brady appealed to the rich and prominent citizens of New York, who lined up to have Brady take their likenesses.

A tireless self-promoter and entrepreneur, in 1845 Brady launched his "Illustrious Americans" project, photographing 24 of the most prominent American citizens of his day. Published in 1850, the book created a sensation in England, where Brady was awarded a medal for his artistic excellence. His prestige and success attracted other photographers to work at Brady's studio. Among them was Alexander Gardner, who introduced Brady to the new "wet plate" process. This method took photography beyond daguerreotype's single-use copper plate and allowed for the production of an unlimited number of positive prints from a fixed negative image on a glass plate, expanding the potential of the craft.

By 1860 Brady had reached the height of his artistic and commercial fame. During a campaign stopover in New

Mathew B. Brady   *(Library of Congress)*

York City that year, presidential candidate ABRAHAM LIN-COLN visited Brady's gallery. Brady produced a flattering photograph that Lincoln claimed helped him win the election. Lincoln would sit for Brady several more times.

When the Civil War began, Brady set out to document the war with photographs. He was convinced that he would reap large profits from such a venture and, at the same time, contribute to history. Brady put all his money into the business, purchasing expensive equipment and hiring many assistants. Brady himself photographed the FIRST BATTLE OF BULL RUN, saying "A spirit in my feet said 'go' and I went." Brady pioneered the idea of a professional force of field photographers going out into the battlefield and into the camps, recording the war in all of its many features. Mathew Brady's haunting series of pictures of the Gettysburg battlefield and town are among his finest efforts.

Brady's primary role, however, was not in the field but consisted of managing the huge project from his WASHINGTON, D.C., studio. Even so, many photographs attributed to Brady were actually those of his most talented assistants, such as Gardner or Timothy H. O'Sullivan. Brady's willingness to take credit for other photographers' work brought him harsh criticism, and many of his assistants abandoned him before the war was over. Overextended financially, Brady was broke by war's end and tried to sell his collection of work to the government. After much pleading for a better price, he agreed to sell his negatives for $2,840. This sum was a fraction of what it cost Brady to produce the 6,176 photographs of the war. In 1875 the government paid Brady another $25,000 and gained exclusive title to his collection. Despite the infusion of funds, Brady, an alcoholic and nearly blind, was ruined. He died alone in a New York charity hospital in 1896.

Further reading: William A. Frassanito, *Early Photography at Gettysburg* (Gettysburg, Pa.: Thomas Publications, 1995); Web Garrison, ed., *Brady's Civil War* (New York: Lyons Press, 2000); Roy Meredith, *Mr. Lincoln's Camera Man: Mathew B. Brady* (1946; reprint, New York: Dover Publications, 1974).

—Rebecca Dresser

Bragg, Braxton (1817–1876)

Braxton Bragg was one of the Confederacy's most prominent generals. Born in Warrenton, North Carolina, on March 22, 1817, Bragg graduated fifth in the UNITED STATES MILITARY ACADEMY AT WEST POINT class of 1837. He served in the Seminole War and the Mexican-American War and became a national hero for his action at the Battle of Buena Vista. He remained in the army until 1856, when he resigned and used his wife's considerable wealth to build a sugar plantation in Louisiana. In March 1861, he was appointed brigadier general in the CONFEDERATE ARMY and assigned to command the defense of the Gulf Coast between Pensacola, Florida, and Mobile, Alabama. At the BATTLE OF SHILOH, Bragg commanded the Second Corps and in June 1862 took command of the Army of the Mississippi (later known as the Army of Tennessee).

While fiercely devoted to the Confederacy and an accomplished administrator, Bragg had a difficult personality. Many of his problems stemmed from a series of illnesses, including migraine headaches, dyspepsia, boils, and rheumatism. Often manifest during active campaigns, Bragg's ailments frequently left him "sick, befuddled, and beleaguered" at moments of crisis. In addition, he failed to build cohesion among his officer corps, and he constantly quarreled with his high-ranking subordinates. These fights were especially problematic during the winter and spring following the BATTLE OF MURFREESBORO and during the siege of Chattanooga. At least one historian claims Bragg's obsession with internal conflicts led to the disaster at Missionary Ridge on November 25, 1863. He was relieved of command December 1, 1863.

In February 1864 JEFFERSON DAVIS appointed Bragg military adviser to the president. He held that position until October, when he was assigned to command the Confederate defenses at the critical port city of Wilmington, North Carolina. After the city fell in February 1865, Bragg helped organize troops to resist Sherman's advance. He was captured May 10, 1865, at Concord, Georgia. After the war, Bragg held a variety of positions in the railroad, utility, and insurance industries. He died in Galveston, Texas, on September 27, 1876.

See also CHATTANOOGA, BATTLE OF.

Further reading: Grady McWhiney, *Braxton Bragg and Confederate Defeat* (Tuscaloosa: University of Alabama Press, 1991).

—James Daryl Black

brothers' war

The CIVIL WAR is frequently portrayed in familial terms, thus a "brother's war," a term used at the time. Often, a group of relatives would enlist together, and some units had so many kinsmen in them that they were known as "cousinwealths." In other instances, families were torn apart as some members decided their loyalties were with the Union while others swore allegiance to the Confederacy.

It was particularly common in the South for military service to be a family affair. Because of manpower shortages, the CONFEDERATE ARMY enlisted virtually its entire white male population. If a family had several sons of military age, most or all of them would join the ranks. For example, the Bledsoe family of Mississippi enrolled 10 sons and five sons-in-law in the Confederate army. Mrs. Enoch Hooper Cook of Alabama saw her husband, 10 sons, and two grandsons go off to join the fight. Eighteen members of the Bell family of Tennessee enlisted in the Confederate army, and only seven returned. There were also Northern families who contributed multiple sons to the Union war effort, although rarely in such large numbers as in the South.

As common as it was for relatives to fight side-by-side in the Civil War, the most oft-repeated stories of the brothers' war have to do with families that were divided by the conflict. This was particularly common in the border states of Missouri, Kentucky, Virginia, and Tennessee. President ABRAHAM LINCOLN was originally from Kentucky, and three of his brothers-in-law served as officers in the Confederate army. Indeed, throughout the war Mrs. Lincoln was hurt by rumors that she was working for the enemy, although there was not a shred of evidence that this was the case. Other high-ranking Northern officials also saw family members join the Confederacy. Two of Union commodore William David Porter's sons enlisted in the Confederate artillery. Kentucky senator John J. Crittenden's son George became a major general in the Confederate army, while his son Thomas was a major general in the UNION ARMY.

Prominent families provide the most famous examples of those split in two by the Civil War. However, there were also thousands of common families who were divided by the conflict. For example, Franklin Buchanan commanded the Confederate ironclad CSS *Virginia* when it sank the USS *Congress.* Among those who were killed when the *Congress* sank was Franklin's brother McKean. At the BATTLE OF GETTYSBURG, hometown boy Wesley Culp returned as a member of the Confederate Stonewall Brigade. He was killed on Culp's Hill, a portion of the family farm named after one of Wesley's relatives, and buried in the basement of the family farmhouse. Perhaps the most well-known monument to the brothers' war is the grave of James Terrill, a brigadier general in the Confederate army, and William Terrill, a brigadier general in the Union army. Both were killed during the war and were buried by their father under a single headstone bearing the inscription "Here lie my two sons. Only God knows which was right."

See also MUSIC.

Further reading: William C. Davis, *Touched By Fire: A National Historical Society Photographic Portrait of the Civil War* (New York: Black Dog and Leventhal Publishers, 1997).

—Christopher Bates

Brown, John (1800–1859)

John Brown was a Northern ABOLITIONist who dedicated himself to doing battle against SLAVERY in the United States. He was born on May 9, 1800, the third child of Owen and Ruth Mills Brown, in Torrington, Connecticut, but was raised in Ohio. Young John, brought up in a devoutly Christian household, was taught that slavery was evil. That upbringing formed Brown into a powerfully persuasive abolitionist. Unlike many abolitionists at the time, he supported the use of violence to end slavery. His battles in Kansas and his raid on HARPERS FERRY significantly hastened the coming of the CIVIL WAR.

In 1820 Brown married Dainthe Lusk. Their union produced 7 children. When Dainthe died in 1831, Brown married 16-year-old Mary Ann Day, with whom he had 13 more children. The family moved from Ohio to Pennsylvania, where Brown opened a tannery. Brown's tannery, like the rest of his numerous business ventures, was a failure. Brown tried his luck at farming, raising cattle and sheep. He even invested others' hard-earned money in canals, usually profitably. The Panic of 1837 foiled his plans to become wealthy once again. By 1856 Brown had amassed a record of 20 failed businesses and a bankruptcy.

But while he was unfit for business, Brown thrived in the antislavery movement. A riveting speaker who used rich biblical imagery to make his points, John Brown impressed the small audiences who heard his antislavery lectures and sermons. Soon he developed a base of support from the movement, including FREDERICK DOUGLASS. In 1837, at an abolitionist meeting in an Ohio church, Brown stood and proclaimed: "Here before God, in the presence of these witnesses, I consecrate my life to the destruction of slavery."

Like Brown, many abolitionists had backgrounds of religiously based antislavery, and many had similarly pledged in their own way to see the "destruction of slavery." Brown, however, was a different breed of abolitionist. He felt his call was directly from a wrathful God and that he personally was an instrument of the Lord's will. Brown often dreamed of inciting violent slave uprisings that would bring a bloody, and just, end to the evil of slavery. Brown's favorite scripture, Hebrew 9:22, attests to this: "Without shedding of blood there is no remission of sin."

While advocating radical means, Brown's methods continued to be practical and useful. Brown helped to found and sustain a free black farming community in North Elba, New York, where he also worked as a conductor in the UNDERGROUND RAILROAD. One of the few white abolitionists who lived and worked with African Americans, Brown enjoyed a rare respect among his fellow black reformers.

John Brown burst on the national scene when his crusade against slavery moved from New York to the Kansas Territory, where five of his adult sons established farms. Brown did not go to Kansas as an ordinary settler; he came

Issued in the North during the Civil War, this melodramatic portrayal of John Brown meeting a slave mother and her child on his way to execution was symbolic and used for propaganda purposes. *(Library of Congress)*

to fight for free soil and abolition. In 1856 Brown joined his sons in the Pottawatomie Rifles, a militia ground dedicated to the defense of the antislavery headquarters town of Lawrence. The Rifles arrived too late to protect Lawrence from a proslavery mob, so Brown collected a small band of men and exacted his own retribution. He and his group, including his sons, used broadswords to hack five proslavery men to death at Pottawatomie Creek late in May 1856. This attack inflamed tensions between the North and South and was the beginning of a violent summer in Kansas.

Brown, filled with anger over what he considered the growing power of slaveholders over the national government, expanded his efforts against slavery. He organized the Kansas Regulars, a Free-Soil militia group whose aim was to fight "border ruffians" from Missouri. In October 1856, Brown began a series of trips between the Kansas Territory and the East Coast, where he raised funds for a free Kansas from the abolitionist lecture circuit.

As Brown traveled across the East, he developed a secret plan to liberate millions of slaves. He would recruit and train a group of committed men in Kansas. With himself in command, Brown would make a raid into Southern territory, thus precipitating a slave uprising. He and his men would then lead the slaves into the North and freedom. Needing money and support for his scheme, he gained the confidence of six prominent and wealthy men, the "Secret Six." Although the backers remained willfully ignorant of the details and violent intent of Brown's mission, they agreed to finance it. In the late 1850s, Brown carried out the first part of his plan, and chose his target, Harpers Ferry, Virginia, a prosperous industrial town and the site of a major federal armory.

At Harpers Ferry, Brown planned to seize the armory and distribute arms to local slaves who would then, in turn, incite many others to join the exodus. Clearly, Brown's scheme was unworkable, something his friend Frederick Douglass pointed out to him in their last meeting prior to the attack. Brown did not listen, and many have claimed that at this point he was simply crazy.

In any event, the plan was set in motion on October 17, 1859. Brown and 21 men, including several of his sons, marched into Harpers Ferry and killed five citizens of the town. They captured the armory and then waited for the slave insurrection to begin. It never did, and a group of U.S. Marines under the command of Col. ROBERT E. LEE easily captured Brown and most of his followers, among them several African Americans.

In November 1859 Brown was convicted by a Virginia court of treason, murder, and insurrection. One month later, on December 2, he was hanged for his crimes. Brown's final message, written shortly before his execution, said, "I, John Brown, am now quite certain that the crimes of this guilty land will never be purged away but with Blood."

John Brown's raid at Harpers Ferry caused a sensation in the country. Although most Northerners condemned his actions, others considered him a martyr to the cause of freedom. Ralph Waldo Emerson called him an "angel of light," and church bells across the North tolled upon his execution. For the slaveholding South, however, he was evil incarnate and proof of a Northern conspiracy to destroy the Southern way of life.

A controversial and disturbing figure, Brown's violent attack at Harpers Ferry widened the gap between North and South and must be counted as one of immediate causes of the Civil War that followed in 1861. Ironically, John Brown finally enjoyed the success in death that had eluded him in life.

See also BLEEDING KANSAS; KANSAS-NEBRASKA ACT.

Further reading: Paul Finkelman, ed., *His Soul Goes Marching On: Responses to John Brown and the Harpers Ferry Raid* (Charlottesville: University Press of Virginia, 1995); Stephen B. Oates, *To Purge This Land with Blood: A Biography of John Brown* (New York: Harper & Row, 1970); Benjamin Quarles, *Blacks on John Brown* (Urbana: University of Illinois Press, 1972); Edward J. Renehan, *The Secret Six: The True Tale of the Men Who Conspired with John Brown* (New York: Crown Publishers, 1995).

—Ruth A. Behling

Brown, Joseph Emerson (1821–1894)

Businessman, four-term governor of Georgia (1857–65), chief justice of the Georgia Supreme Court (1868–70), and U.S. senator (1880–91), Joseph Brown was born April 15, 1821, in Long Creek, South Carolina, to Mackey and Sally Rice Brown. When Joseph was in his early youth, the family moved to Union County in the north Georgia mountains. He attended Calhoun Academy in South Carolina and upon graduation became a teacher and undertook a private study of the law. In 1845 he gained admission to the Georgia bar, and in 1846 he graduated from Yale Law School.

Brown practiced law in Canton, Georgia, throughout the 1840s and early 1850s. During this time he also began a career in politics, serving as a Georgia state senator and as a judge of the Blue Ridge Circuit. In 1858 Georgia's DEMOCRATIC PARTY, hopelessly deadlocked after more than a dozen ballots, nominated Brown as a compromise candidate for governor. Although unknown outside of the north Georgia mountains, his folksy image appealed to a broad segment of the population, and he won election by 10,000 votes.

He quickly established a reputation as a stern, resourceful leader with impressive managerial skills. A strong STATES' RIGHTS advocate, Brown became ardently SECESSIONist upon the election of ABRAHAM LINCOLN. He appealed to nonslaveholders by arguing that the end of SLAVERY would place black people and poor white yeomen in direct competition. Brown argued that black people, desperate to make a living outside the boundaries of slavery, would sell their labor more cheaply than white people. As a result, he claimed, white workers would be reduced to the level of dependent tenants of the wealthy landowning class.

Brown worked hard to prepare Georgia for war by ordering munitions, seizing federal facilities within the state, and using funds borrowed from banks to establish coastal defenses, purchase gun-making supplies, and erect factories for making shoes, clothing, and blankets. His devotion to the state led to early and regular conflicts with the central Confederate government in RICHMOND, Virginia. The conflicts emerged over a variety of issues such as troop recruitment, the election of officers, conscription, the suspension of habeas corpus, taxes, and confiscation of private property without compensation. By 1863 he went so far as to call for the resignation of Confederate president JEFFERSON DAVIS.

After the war, Brown remained an important figure in Georgia politics by adapting to the realities presented by Union victory. He became a Republican, supported both presidential and congressional RECONSTRUCTION, and urged Georgians to accept the FOURTEENTH AMENDMENT. Just as importantly, Brown worked hard to bring Northern businesses—mining and railroad companies—to Georgia to help repair his state's ravaged ECONOMY. In the process, he became wealthy himself. When Republican rule ended, Brown reentered the Democratic Party. He emerged as one of the state's most influential leaders, forming an alliance with John B. Gordon and Alfred Colquitt known as the "Bourbon Triumvirate." The three dominated Georgia politics during the 1880s and 1890s, allowing Brown to be elected to the U.S. Senate in 1890. He died on November 30, 1894, in Atlanta, Georgia.

See also CONFEDERATE STATES OF AMERICA.

Further reading: Joseph H. Parks, *Joseph E. Brown of Georgia* (Baton Rouge: Louisiana State University Press, 1977).

—James Daryl Black

Brown, William Wells (1814–1884)

Born into slavery, William Wells Brown became a conductor of the UNDERGROUND RAILROAD, an antislavery lecturer in the United States and Britain, an author, and a doctor. His work for temperance and for African American people was a lifelong commitment to which he devoted himself without reservation.

William was born near Lexington, Kentucky, to Elizabeth, a slave on the plantation of John Young. William's father was probably one of Young's cousins, George Higgins. William left Kentucky in 1816, when Young relocated to Missouri. Once in St. Louis, William became the slave of three different men in succession, serving in a variety of capacities, including as a house-servant and later a servant in a bar, an errand runner on a steamboat, an assistant to a physician, and a helper to a printing operation. This widely varied experience served him well later, when William drew on his own history to illustrate the evils of both SLAVERY and alcohol.

William escaped bondage on January 1, 1834. Making his way North, he met a Quaker named Wells Brown, whose friendship inspired him to adopt a new name: William Wells Brown. Stopping in Cleveland, Brown met and married Elizabeth Schooner, with whom he had three children, two of whom survived into adulthood. Brown supported himself and his family by working on steamboats, mostly on Lake Erie. Because of his ability to travel freely, he helped numerous slaves reach freedom in Canada via Detroit and Buffalo. His work on the Underground Railroad freed at least 69 slaves in 1842 alone.

Brown also became a familiar face in Buffalo's temperance societies. He spoke publicly about temperance, gaining skills which he put to use in 1843, when he began to lecture for the New York Anti-Slavery Society. Brown remained one of the society's most popular speakers until 1847, when he and Elizabeth separated, and he assumed custody of their two daughters. Brown left New York for Boston, where the Massachusetts Anti-Slavery Society had invited him to begin a lecture tour through New England. In Boston, Brown found a home that would suit him for the rest of his life.

In 1849 the American Peace Society sent Brown to Paris, where he represented their interests at the International Peace Conference, seeking British support for antislavery activism. In Paris, conferees such as Victor Hugo, Alexis de Tocqueville, and Richard Cobden welcomed Brown warmly. On the last day of the conference, Brown spoke to the attendees about the evils of American slavery. His success led Brown to begin a speaking tour of England. Unfortunately, his time there was prolonged by forces outside his control.

Because of the passage of the Fugitive Slave Act in 1850, Brown became concerned that if he returned to the United States he would be reenslaved. Brown had never been "officially" freed, and the issue remained unresolved until 1854. Finally, a group of Brown's English friends collected enough money to buy his freedom, which allowed Brown to return to his work in Boston, where he was active throughout the CIVIL WAR. In 1863 Brown worked with FREDERICK DOUGLASS and others to recruit African-American volunteers for the 54TH MASSACHUSETTS REGIMENT.

In 1860 Brown married Annie Elizabeth Gray (1835–1920) of Cambridgeport, Massachusetts. In addition to Brown's two daughters by his first wife, Annie gave him two more children, neither of whom survived to adulthood. When the war ended, Brown faced the necessity of earning a living that would support his new family. Having been an assistant to a physician while still a slave, and having studied medicine in his leisure time, Brown reinvented himself as a doctor. Still devoted to the numerous causes that had interested him for so long, he remained active in temperance, writing, speaking, and promoting the movement for the rest of his life. In 1880 Brown published *My Southern Home; or the South and Its People,* which encouraged African Americans to work hard and strive for self-improvement.

In 1884 Brown was stricken with bladder cancer. On November 6, 1884, he died in his home in Chelsea, Massachusetts.

See also ABOLITION.

Further reading: William Wells Brown, *The Travels of William Wells Brown, Including the Narrative of William Wells Brown, a Fugitive Slave, and the American Fugitive in Europe, Sketches of Places and People Abroad,* ed. Paul Jefferson (New York: M. Weiner Pub., 1991); Lucille Schulberg Warner, *From Slave to Abolitionist: The Life of William Wells Brown* (New York: Dial Press, 1976).

—Fiona Galvin

Bruce, Blanche Kelso (1841–1898)

U.S. senator, party leader, and educator, Blanche K. Bruce was born into slavery on March 1, 1841, in Farmville, Virginia. A mulatto, Bruce never knew who his father was. Bruce had a relatively privileged childhood as a household slave. As a playmate of his master's only son, he learned to read and write. During the CIVIL WAR, Bruce moved to Hannibal, Missouri, and established the state's first school for African Americans.

After a short stint at Ohio's Oberlin College, he settled in the Delta region in postwar Mississippi. Bruce won the favor of white planters in Bolivar County with his intelligence, eloquence, and moderate politics. He held the offices of sheriff, tax collector, and superintendent of EDUCATION simultaneously. However, as an educated mulatto from out of state, Bruce had little in common with the black masses of the Delta. In 1874 he purchased a 1,000-acre plantation. Regardless, his black constituents were loyal supporters because of his symbolic status as a black political leader and because he turned the school system in Bolivar County into one of the strongest in the state. Bruce's star rose in the REPUBLICAN PARTY as well. With the support of Governor Adelbert Ames, Bruce was selected senator from the state of Mississippi in 1875, the first African American to serve a full term in the U.S. Senate.

As a senator, he strongly defended civil rights for African Americans and demanded that the federal government stop violence against black voters. Bruce was a consistent supporter of federal aid for RAILROADS and an advocate for MISSISSIPPI RIVER improvements. He chaired the committee that investigated the failure of the FREEDMAN'S SAVINGS BANK.

After his career in Congress, he worked with John R. Lynch and James Hill, two other African-American Republicans, to control the state Republican Party. The "Triumvirate's" main interest was patronage. Bruce served as register of the treasury in 1881–85 and again in 1897–98. He was appointed recorder of deeds for the District of Columbia from 1891 to 1893.

Blanche K. Bruce died of diabetes on March 17, 1898.

Further reading: Eric Foner, *Freedom's Lawmakers: A Directory of Black Officeholders during Reconstruction* (Baton Rouge: Louisiana State University Press, 1996); Willard B. Gatewood, *Aristocrats of Color: The Black Elite, 1880–1920* (Fayetteville: University of Arkansas Press, 1990).

—Justin J. Behrend

Buchanan, James (1791–1868)

James Buchanan, who served as president of the United States (1856–60), was born on April 23, 1791, in Stony Batter, Pennsylvania. Although most well-known for his four years as president, Buchanan had a distinguished career in public service long before he entered the White House, serving in the U.S. Senate, as secretary of state, and as minister to Great Britain. Indeed, public service was the sole focus of Buchanan's life; although engaged once as a young man, he never married.

A lawyer by occupation, Buchanan began his political career with two terms in the Pennsylvania State Assembly beginning in 1814. From 1820 to 1830 he served as a congressman for Pennsylvania, first as a Federalist, and then as a Democrat. Buchanan traveled overseas as the appointed minister to Russia, a duty he performed from 1832 to 1833. Upon his return to Pennsylvania, Buchanan was elected U.S. senator from 1834 to 1845. During his third term, he resigned his seat to accept the post of secretary of state under President James K. Polk. Increasingly, Buchanan aspired to the presidency, but the 1852 nomination went to FRANKLIN PIERCE. President Pierce appointed Buchanan as minister to England, and for the next four years, Buchanan represented American interests overseas.

While in England, Buchanan became embroiled in controversy over the 1854 OSTEND MANIFESTO. Issued by Buchanan, along with the U.S. ministers to France and Spain, the manifesto argued that the United States should purchase the island of Cuba from Spain. If Spain refused, they recommended taking it by force. An unstated assumption of the Ostend Manifesto was that Cuba would join the Union as a slave state. While the manifesto came to nothing, it created an uproar. Spain naturally took offense and began preparations for war. Many antislavery Northerners mobilized against it, and support for the fledgling REPUBLICAN PARTY grew.

A good diplomat, Buchanan kept his job as minister. When he returned to the United States, he found himself

James Buchanan, 15th president of the United States *(Library of Congress)*

a hero among Southern Democrats, who applauded his pro-Southern and proslavery sympathies so evident in his support of the manifesto. Buchanan was also acceptable to Northern Democrats and secured his party's nomination easily in 1856. He ran on a platform that promoted the end of further agitation over SLAVERY and supported popular sovereignty in the territories. Buchanan defeated Republican John C. Frémont by a comfortable margin.

Buchanan took office in March 1857, and within days he was embroiled in sectional tensions. On March 6, 1857, the Supreme Court announced its decision in the DRED SCOTT case. Behind the scenes, Buchanan had exercised his influence to see to it that the decision was favorable to the South. He wanted desperately for the Supreme Court to settle the slavery question. It did not, and the Court's ruling nationalizing slavery outraged Northerners.

Sectional tensions worsened further with Buchanan's implementation of a pro-Southern policy in Kansas. The president felt that he had to mollify his Southern base of support, and so he accepted the fraudulent ELECTIONS that led to a proslavery legislature in the Kansas Territory.

Northern Democrats, led by STEPHEN A. DOUGLAS, protested in vain. Buchanan unwisely made support for the Kansas Lecompton Constitution, which legalized slavery, a test of party loyalty. This act destroyed the fragile unity of the Democrats. The beleaguered 67-year-old president recommended the admission of Kansas as a slave state, writing in his message to Congress that Kansas "is at this moment as much a slave state as Georgia and South Carolina."

The growing strength of the Republican Party owed much to the ineptitude of Buchanan's presidency, and in 1860 their candidate, ABRAHAM LINCOLN, captured the White House. An embittered Buchanan blamed the Republicans for the SECESSION of the seven southern states during the days and weeks following Lincoln's election. Nevertheless, he deplored the South's actions, stating that the Union was more than a "mere voluntary association of states." Indeed, Buchanan argued, the United States was a sovereign nation "not to be annulled at the pleasure of any one of the contracting parties." However, his strong defense of unionism was not followed by action during the remainder of his tenure.

In March 1861 Buchanan left WASHINGTON, D.C., and spent his remaining years defending his administration, most prominently in *Mr. Buchanan's Administration on the Eve of the Rebellion,* first published in 1866.

Buchanan died on June 1, 1868, in Lancaster, Pennsylvania.

See also BLEEDING KANSAS; BUSHWHACKERS; FOREIGN POLICY; JAYHAWKERS; KANSAS-NEBRASKA ACT.

Further reading: Michael J. Birkener, *James Buchanan and the Political Crisis of the 1850s* (Selinsgrove, Pa.: Susquehanna University Press, 1996); James Buchanan, *Mr. Buchanan's Administration on the Eve of the Rebellion* (1866; reprint, Scituate, Mass.: Digital Scanning, 2000); Philip Shriver Klein, *President James Buchanan, a Biography* (University Park: Pennsylvania State University Press, 1962).

—John P. Bowes

Bull Run/Manassas, First and Second Battles of
(July 21, 1861 and August 29–30, 1862)
The First Battle of Bull Run, also called First Manassas, was the first major engagement of the CIVIL WAR. The battle took place on July 21, 1861. Southern troops inflicted a humiliating defeat on Northern forces. The Second Battle of Bull Run, or Second Manassas, was fought on August 29 and 30, 1862, with Confederate forces once again defeating the Union troops. Northerners named the battles after Bull Run Creek, while Southerners referred to it by the name of the nearby town of Manassas.

Following the Confederate capture of FORT SUMTER in April 1861, both sides spent the next three months preparing their troops for action in the eastern theater. Men from the North and South responded to the call to arms, and the ranks of both armies swelled with thousands of new and untrained recruits. Northern soldiers enlisted for 90 days, and by July, those enlistments were nearly done. President ABRAHAM LINCOLN pushed his commanders to fight the Confederates before the UNION ARMY lost its recruits. Although Union general Irvin McDowell, head of the eastern Union army, was not sure that his men were truly ready for combat, he complied with Lincoln's wishes.

On July 21, McDowell set out with about 28,000 troops to capture the Confederate capital of RICHMOND, Virginia. Only 2,000 of his men were experienced soldiers, while the remainder had volunteered at the outbreak of hostilities. McDowell expected to encounter about 20,000 Confederate soldiers under the command of Gen. P. G. T. BEAUREGARD. McDowell did not know that 12,000 additional Southern troops had reinforced Beauregard's troops. Word reached WASHINGTON, D.C., that the two sides would meet near the town of Manassas, about 25 miles southwest of the Union capital. A number of Washington residents traveled out to watch what most Yankees expected would be a rout of the Confederate troops.

McDowell's men launched several attacks, pushing back the Confederate forces. Then Confederate resistance stiffened, led by Gen. THOMAS J. "STONEWALL" JACKSON. One Confederate commander told his men, "Look, there is Jackson standing like a stone wall," giving the general his famous nickname. After halting the Union advance, Beauregard ordered a counterattack. The inexperienced Federal troops broke under the pressure and fled the battlefield in panic. The observers from Washington also ran back toward the capital, amazed that the Confederates had defeated the Union forces. The victorious rebels had suffered 1,982 casualties: 387 killed, 1,582 wounded, and 13 missing. Northern losses were greater: 460 killed, 1,124 wounded, and 1,312 missing, for a total of 2,896. President Lincoln responded to the embarrassment by removing McDowell and replacing him with Gen. GEORGE B. MCCLELLAN. The battle also revealed that defeating the South would be much more difficult than many in the North had expected.

By the Second Battle of Bull Run, fought in August 1862, both armies were battle-tested. Gen. ROBERT E. LEE, now in command of Confederate forces, sought to defeat a Union army under the command of Gen. John Pope. Lee knew that two separate Union forces threatened his troops in Virginia. Pope commanded about 55,000 men in central Virginia, while George B. McClellan had about 100,000 men near Washington. President Lincoln had ordered the two Union forces to unify under McClellan's command, a fact known to the Confederates. Realizing that his forces would be outnumbered three to one if the Union plan succeeded, Lee determined to give battle at once to destroy Pope's army before it could join with McClellan's.

Lee sent Stonewall Jackson to observe the Federals, and Jackson won a battle on August 9 at the BATTLE OF CEDAR MOUNTAIN. The Confederate victory did not provoke an immediate Union response, so Jackson led a raid that resulted in the destruction of Pope's supply depot at Manassas on August 27. Angered at the loss of supplies, Pope moved against Jackson's positions and launched his 55,000 troops against Jackson's 12,000 on August 29. The Southerners held out against Pope's poorly coordinated attacks while Lee and Gen. JAMES LONGSTREET, commanding the remainder of Lee's 50,000 men, hurried to

First Battle of Bull Run (Manassas)
July 21, 1861

- Union positions
- Confederate positions
- Union artillery
- Confederate artillery
- Confederate cavalry

Catharpin R.

Bull Run Creek

McDowell

Grover and Sudley Rd.

unfinished R.R.

Mathews Hill

Warrenton Tpk.

Youngs Brook

Chinn Brook

Evans

Stone Bridge

To Centreville →

Warrenton Tpk.

Jackson

Henry Hill

Johnston

Beauregard

Bull Run Creek

N

0   1 Mile
0   1 Km

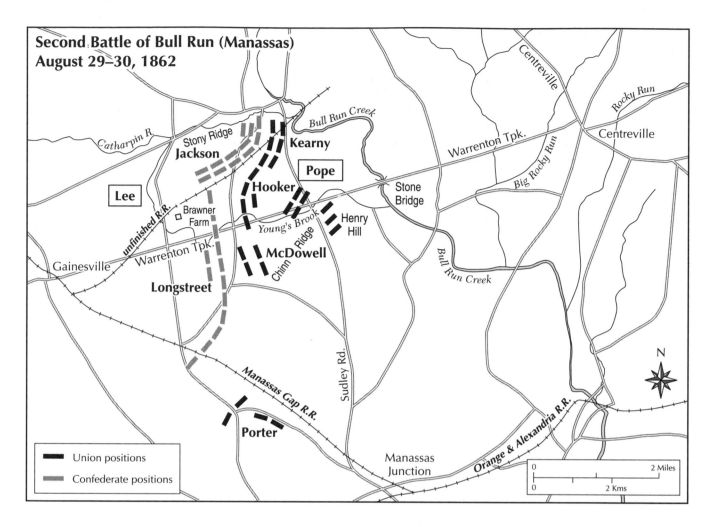

Second Battle of Bull Run (Manassas)
August 29–30, 1862

Union positions
Confederate positions

join forces with Jackson. Pope refused to believe reports that Longstreet had arrived with reinforcements and launched a new attack against Jackson's troops. Longstreet's men raked the advancing Northerners with artillery fire, breaking the attack. Lee then ordered Longstreet to attack and outflank the Union forces. The Confederate troops turned the Union left flank and forced them to retreat. Unlike the First Battle of Bull Run, Northern troops retreated in good order and remained intact. During the campaign, the South recorded 9,200 dead, wounded, or missing in action, while Union casualties numbered 16,000. The Confederate victory dashed Northern hopes for conquering Virginia quickly. Meanwhile, Lee and his army, coming off a string of victories in the summer and fall of 1862, decided to take the war North and invaded Maryland in September.

Further reading: William C. Davis, *Battle at Bull Run: A History of the First Major Campaign of the Civil War* (Gar-

den City, N.Y.: Doubleday, 1977); John J. Hennessy, *Return to Bull Run: The Campaign and Battle of Second Manassas* (New York: Simon & Schuster, 1993).

—Matthew G. McCoy

Burnside, Ambrose E. (1824–1881)

Inventor of the Burnside carbine, a Union general, and three-time governor of Rhode Island, Ambrose Everett Burnside was the commander of the Army of the Potomac between November 1862 and January 1863.

Burnside was born in Liberty, Indiana, in 1824. Originally from South Carolina, his father had freed the family's slaves and moved north shortly before Ambrose's birth. Burnside entered the UNITED STATES MILITARY ACADEMY AT WEST POINT in 1843. Graduating 18th in the class of 1847, he saw action in the Mexican-American War. Remaining in the regular army after the war, he was wounded by Apache warriors while guarding the Southwestern border area.

In 1853 Burnside resigned his army position and moved to Rhode Island. There he started a manufacturing company that produced a breech-loading rifle he himself had designed. When Burnside failed to secure a crucial government contract, his creditors took ownership of his patents. Thousands of Burnside carbines would be produced for the army during the CIVIL WAR.

In the late 1850s Burnside moved from one job and state to another. He worked for GEORGE B. MCCLELLAN, a fellow West Pointer and future commander, on the Illinois Central Railroad, and for the Rhode Island Militia. At the beginning of the Civil War, Burnside rejoined the army and was appointed colonel in the First Rhode Island Volunteers. He fought at the FIRST BATTLE OF BULL RUN and shortly thereafter was elevated to brigadier general by President Lincoln. Burnside's successful campaigns in North Carolina led to the capture of Roanoke Island, New Bern, Beaufort, and Fort Macon.

Promoted to major general in 1862, Burnside commanded the IX Corps in the Army of the Potomac, which he led during the BATTLE OF ANTIETAM in September 1862. On the day of the battle, September 17, Burnside's orders from Gen. George B. McClellan were to move against Lee's right side, which had been seriously weakened during the terrible fighting. Seized with indecision, Burnside delayed moving his corps over a stone bridge (now known as "Burnside's Bridge") that crossed Antietam Creek. That delay allowed Confederate reinforcements to strengthen the lines, and one of the great opportunities for a smashing Union victory was lost forever.

Burnside's boss, George B. McClellan, lost his command a month later, and Lincoln appointed a reluctant Burnside in his place. Burnside had declined Lincoln twice before, not only out of loyalty to his friend but because of an accurate assessment of his lowly generalship capabilities. Predictably, Burnside's command of the Army of the Potomac was a disaster. First, he lost a costly battle in December 1862 at FREDERICKSBURG, Virginia, against Lee's vastly outnumbered army. Then, in a vain attempt to redeem his reputation and uplift his demoralized army, Burnside decided to go "on to Richmond" in the middle of the winter. His troops were dry when they started their march out of the WASHINGTON, D.C., camps on January 19, but soon the rains came, and "Burnside's Mud March" became the laughingstock of the nation.

In January 1863 Lincoln removed Burnside from command of the Army of the Potomac and replaced him with Gen. JOSEPH HOOKER. By March he had been given command of the Department of the Ohio. Away from the battlefield, Burnside proved more successful. He arrested and tried Democratic congressman CLEMENT L. VALLANDIGHAM, a notorious COPPERHEAD. He also managed to direct the capture of Confederate JOHN HUNT MORGAN, whose cavalrymen were threatening southern Ohio. Toward the end of the year, Burnside ably defended Knoxville against Confederate forces, saving the city for the Union.

Burnside joined the 1864 spring campaigns under Gen. ULYSSES S. GRANT. He was placed in charge of his old IX Corps and saw fighting at the WILDERNESS, SPOTSYLVANIA, and North Anna. During the siege of Petersburg, Burnside devised a bold plan that went wrong in the Battle of the Crater, causing the senseless loss of many lives. This time he was gone for good. Burnside resigned from the army on April 15, 1865.

Burnside's postwar years were very successful. He became a prosperous businessman and achieved a solid record in Rhode Island's political history. He was elected three times to the governorship, and in 1874 he was elected to the U.S. Senate, where he served until his death on September 13, 1881, in Bristol, Rhode Island. He is buried in Providence.

Further reading: Edward Hull, *Burnside Breech Loading Carbines, 1853–1866* (Lincoln, R.I.: A. Mowbray, 1986); William Marvel, *Burnside* (Chapel Hill: University of North Carolina Press, 1991).

—Fiona Galvin

Ambrose E. Burnside *(National Archives)*

bushwhackers

During the CIVIL WAR, the term *bushwhacker* was applied to Southerners or Confederate supporters who carried on guerrilla warfare. While the targets of bushwhackers were usually Union soldiers, property, and interests, the name also implied a tendency to plunder private citizens and property.

The violence that plagued Kansas and Missouri in the 1850s spilled over into the 1860s and gave rise to some of the most notorious bushwhackers. One example is WILLIAM CLARKE QUANTRILL, an Ohio native who led a band of bushwhackers into Kansas and sacked the town of Aubry in March 1862. A year and a half later the band raided and burned the city of Lawrence, killing about 150 civilians.

Quantrill attracted men such as Coleman and Robert Younger, Jesse and Frank James, Dave Poole, Arch Clements, "Bloody Bill" Anderson, and George Todd. Anderson and Todd later formed their own bushwhacker bands. Anderson led a bloody attack at Centralia, Missouri, in 1864 in which his guerrillas robbed a train, murdered a number of unarmed Union soldiers, and then scalped and mutilated Union militia casualties in an ensuing fight.

Some Confederate bushwhackers carried on more legitimate warfare, such as JOHN SINGLETON MOSBY, who led guerrilla operations in Union-held northern Virginia. He was commissioned a captain by the Confederate government and organized his small band of guerrillas into the 43rd Virginia Partisan Ranger Battalion. Mosby led many successful guerrilla attacks against Union RAILROADS, supply and communication lines, and bridges. Brig. Gen. JOHN HUNT MORGAN carried on similar operations behind Union lines in Kentucky and Ohio.

Bushwhackers forced the Union to increase troop numbers in vulnerable rear areas and caused several minor logistical problems. In many areas their brutality and disregard for accepted methods of warfare led to bitterness that extended well beyond the end of the Civil War.

See also BLEEDING KANSAS.

Further reading: Michael Fellman, *Inside War: The Guerrilla Conflict in Missouri during the American Civil War* (New York: Oxford University Press, 1989); James A. Ramage, *Gray Ghost: The Life of Col. John Singleton Mosby* (Lexington: University Press of Kentucky, 1999).

—Richard J. Roder

Butler, Benjamin Franklin (1818–1893)

Lawyer, Democratic politician, and businessman, Union general Benjamin Butler was born in New Hampshire but lived most of his life in Massachusetts. Educated at Waterville College in Maine, Butler joined the Massachusetts bar in 1840. Although he practiced criminal law, Butler's real passion was politics, and in 1853 he won a seat in the Massachusetts State House. By 1859 he had worked his way up to the state senate as a Democrat. To support himself, Butler also operated a mill in Lowell, Massachusetts, producing wool cloth.

Although Butler was a Northerner, he hoped a moderate Southern president could avoid sectional strife. Disappointed when war erupted, he stoutly declared himself 100 percent behind the Union. Butler was appointed brigadier general in the Massachusetts Volunteers. For his service in helping to stop the BALTIMORE RIOTS in the spring of 1861, he was promoted to major general. Overall, Butler was valued far more for his political skills than his military talents. In command and in battle, Butler proved to be one of the worst of the so-called political generals, those men whose high army appointments were owed entirely to their ability to marshal support and votes for the government.

Stationed at Fortress Monroe, Virginia, Butler first came to the nation's attention when he declared fleeing slaves "CONTRABAND of war." This circumvented federal authority and antagonized slaveholders in both rebel states and border states like Maryland. Butler's unpopularity with Southern civilians grew during his administration of Louisiana as military governor in 1862. During this time, Butler issued his infamous order that forced Confederate women to treat Union soldiers with respect or to suffer severe penalties.

Although Butler's supporters considered his administration able, he was accused of corruption and even theft by locals, who said that "Spoons" Butler had stolen silverware from the confiscated home in which he lived. Many generals were dismissed or demoted for displaying such breathtaking incompetence. Butler, however, was a wily and popular figure from an important state. Lincoln could not afford to offend him, especially since Butler switched his allegiance to the REPUBLICAN PARTY in 1862.

Butler emerged as a champion of the use of African-American soldiers and, while in New Orleans, raised the Louisiana Native Guard, one of the first two black units to fight in the UNION ARMY. Removed from the Crescent City in early 1863, Butler was placed in charge of the Department of Virginia and North Carolina. In 1864 he led the newly formed Army of the James in the campaign to take RICHMOND, where his battlefield fiascos led to his retirement, courtesy of Gen. ULYSSES S. GRANT. Butler resigned his commission on November 30, 1865.

During RECONSTRUCTION, Congressman Butler joined the RADICAL REPUBLICANS and worked for the impeachment of President ANDREW JOHNSON. He also worked to guarantee the political rights and personal safety of African Americans, including lending his strong support to the CIVIL RIGHTS ACT OF 1875.

Butler served as Massachusetts governor from 1882 until 1884. Always a champion of the working masses, he was nominated for president by the People's Party on an antimonopoly platform. However, Butler's personal and political tactics remained controversial, and he was widely despised for his documented corrupt practices. Nevertheless, in spite of his incompetence on the battlefield and his vain and arrogant demeanor, he was a devoted public servant. He helped to secure a number of important reforms, including many of the progressive race laws of Reconstruction. Benjamin Butler died on January 11, 1893, in WASHINGTON, D.C.

See also NEW ORLEANS, BATTLE OF.

Further reading: Hans Trefousse, *Ben Butler: The South Called Him Beast!* (New York: Twayne, 1957); Richard S. West, *Lincoln's Scapegoat General: A Life of Benjamin F. Butler, 1818–1893* (Boston: Houghton Mifflin, 1965).

—Chad Vanderford

C

Calhoun, John C. See Volume IV

Carney, William Harvey (1840–1908)

William H. Carney was the first African American to receive the Congressional MEDAL OF HONOR during the CIVIL WAR. He was born in 1840 in Norfolk, Virginia, to a slave father who escaped to the North via the UNDERGROUND RAILROAD. The family settled in New Bedford, Massachusetts, one of the major stops for fugitive slaves, and briefly the home of ABOLITIONist FREDERICK DOUGLASS. Carney was working as a laborer when the war broke out. In February 1863, the Massachusetts governor John A. Andrew organized the first all-black regiment and called for volunteers. Carney and 39 other African Americans from New Bedford joined the 54TH MASSACHUSETTS REGIMENT. The New Bedford men were part of the 54th's famed Company C.

Carney was selected to be a sergeant, one of the noncommissioned officers of the unit. After training near Boston, the 54th was sent to Hilton Head, South Carolina, to participate in the Union campaign to reduce the forts and batteries that protected Charleston. On the night of July 18, 1863, the Massachusetts Regiment led an assault on Fort Wagner, the main fortification that protected Charleston Harbor. Commanded by Col. Robert Gould Shaw, the 54th displayed great courage in battle. William H. Carney was one of the few to make it to the top of the fort, where he rescued the regimental flag from the dead color bearer. Injured three times, Carney survived the battle, and upon entering the field hospital for wounded men he told his comrades: "Boys, the old flag never touched the ground."

The regiment saw further action in South Carolina and Florida before disbanding. Carney was officially discharged on June 30, 1864. He returned to New Bedford and worked as a mail carrier and later as an elevator operator in the Massachusetts State House. After the war, William H. Carney gave many speeches recounting his role in the battle of Fort Wagner. He became a symbol of African-American manliness and courage, and he was memorialized in paintings and sculpture. Carney's Medal of Honor was awarded to him in May 1900, nearly 37 years after the attack on Fort Wagner. Carney died on December 9, 1908, in Boston, Massachusetts.

See also AFRICAN-AMERICAN REGIMENTS.

Further reading: Peter Burchard, *One Gallant Rush: Robert Gould Shaw and His Brave Black Regiment* (New York: St. Martin's Press, 1965); Luis F. Emilio, *A Brave Black Regiment: History of the Fifty-fourth Massachusetts Volunteer Infantry* (Boston: The Boston Book Co., 1894).

carpetbaggers

Carpetbaggers were Northerners who either moved to the South or remained in the South after the CIVIL WAR. They were one segment of the Southern Republican coalition that also included SCALAWAGS and African Americans. The carpetbaggers comprised only 16 percent of this coalition, but they dominated Republican politics in the region. They bore primary responsibility for dealing with the practical problems of reconstructing the South. Republican leaders also hoped that carpetbaggers could help to build a permanent presence for the REPUBLICAN PARTY in Southern politics.

The motivations of the carpetbaggers were diverse. Some had humanitarian motives and wanted to help the former slaves make the transition to freedom. This was certainly the case with Republican Adelbert Ames from Maine. A distinguished Union officer, Ames was the RECONSTRUCTION governor and U.S. senator from Mississippi who struggled mightily to help the freedpeople of his adopted state. Other carpetbaggers wanted to help bind the nation's wounds and to facilitate political and economic cooperation between North and South. Still others sensed that the postwar South offered excellent political and economic opportunities.

The carpetbaggers and their Republican allies faced a number of significant obstacles in achieving their goals, however. First, the Republican governments lacked the power to make permanent changes in Southern life. Their hold on office was tenuous at best, and even in the best of circumstances it is difficult for governments to render significant social, economic, and political change in a short period of time. An even greater issue was that the Republican coalition depended on black votes and military rule. White Southerners hated the carpetbaggers for this. Indeed, it was white Southerners who created the term *carpetbagger*, based on a stereotype of carpetbaggers as individuals who had carried their belongings South in the same cheap, carpet suitcases used by salesmen. White Southerners also maintained that carpetbaggers were corrupt and were only interested in their own personal financial and political gains.

The Southern depiction of the carpetbaggers as unscrupulous schemers has found its way into many history books. Certainly, there was some truth to this characterization. There were a number of carpetbaggers who were corrupt and who cared little about the needs of their constituents or their party. These individuals were an exception to the rule, however. Most carpetbaggers did what they could under difficult circumstances, and they achieved a few successes.

Under the carpetbagger-led governments, a public EDUCATION system was set up in every state. This was a major achievement because, before the war, North Carolina was the only Southern state with a public education system. By 1900 African-American literacy had climbed above 50 percent. In addition, civil rights protection was legislated and discrimination was outlawed. The federal CIVIL RIGHTS ACT OF 1866 required that states treat African Americans equally under the law; this was followed by antidiscrimination policies passed by Republican state governments.

As important as the successes of the carpetbagger-led governments were, they must be balanced against their failures. Carpetbaggers focused heavily on building internal improvements, particularly RAILROADS. They thought that the spread of railroads would usher in the "New South," with a modern, industrialized ECONOMY. When it came time to build, however, the railroads were often poorly planned or poorly executed. Contracts were granted to corrupt corporations, sometimes in violation of state law. By the time Reconstruction ended, only 7,000 miles of new railroad track had been laid in the South.

In addition to their belief in the value of railroads, carpetbaggers also came south looking to redistribute Southern land. This was another area in which the Republicans largely failed. With the exception of creating the South Carolina land commission in 1868, nothing was ever done to grant land to the freedmen. Virtually all African Ameri-

Cartoon showing Carl Schurz, a German-born editor, soldier, and politician. Despite the characterization of Schurz as a carpetbagger, he actually opposed the Radical Reconstruction policies. *(Library of Congress)*

cans were forced to work as laborers during Reconstruction. Eventually, this evolved into SHARECROPPING, which trapped African Americans in poverty.

Ultimately, then, the carpetbaggers had a mixed record. They were able to expand educational opportunities for freedmen and also to help secure the passage of important civil rights legislation on the state level. Meanwhile, they made little progress in building internal improvements and in providing land for the freedmen. The carpetbaggers also failed in their larger goal of establishing a unified, politically viable Republican coalition in the South. The era of Reconstruction left most white Southerners with a deep and abiding resentment of the Republicans, which laid the groundwork for the "REDEMPTION" of the South by white Democratic politicians. With the demise of the carpetbaggers and scalawags and the curtailing of African Americans' voting rights, the Republican Party would not again have a meaningful presence in the South for nearly a century.

Further reading: Richard H. Abbott, *The Republican Party and the South, 1855–1877: The First Southern Strategy* (Chapel Hill: University of North Carolina Press, 1986); Eric Foner, *Reconstruction: America's Unfinished Revolution, 1863–1877* (New York: Harper & Row, 1988).
—Christopher Bates

cartography

Cartography is the art of making maps and charts. Throughout the first part of the 19th century, the U.S. government spent a great deal of time and money on expeditions to map the land that the country had acquired, especially the vast Louisiana Purchase. Meanwhile, the older and more heavily settled areas of the country received very little attention from government cartographers. These areas eventually became the battlegrounds for much of the CIVIL WAR, and so the oversight created a major logistical problem for commanders on both sides, necessitating the creation of thousands of new maps.

The Union was better prepared to make the maps that were needed, since it had several experienced mapmaking units already in place, including the U.S. Coastal Survey and the Navy's Hydrographic Office. The most important was the UNION ARMY's Engineering Corps, which included a group of specialists in cartography known as the Topographical Bureau. The bureau had been created in 1816 and by the time of the Civil War had grown to 45 men under the command of Col. William E. Merrill. Only seven of the 45 cartographers resigned their commissions to join the Confederacy when the war broke out, and only two of the seven were senior members of the bureau. In addition to retaining the majority of the nation's experienced military cartographers, the Union also had better technology for duplicating maps. The North's prosperity allowed for the purchase of lithographic presses, which had only been recently developed. Although very heavy, these presses could travel with an army, and they allowed for high-quality reproductions of maps at a rapid pace.

The only real advantage that the Confederacy enjoyed in the creation of maps was that the war was largely fought in their home territory. This made it easier to make accurate maps, since local residents of an area that was being mapped could generally be counted on for assistance. However, this benefit was largely negated by other obstacles confronting Confederate mapmakers. For the first year of the war, the Confederacy had no entity responsible for coordinating mapmaking operations. Not until ROBERT E. LEE took command of the Army of Northern Virginia in June 1862 was a topographical department established, under the command of Capt. Albert H. Campbell.

Campbell's staff was small, and the materials needed for mapmaking were in short supply in the South, so it was impossible for the Confederate mapmakers to produce anywhere near as many maps as their Union counterparts. Even the Confederate capital of RICHMOND was not completely mapped until early 1863, when the war was nearly half over. Campbell also did not have modern technology for duplicating maps, and so the maps given to Confederate field commanders tended to be much cruder than the maps used by the Union field commanders.

Despite the Union's cartographic advantages over the Confederacy, the first months of the war were largely fought without good maps on either side. During the PENINSULAR CAMPAIGN of 1862, for example, leaders on both sides of the conflict were hampered by their poor understanding of local geography. Confederate general Richard Taylor wrote that "Confederate Commanders knew no more about the topography of the country than they did about Central Africa." Union general GEORGE B. MCCLELLAN concurred, noting that "good maps were not to be found." As the war progressed, however, such complaints were less frequent. Indeed, Northern mapmakers in particular became an industry unto themselves. In 1864, the final full year of the war, the Union's various mapmaking bureaucracies produced 43,000 maps and 44,000 nautical charts. By the end of the year, virtually the entire Confederacy had been mapped.

Confederate mapmakers could not approach the level of production achieved by their Union counterparts, although they did have some notable successes. The Confederacy's finest mapmaker was Jedediah Hotchkiss, a self-taught cartographer who was on the staff of Gen. THOMAS J. "STONEWALL" JACKSON. Shortly after joining the CONFEDERATE ARMY in March 1862, Hotchkiss was instructed to make the maps needed for Jackson's SHENANDOAH VALLEY CAMPAIGN. He responded by producing what are arguably the finest maps created by any cartographer on either side of the war. Jackson went on to defeat a numerically superior Union force, and undoubtedly Hotchkiss's maps played an important role in the victory.

Of course, the Union's cartographers had a few successes of their own. Perhaps the most significant occurred in 1864, when a group of mapmakers was ordered to help make the preparations for SHERMAN'S MARCH THROUGH GEORGIA. Under the direct supervision of Colonel Merrill, they completed their "Map of Northern Georgia" on May 2, 1864. The map's level of accuracy was an impressive achievement, given that it was created by men working in enemy territory. And even when it was inaccurate, the map enabled Union commanders to coordinate their actions, since they were all working off of the same map.

Cartographers on both sides played an important role as the Civil War unfolded. By the middle of 1862, mapmakers were providing invaluable intelligence, often at a dizzying pace. Despite their valuable service, however, they received little credit during or after the war. Indeed, they continue to remain largely obscure; their maps are not often reproduced, and mention of their work is rarely incorporated into discussions of TACTICS AND STRATEGY.

Further reading: Jedediah Hotchkiss, *Make Me a Map of the Valley: The Civil War Journal of Stonewall Jackson's Cartographer,* ed. Archie P. McDonald (Dallas: Southern Methodist University Press, 1973); Daniel D. Nettesheim, *Topographical Intelligence and the American Civil War* (Fort Leavenworth, Kans.: U.S. Army Command and General Staff College, 1978); Richard W. Stephenson, *Civil War Maps: An Annotated List of Maps and Atlases in the Library of Congress* (Washington, D.C.: Library of Congress, 1989).

—Christopher Bates

Cary, Mary Ann Shadd (1823–1893)

Born a free African American but compelled by a deeply rooted commitment to activism on behalf of enslaved people, Mary Ann Shadd Cary is best known for an extensive body of written work. A teacher, author, activist, and journalist, Cary spoke out on behalf of fugitive slaves and against both SLAVERY and racism, most famously in the newspaper the *Provincial Freeman.*

Firstborn of 13 children, Mary Ann Shadd spent her earliest years in Delaware and Pennsylvania. Educated by Quakers and raised Roman Catholic, Shadd disliked and distrusted organized mainstream RELIGION because of its role in supporting slavery. In religion, as in everything else, Shadd believed that African Americans should not assimilate but, rather, should develop their own culture while taking full measure of the opportunities of the nation as a whole.

Shadd was a teacher in several Northern cities before she moved with her brother to Canada West, a common Canadian destination (roughly surrounding the Canadian side of the Great Lakes) for escaped slaves. In Canada West, she published a pamphlet, *Notes on Canada West* (1852), intended to help fugitive slaves reach Canada and prosper. Initially, Shadd taught in Canada West. A part of her salary was supplied by the AMERICAN MISSIONARY ASSOCIATION, a relationship she later regretted.

In 1853 Shadd began a career as a writer and editor. Samuel Ringgold Ward offered her a position with the *Provincial Freeman,* a journal written for the men and women of Canada West who had escaped to freedom. Swiftly, Shadd became editor of the paper, and her writing and activism made her a spokesperson for fugitive slaves as a whole. Shadd participated in antislavery politics with zest and vigor, wading right into the often messy fights among

different factions. In 1856 she met and married Thomas G. F. Cary, with whom she had a daughter named Sally in 1862.

In 1863 Mary Shadd Cary accepted a position as a recruiter of African-American soldiers, working in Indiana. She moved again when the conflict ended to WASHINGTON, D.C., where she became a public school principal and a contributor to several African American papers.

Not content with her considerable accomplishments, Cary joined the student body of Howard University, pursuing a degree in the law. It was granted in 1883, when Cary was 60 years old. Although she may have intended to do so, there is no evidence that she practiced law. Cary also joined the National Woman Suffrage Association, for which she returned to Canada in 1881 to organize a suffrage event.

In 1893, Cary died as a result of a cancerous tumor. See also WOMEN'S STATUS AND RIGHTS.

Further reading: Jane Rhodes, *Mary Ann Shadd Cary: The Black Press and Protest in the Nineteenth Century* (Bloomington: Indiana University Press, 1998).

—Fiona Galvin

Catto, Octavius (1839–1871)

Minister, activist, and reformer, Octavius Catto was born and raised in Philadelphia and educated at the Institute for Colored Youth, a Quaker-run school for African Americans. Catto had a great deal of skill as an orator, and after graduation he followed his father William into the ministry. He quickly became a prominent leader of Philadelphia's African-American community and an ardent civil rights activist.

Philadelphia was known in the antebellum era for its hostility toward people of color. After a visit to the city, FREDERICK DOUGLASS wrote, "There is not perhaps anywhere to be found a city in which prejudice against color is more rampant than in Philadelphia." Catto was not deterred, however. He was particularly concerned with voting rights, which had been extended to Pennsylvania's African Americans by the state constitution of 1790 and then revoked by an act of the state legislature in 1838. In hopes of regaining the vote, Catto led petition drives, attended state and national meetings of African-American leaders, gave countless speeches, and organized election day protests. The only tangible result of Catto's efforts was increased violence against Philadelphia's African-American population, including an 1849 riot that received national attention.

During the CIVIL WAR, Catto lobbied for the enlistment of African-American troops, believing that men who had taken up arms for the United States could not possibly be denied their rights as citizens. When the word came in 1863 that government would begin to accept black regiments, Catto organized a group of 100 volunteers. They traveled to Harrisburg and, after some reluctance on the part of Governor Andrew Curtin, were mustered into the UNION ARMY as part of the Sixth U.S. Colored Infantry.

After the war, Catto continued his work, and he was deeply gratified by the passage of the FIFTEENTH AMENDMENT in 1870. In October 1871, Philadelphia's first ELECTIONS after the amendment's passage, Catto traveled around town exhorting all African Americans to vote. As in 1849, there was a riot, and this time Catto was killed. His funeral was attended by thousands of people, and according to one eyewitness, "Not since the funeral cortege of ABRAHAM LINCOLN has there been one as large or as imposing in Philadelphia." Catto's murder was an early indication of what was to become a recurring theme of the RECONSTRUCTION era—legal equality for African Americans did not necessarily translate into actual equality.

See also RACE AND RACIAL CONFLICT.

Further reading: Octavius Catto, *Our Alma Mater: An Address Delivered at Concert Hall on the Occasion of the Twelfth Annual Commencement of the Institute for Colored Youth, May 10th, 1864* (Philadelphia: Historic Publications, 1969); Roger Lane, *William Dorsey's Philadelphia and Ours: On the Past and Future of the Black City in America* (New York: Oxford University Press, 1991).

—Christopher Bates

Cedar Mountain, Battle of (August 9, 1862)

At the Battle of Cedar Mountain, Confederate forces under THOMAS J. "STONEWALL" JACKSON managed to snatch victory from the jaws of defeat. The battle thus became an important step in turning back the Union offensives launched in the summer of 1862, a task that was completed 19 days later at the SECOND BATTLE OF BULL RUN.

By July 1862 GEORGE B. MCCLELLAN's PENINSULAR CAMPAIGN had essentially failed, and he had ordered the withdrawal of Union troops from the area around RICHMOND. To the south, however, Union general John Pope was enjoying a fair amount of success. A portion of Pope's Federal forces, led by Gen. Nathaniel Banks, captured the town of Culpeper and made plans to move further south.

To neutralize the threat, 14,000 troops under Stonewall Jackson were sent to halt the Union's advance. Jackson was not himself aware that Union troops held the town of Culpeper, and so when the Confederates arrived there on the afternoon of August 9, they essentially stumbled into an ambush. Union artillery pounded the Southerners as Gen. JUBAL A. EARLY attempted to organize a line of artillery and infantry with which to fight back. The artillery battle lasted for three hours and claimed the lives of many Confederates.

At 5:00 that afternoon, Banks ordered a pair of infantry attacks against the poorly organized Confederate line. The attacks broke through and trapped many of Jackson's troops on the narrow, winding road leading to Culpeper. In the confusion, a substantial number of Southern soldiers were killed, while others threw down their guns and fled. Jackson arrived on the scene in the midst of this panicked retreat, and he responded swiftly. Jackson drew his sword, the only time this is known to have happened during the war, and he himself led the Confederate countercharge. At the same time, fresh troops under Gen. AMBROSE P. HILL arrived. This gave the Confederates a two-to-one advantage, and the exhausted Union troops were forced to fall back. What would have been a decisive defeat for the Confederates instead became a hard-won victory. The Federal forces suffered 2,381 casualties, the Confederates 1,276. So many men were wounded so quickly that some soldiers called the battle "Slaughter Mountain" in their LETTERS home.

On the next day, August 10, Union leadership decided not to continue the battle and requested permission under a flag of truce to gather their wounded and bury their dead. Jackson and his troops withdrew that evening. Less than a month later, the same armies would meet again at the Second Battle of Bull Run. Victory would be Jackson's on that occasion as well. Pope was forced to join McClellan in withdrawing from Virginia, giving the initiative to ROBERT E. LEE and allowing him to launch an offensive into Maryland in September 1862. It would be two years before Union forces would once again penetrate so deeply into Virginia.

Further reading: Robert K. Krick, *Stonewall Jackson at Cedar Mountain* (Chapel Hill: University of North Carolina Press, 1990).

—Arthur E. Amos

Chamberlain, Joshua L. (1828–1914)

College professor, Union officer, and governor of Maine, Joshua Lawrence Chamberlain was born in Brewer, Maine, on September 28, 1828, to Joshua Chamberlain, Jr., and Sarah Dupee Brastow. Graduating from Bowdoin College in 1852 and Bangor Theological Seminary in 1855, he took a teaching position at Bowdoin and married Frances (Fannie) Caroline Adams.

In 1862, Chamberlain, age 33 and the father of two, took a leave of absence from Bowdoin and accepted a commission as lieutenant colonel of the 20th Maine Volunteer

Infantry. Promoted to colonel after the BATTLE OF FREDER-ICKSBURG, Chamberlain ordered a bayonet charge at Gettysburg on July 2, 1863, that probably saved the Federal position on Little Round Top from being turned by the Confederates. Following a bout with malaria in 1863, he rejoined his regiment at Spotsylvania in May 1864 and was soon given command of a brigade. Chamberlain was officially promoted to brigadier general after he was badly wounded during the PETERSBURG CAMPAIGN. He returned to the army before the BATTLE OF FIVE FORKS, where he was brevetted major general for bravery. Gen. ULYSSES S. GRANT further honored Chamberlain by choosing him to receive the Confederate surrender at APPOMATTOX COURT HOUSE in 1865.

Chamberlain returned to Maine a hero. Uninterested in resuming his professorship, he secured the Republican nomination for governor of Maine and won election in 1866. After a tumultuous four years as governor, he became president of Bowdoin College and set about reforming the curriculum, with mixed results. An attempt to institute military training at the all-male college failed when the students refused to drill.

An increasingly conservative Chamberlain grew nostalgic about the war, expressed sympathy toward ex-Confederates, and applauded the end of RECONSTRUCTION. Having resigned the Bowdoin presidency in 1883, Chamberlain spent his retirement trying to recapture his wartime glory. He lectured on the 20th Maine's heroism at Gettysburg and on the surrender of Lee. He wrote magazine articles, gave Memorial Day addresses, and made frequent trips to old battlefields, especially Gettysburg. In 1893 he was awarded the congressional MEDAL OF HONOR for his leadership at Little Round Top. In his 80s, Chamberlain wrote a history of the Appomattox campaign (published posthumously in 1915 as *The Passing of the Armies*), that revealed his romantic view of war as the ultimate test of character.

Chamberlain died in Brunswick, Maine, on February 24, 1914, of complications from the Petersburg wound he had received 50 years earlier.

See also GETTYSBURG, BATTLE OF; SPOTSYLVANIA, BATTLE OF.

Further reading: Joshua Lawrence Chamberlain, *The Passing of the Armies: An Account of the Final Campaign of the Army of the Potomac, Based upon Personal Reminiscences of the Fifth Army Corps* (1915; reprint, Lincoln: University of Nebraska Press, 1998); Thomas A. Desjardin, *Stand Firm Ye Boys from Maine: The 20th Maine and the Gettysburg Campaign* (Gettysburg, Pa.: Thomas Publications, 1995); Alice R. Trulock, *In the Hands of Providence: Joshua L. Chamberlain and the American Civil War* (Chapel Hill: University of North Carolina Press, 1992).

—Amy J. Kinsel

Chancellorsville, Battle of (April 27–May 6, 1863)
The Confederate victory at Chancellorsville capped a remarkable 11-month period during which ROBERT E. LEE built the Army of Northern Virginia into a self-confident and formidable weapon. The sheer odds against Confederate success at Chancellorsville elevated it to a special position among Lee's victories. Union general JOSEPH HOOKER had rebuilt the Army of the Potomac after AMBROSE E. BURNSIDE's removal from command in late-January 1863. Hooker entered the Chancellorsville campaign at the head of a force with ample equipment, strong discipline, and high morale. He pronounced it "the finest army on the planet."

During the winter of 1862–63, Lee had dispersed his cavalry to secure sufficient fodder and detached two divisions under JAMES LONGSTREET to southeastern Virginia. These measures left him with approximately 61,000 soldiers to face 133,000 Federals. Hooker thus enjoyed the widest margin of manpower of any Union general who had fought against the Army of Northern Virginia to that point in the conflict.

Hooker added an impressive strategic blueprint to his material advantages. He planned marching the bulk of his army up the Rappahannock River in a wide turning movement around Lee's left. At the same time, a sizeable force under John Sedgwick would cross the Rappahannock opposite Lee at Fredericksburg to hold the Confederates in place. As a third element in the plan, Federal cavalry under George Stoneman would swing around Lee's left before striking south toward RICHMOND. If all went well, Lee would be caught between Hooker's powerful turning column to the west and Sedgwick's troops in his front. Confederate options, thought Hooker, would be limited to a retreat toward Richmond or desperate assaults against one or both of the major components of the Army of the Potomac.

The campaign unfolded rapidly after Hooker began his march up the Rappahannock on April 27, 1863. The Federals crossed the Rappahannock and Rapidan Rivers, and by evening on April 30 the flanking force reached the crossroads of Chancellorsville, 10 miles in Lee's rear. There Hooker's soldiers lay in the midst of the Wilderness of Spotsylvania, a scrub forest heavily cut over to feed small iron furnaces in the area. Hooker brimmed with confidence on the night of April 30. He stated that "our enemy must either ingloriously fly, or . . . give us battle on our own ground, where certain destruction awaits him."

Lee responded to Hooker's actions with a series of typically bold moves. Assigning roughly 10,000 men under JUBAL A. EARLY to watch Sedgwick at Fredericksburg, Lee and THOMAS J. "STONEWALL" JACKSON hurried the rest of the Army of Northern Virginia westward to stop Hooker. The decisive moment of the campaign occurred on the morning of May 1, when the vanguards

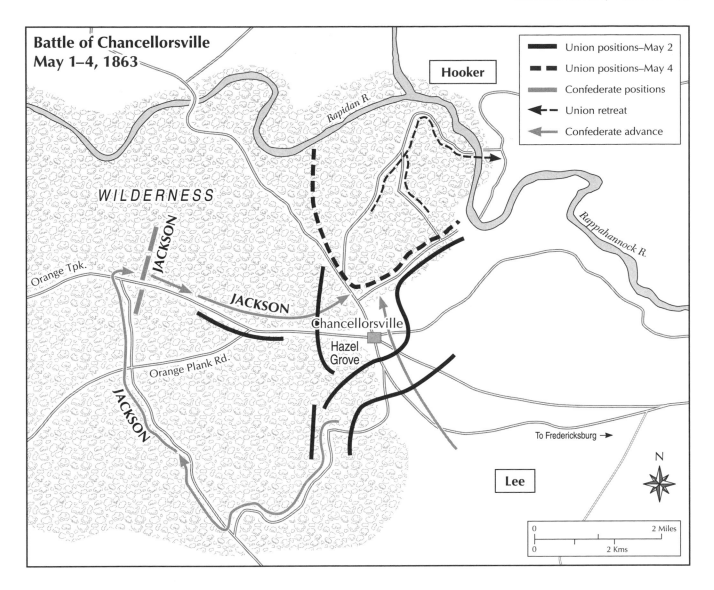

**Battle of Chancellorsville
May 1–4, 1863**

Legend:
- Union positions–May 2
- Union positions–May 4
- Confederate positions
- Union retreat
- Confederate advance

Hooker

Lee

WILDERNESS

JACKSON

JACKSON

JACKSON

Orange Tpk.

Orange Plank Rd.

Chancellorsville

Hazel Grove

Rapidan R.

Rappahannock R.

To Fredericksburg →

N

0   2 Miles

0   2 Kms

of Hooker's and Lee's forces collided near Zoan Church on the road between Chancellorsville and Fredericksburg. Hooker lost all offensive spirit, immediately ordering a withdrawal back to Chancellorsville. Like a frightened child bravely announcing there are no ghosts in the dark, Hooker told a subordinate that he had "Lee just where I want him; he must fight me on my own ground."

On the night of May 1, Lee and Jackson decided on a bold flanking maneuver of their own, which Jackson executed successfully the next day. Jackson's attack on May 2 routed the Federal XI Corps on Hooker's extreme right flank, but the bulk of Hooker's army remained between the two pieces of Lee's force at Chancellorsville. Hooker failed to exploit this opening, pulling his men into a tighter defensive position in the face of heavy Confederate assaults on

May 3. When Lee learned on that day of Sedgwick's success in breaching Early's line at Fredericksburg, he divided his army a third time. Leaving 25,000 men under J. E. B. STUART to keep an eye on Hooker, Lee concentrated the balance of his men several miles west of Fredericksburg at Salem Church, where the Confederates won a fumbling victory against Sedgwick on May 4. By the morning of May 6, the Army of the Potomac had retreated to the north bank of the Rappahannock, returning the strategic situation to precisely where it had been at the outset of the campaign.

Lee had crafted a victory often termed his "masterpiece" but at a cost of more than 12,500 casualties, including Stonewall Jackson, who was shot by his own men in the confusing aftermath of the famous flank attack on May 2 (he died eight days later). Hooker's losses totaled roughly 17,250, a much smaller percentage of his army.

Painting depicting the Battle of Chancellorsville *(Library of Congress)*

Chancellorsville spread optimism throughout the Confederacy and cemented a bond between Lee and his soldiers unrivaled in any other army during the CIVIL WAR. Lee believed his men could accomplish the apparently impossible—a circumstance that would influence his actions two months later at Gettysburg. On the Union side, many officers and soldiers in the Army of the Potomac, disgusted with Hooker's decision to withdraw on May 1, believed they had not been given a chance to win the battle. On the HOMEFRONT, ABRAHAM LINCOLN realized on May 6 that Hooker had failed. A newspaperman recorded the anguished president's reaction: "My God! My God! What will the country say?"

Further reading: Stephen W. Sears, *Chancellorsville* (Boston: Houghton-Mifflin, 1996).

—Gary W. Gallagher

Chase, Salmon P. (1808–1873)

U.S. senator, secretary of the treasury, and Supreme Court justice, Salmon Portland Chase was born on January 13, 1808, in Cornish, New Hampshire. He was educated at Dartmouth and, following a very brief career as a teacher in WASHINGTON, D.C., studied for and passed the bar in 1829. Chase then set up his own practice in Cincinnati, where he soon established a notable reputation and connections to local ABOLITIONists through his work on several cases arguing against the Fugitive Slave Act. Living in a city that bordered the slave state of Kentucky, the young lawyer gained recognition in 1837 when he took on the case of an alleged fugitive. Although he lost this first case, Chase continued to formulate his arguments against the act in particular and

against SLAVERY in general, and in 1841 he acquired even more fame for a victorious decision in a case that paralleled his earlier defeat.

These legal battles not only supported his practice but also fueled his political ambitions. Initially a convert of the Liberty Party in Ohio, he later promoted the Free-Soil Party and entered the U.S. Senate in 1848 on the shoulders of a coalition encompassing the Free Soilers and the Democrats. While in the Senate he vacillated between the two parties but remained steadfast in his views against slavery and its extension, which meant that he voted against all the measures of the Compromise of 1850. Although he served only one term, his political career continued to flourish, and he subsequently affiliated himself with the new party that had risen to challenge the Democrats. In 1856 he was elected governor of Ohio and thus became the first Republican governor of a major state in the Union.

After serving two terms as governor, Chase returned to the U.S. Senate in 1860. Following the presidential election and numerous political maneuverings, Chase abdicated his position when Lincoln selected him to head the Treasury Department despite Chase's lack of a finance background. Over the next several years, the former senator worked hard to support the astronomic costs of the war. His joint efforts with the Philadelphia banker JAY COOKE gained the support of both the banking community and the Northern public for government bonds that enabled the UNION ARMY to remain provisioned with the necessities to continue in the field. Although forever devoted to hard specie, Chase acted based on necessity when he decided to issue GREENBACKS as legal tender in 1862, as the costs of the war continued to put pressure on a somewhat unstable Northern ECONOMY. His tireless efforts to create a system of federally chartered banks also came to fruition in the National Banking Act that became law early in 1864.

Yet for all of his financial responsibilities, Chase never abandoned his political interests and ambitions. He actively advised the president on military affairs in and out of cabinet meetings, and he favored EMANCIPATION long before Lincoln's proclamation became legislation. But the looming election of 1864 and the possibility of a presidential nomination also remained on his mind. This very ambition led to his ill-fated involvement with various schemes with congressional Republicans to promote his position. Chase's constant political maneuverings had often led him into conflict with Lincoln, and in June 1864 he lost his post when Lincoln accepted his impulsive resignation following one of their disputes.

Only six months later Chase returned to the law when Lincoln named him to replace Chief Justice Roger

Brooke Taney on the Supreme Court. In the years that followed, Chase encouraged both universal suffrage and universal amnesty in a moderate RECONSTRUCTION of the South. As chief justice, he presided over the IMPEACHMENT OF ANDREW JOHNSON, and although opposed to Johnson's policies, he was largely responsible for imposing a judicial —as opposed to a partisan legislative—structure on the proceedings. Yet Chase still aspired to the presidency and later in 1868 appeared to compromise many of his principles on equal rights for African Americans in his attempt to gain the Democratic nomination. Once again his reputation suffered and his political aspirations fell short of the mark. Over the next five years, Chase maintained his position as chief justice, striving for universal suffrage and struggling with an ever-deteriorating physical condition.

Salmon Chase died in NEW YORK CITY on May 7, 1873.

Further reading: Frederick J. Blue, *Salmon P. Chase: A Life in Politics* (Kent, Ohio: Kent State University Press, 1987); Salmon P. Chase, *Inside Lincoln's Cabinet; The Civil War Diaries of Salmon P. Chase,* ed. David Donald (New York: Longmans, Green, 1954); John Niven, *Salmon P. Chase: A Biography* (New York: Oxford University Press, 1995).

—John P. Bowes

Chattanooga, Battle of (November 23–25, 1863)

The battle for control of Chattanooga, Tennessee, took place on November 23–25, 1863. The ultimate victory of the UNION ARMY, commanded by Maj. Gen. ULYSSES S. GRANT, placed the strategically important city of Chattanooga, Tennessee, in Union hands for the remainder of the war.

After the BATTLE OF CHICKAMAUGA, fought September 19–20 in northwestern Georgia, the Union army under Maj. Gen. WILLIAM S. ROSECRANS retreated to Chattanooga, while the victorious CONFEDERATE ARMY occupied and fortified the heights of Missionary Ridge and Lookout Mountain to the south and west of the city. President ABRAHAM LINCOLN ordered Maj. Gens. JOSEPH HOOKER and WILLIAM T. SHERMAN with their corps to Chattanooga, bringing the total Union force to about 70,000. Lincoln also ordered Gen. Grant to Chattanooga. The president had just promoted Grant to commander of all western Union forces. Grant immediately replaced the incompetent Rosecrans with Maj. Gen. GEORGE HENRY THOMAS, the "Rock of Chickamauga."

Confederate president JEFFERSON DAVIS sent Lt. Gen. JAMES LONGSTREET and his three divisions from Chattanooga to Knoxville, Tennessee, leaving Bragg with about 40,000 men. Three brigades commanded by Maj. Gen. Carter L. Stevenson were positioned on Lookout Mountain. On November 24, 1863, in what has been romanticized as the "Battle above the Clouds," Hooker's men swept up the northern slope of the steep mountain, causing Stevenson's outnumbered troops to break and retreat to the southern tip of Missionary Ridge.

The day before, Thomas's corps had gained Orchard Knob, a small promontory facing the center of Missionary Ridge. As Hooker moved toward the south of the ridge and Thomas faced the center, Sherman's troops prepared to attack the northern tip, called Tunnel Hill, in what was intended to be the main thrust of the Union army.

The Confederates were positioned with their right flank at Tunnel Hill, protected by the division under Maj. Gen. PATRICK R. CLEBURNE. Stevenson's division held the left flank, at the southern end of Missionary Ridge, while Maj. Gen. John C. Breckinridge's corps held the center. Around 10 A.M. on November 25, Sherman's corps attacked Cleburne's division, which managed to stave off the Federal flank attack.

Thomas's Army of the Cumberland was instructed to take the rifle pits along the base of the ridge in a movement to prevent Bragg from reinforcing his flanks. The Union soldiers, about 20,000 strong, advanced from Orchard Knob and easily overtook the Confederate rifle pits. However, many Federals, unexpectedly and without orders, began moving up the side of the ridge in a charge that is called the "Miracle of Missionary Ridge." The Confederates at the top were overwhelmed and scattered down the eastern side. Only Cleburne's division remained intact enough to complete a successful rearguard action, and soon the entire Confederate Army of Tennessee retreated to Dalton, Georgia. Total casualties numbered 5,824 for the Union and 6,667 for the Confederacy.

Jefferson Davis accepted Bragg's resignation and gave command of the Confederate Army to Gen. JOSEPH E. JOHNSTON. Grant secured Chattanooga for the Union army, and the city served as the supply base for Sherman's army as it advanced toward Atlanta. Almost all of Tennessee was now in Union hands, as well as the vital rail connections that ran from Nashville to Chattanooga.

Further reading: John Bowers, *Chickamauga and Chattanooga: The Battles That Doomed the Confederacy* (New York: HarperCollins, 1994); Peter Cozzens, *The Shipwreck of Their Hopes: The Battles for Chattanooga* (Urbana: University of Illinois Press, 1994); James McDonough, *Chattanooga: A Death Grip on the Confederacy* (Knoxville: University of Tennessee Press, 1984).

—Stacey Graham

Chesnut, Mary B. (1823–1886)

Born March 31, 1823, in Statesboro, South Carolina, diarist and author Mary Boykin Chesnut is best known for her extensive accounts of the CIVIL WAR. The daughter of Mary Boykin and Stephen Decatur Miller, a U.S. congressman and senator, as well as governor of South Carolina, Mary Boykin Miller's life was shaped by Southern politics. Her father, elected governor as a supporter of nullification, returned to the U.S. Senate after his gubernatorial term and continued to support Southern rights.

Mary received an extensive EDUCATION, first at home and in local schools and then at a French boarding school in Charleston. Two years after her father died, Mary married James Chesnut Jr. in 1840. The two moved to WASHINGTON, D.C., in 1858 after James's election to U.S. Senate. There Mary played hostess to many powerful people, including the future leaders of the Confederacy. After Lincoln's election, the Chesnuts returned to South Carolina, where James helped draft the state's December 1860 ordinance of SECESSION.

With the outbreak of war, Mary began keeping an extensive journal to record the historic events occurring around her. As the wife of a Confederate dignitary (James served as a member of the Provisional Congress of the CONFEDERATE STATES OF AMERICA as well as an aide to Gen. P. G. T. BEAUREGARD and President JEFFERSON DAVIS), Mary entertained many Southern leaders. In her diaries, Chesnut commented on meetings and parties with the Confederate elite, including President Davis and his wife Varina. Chesnut also recorded her views on SLAVERY, war, and Southern society in general. The diaries reveal a woman confident in her intelligence and beauty.

After the Civil War, Chesnut attempted to use the information in her wartime diaries to write a Civil War novel. Ultimately, however, she devoted years to the revision of her diaries for publication. Through these heavy edits, Chesnut elaborated on specific topics and eliminated comments that revealed personal flaws. Her diary, first published in 1905 as *A Diary from Dixie, as Written by Mary Boykin Chesnut*, reflected these revisions as well as those by the editors of the volume. The diary reemerged in 1949 as *A Diary from Dixie by Mary Boykin Chesnut*. In 1981 a new edition of the diaries, *Mary Chesnut's Civil War*, proposed to present a fuller picture of Chesnut's edits and original journals. Mary Boykin Chesnut died in 1886 before the publication of her diaries.

Further reading: Mary Boykin Miller Chesnut, *Mary Chesnut's Civil War*, ed. C. Vann Woodward (New Haven, Conn.: Yale University Press, 1981); Mary Boykin Miller Chesnut, *The Private Mary Chesnut: The Unpublished Civil War Diaries*, ed. C. Vann Woodward (New York: Oxford University Press, 1984); Elisabeth Muhlenfeld, *Mary Boykin Chesnut: A Biography* (Baton Rouge: Louisiana State University Press, 1981).

—Lisa Tendrich Frank

Chickamauga, Battle of (September 19–20, 1863)

Chickamauga was a campaign and battle fought in the western theater of operations between Union major general WILLIAM S. ROSECRANS's Army of the Cumberland and Confederate Gen. BRAXTON BRAGG's Army of Tennessee.

Following Rosecrans's successful Tullahoma campaign in June and July of 1863, Bragg's 44,000 soldiers withdrew across the Tennessee River and concentrated near Chattanooga, Tennessee, while the Union's 59,000 forces refitted on the western side of the Cumberland Plateau. Rosecrans advanced on August 16, intending to seize the major TRANSPORTATION center at Chattanooga and force the CONFEDERATE ARMY back toward Atlanta.

Rosecrans crossed the Tennessee River south of Chattanooga at the beginning of September, advancing his army across the rugged terrain and into Georgia with three corps spread across a 40-mile-wide front. Bragg responded by concentrating his forces in a central position around Lafayette. Simultaneously, Confederate reinforcements from Knoxville, Mississippi, and Virginia raised his combat strength to more than 60,000 soldiers, thereby outnumbering Rosecrans's command. Bragg's aborted ambush of Maj. Gen. GEORGE HENRY THOMAS's corps at McLemore's Cove on September 10 alerted Rosecrans to the danger facing his widely scattered army. For the next week both armies raced north to Chattanooga. On September 18, the two armies clashed along Chickamauga Creek as Bragg's forces began attempting to outflank the UNION ARMY.

The fighting on September 19 was essentially a meeting engagement west of Chickamauga Creek. In spite of fierce fighting, neither side gained advantage over the other. By nightfall, Rosecrans had succeeded in concentrating his forces in a strong position along the Lafayette-Chattanooga Road.

During the evening, both sides modified their command structure. George Henry Thomas informally assumed command of four to five divisions in a salient east of Kelly Field on the north of the battle line, while Rosecrans directed the remaining Union forces in the south. Bragg attempted a more formal reorganization into two wings, assigning Lt. Gen. Leonidas Polk to the right and Lt. Gen. JAMES LONGSTREET, who arrived during the night, to the left. From the perspective of subordinate commanders, however, the day began with command arrangements in both armies somewhat confused.

In the north, Polk's attack on September 20 began several hours late. Thomas's troops, massed behind breastworks, slaughtered rebel infantry at close range. Timely Union reinforcements drove back potentially damaging enemy attempts to flank this line from the north. In the center, a dispute between Rosecrans and one of his division commanders around 11 A.M. resulted in a break in the Union line. By coincidence, Longstreet launched three divisions and more than 10,000 men into that gap almost as soon as it appeared. Union forces on the left scattered, and Rosecrans and his staff retreated from the battlefield. Thomas ultimately rallied about half the army on Snodgrass Hill and defeated poorly coordinated Confederate attacks for the remainder of the day. At nightfall, he withdrew all Union forces back to Chattanooga.

Confederate forces lost 18,000, and the Union 16,000 killed, wounded, and missing. While this largest and bloodiest battle in the western theater resulted in a Confederate tactical victory, only two months later the Union had taken Chattanooga, the gateway to the South.

See also CHATTANOOGA, BATTLE OF.

Further reading: Peter Cozzens, *This Terrible Sound: The Battle of Chickamauga* (Urbana: University of Illinois Press, 1992).

—Stephen A. Bourque

Christiana, Pennsylvania, riot (1851)

The Christiana riot was the first well-publicized resistance to the second fugitive slave law, which was passed by Congress as part of the Compromise of 1850. The Fugitive Slave Law was widely hated in the North because it required not only state officials but also ordinary citizens to help recapture runaway slaves.

The chain of events leading to the riot began when four slaves belonging to Edward Gorsuch of Maryland escaped to Christiana, a Quaker village in southeastern Pennsylvania and the home of a number of sympathetic white ABOLITIONists who were part of the UNDERGROUND RAILROAD network. Gorsuch, accompanied by a group of supporters and a U.S. marshal, approached the house of William Parker with warrants for the escaped slaves. William Parker was known in the community as the leader of an African-American self-defense organization, dedicated to helping fugitives liberate themselves.

Gorsuch and the marshal entered the two-story stone house and demanded that Parker turn over the slaves. Outside, Gorsuch's supporters waited with guns loaded; inside, William Parker refused to give up the fugitives. Members of his organization, hiding upstairs, were also armed and ready to resist. A violent clash ensued in which Gorsuch was killed and his son injured. Parker and five others escaped to Canada. In the aftermath, 36 black people and four white people were arrested and charged with treason against the United States. None were convicted, but the trial became the occasion for a full-fledged debate over SLAVERY. One local newspaper described the disturbance as "Civil War, First Blow Struck."

Christiana was one of many such examples of black and white peoples' resistance to the Fugitive Slave Law and the system of slavery in the 1850s. Along with such notable events as the Anthony Burns trial in Boston, Massachusetts, in 1854, the Christiana riot brought what FREDERICK DOUGLASS called "the battle for liberty" to the forefront of the political agenda.

See also SOCIETY OF FRIENDS.

Further reading: Jonathan Katz, *Resistance at Christiana: The Fugitive Slave Rebellion, Christiana, Pennsylvania, September 11, 1851: A Documentary Account* (New York: Crowell, 1974); Thomas P. Slaughter, *Bloody Dawn: The Christiana Riot and Racial Violence in the Antebellum North* (New York: Oxford University Press, 1994).

cities and urban life

Life in American cities changed rapidly between 1856 and 1868. The industrializing country was in a time of transition, as advancements in TRANSPORTATION, manufacturing, and the ECONOMY altered city landscapes dramatically. Factories attracted a growing number of immigrants, swelling the population of cities. Industrialization proceeded at a rapid rate, particularly following the CIVIL WAR, laying the foundation for America's rise to international prominence and making cities such as New York, Boston, Philadelphia, and Chicago some of the most important urban centers in the world.

Improvements in transportation during the Industrial Revolution provided the engine of urban expansion. The ability to move goods cheaply pushed manufacturing to increase its output. In the years leading up to the Civil War, canals and RAILROADS progressively linked more cities together, creating larger markets for products. Most of these new transportation routes linked cities in the North and West, while the more agricultural South lagged behind in terms of economic development. The new connections between northern and western cities brought a more unified economic and political outlook to these regions, leaving the South isolated and aggravating the growing rift between North and South.

Cities expanded in land area. Before 1840 nearly all residents of a city lived within two miles of their place of work. New inventions, including a large horse-drawn carriage known as an omnibus, and expanding rail lines allowed people to move away from the center city and into suburbs. The new advances in public transportation were important because the population of American cities grew to dangerously high levels.

The first great wave of IMMIGRATION from Europe to the United States began in the 1840s. Most of these immigrants came from Germany and Ireland, and they settled in cities in hopes of finding jobs in new factories. Throughout this period, an average of 2.4 million people immigrated to the United States per decade. By the 1870s, an increasing number of immigrants arrived from southern and eastern Europe, bringing new groups, such as Italians, Poles, and Russians, into the United States. Immigrants also came from Asia, with more than 300,000 Chinese immigrating to the western states. Many new Americans settled in ethnic neighborhoods, living in unsanitary tenement houses. Despite these problems, people flocked to the United States in the hope of finding work in the country's exploding industrial economy.

The Industrial Revolution created new social classes in American cities. The middle-class and wealthy members of society could afford to move into larger houses in the suburbs and escape the growing congestion of the cities. Husbands could support a family by working in management or other professional jobs. Their income allowed their wives to shop for the latest goods well as hire servants to help manage the household. Working-class and immigrant families did not have the same advantages. In many cases, all members of the family had to work. Sometimes husbands, wives, and children worked together in the same factory. In other cases, women took jobs as household servants, seamstresses, or laundresses in order to supplement a family's income.

Disposable income, for those who had it, meant manufacturers could produce and sell an ever-increasing number and variety of consumer goods. The first department stores were built in the late 1840s, and by the late 1860s and 1870s shoppers could go to one store and find a wide assortment of goods at reasonable prices. The continued demand for department-store goods helped

Engraving showing underground lodgings for the poor, Greenwich Street, New York City *(Library of Congress)*

fuel the pace of industrialization throughout the 19th century.

As cities became larger, intellectuals and city planners worried that urban residents might lose touch with the natural world. Some cities built large parks in an attempt to preserve some contact with nature as well as to beautify the landscape and give people a place to enjoy outdoor activities. The most famous, New York's Central Park, inspired other American cities to enact their own park-building programs. The creator of Central Park, FREDERICK LAW OLMSTED, designed many other parks around the nation, including San Francisco's Golden Gate Park. Some people disliked the rowdy working-class sports that emerged, but the idea of a small bit of nature in the midst of the expanding city remained popular.

U.S. cities had a seamy underside. Civil War–era America saw rising crime rates make cities even more dangerous places to live. Philadelphia, for example, saw murder rates, indictments, and convictions rise steadily from the 1850s to the 1880s, with the exception of the war years (1861–65). The rise of crime rates was accompanied by a rise in gun ownership and alcohol use. Ethnic tensions between new and old immigrant groups and racial tensions between blacks and whites complicated efforts to unionize workers and accounted for an increase in violent confrontations.

Increasingly professionalized police departments helped to counter crimes committed against both individuals and property. As early as the 1830s and 1840s, cities like Boston, Philadelphia and New York were pushing for efficient and reformed police forces. The London Metropolitan Model was considered a good example for U.S. cities to follow. The London model advocated police to be paid regularly, to be uniformed and organized into a hierarchy, and to be responsible to city officials. From the 1850s onward, the rise in property-based crime generally drove reform in America's urban police departments. Reform was driven by different events, issues, and constituencies in each city across the country. For instance, in Buffalo, New York, the business community began that city's push for a professional police force in 1866 and successfully instituted important changes.

Across urban America, fire departments benefited from the drive to professionalize the police. Indeed, urban businesspeople and concerned property owners were behind many of the drives to professionalize both police and fire services in U.S. cities. Fire fighters changed from volunteer forces to professional forces due largely to two factors: first, consistent pressure from businesspeople, merchants, and insurance companies for stricter protection (including crime prevention, building codes, and fire fighting) of all forms of property interests; and, second, the rise of expensive, steam-powered equipment that demanded fewer personnel to manage but that required more training to operate. Necessarily, the impulse for professionalization of all urban services, including sanitary collection and welfare and hospital institutions, continued to dominate the agenda of urban reformers at this time.

Throughout the Civil War era, economic, political, and social events shaped and were in turn shaped by a remarkable spurt in U.S. urban growth. New immigrant streams, the establishment of shopping centers, the rise of a manufacturing economy, crime and fire prevention, and developments in recreation and transportation all altered the fabric of daily life in American cities.

See also NEW YORK CITY; RACE AND RACIAL TENSIONS.

Further reading: Howard F. Chudacoff and Judith E. Smith, *The Evolution of American Urban Society* (Upper Saddle River, N.J.: Prentice-Hall, 2000); Sidney L. Harring, *Policing a Class Society: The Experience of American Cities, 1865–1915* (New Brunswick, N.J.: Rutgers University Press, 1983); Roger Lane, *Violent Death in the City: Suicide, Accident, and Murder in Nineteenth-Century Philadelphia* (Cambridge, Mass.: Harvard University Press, 1979); Wilbur R. Miller, *Cops and Bobbies: Police Authority in New York and London, 1830–1870* (Chicago, Ill.: University of Chicago Press, 1977); Eric H. Monkkonen, *America Becomes Urban: The Development of U.S. Cities and Towns, 1780–1980* (Berkeley: University of California Press, 1988); Sam Bass Warner, Jr., *The Urban Wilderness: A History of the American City* (New York: Harper & Row, 1972); Sara E. Wermiel, *The Fireproof Building: Technology and Public Safety in the Nineteenth-Century American City* (Baltimore, Md.: Johns Hopkins University Press, 2000).

—Mathew G. McCoy

citizen-soldier

Citizen-soldier is a concept with deep roots in the nation's history. The COMMON SOLDIERs who made up the volunteer armies of the CIVIL WAR knew that previous wars had called upon white male citizens to drop their ordinary occupations and spring into action in the service of their nation. Taking up arms and defending community and country against foreign invaders or domestic threats was an important part of citizenship in a democracy. Afterward, if all went well, the citizen-soldiers would return to their normal lives, secure in the knowledge that they had done their duty. Reasonably, they could expect the country to be grateful for their sacrifices and reward them. This was the case in the American Revolutionary War and in the Mexican-American War of 1846–48.

Glorying in the democratic traditions of their military endeavors, Americans did not trust professional armies, and for good reasons. Britain's "standing army" was associated with the violation of rights endured by the American colonists beginning in the 1760s. The U.S. Constitution provided the power for Congress "to raise and support armies," but the Second Amendment endowed states with the right to maintain militias. A rough-and-ready system of state militias emerged by the 1790s, manned by volunteers as the necessity arose.

Notoriously inefficient and undisciplined, militias composed of citizen-soldiers nonetheless remained the preferred method of waging war throughout the 19th century. Necessarily, the professional army was tiny and viewed with suspicion. Politicians regularly threatened to close the UNITED STATES MILITARY ACADEMY AT WEST POINT. A professional cadre of officers whose loyalty was to the army, not the people, could pose a threat to democratic institutions. On the other hand, the ideal of the citizen-soldier embodied the traditions of popular will and representative government. Both the Union and Confederate armies raised the majority of their men by calling upon the ideal of the citizen-soldier.

Further reading: Eliot A. Cohen, *Citizens and Soldiers: The Dilemmas of Military Service* (Ithaca, N.Y.: Cornell University Press, 1985).

Civil Rights Act of 1866 (April 9, 1866)

With the passage of the THIRTEENTH AMENDMENT in 1865, SLAVERY was abolished. At that point, however, it was not altogether clear what freedom would mean for the ex-slaves. White Southerners quickly tried to answer that question, passing a series of discriminatory BLACK CODES that were designed to keep the freedmen in a subordinate position. Northerners were outraged by the South's unwillingness to change and by President ANDREW JOHNSON's failure to do anything about the situation. Congress felt compelled to act, and the result was the Civil Rights Act of 1866. The act was a landmark, the first time in history that the federal government took responsibility for protecting African Americans' civil rights.

The Civil Rights Act of 1866 was written mostly by moderate Republican senator Lyman Trumbull of Illinois. The bill was not specifically addressed to the problems of African Americans but, instead, was meant to provide a definition of citizenship for all Americans. It enumerated the "fundamental rights belonging to every man as a free man," particularly the rights to inherit, purchase, lease, hold, and sell property. The bill also provided for the prosecution of anyone who tried to interfere with these rights.

Although the Civil Rights Act of 1866 was moderate in its terms, it provoked a great deal of criticism. Radicals felt the bill did not go far enough. They hoped to include pro-

visions for land redistribution and even suffrage. They also did not approve of the fact that courts would be responsible for enforcing the act, as opposed to the military. Ultimately, the RADICAL REPUBLICANS came to realize that the bill was better than nothing, and they lent their support. The act was passed in both houses of Congress by a comfortable margin.

Conservative Democrats also opposed the Civil Rights Act of 1866. They felt it went too far in protecting the freedmen and gave too much power to the federal government. Democrats in Congress could do little to stop the passage of the bill, but President Andrew Johnson could. He promptly vetoed the act, labeling it "another step, or rather stride, toward centralization and the concentration of all legislative powers in the National Government." On April 9 Congress overrode Johnson's veto and the Civil Rights Act of 1866 became law. This was the first time in the history of the United States that a president's veto of a major piece of legislation was overridden.

The Civil Rights Act of 1866 ultimately had little impact on the lives of freedmen. Its provisions were generally ignored by white Southerners, and there was confusion about whether state or federal courts were responsible for enforcement. The act did have a dramatic impact on national politics, however. It demonstrated to congressional leaders that drastic action was needed, and within a decade, the Civil Rights Act of 1866 would be followed by a pair of constitutional amendments and three more civil rights bills. In addition, the debate over the bill served to heighten the tension between Andrew Johnson and Congress, ultimately leading to his impeachment.

See also CIVIL RIGHTS ACT OF 1875; IMPEACHMENT OF ANDREW JOHNSON.

Further reading: Eric Foner, *Reconstruction: America's Unfinished Revolution, 1863–1877* (New York: Harper & Row, 1988); Harold M. Hyman and William M. Wiecek, *Equal Justice under Law: Constitutional Development, 1835–1875* (New York: Harper & Row, 1982); Robert J. Kaczorowski, *The Politics of Judicial Interpretation: The Federal Courts, Department of Justice and Civil Rights, 1866–1876* (Dobbs Ferry, N.Y.: Oceana Publications, 1985).

—Christopher Bates

Civil Rights Act of 1875 (March 1, 1875)

The Civil Rights Act of 1875 was the last major piece of civil rights legislation passed during the RECONSTRUCTION era, following the FOURTEENTH and FIFTEENTH AMENDMENTS as well as three other civil rights acts. The 1875 act was much broader than its predecessors, in that it aimed to bring an end to all forms of racial discrimination.

The bill that became the Civil Rights Act of 1875 was first submitted to Congress in 1870 by RADICAL REPUBLICAN senator CHARLES SUMNER of Massachusetts. Originally, the bill prohibited discrimination in schools, THEATERS, cemeteries, public TRANSPORTATION, hotels, and churches. The provisions for schools and cemeteries particularly angered Democrats and even caused unease among the more conservative Republicans, and so Sumner's proposal was tabled. The bill languished for several years before Speaker of the House James G. Blaine of Maine and Representative James Garfield proposed a compromise version that eliminated schools and cemeteries. President ULYSSES S. GRANT threw his weight behind the Blaine-Garfield proposal, and it was quickly adopted.

Even with the provisions about schools and cemeteries removed, the Civil Rights Act of 1875 had the potential to be a truly groundbreaking piece of legislation. The previous civil rights acts had dealt with specific issues—citizenship, property holding, and voting. The 1875 act, on the other hand, could be read as empowering the federal government to completely remake Southern life. Because the act did not define what constituted discrimination, any issue could be addressed under its terms—politics, economics, law, and so forth.

Unfortunately for African Americans, the impulse for reform was dying out, even among members of the REPUBLICAN PARTY. Hundreds of lawsuits were filed under the terms of the Civil Rights Act of 1875, and most were promptly dismissed. The demise of the act became official in 1883 when the Supreme Court, made up entirely of Republican appointees, ruled eight to one that the act was unconstitutional. The basic spirit of the act would not be revived until nearly a century later, with the passage of the Civil Rights Act of 1964.

See also CIVIL RIGHTS ACT OF 1866.

Further reading: Eric Foner, *Reconstruction: America's Unfinished Revolution, 1863–1877* (New York: Harper & Row, 1988); Harold M. Hyman and William M. Wiecek, *Equal Justice under Law: Constitutional Development, 1835–1875* (New York: Harper & Row, 1982); Robert J. Kaczorowski, *The Politics of Judicial Interpretation: The Federal Courts, Department of Justice and Civil Rights, 1866–1876* (Dobbs Ferry, N.Y.: Oceana Publications, 1985).

—Christopher Bates

Civil War (1861–1865)

The Civil War marked one of the great defining moments in U.S. history. Long-simmering sectional tensions reached a critical stage in 1860–61 when 11 slaveholding states seceded and formed the CONFEDERATE STATES OF AMERICA. Political disagreement gave way to war in April 1861, as Confederates insisted on their right to leave the Union and the loyal states refused to allow them to go. Nothing in the nation's history had prepared Americans for the scale of military fury and social disruption that ensued. Four years of fighting claimed more than 1 million military casualties (of whom at least 620,000 died), directly affected the lives of hundreds of thousands of civilians, and freed 4 million enslaved African Americans. The social and economic system based on chattel SLAVERY that the seceding states had sought to protect lay in ruins. The Union had been preserved, and the supremacy of the national government over the individual states had been confirmed. In the longer term, the North's victory made possible the American economic and political colossus that figured so prominently in 20th-century history.

Also known as "The War of the Rebellion," "The War Between the States," "The War for Southern Independence," and "The BROTHERS' WAR," the conflict continues to fascinate professional historians, novelists, filmmakers, and millions of Americans interested in history. The drama and tragedy of many Civil War battles have been commemorated in a number of national military parks, such as the ones at Gettysburg, Pennsylvania; Antietam, Maryland; and Vicksburg, Mississippi. Many of the major issues of the era—slavery, states' rights, racial equality, the duties and rights of citizenship, and the limits of national authority—continue to provoke debate and dissension.

Before the sectional disruption, the American republic had survived diplomatic and military crises and internal stresses. It weathered tensions with France in the late 1790s, a second war with Britain in 1812–15, and disputes regarding international boundaries. Political debates over economic issues such as the TARIFF, a national bank, and government-supported public works provoked dissension but posed no serious threat to the integrity of the Union. Despite divisions along ethnic and class lines, the majority of Americans had much in common. They were white, Christian, spoke English, and celebrated a shared heritage forged in the crucible of the Revolutionary War.

Questions relating to the institution of slavery led to the sectional strife that eventually erupted in war. Most men and women at the time would have agreed with ABRAHAM LINCOLN's assertion in his second inaugural address that slavery "was, somehow, the cause of the war." Earlier, ALEXANDER H. STEPHENS, the Confederacy's vice president, had proclaimed that slavery "was the immediate cause of the late rupture and the present revolution" to establish Southern independence. The framers of the U.S. Constitution had compromised regarding slavery, creating a democratic republic that sought to ensure its citizenry's freedoms while also reassuring the South that individual states would have the power to maintain and regulate

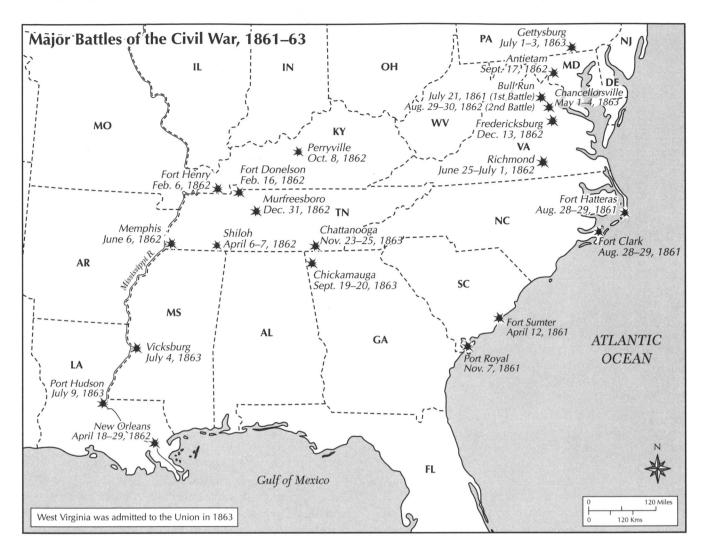

Major Battles of the Civil War, 1861–63

Gettysburg
July 1–3, 1863

PA
NJ

IL
IN
OH

Antietam
Sept. 17, 1862
MD

DE

Bull Run
July 21, 1861 (1st Battle)
Aug. 29–30, 1862 (2nd Battle)

Chancellorsville
May 1–4, 1863

MO
WV

Fredericksburg
Dec. 13, 1862

KY
VA

Perryville
Oct. 8, 1862

Richmond
June 25–July 1, 1862

Fort Henry
Feb. 6, 1862

Fort Donelson
Feb. 16, 1862

Fort Hatteras
Aug. 28–29, 1861

Murfreesboro
Dec. 31, 1862
TN

NC

Memphis
June 6, 1862

Shiloh
April 6–7, 1862

Chattanooga
Nov. 23–25, 1863

Fort Clark
Aug. 28–29, 1861

AR

Mississippi R.

Chickamauga
Sept. 19–20, 1863

SC

MS

AL

GA

Fort Sumter
April 12, 1861

Vicksburg
July 4, 1863

ATLANTIC
OCEAN

LA

Port Royal
Nov. 7, 1861

Port Hudson
July 9, 1863

New Orleans
April 18–29, 1862

FL

Gulf of Mexico

N

0   120 Miles
0   120 Kms

West Virginia was admitted to the Union in 1863

slavery within their boundaries. The paradox of white liberty that rested in part on a foundation of black slavery was thus embedded in the origins of the United States.

Debates over slavery's expansion into federal territories, which were tied to the South's effort to maintain an equal number of free and slave states, created turmoil in national politics. The Missouri Compromise of 1820, the WILMOT PROVISO of 1846 (which sought to prohibit slavery in lands acquired as a result of the Mexican-American War), the establishment of the Free-Soil movement in 1848, the Compromise of 1850 (which ended parity in the Senate with California's admission as a free state), the KANSAS-NEBRASKA ACT of 1854 (which helped foster deadly territorial violence), and the Supreme Court's DRED SCOTT DECISION in 1857 marked mileposts along the road to sectional disruption. Outside the arena of national politics, the rise of the ABOLITION movement, Nat Turner's bloody slave revolt in Virginia in 1831, pub-

lication of HARRIET BEECHER STOWE's antislavery best-seller *Uncle Tom's Cabin* in 1852, and JOHN BROWN's raid on HARPERS FERRY in 1859 fed fears in the South that their slave-based social and economic systems might be in jeopardy.

As sectional divisions deepened, important institutions failed to act as stabilizing forces. Several Protestant denominations, including the Baptists and Methodists, split into Northern and Southern branches. The national political parties, which from the 1830s until the early 1850s had pursued compromise to maintain Northern and Southern wings, fractured along regional lines. The Whig Party collapsed as a national entity after the presidential election of 1852, and many Northern voters came to view the DEMO-CRATIC PARTY as pro-Southern. The REPUBLICAN PARTY, which rapidly gained strength in the North following its creation in the mid-1850s, adamantly opposed extension of slavery into the territories and won virtually no support in the South. The Supreme Court, long venerated by citizens across the nation, lost its reputation an an impartial arbiter of legal questions when the *Dred Scott* decision seemed to open all federal territories—and perhaps free states as well—to slavery.

Historians have debated whether the North and South had become markedly different societies by 1860. Some portray the Free-Soil North, with its commercial and industrial interests, as an emerging capitalist giant at odds with an overwhelmingly agrarian South, where most capital was invested in land and slaves. Others insist that the North and South were far more alike than different. It is clear that by the late 1850s many Americans believed there were fundamental differences between the sections. More ominously, a significant number on each side of the MASON-DIXON LINE had come to distrust those on the other side who disagreed with them about how slavery should figure in the republic's future.

The election of 1860 triggered the SECESSION crisis. Although Lincoln and the victorious Republicans had promised not to interfere with slavery in states where it already existed, they firmly opposed slavery's spread to any federal territories. Between December 1860 and February 1861, the seven Deep South states seceded to avoid what they perceived as a long-term threat to their slaveholding interests. After Confederates fired on FORT SUMTER in mid-April 1861, Lincoln's call for 75,000 volunteers to suppress the rebellion prompted four slave states of the Upper South, including Virginia, to join their Deep South brethren. Four other slave states, typically called the border states—Kentucky, Missouri, Maryland, and Delaware—remained loyal to the Union.

Both sides mobilized on a scale unprecedented in American history. Drawing on an 1860 population of just more than 1 million military-age white males, the Confederacy placed between 800,000 and 900,000 men in uniform

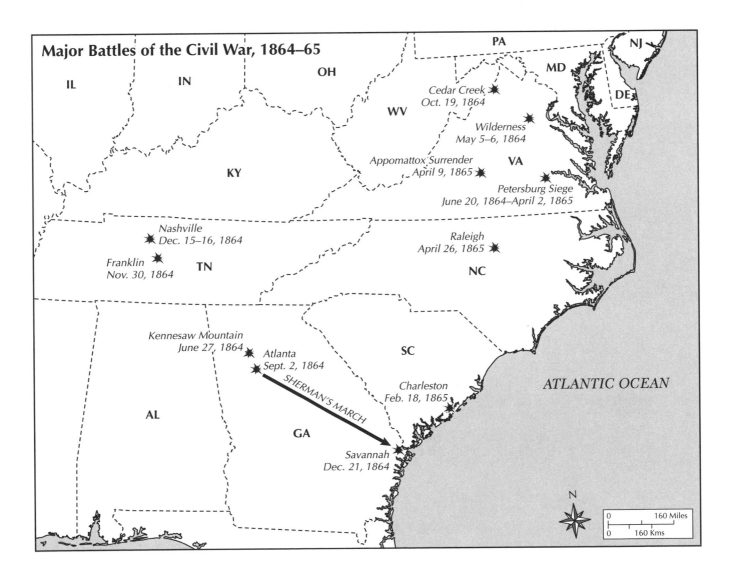

Major Battles of the Civil War, 1864–65

(fragmentary records do not permit a precise count). The North mustered at least 2.1 million men, about half of its 1860 military-age population. More than 180,000 black men served in United States units. Apart from its much larger population, the North held a decided advantage in industrial capacity. In 1860 there were 110,000 Northern manufacturing establishments employing 1,300,000 workers; in the Confederate states, there were just 18,000 establishments employing 110,000 workers.

Yet either side could have prevailed because of the North's more difficult requirements for victory. The Confederacy sought independence and only had to defend itself to prevail. The North sought to compel the seceded states to abandon their hopes to found a new nation. U.S. armies would have to invade the Confederacy, destroy its capacity to wage war, and crush the will of the Southern people to resist. The Confederacy could win by prolonging the war to a point where the Northern people considered the effort too costly in lives and money. Many Confederates appreciated the magnitude of the North's challenge. George Wythe Randolph, who served as Confederate secretary of war, commented in 1861 that Union forces "may overrun our frontier States and plunder our coast but, as for conquering us, the thing is an impossibility."

Union and Confederate leaders adopted very different strategies to achieve victory. Beginning in 1861 with Winfield Scott's so-called Anaconda Plan, the United States pursued a strategy that included a naval blockade to restrict the flow of goods into Southern ports, a combined army-navy effort to divide the Confederacy by seizing control of the MISSISSIPPI RIVER, and major offensives into the Confederate hinterlands. The Confederacy first tried to defend all of its borders, but the futility of such a strategy soon became apparent. For most of the war, JEFFERSON DAVIS and his advisers followed what often is termed a defensive-offensive strategy. Confederate armies generally stood on the strategic defensive, protecting as much of their territory as possible. When circumstances seemed favorable, the Confederacy launched offensives, the most important of which culminated in the BATTLE OF ANTIETAM and Battle of Perryville in 1862 and the BATTLE OF GETTYSBURG in 1863.

Military fortunes ebbed and flowed for more than three years before U.S. forces gained a decisive advantage. The North wavered more than once in its determination, most notably after ROBERT E. LEE frustrated Union offensives in the spring of 1863 and the spring and early summer of 1864. A string of Union successes in the West—won by ULYSSES S. GRANT at Forts Henry and Donelson, Shiloh, Vicksburg, and Chattanooga in 1862–63 and by WILLIAM T. SHERMAN at Atlanta in 1864—more than counterbalanced Lee's successes. By the autumn of 1864, with Grant as the Union general in chief, U.S. armies applied pressure in Virginia, Tennessee, and the Carolinas that eventually forced a Confederate surrender at APPOMATTOX COURTHOUSE in the spring of 1865.

Both sides made use of recent technological advances. RAILROADS moved hundreds of thousands of soldiers and vast quantities of supplies, and TELEGRAPHic communication permitted both governments to coordinate military movements in widely separated areas. The conflict featured numerous applications of recent military technology, among the most important of which were the rifled musket carried by most infantrymen on both sides and IRON-CLAD warships that saw action on a broad scale.

The war touched the lives of almost every American. Women assumed larger responsibilities in the workplace. In the North, they labored as NURSES (previously a male occupation), government clerks, factory workers, and in other ways helped the war effort. Southern white women also worked as clerks and nurses and in factories, and thousands took responsibility for running farms. Several hundred women disguised themselves as men and served in the military. Although the war opened opportunities outside the household for women, its end brought a general return of old patterns of EMPLOYMENT.

Slaves in the South shouldered a major part of the labor burden, as they always had, and made it possible for the Confederacy to put nearly 80 percent of its military-age white men in uniform. No group was more directly affected by the outcome of the war than the 4 million black people who were slaves in 1861. They emerged from the struggle with their freedom (made final by ratification of the THIRTEENTH AMENDMENT to the Constitution in December 1865), though the extent to which they would be accorded equal rights remained unresolved.

The two national governments expanded their powers in an effort to mount sustained war efforts. Ironically, the Confederacy, a republic allegedly devoted to states' rights, witnessed greater governmental intrusions into its citizens' lives. Both sides enacted a series of national taxes, tampered with civil liberties in various ways, and resorted to CONSCRIPTION laws. Many of these measures, especially the drafts implemented by the South in 1862 and by the North the following year, provoked heated political debate and overt antiwar activities. The war produced spending on a scale dwarfing that of any earlier period. In 1860 the federal budget was $63 million; in 1865 U.S. expenditures totaled nearly $1.3 billion—a 200-fold increase that does not include the roughly $1 billion the Confederate government spent.

EMANCIPATION was the war's most revolutionary development. Abolitionists and many RADICAL REPUBLICANS pressed for it from the outset, but the mass of white Northerners considered the conflict a struggle for union rather than for black freedom. As fighting dragged on and casualties mounted, Lincoln presented emancipation as a tool that would undermine the Confederacy. Although many Democrats remained bitter opponents, most white Northerners eventually accepted emancipation as necessary to victory. Hundreds of thousands of slaves in the South did not wait for U.S. politicians to work out their fate, fleeing to Union military lines and thereby applying pressure for governmental action that would transform a struggle for union into a struggle for union and freedom.

The cost of the war was appalling. More Americans were killed than in all other wars combined from the colonial period through the last phase of the Vietnam War. Had American deaths in World War II been proportionately as high, the total would have been 2.6 million rather than the 405,000 actually lost. The war brought wide-scale economic destruction to the Confederate states, which lost two-thirds of their assessed wealth (emancipated slaves accounted for much of this). In contrast, the Northern ECONOMY thrived. Two statistics convey a sense of the relative economic cost: Between 1860 and 1870, Northern wealth increased by 50 percent; during that same decade, Southern wealth decreased by 60 percent.

Human suffering extended beyond the military sphere and continued long after fighting ceased. During the conflict, scores of thousands of black and white Southerners became REFUGEES (far fewer Northern civilians experienced the war so directly). An unknown number of civilians perished at the hands of guerrillas, deserters, and, less frequently, regular soldiers in both armies. After the war, thousands of VETERANS struggled to cope with lost limbs and other physical and emotional scars. Thousands of families faced difficult financial circumstances due to the loss of husbands and fathers. The U.S. government made available minimal support for widows of soldiers, and Southern states did the same for widows of Confederates.

The Civil War was the central event in the lives of most of the soldiers who served. During the postwar years, many joined veterans' organizations such as the Grand Army of the Republic and the United Confederate Veterans. They revisited the sites of their battles, raised MONUMENTS to commemorate their service, and, in significant numbers, wrote reminiscences. For black Union soldiers, the war provided the strongest possible claim for full citizenship. They had risked their lives alongside white comrades, and they justly claimed the right to vote and otherwise live as full members of American society.

Americans remembered the war in different ways. For most white Northerners, it was preeminently a crusade that saved the Union. Black Americans placed freedom at the center of their memories of the conflict. Many ex-Confederates celebrated their failed effort to carve out a distinct destiny. Their arguments, which included an attempt to minimize the importance of slavery as a factor during the

secession crisis and the war, became part of the remarkably durable LOST CAUSE school of interpretation. By the end of the 19th century, a reconciliationist movement united many white Northerners and Southerners in a shared public memory of the war. Reconciliationists rarely spoke of emancipation or black participation and deliberately avoided discussion of the bitter animosities that had divided North and South. They applauded the pluck of white soldiers North and South, often glossed over the question of which side was right, and presented the war as a grand demonstration of American valor and virtue. The reconciliationist vision, with its emphasis on shared courage and its aversion to acrimonious topics, continues to wield a powerful influence on the popular understanding of the Civil War.

See also RECONSTRUCTION; REDEMPTION.

Further reading: James McPherson, *Battle Cry of Freedom: The Civil War Era* (New York: Oxford University Press, 1988).

—Gary W. Gallagher

Clay, Henry   See Volume IV

Cleburne, Patrick R. (1826–1864)

Confederate officer Patrick Ronayne Cleburne was born at Ovens, County Cork, Ireland, on March 16, 1826, to Dr. Joseph and Mary Anne Ronayne Cleburne. Both parents died before Patrick was 15. He attempted to become a physician but was denied admission to Trinity College in February 1846. Later that year he joined the 41st Regiment of Foot of the British Army as a private. After three years service, he bought his discharge and moved with his older brother and two sisters to the United States. Cleburne settled in Helena, Arkansas, and established himself as a druggist. In 1856 he began to practice law and by 1860 had become senior partner in the firm of Cleburne, Scaife, and Mangum.

At the beginning of the CIVIL WAR, he joined the Yell Rifles, a local Rebel infantry company, as a private and was soon elected captain of the company. Upon the organization of the First Arkansas Infantry Regiment, he was elected colonel. In March 1862 he was elevated to brigade command under William J. Hardee, serving in that capacity at the BATTLE OF SHILOH, throughout the Kentucky campaign (where he was shot through the mouth at the Battle of Richmond, Kentucky, on August 30, 1862), and during the BATTLE OF MURFREESBORO.

In early 1863 he was promoted to the rank of major general and given command of an infantry division. He directed the division during the Tullahoma campaign and the BATTLE OF CHICKAMAUGA. His defense of the north end of Missionary Ridge on November 25, 1863, and his rearguard action at Ringgold, Georgia, on November 27 confirmed his reputation as one of the Confederacy's best fighting generals. Cleburne came to be called the "Stonewall Jackson of the West," but his 1864 suggestion to offer freedom to slaves who would join the CONFEDERATE ARMY prevented his elevation to higher command. He led his division with distinction during the ATLANTA CAMPAIGN of 1864 and died leading his men against the Federal earthworks at Franklin, Tennessee, on November 30, 1864.

See also IRISH-AMERICAN REGIMENTS.

Further reading: Mauriel Phillips Joslyn, ed., *A Meteor Shining Brightly: Essays on the Life and Career of Major General Patrick R. Cleburne* (Macon, Ga.: Mercer University Press, 2000); Craig L. Symonds, *Stonewall of the West: Patrick Cleburne and the Civil War* (Lawrence: University Press of Kansas, 1997).

—James Daryl Black

Cold Harbor, Battle of (June 1–6, 1864)

Cold Harbor, Virginia, was the bloodiest in a series of battles that formed the OVERLAND CAMPAIGN, which was undertaken by the UNION ARMY in early May 1864. Besides the carnage, the Battle of Cold Harbor was notable as a turning point when defensive fortifications, siege warfare, and relentless daily fighting characterized the war in the eastern theater.

Gen. ULYSSES S. GRANT's Army of the Potomac marched south into Virginia with hopes of putting an end to the conflict. Northern moral was high, yet ROBERT E. LEE and the Army of Northern Virginia blocked Grant's relentless westward movements toward RICHMOND, inflicting heavy casualties on their opponents. After the Battle of North Anna during May 23–26, Grant moved west again and crossed the Pamunkey River. By month's end, the left wing of the Federal force had reached a tiny crossroads called Cold Harbor, named after a tavern.

Cold Harbor had a road that led into the Chickahominy River and then continued on to Richmond. Grant's plan was to bring his army through Cold Harbor, turn on Lee's right, and pin the Confederates in a vulnerable spot against the river. Unfortunately, the Union forces delayed, and the attack, set for 4 A.M. on June 2, had to be postponed until the same time on the next day. The Confederates, meanwhile, used the extra time to build and extend their fortifications.

By predawn of June 3, 59,000 well-entrenched rebels faced 108,000 Federals across a seven-mile front. Grant's massive frontal assault on Confederate lines failed miser-

ably. That terrible day saw some 7,000 Federal casualties (compared with less than 1,500 for the rebels) that shattered three Union corps. One Northern soldier described some details of the assault: "The time of actual advance was not over eight minutes. . . . In that little period more men fell bleeding as they advanced than in any other like period of time throughout the war." The assault was a disaster, and before the end of the day, Grant stopped the fighting. "I regret this assault more than any one I have ever ordered," he said.

Cold Harbor culminated a month of nonstop campaigning for both armies. The North had experienced 50,000 losses and the South 32,000. In percentages, that represented 41 percent of Grant's forces and 46 percent of Lee's. These losses were a disaster for the South, which could not replenish its armies. Although the Battle of Cold Harbor and the Overland campaign resulted in Northern losses or stalemates on the field, Grant's overall strategy of attrition was working.

Further reading: Louis J. Baltz III, *The Last Battle of Cold Harbor: May 27–June 13, 1864* (Lynchburg, Va.: H. E. Howard, 1994); Ernest B. Furgurson, *Not War but Murder: Cold Harbor, 1864* (New York: Knopf, 2000).

Colored National Labor Union (1869–1872)

Established in 1869, the Colored National Labor Union (CNLU) was the first major attempt on the part of African Americans to organize their labor collectively on a national level. The CNLU, like other labor unions, had as its goal improving the working conditions and quality of life for its members. Unfortunately, in its short life span, the CNLU made precious few inroads for its black constituents.

African Americans had traditionally been excluded from existing labor unions, but when workers sought to capitalize on organizational opportunities created by the CIVIL WAR and formed the NATIONAL LABOR UNION (NLU), black laborers wanted to participate as well. William Sylvis, president of the NLU, made a speech in which he agreed that there should be "no distinction of race or nationality" within the ranks of his organization. In 1869 several black delegates were invited to the annual meeting of the NLU. One of these delegates was a man named Isaac Myers, a prominent organizer of African-American laborers. At the convention, he spoke eloquently for solidarity, saying that white and black workers ought to organize together for higher wages and a comfortable standard of living. But Myers's plea fell on deaf ears. The white unions refused to allow African Americans to enter their ranks. In response to this, Myers met with other African-American laborers to form a national labor organization of their own. In 1869 the Colored

National Labor Union was formed, with Myers as its first president.

The CNLU was established to help improve the harsh conditions facing black workers. Exclusionary white unions and uncooperative employers prevented African Americans from getting highly paid, skilled labor jobs in the North. In the South, the EMANCIPATION of the slaves did not result in social or economic equality. Among the goals of the CNLU, which represented African-American laborers in 21 states, were the issuance of farmland to poor Southern African Americans, government aid for EDUCATION, and new nondiscriminatory legislation that would help black workers who struggled to make ends meet.

The CNLU ultimately made few economic gains for African Americans. A hostile and prejudiced business and labor environment prevented the CNLU from making much headway, and in 1872 the union went under. The CNLU did, however, help raise awareness among many people in the labor movement that all workers deserved adequate representation.

See also EMPLOYMENT; RACE AND RACIAL CONFLICT.

Further reading: William H. Harris, *The Harder We Run: Black Workers Since the Civil War* (New York: Oxford University Press, 1982).

—Troy Rondinone

common soldier

The common soldier of the CIVIL WAR mostly enlisted early, in 1861 and 1862, and stayed to the end, if he lived. He was young, between the ages of 18 to 24. He was most likely to have been born in a rural area and to be the son of a farmer, but many were the sons of businessmen, working-class artisans, intellectuals, and the wealthy. He was white, Protestant, and literate. Indeed, Civil War soldiers were some of the best educated in the history of warfare, and their LETTERS home attested to their ability to express themselves.

The common soldier was not only literate, he was politically astute and knew the reasons why he was fighting. The Northern soldier fought for union and, after 1863, for freedom. "I have no heart in this war if the slaves cannot be free," declared a young Wisconsin private in 1863. The Southern soldier fought to protect his homeland from foreign invaders, for Confederate independence from tyranny, and for STATES' RIGHTS. "We are fighting for the Constitution that our forefathers made," wrote a Confederate soldier, "and not as old Abe would have it." All claimed ideological inheritance from the American Revolution, and all agreed, one way or another, with President ABRAHAM LINCOLN when he said that SLAVERY "was somehow the cause of the war."

Johnny Reb and Billy Yank did not have a lot of money or property but had great ambitions for both. The common soldier was probably not married, although a fair number had already tied the knot. He eagerly accepted the monthly pay, the bonuses, and sometimes even the land that would come to him as part of his service, and rightly so, for these rewards were a part of the rich tradition of the American CITIZEN-SOLDIER. (Although by the second year of the war, the Southern soldier had little expectations of such rewards). He loved the excitement, the martial MUSIC, the parades, and the hoopla that accompanied the earliest calls for men. Often his motives for enlisting were mixed: peer pressure, social expectations, dreams of military glory, and patriotism all played a part in the final decision.

Most of all, the common soldier of the war reflected the deeply held values of individualism, family, community, church, and country in Victorian America. This was not, for the most part, a war fought by the poor for the rich. The families of the Civil War soldiers represented the very heart of the United States as it was in 1861. There were many men, however, who cannot be easily described within the broad depiction of the typical or common soldier. The Irish, German, Italians, and African Americans who served in the war were, in important ways, different from the majority of native-born white volunteers. Draftees, bounty jumpers, and the criminal element that were a part of the armies also departed dramatically from the norm.

Overall, American men shared romantic ideas about being a soldier. The concept of courage was the most important. Men were supposed to be brave in battle and, by doing so, would achieve their manhood, do their duty, and honor their God and their country. Courage was tied to a love of country, a feeling that is commonly called patriotism. The excitement of the early days of the war is reflected in a letter from a Northerner: "The air is full of calls for men who are patriotic to enlist. I really inwardly feel that I want to go do my part as a man." A soldier from Iowa added: "The majority of our Citizens are full of patriotism and express their willingness to stand by the Old Stars and stripes and protect it from dishonor." A Southern counterpart echoed the sentiment: "What is life worth under a government that cannot be enjoyed?"

Shared ideas and feelings created a powerful bond between the volunteer soldier in camp, on the march, and in battlefields and those who stayed back home. Hamlets, towns, and cities followed their "boys" throughout the war. Countless soldiers' newsy letters were printed in hometown newspapers for all to read and comment on. Local and state loyalties were stronger than national, especially in the early days of war.

The Northern and Southern federal governments relied heavily on the common people, the middling classes, to support the war effort through men, supplies, and money. This was not a modern war with a well-oiled CON-SCRIPTION system (the draft accounted for very few soldiers) or a huge propaganda machine. Both the initial enthusiasm and the later dissent for the war came from a grassroots perspective.

In one sense, the young man who served in the war never left home. He joined a local outfit, a company, and regiment that were made up of other young men that he knew well. It was common for brothers, cousins, even fathers and sons to enlist together. In the beginning, soldiers' mothers, wives, sisters, and sweethearts provided UNIFORMS, food, and supplies and sewed the regimental flags. The enlisted men elected the company and regimental officers. The officers themselves, as untrained and innocent in the ways of war as the raw recruits, were only slightly older and better off than the men they were charged with training. When the war became hard and violent, the community suffered the losses together. Replacements would have to come from the same locality. Recruiting became much more difficult everywhere as the losses rose dramatically through the four years of war.

The reality of war hit the common soldier hard. After the initial excitement wore off, the untested farm boys, city clerks, students, and mechanics had to learn how to be soldiers. At first, the typical volunteer had a difficult time accepting the fact that soldiering was a job that required steady discipline, constant drill, and the mastery of skills like the quick loading and firing of a musket. A recruit in the 93rd Illinois summed up his frustrations when he wrote his parents about camp life in 1862: "They keep us very strict here, it is the most like a prison of any place I ever saw. . . . It comes rather hard at first to be deprived of liberty." A rebel from Louisiana echoed that complaint when he commented from a camp in Alabama: "A soldier is not his own man. He has given up all claim on himself."

The common soldier and his comrades learned through experience how to march quickly through heat and cold and rain and snow; how to eat the most unpleasant things under the most challenging conditions; how to go for long periods of time without sufficient food or water; and how to build fortifications at a moment's notice. Most of all, he had to learn to kill his enemy and survive the war.

The biggest test was the first battle. Many have described the early Civil War military clashes as fights between two armed mobs. This was courage tested, and many failed at first. The noise, the smoke, and the fear of death were indescribable, and thousands "skeedaddled" from the battlefield. Who could blame them? They were not professional soldiers; they were volunteers who expected the war to be an adventure that would be over in a few months. A soldier from Tennessee recalled his first time in battle: "I was not much surprised when we received the order to fall in. . . . I can never forget my thoughts as I stood there and looked around. . . . It was the first time I had ever been called upon to face death." Courage for these men was just being able to follow orders and stay in line. "Oh how I wish I was a dwarf, just now, instead of a six-footer," moaned a Mississippian who faced his initial combat experience at the bloody BATTLE OF SHILOH. The best officers were the ones who respected these amateur soldiers and understood that most of the scared ones would come back to the camps chastened and ready to do better next time.

The average soldier became seasoned soon enough at Bull Run, Antietam, Chancellorsville, Shiloh, and Vicksburg. The majority of enlisted men and officers learned their jobs well, and some found they actually enjoyed it. No longer did enthusiasm and a desire to achieve glory in battle drive the soldier. He had seen friends and perhaps a family member or two die horrible deaths in battle. Undoubtedly, he knew many more that died from illnesses like measles and dysentery.

As the war ground on, the soldier bonded with the other men in his company and regiment. He felt estranged from his family back home, and in many ways his fellow soldiers became his family, at least for the duration of the war. Surprisingly, despite the horrors of war, his devotion to his country's cause remained relatively steadfast, although the idealism was replaced with a hard-edged practical side. Often he and his comrades reenlisted late in the war (Rebels by that time had no choice), and when his family protested that he had done enough for the cause, he told them he wanted to see the thing to the end. A young Michigan soldier provided his own common soldiers creed:

> The soldier of '61 was full of life and patriotism, his ardor undampened by hardship and adversity. The soldier of '65 hoped less, but fought and accomplished more. The period of romance had changed to a period of system and endurance. . . . The history of these four years of war has its counterpart in our own lives. In our youth, we acted upon impulse regarding loss of consequences, now we think before we act.

Common soldiers became VETERANS after 1865. After the great conflict, some recalled their experiences with bitterness; most spoke of their service with pride. Individually, thousands published memoirs or contributed to printed regimental histories. Northern veterans, white and black, supported the REPUBLICAN PARTY and joined the Grand Army of the Republic; Southern veterans supported the DEMOCRATIC PARTY and joined the United Confederate Veterans. Most veterans, North and South, preferred to sentimentalize the war, and in their declining years emphasized the positive and patriotic aspects of their experiences. For them, Union soldier Oliver Wendell Holmes's famous utterance was apt: "In our youth, our hearts were touched with fire."

See also BOUNTY SYSTEM; BROTHERS' WAR.

Further reading: James M. McPherson, *For Cause and Comrades: Why Men Fought in the Civil War* (New York: Oxford University Press, 1997); Reid S. Mitchell, *The Vacant Chair: The Northern Soldier Leaves Home* (New York: Oxford University Press, 1993); Bell Irvin Wiley, *The Life of Johnny Reb: The Common Soldier of the Confederacy* (Baton Rouge: Louisiana State University Press, 1978); Bell Irvin Wiley, *The Life of Billy Yank: The Common Soldier of the Union* (Baton Rouge: Louisiana State University Press, 1978).

Compromise of 1850   See Volume IV

Confederate army

The Confederate army consisted of a regular force, the Army of the CONFEDERATE STATES OF AMERICA, and a volunteer force designated the Provisional Army of the Confederate States. Created by the Confederate Provisional Congress on March 6, 1861, the Confederate regulars imitated the U.S. Army's organizational structure and its operational manual. Regulations for the Army of the Confederate States were, with two minor revisions, a copy of the U.S. Army Regulation, 1857.

While very few enlisted men from the U.S. Army joined the Confederate cause, as many as one-fourth of the officers took commissions in the rebel regulars. These men exerted significant influence over the operations of volunteer military forces as senior general officers, engineer officers, staff officers, and supply bureau officers. In numbers, however, the Confederate regular army proved insignificant. Authorized to enlist 15,000 men in eight regiments of infantry, two regiments of cavalry, a corps of artillery, a corps of engineers, and a company of sappers and bombardiers, during the entire 1861–65 period a mere 1,650 men served in the regulars. Of these, half were officers.

Numerically, the volunteer force proved the most significant element of the Confederate military. Created by the Confederate Congress February 28, 1861, the provisional army provided a temporary force to deal specifically with the threat of Northern attempts to stop SECESSION by force. The enabling legislation granted the president the power to accept into Confederate service any units in state service for a period of 12 months. The legislation also allowed a call for 100,000 volunteers and the enrolling of the various state militias into Confederate service. In August 1861, Congress authorized a second call for 400,000

volunteers to serve enlistments ranging from one to three years. These troops remained in the service of their respective states until April 1862, when as part of the first CONSCRIPTION act, they became a part of the provisional army. Throughout the war, between 600,000 and 1,500,000 men served in the provisional army.

Recruiting the Confederate military forces took place at various levels. The regular army created recruiting stations at Baton Rouge Barracks, Louisiana; San Antonio Barracks, Texas; Mount Vernon Arsenal, Alabama; Augusta Arsenal, Georgia; Castle Pinckney, South Carolina; Fort Johnston, North Carolina; and Bellona Arsenal, Virginia. At these stations, recruitment officers attempted to obtain men. However, the recruiting of regular army enlisted men failed miserably, and most of the stations suspended operations by the end of 1861.

More successful during 1861 was the creation of various volunteer military companies throughout the towns and countryside of the Confederate states. Prominent citizens who called on their neighbors to join in creating small military units (e.g., an infantry company, an artillery battery, a company of cavalry, and so on) often organized this local recruiting. These units then consolidated into regiments with others from the same state. During 1861, more volunteers presented themselves than could by law be accepted into Confederate service. The emotional response was so great that, in many cases, hopeful soldiers in units not accepted for field service grew furious at the thought of missing out on the action. They despaired that they would never get a chance to fight, since the war would end after the Yankees got a taste of Southern fighting.

There were three primary branches in the provisional army: infantry, cavalry, and artillery. The largest number of men served in the infantry. Organized into regiments of 10 companies totaling 1,000 men, this branch of the service constituted the main fighting force of the Confederate military. Infantry training proceeded unevenly and depended in many instances on the ability of the local unit commanders to teach themselves (while simultaneously teaching their men) the mysteries of tactics. The work proved difficult and seemed unending to the volunteers. As one Virginian put it, drill "was arduous labor, harder than grubbing, stump-pulling, or cracking rocks on the turnpike." While difficult, it was also necessary because the period's infantry fighting tactics required a complex evolution of movements made by men standing in line elbow to elbow in two ranks. To help facilitate the training of the CITIZEN-SOLDIERS, the Confederate government assigned professional soldiers and, in some cases, the cadets of the state military schools to instruct the recruits. Slowly, the men learned the drills and the officers learned how to control their units. In the two main Confederate armies serving in northern Virginia and Tennessee, drill proficiency reached high levels within a fairly short time. By early 1862, most of the incompetent elected officers had been removed and replaced by more highly skilled tacticians and administrators.

In the secondary branches, artillery and cavalry, the Confederates achieved mixed success in training and tactics. In the artillery, the lack of experienced officers and enlisted men created problems throughout the war. One Rebel gunner remembered after the CIVIL WAR that "whole battalions of artillery went into active service without a single man, whether officer, non-commissioned officer, or private, who knew anything about artillery." In a service where technical knowledge played a major role, the lack of skilled men resulted in a tactically inferior force.

In cavalry, the Confederates held an early advantage in leadership and in rank and file. Bold leaders such as J. E. B. STUART, NATHAN BEDFORD FORREST, JOHN SINGLETON MOSBY, and JOHN HUNT MORGAN used their mounted troops aggressively and imaginatively. The skill of many Southern horsemen contributed to the success of the cavalry, which maintained its superiority to Union mounted troops until 1864, when declining supplies of horses limited rebel mobility and the employment of rapid-fire shoulder arms gave Federal cavalry troops firepower advantage.

While many volunteer units struggled to organize and train, the presence of state militias and military schools, such as the Citadel in Charleston and the Virginia Military Institute in Lexington, Virginia, improved the state of military preparedness. Although many Southern militia units were little more than glorified social clubs, some units, such as the Washington Artillery of New Orleans, the Oglethorpe Light Infantry of Savannah, the Kentucky State Guard, and various state militias, provided a small core of trained soldiers. These prewar institutions impacted most strongly the army forming in Virginia, where many of the officers who led the rebel forces had served in some of the South's best militias. Throughout the war, their experience provided the foundation of a well-led force. In other regions, where the militia influence was less (such as the army forming in Tennessee), the officer corps remained weak and leadership less than ideal.

The task of supplying the vast number of volunteers created major problems for the Confederate government. With no formal military supply apparatus in place and with limited production capabilities, the Confederate War Department faced a seemingly impossible task.

Arming the volunteers presented the most pressing problem for the secessionist war department. At the war's outset, Southern arsenals contained roughly 296,000 shoulder weapons of all types. Many of them were old smoothbore muskets, some still using the outdated flintlock ignition system. In all, only about 24,000 modern rifles and rifle muskets were available. Regiments were unable to take the field in many instances because they had no weapons. By 1862, through a combination of domestic production, battlefield captures, and imports from Europe, the supply problem lessened. Throughout the Confederacy, increasing numbers of rebel troops obtained long-range, efficient weapons, thus improving their combat effectiveness. Still, mixed supplies of weapons within regiments and brigades led to problems in the field and limited the overall efficiency of some units. In the artillery service, weapons proved an even greater problem. Unable to produce adequate numbers of cannons and reliable ammunition, the Confederate artillery almost always fought at a tactical disadvantage.

Clothing varied at the war's outset, from the fine UNIFORMS worn by the former militia companies and provided by friends, to the mismatched civilian clothing worn by many volunteers. However, problems appeared early as the clothes worn by the troops began to wear out. The central government responded by creating a system called "commutation." In this system, soldiers either bought clothes or were supplied by their home states at the expense of the RICHMOND government. Slowly, the quartermaster department established a series of depots throughout the South where clothing was produced for issue to all troops in Confederate service. This system worked with varying degrees of success through 1862–65.

Food and TRANSPORTATION also presented operational challenges to the emerging armies. Shortages of grain and meat, and the inability to transport these vital supplies, were serious problems. So severe were the shortages that the Confederate government resorted to the practice of IMPRESSMENT to obtain sufficient supplies of flour and meat. While this did little to ease the problem, it underscored the degree of shortage in the Southern armies. Inadequate supplies of horses and vehicles to transport ammunition, clothing, and food compounded all of the supply problems. As the number of horses declined, so did the ability of the armies to take offensive actions or even feed themselves.

Operationally, the volunteer force was divided into several organizations known as armies. These forces were generally arrayed to protect the Southern territory. During 1861, the government spread its military forces widely in an attempt to protect as many points as possible. This resulted in troops being scattered along the Gulf Coast, in northern Virginia, and across the northern border of Tennessee. The nature of the Federal invasion of the South in some ways dictated the emerging shape of the two main rebel forces. In Virginia, the front of the Union advance in July 1861, the forces assigned to protecting the Shenandoah Valley consolidated with Southern troops at Manassas. This army successfully defended Richmond in the summer of 1862 and became famous as ROBERT E. LEE's Army of Northern Virginia (so named shortly after Lee took command). As the threat to the Confederate capital increased, more and more troops from the Atlantic coast and western Virginia were funneled to Lee's army. By far the most successful of the Confederate armies, the Army of Northern Virginia fought at the BATTLES OF BULL RUN, the Seven Days' campaign, ANTIETAM, FREDERICKSBURG, CHANCELLORSVILLE, GETTYSBURG, the OVERLAND CAMPAIGN of 1864, and the PETERSBURG CAMPAIGN. Some of the most famous secessionist generals including JOSEPH E. JOHNSTON, THOMAS J. "STONEWALL" JACKSON, J. E. B. Stuart, JAMES LONGSTREET, and GEORGE E. PICKETT served in the Army of Northern Virginia. Indeed, by 1863, Gen. Robert E. Lee and his army had come to symbolize the heart and soul of the Confederate cause for most of the Southern people.

The second major Confederate force coalesced in northern Mississippi as Union forces advanced along the Tennessee River and into the Confederate heartland. Several scattered corps under Leonidas Polk and William J. Hardee held the southern part of Kentucky in 1861 and early 1862. These Confederate troops retreated into northern Mississippi following the fall of Fort Donelson in February 1862. Directed by ALBERT SIDNEY JOHNSTON, the forces concentrated at Corinth, Mississippi, in March 1862 and were bolstered by reinforcements under BRAXTON BRAGG from the Gulf Coast. The concentrated army struck back and met the invading force at the BATTLE OF SHILOH in southwestern Tennessee.

Having lost the battle and its commander, Albert Sidney Johnston, the army retreated to northern Mississippi where it worked to perfect its organization under P. G. T. BEAUREGARD and later Bragg. First called the Army of the Mississippi, and later the Army of Tennessee, this force under Braxton Bragg proved much less successful than Lee's army. Under Bragg, the command failed to protect the valuable food- and supply-producing regions of Tennessee and Georgia. With Bragg as commander, the Army of Tennessee fought at the Battles of Perryville, Kentucky; MURFREESBORO, Tennessee; CHICKAMAUGA, Georgia; and CHATTANOOGA, Tennessee. Following the rebel rout at Chattanooga in November 1863, Bragg resigned from active command and was replaced by Joseph E. Johnston. Johnston commanded the army in July 1864 but was fired for his inability to defend Atlanta. JOHN BELL HOOD took command, lost the ATLANTA CAMPAIGN, and destroyed the Army of Tennessee's effective field capabilities by hurling it against the Federal trenches at Franklin, Tennessee, on November 30, 1864. The army essentially dissolved in the face of fierce Federal attacks at Nashville on December 16, 1864.

Other significant armies created by the Confederate government included Earl Van Dorn's Army of the West that was defeated at Pea Ridge, Arkansas, in March 1862; H. H. Sibley's Army of New Mexico that attempted but failed to take and hold Arizona and New Mexico for the Confederacy; John C. Pemberton's Army of Vicksburg that, in July 1863, surrendered to ULYSSES S. GRANT; and Kirby Smith's Army of the Trans-Mississippi that served in the Confederate territory west of the MISSISSIPPI RIVER.

See also BOUNTY SYSTEM; DESERTION.

Further reading: Thomas L. Connelly, *Army of the Heartland; The Army of Tennessee, 1861–1862* (Baton Rouge: Louisiana State University Press, 1967); Douglas Southall Freeman, *Lee's Lieutenants: A Study in Command* (New York: Scribner, 1998); Gary W. Gallagher, *Lee and His Army in Confederate History* (Chapel Hill: University of North Carolina Press, 2001); J. Tracy Power, *Lee's Miserables: Life in the Army of Northern Virginia from the Wilderness to Appomattox* (Chapel Hill: University of North Carolina Press, 1998); Bell Irvin Wiley, *The Life of Johnny Reb: The Common Soldier of the Confederacy* (Baton Rouge: Louisiana State University Press, 1978).

—James Daryl Black

Confederate navy

Nonexistent in 1860, the Confederate navy played an invaluable role in the Southern war effort during the CIVIL WAR. The navy was created by an act of the Confederate Provisional Congress on February 20, 1861. At that point it was only a paper navy: It had few boats, and it had no sailors. It fell upon STEPHEN R. MALLORY, appointed Confederate secretary of the navy on February 21, to address these issues. Mallory, a senator from Florida before resigning from the U.S. Congress, had served as chairman of the Senate Naval Affairs Committee. This experience would prove to be vital, as he personally oversaw almost all of the Confederacy's maritime policy and naval strategy during the war.

Mallory's first concern upon assuming office was to build a fleet. At the outset of the war, the Confederate government could claim ownership of roughly a dozen vessels, none of them warships. Mallory was determined to turn this into an advantage. Since he was starting from scratch, he hoped to build a navy that utilized the latest technology—ironclad warships, steam engines, and powerful, new guns. The Confederacy did not have the capacity to build its own ships, so Mallory began by trying to purchase ships from Europe. The Lincoln administration quickly brought diplomatic pressure to bear upon the European powers, and so Mallory was only able to acquire a handful of wooden ships. As such, the Confederacy was largely forced to make do with its own resources. Under Mallory's direction, the Southern navy was able to develop a limited capacity for producing its own ships. The Confederates were also able to salvage numerous Union warships, converting most of them to IRONCLADS. The Confederacy also innovated, developing ironclad rams, submarines such as the CSS *H. L. Hunley,* and underwater mines called torpedoes. These efforts were fairly successful. Over the course of the war, the Confederate navy managed to put more than 100 ships into service.

Ships required sailors aboard, so while Mallory was working to piece together a fleet, he was also trying to recruit seamen. The officer corps was easier; 250 naval officers, including the talented RAPHAEL SEMMES, Matthew Maury, Franklin Buchanan, and John Mercer Brooke, had resigned from the U.S. Navy to join the Confederate ranks. Filling out the rank and file, however, proved a much more challenging task. The Confederate navy set up recruitment centers in each of the major Southern cities and offered enlistment bonuses of $50. There were also attempts to force the army to reassign men to the navy. Mallory even agreed to use convicts on Confederate ships, although he refused to allow African Americans into the naval ranks. In the end, the Confederate navy was never really able to raise enough men, and at its height in 1865 it only had a strength of about 4,000 enlisted men and officers.

Due to lack of manpower and ships, the Confederate navy could not hope to compete directly with its Union counterpart. Given the Union's edge in resources and technology, head-to-head confrontations tended to prove disastrous for the Confederates. Over the course of the war, only a half-dozen Union warships were sunk in action by Confederate warships. As such, the Southern navy's efforts were focused on three main activities: defense of rivers and coastal fortifications, blockade running, and commerce raiding.

The Confederates had a fair amount of success in defensive warfare. The navy helped keep the southern MISSISSIPPI RIVER in Confederate hands until mid-1863. Confederate ironclads also protected small rivers, including the Roanoke, the Neuse, the Chattahoochee, and the Red. Most of the Confederacy's major cities were on the seacoast and were dependent on Confederate ships for protection. In particular, the navy played a critical role in defending RICHMOND, Charleston, Savannah, and Mobile.

River and coastal defense may have been the most important task performed by the navy, but blockade running has received a great deal more attention from historians. Blockade runners were usually small, fast boats designed to sneak past the Union warships responsible for preventing any vessels from entering or leaving Southern ports. The blockade runners were critical to the Confederate war effort because they were the only way for the South to export cot-

ton and to import raw materials and manufactured goods from European countries. Although most blockade runners were privately held and were operated for profit, the Confederate navy also owned and operated several dozen of the ships. Blockade runners were very effective. Over the course of the war an estimated 92 percent of attempts to run the Union blockade were successful. The odds of success were much higher in the early years of the war than in the latter years, however, as the UNION NAVY learned how to patrol the Southern coast more effectively.

Blockade running's counterpart was commerce raiding—the attack and capture of Union merchant ships. The former was undertaken to sustain the Southern ECONOMY, while the latter was meant to disrupt the Northern economy. Commerce raiding was much riskier than blockade running due to the 1856 Treaty of Paris, an international agreement that made the practice illegal. The existence of the treaty meant that the rewards of commerce raiding were minimal, because captured ships and goods could not be easily sold. Meanwhile, penalties were severe: Commerce raiders risked imprisonment or execution as pirates. Private interests invested their money in blockade runners, while commerce raiding became almost exclusively the responsibility of the Confederate navy. There were several successful commerce raiders, most notably the *Shenandoah,* which captured or destroyed 36 ships, and the *Alabama,* which was responsible for the demise of 71 Northern vessels. Roughly 5 percent of Northern merchant ships fell victim to commerce raiders over the course of the war. In addition, it is estimated that for every one ship captured or destroyed, another eight ships had to remain in port due to the threat of commerce raiding. Altogether, 1,616 Northern vessels with a total capacity of 774,000 tons were rendered unavailable during the war, with a consequent negative impact on the Northern economy.

Despite the fact that the Confederate navy began with almost nothing, it played a very important role in the Confederate war effort, with an impact on both military and economic affairs. The Confederate navy was no match for its Union counterpart, but it must nonetheless be judged at least a partial success.

See also FOREIGN POLICY; *MONITOR-MERRIMACK*; VICKSBURG CAMPAIGN.

Further reading: William M. Fowler, *Under Two Flags: The American Navy in the Civil War* (New York: Norton, 1990); Raimondo Luraghi, *A History of The Confederate Navy* (Annapolis, Md.: Naval Institute Press, 1996); William N. Still, ed., *The Confederate Navy: The Ships, Men and Organization, 1861–1865* (Annapolis, Md.: Naval Institute Press, 1996).

—Christopher Bates

Confederate States of America

The Confederate States of America was established under a constitution signed on March 11, 1861. The new republic consisted of the Deep South states of Alabama, Florida, Georgia, Louisiana, Mississippi, South Carolina, and Texas. The number of Confederate states eventually grew to 11 when Arkansas, North Carolina, Tennessee, and Virginia left the Union following ABRAHAM LINCOLN's post–FORT SUMTER call for 75,000 volunteers to suppress the Southern rebellion. Four years of CIVIL WAR failed to secure Confederate independence, and the nation ceased to exist after the surrender of its principal armies in April and May 1865.

Abraham Lincoln's election on the Republican presidential ticket in 1860 caused many white Southerners to fear for the future of their slave-based society and provided the trigger for South Carolina's SECESSION convention. On December 20, 1860, South Carolina's 169 convention delegates voted unanimously to leave the Union. Similar conventions soon met in the other states of the lower South. By February 1, 1861, the first wave of secession was completed.

Delegates from the seceded states met in Montgomery, Alabama, during the first week of February 1861. Moderates controlled the convention and quickly drafted a provisional, or temporary, constitution closely modeled on the U.S. Constitution. JEFFERSON DAVIS of Mississippi, a moderate secessionist, and ALEXANDER H. STEPHENS of Georgia, who had been opposed to secession, were chosen as president and vice president. The delegates in Montgomery, selected by their respective state conventions rather than in popular ELECTIONS, converted themselves into the new nation's unicameral Congress. Together with Davis and Stephens, members of the Congress would serve until national elections could be held in November 1861. Congress also set up executive departments similar to those in the United States, as well as a postal system and other elements of a national government.

The Davis administration soon faced a crisis at FORT SUMTER in Charleston, South Carolina. Under increasing pressure to assert Confederate nationality, Davis ordered Southern forces to bombard and seize the United States's last remaining Southern fort during the second week of April 1861. Abraham Lincoln responded to the loss of Sumter by issuing a call for 75,000 volunteers to suppress the rebellion. That threat convinced four more slave states, Virginia, Arkansas, North Carolina, and Tennessee, to secede from the Union. The slave states of Missouri, Kentucky, Maryland, and Delaware remained loyal to the Union, although some of their citizens were active in support of the Confederacy.

The Confederate government operated under a temporary constitution for one month. The permanent constitution, written and approved by the Montgomery delegates, generally followed the U.S. Constitution except for a few important differences. The Confederate Constitution limited national power and stressed STATES' RIGHTS. Most importantly, it protected SLAVERY in the states and all territories. The new document's preamble affirmed that each Confederate state acted "in its sovereign and independent character." The first 12 amendments to the U.S. Constitution appeared in the body of the Confederate version. The Confederate constitution created a national executive and bicameral legislature very similar to those of the United States, although it departed from the U.S. model in limiting the president to one six-year term.

The Confederate executive department included President Davis, Vice President Stephens, and the cabinet secretaries of state, war, the navy, and the treasury, a postmaster general, and an attorney general. The brilliant JUDAH P. BENJAMIN served as attorney general, secretary of state, and secretary of war at different times. STEPHEN R. MALLORY worked at the head of the Navy Department, and John H. Reagan was postmaster general. George Wythe Randolph and James A. Seddon stood out as the most important among several men to hold the post of secretary of war, while Christopher G. Memminger directed affairs at the Treasury Department for more than three years. Cabinet members faced huge problems as they sought to plan and pay for war while also overseeing day-to-day governmental operations.

RICHMOND, Virginia, replaced Montgomery as the capital of the Confederacy in 1861 and became the nation's most visible geographic symbol. The move was made because it was the capital of Virginia, the most populous Confederate state, and also the leading manufacturing center in the South. The first permanent Congress convened in Richmond on February 18, 1862. Elected by voting-age white male citizens the preceding November, congressmen and senators had not run on specific political party tickets, like the Democratic or Republican parties of the North. The Confederacy deliberately sought to avoid partisan politics. Although parties never developed, bitter divisions soon arose between congressional supporters and opponents of Jefferson Davis and his policies.

The burden of conducting a protracted war against a powerful opponent placed enormous strains on Confederate society. Well before the end of the conflict, the South underwent changes and confronted challenges no one could have anticipated in 1861. Moreover, the Davis government passed laws and regulations that conflicted with the states' rights philosophy so often associated with the Confederacy. Still, the Confederacy held some advantages over the North. It sought to win independence and could achieve that by defending itself and persuading the Northern people that the effort to restore the Union would be too

Confederate president Jefferson Davis with his cabinet and, center, General Robert E. Lee *(Hulton/Archive)*

expensive in lives and money. The North, in contrast, had to invade the Confederacy, destroy its capacity to make war, and crush the Southern people's will. Many Confederates looked to the American Revolution as proof that a weaker power could defeat a more powerful foe. They expected the great size of the Confederacy and the unity of its people to be crucial factors in bringing Southern victory.

First, the nation needed soldiers. Hundreds of thousands of men volunteered for Confederate service in 1861, after which the rate of enlistment drastically declined. The CONSCRIPTION Act of 1862 made all white males between the ages of 18 and 35 eligible for service but exempted men in several occupations deemed essential to the war effort (the most controversial exemption allowed one white man on each plantation with twenty slaves or more to avoid service). Later acts extended the age limits to 18 and 45 and then to 17 and 50 and modified the roster of exemptions. Until December 1863, any man drafted could pay a substitute to serve for him. The conscription acts were designed to promote volunteering rather than to draft men directly, and they generally worked well. Severe manpower short-

ages caused Congress to approve the enrollment of slaves into the CONFEDERATE ARMY very late in the war, but the legislation came too late to have any impact on the war.

Both the Davis and Lincoln governments understood that French aid had tipped the balance in favor of the colonists during the American Revolution. Confederate diplomatic efforts therefore concentrated on achieving recognition from Great Britain or France. Initial hopes rested on the belief that by withholding cotton exports, the Confederacy could produce such economic hardship among British textile manufacturers and their employees that the London government would intervene to assure a steady flow of cotton. Among other things, such intervention likely would bring the Royal Navy into conflict with the United States's naval blockade of the Confederacy. But "King Cotton" diplomacy failed miserably because Britain had a surplus of cotton on hand in 1861, rapidly developed new sources of cotton in India and Egypt, and saw increased production in arms manufacturing and other areas boost EMPLOYMENT when textile production lagged in the summer and fall of 1862.

During the war, the Confederacy suffered immense economic dislocation. Much of the problem was due to the fact that the antebellum Southern ECONOMY was not prepared to wage war. With most capital tied up in land and slaves, the Confederacy struggled to pay for its war effort. The Davis administration relied on three sources of income: taxes that raised about 5 percent of revenues, bonds that raised another 35 percent, and paper treasury notes that raised the remaining 60 percent. This overproduction of paper money helped fuel inflation that eventually reached 9,000 percent. Shortages of goods contributed to inflation, as the Union blockade limited trade with Europe. Union military successes throughout the war also played a role in disrupting industrial and agricultural production and TRANSPORTATION networks.

Richmond adjusted to growing economic problems with a number of measures, such as IMPRESSMENT, which allowed the national government to seize goods—food, supplies, and slaves—for the war effort. Impressment caused considerable dissension but also provided invaluable war-related goods that helped keep the Confederate armies in the field.

The Confederacy registered impressive accomplishments in the area of war industry as well. The government created the largest powder works in North America at Augusta, Georgia, and established arsenals and ironworks in Richmond; Charleston; Selma, Alabama; and elsewhere. During 1863, war-related industries in Selma employed more than 10,000 people. No Confederate army ever lost a battle because it lacked weapons, ammunition, or other materiel.

The demands of fighting a war created serious political tensions in the Confederacy. In the absence of formal parties through which disagreements could be expressed, Confederate political opinion divided into pro– and anti–Jefferson Davis factions. Davis and military figures such as ROBERT E. LEE insisted that winning the war should take precedence over everything else. Other political figures insisted that the central government must protect essential state and individual rights, even if doing so hindered the Confederate war effort. Relations between Davis and the national Congress were tense. Disagreement over conscription, the suspension of HABEAS CORPUS, and policies that promoted economic centralization divided the leadership of the Confederacy. Congressional critics blasted Davis as a dictator and warned that winning independence would be worthless unless the values that made the new nation distinctive were preserved.

Vice President Stephens broke with Davis in 1862 over conscription and other issues, becoming another outspoken critic. GOVERNORS such as JOSEPH E. BROWN of Georgia and Zebulon Vance of North Carolina deliberately withheld supplies from the government and flaunted or circumvented national laws. Despite great opposition, President Davis worked extremely hard, set an example of selfless service, and created and sustained a national army and government. At the same time, Davis's inability to delegate military responsibilities hurt the war effort. In addition, Davis was not an eloquent public speaker and failed to inspire public faith in the Southern cause. For that, the nation turned to Gen. Robert E. Lee and the Army of Northern Virginia. Victories over the Union's army of the Potomac helped to maintain the Confederacy after public support of Davis's government died. As the war continued, the Southern government suffered from divisions that prevented the most effective use of limited resources. Many historians argue that the Confederacy's inability to resolve the contradiction of nationalism versus states' rights and individualism caused the ultimate defeat of the South.

Military losses, particularly during and after the summer of 1863, along with inflation, scarcity of goods, and loss of loved ones led to dissent and disaffection behind the lines. DESERTION from Southern armies escalated dramatically during the winter of 1864–65. In early April 1865, Robert E. Lee and the Army of Northern Virginia abandoned Richmond. On April 9, Lee surrendered to ULYSSES S. GRANT at APPOMATTOX COURT HOUSE. Appomattox marked the end of the war for most Confederates, though additional surrenders of large forces would take place over the next month. Jefferson Davis, who fled southward with part of his cabinet just before the fall of Richmond, was captured on May 10 near Irwinville, Georgia.

The South paid a high price for its rebellion. Nearly 260,000 Confederate soldiers died from wounds or disease and another 200,000 were wounded in combat. Two-thirds of the region's assessed wealth was destroyed. Approximately 40 percent of all Southern livestock perished. Much of the infrastructure of the region—banks, factories, RAILROADS, bridges, levees, and the like—lay in ruins. One comparative figure is especially revealing: Between 1860 and 1870, Northern wealth increased by 50 percent while Southern wealth decreased by 60 percent.

The Confederate States of America failed because of internal dissent and military defeat. No other white group in U.S. history suffered the kind of catastrophe that was the fate of white Southerners. This regionally distinctive legacy has been, and continues to be, explored in LITERATURE, song, political culture, and symbols, such as the conflict over the Confederate battle flag.

See also FOREIGN POLICY; INDUSTRIAL DEVELOPMENT; MUSIC; TREDEGAR IRON WORKS.

Further reading: William J. Cooper Jr., *Jefferson Davis, American* (New York: Knopf, 2000); William C. Davis, *Look Away: A History of the Confederate States of America*

(New York: Free Press, 2001); Gary W. Gallagher, *The Confederate War* (Cambridge, Mass.: Harvard University Press, 1997).

Confiscation Acts (August 6, 1861, and July 17, 1862)
The Confiscation Acts authorized Union troops to seize private property from individuals supporting the Confederacy during the CIVIL WAR. This provided valuable supplies for the Union war effort while undermining the Southern will to fight. At the same time, the Confiscation Acts played an important role in bringing an end to the institution of SLAVERY.

In the first Confiscation Act, passed on August 6, 1861, Congress authorized the UNION ARMY to seize any property used in "promoting . . . insurrection or resistance to the laws." On its face, the act might have aroused little controversy in the North, because seizure of such "contraband" occurred in most wars. However, Southern property included slaves. This opened up an important question: If soldiers confiscated slaves, would those slaves be free?

Certain Union commanders, most notably Gens. John C. Frémont and BENJAMIN F. BUTLER, believed that confiscated slaves were indeed free. President ABRAHAM LINCOLN, however, forbade Union officers from freeing slaves on their own authority. Lincoln's 1861 repudiation of Frémont and Butler stemmed from his fear that any action that hinted at the ABOLITION of slavery would enrage the citizens and soldiers of Maryland, Delaware, Kentucky, and Missouri. Though none of these "border states" had joined the Confederacy, all of them still permitted slavery. Any perceived threat to the institution created the possibility that the states would throw their support to the Confederacy. Lincoln also worried that freeing captured slaves would cost him significant political support in Congress.

As the war dragged on through 1862, however, Lincoln's position changed. Southern resistance proved stronger than most Northerners had anticipated. By the spring of that year, both Lincoln and most congressional Republicans had concluded that victory would require a more determined and ruthless policy. In this new mood, Congress passed the second Confiscation Act on July 17, 1862. The act required that Union soldiers free any slaves that came into their hands. The act also authorized Lincoln to "employ as many persons of African descent as he may deem necessary and proper for the suppression of this rebellion . . . and use them in such manner as he may judge best." Lincoln was now free to arm former slaves to fight against the Confederacy.

The second Confiscation Act was not an abolitionist measure. Instead, it was a military tactic intended to undermine the South's ECONOMY and social institutions. However, it took no great leap of imagination to predict that if Union forces advanced far enough into Confederate territory, slavery might actually collapse.

The second Confiscation Act thus paved the way for Lincoln's EMANCIPATION PROCLAMATION in January 1863. The Proclamation took the next logical step, declaring that all slaves in rebellious states were free, whether they had been captured by Union soldiers or not. The Emancipation Proclamation, in turn, was superseded after the war by the THIRTEENTH AMENDMENT, ending slavery forever. And so the end of slavery came not in one great stroke, but in steps; the Confiscation Acts were an important part of this process.

Further reading: Herman Belz, *A New Birth of Freedom: The Republican Party and the Freedmen's Rights, 1861–1866* (Westport, Conn.: Greenwood Press, 1966); Louis S. Gerteis, *From Contraband to Freedmen: Federal Policy toward Southern Blacks, 1861–1865* (Westport, Conn.: Greenwood Press, 1973); Bell Irvin Wiley, *Southern Negroes, 1861–1865* (New Haven, Conn.: Yale University Press, 1938).

—Tom Laichas

conscription

Conscription, or "the draft" as it is more generally known, is the practice of compelling citizens to serve in the military. With the CIVIL WAR, the United States began a transition from the limited warfare of the past, in which a relatively small number of men were mobilized as soldiers, toward modern "total war." A total war mobilizes the entire populace and is fought on a much broader scale. The Civil War was not a modern war in every way, but it certainly was modern in terms of its scale. In the Revolutionary War, roughly 200,000 soldiers took the field for the United States. In the War of 1812, 286,000 soldiers fought, and in the Mexican-American War a mere 79,000 soldiers participated. These numbers were dwarfed during the Civil War, when nearly 4 million men donned the uniform of either the Confederacy or the Union.

Early in the Civil War, there were more than enough volunteers on both sides to fill the ranks. This reflected the populace's excitement over the impending conflict as well as their sense that the war would not last more than a few months. When it became clear that this was not to be the case, the number of volunteers dropped dramatically, and leaders quickly realized that they would have to do something to fulfill their armies' manpower needs.

The Confederacy was the first to act. Most of the CONFEDERATE ARMY's early volunteers signed up for one-year enlistments that expired in spring of 1862. While some of these men extended their enlistments, many others made clear their intentions to return home. In response, on April 16, 1862, the Confederate Congress passed the first of three conscription acts, establishing the first national draft in American history. The first Conscription Act extended the one-year enlistments to three years or until the end of the war. To soften the blow, these VETERANS were to be granted 60-day furloughs before finishing their time. The act also required men between the ages of 18 and 35 who were not already in the ranks to serve for three years, although there was a grace period before the act took effect so that these individuals would have the opportunity to "volunteer." The second Conscription Act, passed in October 1862, refined the terms of the first, most notably extending the upper end of the eligible age range from 35 to 45. The third Conscription Act, passed in February 1864, went even further, declaring the eligible age range to be 17 to 50 years.

The Union was in the same position as the Confederacy, and the Union leadership responded in a similar fashion. In August 1862, President ABRAHAM LINCOLN used the terms of the Militia Act of 1862 to require states to furnish 300,000 troops, with each state being assigned a quota based on its population. This system proved to be very inefficient, and so in March 1863 Congress passed the Enrollment Act, which was similar to the Conscription Act that had been adopted by the Confederate government. The act made men between the ages of 20 and 45 liable for up to three years of service. Unlike the Confederate version, however, the Union's Enrollment Act did not automatically draft all eligible men into the army. Instead, it set up quotas for how many soldiers each state was expected to provide. If states could meet their quota with volunteers, then no draft was held. If not, then federal officials would go from district to district within the state and set up a wheel in a public place containing the names of all eligible men in the district. At the appointed time, a draft officer would put on a blindfold and choose the required number of names from the wheel.

The draft was not received well in either the North or the South. One of the most common objections was that a draft was not within the authority of the government. President Lincoln was regularly asked to suspend the draft or to reduce state quotas. The president faced particularly vocal opposition from New York governor Horatio Seymour, who threatened to take the case to the Supreme Court. Lincoln usually managed to deflect these challenges by making minor concessions when he felt it necessary. JEFFERSON DAVIS faced similar objections in the South, where it was felt that the draft was not only unconstitutional but also contrary to the STATES' RIGHTS philosophy of the Confederacy. Among the prominent critics who faced off against Davis were GOVERNORS, including

JOSEPH E. BROWN of Georgia and Zebulon Vance of North Carolina. The supreme courts of several states sustained Davis's position.

The biggest objections to the draft laws centered on the exemption clauses contained in both the Northern and Southern acts. Union draftees were allowed to pay a $300 commutation fee, or to hire a substitute, in acknowledgement of the fact that some men had responsibilities that made military service impossible. In the Confederacy, a draftee could also hire a substitute. In addition, certain classes of men necessary on the HOMEFRONT were exempt from the Confederate draft: government employees, contractors, shoemakers, blacksmiths, millers, and so forth. The most controversial exemption was included in the second Conscription Act: The so-called Twenty-Negro Law added any slaveholder with more than nineteen slaves to the list of exempt classes. Officially, this was because these individuals were needed to keep the ECONOMY running, but many Southerners felt that the clause was included because of the large plantation owners' political connections.

The exemption clauses gave rise to complaints on both sides that the conflict was a "rich man's war, poor man's fight." Scholarly studies have shown that this was not true, but the perception held by some groups was strongly felt. Resentful draftees failed to appear when called, or they deserted shortly after joining the ranks. Anti-draft violence was also a common phenomenon in both the North and South. The most well-known uprising was the NEW YORK CITY DRAFT RIOTS in July 1863. A mob made up mostly of poor Irishmen and women went on a two-day rampage. These Irish workers were angry not only about the draft but also about EMANCIPATION, which they opposed due their fears that freedmen would provide unwanted competition for jobs. The rioters inflicted $1.5 million in damage while killing many African-American men. The situation was finally resolved when NEW YORK CITY's government came up with enough money to purchase exemptions for all of the draft spots the city was expected to fill. Eventually, incidents like the draft riots convinced leaders on both sides to eliminate some of the exemptions. In 1863 the Southern Congress disallowed any further hiring of substitutes. In 1864 President Lincoln and the Northern Congress did away with the $300 exemption.

If judged by the number of soldiers added to the ranks, the draft was not very successful in either the North or the South. There are no reliable numbers for the South, but the statistical story of the North is probably representative of what happened on both sides. Of the 776,000 men drafted, 161,000 failed to report, and another 391,000 had to be sent home due to disability or because being drafted would be an undue hardship on their families. Of the remaining 207,000 men, 87,000 paid the commutation fee and another 74,000 furnished substitutes. Only 46,000 men, less than 7 percent of the total drafted, actually went into the army. If the substitutes are taken into account, then drafting accounted for the addition of a total of 120,000 men to the UNION ARMY, only about 4 percent of the total number of Yankee soldiers. And since draftees tended to be poor soldiers, their impact was likely even less substantial than their modest numbers would suggest.

The purpose of the draft was not to force men to fight. Instead, the goal was to motivate able-bodied men to volunteer on their own. At roughly the same time the Conscription and Enrollment Acts were passed, the respective governments set up incentive programs for new volunteers. Men were given cash bounties of as much as $1,000 or more and granted other concessions designed to ease their service in the army. If a man was drafted, however, all benefits for enlisting were forfeit, and he was forever branded with the stigma of having been forced to fight rather than volunteering. It is impossible to say exactly how many men were motivated to enlist or to reenlist by the combination of negative and positive reinforcement.

Once again, there are no reliable statistics for the Confederacy, but in the Union more than 750,000 men volunteered to join the ranks in the years after the passage of the Enrollment Act. If even a modest percentage of those men joined out of fear of being drafted, then the draft has to be considered at least a qualified success.

Further reading: James W. Geary, *We Need Men: The Union Draft in the Civil War* (DeKalb: Northern Illinois University Press, 1991); Albert Moore, *Conscription and Conflict in the Confederacy* (New York: Hillary House, 1963); Eugene Murdock, *One Million Men: The Civil War Draft in the North* (Westport, Conn.: Greenwood Press, 1980).

—Christopher Bates

contrabands

Contrabands was the term used for fugitive slaves who crossed over UNION ARMY lines during the CIVIL WAR. Before the Union developed a coherent policy on EMANCIPATION, slave REFUGEES were neither in bondage nor free, but somewhere in between, recognized legally as confiscated enemy property.

About a month after the Confederate attack at FORT SUMTER, three slaves crossed the Union picket lines at Fortress Monroe, Virginia, where they offered their services to the Union army and sought protection from their masters. Thus began a spontaneous and grassroots effort by slaves across the South to escape bondage. Within a few months, thousands of slaves poured over Union lines. Wherever the army went, SLAVERY seemed to disintegrate

in the immediate vicinity. Because there were so many fugitive slaves in army camps, Union military leaders were forced to confront the future of slavery.

Gen. BENJAMIN F. BUTLER, the commander at Fortress Monroe, freed the first three slaves and put them to work as army laborers. Butler learned that Confederates used slaves to construct fortifications; thus, he declared that fugitive slaves were enemy property—in other words, "contraband of war." Butler's actions were some of the first steps toward emancipation. Nevertheless, the Union had not yet formulated a policy toward fugitive slaves. Other military officers, including Butler when he administered captured lands in Louisiana, returned runaways because they did not have a system to care for them.

Congress attempted to clarify the emerging problem of contrabands with the CONFISCATION ACT of August 6, 1861. It stated that slaveholders forfeited their rights to any slave that had been employed by the Confederate military. While the law did not address emancipation, it did recognize the fact that slaves could be used as weapons of war. Consequently, it was in the best interests of the Union military to weaken the institution of slavery.

A preliminary and uncertain federal policy did not deter slaves from seeking their freedom, but Union forces were ill-equipped to deal with thousands of fugitive slaves. Male slaves were put to work, but the army had little to offer slave women and children. Northern benevolent associations rushed in food and clothing for the destitute, and teachers arrived to educate freed families in the contraband camps.

In 1862 Congress continued to refine its policy toward fugitive slaves and to inch ever closer toward emancipation. An article of war was added in March forbidding the army or the navy from returning fugitive slaves to their owners. Slavery was abolished in WASHINGTON, D.C., in April and in the U.S. territories in June. A second Confiscation Act passed on July 17, 1862, freed the slaves of any person who aided the rebellion and authorized the seizure and sale of any other property from disloyal citizens. On the same day, Congress recognized the labors of the contrabands at army camps. According to the Militia Act, any fugitive slave who worked for the military was freed, as was his or her family.

Lincoln and Union military leaders entered the Civil War with the desire to not interfere with the slave system in the South, but the slaves and the lengthening war forced the issue. More than 10,000 contrabands crossed Union lines in Virginia by mid-1863. Along the MISSISSIPPI RIVER, similar large encampments of contrabands stretched the limits of Union supply lines. Crowded into unhealthy camps, thousands died from disease, exposure, and even starvation. In spite of the degradation, most refugees stayed in the camps. If they ventured from the protection of the

Union lines, contrabands were subject to marauding guerrilla bands of Confederate soldiers or recapture by their owners.

Facing a humanitarian crisis, Union leaders began to develop a policy of refugee settlement on abandoned lands. Some were hired out to Unionist planters, while others were placed on U.S. government-run PLANTATIONS on a wage-labor basis. After 1863, male contrabands were encouraged to enlist in the Union army. At the end of the war, Congress created the FREEDMEN'S BUREAU to formally help ex-slaves make the transition to freedom.

Contrabands played a crucial role in forcing the Union to confront the issue of slavery and emancipation. As the war persisted, the value of fugitive slaves as military laborers and as soldiers helped to convince President Lincoln and Congress to emancipate all of the slaves. Unfortunately, far too many contrabands met an untimely death at disease-ridden camps, demonstrating the uncertainty that accompanied freedom.

See also DAVIS BEND, MISSISSIPPI, FREEDMEN'S COLONY; EMANCIPATION PROCLAMATION; PORT ROYAL, SOUTH CAROLINA EXPERIMENT; SPECIAL FIELD ORDER NO. 15.

Further reading: Louis S. Gerteis, *From Contraband to Freedman: Federal Policy towards Southern Blacks, 1861–1865* (Westport, Conn.: Greenwood Press, 1973).

—Justin J. Behrend

Cooke, Jay (1821–1905)

Known as "the financier of the CIVIL WAR," Jay Cooke was the most influential investment banker of his day. Born in Sandusky, Ohio, to a prosperous family (his father was a lawyer, a businessman, and a politician), Cooke started his working life as a clerk in a dry goods store at age 14. In 1838 his brother-in-law offered him a similar position in Philadelphia, but after the company's failure and a short stint as a hotel clerk, he moved back to Sandusky.

In 1839 Cooke began his long career in the banking business with a position at E.W. Clark & Company. His skills soon rapidly advanced him up the corporate ranks. By age 21, he was made a full partner in the firm. In 1844 he married Dorothea Elizabeth Allen, sister of the president of Allegheny College in Pennsylvania, where his brother Henry was a student.

Cooke went on to become a successful investment banker with E.W. Clark & Company, which helped to finance the Mexican-American War and a few railroad companies. The firm went bankrupt during the financial PANIC OF 1857, and Cooke retired. The Civil War would soon provide new opportunities for him.

In 1861 as the war broke out, Cooke ended his brief retirement and opened his own firm, called Jay Cooke & Company. Vigorously and shrewdly marketing Civil War bonds, he made a great success of the firm. Using a patriotic advertising campaign, Cooke convinced Americans to invest in their government during the darkest days of the war. The money used to purchase these bonds helped to keep the war effort alive for the Union, particularly when resources were most desperately needed.

Following the war, Cooke expanded his investments into new ventures. The largest of these was the Northern Pacific Railroad, a new transcontinental railroad that was to run from the Great Lakes to the Pacific Ocean. Cooke needed to raise $100 million for the railroad, and he sought both American and European investors to back the scheme. Money was not easily forthcoming, and the investment quickly turned bad because there was not enough rail traffic or people along the line for the road to attract new investors. Cooke spent unwisely in order to keep the project alive, and on September 18, 1873, his company went bankrupt.

The failure of Jay Cooke & Company, which was the leading brokerage firm in the country in 1873, played an important role in ushering in the Panic of 1873 and the depression that followed. Cooke afterwards spent a few years away from the world of banks and finance, only to return once more as an investor in silver mines and real estate in Minnesota. He proved to be a success a final time, purchasing, among other things, an estate near his adopted city of Philadelphia. He spent the last years of his life living with his daughter and her family after converting his estate into a school for girls.

Cooke's influence extended far beyond his own lifetime. His innovations in investment banking and marketing of war bonds set precedents that resonated well into the next century.

See also ECONOMY.

Further reading: John Lewis Harnsberger, *Jay Cooke and Minnesota: The Formative Years of the Northern Pacific Railroad, 1868–1873* (New York: Arno Press, 1981); Ellis Paxson Oberholtzer, *Jay Cooke, Financier of the Civil War* (New York: A. M. Kelley, 1968).

—Troy Rondinone

Copperheads

There were a number of groups in the North who opposed the CIVIL WAR. The most prominent of these was the peace wing of the DEMOCRATIC PARTY, derisively called Copperheads by their detractors, likely after the poisonous snake of the same name. The Copperheads came to exercise substantial influence among important segments of the Northern population over the course of the war before finally fading from the political scene in 1864.

In the first months after the firing on FORT SUMTER, Democrats and Republicans were generally united in their desire to crush SECESSION and reunite the country. As the war dragged on, however, a number of Democrats were increasingly critical of President ABRAHAM LINCOLN and the Union war effort. RADICAL REPUBLICANS, firm advocates of the war, wanted to discredit and silence these Democrats. *Cincinnati Gazette* editor Whitelaw Reid began to call them Copperheads in the pages of his newspaper. The term quickly gained wide usage.

The majority of individuals who were called Copperheads were simply political conservatives who opposed the war effort for any one of a number of reasons. Radicals, however, were willing to stretch the truth to maximize the propaganda value of their attacks. Radical newspaper editors and political leaders told Americans that Copperheads not only opposed the war but that they were secretly providing financial and logistical support for the Southern war effort.

Many Northerners, particularly Northern soldiers, were enraged by this propaganda. A captain in the 46th Pennsylvania wrote, "My *first* object is to crush this infernal Rebellion, the *next* to come North and bayonet such fool miscreants as Vallandigham." The Radicals' depiction of the Copperheads has found its way into many history books, but the charges were almost entirely untrue. Copperheads opposed the war, but they were not conspiring with the South.

There were a number of important political leaders who came to be identified as Copperheads. Most prominent was Ohio congressman CLEMENT L. VALLANDIGHAM. Others included Fernando Wood of New York, William A. Richardson of Illinois, Daniel W. Voorhees of Indiana, and George Woodward of Pennsylvania. A number of newspapers also became vocal supporters of antiwar politics, including the *Illinois State Register,* the *Lacrosse Democratic,* and the *Dubuque Herald.*

The Copperheads rallied around a number of issues. They were angered by Lincoln's suspension of the writ of HABEAS CORPUS, which they felt was unconstitutional. Copperheads became increasingly vocal about this issue as a number of them, including Vallandigham, were jailed for their opposition to the war. In the Midwest, antiwar sentiment was strong because the closure of the MISSISSIPPI RIVER compelled farmers to send their crops via RAILROADS, which were generally controlled by eastern businessmen. Copperheads thus found much support for their argument that the war was being fought to enrich eastern capitalists at the expense of Western farmers. The Copperheads also enjoyed the backing of substantial numbers of German Americans and Irish Americans in the Midwest and in eastern cities. Many members of these ethnic groups opposed administration policies, especially the draft and EMANCIPATION. Indeed, emancipation was the central issue that crystallized opposition to the war. Copperhead leaders strongly opposed any change in the nation's strictly defined racial order. Their supporters shared this attitude and also had an additional, more practical concern. Freed slaves, they feared, would move north and compete for jobs.

These issues generated a great deal of support for the Copperheads. Just as important in determining Copperhead fortunes, however, were Union successes on the battlefield. When the Northern military failed to make progress, antiwar sentiment was high. Northern victories, on the other hand, undermined support for the Copperheads. The so-called high point of Copperheadism occurred in the first months of 1863. Lincoln issued the EMANCIPATION PROCLAMATION in January of that year, and at the same time, the Union armies were struggling on the battlefield. A number of prominent Copperhead leaders, including Clement L. Vallandigham, took advantage of the situation and ran for the governorships of their states. They were heavily favored in these gubernatorial contests until the Union won victories at GETTYSBURG and VICKSBURG. This rallied support for the war among the Northern populace, and when the ELECTIONS came, the Copperheads were all defeated.

The same pattern played itself out in 1864. Early in the year, the Union military was not having a great deal of success. At the Democratic convention, Copperheads were able to secure control of the committee charged with drafting the party platform, and they included a plank calling for an immediate end to the war. Two things ultimately conspired to undermine them. The first was that the convention chose Gen. GEORGE B. MCCLELLAN as its candidate, and he immediately rejected the plank. The second was that Gen. WILLIAM T. SHERMAN captured Atlanta. These reverses ultimately brought an end to the power of the Copperheads.

Although the Copperheads essentially disappeared after 1864, their influence on the Democratic Party lasted a great deal longer. The actions of the Copperheads during the war made it much easier for Republicans in the postwar era to disparage the Democrats as the party of treason. "Waving the bloody shirt," as this was called, was a common feature of political contests for most of the rest of the 19th century.

See also CITIES AND URBAN LIFE.

Further reading: Frank L. Klement, *The Copperheads in the Middle West* (Chicago: University of Chicago Press, 1960); Frank L. Klement, *Lincoln's Critics: The Copperheads of the North,* ed. Steven K. Rogstad (Shippensburg, Pa.: White Mane Books, 1999); Joel A. Silbey, *Respectable Minority: The Democratic Party in the*

Civil War Era, 1860–1868 (New York: W. W. Norton, 1977).

—Christopher Bates

Corinth, Battle of (October 3–4, 1862)

Determined to regain the ground lost during winter and spring 1862, Confederate forces in the west embarked on a late summer offensive designed to regain control of northern Mississippi and Tennessee. Gen. BRAXTON BRAGG's Army of the Mississippi and E. Kirby Smith's troops in east Tennessee constituted the primary offensive force. Together, they launched an invasion of Middle Tennessee and central and eastern Kentucky. Bragg, whose army had protected Mississippi previous to taking the offensive, left behind two small forces of 16,000 men each under Earl Van Dorn and Sterling Price. Strategically, these forces were to support Bragg's invasion by either moving into middle Tennessee, threatening Corinth, Mississippi, (the site of a major railroad junction) and thus preventing Grant from sending troops to counter the main Confederate offensive, or, in the case that Grant diminished his force by sending reinforcements to counter Bragg, attack Corinth.

By early August it was clear that Grant had sent troops toward Nashville, weakening his hold on northern Mississippi. Price called on Van Dorn, who had been operating against Baton Rouge, Louisiana, to move north and unite in an effort to either move into middle Tennessee or capture Corinth. Not until late August did Van Dorn agree to cooperate with Price. Van Dorn moved slowly toward Price's army and by mid-September had not yet joined it. Frustrated by the delays, Price moved alone and captured the town of Iuka on September 14. A column under WILLIAM S. ROSECRANS struck Price on September 19 in a fiercely contested battle. Price abandoned the town on September 20 and with it any hope of moving into Tennessee. On September 28 Price's army arrived at Ripley, where he united with Van Dorn, who assumed command of the united armies. A thrust at Corinth was quickly planned, and the small rebel army of just over 20,000 moved rapidly to the northwest of the town. Union troops under Rosecrans were prepared for the attack and had created a series of light defensive earthworks designed to maximize the defensive capabilities of his 22,000 men. On the morning of October 3, Van Dorn launched his attack. Although successful in his drive against the Federal pickets, hot weather, rugged terrain, and stubborn fighting on the part of Union troops limited rebel gains. At 9:00 A.M. October 4, the Confederates attacked the Federal line. Described as "irregular" by one Federal officer and containing a gap of nearly 500 yards in its center, the defense seemed to be imperfect. Advancing Confederates, however, were met with converging fire from Northern artillery and infantry. While bravely executed, the Southern attacks (which in some isolated spots broke through into the town itself) were uncoordinated and lacked sufficient weight in any one place to make an effective breakthrough.

Federal victory resulted from a combination of poorly orchestrated rebel attacks, a well-conceived series of defensive works, the steadfastness of the Union infantry, and the terrible effectiveness of the Yankee artillery. The Confederates left on October 5, unable to achieve either their tactical or strategic goals. Losses on the Confederate side included 505 killed, 2,150 wounded, and 2,183 missing. The Federals counted 355 killed, 1,841 wounded, and 324 missing.

Further reading: Peter Cozzens, *The Darkest Days of the War: The Battles of Iuka and Corinth* (Chapel Hill: University of North Carolina Press, 1997); Earl J. Hess, *Banners to the Breeze: The Kentucky Campaign, Corinth, and Stones River* (Lincoln: University of Nebraska Press, 2000).

—James Daryl Black

Corps d'Afrique

The story of the Corps d'Afrique, a black regiment, was among the most unusual of any unit in the CIVIL WAR. Originally known as the First Louisiana Native Guards, the Corps began life as part of the CONFEDERATE ARMY on November 23, 1861, and at that time comprised 33 officers and 731 enlisted men, all of them African American. The members of the Corps d'Afrique were from New Orleans and its surrounding areas, and their initial purpose was to defend the city against the UNION ARMY.

During the Civil War and afterward, the fact that black soldiers were willing to fight for the Confederacy was used as evidence that African Americans were happy with their life in the South, so much so that they were willing to take up arms to defend it. However, the men who made up the Corps d'Afrique were not in any way representative of the general African-American population of the South. Most were mulattoes, were educated, and were financially well off. Some were even slave owners. As residents of New Orleans, all were afforded rights that were not available to African Americans in the rest of the South, or even in the North.

Even if they had initially been willing to support the Southern cause, the Corps d'Afrique's enthusiasm soon began to wane. Not surprisingly, Confederate authorities did not give them the support or respect that was afforded to white units. Also, it became clear to corps members that their purpose was to serve as propaganda and not to fight. At the same time, a number of escaped slaves joined the ranks. When the Union army captured New Orleans in

1862, the disillusionment of the unit's membership was complete, and most of its members consented to join the Union army as the First Corps d'Afrique.

The First Corps d'Afrique was officially mustered into service on September 27, 1862. As such, it was the first African-American regiment to be formally recognized as part of the Union Army, predating the famous 54TH MASS-ACHUSETTS REGIMENT by eight months. The unit provided valuable service—guarding prisoners, building fortifications, and fighting at Port Hudson, Mansura, and Mobile. Eventually rechristened the 73rd U.S. Colored Infantry, the regiment continued to serve after the war, often being utilized to make certain that the government's RECON-STRUCTION policies were being properly observed. Thus, a unit that had been formed to defend the Old South became an instrument in its destruction.

Further reading: Nathan W. Daniels, *Thank God My Regiment an African One: The Civil War Diary of Colonel Nathan W. Daniels,* ed. C. P. Weaver (Baton Rouge: Louisiana State University Press, 1998); James G. Hollandsworth, *The Louisiana Native Guards: The Black Military Experience during the Civil War* (Baton Rouge: Louisiana State University Press, 1995).

—Christopher Bates

Crédit Mobilier

The Crédit Mobilier was a company set up in the 1860s by the principals of the Union Pacific Railroad to contract for the construction of the westward portion of the transcontinental railroad. These construction contracts inflated the price, which ensured a profit for Crédit Mobilier but jeopardized the financial health of the Union Pacific. The Union Pacific passed cash, its own stock, and government subsidies to Crédit Mobilier as payment for the construction. The Crédit Mobilier scandal shocked the nation, and involved many politicians, government officials, and businessmen.

The transcontinental RAILROAD was the most challenging engineering project of its day. Authorized by Congress in the PACIFIC RAILROAD ACT of 1862, the Union Pacific Railroad was built westward from Omaha, Nebraska, to meet the eastward-building Central Pacific Railroad, which began its line in Sacramento, California. Congress provided for financial incentives to be transferred to the RAILROADS as portions of track were completed, including grants of land along the track, cash reimbursements, and government-guaranteed bonds that the railroads could sell to investors.

In order to limit their financial risk as well as to benefit from the construction phase, major directors and shareholders of the Union Pacific created a "dummy" construction company, a common practice for railroads in the 19th century. When the Union Pacific began construction in 1864, Herbert M. Hoxie, a shady Republican wheeler-dealer from Des Moines, Iowa, was offered a fee plus Union Pacific stock. In exchange, he agreed to sign a construction contract with the Union Pacific for the first 100 miles of track and then assign the contract to Crédit Mobilier. The onsite engineer for the Union Pacific estimated the costs of construction to be between $20,000 and $30,000 per mile, but he was ordered by Union Pacific officials to contract with Hoxie at a cost of $50,000 per mile. Similar arrangements covered the remainder of the Union Pacific line.

Early efforts to sell Crédit Mobilier stock were largely unsuccessful. Investors questioned the ability of any organization to complete this large undertaking, and the risk was increased by the lack of government regulation of capital markets. However, after Crédit Mobilier's December 1867 distribution to shareholders of assets worth 76 percent of the initial cost of the stock, investors were anxious to hold the stock. One shareholder marketing Crédit Mobilier stock to friends was Massachusetts Republican congressman Oakes Ames. Ames found willing holders in nine representatives and two senators, including the Speaker of the House, two future vice presidents, and future president James Garfield. Many of the politicians received preferential terms for acquiring their stock, and some placed the shares in the names of relatives to hide their relationship to Crédit Mobilier. A lucrative investment, Crédit Mobilier made distributions worth 280 percent of the original investment by the end of 1868.

The good times for the investor were short-lived, however. Evidence in documents and court cases between factions of shareholders supported rumors on Wall Street and in WASHINGTON, D.C., that prominent politicians were involved with Crédit Mobilier and that large profits flowed to its shareholders while the Union Pacific was struggling financially. When newspapers began covering the story in the late 1860s, Crédit Mobilier was criticized for receiving government benefits supported by some of its congressional shareholders and for diverting the profits from the Union Pacific.

The news coverage expanded as the 1872 election neared. Although most of the politicians involved with Crédit Mobilier were Republicans, the growing scandal did not hinder President ULYSSES S. GRANT's bid for reelection. A lame-duck Congress reconvened in December 1872, and Speaker of the House James Blaine moved for an investigation to clear the names (including his) mentioned in the extensive press coverage of Crédit Mobilier. Congressman Ames supported his testimony with records of which politicians held interests in Crédit Mobilier and the terms of their investments. Ames's correspondence indicated that he had offered stock to politicians who could further the corporation's interests.

However, the other politicians involved distanced themselves from Ames, leaving him and the only Democrat involved, James Brooks, to bear the burden of the scandal. On February 28, 1873, with four days remaining of the 42nd Congress, Ames and Brooks were censured. While acknowledging that the other congressmen had been indiscreet, the investigative committee found they were not guilty of accepting bribes. A separate committee investigating the financial dealings of Crédit Mobilier recommended that the government sue to recover Crédit Mobilier's illegal profits. Investigative measures began to expand, but attempts to investigate the Central Pacific Railroad (the other half of the transcontinental railroad) were hampered by a fire that destroyed the records of the construction company owned by its major shareholders.

Crédit Mobilier was one of the most publicized examples of the financial and political scandals of the post–CIVIL WAR era. Economic frauds were commonplace as people scrambled to take advantage of the postwar economic boom and the technological advances of the era, and corruption was not uncommon.

Further reading: David Haward Bain, *Empire Express: Building the First Transcontinental Railroad* (New York: Viking, 1999); Jay Boyd Crawford, *The Crédit Mobilier of America: Its Origin and History, Its Work of Constructing the Union Pacific Railroad and the Relation of Members of Congress* (New York: AMS Press, 1980); Elisabeth Paulet, *The Role of Banks in Monitoring Firms: The Case of the Crédit Mobilier* (New York: Routledge, 1999).

—Martha Kadue

Cumming, Kate (1833–1909)

Born in Edinburgh, Scotland, in 1833, Kate Cumming served as a nurse for the Army of Tennessee during the CIVIL WAR.

As a child, Kate immigrated with her family to Mobile, Alabama, where her father, David Cumming, became a successful merchant. When her mother and two sisters left for England in the spring of 1861, Kate remained with her father and brother in Mobile. After her brother enlisted in the CONFEDERATE ARMY, Kate volunteered for hospital duty. On April 7, 1862, she departed from Mobile with a group of women volunteers heading to a command post hospital in Corinth, Mississippi. Cumming served as a nurse with the Army of Tennessee at the BATTLE OF SHILOH and continued until the end of the Civil War. Early in her career, Cumming became a hospital matron and, like others in her position, constantly struggled against hostility from men to effectively do her job. Cumming's assignment as hospital matron arose, in part, from her status as a mature, unmarried woman, which allowed her some freedom from male control and domestic obligations.

In 1866 Cumming became one of the first Southern NURSES to publish her story, *A Journal of Hospital Life in the Confederate Army of Tennessee*. This account of Cumming's nursing career included her impressions of wartime life in the Confederacy. In her journal, Cumming criticized the inadequate supplies, lack of competency by male nurses and hospital heads, and the chaos of Civil War hospitals. In addition to accounts of her constant frustration with male doctors who refused to value women's ideas or contributions, Cumming also recorded her exasperation with those Southern women too timid to become nurses. Cumming's memoir, *Gleanings from the Southland*, published in 1895, retold the story of her diary but incorporated the outcome of the war, events in postwar America, and stressed national reconciliation.

In 1874 Kate and her father moved to Birmingham, Alabama, where she taught school and MUSIC. She also took an active role in the activities of the UNITED DAUGHTERS OF THE CONFEDERACY and the United Confederate Veterans.

Kate Cumming died June 5, 1909, in Birmingham and was buried in Mobile.

See also DISEASES AND EPIDEMICS; MEDICINE AND HOSPITALS; VETERANS; WOMEN'S STATUS AND RIGHTS.

Further reading: Kate Cumming, *The Journal of Kate Cumming: A Confederate Nurse, 1862–1865*, ed. Richard Harwell (Savannah, Ga.: Beehive Press, 1975).

—Lisa Tendrich Frank

D

Dahlgren, John A. B. (1809–1870)

Union naval officer John A. B. Dahlgren is best known for his research in naval TACTICS, his innovation in naval weaponry, and during the CIVIL WAR, his successful prosecution of the blockade against Confederate ports.

Born in Philadelphia, Dahlgren became a sailor, joining the Navy as a midshipman in 1826. In 1834 his mastery of mathematics and survey technique won him a position in the U.S. Coastal Survey. During the 1840s, Dahlgren took an interest in naval weaponry, urging that the navy test, design, and manufacture its own weapons. Dahlgren, now a lieutenant, got his chance in 1847 when the navy made him chief of the Bureau of Ordnance.

Dahlgren tested his weapons designs extensively at his Navy Yard workshop and foundry. For instance, he bored holes in the metal walls of cannon, inserting gauges to measure air pressure as weapons were fired. Dahlgren then redesigned the cannon, thickening the walls where the internal pressure was greatest. This gave the "Dahlgren gun" a distinctive shape (gunners also called it the "soda-water bottle") but made the weapon particularly reliable. By the Civil War, most naval vessels carried Dahlgren's guns, including Union IRONCLADS armed with Dahlgren's 15-inch smoothbores.

In 1861 Lincoln promoted Dahlgren to captain after all but three of the Navy Yard's officers resigned their commissions to join the Confederacy. In charge of the Washington Navy Yard in the war's first two years, Dahlgren took command of the South Atlantic Blockading Squadron shortly after his 1863 promotion to rear admiral. Under his leadership, the squadron successfully blockaded Charleston Harbor, which assisted Sherman's capture of Savannah, Georgia.

With the end of the Civil War, Dahlgren was given command of the South Pacific Squadron. He returned to the Navy Yard in 1868 and died in 1870.

Rear Admiral John A. Dalhgren standing by a Dahlgren gun on the deck of the USS *Pawnee* *(Library of Congress)*

Further reading: Madeleine Vinton Dahlgren, *Memoirs of John A. Dahlgren* (Boston: J. R. Osgood, 1882); Robert J. Schneller, *A Quest for Glory: John A. Dahlgren, American Naval Ordinance and the Civil War* (Annapolis, Md.: Naval Institute Press, 1995).

—Tom Laichas

Dana, Charles A. (1819–1897)

Newspaper owner and journalist, Charles Anderson Dana played a prominent role during the CIVIL WAR as an assistant secretary of war. Born in New Hampshire in 1819, Dana attended Harvard and later joined a group of utopian intellectuals at Brook Farm, Massachusetts. When Brook Farm dissolved in 1845, Dana traveled widely in Europe. Upon his return in 1849, he assumed the position of managing editor of HORACE GREELEY's *New York Tribune*. A passionate ABOLITIONist, Dana used the *Tribune* as a forum to denounce the policies and positions of the slave-owning South.

In 1862 Dana resigned over differences with Greeley about the newspaper's editorial positions on the Civil War. Shortly thereafter, Secretary of War EDWIN M. STANTON assigned Dana as a frontline investigator with the title of second assistant secretary of war. Serving in the western theater, Dana investigated pay irregularities, fraud, and was unofficially assigned to report on Gen. ULYSSES S. GRANT's conduct. Dana sent many admiring reports to WASHINGTON, D.C., reinforcing the president's confidence in Grant. ABRAHAM LINCOLN lauded Dana for being the "eyes and ears of the government at the front." In 1864 he was promoted to assistant secretary of war.

In 1868 Dana bought the *New York Sun*. He wrote that he wanted to publish news that was "the freshest, most interesting and sprightliest." Under Dana's guidance, the *Sun* gained renown for its young, college-educated reporters, human-interest stories, and varied editorials. The *Sun* opposed President ANDREW JOHNSON's impeachment and supported Grant's run for the presidency in 1868, but it backed the Liberal Republicans in 1872 and their candidate, Dana's former boss and competitor, Horace Greeley. *The New York Sun*, which sold 130,000 papers a day, became a major national newspaper by the late 1870s. In the Gilded Age, Dana and the *Sun* were known for their support of laissez-faire business.

Dana died in 1897. His *Recollections of the Civil War* was published shortly thereafter.

See also JOURNALISM.

Further reading: Charles A. Dana, *Recollections of the Civil War: With the Leaders at Washington and in the Field in the Sixties* (1898; reprint, Lincoln: University of Nebraska Press, 1996); Janet E. Steele, *The Sun Shines for All: Journalism and Ideology in the Life of Charles A. Dana* (Syracuse, N.Y.: Syracuse University Press, 1993).

—Scott L. Stabler

Davis, Jefferson (1808–1889)

Confederate president Jefferson Davis was born in Christian (subsequently Todd) County, Kentucky, on June 3, 1808, the 10th and last child of Samuel Emory and Jane Cook Davis. His father, a farmer who owned a few slaves, moved the family more than once, eventually settling near Woodville, Mississippi, when Jefferson was about three years old.

Jefferson Davis received a far better than ordinary EDUCATION. Between the ages of 8 and 16, he attended St. Thomas College in Springfield, Kentucky, two academies in Mississippi, and, in 1823, Transylvania University in Lexington, Kentucky. After a year at Transylvania, Davis followed the advice of his brother, Joseph Emory Davis, a successful planter in Warren County, Mississippi, and entered the UNITED STATES MILITARY ACADEMY AT WEST POINT. Davis compiled a career at West Point more memorable for the number of rules he violated than for his academic record, graduating 23rd of 33 cadets in the class of 1828.

Davis spent nearly seven years as an army officer. Commissioned a second lieutenant on July 1, 1828, he served on the frontier in Wisconsin and Illinois. Like ABRAHAM LINCOLN, he played a minor role in the Black Hawk War of 1832 and on May 10, 1834, was promoted to first lieutenant in the dragoons. The tedium and relative lack of opportunity in the army frustrated Davis, who resigned his commission on May 12, 1835. Shortly more than a month later, he married Sarah Knox Taylor, the daughter of Zachary Taylor, under whom Davis had served for a time in Wisconsin.

The young couple moved to Mississippi, where Joseph Davis provided land and advice to assist his brother in establishing himself as a planter. Less than three months into the marriage, "Knoxie" Davis died of a fever, and Jefferson, stricken by the same malady and prostrate with grief, left Mississippi for a few months. Upon his return, he secluded himself at "Brierfield," as he called his property, where he looked to his brother as a mentor in learning the business of running a plantation. Davis also read widely about politics, developing a staunch belief in STATES' RIGHTS and a devotion to the DEMOCRATIC PARTY. His first bid for office ended in failure when he lost a race for the Mississippi state legislature in 1843, but two years later he won election to the U.S. House of Representatives. Several months before his election, on February 25, 1845, he had married Varina Howell, a well-born, intelligent, 19-year-old woman from Natchez. They had four sons and two daughters during the course of a sometimes tumultuous marriage.

Military rather than political glory marked the next phase of Davis's career. Elected colonel of the First Mississippi Volunteers after the outbreak of the Mexican-American War, he fought in northern Mexico under his former father-in-law, Gen. Zachary Taylor. He and his regiment distinguished themselves, and Davis was wounded at the

Battle of Buena Vista in February 1847. Widely praised in the American press, he returned a hero to Mississippi, where the legislature presented him with a sword and, in August 1847, named him to an unexpired term in the U.S. Senate.

Once in WASHINGTON, D.C., Davis quickly gained stature as an important advocate of slaveholders' interests and Southern rights. He supported the expansion of SLAVERY into the federal territories, calling for an extension of the Missouri Compromise line of 1820 to the Pacific Ocean. He also opposed the admission of California to the Union as a free state. Within the Senate, Davis chaired the committee on military affairs and took an active interest in, among other topics, the weaponry of the U.S. Army. Reelected to a full Senate term in 1850, he resigned the next year to run for the governorship of Mississippi, losing a close race to Henry Stuart Foote, a moderate on sectional issues who was much loathed by Mississippi's Democrats.

FRANKLIN PIERCE, elected president on the Democratic ticket in 1852, summoned Davis back to Washington to serve as secretary of war. Davis compiled a solid and innovative record as a cabinet officer. Under his stewardship, the army improved the quality of its arms, purchased camels for use in the arid southwestern territories, adopted revised infantry tactics designed to deal with rifled weaponry, and conducted surveys for transcontinental RAILROAD routes.

Davis returned to the Senate in 1857, immediately assuming a position in the front rank of Southern politicians. Many people considered him the successor in this regard to John C. Calhoun, who before his death in 1850 had been the most prominent Southern statesman. Throughout the late 1850s, Davis strongly advocated the slaveholding position on a cluster of issues. He came to oppose STEPHEN A. DOUGLAS's doctrine of popular sovereignty, most famously expressed in the KANSAS-NEBRASKA ACT of 1854, because it left open the door for a territory to bar slavery. Insisting that slavery benefited slave and master alike, Davis also maintained that states had willingly come together to form the Union and could choose at any time to reclaim their sovereignty by withdrawing from the compact. He saw the emerging REPUBLICAN PARTY, which he identified with ABOLITIONists in the North, as a major threat to the slaveholding South. As the decade drew to a close, he declared that no "abolition president" should be allowed to take office. Life under Republican rule would be intolerable, and he "would rather appeal to the God of Battles at once than attempt to live longer in such a Union."

Abraham Lincoln's election in 1860 precipitated a political crisis that prompted Davis, who did not stand among the most ardent SECESSIONists, to eventually support secession. On January 21, 1861, shortly after Missis-

Jefferson Davis *(National Archives)*

sippi seceded, he delivered a farewell speech to the Senate in which he asserted that the South's constitutional rights were at risk. Davis journeyed from Washington to Brierfield, where, on February 9, he learned that a constitutional convention of delegates from the Deep South states had selected him to be the first president of a new slaveholding republic christened the CONFEDERATE STATES OF AMERICA. Davis accepted the position, though he would have preferred a military command. Widely perceived as a moderate within the context of Deep South slaveholding sentiment, Davis seemed a logical choice for his new position. Apart from his political reputation, his presence at the head of the new government would reassure states of the Upper South that the Confederacy meant to chart a responsible course.

Davis's first major test as president came in April 1861 when he faced a crisis regarding FORT SUMTER. Held by a small garrison of U.S. troops, the fort guarded the approach to Charleston harbor in South Carolina. After Lincoln made it clear that he intended to resupply and hold Sumter, Davis approved a bombardment that commenced on April 12 and quickly forced the fort to surrender.

Lincoln's subsequent call for volunteers to suppress the rebellion led four states of the Upper South to join the seven Deep South states already in the Confederacy, and events moved rapidly toward a full-scale military conflict. In a message to the Confederate Congress on April 28, Davis left no doubt about the centrality of slavery to the establishment of the Confederacy. Lincoln and the Republicans would exclude slavery from the territories, he remarked, and that in turn would render "property in slaves so insecure as to be comparatively worthless . . . thereby annihilating in effect property worth thousands of millions of dollars."

Davis embarked on his career as Confederate commander in chief in poor health. Suffering from stomach ailments, a virus that repeatedly attacked his left eye, and other physical problems, he would struggle against illness even as he labored hard to manage a war that mushroomed beyond what anyone could have imagined in 1861. He pursued Confederate independence with a single-minded energy and impatience toward those unwilling to sacrifice for the cause. Although a vocal supporter of states' rights in the antebellum years, he understood that Confederate victory would require enormous mobilization of the South's manpower and material resources at the federal level. Together with ROBERT E. LEE, his chief military adviser in early 1862 and later his only successful field commander, Davis called for the subordination of state and local needs to those of the national war effort.

Against increasingly passionate opposition from states' rights advocates, including Confederate vice president ALEXANDER H. STEPHENS, Davis pressed for measures that greatly enhanced central power. A national CONSCRIPTION ACT in the spring of 1862 (the first such legislation in American history), wide-scale IMPRESSMENT of farm products, and an array of national taxes helped keep armies in the field but convinced critics that Davis, who also called for a limited suspension of the writ of HABEAS CORPUS on several occasions, was willing to tolerate a systematic assault on personal liberties. Opponents often attacked Davis personally, as when the influential Georgia politician Robert Toombs referred to him as a "false and hypocritical . . . wretch." Davis's administration eventually shaped a war effort that placed roughly 80 percent of all military-age white males in uniform and witnessed the growth of government-sponsored industries (including munitions and saltworks) that employed thousands of workers.

Davis spent much of his time dealing with generals, strategy, and other military affairs. Although he may have been too loyal to commanders such as BRAXTON BRAGG, he wisely granted considerable latitude to Robert E. Lee, whose Army of Northern Virginia supplied most of the Confederacy's major victories. Davis felt pressure from all parts of the Confederacy to provide military protection against invading Union forces, but he sought to concentrate manpower in field armies that would act broadly on the defensive while seeking openings to launch counteroffensives. The Confederate movements into Kentucky and Maryland in the late summer and autumn of 1862 provide excellent examples of Southern strategic counterpunches. In the end, only Lee developed as a capable CONFEDERATE ARMY commander, a circumstance that severely limited Davis's options.

Northern military and industrial power, internal divisions within Confederate society, and escalating material hardship on the HOMEFRONT left scant prospects for Southern success by the autumn of 1864. Davis remained more resolute than most, urging his fellow citizens to fight on and even recommending, along with Lee, that slaves be placed in the Confederate army and freed if they served well (after a bitter national debate, the Confederate Congress approved a watered-down version of what Davis and Lee sought). For Davis, Confederate independence had come to mean everything, overshadowing even the importance of maintaining the institution of slavery as it had existed at the time of secession. After the fall of RICHMOND on April 2, 1865, Davis fled southward, falling into Union hands at Irwinville, Georgia, on May 10.

Davis spent two years as a prisoner at Fort Monroe but was never formally charged with treason or brought to trial. Released in May 1867, he steadfastly maintained that secession had been a constitutional and logical Southern response to the threat of Northern domination. He presented his version of the momentous events through which he had lived in *The Rise and Fall of the Confederate Government* (1881), two thick volumes that mounted an unapologetic defense of the South and his own actions. Never a success financially after the war, Davis also endured a great deal of personal tragedy. All four of his sons preceded him in death, and his ill health continued. He died on December 5, 1889, having been, since Lee's death 19 years earlier, the most visible symbol of the failed Confederate cause.

See also DAVIS, VARINA HOWELL; LOST CAUSE.

Further reading: William J. Cooper, *Jefferson Davis, American* (New York: Knopf, 2000); Jefferson Davis, *The Rise and Fall of the Confederate Government* (1881; reprint, Gloucester, Mass.: Peter Smith, 1971); William C. Davis, *Jefferson Davis: The Man and His Hour* (New York: HarperCollins, 1991).

—Gary W. Gallagher

Davis, Varina Howell (1826–1906)

Author and wife of Confederate president JEFFERSON DAVIS, Varina Anne Banks Howell Davis was born May 7, 1826, near Natchez, Mississippi. Varina's parents, Margaret Kempe and William Burr Howell, both came from distinguished Southern families.

As the daughter of a wealthy slaveholding planter, Varina attended an elite girls' academy in Philadelphia for a few terms. She also received private tutoring at home from Harvard graduate Judge George Winchester. In 1843 Varina met Jefferson Davis, a rich planter and slaveowner. Despite the 17-year age difference, they married in February 1845.

Soon after the wedding, Jefferson left to fight in the Mexican-American War. He returned in 1847 and was elected to the U.S. Senate. He moved to WASHINGTON, D.C., leaving Varina behind in Mississippi for the next year and a half. She joined him in 1849 and spent most of the next 12 years in Washington, where they did a lot of entertaining and cultivated friendships with many powerful people. During this period, the couple had four children.

Varina, who often sat in the galleries with other congressional wives, shared many of her husband's views on SLAVERY, Southern rights, and the REPUBLICAN PARTY. Both feared the consequences of CIVIL WAR but embraced their roles as Confederate president and first lady, although Varina's shrewd political sense and outspoken nature provoked criticism. The Davises had two more children while in the Confederate White House.

The Davis family faced many problems in the postwar years. Jefferson Davis spent two years in federal prison on treason charges. After sending the older children to Canada, Varina remained in Georgia with their youngest daughter, Winnie, to be close to Jefferson. Varina helped secure Jefferson's release in May 1867. The family reunited in Canada and moved to England for a few years beginning in late 1868. Although Jefferson tried his hand at several business ventures, the family struggled to make ends meet. In the fall of 1870, the family moved to Memphis, Tennessee, where Jefferson headed an insurance company and Varina worked part-time as a seamstress.

After her husband died in 1889, Varina worked on a two-volume biography of his life. The book, published in 1890, did not sell well. She moved to Manhattan in 1892, where she worked as a journalist for the *New York World* and remained loyal to the memory of the Confederate cause.

Varina Davis died on October 16, 1906, in NEW YORK CITY. She was buried beside her husband in RICHMOND.

See also DAVIS, JEFFERSON; UNITED DAUGHTERS OF THE CONFEDERACY.

Further reading: Gerry Van Der Heuvel, *Crowns of Thorns and Glory: Mary Todd Lincoln and Varina Howell Davis, the Two First Ladies of the Civil War* (New York: Dutton, 1988); Bell Wiley, *Confederate Women* (Westport, Conn.: Greenwood Press, 1975).

—Lisa Tendrich Frank

Davis Bend, Mississippi, freedmen's colony

Located just south of Vicksburg along the MISSISSIPPI RIVER, Davis Bend was the site of one of the first experiments in African-American free labor during the CIVIL WAR. Originally designed as a model for antebellum slave PLANTATIONS, Davis Bend, instead, became a model for how to transform slave labor to a free labor system while still maintaining profitability. In addition, the plantations at Davis Bend attempted to create a community of cooperation, whereby black farmers and laborers were given more autonomy over production and their daily lives.

Joseph Davis, a successful Mississippi lawyer, founded Davis Bend in 1827. Influenced by utopian thinkers, Davis sought to create a model plantation, whereby slaves were given more freedom and responsibility. Davis provided his slaves with better food and housing. He encouraged the development of skilled labor and rewarded superior work with gifts and other financial incentives. Moreover, a slave jury authorized punishments on the plantation, not the overseer.

Within this environment, Davis encouraged the development of individual slaves, most notably Benjamin Montgomery. Montgomery, a self-educated and skilled engineer, oversaw levee construction and served as a cotton gin mechanic. He quickly distinguished himself as a leader and an entrepreneur by establishing a store on the Davis plantation, selling goods to white people, and even establishing a line of credit with New Orleans wholesalers. With the help of Montgomery, the Davis Bend plantation prospered in the antebellum era.

The Civil War, however, fundamentally transformed Joseph Davis's dream of a community of cooperation. Davis abandoned the Davis Bend plantations ahead of the advancing UNION ARMY. Most of his slaves, though, resisted Davis's entreaties to flee with him and some even looted the plantation's mansions after his departure.

Union military leaders hoped to transform Davis Bend into a black colony that would serve as a model for the transition from slave to free labor and operate as a haven for freedmen. Blessed with rich soil and a preexisting labor force, Davis Bend was a prime location for an experiment that hoped to prove the superiority of a free labor system. There also were political motives for establishing a black colony. JEFFERSON DAVIS, the president of the Confederacy, was Joseph Davis's younger brother and had administered one of the plantations (Brierfield) on Davis Bend before the war.

The FREEDMEN'S BUREAU assumed control of Davis Bend in 1865 and leased land to freedmen who in turn planted cotton. Black lessees turned a profit and benefited from the protection of the Union army. Self-government was reestablished, including a court system, an elected sheriff, and a board of EDUCATION. Overall, the experiment was a success.

Carrying on a revised vision of Joseph Davis's dream, Ben Montgomery believed that in order for Davis Bend to become a utopian community, black people needed to be in control of the plantations. In 1866 Montgomery purchased (under favorable terms) the Davis Bend plantations from Joseph Davis. Although damaging floods and pests plagued the first couple of years, the all-black Davis Bend plantations thrived during RECONSTRUCTION, producing some of the highest quality cotton in the country. To defuse white opposition, Montgomery emphasized the utopian ideal of Davis Bend and publicly discounted the importance of African-American political activity. Nonetheless, the sizable population of freedmen in Davis Bend attracted Republican politicians who depended on their votes in statewide offices.

The freedmen benefited from fertile land, favorable credit terms, and protection from white intrusion, but by 1875, the Davis Bend community began to decline as Reconstruction came to an end. Jefferson Davis sued and reclaimed the Brierfield plantation. Poor cotton crops in 1875 and 1876 depleted Montgomery's capital reserves, forcing him to turn over to creditors one of the remaining two plantations.

Unlike other experiments with black free labor, such as the PORT ROYAL EXPERIMENT, the Davis Bend freedmen were adept at raising cotton and turning a profit. Their success owed to the unique leadership of Ben Montgomery and his prior experience in plantation management. It was his commitment to an all-black community, however, that enabled him to win the trust of the freedmen and attract the opposition of white Mississippians. The postwar community succeeded because the freedmen were given more autonomy and control over their crops and their persons.

Further reading: Janet Sharp Hermann, *The Pursuit of a Dream* (Jackson: University Press of Mississippi, 1999).

—Justin J. Behrend

De Forest, John William (1826–1906)

Author and soldier John William De Forest was born in Humphreysville, Connecticut, in 1826. As a young adult, De Forest traveled extensively throughout Europe and the Middle East. By the time of the CIVIL WAR, De Forest was a well-known writer of travel books and novels.

Immediately after the outbreak of war, De Forest raised a company in support of the Union. He was sworn into service on January 1, 1862, and served as captain of Company I, 12th Connecticut Volunteer Infantry. During the war, De Forest and his regiment saw action in Louisiana at the siege of Port Hudson, as well as in the Virginia countryside in 1864. He was particularly affected by his experience at the Battle of Cedar Creek in October 1864. After the war, De Forest famously wrote that, "I never on any other battlefield saw so much blood as on this of Cedar Creek. The firm limestone soil would not receive it, and there was no pitying summer grass to hide it." He was discharged from the 12th Connecticut on December 2, 1864.

After the war De Forest resumed his writing career, penning his memoirs along with a number of fictional works. In the many short stories and novels that flowed from his pen, De Forest portrayed soldiers' lives with emotion, accuracy, and respect. Determined to faithfully chronicle the war from the ordinary volunteer's point of view, De Forest helped to pioneer the "realistic" genre of combat writing. De Forest's most famous novel, *Miss Ravenel's Conversion from Secession to Loyalty* (1867) combined a realistic view of combat with a romantic story of sectional reconciliation. The theme of reunion became increasingly prominent in De Forest's later works, as the nation came to view the South with an increasing sense of romanticism.

Productive well into his 70s, John William De Forest died in 1906 at the age of 80 in New Haven, Connecticut.

See also LITERATURE.

Further reading: John William De Forest, *A Union Officer in the Reconstruction* (1868–69; reprint, Hamden, Conn.: Archon Books, 1968); James F. Light, *John William De Forest* (New York: Twayne, 1965).

—Megan Quinn

Delany, Martin Robinson (1812–1885)

Born in Charles Town, Virginia (now West Virginia), on May 6, 1812, Martin Robinson Delany became a well-known writer and a leader of the black colonization movement. Delany initially fought for racial equality, but later he concluded that this goal was no longer possible in the United States. Thereafter, he pursued the idea of colonization in territories outside of the country.

Delany's formal EDUCATION began when he attended an African-American high school in Pittsburgh, Pennsylvania. Afterward, he served as a doctor's apprentice, and in 1836 he set up his own medical practice. While in Pitts-

Martin Robinson Delany *(Hulton/Archive)*

burgh, Delany founded a temperance society and actively worked with a slave rescue and transport group. In 1843 Delany married Catherine A. Richards, with whom he had seven children. In the years immediately after his marriage, Delany wrote on the condition of African Americans in the United States. From 1843 to 1847, he published a newspaper entitled *The Mystery* (1843–47). For a short time, he also coedited the *Rochester North Star* with FREDERICK DOUGLASS.

Two experiences in the early 1850s made Delany a proponent of African colonization. The first was the passage of the Fugitive Slave Act in 1850. The second was the decision of Delany's classmates to dismiss him and two other African-American students from Harvard Medical School in 1851. These two events vastly increased Delany's frustration with the condition of race relations in the United States. In 1852, after his expulsion from Harvard, Delany published his first book, entitled *The Condition, Elevation, Emigration, and Destiny of the Colored People of the United States.* In it, Delany said he believed that African Americans could not successfully "elevate" their sit-

uation to attain "equality with the white man" if they continued to live within the United States. Delany recommended that black people seek new territory in Central and South America. He would later promote emigration to Africa and would make several trips to Liberia to coordinate emigration efforts.

During the CIVIL WAR, Delany recruited African-American troops in New England. In 1865 he was commissioned, becoming one of the first African-American field officers in the UNION ARMY. Major Delany served as a physician in the Union army for only three months, however, before the war ended. After the war, Delany worked in the FREEDMEN'S BUREAU in South Carolina for three years. Later he became a trial judge in Charleston, South Carolina. Racial extremists ultimately forced Delany to leave this post once RECONSTRUCTION had ended. Despite this setback, Delany continued to publish books and articles until his death on January 24, 1885.

See also RACE AND RACIAL CONFLICT.

Further reading: Robert S. Levine, *Martin Delany, Frederick Douglass, and the Politics of Representative Identity* (Chapel Hill: University of North Carolina Press, 1997); Dorothy Sterling, *The Making of an Afro-American: Martin Robison Delany, 1812–1885* (Garden City, N.Y.: Doubleday, 1971).

—Courtney Spikes

Democratic Party

The Democratic Party is the nation's oldest existing political party. Officially founded as the Democratic-Republican Party by Thomas Jefferson and James Madison in 1800, it played a critical role in the political and economic history of the 19th-century United States. Immigrants, the urban working class, subsistence farmers, and Southern plantation owners formed the core groups that supported the Democrats in the CIVIL WAR and RECONSTRUCTION eras.

Democrats generally believed in a narrow construction of the U.S. Constitution, limited powers for the federal government, and economic policies that led to expansion and settlement of the nation's vast territories for the benefit of ordinary white people. Democrats controlled the political system in the country from 1828 through 1856 by winning six of the eight presidential ELECTIONS and dominated Congress for much of the 1840s and 1850s. The party's power and prestige greatly diminished when it split into Northern and Southern wings over the SLAVERY issue in 1860. From 1860 to 1928 the Democrats controlled the White House only 4 out of 18 times.

The modern Democratic Party emerged from the presidential election of 1828 under the leadership of President

Andrew Jackson of Tennessee and Martin Van Buren of New York. Van Buren, a talented and dedicated professional politician, forged a national network of strong ties between Democratic political leaders that stressed commonalities between the humble farmers and working class of the North and the yeomanry and cotton growers of the South. They were adamantly opposed to the new Whig Party's strongly pro-manufacturing economic plan and especially to a national banking system. A central bank, Jackson and other Democrats asserted, represented a dangerous and unprecedented concentration of power that threatened STATES' RIGHTS and the vision of a "small" democracy articulated by Jefferson.

Jackson, an ardent supporter of the political philosophy of Thomas Jefferson, was, like Jefferson, a Southern slaveholder. Despite their undeniable appeal to Northerners and Southerners of more modest means, Democrats soon became identified with a proslavery agenda. In 1828 Congress decided to increase TARIFF rates. Outraged wealthy Southern plantation owners attacked the "Tariff of Abominations." South Carolina's John C. Calhoun, then serving as vice president, published a series of anonymous letters criticizing the tariff.

When an even higher tariff was adopted in 1832, Calhoun resigned his office and reentered the Senate, where he could openly express his opposition. Calhoun argued that South Carolina should "nullify" the tariff, in essence declaring it void in their state. The conflict was ultimately resolved with a compromise tariff, but nullification became an important argument used by the South to derail proposed action against slavery, and a disturbing reminder that Democrats were divided by regional interests.

Throughout the 1840s and 1850s, the identification of the Democratic Party with Southern slavery became even stronger. Democrats worked for the successful annexation of Texas and the unsuccessful annexation of Cuba as slave states. Led by President James Polk, a Tennessee Jacksonian, Democrats supported the Mexican-American War and refused to ban slavery in the territory acquired as a result of the war. Democrats insisted on the inclusion of a stricter Fugitive Slave Act in the Compromise of 1850.

Slavery was responsible for the death of the Democrats' major opposition party, the Whigs, as well as the birth of its new opposition, the REPUBLICAN PARTY. Slavery was also a deeply divisive issue among Democrats themselves, especially after the Mexican-American War. Senator STEPHEN A. DOUGLAS of Illinois tried very hard to satisfy both wings and ended up destroying the party that he loved. Douglas was the driving force behind the KANSAS-NEBRASKA ACT of 1854, which abolished the traditional slave-versus-free line between North and South and opened up the territories to slavery. Democratic president JAMES BUCHANAN's administration created a firestorm of protest with his overtly pro-Southern policies in Kansas and elsewhere from 1856 to 1860.

In the election of 1860, the Democratic Party finally split between proslavery SECESSIONists and more moderate Unionists. At the Democratic convention in Charleston, South Carolina, the party failed to nominate a candidate due to disruptions by secessionist Southern delegates. Northern and Southern Democrats then met separately several weeks later, with Northern Democrats choosing Stephen A. Douglas as their presidential candidate, while Southern Democrats nominated John C. Breckenridge to carry their banner. This split effectively guaranteed victory for Republican candidate ABRAHAM LINCOLN. With Lincoln's victory, South Carolina seceded from the United States on December 20, 1860, and by February 1, 1861, was followed by six additional states. Delegates from these states met soon after at Montgomery, Alabama, to draft the Constitution of the CONFEDERATE STATES OF AMERICA and elect as president the former U.S. Senator JEFFERSON DAVIS.

During the Civil War, Confederate politics and government led to the development of a single party system, made up of former Democrats and Whigs, that was highly disorganized and ineffective. In the North, Democrats became the opposition party. The party divided into two wings, "War Democrats" and "Peace Democrats." The War Democrats were the majority for most of the years between 1861 and 1865. They supported Lincoln and the war and were careful not to bring the dreaded name of "traitor" down upon their organization.

As the war went on, however, more and more Democrats criticized what they thought to be the Lincoln administration's unconstitutional abuse of power in the prosecution of the conflict. Two issues particularly were successful in mobilizing Democratic voters against Republicans during the war: Lincoln's unpopular suspension of HABEAS CORPUS and his EMANCIPATION of Southern slaves. Although the Republicans kept a majority in the Congress, there were significant Democratic gains in the House and Senate in the elections of 1862.

Some Democrats went so far as to argue that the war should be brought to an end, even if that meant accepting secession. These Peace Democrats, or COPPERHEADS, felt the war victimized working-class and immigrant families. They also feared that freedmen would compete with white laborers for the same jobs. By 1864 the Copperheads were a powerful faction in the Democratic Party, and they were able to insist that a peace plank be included in the party's platform for the presidential elections in that year. Renewed Union successes on the battlefield caused Democratic nominee GEORGE B. MCCLELLAN to repudiate the plank, and thereafter the Copperheads waned in importance.

After the war, the Democratic Party remained in the minority and, indeed, reached the lowest point in its history. Republicans regularly, and successfully, attacked Democrats as acting disloyally during the war. "Not every Democrat was a traitor," crowed Republicans, "but every traitor was a Democrat." During the first year of Reconstruction, a bitter dispute developed between Democrats and Republicans over the extension of citizenship and the franchise to African Americans. Encouraged by President ANDREW JOHNSON, many Democrats opposed what they called the "Africanization" of the South.

Democrats continued to attack Republican-led Reconstruction. In the years immediately after the Civil War, Democratic Southern state legislatures passed a series of restrictive racial laws known as the BLACK CODES. The primary purpose of the codes was to keep African Americans subordinate by controlling freedmen and keeping them in a state close to slavery. Northern Republicans, particularly a militant faction of the party known as the RADICAL REPUBLICANS, were outraged.

Congressional Radicals were able to impose an especially harsh Reconstruction on the South that effectively kept Southern Democrats out of positions of power. Barred from participating in the political system through legal means, a great number of Southern Democrats worked to reestablish a system of white supremacy through illegal means, namely terrorism. The KU KLUX KLAN and other groups kept African Americans from voting by harassing and even killing those individuals who presumed to exercise their civil rights.

As the decade of the 1860s closed, support for congressional Reconstruction was waning. ULYSSES S. GRANT won the election of 1868 handily and overcame a serious challenge from anti-Reconstruction Democrats and Republicans to win a second term in 1872. Increasingly, the Democratic cry that Republicans had denied votes to competent white Southern voters while enabling "unfit" African Americans to vote resonated with Northerners. Perhaps the biggest boost for the Democrats, however, was the depression of 1873. Dissatisfied with the Republican handling of the ECONOMY, voters returned Democratic majorities to Congress in 1874. Two years later, a disputed election between Democrat Samuel J. Tilden and Republican Rutherford B. Hayes led to a series of compromises that awarded Hayes the presidency while bringing an end to Reconstruction.

The election of 1876 solidified a status quo that remained in place for the remainder of the 19th century. The Republicans controlled the majority of Northern voters and had a virtual monopoly on the presidency. Every president elected between 1860 and 1912, with the exception of Grover Cleveland, was a Republican. The Democrats, meanwhile, dominated the "Solid South" and were powerful in a number of Northern localities, particularly NEW YORK CITY. African Americans, most of them still living in the South, were largely denied a voice in politics. It would take another depression, in 1932, to begin the historic transformation of the Democratic Party from its 19th-century origins as a proslavery and states' rights political organization to its current liberal incarnation.

Further reading: Jean Baker, *Affairs of Party: The Political Culture of Northern Democrats in the Mid-Nineteenth Century* (New York: Fordham University Press, 1998); Joel Silbey, *A Respectable Minority: The Democratic Party in the Civil War Era, 1860–1868* (New York: Norton, 1977).

—Michael Ward

desertion

Desertion is defined as a soldier being "absent without leave" from his post. It can have a devastating impact on an army's morale and on an army's chances for success on the field of battle. Desertion has been a problem for armies throughout history, but CIVIL WAR armies proved especially susceptible because the majority of the soldiers were volunteers. Untrained, untested, and sure that the war would last at most a few months, the reality of camp life and battle drove many young men to "skeedaddle."

There were other factors when considering desertion during the Civil War. It was easy to escape both on the march and approaching the battlefield. A deserter could easily blend in with the countryside simply because he spoke the same language as his enemies. Many battles were fought in states with heavily divided loyalties, like Tennessee. Deserters would not find it difficult to locate a friendly refuge.

Beyond that, Civil War combat was extremely violent and bloody, arguably more so than any war before or since. Even the bravest and most loyal of men could easily lose their stomach for battle when faced with the carnage that was inflicted on a regular basis. As 1861 turned into 1862 and 1863, the early volunteers became tested soldiers, and desertion rates dropped. The payment of enlistment bounties, however, later in the war brought another wave of desertion, especially to the Union armies. "Bounty jumpers" would enlist, collect their bonus, and then promptly desert so that they could enlist again for another bounty.

There were a variety of motives for desertion. The most common were lack of success on the battlefield and problems at home. Historian Bell Wiley has combed through the LETTERS written by soldiers and identified poor rations, sickness, incompetent or overbearing officers, failure to receive pay, and boredom as reasons why men deserted. Because of the Confederate government's poor resources, Southern soldiers were more likely to suffer these kinds of aggravations and so were more likely to desert. This was a major concern for Confederate leadership, for the much smaller CONFEDERATE ARMY, which never exceeded 500,000 men at any one time, could ill afford the defections. ROBERT E. LEE thought that desertion played a prominent role in the Confederate army's defeats at ANTIETAM and GETTYSBURG.

The Union leadership was also concerned about deserters, and both sides took steps to try to stem the tide of deserters. It was necessary to tread lightly, however. Excessive punishments, such as lashings and executions, deprived the army of a soldier's services and tended to have a negative impact on morale in the army as a whole. Union and Confederate military and civilian leaders addressed the problem of desertion with a combination of negative and positive reinforcements. When deserters were caught, they were punished. The most severe punishment, death by hanging, was rare, reserved for extreme cases when an example needed to be made.

Meanwhile, at times when desertion was especially likely, both armies took steps to try and stop soldiers from leaving. Some officers would resort to frequent roll calls, as many as three or four an hour. Another common strategy, especially in the Rebel army, was to distribute extra rations. When possible, Northern and Southern leaders would grant their soldiers furloughs, which in most cases guaranteed their return.

At the same time that Union and Confederate leaderships were struggling to combat desertion in their own ranks, they were making every effort to convince enemy soldiers to desert. The Confederacy offered Union deserters sanctuary in the South, jobs, and sometimes land. The Northern government offered even more generous terms. Confederate deserters were given amnesty, payment for any equipment they brought with them, and free TRANSPORTATION back to their homes if it was in an area under Union control. Those who could not return home, or did not wish to do so, were given jobs in the North or allowed to serve in the U.S. Army on the western frontier.

It is difficult to say how many soldiers deserted over the course of the war. The official estimates by the two sides place the number at 200,000 for the North and 104,000 for the South. These numbers, however, are not especially trustworthy. Many men killed in action were classified as deserters because their bodies were never identified. Other men were incorrectly identified as deserters because they were temporarily separated from their units, either deliberately or inadvertently. Also, toward the end of the war, Northern authorities began to classify lesser offenses, such as dereliction of duty, as desertion. After January 1865, so many men were fleeing the Confederate ranks that Southern officials stopped bothering to count them.

Indeed, Southerners in particular became quite nonchalant about deserters by the end of the war. In 1865 Gen. John S. Preston, commissioner of the Confederate Bureau of CONSCRIPTION, commented that "so common is the crime, it has in popular estimation lost the stigma which justly pertains to it." To an extent, a relaxed attitude toward desertion has filtered down to the present. Since the Civil War, only one American soldier has been executed for the crime.

See also BOUNTY SYSTEM.

Further reading: Ella Lonn, *Desertion during the Civil War* (Lincoln: University of Nebraska Press, 1998); Mark A. Weitz, *A Higher Duty: Desertion among Georgia Troops during the Civil War* (Lincoln: University of Nebraska Press, 2000); Bell Irvin Wiley, *The Life of Johnny Reb: The Common Soldier of the Confederacy* (Baton Rouge: Louisiana State University Press, 1978).

—Christopher Bates

disease and epidemics

During the CIVIL WAR, at least twice as many soldiers died from disease as from combat wounds. This staggering statistic points to both the horrors of living conditions and to medical ignorance. Disease hit soldiers hardest during their first years of fighting. When camped together, thousands of men from various backgrounds caught contagious diseases from each other. Especially affected were men from rural areas, who might not have been exposed to common childhood ailments such as measles that affected a greater proportion of city dwellers. Smallpox also had devastating effects on those who were previously unexposed to an outbreak.

Cramped living conditions and extremely poor sanitation also led to the spread of three diseases that frequently appear during times of war. Dysentery/diarrhea, typhoid, and pneumonia plagued troops who faced bad weather and unclean water supplies. Malaria also raged during the warmer months, especially in the hot, mosquito-laden areas of the South. Socially spread diseases also affected both Union and Confederate troops. Venereal diseases hit both armies hard and were most widely reported by regiments camped near cities.

Medical practices during campaigns also inadvertently led to many deaths. Unclean wounds, for instance, often caused gangrene, which in turn dealt a fatal blow to an otherwise slightly injured soldier. Doctors in field hospitals often administered massive doses of narcotics to patients for every injury and ailment. Such dosing did more to cause shortages for those who really needed morphine, such as an amputee, than it did to cure ailments such as pneumonia.

Lack of knowledge about bacteria had perhaps the greatest impact on the health of a Civil War soldier. The regular exposure to microscopic invaders and the lack of any antibiotics caused deaths by the thousands. In fact, at the very time that war raged in America, Europeans such as Louis Pasteur and Joseph Lister led the beginnings of a medical revolution when they drew the first connections between microscopic organisms and disease.

These medical breakthroughs, however, did not reach the United States in time to help Civil War soldiers. The relationship between water and typhoid and between mosquitoes and the blood-borne illnesses yellow fever and malaria remained a mystery. Doctors also did not know the importance of sterilizing medical equipment and routinely operated on more than one soldier with the same dirty instrument. Not until after the war did the American medical profession connect what had happened to soldiers during the 1860s with the European advancements in science made at the same time.

Although doctors did not know exactly what caused the diseases they attempted to treat, they did recognize the problem. Along with the doctors themselves, private citizens, the government, and especially women founded groups to tackle the medical challenges and to care for the ill and injured. For example, Elizabeth Blackwell, M.D., led a meeting of 3,000 women to form the Women's Central Association for Relief (WCAR) in New York in 1861. The WCAR later evolved into the government-sponsored UNITED STATES SANITARY COMMISSION. Women, acting as NURSES, played a central part in each of the organizations treating and caring for the ill and wounded. One independent nurse, CLARA BARTON, eventually founded the American branch of the International Red Cross after her experiences during the Civil War.

Nursing developed as a profession during the war years, and after the war the profession emerged as a predecessor to women-led reform movements. Many of these movements in the latter 19th century focused on the problems of disease. Targeted especially at densely populated urban settlements, some groups led crusades promoting better hygiene among the immigrants who lived in crowded tenements. Communicable diseases such as typhoid and tuberculosis often affected these urban dwellers at a greater proportion than the rest of the population. Progressive women reformers lobbied for solutions to such health issues. Although not always successful or even always scientifically correct, reformers raised awareness and concern over the spread of diseases. That attentiveness came directly from experiences during the Civil War and from advancements made because of it.

The understanding of disease made enormous leaps during and after the Civil War. Because of the horrors that soldiers endured, the medical profession strengthened both its social and scientific awareness of contagion.

See also HOSPITALS AND MEDICINE.

Further reading: George Worthington Adams, *Doctors in Blue: The Medical History of the Union Army in the Civil War* (Baton Rouge: Louisiana State University Press, 1996); Horace H. Cunningham, *Doctors in Gray: The Confederate Medical Service* (Baton Rouge: Louisiana State University Press, 1993); Frank R. Freeman, *Gangrene and Glory: Medical Care during the Civil War* (Urbana: University of Illinois Press, 2001); Bell Irvin Wiley, *The Life of Johnny Reb: The Common Soldier of the Confederacy* (Baton Rouge: Louisiana State University Press, 1978).

—Samantha Holtkamp Gervase

Douglas, Stephen A. (1813–1861)

Lawyer and U.S. senator, Stephen Arnold Douglas played a key role in the sectional politics that led to the outbreak of the CIVIL WAR. Best known for his famous debates against ABRAHAM LINCOLN in the 1858 Illinois senatorial contest and as Lincoln's opponent in the 1860 presidential race, Douglas was affectionately called the "Little Giant" for his widely admired oratory skills and small stature. Douglas, considered the most talented politician of his generation, saw his ambitions for higher office destroyed in the bitter debates and violent struggle between pro- and antiSLAVERY forces over the Kansas-Nebraska territory. Douglas's failure to gain the support of Southern Democrats in 1860 split the party and led to Republican Abraham Lincoln's victory.

Stephen Arnold Douglas was born on April 3, 1813, in Brandon, Vermont, the son of a doctor. Douglas enjoyed an excellent EDUCATION at the Canandaigua Academy in upstate New York, where he moved with his family in 1830. There, Douglas trained in the Latin and Greek classics that would give his political speeches sparkle, spirit, and a learned quality. As a youth he was already endowed with the remarkable energy and ambition that led a friend to describe him as a "steam engine in breeches." After training in law, Douglas moved west to Jacksonville, Illinois, in 1833, where he quickly proclaimed: "I have become a *Western* man."

At age 21 he entered state politics, rising to the state supreme court by the age of 27. At court, he earned and kept the nickname "Judge" Douglas. Hard-working and innovative, Douglas is credited with building the Illinois DEMOCRATIC PARTY from the bottom up. His hero was Andrew Jackson, and he supported the principles of Jacksonian democracy that stood for the betterment of the common person. Douglas prospered in the tough world of

Stephen Douglas *(Library of Congress)*

frontier politics. In 1843 he won the first of three terms in the U.S. House. He was elected to the U.S. Senate in 1847, where he served until his death in 1861.

Douglas married a North Carolinian, Martha Martin, in 1847. Martha was the heiress to a large plantation with 100 slaves that Douglas managed. Shortly after bearing two sons, Martha died in 1853. The lonely widower remarried in 1856 to the 21-year-old Adele Cutts. They lived in WASH-INGTON, D.C., for most of the year. While in Congress, Douglas was a major proponent of westward expansion and the idea of Manifest Destiny. Leader of the "Young Democrat" movement, he was a tough-minded politician who usually got his way.

After the end of the war with Mexico in 1848, the settlement of the territories acquired from that war became a controversial national issue. Should they be reserved for free or slave labor? Douglas helped push through the various pieces of legislation that made up the Compromise of 1850, including the completion of the Illinois Central Railroad, his pet project. He was absent for the vote on the controversial Fugitive Slave Act but supported its passage. As a Westerner, he promoted westward expansion, negotiating

the slavery issue to his constituents' benefit. He was neither strongly proslavery nor antislavery, but his position as chairman of the Senate Committee on Territories put him in the middle of the coming political firestorm.

In 1854 Douglas promoted the idea of popular sovereignty as a democratic method to decide the issue of expansion in the Kansas and Nebraska Territories. Douglas's ultimate goal was the building of a northern route for a transcontinental RAILROAD that would have to cross these territories, but he needed Southern congressional support to fund its construction. This need led to the passage of the KANSAS-NEBRASKA ACT, which abolished the 1820 Missouri Compromise (banning slavery in all territories north of the 36'30' parallel) and allowed the Kansas and Nebraska Territories to decide their status as either free or slave territory via popular mandate.

Upon the passage of the act, both Free-Soil and proslavery proponents flooded Kansas Territory in anticipation of a vote on the territory's status. The influx of a divided population led to the conflict known as "BLEEDING KANSAS," which served as a preview to the Civil War. The 1854 act had many more effects than just local conflict. It destroyed the last remnants of the Whig Party and helped boost the popularity of the newly formed REPUBLICAN PARTY. The act was so divisive and unpopular in the North that Douglas joked that he could go from his home in Washington, D.C., to his home in Illinois by the light of his burning effigies.

Controversy aside, Douglas commanded the loyalties of many Democrats and only narrowly lost the 1856 presidential nomination to JAMES BUCHANAN. Buchanan and Douglas, however, were increasingly at odds over Kansas's proslavery Lecompton Constitution. Their split reduced Douglas's influence with the Southern Democrats that he hoped to recover in his Senate reelection bid. In 1858 Republican lawyer Abraham Lincoln challenged Douglas for his Senate seat. The famous Lincoln-Douglas debates drew the entire nation's attention. As the candidates "stumped" throughout the state, their debates were followed closely because of the important issues at stake and because Douglas was the leading candidate for the Democratic Party's 1860 presidential nomination.

The debates' focus was on slavery. Southerners were very interested in what Douglas had to say. During his speech in Freeport, Illinois, Douglas articulated his famous "Freeport Doctrine." In it, Douglas sought to reassure Southerners that he would not use federal power to stop slavery, while at the same time pointedly informing Northerners that no court, supreme or otherwise, could impose slavery where it was not wanted. He had a tough position to stake out, because he could not win nationally without the support of the proslavery South, and he could not win a statewide election without free-labor votes. Ultimately, he failed to persuade Southerners that Northern Democrats would protect their property, but he did win the election in Illinois.

Douglas's beloved Democratic Party had split in half by the time the Democratic National Convention met in Charleston, South Carolina, in the spring of 1860. With little agreement between the Northern and Southern wings, many delegates from the slave states stormed out, and the convention adjourned without a candidate. Two months later, a new Democratic Party convention was called in Baltimore, where Douglas won the party's nomination. The convention did not attract delegates from the Deep South; that group nominated John C. Breckenridge as their Democratic candidate.

Douglas campaigned nonstop during the fall ELECTIONS. Unlike the other candidates, Douglas took his message to the public. He toured New England and the Deep South, where he was greeted with hostility. His message was simple and straightforward: Save the Union. No issue, he argued, even slavery, should break up the country, but it was too late for that message to appeal to the voters. In the election, Douglas won only Missouri outright, but came in second in the popular vote with nearly 30 percent.

When hostilities broke out in April 1861, Douglas stood firmly in support of President Lincoln and decried any attempts at disunion. Just after FORT SUMTER, Douglas made a speech in which he said: "It is with a sad heart—with a grief that I have never before experienced, that I have to contemplate this fearful struggle." Months of tireless campaigning had taken their toll on the "Little Giant," and he died in a hotel room in Chicago on June 3, 1861.

Stephen A. Douglas was an important figure in U.S. political history, and although an intelligent and talented man, he never grasped fully the power of the forces he unleashed when he signed the Kansas-Nebraska Act into law. On his deathbed, he sent a last message to his two sons: "Tell them to obey the laws and support the Constitution of the United States."

Further reading: Robert W. Johannsen, *Stephen A. Douglas* (New York: Oxford University Press, 1973); Damon Wells, *Stephen Douglas; The Last Years, 1857–1861* (Austin: University of Texas Press, 1971).

—Scott L. Stabler

Douglass, Frederick (1817–1895)

Slave, ship's caulker, orator, journalist, autobiographer, ABOLITIONist, and women's rights activist, Frederick Douglass was the most important African-American leader of the 19th century. He was born Frederick Bailey on a plantation in Tuckahoe, Maryland, in 1817. Douglass knew his mother only for a short time and assumed that his absent father was his master, a white plantation owner. As a young boy, Douglass was raised by his grandmother after his mother's death, and at the age of eight he was "hired out" to work as a servant for a family in Baltimore, Maryland. It is there that he learned to read, first under his mistress's tutelage and then by way of the neighborhood children.

After eight years, Douglass was sent back to the plantation in Tuckahoe. He found rural SLAVERY a sharply unpleasant contrast to his experience as an urban houseboy. More than once, he tried to escape, but he was caught and sent back to Maryland, where, after working in the shipyards as a caulker, he did in fact escape in 1838 with papers borrowed from a sailor.

Settling in New Bedford, Massachusetts, after marrying Anna Murray, a free woman of color, Frederick Bailey chose a new name for his life of freedom, Douglass. Prejudice made EMPLOYMENT as a caulker impossible, so in New Bedford Douglass took any job he could find. In 1841 his oratorical skills made him an object of national attention, and he was invited to attend the Nantucket convention of the Massachusetts Anti-Slavery Society. After being called

Frederick Douglass *(National Archives)*

on to speak, Douglass's powerful voice, emotive style, and command of the language riveted the audience. He soon became one of the most asked-for speakers on the abolitionist lecture circuit. Douglass lectured on behalf of the society, but he also cultivated his writing skills for WILLIAM LLOYD GARRISON's newspaper, the *Liberator.*

For the next 10 years, Douglass was associated with the "Garrisonians," the branch of radical abolitionism, led by William Lloyd Garrison, that advocated immediate EMANCIPATION and full citizenship rights for slaves. They rejected politics and political parties and emphasized "moral suasion" as the method to achieve their goals.

In 1845 Douglass published *Narrative of the Life of Frederick Douglass, an American Slave.* Describing life under slavery in gruesome and bitter detail, Douglass noted the evil effects on white people as well as African Americans from the indignity of slavery. With prefaces written by William Lloyd Garrison and Wendell Phillips, the *Narrative* was well received in antislavery circles in the United States and abroad. Unlike other slave narratives, Douglass's was written without the aid of a ghostwriter. His story was infused with a remarkable sense of honesty and candor. In 1855 Douglass published another, larger version of his autobiography, *My Bondage and My Freedom.* Douglass's fame was so great that he feared that he would be recaptured and sent back into slavery, so he went to England for two years.

With the earnings from the *Narrative* and his lecture tours, Douglass resettled in Rochester, New York, where he bought a newspaper in 1847, the *North Star,* which he coedited with the help of MARTIN R. DELANY. The masthead of the paper proclaimed its goals: "Abolish slavery in all its forms and aspects, advocate universal emancipation, exalt the standard of public morality, and promote the moral and intellectual improvement of the colored people, and hasten the day of freedom to the Three Millions of our enslaved fellow countrymen." Douglass and the *North Star* also supported women's rights. Indeed, Douglass spoke at the 1848 Seneca Falls Convention and was one of the official signers of the manifesto of women's rights.

As Douglass turned increasingly toward political action, he split with William Lloyd Garrison's group over the latter's refusal to engage in politics. Personally advocating nonviolence, Douglass, a friend of JOHN BROWN, called him "a noble old hero" after his hanging for his role in the raid at HARPERS FERRY in 1859. By the 1860 presidential election, Douglass had identified himself with the REPUBLICAN PARTY and supported candidate and president-elect ABRAHAM LINCOLN.

Douglass believed that the Union's primary goal in the war should be to end slavery. Unhappy with Lincoln's slow moves toward emancipation, he pushed the president and the Republican Party toward progressive policies. Douglass

and other abolitionists also pressed hard for the mobilization of African-American soldiers, a dream that came true after January 1, 1863. Douglass gloried in his role of recruiter for colored regiments, especially the 54TH MASSACHUSETTS REGIMENT. Among the first to enlist in that famous all-black regiment were his two sons, Lewis and Charles. Unfortunately, equality in the army could not be assured for African-American troops. Douglass protested gross inequalities of pay and treatment and was able to bring some improvement in the lives of the black soldiers.

The CIVIL WAR brought freedom to 4 million slaves, but it did not bring the equality, justice, and economic opportunities that Douglass had hoped for. The THIRTEENTH, FOURTEENTH, and FIFTEENTH AMENDMENTS were passed, providing for emancipation, citizenship, and suffrage for African Americans, but too often the laws were not enforced. Douglass dedicated himself in the postwar years to fighting to make the dreams of political and economic freedom for African Americans a reality.

He was a firm supporter of the Republican Party and was rewarded by President ULYSSES S. GRANT with an appointment as secretary to the Santo Domingo Commission. He subsequently served in a number of party-appointed positions, such as recorder of deeds for the District of Columbia and as a minister plenipotentiary to Haiti.

Douglass retained his stature as the most important political leader of the African-American community into his old age. He continued his tireless agitation for racial equality through newspaper writing and lecturing. Douglass frequently traveled to Europe with his second wife, Helen. In 1881 the third revision of his autobiography was published, *The Life and Times of Frederick Douglass.*

Douglass died of a heart attack on February 10, 1895, in WASHINGTON, D.C.

Further reading: David Blight, *Frederick Douglass's Civil War: Keeping Faith in Jubilee* (Baton Rouge: Louisiana State University Press, 1991); Frederick Douglass, *Narrative of the Life of Frederick Douglass, an American Slave,* ed. Deborah E. McDowell (New York: Oxford University Press, 1999); William S. McFeely, *Frederick Douglass* (New York: W. W. Norton, 1991).

—Lee Ashley Smith

Dred Scott decision (1856)

Few Supreme Court decisions outweigh *Dred Scott v. John F. A. Sandford* (the name *Sanford* was misspelled in the formal reports) in legal and historical importance. With its decision in *Dred Scott,* the Court denied citizenship to African Americans, denied that Congress had the right to legislate on the issue of SLAVERY in the territories, and ultimately affirmed the place of slavery in America. The decision was a major milestone on the road to the CIVIL WAR.

Dred Scott was born into slavery in Virginia between 1795 and 1809. His owner, Peter Blow, sold Scott to Dr. John Emerson in St. Louis in 1833. Emerson, an army surgeon, took Scott with him on his first assignment at Fort Armstrong, Illinois, and then in 1836 to Emerson's next posting, Fort Snelling, Wisconsin Territories (present-day Minnesota). In both the free state of Illinois and the Wisconsin Territories (free by the Missouri Compromise), Scott served as Emerson's slave.

In 1836 or 1837, while still at Fort Snelling, Scott met and legally married Harriet Robinson, who was the slave of Indian Agent Maj. Lawrence Taliaferro. A justice of the peace, Taliaferro conducted the ceremony, and apparently "gave" Robinson to Emerson so that the new couple could remain together.

As Emerson's career dictated, he moved about the country, sometimes taking Mr. and Mrs. Scott with him (including, for a time, on a posting back to the slave state of Missouri), and sometimes hiring them out to other people while he traveled. On one of his assignments, Emerson married Irene Sanford. Emerson died in 1843 and left his estate, including Dred and Harriet Scott and their two children, Eliza and Lizzie, to Irene Sanford Emerson.

Three years later, in December 1846, Dred Scott filed suit in Missouri against Irene Emerson for his freedom. His case rested on the contention that living in free areas made him a free man. When he lost the case in the Missouri State Court, Scott sued again, this time in the state of New York, which also denied his claim. Irene Emerson's brother, John F. A. Sanford, who was the manager of her estate, was now the owner of the Scott family. By the time the case arrived at the Supreme Court, Scott's suit was against Sanford (spelled incorrectly in the official court records as Sandford).

Chief Justice Roger B. Taney, a Maryland slaveholder and a strong defender of the institution, wrote for the seven-justice majority on the decision. He declared that there were two main questions before the Court: Did the lower courts have jurisdiction to hear the case? Were the decisions of the lower courts correct? In answering the former, Taney found that the lower courts did not have jurisdiction to hear the case because Scott was not a citizen and therefore not entitled to bring suit.

Taney further stated that at the time of the founding of the nation, African Americans were considered "beings of an inferior order" and that, even at the time of the writing of the Declaration of Independence, it was common belief that black people had "no rights which white men were bound to respect." This was true, Taney explained, even though a few states had allowed African Americans to exercise voting rights. There were different levels of citizen-

ship—state and national, Taney wrote—and the rights of citizenship in individual states did not confer national citizenship rights. If African Americans had no rights at the time of the founding of the United States, then they could not be considered citizens, ever.

The decision could have, and many argue should have, ended there. After all, if African Americans were not citizens and therefore not entitled to bring suit, then Dred Scott's case was over. But Taney went further and ruled on whether or not the lower courts had been right. The remainder of his opinion was considered *obiter dictum* (incidental remarks) and therefore not truly part of the legal precedent of the case. The impact, however, was immense. Taney declared that Scott's claim to freedom based on living in the free territory of Wisconsin was worthless because the Missouri Compromise, passed by Congress, was unconstitutional. Taney's decision destroyed the shaky foundations of African-American rights and denied Congress the right to legislate slavery out of the territories.

Two justices, Benjamin Curtis and John McClean, dissented from the opinion. Curtis pointed out that the public records of many states demonstrated without a doubt that African Americans enjoyed the benefits of citizenship and that they were shown capable of exercising those rights from the time of the U.S. Constitution. McClean added to Curtis's dissent by writing that Scott was free due to the time he spent in Illinois and the Wisconsin Territory because a "slave is not mere chattel. He bears the impress of his Maker and he is amenable to the laws of God and man." McClean and Curtis were not the only people who disagreed with the majority Court's decision.

A chorus of Northern-based denunciations began as soon as the press reported on the decision. Republican senator WILLIAM H. SEWARD of New York claimed that with "this ill-omened act, the Supreme Court forgot its own dignity." The *Chicago Tribune* went even further by stating that they were "shocked at the violence and severity of the Judicial Revolution caused by the decision . . . and [could scarcely] fathom the wicked consequences which may flow from it."

Northerners tended to view the *Dred Scott* decision as shocking evidence of a widespread slaveholding conspiracy. If Congress could not legislate against slavery in the territories, then certainly a territorial legislature, who drew their authority from a congressional grant, could not ban slavery either. Popular sovereignty, the last tie holding the Northern and Southern wings of the DEMOCRATIC PARTY together, was severed. Republicans had yet another issue with which to continue their drive toward the presidency in 1860.

The outcry against the Court's opinion was analyzed in the popular press. *Harper's Weekly* remarked: "However repugnant the *Dred Scott* decision may be to the feeling of a portion of the Northern States, it can have no practical effects injurious to our tranquility." The South Carolina *Charleston Daily Courier* echoed a similar sentiment when it declared that *Dred Scott* would "settle these vexed questions forever, quiet the country, and relieve it of ABOLITION agitation." Neither statement could have been further from the truth. *Dred Scott*—combined with BLEEDING KANSAS, the caning of CHARLES SUMNER, and JOHN BROWN's raid on HARPERS FERRY—only served to divide the nation further. More and more Northerners believed the South had corrupted a Court that was determined to nationalize slavery; more and more Southerners believed that the North was intent on destroying their property and inciting their slaves to violence and mayhem.

Dred Scott and his family were freed through private means. Scott became a Northern celebrity, and the family was photographed for *Frank Leslie's Illustrated Newspaper.*

His immediate fame was short lived, as was his time as a free man. On September 17, 1858, Dred Scott died in St. Louis.

Dred Scott had an incredible impact on the course of the history of 19th-century America, and *Dred Scott v. John F. A. Sandford* electrified a divided nation. Despite his controversial decision, Chief Justice Taney had not defused the slavery debate but had fanned the flames of sectionalism even higher.

Further reading: Walter Ehrlich, *They Have No Rights: Dred Scott's Struggle for Freedom* (Westport, Conn.: Greenwood Press, 1979); Paul Finkelman, *Dred Scott v. Sandford: A Brief History with Documents* (Boston: Bedford Books, 1997); Kenneth Stampp, *America in 1857: A Nation on the Brink* (New York: Oxford University Press, 1990).

—Ruth A. Behling

E

Early, Jubal A. (1816–1894)

Lawyer, Confederate general, and architect of the "LOST CAUSE" ideology, Jubal Anderson Early was born on November 3, 1816, near Rocky Mount, Franklin County, Virginia. The son of Joab Early, a substantial holder of land and slaves, and Ruth Hairston Early, Jubal Early entered the UNITED STATES MILITARY ACADEMY AT WEST POINT in 1833 and graduated 18th of 50 in the class of 1837. He resigned in 1838 to return to Rocky Mount, where he practiced law for the next 20 years. As a delegate to the Virginia SECESSION convention in 1861, he maintained a strong Unionist stance until ABRAHAM LINCOLN's call for 75,000 volunteers to suppress the rebellion. Virginia's secession on April 17 galvanized Early, who immediately accepted a colonel's commission in the CONFEDERATE ARMY. Early quickly displayed marked aptitude as a soldier, playing an important role as a brigade commander at the FIRST BATTLE OF BULL RUN and winning promotion to brigadier general in August 1861. Badly wounded at the Battle of Williamsburg on May 5, 1862, he returned to the army to fight with distinction at the Battles of Malvern Hill, SECOND BULL RUN, ANTIETAM, and FREDERICKSBURG. Promotion to major general in April 1863 rewarded Early's excellent service.

ROBERT E. LEE demonstrated confidence in Early by assigning him difficult tasks. During the Chancellorsville campaign, for example, Early held the front at Fredericksburg while most of the army marched west to confront JOSEPH HOOKER's flanking force. At the BATTLE OF GETTYSBURG, Early participated in the successful Confederate assaults on the afternoon of July 1 and advocated a joint attack against Cemetery Hill by the corps of A. P. HILL and RICHARD S. EWELL that evening. Strong and steady leadership at the BATTLES OF THE WILDERNESS and SPOTSYLVANIA in May 1864 brought him promotion to lieutenant general and command of the Second Corps in Lee's army. Poised to start his most famous operations, Early was a respected if not beloved officer. A soldier described him in 1864 as "one of the greatest curiosities of the war," a man "about six feet high" whose "voice sounds like a cracked Chinese fiddle, and comes from his mouth . . . with a long drawl, accompanied by an interpolation of oaths." His men called him "Old Jube," while Lee affectionately referred to him as "my bad old man."

In mid-June 1864, Lee sent Early and his command to the Shenandoah Valley. Over the next month, Early cleared the valley of Federal troops, crossed the Potomac, won the Battle of the Monocacy near Frederick, Maryland, on July 9, and menaced WASHINGTON, D.C. A second phase of the valley campaign began in August, when ULYSSES S. GRANT ordered PHILIP H. SHERIDAN to crush Early and lay waste to the valley. Early's small army, which never numbered as many as 18,000 men, lost decisively to Sheridan's 35,000–40,000-man force at Third Winchester on September 19, at Fisher's Hill three days later, and at Cedar Creek on October 19. Early suffered a final defeat at Waynesboro on March 2, 1865, which ended his career as a Confederate soldier.

After the war, Early remained thoroughly unreconstructed and devoted most of his energy to creating a favorable written record of the Confederate military experience. He wrote to Lee in 1868: "The most that is left to us is the history of our struggle. . . . We lost nearly everything but honor, and that should be religiously guarded." As a leading proponent of the LOST CAUSE interpretation of Confederate history, Early stressed Lee's greatness and the valor of outnumbered Confederates while also insisting that only superior numbers allowed the North to triumph. Early died on March 2, 1894, in Lynchburg, Virginia.

See also SHENANDOAH VALLEY: SHERIDAN'S CAMPAIGN.

Further reading: Jubal A. Early, *Jubal Early's Memoirs: Autobiographical Sketch and Narrative of the War Between the States* (1912; reprint, Baltimore: Nautical & Aviation, 1989); Charles C. Osborne, *Jubal: The Life and Times of*

General Jubal A. Early, CSA, Defender of the Lost Cause (Chapel Hill, N.C.: Algonquin Books, 1992).

—Gary W. Gallagher

Eaton, John, Jr. (1829–1906)

John Eaton, Jr., is best known for his work as superintendent of freedmen in the Mississippi Valley during the CIVIL WAR and later as commissioner of the Bureau of EDUCATION. Born on December 5, 1829, in rural New Hampshire, his early life revolved around chores on the family farm and the occasional schooling common in the antebellum era. A job teaching in a nearby school at the age of 16 allowed him to attend Thetford Academy in Vermont and later to enroll at Dartmouth College. Graduating from Dartmouth in 1854, Eaton became principal of the Ward School in Cleveland, Ohio. In 1856, at the age of 27, Eaton accepted the position of superintendent of the city schools in Toledo, Ohio. Resigning the school superintendence in 1859, he entered a seminary and was ordained in the spring of 1861.

Eaton joined the Union cause in August 1861 as chaplain of the 27th Ohio Volunteer Infantry. In November 1862 Gen. ULYSSES S. GRANT appointed Chaplain Eaton superintendent of CONTRABANDS for the Department of the Tennessee, a post he held for the remainder of the war. Eaton displayed extraordinary organizational ability in providing for the relief of thousands of liberated slaves and, following EMANCIPATION, coordinating the relief efforts of the Freedmen's Aid Societies and organizing schools for the freedpeople. Eaton assumed command of the Ninth Louisiana Volunteers African Descent (later redesignated 63rd U.S. Colored Troops) in October 1863. Col. Eaton's unstinting work on behalf of freed people in the Mississippi Valley earned him a brevet to brigadier general of volunteers in March 1865. John Eaton married Alice Shirley, the daughter of a Vicksburg Unionist in September 1864. Following the war, Eaton served as assistant commissioner of the FREEDMEN'S BUREAU and as state superintendent of schools for Tennessee.

When in 1867 Congress created the Department of Education, Dr. Henry Barnard was named its first commissioner, but Congress never appropriated the funds to print the department's reports. Dr. Barnard spent much of his personal fortune printing the reports privately, but despite his best efforts, by 1879, the Department of Education had not only been reduced to a bureau in the Department of the Interior but its very existence was threatened. In 1870 President Grant appointed Eaton commissioner of the bureau, and Eaton set about a revitalization campaign. He established the annual collection of vital statistics on education as the bureau's chief function and secured funds from Congress for printing annual reports. Under Eaton's

leadership, the Bureau of Education supported efforts to expand education for African Americans in the South, organized a training school for NURSES, and promoted agricultural, commercial, and industrial training. In 1886 Eaton also took a special interest in the educational opportunities available to NATIVE AMERICANS.

Eaton resigned as commissioner due to failing health, although, at the request of the administration, he remained for nearly a year after his official resignation. He later served as president of Marietta College in Ohio (1886–91) and Sheldon Jackson College in Salt Lake City (1895–99). In January 1899 the military appointed General Eaton superintendent of schools for Puerto Rico. During his brief tenure he established the first free school system for all children on the island and worked to ensure adequate educational opportunities for girls, particularly in rural areas. Eaton resigned the following May due to ill health and died on February 9, 1906, at the age of 76.

Further reading: John Eaton, *Grant, Lincoln, and the Freedmen: Reminiscences of the Civil War, with Special Reference to the Work for the Contrabands and Freedmen of the Mississippi Valley* (1907; reprint, New York: Negro Universities Press, 1969).

—Mark Groen

economy

In 1850 the economy of the United States was booming. The South was exporting more than $150 million worth of agricultural products a year. The North's factories were growing as the region industrialized. The nation's railroad mileage tripled between 1850 and 1855 to 30,000 miles. Meanwhile, thousands of new schools and churches were founded.

For the North, the bubble burst in the summer of 1857. In August, the Ohio Life Insurance Company of Cincinnati closed its doors. The unexpected collapse of one of the nation's most prominent businesses started a run on banks across the country and sent the nation into a depression that would last into the CIVIL WAR. The PANIC OF 1857 had a number of root causes: First, state banks, operating with only minimal oversight, had failed to keep their capital reserves at a high enough level. Second, RAILROADS had expanded too much and were unable to meet their costs. Third, the end of the Crimean War in Europe led to a resurgence of AGRICULTURE on that continent, with a resulting drop in the prices being paid for the crops of Midwestern farmers. Finally, gold prices had dropped due to an influx of gold from California.

The South was largely unaffected by the Panic of 1857, since European demand for cotton remained high. At the same time, the South took advantage of new forms of

TRANSPORTATION and new kinds of cotton seeds. As a result, cotton production doubled during the 1850s. In 1860 alone, the South grew 2 billion pounds of cotton with a value of $250 million. The incredible profitability of "King Cotton" encouraged Southerners to invest nearly all of their money in more land and more slaves. As a result, the region failed to develop industrially and failed to build up meaningful cash reserves.

When the Civil War broke out, then, neither the Northern nor the Southern economies were ready for the financial demands of a war. The North was still suffering the effects of the Panic of 1857 and was also handicapped by an antiquated banking system. The South had very little capital or credit and very little industrial capacity. Ultimately, the Union was able to overcome the economic obstacles it faced, and this success played an important part in the Northern victory. The Confederacy, on the other hand, made very little progress in addressing its economic challenges, and this failure played a major role in the South's defeat.

During the Civil War, the main economic issue that both the Union and Confederate governments faced, naturally, was paying for the war. There were three main options available for raising funds to pay the government's bills: TAXATION, bond issues, and printing currency. Northern authorities used all of these tools in an effective fashion. Early in the war, the Northern Congress authorized several bond issues. A bond is an agreement between the government and private businesses or citizens; money is loaned to the government with the promise that it will be repaid with interest at some agreed-upon point in the future. Before the Civil War, bonds had been sold only to bankers, but Treasury Secretary SALMON P. CHASE decided to open up bond purchases to the general public. This was a stroke of genius for two reasons: First, it gave the government access to a vastly larger pool of money. Second, it gave the citizenry a vested interest in the success of the Northern war effort and the Northern economy. The public responded slowly at first, but eventually talented bond salesmen, most notably JAY COOKE, succeeded in winning the people over. One family in four purchased at least one bond during the war, adding $1.5 billion to the Union government's coffers.

The Congress also moved to increase taxation fairly early in the war. In March 1861, before the war had even begun, Congress passed the Morrill Tariff Act. The Morrill Act more than doubled the rates on goods coming into the country, raising them from 20 percent to 47 percent. In August 1861, Congress levied a tax of 3 percent on incomes more than $800, the first income tax in American history. A succession of bills eventually expanded the tax to 5 percent on incomes more than $600 up to 10 percent on incomes more than $10,000. Income taxes and the high tar-

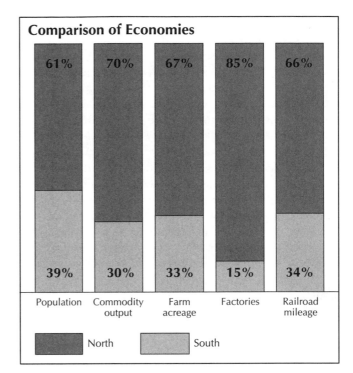

iff helped keep inflation down in the North while adding $600 million to the Union government's balance sheet.

The most controversial step the Northern Congress took in order to finance the war was the passage of the Legal Tender Act of 1862. Prior to the Civil War, currency was almost invariably backed by a quantity of silver or gold, known as specie, being held in a bank vault. At any time, paper money could be exchanged at the institution that had issued it for specie of equal value. By 1862, however, there was not enough specie in the North to keep this system viable. As such, the Legal Tender Act provided for the printing of $150 million worth of what is known as fiat currency, which is backed not by specie but instead by the good credit of the government. The act also specified that this fiat currency would be legal tender, which meant that people and businesses were legally required to accept it as payment for debts.

There were a number of objections to the printing of fiat currency. Some congressmen argued that Congress was not empowered to print money that was not backed by gold or silver. Others felt that it was immoral to force Americans to accept this money. Still others argued that fiat currency would create runaway inflation. These fears proved to be unfounded. Most Northern citizens proved willing to accept GREENBACKS as a medium of exchange, and inflation was kept within reasonable limits. In total, the printing of greenbacks provided $447 million for the Union war effort.

As it worked to finance the war, the Union government also took steps to shore up the foundations of its financial system. The National Banking Act of 1863 created a system of banks chartered by the federal government. These banks were allowed to print currency, as long as the currency was backed by government bonds. This created a market for government bonds and strengthened the Union's greenback currency by tying it to those bonds. It also gave the Union government more control over banks and the nation's money supply. The Congress went even further in this direction in 1864 when it passed a law establishing a 10 percent tax on money printed by state-chartered banks. This action effectively took these banks out of the business of printing money. By the end of 1865, a total of 1,294 national banks had been chartered, and they had more than five times the assets of the 349 state banks still in existence. This banking system would remain in place throughout the Civil War and RECONSTRUCTION.

Northern leaders, then, struck a balance between taxation, bond issues, and the printing of currency while taking steps to rectify problems within their financial system. Confederate authorities had the same options available to them, but under the leadership of Treasury Secretary Christopher Memminger, they proved far less able to maintain an effective balance. The results were devastating for the Confederate economy.

Early in the war, the Confederate Congress considered the possibility of taxing its citizens. There was widespread opposition to the idea, however. Some congressmen opposed taxation because of their dislike of a strong central government. Others felt that such a step would undermine support for the war. Still others saw a tax as unnecessary, believing the war would end quickly. In August 1861, proponents of taxation finally persuaded the Congress to exact a nominal property tax, but it ended up adding very little money to the Confederate bottom line. In 1863 the poor state of the Confederate economy allowed for the passage of a more comprehensive tax, but it also did little to help the Confederate cause. The bill taxed incomes at rates from 1 percent to 15 percent and established a "tax-in-kind" for farmers that required them to turn over 10 percent of their crops to the government. Due to evasion and poor enforcement, these taxes provided less than $150 million for the war effort, most of it in depreciated currency late in the war.

Among Confederate officials, the preferred means for financing the war was bond issues. An initial offering of $15 million in 1861 was quickly purchased by patriotic Southerners. After that, however, bonds became increasingly difficult to sell as the available money in the South dried up. The Confederate Congress then authorized a "produce loan" of $100 million, wherein farmers would be allowed to pledge a portion of their crops in exchange for bonds. Although an innovative idea, the produce loan failed to produce the desired results. Farmers were reluc-

tant to take advantage of the program, preferring instead to hoard their crops or sell them to the Union soldiers. And when pledges were made, the Confederate government often had difficulty collecting the crops that were due. By the end of the war, the produce loan had generated only $34 million.

Given how little money was being raised through taxes and bonds, the Confederate government had little choice but to begin printing fiat currency. The Congress authorized the printing of $119 million worth of "bluebacks" in 1861 and $400 million worth in 1862. This money quickly lost value, for a variety of reasons. The Confederate government was not nearly as stable as the Union government, thus Confederate fiat currency was far less trustworthy than Union fiat currency. Beyond that, there was far too much currency in circulation. By the end of 1862 the Confederate government had printed almost as much money as the Union government would print over the course of the entire war. The glut of paper money was made even worse by the fact that state and local governments were also compelled to print money to meet their obligations. Yet another problem was that the Confederate government chose not to make Confederate currency legal tender; Southern citizens and businesses were not legally required to accept it as payment for goods and services. The purpose of this decision was to inspire confidence in Confederate paper money, but in the end it had the opposite effect. Southerners avoided Confederate money whenever possible, relying mostly on barter, on specie when it was available, and sometimes on Union currency.

In addition to establishing a poor balance between sources of money, the Confederate government also took steps that undermined its financial system. At the start of the war, the South had a system of branch banks that was much more stable and much more modern than the decentralized banking system of the North. Early in the war, the Confederate Congress required Southern banks to provide loans to the government, exchanging specie and bank notes for bonds. As the government's bonds declined in value, the banks were effectively drained of capital. The government continued to exacerbate the situation throughout the war through excessive taxation on banks and additional forced loans. Union armies also contributed to the banks' woes. A large portion of the assets of Southern banks was invested in land and slaves, and these assets were lost as the UNION ARMY marched across the South. By the end of the war, the Southern banking system had effectively collapsed.

The failure of the Confederate government's economic policies was evident on both the war front and the HOME-FRONT. Confederate soldiers were notoriously undersupplied, often going without proper UNIFORMS, modern weapons, sufficient ammunition, or adequate rations. In desperation, they took whatever steps possible—stealing, utilizing captured goods, even trading with the enemy—to obtain the needed supplies.

On the homefront, the situation was arguably even worse. Inflation was out of control in the Confederacy— 9,000 percent over the course of the war. By 1865 flour cost as much as $500 a barrel, and a suit of clothes cost $2,500. The Union's naval blockade contributed to the Confederacy's economic problems by curtailing the amount of goods flowing into the South while denying Southerners the opportunity to sell their cotton. Although the South had an agricultural economy, many Southerners starved over the course of the war. Railroads were in a state of disrepair, and food rotted in storage because it could not be transported to the locations where it was needed. The privations felt by the Southern people created DISEASE AND EPIDEMICS and even resulted in occasional rioting. The largest riot occurred in RICHMOND on April 2, 1863, when several hundred women marched through the streets smashing store windows and chanting "Bread or Blood!" JEFFERSON DAVIS himself had to speak to the mob and convince them to disperse.

The failures of the Southern economy stood in stark contrast to the successes of the Northern economy. By 1862 the North had entirely recovered from the Panic of 1857, and its economy was thriving. While the CONFEDERATE ARMY struggled to survive, the Union army was the best-supplied military force in history. Inflation in the North was kept in check as much as was possible in a wartime economy, only 80 percent compared with the South's rate of inflation, which exceeded 9,000 percent over the course of the war. A few Northern industries struggled due to the loss of Southern raw materials and customers, but others prospered. The agricultural sector performed especially well, with Northern farmers producing more wheat and corn in both 1862 and 1863 than the entire nation had produced in 1859. Between 1861 and 1865, American agricultural exports doubled, a remarkable accomplishment given that one-third of the workforce was in the army.

The successes of the Northern economy and the failures of the Southern economy had a clear impact on the outcome of the war. The Union government was able to put an extremely well-equipped army into the field throughout the course of the war while still satisfying the needs of civilians on the homefront. Meanwhile, the Confederacy was increasingly unable to provide for the needs of its soldiers and its civilians. This drained an already outnumbered Southern army of manpower as some soldiers succumbed to disease or starvation and others deserted to take care of needy family members. Meanwhile, suffering on the homefront deprived the Confederacy of valuable labor and undermined support for the war.

The long-term economic effects of the Civil War are harder to nail down. Some historians argue that the Civil War started the United States on the path to industrialization; others suggest that the Civil War simply hastened trends already in progress. What is certain is that the Civil War caused a major redistribution of wealth from the South to the North. In 1860 the South's share of national wealth had been 30 percent; by 1870 it was 12 percent. This disparity would endure for decades after the Civil War creating an almost constant state of economic deprivation in the South throughout the Reconstruction period and extending into the late 19th and early 20th centuries.

While the Southern economy struggled in the years immediately after the Civil War, the Northern economy prospered. Industrialization continued, and the national banking system established during the Civil War kept currency stable. A number of measures adopted by the Republican Congress during the war, particularly the PACIFIC RAILROAD ACT, pumped government money into the economy. Meanwhile, Northern farmers continued to fetch high prices for their crops as Europe suffered through a series of poor harvests.

In 1873 a financial panic once again undermined Northern prosperity. The Panic of 1873 began with the closure of Jay Cooke and Company and resulted in a lengthy depression. Overextension of the RAILROADS once again played a part, as did the collapse of several European economies and the damage done by the great Chicago Fire of 1871. Ultimately, the Panic of 1873 left 3 million people unemployed while causing the failure of businesses valued at $500 million. The economy would not recover until 1878, when industrialization would once again begin to drive the economy forward at a breathtaking pace.

See also BANKING AND CURRENCY.

Further reading: Douglas D. Ball, *Financial Failure and Confederate Defeat* (Urbana: University of Illinois Press, 1991); Stuart Weems Bruchey, *The Wealth of the Nation: An Economic History of the United States* (New York: Harper & Row, 1988); J. Matthew Gallman, *The North Fights the Civil War: The Home Front* (Chicago: I. R. Dee, 1994); Paul W. Gates, *Agriculture and the Civil War* (New York: Knopf, 1965).

—Christopher Bates

education

Americans of the 19th century believed that the success of the Republic depended upon an educated citizenry. Education was a key component of national identity in the CIVIL WAR era. A unique program of education emerged, encompassing democratic hopes, Protestant piety, and utilitarian values.

The meaning of education and the types of schools changed dramatically over the course of the 19th century. In the early decades of the century, children and young adults acquired education in a variety of settings. Many received a rudimentary education at the kitchen table in the home. Girls obtained domestic skills there as well. Boys learned crafts such as carpentry, and young men studied law through a system of apprenticeships. Charity schools in cities taught the children of the poor. Small "dame" schools (usually taught by an unmarried female instructor) were opened for young children. Academies, usually boarding, offered higher education to those who could pay. And in church-sponsored schools, children learned religious tenets and how to read the Bible.

By the time of the Civil War, a more systematic and uniform public school system had become the backbone of American education in the North and Midwest. Horace Mann has been credited with the emergence of the public school in the United States. As head of the Massachusetts Board of Education from 1837 to 1849, he advocated schools that were publicly supported, publicly controlled, and available to children of all classes and races. In Mann's optimistic reform vision, the inclusiveness of the common schools would have a positive effect on the country as a whole by fostering social harmony and morality.

Although there were some regional differences, the public school movement spread across the country before and after the Civil War. New England was ahead of the nation in public schools, with more than 75 percent of school-age boys and girls attending school at mid-century. In most of the rural United States, the one-room schoolhouse prevailed, with one teacher responsible for instructing between 40 and 60 boys and girls. Strains on the teachers and students in this setting school were enormous. The teacher usually lived with his or her pupils, and disciplining the rowdy students was a trial, as was teaching a variety of age and skill levels.

Urban centers had designed a unitary system of education that gradually spread to other areas over the course of the century. A child was assigned to a grade according to age. Then the student would proceed from a primary school to some kind of intermediate school, to a high school or academy. The schools stressed reading, spelling, writing, arithmetic, geography, and history. Teaching was centered on textbooks such as McGuffey's readers. High schools began to develop an expanded curriculum, offering vocational education such as bookkeeping in addition to their traditional subjects.

Advanced education was less available to girls than to boys, and those girls who sought an education usually went to a sex-segregated institution. Private female academies or seminaries offered a secondary education to middle-class girls who could afford to pay. Not only did girls go to separate schools, but the subjects they were taught were different than those taught boys, reflecting prevailing notions of girls' abilities and the female role in society.

In the South, most states did not adopt tax-supported, state-regulated common schools by the time of the Civil War. A number of factors worked against public education in the South, including the perception that education was for the elite. Aristocratic PLANTATION owners regarded education their private concern and thus left it to tutors. It was illegal in the Southern states to teach slaves to read and write. There was also little support in the South for TAXATION for education purposes. Then too, much of the South was rural and sparsely populated, with a poor system of communication making education reform difficult.

The Civil War and RECONSTRUCTION brought dramatic changes to education in the South. During the war, education nearly came to a standstill. Schoolhouses were commandeered for military purposes; teachers and students were scattered. After the war, the most dramatic change in the South was the education of African Americans. Under the auspices of the FREEDMEN'S BUREAU, established in 1865, Northern teachers came to the South to teach thousands of eager black children and adults. Ex-slaves were determined to learn, but white Southerners were unwilling to pay for their education. There was a drive to build colleges to provide higher education for African Americans, but the idea of universal public education continued to lag in the South after the war, in part because it was seen as a Northern concept imposed upon the defeated South.

Colleges, too, were transformed in the 19th century. At the beginning of the century there were only 18 colleges in the United States; 100 years later, there were more than 450 colleges and universities. The upsurge in colleges occurred after the Civil War. In 1862 the government set aside funding for land-grant colleges in the Morrill Act. Private colleges also expanded after the war as men who had accumulated large fortunes endowed private institutions. The number of women's colleges, such as Vassar, Wellesley, Smith, and Bryn Mawr, also increased after the war.

Although the number of colleges grew dramatically, only 1 percent of college-age Americans actually attended college in 1870. Men found more opportunities entering business or farming than in pursuing professions that demanded a liberal arts education. College reformers attempted to make colleges more relevant over the century. Choice was introduced in the curriculum, and some schools added utilitarian subjects such as chemistry, law, and the principles of AGRICULTURE.

See also SCIENCE AND TECHNOLOGY.

Further reading: Lawrence Cremin, *American Education: The National Experience, 1783–1876* (New York: Harper & Row, 1980).

—Jaclyn Greenberg

elections

Elections occur when qualified individuals choose candidates for public office. They are the principal mechanism through which a democratic system of government is instituted. National elections are governed by the rules laid down in the U.S. Constitution, but each state constitution contains provisions for its own voting procedures. Thus, every four years a president must be elected, and every two years congressional elections are held to elect all 435 members of the House of Representatives. U.S. senators are elected for six-year terms.

There are conditions for voting, which is a privilege and not a right. All voters must be U.S. citizens, have lived in the country for a specified period, and be of a certain age. For most of the 19th century, the right to vote was granted to most white male citizens and was expanded to include African-American males with the addition of the FIFTEENTH AMENDMENT, passed in 1872. Even though women were excluded from voting until the early 20th century, the United States still had by far the largest number of voters in the world. By the election of 1860, Americans had developed a powerful tradition of partisan and colorful campaigns and electioneering.

Elections tend to produce opposing groups, and early in American history, these groups organized themselves into political parties. Lacking any official constitutional basis, political parties became vital to the workings of government on a national, state, and local level. Party organizations helped in the selection and nomination of candidates, supported their own candidates, and identified the issues around which each election revolved. Their goal was, and is, to win elections and control the government. Political parties in the 19th century relied upon a huge base of volunteer support that provided the "foot soldiers" in massive electoral campaigns marked by parades, demonstrations, and rallies. This kind of enthusiasm meant that for many of the national presidential elections in the 19th century, voter turnout reached incredibly high percentages, between 75 percent and 90 percent.

In the 1850s the two major political parties were the Whigs and the Democrats. The Whigs advocated a strong program of federally sponsored economic development, such as a transcontinental RAILROAD, a central bank, and a national currency. The REPUBLICAN PARTY later adopted this program. The Whigs's message appealed to the growing urban and capitalist class and commercial farmers, especially in the Northeast and many parts of the Midwest. The Democrats, on the other hand, viewed all government with suspicion and supported STATES' RIGHTS and individual liberties. The party of Southern slaveholders, yeoman farmers, and urban immigrants, Democrats for the most part controlled the presidency and Congress up until 1860. That election was the culmination of a reordering of the American political system. In the 1850s the North and South engaged in increasingly bitter debates over SLAVERY in the territories. The Whigs disbanded over internal dissension around slavery, and a new political party was born in 1854, the Republican Party.

The presidential election of 1860, which featured four candidates, shaped the course of national politics for a long time to come. ABRAHAM LINCOLN campaigned on an antislavery platform that appealed greatly to Northerners but was so abhorrent to Southern interests that his name did not even appear on the ballot there. The Democrats divided up into Northern, Southern, and Unionist wings and lost the election. Lincoln carried the North with a solid majority of 180 electoral votes. Southern states seceded because they were convinced that slavery would not be protected under a Republican administration. The outbreak of the CIVIL WAR brought many changes, but the governance of the United States by political parties marked by regular elections of public officials on every level remained in place.

The Northern wartime elections brought spirited, at times violent, discussion and debate over Lincoln's and the Republican Party's policies. Lincoln enjoyed the near-unanimous support of the public in the first year of the war. Defeat after defeat on the battlefield, however, gave rise to Democratic criticism of the way in which the war was being waged. Specifically, Northern Democrats, who were split into "war" and "peace" wings, expressed outrage at Lincoln's assumption of wartime powers that in their view violated the basic civil liberties of all citizens. The suspension of the writ of HABEAS CORPUS, the arrests of Southern sympathizers, the use of military trials, and EMANCIPATION provided Democrats with the issues they needed to mobilize voters against the Republican Party in 1862.

When the votes were tallied in 1862, Democrats gained 32 seats in the House of Representatives, won the governorships of New York and New Jersey, and achieved majorities in the state legislatures of Indiana and Illinois. Historians have traditionally described the outcome as a triumph for the Democrats, yet a closer look at the election results yields a different slant. The Republicans' loss in the House was smaller than expected, enabling them to retain a comfortable majority. They also remained very strong in New England, the upper North, and the border states. As the next set of elections approached, however, the opposition to Lincoln's policies increased as draft resistance turned into draft riots, and worries about emancipation among traditional Democratic groups, like the Irish, contributed to the antiwar feeling. "No ABOLITIONism, No Emancipation, No Negro Equality" became the rallying cry for many Democrats in the 1863 elections. DEMOCRATIC PARTY leaders, such as CLEMENT L. VALLANDIGHAM of Ohio, openly called the war a failure and demanded that it be stopped. Shortly before the elections, however, the Northern military achieved a series of stunning successes, including victories at VICKSBURG and the BATTLE OF GETTYSBURG. When the elections came, Northern voters once again decisively supported the Lincoln administration, as they would in the last major election to be held during the war, the presidential election of 1864.

That election pitted Lincoln against Gen. GEORGE B. MCCLELLAN, the Democratic candidate. In an odd twist, McClellan, a self-proclaimed "War Democrat," was asked by his party to run on a "peace" platform that advocated an immediate suspension of hostilities. He repudiated the platform and pledged Democrats to fight the war to victory over the South. Throughout the summer and fall of 1864, Northerners were asked if they wanted to continue the sacrifices of the war for union and emancipation. They also were asked to support, or denounce, Lincoln's plans for RECONSTRUCTION. Few campaigns in U.S. history have been as dramatic. The war had been going badly for the North, and many, including Lincoln himself, believed throughout the summer that he would be defeated. A string of brilliant Union victories—beginning in August with Adm. DAVID GLASGOW FARRAGUT's victory at Mobile Bay, the September 1 fall of Atlanta engineered by Gen. WILLIAM T. SHERMAN, and later in the autumn, Gen. PHILIP H. SHERIDAN's sensational exploits in the Shenandoah Valley—helped to ensure Republican victory.

On November 8, 1864, Northern voters went to the polls and gave Lincoln a tremendous majority of 212 to 21 in the electoral college and 55 percent of the popular vote. The soldier vote was critical in reelecting Lincoln. Many states during the war had arranged for their "boys" to vote on the battlefield. For those states that did not, the federal government granted furloughs so that soldiers, by the thousands, could go home to cast their vote. Most chose Lincoln. "We can not have free government without elections," Lincoln stated, "and if the rebellion could force us to forego, or postpone a national election, it might fairly claim to have already conquered and ruined us."

The Confederacy continued to hold regular elections as well. In May 1861, the Provisional Confederate Congress announced that general elections—for president and for the national legislature—would be held the following November. This first national election, it was assumed,

would confirm by popular vote the appointment of JEFFERSON DAVIS and other politicians that had taken place earlier. And so it did. The new government in RICHMOND enjoyed an overwhelming level of support from every Confederate state. If there was controversy in the elections of 1861, it arose out of local issues. One of the major differences between the Confederate States and the United States was the absence of formal political parties in the South. Voters tended to support or oppose candidates for office on the basis of their prewar political preferences—Whigs or Democrats—and whether or not the candidates were strong in their support of the current military effort. This favorable set of circumstances for the Davis government began to change for the worse by the spring of 1862 and affected the second set of national elections, held from June through November 1863.

By the summer of 1863, Davis was being attacked severely by critics of his war policy and called a dictator. Popular support for his government had declined dramatically from the early days of the war. Instead of political parties, dissent was organized around pro- and antiadministration issues, with Jefferson Davis the lightning rod for criticism. He was accused of violating STATES' RIGHTS through his support for the CONSCRIPTION laws, his policy on exempting slave owners from military service, his imposition of martial law, and his economic policies of IMPRESSMENT and TAXATION. All of the above together, Davis's opponents claimed, spelled out an extreme centralization of national power. This ran counter to the principles of states' rights and limited government upon which the Confederacy was founded. Davis's own vice president, ALEXANDER H. STEPHENS, and the powerful GOVERNORS of North Carolina and Georgia, Zebulon Vance and JOSEPH E. BROWN, joined the swelling chorus of dissent, which included advocates of a truce with the North.

President Davis was not a noticeably eloquent speaker, but he ably defended his policies. He enjoyed a strong base of support throughout the South, especially in Virginia and his home state of Mississippi. Davis and his supporters made their message simple in the 1863 elections. They called upon the Southern population to remain loyal to the Confederate cause by supporting the government.

Traditional campaign practices had to be altered in time of war. The Confederate Congress passed a law approving voting by general ticket in areas such as Louisiana, Arkansas, and Tennessee, where federal troops occupied large amounts of territory. The government also arranged for the many thousands of REFUGEES to vote by absentee ballots. Finally, special arrangements were made for every soldier to have his vote count. The election results were mixed. Twelve of 26 senators who entered the second regular Congress in May 1864 were elected on the opposition platform. Jefferson Davis, however, still controlled the Congress and would maintain control until the ultimate collapse of the Confederacy in April 1865. Like his Northern counterpart, Davis owed his victory to the overwhelming support of the soldiers in the field. The votes from the occupied areas were also heavily pro-Davis.

In the 12 years after 1865, national elections revolved around Reconstruction issues. In 1868 and 1872, Republican ULYSSES S. GRANT won the presidency and promised to bring peace and reconciliation to the South and fairness and political equity to African Americans. Northerners attempted to uphold the political rights of the freedmen, which placed them on an equal basis with white people. Southerners resisted this equality, often with extreme violence surrounding elections, as evidenced by the growth of the KU KLUX KLAN. In the 1870s, white Southerners regained control of state governments while Democrats regained control of the House of Representatives. Combined with growing Northern indifference to Southern problems, the resurgence of the Democratic Party in the South resulted in the abandonment of the Republican Reconstruction program. That abandonment was cemented in the presidential election of 1876, in which Republican Rutherford B. Hayes of Ohio won a disputed election. The 1876 election brought an end to the bitter sectional dispute among white people with Hayes's peaceful inauguration. The national electoral process, which had failed to prevent war in 1860 and which had been dangerously unstable after the war, emerged validated and strengthened by the late 1870s.

Further reading: Robert J. Dinkin, *Campaigning in America: A History of Election Practices* (New York: Greenwood Press, 1989); Joel H. Silbey, *The American Political Nation, 1838–1893* (Brooklyn: Carlson Publications, 1991).

Elliot, Robert Brown (1842–1884)

Robert B. Elliot was one of the most respected and distinguished African-American legislators of the RECONSTRUCTION era. He was born a free man, either in Boston or England, to parents of West Indian heritage. Well-educated and ambitious, Elliot decided to move to South Carolina after the CIVIL WAR. Shortly after settling in the Palmetto State, he married, opened a law office, and was employed as an associate editor of the *South Carolina Leader*. A Republican, Elliot staked out a political agenda that promised EDUCATION, equality, and prosperity for his race.

First as a member of the state's constitutional convention in 1868 and then as both a state and national legislator, Elliot pressed for laws that would enable all African-American children to receive the benefits of education, guarantee equal treatment to black citizens in public facilities, and ensure unrestricted male suffrage. Elected to Congress in 1870, Elliot was known for his passionate and eloquent speeches in favor of the KU KLUX KLAN ACT and Senator CHARLES SUMNER's Civil Rights bill.

As much as Elliot enjoyed the national spotlight, he became increasingly concerned with the fate of the REPUBLICAN PARTY in South Carolina. In 1874 he returned to that state and served as speaker of its state legislature until 1876. Faced with the withdrawal of Northern support for Reconstruction, Elliot fought desperately to save the only party that welcomed black participation. His fight was to no avail, however. Amid rising incidents of terrorism sponsored by the DEMOCRATIC PARTY, and plagued by corruption and internal dissension, the South Carolina Republican Party was finished when President Rutherford B. Hayes withdrew federal troops from the South in 1877.

Robert B. Elliot continued to practice law in South Carolina, and in 1879 he was appointed a special inspector of customs. He died in New Orleans in 1884.

Further reading: Peggy Lamson, *The Glorious Failure: Black Congressman Robert Brown Elliot and the Reconstruction in South Carolina* (New York: Norton, 1973).

emancipation

Emancipation, the liberation of 4 million slaves, was a major legacy of the CIVIL WAR. The fundamental difference between the South and the North in 1861 was that one was a slave society and the other was not. At first, the Northern goal in the Civil War was to preserve the status quo, that is, to maintain the Union as it was, which meant without interfering with Southern SLAVERY. As the war dragged on unexpectedly, and as Southern resistance seemed to grow stronger, emancipation for the slaves became both a military necessity and a moral imperative.

African Americans from the beginning realized that the war brought opportunity to gain their freedom. Both slaves in the South—and free African Americans in the North—agitated, lobbied, and fought for freedom, and in so doing, they challenged Northern leaders to end the institution of slavery. President ABRAHAM LINCOLN ensured slavery's doom when he issued the EMANCIPATION PROCLAMATION, and the UNION ARMY put the force behind the proclamation by defeating the Confederacy on the battlefield. The THIRTEENTH AMENDMENT finally completed the work that slaves, free African Americans, and ABOLITIONists had begun so long before: the destruction of slavery in the United States of America.

A revolution bringing freedom to enslaved peoples emerged from the bloody battlefields of the Civil War, but the meaning of that freedom was not clear. Freed people of the South, African Americans living in the North, and white people across the country had very different ideas about what black freedom should entail. In the decades following emancipation, the outward signs of freedom—civil rights, citizenship, suffrage, and economic independence—would become battlegrounds of a different kind.

At the time of the FORT SUMTER bombardment, Lincoln was clear that the Civil War would be fought only to restore the Union. Slaves, on the other hand, took advantage of the social disruption that the war engendered by fleeing from bondage. Wherever the Union army moved, slaves flocked to their lines. At first, some military leaders returned slaves to their owners, but others realized that these men constructed Confederate fortifications and provided many other services for the CONFEDERATE ARMY. To return fugitive slaves, then, would aid the Confederate cause and harm the Union's.

Thus, Gen. BENJAMIN F. BUTLER declared fugitive slaves "contraband of war" and put them to work for the Union army. In the following months, thousands of slaves sought refuge with the army, which needed help in caring for them. Northern missionaries and benevolent associations provided aid and EDUCATION to fugitive slaves in crowded and filthy contraband camps. The sheer numbers of CONTRABANDS, however, soon demanded that the political and military leadership address the issue of slaves and slavery.

Congress helped push the Union toward emancipation. The first CONFISCATION ACT declared that slave owners would forfeit their rights to slaves if their slaves were used for Confederate military service. An article of war was adopted in March 1862 prohibiting the military from returning fugitive slaves to their owners. A month later, Congress banned slavery in the District of Columbia, the only area under direct jurisdiction by Congress. Slavery was also banned in all territorial land out west.

In a second Confiscation Act, Congress freed the slaves of any person who aided the rebellion while also authorizing the seizure and sale of any other property from disloyal citizens. Congress also issued a Militia Act, which

Thomas Nast's engraving celebrates the emancipation of the Southern slaves with the end of the Civil War. *(Library of Congress)*

stated that any slave who gave service to the U.S. military would be free, as would his family. For all of these measures, Lincoln and others doubted that Congress had the legal authority to make emancipation stick once the war ended.

Lincoln's greatest fear was that emancipation would provoke the border states to join the Confederacy, but by the summer of 1862, he had come to believe that the war could not be won without freeing the slaves. He favored compensated emancipation (paying owners for freeing their slaves) and colonization (the removal of African Americans to another part of the country or overseas), but the border states rejected both emphatically. On September 22, 1862, Lincoln issued a preliminary Emancipation Proclamation. It declared that slaves in states still in rebellion as of January 1, 1863, would be freed.

The final Emancipation Proclamation, issued on New Year's Day, 1863, declared all slaves in the Confederate states to be free except for those areas under Union control. It did not apply to slaves in the border states. As such, the proclamation did not immediately free many slaves. Nonetheless, abolitionists and their supporters across the country hailed the Emancipation Proclamation as a document of freedom that signaled the end of slavery. For the first time, the interests of African Americans became the interest of the national government. Lincoln justified his emancipation order under his military powers, but he acknowledged the morality of his decision, declaring it "an act of justice." The Emancipation Proclamation changed the tenor of the Civil War. Instead of preserving the status quo, the goal of the war became the establishment of a new social order, what Lincoln called in his address at Gettysburg "a new birth of freedom."

In one of its most radical provisions, the Emancipation Proclamation declared the Union's intention to enlist black soldiers and sailors. Lincoln worked hard to make sure that all Union commanders would aid in forming black units. This opportunity gave African Americans a chance to fight for their freedom and their family's freedom. Now, the Union army was explicitly an army of liberation. No other army in the history of warfare had such immense responsibilities thrust upon it. Among other things, emancipation would allow for the spread of free labor to the South. The Union army became an employer of sorts as it experimented with black free-labor colonies in PORT ROYAL, South Carolina, and DAVIS BEND, Mississippi. The results were mixed and demonstrated the complexities of trying to conduct a social revolution in the middle of a violent war.

Important as the agency of slaves was in forcing the issue of emancipation on the North, the fact remained that the vast majority of slaves could not, and did not, free themselves. Slavery was ultimately defeated through the force of arms first and then through the legal process, and the latter depended heavily on the former. Gen. WILLIAM T. SHERMAN's capture of Atlanta on September 2, 1864, provided the needed boost for Lincoln to defeat his Democratic opponent in the fall election. The Northern people voted in overwhelming numbers not just for Lincoln's reelection but for the war's twin goals of union and emancipation. The election's mandate meant that Lincoln would prosecute the war until all the Confederate armies were defeated. The new social order brought by emancipation would be enforced by the Union army, both during the war and for some time afterward.

Final emancipation came with the ratification of the Thirteenth Amendment on December 18, 1865. The story of freedom did not end there, because its meaning had not yet been agreed upon. Many white people in the North held to a narrow interpretation of freedom that did not include equal rights and suffrage privileges. Needless to say, white Southerners were horrified by the realities of freedom for their ex-slaves. Eliza Andrews, a Georgia plantation mistress, complained bitterly when a former slave would not move aside for her: "It is the first time in my life that I have ever had to give up the sidewalk to a man, much less to negroes!"

The freedmen and freedwomen held to an expansive interpretation of freedom. For black people recently enslaved, freedom first meant the absence from white control—the ability to go wherever, whenever, and do whatever they wanted. Consequently, thousands of freedmen clogged Southern roads, many searching for family members, others looking for a better place to settle down and make a living. In short, the freedpeople did all the things they could not do under slavery: hold mass meetings, learn to read and write, buy guns, and own dogs.

African Americans rushed to establish their own churches, schools, and re-form broken families. For example, ex-slaves were eager to marry legally in the months after emancipation. By 1870 the two-parent household was common among a majority of African Americans. Legal recognition also meant control over one's household and prevented the removal of family members. Many thousands of emotional reunions took place. William Curtis of Georgia, whose father had been sold away, remembered, "That was the best thing about the war setting us free, he could come back to us." For Southern African Americans, freedom was especially to be found in independent ownership of land. Freedmen fought for land redistribution, believing that land would provide a solid foundation for lasting freedom.

Always trying to restrict and confine the meaning of freedom, or emancipation, Southern planters desired to return the freedmen to the fields as laborers in a system as close to slavery as possible. Northern officials, worried that the cotton crop would be wasted, collaborated with the planters, although always insisting on wages for the freedmen.

African-American leaders like FREDERICK DOUGLASS helped flesh out the meaning of freedom. Douglass, the famed abolitionist, asserted that the sacrifices made by African Americans in the war to bring emancipation entitled them to equality before the law. He worked toward an end of racial discrimination, the passage of black suffrage, and acceptance of black people as a part of American society and culture. African Americans did not struggle alone to make freedom work for themselves and their families; Congress created the FREEDMEN'S BUREAU in March 1865 to help ease the transition from slavery to freedom.

Emancipation was a fundamental change in Southern society and altered dramatically the position of African Americans in U.S. society and culture. Emancipation was also a part of a broader change in the Atlantic world. Within the span of a few decades, all of the slave regimes of the Western Hemisphere fell. Since the 1830s, the United States had ranked as the largest and most powerful slaveholding society. In 1834 Great Britain abolished slavery in its Caribbean colonies. Slavery persisted in Cuba and Brazil after the Civil War, but it was already a dying institution, lasting only into the 1890s.

When the peace agreement was signed at APPOMATTOX COURT HOUSE in April 1865, the two goals of the North's Civil War were achieved: reunion and emancipation. The guns had fallen silent, but both RECONSTRUCTION and freedom would remain deeply problematic issues for the reunited nation. The most fundamental change wrought by the war was the rapid transformation of 4 million people from chattel property to citizens. This revolutionary change brought with it a host of problems regarding how the freedmen would establish new lives and how emancipation would change the social, political, and economic future of a nation reeling from a devastating civil war. Emancipation was the process of obtaining freedom. African Americans attained legal status as free and equal citizens of the United States, but this status, though enshrined in the Thirteenth, FOURTEENTH, and FIFTEENTH AMENDMENTs to the Constitution, would be contested and challenged well into the 20th century.

Further reading: Eric Foner, *The Story of American Freedom* (New York: Norton, 1998); Leon F. Litwack, *Been in the Storm So Long: The Aftermath of Slavery* (New York: Vintage Books, 1980); David G. Sansing, *What Was Freedom's Price?: Essays* (Jackson: University Press of Mississippi, 1978); Michael Vorenberg, *Final Freedom: The Civil War, the Abolition of Slavery and the Thirteenth Amendment* (New York: Cambridge University Press, 2001).

—Justin J. Behrend

Emancipation Proclamation

The Emancipation Proclamation, issued on January 1, 1863, by President ABRAHAM LINCOLN, has proven to be one of the landmark documents of American history. In it, Lincoln freed all of the slaves residing in Confederate territory not under UNION ARMY occupation. The Emancipation Proclamation changed the tenor of the CIVIL WAR by linking the Union cause with the liberation of the slaves.

The idea for an Emancipation Proclamation originated in the actions of slaves during the war. From the beginning of armed conflict, slaves near the battle lines crossed over to the Union army camps. Unwilling to return the slaves because the CONFEDERATE ARMY was using them to build forts and other armaments, Union army officials did not know at first what to do with fugitive slaves. Congress stepped in and passed the first Confiscation Act in August 1861. It declared that slave owners forfeited their rights to slaves if their slaves were used in military service. Nearly a year later, Congress passed a second Confiscation Act. This one was more emphatic, claiming that slaves of any person actively supporting rebellion would be "forever free of their servitude." Congress also issued a Militia Act, which stated that any slave who gave service to the military would be free, as would his family. Still, by the summer of 1862, there was no official EMANCIPATION, or freeing of slaves. The war was still for "union."

Lincoln detested SLAVERY, but early in the conflict, he feared that emancipation would provoke the border states into joining the Confederacy. He also had doubts about the legality of an emancipation act from Congress and hoped to provide monetary compensation to slave owners as a compromise measure. In the period between the two CONFISCATION ACTS, ABOLITIONists, Republican politicians, newspaper editors, and various citizen groups pressured Congress, and especially President Lincoln, to emancipate the slaves.

During the spring and summer of 1862, FREDERICK DOUGLASS, the most influential African American at the time, and CHARLES SUMNER, the abolitionist senator from Massachusetts, met with Lincoln, hoping to push him toward immediate and unconditional emancipation, but Lincoln remained steadfast. In a famous reply to newspaper editor HORACE GREELEY, Lincoln wrote, "If I could save the Union without freeing *any* slave I would do it, and if I could save it by freeing *all* the slaves I would do it, and if I could save it by freeing some and leaving others alone I would also do that." But even as he reaffirmed his primary public commitment to preserving the Union, privately Lincoln was beginning to fashion an emancipation order. He read an early draft to his cabinet in July 1862. Most cabinet members favored emancipation, but a few questioned the timing of the order. There was pressure for immediate emancipation to forestall foreign (especially British) aid and recognition of the Confederacy, but with the poor showing of the Union army in the field, the cabinet did not want emancipation to be seen as an act of desperation. Lincoln decided to wait for a military victory.

Lincoln got his victory at the BATTLE OF ANTIETAM, and issued a preliminary Emancipation Proclamation five days later on September 22, 1862. Under his authority as commander in chief, Lincoln declared that as of January 1, 1863, slaves in those states still in rebellion would be freed. As a compromise measure, the preliminary proclamation included a compensation provision for loyal slave owners and suggested colonizing ex-slaves in another part of the country or overseas. Nonetheless, the impact of the proclamation was polarizing. Slaves in the border states, though unaffected by the terms of the order, began to act like freedmen, refusing to do work and demanding respect from white people. Abolitionists praised Lincoln's decision, but many more in the North were critical, contributing to Republican defeats in the fall ELECTIONS.

On New Year's Day 1863, Lincoln issued a final Emancipation Proclamation. "I do order," it stated, "and declare that all persons held as slaves within said designated States and parts of States are and henceforward shall be free." Unlike the preliminary proclamation, this one specified which areas were included by the order. All of Arkansas, Texas, Mississippi, Alabama, Florida, Georgia, South Carolina, and North Carolina fell under the authority of the Emancipation Proclamation, but Lincoln excluded 12 parishes in Louisiana, 53 counties in Virginia, all of Union-occupied Tennessee, and the border states of Delaware, Kentucky, Maryland, and Missouri.

Hundreds of thousands of African Americans remained in bondage, but the legalities of the Emancipation Proclamation made little difference to slaves across the country. The document actually freed very few slaves, since most areas under Union occupation were exempt and those under Confederate control were out of reach. However, the proclamation encouraged slaves to assert their freedom everywhere. Wherever the Union army moved, slavery effectively ended.

Besides the geographic boundaries, there were two other significant changes in the final Emancipation Proclamation. First, Lincoln left out any mention of compensation and colonization. Second and more important, the Emancipation Proclamation called for the enlistment of African-American soldiers: "And I further declare and make known that such persons, of suitable condition, will be received into the armed service of the United States, to garrison forts, positions, stations, and other places, and to man vessels of all sorts in said service." Recruiters spread across the country, and by the war's end 180,000 African Americans had served in the Union armed forces. Lincoln had turned Confederate slave labor into Union fighting power.

The Emancipation Proclamation also represented a shift in focus for the war effort. By the time it was issued, Lincoln believed that the Civil War could not be won without emancipating the slaves. By arming former slaves, Lincoln gave them an opportunity to fight for their own freedom and, in so doing, to fight for their country. More than just adding muscle to the armed services, enrolling black soldiers implied that, at war's end, they would receive full citizenship rights by virtue of their service.

Celebrations erupted across the North to praise the Emancipation Proclamation. Few stopped to consider that only a tiny number of slaves were officially freed, since the Confederate government controlled most of the areas detailed in the document. Instead, the celebrants, mostly African Americans and abolitionists, insisted that the Emancipation Proclamation had injected a moral element into the war, giving it a new cause. Lincoln noted the morality of his decision, writing that he believed emancipation to be "an act of justice, warranted by the Constitution, upon military necessity." The document had immediate practical benefits as well, as the British government backed away from recognizing the Confederacy soon after Lincoln issued the Proclamation.

The THIRTEENTH AMENDMENT officially ended slavery in the United States in December 1865, but the Emancipation Proclamation was the crippling blow to the slave system in the United States.

Further reading: John Hope Franklin, *The Emancipation Proclamation* (Wheeling, Ill.: Harlan Davidson, 1995); Michael Vorenberg, *Final Freedom: The Civil War, the Abolition of Slavery and the Thirteenth Amendment* (New York: Cambridge University Press, 2001).

—Justin J. Behrend

Emerson, Ralph Waldo   See Volume IV

employment

The importance of labor to the CIVIL WAR can hardly be overstated. Workers served in the ranks and provided the materiel used to wage the war. Moreover, ideological and political conflicts over what form of labor was best for the United States played a critical role in precipitating the conflict.

For the first half-century or so of the United States's existence, two labor systems existed in a general state of harmony. Although not all of the laborers in the South were slaves, SLAVERY certainly formed the backbone of the Southern ECONOMY. Meanwhile, Northern factories and farms were worked by free laborers. The balance between these two systems was upset in the 1840s and 1850s as the North became increasingly industrialized. Northerners took pride in the freedom and upward mobility that being a free laborer could provide. Slavery came under attack for its inefficiency more than for its inhumanity. Southerners tried to defend slave labor, emphasizing how much more humanely slaves were treated in comparison with factory workers.

Ultimately, free labor versus slave labor became the dominant political issue of the 1850s. Over the course of the decade, advocates of free labor gathered into the REPUBLICAN PARTY, which celebrated free labor as its main issue. Prominent Republicans traveled around the country, arguing that the strength of the United States derived from the opportunity for advancement provided by the free-labor system. Slavery, meanwhile, posed a threat to the continued existence of free labor. WILLIAM H. SEWARD described the tension between the two as an "irrepressible conflict," and ABRAHAM LINCOLN warned that "a house divided upon itself cannot stand." The Republican platforms of 1856 and 1860 committed the party to a specific plan with regard to the future of slave and free labor. Both stated that the party had no intention of interfering with slavery where it existed, but the platforms also avowed that the institution would not be allowed to spread elsewhere in the country. When Republican Abraham Lincoln was elected president in 1860, Southerners correctly perceived this as a sign that slavery's future was in question, and SECESSION soon followed.

Ironically, as the country's focus was on a philosophical debate about labor, actual laborers themselves were not doing especially well. Although the conditions of their work varied widely, slaves in the South were often subject to great cruelties. In both the North and the South, the PANIC OF 1857 had undermined wages and cost thousands of workers their jobs.

The South's white labor force was the first to feel the influence of the Civil War. Although many skilled laborers enlisted in the army, a substantial number took advantage of the draft exemption provided them and remained on the HOMEFRONT. Those who remained behind found themselves very busy with construction and manufacturing projects, and they helped to keep the Confederate war effort on track. The wages paid by both government and private jobs were quite good, but ultimately they did not match the runaway inflation that gripped the South in the latter half of the war. This resulted in a number of STRIKES, including an 1864 incident where workers from every branch of the government went on strike at the same time.

While white workers continued to provide most of the South's skilled labor during the Civil War, unskilled labor was increasingly the responsibility of slaves, women, and children. Agricultural work was the most important form of unskilled labor they performed, but they also played significant roles in the manufacturing sector. As much as skilled labor suffered from inflation, unskilled labor suffered even more. Slaves availed themselves of the opportunity to escape when they could. Other unskilled laborers, especially white women, did not have the option of escape, nor did they generally have the leverage to organize and go on strike. Sometimes the only recourse available was violence. The most famous incident in the Confederacy was the RICHMOND bread riots of 1863, when a mob of women marched through the capital, inflicting a great deal of damage along the way. JEFFERSON DAVIS intervened personally and broke the demonstration up.

The North also had its share of labor tension during the Civil War, although it was generally longer in coming. The economic malaise precipitated by the Panic of 1857 lasted until the middle of the war, which meant that unemployment rates remained high in 1861 and 1862. As the North recovered, a similar division developed in the workforce there as in the South. Skilled jobs were monopolized by white Protestant men, and unskilled jobs went to Irish Catholics, African Americans, women, and children.

For most of the war, wage increases for both skilled and unskilled workers lagged 25 percent or more behind inflation-related price increases, despite the fact that Northern industry was doing a remarkably good job of sustaining the Union war machine. Between this and the high rates of unemployment, the North had a great deal of labor unrest during the war. Skilled workers generally chose to organize into unions and to strike. Their strikes were often successful, and by 1864 the wages of skilled workers generally paced increases in the cost of living. Unskilled workers, on the other hand, fell further and further behind. Sometimes there were attempts to organize these workers. One notable example was the 1863 formation of the Workingwomen's Protective Union, a group of New York seamstresses. The union struck and was rewarded with a wage increase by order of Abraham Lincoln. This was the exception to the rule, however. In general, the only choice for unhappy unskilled workers was protest. The NEW YORK CITY DRAFT RIOT of 1863, for example, was in part caused by Irish workers who resented the threat posed by free African-American labor.

For many workers, the postwar era marked a return to the status quo. The number of women in war-related jobs dropped as men returned from the military. One exception was the white-collar jobs that women flocked to in WASHINGTON, D.C., and Richmond. African Americans in the North were still relegated to underpaid unskilled jobs, while a majority of African Americans in the South went from slavery to SHARECROPPING. Sharecropping may have been an improvement over slavery, but it still retained as many vestiges of the "peculiar institution" as white Southerners could get away with under the terms of the THIRTEENTH AMENDMENT.

The Civil War did bring one important change to employment patterns, namely the increased strength of the labor movement. Skilled laborers had organized frequently during the war, with some success. Their labor organizations survived the war and continued to grow. The most prominent was the NATIONAL LABOR UNION, which eventually came to be known as the American Federation of Labor. By the early 1870s, a larger percentage of the workforce was unionized than at any other point in the 19th century.

For the Republicans, the postwar relationship with labor was mixed. Although they had triumphed in the Civil War, and the free-labor ideology had won the day, there was an increasing divide between the party and labor. By 1870, two-thirds of Americans were wage earners, and they increasingly came to see the social and financial mobility promised by the free-labor ideology as an illusion. Through the rest of the 19th century, the Republican party became increasingly identified with the interests of the managerial class, while laborers moved into the Democratic fold, an arrangement that has lasted to the present day.

Further reading: Eric Foner, *Free Soil, Free Labor, Free Men: The Ideology of the Republican Party before the Civil War* (New York: Oxford University Press, 1970); J. Matthew Gallman, *The North Fights the Civil War: The Home Front* (Chicago: I. R. Dee, 1994); David Montgomery, *Beyond Equality: Labor and the Radical Republicans, 1862–1872* (New York: Knopf, 1967).

—Christopher Bates

Enforcement Acts (1870–1871)

At the conclusion of the CIVIL WAR, Congress moved to grant citizenship to African-American men. In ratifying the THIRTEENTH, FOURTEENTH, and FIFTEENTH AMENDMENTs to the Constitution, Congress ensured freedom, civil rights, and suffrage for former slaves but failed to anticipate the violent opposition of white Southerners. That opposition led to the passage of three measures, known as the Enforcement Acts, that protected the newly granted rights of African Americans in the South.

The first measure, passed on May 31, 1870, consisted of four parts: It provided considerable penalties for those who interfered with a citizen's right to vote; it turned cases pertaining to congressional ELECTIONS over to the jurisdiction of the federal courts; it assured impartial voting by outlawing conspiracies; and it gave President ULYSSES S. GRANT the power to use American armed forces to assist in protecting civil rights.

The second measure, passed on February 28, 1871, was an amendment to the first. Rather than give the federal courts complete control over congressional elections, this measure authorized federal supervisors to observe and intervene in congressional elections in towns with more than 20,000 inhabitants. In order to prevent these supervisory officers from taking too much control, the second measure also defined their role and specified their powers.

Congress passed the third, and last, measure, also known as the KU KLUX KLAN ACT, on April 20, 1871. This measure prohibited terrorist conspiracies, by which Congress meant the new groups of racist vigilantes calling themselves the KU KLUX KLAN. In addition, it gave the president the authority to suspend the writ of HABEAS CORPUS in areas where terrorist conspiracies took place.

The Enforcement Acts proved ineffective, except in breaking the power of the Ku Klux Klan in South Carolina. Throughout the decade after the passage of the acts, Southern resistance to voting by African-American people only intensified.

By 1876 support for the Enforcement Acts was beginning to fade. Two cases argued before the Supreme Court (*United States v. Reese et al.* and *United States v. Cruikshank*) challenged the constitutionality of aspects of the first enforcement measure. The Court declared that voting rights were best regulated by state power, not federal authority. In addition, the Court claimed that the language of the statutes was too vague. In 1890 Senator Henry Cabot Lodge of Maine made one last effort to strengthen the Enforcement Acts. His bill would have bolstered some provisions of the Enforcement Acts, but the Senate rejected the measure. The federal government would not again take an active role in protecting freedmen's rights in the South until the 1960s.

Further reading: David Donald, *Charles Sumner and the Rights of Man* (New York: Knopf, 1970); William Gillette, *Retreat from Reconstruction, 1869–1879* (Baton Rouge: Louisiana State University Press, 1979).

—Megan Quinn and Fiona Galvin

espionage

For both the Union and the Confederacy, information was essential to political and military strategy. Although espionage was an evolving art during the CIVIL WAR, it proved invaluable and was actively undertaken throughout the war.

Initially, Union forces did not organize an official intelligence-gathering effort. Espionage was not a part of the art of war as understood and taught at military academies, such as the UNITED STATES MILITARY ACADEMY AT WEST POINT. As such, spying was initially left to civilians. A private detective agency, operated by Scottish immigrant

Allan Pinkerton, organized the first Union espionage, and eventually the foundation he built became the United States Secret Service.

Pinkerton's agents were best at identifying Confederate spies in WASHINGTON, D.C., where they mounted counterintelligence operations. Less effective was their military work, especially in the field. Pinkerton's inflated estimates of Confederate troop strength played to the fears of Lincoln's "do nothing" Gen. GEORGE B. MCCLELLAN. When Lincoln removed McClellan from command of the Army of the Potomac in November 1862, Pinkerton, too, was removed from battlefield intelligence.

At roughly the same time, Gen. ULYSSES S. GRANT commissioned Brig. Gen. Grenville M. Dodge to gather intelligence in the western theater. Dodge assembled an assortment of civilian agents and assigned them to various positions throughout the Confederacy. These men supplied information to Grant regarding Confederate troop movements and sometimes engaged in counterintelligence work as well.

In 1863, when Grant moved east, he appointed Col. George H. Sharpe to oversee espionage in the eastern theater. Sharpe proved much better than Pinkerton at determining Confederate troop strength and location. Utilizing female operatives, Sharpe gained valuable information from within the Confederacy. RICHMOND aristocrat ELIZABETH VAN LEW, for example, smuggled information to Northern officials in her clothing and in the shoes of her slaves. S. Emma E. Edmonds used her skill at impersonation to obtain information. She disguised herself as both an African-American slave and a soldier, experiences she wrote about after the war in her memoir *Nurse and Spy in the UNION ARMY.* Toward the end of the war, Edmonds became a counterintelligence operative in St. Louis, Missouri.

Confederate efforts at espionage surpassed those of the Union in some respects. The Confederacy established a "Special and Secret Service Bureau" that managed both their spy network in Washington as well as other clandestine activities. Through this bureau, the Confederacy spent approximately $2 million on intelligence activities during the war. The bureau also helped the CONFEDERATE ARMY and NAVY preserve secrecy on major technological advancements such as their development of underwater mines.

Confederate investments in espionage proved essential in several respects. Because of operatives in Washington, the Confederate military knew in advance that Union forces were moving toward Manassas, and this helped the Confederates to secure a victory there in 1861. It was a female spy, ROSE O'NEAL GREENHOW, who gathered the information that so hurt the Union at the FIRST BATTLE OF BULL RUN. She was a Washington hostess with wide social connections that she used to help the Confederacy. Later,

Pinkerton's men discovered her work and arrested her. Greenhow was by no means the only female spy for the Confederacy, however. Another prominent woman to engage in espionage was BELLE BOYD, who was famous for her ability to avoid capture and cross back and forth across enemy lines. She spied for the South throughout the war and was especially valued by THOMAS J. "STONEWALL" JACKSON.

The most elaborate and expensive Confederate secret operations were those headed by the Confederacy's official representative to Canada, Jacob Thompson. With $1 million in gold, Thompson funded a Northern peace movement run by the Knights of the Golden Circle, a secret organization. He also attempted to free Confederate prisoners held in PRISONS near the Canadian border. Thompson even contacted JOHN WILKES BOOTH in 1864 with a plan to kidnap President ABRAHAM LINCOLN and ransom him in exchange for Southern prisoners.

Although the Union was not as quick to organize its intelligence-gathering efforts as the Confederacy, it succeeded in establishing a variety of sources for secret information by the end of the war. Southern espionage, too, proved useful repeatedly. Most importantly, the idea of spying itself was made acceptable by the recognition that the pragmatism of war required the use of all available tools.

See also ASSASSINATION OF ABRAHAM LINCOLN.

Further reading: Alan Axelrod, *The War between the Spies: A History of Espionage during the Civil War* (New York: Atlantic Monthly Press, 1992); John Bakeless, *Spies of the Confederacy* (Philadelphia: J. B. Lippincott, 1970); S. Emma E. Edmonds, *Nurse and Spy in the Union Army: Comprising the Adventures and Experiences of a Woman in Hospitals, Camps, and Battle-fields* (1865; reprint, DeKalb: Northern Illinois University Press, 1999).

—Chad Vanderford

Ewell, Richard Stoddert (1817–1872)

Confederate general Richard Stoddert Ewell was born in Virginia. He attended the UNITED STATES MILITARY ACADEMY AT WEST POINT as a member of the Class of 1840, graduating 13th. In the U.S. Army, Ewell served mostly with the cavalry in the West, including limited action in the Mexican-American War. In 1861 he resigned his commission in the U.S. Army to join the Confederacy.

Although Ewell eventually reached the rank of lieutenant general, he began his service as a relatively low-ranking division commander under Gen. THOMAS J. "STONEWALL" JACKSON. Ewell's units distinguished themselves in 1862 in both the SHENANDOAH VALLEY CAMPAIGN and in the defense of RICHMOND, Virginia. In August of that year, Ewell traveled north with Jackson to the SEC-

OND BATTLE OF BULL RUN. There he was shot in the right knee, an injury that eventually resulted in the loss of his leg. Recuperating in Richmond, Ewell, called "Old Bald Head" by his soldiers, was reunited with his childhood sweetheart, Lizinka Campbell Brown, who nursed him back to health. On May 24, 1863, Ewell married Brown and then returned to duty with the army.

In early May, while Ewell was recovering in Richmond, Stonewall Jackson was wounded at the BATTLE OF CHANCELLORSVILLE. He died on May 10, and as a result Ewell assumed command of Lee's Second Corps. On June 14, 1863, in his first battle after returning to duty, Ewell won a spectacular victory at Winchester, Virginia. He was then ordered to join Gen. ROBERT E. LEE's army in Pennsylvania.

Ewell's corps successfully drove back Union forces on July 1, 1863, but his failure to attack Union troops on Cemetery Hill led to severe criticism of his generalship. By the third day, the Union victory at the BATTLE OF GET-TYSBURG was secured, and Lee returned to Virginia. Ewell served in the OVERLAND CAMPAIGN of 1864, but illness led to his temporary retirement in May 1864. His last assignment was to command the defenses of Richmond. Ewell was captured at Sayler's Creek on April 5, 1865, in the Appomattox campaign.

Released in July 1865, Ewell retired to Spring Hill, Tennessee. There, on a farm owned by his wife, Ewell lived the life of a gentleman farmer until contracting pneumonia in the winter of 1872. Lizinka tried again to nurse him back to health, but instead she fell ill and died on January 22. Ewell followed her two days later.

Further reading: Douglas Southall Freeman, *Lee's Lieutenants: A Study in Command* (New Yok: Scribner, 1998); Donald Pfanz, *Richard S. Ewell: A Soldier's Life* (Chapel Hill: University of North Carolina Press, 1998).

—Megan Quinn

F

Farragut, David Glasgow (1801–1870)
Widely admired for his innovative tactics and operational skills, Union admiral David Glasgow Farragut was born near Knoxville, Tennessee, on July 5, 1801. The family moved to New Orleans in 1807, where Farragut's mother died. After his father enlisted in the navy, Comdr. David Porter (head of the New Orleans Naval Station) adopted the boy. Destined for the sea, the nine-year-old Farragut began working as a midshipman with the U.S. Navy Department. Most of his youth was spent on board various ships in the Pacific, the Mediterranean, and the West Indies, and he saw action in the War of 1812. Farragut assumed his first naval command in 1842, and during the Mexican-American War he commanded the *Saratoga*.

Farragut's loyalty was questioned early in the CIVIL WAR, but he remained steadfastly attached to the Union. To his SECESSIONist friends, Farragut said: "Mind what I tell you. You fellows will catch the devil before you get through with this business." In January 1862 he was placed in charge of the West Gulf Blockading Squadron with two goals in mind. The first was to assure Union control of the MISSISSIPPI RIVER, and the second was to take the South's greatest port city, New Orleans.

Farragut captured New Orleans in a dazzling display of Union naval power. After passing the heavily armed Fort Jackson and Fort Saint Phillip and defeating Confederate defenses, Farragut arrived at New Orleans on April 25, 1862. The victory, a rare bloodless affair, was critical to controlling Louisiana and the Mississippi River. Now a rear admiral, he turned his attention to the "river war." In June and July 1862 Farragut attempted to fight the Vicksburg defenses for the Mississippi above Port Hudson, but to no avail. He returned to the Gulf Coast to implement and strengthen the naval blockade from August to February 1863. In March, Farragut's ships attacked the batteries at Port Hudson, Louisiana. By July and August 1863 the Mississippi River was under Union control.

Perhaps his finest moment as a naval strategist came on August 5, 1864, at the Battle of Mobile in Alabama. Three impressive forts protected the last major port still in Confederate hands. Farragut sailed 18 ships into Mobile Bay and smashed into the enemy fleet. At this point Farragut was so afflicted with vertigo that he had himself lashed to the rigging of his flagship, the *Hartford*. It was at this battle that he uttered his immortal phrase. After a mine

David G. Farragut   *(National Archives)*

(called torpedoes during the Civil War) had sunk one of the ships ahead of Farragut's, several men expressed great reservations about proceeding. Farragut responded by saying, "Damn the torpedoes, full speed ahead!" The Confederate fleet surrendered, and Farragut had another magnificent victory to his credit.

Farragut was promoted twice after the war, making him the navy's first full admiral. He died at age 69 in Portsmouth, New Hampshire, on August 14, 1870.

See also UNION NAVY.

Further reading: Chester G. Hearn, *Admiral David Glasgow Farragut: The Civil War Years* (Annapolis, Md.: Naval Institute Press, 1998); Charles Lee Lewis, *David Glasgow Farragut* (Annapolis: United States Naval Institute, 1941).

—Arthur E. Amos

fashion

Mid-19th century American women in the countryside and in the cities were eager to learn of fashion trends. European, especially French, style dominated fashion. One of the most popular features of women's magazines were fashion plates, illustrations of the latest styles of clothing. Some of the most popular magazines of the mid-19th century, like *Godey's Lady's Book, Harper's Bazaar,* and *Frank Leslie's Gazette of Fashion,* focused most if not all of their attention on fashion. Despite the great popularity of these publications, the extent to which these fashion dictates were followed in 19th-century America depended largely on economics and geography.

In the 19th century men's fashions, which received less public notice or press attention than women's fashions did, underwent a significant change. In earlier eras, fashionable men's clothing was as showy and decorative as women's, but by the mid-19th century, men's fashions had settled into a more staid and somber appearance. The standard costume for America's gentlemen from the 1850s through the 1860s included a redingote or frock coat (long, tailored jackets with wide, sometimes rolled lapels, and flared hems), usually worn over a fitted vest. Trousers were worn long and over boots. By the 1870s the big transformation in men's clothing was the rise in popularity of the sack coat, a less-fitted option to the tailored lines of the redingote and frock coat for the "modern man." But tailored or not, not all men wore the typical gentleman's outfit. Slaves, as well as working men in American cities and farms, had costumes more appropriate to the daily rigors of butchering, manufacturing, blacksmithing, and plowing —coarser, more hard-wearing fabrics, bibbed trousers, and loose shirts were more conducive to their daily labors. Also, the westward movement of American settlers and entrepreneurs brought to men's clothing the "Western style" more suitable to life on the frontier. Leather trousers and shirts and hard-wearing fabrics were necessities for trappers, miners, railroad workers, and frontier settlers.

While men's clothing became more somber over the 19th century, upper-middle-class women's fashion continued to be fanciful and decorated. Mainstream fashion for women before the Civil War dictated in physical appearance a slight, rounded, submissive figure. The ideal female, according to portrayals in lithographs, journals, and fiction, was dark-haired with a small oval-shaped face, a soft chin, cupid bow lips, pale white skin, and a frail and delicate physique. According to the ideal, a woman's hands and feet were delicate and tapered and no part of her body should be strong or forceful. Even her movements and posture were to be curved and bent.

Clothing emphasized these physical ideals. Dresses created a curved, bell-shaped figure, with the overall appearance of a triangle from the tiny hats or hair ornaments trailing outward, with the interruption of a tiny, cinched-in waist, to a wide, belled-out hem. Necklines were wide and rounded. The waist was tightly constricted by using corsets that could be tightened by stays that tied in the back. In contrast to the small waist, skirts were long, touching the floor, and were capacious, using yards of fabric. In 1856 hoops, metal frames worn under the skirt to enhance its fullness, came into fashion. Despite its weight, the hoop was considered a fashion boon for women because it replaced the innumerable layers of crinoline petticoats that were even heavier and more restrictive of movement. In the 1860s skirts were at their widest, held out by a few layers of crinoline underskirts over the hoop. With her hoop, the well-dressed woman wore a shawl, rather than a coat. Women were counseled by *Godey's* to wear their shawls to their best advantage—generally to be seen as if they were just putting the shawl on, which ostensibly gave the most pleasing presentation of perfect, rounded shoulders.

After the Civil War, the ideal silhouette changed. *Harper's Bazaar* counseled women in 1875 that the "ideal at present is the greatest possible flatness and straightness: a woman is a pencil covered with raiment." Clothes were tighter fitting in the front with a bustle in the back, beginning a trend away from voluminous skirts. The rising popularity of bustles created in the 1870s a distorted appearance of women's posture—pushing the bust up, flattening the front of the woman's figure from the bust down to the feet, and swaying out the woman's back in an exaggerated bubble of crinolines and bows.

Alongside the ideal fashion was a range of alternatives for women that largely hinged on the geography and economic position of the women involved. Like men, women of the working classes invented their own styles to meet

Woman and girl in fashionable clothing, 1862 *(Library of Congress)*

their needs. Some working women had strict constraints about the fashions available to them; for instance, women working in U.S. textile mills were forbidden from wearing hoops because they posed a danger around the manufacturing machinery. Rural and frontier women were also generally hoopless and bustleless and made clothing of sturdy, wearable fabrics including canvas, muslin, and calico. The 1870s saw the rise of paper-pattern publication and the ever-increasing availability of sewing machines for women of most economic levels, thus allowing women across the expanding nation to fashion their own versions of the magazine ideals.

Notwithstanding the general acceptance of the "ideal" figure and fashion for women in the mid-19th century, mainstream women's fashion did have its detractors. From the 1820s through the end of the 19th century, the United States had a burgeoning "dress reform movement." Feminists and health reformers criticized fashion trends and advocated less restrictive clothing for women. They were largely concerned about the harmful health effects of cinching at the waist, which constricted breathing, and of the impact of the heavy underskirts. Also, feminists argued for a less gender-segregated fashion standard. Reformers advocated the shortened dress with long pantaloons (to be cut like men's trousers) for women; the outfit generally became known as the "bloomer costume." One of the health publications of the day, the *Water-Cure Journal* summed up reform attitudes and poked fun at the restrictiveness of the ideal for women's attire in 1853 with a bit of verse:

> To breathe, or not to breathe; that's the question
> Whether 'tis nobler in the mind to suffer
> The slings and arrows of outrageous fashion,
> Or to bear the scoffs and ridicule of those
> Who despise the Bloomer dresses.

A coalition of dress reformers formed the National Dress Reform Association (NDRA), which met for the first time in New York in 1856. The NDRA used their association magazine, *The Sybil: A Review of the Tastes, Errors and Fashions of Society*, to promote their campaign on the health aspects of the bloomer costume. By 1866, however, the NDRA had dispersed, and support for the bloomer movement was dwindling.

See also MARRIAGE AND FAMILY LIFE; WOMEN'S STATUS AND RIGHTS.

Further reading: Stella Blum, ed., *Victorian Fashions and Costumes from Harper's Bazaar, 1867–1898* (New York: Dover Publications, 1974); Gayle V. Fischer, *Pantaloons & Power: A Nineteenth-Century Dress Reform in the United States* (Kent, Ohio: Kent State University Press, 2001); Robert Kunciov, ed., *Mr. Godey's Ladies: Being a Mosaic of Fashions & Fancies* (Princeton, N.J.: Pyne Press, 1971); Joan L. Severa, *Dressed for the Photographer: Ordinary Americans and Fashion, 1840–1900* (Kent, Ohio: Kent State University Press, 1995); Estelle Ansley Worrell, *American Costume, 1840–1920* (Harrisburg, Pa.: Stackpole Books, 1979).

—Ruth A. Behling and Jaclyn Greenberg

Fifteenth Amendment (March 30, 1870)

The Fifteenth Amendment to the U.S. Constitution, ratified on March 30, 1870, specifically guaranteed the right to vote to all males regardless of "race, color or previous condition of servitude." Section 2 of the amendment also firmly locates the power "to enforce this article by appropriate legislation" in Congress. While Section 2 of the FOURTEENTH AMENDMENT dealt with the denial of suffrage, the Fifteenth Amendment stated Congress's position on African-American voting rights more clearly and forcefully.

African Americans began agitating for the right to vote immediately after the end of the CIVIL WAR. Black citizens organized mass meetings, marched in parades, and signed petitions insisting that freedom meant suffrage and civic equality. They went to WASHINGTON, D.C., to lobby for suffrage, reminding congressmen that those who took up arms in defense of their nation deserved the right to vote. In the South, African-American conventions made public their request for suffrage, and thousands deluged the FREEDMEN'S BUREAU, military leaders, and state officials with petitions and LETTERS.

These protests for black suffrage made little progress at first. Only five states allowed African-American men to vote by the end of 1865, and in those states there were additional qualifications that white males did not have to meet. For instance, New York had a property requirement. However, the BLACK CODES, racial violence, and an upsurge of unrepentant Southern nationalism encouraged congressional Republicans to take RECONSTRUCTION into their own hands and make black suffrage a hallmark of the radical effort. The attainment of the vote for freedmen seemed to be the answer to several problems. Some supporters liked the idea because it removed the federal government from the primary responsibility of providing for the welfare of African Americans; others envisioned black voters as a key Republican voting bloc and a barrier to Democratic domination in the South. The challenge was how to best establish black suffrage.

Republicans recognized the importance of black voters in the election of 1868, in which freedmen participated, thanks to the Fourteenth Amendment. Without black votes, ULYSSES S. GRANT would have lost the popular vote. Facing violence and intimidation from white Democrats, Southern African Americans voted overwhelmingly for the REPUBLICAN PARTY. Constitutional protection of black suffrage would help Republican candidates while ending the party's hypocrisy of supporting voting rights in the South when most Northern African Americans also faced racial restrictions on voting rights. In addition, a constitutional amendment would hopefully establish black political power in the South.

In its final form, the Fifteenth Amendment was a moderate measure. The Senate rejected language that would have prohibited discrimination based on nativity, RELIGION, property, and EDUCATION, as well as a provision claiming the right to hold political office. While most states seemed content to allow African Americans to vote, others wished to keep restrictions on certain immigrant groups. California, for instance, denied Chinese immigrants the right to vote.

Reaction to the amendment was mixed. Ratification was fiercely contested in the border states, the Midwest, and the mid-Atlantic states. Feminists opposed ratification and were incensed by the language of ABOLITIONist reformers. "One question at a time," declared Wendell Phillips, "This hour belongs to the Negro." By advocating universal manhood suffrage, the amendment implicitly recognized suffrage discrimination based on sex. Abolitionists were elated by its results. Constitutional protection for black male voters was almost unthinkable just five years before. However, the traditional alliance of abolitionist and feminist reformers permanently split over the ratification of the Fifteenth Amendment.

Though secured in the Constitution, black suffrage had a short life in the 19th century. Violence and intimidation continued in Southern ELECTIONS because the federal government failed to protect black voting rights: With the rise of REDEMPTION governments beginning in the 1870s, Southern states took steps to systematically disenfranchise black voters through literacy tests, poll taxes, and other measures. With the end of Reconstruction in 1876–77, white Democrats were well on their way to once again controlling Southern politics, and African Americans would not vote again in large numbers in the South until the late 1960s.

Further reading: William Gillette, *The Right to Vote: Politics and the Passage of the Fifteenth Amendment* (Baltimore, Md.: Johns Hopkins Press, 1969).

—Justin J. Behrend

54th Massachusetts Regiment

Few stories about the CIVIL WAR carry more emotional importance for African Americans than the assault on Fort Wagner, Morris Island, South Carolina, on July 18, 1863. The assault was led by the 54th Massachusetts Colored Volunteer Infantry Regiment under the command of 26-year-old Col. Robert Gould Shaw. Like many massed infantry charges, it failed, and the soldiers fell back after suffering heavy losses. But the courage of the 54th's African-American troops and the heroic death of Colonel Shaw made the regiment instantly famous, and its history is the subject of poems, songs, books, documentaries, and a movie. Augustus Saint-Gaudens, a well-known American sculptor, designed a beautiful monument to honor the regiment that was unveiled in Boston in 1897. Ralph Waldo Emerson wrote a poem that is inscribed on the monument's granite base: "So nigh is grandeur to our dust, So near to God is man, When Duty whispers low, THOU MUST, The youth replies, I can."

The origins of the 54th lie with Massachusetts's wartime ABOLITIONist governor, Republican John A. Andrew. His dream was to see AFRICAN-AMERICAN REGIMENTS in battle, fighting for their rights as citizens and their dignity as men. He wanted to prove wrong the commonly held stereotype of black incapacity to train and fight as soldiers. Andrew had plotted and agitated for an all-black regiment from the beginning of the war, to no avail for nearly two years. But finally the EMANCIPATION PROCLAMATION, issued on January 1, 1863, made the enrollment of African-American soldiers possible. The majority of African-American regiments were organized under the auspices of the federal government and were called the United States Colored Troops. Three colored regiments, however, were raised in the same fashion as the majority of white regiments, that is, by state. Two were from Massachusetts and one was from Connecticut. The 54th was the first of the three.

In early January 1863 Andrew received permission from President ABRAHAM LINCOLN and Secretary of War EDWIN STANTON to raise an all-black Northern regiment from men living in the Bay State. For the officers, Andrew was required to choose white men only. Lincoln had refused his request to commission black officers in fear that Northern public opinion would not support that advancement. Andrew was disappointed but did what he thought was the next best thing: He recruited officers with an anti-SLAVERY background. "Such officers," Andrew explained, "must be necessarily gentlemen of the highest tone and honor; and I shall look for them in those circles of educated Anti-Slavery Society, which next to the colored race itself have the greatest interest in the success of this experiment." True to his words, Andrew offered the colonelcy of the regiment to Bostonian Robert Gould Shaw of the Second Massachusetts, with the lieutenant colonelcy going to a captain of the 20th Massachusetts, Norwood Hallowell of Philadelphia. Both were sons of prominent abolitionist families. Other white officers included Lts. Edward Emerson and Wilkie James and Capts. Luis F. Emilio and Cabot Russel.

It soon became clear that Massachusetts alone could not begin to fill the regimental requirement for 1,000 men. Andrew formed a committee of concerned citizens, headed by George L. Stearns, a wealthy Boston industrialist, to raise money for the hiring of speakers who would travel across the North to recruit for the regiment. Andrew needed the wholehearted support of the black Northern leadership for this task, and he received it. WILLIAM WELLS BROWN, John Mercer Langston, MARTIN R. DELANY, Robert Purvis, Henry Highland Garnet, and FREDERICK DOUGLASS all persuaded men from the tiny Northern population of free African Americans to become Union soldiers. In a stirring speech, Douglass explained to his audiences why African Americans should fight in what had previously been a white man's war: "Once let the black man get upon his person the brass letters, U.S., get an eagle on his button and a musket on his shoulder and bullets in his pocket; and there is no power on the earth or under the earth which can deny that he has earned the right of citizenship in the United States." The recruiters had other, more tangible, rewards to offer, namely a generous bounty, $8-per-month salary from the state, and $13-per-month salary from the federal government, the same as for white soldiers.

By February 1863, volunteers were pouring into the 54th's training camp in Readville, near Boston. The bulk of them hailed from Massachusetts, Pennsylvania, New York, Ohio, Michigan, Illinois, and Indiana. There were more than 1,000 men; the rest filled up the ranks of the 55th Massachusetts Colored Regiment. The men of the 54th represented the cream of the black Northern society. Most could read and write, and many were married with families. They were barbers, cooks, teamsters, farmers, laborers, and students. Pennsylvanian George E. Stephens was a cabinetmaker, while Joseph Sulsey from New Jersey was a dentist. The vast majority of enlisted men in the 54th were working class. More than a quarter were born into slavery, and their average age was 24. Several men achieved distinction as noncommissioned officers. One of the two sons of Frederick Douglass who volunteered for the 54th was Sgt. Maj. Lewis Douglass, the highest-ranking noncommissioned officer in the unit. Sgt. WILLIAM H. CARNEY of New Bedford, Massachusetts, won the congressional MEDAL OF HONOR for his courage in rescuing the regimental flag at Fort Wagner, and Sgt. Robert J. Simmons of New York was also cited for his bravery in that battle.

The young men in the 54th naturally shared a sense of pride in themselves and their mission, which was to serve as an example for all other black units. No expense was spared for the 54th. They received UNIFORMS, shoes, rifles, and a great deal of training. Although difficult and sometimes discouraging, the effects of discipline and daily drill made the 54th come together as a group. Thousands flocked to view their dress parades, which demonstrated the capability of the black man to be a soldier. There was great disappointment in the ranks when the federal government went back on its promise to pay African-American soldiers equally for their service. White soldiers received $13 per month in addition to clothing; black soldiers received $10 per month, from which they were expected to deduct $3 for clothing. Most of the enlisted men in the 54th refused to accept their pay until Congress corrected the injustice in early 1865.

After several months of training, orders arrived in May 1863 requiring the 54th Massachusetts to report to Maj. Gen. David Hunter, commander of the Department of the South, in Hilton Head, South Carolina. Before they left, a huge parade was held in honor of the 54th in Boston. In his parting words, Governor Andrew said "I know not . . . when, in all human history, to any given thousand men in arms there has been committed a work at once so proud, so precious, so full of hope and glory as the work committed to you." From the Boston harbor, the men of the 54th sailed down to the South Carolina seacoast and disembarked at St. Simons Island. The regiment was to take part in a movement of Union forces to seize FORT SUMTER and conquer Charleston, South Carolina, where the rebellion had begun. Eager to participate in combat action, the men of the 54th were instead relegated to labor duties as May turned into June and July. Col. Robert Gould Shaw was furious and began a letter-writing campaign to members of his influential family, who in turn, forwarded his letters to President Lincoln and other major political leaders. For Shaw, the reputation of black units would be irreparably harmed if the flagship regiment did not experience combat, and soon.

Finally, on July 16, 1863, three companies of the 54th were ordered to proceed to nearby James Island, where they met, fought, and defeated a much larger Confederate force. Exhausted but extremely proud, the men, now joined by the rest of the regiment, marched straight to Morris Island, the site of battery Wagner, one of the forts that offered protection to Charleston. Arriving with their colonel on the morning of July 18, the men of the 54th learned that heavy federal artillery had been shelling Fort Wagner for hours. Wrongly assuming that the Confederates within the battery were wounded, killed, or demoralized, the Union commander planned an assault for that evening. Colonel Shaw reported for duty and was asked by the commanding general if the 54th would consider leading the infantry charge. Shaw did not hesitate in accepting and was pleased that the good fighting reputation of his men had already reached the general's ears. "I trust God will give me the strength to do my duty," he confided to a friend.

Shaw positioned his regiment at the front of the line, and as they marched up the shore the men were cheered loudly by thousands of Union soldiers who were to follow them in battle. Shaw made a speech in which he told the soldiers to "prove themselves as men." The signal to begin the charge was given, and Colonel Shaw led the 54th to the top of the fort, where an enemy bullet killed him. Nearly half of the regiment made it inside the fort, and the soldiers outside held their ground for over an hour. Shortly after, the Federals were forced to withdraw, paying a heavy price for the failed assault. Seventy-five men of the 54th died at the battle of Fort Wagner, including Shaw and two other officers; overall the unit's casualty rate was 272 out of 650 men. Total Union losses were also severe: 1,505 dead, wounded, or captured, while the Rebels lost 174 men. Charleston was not captured until the end of the war.

The performance of the 54th was widely covered by the Northern press. All agreed that Colonel Shaw and his men, both officers and enlisted, had conducted themselves with an impressive display of courage and daring. Overnight, the regiment became a powerful symbol for African-American manliness and readiness for citizenship. After Fort Wagner, the men of the 54th Massachusetts were used in campaigns in Florida, most notably the Battle of Olustee, waged in early 1864. In total, they fought in four battles and several skirmishes. When the war ended, a little over half of the regiment returned to Boston. The men of the 54th happily resumed their normal lives, confident that they had fulfilled the bright promise of the regiment envisioned by Governor Andrew and others. VETERANS of the 54th commemorated their wartime achievements by voting Republican, and many joined the Grand Army of the Republic. The fight for justice and equality for African Americans was not by any means secured after the Civil War, but the soldiers of the 54th Massachusetts Colored Regiment advanced the cause considerably.

See also AFRICAN-AMERICAN REGIMENTS; CORPS D'AFRIQUE.

Further reading/viewing: Russell Duncan, *Where Death and Glory Meet: Colonel Robert Gould Shaw and the 54th Massachusetts Infantry* (Athens: University of Georgia Press, 1999); Luis F. Emilio, *A Brave Black Regiment: History of the Fifty-Fourth Regiment of Massachusetts Volunteer Infantry, 1863–1865* (New York: Da Capo Press, 1995); *Glory* (Los Angeles: Tristar Pictures, 1989); Robert Gould Shaw, *Blue-Eyed Child of Fortune: The Civil War Letters of Colonel Robert Gould Shaw* (Athens: University of Georgia Press, 1992); Joan Waugh, "A Sacrifice We Owed: The Shaw Family and the Fifth-fourth Massachusetts," in *Hope and Glory: Essays on the Legacy of the Fifty-fourth Massachusetts Regiment*, eds. Marvin H. Blatt, Thomas J. Brown, and Donald Yacovone (Amherst: University of Massachusetts in association with the Massachusetts Historical Society, 2000).

filibustering

Filibustering was a term used in the antebellum period to describe privately organized military expeditions into the Caribbean and Central America in the 19th century. Though most participants in filibustering expeditions of the 1840s and 1850s were generally sympathetic to Manifest Destiny and Southern proSLAVERY extremism, filibustering also attracted men who hoped to make their fortunes or who simply needed work.

The most famous of the filibusterers was Tennessean William Walker. While studying medicine in Europe, Walker was deeply influenced by the first flowering of European revolutionary nationalism. Though he briefly practiced medicine, he became an impassioned advocate of further U.S. expansion into Mexico, resolving that if the

U.S. government would not build on its successes in the Mexican-American War, he would do so personally.

Moving to San Francisco in the early 1850s, Walker made good on his commitment. He gathered a volunteer force, journeyed south, and took control of the northwestern Mexican town of La Paz. There he proclaimed the establishment of the Republic of Lower California. When Mexican forces threatened his position in La Paz, Walker moved his men north to Ensenada, declaring that he had founded the Republic of Sonora. Though Mexico had abolished slavery, Walker's would-be countries both protected it.

The U.S. government, wary of renewing its divisive conflict with Mexico, did not provide Walker with any assistance. DESERTION, poor organization, and harsh conditions all undermined Walker's efforts, and he finally fled Mexico. U.S. officials sympathetic with Walker's venture saw to it that the federal government did not charge Walker with any crime.

Several years later, Walker led another expedition, this time to intervene in a Nicaraguan civil war. Victories there led Walker to declare himself Nicaragua's president. To the delight of Southern plantation owners, Walker repealed the country's antislavery laws. Southern advocates of Manifest Destiny now spoke of annexing Nicaragua and perhaps all of Central America.

While Walker's proslavery stance thrilled many Southerners, it infuriated most Nicaraguans and deeply concerned other Central Americans who feared that Walker—or the United States itself—might threaten the entire isthmus. Walker made his situation more precarious when he angered RAILROAD financier Cornelius Vanderbilt, who had contracted with Nicaragua's previous government to build and manage a railroad that would carry passengers and freight between Nicaragua's Caribbean and Pacific coasts. Believing that the contract had benefited Vanderbilt more than it had Nicaragua, Walker canceled the arrangement. When Costa Rica declared war against Walker's Nicaragua, Vanderbilt lent his support. In 1857 Walker was forced out of Nicaragua.

Walker's Nicaraguan adventure deeply divided American officials. Some, like Secretary of War JEFFERSON DAVIS, openly sympathized with Walker's objectives. Some proslavery officials saw Walker as taking the first necessary steps toward the U.S. conquest of the entire Caribbean, creating a "golden circle" of slavery.

At the same time, a number of American politicians, even those sympathetic to the expansion of slavery within U.S. territory, worried that Walker and other filibusterers might entangle the United States in dangerous conflicts, not only with Latin American and Caribbean states but also with Britain and France. In addition, the prospect of an aggressively expanding "slaveocracy" hardened antislavery

opinion in the North and contributed to the growth of the new REPUBLICAN PARTY. It was for such reasons that President JAMES BUCHANAN, a Pennsylvania Democrat allied with proslavery Southerners, ultimately refused U.S. support for Walker.

Walker returned to Central America twice, but each time he was repulsed. After his last incursion, into Honduras, Walker surrendered to a British naval commander, who turned the prisoner over to Honduran authorities. In 1860 the Hondurans executed Walker before a firing squad.

With a Union victory in the CIVIL WAR, much of the impetus for filibustering ended. Though some American politicians continued to harbor ambitions for Central America and the Caribbean, privately financed attacks ceased. For the peoples of Central America and the Caribbean, however, the image of Americans shooting their way into power persisted, influencing their response to American intervention in regional affairs well into the 20th century.

See also FOREIGN POLICY.

Further reading: Merritt Parmelee Allen, *William Walker, Filibuster* (New York: Harper & Bros., 1932).

—Tom Laichas

fire-eaters

The term *fire-eaters* was applied by Northerners to PROSLAVERY extremists in the South during the two decades prior to the outbreak of the CIVIL WAR in 1861. Fire-eaters attempted to use the political process to protect the South from what they perceived as Northern political aggression. They consistently promoted SECESSION as the only solution to what Southern moderates and conservatives considered at the time a temporary problem of sectional discord.

The most notable of this group of radical Southern nationalists were Edmund Ruffin, Robert B. Rhett, and WILLIAM LOWNDES YANCEY. Ruffin, a Virginian, was an ardent supporter of STATES' RIGHTS and the secession of the South. Prior to the outbreak of the Civil War, Ruffin left Virginia for the more congenial political milieu of South Carolina, and on April 12, 1861, he was given the privilege of firing the first shot against FORT SUMTER, thus starting the Civil War. The ultimate fire-eater, a devastated Ruffin committed suicide when ROBERT E. LEE surrendered at APPOMATTOX COURT HOUSE in 1865.

Rhett, from South Carolina, was known as the "father of secession." He was one of the earliest proponents of secession in his home state of South Carolina and spent much of his life working for an independent South. Convinced that the Southern way of life was doomed if the South remained in the Union after ABRAHAM LINCOLN and the REPUBLICAN PARTY won the presidential election in 1860, Rhett drafted South Carolina's Ordinance of Secession. In 1861 Rhett took part in writing the Confederate Constitution. Because of his extremist position, Rhett was not selected for the presidency of the Confederacy, and in 1863 he was defeated in a race for a seat in Congress. When the Civil War ended he refused to apply for a pardon from his Yankee enemies.

The third big gun in the fire-eater arsenal, William Yancey, the "orator of secession," was one of the most fervent advocates of states' rights and slavery. Yancey demanded that Southerners have the right to take their slaves into western territories and, as the years passed, his belief in the inalienable rights of states grew. He strongly opposed the Compromise of 1850 and proposed a Southern Confederacy as early as 1858. Yancey helped create Alabama's Secession Ordinance after Lincoln was elected president, and he served as a Confederate senator.

As early as 1850, at a convention held in Nashville, Tennessee, these three men along with the rest of the fire-eaters urged secession upon the South. However, after the Compromise of 1850, a more moderate council met and managed to compromise enough to postpone that event for another 10 years. Although the fire-eaters were in large measure responsible for the movement to organize a separate Southern government, they filled only minor offices under the Confederacy.

See also CONFEDERATE STATES OF AMERICA.

Further reading: William C. Davis, *Rhett: The Turbulent Life and Times of a Fire-Eater* (Columbia: University of South Carolina Press, 2001); David S. Heidler, *Pulling the Temple Down: The Fire-Eaters and the Destruction of the Union* (Mechanicsburg, Pa.: Stackpole Books, 1994); Eric H. Walther, *The Fire-Eaters* (Baton Rouge: Louisiana State University Press, 1992).

—Emily E. Holst

Fitzhugh, George (1806–1881)

Staunch proSLAVERY advocate, writer, and lawyer, George Fitzhugh was born in Prince William County, Virginia, on November 4, 1806. He married Mary Metcalf Brockenbrough in 1829 and obtained a small plantation in Virginia.

In the 1850s Fitzhugh became known as one of the fiercest defenders of slavery. He wrote dozens of essays for the RICHMOND *Enquirer* and *De Bow's Review* that attacked modern capitalist society and defended slavery. Fitzhugh republished several of these essays in *Sociology for the South: or the Failure of Free Society* (1854) and later expanded on other articles in *Cannibals All!, or, Slaves without Masters* (1857). These writings defended and promoted the institution of slavery on moral and economic terms.

In *Sociology for the South,* Fitzhugh argued that not only had slavery "produced the same results in elevating the character of the master that it did in Greece and Rome" but that slavers were "as happy as a human being can be" under the Southern slave system. Fitzhugh contended that, unlike the free-labor North, in "the slaveholding South all is peace, quiet, plenty and contentment. We have no mobs, no trades unions, no strikes for higher wages, no armed resistance to the law, [and] but little jealousy of the rich by the poor." In *Cannibals All!,* Fitzhugh continued his argument against free labor, contending that a "free laborer must work or starve. He is more of a slave than the Negro, because he works longer and harder for less allowance."

Fitzhugh's theories about slavery stemmed from his personal experiences as a slaveowner, his reading about the conditions in English factories, and a trip to Boston, Massachusetts, in 1855. There, after delivering a series of lectures and discussing slavery with ABOLITIONists such as HARRIET BEECHER STOWE, Fitzhugh became even more convinced of the virtue of slavery. Fitzhugh used his writings to explain the evils of the Industrial Revolution and the comparative morality of slavery over free-labor systems.

Fitzhugh did not devote his entire life to the writings for which he is most remembered. In 1857 and 1858 he worked as a law clerk in WASHINGTON, D.C., for Attorney General Jeremiah Sullivan Black. When the CIVIL WAR began, Fitzhugh supported the Confederacy, and in 1862 he moved to Richmond, Virginia, where he served as a clerk in the Confederate Treasury Department.

When the war ended, he worked for the FREEDMEN'S BUREAU as a judge and continued to write articles on agriculture for *De Bow's Review* and other periodicals. Fitzhugh died on July 30, 1881, after suffering from near-blindness and insomnia.

See also PLANTATIONS.

Further reading: George Fitzhugh and Hinton Rowan Helper, *Antebellum Writings of George Fitzhugh and Hinton Rowan Helper on Slavery,* ed. Harvey Wish (New York: Capricorn Books, 1960); Harvey Wish, *George Fitzhugh: Propagandist of the Old South* (Gloucester, Mass.: Peter Smith, 1962).

—Andrew K. Frank

Five Forks, Battle of (March 30–April 1, 1865)

The Battle at Five Forks, Virginia, was the first engagement in Gen. ULYSSES S. GRANT's Appomattox campaign. The goal of the battle was to cut Gen. ROBERT E. LEE's supply lines coming down the South Side Railroad into Petersburg. If the Union succeeded, they would gain Petersburg, force the evacuation of RICHMOND, and place themselves between Lee and JOSEPH EGGLESTON JOHNSTON's Confederate armies, thus preventing Lee from moving south. Grant placed Maj. Gen. PHILIP H. SHERIDAN at the head of the Union forces, while Maj. Gen. GEORGE E. PICKETT was placed at the head of the Confederate forces. Lee's instructions to Pickett were clear: "Hold Five Forks at all hazards."

Lee positioned 19,000 soldiers at the Five Forks road junction, a mere three miles from the South Side Railroad. Pickett had at his command a division of his own along with three mounted cavalry divisions commanded by Maj. Gen. Fitzhugh Lee (nephew of Gen. Robert E. Lee). Sheridan commanded the Union cavalry as well as being given the V Corps, which was commanded by Maj. Gen. Gouverneur K. Warren, totaling almost 50,000 men.

At 1 P.M. on April 1, Sheridan ordered the cavalry divisions of Brig. Gens. George A. Custer and Thomas A. Devin to attack Pickett's right flank, which was held by Confederate cavalry. The plan was to then have the V Corps jointly attack on Pickett's left, which was held by his own infantry division. Unfortunately, Warren was slow to act and the opportunity to crush Pickett nearly slipped by. By 4 P.M., out of Warren's three divisions, commanded by Generals Ayers, Griffen, and Crawford, only Ayers's division was in place to attack the 90-degree angle in Pickett's line. Griffen's and Crawford's divisions had swung too far to their right to be effective. In a moment of overconfidence during the battle, Pickett and Fitzhugh Lee left the battle briefly to have a drink, only to return to a surprise. Ayers' division had been enough to breach Pickett's line.

The rebels were captured in large numbers, and Grant was able to interpose his force between the two main Confederate armies. The victory, which came to be called the "Confederate Waterloo," was such a great success for the Union that when on April 2 Gen. Grant ordered an attack on the center of the rebel lines at Petersburg, they broke easily, and the Confederates were forced to evacuate the city in a rush. Five Forks also caused Lee to remove Pickett from command, while Sheridan, despite the Union victory, removed Warren from command due to his sluggish action in the battle.

See also OVERLAND CAMPAIGN.

Further reading: Edwin C. Bearss, *The Battle of Five Forks* (Lynchburg, Va.: H. E. Howard, 1985).

—Arthur E. Amos

food riots

One of the most serious problems facing the CONFEDERATE STATES OF AMERICA during the CIVIL WAR was supplying its armies and its civilians. Although most Southerners lived on farms and PLANTATIONS, by the end of the war many parts of the Confederacy simply did not have enough food.

There were a number of reasons for shortages in cities and specific regions of the Confederacy. A major factor was simply the occupation of farming country and the destruction or confiscation of crops and livestock by Union troops. Other important reasons included the presence of hundreds of thousands of hungry Union and Confederate soldiers in places such as northern Virginia, western Tennessee, and central Mississippi, making it almost impossible for civilians living in those areas to get enough food; the inability of the South to keep roads open and RAILROADS operating; the crowding of thousands of REFUGEES into towns and cities; the enrollment of many farmers in the CONFEDERATE ARMY; and the tightening blockade of Southern ports. All of these caused people to go hungry and, in some cases, to starve in many parts of the Confederacy. To make matters worse, rising prices made it hard for people to buy the goods that were available. With inflation rates in the four figures, one Virginia woman discovered late in the war that $100 in Confederate money bought a few pounds of fatty bacon, three candles, and a pound of poor butter.

The Confederate government tried to force planters to raise food crops rather than cotton, and local governments sometimes set up markets at which poor people or the families of soldiers could buy necessities at relatively low prices. In addition, Southerners found a number of clever substitutes for their normal diet, with unusual replacements for coffee, salt, sugar, and other basics. But none of these actions solved the problem of hunger in the Confederacy. Not surprisingly, many Southern civilians grew angry about this state of affairs. When residents of towns or cities believed that Confederate government or military officials were keeping food from them, riots broke out. Disturbances occurred in large cities such as Atlanta, Macon, Columbus, and Augusta, Georgia, and in smaller towns like Salisbury and High Point, North Carolina, and Sherman, Texas. Even in Mobile, Alabama, one of the last ports in the Confederacy to be captured by the Union, residents feared in the fall of 1864 that there would not be enough food to last through the winter. A mob waving signs that demanded "bread or blood" looted the stores on one of the city's main streets. Eventually, almost every Confederate state had experienced at least one riot over food shortages.

The most famous food riot took place in RICHMOND, Virginia, in April 1863. With a population that grew larger every week, with its nearby farmland frequently occupied or fought over by both armies, and with sometimes unreliable TRANSPORTATION links to other parts of the Confederacy, Richmond was one of the most crowded and most expensive cities in the Confederacy. A complicated pass system—the army wanted to make sure that spies did not enter the Confederate capital—discouraged farmers from coming into the city to sell their products. A heavy snowfall in mid-March was the last straw, and hard-pressed women, desperate to feed their families, began gathering at a Baptist church on April 2. They decided to march to the state capital to ask for help from Governor John Letcher. Along the way, other women—and a number of men and boys—joined them. Letcher spoke briefly to the several hundred people gathered outside the governor's mansion, but when he went back inside without giving them any answers, the crowd turned violent: Some took out hatchets, a few pulled pistols out of their pockets. The mob spread over a 10-square-block area, breaking into stores, taking not only bread and meat but also jewelry, clothes, and other items. The governor and mayor failed to calm them, and the mob did not pause until a small unit of Confederate troops and President JEFFERSON DAVIS appeared in their path. Davis threw all of the money he had in his pockets at the rioters, then took out his pocket watch and declared that if they did not disperse in five minutes, the soldiers would fire on them. When the captain commanding the men loudly ordered them to load their rifles, the rioters went home.

Sometimes riots did not end so peacefully. Late in the war, when a group of Galveston, Texas, residents and a few soldiers stationed in the city demanded that local officials share the military provisions stored in the city, a Confederate regiment fired over the heads of the protesters, accidentally killing one of the protesting soldiers.

The food riots were minor episodes in the history of the Confederacy, but they exemplify how economic problems and political and social differences weakened the Confederate war effort.

See also ECONOMY.

Further reading: Mary Elizabeth Massey, *Ersatz in the Confederacy: Shortages and Substitutes on the Southern Homefront* (Columbia: University of South Carolina Press, 1952).

—James Marten

foraging

Foraging during the CIVIL WAR was widespread and controversial. There are two kinds of foraging: unofficial and official. The unofficial occurred when soldiers on the march or in camp indulged in unauthorized raids on civil-

ian property. For example, soldiers would seize pigs, chickens, eggs, and other foodstuffs to ease their hunger. This type of foraging occurred with as much regularity in the CONFEDERATE ARMY as it did in the UNION ARMY, and often with little care as to whether the civilians were friends or enemies. Southern families at times had as much to fear from their own countrymen as from Union soldiers. ROBERT E. LEE's men foraged liberally off the rich Pennsylvania farming countryside during the Gettysburg campaign of June and July 1863, as did ULYSSES S. GRANT's soldiers in Mississippi during the VICKSBURG CAMPAIGN at exactly the same time. Occasionally, groups of soldiers would go far beyond feasting and plunder the countryside. They would deliberately steal money, jewels, silver, and other valuables from helpless civilians. This type of behavior was branded as criminal, and soldiers caught in such acts were punished by military courts.

Official foraging, by contrast, was allowed under the international RULES OF WAR. Military commanders had the right to sustain their armies from goods taken from the countryside. This type of foraging was supposed to be conducted under strict rules and regulations. Even so, in the first two years of the war most Union commanders discouraged or prohibited foraging, fearing rightly that the behavior could degenerate into simple theft. WILLIAM T. SHERMAN, the Northern general most associated with the successful use of foraging, commented on the dangers: "The feeling of pillage and booty will injure the morale of the troops, and bring disgrace to their cause." As the war became harder, however, foraging became much more of a military necessity than expected and especially affected the TACTICS of the Northern side.

The most famous example of the dramatic expansion of the use of authorized foraging was in Sherman's "March to the Sea," begun in September 1864. His western soldiers confiscated and/or destroyed crops, food, livestock, and other valuables in an attempt to end the war by undermining the Southern ECONOMY and morale. Although Sherman's March became notorious for its supposedly wanton destruction, his raid was conducted under strict guidelines. The Union policy was to differentiate between sympathetic and hostile Southerners and act accordingly. It mattered, therefore, whether families in any one area were Unionist, took a neutral stance, or professed to be rabid SECESSIONists. The "secesh" fared by far the worst. Admittedly, there were times when soldiers ignored their orders and engaged in behavior far outside the regulations, sometimes with the approval of their officers. This was especially true in South Carolina, where many Union soldiers expressed an intense desire to punish the place "where treason began." Yet most historians now agree that far from being an uncontrolled spree, Sherman's soldiers acted with restraint and well within the bounds of the rules of war.

See also GETTYSBURG, BATTLE OF; SHERMAN'S MARCH THROUGH GEORGIA.

Further reading: Joseph T. Glatthaar, *The March to the Sea and Beyond: Sherman's Troops in the Savannahs and Carolinas Campaigns* (Baton Rouge: Louisiana State University Press, 1995); Bell Irvin Wiley, *The Common Soldier of the Civil War* (New York: Scribner, 1973).

foreign policy

Historians of American diplomatic affairs tend to use 1898, the date of the Spanish-American War, as the beginning date for the history of U.S. foreign policy. While it is true that the contours of U.S. diplomacy after this point are more familiar to modern Americans, the mid-19th-century United States was no stranger to foreign affairs. U.S. foreign policy from 1850 to 1880 was concerned with two main issues: American expansion and the CIVIL WAR.

As was the case with much of antebellum American politics, U.S. foreign affairs before the Civil War focused on territorial expansion. In the 1850s, while domestic political debates surrounded the potential expansion of SLAVERY in the West, U.S. diplomatic efforts focused on expanding the United States's influence and territorial holdings beyond continental boundaries. Throughout the mid to late 19th century, U.S. diplomatic overtures concentrated on three main areas: Hawaii, the Caribbean, and Latin America.

In Hawaii, the United States was interested in annexing the island kingdom or at the very least establishing favorable trade agreements and possibly a naval base and coaling depot for the United States in the Pacific. In August 1854, a treaty allowing for the annexation of the island chain was signed but later withdrawn by Hawaii's King Kamehameha IV. Hawaii would eventually be annexed, but not until the end of the century.

While the Hawaiian negotiations were souring, the United States was also making overtures in the Caribbean, especially Cuba, for a similar deal but with more emphasis on an American naval installation and coaling depot. In November 1854 the OSTEND MANIFESTO, a note to the secretary of state from the American foreign ministers to Britain, Spain, and France, suggested that the United States make every effort to secure Cuba from Spain. Shortly thereafter, the minister to Britain returned to the United States and was elected to the presidency. In his annual message to Congress in 1858, President JAMES BUCHANAN reiterated his belief that the United States should buy Cuba from Spain. The next year, Louisiana senator John Slidell proposed a plan to buy Cuba for $30 million, but his plan was soundly defeated.

The third area of American diplomatic concern, Latin America, saw the most action and intrigue in the years before the Civil War. In 1848 the U.S. Senate approved a treaty with Colombia, which was then called New Grenada. A year later, a treaty with Nicaragua was signed. In April 1850, the United States signed the Clayton-Bulwer Treaty in hopes of constructing an isthmian canal linking the Atlantic and Pacific Oceans. The treaty guaranteed the neutrality of the proposed canal and declared that neither the United States nor Britain would have solitary control of the project. Ultimately, the canal plan did not come to fruition as quickly as hoped. The canal proposal was a tremendous undertaking whose location and engineering had yet to be worked out. At the same time, the actions of the FRANKLIN PIERCE and Buchanan administrations left many Northerners convinced that the plan was just an excuse to spread slavery.

With the outbreak of the Civil War, U.S. foreign policy had one goal: reuniting the Union. To this end, the United States worked diplomatically to see that foreign nations recognized the war as an internal affair and did not support the efforts of the Confederacy. The CONFEDERATE STATES OF AMERICA, on the other hand, lobbied the powers of Europe diligently, first for "belligerent status," then for recognition, and finally for assistance and supplies.

The chief architect of the United States's foreign policy during the war years was Secretary of State WILLIAM H. SEWARD. Seward was entrusted with the important and often difficult task of keeping the French and British, Europe's two main superpowers, from aiding the Confederacy. Among Seward's first and most important goal was attaining British and French recognition of the U.S. blockade of Southern ports. The 1856 Declaration of Paris stated that only effective blockades would be honored, and the debate raged between the North, the South, and Europe as to whether or not the Union blockade was effective. In the early years of the war, blockade running was frequent and lucrative, and this seemed proof enough of Southern claims that the blockade need not be honored. But the South hurt its case by playing its "King Cotton" card. The Confederacy felt that its strongest international bargaining chip was its cotton crop, because Southern cotton fueled the British textile industry and kept Europe supplied with cotton cloth. As such, the Confederacy embargoed cotton, refusing to export it to the European market until Britain and France agreed to ignore the blockade. Unfortunately for the Confederacy, bumper cotton crops in previous years had left Europe with an abundance of warehoused cotton, and the Civil War was well underway by the time the embargo had any impact. Ultimately, rather than gaining the support of Britain and France, the embargo motivated Europe to explore other options, including cotton from Egypt, to fill their needs.

Confederate missteps played into the hands of the United States, which, under the leadership of Seward, worked to keep Europe from coming into the war by alternately threatening and cajoling. Seward advised Britain and France that war would be declared if they recognized or assisted the Confederacy. Seward also rebuffed European efforts to mediate the conflict early in the war, arguing that this was an internal dispute and not a case for international arbitration. The United States's concern was that any movement to arbitrate the war would give, at the very least, unofficial recognition to the Confederacy. Ultimately, in mid-1861, both Britain and France declared themselves to be neutral. These decisions were not welcomed by either the Union or the Confederacy, since Seward had fought hard for European powers to support the Union's cause alone, while the Confederacy badly needed European backing to make their war effort tenable.

Shortly after Britain and France declared their neutrality, a dramatic incident occurred that could have drastically altered the course of international relations during the Civil War. The "Trent affair," as it came to be called, began in the summer of 1861 with French pressure on the United States to ease the blockade restrictions, thus allowing an exchange of goods between the Confederacy and Europe. The French sought British assistance on the issue, but at that point the British were more dependent on Northern exports of grain than they were on Southern cotton, and so the French were on their own.

Confederate officials put further pressure on France by sending former U.S. senators James Mason and John Slidell to France to negotiate for formal recognition and assistance. Slidell and Mason's ship out of Charleston successfully evaded the Northern blockade ships, but once they transferred to the British ship *Trent* in Cuba, their luck ran out. The *Trent* was captured on November 8, 1861, by the USS *San Jacinto*, captained by Charles Wilkes. Wilkes claimed the ship as a prize of war and arrested Mason, Slidell, and their secretaries. The British were outraged, but the North lionized Wilkes as a hero. Tempers flared as the British made plans to bolster troop strength in Canada and send warships to the West Indies. Britain threatened to sever relations, and for some time it appeared as if they were on the brink of joining the war against the North. Seward convinced President ABRAHAM LINCOLN that complying with British demands for the Confederate officials' release was the wisest course of action, and the tensions passed.

Beyond recognition and issues of neutrality, Seward also had to prevent Britain and France from helping the Confederacy to build a navy. One of the key concerns of foreign ministers for the Confederacy was to secure naval-class ships for their war effort. With the seeming inability of Gen. GEORGE B. MCCLELLAN to secure Union victories early in the war, some British officials began to doubt that the North would prevail. In that climate, it seemed prudent to help outfit a rebel navy. Confederate president JEFFERSON DAVIS sent James D. Bulloch to England in 1861 to gain British help in refitting existing Confederate vessels into IRONCLADS and to commission new battleships. British shipbuilding concerns built the commerce raiders, *Alabama* and *Florida,* and converted an existing vessel into the rebel ram CSS *Atlanta.*

Such actions on the part of British manufacturers were in direct violation of Britain's declaration of neutrality, but they continued nonetheless. The *Alabama* eventually became extremely successful as a commerce raider, so much so that its name was given to the postwar claims lodged by the United States against Britain for losses due to commerce raiding. The "*Alabama* claims" went to an arbitration panel in Geneva in 1871. The United States argued that Britain should be held accountable for the entire cost of the Civil War from the BATTLE OF GETTYSBURG forward plus seven percent interest. The British, appalled at the American claim, were angry when the tribunal awarded the United States $15 million in 1872.

Seward regularly leveraged the United States's status as a member of the international community, as well as the country's economic might, to his advantage. He also had one other card to play: the slavery issue. Both Britain and France took issue with the Southern slave system, and once Lincoln issued the EMANCIPATION PROCLAMATION, British and French politicians found their ability to support the Confederacy circumscribed.

Even with all of the advantages the United States enjoyed, the Union faced a difficult road in European affairs. England and much of the rest of Europe wanted peace and the restoration of prewar trading. France had designs on Mexico, and it seemed to Napoleon III that the Confederacy would be willing to let him "have" Mexico in exchange for formal recognition. Mexico, in the mid-19th century, was having internal political trouble and was facing problems with foreign debt. In June 1863, Napoleon's 35,000 troops in Mexico captured Mexico City. In 1864, Archduke Maximilian was installed as emperor of Mexico with Napoleon's support. France might well have recognized the Confederacy at this point, but the war had turned against the South. By 1867, with continuing U.S. pressure, French support of Maximilian was removed, and the emperor was deposed and executed.

With the Civil War at an end and RECONSTRUCTION underway, U.S. diplomatic efforts once again focused on expansion and trade. With Secretary of State Seward still managing matters, the United States redoubled its efforts to gain bases and an isthmian canal. Seward wanted to build an American commercial empire, and for that he required strategic bases, trade treaties, and the ability to transport goods safely. Most notable of Seward's diplomatic maneuvers was the purchase of Alaska from Russia in 1867. Although the deal seemed rife with scandal, Seward pushed it through and the Senate ratified the purchase in April 1867. The acquisition of "Russian America" was attacked by some in the press, and the new territory was often labeled "Seward's Folly" or "Seward's Ice Box." The *New York Herald* called Alaska a "worthless desert," while the *New York World* ran headlines proclaiming "A Great Opening for Soda-Water Fountains and Skating Ponds." But Seward ran a countercampaign of LETTERS to the press, extolling the virtues of Alaska.

Seward's postwar diplomatic maneuvers were complicated by strained British-American relations. Not only was there anger over the *Alabama* claims and unofficial British support for the Confederate cause but Irish-American "Fenians" twice invaded British Canada after the Civil War, first in 1866 and then again in 1870. Despite these problems with Britain, by the 1870s the United States was attempting to make progress in all three of its key regions of interest. In 1870 the ULYSSES S. GRANT administration began its campaign for an American base in the Caribbean by attempting to buy Santo Domingo. Grant's representative, General Orville E. Babcock, successfully negotiated a treaty of annexation in November 1869, but CHARLES SUMNER, chairman of the Foreign Relation Committee, saw to it that the treaty was voted down by the Senate.

Defeated on the Santo Domingo issue, the Grant administration turned its attention to Cuba. From 1868 to 1878, Cuban insurgents rebelled against Spanish control with the help of the Cuban-American community. On several occasions, the United States and Spain came to the brink of war over Cuban insurgency. Tensions peaked in 1873 when Spain captured what the United States believed to be an American ship, killing her captain and some of the passengers and crew. An investigation later proved it was a Cuban ship, but Spain defused the situation by releasing the ship and paying $80,000 in reparations. Tensions between the United States and Spain over Cuba ultimately led to the 1898 Spanish-American War.

Also in the post–Civil War years, the United States continued to work on plans for an isthmian canal. In 1867 the Dickinson-Ayon Treaty with Nicaragua granted the United States transit rights through Nicaragua. In 1869 the United States secured a treaty with Colombia that allowed the United States the right to build a canal across the Colombian state of Panama. In 1872 President Grant appointed the Interoceanic Canal Commission to recommend a route for the canal. The Commission's report, released in 1876, said that the route through Nicaragua was preferable, but the United States lacked building rights to the Nicaragua route. Ultimately, the canal would not be built until the early 20th century.

In the Pacific, the United States continued to pursue its interest in Hawaii after the Civil War. In 1870 and 1871, Secretary of State Hamilton Fish once again laid the groundwork for the annexation of Hawaii by the United States. In 1873, when annexation plans fell through, Hawaii offered to cede Pearl Harbor to the United States for use as a base and coaling station in exchange for preferential tariff rates. In January 1875, the United States finally signed a treaty of reciprocity with Hawaii, although the treaty lacked an agreement about Pearl Harbor due to growing Hawaiian opposition to American control.

The mid-19th century, then, was a busy time in America's diplomatic history. The United States managed to keep the great powers of Europe at bay while settling the difficult issues of what "United States" really meant. The United States also made forays into expansionism, which laid the groundwork for subsequent moves in the Caribbean, Latin America, the Pacific, and Asia.

See also FILIBUSTERING.

Further reading: Eugene H. Berwanger, *The British Foreign Service and the American Civil War* (Lexington: University Press of Kentucky, 1994); Charles S. Campbell, *The Transformation of American Foreign Relations, 1865–1900* (New York: Harper & Row, 1976); Lynn M. Case and Warren F. Spencer, *The United States and France: Civil War Diplomacy* (Philadelphia: University of Pennsylvania Press, 1970); Howard Jones, *Abraham Lincoln and a New Birth of Freedom: The Union and Slavery in the Diplomacy of the Civil War* (Lincoln: University of Nebraska Press, 1999); Frank L. Owsley, *King Cotton Diplomacy: Foreign Relations of the Confederate States of America* (Chicago: University of Chicago Press, 1966); Ernest N. Paolino, *The Foundations of the American Empire: William Henry Seward and U.S. Foreign Policy* (Ithaca, N.Y.: Cornell University Press, 1973).

—Ruth A. Behling

Forrest, Nathan Bedford (1821–1877)

Businessman, planter, slave trader, politician, CONFEDERATE STATES OF AMERICA general, cavalry commander, and first grand wizard of the KU KLUX KLAN, Nathan Bedford Forrest has long been regarded as both a military genius and one of the most controversial figures of the CIVIL WAR. Although overrated in military skills, Forrest's cavalry consistently represented a major thorn in the side of Union forces. At one point, General WILLIAM T. SHERMAN exclaimed that Union soldiers must capture and kill Forrest even "if it costs ten thousand lives and breaks the treasury." At the end of the war, Forrest boasted that he had killed

30 men in hand-to-hand combat while having had only 29 horses shot out from under him. Forrest noted with pride that he remained one horse ahead.

Forrest was born in Tennessee and moved to Mississippi at the age of 21. His roots were in the Southern yeomanry and his EDUCATION was scanty, but his ambitious nature and his activities as a slave trader and planter brought him a large fortune. Immediately upon Tennessee's SECESSION from the Union, the 40-year-old Forrest enlisted as a private in the Seventh Tennessee Cavalry. However, under protest from the governor of Tennessee, Forrest was given the rank of lieutenant colonel and the opportunity to raise his own cavalry battalion. Forrest recruited and equipped a command at his own expense.

Forrest distinguished himself in battles at Fort Donelson and Shiloh, both Union victories, and in a raid directed at Union forces in the area of Murfreesboro, Tennessee. In late 1862, Forrest and his men devoted their energies to disrupting Grant's line of supply in west Tennessee. It was this raid, along with two others later that year, that made Forrest a hero throughout the South. His simple motto, "get there first with the most men," belied his growing reputation as a brilliant and daring commander who could strike fear into the heart of numerically superior forces.

In spite of Forrest's successful raids in Tennessee, the Confederate forces led by BRAXTON BRAGG retreated from the area. Forrest resented Bragg's decision to evacuate Tennessee. Moreover, he swore that if he ever met Bragg he would kill him. Because of the mutual animosities between these men, JEFFERSON DAVIS gave Forrest an independent command in Mississippi.

In April 1864, Forrest and his men attacked FORT PILLOW in Tennessee. The sacking of Fort Pillow marks the most controversial moment in Forrest's career. On April 12, Confederate marksmen had surrounded the fort and made life extremely difficult for the Union soldiers inside. After Forrest's men had control of the perimeter of the fort, Forrest offered the Union commander an opportunity to surrender. Forrest also stated that he could not be responsible for the safety of the Union soldiers if their commander refused. Since no surrender seemed forthcoming, Forrest's men seized the fort. In the ensuing melee, the 262 black Tennessee Unionists who composed the majority of the garrison suffered the most. Forrest's soldiers took 58 black prisoners; they killed the remainder, many of whom tried to surrender.

In June 1864, Forrest was victorious in two notable battles waged in the northeastern part of Mississippi. Historians generally regard these battles, known as Brice's Crossroads and the Battle of Tupelo, as Forrest's masterpieces. In the latter battle, Forrest was injured and unable to lead his men from horseback. Instead, he moved about the battlefield in a horsecart, giving orders that kept his men one step ahead of all Union movements.

After the battle at Tupelo, Forrest and his men ranged over northern Alabama and Tennessee harassing Union soldiers, raiding various supply depots, and destroying RAILROADS. Forrest also accompanied Confederate Gen. JOHN BELL HOOD in his unsuccessful attempt to take back Tennessee for the Confederacy. When Hood's men retreated from Nashville, Forrest displayed his ferocity in protecting the Confederate retreat.

Forrest was promoted to lieutenant general in February 1865 and spent the last months of the war trying to put together a force of men in Mississippi. However, Union cavalry outnumbered his command to such an extent that it was no longer possible to engage them successfully. Forrest finally surrendered his forces in May 1865, a little over a month after Appomattox. "I went into the army worth a million and a half dollars," he said, "and came out a beggar."

Forrest's postwar career is nearly as controversial as his wartime career. Forrest tried to regain his fortune through railroad building and insurance enterprises, but he was not successful. In 1867 Forrest became the first grand wizard

Nathan Bedford Forrest *(Library of Congress)*

of the Ku Klux Klan. Forrest demanded that the Klan operate to defend the people of Tennessee, that it only use violence in self-defense, and that it keep within the bounds of chivalry. Because he was unable to control Klan activity within those guidelines, Forrest disbanded the organization and gave up his command. His disbandment order had little effect outside Tennessee, and the Klan has continued to exist in one form or another ever since. In 1871 Congress called an uncooperative Forrest to testify concerning his involvement with the Klan.

In his last years, Forrest's physical health deteriorated, in particular due to diabetes. He died in Memphis on October 29, 1877, at the age of 56.

See also SHILOH, BATTLE OF.

Further reading: Jack Hurst, *Nathan Bedford Forrest: A Biography* (New York: Knopf, 1993); Brian Steel Willis, *Battle from the Start: The Confederacy's Greatest Cavalryman: Nathan Bedford Forrest* (Lawrence: University Press of Kansas, 1992).

—Chad Vanderford

Fort Pillow, Tennessee (April 12, 1864)

Fort Pillow was the site of an 1864 massacre of mostly African-American Union soldiers by troops under the command of Confederate general NATHAN BEDFORD FORREST. Located 40 miles north of Memphis on the Chickasaw Bluffs, Fort Pillow was built in 1861 as a Confederate fortification overlooking the MISSISSIPPI RIVER. Confederate troops abandoned the fort in June 1862 after Union victories in the area jeopardized their position. For the next two years Union troops intermittently occupied the site.

On April 12, 1864, Confederate general Nathan Bedford Forrest led about 1,500 troops in an attack on the fort, then garrisoned by just over 500 Union soldiers, nearly half of them black. During the initial fighting, Forrest's sharpshooters killed Maj. Lionel F. Booth, the fort's commander. Forrest then demanded that the fort surrender, guaranteeing the safety of Union soldiers inside—an offer which, Forrest's representatives avowed, included black soldiers as well. Maj. William E. Bradford, who took command on Booth's death, refused to give up the fort. Forrest's men, positioned in well-protected ravines below the fortification's low earth walls, now attacked. In about 20 minutes they had overrun the works.

As Union soldiers surrendered, Bedford ordered that they be cut down. Wrote one Confederate soldier, "The poor deluded Negroes would run up to our men, fall upon their knees . . . for mercy, but they were ordered to their feet and then shot down. . . . The fort turned out to be a great slaughter pen. . . . Gen. Forrest ordered them shot down like dogs. . . . Finally our men became sick of blood

and the firing ceased." By the end of the battle, 64 percent of black and 33 percent of white Union soldiers had been killed. Bedford had lost 14 men.

The massacre instantly outraged Northerners. Congressman BENJAMIN WADE demanded an investigation, while President ABRAHAM LINCOLN considered executing selected Southern prisoners of war. Fearing a cycle of retaliatory violence, Lincoln decided against that extremity; even so, the phrase "Remember Fort Pillow!" became a battle cry among white soldiers as well as black.

Forrest later denied any massacre had taken place, claiming that his troops faced gunfire even after the fort had raised the white flag of surrender and that he had acted accordingly. Some historians have argued that Forrest and his soldiers were enraged at the extortion, lawlessness, and destruction they believed that Union soldiers had visited on Tennessee. Some of the worst offenders, Forrest believed, were Tennessee Unionists at Fort Pillow. Others argue that Forrest himself tried to halt the bloodshed but was unsuccessful.

Historians note that it was Confederate policy to execute African Americans wearing the Union blue. Though enforced inconsistently, many Confederate officials believed the policy was a necessary defense against "servile rebellion" and a rebuke to Northerners intent on sending "savages" against the South. The policy extended to white officers commanding black regiments, a fact that may explain the shooting death of Major Bradford in Confederate custody a few days after the battle.

No one disputes that it was Forrest's practice to offer protection to besieged adversaries if they surrendered, while promising dire consequences if they refused. At Fort Pillow, Forrest was true to his word.

Further reading: Richard L. Fuchs, *An Unerring Fire: The Massacre at Fort Pillow* (Rutherford, N.J.: Fairleigh Dickinson University Press, 1994).

—Tom Laichas

Fort Sumter, South Carolina (April 11–12, 1861)

Located on a man-made island at the entrance to Charleston Harbor, Fort Sumter was the site of the first shots of the CIVIL WAR. Attention was first drawn to this federal outpost immediately following the election of ABRAHAM LINCOLN in November 1860. Fort Sumter was owned by the federal government but was not yet occupied by U.S. troops due to its construction having just been completed. South Carolinians, who had recently seceded from the Union, found the garrison to be a threat to their security and a challenge to their sovereignty. The *Charleston Mercury* explained to its readers that other Southern states would never take the cause seriously until "we have proven

Interior view of Fort Sumter on April 14, 1861, after its evacuation *(National Archives)*

that a garrison of seventy men cannot hold the portal of our commerce."

South Carolina's governor, Francis Pickens, claimed he had an unwritten agreement with President JAMES BUCHANAN. The agreement was that U.S. major ROBERT ANDERSON (who commanded the federal forces in Charleston harbor) and his men would remain at Fort Moultrie, another fort in the Charleston Harbor. Anderson, however, viewed Fort Moultrie as indefensible from land and therefore considered moving his men to the more secure location provided by Fort Sumter. Immediately after Anderson received authorization to do just that from the Buchanan administration, he moved his small force onto boats and occupied Fort Sumter on the night of December 26, 1860.

When the news broke, Governor Pickens immediately sent his military aide, Col. J. Johnston Pettigrew, to meet with Anderson and to request that he and his men return to Fort Moultrie. Anderson refused his request, and in response Pickens assembled battery units on Morris Island. Anderson sent word to the Buchanan administration that his men needed reinforcements and supplies if they were to hold Fort Sumter. Buchanan decided to send

an unarmed merchant ship, the *Star of the West*, loaded with 200 civilian-dressed recruits, thus reinforcing the fort without overtly threatening South Carolina authorities. However, despite the efforts to remain secret, news about the ship's mission and destination quickly spread after its departure from NEW YORK CITY on January 5, 1861. As a result, when the ship neared the Charleston Harbor on January 9, it was unable to make it past the guns at Fort Moultrie, and it was forced to turn back and leave Anderson and his men without their reinforcements and supplies. Following the *Star of the West* incident, Pickens added to the ring of battery units that surrounded Fort Sumter. On January 11, Pickens sent a note to Anderson requesting the surrender of the fort. Once again, Anderson refused, and the opposing forces remained stalemated for two months.

On March 1, 1861, three days before Abraham Lincoln took his oath of office, Confederate president JEFFERSON DAVIS assigned Confederate brigadier general P. G. T. BEAUREGARD command of the military situation in Charleston. Immediately, Beauregard strengthened the defenses of both the harbor entrance and the battery units facing Fort Sumter. Shortly after Lincoln's inauguration,

Anderson reported to the president that the garrison was very low on supplies and would need reinforcements as well as naval support to successfully hold the fort. Meanwhile, the Lincoln administration could not come to an agreement about the current situation at Fort Sumter. WILLIAM H. SEWARD, Lincoln's secretary of state, and Gen. Winfield Scott, commanding general of the U.S. Army agreed that Anderson and his men should evacuate the island, but Lincoln felt he needed to learn more about the situation before making a decision. As a result, the Lincoln administration sent a number of unofficial delegates to determine the situation of the fort and its occupants.

Despite the pleas of many of his advisors, President Lincoln decided to send relief to Fort Sumter. On April 6, Lincoln sent word to Governor Pickens that reinforcements were being sent to Fort Sumter. The administration felt that this warning left it up to the Confederate authorities as to whether or not a war would take place, therefore supporting their defensive strategy concerning the outbreak of the war. On April 10, the USS *Powhatan* left for Fort Sumter.

Following Lincoln's message to Pickens, the Confederate secretary of war, Leroy Pope Walker, instructed Beauregard to demand that Anderson surrender the fort and to conquer the fort if Anderson refused the request for surrender. Upon receiving these instructions, Beauregard began positioning his men and equipment to prepare adequately for an artillery assault on Fort Sumter as well as to prevent any reinforcements from successfully landing and resupplying the fort.

On the afternoon of April 11, 1861, a Confederate delegation was sent by Beauregard to Fort Sumter to demand the immediate surrender of the fort. After a unanimous vote by the federal officers, Anderson once again refused to evacuate. The rebels advised Anderson that firing would begin early the next morning. At 4:30 A.M. on April 12, 1861, a signal gun was fired, alerting all the batteries to begin firing—the Civil War had begun.

Despite a hard first day's fight for Anderson and his men, the end seemed in sight when the garrison spotted three U.S. ships off the harbor. However, unbeknownst to them at the time, the reinforcement ships would never be able to make it past the harbor entrance batteries and, therefore, would not be able to assist Anderson. As a result, after deliberating with Beauregard's delegates, Anderson set the time for the surrender for the following day, April 14, 1861.

The first shots had been fired in the Civil War. Though the opening volleys were not deadly, they opened the door to a conflict that cost both North and South dearly in both lives and money. On April 15, 1861, President Lincoln issued a call for 75,000 volunteers to help restore the Union, and Jefferson Davis responded in kind. Preparations began in earnest for America's Civil War.

Further reading: Richard N. Current, *Lincoln and the First Shot* (Philadelphia: Lippincott, 1963); William A. Swanberg, *First Blood: The Story of Fort Sumter* (New York: Scribner's, 1957).

—Megan Quinn

Foster, Stephen C. (1826–1864)

Songwriter and composer Stephen Collins Foster wrote MUSIC that represented the heartfelt sentiments and folksy way of life of most 19th-century Americans. Enduring classics such as "Oh! Susannah" ("I come from Alabama, with my banjo on my knee") and "Camptown Races" remain beloved tunes to the present day. Among other distinctions, Foster was the first "professional" songwriter in the United States. From 1850 to his death, he lived only off the income he earned from the sale of his music. A contemporary critic summed up Foster's impact in this way: "The air is full of his melodies. They are our national music."

Foster was born on July 4, 1826, in Lawrenceville, Pennsylvania, the 10th of 11 children. His father was a politician and merchant who fell on hard times but managed to maintain his family's middle-class existence. Foster's parents encouraged their children's love of music with piano lessons and recitals. Stephen received a good EDUCATION and was tutored in music by a teacher in Pittsburgh.

Foster's parents expected their talented son to take a job in the business world, which he did, at first. Hired as a bookkeeper, Foster felt out of place in an office. He quit and dedicated himself to music. Foster's first published song, "Open Thy Lattice Love," was in print by the time he was 20. In 1850 he had 12 compositions in print and felt secure enough to marry his sweetheart, Jane MacDowell, with whom he had a daughter, Marion. His income was based on 10 percent royalties of his sheet-music sales. Foster's compositions were not protected by copyright. Thus, while arrangers and publishers made thousands of dollars from his music, his own income remained limited, and he and his family struggled at near-poverty levels for much of the time.

Possessed of a sensitive ear for the cadence of language and style, Foster began his career in Pittsburgh, where he lived for most of his short but productive life. Writing tender, lyrical ballads for parlor singers and pianists, such as "Jeanie with the Light Brown Hair," Foster studied the various musical and poetic styles of immigrant populations. The first songwriter to weave African-American, German,

Irish, Italian, Scottish, and English music into one style, Foster created a distinctly American type of song.

Soon, Foster's music was wildly popular among the growing middle-class families who had a piano in their newly added parlor. But his influence was also widely felt in the musical THEATER, as well, and reached out to large immigrant and working-class audiences. Many of his most well-known songs were composed for minstrel shows, where white actors posed as African Americans in black face. Foster's songs for minstrel shows were written in dialect. This genre of songs exposed white audiences to the slaves' point of view, to their cruel treatment, and to the fact that African Americans were capable of the same feelings as white people. "My Old Kentucky Home, Good Night" is deeply evocative of the pain slaves endured. Another famous example is "Way Down upon the Swanee River."

Foster was the first songwriter to refer to an African-American woman as a "lady" in "Nellie Was a Lady" (1849). Although the dialect he created for minstrel shows was vulgar, Foster attempted to provide a more human view of African Americans to counteract the racism of the time. With this approach, Foster also made minstrel music more acceptable to the middle class and to female audiences.

When the approach of the CIVIL WAR found Foster bankrupt, he combined forces with George Cooper to produce two Civil War songs, "Willie Has Gone to War" and "For the Dear Old Flag I Die." However, by the age of 37, Foster was separated from his family, in ill health, penniless, and living alone in NEW YORK CITY. Weakened by fever, he fell and cut himself on his washbasin, which led to his death on January 13, 1864.

Further reading: Ken Emerson, *Doo-Dah!: Stephen Foster and the Rise of American Popular Culture* (New York: Simon & Schuster, 1997); John Tasker Howard, *Stephen Foster, America's Troubadour* (New York: Crowell, 1953).

—Gina Ladinsky

Fourteenth Amendment (July 28, 1868)

The Fourteenth Amendment to the U.S. Constitution was ratified July 28, 1868, and was designed to extend the rights of citizenship to African Americans and to enfranchise black men. Section 1 was the key to the amendment; it declared that

> All persons born or naturalized in the United States, and subject to the jurisdiction thereof, are citizens of the United States and of the State wherein they reside. No State shall make or enforce any law which shall abridge the privileges or immunities of citizens of the

United States; nor shall any State deprive any person of life, liberty, or property, without due process of law; nor deny to any person within its jurisdiction the equal protection of the laws.

Section 2 enforced Section 1 by stating that any denial or abridgement of voting rights to eligible men would lead to a reduction in the offending state's national political representation.

Beyond the rights of citizenship and their bearing on suffrage, the other provisions of the Fourteenth Amendment barred any person from office who had previously held office and later "engaged in insurrection or rebellion." It targeted those individuals who had violated their oaths of office; however, such persons could be pardoned by a two-thirds vote from each house of the Congress. Section 4 rejected the Confederate debt while acknowledging the "validity" of the U.S. debt from the CIVIL WAR. It also invalidated claims for the "loss or emancipation of any slave." Finally, Section 5 gave Congress power to enforce these provisions.

The first two sections of the Fourteenth Amendment were enormously important because they moved to guarantee equality before the law. The intent of Section 1 was to reinforce and give meaning to the THIRTEENTH AMENDMENT by making states accountable for upholding all of the rights set forth in the Constitution. The Republican-dominated Congress was motivated by ideals of equality before the law and outrage at the BLACK CODES, legislation passed by Southern governments that deprived African Americans of their basic civil rights. Section 1 also superseded the notorious DRED SCOTT DECISION, where the Supreme Court declared that black people were not citizens of the United States. Suddenly, with the African-American population of the South no longer being counted as three-fifths of a person (as set forth in the Constitution's three-fifths clause) in population apportionments for seats in the House of Representatives, the South's population exploded, allowing them far greater representation in the House. Northern Republicans feared these additional Southern seats in the House and were wary that this resurgent power would come at the cost of denying the vote to African Americans in the South. Section 2 was designed to counter this perceived Southern advantage. Representation now would be based upon the number of actual voters and not just the potential number of voters. This was a roundabout way of encouraging Southern states to allow black suffrage, but it also implied that states could determine who qualified to vote, earning the anger of ABOLITIONists campaigning for universal suffrage.

Abolitionists were not the only angry voices raised over the wording of the Fourteenth Amendment. Feminists were outraged because for the first time the word "male" was added to the Constitution. Since representation was to be based on "male inhabitants," it indirectly sanctioned sexual discrimination at the ballot box. For many suffragists, the Fourteenth Amendment marked a critical moment in the history of feminism. It taught leaders, such as ELIZABETH CADY STANTON and Susan B. Anthony, that women could not rely upon men for the advocacy of their rights.

The far-reaching consequences of the Fourteenth Amendment's equal protection clause, privileges and immunities clause, and due process clause were blunted by the Supreme Court's early interpretations of the amendment. In the *Slaughterhouse* cases (1873), the Court ruled that basic civil rights and liberties fell under the authority of state governments, not the federal government. The Court further limited the scope of the amendment in *United States v. Cruikshank* (1876) by ruling that the federal government could only prohibit state government violations of black rights, not the actions of individuals. In 1896 the Fourteenth Amendment was further weakened; in *Plessy v. Ferguson*, the Court held that segregated railroad cars did not violate the equal protection clause. However, in the 20th century, the Supreme Court has reevaluated the Fourteenth Amendment. Though still controversial, it is considered one of the strongest Constitutional bulwarks in the defense of freedom and equality for all citizens.

Further reading: James Edward Bond, *No Easy Walk to Freedom: Reconstruction and the Ratification of the Fourteenth Amendment* (Westport, Conn.: Praeger, 1997); Joseph B. James, *The Ratification of the Fourteenth Amendment* (Macon, Ga.: Mercer University Press, 1984).

—Justin J. Behrend

Fredericksburg, Battle of (December 11–15, 1862)

The Battle of Fredericksburg in December 1862 was a tactical victory for the South. But rather than being a major cause for celebration, Fredericksburg only slowed rather than stopped the Union push toward RICHMOND.

The battle had its origins in a change in leadership on the Union side of the war effort. Frustrated with Gen. GEORGE B. MCCLELLAN's sluggishness in moving against ROBERT E. LEE's Army of Northern Virginia in the weeks following the Northern victory at the BATTLE OF ANTIETAM in September 1862, Lincoln decided to replace him as commander of the Army of the Potomac for the second and final time. His successor, Gen. AMBROSE E. BURNSIDE, assumed command on November 7. Urged on by impatient superiors, Burnside converted the army's cautious march southwest into a 40-mile quick march across the Vir-

ginia countryside to Fredericksburg in an attempt to secure a direct route to the Confederate capital at Richmond before Lee could re-form his army and respond. Burnside was quick to implement his plans, and by November 17 the lead units of his army arrived on Stafford Heights on the north bank of the Rappahannock River, opposite the town of Fredericksburg.

Burnside called for pontoon bridge equipment; however, due to a combination of bad weather and bureaucracy, the pontoons did not arrive until November 25. The delay gave Lee the time necessary to move Gen. JAMES LONGSTREET's corps to take up positions along the terraced slopes south of town. Lee did not know where the Union army would cross the river, so, when Gen. THOMAS J. "STONEWALL" JACKSON's troops arrived a few days later, he sent them as far as 20 miles downriver to cover all potential crossings.

Reasoning that if he moved quickly he could concentrate his superior force on Longstreet's corps alone, Burnside ordered two pontoon spans erected opposite the city and another a mile downstream. In the early morning hours of December 11, Union engineers began laying pontoons but soon gave up the effort in the face of withering musket fire from Mississippians on the southern bank. After nine unsuccessful attempts to complete the bridges throughout the day, a small force of volunteers finally managed to cross the river at dusk and drive the rebel sharpshooters from the town. Burnside's army began crossing into Fredericksburg during the night.

Burnside issued no orders for an attack on the morning of December 12; instead, the Union troops spent the day looting the town. Meanwhile, having observed the enemy crossing, Lee sent for Jackson's scattered corps. A quick march brought the corps to the field and in position on Longstreet's right by dawn on December 13.

Painting depicting the Battle of Fredericksburg *(Library of Congress)*

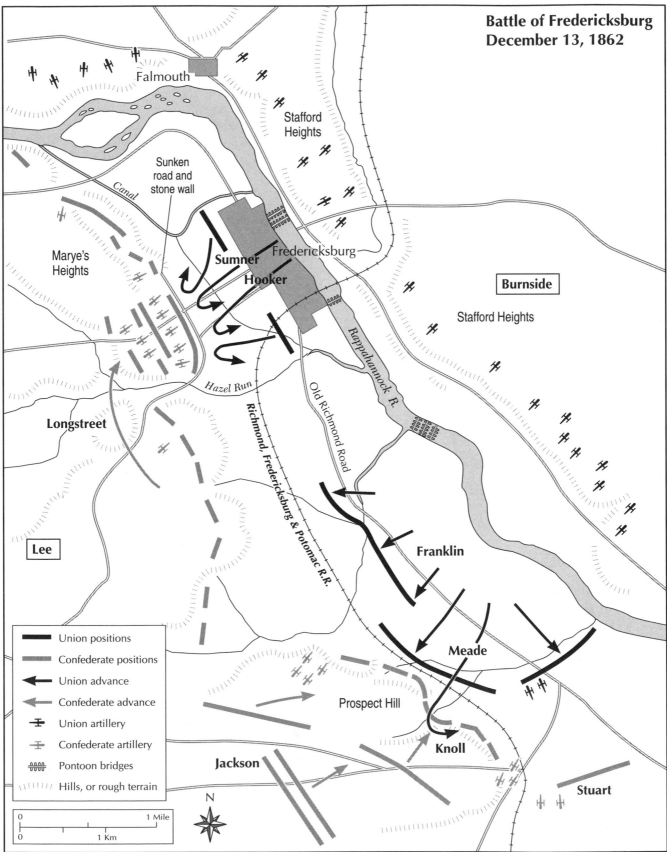

**Battle of Fredericksburg
December 13, 1862**

Falmouth

Stafford
Heights

Sunken
road and
stone wall

Canal

Marye's
Heights

Sumner

Fredericksburg

Hooker

Burnside

Stafford Heights

Rappahannock R.

Longstreet

Hazel Run

Old Richmond Road

Richmond, Fredericksburg & Potomac R.R.

Lee

Franklin

Meade

Prospect Hill

Knoll

Jackson

Stuart

	Union positions
	Confederate positions
	Union advance
	Confederate advance
	Union artillery
	Confederate artillery
	Pontoon bridges
	Hills, or rough terrain

0   1 Mile

0   1 Km

N

Burnside planned to attack Longstreet's positions with part of his army while launching a strong flanking attack on Lee's right with 55,000 men. At 8:30 A.M., Gen. GEORGE G. MEADE's brigade of Pennsylvanians moved against Jackson, only to be beaten back by both frontal and flanking artillery fire. Resuming their attack, Meade's men stumbled into a section of woods that had been left unprotected by Jackson and briefly managed to pierce the rebel lines. Having anticipated the possibility of a break along his lines, Jackson counterattacked with his reserves, driving the Federals back to their original positions.

On the Union right, Burnside ordered a series of assaults over the plain south of town toward a sunken road and stone wall along the base of Marye's Heights. Over the course of the afternoon, one Union brigade after another was hurled against the stone wall, only to be shattered and repulsed by the artillery on the crest of Marye's Heights and the musketry of Longstreet's infantry, standing four deep in the sunken road along its base. In one 600-yard section of the line, more than 30,000 Federals were sent against a position occupied by 7,000 Confederates, who shot them down en masse, leaving 9,000 dead and wounded in their front. It was at this point in the battle that Lee turned to Longstreet and uttered his famous comment, "It is well that war is so terrible! We should grow too fond of it!"

As the day came to a close, Burnside withdrew his battered brigades to the town while the cries of the wounded, "weird, unearthly, terrible to hear and bear," rose in the bitter-cold winter night. Burnside's determination to personally lead a resumption of the attacks the next day met with stubborn resistance from all of his subordinates, who saw no better prospects for success. Burnside reluctantly withdrew his army across the river over the next two days, pulling up his bridges behind him.

As the armies settled into winter camps, the tactical victory of the Battle of Fredericksburg belonged to Robert E. Lee. However, the Confederates had lost more than 5,000 men whom they could not easily replace. While the Federals had lost more than twice that number, the steady stream of replacements from the North soon brought the Army of the Potomac back to its original strength. The real legacy of the battle was the devastating impact on the morale of the Northern populace and its army. Hearing of the terrible, tragic losses of men, Lincoln sadly remarked, "If there is a worse place than Hell, I am in it." Seven months would pass, two more commanders would succeed Ambrose E. Burnside, and the BATTLES OF CHANCELLORSVILLE and GETTYSBURG would be fought before the Army of the Potomac would regain its esprit de corps.

Further reading: Gary Gallagher, ed., *The Fredericksburg Campaign: Decision on the Rappahannock* (Chapel Hill: University of North Carolina Press, 1995); William Marvel, *Burnside* (Chapel Hill: University of North Carolina Press, 1991).

—Don Worth

Free-Soil Party   See Volume IV

Freedman's Saving Bank (1865–1874)

Also known as the Freedman's Saving and Trust Company, the Freedman's Saving Bank was chartered as a private corporation in March 1865. The bank was the first financial institution specifically meant for the savings of recently emancipated African Americans. The mutual savings bank was undertaken with a dual mission of providing financial stability for freedpeople and inculcating the middle-class habits needed for them to succeed in a system of free labor. As such, many prominent African Americans and their supporters in Congress welcomed the bank and its educative agenda. Henry Wilson, vice president of the United States under ULYSSES S. GRANT, remarked enthusiastically that the hard-earned dollars of freed people were "just as safe there as if it were in the Treasury of the United States."

Headquartered in WASHINGTON, D.C., the Freedman's Saving Bank opened 37 branches throughout the South. Each office employed African-American tellers and appointed leaders of the local community to the advisory boards of the various branches. The bank worked hand in hand with other respected black institutions, such as the FREEDMEN'S BUREAU and churches, to encourage customers to use its services. Newspaper advertisements often prominently featured ABRAHAM LINCOLN in the background, giving the distinct impression of government endorsement. John W. Alvord, president of the bank, presided over a conservative institution that received depositors' money and invested in government securities but did not make any loans. This sensible policy won the respect and the business of 100,000 customers and assets of $4 million. Deposits ranged anywhere from a few pennies to around $50, but all were welcomed. In addition to individual deposits, many African-American organizations eagerly put their treasuries into the bank.

In 1870 Congress amended the bank's charter to allow speculative investments and loans. Unfortunately, a combination of bad investments, corrupt practices, and the effects of the Panic of 1873 led to financial insolvency. In 1875 the Freedman's Saving Bank closed its doors forever. Attempts made by friends of the bank failed to secure full financial restitution to investors. "I pray you to consider us old People," wrote one former customer, "our best life spent in Slavery. . . . Just asking for what we worked for." The failure of the Freedman's Bank, and the inability of former slaves to regain their deposits, explained why many African Americans distrusted financial institutions for decades afterwards.

See also RECONSTRUCTION.

Further reading: Carl R. Osthaus, *Freedmen, Philanthropy, and Fraud: A History of the Freedman's Saving Bank* (Urbana: University of Illinois Press, 1976).

Freedmen's Bureau (Bureau of Freedmen, Refugees, and Abandoned Lands) (1865–1872)

Congress created the Bureau of Refugees, Freedmen, and Abandoned Lands, commonly known as the Freedmen's Bureau, on March 4, 1865, to help ex-slaves negotiate the transition from SLAVERY to freedom. The primary task of the Freedmen's Bureau was to transform the South into a free-labor society. The Bureau's 900 agents had the nearly impossible task of introducing a free-labor system; educating the freedmen; aiding the ill, insane, aged, and poor; passing judgment on interracial quarrels; and instituting an impartial justice system. The bureau was continually understaffed, underfunded, and subject to opposition from hostile Southern whites. For all of its limitations and weaknesses, however, the Freedmen's Bureau demonstrated the federal government's commitment to making freedom a reality for ex-slaves.

The bureau was designed to meet the needs of ex-slaves at the end of the war. CONTRABAND camps throughout the South strained under the burden of provisioning thousands of freedpeople who had fled their masters. In 1863 the American Freedmen's Inquiry Commission suggested the creation of a permanent institution to meet the needs of war REFUGEES and to help ex-slaves become self-reliant. As a measure of the enormity of the endeavor, more than 21 million rations were distributed to destitute black and white Southerners over the life of the Freedmen's Bureau.

Attached to the War Department, the bureau was charged with distributing aid and helping the former slaves attain land ownership. Commissioner General O. O. HOWARD headed the agency and was assisted by 10 assistant commissioners, one commissioner for each of the 11 former Confederate states. Howard was a CIVIL WAR general, a devout Christian, and a strong advocate of civil rights for recently emancipated slaves. The Freedmen's Bureau legislation authorized Howard, as commissioner, to divide abandoned lands into 40-acre plots for settlement by freedmen families and to set up lease agreements for a term of three years at a low interest rate. At the end of the term, the freedman could purchase the land.

In the South Carolina Sea Islands and along the MISSISSIPPI RIVER, experiments in black landownership during the war sought to establish patterns for settlement. On January 16, 1865, Gen. WILLIAM T. SHERMAN issued SPECIAL FIELD ORDER NO. 15, which set aside the coastal areas of South Carolina, Georgia, and Florida for the freedmen. Within six months, 40,000 freedmen had been settled on 400,000 acres. In DAVIS BEND, Mississippi, the Freedmen's Bureau established a black colony by leasing land that ex-Confederate president JEFFERSON DAVIS had once occupied to ex-slaves. In Louisiana, bureau agents converted abandoned PLANTATIONS into black communities. Though these settlement plans were temporary measures, the freedmen worked the land, produced profits, and claimed ownership.

Land redistribution was the single most contentious issue during the existence of the Freedmen's Bureau. Not only was land an economic asset and a means for self-sufficiency, but in the mid-19th century, land ownership was equated with independence and citizenship. At its peak, however, the Freedmen's Bureau controlled only 800,000 acres of land, enough to settle just 20,000 families on 40-acre plots, not nearly enough for 4 million former slaves. Compounding the problem of land redistribution was a vigorous campaign by white Southerners to regain titles to the small amount of land that the bureau did possess.

Plans to place freedmen families on 40-acre plots also ran into significant opposition from President ANDREW JOHNSON, who issued an Amnesty Proclamation on May 29, 1865, pardoning former Confederates (except the wealthy and certain political leaders) and restoring their confiscated land. The proclamation specifically ignored the fact that freedmen already occupied much of this land and were working it for themselves. This decision also threatened the solvency of the bureau, since much of its revenue was derived from leased land. Commissioner Howard moved to absorb all confiscated land controlled by other federal agencies into the Freedmen's Bureau and to immediately distribute the land. President Johnson, however, countered by issuing executive orders to restore the land to the original owners.

Understandably, the freedmen felt betrayed by the rescinding of their land grants. They believed that the land belonged to them, since they had made it productive. Congress subsequently took up the issue of land redistribution in the Southern Homestead Act of 1866. It set aside more than 3 million acres of federal land for settlement by the freedmen; however, few were able to secure a homestead. When the law went into effect on the first day of 1867, many freedmen were already tied to yearlong labor contracts that prevented them from making a claim. Others

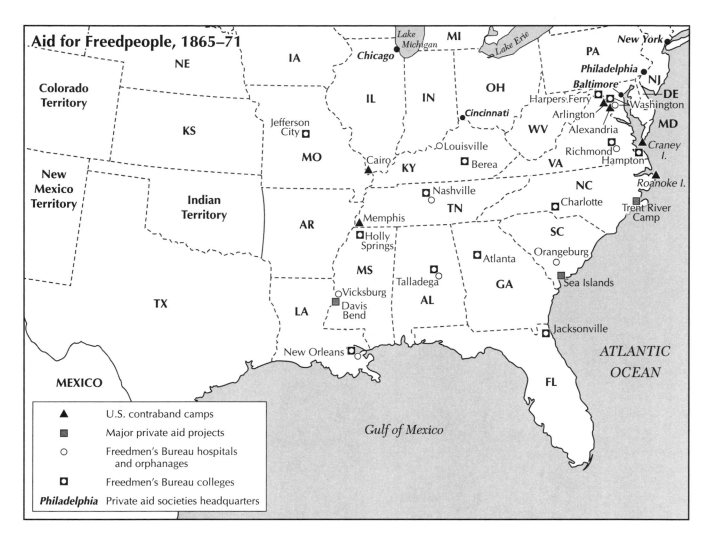

Aid for Freedpeople, 1865–71

Legend:
- ▲ U.S. contraband camps
- ■ Major private aid projects
- ○ Freedmen's Bureau hospitals and orphanages
- ☐ Freedmen's Bureau colleges
- *Philadelphia* Private aid societies headquarters

lacked the capital needed for tools and animals or the time needed to clear unimproved land. BLACK CODES also forbade black land ownership and, in some states, restricted leasing. Even the actual land held problems for the freedmen, since most of the federal land was of poor quality. In the end, only 4,000 families settled in Southern homesteads.

Despite failed attempts at land redistribution, the freedmen remained loyal supporters of the Freedmen's Bureau. Although most agents deferred to local planters in disputes over working conditions or labor contracts, agents like the ones in the South Carolina Sea Islands had the true interests of the freedmen in mind and consistently sided with them against the planters. The freedmen used the bureau as their advocate to resist the power of planters and local white people. Planters pushed for a labor system similar to slavery, with yearlong contracts that tied freedmen to the land. The freedmen resisted by withholding their labor and eventually settling on a system of SHARECROPPING. The Freedmen's Bureau attempted a moderate approach

in the transition to free labor. They placed African Americans at work on plantations while providing for schools and protecting them from white violence.

EDUCATION was the greatest achievement of the Freedmen's Bureau. Although it was not among the original directives from Congress, the bureau, along with Northern benevolent societies and state governments, funded black education because the freedmen demanded it. Three thousand schools were constructed by 1869, enrolling 150,000 students. The bureau also assisted in establishing black colleges designed to train African-American teachers for the new schools. The bureau's attempt to protect African Americans from white violence was less successful than its educational program; they were never able to assemble enough troops to prevent violence against African Americans. Furthermore, they relied on Southern state courts for judicial proceedings instead of Freedmen's Bureau courts, which were authorized to intervene in civil rights cases when African Americans were not treated equally.

The Freedmen's Bureau lasted until 1872. However, with the passage of the RECONSTRUCTION ACTS of 1867, most of the responsibilities of the bureau passed over to the military. Foreshadowing the shift toward Radical Reconstruction, Congress passed a bill extending the life of the Freedmen's Bureau over President Johnson's veto in 1866. In one of its last major initiatives, the bureau registered thousands of black voters across the South. The Freedmen's Bureau and the federal government failed to provide land for freedpeople, but many hoped that acquiring the vote would provide the foundation for lasting freedom.

Institutionally, the Freedmen's Bureau was an example of the expanding powers of the nation-state in the wake of the Civil War. It marked one of the first times that federal power was used to provide for the general welfare of a segment of the population. Despite its pioneering mandate, the bureau was less than successful in its goal to help freedmen make themselves into free and equal citizens. In fairness, material resources and manpower were never sufficient to meet the needs of the 4 million ex-slaves, and most white Southerners fought the bureau's efforts to uplift the freed people at every step. Though slavery was destroyed, white planters hoped to recreate a subservient labor force to work the cotton fields. Even Freedmen's Bureau agents denigrated the capacity of freedmen to become independent proprietors. Nevertheless, the bureau established a legacy of federal commitment to the welfare of African Americans.

See also KU KLUX KLAN.

Further reading: Eric Foner, *Reconstruction: America's Unfinished Revolution, 1863–1877* (New York: Harper & Row, 1988); William S. McFeely, *Yankee Stepfather: General O. O. Howard and the Freedmen* (New Haven, Conn.: Yale University Press, 1968); Claude F. Oubre, *Forty Acres and a Mule: The Freedmen's Bureau and Black Land Ownership* (Baton Rouge: Louisiana State University Press, 1978).

—Justin J. Behrend

Fugitive Slave Law   See Volume IV

G

Galveston, Battle of (January 1, 1863)

At the outset of the CIVIL WAR, Galveston was the second largest city in Texas. Home to 7,000 people, the seaport was a major exporter of cotton—more than 200,000 bales in 1860. It was also one of the South's leading industrial centers, with two iron foundries and several facilities capable of manufacturing boats and other equipment for shipping and fishing.

During the Civil War, Galveston continued to be economically important, serving as a major port for receiving imported goods from blockade runners. Galveston also had strategic importance to both the Confederacy and the Union: As the South's westernmost major port, it had the potential to be an important base of operations for the UNION NAVY's blockade, if captured. Despite its significance, Galveston received scant military attention for the early part of the war. Given the Confederacy's manpower needs, there were no troops to spare for the town's defense, and by late 1861 it was guarded by only a handful of local militiamen. Union ships would occasionally bombard the town, but they made no serious attempt at capture until October 1862. Finally, in that month, a small contingent of Union ships and soldiers managed to overtake Galveston with relatively little bloodshed.

Once Galveston had been taken, 260 members of the 42nd Massachusetts Infantry Regiment were sent to fortify the town and prepare for a Confederate counterattack, which came in the early hours of New Year's Day, 1863. A small and disorganized group of Confederate troops and ships under Maj. John Magruder invaded from both land and sea. After a brief period of intense fighting, the Battle of Galveston ended with a Union retreat. The Confederate losses were 30 killed, 130 wounded. The Union had 21 killed, 36 wounded, and 250 captured.

Confederate troops held the city for the rest of the war. The last two years of the war were marked by a series of crises in Galveston: There were two near-revolts of under-fed and undersupplied Confederate troops and a severe outbreak of yellow fever in 1864 that killed 250 people. Nonetheless, it continued to be an important port for blockade runners, with as many as nine or 10 ships in port at any given time. Galveston remained open for business until it surrendered on June 5, 1865. The town's story illustrates the logistical difficulties the Union faced in effectively blockading a coastline as long as the Confederacy's.

See also CONFEDERATE NAVY.

Further reading: Edward T. Cotham Jr., *Battle on the Bay: The Civil War Struggle for Galveston* (Austin: University of Texas Press, 1998).

—Christopher Bates

Garrison, William Lloyd (1805–1879)

Militant ABOLITIONist William Lloyd Garrison was born in 1805 in Newburyport, Massachusetts, the son of Abijah Garrison and Frances "Fanny" Lloyd. Abijah abandoned the family when William was young, and Fanny was left to raise three young children on her own. The family's finances were tight, and young William was regularly dispatched to beg for scraps from neighbors' tables. From this he developed a strong sense of compassion for the poor. He was also heavily influenced by his mother's devout Baptist convictions.

In 1818 the 13-year old William was apprenticed to the editor of the *Newburyport Herald*. He completed his apprenticeship in the mid-1820s and moved on to serve as editor of a series of newspapers in Massachusetts and Vermont. Each of these ventures failed, as readers were put off by Garrison's antigovernment editorials. In 1829 Garrison accepted a post as the editor of *The Genius of Universal Emancipation*, published in Baltimore. In that capacity, Garrison wrote an editorial that condemned Massachusetts businessman Francis Todd as a "murderer" because he had participated in the slave trade. Todd sued, and Garrison was jailed.

Garrison's imprisonment changed his fortunes. For 49 days, Garrison remained in his cell, publicizing his "martyrdom." By the time he was released, he had become a hero among New England's rapidly growing abolitionist community. Garrison returned to Boston and promptly founded a newspaper, *The Liberator*. In his first issue, published in January 1831, Garrison promised to be "harsh as truth, and uncompromising as justice." He served notice that "I will not retreat an inch, AND I WILL BE HEARD." *The Liberator* quickly became the preeminent abolitionist newspaper, and it would remain so throughout the 1840s and 1850s.

Garrison's message to readers of *The Liberator* was that SLAVERY had to be eliminated through immediate EMANCIPATION of the slaves. He believed that to enslave human beings was a sin and that both Northerners and Southerners were complicit. Garrison rejected colonization, which was the relocation of freed slaves back to Africa. In his 1832 pamphlet "Thoughts on African Colonization," Garrison explained that he found colonization to be both impractical and racist. Instead, he thought the slave problem should be solved through "moral suasion," the use of

William Lloyd Garrison *(Library of Congress)*

petitions, speeches, newspapers, and pamphlets to peacefully turn public opinion against slavery.

In 1833, Garrison reached the height of his influence. He helped to found the American Anti-Slavery Society, a biracial, gender-inclusive organization dedicated to promoting abolitionist activities throughout the United States. Garrison authored the society's Declaration of Sentiments, which emphasized nonviolence and urged abolitionists to do whatever necessary to cause their message to be heard. In 1834, shortly after completing the Declaration of Sentiments, Garrison married Helen Benson.

During the latter part of the 1830s, Garrison grew increasingly radical. He was attacked by a mob in 1835 and had to be rescued from being lynched. A number of other events—including the murder of abolitionist Elijah Lovejoy, Congress's tabling of all antislavery petitions, and the failure of church leaders to join in the abolition movement—left Garrison disillusioned. He came to believe that government and religious institutions had become corrupted and needed to be overthrown. He condemned Christian scripture as "superstition" and vowed that he would only follow the "pure religion of Jesus' perfect example." He called the U.S. Constitution "a covenant with death—an agreement from hell" and suggested that the states without slavery should secede from the Union.

Garrison's increased militancy created serious tensions within the abolitionist movement. A number of prominent Garrison supporters were put off by what they saw as blasphemy. Others disagreed with Garrison's unwillingness to work within the political system. Some abolitionists did not approve of Garrison's belief in women's suffrage. And a number of African-American abolitionists, including FREDERICK DOUGLASS, were angered by Garrison's paternalism. He was willing to fight for African-Americans' freedom but was generally unwilling to make them equal partners in the struggle by appointing them to leadership positions within the American Anti-Slavery Society.

In 1840 the split between "Garrisonian" and "anti-Garrisonian" factions became official, as a number of prominent abolitionists resigned from the American Anti-Slavery Society and founded the Foreign Anti-Slavery Society. Others left to found the Liberty Party, the United States's first antislavery political party. In seven years, Garrison had gone from being the leader of the abolition movement to being on the fringes. He continued to generate attention with *The Liberator* and with outrageous gestures like publicly burning copies of the U.S. Constitution, but he had little influence on the antislavery movement.

During the CIVIL WAR, Garrison began to back off from his nonviolent philosophy, conceding that the use of force was sometimes necessary. He also came to be a supporter of ABRAHAM LINCOLN. When the war ended and the THIRTEENTH AMENDMENT was adopted, Garrison told the readers of *The Liberator* that his work was at an end. Although he supported Radical RECONSTRUCTION, he evinced little interest in joining the fight for African-American civil rights. At the end of 1865, Garrison shut down his newspaper and resigned from the American Anti-Slavery Society. By 1866 his career as a public figure was essentially over. Garrison devoted the rest of his life to the care of his wife and four sons before dying in New York in 1879.

See also AFRICAN METHODIST EPISCOPAL CHURCH.

Further reading: William Lloyd Garrison, *William Lloyd Garrison and the Fight against Slavery: Selections from The Liberator*, ed. William E. Cain (Boston: Bedford Books of St. Martin's Press, 1995); Henry Mayer, *All on Fire: William Lloyd Garrison and the Abolition of Slavery* (New York: St. Martin's Press, 1998).

—Christopher Bates

German-American regiments

In 1860 ethnic Germans in the United States numbered about 1.3 million, the large majority of whom lived in Northern urban areas, and many thousands of whom were recent immigrants. The substantial and visible participation of German-Americans in the CIVIL WAR helped to unite the German-speaking communities in many cities and contributed substantially to the preservation of the German identity in America.

Perhaps the largest impetus in the formation of all-German military units in the Union was the persuasion of ethnic political leaders, although language, social ties, community spirit, and location surely contributed. Immigrants who were not actually from Germany but who spoke German or Germanic languages (such as Swiss, Austrians, Poles, Hungarians, Czechs) had similar experiences or participated in the larger "German" context. German-American sports clubs, or Turnvereine, were particularly active in the formation of ethnic German units. "Turners," as members were called, were well geared for the task; they were men of youthful vigor, used to physical training, organized, and involved. Some all-German units were composed solely of Turners.

The vast majority (85 percent) of ethnic Germans who served the Union cause fought in nonethnic units under American officers. However, at least 145 units were either all German or nearly so. They were formed mostly in Northern American cities, namely New York, Chicago, St. Louis, Cincinnati, Pittsburgh, Philadelphia, Milwaukee, and Indianapolis. Of the approximately 200,000 Germans who participated in the Civil War for the Union, about 5,000 were known as "48ers." These men had fought for German unification and democracy in Europe during insurrections of 1848–49. Several 48ers rose through the

ranks of the UNION ARMY and led all-German regiments. Friedrich Hecker led the 24th and 82nd Illinois Infantries, raised in Chicago. August Willich commanded the 32nd Indiana, possibly the most distinguished German unit. Franz Sigel led the Third Missouri Infantry and eventually rose to the rank of brigadier general. He was a hero to the ethnic Germans, who often sang, "I fights mit Sigel." Peter Osterhaus's 12th Infantry, perhaps the most distinguished of the 18 German units of Missouri, included Henry Kircher, who left LETTERS written in German and English revealing daily life in a German unit.

Although Germans were the second-largest ethnic group in the Confederacy, behind the Irish, there were no all-German Confederate units. However, many units, especially from New Orleans, Charleston, RICHMOND, and Memphis, contained large numbers of Germans.

The ethnic German units of the Union received both criticism and praise. At Chancellorsville, two-thirds of the XI Corps were German or "mixed nationality" regiments and, when routed, they were tagged the "Flying Dutchmen," non-Germans included. The *New York Times* credited German soldiers from preventing a total rout at the SECOND BATTLE OF BULL RUN by remaining to fight amidst a chaotic retreat, and WILLIAM T. SHERMAN singled out the 32nd Indiana at the BATTLE OF SHILOH for its valiant efforts.

See also IMMIGRATION.

Further reading: William L. Burton, *Melting Pot Soldiers: The Union's Ethnic Regiments* (New York: Fordham University Press, 1988).

—Richard J. Roder

Gettysburg, Battle of (July 1–3, 1863)

In a major battle at Gettysburg, Pennsylvania, the UNION ARMY of the Potomac under Gen. GEORGE GORDON MEADE defeated the CONFEDERATE ARMY of Northern Virginia commanded by Gen. ROBERT E. LEE. By reputation the most important Union victory of the war and the most crushing Confederate defeat, Gettysburg was dubbed "The High Water Mark of the Confederacy" and was seen by many observers as a turning point in the fortunes of both sides.

In June 1863, Lee marched his army into Maryland and Pennsylvania to forage for supplies and to draw the Army of the Potomac, then under Gen. JOSEPH HOOKER, away from Virginia. Lee hoped to win a decisive battle on Northern soil that would undermine Northern morale and hasten the end of the war. His army of about 75,000 men consisted of three infantry corps (each with five artillery battalions attached) under the command, respectively, of Gens. JAMES LONGSTREET, RICHARD S. EWELL, and A. P.

HILL, along with two cavalry brigades (each with artillery attached) under Gen. J. E. B. STUART.

Hooker's army numbered roughly 90,000 men organized into seven corps of infantry and artillery, one corps of cavalry and artillery, and 21 batteries of reserve artillery. When Lee moved north, Hooker cautiously followed, keeping his forces between Lee and WASHINGTON, D.C. The Confederates, their morale high, marched up the Shenandoah Valley and captured the Union garrison at Winchester on June 14. Ewell's infantrymen crossed the Potomac River at Williamsport on June 15, advancing toward the Cumberland Valley and plundering Northern towns and farms as they went.

Although its cavalry corps nearly defeated Stuart's troopers in the Battle of Brandy Station on June 9, the Union army was not able to impede Lee's northward movement. On June 25, Hooker sent three corps into Maryland under the command of Gen. John F. Reynolds, but he had moved too late, and by June 27, Hill's and Longstreet's corps reached Pennsylvania. However, Lee had lost track of Stuart, whose cavalry took an indirect route around the Union army and failed to provide Lee with intelligence about enemy movements.

On June 28 President Lincoln replaced Hooker with Gen. George Gordon Meade, the able Fifth Corps commander. While Meade gathered his forces in northern Maryland, Lee ordered his own corps to concentrate in southern Pennsylvania. On June 30 Confederate infantry encountered Union cavalry in Gettysburg, a town of about 2,400. Two Confederate divisions, commanded by Gens. Henry Heth and William Dorsey Pender, returned to Gettysburg on July 1. At about 10 A.M., Heth's men exchanged fire with dismounted Union cavalry, commanded by Gen. John Buford, west of town. Meade's field commander, Gen. John Reynolds, who had ordered the First and 11th Corps to Gettysburg in support of Buford, was killed while hurrying his infantry into action near Herbst's Woods. Gen. Abner Doubleday, commander of the Third Corps, assumed command of the First Corps. Gen. O. O. HOWARD of the 11th Corps, who had not yet reached Gettysburg, assumed field command of the Union left wing.

Reynolds had earlier sent word to Meade that he would hold off the Confederates as long as possible to allow the Union infantry time to arrive in force and occupy a defensive position on the hills south and east of Gettysburg. Gen. Howard, arriving with the 11th Corps at about noon, sent two First Corps divisions to reinforce Doubleday on McPherson's Ridge, positioned two 11th Corps divisions to guard the approaches north of town, and kept a third division in reserve on Cemetery Hill. Like Reynolds, Howard recognized that in a full-scale battle the advantage would go to the side that held the hills south of Gettysburg.

Gen. Lee, arriving on the field at about 2 P.M., ordered Heth and Pender to renew their assault on McPherson's Ridge. In some of the deadliest fighting of the war, Union forces stoutly resisted successive Confederate attacks before falling back. Reaching Gettysburg from the north, two divisions of Ewell's corps launched coordinated assaults on divisions from the Union I and XI Corps. With his lines hard pressed and no sign of reinforcements, Howard ordered a Union retreat through town to Cemetery Hill. Gen. WINFIELD SCOTT HANCOCK of the Second Corps, Meade's choice to replace the fallen Reynolds as field commander, arrived in time to help rally the Union troops against a renewed Confederate attack. In light of the battered condition of Hill's corps, however, Ewell decided to forgo an assault.

Meade reached the field late on July 1. By the next morning, all of the Union army except for the Sixth Corps was at or near Gettysburg. The Union forces occupied an excellent defensive position—a hook-shaped line extending from Culp's Hill southeast of town, north and west through Cemetery Hill, then south down the length of Cemetery Ridge, and ending on a rocky prominence called Little Round Top. A mile to the west, two Confederate corps, those of Hill and Longstreet, occupied Seminary Ridge, which paralleled Cemetery Ridge, while Ewell's corps occupied the town of Gettysburg itself. Determined to remain on the offensive after the success of the previous day, on July 2 Lee ordered Longstreet to attack the Union left with two fresh divisions. Ewell was ordered to launch a simultaneous assault against the Union right.

In a vain attempt to avoid detection by Union signalmen, Longstreet's divisions took a circuitous route to the south end of the field that delayed the Confederate assault until late afternoon. When Longstreet's men finally attacked the enemy's left, they unexpectedly encountered Gen. DANIEL E. SICKLES's Third Corps at the Peach Orchard and the Emmitsburg Road. Against orders, Sickles had advanced his corps to what he believed was a better defensive position than the one Meade had assigned him on Cemetery Ridge. Discovering the situation as the Confederate attack began, Meade ordered George Sykes's Fifth Corps to support Sickles's vulnerable line. When Meade's chief engineer, Brig. Gen. Gouverneur K. Warren, reported that Little Round Top was undefended, Sykes quickly sent Col. Strong Vincent's brigade to occupy the hill. This critical position was saved for the Union by the courageous stand of Vincent's outnumbered brigade, including Lt. Col. JOSHUA LAWRENCE CHAMBERLAIN's 20th Maine Regiment, which held the hill until reinforcements arrived.

In front of Cemetery Ridge, Sickles's infantry was overwhelmed by the Confederate onslaught and suffered heavy casualties. Reinforcements from the Fifth Corps

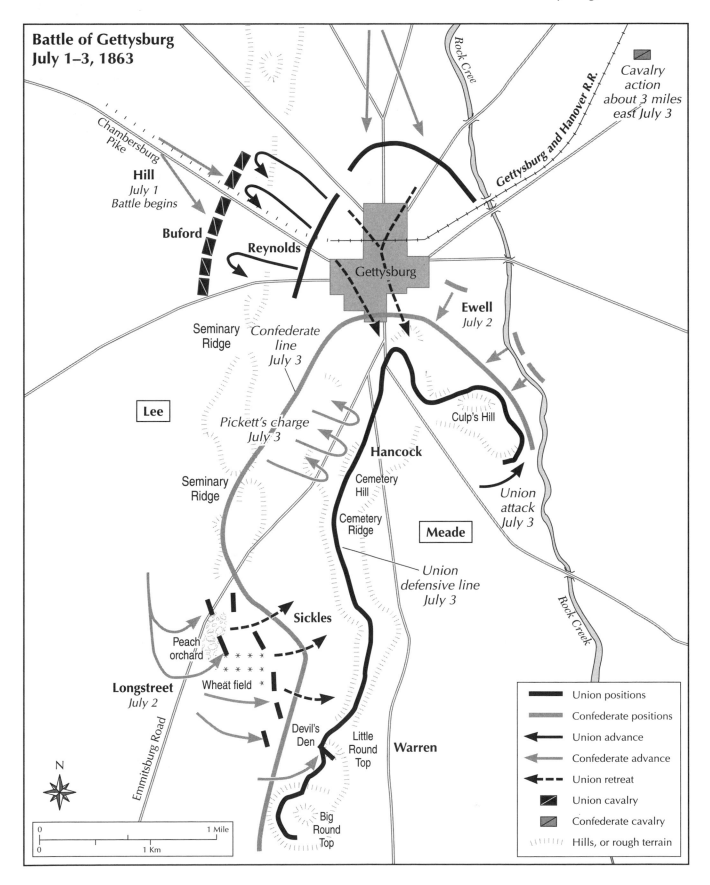

**Battle of Gettysburg
July 1–3, 1863**

Rock Cree

Cavalry
action
about 3 miles
east July 3

Gettysburg and Hanover R.R.

Chambersburg
Pike

Hill
*July 1
Battle begins*

Buford

Reynolds

Gettysburg

Ewell
July 2

Seminary
Ridge

*Confederate
line
July 3*

Lee

*Pickett's charge
July 3*

Culp's Hill

Hancock

Seminary
Ridge

Cemetery
Hill

Cemetery
Ridge

Meade

*Union
attack
July 3*

*Union
defensive line
July 3*

Sickles

Peach
orchard

* * *
* * *

* * * *

Longstreet
July 2

Wheat field   *

Rock Creek

Emmitsburg Road

Devil's
Den

Little
Round
Top

Warren

N

Big
Round
Top

0	1 Mile
0	1 Km

▬	Union positions
▬	Confederate positions
◄—	Union advance
◄—	Confederate advance
◄- -	Union retreat
▨	Union cavalry
▨	Confederate cavalry
⑊⑊⑊	Hills, or rough terrain

delayed the Third Corps's retreat from its forward position long enough for Meade to reestablish a thin defensive line on Cemetery Ridge. Gen. Hancock sent regiments from his Second Corps into the fray to stem the Confederate charge on the left, leaving an opening in the Union line that the Confederates were unable to exploit. Hancock and Meade rushed troops from the First and Second Corps to repair the broken Union line and turn back the Confederate assault.

On the Union right, Ewell was unable to coordinate his attack with Longstreet's and so his troops did not take advantage of weaknesses in the federal line. Henry Slocum's 12th Corps had occupied breastworks on Culp's Hill, but Meade borrowed two of its divisions to help shore up his line on Cemetery Ridge, leaving a single brigade to defend the Union works. When Ewell finally attacked at 8 P.M., darkness and the inherent strength of the Union position allowed the outnumbered Federals to hold off three Confederate brigades until reinforcements from the First and 11th Corps arrived. Meanwhile, on Cemetery Hill, Union defenders turned back an attack by Early's division.

The Confederates had fought hard on July 2 but could not dislodge the Union army from its strong defensive position. Lee intended to try again on the following day to launch simultaneous assaults on Culp's Hill and on the Union left. Meade disrupted Lee's plan by attacking first. The Union 12th Corps, reinforced by men from the First and Sixth Corps, had reoccupied the breastworks on Culp's Hill, and at dawn Union guns opened a barrage on the Confederates at their front.

Forced to change course, Lee decided to attack the Union center, which had been briefly breached the day before. Preparations for an artillery barrage and infantry assault took all morning. At 1 P.M., as many as 170 Confederate guns opened a massive two-hour barrage on the Union line. Confederate gunners damaged some of their targets in the Union center, but many shells overshot their targets. Returning fire, Union gunners caused significant casualties among Confederate infantry massed for the assault. When Union artillery chief Henry J. Hunt stopped firing to conserve ammunition, Confederate artillery commander Col. E. P. ALEXANDER signaled Longstreet to begin the assault.

Longstreet reluctantly sent the infantry forward across nearly a mile of open ground. Three Confederate divisions—commanded by Gens. GEORGE E. PICKETT, James Pettigrew, and Isaac Trimble—took part in the attack, which became known to history as "Pickett's Charge." The 12,000 men who participated in the famous assault suffered casualties in excess of 50 percent. Faced with deadly canister fire the moment they came within range of Union artillery, only a few thousand Confederates made it to the Union line on Cemetery Ridge. Those who did make it were met with rifle fire and double canister. As his infantry retreated back toward Seminary Ridge, Lee told them, "The fault is mine, but it will be right in the end."

The Battle of Gettysburg ended with a cavalry engagement three miles east of town. At about 3 P.M. on July 3, Stuart's cavalry, which had arrived the day before, attempted to attack the Union rear. In one of the largest cavalry fights of the war, Brig. Gen. David M. Gregg's Union troopers fought Stuart's brigades to a draw.

On July 4, Lee's army waited in the rain for a possible counterattack. After none materialized, the Confederates began their retreat to Virginia that night. By July 7 Lee had reached the rain-swollen Potomac River but was unable to cross. Meade followed Lee by way of Frederick, Maryland, where he met his supply trains. The slow-moving Union army reached the Potomac too late to prevent the Confederates from crossing on July 14.

Casualties during the Gettysburg campaign totaled more than 20,000 for the Confederate army and more than 23,000 for the Union army. In the battle's aftermath, the question of why the Confederate army lost took precedence over the question of how the Union army won. Southern loyalists were slow to blame Lee for his costly decision to take the tactical offensive. Lee apologists condemned Stuart for being absent during most of the campaign and criticized Longstreet for launching his July 2 attack on the Union left later than Lee had intended. Confederate blunders do not entirely explain the Union victory, however. Meade and his army won the battle because of effective leadership and tenacious fighting. Wrongly accused of wanting to abandon the field, criticized for allowing Lee's defeated army to return to Virginia, and embroiled in controversy over the merits of Sickles's actions on July 2, Meade never received the credit he deserved for his leadership at Gettysburg.

In November 1863, the Union states established a federal cemetery at Gettysburg that was dedicated by PRESIDENT ABRAHAM LINCOLN. After the war, the battlefield became a popular tourist site, covered with MONUMENTS and preserved as a national military park.

See also GETTYSBURG ADDRESS.

Further reading: Edwin B. Coddington, *The Gettysburg Campaign: A Study in Command* (New York: Scribner, 1984); William A. Frassanito, *Gettysburg: A Journey in Time* (New York: Scribner, 1975); Gary W. Gallagher, ed., *Three Days at Gettysburg: Essays on Union and Confederate Leadership* (Kent, Ohio: Kent State University Press, 1999); Michael Shaara, *The Killer Angels* (New York: Ballantine Books, 1996).

—Amy J. Kinsel

Gettysburg Address (November 19, 1863)

President ABRAHAM LINCOLN delivered the Gettysburg Address, one of his most memorable public speeches, on November 19, 1863. Lincoln's brief remarks officially dedicated the Soldiers' National Cemetery at Gettysburg, Pennsylvania, where in July 1863 the UNION ARMY of the Potomac had won a major victory over the CONFEDERATE ARMY of Northern Virginia. The federal cemetery that Lincoln dedicated on the battlefield would hold the bodies of thousands of Union soldiers who had died as a result of the fighting.

Contrary to popular myth, Lincoln wrote his address several days in advance of his trip to Gettysburg, carefully crafting his remarks in the full knowledge that they would be widely reported in the Northern press. Published accounts of the speech contained slight variations in wording, and Lincoln continued to edit the text when he copied it out for admirers. Lincoln's final version read:

> Four score and seven years ago our fathers brought forth on this continent a new nation, conceived in Liberty, and dedicated to the proposition that all men are created equal.
>
> Now we are engaged in a great civil war, testing whether that nation, or any nation so conceived and so dedicated, can long endure. We are met on a great battle-field of that war. We have come to dedicate a portion of that field, as the final-resting place of those who here gave their lives that that nation might live. It is altogether fitting and proper that we should do this.
>
> But in a larger sense we can not dedicate—we can not consecrate—we can not hallow this ground. The brave men, living and dead, who struggled here, have consecrated it, far above our poor power to add or detract. The world will little note, nor long remember what we say here, but it can never forget what they did here. It is for us the living, rather, to be dedicated here to the unfinished work which they who fought here have thus far so nobly advanced. It is rather for us to be here dedicated to the great task remaining before us—that from these honored dead we take increased devotion to that cause for which they gave the last full measure of devotion—that we here highly resolve that these dead shall not have died in vain—that this nation, under God, shall have a new birth of freedom—and that government of the people, by the people, for the people, shall not perish from the earth.

Lincoln used the Gettysburg Address to place his interpretation of the battle and the war before the American people. He framed the war with his own vision of the future—a reunited country grounded in its Revolutionary heritage but different from what had gone before. By proclaiming a devotion to freedom, equality, and republican government as the nation's guiding philosophy, he defined the principles for which Union soldiers had died and around which he hoped the country might be rebuilt. In speaking of "the unfinished work" that the soldiers at Gettysburg had begun, he expressed optimism that something profoundly good might yet come from the CIVIL WAR's horrible devastation.

This good, though, would result only from Americans' commitment to the cause of freedom within a restored republic. Lincoln admonished his fellow Americans that preserving the Union through victory on the field would not be enough. A rededication to first principles, "a new birth of freedom," would be required to make the victory worthy of its awful price. Americans, Lincoln urged, must resolve to fight on in the cause of freedom so that Gettysburg's dead "shall not have died in vain."

If Lincoln sought to rededicate the United States to the ideals of liberty and equality, however, his expansive constitutional interpretation quickly foundered on the political compromises of the postwar period and the romantic lure of sectional reconciliation. In the end, Lincoln's attempt to remake the country on the basis of a broad interpretation of the Declaration of Independence faltered in the face of white Americans' eagerness to remember the war as a tale of glory rather than a struggle for freedom.

See also GETTYSBURG, BATTLE OF.

Further reading: Garry Wills, *Lincoln at Gettysburg: The Words That Remade America* (New York: Simon & Schuster, 1992).

—Amy J. Kinsel

Gorgas, Josiah (1818–1883)

Confederate brigadier general and educator, Josiah Gorgas was born on July 1, 1818, in Running Pumps, Pennsylvania, to Joseph Gorgas and Sophia Atkinson Gorgas. He graduated from the UNITED STATES MILITARY ACADEMY AT WEST POINT in 1841, ranking sixth in his class, and was assigned to the Corps of Ordnance, the branch of the army concerned with military supplies and materials. In the Mexican-American War he played a major role in positioning the American guns used to bombard Mexican positions at Vera Cruz, and he also commanded the Ordnance Depot supporting Scott's campaign to Mexico City.

Following the war, he served at several arsenals including Mount Vernon, Alabama, where he met and married Amelia Gayle, daughter of a prominent state politician. Dissatisfied by internal U.S. Army politics and strongly pro-Southern, he resigned his commission in the U.S. Army and accepted appointment as Confederate chief of ordnance in April 1861.

Faced with major difficulties from the beginning, Gorgas worked hard to coordinate the several Southern states' ordnance agencies into a unified system. He worked quickly to establish Confederate-controlled arsenals and armories and to coordinate the contracts of various private firms. He based his department on a decentralized model that depended on the talents of subordinate officers who had wide discretion in the administration of their depots and arsenals. By 1863 Gorgas had done as well as anyone could to supply the Confederacy with arms and equipment. Proudly, he recorded in his diary: "Where three years ago we were not making a gun, pistol nor a sabre, no shot nor shell—a pound of powder—we now make all these in quantities to meet the demand of our large armies." As the war dragged on, however, Gorgas encountered increasingly difficult problems as raw materials became less available, labor shortages became acute, and important sites of production fell to Union advances.

Following the war, Gorgas purchased and ran the Brierfield Iron Works in Alabama. He sold the facility in 1869 and accepted appointment at the University of the South, where he played a vital role in establishing the school's curriculum and physical plant. In August 1878 he accepted the presidency of the University of Alabama. Gorgas died in Tuscaloosa, Alabama, on May 15, 1883.

See also CONFEDERATE STATES OF AMERICA.

Further reading: Richard D. Goff, *Confederate Supply* (Durham, N.C.: Duke University Press, 1969); Josiah Gorgas, *The Journals of Josiah Gorgas, 1857–1878*, ed. Sarah Woolfolk Wiggins (Tuscaloosa: University of Alabama Press, 1995); Frank Vandiver, *Ploughshares into Swords: Josiah Gorgas and Confederate Ordnance* (College Station: Texas A&M University Press, 1994).

—James Daryl Black

Gould, Jay   See Volume VI

governors

The chief executives of a state, governors are elected every four years (in a few states, every two years), and the position involves a combination of executive, legislative, and judicial duties. Like most of the top political leadership during the 19th century, governors were likely to be former lawyers, with extensive political experience in local and state offices, and more than a few would have seen some military action. Every governor had control over his state's militias, and during the CIVIL WAR, this power made them indispensable to the national war effort in both the CONFEDERATE STATES OF AMERICA and the United States of America.

Governors, Northern and Southern, exercised great power during the war. Among other duties, they were commanders in chiefs of their state forces. As such, they were responsible for marshalling the state's manpower, resources, and population for the war effort. The midwestern governors were notable for their drive to enlist troops for the Union. In 1861 early volunteer regiments raised by Governor William Dennison of Ohio and Governor Oliver Morton of Indiana entered western Virginia. GEORGE B. MCCLELLAN of Ohio led the force, which helped West Virginia separate itself from Virginia during the war. The fact is that going into the war, most CITIZEN SOLDIERs had a stronger allegiance to their state than the national government. The regiment, identified by state, was the basic fighting unit of the Civil War.

Just like President ABRAHAM LINCOLN in WASHINGTON, D.C., and President JEFFERSON DAVIS in RICHMOND, the governors were also charged with explaining to the people of the state why men should enlist, why they should continue to fight, and why they should continue to support and to pay for the war. In the four years of the Civil War, governors raised money and troops, appointed officers, fostered and encouraged manufacturing, and enlarged and expanded social welfare programs for soldiers and soldiers' families.

Southern governors were mainly former Democrats who were strong SECESSIONists before the war. Several Southern governors seized federal property in their state, such as Governor Henry Rector of Arkansas, who captured a federal arsenal and allowed the placement of Confederate guns even before his legislature convened to consider secession. The governor of North Carolina seized three forts and the arsenal in Fayetteville.

On the other hand, in slave Maryland, Unionist governor Thomas Hicks delayed action by the Southern-rights legislature by refusing to call it into session, thus helping to save his state for the Union. In the border state of Missouri, proSLAVERY governor Claiborne Fox Jackson squared off with Congressman FRANCIS P. BLAIR, a Unionist; violence and confusion reigned in the divided state. In fact, Jackson's government existed in exile for most of the Civil War, and Missouri remained in the Union column. Governor Beriah Magoffin of Kentucky hoped to uphold his state's tradition of mediation by requesting a conference of border states that could seek a peaceful solution. Southern invasion early in the war brought the state over to the North's side.

The powerful STATES' RIGHTS sentiments that led to secession from the Union hindered centralization efforts by President Davis and the Confederate command. Governors such as JOSEPH E. BROWN of Georgia and Zebulon Vance of North Carolina supported the war aims of the Confederacy but vigorously opposed several of the total-war measures used to attain them, which each man saw as occurring at the expense of his state and its population. Despite their resistance to many of President Jefferson Davis's nationalizing ordinances, both Brown and Vance were popular and effective governors of their respective states. In particular, they took excellent care of their states' soldiers and the folks left behind by dramatically expanding programs for relief and welfare.

When Davis enacted the first CONSCRIPTION law in American history (1862), it exempted certain civil servants. Brown and Vance vociferously opposed the draft and vastly increased the number of exempt civil servants in their states. In fact, the two states eventually contained 92 percent of all such exemptions. Brown went even further by unilaterally extending the exemption clause of the draft, insisting that militia officers be included. He then appointed hundreds of new officers.

States' rights governors often refused to share their resources and supplies with the national army. Armaments seized from federal arsenals were a particular sore point. Southern governors maintained that they needed to keep guns and troops in their own states to guard their borders and deter slave uprisings rather than sending them to the fronts in Virginia or Tennessee. The same was true with food, clothes, and other military necessities.

The governors often insisted that they were acting in defense of the people against Davis's "despotism." Governor Brown led others against Davis's harsh martial law in Richmond and other Virginia cities. He strongly advocated aid to families of poor soldiers and decried mistreatment of civilians by Confederate cavalry and other military units. Conversely, the two wartime governors of Virginia, John Letcher and "Extra Billy" Smith, strongly supported Davis's policies. It was in their states' interest to do so, as so much of the war was fought in Virginia; the same was true for the governors of Louisiana and Mississippi.

Unlike his counterpart, President Abraham Lincoln could depend upon the strong support and cooperation of the majority of governors in the North. Mainly Republican, the governors knew that their political fortunes rested upon the course of the war going as smoothly as possible. Upon setting quotas for volunteer regiments at the beginning of the war, several governors sent pleas to increase their quotas so that they could accept all those seeking to enlist. While Lincoln mobilized the national army and the government on war-alert status, the governors convened their legislatures and appropriated funds to supply regiments at state expense until late 1861, when the army could incorporate the troops.

The main problem in the Union in the beginning (as in the Confederacy) was the clash of local fervor with national disorganization. Recruitment was so successful, in fact, that it was temporarily suspended in the spring of 1862. This proved a mistake later in the year, when ROBERT E. LEE defeated GEORGE B. MCCLELLAN in the PENINSULAR CAMPAIGN, creating a severe manpower shortage. Coming on the heels of loss in battle, a drive for recruitment was especially difficult. Northern governors quickly joined forces with Secretary of War EDWIN M. STANTON to backdate a statement asking Lincoln to follow up recent successes with another call to arms. Lincoln pretended compliance with the request in calling for 300,000 new volunteers.

The president did encounter political setbacks and difficulties regarding challenges to key Republican governorships, mainly after the 1863 EMANCIPATION PROCLAMATION, especially in New York, Illinois, and Indiana. For example, antiEMANCIPATION sentiment in Indiana led to the election of a majority Democratic legislature that threatened to cut off support for the war. Republican governor Oliver P. Morton consulted the state constitution and found that a two-thirds quorum was necessary for the legislature to conduct its business. Dismissing Republican legislators, he ran the state for two years with the help of loans from the federal government. This kind of extraordinary (and, in Morton's case extralegal) action on the part of most Northern governors ensured that problems arising in the states never significantly affected Lincoln's national leadership.

The increased prominence of governors during the Civil War set a precedent from which few states retreated. Today, governors wield much more power than they did in the past, and at least some of that authority began to be shaped when they were called upon to serve their states' interests during the sectional conflict.

See also ELECTIONS.

Further reading: William B. Hesseltine, *Lincoln and the War Governors* (New York: Knopf, 1955); George C. Rable, *The Confederate Republic: A Revolution against Politics* (Chapel Hill: University of North Carolina Press, 1994); Wilfred Buck Yearns, ed., *The Confederate Governors* (Athens: University of Georgia Press, 1985).

—Richard J. Roder

Grand Army of the Republic   See Volume VI

Grant, Julia Dent   (1826–1902)

Wife of General and President ULYSSES S. GRANT, Julia Dent was born at White Haven, Missouri, on January 26, 1826. Daughter of a slaveholding planter, Julia grew up in a close and affectionate family that included seven siblings. After attending an elite boarding school in nearby St. Louis, the 18-year-old Julia was introduced to her older brother's West Point roommate, Ulysses S. Grant, aged 22.

Their two-year courtship and four-year engagement were conducted in the midst of Grant's frequent absences in army service, including the Mexican-American War. Finally married in 1848, Julia accompanied Ulysses to an obscure military outpost near Sackets Harbor, New York. The life of an army wife was filled with uncertainty and loneliness, but Julia worked hard to ensure a happy family. A fun, lively, and charming woman, her great love and affection for Ulysses was returned in full. Within 10 years of their marriage she was busy raising four children.

Julia experienced many disappointments in the 1850s. Bored and frustrated with the professional military life, Ulysses resigned from the army in 1854. Returning to St. Louis, he tried his hand at various occupations, including farming. Almost totally dependent upon her father's charity, Julia and Ulysses struggled with poverty and his depression. Despite a record of failure, Julia stoutly defended her husband, believing that one day his talent and intelligence would find an outlet. In 1859 they moved their family to Galena, Illinois, so that Ulysses could work in his father's leather-goods store. When the war broke out in 1861, Ulysses volunteered his services immediately, and the next few years saw his swift rise to fame and glory as the Union's top general.

If everyone else was surprised by her husband's rapid elevation to hero of the Northern army, the ever-loyal Julia was not. She basked in his reflected glory and expanded her role as his helper and confidante. No other wife of a prominent general spent more time with her husband on campaigns. At the end of the war, Julia had developed a confidence that would impress citizens when she served as first lady during the eight years of her husband's presidency, 1868–76. "My life at the White House was like a bright and beautiful dream and we were immeasurably happy," she later wrote. The Grants and their young children became the object of a country's adoration as they set a new style of friendly, casual, and constant entertaining. Julia also shared the setbacks of the Grant presidency as corruption and scandal marked their last years in WASHINGTON, D.C.

A few years after leaving the White House, the Grants retired to New York, where they expected to live out their lives in comfort. Unfortunately, in 1884, Grant lost all the family money in a financial disaster. Shortly afterward, he developed the throat cancer that led to his death in 1885. In his dying days, Grant completed his *Personal Memoirs*, which left Julia and the children financially secure. After his death, Julia lived for 17 years with her daughter in Washington, D.C., where she wrote her own *Memoirs*. She died on December 14, 1902. Julia Dent Grant is interred alongside her husband in General Grant's National Monument (Grant's Tomb) in NEW YORK CITY.

Further reading: Julia Dent Grant, *The Personal Memoirs of Julia Dent Grant*, ed. John Y. Simon (Carbondale: Southern Illinois University Press, 1988); Ishbel Ross, *The General's Wife: The Life of Mrs. Ulysses S. Grant* (New York: Dodd, Mead, 1959).

Grant, Ulysses S. (1822–1885)

Commanding general of the UNION ARMY and 18th president of the United States, Ulysses S. Grant was born on April 27, 1822, in Point Pleasant, Ohio. The oldest child of Jesse and Hannah Simpson Grant was raised on the rough-hewn Ohio frontier, first in Point Pleasant and then in nearby Georgetown. The young Hiram Ulysses (his first and middle names were later changed to Ulysses Simpson) struggled to live up to his ambitious father's high expectations. Hiram was sensitive, moody, and well educated for his time and place. The decision to send "Lyss" to the UNITED STATES MILITARY ACADEMY AT WEST POINT was ultimately a wise one. During his four years at the U.S. Military Academy (1839–43) Grant was a middling student but a superb horseman. He clearly enjoyed the military life. A few years after graduation from West Point, Lieutenant Grant fought in the Mexican-American War, where he showed great courage and skill as a soldier, winning promotion and accolades. The young soldier had a talent for fighting and, even more, an impressive knowledge of the strategy and tactics of warfare learned from experience, not textbooks.

Despite his good record in the war and a solid marriage to the sister of one of his West Point classmates, Grant did not do well in the peacetime army of the late 1840s and early 1850s. Assigned to remote forts, Grant took to drinking and resigned from the army under a cloud of suspicion. The civilian world proved just as difficult. Grant failed as a provider for his family, as a farmer, and as a businessman. He lived on his father-in-law's land outside of St. Louis, Missouri, until moving in 1859 to Galena, Illinois, to work as a clerk in his father's store. Although these years were a low point in his life, there were some happy times. He was a loving husband to JULIA DENT GRANT and an unusually attentive and affectionate father to their four children. When the guns of FORT SUMTER fired, Grant was eager to serve his country.

After briefly holding a series of low-level positions, Lt. Col. Grant was given command of the 21st Illinois Volunteer Infantry Regiment. Rising swiftly through the ranks, Brigadier General Grant was placed in command of the large Union supply and training camp at Cairo, Illinois. In the fall and winter of 1861–62, Grant used his troops aggressively and, in conjunction with the U.S. Navy, captured the strategically important Fort Henry on the Tennessee River and Fort Donelson on the Cumberland River. When the Confederate commander of Fort Donelson sent

Ulysses S. Grant *(National Archives)*

Grant a note to discuss the terms of surrender for his army of 21,000 men, Grant replied: "No terms except unconditional and immediate surrender can be accepted." Now famous as "Unconditional Surrender" Grant, he continued to display the winning ways that would bring him to the favorable attention of President ABRAHAM LINCOLN and the victory-starved North. Grant's hard-won victories at Shiloh, Tennessee (April 6–7, 1862); Vicksburg, Mississippi (January–July 1863); and Chattanooga, Tennessee (October–November 1863) made him the leading Northern general of the CIVIL WAR.

Grant and Lincoln enjoyed an unusually close relationship, and Grant developed political skills that complemented his military abilities. Unlike many Union generals, Grant believed firmly that the president's role as commander in chief of the war was never to be questioned, even if he disagreed with an order. For example, Grant did not like the fact that many "political" generals were appointed simply because they were popular figures back home whose support Lincoln thought important to cultivate. Nevertheless, he accepted the reality and worked with the situation. Grant was an enthusiastic supporter of most of Lincoln's policies, however, especially the use of black soldiers. Most importantly, the popular Grant denied emphatically that he had any interest in running for the office of the president. By the end of 1863, Lincoln realized that he had found the general that would lead the country to victory. In January 1864, Lieutenant General Grant came to WASHINGTON, D.C., to accept command of all the Union armies.

Grant did not rise to his position without controversy. As he progressed up the chain of command, he was increasingly subject to attacks on his character and generalship. Charges of drinking, incompetence, and a brutal indifference to death and suffering dogged him throughout his career and affected his reputation after the war as well. There is no doubt that Grant did make mistakes. He was caught unprepared for the Confederate attacks at Shiloh, for example. He also quickly regretted an ill-advised order that banned Jews from trading cotton. As to the reports of Grant's drunkenness, the historical evidence on his drinking shows that he rarely imbibed during the Civil War and never when it counted.

Grant began to implement his grand strategic vision during the spring and summer campaign of 1864. The plan, which involved the movement of all Union armies at the same time to attack and defeat the Confederates, drew Lincoln's warm support and raised the hopes of the Northern nation for a quick end to the war. Unfortunately, it took longer than expected. The battles of the OVERLAND CAMPAIGN, where Grant and ROBERT E. LEE's armies fought to bloody stalemate in the BATTLES OF THE WILDERNESS, SPOTSYLVANIA, and COLD HARBOR, gave rise to the nickname of "butcher" for the general in chief whose main strategy seemed to be throwing bodies at the enemy. Subsequent military historians have ably defended Grant against the butcher charge, pointing out that Lee lost many more men in proportion than did Grant, but Northern citizens were unaware of this fact. Fortunately, Grant's trusted western comrades, Gen. WILLIAM T. SHERMAN and Gen. PHILIP H. SHERIDAN, under Grant's direction, led victorious armies that made possible Lincoln's reelection in the fall of 1864. On April 9, 1865, at APPOMATTOX COURT HOUSE, Virginia, Grant dictated the terms upon which the war ended and upon which the nation could begin the process of reconciliation.

Having led the Union army to victory, Grant emerged from the Civil War a popular hero, appearing to most of the people as a man who had character and upright morality. Like many, if not most, of his fellow countrymen, Grant had tasted the bitterness of defeat and failure. He also had a sharp intelligence that served him well in both plotting strategy and in dealing with the CITIZEN-SOLDIER of the Civil War. Grant had made many mistakes, but he had learned from them. Moreover, he had a deep and abiding faith in democracy and democratic institutions. Even his lack of political experience was, in the eyes of those who viewed politicians with contempt, a virtue. By 1866, the battles between President ANDREW JOHNSON and Congress had left Grant as the most powerful man in the country. Nominated for president by the REPUBLICAN PARTY in 1868, Grant swept to victory. He was aided by newly enfranchised Southern African Americans in states reconstructed by Congress as well as by his famous campaign slogan "Let Us Have Peace."

When Grant took office in 1869, RECONSTRUCTION governments in which African Americans participated existed in all of the former Confederate states except Tennessee. Although Grant did his best to uphold these "Black Republican" governments, violence-prone white supremacists gradually overthrew them everywhere except in South Carolina and Louisiana before Grant left office. Even in South Carolina and Louisiana, which had black majorities, the Republican governments were sustained only by the presence of army detachments. Black Republicanism during Reconstruction failed not because of Grant but because of growing Southern white resistance matched by growing Northern white apathy.

In foreign affairs, Grant was obsessed with the idea of annexing Santo Domingo but was frustrated by opposition in the Senate. Grant's greatest success in this area came when Secretary of State Hamilton Fish negotiated the Treaty of Washington (1871) and prevented intervention in a Cuban revolution before and after the *Virginius* affair (1873).

Although rank-and-file Republicans stuck by Grant, Republican intellectuals were disillusioned by his presidency. They had hoped that he would be above partisanship and appoint the "best people" (like themselves) to office. Indeed, Grant did ignore politics initially in his cabinet and other major appointments, but having gratified no one in particular by his independent course, he soon learned to please spoils-minded Republican senators like Roscoe Conkling of New York and representatives like BENJAMIN F. BUTLER of Massachusetts. Grant also proved to be too trusting, and while personally honest, he could be duped by unscrupulous friends and relations.

Reform Republicans were hostile to the spoilsmen and thus increasingly hostile to Grant. They disliked corruption in government circles and were opposed to special favors to corporations, whether in the form of land grants for RAILROADS or protective TARIFFS for manufacturers. Ultimately, the reform Republicans split with the administration and formed a new Liberal Republican Party. The party's laissez-faire program included civil service reform, low tariffs, gold-backed currency, and no legislation aiding special groups, be they wealthy corporations or poor African Americans. Grant could not stand the self-righteousness and superior airs of many reformers, but he recognized that some civil service reform would benefit the nation. He approved tariff reductions, and he endorsed gold-backed "sound money." These actions somewhat undermined the Liberal Republicans. To the dismay of the party's leaders like Carl Schurz, the 1872 Liberal Republican convention nominated for president HORACE GREELEY, the eccentric editor of the *New York Tribune*. Although the Democrats also nominated Greeley, Grant triumphed handily in the election.

Grant's second term was marred by a severe economic depression following the Panic of 1873 and by the exposure of widespread corruption. For example, Orville E. Babcock, Grant's personal secretary, was implicated in the WHISKEY RING that defrauded the government of millions of dollars in internal revenues. Grant's secretary of war, William Worth Belknap, illegally sold an Indian-post tradership. The Republican Party was already disintegrating in the South, and the scandals and economic stagnation also caused it to decline in the North. Grant backed two important measures that bucked the ebbing tide: Despite financial struggles, Grant opposed even mildly inflationary measures and approved the Specie Resumption Act (1875) that would put the United States back on the gold standard on January 1, 1879. And despite flagging interest in aiding African Americans, he signed the Civil Rights Act (1875) that guaranteed African Americans equal rights in public places such as streetcars, THEATERS, and hotels and prevented their exclusion from juries. When the outcome of the presidential election of 1876 was in dispute from November 1876 to March 1877, Grant behaved circumspectly, supported the Electoral Commission Act (1877), and never once hinted that he would use his control of the army to declare fellow Republican Rutherford B. Hayes the winner.

Throughout his presidency, Grant remained steadfast in the belief that the goals of the war should be preserved, even as the country's enthusiasm for Reconstruction of the South in the North's image faded away. Grant's final task as president harked back to his first, and perhaps most important, achievement: to ensure a stable transition between presidents. He succeeded in 1876, just as he had succeeded in 1868, and the country was reconciled for good. Few professional politicians could have done better, and most might have done far worse.

In retirement, Grant went on a world tour (1877–79), lobbied unsuccessfully for nomination to a third term as president, and went into the brokerage business. His firm, Grant & Ward, went bankrupt in 1884, leaving him broke. Mortally ill with throat cancer, Grant retreated to his home to write his *Personal Memoirs*, regarded by many as the greatest military memoirs since Caesar's *Commentaries*. Grant was in a great deal of pain as he raced against the clock to complete his book, and he died within weeks of finishing the task. Upon publication, Grant's memoirs sold hundreds of thousands of copies and recouped his fortune for his family. His memory as one of America's greatest generals, if not one of its greatest presidents, was secured.

Grant's legacy is deep and wide. By the time of his death on July 23, 1885, at Mount McGregor, New York, Ulysses S. Grant was an icon in the historical memory of the Civil War shared by a whole generation of men and women. Americans of that time compared Grant favorably to Washington and Lincoln. They believed that an appreciation of Grant could only come with the recognition that he was both the general that saved the Union and the president who made sure that it stayed together. On the same day that 1.5 million Americans attended Grant's funeral in NEW YORK CITY and countless others commemorated his life in cities and towns across the country, a newspaper headline provided the perfect epitaph for the accomplishments of General and President Ulysses S. Grant: "The Union, His Monument."

See also CHATTANOOGA, BATTLE OF; SHILOH, BATTLE OF; VICKSBURG CAMPAIGN.

Further reading: Bruce Catton, *Grant Moves South, 1861–1863* (Boston: Back Bay Books, 1990); Bruce Catton, *Grant Takes Command, 1863–1865* (Boston: Back Bay Books, 1990); Ulysses S. Grant, *The Personal Memoirs of U. S. Grant* (1885; reprint, New York, Penguin Books, 1999); William S. McFeely, *Grant: A Biography* (New York: Norton, 1982); Brooks D. Simpson, *Ulysses S. Grant: Triumph over Adversity, 1822–1865* (Boston: Houghton Mifflin,

2000); Jean Edward Smith, *Grant* (New York: Simon & Schuster, 2001).

Greeley, Horace (1811–1872)

Newspaper editor Horace Greeley was born in Amherst, New Hampshire, on February 3, 1811. In 1826 he entered into the world of JOURNALISM, serving as a printer's apprentice for the *Northern Spectator* of East Poultney, Vermont. Over the next several years, Greeley worked for many different newspapers in the Northeast, editing several and forming a political partnership with two powerful figures in New York state politics, Thurlow Weed and WILLIAM H. SEWARD. Greeley's most important opportunity, however, arrived in 1841 when he founded and became editor of the *New York Tribune.*

Greeley's role as editor of the *Tribune* not only established his legacy but also allowed him to promote his interests in reform, writing, and politics. He used his editorials over the course of three decades to battle against numerous vices and social problems, including tobacco, alcohol, gambling, PROSTITUTION, and SLAVERY. He also pushed for land reform and a protective TARIFF that would aid the American worker. Above all else, he strove for his vision of national unity and harmony. As a result, his support for labor did not encompass the encouragement of what he saw as divisive STRIKES. He stood for freedom and against slavery, yet in the 1840s and early 1850s he expressed his opinions carefully, for he saw radical ABOLITIONism as a threat that could destroy the nation.

Greeley's expansive nationalism found expression in his vision for the western lands. Although he did not invent the phrase, Greeley has long been credited with first saying, "Go west, young man." He became a strong proponent of the development of RAILROADS. In his mind, the open lands of the West would provide land for numerous free-labor settlers and bring prosperity for all, as long as the Southern institution of slavery was not allowed to expand as well. Long a "Conscience" Whig who stood against the "Cotton" Whigs, Greeley helped found the REPUBLICAN PARTY in 1854. His newspaper took a powerful stand against the KANSAS-NEBRASKA ACT and popular sovereignty, which he believed would aid in the growth of slavery. Heading into the crisis of the late 1850s, Greeley promoted peace and harmony above all else. Greeley was intent on keeping the nation together, even as he attacked slavery.

While he remained involved in New York state politics throughout his life, Greeley ended his partnership with Weed and Seward in 1854. He campaigned for John C. Frémont in 1856, and although he did not initially support ABRAHAM LINCOLN in 1859 for the Republican nomination, neither did he support Seward, whom he believed lacked the necessary national appeal. Throughout the years of the CIVIL WAR, Greeley maintained an alternately supportive and adversarial relationship with Lincoln through his editorials in the *Tribune.* In the hope of avoiding war in 1860, Greeley advocated letting the Southern states secede, for he believed that most Southerners did not support SECESSION and that these "erring sisters" would soon be forced to return.

After the war began, the *Tribune* editorials revealed a shift in Greeley's thinking. He began to advocate the abolition of slavery as a primary war objective and encouraged Lincoln to formulate an EMANCIPATION policy. Although his political positions aligned him with the RADICAL REPUBLICANS, Greeley still looked to find a compromise to end the war. As a result, in July 1864, he found himself in Niagara Falls, meeting with several Southern "peace commissioners." Given permission to participate by an extremely skeptical President Lincoln, the *Tribune* editor failed to bring anything but derision upon himself for his efforts. As the war came to a close, Greeley stated his support for a moderate RECONSTRUCTION, one that allowed for universal amnesty and impartial suffrage while promoting the long-range goal of Republican predominance in national politics.

A man of principles, Greeley helped post bail for JEFFERSON DAVIS in 1867. This decision not only hurt his standing in the public eye but also dealt a blow to sales of the second volume of his history of the Civil War, *The American Conflict.* In the last years of his life, Greeley grew disenchanted with the Republican Party and was only a reluctant supporter of ULYSSES S. GRANT in the 1868 election. In 1871 he completely broke ranks with the party he helped found and joined the rising Liberal Republican movement. With his principles and national recognition firmly in place, Greeley became the Liberal Republican and Democratic nominee for president in 1872. In two emotionally crushing losses, Greeley suffered the death of his wife and defeat at the hands of Grant in early November.

Horace Greeley died in Pleasantville, New York, on November 29, 1872.

Further reading: Coy F. Cross, *Go West, Young Man!: Horace Greeley's Vision for America* (Albuquerque: University of New Mexico Press, 1995); Ralph Ray Fahrney, *Horace Greeley and the Tribune in the Civil War* (New York: Da Capo Press, 1970); Horace Greeley, *The Autobiography of Horace Greeley, or, Recollections of a Busy Life* (New York: Treat, 1872).

—John P. Bowes

greenbacks

In early 1862, after the CIVIL WAR caused a great crisis for the Northern ECONOMY, the U.S. government began printing "greenbacks," a legal-tender currency that partially underwrote the costs of the Civil War.

Throughout the country, citizens used various paper currencies issued by many different banks and redeemable in specie (gold and silver), but the federal government was required by law to pay its debts in specie only. The enormous costs of the war seriously depleted the Treasury's reserves of gold, and the uncertainties of the military conflict were causing private citizens to hoard vast amounts of the precious metals. When the dwindling precious metal reserves of banks in New York, Philadelphia, and Boston caused those institutions to suspend paying out specie to back their notes, the Union was on the verge of a terrible financial disaster. This, in turn, would result in a shutdown for the war effort, and then the Union.

Treasury Secretary SALMON P. CHASE recognized the urgency of the situation and told Congress on February 3, 1862, that America's financial policies must be altered quickly. New York congressman Elbridge G. Spaulding suggested that the government begin issuing its own paper currency. This newly created currency would be "fiat money," meaning that it was not redeemable in gold or silver of equivalent value but would act as legal tender for all public and private debts except import duties and interest due on government bonds, both of which would continue to be paid in specie. Because the Constitution empowered Congress only to "coin money," there was much debate over the legality of Spaulding's proposal. There was also concern that a national paper currency would initiate rampant inflation.

Nevertheless, those were extraordinary times, and exceptions had to be made. Spaulding's proposal passed Congress on February 12, 1862, and became known as the first Legal Tender Act. It authorized the printing of $150 million in Treasury notes. The currency was issued in denominations ranging from $1 to $10,000. The bills were printed on one side only with green ink and quickly became known as "greenbacks." The value of greenbacks fluctuated with the Union's fortunes in the war. At one point after the Union had suffered a great defeat, they were worth no more than 40 cents in gold. For the most part, however, greenbacks proved to be universally popular and remarkably sound.

See also BANKING AND CURRENCY.

Further reading: Milton Friedman and Anna Jacobson Schwartz, *Monetary History of the United States, 1867–1960* (Princeton, N.J.: Princeton University Press, 1971); Wesley Clair Mitchell, *A History of the Greenbacks,* *with Special Reference to the Economic Consequences of Their Issue, 1862–65* (Chicago: University of Chicago Press, 1960).

—Emily E. Holst

Greenhow, Rose O'Neal (ca. 1815–1864)

Confederate spy Rose O'Neal Greenhow was born in Montgomery County, Maryland, and grew up in WASHINGTON, D.C. In 1835 she married Virginian Robert Greenhow, and the couple had four children. As the wife of a politician in the State Department, Rose entertained diplomats and cultivated relationships with future politicians. Rose's work with Robert researching American land claims in the Pacific Northwest gave her experience with map skills and analysis. In 1850 she supported John C. Calhoun's efforts against sectional compromise. Robert left the State Department in 1850, and the family moved to San Francisco. Rose returned to Washington after his death in 1854.

Once the CIVIL WAR began, Thomas Jordan, Confederate general P. G. T. BEAUREGARD's adjutant, recruited Greenhow to head an ESPIONAGE ring in Washington. As a socially prominent widow, Greenhow easily gathered information from new officers and government workers, all eager to show their importance. This information proved particularly valuable in July 1861, when intelligence Greenhow relayed to Beauregard at the FIRST BATTLE OF BULL RUN contributed to Confederate victory.

The Union secret service placed Greenhow under house arrest on August 23, 1861, but she continued to send information South and published LETTERS criticizing the Union's treatment of women. To stop these activities, the federal government transferred Greenhow to the Old Capitol Prison in January 1862. In June she was exiled to the Confederacy in a prisoner exchange. Greenhow departed for RICHMOND wrapped in a Confederate flag and carrying a diary of her imprisonment. President JEFFERSON DAVIS and Beauregard rewarded her espionage activities.

Greenhow traveled to Europe in August 1863 as an unofficial diplomat for the Confederacy. There she published her diary, *My Imprisonment and the First Year of Abolition Rule in Washington.* After unsuccessfully pleading her case for Confederate support, she started home in August 1864. Chased by Union blockaders, Greenhow's ship ran aground near North Carolina on October 1, 1864; Greenhow insisted on being rowed ashore. Her boat overturned and she drowned, weighed down by the gold she was carrying for the Confederate government. Greenhow was buried with military honors.

See also ABOLITION.

Further reading: Rose O'Neal Greenhow, *My Imprisonment and the First Year of Abolition Rule in Washington* (London: R. Bentley, 1863); Ishbel Ross, *Rebel Rose: Life of Rose O'Neal Greenhow, Confederate Spy* (New York: Harper, 1954).

—Lisa Tendrich Frank

Grimké, Charlotte Forten (1837–1914)

African-American author, educator, and civil rights advocate, Charlotte Forten was born on August 17, 1837, into a prominent and wealthy ABOLITIONist family in Philadelphia. The family wealth allowed Forten to be tutored at home until she was 16 years old, at which time she was sent to Higginson Grammar School in Salem, Massachusetts. Upon graduation from Higginson, Forten enrolled at Salem Normal School to become a teacher. In 1856 Forten accepted a teaching position at Epes Grammar School in Salem. Ill health caused her to return to Philadelphia in 1858. Besides teaching, Forten was a gifted poet, with antiSLAVERY the most common subject of her poetry.

By the spring of 1862, Union forces had pushed Confederate planters out of the South Carolina Sea Islands. Left behind upon the rebel retreat were thousands of slaves. On October 21, 1862, Forten received her assignment as the first black teacher hired for the Sea Islands Mission. From noon until 3 P.M., nearly 100 students attended the school. Classes resumed in the evening. In 1864 Forten's continued poor health caused her to leave the mission, but she published essays about her experiences in the South Sea Islands in *Atlantic Monthly*.

During RECONSTRUCTION, Forten worked as secretary of the Freedmen's Relief Association, and she continued to write. She also taught high school and was one of 15 people selected for a position as a clerk at the U.S. Treasury Department out of a field of nearly 500 candidates. At age 41, she married Frances J. Grimké, a Presbyterian minister from a prominent abolitionist family.

When Charlotte Forten died in 1914, she had served as a groundbreaker and a role model for her generation. Her diaries, probably her greatest legacy to history, were first published in 1953 and tell the story of a well-educated, self-possessed, and motivated woman who did much to forward the cause of African-American rights.

Further reading: Charlotte L. Forten, *The Journals of Charlotte Forten Grimké*, ed. Brenda Stevenson (New York: Oxford University Press, 1988).

—Gina Ladinsky

H

habeas corpus, writ of

According to the U.S. Constitution, when any citizen is imprisoned, a court must issue a writ of habeas corpus, which requires the government to produce the suspect in open court and to charge him or her with a specific crime. The Confederate Constitution had a similar clause. Intended to prevent arbitrary and indefinite imprisonment, habeas corpus was suspended by both the Confederacy and the Union during the CIVIL WAR.

In the CONFEDERATE STATES, the suspension of habeas corpus was short lived and usually ineffective. JEFFERSON DAVIS, motivated partly by his personal commitment to having a weak central government, refused to suspend habeas corpus without congressional approval. Violence by Union sympathizers and a general perception that opposition to the Confederate cause required repression led the Confederate Congress, in early spring 1862, to give Davis that power. Moving quickly, Davis enacted martial law, including the right to hold suspects indefinitely without charge in Norfolk, Portsmouth, and RICHMOND. In those cities, the suspension of habeas corpus was intended to legitimize the existing practice of imprisoning Union sympathizers in the "Castle Thunder" Prison at Richmond and to free Confederate military governors to destroy local dissent.

Because the Confederate Congress had only provided Davis with suspension power for a limited period, the president lobbied repeatedly for votes to renew his authority. In addition to Unionist sentiment, the Confederate government pointed to local opposition as a reason why suspension was necessary. In several states, especially North Carolina and Georgia, GOVERNORS and local judges opposed the use of various federal powers, including CONSCRIPTION. Using writs of habeas corpus, judges freed local men from the control of military recruiters and military courts. In effect, habeas corpus served as a way for state judicial authority to override military power. Although the Confederate Congress enacted legislation, in February 1864, intended to prevent local judges from interfering with military tribunals or martial law, it was never able to assert federal control completely.

Ultimately, the suspension of habeas corpus in the Confederacy had little beneficial effect. Unlike ABRAHAM LINCOLN, Davis was unwilling to act zealously in this regard. He was caught—as he was in policies on BANKING AND CURRENCY and conscription—between what was expedient and what served the philosophical purpose of SECESSION. If the purpose of the Confederacy was to protect the right of states to avoid domination by a central government, then Davis could hardly use federal power to impose a national view on municipalities and local judiciaries. Instead, the suspension of habeas corpus was used sparingly and rarely made a positive difference for the Confederate cause.

In the Union, by contrast, habeas corpus was suspended for much of the war, and thousands of people were imprisoned. Before the Civil War, only once had a president suspended habeas corpus. Even then, the suspension had been short lived. President Lincoln, however, sought to use his executive power in a much more expansive and pragmatic way. Arguing that no single law was worth the failure of the Union, Lincoln believed that suspending habeas corpus allowed him to achieve several goals.

The first goal, and the reason for which the writ was suspended initially, was keeping Maryland in the Union. Faced with the possibility that Maryland would secede, which would cut WASHINGTON, D.C., off from the rest of the North, Lincoln allowed Winfield Scott to arrest Confederate sympathizers at every level of Maryland society, including Baltimore's chief of police and mayor. One of those arrested was John Merryman, who sued for release based on his constitutional right to be charged or released. Although the Supreme Court agreed that he should be freed (in *Ex Parte Merryman*), Merryman remained in prison.

Throughout the war, the issue of whether the executive branch was empowered to suspend habeas corpus or whether it required the approval of another branch remained unclear. The Constitution says that the writ can be suspended, but not by whom, in what circumstances, or how. While lawyers, congressmen, and citizens debated executive authority, at least 13,535 Americans were arrested. Finally, in March 1863, Congress passed the Habeas Corpus Indemnity Act, which gave Lincoln the power to suspend the writ. By assenting to the power of the president, however, Congress effectively moved to assert its own power to approve any executive use of suspension. In addition, Congress insisted that all those arrested must be identified in regular lists of prisoners within 20 days of their arrest.

While the Confederacy had used the suspension of habeas corpus to prevent ESPIONAGE and to assert its right to conscription, the Union's suspension of habeas corpus served mostly to suppress political dissent. Although some Confederate collaborators and spies were arrested, the majority of those detained were Democrats and other opponents of Lincoln administration policies. Democratic candidates for office were quick to label Lincoln a tyrant, and in some cases their rhetoric hurt Republicans, including the president, at the ballot box. For his part, Lincoln perceived the value of a unified HOMEFRONT, and he was willing to silence some dissenting voices to achieve that unity, at least on the surface.

See also STATES' RIGHTS.

Further reading: Mark E. Neely, *The Fate of Liberty: Abraham Lincoln and Civil Liberties* (New York: Oxford University Press, 1991).

—Fiona Galvin

Halleck, Henry Wager (1815–1872)

A renowned military theoretician, Henry W. Halleck served the Union as field general, general in chief, and army chief of staff. While he failed to provide innovative and decisive leadership in battlefield strategy, Halleck excelled at organizing the army. Born on January 16, 1815, in New York, Halleck became discontented with farm life and left home to attend the UNITED STATES MILITARY ACADEMY AT WEST POINT, where he graduated third in the class of 1839.

After a six-month tour of European military establishments, Halleck published *Elements of Military Art and Science* in 1846, a text that incorporated ANTOINE-HENRI DE JOMINI's approach to war. Halleck's work spread Jomini's theories beyond the professional military when it was read by President ABRAHAM LINCOLN and volunteer officers during the CIVIL WAR.

During the Mexican-American War (1846–48), Halleck was assigned to California. He resigned from the army in 1854 to focus on his law practice and land and mining interests. By 1861, Halleck had amassed a fortune of $500,000. But in August 1861, Halleck left his successful private pursuits and returned to the army. He replaced Gen. John Frémont in the Department of the Missouri, where he quickly instilled order to the disorganized and corrupt command. His curt manner facilitated rapid reform but did not foster positive personal relationships, traits that continued to shape Halleck's reputation during the Civil War. Halleck proved to be a tentative commander, reluctant to authorize advances until all risks could be minimized. Yet when General ULYSSES S. GRANT's forces captured Forts Henry and Donelson in early 1862, Halleck eagerly claimed credit for the victories of his subordinate, who had operated beyond Halleck's orders.

Lincoln brought Halleck to WASHINGTON, D.C., as general in chief of the army in July 1862 in the hope that Halleck's theoretical expertise would provide much needed coordination to the Union war effort. Halleck relayed Lincoln's desires for more aggressive efforts against Confederate troops, but his lack of innovative battlefield strategies and his deference to the field generals disappointed Lincoln. Halleck convinced Lincoln that Grant's forces in the western theater should continue to follow Jomini's principle of seizing strategic property, but by 1863 he was willing to compromise Jomini's genteel method of war and concentrate on destroying ROBERT E. LEE's Army of Northern Virginia.

Lincoln utilized Halleck as an intermediary to avoid conflicts with field generals, to deflect criticism when popular officers were dismissed, and to avoid responsibility when victory eluded Union troops. Much criticism was directed at Halleck by the press, politicians, dissatisfied officers, and the general public, even when disappointing results were due to the failure to follow Halleck's orders.

Ultimately, Grant's successes led to his promotion to general in chief of the army on March 9, 1864. Halleck became chief of staff and continued his duties: forwarding orders from Lincoln and Grant; overseeing the administrative aspects of the army; and bearing the brunt of criticism from soldiers, politicians, and the public.

Halleck's successes were less publicized. He instilled order, efficiency, and discipline in a largely VOLUNTEER ARMY. Halleck organized the mobilization of troops; the TRANSPORTATION of men and material; and the acquisition and distribution of food, clothing, and ammunition. He centralized the administration of an army that had been formed largely through state-sponsored units, and he professionalized the army by working for the replacement of political generals with West Point graduates.

After Lincoln's death, Halleck was stripped of his chief of staff title and ordered out of Washington. Assigned first to RICHMOND, then to San Francisco, and finally to Louisville, Kentucky, Halleck remained with the army until his death on January 9, 1872. He was vilified in the memoirs of Union generals, with few people defending his contributions. While Halleck was not a great military strategist, his administrative efforts made many Union victories possible and created the first national army in the United States.

Further reading: Stephen E. Ambrose, *Halleck: Lincoln's Chief of Staff* (Baton Rouge: Louisiana State University Press, 1962); Henry W. Halleck, *Elements of Military Art and Science* (1864; reprint, Westport, Conn.: Greenwood Press, 1971).

—Martha Kadue

Hancock, Winfield Scott (1824–1886)

Union general and Democratic politician, Winfield Scott Hancock was born on February 14, 1824, in Montgomery County, Pennsylvania, to Elizabeth and Benjamin Franklin Hancock. Hancock used his family's DEMOCRATIC PARTY connections to secure an appointment to the UNITED STATES MILITARY ACADEMY AT WEST POINT, graduating in 1844 in the bottom third of his class. Breveted a second lieutenant, Hancock served effectively as an infantry recruiter on the western frontier. He first experienced combat in 1847 during the Mexican-American War. Hancock commanded a company at Chapultepec and discovered that he enjoyed battle. Breveted first lieutenant, the gregarious Hancock became friends with his fellow officers, including Virginian LEWIS A. ARMISTEAD. Returning to garrison duty in St. Louis, Hancock married Almira Russell, a supportive wife who saw him through the disappointments of peacetime army service. In 1861 Hancock, a captain of infantry, was stationed in Los Angeles as chief quartermaster for the southern district of California.

A Democrat and Southern sympathizer, Hancock favored STATES' RIGHTS, but he never considered taking up arms against the Union. After hosting a bittersweet farewell dinner for friends who had decided to fight for the Confederacy, Hancock traveled east to seek an infantry command. Fellow Democrat Gen. GEORGE B. MCCLELLAN gave Hancock the Third Brigade, Smith's division, army of the Potomac, which in 1862 was assigned to the Second Division, Fourth Corps. In May, the new brigadier general skillfully led his men at the Battle of Williamsburg, earning the nickname "Hancock the Superb." In September, he assumed command of the First Division, II Corps, when its senior officer was mortally wounded at the BATTLE OF ANTIETAM.

Breveted to major general, Hancock was a stickler for military procedure whose men admired his geniality and dashing appearance. In December 1862, he demonstrated his outstanding leadership abilities and conspicuous personal bravery during the futile Union assault on Marye's Heights at the BATTLE OF FREDERICKSBURG. In May 1863, he valiantly held his division in an exposed position while the rest of the UNION ARMY retreated from the BATTLE OF CHANCELLORSVILLE. Hancock succeeded to the command of II Corps in June, just before the Army of the Potomac, under Gen. GEORGE GORDON MEADE, marched north in pursuit of the Army of Northern Virginia and Gen. ROBERT E. LEE.

Word arrived at Meade's Maryland headquarters on July 1 that the Confederates had been engaged near Gettysburg, Pennsylvania, and that Union First Corps commander, Gen. John F. Reynolds, had been killed. Meade, ignoring military protocol, sent Hancock ahead to take command on the field while the rest of the army came up. Hancock's main contribution that day was to restore order to the Union forces and place the troops in defensive positions along Cemetery Ridge and Culp's Hill. His steadiness under fire was evident the next day, when he commanded his own Second Corps at the center of the Union line and shored up the exposed Third Corps to his left. On July 3 Hancock was again in the thick of the action, commanding the Union defense during Pickett's Charge, an assault in which his friend, Confederate general Lewis Armistead, was mortally wounded. Hancock, also wounded, refused to leave the field until victory was assured.

Despite nursing a painful, unhealed thigh wound, Hancock returned to the Second Corps in March 1864. He fought well in the WILDERNESS campaign and the BATTLES OF SPOTSYLVANIA, but his corps suffered heavy losses at the BATTLE OF COLD HARBOR during frontal attacks on entrenched Confederate positions. Hancock uncharacteristically declined to assume field command at Petersburg on June 15, missing a potential opportunity to overrun the then lightly defended city. Hancock gave up his Second Corps command in November 1864, and after attempting unsuccessfully to recruit volunteers for a new veteran corps, he finished the war as commander of the Department of West Virginia and the Middle Military Division.

In 1866 Congress awarded Hancock the postwar rank of major general. He returned to the regular army, serving stints as commander of the Military Department of the Missouri and the Fifth Military District. Stationed in New Orleans, Hancock, an opponent of Radical RECONSTRUCTION, issued orders designed to keep free African Americans off juries and voter-registration lists. Gen. ULYSSES S. GRANT recalled Hancock to WASHINGTON, D.C., and briefly appointed him commander of the Division of the Atlantic. After Grant became president in 1869, Hancock was assigned to the remote Department of Dakota. Meade's death in 1872 entitled Hancock, as the army's senior major general, to reclaim command of the Division of the

Atlantic. From division headquarters in NEW YORK CITY, Hancock pursued his long-standing political ambitions. In 1880 Hancock won the Democratic presidential nomination but lost the general election to Republican James A. Garfield. During the campaign, Grant condemned Hancock's postwar administration of the Fifth District, so it was ironic that Hancock's last public duty was to plan and direct Grant's 1885 funeral. Hancock died in New York on February 9, 1886.

See also GETTYSBURG, BATTLE OF; PETERSBURG CAMPAIGN.

Further reading: David M. Jordan, *Winfield Scott Hancock: A Soldier's Life* (Bloomington: Indiana University Press, 1988); Glenn Tucker, *Hancock the Superb* (Dayton, Ohio: Press of Morningside Bookstore, 1980).

—Amy J. Kinsel

Harper, Frances Ellen Watkins (1825–1911)

An advocate of African-American civil rights, EDUCATION, temperance, ABOLITION, and civic morality, poet and author Frances Ellen Watkins Harper was also a prominent leader of the women's club movement of the late 19th century. Born in Baltimore, Maryland, in 1825, Frances Watkins was the only child of free African-American parents. At three years of age, Frances was orphaned and adopted into the family of her uncle, Reverend William Watkins. Frances attended her uncle's school, where she received significantly more intellectual training than was common for African-American children at the time. At 14 years of age, Watkins began an informal apprenticeship in sewing with a Baltimore man named Armstrong. Sewing provided an income for Watkins, who taught the craft at the Union Seminary in Columbus, Ohio, and in Little York, Pennsylvania. By the time she began teaching in the late 1840s, she had also achieved her first major success as an author, publishing a collection of poetry, *Forest Leaves* (1845).

Although sewing provided an adequate income, teaching became unnecessary once Watkins began to speak publicly about her strong antiSLAVERY sentiments. Her first public comment was a lecture in New Bedford, Massachusetts, in 1854. Watkins's passionate speeches quickly made her popular on the speaking circuit. She also became one of the most widely read African-American poets in America. She would continue to be a prolific and popular writer for the next half century, publishing a number of volumes of poetry as well as novels, most famously *Iola Leroy* (1892).

On November 22, 1860, Frances Watkins married Fenton Harper, and the couple began farming a property in Columbus, Ohio. Following his death in May 1864,

Frances Harper resumed lecturing, focusing in particular on the effects of the CIVIL WAR on African-Americans. While lecturing, Harper stressed the importance of education, moderation in alcohol consumption, and morality within the African-American community.

In 1871 Harper and her daughter Mary moved to Philadelphia, Pennsylvania. There, Harper continued to lecture, concentrating largely on two subjects: moral issues among African Americans and temperance. Joining the National Woman's Christian Temperance Union (WCTU), Harper spearheaded work among African Americans. In addition, she established Sunday schools for African-American children in Philadelphia. In 1894, at age 69, she became the director of the American Association of Education of Colored Youth. She was also a member, and later vice president, of the National Association of Colored Women. Like many of the most prominent reformist women of her time, advancing age did not deter Harper from participating in civic causes. She continued to fight for a variety of reforms until her death in 1911.

Further reading: Melba Joyce Boyd, *Discarded Legacy: Politics and Poetics in the Life of Frances E.W. Harper, 1825–1911* (Detroit, Mich.: Wayne State University Press, 1994); Frances Ellen Watkins Harper, *Iola Leroy, or, Shadows Uplifted* (1892; reprint, New York: Oxford University Press, 1988).

—Megan Quinn

Harpers Ferry, West Virginia (Harper's Ferry, Virginia)

Best known as the site of JOHN BROWN's raid in 1859, Harpers Ferry (then in Virginia) was an essential strategic possession for both the Union and Confederate armies during the CIVIL WAR, changing hands eight times between 1861 and 1865.

A place of great natural beauty, Harpers Ferry is located on a wedge of land that separates the Shenandoah and Potomac Rivers at the northern end of Virginia's rich Shenandoah Valley. In 1796 President George Washington selected the town for one of the federal armories, and the manufacture of weapons became the basis of its ECONOMY.

Bordering on Pennsylvania and Maryland, Harpers Ferry in the late 1850s was a prosperous and growing place of nearly 3,000 people. The U.S. Armory was the biggest employer, and the 250 men who worked in the factories turned out roughly 10,000 rifles and muskets per year. There were other industrial concerns as well—an iron foundry, a flour mill, and cotton mill—all powered by the water flowing from the Shenandoah River. Goods and people were transported in and out of town courtesy of the Baltimore and Ohio Railroad. In short, Harpers Ferry was one of the rare industrial villages in the South. Its citizens were a diverse group of small businessmen, native-born working class, immigrants, slaves, and 150 free African Americans. PLANTATIONS and farms were in the surrounding countryside.

Harpers Ferry was also a quiet and harmonious place until 1859, when radical ABOLITIONist John Brown selected it as the target for his infamous raid. Attracted by the armory, the slaves, and the geography, Brown and his men planned to seize the munitions and ignite a revolution that would end SLAVERY. His scheme was cut short when armed townsmen, local militia, and the U.S. Marines led by Lt. Col. ROBERT E. LEE ended the ill-fated invasion. Brown and several members of his party were tried and hanged for the attack. The incident at Harpers Ferry gripped the nation and further polarized North and South.

When the Civil War broke out, Harpers Ferry became a tragic victim of the "BROTHERS' WAR." Forced to choose between fighting for the North or the South, most of its citizens fled, leaving the town almost empty. In April 1861 Union forces decided to abandon the arsenal. Union lieu-tenant Roger Jones, garrison commander at Harpers Ferry, ordered his men to set the armory on fire and retreat to the north. Jones and his men successfully destroyed the main arsenal and 15,000 guns. However, the local citizens put out the fire before it spread to the remainder of the armory. Virginia forces led by THOMAS J. "STONEWALL" JACKSON entered the town and saved the remaining firearms and factory equipment. They shipped the valuable materials to the Confederate armories in RICHMOND, Virginia, and Fayetteville, North Carolina.

Harpers Ferry would change hands seven more times over the course of the war. The Battle of Harpers Ferry on September 15, 1862, was a vital part of Robert E. Lee's Maryland campaign. Stonewall Jackson, Maj. Gen. Lafayette McLaws, and Brig. Gen. John G. Walker directed a successful assault on Harpers Ferry, which was occupied by thousands of Union soldiers. The largest surrender of Union forces during the war, Confederate troops captured 12,419 men, thousands of firearms, and 70 artillery pieces. The Battle of Harpers Ferry proved a crucial morale boost for the Confederates, who would lose the BATTLE OF ANTIETAM two days later.

Engraving of the Harper's Ferry (as it was then known) insurrection depicting the U.S. Marines storming the engine house while John Brown and his followers fire through holes in the doors *(Library of Congress)*

The rebels moved out of Harpers Ferry after Antietam, and Union troops again occupied the town. On October 1–2, 1862, President ABRAHAM LINCOLN visited Harpers Ferry, as well as his troops positioned on the craggy mountains called Maryland Heights above the town. Toward the end of the war, Harpers Ferry became an important supply base for Union operations in the Shenandoah Valley.

After 1865 Harpers Ferry was abandoned, since the war had left the town in ruins. By the late 19th and early 20th centuries, Harpers Ferry had become an important stop for African-American leaders such as FREDERICK DOUGLASS and W. E. B. Du Bois, who proclaimed the importance of black people's contribution to the Civil War and to the American nation. Significantly, the memory of John Brown as an abolitionist hero and martyr to the cause of freedom was commemorated in positive ways. Today, the National Park Service preserves the past of Harpers Ferry by operating museums, tours, and demonstrations for the thousands of tourists who crowd the narrow winding streets of this historic place.

Further reading: Paul Finkelman, ed., *His Soul Goes Marching On: Responses to John Brown and the Harpers Ferry Raid* (Charlottesville: University Press of Virginia, 1995); Chester G. Hearn, *Six Years of Hell: Harper's Ferry during the Civil War* (Baton Rouge: Louisiana State University Press, 1996); James V. Murfin, *The Gleam of Bayonets: The Battle of Antietam and the Maryland Campaign of 1862* (Baton Rouge: Louisiana State University Press, 1982); Truman John Nelson, *The Old Man: John Brown at Harpers Ferry* (New York: Holt, Rinehart and Winston, 1973).

—Fiona Galvin

Hayes, Rutherford B.   See Volume VI

Herndon, William H. (1818–1891)

William Henry Herndon was best known as ABRAHAM LINCOLN's law partner and biographer. He was born on Christmas Day in 1818 in Greensburg, Kentucky, and in 1820 his family moved to Illinois. Herndon attended Illinois College, where he learned strong antiSLAVERY principles. To earn money, he worked briefly as a clerk in a Springfield store, renting the room above the store for living quarters, which he shared with a number of friends at different times, including Abraham Lincoln.

Herndon was admitted to the Illinois bar and in 1844 joined Lincoln's law firm. They remained partners until 1861, when president-elect Lincoln left Springfield for WASHINGTON, D.C. Lincoln and Herndon complemented each other well. Herndon managed the office and provided stability while Lincoln was for gone months at a time working the law circuit. They shared similar political convictions. Both were passionate Whigs and then Republicans; both were also protemperance, supported federal programs to aid economic growth, and opposed the expansion of slavery into the territories. Indeed, Herndon was one of Lincoln's most enthusiastic political supporters.

After Lincoln's death in 1865, Herndon's business failed. Married with eight children, he struggled with alcoholism and depression. He became obsessed with the idea of writing a "true" history of Lincoln's life, as opposed to the worshipful biographies so popular at the time. Determined to publish an accurate representation, he traveled to Kentucky and Indiana, where he recorded numerous oral interviews with surviving Lincoln relatives and friends. His three-volume biography, *Herndon's Lincoln: The True Story of a Great Life*, was published in 1889.

Many people attacked *Herndon's Lincoln*. Herndon claimed that Lincoln loved only one woman in his life, Ann Rutledge. Her early death, according to Herndon, caused Lincoln's lifelong melancholy. Family members, including Mary Todd Lincoln, denied this story. Other controversies erupted over Herndon's revelation that Nancy Hanks Lincoln was illegitimate. Historians have proved this assertion to be erroneous and found many other errors as well. Nevertheless, the collected reminiscences have been invaluable to generations of Lincoln scholars. Herndon died on March 18, 1891.

Further reading: David Herbert Donald, *Lincoln's Herndon* (New York: A. A. Knopf, 1948).

Higginson, Thomas Wentworth (1823–1911)

During his long life, Thomas Wentworth Higginson was a Unitarian minister, educator, writer, and public speaker. He published numerous books and countless articles on a many different subjects. He led riots, wrote about children's books and slave spirituals, edited a magazine, and introduced the poems of Emily Dickinson to the world. He was also a colonel in the UNION ARMY.

Higginson was born in Cambridge, Massachusetts, and attended Harvard College and Harvard Divinity School. In the 1850s he served churches in Newburyport and Worcester, Massachusetts. He made his mark as a radical ABOLITIONist—in fact, he left his first church because his antiSLAVERY lectures were unpopular with the congregation. He traveled to "BLEEDING KANSAS" in 1856, where he approved of the sometimes violent actions of fellow abolitionists; he helped lead the attempt to free a fugitive slave named Anthony Burns from the Boston Court House (he was wounded in the fight that broke out); and he helped finance JOHN BROWN's raid on HARPERS FERRY.

His commitment to racial justice made him an enthusiastic supporter of the Union when the CIVIL WAR began. He was also in favor of allowing African Americans to join the Union army. In the fall of 1862, he took command of the First South Carolina Volunteer Infantry (later called the 33rd U.S. Colored Troops), one of the first regiments composed of black troops. Most of the men in his unit were former slaves from South Carolina. In fact, the First South Carolina had been formed just before Higginson joined it. With the new colonel in command, the regiment reached its full strength and became a well-trained and effective military force. During the year or so that Higginson was in charge, the regiment made a raid up the St. Mary's River on the Georgia-Florida state line, where Higginson and his men fought their first skirmish. They suffered several casualties but won the short fight. During the winter they served on the picket line for the Union army and, in March 1863, briefly occupied Jacksonville, Florida. Although they fought off several Confederate attacks, the regiment eventually abandoned the town.

Higginson was wounded during a raid in the spring of 1863, and although he returned to the regiment later in the year, he left the army in 1864. He spent the next 40-plus years lecturing all over the country on behalf of social justice and writing literary and other articles for magazines like *The Nation, Atlantic Monthly,* and *Harper's Bazaar.* He remained interested in the plight of the former slaves, advocating voting rights and economic equality for them. Shortly after the war, he lost an election for a seat on the local school board because he wanted to end the practice of teaching white and black students in separate schools. Unlike most men, he also argued in favor of extending the vote to women.

His experiences as a Civil War commander led him to write the book for which he is best remembered—*Army Life in a Black Regiment* (first published in 1870 and still in print more than a century later). Although Higginson published 30 books in his lifetime—including novels, literary criticism, and several autobiographies—*Army Life in a Black Regiment* stands out for its kindness, humor, and sympathetic descriptions of the African-American men who served under him during the war. Although the former colonel accepted some of the negative racial stereotypes shared by most Americans at the time—he suggested that African Americans were quite emotional and less able to think independently than white soldiers—he generally presented a very positive image of the former slaves serving in the Union army. They made brave and disciplined soldiers and were less likely to cause problems than white soldiers. They were extremely religious, and Higginson loved to listen to the men sing old plantation spirituals around camp-

fires at night. They were polite and kind to him and to everyone else they met, including—to Higginson's surprise—former slave owners. Higginson's book was intended to show that African Americans were hardworking, as capable of learning as any other person, and certainly deserving of their freedom.

Despite accomplishing many things during his 88 years, Higginson is probably best remembered for his year of service during the Civil War and for his classic description of the African-American men who fought for the union.

Further reading: Tilden G. Edelstein, *Strange Enthusiasm: A Life of Thomas Wentworth Higginson* (New Haven, Conn.: Yale University Press, 1968); Thomas Wentworth Higginson, *The Complete Civil War Journal and Selected Letters of Thomas Wentworth Higginson,* ed. Christopher Looby (Chicago: University of Chicago Press, 2000); James W. Tuttleton, *Thomas Wentworth Higginson* (Boston: Twayne, 1978).

—James Marten

Hill, Ambrose P. (1825–1865)

Confederate general Ambrose Powell Hill was born in Culpepper, Virginia, on November 9, 1825. In 1842 he was accepted to the UNITED STATES MILITARY ACADEMY AT WEST POINT, where he trained as an artillery officer. After having to repeat his third year due to illness, he graduated 15th in a class of 38. Hill's original graduation class included such notables as GEORGE B. MCCLELLAN, GEORGE E. PICKETT, and THOMAS J. "STONEWALL" JACKSON. Leaving West Point, Hill was commissioned as a second lieutenant in the First Artillery.

Like so many West Point graduates of his era, A. P. Hill's first experience of battle was as a commissioned officer in the Mexican-American War. During the last moments of the war, Hill participated in the capture of Mexico City. He was then stationed at Fort McHenry, Maryland. Later, he would put down an insurrection by the Seminole Indians in Florida. At the outbreak of the CIVIL WAR, Hill felt obligated to defend his home state, and he resigned his commission on March 1, 1861. He was made colonel of the 13th Virginia Volunteer Infantry. In February 1862, Hill was promoted to brigadier general. In command, Hill saw action at Williamsburg, Virginia, and in the PENINSULAR CAMPAIGN. He was promoted in May 1862 to major general and was made a division commander in the new Army of Northern Virginia.

A. P. Hill's division came to be known as "Hill's Light Division" because they could quickly move into emplacements and organize into fighting positions. Hill distinguished himself and his command at engagements such as the BATTLES OF CEDAR MOUNTAIN, SECOND BULL RUN, ANTIETAM, FREDERICKSBURG, and CHANCELLORSVILLE. Throughout all these engagements, Hill became famous for leading his division wearing his bright red battle shirt.

After the death of Stonewall Jackson at the BATTLE OF CHANCELLORSVILLE, Hill was promoted to lieutenant general and was given command of the III Corps. As a corps commander, Hill enjoyed limited success. Due to constant illness, Hill was often lacking the fervor that had previously distinguished him. His leadership in the BATTLES OF GETTYSBURG and THE WILDERNESS campaigns was seriously flawed. Due to his continuing health problems, Hill took a leave of absence in May 1864 and missed the BATTLES OF SPOTSYLVANIA. He reclaimed command during the Battles of North Anna and COLD HARBOR.

On April 2, 1865, at the siege of PETERSBURG, when his command's lines had collapsed, Hill charged a group of Pennsylvania volunteers. After drawing his pistol he was shot dead. Hearing of his death, ROBERT E. LEE said, "He is at rest . . . and we who are left are the ones to suffer."

Further reading: Douglass Southall Freeman, *Lee's Lieutenants: A Study in Command* (New York: Scribner, 1998); James I. Robertson Jr., *General A. P. Hill: The Story of a Confederate Warrior* (New York: Random House, 1987).

—Arthur E. Amos

homefront

Northerners and Southerners living far from the fighting— on the "homefront," as it is called—shared a number of experiences and proved critical to their nation's war efforts. Food and other supplies became more expensive during the war. Because so many men were in the army, women and children worked on farms and in factories, and thousands of wives became widows and thousands of children became orphans. But there were vast differences between the regions as well. These differences are clearly demonstrated in the diaries of two children.

Gerald Norcross, who turned seven when the CIVIL WAR started, lived in Boston, Massachusetts, where his father owned a store. The war barely affected him; he continued going to school, his family went on long summer vacations, and he never mentions a relative or friend being killed or wounded in the army. Gerald experienced the war through books and games and exciting events held in Boston. He read about the war in "dime novels" (cheaply made paperbacks that cost only a dime) with names like *Old Hal Williams; or, the Spy of Atlanta* and *The Vicksburg Spy; or Found and Lost.* He and his classmates sang war songs and read war news from the newspapers at school. He bought and made an army of paper soldiers, whom he named after famous officers from Massachusetts.

Gerald also took part in all sorts of activities related to the Civil War. He watched army regiments parade through the city and drill on Boston Common; he went to Boston Harbor to view an ironclad ship; he attended a huge "Soldiers and Sailors' Fair," which had exciting displays of guns and flags and lots of food and toys to buy; and he played soldier. The war was an important part of Gerald's life, but it was a source of excitement and interest rather than danger and loss.

The Southern homefront was very different for many children. During the siege of Atlanta in 1864, 10-year-old Carrie Berry wrote about hiding from Yankee shells in her family's "bombproof." Her school and church were frequently disrupted; she was rarely able to play with her friends, and on her birthday she wrote that "I did not have a cake times were too hard." Food was in such short supply that one day she was thrilled when her aunt gave her a bunch of grapes. After the battle for Atlanta ended and much of the city had burned to the ground, she helped out by combing through the ashes of destroyed buildings, looking for nails or anything else that might be of use.

Gerald's and Carrie's wartime lives symbolized the homefront experiences of all Americans. In the South, although cities like Atlanta and RICHMOND briefly prospered because of military and government activities, in general life got steadily harder. Food became so scarce in some places that residents rioted, roads and RAILROADS wore out, inflation made it difficult to buy even the most basic goods, schools often closed, many newspapers had to stop publishing, and a large percentage of women and children had to go to work simply to survive. The North, on the other hand, generally prospered during the war. Although there was a period of economic distress in the first year and a half of the war, factories and farms produced record quantities of manufactured goods and food. In fact, they grew so much wheat and corn that Northern farmers exported more grain to Europe during the war than the entire country had before the war. Schools and universities flourished, fast-growing cities like Chicago expanded their street and sewer systems, and migrants continued to move to the West. By the end of the war, many Southern cities lay in ruins, the plantation ECONOMY was destroyed, and most people were living a hand-to-mouth existence. In contrast, most Northerners, aside from those families who had lost loved ones, were probably better off at the end of the war than at the beginning.

Although differences between the Union and Confederate homefronts were vast, there were also important similarities. Northerners and Southerners worked to aid the soldiers in their respective armies, often disagreed over military strategy and government policies, and found their morale changing drastically depending on how well their armies did in the field.

Most Northerners and Southerners worked to help the soldiers. Churches, schools, and soldiers' aid societies raised money, collected supplies, and sewed and knitted clothes and socks for the soldiers. Children in both sections spent some of their spare time "picking lint" from rags for packing around wounds. Although Southerners' efforts to aid the soldiers remained locally controlled, in the North a number of prominent men created a national organization called the UNITED STATES SANITARY COMMISSION (USSC) to coordinate fund-raising and other activities on behalf of the soldiers. The USSC sent supplies to the army, hired NURSES and doctors and sent them to army hospitals, and helped soldiers get mail and fill out discharge forms. To support this work, giant "Sanitary Fairs" were held in towns and cities all over the North. Attendees bought homemade food, clothing, toys, and other goods donated by businessmen and by individuals; attended concerts and demonstrations by schools and churches; marveled at the huge displays of historical artifacts and war-related relics from the American Revolution as well as the current "Rebellion;" and enjoyed appearances by famous generals and politicians. Altogether, the Sanitary Fairs raised more than $4 million for the Union war effort.

Even though the North and South were engaged in a desperate war, there were many people in each region who disagreed with the policies of their governments. In the North, the DEMOCRATIC PARTY continued to oppose the Republicans. Without their Southern allies, the Democrats had little power in Congress, but they did demonstrate considerable strength in parts of the Midwest and in cities like NEW YORK CITY. Most Democrats remained loyal to the U.S. government, but some, like Ohio congressman CLEMENT L. VALLANDIGHAM, were so extreme in their criticism that Republicans nicknamed them COPPERHEADS, after the poisonous snake. Also causing problems for President ABRAHAM LINCOLN were the "radicals" in his own REPUBLICAN PARTY, who believed for the first year or two of the war that the government was moving too slow in attacking SLAVERY. Political parties never actually formed in the Confederacy, but an opposition to the administration of JEFFERSON DAVIS arose by 1863.

The opponents of Lincoln and Davis expressed similar complaints: They did not like the way that the central governments were conducting the war. In both regions, the governments wielded far more power than the antebellum federal government had ever exerted. Both governments resorted to CONSCRIPTION to raise troops, levied high taxes to pay for the war, and jailed men who criticized the government.

The most serious resistance in the Confederacy came after the military draft went into effect in spring 1862. By the end of the Civil War, thousands of deserters and draft evaders were hiding in isolated parts of the South. The Union waited another year before beginning to conscript soldiers, but the reaction was the same. Public meetings condemned the policy and riots broke out around the country. The biggest was the NEW YORK CITY DRAFT RIOTS in July 1863, which resulted in the deaths of more than 100 people. Attacks on African Americans during the riot indicated the extent to which many Northerners opposed the EMANCIPATION PROCLAMATION. In fact, the Democratic Party gained a number of seats in the U.S. Congress in 1862, largely because of Lincoln's decision to issue the Preliminary Emancipation Proclamation in the fall of that year. Many Southerners also opposed the centralization of power as the Confederate government, in addition to raising taxes and drafting soldiers, limited the freedom of planters to grow cotton and, by the end of the war, had begun the process of recruiting and arming African Americans for the CONFEDERATE ARMY. The most organized resistance groups in the Confederacy were the so-called Peace Parties that appeared during the 1864 election, most notably in North Carolina. A few members of these groups won election to state legislatures and to the Confederate Congress.

Opposition to the Lincoln administration also grew in strength as the war progressed, and by the late summer of 1864 the president believed that he would lose the election to the Democratic candidate Gen. GEORGE B. MCCLELLAN in November, primarily because Lincoln's armies were doing so badly. The Army of the Potomac had failed to capture Richmond in its OVERLAND CAMPAIGN, losing tens of thousands of men in the BATTLES OF THE WILDERNESS, SPOTSYLVANIA, and COLD HARBOR. Gen. WILLIAM T. SHERMAN's summer campaign to capture Atlanta had also gotten bogged down in northwestern Georgia. Nothing seemed to be going right, and the Democratic "peace platform" seemed attractive to Northern voters. Ultimately, Lincoln won reelection by a comfortable margin, mainly because of the soldiers' vote and because Sherman and his army captured Atlanta while Grant laid siege to Petersburg, causing Northern morale to rise. Similar swings in morale occurred in the Confederacy, where victories in the FIRST and SECOND BATTLES OF BULL RUN, the Seven Days' Battles, and the BATTLE OF CHICKAMAUGA brought confidence and high levels of patriotism, while defeats at the BATTLE OF SHILOH and the VICKSBURG CAMPAIGN and the deaths of popular generals like THOMAS J. "STONEWALL" JACKSON caused morale to fall.

As the ups and downs of civilian morale show, the Civil War homefront, rather than being removed from the military events of the war, was closely linked to its battles and campaigns. Some historians have called the Civil War the first "total war," and to the extent that the Confederate and Union homefronts—their economies, their political systems, and their societies—were part of the war efforts of the North and South, that label is accurate.

See also BANKING AND CURRENCY; FOOD RIOTS; HABEAS CORPUS, WRIT OF.

Further reading: E. Merton Coulter, *The Confederate States of America, 1861–1865* (Baton Rouge: Louisiana State University Press, 1950); J. Matthew Gallman, *The North Fights the Civil War: The Home Front* (Chicago: I.R. Dees, 1994); James Marten, *The Children's Civil War* (Chapel Hill: University of North Carolina Press, 1998); Phillip Shaw Paludan, *"A People's Contest": The Union and Civil War, 1861–1865* (Lawrence: University Press of Kansas, 1996).

—James Marten

homespun

As materials became increasingly scarce, Confederate women turned to homemade thread and cloth during the CIVIL WAR. Women who had previously engaged only in ornamental sewing and embroidery found themselves learning how to spin thread and weave cloth to keep their families clothed. These methods, which in antebellum years had been used primarily by slaves, became commonplace for all women in the Confederacy, white and black. The materials manufactured by Southern women during the war served as the basis for clothing, undergarments, shoes, and other cloth items.

Homespun cloth had many different forms. Some women made it in solids, some in stripes or plaids. In addition, the quality of homespun cloth varied widely, ranging from very tight weaves to extremely coarse materials. Opinions on the FASHIONS created from these materials varied, with some decrying the shabby look of wartime women and others praising the ingenuity and creativity of the homespun weavers and seamstresses.

White Southern women took pride in their manufacture of homespun as well as in their use of it. Indeed, the wearing of Confederate homespun became a badge of patriotism throughout the South because it represented a sacrifice of luxury for the benefit of the war effort. It also demonstrated the resourcefulness of Southern women. In 1862 one Southern woman wrote "The Homespun Dress," a song that exulted in women's use of the homemade fabric; according to the lyrics, the wearing of homespun "shows what Southern girls / For Southern rights will do."

Men, too, proudly wore outfits made from homespun cloth. Vice President ALEXANDER H. STEPHENS wore a homespun suit to his inauguration. Other dignitaries—including North Carolina governor JOSEPH E. BROWN, Edmund Ruffin, and other members of the Confederate Congress—commonly wore homespun as a symbol of their dedication to the Confederate war effort.

See also HOMEFRONT.

Further reading: Mary Elizabeth Massey, *Ersatz in the Confederacy* (Columbia: University of South Carolina Press, 1952); Laurel Ulrich, *The Age of Homespun: Objects and Stories in the Creation of an American Myth* (New York: Knopf, 2001).

—Lisa Tendrich Frank

Homestead Act (1862)

The Homestead Act, adopted by Congress in 1862, provided for the settlement of the nation's vast public western lands by farmers.

During the first half-century of its existence, the American government used the sale of public lands as one of its primary sources of income. Officials encouraged settlers to move to western lands and used the sale of those lands to fund numerous government activities. As farmers struggled to deal with the costs of purchasing and settling these new areas, and as the eastern populations grew, land reformers sought to make the government change its policies. Men like HORACE GREELEY wanted to make it easier and less expensive for settlers to occupy the West and kept the issue before Congress from 1845 to 1862. Although the House of Representatives passed homestead bills three times in the 1850s and twice in 1860 alone, the bills either died in the Senate or at the hands of the president.

However, JAMES BUCHANAN's veto of the Homestead Bill in 1860 raised the ire of land reformers and settlers throughout the country, and the passage of this legislation became a central piece of the Republican platform in the 1860 ELECTIONS. The resulting support of Westerners for this measure contributed in no small part to Lincoln's victory in November of that year. Representative Galusha Grow reintroduced the Homestead Bill in Congress early in Lincoln's first term, and on May 20, 1862, the president officially signed it into law. As written, the Homestead Act provided 160 acres for any head of household and the right to acquire title to that land for a minimal fee once the individual had occupied the land for five years. In theory, the act provided the means for farmers to obtain land virtually free, and it also created an outlet for the growing populations in the cities and towns throughout the East.

While the number of homesteaders grew at a slow pace during the years of the CIVIL WAR, their numbers increased significantly following the surrender at APPOMATTOX COURT HOUSE. However, land reformers soon realized that the bill contained several deficiencies.

Engraving showing potential homesteaders scoping out plots of land on a map of a county in Kansas *(Library of Congress)*

First, designed to avoid the avid speculation that occurred throughout the 19th century, the bill contained a loophole that allowed the homesteader to acquire a pre-emption claim to his property after only six months residence. Such a claim conferred the title to the land and thus allowed the homesteader to sell to private interests long before the designated five-year period elapsed. Cattle ranchers, lumber companies, and speculators all participated in the process of hiring agents to obtain titles or bribing government employees to ignore the activity.

Second, the designation of 160 acres had been sufficient for lands settled in more humid regions, but for the semiarid lands of the West, such a small amount of land maximized the room for error for prospective farmers. Third, a significant amount of the land designated for settlers had already been apportioned to various private and public interests by the time the act went into effect in the beginning of 1863. Railroad companies, state schools, and universities occupied and utilized acreage sufficient for almost 2 million individual homesteads. Finally, by encouraging settlement throughout the western territories, the act created conflict between the settlers and the American Indians who lived in the western plains, resulting in warfare and ultimately government-sponsored removal of the Indians from reservation lands.

The Homestead Act and subsequent legislation continued to provide public lands for individuals looking for a new start in the West well into the 20th century. By 1900, approximately 70 million acres of land had been claimed under the auspices of the 1862 edict.

See also NATIVE AMERICANS; PACIFIC RAILROAD ACT.

Further reading: Coy F. Cross II, *Go West, Young Man!: Horace Greeley's Vision for America* (Albuquerque: University of New Mexico Press, 1995); Paul Wallace Gates, *Free Homesteads for All Americans: The Homestead Act of 1862* (Washington, D.C.: Civil War Centennial Commission, 1962).

—John P. Bowes

Hood, John Bell (1831–1879)

Confederate general John Bell Hood was born to a prominent family in rural Owingsville, Kentucky, on June 29, 1831. Hood's parents had high expectations for him. At the UNITED STATES MILITARY ACADEMY AT WEST POINT, Hood proved a mediocre student and barely managed to graduate. ROBERT E. LEE commented that "Hood is a bold fighter . . . very industrious on the battlefield, careless off . . . I am doubtful as to the other qualities necessary." Confederate president JEFFERSON DAVIS nonetheless selected Hood to command the Army of Tennessee in July 1864. Lee's evaluation, however, proved both accurate and prophetic. Despite his early successes at the brigade and divisional levels, Hood was unable to meet the challenges of higher responsibility. Hood's battlefield errors destroyed the Army of Tennessee and ruined Confederate aspirations in the West. Perhaps no other commander during the CIVIL WAR experienced such adulation only to be followed by utter disgrace.

The outbreak of the Civil War found First Lieutenant Hood in Texas, serving with the Second Cavalry. After resigning his U.S. Army commission, Hood traveled east as a Confederate major in the Fourth Texas Infantry Regiment. Over the next five months Hood's aggressive fighting earned him the favor of President Davis and a promotion to colonel, in command of his own regiment. When the position of brigade commander became available in March 1862, Hood was elevated to brigadier general.

Hood's reputation continued to grow as he and his "Texas Brigade" impressed Gens. Robert E. Lee and THOMAS J. "STONEWALL" JACKSON with outstanding performances at the BATTLES of Gaines Mill, SECOND BULL RUN, and ANTIETAM. Promotion to major general followed, and Hood and his Texans became heroes throughout the South.

A ferocious fighter, Hood's reputation continued to grow. At the BATTLE OF GETTYSBURG in July 1863 his left arm was permanently disabled during the assault on the Devil's Den. The following September, Hood's division spearheaded Gen. JAMES LONGSTREET's successful attack at the BATTLE OF CHICKAMAUGA, Georgia. Hood was again seriously wounded, losing his right leg. His bravery was recognized a few weeks later with a promotion to lieutenant general when he returned to RICHMOND. During this time Hood became a close confidant to Jefferson Davis, a friendship that would yield negative consequences for their nation.

Requesting reassignment, Hood was appointed a corps commander under Gen. JOSEPH E. JOHNSTON in the Army of Tennessee. As Gen. WILLIAM T. SHERMAN pushed the Confederates south through Georgia, Hood used his influence with Jefferson Davis to argue for Johnston's removal, making the case that he, Hood, would conduct a more aggressive campaign. Davis eventually acquiesced, naming Hood commander of the Army of Tennessee in July 1864.

Hood lost no time in taking the initiative, with disastrous results. Suffering the loss of one-third of his army in a series of reckless assaults on Gen. William T. Sherman's army, Hood was forced to abandon Atlanta by late August 1864. As Sherman embarked on his famous "march to the sea," Hood led his army in the opposite direction, intending to threaten Sherman's supply lines in Tennessee. After missing an opportunity to destroy a portion of Gen. GEORGE HENRY THOMAS's forces at Spring Hill, Tennessee, Hood recklessly threw his army against the Federals at Franklin, Tennessee, on November 30, 1864. Suffering crippling casualties, Hood would not give up his campaign. Instead, he moved to Nashville with a force that was no longer adequate to the task. On December 15 and 16 Thomas attacked and destroyed the Army of Tennessee. Hood was relieved of command at his own request and returned to Richmond in February 1865.

After the war, Hood established an insurance business in New Orleans, where he married and had 11 children. In the mid-1870s his business failed and a yellow-fever epidemic swept through New Orleans, taking his wife and eldest daughter before claiming the general himself on August 30, 1879, at the age of 48.

See also SHERMAN'S MARCH THROUGH GEORGIA.

Further reading: John Bell Hood, *Advance and Retreat: Personal Experiences in the United States & Confederate States Armies,* ed. Richard N. Current (New York: Kraus Reprint, 1969); Richard M. McMurry, *John Bell Hood and the War for Southern Independence* (Lexington: University Press of Kentucky, 1992).

—Don Worth

Hooker, Joseph

Union general and commander of the Union's Army of the Potomac for a brief time, Joseph Hooker was born on November 13, 1814, in Hadley, Massachusetts. Hooker was educated at the UNITED STATES MILITARY ACADEMY AT WEST POINT, where he graduated 29th of 50 in the class of 1837. Shortly afterward, he received his first army combat assignment as a staff officer during the Mexican-American War. A tall, well-proportioned man, Hooker possessed a contentious and prickly personality. After several arguments marred his early career, he resigned from the military and settled in California as a farmer and landowner in the 1850s.

Hooker reentered the army after the FIRST BATTLE OF BULL RUN. Appointed a brigadier general, Hooker commanded a brigade of U.S. volunteers charged with the defense of WASHINGTON, D.C. He demonstrated great competence in battle and was rewarded for his performance during the PENINSULAR CAMPAIGN and the SECOND BATTLE OF BULL RUN in spring and summer of 1862 with the grade of major general.

Called "Fighting Joe" by a newspaper correspondent, Hooker led the I Corps of the Army of the Potomac in the Antietam campaign, again demonstrating his military capabilities. His action in charge of a division was one of the few bright spots during the Union loss at the BATTLE OF FREDERICKSBURG. As a result of the disaster there, Lincoln turned to Hooker to command the Army of the Potomac, despite rumors of his heavy drinking and womanizing. Lincoln knew of Hooker's rash remark that what the country needed was a good dictator to run the war. He wrote "I have heard, in such a way as to believe it, of your recently saying that both the Army and the government needed a dictator. Of course it was not for this, but in spite of it, that I have given you the command. Only those generals who gain success can set up dictators. What I now ask of you is military success, and I will risk the dictatorship."

Unfortunately, Hooker would prove as ineffective against Lee as many of his predecessors had. Despite reinvigorating the morale of the Army of the Potomac and planning an excellent campaign, Hooker was outthought, outflanked, and outfought by Lee. One reporter commented: "Not the Army of the Potomac was beaten at Chancellorsville, but its commander." On June 28, 1863, Hooker resigned as commander of the Army of the Potomac and was replaced by Gen. GEORGE GORDON MEADE, who led the army to its greatest victory at the BATTLE OF GETTYSBURG.

Hooker was reassigned to command of the XI and XII Corps of the Army of the Cumberland in September 1863. In a well-executed attack, Hooker and his men took the

Confederate position on Lookout Mountain during the BATTLE OF CHATTANOOGA. Hooker played a part in the ATLANTA CAMPAIGN, but after being passed over for the command of the Army of the Tennessee, he resigned and spent the rest of the war carrying out administrative duties. Hooker retired from the professional military in 1868 and died on October 31, 1879, in Garden City, New York.

See also ANTIETAM, BATTLE OF; CHANCELLORSVILLE, BATTLE OF.

Further reading: Walter H. Hebert, *Fighting Joe Hooker* (Indianapolis: Bobbs-Merrill, 1944); Stephen W. Sears, *Chancellorsville* (Boston: Houghton-Mifflin, 1996).

—Arthur E. Amos

Howard, Oliver Otis (1830–1909)

Major general in the CIVIL WAR, commissioner of the FREEDMEN'S BUREAU, and MEDAL OF HONOR winner O. O. Howard was born in Leeds, Maine, on November 8, 1830. Graduating from Bowdoin College in 1850, Howard also attended the UNITED STATES MILITARY ACADEMY AT WEST POINT, where he taught mathematics until 1861. A strikingly handsome man, Howard served as colonel of the Third Maine Infantry at the FIRST BATTLE OF BULL RUN and then was promoted to brigadier general and assigned to the II Corps in the Army of the Potomac. Accompanying Gen. GEORGE B. MCCLELLAN on the PENINSULAR CAMPAIGN, he lost an arm fighting in the battle of Fair Oaks on May 31, 1862. Returning to duty in time to fight at the BATTLE OF ANTIETAM, Howard distinguished himself enough to be appointed, at age 32, major general in command of the XI Corps. Howard's leadership was criticized in the BATTLE OF CHANCELLORSVILLE, in May 1863, and at the BATTLE OF GETTYSBURG, in July of the same year. At the former, Howard's evident inattentiveness led to a rout of his men by THOMAS J. "STONEWALL" JACKSON's famous flank attack and was a major factor in the devastating defeat of the UNION ARMY.

After the death of Gen. John Reynolds, Howard was in command of all Union forces at Gettysburg, Pennsylvania, on the afternoon of July 1, 1863. Outnumbered and increasingly outflanked by the Confederates, Howard made a number of ill-advised decisions that resulted in the collapse of the IX Corps and then the rest of the Union forces on Oak Ridge. Driven back through the town to Cemetery Hill, thousands of panicked soldiers were re-formed by Howard and others for a new stand against their attackers. Howard subsequently claimed credit for the excellent Union defensive position along Cemetery Hill and Ridge, although the new commander on the field, Gen.

WINFIELD SCOTT HANCOCK, disputed this. The following September, Howard was sent to the western army, where he was a corps commander under Gen. ULYSSES S. GRANT and Gen. WILLIAM T. SHERMAN in several notable battles, including the BATTLE OF CHATTANOOGA. Sherman appointed Howard commander of the Army of the Tennessee before the march through Georgia and the Carolinas. Despite his high rank and continued advancement, Howard was never particularly well regarded either by his men or his peers and was judged at best a mediocre general.

After the war, Howard continued to serve the country. A devout Christian and a strong supporter of African-American freedom and advancement, Howard was singled out by President ABRAHAM LINCOLN to head the newly created FREEDMEN'S BUREAU in 1865. Howard had a strong vision for the bureau that included providing EDUCATION, protection, and economic security in the form of land for the masses of freed people in the South. Disappointed by the lack of enthusiasm and support from the Johnson administration, Howard struggled to maintain the integrity of the bureau's work against a hostile and oftentimes violent environment in the Southern states. His administration was attacked for inefficiency, and some of his financial dealings were subject to congressional investigations. Despite immense difficulties, the bureau under Howard's direction was able to establish and support schools and provide some protection for black freedom through its system of courts. Howard personally expanded opportunities for African Americans when he helped to found Howard University, becoming its first president in 1869 and serving in that capacity until 1874. Later, he also founded Lincoln Memorial University in Harrowgate, Tennessee.

The demise of the Freedmen's Bureau in the early 1870s brought Howard, still in the regular army, out West again, this time to serve in the frontier wars against the Indians. He was peace commissioner to the Apache, and in 1877 he led the campaign against Chief Joseph and the Nez Perce, earning criticism for his inept handling of men and supplies. Before Howard ended his military career in 1894, he served as superintendent of West Point and commanded the Division of the East. An active supporter of the REPUBLICAN PARTY and of educational and philanthropic organizations and a popular speaker on the lecture circuit, Howard kept himself busy in retirement. He was an accomplished writer and published widely on many military and historical topics. Oliver Otis Howard died on October 26, 1909, in Burlington, Vermont.

Further reading: O. O. Howard, *Autobiography of Oliver Otis Howard, Major General, United States Army* (1907;

reprint, Freeport, N.Y.: Books for Libraries Press, 1971); William S. McFeely, *Yankee Stepfather: General O. O. Howard and the Freedmen* (New Haven, Conn.: Yale University Press, 1968).

Howe, Julia Ward (1819–1910)

Julia Ward Howe was a poet, lecturer, ABOLITIONist, and advocate for women's rights, but she is best remembered for writing the song "Battle Hymn of the Republic."

Howe was born into a respected family, descended from Revolutionary War heroes and Rhode Island GOVERNORS. She lost her mother at a young age but enjoyed the benefits of a privileged upbringing. She threw herself wholeheartedly into her studies as well as a social life that included visits to and from many noted authors, politicians, and scholars. While still very young, Howe began her career as an author, publishing several articles and reviews.

She married Dr. Samuel Howe in 1843. The couple made their home at an estate Howe called "Green Peace" in Boston, where she had six children. The Howes were actively involved in the abolitionist movement and edited an antiSLAVERY newspaper. Dr. Howe disapproved of his wife's writing, however, and to try to hide it from him she began to publish anonymously. In 1854 he discovered that she was the author of *Passion Flowers,* her first full volume of poems. The couple separated soon after, although they never divorced.

In 1861 Howe wrote the "Battle Hymn of the Republic" after a friend suggested that she compose "good words" for the tune of "JOHN BROWN's Body," which was already a popular song. As Howe described it afterward, she awoke in her room at the Willard Hotel in the nation's capital with the words in her head. Getting up, she "began to scrawl the lines almost without looking." She then went back to sleep, "but not without feeling that something important had happened to me."

The "Battle Hymn of the Republic" was published in 1862. Chaplain Charles McCabe became linked with the poem, singing it before President ABRAHAM LINCOLN and at many public occasions. It continued to grow in popularity long after the war had ended and is as well known today as it was in the 1860s.

After the CIVIL WAR, Howe became active in the struggle for women's voting rights. The war, she said, had "brought many of us out of the ruts of established ways" and "forced us to take a larger outlook into the possibilities of the future." Howe founded and led several women's organizations on both the local and national level. She continued to write, travel, and speak on many issues. Her prominence led to her being the first woman elected to the American Academy of Arts and Sciences in 1908. Howe served only briefly before dying in 1910 at the age of 91.

See also MUSIC.

Further reading: Julia Ward Howe, *Reminiscences, 1819–1899* (Boston: Houghton, Mifflin, 1899).

—Vickey Kalambakal

I

immigration

Between 1850 and 1880, nearly 8 million immigrants arrived in the United States, and as a percentage of the population, the foreign-born rose from 9.7 to 13.3 percent. Immigration on that large a scale had important impacts, not only on the immigrants but also on American political, social, and economic life.

The immigrants of the mid-19th century were largely northwestern European, with the majority coming from Germany and Ireland. In the decades between 1851 and 1880, Irish and German immigrants combined were never less than 40 percent of America's total immigration pool, and they constituted more than 70 percent of America's immigrants between 1851 and 1860. The demographics of the immigrant stream changed over time and varied among national-origin groups, but, generally, immigrants were male, single, and between 18 and 40 years of age. Some came highly skilled, like the Jewish tailors of eastern Europe and the potters of Staffordshire, England, while some came seemingly unprepared to make a life in America. The demographic profile of those who immigrated shifted in reaction to current conditions. For instance, the Irish potato-famine migrants generally came as families rather than single individuals, but in the mid-1850s, legal developments in land policies in Ireland brought proportionately more single women than the Irish or other immigrant groups had previously sent.

Unlike the fanciful tales of immigrants seeking refuge in the United States after dreaming for their entire lives of riches and freedom, historians have come to understand that immigrants to the United States were generally very shrewd and took into account conditions not only in their homeland but also in potential destinations. For instance, the number of immigrants arriving in the United States during the CIVIL WAR dropped significantly, just as they did during depressions and panics in the American ECONOMY. Immigrants generally made the choice to come to the United States when that choice was advantageous to them. Thus, the motivations of immigrants are complex and individual. Among the key reasons for immigration during the mid-19th century were rapidly changing conditions in Europe, the economy, religious persecution, and political strife.

In the middle of the 19th century, Europeans were caught in a nexus of events and developments that made the likelihood of immigration greater. Famines, like the potato famine that decimated Irish and German potato crops from the 1840s through the 1850s, forced many people to leave their homes merely in an effort to survive. Religious persecutions brought more immigrants to America's ports. For example, in the late 19th century nearly 2 million Jews came to the United States to escape pogroms in Europe. Political persecution, or fear of it, brought another flood of immigrants, especially the German "48ers" who came in large numbers to the United States after the failed revolutions of 1848 in Europe. On a larger scale, a dramatic increase in European populations meant more people needed food, land, and EMPLOYMENT, while at the same time the spread of commercial AGRICULTURE consolidated land holdings and pushed smaller farmers off the land. The rise of the factory system in Europe moved people from the rural areas to the cities and put them in contact with the growing proliferation of relatively inexpensive TRANSPORTATION.

Transportation developments played an important role in the process of immigration. The 1850s began the age of steamships. As late as 1856, 95 percent of European immigrants to the United States arrived by sailing ship after an arduous journey of anywhere from one to three months. By 1873, 95 percent of European immigrants were arriving in America's ports on steamships, whose passage time was generally 10 days. It was a difficult trip nonetheless, as immigrants' accommodations were generally cramped, dark, and lacking in ventilation and amenities, sometimes with tragic consequences. For instance, in 1866 cholera killed hundreds of German immigrants on National Line ships out of Rotterdam.

Other developments in transportation also helped fuel immigration to the United States. The improved European rail network that helped change landholding patterns also allowed for easier and cheaper transportation within Europe, especially the port cities. Some businesses, particularly settler-hungry American railroad companies with land grants and steamship companies seeking to fill all their berths, set up easily accessible ticketing agencies in Europe and America. The most popular ticketing option was for immigrants who had made their "fortune" in the United States to buy prepaid travel packages for their family and friends back home, developing what historians refer to as a "chain migration." U.S. land-grant RAILROADS heavily promoted this scheme of migration, which ultimately had a significant impact on the settlement of the American West and Midwest. Railroad ticketing agents facilitated what amounted to the transfer of whole European villages to the American territories, thus developing enclaves of Welsh, Norwegian, German, and Russian settlers across America's heartland. In addition, states and territories in the United States, campaigned in Europe for settlers. They advertised cheap or even free land, plentiful resources, and a harmonious environment, all waiting to be selected by a willing immigrant as his or her own.

The first sight most immigrants had of the United States in the mid-19th century was Castle Garden, New York, which served as the East Coast's main immigrant entry port until Ellis Island opened in 1892. For West Coast immigrants, Angel Island in San Francisco was the general port of entry. Beyond the gates of the processing centers at the ports, immigrants faced a United States that was not hospitable. Americans wanted immigrants to easily assimilate into their culture, to work hard for whatever wages were offered, and to be literate.

America's largest immigrant groups of the mid-19th century, the Germans and Irish, were generally Catholic and imbibers of alcohol, both character flaws as far as "old" Americans were concerned. The largely Protestant United States had an overwhelmingly negative opinion of Catholicism. Native-born American distrust of the immigrants' ties to the Catholic Church was only exacerbated when German-Americans placed such great emphasis on parochial school development, and Irish-Americans poured millions of dollars into building towering cathedrals like St. Patrick's in NEW YORK CITY. Beyond their suspicions of immigrants' Catholicism, alcohol use by immigrants became a key target of protesters in the mid-19th century. In 1851 Maine passed a statewide prohibition law, and other states followed with their own version of what came to be known as "Maine laws," but the restrictions of alcohol were rarely enforced effectively.

With two strikes against them already, Irish and German immigrants inspired even more animosity by affiliating themselves with urban political machines. Both immigrant groups were adopted by Democratic political machines, who came to depend on the votes of immigrants to stay in power. Most notorious of the urban machines was New York's Tammany Hall, which reached the height of its power under the leadership of the notorious William "Boss" Tweed. Despite their political skullduggery and unsavory reputations, however, the urban machines offered immigrants an important support network—jobs, assistance in times of need, and a chance to rise in the machine and the city. Because of their affiliation with the machines, Catholicism, and alcohol, German and Irish immigrants were the targets of rising tides of anti-immigrant sentiment, or NATIVISM. Newspapers portrayed them as baboons and drunkards who stole ELECTIONS and defiled democracy. Many argued that these immigrants could never be real American citizens.

The assimilation of these "unassimilable" immigrants came in a drastic way. With the advent of the Civil War, many immigrant groups seized their chance to prove their allegiance to the United States. Immigrants of all ethnicities answered calls like that of the Irish-American newspaper, the *Boston Pilot*, which urged its readers to "Stand by the Union; fight for the Union; die for the Union." Across the North, ethnic units like the 79th New York Infantry (Scottish), the 55th New York Infantry (French), the 15th Wisconsin Infantry (Scandinavian), and the famed "Irish Brigade" formed. The Confederacy had its ethnic regiments as well, such as the "Emerald Guards" and the "New Orleans Jägers," but most immigrants in the preceding decades had settled in the North because of the limited employment opportunities open to them in the Southern slave system.

Many members of these ethnic units signed on for less lofty reasons than saving the Union or the Confederacy. Many were moved, just as their native-born fellow soldiers had been, to sign up for adventure and for the economic opportunities enlistment provided. For the typical immigrant worker in Northeastern cities or on Midwestern farms, the monthly soldier's salary was good money in comparison to their own laborer's earnings. Few immigrants enlisted with the aim of freeing the slaves, since most immigrants were on the bottom of the labor ladder and thus would be competing with freedmen for jobs. For this reason, many immigrants declined to participate in the Civil War, particularly after Lincoln's issuance of the EMANCIPATION PROCLAMATION. The most notable example of racial tensions during the war came with the NEW YORK CITY DRAFT RIOTS of 1863, when mobs of angry Irish New Yorkers ransacked African-American neighborhoods. The negative impact of the draft riots, however, was far outweighed by the positive contribution that immigrants made to the Union war effort. Over the course of the Civil War, more than 200,000 German-Americans and 160,000 Irish-Americans served in the Union and Confederate armies. Other immigrant groups provided troops in lesser, but still substantial, numbers. Throughout the war, immigrants' enlistment rates remained high, and their battlefield prowess and bravery won them great acclaim and a significant measure of respect from old-stock, native-born Americans.

Even after dedicated military service, however, immigrant life was not easy in the United States. In employment, immigrants were always near the bottom of the ladder, generally only advancing when a new wave of immigrants came along and pushed them up. Along with a reliance on machine politics, some immigrant groups formed alliances with organized labor to assist their rise in the United States. Association with organized labor, however, generally put immigrants once again at odds with the larger American society. The Knights of Labor, one of the foremost unions of the late 19th century, exemplified the connections between the immigrant, his homeland, and the United States. The Knights forged links to the Land League, a nationalist movement for Irish independence and land reform, and Clan na Gael, an Irish nationalist society. In the 1860s a controversial and "secret" labor organization of the Pennsylvania mining region, the Molly Maguires, was said to be an offshoot of the Irish-American association, Ancient Order of Hibernians.

Other American immigrant groups also found the postwar United States to be a difficult place. Chinese immigrants, who originally came to work the California gold fields in the 1850s and then worked for the Union Pacific half of the transcontinental railroad in the 1860s, made up 9 percent of the California population from 1860 through 1880. The work they did in the labor gangs of the Union Pacific was invaluable to the success of the line, but their sacrifice was not rewarded upon its completion. When the transcontinental railroad was finished in 1869, large numbers of unemployed Chinese immigrants were left in its wake. Anti-Chinese sentiment rose throughout the West, culminating in riots and expulsions of immigrants through the 1880s. The federal government was constrained in its actions by the Burlingame Treaty of 1868, which allowed unrestricted Chinese immigration, but in 1882 Congress finally passed an act suspending Chinese immigration for ten years. The act was renewed several times.

For all the trials and tribulations, immigration to the United States continued unabated. Through the end of the 19th and into the 20th century, it followed time-worn patterns of largely economic push-pull factors, but in the 1880s and 1890s "new" immigrants from southern and eastern European nations like Russia, Italy, Turkey, and Greece replaced the "old" northwestern European immigrants. The rise of southern and eastern European immigrant streams fed the fires of nativist concerns once again, and a new group of immigrants were subject to American suspicion and attack. In 1896 "new" immigrants outnumbered "old" ones for the first time in U.S. history. For all that immigrants had accomplished for themselves and on behalf of the Union in the mid-19th century, Americans had learned very little as a nation about the benefits of new citizens.

See also GERMAN-AMERICAN REGIMENTS; IRISH-AMERICAN REGIMENTS.

Further reading: Charles J. Hoflund, *Getting Ahead: A Swedish Immigrant's Reminiscences, 1834–1887*, ed. H. Arnold Barton (Carbondale: Southern Illinois University Press, 1989); Bruce Levine, *The Spirit of 1848: German Immigrants, Labor Conflict, and the Coming of the Civil War* (Urbana: University of Illinois Press, 1992); Kerby Miller, *Emigrants and Exiles: Ireland and the Irish Exodus to North America* (New York: Oxford University Press, 1988); Alexander P. Saxton, *The Indispensable Enemy: Labor and the Anti-Chinese Movement in California*, rev.ed. (Berkeley: University of California Press, 1995); William E. Van Vugt, *Britain to America: Mid-Nineteenth-Century Immigrants to the United States* (Urbana: University of Illinois Press, 1999).

—Ruth A. Behling

impeachment of Andrew Johnson (1868)

On February 25, 1868, the House Managers of Impeachment, led by THADDEUS STEVENS, appeared before the U.S. Senate to present 11 articles of impeachment against President ANDREW JOHNSON. Their case rested on Johnson's removal of Secretary of War EDWIN M. STANTON from office, but the action really grew out of a political struggle between Johnson and Congress over RECONSTRUCTION. The sensational trial brought the national government to a halt for three months. On May 26, 1868, the Senate voted 35 to 19 to convict Johnson, only one vote short of the two-thirds necessary to remove him from office. Johnson was acquitted, but his effectiveness as a leader was destroyed.

When Vice President Andrew Johnson assumed the office of president in April 1865 after the ASSASSINATION OF ABRAHAM LINCOLN, he enjoyed the united support of the Northern leaders and citizenry. Johnson, a Democrat who was the wartime governor of Tennessee, appeared on the 1864 ticket to broaden the appeal of the REPUBLICAN PARTY beyond its traditional base. Johnson's deep hatred of the Southern slaveholding class was widely known. RADICAL REPUBLICANS, a strong wing of the party led by CHARLES SUMNER of Massachusetts, had good reason to assume Johnson agreed with their harsh position on Reconstruction. They believed, as did the majority of more moderate Republicans, that Congress and the executive would work together well to determine the process of incorporating the Southern states back into the Union.

Johnson was no stranger to Congress. He had served on the JOINT COMMITTEE ON THE CONDUCT OF THE WAR with BENJAMIN WADE, Zechariah Chandler, and GEORGE W. JULIAN, all Radical Republicans. Ominously, although a staunch Union man who favored EMANCIPATION, he had never supported an agenda that included black suffrage and civil rights. His sympathies were for the plain white farmers of the South, and his beliefs were those of a typical Democrat, including the desire for a small national government and the upholding of STATES' RIGHTS. He loudly proclaimed that he would follow in his predecessor's footsteps, with a lenient and merciful Reconstruction policy. Unfortunately, Johnson was sorely lacking in Lincoln's political skills. Called by some the "accidental president," he was inflexible, stubborn, and, in the end, self-destructive. Understandably, Johnson wanted to control Reconstruction from the White House, but his many vetoes, together with his adamant refusal to compromise with congressional Republicans, brought catastrophic results for the nation.

Johnson's earliest policy moves alarmed the Republican-dominated Congress. He readmitted Virginia with only a few restrictions and on May 29, 1865, issued a Proclamation of Amnesty, setting in motion liberal policy of pardons for ex-Confederates.

The new president had initiated a heated struggle over the control of Reconstruction that eventually led to his impeachment. Johnson supported the restoration of landed property to ex-Confederates, and early in 1866 he vetoed the FREEDMEN'S BUREAU bill. Throughout this period many Republicans grew increasingly alarmed but did not break with the White House, hoping to work out an agreement before the fall ELECTIONS. Only when the president vetoed the CIVIL RIGHTS ACT OF 1866 and made known his opposition to the proposed FOURTEENTH AMENDMENT did congressional Republicans declare an open war and take their case to the voters.

The fall elections of 1866 went badly for Johnson and his supporters. Radical and moderate Republicans were united and now had the power to act on their desire to end Johnson's obstructionist stance on Reconstruction. Congress intended to halt the widespread removal of Republicans from government positions by Johnson. The first step was to deprive the president of his patronage powers. Early in 1867, the Tenure of Office Act passed. In the same session, Congress also passed legislation to limit Johnson's influence over the military. Still not finished, Congress, over a presidential veto, initiated the RECONSTRUCTION ACT that established military governments throughout the South. Congress and the president were declared enemies. Republicans hoped to force the South to

accept universal male suffrage and the Fourteenth Amendment. Johnson, horrified by what he described as a blatant violation of the Constitution, fought hard to stop the legislation and employed the veto. These policies, the president also believed, would severely hinder the South's recovery. Congress overrode his veto with ease. Johnson's fierce opposition, however, threatened their future Reconstruction plans. Impeachment talk was becoming common within congressional chambers.

In December 1867 the House of Representatives began the impeachment proceeding against Johnson. For the moment, they were unsuccessful, but the newly elected president of the Senate, Radical Republican Benjamin Wade, was determined to pursue the issue. Over the following year, Wade directed a Congress that set its Reconstruction policy in motion without hesitation. Yet another Reconstruction bill passed over Johnson's veto. The president's response was twofold. First, he outwardly complied with their policy, but he made sure that the military GOVERNORS of the reconstructed South were conservative and effectively blocked the Republican's agenda. Second, Johnson removed Radical sympathizer Secretary of War Edwin M. Stanton from office, a defiant challenge to the Tenure of Office Act. Every Republican felt that the president had gone too far. Despite the seriousness of the situation, a comic element surfaced as Congress and the president alternately fired and rehired Stanton.

Congress reinstated Stanton to his cabinet post in February 1868. Johnson brazenly defied that body by again ordering the secretary's dismissal, replacing Stanton with former Union general Lorenzo Thomas. His bold action brought swift reaction. Within days, the House of Representatives voted for impeachment of President Andrew Johnson for "high Crimes and Misdemeanors." Naturally, the vote was along strict party lines. The first eight articles of impeachment, which were the heart of the case, focused on the president's alleged violations of the Tenure of Office Act. On February 25, the Senate initiated its proceedings, and the trial began on March 30. Chief Justice SALMON P. CHASE presided over the trial and, to his credit, tried to govern the process in a fair and impartial manner.

The political subtext of the trial was the fight over Reconstruction policy. Johnson's able defenders, including former associate justice Benjamin R. Curtis, argued correctly that the Tenure of Office Act was clearly unconstitutional. The Republicans, meanwhile, attacked the president's opposition to their policies for the Southern states. Their primary concern was that Johnson was subverting the Union victory in the war. By May 6, the arguments had concluded, and only the vote remained. As it turned out, none of the articles of im-

Sketch showing the U.S. Senate as a court of impeachment for the trial of Andrew Johnson *(Library of Congress)*

peachment passed, and a motion to adjourn the trial was offered and adopted. Seven Republicans voted against impeachment.

Johnson had survived the trial, and the Republicans searched for explanations. Many congressmen came to believe that the case against Johnson lacked proof that he had undermined the Constitution, since Lincoln had appointed Stanton. Others distrusted the intentions of Benjamin Wade, next in line for the presidency should Johnson's impeachment be successful. Wade's extreme position on Reconstruction and his almost obsessive pursuit of Johnson worried many of the moderate Republicans. In the end, the spectacle of the trial and Johnson's acquittal had serious consequences. The Radicals' moment had ended. Northerners felt sorry for Johnson and preferred a more modest approach to Reconstruction. ULYSSES S. GRANT, the choice of the moderate majority of the Republican Party, was the candidate for president in 1868. Johnson's acquittal, then, signaled the beginning of the Radicals' quick political decline. Significantly, the fact that Johnson remained in office emboldened ex-Confederate leaders to oppose the Reconstruction of their states that began to be imposed in 1868.

Further reading: Michael Les Benedict, *The Impeachment and Trial of Andrew Johnson* (New York: Norton, 1973); (Hans L. Trefousse, *Impeachment of a President: Andrew Johnson, the Blacks, and Reconstruction* (Knoxville: University of Tennessee Press, 1975).

—John P. Bowes

impressment

During the 19th century, impressment, or the appropriation of private property during emergencies for military use, was recognized by American military precedent as a power granted both civilian and military leadership. During the first year of the CIVIL WAR, the Confederate government used this policy to obtain needed supplies. However, public outcry against it led to severe limits on the practice, and the government quickly rejected it as a regular means of obtaining supplies.

By late 1861, however, the Confederate supply agencies experienced increasing shortages of raw materials. The lack of available materials was compounded by the hoarding of supplies by speculators. As a result, Quartermaster General Abraham C. Myers and Commissary General Lucius B. Northrup requested Secretary of War JUDAH P. BENJAMIN to grant them and their bureau purchasing agents impressment powers. In November 1861, Myers granted his subalterns the authority to impress if "absolutely demanded by the public necessities." Still, the practice of impressment remained limited through spring 1862.

During the first half of 1862, however, instances of impressment became more common as the government seized medical supplies from blockade runners and speculators, took quartermaster hardware, appropriated forage, and forced the sale of horses held by reluctant sellers. In a sweeping and unprecedented move, the secretary of war began impressing major items such as railroad iron and distilleries.

While such seizures created some public opposition, it was the extension of policy to foodstuffs that created widespread resistance. This step was believed necessary by commissary officers unable to feed the soldiers in the field. Outraged private citizens and speculators evaded impressing officers and in some cases destroyed food items rather than turn them over to commissary officials. The War Department attempted to defuse the conflict by creating formal rules for impressing. For example, they devised a universal price schedule for foods like flour and sugar. Individuals were given the option to accept the price offered or face impressment. Agents provided evidence of authorization from their commanding officer, paid on the spot, left enough subsistence for the family, and provided written forms detailing the transaction. To ensure that no abuses occurred, the supply bureaus maintained records open to the public. Even this more formalized policy brought a loud protest from Confederate newspapers and citizens.

In March 1863, Virginia speculators challenged War Department rules in state courts and forced the Confederate Congress to take action to uphold the system. Congress enacted legislation that legally established in civil law the practice of military impressment. They strongly agreed that only extreme measures could keep the rebel armies in the field.

War Department officials worked to soften the impact of impressments, promising in one general order that "wherever the requisite supplies can be obtained by the consent of the owner at fair rates, and without hazardous delay, the military authorities will abstain from the harsh proceeding of impressment." Yet, through 1863, the seizures continued.

Increasingly, field agents resorted to arbitrary actions to obtain raw goods. As a result, civilian opposition hardened, and as the war dragged on the program lost much of its utility. The failure stemmed in large part because the law enacted by Congress lacked any punitive provisions. Coupled with the open resistance of local police and civil authorities to impressing officers, the program yielded smaller and smaller returns. By 1864, it became clear that impressment had failed as a means of domestic procurement of military supplies, and the government rescinded it as an official policy.

See also FORAGING; HOMEFRONT; RULES OF WAR.

Further reading: Richard D. Goff, *Confederate Supply* (Durham, N.C.: Duke University Press, 1969).

—James Daryl Black

industrial development

Historians Charles Beard and Mary Beard, writing in the 1920s, described the CIVIL WAR as "The Second American Revolution." They believed that the Civil War started the United States on the path to industrialization, a development that transformed the face of American society. This may be an overstatement—the forces that gave rise to industrialization were already present in the United States before the war started. However, it is certainly the case that the Civil War sped up the move toward industrialization while solidifying the North's dominance in American manufacturing.

In a wartime ECONOMY, some industries suffer while others prosper. The North's largest industry at the start of the war was cotton textiles, but manufacturers of cotton goods saw a 74 percent decline in business during the war due to the loss of Southern raw material and Southern customers. Shoe manufacturers were also negatively affected by the loss of the Southern market, although to a lesser extent because military contracts made up for much of the shortfall. The profits of the coal and iron industries dropped precipitously in the first two years of the war before finally rebounding in 1863 and 1864.

Not all Northern industries struggled, however. War-related businesses naturally did well throughout the war. These included the manufacturers of gunpowder and firearms, wool clothing, leather, copper, and packaged foods. The strength of these industries allowed the North to produce 13 percent more goods in 1864 than the entire nation had produced in 1860. For the entire course of the war, there was actually a slight drop in national output, likely because more than one-third of the workforce was in the army. A burst of productivity in the 1870s made up for the shortfall, and by 1880 America's level of production stood almost exactly where it would have if the Civil War had never happened.

Although the Civil War did not cause tremendous growth in the Northern economy, it did accelerate the process of industrialization. The TRANSPORTATION industry underwent a boom during the war. The four years of the war saw the construction of twice as many merchant boats as had been built in the four years before the war. At the same time, railroad traffic doubled, and thousands of new miles of track were built. These boats and RAILROADS would be utilized to move goods between markets in the postwar era and would therefore play an important part in the industrialized economy.

The demands of the UNION ARMY also helped to speed up the move toward mechanization and the factory system. For example, the need for millions of army UNIFORMS transformed the clothing industry. The sewing machine had been invented in the 1850s, and the number of sewing machines in use in the North doubled between 1860 and 1865. As clothing production became increasingly mechanized, it also became standardized. The War Department provided manufacturers with a set of graduated measurements for soldiers, thus creating the concept of "sizes" for uniforms and, after the war, civilian clothes.

By compelling large numbers of Northern businessmen to expand transportation networks, invest in machinery, and adopt standardization, the Civil War helped hasten the onset of the industrial era in the North. In part, this was possible because the North had the capital resources and labor necessary to make such changes. The South, on the other hand, enjoyed no such advantages. More than 90 percent of the nation's manufacturing capacity in 1860 was located in the North. The South had some modern manufacturing facilities, notably the TREDEGAR IRON WORKS in Virginia, but they were few in number. The North also had the majority of the nation's capital in 1860. What capital the South did have was tied up in land and slaves and could not easily be converted into the equipment needed for manufacturing.

Given the scarcity of privately held factories in the South, the Confederate government was compelled to go into the manufacturing business for itself. By 1863, publicly owned firms were producing virtually every manufactured good needed to wage war—ships, guns, bullets, blankets, wagons, and uniforms. However, when the war ended and the Confederate government collapsed, these industries disappeared, and the South was once again left with almost no manufacturing capacity. Meanwhile, over the course of the war and RECONSTRUCTION, a major redistribution of wealth took place. The South had 30 percent of the nation's wealth in 1860 but only 12 percent in 1870. The war had also caused the collapse of the Southern banking system. With no factories, no capital, and no source of credit, Southern businessmen could hardly hope to develop any sort of manufacturing capacity in the postwar era. While there were some Southern leaders who called for an industrialized "New South," this was not an easily realized possibility, although cotton textile mills flourished in several Southern states by the 1880s.

The Civil War, then, did not spark a revolution. However, as Northern manufacturers struggled to be profitable and to respond to the needs of the Union army, they made choices that accelerated the pace of industrialization. They built more railroads, invested heavily in the new machinery that had been developed in the 1840s and 1850s, and utilized standardization with increasing frequency. Meanwhile, wealth flowed from South to North, creating an imbalance that would exist long after Reconstruction had ended. These trends would, in the late 19th century, culminate in an economy dominated by manufacturing and by the North.

Further reading: Fred Bateman and Thomas Weiss, *A Deplorable Scarcity: The Failure of Industrialization in the Slave Economy* (Chapel Hill: University of North Carolina Press, 1981); J. Matthew Gallman, *The North Fights the Civil War: The Home Front* (Chicago: I.R. Dee, 1994); Patrick O'Brien, *The Economic Effects of the American Civil War* (Basingstoke, UK.: Macmillan Education, 1988); Phillip Shaw Paludan, *A People's Contest: The Union and Civil War, 1861–1865*) (Lawrence: University Press of Kansas, 1996).

—Christopher Bates

Irish-American regiments

The famous "Irish Brigade," one of the most important and brave combat units in the UNION ARMY, epitomized Irish-American participation in the CIVIL WAR. The brigade began as the 69th New York Militia under Irish-born Col. Michael Corcoran. The unit fought with distinction at the FIRST BATTLE OF BULL RUN in July 1861. After serving out its 90-day federal enlistment, most of its members reenlisted in what became the 69th New York Volunteer Regiment. The idea for and formation of the all-Irish brigade was largely attributed to Thomas Meagher. He anticipated that such a brigade would silence the Know-Nothing attacks on Irish Americans and would emulate the glory of Irish brigades that fought in the Catholic armies of France and Spain. After the brigade was formed, President ABRAHAM LINCOLN appointed Meagher its brigadier general.

The Irish Brigade saw its first action under GEORGE B. MCCLELLAN in the PENINSULAR CAMPAIGN, gaining quick notoriety for bravery at Gaines's Mill, Savage's Station, and Malvern Hill in June and July 1862. That September, as the brigade prepared to take part in a desperate frontal assault at the BATTLE OF ANTIETAM, Father William Corby (later

Photograph showing a group of soldiers from the Irish Brigade during the Peninsular campaign, 1862 *(Library of Congress)*

the president of the University of Notre Dame) rode along their line granting general absolution. The Irish Brigade fiercely attacked the strong Confederate position at the "Bloody Lane." Though decimated by horrendous fire, they held their position until relieved by another brigade. They participated in an even more famous and deadly assault (Marye's Heights) at the BATTLE OF FREDERICKSBURG in December 1862. Following two failed assaults, the Irish Brigade surged forth while shouting an old Irish cheer, "Faugh-a-Bellagh," or "Clear the Way." The brigade was shattered, reduced to less than 400 men. However, the Irish Brigade persisted, serving vital roles at the BATTLES OF CHANCELLORSVILLE, GETTYSBURG, SPOTSYLVANIA, COLD HARBOR, and the assault on St. Petersburg. The Irish Brigade stood at APPOMATTOX COURT HOUSE, having suffered the third-highest casualty rate of any brigade in the U.S. Army.

See also IMMIGRATION.

Further reading: Joseph G. Bilby, *The Irish Brigade in the Civil War: The 69th New York and Other Irish Regiments in the Army of the Potomac* (New York: Da Capo Press, 1998); William L. Burton, *Melting Pot Soldiers: The*

Union's Ethnic Regiments (New York: Fordham University Press, 1988).

—Richard J. Roder

ironclad oath

The "ironclad test oath of loyalty" was the oath of allegiance to the Union required by the U.S. government of citizens and Southerners in Union-occupied areas. Instituted in the summer of 1862, the ironclad oath remained in place until the 1880s.

The ironclad oath incorporated and merged the various civil and military oaths of allegiance that had been in place from the beginning of the CIVIL WAR. It required the person taking it to proclaim that he or she had "never voluntarily borne arms against the United States." In addition, this oath required the taker to swear to uphold the U.S. Constitution, defend the United States from foreign and domestic enemies, and forsake state allegiance. In essence, the ironclad oath forced takers to renounce any affiliation to any entity other than the U.S. government. It also asked Southerners to deny an active role in SECESSION and the war against the United States.

Federal authorities required that everyone in areas under Union control during the Civil War swear to the ironclad oath. Northerners readily swore to the terms of the oath as they supported the Union through military or material means. So did Unionists throughout the Confederacy as their areas came under federal control. Those in occupied areas gained special protection and rights from their status as loyal U.S. citizens. Some Unionist Southerners took the ironclad oath multiple times, as different Union detachments marched through their towns, hoping for the protection and rights the oath promised to grant them.

Other Southerners were forced to take the oath despite their continued support for the Confederacy. People living in Union-occupied areas were required to take the ironclad oath to do business in the occupied city or with the federal government. As a result, many unwilling Confederates swore to the oath to support their families. Other Southerners took the oath because doing so entitled them to reimbursement for property taken by Union troops. Other Confederates refused to take the oath under any circumstances, arguing that it denied their commitment to Southern independence and their right to secede. Even so, many Confederates found themselves in a position that required them to take the oath, despite their protests. In these instances, some took the ironclad oath only under duress and without necessarily following its guidelines.

Union officials also required that Confederate prisoners of war take the oath before they were released on parole. Confederate soldiers who took the ironclad oath did not always follow its rules against taking up arms against the United States. Many gained parole only to return to the ranks of the CONFEDERATE ARMY and continue fighting Union troops. The Union terminated its practice of exchanging Confederate prisoners by the end of 1863, in part due to the persistent reenlistment of paroled prisoners.

The ironclad oath's strict prohibitions against takers having "voluntarily" fought against the Union caused problems after the Civil War. In a highly charged atmosphere of sectional tensions and resentments, this stress on a renunciation of Southerners' roles in the Confederate fight for independence impaired the effort for national reunification. Many Southerners who played roles in military and civilian capacities refused to renounce their support of the Confederacy. Those who did so and did not take the ironclad oath were prohibited from holding local, state, or federal office or serving in the military. In response, many Confederate military leaders appealed to the president for pardons and had their federal rights and citizenship restored without a renunciation of their roles in the war effort. In 1884 the United States replaced the ironclad oath with an oath of allegiance that only required oath takers to support and uphold the U.S. Constitution.

See also AMNESTY, ACTS OF; HOMEFRONT.

Further reading: Eric Foner, *Reconstruction: America's Unfinished Revolution, 1863–1877* (New York: Harper & Row, 1988); Eric L. McKitrick, *Andrew Johnson and Reconstruction* (New York: Oxford University Press, 1988).
—Lisa Tendrich Frank

ironclads

An ironclad is a warship that is partially or fully shielded with iron plating. Some textbooks incorrectly state that ironclad ships were invented during the CIVIL WAR. In fact, the first ironclads were constructed more than 250 years prior by Korean admiral Yi Sun Shin, who led a fleet of armored ships to victory over Japanese naval forces in the late 16th century. Shin was ahead of his time; after his death ironclads were not utilized by any of the world's navies until the Crimean War of the 1850s. During the conflict, both the British and French navies relied upon ironclads, demonstrating their superiority over wooden ships to the rest of the world.

When the Civil War broke out, it was clear to leaders on both sides of the conflict that they needed ironclad technology. The Union, with its superior industrial capacity, was the first to act. In the first few months of the war, the UNION NAVY commissioned and began construction on

three ironclad warships: the *New Ironsides*, the *Galena*, and the *Monitor*. These ships were finished by early 1862, and numerous others followed. By the end of the Civil War, the Union navy had constructed 71 ironclad ships, vastly more than any other naval power of that era.

The CONFEDERATE NAVY did its best to keep up with the Union, but they faced several handicaps. Raw materials were in short supply in the South. This was particularly true of iron, which was needed not only for ships but for railroad rails and for armaments. Even if supplies had been abundant, the South did not have any factories capable of manufacturing all of the parts necessary to build an ironclad ship. So, the Confederate navy was compelled to modify existing vessels, usually damaged ships that had been abandoned by the Union navy. The Confederates had some success doing this, and by the end of the war their navy had 25 ironclads in service that had been constructed in this fashion. Southern leaders also tried to purchase some European-made ironclads, which utilized technology vastly superior to that possessed by the Union navy. However, diplomatic pressure from Northern authorities largely compelled France and Britain to turn a deaf ear to the Confederates. The rebel navy did manage to purchase one ship from France, the *Stonewall*, but it did not arrive in the United States until after the war was over.

There was a great deal of variety among Civil War ironclads, but most can be grouped into two basic classes: Casemates like the USS *New Ironsides* were iron boxes, usually with slanted sides, placed on top of a wooden hull. Sailors and guns would be contained within the iron box, which protected them from enemy fire. Casemates were typically very large and not very maneuverable, so they were most effective when used for defensive purposes or for bombardment of targets on land. Most Southern ironclads were casemates.

The other class of ironclad was the monitors, named after the USS *Monitor*. Monitors were low-freeboard steamships, meaning that their decks were very close to the water. While casemates tended to have fixed guns, monitors had turrets that could be rotated to aim their guns. The majority of Union ironclads were monitors, although most Northern naval leaders, including Adm. DAVID GLASGOW FARRAGUT, preferred casemates.

Ironclad ships played a role in most of the major naval battles of the Civil War. They achieved their greatest fame, however, in an engagement that had very little to do with the outcome of the war. In March 1862, several Union warships were destroyed or severely damaged by the CSS *Virginia*, a casemate ironclad that had been built by converting the abandoned USS *Merrimack*. In order to save the remaining Union ships, John L. Worden, commander of the recently completed USS *Monitor,* was ordered to engage the *Virginia* at Hampton Roads, Virginia. The *Monitor* arrived early on the morning of March 9, just as the *Virginia* was preparing to finish off the USS *Minnesota*, a wooden ship. The two ironclads fired at one another all day, inflicting very little damage. Finally, Worden was wounded, and the *Monitor* had to withdraw temporarily so he could be relieved. By the time the ship had returned to the fray, the *Virginia* had backed off, ending the engagement.

Although Hampton Roads did not impact the Civil War, it was still among the war's most significant engagements. Ironclads had been used in warfare before, but Hampton Roads marked the first time that two ironclad ships had faced off against one another. Both Northerners and Southerners took pride in the accomplishment, and a wave of songs, poems, and newspaper articles praising the ironclads swept across the country. Union and Confederate naval leaders knew from the outset that wooden ships would soon be replaced by ships made of metal, and now the general populace knew it too. The value of existing wooden ships was vastly reduced in popular and professional opinion, setting the stage for an arms race in the construction of iron and, eventually, steel ships, a trend that would last for nearly a century.

See also MONITOR-MERRIMACK.

Further reading: Jack Greene and Alessandro Massignani, *Ironclads at War: The Origin and Development of the Armored Warship, 1854–1891* (New York: Da Capo Press, 1998); David A. Mindell, *War, Technology, and Experience Aboard the U.S.S. Monitor* (Baltimore: Johns Hopkins University Press, 2000); Arthur Mokin, *Ironclad: The Monitor and the Merrimack* (Novato, Calif.: Presidio, 1991).

—Christopher Bates

J

Jackson, Thomas J. (Stonewall) (1824–1863)

Thomas Jonathan "Stonewall" Jackson was born in Clarksburg, Virginia (now West Virginia), on January 21, 1824, to Jonathan and Julia Beckwith Neale Jackson. He lost both parents as a child and spent much of his youth in the household of an uncle who owned lumber mills in Lewis County. Educated by tutors as a youth, he entered the UNITED STATES MILITARY ACADEMY AT WEST POINT in 1842. Poorly prepared for the rigorous coursework at West Point, he succeeded only by working resolutely on his studies. He improved his class standing to 17th of 59 by the time of his graduation in the class of 1846.

War had erupted with Mexico before Jackson's graduation, and he soon found himself a second lieutenant of artillery with the invading U.S. Army commanded by Winfield Scott. During Scott's campaign against Mexico City in 1847, he fought at the siege of Vera Cruz and in the Battles of Cerro Gordo, Contreras, and Chapultepec, so distinguishing himself that he won brevets (honorary rank for exceptional service) to the rank of major. After a year with the American army of occupation in Mexico, he saw peacetime service in New York and Florida.

In 1851 Jackson accepted a professorship in artillery TACTICS and natural philosophy at the Virginia Military Institute in Lexington, Virginia. He taught there for the next 10 years, earning a reputation as an inflexible and often boring instructor. He married twice while in Lexington—in 1853 to Eleanor Junkin, who died in childbirth after just more than a year, and in 1857 to Mary Anna Morrison. Both women were daughters of Presbyterian clerics, and Jackson himself became a devoted member of that church. His extreme piety caused considerable comment when he achieved military fame.

Jackson remained loyal to Virginia in the SECESSION crisis of 1861. A Democrat who owned a few slaves, he harbored fewer doubts about secession than many people in his native western region of the state. Commissioned a Confederate colonel and given a command at HARPERS FERRY, he was promoted to brigadier general on June 17, 1861. He made a dramatic military debut at the FIRST BATTLE OF BULL RUN on July 21, where his brigade helped stop a Union assault and turned the tide in the war's first big battle. Jackson also won his famous nickname that hot July afternoon when a South Carolina officer pointed toward him and shouted, "There is Jackson standing like a stone wall." Promoted to major general on October 7, 1861, he shortly thereafter assumed command in the Shenandoah Valley and mounted a largely ineffective campaign into western Virginia that winter.

On the eve of his celebrated SHENANDOAH VALLEY CAMPAIGN, Jackson was known as a good soldier but had yet to gain wide fame. ROBERT E. LEE sketched the broad outline of the Shenandoah operation, hoping Jackson would tie down Northern forces under Nathaniel P. Banks and John C. Frémont in the valley and farther west in the Allegheny Mountains, so they could not reinforce the UNION ARMY menacing RICHMOND. An initial clash at First Kernstown on March 23, though a tactical defeat for Jackson, prompted the Federals to retain troops in the lower valley. Reinforced to 17,500 by early May, Jackson embarked on a whirlwind of action. He struck part of Frémont's force west of Staunton at McDowell on May 8, then marched back to the valley and turned northward to capture a Union garrison at Front Royal on May 23 and defeated Banks in the Battle of First Winchester two days later. Continuing on to the Potomac River, he subsequently moved south to the vicinity of Harrisonburg, eluding Union forces under Frémont and James Shields. In early June, he turned to meet his pursuers, defeating Frémont at Cross Keys on June 8 and Shields at Port Republic the next day. The Federals withdrew northward, freeing Jackson to reinforce Lee's army outside Richmond. Jackson had used rapid movement and boldness to craft a memorable success. His victories, which came in the midst of a run of Southern defeats, not only prevented a concentration of Union forces at Richmond but also lifted Confederate civilian morale. Typical of reactions behind the lines was that of a diarist in Richmond, who wrote that "General Jackson is performing prodigies of valor in the Valley."

Jackson participated in all of the great battles in the eastern theater during the remainder of 1862. He stumbled badly at the Seven Days' Battle and also failed to carry out his assigned roles at Mechanicsville, Gaines's Mill, and White Oak Swamp. Detached by Lee from the army at Richmond in early August, he defeated a portion of John Pope's Army of Virginia on August 9 near Culpeper in the BATTLE OF CEDAR MOUNTAIN. Later that month, he carried out a memorable march around Pope's right flank, destroying a vast Union supply depot at Manassas Junction and setting the stage for Lee's victory at the SECOND BATTLE OF BULL RUN on August 28–30. He played a key role in the Maryland campaign in September, capturing the 12,500-man Union garrison at Harpers Ferry on September 15 and then joining the rest of the army near Sharpsburg, Maryland, for the bloody fighting at the BATTLE OF ANTIETAM two days later. Promoted to lieutenant general on October 10 and given command of the Second Corps in the Army of Northern Virginia, he defended Lee's right flank in the Confederate victory at the BATTLE OF FREDERICKSBURG on December 13.

Jackson's reputation reached new heights during the BATTLE OF CHANCELLORSVILLE in May 1863. Confronting a superior Union force, he and Lee decided on a bold response. On May 2, Jackson took his corps on a flank march around the Army of the Potomac, launching an attack that routed the Federal 11th Corps. In the confusion of battle and darkness that evening, he was wounded by his own men. His left arm was amputated that night, and though it seemed at first that he would recover, he died eight days later. President JEFFERSON DAVIS spoke for the Confederate people in describing Jackson's death as a "great national calamity," and Robert E. Lee remarked that the army would miss "the daring, skill and energy of this great and good soldier."

Further reading: James I. Robertson, *Stonewall Jackson: The Man, the Soldier, the Legend* (New York: Macmillan, 1997); Frank E. Vandiver, *Mighty Stonewall* (College Station: Texas A&M University Press, 1989).

—Gary W. Gallagher

Thomas J. "Stonewall" Jackson *(Library of Congress)*

jayhawkers

Officially, the CIVIL WAR began on April 12, 1861, with the firing on FORT SUMTER. However, armed combat had been underway for years before that along the Kansas-Missouri border. In 1854 the KANSAS-NEBRASKA ACT had opened up the Kansas Territory to popular sovereignty, which was supposed to allow the people of Kansas to decide for themselves if they wanted SLAVERY. Whenever a vote on the issue came up, however, proslavery Missourians would cross the border to Kansas and vote illegally in hopes of getting Kansas admitted to the Union as a slave state. Armed violence between proslavery and antislavery guerrillas regularly occurred on these occasions, and eventually a state of near-constant warfare developed. The proslavery guerillas were known as "BUSHWHACKERS," and the antislavery forces were called "jayhawkers."

The jayhawkers, like the bushwhackers, had few scruples when it came to enforcing their will. They supplied themselves almost entirely by stealing. They usually killed any enemies they encountered, women and children included. Their leader was "Doc" Charles Jennison, who had given up medicine for a career as a horse thief. The ranks of the Jayhawkers also included Senator James Henry Lane, Susan B. Anthony's brother Dan Anthony, and JOHN BROWN's son John Brown Jr. Between 1855 and 1860, more than 200 people were killed by the jayhawkers, and countless thousands of dollars worth of goods were stolen.

When Civil War finally came to the rest of the nation, the jayhawkers were accepted into the Union ranks as the

Seventh Kansas Volunteer Cavalry Regiment, with Jennison as colonel and Anthony as lieutenant colonel. Mustered into service on October 28, 1861, the jayhawkers had only loose ties to the UNION ARMY. They continued to supply themselves by stealing, and they generally operated independently of any Union command. They also continued to operate mostly in Missouri. This was a problem for Union leadership, because Missouri had remained with the Union, and many of the people killed by the Jayhawkers in 1861 were loyal Unionists. Concerned that the unit was creating more rebels than it was conquering, the jayhawkers were transferred to Kentucky and then to Tennessee. They performed well in these new assignments, particularly after Jennison and Anthony resigned and were replaced by more able officers. The jayhawkers did not return to Kansas until they were mustered out in 1865.

See also BLEEDING KANSAS.

Further reading: Stephen Z. Starr, *Jennison's Jayhawkers: A Civil War Cavalry Regiment and Its Commander* (Baton Rouge: Louisiana State University Press, 1974).
—Christopher Bates

Andrew Johnson *(Library of Congress)*

Johnson, Andrew (1808–1875)

Tailor, merchant, governor, U.S. senator, vice president, and 17th president, Andrew Johnson took office upon the ASSASSINATION OF ABRAHAM LINCOLN in April 1865. An "accidental president," Johnson's tenure as chief executive was marked by turmoil and controversy, some of it due to his political blunders and incompetence. He enjoys the dubious distinction of being the first president to be impeached while in office.

Born on December 29, 1808, in North Carolina to parents of humble means, Johnson had virtually no schooling. As a young boy, Johnson was apprenticed to a tailor but fled at the first opportunity, landing in Greenville, Tennessee. There, he opened a thriving tailor business and established himself as a wealthy merchant. Married and successful, Johnson turned to politics, where he followed in the footsteps of his hero, Democrat Andrew Jackson. Although a slaveholder himself, Johnson detested the wealthy planters who dominated Southern politics and economic power. As he moved up the political ladder from local to state to national office, Johnson became known as a champion for the ordinary white Southern yeoman farmer.

When the CIVIL WAR broke out, Johnson had for three years been the U.S. senator from Tennessee. A decided Unionist, he followed the U.S. flag, the only member of Congress's upper house from a seceded state to remain loyal. Labeled a traitor throughout the South, he was a hailed as a hero in the North. The UNION ARMY captured

Nashville and occupied SECESSIONist western Tennessee in March 1862. Shortly afterward, ABRAHAM LINCOLN appointed Johnson to serve as the state's wartime governor.

Johnson worked hard to restore his state to the Union, something that was made more difficult because the Confederates controlled eastern Tennessee. By summer of 1863 Johnson endorsed EMANCIPATION and supported strongly Lincoln's efforts to end SLAVERY in the border states. Due to Johnson's persistence, in January 1865 a Tennessee state convention approved the ABOLITION of slavery, and the voters quickly ratified the measure.

In 1864 the Republicans (temporarily renamed the American Union Party) wished to attract War Democrats by placing Andrew Johnson, the popular Unionist, on the ticket with Lincoln. The party won handily, and Johnson was inaugurated as vice president on March 4, 1865. Feeling ill on inauguration day, Johnson fortified himself with several glasses of whiskey before his speech. The result was a rambling, incoherent tirade that embarrassed all who witnessed it. Johnson created a more favorable impression when, after Lincoln's death early in the morning of April 15, he took the oath of office at the Kirkwood House in a dignified and calm manner. The shocking aftermath of the assassination gave Johnson a period of overwhelming support among Northern politicians and voters. He presided competently over the pursuit, capture, and trial of Lincoln's assassins and created an atmosphere of friendly relations between the executive and congressional branches as the problems of RECONSTRUCTION loomed.

"Treason must be made infamous and traitors must be impoverished," declared Johnson. RADICAL REPUBLICANS could be forgiven if they thought the new president would stand with them in implementing a harsh Reconstruction policy. They were wrong. Johnson, like Lincoln, believed that secession was illegal, and thus the rebel states were never actually out of the Union. Johnson's vision was a harmonious "restoration," directed by the executive branch. His plan was simple. The seceded states had to ratify the THIRTEENTH AMENDMENT, nullify the secession laws, and repudiate the Confederate debt. Once those requirements were met, ELECTIONS could be held, civil governments restored, and elected officials could take their places at all levels, including the national legislature.

Johnson ignored requests from Radicals that he include suffrage for African Americans as part of the restoration plan. A typical STATES' RIGHTS Democrat, he feared the intrusion of the federal government into areas that trespassed on state sovereignty. In addition, he was a fierce opponent of black voting and civil rights measures. The fact that the dominant Republican Congress would not come into session until December 1865 meant that Johnson could push through his measures with executive decrees.

Johnson busied himself in obstructing all congressional policies designed to assist ex-slaves. In September 1865, Johnson virtually ended land redistribution to freedmen and poor white people. He ordered the FREEDMEN'S BUREAU commissioner, Gen. O. O. HOWARD, to return all confiscated lands to white Southerners who had been pardoned. Under Johnson's May 1865 plan, only rebellious Southerners who owned more than $20,000 in taxable property had to receive a presidential pardon personally; the rest were pardoned automatically. Nearly all, more than 6,000, in need of a presidential pardon received one after a short visit with Johnson. By the end of 1865, all of the Southern states except Texas had followed Johnson's plan and applied for reentry into the Union. Johnson considered "restoration" complete.

The consequences of Johnson's acting unilaterally were deeply unsettling. Northerners reacted with horror as ex-Confederates blatantly assumed power as if there had never been a war at all. In state after state, BLACK CODES were passed, which made emancipation a dead letter. Republicans of all backgrounds in Congress supported a more stringent Reconstruction and pushed for protection of African Americans' economic and basic civil rights.

In December, the hostility between the executive and the legislative branches deepened when the "restored" Southern congressmen arrived in the Capitol to take their places in the Senate and House chambers. The newly elected officials included four ex-Confederate generals, eight colonels, six ex-cabinet members, and the Confederacy's vice president, ALEXANDER H. STEPHENS. Congress refused to seat the Southerners, in effect rejecting presidential Reconstruction. The best both sides could hope for now was a serious session of compromise. Johnson, however, refused to negotiate with the Republicans on Reconstruction.

In early 1866, Congress passed two bills, one extending the Freedmen's Bureau and the other the CIVIL RIGHTS ACT OF 1866. Johnson vetoed both bills. Congress would later override his vetoes, and the bills became law. Even the most moderate Republicans moved into alignment with the Radical Republicans (so-named for their support of the freedmen) after Johnson's policies had rendered emancipation and civil rights essentially meaningless.

Republicans implemented a plan that set strict requirements for states reentering the Union. These requirements mandated military occupation for all Confederate states (with the exception of Tennessee) until a state convention recognized freedmen's rights to citizenship and all the other provisions of the FOURTEENTH AMENDMENT and ended the racially discriminatory black codes. Eventually, Congress even called for African-American male suffrage. Johnson vetoed nearly every bill but was again overridden nearly every time.

Johnson, who thought he enjoyed the support of most Northerners, fought hard for his restoration plan. He still controlled the military, which was responsible for carrying out congressional Reconstruction. As commander in chief, he appointed politically conservative, pro-Southern officers to military posts in the South. This further alienated his few supporters left in Congress. Increasingly, his pronouncements were controversial. Terrible race riots in Memphis and New Orleans in the spring and summer of 1866 belied Johnson's assurances that conditions in the South were returning to normal. Congress further turned against the president.

Before the 1866 congressional elections, Johnson undertook a controversial speaking tour known as the "Swing around the Circle." His goal was to rally voter support for his policies. Instead, Johnson's speeches were divisive, rude, and often confrontational. He received much negative publicity, and many in the crowds booed his appearances. Gossips whispered that the president had been drunk for much of the tour. Drunk or not, the tour was a disaster at the polls, and a large, "veto-proof" Republican majority was returned to Congress.

In March 1867, the House and Senate passed the Tenure of Office Act over Johnson's veto. The act required Johnson to obtain the Senate's approval before dismissing any of his cabinet members. It was designed to protect Secretary of War EDWIN M. STANTON, a leftover from Lincoln's cabinet and a Radical Republican. Citing his executive powers, Johnson suspended Stanton in August 1867 without the Senate's consent. After much political wrangling, the House impeached Johnson in February 1868 for committing high crimes and misdemeanors in office, the first ever impeachment in U.S. history. However, the Senate failed to convict him by one vote. Vindicated but powerless, Johnson did not accomplish anything of significance for the rest of his term.

In 1868 the Democrats chose Horatio Seymour to run for president against ULYSSES S. GRANT. Johnson was quite bitter over his treatment in WASHINGTON, D.C., and refused to attend Grant's inauguration. Andrew Johnson retired to Tennessee but reentered politics, returning to the U.S. Senate in 1875. He served for only a few months before his death on August 31, 1875.

See also IMPEACHMENT OF ANDREW JOHNSON.

Further reading: Eric McKitrick, *Andrew Johnson and Reconstruction* (New York: Oxford University Press, 1988); Brooks D. Simpson, *The Reconstruction Presidents* (Lawrence: University Press of Kansas, 1998); Hans L. Trefousse, *Andrew Johnson: A Biography* (New York: Norton, 1989).

—Scott L. Stabler

Johnston, Albert Sidney (1803–1862)

At the beginning of the CIVIL WAR, Albert Sidney Johnston was perhaps the Confederacy's most renowned and well-respected soldier. Johnston was born in Washington, Kentucky, on February 2, 1803, to John and Abigail Johnston. He was appointed to the UNITED STATES MILITARY ACADEMY AT WEST POINT from Louisiana and graduated eighth in the class of 1826. Johnston served at Sackett's Harbor, New York, in 1826; with the Sixth Infantry at Jefferson Barracks, Missouri, in 1827; and as regimental adjutant in the Black Hawk War. He married Henrietta Preston in 1829 and resigned his commission in 1834 due to her grave illness. After Henrietta's death in 1836, he went to the Southwest and fought for Texas's independence. This appointment resulted in a duel with Felix Huston, the man he replaced. Due to an injury suffered in the duel, however, Johnston was unable to take his new post. On December 22, 1838, he was appointed secretary of war for the Republic of Texas by President Mirabeau B. Lamar. In 1840 Johnston returned to Kentucky, where, on October 3, 1843, he married Eliza Griffin, a cousin of his first wife. They returned to Texas to settle at China Grove Plantation in Brazoria County.

During the Mexican-American War Johnston served as colonel of the First Texas Rifle Volunteers and then served with W. O. Butler as inspector general at Monterrey, Mexico. Johnston reentered the regular army in 1849 and by 1855 had risen to the rank of colonel. In 1857 he was promoted to brigadier general.

When the Civil War began, Johnston returned to the army as a Union brigadier general in command in California, but when his "home state" of Texas seceded from the Union, he resigned from the U.S. Army and joined the Confederacy. JEFFERSON DAVIS placed him in command of the western theater as a full general. As commander of this department, his area of responsibility was massive, extending from the Appalachian Mountains in the east to the Indian Territory in the west. When Fort Henry and Fort Donelson were lost in February 1862, Johnston was forced to retreat from Kentucky and most of Tennessee. Johnston joined forces with Gen. P. G. T. BEAUREGARD and massed in Corinth, Mississippi, where he planned to launch a surprise attack on the UNION ARMY in Tennessee.

Early on the morning of April 6, 1862, Johnston assaulted ULYSSES S. GRANT's army at its camp on Pittsburg Landing on the Tennessee River. The two-day BATTLE OF SHILOH, named for a small church near the landing, had begun. As hoped, Johnston's attack caught the Federals completely by surprise. However, momentum was lost when raw recruits paused to loot the overrun Union encampments, but by late morning Johnston believed victory was his. "We are sweeping the field," he told Beauregard, "and I think we shall press them to the river." But the Federals held the Confederate forces for a time at what became known as the "Hornet's Nest." There was also hard fighting in a peach orchard, where Johnston himself led the final charge that drove the Union defenders out of it. While directing operations at Shiloh, Johnston was hit in the leg by a bullet that severed his femoral artery. Johnston had sent his surgeon to tend to a group of wounded Union prisoners, and he bled to death for lack of medical attention. He was temporarily buried in New Orleans, but his remains were later transferred to Texas for burial in the state cemetery in Austin.

Further reading: Charles P. Roland and Gary Gallagher, *Albert Sidney Johnston: Soldier of Three Republics* (Lexington: University Press of Kentucky, 2001).

—Arthur E. Amos

Johnston, Joseph E. (1807–1891)

A career soldier, Gen. Joseph Eggleston Johnston was one of the top military commanders for the Confederacy. For him, the CIVIL WAR was alternately marked by failure and success. His predisposition toward defensive warfare placed him at odds with President JEFFERSON DAVIS, and his critics attacked him for wasting many opportunities for Confederate victory. Like many of his contemporaries,

Johnston's postwar years were spent in justifying his wartime record and casting doubt on the record of his many detractors.

Johnston was born on February 3, 1807, into a distinguished family in Prince Edward County, Virginia. His father, Peter Johnston, served in the American Revolution, and his mother was a niece of Patrick Henry. Educated at the UNITED STATES MILITARY ACADEMY AT WEST POINT, he graduated in good standing with the class of 1829. Commissioned as a second lieutenant, Johnston participated in the Black Hawk War of 1832, the Seminole War of 1836–37, and the Mexican-American War of 1846–48. From the 1830s to the eve of the Civil War, Johnston compiled an excellent record as a topographical engineer in the Southwest, a lieutenant colonel of the U.S. First Cavalry, and quartermaster general of the U.S. Army, a position he resigned from in 1861 to join the Confederate forces.

The highest ranked officer from the "old army," Johnston was appointed brigadier general by President Jefferson Davis. Along with P. G. T. BEAUREGARD, Johnston directed the Confederate victory at the FIRST BATTLE OF BULL RUN in July 1861. The victory was marred shortly thereafter by a bitter argument over Johnston's ranking in the Confederate military hierarchy. He believed that he should be ranked first, but President Davis disagreed, and Johnston was placed fourth. This was the first of many personal and professional disagreements between the two proud and stubborn men, much to the detriment of the Confederate armies in the western theater.

In the spring of 1862, Johnston was given the task of defending RICHMOND against the Northern invasion led by his former Mexican-American War comrade, GEORGE B. MCCLELLAN. In late May, Johnston was severely injured during the Battle of Seven Pines, and the command of the main CONFEDERATE ARMY was given to Gen. ROBERT E. LEE. Johnston resumed his field career in December, commanding the Confederate forces in Tennessee and Mississippi. Expected to defend a huge amount of land against the Federals, Johnston assumed a defensive stance whenever possible. For his bloodless approach to war and more, Johnston's men loved him as few other generals. "In appearance," an observer remarked, "he is small, soldierly and graying." To his superiors, Johnston appeared arrogant, affecting a superior attitude about all things military. Jefferson Davis also considered himself a military expert and deferred to no one except Robert E. Lee, whose record of victory was second to none. Davis was especially overbearing in his dealings with the western generals, and Johnston in particular.

When the Mississippi citadel of Vicksburg fell in July 1863, Johnston was blamed for his apparent slowness in supporting John Pemberton's beleaguered forces. Davis and the press criticized Johnston's cautious nature harshly after the surrender of Vicksburg, and he was temporarily relieved of his command for failing to stem the Union advance.

Davis could not afford to retire a competent and respected general like Johnston for long, however. December of 1863 found him in charge of the Army of Tennessee after BRAXTON BRAGG lost Chattanooga to the Federals. This time, Johnston faced WILLIAM T. SHERMAN in the ATLANTA CAMPAIGN of the spring and summer of 1864. Leaving Dalton, Georgia, under heavy pressure from Sherman, Johnston executed a textbook series of backward maneuvers until he entrenched just outside of Atlanta. Once again, Davis, impatient with Johnston's timid generalship, removed him from command. His replacement was the feisty Texan JOHN BELL HOOD, whose willingness to do battle with Sherman's troops led to defeat and the surrender of Atlanta on September 2, 1864. By now the master of thankless tasks, Johnston squared off against Sherman again in February 1865 in the Carolinas campaign. Johnston surrendered the Army of Tennessee to Sherman on April 26, 1865.

Johnston's postwar career was more successful. A prosperous businessman in railroad and insurance, he also dabbled in politics as a congressman from Virginia (1878–80). Johnston, who published his memoirs in 1874, was a popular speaker at VETERANS reunions throughout the South. He also was invited on a regular basis to speak to Northern veterans organizations, where he spread a message of reconciliation and harmony between the sections. At 84, he became a tragic symbol of reunion when, after serving as a pallbearer at Sherman's funeral on a cold wintry day, he caught pneumonia. Shortly thereafter, on March 21, 1891, Johnston died at his home in WASHINGTON, D.C.

See also VICKSBURG CAMPAIGN.

Further reading: Joseph E. Johnston, *Narrative of Military Operations Directed during the Late War between the States* (1847; reprint, Milwood, N.Y.: Kraus Reprint, 1969); Craig L. Symonds, *Joseph E. Johnston: A Civil War Biography* (New York: Norton, 1992).

Joint Committee on the Conduct of the War

Formed in December 1861, the congressional Joint Committee on the Conduct of the War (CCW) held the broadly interpreted power to inquire into the conduct of the Northern war effort through the investigation and examination of military persons and maneuvers. The CCW began in obscurity in the months following the FIRST BATTLE OF BULL RUN but remained in existence for the length of the CIVIL WAR, making a name for itself through its harassment of Gen. GEORGE B. MCCLELLAN and its efforts to influence the military policies and appointments of President ABRAHAM LINCOLN.

Following the disastrous Union defeat at the First Battle of Bull Run and the subsequent loss at Ball's Bluff, Senator Zachariah Chandler of Michigan introduced a resolution in the Senate to create a joint committee with the House of Representatives to probe the causes for these military catastrophes. The resolution passed in both chambers without significant debate, and the respective leaders of Congress appointed the following members to the committee: Senator Chandler (R-Mich.), Senator BENJAMIN WADE (R-Ohio), Senator ANDREW JOHNSON (D-Tenn.), Representative GEORGE W. JULIAN (R-Ill.), Representative Moses Odell (D-N.Y.), Representative John Covode (R-Pa.), and Representative Daniel Gooch (R-Mass.). The president of the Senate selected Wade as chairman, and the CCW initiated its first investigation in January 1862.

Over the course of the Civil War, the committee's scope included not only the Battles of Bull Run and Ball's Bluff but also the BATTLES OF FREDERICKSBURG, Fort Fisher, and the Crater, as well as the atrocities committed by Confederate soldiers at FORT PILLOW. While the CCW and its supporters in Congress made sure that the scope of its mission statement remained broad, the overall agenda of the committee's members remained narrow throughout its tenure. Led in name and spirit by the RADICAL REPUBLICANS Wade, Chandler, and Julian, the committee sought to place a definitive spin on their investigations, and by war's end the CCW had earned a deserved reputation for doggedly pursuing their partisan goals. These men held very strong ABOLITIONist beliefs and felt that the war effort required an aggressive approach regarding SLAVERY and the Confederacy. As a result, they used the committee's powers in numerous attempts to influence both the use and the leadership of the UNION ARMY.

Beginning with the investigation of Bull Run and Ball's Bluff in January 1862, the CCW established a pattern that defined its procedures until its disbandment in June 1865. First, in their attacks on Brig. Gen. Charles P. Stone and General McClellan, the Radical Republicans expressed their dissatisfaction with West Point military men and, more importantly, with Democratic officers. By examining Stone in secret without allowing him representation and subsequently influencing his military arrest and solitary confinement, the members of the CCW also displayed a willingness to use extralegal means to accomplish their goals. Finally, as evidenced by their meetings with Lincoln and their calls for military activity against the Confederacy in the early months of 1862, Wade and his cohorts revealed their desire to influence the way in which Lincoln and his generals chose to direct the Union war effort.

From 1862 to 1865, the machinations of the CCW remained barely hidden beneath their investigative actions. While the initial inquiries into Ball's Bluff and Bull Run targeted particular officers negatively, the committee's report on Fredericksburg sought to bolster the reputation of Gen. AMBROSE E. BURNSIDE in an effort to indirectly end McClellan's military career. Similarly, the conclusions reached by Wade and his colleagues on Fort Fisher supported the actions of one of their favorites, Gen. BENJAMIN F. BUTLER, a man who had not found similar support in the White House. The committee at times even went beyond the scope of its mission statement, and Wade and Chandler in particular often besieged Lincoln in their efforts to push for a more aggressive military strategy.

Yet not all of the CCW's investigations focused on the failures of various Union military endeavors. It also exposed corruption in military contracts and facilitated reform. Further, the CCW's reports on Fort Pillow and on Union prisoners of war highlighted some of the atrocities of the war that the Northern public may not have been completely aware of. Their investigation of the inhumane treatment of black soldiers and military prisoners brought the CCW's focus squarely on the Confederacy's conduct of the war and provided the evidence the Radical Republicans needed for pursuing a strict RECONSTRUCTION of the South. By demonstrating the cruelty of the rebels in warfare, the CCW hoped to destroy the hopes of those individuals, including Lincoln, who sought to create a harmonious plan for the reunion of the two warring sides.

Over a period of approximately three and a half years, the CCW compiled an impressive record of investigations and reports. Its members vociferously presented their opinions and conclusions on military strategy, military appointments, and the plans for the Reconstruction that would follow the war. Their impact on the Northern war effort and on Lincoln's policies cannot be neatly summarized. While their attacks eventually influenced the president's dismissal of McClellan, the general's record in the field also played a significant role. In their fervent support of abolition, the CCW prodded the administration toward declaring EMANCIPATION. However, their contempt for West Point and Democratic officers also led the committee to promote several officers, such as Benjamin F. Butler and JOSEPH HOOKER, long after they had proven themselves liabilities in battle. And in the last year of the war, the CCW also found itself unable to force Lincoln to dismiss ULYSSES S. GRANT or GEORGE GORDON MEADE. In the end, the Joint Committee on the Conduct of the War served as a strong voice of the Radical Republicans and their agenda throughout the Civil War, and Lincoln could never completely ignore its influence.

See also ANDERSONVILLE PRISON; PRISONERS; UNITED STATES MILITARY ACADEMY AT WEST POINT.

Further reading: Bruce Tap, *Over Lincoln's Shoulder: The Committee on the Conduct of the War* (Lawrence: University Press of Kansas, 1998); T. Harry Williams, *Lincoln and the Radicals* (Madison: University of Wisconsin Press, 1960).

—John P. Bowes

Jomini, Antoine-Henri, baron de (1779–1869)

Baron Antoine-Henri de Jomini was a widely read military theorist whose textbook on strategy is believed to have influenced many generals in the American CIVIL WAR. Born in Payerne, Switzerland, he served in the French army under Napoleon and in the Russian army under both Alexander I and Nicolas I. His books on the campaigns of Frederick the Great of Prussia and Napoleon Bonaparte of France were used throughout the Western world to promote an increasingly scientific curriculum of military education.

At the UNITED STATES MILITARY ACADEMY AT WEST POINT, an entire generation of cadets, many of whom would become officers on both sides of the Civil War, absorbed Jomini's scientific approach to strategy. At the heart of Jomini's theory of warfare was the idea that war should be contained on the battlefield and its violence limited whenever possible. This led to an emphasis on a war of maneuver rather than battle, something that was particularly notable in the campaigns of Union general GEORGE B. MCCLELLAN.

Historians are still debating how powerful Jomini's ultimate influence on Civil War strategy was, but it is certain that his writings informed the military TACTICS AND STRATEGY of both Union and Confederate armies.

Further reading: Peter Paret, ed., *Makers of Modern Strategy: from Machiavelli to the Nuclear Age* (Princeton, N.J.: Princeton University Press, 1986).

—Fiona Galvin

journalism

The CIVIL WAR played a critical role in changing the role of journalism and journalists in American society, but the stage was set for change well before the guns thundered at FORT SUMTER in 1861. The newspapers of the early 19th century bore little resemblance to their modern counterparts. Largely supported by political groups and expensive subscriptions, their circulations were usually limited to a few thousand people or less. Content was mostly composed of highly partisan editorial opinion addressing the topics of the day. Coverage of current events was limited and was generally buried on the inside pages of the paper.

This began to change in the 1840s, thanks in part to innovations in technology. The most important new development was the TELEGRAPH. Previously, news of faraway events could take days, weeks, or even months to travel to the cities of the United States. The telegraph reduced this time significantly. The Mexican-American War, fought from 1846 to 1848, became the first American war where a person living in NEW YORK CITY or Philadelphia could stay largely up-to-date on events as they occurred. In addition to the telegraph, new types of printing presses and new printing techniques dramatically increased the speed with which copies of newspapers could be produced while reducing costs, allowing publishers to reach a much broader audience each day.

Technological innovations are only a part of the story, however. A significant portion of the credit for reinventing the American newspaper belongs to James Gordon Bennett, perhaps the greatest innovator in the history of journalism. Bennett founded the *New York Herald* in 1835 and served for decades as its publisher and editor. Bennett disdained the papers of his day as elitist, and he made it his goal to attract as many readers as possible. To start, he charged only two cents for a copy of his paper, and eventually he reduced the cost to one penny. At a price that low, daily newspapers could fit within the budget of almost all Americans.

The *Herald's* coverage was also designed to stimulate readership. While Bennett did not dispense with opinion pieces, he moved them inside the paper and instead used the front page exclusively for news. Bennett based his choice of coverage on what he thought would interest the largest number of people, which often meant that the most sensational stories grabbed the headlines. Because news-gathering was expensive, Bennett formed a partnership with other New York papers to share costs, and thus the Associated Press was born. Bennett also developed entirely new areas of coverage. His boxing stories made the *Herald* the first newspaper in the country to have a sports section. Bennett also incorporated daily coverage of the stock market into the *Herald,* even coining the terms "bull" and "bear" market.

Thanks to these and numerous other innovations, the *Herald* became the most widely read newspaper in America, with a circulation in excess of 100,000 by the start of the Civil War. However, despite this success, papers outside of New York largely avoided adopting Bennett's model prior to 1860. Editors in Chicago, Philadelphia, and other smaller cities throughout the country either were not confident that a paper like Bennett's could work for them, or they did not have the resources that New York papers had. This all changed with the Civil War. Americans demanded up-to-the-moment news coverage, and they bought the papers that would provide it. This compelled newspapers across the nation to make news the centerpiece of their papers, the way Bennett had, thus rendering opinion-centered papers obsolete.

Indeed, the period from 1861 to 1865 was so significant in the history of journalism that it is sometimes referred to as the "news revolution," because at the same time that the Civil War was reshaping the face of journalism, newspapers were helping to reinvent warfare. The Civil War has been called the first modern war. It may not have been so in all regards, but it was modern in the fact that the HOMEFRONT and the war front were intimately connected. Newspapers played an integral role in developing and maintaining that connection.

More than 200 correspondents roamed the various theaters of the war, and reporters were on hand from the beginning to witness every major engagement of the conflict. "The ball is opened," reported correspondent B. S. Osbon from Fort Sumter, "War is inaugurated." Serving as a reporter during the Civil War could be a tricky and even dangerous business. Editors demanded the latest news, and if a correspondent found himself too far away from the action, he risked losing his story or even his job to a rival reporter. This meant that reporters had to stay as close as possible to the army, which often put them in harm's way. Eight reporters were killed during the war, and numerous others were captured and detained for varying lengths of time.

The 200 reporters who covered the CIVIL WAR were joined in the field by several dozen illustrators. The technology to reproduce photographs in newspapers would not be developed until a decade after the Civil War, and so editors used woodcut carvings to provide images of the war for their readers. Illustrations were difficult and expensive to produce, and they were mostly limited to more expensive publications, particularly *Frank Leslie's Illustrated Newspaper* and *Harper's Weekly.* Despite their ten-cent price tag, however, both publications found a wide readership during the Civil War, and the circulation of each exceeded 100,000 by the end of the war. Particularly popular were the portraits of camp life drawn by Winslow Homer and the work of THOMAS NAST, both of whom were employed by *Harper's Weekly.* Nast was avowedly Republican, and his illustrations were designed to bolster Northern morale and rally support for the Lincoln administration. In this he was very successful, so much so that Lincoln remarked at the end of the war that "Thomas Nast has been our best recruiting sergeant."

The vast majority of correspondents during the Civil War worked for Northern newspapers, particularly the powerful triumvirate of New York papers: the *Times,* the *Herald,* and the *Tribune.* Southern newspapers suffered from shortages of paper and money, and so they had a much more difficult time covering the war. This is not to say that there were no Southern newspapers, however. To save money, Confederate newspapers pooled their resources and formed the Press Association of the Southern States, or PA. The PA's stories were available to almost all Southern newspapers, because the Confederate military leaders allowed use of their telegraph lines free of charge. Thanks to cost-saving measures like these, as well as a willingness to print on almost any scraps of paper that could be found, most Southern papers continued publication up to the point that their city was captured by the UNION ARMY.

Through their reporting, their editorials, and their pictures, newspapers naturally had a powerful impact on public opinion. They could influence the populace's outlook on how the war was progressing and on what should happen next. Shortly after the firing on Fort Sumter, the *New York Tribune* urged the Union army to move "On to Richmond!" The *Tribune* continued to put the slogan below its masthead until an attempt to capture the Confederate capital ended in disaster in the summer of 1862. Southern newspapers also expressed their points of view on military affairs, regularly calling for the head of one general or another. JEFFERSON DAVIS and ABRAHAM LINCOLN were popular targets for both praise and criticism, although they generally attracted more of the latter than the former. The abuse heaped on Lincoln was particularly vitriolic. The *Herald,* for example, regularly described Lincoln as "that hideous baboon at the other end of the avenue."

Despite this mistreatment, both Lincoln and Davis understood the importance of cultivating good relations with the press. Davis knew that keeping the homefront apprised of events helped sustain morale, and he did what he could to help reporters. Lincoln wrote LETTERS to newspaper editors on a fairly regular basis, even those editors that disagreed with his policies, knowing that he was being given an opportunity to present his case to thousands of readers free of cost. Lincoln also gave special treatment to papers that supported him, favoring them with interviews and government printing contracts. For the most part, Lincoln did not take steps to suppress unfriendly newspapers.

In contrast to political leaders like Lincoln and Davis, military leaders generally had little use for reporters. It is true that an ambitious officer seeking promotion could curry favor with a reporter and perhaps earn some good coverage in return. But reporters could also do serious damage to a career by reporting and magnifying even the slightest mistakes. Early in the war, Gen. WILLIAM T. SHERMAN made a request for a larger number of troops than could possibly be provided to him. A Union official related the request to a reporter, offhandedly describing it as "crazy." The next day, headlines across the nation read "Sherman is Insane!" The ensuing publicity caused Sherman to lose his command temporarily and fostered his hatred of reporters. Similar reports of ULYSSES S. GRANT having problems with alcohol caused personal anguish and raised doubts about his professional competence. Of course, as much as Grant and Sherman resented the personal wrongs that had been done to them, they were even more concerned about reporters' ability to reveal sensitive information to the enemy. Typically, their only recourse was censorship, and Northern military leaders in particular did so regularly. On occasion, reporters were banished or arrested, and on one occasion a correspondent came within hours of being executed by an angry Union general.

Despite the military's misgivings, there would be no going back. The press had brought the realities of combat to the American people. No longer would people on the homefront be willing to support a war without being informed as to what decisions were being made and why. In the years immediately after the war, newspapers continued to have an important role in informing the public and shaping peoples' opinions. For example, newspaper reports of violence against former slaves in 1866 and 1867 rallied support for the RECONSTRUCTION plans of the RADICAL REPUBLICANS. At the same time, revelations of corruption in newspapers, coupled with the drawings of THOMAS NAST, helped to end the career of NEW YORK CITY political boss William Marcy Tweed. Due in large part to their service during the CIVIL WAR, journalists came to see themselves as having an important role in democracy, namely making certain that people were kept informed about the activities of their leaders and of their fellow citizens. As such, the "news revolution" is one of the most significant developments to come out of the Civil War.

Further reading: J. Cutler Andrews, *The North Reports the Civil War* (Pittsburgh, Pa.: University of Pittsburgh Press, 1955); J. Cutler Andrews, *The South Reports the Civil War* (Princeton, N.J.: University of Princeton Press, 1970); Ford Risley, "The Confederate Press Association: Cooperative News Reporting of the War," *Civil War History* 47 (Sept. 2001): 222–239; Louis Morris Starr, *The Bohemian Brigade: Civil War Newsmen in Action* (Madison: University of Wisconsin Press, 1987).

—Christopher Bates

Julian, George Washington (1817–1899)

Radical Republican congressman George W. Julian was born in Centreville, Indiana, on May 5, 1817. He began studying law in 1840 after teaching for several years. The law led him to the state legislature in 1845, where he served as a member of the Whig Party. In the late 1840s, Julian, attracted by the Free-Soil Party, left the Whigs and became a fervent spokesman against SLAVERY. His first term as a

U.S. congressman began in 1849, and his principles made him an opponent of the Compromise of 1850. Defeated in his reelection bid because of this stand, Julian became the vice presidential candidate for the Free-Soil Party in 1852. Following FRANKLIN PIERCE's victory, Julian remained an advocate of ABOLITION when he returned to Indiana and joined the REPUBLICAN PARTY.

Julian returned to the U.S. Congress in 1859, where his support of abolitionism made him a prominent spokesman for the RADICAL REPUBLICANS. He served as a member of the JOINT COMMITTEE ON THE CONDUCT OF THE WAR, and in his second term he was named the chairman of the Committee on Public Lands. Both committees represented his interests for the remainder of his years in the legislature: an aggressive war policy, a harsh RECONSTRUCTION, African-American suffrage, and a democratic homestead policy that would keep public lands out of the hands of monopolists and speculators. Following his departure from Congress in 1870, Julian again changed parties but remained reform minded. He affiliated himself with the Liberal Republicans in 1871 but ended up as a Democrat, stumping for Samuel Tilden in 1876. In his last decades he consistently advocated land and currency reform, as well as woman suffrage.

Julian died in Irvington, Indiana, on July 7, 1899.

Further reading: Patrick W. Riddleberger, *George Washington Julian, Radical Republican: A Study in Nineteenth-Century Politics and Reform* (Indianapolis: Indiana Historical Bureau, 1966).

—John P. Bowes

Juneteenth (June 19th)

"Juneteenth" is an annual African-American celebration commemorating the 1865 ABOLITION of SLAVERY in Texas.

Though cut off from the rest of the South in 1863, much of Texas remained unoccupied by Union troops until Union general Gordon Granger arrived at Galveston, Texas, 10 weeks after Lee's surrender. On June 19, 1865, Granger issued General Order No. 3, declaring: "The people of Texas are informed that all slaves are free. This involves an absolute equality of rights of property between masters and slaves and the connection heretofore existing between them becomes that between employer and free laborer." Thus, two and a half years after ABRAHAM LINCOLN issued the EMANCIPATION PROCLAMATION, Granger made it the law in Texas.

As word of Granger's order spread, African Americans joined in spontaneous celebration of "Juneteenth." Beginning in 1866, the anniversary of Juneteenth became an occasion for picnics, baseball games, family reunions, and other revelry. By the turn of the 20th century, Juneteenth celebrations also featured prayer services and oratory. Speakers typically urged celebrants to dedicate themselves to EDUCATION and spiritual uplift.

As late as the 1930s, tens of thousands of people participated in Juneteenth celebrations across Texas. With the number of former slaves dwindling, however, Juneteenth shrank in importance after World War II. The rise of public education may have also played a role; history textbooks dated the end of slavery to ABRAHAM LINCOLN's 1863 proclamation rather than to events in Texas.

In the late 1960s, Juneteenth celebrations began again to grow as African Americans reclaimed their history. Juneteenth was prominent, for instance, on the buttons and banners Texans carried to the June 1969 Poor Peoples March on WASHINGTON, D.C. As interest revived, pressure mounted to declare Juneteenth a state holiday in Texas, a goal achieved in 1980. Juneteenth has since become a national symbol of slavery's demise, a fact marked by the 1999 publication of Ralph Ellison's posthumous novel *Juneteenth,* set in early 20th-century Texas. Says one of Ellison's characters, "There've been a heap of Juneteenths gone by and there'll be a heap more before we're free."

See also EMANCIPATION.

Further reading: Francis Edward Abernethy, ed., *Juneteenth Texas: Essays in African-American Folklore* (Denton: University of North Texas Press, 1996); Charles A. Taylor, *Juneteenth, A Celebration of Freedom* (Madison, Wis.: Praxis Publications, 1995).

—Tom Laichas

K

Kansas-Nebraska Act (1854)

Many historians believe that the passage of the Kansas-Nebraska Act on May 30, 1854, was the single most important event pushing the United States on the road to the CIVIL WAR. This act superseded the Missouri Compromise and undid much of the Compromise of 1850. The passage of the Kansas-Nebraska Act also had a major effect on the reconfiguration of America's political parties. It divided the DEMOCRATIC PARTY, played an instrumental role in the demise of the Whig Party, and contributed to the rise of a new, exclusively Northern and antiSLAVERY party, the REPUBLICAN PARTY. The passage of the act also triggered guerrilla fighting in Kansas.

Senator STEPHEN A. DOUGLAS of Illinois played the single most important role in the formation of the Kansas-Nebraska Act. Douglas, serving as chairman of the Senate Committee on Territories, used his position to promote the development of the western part of the United States. Douglas hoped that Western development would have a chastening influence upon the growing sectional enmities between the North and the South. Instead, it had the opposite effect.

Douglas knew that entrepreneurs could not complete a transcontinental railroad without the prior political organization of the West. In February 1853, a bill calling for the admission of Nebraska as a state passed the House. However, when Douglas brought the bill before the Senate, it failed. Douglas could not obtain Southern support for the development of Nebraska so long as the Missouri Compromise prohibited slavery in the area. Douglas knew that if he incorporated the idea of popular sovereignty—of territories deciding for themselves whether to be free or slave—into the bill, he had a better chance of gaining the support of Southern Democrats.

For his first step, Douglas had to persuade four key Democrats: Andrew Butler of South Carolina, David Atchison of Missouri, and James Mason and Robert Hunter of Virginia, known collectively as the "F Street Mess" (for the house on F Street in which they boarded while in WASHINGTON, D.C.). These four senators, like Southern Democrats in general, viewed the organization of the Kansas territory under the Missouri Compromise restrictions as a grave threat to SLAVERY. But, in negotiation with Douglas, the F Street Mess saw an opportunity, in a modified bill of territorial organization, to strengthen slavery's position in the United States by repealing the Missouri Compromise line and instituting popular sovereignty instead.

In January 1854, Douglas inserted the language of popular sovereignty into the bill for Nebraska statehood and added the Kansas Territory to the Nebraska Territory already under consideration. Unfortunately, the idea of popular sovereignty for this region violated the Missouri Compromise, which forbade slavery north of the 36° 30' line. Southern Whigs called for explicit repudiation of the Missouri Compromise. In the South, the Whigs and the Democrats were in a contest to show their dedication to slavery. Neither party could allow the other to appear to be more favorable to it, so Southern Democrats also called for the repeal of the Missouri Compromise.

Congressional debate on the Kansas-Nebraska Act revealed great concern from Northerners and many Southerners. Debates raged over the legislation. Northerners argued that the act was too vague on when a vote on slavery ought to take place. Their claim was that the longer a vote waited, the more likely it was that slavery would exist ipso facto. Slaveholders would bring their property with them, so as soon as Southern settlers moved in, Kansas would become a slave territory. Southerners in turn viewed the Northern reaction as yet more proof that they were under siege by Yankee ABOLITIONists, and Northern rhetoric gave them no cause to doubt this. For instance, in October 1854 ABRAHAM LINCOLN, then an up-and-coming young Illinois lawyer, stated about popular sovereignty that "[w]hen the white man governs himself, and also governs *another* man, that is *more* than self-government—that is despotism."

Political parties were just as angry and just as divided as individuals and interest groups over the Kansas-Nebraska Act. Several members of the Ohio congressional delegation, including Senators BENJAMIN WADE and SALMON P. CHASE, believed that the act was "a gross violation of a sacred pledge." They implored their fellow members of Congress to vote against the act on the grounds that "[w]hatever apologies may be offered for the toleration of Slavery in the states, none can be urged for its extension into Territories where it does not exist." Northern Whigs were upset with the act as well. They were afraid that the Kansas-Nebraska Act might resurrect the Northern Free-Soil Party that had previously caused many problems for them. Northern Whigs also believed that Southerners would take advantage of this opportunity to expand plantation slavery into the Northern United States. This was unlikely, since Southerners believed that the climate of the more northern latitudes prohibited the rise of further slave states in these parts of the West. Correspondingly, Southerners were unenthusiastic about any measure that could, under the tenets of popular sovereignty, lead to the existence of more free states.

On March 3, 1854, the Senate voted 37 to 14 in favor of the passage of the Kansas-Nebraska Act, with Southern Democrats and Whigs voting nearly in lockstep. However, in the House the story was quite different. ALEXANDER H. STEPHENS, the future vice president of the Confederacy, brought 13 Southern Whig representatives across party lines and assured the passage of the act on May 22, when the House voted 113-100 in favor of the bill.

Northern Whigs of both houses had generally opposed the bill. In fact, a large portion of the Northern Whig Party had hoped to convince Southern Whigs to oppose the bill as well. The Whigs hoped to generate a Whig "renaissance" in 1856 and perhaps even to recapture the White House. These hopes were extremely unrealistic, for they failed to take into account that for a Southern Whig to oppose the Kansas-Nebraska Act would be to commit political suicide, since voting against slavery's interests doomed any Southern political career. Still, the Kansas-Nebraska Act energized Northern Whigs such as Abraham Lincoln to redouble their political efforts against slavery's spread.

The response to the passage of the Kansas-Nebraska Act was violent. Proslavery and antislavery forces flooded into Kansas. Once there, they established themselves in mutually hostile communities. In 1855, amidst pitched battles that earned the period the name *BLEEDING KANSAS*, the doctrine of popular sovereignty failed its initial test when the Kansas territory held its first election. The proslavery forces were victorious, but antislavery forces refused to accept the results of the election. They claimed that proslave forces from Missouri had illegally stuffed the ballot boxes. President FRANKLIN PIERCE accepted the proslave victory as legitimate and sent government troops into the area to restore order. Congress, however, refused to accept Kansas as a slave state. A crisis over slavery once again shook the entire nation. It was not until 1861, with the South gone from the Union, that Kansas was finally admitted to the Union as a free state.

Further reading: Thomas Goodrich, *War to the Knife: Bleeding Kansas, 1854–1861* (Mechanicsburg, Pa.: Stackpole Books, 1998); Kenneth Stampp, *America in 1857: A Nation on the Brink* (New York: Oxford University Press, 1990).

—Chad Vanderford

Kelley, William D. (1814–1890)

Born in Philadelphia in 1814, William Darrah Kelley was a congressman who advocated racial equality in the postwar years.

When Kelley was 13, he was apprenticed to a jeweler, moving to Boston to become an enameler in 1834. His gregarious and open personality soon manifested itself as he spent his time off writing and debating the issues of his day. In 1838 he moved back to his hometown of Philadelphia and learned the law, passing the bar exam in 1841. After becoming a prosecuting attorney, he quickly rose up the ranks of Philadelphia's legal system and was elected as a judge in 1851.

Politically, Kelley started out as a member of the DEMOCRATIC PARTY, but after the Missouri Compromise was repealed in 1854 (allowing SLAVERY to extend further than had previously been agreed), he became an influential founding member of the antislavery REPUBLICAN PARTY of Pennsylvania. His first famous speech was delivered that same year, an antislavery oration entitled "Slavery in the Territories."

Kelley was an excellent speaker whose loud voice carried audiences along with him. He decided to capitalize on his asset, running for Congress in 1856. Although he lost, he ran again four years later and won, holding his seat for the next 20 years.

When the CIVIL WAR broke out, Kelley enlisted in the artillery, although he never saw combat. When he returned to Congress he voted for every EMANCIPATION or war-related bill that he could. He supported arming African Americans to fight for the Union, and after the war he voted for the establishment of the FREEDMEN'S BUREAU and endorsed military RECONSTRUCTION. He became well known as an advocate of black suffrage and an avowed enemy of segregation.

Kelley died in 1890, after spending many years in Congress fighting for those issues he believed in. His daughter Florence Kelley later become well known as a reformer in her own right.

Further reading: Kathryn Kish Sklar, *Florence Kelley and the Nation's Work: The Rise of Women's Political Culture, 1830–1900.* (New Haven, Conn.: Yale University Press, 1995).

—Troy Rondinone

Knights of Labor   See Volume VI

Know-Nothing Party   See Volume IV

Ku Klux Klan

A white supremacist terrorist group in the postbellum South, the Ku Klux Klan began in May and June 1866 in Pulaski, Tennessee. Soon after its creation, the Klan had chapters in every Southern state and attracted support from all segments of Southern white society. Former Confederate officers, like Gen. NATHAN BEDFORD FORREST, who is widely believed to have been the organization's first grand wizard, helped turn the informal social-club Klan into a paramilitary force.

By 1868, the fraternal organization donned white hoods and dedicated itself to the overthrow of RECONSTRUCTION and the preservation of white supremacy. Like other vigilante groups in the region (such as the Knights of the White Camelia and the White Brotherhood), the Klan used violence to intimidate freedmen and their white supporters. Klansmen whipped and lynched Southern African Americans for any conceivable reason. All signs of African-American autonomy and power became targets for Klan activities. Klansmen burned schools and churches and lynched ministers, students, and teachers. Klansmen also attacked black sharecroppers who disputed their portions of the crop, refused to work for white employers, tried to change employers, or showed any signs of economic success.

The Klan directed most of its energy at the political sphere, especially at black politicians and other supporters of the South's REPUBLICAN PARTY. In many ways, it served as the military arm of the South's DEMOCRATIC PARTY. Klansmen whipped and often murdered African-American officeholders and local leaders for their political beliefs and actions. Hundreds of black leaders fled their homes after the beatings, and countless others withdrew from politics. Prior to the election of 1868, the Klan killed more than 200 Republican supporters in Arkansas and more than

1,000 in Louisiana. The intimidation intensified on election day. Armed mobs prevented many polls from opening while others scared black voters away. In 11 counties with African-American majorities in Georgia, Klan violence prevented Republican presidential candidate ULYSSES S. GRANT from receiving any votes.

Klan terror continued after the 1868 election, provoking responses from state and federal governments. Several states made it a crime to travel in disguise, raised the penalties for mob activities, and even authorized ordinary citizens to arrest suspected Klansmen. Republican sheriffs led posses and a few GOVERNORS sent militia companies to track Klansmen down. Most Southern governors, however, were reluctant to act, and when they did their efforts enjoyed little success. Even when they captured Klan members, conviction in the local courts proved impossible, as the routine killing and intimidation of jurists and witnesses prevented successful prosecutions. During Reconstruction, local prosecutors obtained no convictions in the civil courts.

Prosecutors enjoyed more success in the military courts. In 1868 and 1869, Arkansas governor Powell Clayton declared martial law in 10 counties, formed segregated militias, sent undercover agents to infiltrate the Klan, and tried and executed Klansmen in military courts. Law and order returned to the state by the end of 1869, and the state's Klan was effectively silenced. Texas governor Edmund J. Davis proceeded similarly by organizing a 200-member state police. This force arrested more than 6,000 men and effectively suppressed the Klan. The effectiveness of martial law led Klansmen in Tennessee to disband almost immediately after Governor William G. Brownlow declared martial law in nine counties.

Attempts in North Carolina to shut down the Klan proved less successful. In 1879 Governor William W. Holden responded to a wave of terror and the murder of Senator John W. Stephens by declaring martial law without the constitutional authority to do so. Holden sent white militia units, under the command of former Union officer George W. Kirk, to patrol the western counties and subdue the Klan. Kirk arrested about 100 men, but Holden backed down from his desire to try the Klansmen in military courts. The resulting trials took place in the Klan-controlled local courts and resulted in no convictions. The Kirk-Holden war crippled the state's Republican Party just prior to the legislative election of 1870. Democrats swept into power, and in 1871 they impeached and convicted Holden for illegally declaring martial law.

As the death tolls rose, Southern Republicans called on the federal government for assistance. Congress responded with a series of ENFORCEMENT ACTS. The first act, passed in 1870, allowed for the federal supervision of voting and authorized the president to appoint election supervisors

A Thomas Nast cartoon commenting on violence toward African Americans shows a member of the White League and a Ku Klux Klansman joining hands over a terrorized black family *(Hulton/Archive)*

with the power to bring federal charges for election fraud and voter intimidation. In January 1871, the violence initiated by the Klan reached a feverish pitch in South Carolina when 500 masked men attacked a Union county jail and lynched eight black prisoners. In April, after several

months of sustained violence, Congress issued the KU KLUX KLAN ACT. This law turned several criminal offenses (such as participating in conspiracies designed to deprive citizens of their right to vote, hold office, or serve on juries) into federal crimes, authorized the president to use the army to enforce this and the earlier Enforcement Act, and gave him the authority to suspend the WRIT OF HABEAS CORPUS in areas under a state of insurrection. The act further gave the courts the power to eliminate suspected Klansmen from juries.

The Enforcement and Ku Klux Klan Acts allowed Attorney General Amos Akerman and President Ulysses S. Grant to respond vigorously to the Klan. While Congress held investigative hearings and recorded the outrages that the Klan sponsored throughout the region, Grant sent several cavalry companies to shut the Klan down. Grant suspended the writ of habeas corpus in nine South Carolina counties, where federal troops arrested hundreds of suspected Klansmen and federal grand juries issued thousands of indictments. Most of those who were convicted received fines or light prison sentences, but the arrests effectively shut South Carolina's Klan down. Grant never extended the military provisions of the KU KLUX KLAN ACT outside of South Carolina, but federal prosecutors also indicted more than 1,000 Klansmen in Mississippi and North Carolina.

The legal offensive of 1871 effectively destroyed the Reconstruction-era Klan. The Klan disappeared from American and Southern society for more than 40 years before it revived itself in a national organization in 1915 and again during the Civil Rights movement.

Further reading: Everette Swinney, *Suppressing the Ku Klux Klan: The Enforcement of the Reconstruction Amendments, 1870–1877* (New York: Garland, 1987); Allen W. Trelease, *White Terror: The Ku Klux Klan Conspiracy and Southern Reconstruction* (Baton Rouge: Louisiana State University Press, 1995).

—Andrew K. Frank

Ku Klux Klan Act (April 20, 1871)

The Ku Klux Klan Act, also known as the Third ENFORCEMENT ACT, was passed by Congress on April 20, 1871, over strong objections by Democrats. The act was meant to stop white violence against freedmen in the former Confederate states. It gave the president, ULYSSES S. GRANT, the ability to stop "insurrection" by using military force or by suspending HABEAS CORPUS, which meant he could place people in jail without charging them.

In 1866 the KU KLUX KLAN (KKK) was founded as a social club for former Confederate soldiers. The organization quickly evolved into a vigilante group that opposed freedmen's rights. The Klan often terrorized African Americans and their white sympathizers by intimidating voters, bullying politicians supportive of Radical RECONSTRUCTION, burning African-American schools and churches, and even committing murder. Because law enforcement was generally a local matter, and because local authorities in the South sympathized with the Klan's racial agenda, crimes against Republicans and freed people in the South generally went unpunished by local authorities.

When Congress convened in March 1871, Grant condemned what was happening in the South and called for action by the federal government. The act was passed in April, and habeas corpus was suspended in nine South Carolina counties in May. Hundreds of arrests were made, and an estimated 2,000 Klansmen fled the state. Eventually, federal grand juries indicted 3,000 people throughout the South, bringing the worst offenders to trial and obtaining 600 convictions.

The Ku Klux Klan Act had some impact in lessening violence in the South. However, in 1876's *UNITED STATES V. CRUIKSHANK*, the Supreme Court ruled that the act only applied to wrongdoing by state and local governments, not to acts by individual citizens. Since the Klan was not a part of the government, the Supreme Court's decision effectively meant that the Ku Klux Klan Act could no longer be used to stop the Klan. The act is thus another example of a seeming victory for the freed people ultimately being transformed into a defeat.

Further reading: George C. Rable, *But There Was No Peace: The Role of Violence in the Politics of Reconstruction* (Athens: University of Georgia Press, 1984); Allen W. Trelease, *White Terror: The Ku Klux Klan Conspiracy and Southern Reconstruction* (Baton Rouge: Louisiana State University Press, 1995).

—Scott L. Stabler

L

ladies aid societies

With the fall of FORT SUMTER in April 1861, women North and South responded by supplying volunteers with blankets, clothes, and food. In villages, hamlets, cities, and towns, women packed lunches, mended shirts and socks, sewed UNIFORMS and flags, and collected family quilts. Women equipped their relatives, friends, and townsmen with supplies to get them to the front, believing that the government would then take over the provisioning of the troops. But neither the United States nor Confederate governments had the military infrastructure with which to organize and equip a large army. As a result, at the beginning of the CIVIL WAR, individuals and local governments provided their own uniforms, weapons, food, and general equipment such as knapsacks, blankets, and tents. Even after the U.S. government had a system in place that combined federal production with private enterprise, there was plenty of room for the assistance of ladies aid societies.

In both the North and the South, women's efforts quickly evolved into soldiers' aid societies. The organizers had been active in benevolence work before the Civil War and transformed their groups to accommodate the soldiers, or they simply established new associations. Women wrote organization constitutions, elected officers, established dues, and created work committees to cut, sew, and pack, as well as solicit funds. Women volunteered their time and talents with the patriotic sentiment that they were doing their part for the cause. "We never knew before how much we loved our country," wrote Josephine Shaw, the sister of Col. Robert G. Shaw of the 54TH MASSACHUSETTS. A devoted volunteer, she added: "We can work though we can't enlist. It is very pleasant to see how well the girls and women do work everywhere, sewing meetings, sanitary hospitals and all." The societies provided the soldiers with comforts when well and with hospital supplies and NURSES when wounded and sick. In the North, it is estimated that more than 20,000 ladies aid societies operated throughout the war. In the South, women established more than 1,000 societies by the end of 1861, but Confederate ladies never organized on a national scale, and they faced an array of problems that doomed the smooth and continuous operation of their associations.

First, Southern ladies aid societies remained the domain of the elite ladies. This discouraged working-class women, who held the domestic skills, from participating, thus hampering society relief efforts. Southern women turned much of their time to fund-raising when they realized that many supplies needed to be purchased. Along with the basic medical and domestic goods like bandages, scissors, and Bibles, societies in Charleston, Mobile, Norfolk, and Savannah raised money for the purchase of ships. However, the Confederacy also lacked the overall resources that were available to Northern women as goods became scarce with intensifying war activities and the successful Union naval blockade of Southern ports. Southern ladies aid societies finally collapsed when the Union troops invaded the Confederacy. Federal soldiers stole the societies' supplies, thus ending their operations.

In contrast, Northern women established a national network of ladies aid societies that were able to support the troops for the duration of the hostilities. While the societies began at a grassroots level, it became apparent to several women, particularly in the East, that a more efficient system was needed to identify and locate misplaced boxes and to rationalize management to prevent the overlapping of efforts in one area and the lack of supplies in another area. Creating such an organized system, they thought, would help rather than hinder the army. Dr. Elizabeth Blackwell of New York was the first to recognize the need for organization and called a meeting for April 26, 1861, at the Cooper Union in NEW YORK CITY. She invited some of the city's most prominent women as well as Dr. Henry Bellows, the Unitarian minister of All Souls Church. Before the meeting adjourned for the day, the ladies and men present formed the Women's Central Association of Relief (WCAR). They proposed that they would "give organization and efficiency to the scattered efforts" already in progress, that they would establish a relationship with the medical staff of the army, and a central depot for supplies, and that they would investigate the needs of the soldiers. Blackwell also began a program to train and register female nurses. In the short term, the WCAR proved to be a success. The ladies aid societies of the Northeast responded by funneling their supplies into the office of the WCAR in New York. Other women around the area who had not yet organized were inspired to establish soldiers' aid societies in their towns and began a relationship with the WCAR.

The achievements of the WCAR were somewhat overshadowed by the creation of the UNITED STATES SANITARY COMMISSION (USSC). Dr. Henry Bellows feared that the War Department's announcement that they would not accept the nursing trainees was the first of many military rejections of the WCAR. Bellows proposed that a centralized, national organization separate from the WCAR was needed to combine all of the efforts of the nation's relief associations, help the army operate the hospitals, and determine the needs of the soldiers. Bellows suggested that the new organization have government sanction but operate on private funds. On June 13, 1861, Bellows gained official authority from President ABRAHAM LINCOLN, who believed the USSC would prove to be as useful as a "fifth wheel on a coach," but who gave his approval anyway.

In Chicago, ladies like Mary A. Livermore helped establish the Northwestern Sanitary Commission, which became the main depot for Wisconsin, Michigan, Illinois, and Iowa supplies. In Cleveland, women formed the Soldiers' Aid Society of Northern Ohio. In Boston, they became known as the New England Women's Aid Association and received goods from Maine, New Hampshire, Vermont, and Massachusetts. And in Pennsylvania the Ladies Aid Society of Philadelphia received goods from around the state. All of these groups became affiliates of the United States Sanitary Commission and sent their supplies through their regional USSC channels.

The USSC and their chapters expanded their work to include sanitary inspection of camps and instruction of soldiers on matters of water supply, placement of latrines, and safe cooking methods. They provided meals, housing, and TRANSPORTATION to soldiers on furlough and nursed those who were too sick or wounded to continue. After the BATTLE OF GETTYSBURG, a grateful doctor wrote of the USSC ladies aid: "I . . . get plenty to eat and of excellent quality from the Sanitary Commission, eggs, chickens, crackers of every kind. They are doing noble work." They helped soldiers obtain their pay and also established a messenger service that employed disabled VETERANS. They maintained hospital records and helped locate wounded, captured, and dead soldiers for the distraught parents and relatives. The

ladies sustained these multifaceted programs through a variety of fund-raising activities. The most popular form was the sanitary fair, which usually lasted about two weeks and included displays, entertainment, auctions, and restaurants. The fair was the brainchild of Mary A. Livermore and Jane C. Hoge, who held a successful Chicago fair in October 1863 in which the Northwest Commission raised more than $100,000.

In spite of these successes, the USSC never attained its goal of creating an all-inclusive national system. Other women like those who formed the Western Sanitary Commission in St. Louis and the Cooper Shop Volunteer Refreshment Saloon and the Union Volunteer Refreshment Committee, both of Philadelphia, chose to operate independent of the USSC. These groups and hundreds of smaller societies across the North contributed supplies to the USSC but maintained their independence, believing autonomous societies could better meet the needs of their local soldiers.

The USSC also vied for supplies with the UNITED STATES CHRISTIAN COMMISSION (USCC). Organized by the Young Men's Christian Associations across the North with the ideal of caring for the soldiers' spiritual needs, the USCC quickly became the USSC's arch rival. Independent societies and USCC actions frustrated men and women dedicated to the national goals of the USSC, who saw their agency as the symbol of Northern unity. Although there was much infighting among the benevolent communities of the North during the war, the ladies aid societies were able to supply troops and hospitals and consequently saved thousands of soldiers' lives.

In short, ladies aid societies, whether independent or chapters of the USSC or its Southern counterparts, were in the business of aiding the soldiers with whatever means available. Northern and Southern women volunteered their services with the call for troops in 1861, helped their causes by assisting the soldiers, and in this way became patriots of the war.

See also COMMON SOLDIER; HOMEFRONT.

Further reading: Jeanie Attie, *Patriotic Toil: Northern Women and the American Civil War* (Ithaca, N.Y.: Cornell University Press, 1998); Drew Gilpin Faust, *Mothers of Invention: Women of the Slaveholding South in the American Civil War* (Chapel Hill: University of North Carolina Press, 1996); Judith Ann Giesberg, *Civil War Sisterhood: The U.S. Sanitary Commission and Women's Politics in Transition* (Boston, Mass.: Northeastern University Press, 2000); Joan Waugh, *Unsentimental Reformer: The Life of Josephine Shaw Lowell* (Cambridge, Mass.: Harvard University Press, 1998).

—Patricia Richard

Lee, Robert E. (1807–1870)

West Pointer and Confederate general Robert Edward Lee was born on January 19, 1807, at "Stratford Hall," Virginia, the fifth child of Henry "Light-Horse Harry" Lee and Ann Hill Carter Lee. His father, a Revolutionary War hero and later governor of Virginia, left home when Robert was six and never returned. With few financial resources, the family settled on a career in the army for Robert. Political connections helped secure an appointment to the UNITED STATES MILITARY ACADEMY AT WEST POINT in 1825.

Lee completed four years at the academy without any demerits and graduated second in the class of 1829. Apart from his exceptional academic record and conduct, he also exhibited qualities of leadership. Cadets referred to him as the "Marble Model," a nickname that probably reflected some envy as well as admiration. Just under six feet tall, handsome, and with black hair and brown eyes, Lee cut a striking figure. He entered the Engineer Corps as a second lieutenant on July 1, 1829.

More than a decade and half passed before Lee saw a battlefield. Promotions to first lieutenant and captain punctuated this long stretch of peacetime service. In June 1831, Lee married Mary Anna Randolph Custis, the only daughter of George Washington Parke Custis, himself the grandson of Martha Washington. Mary Anna and Lee would share a 39-year marriage that produced four daughters and three sons. Lee took seriously the ties to Washington, whom he sought to emulate throughout his life. The Confederate people later would often compare the two Virginians, viewing Lee and his Army of Northern Virginia much as the American colonists had viewed Washington and the Continental army.

On May 13, 1846, the United States declared war on Mexico. Between March and September 1847, Lee served on the staff of Winfield Scott during a brilliant campaign from Vera Cruz to Mexico City. Lee performed exemplary service and impressed his superiors—none more so than Scott, who came away from Mexico filled with admiration for the younger officer.

In the 1850s, Lee held the superintendence of the United States Military Academy from 1852 to 1855 and later served as lieutenant colonel of the Second Cavalry in Texas. In late October 1859, he chanced to be in WASHINGTON, D.C., when JOHN BROWN attacked HARPERS FERRY. Summoned to the War Department on October 17, Lee proceeded to Harpers Ferry with a detachment of marines and the next morning captured Brown.

By the time of Lee's promotion to colonel of the First Cavalry on March 16, 1861, seven southern states had seceded. Confederates fired on FORT SUMTER on April 12, and ABRAHAM LINCOLN issued a call three days later for 75,000 volunteers to suppress the rebellion. On April 18,

Lee was offered command of the U.S. Army being raised to put down the rebellion. He declined with the explanation that he could not take the field against the Southern states. "Save in the defense of my native State," he wrote to Winfield Scott, "I never desire again to draw my sword."

In late April, Lee accepted appointment as major general of Virginia's state forces and shortly thereafter transferred to the CONFEDERATE ARMY. He was made a full general on August 31, 1861, ranking third in seniority among Confederate generals. Lee's first year in command, which included duty in western Virginia and along the South Atlantic coast, yielded no dramatic victories and created the impression that he was a timid commander. In early March 1862, he became military adviser to President JEFFERSON DAVIS in RICHMOND, capital of the Confederacy. On May 31 JOSEPH E. JOHNSTON, who commanded the Confederate army defending Richmond, was wounded in the Battle of Seven Pines. Lee took his place the next

Robert E. Lee *(National Archives)*

day, an appointment that provoked a mixed reaction. Many Confederates approved, but others doubted Lee's ability. A member of Lee's staff recalled that some Southern newspapers predicted that with Lee in charge "our army would never be allowed to fight."

Lee immediately sought to take the initiative. Reinforcements under THOMAS J. "STONEWALL" JACKSON from the Shenandoah Valley boosted his army's strength to more than 85,000. Between June 25 and July 1, Lee and GEORGE B. MCCLELLAN fought the Seven Days' Battle. The Confederates pushed McClellan's army southward, away from Richmond and toward the James River. Lee's victory was not a masterpiece. His plans had been too complicated, and the Confederates suffered more than 20,000 casualties to McClellan's 16,000. Yet Lee's first major campaign as a field commander lifted civilian spirits across the Confederacy and greatly enhanced his reputation.

Lee reorganized the Army of Northern Virginia after the Seven Days, dividing its infantry between Stonewall Jackson and JAMES LONGSTREET. The revamped army defeated Union general John Pope at the SECOND BATTLE OF BULL RUN on August 28–30, an engagement that tallied more than 9,000 Confederate and 16,000 Union casualties. Since taking command in June, Lee had restored the Confederacy's eastern military frontier to where it had been in April 1861. His decisive leadership and victories won praise from across the Confederacy. A colonel from Georgia reflected this attitude, observing on September 5, 1862, that "Genl Lee stands now above all Genls in Modern History."

After SECOND BATTLE OF BULL RUN, Lee decided to take the war out of Virginia and into the Union. The Army of Northern Virginia, a ragged force some 55,000 strong, crossed the Potomac on September 4–7. GEORGE B. MCCLELLAN, reinstated after Pope's defeat, opposed Lee on September 17 in the campaign's climactic BATTLE OF ANTIETAM. Lee's army had suffered from severe straggling and DESERTION while in Maryland, leaving only about 35,000 men to face McClellan's 80,000. During a day of savage combat that ended with an uneasy standoff, more than 10,000 Confederates and 12,500 Federals fell, making Antietam the bloodiest day in U.S. history. The Army of Northern Virginia retreated to the Potomac on the night of September 18.

The Maryland campaign ended a three-month drama that had begun with the Seven Days' Battle. Although turned back at Antietam, Lee had crafted an overall Confederate success. His victories had driven major enemy forces from Virginia, raised Confederate civilian morale, sent tremors through the North, and laid the foundation for a memorable bond between himself and his soldiers.

A victory at the BATTLE OF FREDERICKSBURG on December 13, 1862, increased public confidence in Lee.

This unusual winter campaign pitted 75,000 Confederates against more than 125,000 Union soldiers under Gen. AMBROSE E. BURNSIDE, who had replaced McClellan. At one point in the battle, an admiring Lee watched his VETERANS drive back the Federals. Turning to James Longstreet, he said in an even voice, "It is well that war is so terrible! We should grow too fond of it!" The battle claimed 12,653 Northern and 5,309 Southern casualties. Behind the lines in the Confederacy, the victory spread optimism and heightened faith in Lee.

In late April 1863 Gen. JOSEPH HOOKER, Burnside's successor, commenced a new Union offensive along the Rappahannock River that ended with the BATTLE OF CHANCELLORSVILLE. Lee had detached half of Longstreet's troops to southern Virginia, leaving him with about 60,000 men to oppose Hooker's 120,000. Lee reacted to Hooker's movements with a series of daring decisions that involved dividing his outnumbered force three times. Four days of fighting commenced on May 1, at the end of which Hooker retreated to the north bank of the Rappahannock. Utterly dominating Hooker psychologically, Lee had wrested victory from circumstances that would have undone most generals. He also lost more than 12,500 men, among them Stonewall Jackson, who died on May 10 after being wounded on the evening of May 2.

Chancellorsville uplifted the Confederate people, who made Lee their unquestioned military idol, and sent waves of disappointment rippling across the North. It also completed the process by which the Army of Northern Virginia became almost fanatically devoted to Lee. In language echoed by countless others, a Georgia soldier described this deep attachment: "Wherever he leads they will follow. Whatever he says do, can and must be done."

The next test for Lee came on Northern soil. His army, with Longstreet back, marched northward in June 1863 numbering 75,000 men. By the end of June, Confederates had penetrated well into Pennsylvania. The greatest battle of the war opened on July 1 just west of Gettysburg. Confederates carried the field on the first day, then continued their offensive during the next two days. Fighting raged at such places as the Peach Orchard and Little Round Top on July 2, and the battle closed on July 3 with the famous Confederate attack known as Pickett's Charge. During the three days, more than 23,000 Federals and at least 25,000 Confederates fell. Many critics have pointed to the BATTLE OF GETTYSBURG as proof that Lee's aggressiveness sometimes overcame his better judgment. Others have argued that several subordinates performed poorly and frustrated Lee's plans. Lee typically took full responsibility for the defeat. In the wake of Pickett's Charge, he told a subordinate, "Never mind General, all this has been my fault—it is I that have lost this fight."

Nearly 10 months passed before Lee faced another serious Union offensive. In the spring of 1864, Gen. ULYSSES S. GRANT assumed command of operations in Virginia. His presence raised hopes among Northerners that they finally had a champion who could vanquish Lee. The Confederate people held an equally firm belief that Lee would triumph against Grant. The Army of Northern Virginia mustered about 65,000 men to face roughly 120,000 Federals in what would be called the OVERLAND CAMPAIGN.

Six weeks of unprecedented fury opened when Lee and Grant tested each other on May 5–6 in the BATTLE OF THE WILDERNESS. Two days of combat felled more than 18,000 Federals and 11,000 Confederates. Unlike previous Union generals in Virginia, Grant ignored his losses and pressed southward. The armies fought again during May 8–21 in the BATTLES OF SPOTSYLVANIA, piling up another 18,000 Federal and 12,000 Confederate casualties. By June 1, the armies had shifted southeast to the vicinity of Cold Harbor. More than 50,000 Federals struck Lee's well-engineered positions on June 3. Confederates lost just 1,500 men while inflicting 7,500 casualties. On June 12, Grant began a movement that fooled Lee completely. The Federals crossed the James River and hastened toward Petersburg, where on June 15–18 a series of disjointed assaults failed to take the city. Once certain that Grant had crossed the river, Lee shuttled troops to the Petersburg defenses.

The Overland campaign ended on June 18 as the armies settled into their lines around Petersburg for a siege that would last more than nine months. The final period of the war offered little good news to Lee and his army. Although many Confederates took heart at Lee's appointment as general in chief of all national forces on February 6, 1865, the promotion came too late to have any practical effect. On March 25, Lee made a final unsuccessful attempt to break Grant's encircling grip. Federals turned Lee's right flank at the BATTLE OF FIVE FORKS a week later, and on the night of April 2–3 Confederates abandoned the Richmond-Petersburg lines.

A weeklong retreat westward from Richmond and Petersburg ensued. Lee hoped to join Joseph E. Johnston's army in North Carolina, but Grant's pursuit denied him an opening. On April 9, hemmed in by powerful Northern forces, Lee remarked, "There is nothing left me to do but to go and see General Grant, and I would rather die a thousand deaths." The war's two most famous generals met in the parlor of Wilmer McLean's home in APPOMATTOX COURT HOUSE that day. Grant extended generous terms; Lee accepted them; and the two men signed the document of surrender.

Nearly four months passed between Lee's surrender and the arrival of an offer that would define the work of his last years. In August 1865, he became president of Washington College in Lexington, Virginia. He proved to be an able educator who improved the faculty, increased the size of the student body, and broadened the curriculum by adding courses in science and engineering to the traditional offerings in classical subjects.

Plagued by various physical ailments during the postwar years, Lee was stricken on September 28, 1870, with a stroke. He lingered for two weeks, uttering an average of just one word a day, until he died peacefully on October 12.

See also COLD HARBOR, BATTLE OF; PETERSBURG CAMPAIGN.

Further reading: Gary W. Gallagher, *Lee and His Army in Confederate History* (Chapel Hill: University of North Carolina Press, 2001); Emory M. Thomas, *Robert E. Lee: A Biography* (New York: W. W. Norton, 1995).

—Gary W. Gallagher

letters

Written correspondence was an important way of communicating for 19th-century Americans. Early in the century, as the country expanded westward and people left their communities, letters were the only method of keeping in touch with their now-distant kin. Frontier settlers could read letters about the latest FASHIONS, the newest books, and the recent political controversies, as well as local gossip. Their letters would provide fascinating information to the folks back home about the pioneering experience. With the outbreak of the CIVIL WAR, the importance of letter writing was magnified tremendously. Letters became the most important link between the volunteer soldiers and their friends and relatives back home.

The Union maintained this lifeline more easily than the Confederates. The North sustained an efficient mail service throughout the war and delivered mail to Yankee soldiers in Virginia and Tennessee within a couple of days. The U.S. Postal Service saw an unprecedented number of letters, with approximately 180,000 passing through its doors daily, as civilians and soldiers kept in touch. The South was not quite as successful. The Confederates kept letters moving as long as they could, but occupying Northern troops disrupted increasingly large segments of the railroad system and with it the postal service.

Corresponding was not always an easy task for soldiers on either side. Stationery was sparse, and soldiers wrote on any scrap of paper they could find, while regularly asking relatives to send them paper and stamps. Federal soldiers were more fortunate. Civilian organizations like the UNITED STATES CHRISTIAN COMMISSION distributed free stationery, pens, and stamps. Confederates had a more difficult time finding stationery, but they supplemented their supplies by scavenging through the knapsacks abandoned by retreating Yankees.

Writing was well worth the difficulties, however, as wartime correspondence took on new importance for both the soldiers and the civilians on the HOMEFRONT. For the civilians, letters kept them informed about the health and well-being of their kin and friends in the army. They learned about the hardships of camp life and the thrills and brutality of battle. "I do not know what is getting into me but I am getting more and more scary every fight I go into," declared a soldier from Georgia. Through these frontline reports, civilians felt connected to the cause and gained a renewed sense of patriotism.

For the soldiers, mail call was generally the brightest part of their day. "After long marches and great exposure," wrote one Union soldier who was in the Gettysburg campaign of 1863, "when you have gone through all that a man can go through, to get into camp at last and hear that a mail has come! You should see the news fly round the camp and the men's faces light up." Friends and relatives kept the soldiers connected to the home through their letters. Soldiers learned about hometown gossip of weddings, funerals, local politics, and the daily routines of their friends and families.

Letters were so prized by the soldiers that they read and reread them and literally wore them out. Soldiers found reading and writing letters to be wholesome diversions from the dullness of camp. Receiving letters could have either a good or a bad impact on the soldiers. *Not* receiving a letter from a wife drove this soldier into despair: "It seems so lonely to me not get any [*sic*] letters at all from you as I have had none of but about one for about 4 weeks. Perhaps you are sick & cant write but a neighbor could. I feel very anxious to know what is the trouble or if you have got mad at me."

Cheerful letters could boost morale and remind the men that their friends and families loved them and supported the cause for which the soldiers fought. One wife wrote longingly to her soldier-husband: "My heart is full of love for you tonight and my earnest prayer ascends for your safety and happiness." Civilians used correspondence to keep in touch, but they also counseled and guided the soldiers. Advice was a two-way street, as married soldiers also counseled and guided their children and spouses from the camp. A Confederate from Mississippi wrote his wife: "I often ask myself whether our little Callie speaks of her Pa. Does she remember me? You must not whip her. I have a perfect horror of whipping children." Most soldiers accepted and appreciated the concern of their family.

Just as letters containing happy news could boost morale, letters filled with financial woes, family deaths, or crop problems had the opposite effect on the men. Volunteers felt torn between their duty to their country and their responsibility as breadwinners for their families. James Colwell of Pennsylvania left his wife and four small children to volunteer for the Union. Responding to her anger at his leave-taking, he tried to console her: "I feel sorry that you permit hard thoughts to possess your heart at our separation . . . I did it from a sense of right and duty . . . Now I am sure my own Annie would not wish me to come back with dishonour, and thus bring disgrace on her and our children." Receiving several hardship letters created poor morale and hurt the combat effectiveness of the troops. Confederate soldiers were most susceptible to bad news because the Yankees had invaded their homeland and devastated their ECONOMY.

Letters did not determine the outcome of the war, but historians believe that such correspondence was an essential part of an army's positive morale. Letters connected soldiers to their families who were the main base of their support and gave the men courage and conviction to fight for their cause.

See also COMMON SOLDIER.

Further reading: K. M. Kostyal, ed., *Field of Battle: The Civil War Letters of Major Thomas J. Halsey* (Washington, D.C.: National Geographic Society, 1996); James M. McPherson, *For Cause and Comrades: Why Men Fought in the Civil War* (New York: Oxford University Press, 1997); Reid S. Mitchell, *The Vacant Chair: The Northern Soldier Leaves Home* (New York: Oxford University Press, 1993); Bell Irvin Wiley, *The Life of Johnny Reb: The Common Soldier of the Confederacy* (Baton Rouge: Louisiana State University Press, 1978).

—Patricia Richard

Lincoln, Abraham (1809–1865)

Abraham Lincoln is widely considered the greatest president in U.S. history. As head of the REPUBLICAN PARTY, leader of the Union, and commander in chief of the largest army ever assembled, Lincoln ended SLAVERY and reunited the North and South. For those accomplishments, he is called "The Great Emancipator" and the "Savior of the Union." Lincoln's limited political experience as he assumed the presidency caused many to question his leadership abilities. Despite making mistakes, his growth as a man, a politician, and as chief executive was remarkable. His tragic assassination just days after the South's surrender at APPOMATTOX COURT HOUSE plunged the country into mourning and ensured his apotheosis as a martyr for the cause of freedom and union.

From the time of his death, Abraham Lincoln has been the subject of numerous paintings, books, poems, plays, and, later, movies, documentaries, and web sites. The Lincoln Memorial in WASHINGTON, D.C., is one of the most visited MONUMENTS in the country. Indeed, more books have been written about Abraham Lincoln than any other historical figure, except Jesus of Nazareth. He stands as a national and international symbol for freedom and democracy.

Lincoln's rise from a humble pioneer background to the highest office in the land began with his birth in a one-room log cabin near Hodgenville, Kentucky, on February 12, 1809. Abraham's parents, Thomas Lincoln and Nancy Hanks Lincoln, were illiterate farming folk. Thomas Lincoln was not a particularly successful farmer, but he worked hard and had ambitions for himself and his family. In 1816 Thomas and Nancy moved to the Indiana Territory, where land was cheaper and the land titles more secure than in Kentucky. Lincoln's parents had another reason to move out of Kentucky, and that was their opposition to slavery. Members of an antislavery Baptist group, they believed that going to a free-labor land would boost their chances for prosperity.

Like the children of most pioneer families, Abraham and his older sister Sarah were expected to pitch in and help on the farm. The young Abe labored side by side with his father, learning how to use the axe and the plow as they cleared the forest to build the family's simple cabin and prepare the fields for planting. Abraham grew into an unusually strong youngster who was adept at splitting rails and winning wrestling contests against older and more experienced men. His early life was marked by tragedy. Nancy Hanks Lincoln died suddenly in 1818, leaving Thomas and the children to fend for themselves for a year. Thomas Lincoln remarried widow Sarah Bush Johnston. Sarah and her three children moved in with the Lincolns and brought a measure of stability and affection to Abraham's life. He always remembered with fondness Sarah's kindly ways, which provided a contrast to his strained relations with Thomas Lincoln. Abraham, his father complained, was "lazy" because he preferred reading books to farm chores.

As Abraham matured, he was drawn to the life of the mind over the life of labor that was his father's lot. A few months in a rural schoolhouse was his only "formal" EDUCATION, but Abraham borrowed heavily from the small libraries of Pigeon Creek, Indiana. From books, Abraham trained his mind and developed a love of language and an appreciation for rhetoric and oratory. Calculating and ambitious, Lincoln earned money in a variety of working-class jobs, including taking a flatboat loaded with produce down the Ohio and MISSISSIPPI RIVERS to sell in the market at New Orleans. He recoiled in horror at the busy slave markets of the Southern port city. In 1830 the 21-year-old Lincoln moved with his family to central Illinois. Anxious to be on his own, he set out for New Salem, Illinois, a small commercial river town. Here Lincoln made his home for

Abraham Lincoln *(Library of Congress)*

the next six years, boarding with various families and working as a clerk in a store, a partner in a general store (that went bankrupt), and a postmaster, among other jobs. In New Salem, Lincoln continued his program of self-education, studying mathematics and LITERATURE (he especially loved Shakespeare) with the local schoolmaster.

Lincoln developed an enthusiasm for politics and joined the local debating society. In 1832 he participated in the Black Hawk War and was elected a captain of the militia. This brief and bloodless experience would be his only brush with the military before 1861. Lincoln ran for the state legislature in 1832 and lost. On his second try in 1834, he won handily as a member of the Whig Party. Quickly mastering the ways of the lower legislature in Vandalia, Illinois, Lincoln became a prominent member of the tiny but influential Whig faction, serving four terms in the lower house. An admirer of Henry Clay's "American system," Lincoln supported a national bank and government-sponsored economic development for Illinois. While serving in the legislature, Lincoln studied law with his political mentor, John Todd Stuart, a prominent Whig lawyer and resident of Springfield, Illinois. When the state capitol was moved to Springfield, Lincoln happily followed and in 1837 began his legal practice. In 1844 he formed a partnership with WILLIAM H. HERNDON. Within a decade

Lincoln had established himself as a respected and prosperous lawyer.

As a young professional in Springfield, Lincoln had come a long way from his backwoods upbringing, but the rough edges were still very much present. Extremely tall, the six-foot, four-inch Abraham had a thick shock of black hair and a face that many found ugly. Lincoln often joked about his looks. In response to a critic's attack that he was a "two-faced" politician, Lincoln responded humorously, "If I had two faces, do you think I would use this one?" He was most comfortable within his wide circle of male colleagues, friends, and supporters in the political and legal world in which he lived and worked. They knew him as a master storyteller, a humorist and wit, and, occasionally, as someone who fell into melancholic moods. Death was a constant presence in Lincoln's life, and in 1828 his beloved sister Sarah died in childbirth. In 1835 a young woman he was courting, Ann Rutledge, died, and Lincoln became depressed, withdrawing temporarily from his active life. A few years later, Lincoln began an on-and-off relationship with Mary Todd from a wealthy slaveholding family in Lexington, Kentucky. In 1842 Abraham Lincoln and Mary Todd married. Two years later, the Lincolns bought their first house in Springfield, Illinois. They remained in the attractive, spacious home until they moved to the White House in 1861.

Abraham and MARY TODD LINCOLN had four sons together between 1843 and 1853: Robert Todd, Edward Dickinson, William Wallace (Willie), and Thomas (Tad). Both parents were devoted to their children and grieved deeply when the four-year-old Edward died of tuberculosis. Twelve years later, in 1862, they lost Willie to typhoid fever. The Lincolns' marriage has been the subject of much speculation. Evidence suggests that despite many rocky periods they loved and respected each other. Mary's high-strung nature was tested by Abraham's constant absences due to his law practice and his inattentiveness to the details of daily life, including his well-known tendency to be careless about his appearance. Yet, she provided intelligent and enthusiastic support for her husband and boosted his career through her familial and social connections.

Lincoln made his living by the law, but his true passion was for politics. In 1847 he was elected to the U.S. House of Representatives where, during a single two-year term, he was principally known for opposing the Mexican-American War and the extension of slavery. Lincoln returned to Springfield determined to run for higher office. In the meantime, his political career as a Whig had come to an end with the dissolution of the party in the wake of the KANSAS-NEBRASKA ACT of 1854. In 1856 Lincoln joined the Illinois Republican Party and quickly became one of its most prominent spokesmen. Two years later, when accepting the Republican Party's nomination for senator, Lincoln declared: "A house divided against itself cannot stand. I believe that this Government cannot endure, permanently, half-slave and half-free."

In 1858 Abraham Lincoln ran against STEPHEN A. DOUGLAS for the Illinois Senate seat. The campaign drew national attention. The seven Lincoln-Douglas debates set out clearly the differences between the Republican and Democratic Parties on slavery. Although Douglas captured the Senate seat, Lincoln had established for himself a modest fame as an up-and-coming Republican. After the election, he expanded his political base when he embarked on a speaking trip in the North. On February 27, 1860, Lincoln gave a brilliant speech at Cooper Union in NEW YORK CITY. This speech, repeated many times in the upcoming months, explained clearly and convincingly why the federal government had the constitutional right to stop extension of slavery in the territories. Lincoln reassured the South that the Republicans did not intend to threaten slavery where it was protected, just to stop it from spreading. In May 1860, the Republican Party nominated Lincoln for president of the United States. Lincoln won the three-way election by receiving 40 percent of the popular vote and more than 60 percent of the electoral votes. Immediately, seven Southern states seceded.

By the time Lincoln was sworn into office on March 4, 1861, as the 16th president of the United States, the CONFEDERATE STATES OF AMERICA were established. Lincoln's First Inaugural Address offered a stern warning to the rebellious states but also spoke in reassuring terms of his intention to preserve slavery in the South. After the Confederate bombardment of FORT SUMTER on April 12, Lincoln called for 75,000 militiamen to defend the Union. No other president had ever had to face the gravity of a CIVIL WAR, and Lincoln acted quickly, and without constitutional authority, to stem the rebellion. In addition to calling the state militias to national service, Lincoln ordered a blockade of the Southern ports and suspended the writ of HABEAS CORPUS in SECESSIONist-leaning Maryland. Called a dictator for seizing war powers, Lincoln's paramount goal for the first year and a half of the war was to save the Union, with a minimum amount of bloodshed. He hoped that the seceded states would rejoin the nation and come to their collective senses once they realized the true cost of the war. This rosy and unrealistic scenario did not occur, and with the conflict dragging on, Lincoln made the decision in the summer of 1862 to emancipate the slaves as a military measure. Personally opposed to slavery and racism, Lincoln moved slowly on EMANCIPATION to keep the loyal boarder states within the Union and dampen the inevitable outcry that would follow the EMANCIPATION PROCLAMATION. On January 1, 1863, Lincoln signed the historic document that freed the slaves in the Confederate states in areas not occupied by Federal forces, and with a stroke of his pen he changed the war into a revolution that would forever end slavery in the United States.

Lincoln waged the war in a steadfast and vigorous manner, always with a passion for saving the Union. He exhibited surprising skill in foreign relations and kept European nations from endorsing the Confederate nation. He became a student of military TACTICS AND STRATEGY, learning from his mistakes and the mistakes of his leading generals. As the casualty lists grew longer and the political opposition from War Democrats, COPPERHEADS, and RADICAL REPUBLICANS mounted, Lincoln was subjected to constant criticism for his policies. Even members of his own cabinet worked against him. Lincoln steered the middle course, always trying to find the compromise position and explain to the citizens and soldiers why it was important to preserve the Union, which he considered to be the world's one hope for democracy. "This is essentially a People's contest," Lincoln declared, "On the side of the Union, it is a struggle for maintaining in the world, that form, and substance of government, whose leading object is, to elevate the condition of men—to lift artificial weights from all shoulders—to clear the paths of laudable pursuit for all—to afford all, an unfettered start, and a fair chance, in the race of life." Lincoln demonstrated the skills of a master politician and a strong and able commander in chief. His administration was necessarily primarily concerned with military matters, but he also presided over the passage of the Republican economic package in Congress, including one of the key pieces of legislation in the 19th century, the HOMESTEAD ACT of 1862.

By 1864, despite the great Northern victories the previous summer and spring, Lt. Gen. ULYSSES S. GRANT's OVERLAND CAMPAIGN did not bring final victory but, rather, more losses and stalemate. Lincoln stood loyally by Grant and prepared to suffer the political consequences of military defeat. For a while, it looked like he was going to lose the critical election of 1864. Success on the battlefield and the overwhelmingly favorable soldiers' vote returned him to the White House with a large majority. With the war's end in sight, Lincoln prepared for a mild RECONSTRUCTION that would heal the wounds of the broken nation. He also pushed hard for the passage of the THIRTEENTH AMENDMENT as a signal to all Americans that the reuniting of the North and South would also ensure the permanent freedom and civil rights of the ex-slaves, although at this stage Lincoln was more concerned with resecuring the loyalty of white Southerners. "With malice toward none; with charity for all," said Lincoln in his Second Inaugural Address on March 4, 1865. Doubtless the knowledge Americans had of Lincoln's deeply felt desire to reconcile the sections peacefully accounted for the lack of violence after

his assassination on April 14 and his death early the next morning. Abraham Lincoln is buried in Springfield, Illinois.

See also ASSASSINATION OF ABRAHAM LINCOLN; GETTYSBURG ADDRESS.

Further reading: Roy P. Basler, ed., *The Collected Works of Abraham Lincoln* (New Brunswick, N.J.: Rutgers University Press, 1953); LaWanda Cox, *Lincoln and Black Freedom* (Columbia: University of South Carolina Press, 1994); David Herbert Donald, *Lincoln* (New York: Simon & Schuster, 1995); Allen C. Guelzo, *Abraham Lincoln: Redeemer President* (Grand Rapids, Mich.: William B. Eerdman, 1999); Harold Holzer, *Dear Mr. Lincoln: Letters to the President* (Reading, Pa.: Addison-Wesley, 1993); James McPherson, *Abraham Lincoln and the Second American Revolution* (New York: Oxford University Press, 1990); Stephen B. Oates, *With Malice toward None: The Life of Abraham Lincoln* (New York: Mentor Books, 1977); Phillip S. Paludan, *The Presidency of Abraham Lincoln* (Lawrence: University Press of Kansas, 1994); Merrill D. Peterson, *Lincoln in American Memory* (New York: Oxford University Press, 1994); Ronald C. White Jr., *Lincoln's Greatest Speech: The Second Inaugural* (New York: Simon & Schuster, 2002); Douglas L. Wilson, *Honor's Voice: The Transformation of Abraham Lincoln* (New York: Knopf, 1998); Kenneth J. Winkle, *The Young Eagle: The Rise of Abraham Lincoln* (Dallas: Taylor Trade Publishing Co., 2001).

Lincoln, Mary Todd (1818–1882)

Wife of President ABRAHAM LINCOLN, Mary Todd Lincoln was born into a wealthy and powerful family of slaveholders near Lexington, Kentucky, in December 1818. Although the Lincolns' marriage was a loving one, Mary never succeeded in winning much popular support while she was first lady, and in the wake of her husband's assassination she descended into mental instability.

Because Mary Todd's father, a prominent Whig politician, strongly supported female EDUCATION, Mary enjoyed a wide ranging intellectual training unusual for girls in the 19th century. In 1839 Mary Todd joined her sister's household in Springfield, Illinois. There, she met the young attorney Abraham Lincoln. Although Lincoln was an ambitious professional man, he lacked education and his manners were unpolished. By 19th-century Victorian standards, his behavior was occasionally rude and countrified. Nevertheless, Lincoln and Mary Todd were married in 1842. Mary supported Abraham's political aspirations and matched his ambition with her own from the very start of their married life. As a measure of their political partnership, Lincoln exclaimed, when he first heard of his election to the presidency in 1860, "Mary, Mary, *we* are elected."

When Lincoln assumed the presidency, the White House was in disrepair, its furnishings old and shabby and its structure in need of refurbishing. Mary Todd Lincoln took it upon herself, as first lady, to make drastic improvements to the public rooms of the White House. She believed that the home represented the power of the Union and therefore that it was required to be impressive and opulent. As a result, when replacing the peeling wallpaper, worn furniture, and cheap decorations, Mary purchased goods of exceptionally high quality and cost. Although Washingtonians agreed that the White House required some renovation, some of her purchases were considered too extravagant, and she suffered criticism from a number of sources. To show off the new rooms, Mary Todd Lincoln hosted a number of dinner parties for official Washington, and her invitations were highly prized. Socially, she was a success.

However, her tenure in WASHINGTON, D.C., was not without both tragedy and controversy. A devoted mother and wife, Mary suffered the losses of many of her family during the war, including two of her half brothers, who were Confederate soldiers. In 1862 the Lincolns lost their 12-year-old son, Willie, to typhoid fever. In spite of her position as the wife of the commander in chief, Mary was criticized by many people for her strong ties to the South. She was even accused of being a rebel spy and of passing Union secrets to the Confederates.

The greatest loss to Mary Todd Lincoln, however, was the death of her husband by an assassin's bullet on April 15, 1865. In both material and personal terms, she never recovered from his death. Abraham Lincoln had left an estate that was $70,000 in debt from his wife's lavish spending in the White House. Mary Todd Lincoln was unable to control her spending even after her husband's death, accumulating huge debts of her own.

Unstable and grief-stricken, Mary Todd Lincoln and her son Tad sought solace in travels to Europe. When Tad died in 1871, Mary's mental condition worsened, and her final surviving son, Robert, committed her to a private mental institution outside of Chicago in 1875. She remained there for four months but found it unbearable and fled to France. In 1882 Mary returned to Springfield, Illinois, where she died and was buried beside her husband at Oak Ridge cemetery.

See also ASSASSINATION OF ABRAHAM LINCOLN.

Further reading: Jean H. Baker, *Mary Todd Lincoln: A Biography* (New York: Norton, 1987); David Herbert Donald, *Lincoln* (New York: Simon & Schuster, 1995).

—Megan Quinn

literature

For most of its existence, the United States has been among the most literate societies in the world. The generation that fought the CIVIL WAR was no exception. As such, individuals who had a message to convey to the American populace in the antebellum era turned to books, articles, and pamphlets. In the North, antiSLAVERY writers penned countless works criticizing the "peculiar institution." Noteworthy among them were the autobiographical *Narrative of the Life of* FREDERICK DOUGLASS and the fictional *Uncle Tom's Cabin* by HARRIET BEECHER STOWE, the best-selling novel of its time. Southern writers responded with books of their own defending slavery, most prominently GEORGE FITZHUGH's books, *Sociology for the South* and *Cannibals All!* These works, and countless others, played an important role in plunging the nation into civil war. ABRAHAM LINCOLN acknowledged as much when he met Harriet Beecher Stowe during the war, greeting her by saying, "So you're the little woman who wrote the book that made this great war."

During the war itself, the nation's attention was occupied with the prosecution of the conflict. Nonetheless, new literary works were still produced and read, especially in the North, where the publishing industry throve. Once the war was over, the American public was even more enthusiastic about reading. The Civil War had a tremendous impact on postwar American culture and shaped the literature created in the 35 years between Appomattox and the turn of the century.

Autobiographical accounts of the war were the most popular and ubiquitous form of literature in the years immediately after the war. Virtually every important general and political leader who survived long enough to do so penned a book or article about their experiences during the war. Between 1884 and 1887, *Century* magazine commissioned a series of personal accounts by Civil War generals entitled "Battles and Leaders of the Civil War." The articles were widely read throughout the North and South, and in particular the popularity of ULYSSES S. GRANT's contribution to the series convinced him to write his lengthy *Personal Memoirs* (1885–86) just before his death. Grant's *Memoirs* was a best-seller, as popular in the North as JEFFERSON DAVIS's two-volume *Rise and Fall of the Confederate Government* (1881) was in the South.

The articles and books written by the leaders of the Civil War, especially the Southern leaders, reflected an important debate over the Southern war effort. The ex-Confederates justified their actions to the victorious North, and in so doing, they pleaded their case for acceptance back into mainstream American life. These writers, particularly General JUBAL A. EARLY, downplayed the role of slavery in the conflict and emphasized the virtue of Southern soldiers in general and of ROBERT E. LEE in particular.

Eventually, this vision of the Civil War came to be called the LOST CAUSE, and it has exercised a great deal of influence over how Americans viewed the war up to the present day.

The books and articles written by the leaders of the war were both popular and influential. However, they were by no means the only autobiographical accounts published in the postwar years. Many COMMON SOLDIERS published histories of their regiments or personal recollections of the war. Some of these received a wide readership and are still considered classics, among them Sam Watkins's *Co. Aytch* (1882), John Billings's *Hardtack and Coffee* (1888), and William Fletcher's *Rebel Private: Front and Rear* (1907). Women contributed to the body of Civil War nonfiction, and some writing memoirs with others publishing the diaries they wrote during the war or during a particular battle. Prominent among them are Emma Edmonds's *Nurse and Spy in the Union Army* (1865) and BELLE BOYD in *Camp and Prison* (1865). There were also a number of memoirs of slavery written by African Americans in the postwar era. Rather than emphasize the evils of slavery, they stressed the necessity of self-reliance and independence. The best known of these accounts is Booker T. Washington's *Up from Slavery* (1901).

Novels about the Civil War were also popular. The most notable Civil War fiction of the period was written by JOHN WILLIAM DE FOREST, whose work presents warfare in a very realistic fashion that would have been unthinkable in the antebellum era. De Forest's most popular book was *Miss Ravenel's Conversion from Secession to Loyalty.* Published in 1867, the novel combines a romantic story of sectional reconciliation with vivid descriptions of the brutality of combat. Author Nathaniel Hawthorne saw a direct correlation between the war and the realist movement, arguing that the Civil War "introduced into the national consciousness a certain sense of proportion and relation, of the world being a more complicated place than it had hitherto seemed." The work of De Forest had a profound influence on the generation of writers that came after him, including Ambrose Bierce, Stephen Crane, Edward Bellamy, and William Dean Howells.

Other literary movements of the postbellum era had their roots in the Civil War as well. The most notable was regionalism. Paradoxically, a war fought to reunite the nation gave Americans a heightened, highly romanticized sense of their regional differences. Western fiction became an established genre. Western authors, most prominently Bret Harte, excited readers' imaginations with images of a "Wild West" filled with endless adventure and excitement. At the same time, the South experienced a literary renaissance led by Mark Twain, arguably the most famous author in American history. Twain's career began with "The Celebrated Jumping Frog of Calaveras County" (1865) and continued through such classics as *The Adventures of Tom Sawyer* (1876), *The Adventures of Huckleberry Finn* (1884), and *A Connecticut Yankee in King Arthur's Court* (1889). Twain developed a distinctive style that reflected a number of influences, among them slave narratives, folk tales, and political satire.

By 1900, the overwhelming influence of the Civil War on American popular culture subsided as the generation that had lived through the war faded away. Nonetheless, the war had assumed a permanent place in American memory, and it continues to be a popular subject among American authors. Margaret Mitchell's *Gone with the Wind* (1936), Shelby Foote's *Shiloh* (1952), Michael Shaara's *The Killer Angels* (1974), and Charles Frazier's *Cold Mountain* (1997) are among the modern works on the Civil War to tally sales in the millions of copies. Clearly, the war continues to resonate with Americans.

Further reading: Daniel Aaron, *The Unwritten War: American Writers and the Civil War* (Madison: University of Wisconsin Press, 1987); Emory Elliott, ed., *The Columbia History of the American Novel* (New York: Columbia University Press, 1991); Alice Fahs, *Popular Literature of the North and South, 1861–1865* (Chapel Hill: University of North Carolina Press, 2001); Edmund Wilson, *Patriotic Gore: Studies in the Literature of the American Civil War* (New York: W. W. Norton, 1994).

—Christopher Bates

Little Bighorn, Battle of (June 25–26, 1876)

One of the last victories by the Plains Indians over the United States, the Battle of Little Bighorn took place in southeastern Montana between June 25 and June 26, 1876. It is largely remembered as Custer's Last Stand. Teton Sioux (Lakota), Cheyenne, and Arapaho Indians routed the Seventh Cavalry of the United States, which was under the command of Lt. Col. George Armstrong Custer. The United States responded to its overwhelming defeat with a relentless military pursuit of the NATIVE AMERICANS.

The origins of the battle, which took place on the Greasy Grass River, or the Little Bighorn, lay in the refusal of many Cheyenne, Arapaho, Blackfeet, and especially Sioux bands (Hunkpapa, Oglala, Miniconjou, Sans Arcs) to be confined to reservations. The 1868 Treaty of Fort Laramie provided the Sioux a permanent reservation, guaranteed them the right to hunt buffalo in the Black Hills west of the Missouri River, and prohibited white settlements on the land. Between 1871 and 1874, however, the United States routinely violated the terms of the treaty. Surveyors charted routes through the hunting lands, and gold seekers and prospectors threatened to invade the territory. Rather than enforcing the provisions of the Treaty of Fort Laramie, the United States tried unsuccessfully to purchase the Black Hills from the Sioux.

In late 1875, the free-roaming Sioux were drawn into a war. The conflict served as a pretense to remove them from the unceded territory and open the lands to American settlement and gold prospectors. The United States ceased enforcing the ban limiting the presence of speculators in the Black Hills, and rumors of atrocities committed by Sioux and other native buffalo hunters spread rapidly. Finally, in December 1875, the U.S. War Department ignored the Treaty of Fort Laramie and ordered all of the Sioux Indians to surrender themselves at the Dakota agencies by January 31, 1876. All of those who refused to settle on the Great Sioux Reservation in present-day South Dakota would be deemed hostile and subject to a military response.

The Native Americans, in a coalition formed by Sitting Bull, refused to accept this ultimatum, and the United States declared them hostile. In May 1876, Gen. Alfred H. Terry decided to settle the matter by ordering Custer to disperse or capture the defiant natives. Custer led 12 companies of the Seventh Cavalry, 655 soldiers in all, along with an Indian camp of mostly Sioux (with some Northern Cheyenne and Arapaho) Indians along the south bank of the river.

Upon learning that his forces had been spotted, Custer decided to attack before the warriors had time to vacate the valley. He divided his units and ordered an immediate attack. Custer sent three companies under the command of Maj. Marcus Reno across the upper ford of the river. Capt. Frederick Benteen, who was ordered to make sure that no Indians escaped, took three companies to the left of Reno. Finally, Custer himself led five companies to cross the lower ford and ordered one company to bring up the pack train.

Intended to hit the Sioux warriors from two directions simultaneously, Custer's plan deteriorated almost immediately. Major Reno crossed the river and faced an enemy significantly stronger than he expected. Recognizing that his forces were outnumbered, Reno ordered his men to retreat from the valley. The retreat turned chaotic and the native warriors killed at least 40 of Reno's soldiers. Reno's men then took a defensive position on the east side of the river on the high bluffs.

The estimated 2,000 to 3,000 Sioux warriors, including Crazy Horse, Hump, Two Moon, Gall, and Rain-in-the-Face, turned their full attention to Custer's forces that were on the northern end of the village. Custer and some of his men retreated to the top of Custer Hill, and within an hour all of Custer's 212 men were dead. Their bodies were later found in what may have been battle lines. Historians disagree about these final moments, but it remains clear that this was one of the greatest disasters in American military history.

Benteen's forces came to battle too late and ended up joining Reno four miles away from the battle. The following day, General Terry arrived from the north with reinforcements, and most of the Indian warriors withdrew to the south. It was too late. Army casualties included 263 dead and 59 wounded.

The United States responded to the defeat of Custer with an intensified effort to obtain vengeance, and by 1877 most Sioux bands either surrendered or fled to Canada. The U.S. government forced the natives to cede their claims to the Black Hills, and most Cheyenne and Sioux were confined to the reservations.

Further reading: Paul Goble, *Red Hawk's Account of Custer's Last Battle: The Battle of the Little Bighorn, 25 June 1876* (Lincoln: University of Nebraska Press, 1992); Mari Sandoz, *The Battle of the Little Bighorn* (Philadelphia: J. B. Lippincott, 1978); James Welch, *Killing Custer: The Battle of the Little Bighorn and the Fate of the Plains Indians* (New York: Norton, 1994).

—Andrew K. Frank

Longstreet, James (1821–1904)

Confederate general James Longstreet was born January 8, 1821, in Edgefield District, South Carolina. He grew up in Georgia, on his father's farm near Gainesville and at Westover, his uncle's Augusta cotton plantation. After his father died in 1833 and his mother moved to Alabama, the boy remained with his uncle, Augustus Baldwin Longstreet, a lawyer, STATES' RIGHTS advocate, and prominent Georgia intellectual. With an appointment from Alabama Longstreet entered the UNITED STATES MILITARY ACADEMY AT WEST POINT in 1838. Among his classmates were ULYSSES S. GRANT, Lafayette McLaws, and GEORGE E. PICKETT. Longstreet first experienced battle in the Mexican-American War and was seriously wounded at Chapultepec. After the war, he married Maria Louisa "Louise" Garland, daughter of Bvt. Brig. Gen. John Garland.

With the coming of the CIVIL WAR Longstreet opposed SECESSION. In 1861, however, he resigned his commission and traveled to RICHMOND from his western post to offer his services to the South. Despite having no connection to the state, he received command of a brigade of Virginia volunteers. While Longstreet's lack of identification with a single state would later be a political liability, in July 1861, he led his brigade well at Blackburn's Ford, winning the confidence of Gen. JOSEPH E. JOHNSTON and promotion to major general.

Longstreet suffered personal tragedy in January 1862, when three of his four living children died in Richmond of scarlet fever (two others had previously died in infancy). He performed inconsistently during the spring campaigns of 1862, skillfully commanding a rearguard action at Williamsburg on May 5 but badly bungling an attack at Seven Pines on May 31. After Seven Pines, Gen. ROBERT E. LEE replaced the seriously wounded Johnston as commander of what was now the Army of Northern Virginia. During the Seven Days' Battle, Longstreet impressed Lee with his hard fighting, and in July he became Lee's second in command. At the SECOND BATTLE OF BULL RUN in late August, Longstreet counseled Lee to adopt defensive battle TACTICS, demonstrating the wisdom of this advice with a devastating flank assault on the attacking Federals. At the BATTLE OF ANTIETAM in September, Longstreet fought tenaciously, earning promotion to lieutenant general and formal command of the First Corps.

The BATTLE OF FREDERICKSBURG in December 1862 confirmed the advantage of holding a good defensive position. Longstreet's entrenched corps took the brunt of the Union army's futile assault on Marye's Heights while suffering only minimal casualties. Briefly commanding two detached divisions in early 1863, Longstreet rejoined Lee's army after its May victory at the BATTLE OF CHANCELLORSVILLE. Lee reorganized his troops into three corps following Gen. THOMAS "STONEWALL" JACKSON's death. Longstreet commanded the first, Gen. RICHARD S. EWELL the second, and Gen. A. P. HILL the new third corps. In May, Longstreet (who thought the key to Confederate victory lay in the western theater) agreed with Lee's plan to invade Pennsylvania, but he urged Lee to adopt defensive tactics should a battle occur. In late June, when Lee's army came in contact with Union forces (commanded by Gen. GEORGE GORDON MEADE) near Gettysburg, Lee ignored his advice.

On July 1 Ewell's II Corps forced the I Corps and XI Corps of the Army of the Potomac to retreat south through the town. While the disorganized Union troops waited on Cemetery Hill for reinforcements, Ewell and his subordinate, Gen. JUBAL A. EARLY, hesitated to press their numerical advantage by attacking the hill. When Longstreet arrived on the field, he noted the strong position held by the newly reinforced Union troops and advised Lee to occupy a defensive position and force Meade to assume the offensive. To Longstreet's dismay, Lee indicated his intention to attack the Union army at Gettysburg the following day. Lee ordered Longstreet to use the two divisions that he had on the field to attack the Union's left on the morning of July 2. Confederate reconnaissance proved unreliable, however, and to avoid detection by the enemy Longstreet led his troops on a time-consuming countermarch. His attack, which was to have occurred simultaneously with an assault on the Union's right flank, did not begin until late afternoon. By that time, the UNION ARMY had extended its line south of Cemetery Ridge, and Longstreet found himself directing a frontal rather than a flank attack. His two divisions took the low ground in front of the Union position, inflicting serious damage on the Union Third Corps. Longstreet blamed his failure to occupy the high ground on lack of reinforcements and poor coordination with Lee's other two corps.

Over Longstreet's objections, Lee decided to launch a frontal assault against the Union position on July 3. Longstreet reluctantly directed the attack, which consisted of a ferocious artillery bombardment followed by a massed infantry assault, and claimed later that he would have prevented it if he had been able to do so. "Pickett's Charge" was a disaster for the CONFEDERATE ARMY, which lost more men and officers than it could replace.

After Gettysburg, Longstreet maneuvered himself into a western command in Gen. BRAXTON BRAGG's Army of Tennessee and directed a rout of the Union forces at the BATTLE OF CHICKAMAUGA on September 20, ironically employing a frontal assault. The Federals retreated to Chattanooga, where Longstreet's misjudgment of the tactical situation at the BATTLE OF LOOKOUT MOUNTAIN allowed the Federals to reopen their supply lines. His relationship with Bragg deteriorating, Longstreet detached his corps and laid siege to Knoxville, remaining there until April 1864.

In East Tennessee he became embroiled in bitter internecine disputes over his choice to succeed Lt. Gen. JOHN BELL HOOD, who had been wounded at Chickamauga, and his decision to relieve Maj. Gen. McLaws for poor conduct. Searching for a way to alter the Confederacy's grim prospects, he unsuccessfully proposed an invasion of Kentucky as a means of demoralizing the North and boosting opposition to President ABRAHAM LINCOLN's reelection. Longstreet returned to Virginia at Lee's request and was accidentally shot by his own troops in the BATTLE OF THE WILDERNESS on May 6. He resumed his command in October after recuperating in Georgia from serious throat and shoulder wounds. Longstreet remained in Virginia during the rest of the Civil War and was with Lee at APPOMATTOX COURT HOUSE.

Controversy marked Longstreet's postwar years. In 1865 he moved to New Orleans with his family (which included four children born after 1863) and successfully entered the insurance and RAILROAD businesses. He soon infuriated Confederate VETERANS by publishing his recommendation that they cooperate with federal RECONSTRUCTION policies. In a move that branded him forever as a SCALAWAG traitor to the South, Longstreet reacted to his critics' outrage by joining the REPUBLICAN PARTY.

Lee's death in 1870 made the unpopular Longstreet vulnerable to false accusations. In 1872 ex-Confederate general Jubal Early launched a self-serving campaign to blame Longstreet for Lee's defeat at Gettysburg. In Early's distorted history, Lee had intended Longstreet to attack at dawn on July 2, and by failing to do so Longstreet had cost the Confederacy the battle and the Civil War. Longstreet's belligerent attempts to clear his name backfired, and his criticism of Lee's offensive battlefield tactics prompted Lee's former staff officers—who had refuted the dawn attack accusation—to charge that Longstreet's failings at Gettysburg included deliberate slowness on July 2 and insubordination on July 3.

The "Gettysburg Series," published in Early's *Southern Historical Society Papers* in the late 1870s, sealed Longstreet's lasting reputation as scapegoat and traitor, as did his acceptance of Republican patronage. Longstreet's five articles for the *Century* magazine Civil War series criticized Jackson and Lee and inflated his own military accomplishments. A pariah in the South, he became a sought-after speaker at Northern VETERANS reunions.

Longstreet's memoirs, published in 1894, represented his final, futile attempt to settle scores and right the wrongs he had endured. In 1897, retired and aged 76, the widowed Longstreet married a second wife, the vivacious Helen Dortch, who was less than half his age. He died on January 2, 1904, in Gainesville, Georgia. His devoted young widow spent her remaining 58 years attempting to restore his reputation.

See also GETTYSBURG, BATTLE OF.

Further reading: H. J. Eckenrode and Bryan Conrad, *James Longstreet: Lee's War Horse* (Chapel Hill: University of North Carolina Press, 1986); James Longstreet, *From Manassas to Appomattox: Memoirs of the Civil War in America* (1896; reprint, Secaucus, N.J.: Blue & Grey Press, 1984); Jeffry D. Wert, *General James Longstreet, The Confederacy's Most Controversial Soldier: A Biography* (New York: Simon & Schuster, 1993).

—Amy J. Kinsel

Lookout Mountain, Battle of (November 24, 1863) The Battle of Lookout Mountain, also known as the "Battle above the Clouds," was one of two (the other was the Battle of Missionary Ridge) resounding Union victories that occurred within a day of each other and that helped secure Tennessee for the Union. General ULYSSES S. GRANT had come to Chattanooga with the intent of breaking the Confederate siege of that city. His ultimate success in the BATTLE OF CHATTANOOGA prompted President ABRAHAM LINCOLN to invite him to WASHINGTON, D.C., to take command of all Union armies and marked an important turning point in the war for the North.

After the defeat of Northern forces at the BATTLE OF CHICKAMAUGA in September 1863, Union general WIL-LIAM S. ROSECRANS had withdrawn his demoralized soldiers to Chattanooga. Meanwhile, Rosecrans's opponent at Chickamauga, BRAXTON BRAGG, moved his men onto the heights that rose above the city of Chattanooga, from Lookout Mountain on the southwest to Missionary Ridge to the east. In Rosecrans's view, Chattanooga was beginning to look "more like a prison than a prize." Bragg had effectively encircled the Yankees and cut off their supply lines.

Shortly thereafter, Lincoln replaced the incompetent Rosecrans with Maj. Gen. GEORGE HENRY THOMAS, whose bravery at Chickamauga had earned him the title "Rock of Chickamauga." Thomas swore to Grant that he and his men would hold Chattanooga "until we starve," and they very nearly did. Grant, who had been put in control of the new Division of the Mississippi in October 1863, called for reinforcements and moved to break the Confederate siege of Chattanooga. By mid-November of 1863, Gen. WILLIAM T. SHERMAN had brought 17,000 men from the Army of the Tennessee and Gen. JOSEPH HOOKER had brought 20,000 men from the Army of the Potomac to supplement the 35,000 men in Thomas's Army of the Cumberland.

It was clear to Grant and his subordinates that the siege on Chattanooga would have to be broken, and quickly, or the Federals would be forced to surrender. It was also clear that the Confederate position on rugged Lookout Mountain would have to be taken for Union troops to have any chance at breaking the siege. This appeared to be an impossible task, however. The formidable heights of Lookout Mountain, rising some 1,100 feet above the valley, were filled with what seemed like thousands of well-entrenched Confederates, with supporting units nearby.

On the evening of November 23, Union troops began massing underneath Lookout Mountain. Confederate major general Carter L. Stevenson wrote in code to his commander, Braxton Bragg, that he doubted his small division (numbering 2,694 on the mountain, plus cavalry and cannon) had the strength to hold off an assault. Unknown to the Confederates, the Union had broken their special code. The Union's leaders realized that the number of Confederates holding Lookout Mountain was not nearly as great as they had imagined.

With this information, Grant launched an attack upon the Confederate position on Lookout Mountain on November 24. At 8:00 A.M. Gen. Joseph Hooker directed the forces, consisting of one division from each of the Union armies taking part in the Chattanooga campaign, up the mountain. Repeated Union assaults were successful in driving the Confederates from the lofty summit, with the last Southern units withdrawing by 8:00 P.M.

An unusual feature of the battle was that a swirling mist of fog and clouds obscured much of the fighting during the day from the thousands of soldiers watching intently from the valley below. Only occasional flashes of red light penetrating the thick cover gave indication of an ongoing battle. When the clouds finally broke, Union soldiers cheered when they saw the retreating Confederates.

Early the next morning, Union soldiers swiftly climbed the now-vacant summit and planted the Stars and Stripes on the top. Union general Montgomery C. Meigs, who watched the action from Grant's headquarters, declared Hooker's attack the "Battle above the Clouds." Few who were there ever forgot the eerie experience, including Ulysses S. Grant, who later wrote, "The Battle of Lookout Mountain is one of the romances of the war. There was no such battle and no action even worthy to be called a battle on Lookout Mountain. It is all poetry."

Casualty (killed, wounded and captured) figures for both sides were never given precisely, only the total numbers for the Chattanooga campaign. Out of 64,165 Confederates, losses were 6,667; Union casualties were 5,824 out of 56,359 engaged.

Further reading: Peter Cozzens, *The Shipwreck of Their Hopes: The Battles for Chattanooga* (Urbana: University of Illinois Press, 1994); Jerry Korn, *The Fight for Chattanooga: Chickamauga to Missionary Ridge* (Alexandria, Va.: Time-Life Books, 1985); James Lee McDonough, *Chattanooga: Death Grip on the Confederacy* (Knoxville: University of Tennessee Press, 1984).

—Ruth A. Behling

lost cause, the

The phrase *lost cause* refers to an ideology that developed among white Southerners in the last decades of the 19th century and continued through the First World War. Although the South had decisively lost the CIVIL WAR, in the years after defeat, Southerners began to look back on the war years nostalgically and to celebrate them as the years of the South's greatest glory. This romanticization of the Confederacy was expressed in an outpouring of sentimental LITERATURE, memoirs, and historical accounts, as well as in numerous MONUMENTS and public ceremonies.

Although the roots of the lost cause can be traced back to the war and its immediate aftermath, the first formal organizations did not emerge until the 1870s. In that decade, a group of Virginia elites and military leaders, centered on Gen. JUBAL A. EARLY, founded such organizations as the Association of the Army of Northern Virginia and the Southern Historical Society. There, they developed a justification for the South's defeat that glorified Southern military leaders, particularly ROBERT E. LEE, and argued that the Civil War had been lost not because of a lack of will or insufficient military acumen but simply because Southern forces had been overwhelmingly outnumbered. Thus, defeat thus involved no shame or dishonor. In fact, the Southern cause remained a noble one, irremediably doomed from the start, but for that very reason, all the more heroic.

During the 1880s and 1890s the beliefs of the lost cause spread far beyond the circle of elites who had originally propounded it. The United Confederate Veterans (1889), the UNITED DAUGHTERS OF THE CONFEDERACY (1894), and the Sons of the Confederate Veterans (1896) were led by elites but included large numbers of white members from less exclusive backgrounds. Its monthly publication, the *Confederate Veteran,* was directed toward a popular audience and offered accounts of the experiences of COMMON SOLDIERS. Moreover, even white Southerners who did not belong to a lost-cause organization or subscribe to its publications participated in the general enthusiasm for the vanished Confederacy by attending the monument dedications, public ceremonies, and museums sponsored by the Daughters of the Confederacy. Yet, however many Southerners participated in lost-cause activities, the overall purpose of such activities was decidedly exclusionary. Although during the conflict itself Southerners had freely acknowledged that the Civil War was a struggle over SLAVERY, under the lost-cause scenario, the South's defense of slavery was conveniently transformed into a defense of STATES' RIGHTS.

Though the lost cause was celebrated most vehemently in the South, its effects extended well beyond the MASON-DIXON LINE. The VETERANS' reunions, which began in the 1880s, brought white veterans from both North and South together in celebration of a newly discovered camaraderie that strove to recognize both sides as somehow "right" and erased references to slavery even as black soldiers were excluded from the reunions themselves. Nor was the celebration of the Southern cause confined to commemorations of the battlefield. The novels of Thomas Nelson Page, for example, sold widely in both North and South and disseminated an escapist image of an idyllic prewar South in which masters were unfailingly benevolent and slaves unceasingly loyal.

It is perhaps tempting to dismiss the lost cause as simply a trivial and misplaced nostalgia. However, it is also worth noting that it has had enduring political consequences. The legacy has persisted through to our own time, for example, in the continuing popularity of *Gone with the Wind* and similar works. Nowhere is that legacy more evident than in the ongoing struggle over the display of the Confederate flag, for it was during the years of the lost cause that what might have become merely a historical artifact was reinstated as an object of passionate devotion. And it was also in those years that the flag's racist meanings were suppressed. Those who demand that the Confederate flag be flown above state capitol buildings as a symbol of states' rights are heir to a century-old ideology that systematically denied what that flag meant during the Civil War itself and indeed the very reasons the war was fought at all.

Further reading: David W. Blight, *Race and Reunion: The Civil War in American Memory* (Cambridge: Belknap Press of Harvard University Press, 2001); Gary W. Gallagher and Alan T. Nolan, eds., *The Myth of the Lost Cause and Civil War History* (Bloomington: Indiana University Press, 2000).

—Teresa Barnett

Louisiana Tigers

Renowned both for their courage and skill in battle and for their uncontrolled looting, vandalism, and violence, the Louisiana Tigers were one of the most effective and most feared Confederate battle units.

The term *Tigers* was first applied to the Tiger Rifles, a company in the First Special Battalion, Louisiana Infantry, which adopted slogans such as "Lincoln's Life or a Tiger's Death." The term eventually came to refer to all of the 12,000 Louisiana Infantrymen who joined the Army of Northern Virginia in 1861. The Tigers generally operated on the very front of the offensive lines, often executing particularly dangerous and important offensive missions. The Tigers also distinguished themselves at the SECOND BATTLE OF BULL RUN/MANASSAS and the BATTLES OF SPOTSYLVANIA.

The Tigers' reputation for courage was marred, however, by the repeated acts of violence and theft that characterized their ranks and by the high DESERTION rate within the units. The desertion rate was partly the result of the high proportion of foreign-born recruits, many of whom had little commitment to the war and a few of whom had been forced into service. The soldiers who remained, however, became infamous, especially in Virginia, for their drunkenness and rioting. On a train ride from New Orleans to RICHMOND in 1861, for example, various Louisiana regiments, drunk on barrels of alcohol that they had smuggled onto their train, shot at livestock, broke into saloons, and destroyed property.

By 1865, the mixed reputation of the Tigers was shared by relatively few men, as the Tigers sustained some of the greatest casualty rates of the war. The Louisianans' units had been organized and reorganized so many times that most of the Tigers felt they had lost their identity. By the time the Army of Northern Virginia surrendered at APPOMATTOX COURT HOUSE, only 373 of the original Louisiana Tigers were present.

Further reading: Terry Jones, *Lee's Tigers: The Louisiana Infantry in the Army of Northern Virginia* (Baton Rouge: Louisiana State University Press, 1987).

—Fiona Galvin

loyalty oaths

Although swearing loyalty to the Constitution and to the United States had always been a part of government service, the CIVIL WAR and RECONSTRUCTION era witnessed an increased devotion to that practice as a way to determine the fidelity of both citizens and officials. The need to draw a firm line between traitor and patriot defined these actions, and during this period loyalty oaths served as a federal job requirement, a weapon of war, and an effective tool in partisan politics.

In August 1861, Congress passed legislation that prescribed a new oath for federal employees. By the middle of 1862, those working in federal positions had taken two different pledges swearing loyalty to the Union and its efforts. As the desire to identify treason grew, pensioners and postal contractors also found themselves required to avow their fidelity. In order to submit a bid on any federal contract in the summer of 1862, businessmen had to affirm their support for the United States. Wisconsin congressman John Potter headed a committee that searched for traitors in government offices, and much of the committee's work focused on those who failed to take the prescribed oath. This drive to confirm the patriotism of any person connected to the government reached its peak in June 1862. At that time, Congress debated the necessity of a loyalty oath that would include senators and would require them to swear their allegiance for the past, present, and future. Subsequently known as the "ironclad test oath," or IRONCLAD OATH, this measure failed to pass the Senate, but later became a fixture of Reconstruction.

The Northern military also played a significant role in the demarcation of loyalty among citizens and prisoners. Southern residents of Union-occupied territories dealt with restrictive conditions but received a measure of freedom as soon as they pledged their faithfulness to the cause of the Union. However, the federal administration did not regulate this system, and as a result the impact and enforcement of these oaths varied. The Northern military governments in Missouri, Louisiana, and Tennessee in particular enraged Confederate sympathizers, for in those areas men like BENJAMIN F. BUTLER enforced the loyalty oaths with tremendous zeal. Southern citizens received relative freedom with their pledge, but ABRAHAM LINCOLN also felt strongly about the condition of prisoners of war, and he favored oaths that testified to the future fidelity of the individual as opposed to a more restrictive oath that encompassed the past. The president believed that the willingness to state allegiance definitively determined a person's loyalty. As a testament to this idea, Lincoln issued an amnesty proclamation on December 8, 1863, that became the standard prisoner's oath for the remainder of the war. This oath required the future support of the Union effort and EMANCIPATION but also protected the individual's property, with the exception of slaves, from confiscation. Such relative leniency served as a powerful temptation for Southern soldiers and prisoners in the final years of the war.

The loyalty oath soon became an integral and controversial piece of Reconstruction policy. For both Lincoln and ANDREW JOHNSON, the oath, while important, did not need to be any more than a profession of future fidelity. For the RADICAL REPUBLICANS seeking a strict Reconstruction, the oath needed to be true to the ironclad test oath created in 1862. This struggle, especially between Johnson and the Radicals, most seriously affected the resumption of numerous federal activities in the South. In requiring federal employees to attest to their past, present, and future loyalty to the federal government, the ironclad test oath made it extremely difficult to find Southern citizens willing and able to work for the government. Treasury Secretary Hugh McCulloch, in order to fill numerous revenue positions in the South, found it necessary to hire individuals even if they could not take the oath. This action, though taken with the approval of the president and the cabinet, enraged the Radicals in Congress and set the stage for the battles over the test oath in the years that followed.

As the Republicans in Congress worked to impose their idea of Reconstruction on the president and the South, they used the ironclad oath as a tool to keep Confederate sympathizers out of Congress as well as administrative posts. When Southerners demonstrated their intransigence by electing men to Congress who could not and would not take the oath, the Radicals rallied against them and made sure that the newly elected officers were not officially seated when they arrived in the Capitol. Although the Radicals scaled back their opposition in 1870 as their political strength waned, and the ironclad oath for Southerners was repealed in 1871, members of Congress repeatedly defeated measures to remove the test-oath law. The loyalty tests remained in force until May 13, 1884.

Further reading: Harold Melvin Hyman, *Era of the Oath: Northern Loyalty Tests during the Civil War and Reconstruction* (Philadelphia: University of Pennsylvania Press, 1954).

—John P. Bowes

M

Mallory, Stephen R. (1811–1873)

Lawyer, judge, U.S. senator, and secretary of the navy for the CONFEDERATE STATES OF AMERICA, Stephen Russell Mallory was born in Trinidad in 1811 and raised in Key West, Florida. His father was an engineer from Connecticut, and his mother was Irish. After briefly attending schools in Alabama and Pennsylvania, Mallory returned to Florida to study law and was admitted to the bar in 1834. His early career demonstrated an impressive record of public service. Appointed the inspector of customs, Mallory also served as town marshal and was the collector of the port at Key West in 1845. He enlisted in the Florida militia during the Seminole War of 1836–38.

Mallory's experience and excellent reputation recommended him to Florida's DEMOCRATIC PARTY, where he made a name for himself as a promising young politician. In 1850 Florida's legislature elected him to the U.S. Senate. As chairman of the Senate's Naval Affairs Committee from 1853, Mallory pushed for the construction of new warships and for the modernization of the ordnance department. He was especially interested in developing IRONCLAD vessels for the navy's use.

Mallory was a strong supporter of Southern rights during his decade-long term in WASHINGTON, D.C. He advocated SLAVERY's expansion and argued for a strict enforcement of the Fugitive Slave Act. When the SECESSION crisis gripped the country after ABRAHAM LINCOLN's election, Mallory joined with several of his Senate colleagues in trying to persuade the North to let the South go in a peaceful manner. Persuasion failed, and Florida left the Union in January 1861. Mallory resigned his Senate seat shortly thereafter and returned to his home in Pensacola.

On February 21, 1861, Mallory received word that his close friend and former fellow U.S. senator, President JEFFERSON DAVIS, had appointed him as the Confederate States' secretary of the navy. Only Mallory and John H. Reagan, postmaster general, kept their cabinet positions throughout the war, a testament to their political skills and resourcefulness. A daunting task awaited Mallory as he assumed his duties in RICHMOND, Virginia. The CONFEDERATE NAVY was practically nonexistent in 1861, possessing only 12 boats and 300 officers who had resigned from the U.S. Navy. Mallory's job was to raise a navy, build and sustain a fleet of warships, and undermine the Union blockade of the Southern coast. Through a combination of hard work, dedication, and intelligence, Mallory oversaw the successful recruitment and training of the sailors and the purchase and construction of ships abroad and in the South. Perhaps most importantly, he articulated and implemented Confederate naval strategy.

In order to break the Union blockade, Mallory got the Confederate Congress to approve the sum of $2 million to use to purchase or build ships in Europe. At home, he urged the construction of foundries and shipyards to build ironclads. Additionally, he used commerce raiders to confuse and divert Yankee commercial ships and hoped to draw Union ships from the blockade. Mallory was in the forefront of the drive to develop and use torpedoes in naval warfare. By the end of the war, Confederate torpedoes had sunk or severely damaged 43 Union ships. Elaborate minefields prevented the Union navy from entering Charleston harbor, and delayed the capture of Mobile Bay until near the end of the conflict.

Despite these herculean efforts, the South simply did not have the industrial capacity or financial resources to produce the ships and weaponry needed to sustain a modern navy. Mallory came under heavy and constant attack in the Confederate Congress and in the press for the losses of New Orleans, Norfolk, and Memphis in 1862. Investigations cleared him of wrongdoing, but criticism continued as losses mounted. Despite ultimate failure, historians have given Mallory's stewardship of the Confederate navy high marks.

Stephen R. Mallory fled Richmond with the rest of the Confederate cabinet in April 1865. Captured and arrested in Georgia, he was imprisoned at Fort Lafayette, in NEW YORK CITY, until 1866. After his release from prison, Mallory returned to Pensacola, Florida, where he resumed the practice of law. He was a bitter opponent of Radical RECONSTRUCTION and denounced African-American suffrage in many newspaper editorials. He died on November 12, 1873.

See also WELLES, GIDEON.

Further reading: Joseph T. Durkin, *Confederate Navy Chief: Stephen R. Mallory* (Columbia: University of South Carolina Press, 1987); Raimondo Luraghi, *A History of the Confederate Navy* (Annapolis: Naval Institute Press, 1996).

marine corps

In modern warfare, marines are used for amphibious combat—attacks on coastal installations, raiding ships, and so forth. At the time of the CIVIL WAR, however, marines were generally used for more mundane purposes: guarding ships, maintaining discipline among sailors, and occasionally manning naval guns. They rarely participated in combat, and when they did it was in a supporting role, which is why the Union and Confederate marine corps played a minimal role in the Civil War.

At its height, the Union's marine corps numbered about 4,000 enlisted men and officers. Throughout the war, the corps was handicapped by poor leadership, because most of the best young officers in the marines had resigned and joined the Confederacy. The officers who remained were older and found it hard to adapt to the new realities of the Civil War. U.S. Marines did see some combat action, notably at New Orleans, Fort Wagner, and Drewry's Bluff. However, the majority of U.S. Marines spent the war serving aboard ships as guards and artillerists. Over the course of the Civil War, the U.S. Marine Corps' battle casualties numbered 175 wounded and 78 killed.

The Confederate marine corps was very small, never numbering more than 500 men. For the entire Civil War, the commandant of the Confederate corps was Lloyd J. Beall, who proved to be an able leader. He also benefited greatly from the services of the 19 officers that had resigned from the Union marine corps. Despite their limited numbers, Confederate marines tended to see combat action much more frequently than Union marines. In addition to performing shipboard duty, Confederate marines fought at Hampton Roads, Drewry's Bluff, Mobile Bay, Fort Gaines, Savannah, and Charleston. A large segment of the Confederate marine corps was killed in action at the Battle of Sayler's Creek on April 6, 1865; most of the rest surrendered at APPOMATTOX COURT HOUSE a few days later.

The fact that marines, and U.S. Marines in particular, never found a clearly defined role to play during the Civil War nearly led to the elimination of the marine corps. On several occasions the U.S. Congress considered disbanding the corps or consolidating it into the army. It was not until the 20th century that marines would come to play an important role in military TACTICS AND STRATEGY.

Further reading: Ralph Donnelly, *Confederate States Marine Corps: The Rebel Leathernecks* (Shippensburg, Pa.: White Mane, 1989); Bernard Nalty, *The United States Marines at Harpers Ferry and in the Civil War* (Washington, D.C.: Historical Branch, G-3 Division, Headquarters, U.S. Marine Corps, 1966).

—Christopher Bates

marriage and family life

Marriage and family life in the mid-to-late 19th-century United States represented the stability needed to anchor a dynamic and fluid society. The home represented a "haven in a heartless world" and was dominated largely by women and children. Moreover, law, custom, and social practices protected the institution of marriage and family life. Divorce was rare and difficult to obtain, and the vast majority of people were married and had children. Although the family was not strictly "political," it was considered the main foundation for sustaining the uniquely democratic republic that was the United States of America.

As market capitalism spread throughout much of the country, more and more families were drawn into commercial farming or moved into the rapidly expanding urban areas. Men and women were no longer working side by side on the farm, growing their own food, and making all or most of their necessities. Increasingly, men were characterized as rugged individualists, up-and-coming ambitious capitalists expected to succeed in the public sphere. Women, on the other hand, assumed a powerful role in the home, defined as the private sphere. They had more time now because they could buy their own and the families' clothes and many other luxuries that did not require physical labor. Women were expected to use that extra time to instruct their children in Christian morality and values. From this kind of benevolent but educative home, the children would emerge as moral upright citizens.

Thus, the economic changes that swept the country also shaped the cultural traditions of its citizens. Courtship, marriage, and the family became individualized and private to a much larger degree than had previously existed. This spirit of individualism affected marriage practices. The ideal of romantic love combined with the market system seemed to offer young men and women greater freedom in their marriage choices.

Middle-class husbands and wives viewed one another as partners in a "companionate marriage." Children were regarded as individuals who required love, nurture, and special EDUCATION. Parents were very conscientious about child rearing and child development. The father assumed the position of sole breadwinner for the family, and the wife reared the children. Women were defined as morally superior to men and were now looked to as the guardians of civilization.

Mothers played an active role in the lives of their sons by instilling in them a moral conscience. Although the middle-class household became the domain of the mother, fathers continued to play an active role in their children's lives. Fathers were also advisers and disciplinarians, especially to their sons. The primary goal of both parents was to develop the child's conscience and his and her ability for self-government.

During an earlier period, children were trained to fear authority; in the 19th century, more indulgent and kindly parents taught their children to have the capacity for self-control but also to enjoy the fruits of their labor. Several historians have argued that with the emergence of individualism and society's new focus on personal advancement, 19th-century couples actively practiced contraception to ensure that they produced a smaller family for whom they could provide materially and emotionally.

At the same time, the family slowly lost its productive function as subsistence farming gave way to a reliance on factory-produced goods and a growing consumer ECONOMY. This change neither happened overnight nor did it occur at the same speed everywhere in the United States. Large numbers of people, including pioneer families, working-class and immigrant families in both the cities and the countryside, and slave families, had very different expectations and experiences. In general, however, middle-class marriage and family patterns were influential on every social stratum.

The small nuclear family fostered intense emotional ties between its members, especially as the line between public and private became more defined and as society and the economy became more specialized. The home became a place where mothers, fathers, and children found spiritual guidance, emotional support, and physical sustenance. The home became a place that nurtured and protected its members from a possibly immoral and definitely acquisitive world. This sentiment was summed up perfectly in one of the most popular songs of the era, "Home! Sweet Home!": "'Mid pleasure and Palaces though we may roam; Be it ever so humble there's no place like home!"

Further reading: Norma Basch, *Framing American Divorce: From the Revolution to the Victorians* (Berkeley, Ca.: University of California Press, 1999); Karen Lystra, *Searching the Heart: Women, Men, and Romantic Love in Nineteenth-Century America* (New York: Oxford University Press, 1989); Steven Mintz and Susan Kellogg, *Domestic Revolutions: A Social History of American Family Life* (New York: Free Press, 1988).

—Patricia Richard

Marx, Karl (1818–1883)

Writer and political philosopher Karl Marx offered a powerful critique of industrial capitalism and called for socialism. His ideology, known as marxism, had widespread influence both in his own era and later in communist regimes, notably in Russia and China. Less well known is Marx's short stint as a journalist covering the American CIVIL WAR.

Born in the Rhineland, (now Germany) to a comfortable middle-class family, he attended the universities in Bonn and Berlin. When he was banned from universities because of his participation in extremist political organizations, he turned to JOURNALISM. Throughout his life he wrote for and edited many different radical journals. Moving to France in the 1840s after one such journal was banned, he continued researching, writing, and working out his theories on the one hand and organizing European social movements on the other. He formed a lifelong partnership with fellow revolutionary theorist Frederick Engels. Exiled in 1849, he moved to London with his wife and children, where he lived the rest of his life.

Marx spurned religious explanations in favor of a detailed scientific system based on the material conditions of production. His work contained the idea of predictable stages. Workers, he argued, were economically exploited and morally alienated. These wrongs would lead to a class struggle and the overthrow of capitalism. In a more humane communist society, which he considered the last stage of civilization, human beings could develop their natural gifts freely in cooperation with others. A prodigious writer, his evolving ideas were published in more than 50 volumes. Among his most noteworthy books are *Communist Manifesto* (1848) and *Das Capital* (1867). His activist legacy was the First International.

Marx's work was an inspiration to U.S. anarchist and socialist groups active in the late 19th-century protest movements, such as the labor rally for the eight-hour day. Marx, who for 10 years was a foreign correspondent for the *New York Daily Tribune*, wrote trenchant essays on the political and economic causes of the Civil War as well as the military campaigns. A strong Unionist, he believed that ABRAHAM LINCOLN and the REPUBLICAN PARTY would bring a new hope for the working-class people in the United States and throughout the world. In an address to Lincoln, Marx wrote: "The workingmen of Europe feel sure that, as the American War of Independence initiated a new era of ascendancy for the middle class, so the American antislavery war will do for the working classes. They consider it an earnest of the epoch to come that it fell to the lot of Abraham Lincoln, the single-minded son of the working class, to lead the country through the matchless struggle for the rescue of an enchained race and the reconstruction of a social world."

Further reading: Saul K. Padover, ed., *Karl Marx on America and the Civil War* (New York: McGraw Hill, 1972); Francis Wheen, *Karl Marx: A Life* (New York: W. W. Norton, 2000).

—Jaclyn Greenberg

Mason-Dixon Line

The Mason-Dixon Line was the result of a 1760s survey that resolved a boundary dispute between the Penn family, the founders of the Pennsylvania colony, and the Calvert family, who founded Maryland. While the line is technically the northern boundary of Maryland, it has had greater significance as a legal and cultural divide. During the antebellum years, the line signified the division between the slave South and the free North. After the CIVIL WAR, the line continued to denote a cultural and emotional boundary between North and South.

After three generations of boundary disputes, the Penn and Calvert families hired British surveyors Charles Mason and Jeremiah Dixon, who used celestial navigation tools from 1765 to 1768 to mark a negotiated latitudinal boundary between Pennsylvania and Maryland at 39 degrees, 43 minutes, 17.4 seconds north. Once set, the Mason-Dixon Line became a significant American demarcation line.

Previously referred to by Thomas Jefferson as the geographical line that reflected a moral and political divide, the Mason-Dixon Line became the symbolic division between free states and slave states during the congressional debates over the Missouri Compromise of 1820. The line represented freedom for escaped slaves, and free African Americans and escaped slaves formed communities north of the line. As with many boundary areas, PROSLAVERY and ABOLITIONist views existed on both sides. Slave catchers had allies in Pennsylvania, while sympathetic Maryland residents assisted runaway slaves. Especially after the Fugitive Slave Act of 1850, the area saw activity by both the UNDERGROUND RAILROAD and slave catchers.

However, the Mason-Dixon Line was not the boundary between the Union and the Confederacy. While Maryland allowed slavery and contained many Confederate sympathizers, it remained part of the Union.

After the Civil War, the Mason-Dixon Line had diminished legal significance but retained its symbolic role as the cultural division between North and South.

Further reading: William Ecenbarger, *Walkin' the Line: A Journey from Past to Present along the Mason-Dixon* (New York: M. Evans, 2000).

—Martha Kadue

McClellan, George Brinton (1826–1885)

George B. McClellan, called "the Young Napoleon" during the CIVIL WAR, was known more for his organizational skills than his fighting ability or political talent. McClellan was born to a wealthy and distinguished family in Philadelphia, Pennsylvania. A brilliant student, McClellan entered the UNITED STATES MILITARY ACADEMY AT WEST POINT at the age of 15 and graduated second in his class in 1846. Like many of his classmates, McClellan served in the Mexican-American War, where he earned promotion for courage on the battlefield. In 1857 McClellan resigned his commission to accept a position as chief engineer and president of the Illinois Central RAILROAD. In this capacity, he honed his considerable skills as a businessman. He also became acquainted with his future commander in chief, ABRAHAM LINCOLN, who was working as a lawyer for the Illinois Central.

When the Civil War broke out, McClellan was appointed commander of the Department of the Ohio. Now a major general, he quickly won fame with a minor victory in West Virginia, 10 days before the Union defeat under General Irvin McDowell at the FIRST BATTLE OF BULL RUN. When Lincoln looked for replacements for the bumbling McDowell, he turned to McClellan, one of the rare heroes of the early war. Shortly afterward, the handsome and charismatic 35-year-old was given command of the armies around WASHINGTON, D.C. In November, McClellan replaced the elderly and ailing Winfield Scott as general in chief of all of the Union forces in the country. It seemed to the arrogant young general that he was destined for greatness. "I can do it all," he said. He wrote his wife: "All tell me that I am held responsible for the fate of the nation, and that all its resources shall be placed at my disposal." While that was true enough, personality clashes, political blunders, and bad generalship would soon dim McClellan's bright future as the nation's "savior."

At first, McClellan vindicated Lincoln's appointment. In the fall and winter of 1861 he disciplined, drilled, and organized the Army of the Potomac, the main army of the eastern theater. More than that, he instilled pride into the men under his command. Washingtonians thrilled to the parades and reviews that displayed the power of the United States. "On to RICHMOND!" was the cry accompanying the superbly executed marches of McClellan's devoted men. As late summer turned to autumn and autumn to winter, however, McClellan was increasingly criticized for inaction. Press, public, and politicians alike openly wondered if the Army of the Potomac was ever going to leave Washington to attack the CONFEDERATE ARMY in northern Virginia. Congressional investigations tarnished McClellan's reputation. A frustrated Lincoln remarked that if McClellan did not intend to use the army, he (Lincoln) wanted to borrow it.

McClellan responded by attacking his critics. In the process, he alienated many of his former supporters, including the president, whom he derided as "the original gorilla." Increasingly suspicious of his detractors, McClellan cultivated friendly politicians and reporters. A Democrat, he appointed many generals who shared his political beliefs, including the idea that the war should not be fought to end SLAVERY. These actions angered many Republicans in Congress and created friction between McClellan and Lincoln, particularly given the fact that the longer the war went on, the more EMANCIPATION was considered as a serious option.

McClellan defended his inaction, arguing that the enemy was higher in number and better prepared than his own, even when confronted with incontrovertible evidence to the contrary. He unwisely preferred to keep his strategic plans a secret and bitterly resented any political interference with what he considered purely military matters. Some of McClellan's modern biographers have even advanced the argument that he was psychologically incapable of taking decisive action.

McClellan finally presented a plan of invasion to Lincoln, and it was a good one. He envisioned one huge offensive movement to capture the Confederate capital, Richmond, by transporting the Army of the Potomac down the Chesapeake Bay to the tip of the Virginia Peninsula. If Richmond fell and the Confederate army was decisively defeated, the war would be over. Finally, in the spring of 1862, after many months of prodding and pushing, McClellan's army was on the move for the PENINSULAR CAMPAIGN. McClellan laid siege against the vastly outnumbered Confederates at Yorktown for a month. McClellan's unnecessary delay allowed the Southern army precious time to prepare the defense of Richmond. As always, McClellan sincerely believed that he was facing a more powerful and numerous army than his own. He constantly asked Lincoln for more men and supplies, prompting Lincoln's famous observation that "sending reinforcements to McClellan is like shoveling flies across a barn."

McClellan slowly but surely advanced toward Richmond and came within five miles of capturing the city. His forward movement was permanently stopped when, after the Battle of Seven Pines (May 31–June 1, 1862), ROBERT E. LEE assumed command of the Army of Northern Virginia. General Lee launched a counterattack that drove

George B. McClellan *(National Archives)*

the Army of the Potomac back to the James River in the Seven Days' Battle (June 25–July 1, 1862). Defeated but defiant, McClellan blamed his loss on the politicians in Washington who refused him the support he requested. Lincoln, disappointed by the lackluster performance of his general, ordered him back to northern Virginia to join with Gen. John Pope's new army. Lincoln also removed McClellan from his position as general in chief, replacing him with HENRY W. HALLECK. Unfortunately, Pope was far worse than McClellan and suffered one of the most humiliating defeats of the war at the SECOND BATTLE OF BULL RUN (August 29–30, 1862). Lincoln had no choice but to reappoint McClellan to rebuild the shattered remnants of the Army of the Potomac, a task he eagerly accepted.

Meanwhile, buoyed by his recent victories over the UNION ARMY, Robert E. Lee brought the war to the North when his army entered Frederick, Maryland, on September 4, 1862, prompting fears that an attack on Washington, D.C., was near. "Little Mac" slowly moved the Army of the Potomac into position between Washington and the Confederates. The audacious Lee then split his army in the face of a much larger foe and sent Gen. THOMAS J. "STONEWALL" JACKSON to capture the Union garrison at HARPERS FERRY, West Virginia. By accident, a Union soldier found a copy of Lee's official orders directing Jackson away from the main body of the Army of Northern Virginia. This vital information was in McClellan's hands within hours. "Here is a paper," exulted McClellan, "with which if I cannot whip Bobbie Lee, I will be willing to go home." Few commanding generals have possessed such precise information about their opponents' intentions, but McClellan did not strike quickly enough to destroy portions of Lee's divided army. Another opportunity to bring the war to an end was lost. Instead, the two armies met on ground of Lee's choosing, just north of Sharpsburg, Maryland.

On the morning of September 17, the Federals attacked the Confederates along Antietam Creek, which gave the battle its name in the North. Critics then and now of McClellan's generalship on the bloodiest one-day battle in U.S. history (23,000 casualties) claim that his plan was poorly executed and that he failed to use the thousands of Union troops who were held in reserve, thus minimizing the Northern advantage in numbers. The battle was a tactical draw. Nevertheless, General Lee's invasion failed, and the Army of Northern Virginia retreated across the Potomac to its Virginia camps. The North claimed the BATTLE OF ANTIETAM as a victory, and on September 22, 1862, Lincoln issued the preliminary EMANCIPATION PROCLAMATION.

After the battle, Lincoln urged McClellan to fight aggressively against Lee. Characteristically, McClellan felt a new campaign required many more men and more supplies. Finally, in November 1862, the president relieved McClellan of his command and replaced him with Gen. AMBROSE E. BURNSIDE. After a tearful farewell to his soldiers, McClellan moved to NEW YORK CITY and never commanded an army in the field again.

McClellan remained popular with his men, and for that reason he was an attractive candidate for the DEMOCRATIC PARTY in the 1864 presidential election. Although strongly pro-Union, McClellan was tainted by the peace wing of his party, which advocated an end to the war through negotiation. Lincoln was reelected by a substantial margin, including most of the soldiers' vote. After the war, McClellan worked as the chief engineer of the New York City Department of Docks (1870–72) and later was elected governor of New Jersey. Like many other Civil War generals, McClellan published an autobiography, *McClellan's Own Story* (1887), a strong defense of his war record. He died in Orange, New York, on October 29, 1885.

Further reading: Thomas J. Rowland, "In the Shadows of Grant and Sherman: George B. McClellan Revisited," *Civil War History* 40 (Sept. 1994): 202–225; Stephen W. Sears, *George B. McClellan: The Young Napoleon* (New York: Da Capo Press, 1999); T. Harry Williams, *Lincoln and His Generals* (Westport, Conn.: Greenwood Press, 1981).

Meade, George Gordon (1815–1872)

Union general George Gordon Meade was born on December 31, 1815, in Cadiz, Spain, to Margaret Butler and Richard Worsam Meade (a prominent Philadelphia merchant). The ninth of 11 children, Meade spent much of his boyhood in Pennsylvania. His father's financial losses and premature death forced Meade to pursue a military EDUCATION and a career in engineering. Graduating from the UNITED STATES MILITARY ACADEMY AT WEST POINT in 1835, he served in the Seminole War, subsequently leaving the army for eight years to work as a civil engineer. Marriage (to Margaret Sergeant, the daughter of Representative John Sergeant of Philadelphia) and fatherhood prompted Meade to return to the service in 1842. With the assistance of his brother-in-law, Representative Henry A. Wise of Virginia, he was appointed second lieutenant in the Corps of Topographical Engineers, where his duties included construction of lighthouses and breakwaters.

Meade fought in the Mexican-American War (alongside fellow engineers ROBERT E. LEE and JOSEPH E. JOHNSTON), earning a brevet to first lieutenant for his work during the siege of Vera Cruz. In August 1861, Meade (a captain with influential political connections in his home state) received command of a Pennsylvania brigade.

Meade's brigade joined the Army of the Potomac in June 1862 for Gen. GEORGE B. MCCLELLAN's ill-fated PENINSULAR CAMPAIGN. Serving in the same division as friend and fellow Pennsylvanian General John F. Reynolds, Meade fought at Mechanicsville and Gaines's Mill and was seriously wounded at Glendale, Virginia. He returned to the army in August 1862 to take charge of Reynolds's former brigade at the SECOND BATTLE OF BULL RUN, where Reynolds commanded the division. Meade inherited the division after Reynolds departed for recruiting duties and led the reserves with skill and conspicuous bravery at the September BATTLES OF South Mountain and ANTIETAM, Maryland.

In December at the BATTLE OF FREDERICKSBURG, with Reynolds now commanding the First Corps, Meade directed the reserves in a vigorous but unsupported attack on the Confederate right. Following disastrous losses in the Union attack on Marye's Heights, Gen. JOSEPH HOOKER assumed command of the Army of the Potomac and Meade took over the Fifth Corps. At the BATTLE OF CHANCELLORSVILLE in May 1863, he was among a minority of corps commanders who advised Hooker to stay and fight rather than withdraw across the Rapahannock River. Hooker, deciding to retreat, crossed the river ahead of his men while Meade's corps covered the army's rear.

On June 28, with the Army of the Potomac on the move and preparing for battle, President ABRAHAM LINCOLN, having lost patience with generals who refused to fight, appointed Meade to replace Hooker after Reynolds had declined the promotion. Meade directed the most important campaign of his career during his first week as army commander. In early June, General Lee had marched the Army of Northern Virginia through Maryland into Pennsylvania. In pursuit, the Army of the Potomac's forward wing (commanded by Reynolds) made contact with Confederate forces on July 1, 1863, near Gettysburg. The outnumbered Federals retreated south through town and took up a defensive position on Cemetery Hill. Learning that Reynolds had been killed, Meade ignored military protocol and sent Gen. WINFIELD SCOTT HANCOCK, another Pennsylvanian, to assume field command. When he reached Gettysburg, Hancock calmly restored order to the retreating troops and secured the Union position.

Meade ordered the army to concentrate at Gettysburg. Arriving on the field around midnight on July 1, he placed his available troops in an arc that extended from Culp's Hill southeast of Gettysburg, around Cemetery Hill to its west, and south along Cemetery Ridge. Meade instructed his Third Corps commander, Gen. DANIEL E. SICKLES, a New York politician, to extend the Union line to Little Round Top, a prominent hill suitable for artillery. Hearing on the morning of July 2 that the Third Corps was not yet in position, Meade sent messages to Sickles directing him to take up his assigned line. Sickles, who erroneously believed that the slightly higher but longer rise along the Emmitsburg Road would make a better defensive position than Cemetery Ridge, ignored Meade's instructions and advanced his corps about three-quarters of a mile in front of the designated Union line. Confederate forces attacked the Union left just as Meade rode over to Sickles in person to order him back to Cemetery Ridge. The Third Corps was forced to retreat under fire while Meade hurried men from Culp's Hill to Cemetery Ridge to fill the gaps left by Sickles's ill-considered advance. The Union left secured, he then rushed men back to the right to meet a Confederate attack on Cemetery Hill. A brigade from the Fifth Corps had occupied Little Round Top in time to save it for the Union, but Sickles's mistake on July 2 cost the Third Corps dearly.

Late on July 2, Meade called a council of war among his top officers. There was no question he intended to remain at Gettysburg, but soliciting his corps commanders' opinions about the best course of action for the next day, whether offensive or defensive, left him vulnerable to later charges of weak leadership. In the event, Meade ordered a dawn attack to remove Confederate troops from the foot of Culp's Hill, and he prepared the army for an expected enemy assault on the Union center. That assault began around 1:00 P.M. with a terrific artillery barrage followed by an impressive infantry assault. The Confederates, facing devastating artillery and rifle fire, were unable to carry the strong Union position. Meade had won a resounding victory, but he decided against an immediate counterattack, and Lee retreated south late on July 4 with the UNION ARMY in pursuit.

Lincoln was reportedly dismayed that Meade allowed Lee and his army to escape across the Potomac River, but more biting and politically motivated criticisms would follow. Disgruntled corps commanders Gen. Abner Doubleday and Gen. O. O. HOWARD complained that Meade had favored Hancock over higher-ranking officers. Meade's disloyal chief of staff, Gen. Daniel Butterfield (a Hooker partisan), falsely charged in testimony to the congressional JOINT COMMITTEE ON THE CONDUCT OF THE WAR that Meade had wanted to retreat from Gettysburg on July 1. General Sickles, motivated by the need to repair his own reputation, made outrageous claims in print and before the joint committee that moving the Third Corps to a forward position on July 2 had forced Meade to stay put, thereby saving the Union army from defeat. Stung by unwarranted attacks, Meade nevertheless retained his position as commander of the Army of the Potomac throughout the rest of the war. Changes in the Union command structure reduced his authority, however. In the spring of 1864, Lincoln selected Gen. ULYSSES S. GRANT to command all of the Northern armies. Grant chose to make his headquarters with the Army of the Potomac, an uncomfortable arrangement for Meade but one that he accepted. Meade was the nominal commander of the Army of the Potomac at the BATTLES OF THE WILDERNESS, SPOTSYLVANIA, and COLD HARBOR and during the PETERSBURG CAMPAIGN.

Following the war, Meade headed military departments in the East and South and, promoted to major general, was stationed in Philadelphia as commander of the Division of the Atlantic, where he died of pneumonia on November 6, 1872.

See also GETTYSBURG, BATTLE OF.

Further reading: Freeman Cleaves, *Meade of Gettysburg* (Dayton, Ohio: Press of Morningside Books, 1980); George Gordon Meade, *The Life and Letters of George Gordon Meade, Major-General United States Army* (New York: Charles Scribner's Sons, 1913).

—Amy J. Kinsel

Medal of Honor

A Medal of Honor is an award for valor on the battlefield. Such awards were uncommon in the U.S. military before the CIVIL WAR and were even frowned upon in some quarters. During the Revolutionary War, a few officers were awarded medals for leadership or received decorations from foreign powers. Late in the war, when morale was flagging, George Washington created the Purple Heart to recognize bravery among his troops, but the commendation was given only three times before 1800. In later wars, officers were sometimes given brevet promotions in recognition of meritorious service or political connections, while enlisted men were occasionally awarded extra pay. Nonetheless, when the Civil War started, there was no standard means by which exemplary military service was recognized.

Shortly after the war began, several congressmen proposed creating a medal for valor in combat, but General in Chief Winfield Scott stopped their efforts because he felt that such a measure was unnecessary. Once Scott retired, however, medal proponents were able to proceed without serious opposition. Iowa senator James W. Grimes, chairman of the Senate Naval Affairs Committee, quickly moved a bill through Congress instructing that the Medal of Honor be presented to enlisted personnel in the navy and marines who "most distinguish themselves by their gallantry in action." ABRAHAM LINCOLN signed the bill into law on December 21, 1861. On July 12, 1862, he signed a similar bill, sponsored by Massachusetts senator Henry Wilson, establishing the Medal of Honor for army enlisted personnel. A later act extended eligibility to army officers, although navy officers had to wait until World War I for inclusion.

The actual medal was designed by a private firm, Philadelphia silversmith William Wilson & Son Company, and struck by the U.S. Mint. The front of the medal was a five-pointed star depicting images of the Union defeating SECESSION. The reverse had space to be engraved with the recipient's name and unit and date and place of action. A red, white, and blue ribbon was attached to the medal, enabling it to be worn by the recipient.

The first Medals of Honor were awarded by Secretary of War EDWIN M. STANTON on March 25, 1863, to six surviving members of ANDREWS'S RAID. The first African American to win the medal was Sgt. WILLIAM H. CARNEY of the 54TH MASSACHUSETTS REGIMENT. Lt. Tom Custer, the brother of Gen. George Armstrong Custer, was the only person to win two Medals of Honor during the Civil War. There was also one female recipient, surgeon MARY EDWARDS WALKER, whose medal was eventually rescinded in 1917 and then restored by President Jimmy Carter in 1976. A total of 1,527 Medals of Honor were awarded during and after the Civil War, five times more than any war since. Of these, 1,195 were presented to army soldiers, 307 were given to navy sailors, and 17 were presented to marines. A handful were also presented to nonmilitary personnel.

There was no corollary to the Medal of Honor in the CONFEDERATE ARMY. For a while, a "Roll of Honor" system was tried, but it failed due to lack of support in the ranks. Medals were ordered struck for the famous Stonewall Brigade, but they were never awarded. The only Confederate soldiers to actually receive decorations were 43 members of the First Texas Heavy Artillery, who were given special "Davis Guard" medals by President JEFFERSON DAVIS in recognition of their defense of the Sabine Pass in Texas in 1863.

After the Civil War, several changes were made to the Medal of Honor. It was redesigned in 1904, and eventually different versions were created for the army, the navy, and the marines, and, in 1956, the air force. The rules for awarding the Medal of Honor were clarified so as to make the award much more selective. In addition, a review board composed of five retired generals was convened in 1916 and instructed to review every Medal of Honor that had been awarded to that date. They eventually revoked 911 of them, mostly those that had been given for lesser acts of bravery not deemed worthy of America's highest military decoration.

Further reading: Joseph B. Mitchell, *The Badge of Gallantry; Recollections of Civil War Congressional Medal of Honor Winners* (New York: Macmillan, 1968); R. J. Proft, ed., *United States of America's Congressional Medal of Honor Recipients and Their Official Citations* (Columbia Heights, Minn.: Highland House II, 1994).

—Christopher Bates

medicine and hospitals

Both hospitals and medical processes were rudimentary in the 19th century. Before the CIVIL WAR, hospitals played a small role in American medical care and were generally run not by doctors but by "civic-minded" leading citizens of the community where the hospital was located. The Civil War, which brought great numbers of people together into squalid military camps and brutal combat, only served to accentuate the shortcomings of medical care in the era. The doctors who treated soldiers had received their training almost exclusively from mentors who used the antiquated methods standard in American medicine at the time. While university and college courses of instruction were on the rise, even the most prestigious schools frowned upon clinical and laboratory work.

Adding to the health challenges facing the United States was the fact that medical methodology much more closely resembled medieval practices than anything "modern." Pharmacology was primitive and employed medicines that, in large doses, created the same symptoms as the targeted disease. In fact, several outright poisons, such as mercury, were commonly prescribed. Modern antibiotics were unavailable, and sterilization by heat was unknown. The concept of antiseptic surgery was introduced in Europe by Joseph Lister in 1867, but it took 10 to 15 years for its practice to become generally adopted. Training by apprenticeship perpetuated methods of diagnosis and treatment that fixated on bodily fluids, methods that dated back to Aristotle. Doctors observed urine, feces, blood, and pus to determine the nature of the problem. The prevailing medical opinion was that the body sought to cure itself by excreting toxins. Thus, diarrhea, vomiting, bleeding, or secretions resulting from infection were to be encouraged or induced. It is little wonder that the soldiers of the Civil War hid all but the most dreadful maladies from physicians.

As soon as the fighting broke out in earnest in 1861, the inadequacies of the respective medical corps of both the Union and the Confederacy became quickly and ominously evident. Clement A. Finley, the newly appointed head of the Union's Army Medical Bureau, was widely regarded as grossly incompetent. Health examinations of recruits and volunteers were not a priority, and as soon as the camps formed, the federal officials found that nearly a quarter of their men were unfit to enter battle. Samuel Preston Moore was responsible for building the Confederate Medical Department, but he was hindered by drastic shortages of supplies. Neither the Confederate national government nor the individual states had a method for commissioning physicians.

At the first major clash of the war, the FIRST BATTLE OF BULL RUN in July 1861, most of the doctors on both sides were regimental physicians supplied by the states, and their scant numbers left them no chance of effectively tending to the wounded. Ambulances were nearly nonexistent; addi-

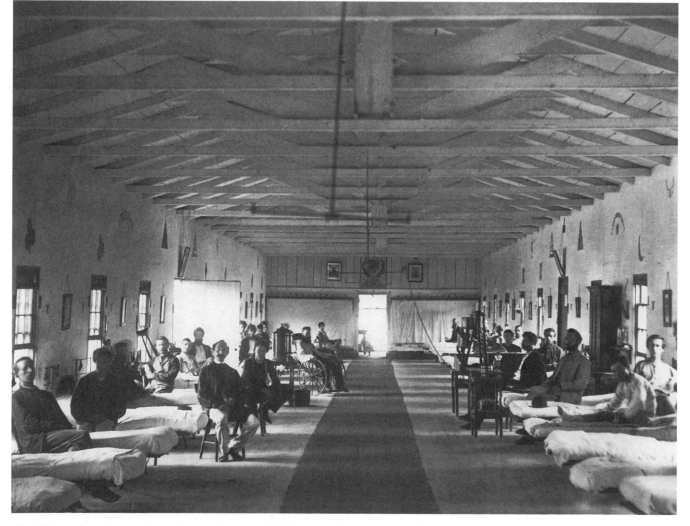

Civil War patients in the Amory Square Hospital, Washington, D.C. *(Library of Congress)*

tionally, there was no system in place for their use. Horribly injured soldiers mostly had to fend for themselves wherever they happened to fall.

The Union created the UNITED STATES SANITARY COMMISSION in June 1861 with official duties limited to conducting investigations and providing advice. Staffed by dedicated and diligent workers, the commission quickly became vital in improving conditions in the military camps. The commission submitted a scathing report of Clement Finley and his medical bureau in September 1861 and persuaded Congress to fully reorganize the army's medical services. Dr. William A. Hammond, Finley's replacement, established an excellent working relationship with the commission. He assigned Jonathon Letterman as medical director of the Army of the Potomac. Letterman was largely responsible for initiating the structure of the Army Medical Department that existed through World War II. Of immediate importance to the men in the field was the ambulance corps, which, by the BATTLE OF ANTIETAM in September 1862, was providing vital service in the evacuation of the injured to field hospitals. Letterman also authorized the assignment of a medicine wagon to each brigade.

Dr. Samuel Moore worked from within the blockaded Confederacy to build a military medical establishment comparable with that of the Union. He developed domestic pharmaceutical resources, recruited and trained NURSES, established a systematic method for treating casualties, experimented with the manufacture of surgical instruments, and implemented a system for military evacuation and hospitalization. However, due to limited resources, his effectiveness in treating the sick and wounded fell short of his rivals in the North.

Timely treatment of wounded and sick soldiers in camp and in field hospitals was implemented widely by 1862 in many areas. Large hospitals in cities were also built. A prevailing antebellum societal opinion was that hospitals were dangerous and were to be avoided at any cost. Hospitals were considered necessary for free or low-cost care for the poor, and for teaching, research, and war, but not for the treatment of the middle or upper classes. The terrible sights and sounds that one encountered (probably similar to those of a military field hospital) greatly deterred admissions. It was believed that most diseases came from "bad air," so Civil War hospitals were designed for maximum ventilation, emulating the success of military barracks hospitals operated by Florence Nightingale during the Crimean War. Peacetime citizens of the United States considered home medical care to be safer and more comfortable, and doctors obliged.

Both the Union and the Confederacy built large temporary military hospitals that became models of organization and models for "fresh air" ideas. The disparity in the availability of resources to the North and South that marked so much of the Civil War found astounding expression in the number and quality of hospitals. The North had erected 151 hospitals by 1863 and added another 53 by the end of the war with a total capacity of nearly 137,000 beds. The Confederacy had about 150 hospitals, although the number included improvised houses and barns. RICHMOND had the best of the Confederate facilities, including what may have been the largest military hospital ever, the 8,000-bed establishment at Chimborazo Heights. Hospital construction halted with the end of the Civil War, and the lessons learned both North and South in construction and efficiency were not to be applied for nearly two decades. In fact, the United States had only 178 hospitals in 1873, but by 1909, the number grew to 4,359.

While hospitals had promoted some great medical leaps before—for instance, anesthesia—many of those benefits were not available to soldiers in the field. For example, in 1846 William Morton first demonstrated ether as an anesthetic in surgery at Massachusetts General Hospital, but the supplies and equipment necessary to make ether were not something armies generally carried with them into the field. (Even on the HOMEFRONT, anesthesia use was circumscribed. While many physicians used anesthesia for "major" surgeries, most also refused to use it for "minor" operations.)

And while surgery without anesthesia was dreaded, a Civil War soldier's deadliest and most invincible enemy was disease. Union men actually had an almost two and a half times better chance of dying from disease than from combat; for Confederates, the chances were three to one. Contributions to a soldier's breakdown in health were many, including poor diet, bad weather, insects, and unsanitary camps. Diarrhea in its many forms, including dysentery, claimed more lives than battlefield wounds. Other chronic problems included pneumonia, bronchitis, scurvy, and "camp itch." Added to the equation were sporadic outbreaks of measles, smallpox, and malaria. Outbreaks of disease were known, especially in the earlier war years, to slow or halt entire military operations. The fate of Civil War military campaigns often hinged on the general health of the troops. ROBERT E. LEE's first field command in western Virginia experienced incessant, bone-chilling rains, and the resulting sickness nearly crippled his army. The putrid swamps of Chickahominy contributed typhus, diarrhea, and scurvy to the list of problems encountered by GEORGE B. MCCLELLAN during his PENINSULAR CAMPAIGN. ULYSSES S. GRANT's siege of Vicksburg was considerably slowed by disease.

Alcohol, in whiskey or brandy form, was the most commonly used "cure-all." Letterman's Union medicine wagons generally tried to contain some form of anesthetic (chloroform, ether, morphine, or opium) as well as alcohol, asafetida, calomel, castor oil, digitalis, spirits, turpentine, and assorted acids. And even with anesthetics and drugs, many doctors were educated to believe that pain in treatment was a good thing. The 1862 *Manual of Military Surgery for the Use of Surgeons in the Confederate States Army* argued that "the lusty bawling of the wounded" during surgery was a "powerful stimulant."

Though the Civil War did not produce any new "wonder drugs," it gave rise to the pharmaceutical industry that eventually made tremendous contributions to the medical advances of the 20th century. Since the Union relied heavily on imported drugs, readily accessible throughout the war, the majority of the advances were made out of necessity in the South. As the Confederacy began to feel the effects of the Union blockade, it depended on medicines captured in battle or provided by blockade-runners. Scientist-physicians were dispatched to find naturally occurring substitutes for unobtainable medicines. Francis P. Porcher subsequently discovered that green persimmon juice could be used as styptic, wood turpentine as an antiseptic, and red garden-poppy opium as an anesthetic. Joseph Le Compte used native plants to produce alcohol, silver chloride, sulfuric ether, and nitric ether. Despite the domestic alternatives, war drugs continued to run out. In the later years of the war, Confederate soldiers often endured illness, wounds, and amputations without medication.

Within the scope of the war effort were several medical advancements. Dentistry was singled out for the first time as an allied health profession. Early on, the Confederacy recognized the value of the discipline; it set up special pay for dentists serving in its ranks, gave dentists dispensations from the draft, and commissioned them to work in the medical corps. One such man commissioned was James Baxter Bean, who developed a system for immobilizing fractured jaws by use of inter-dental wiring and splinting.

The first women officers were also commissioned. The Confederacy desperately needed trained NURSES, and many women's organizations were formed to help establish private hospitals. The Confederacy, desiring a method to ensure the quality of care in its hospitals, passed a law requiring that Confederate soldiers be treated only in hospitals directed by commissioned military officers of at least the rank of captain. Subsequently, Capt. Sally Louisa Tompkins was commissioned in September 1861, enabling her continued direction of her excellent hospital. A sign of the times, her letter of appointment from the secretary of war began, "Sir: You are hereby informed that the President has appointed you Captain in the army of the Confederate States. . . ." On the Union side, MARY EDWARDS WALKER, a physician and winner of the MEDAL OF HONOR, was commissioned in October 1864.

Typical of this era were advertisements for medicines that promised relief from pain. *(Library of Congress)*

Modern public health was energized as specialized doctors on both sides of the lines were sent out to look for causes of disease outbreak in troops. Joseph Jones, a Confederate surgeon, was the first physician in the United States to use a clinical thermometer and one of the first to employ a microscope for clinical research.

After the Civil War the professionalization of America's hospitals and medical profession continued. In 1873 three schools for the training of nurses were opened in the Northeast, greatly improving the care available in America's hospitals. By the 1880s Lister's antisepsis techniques were in use in U.S. hospitals, but they were quickly replaced by aseptic surgery practices, thus making surgical procedures safer. With these processional developments came a growth in both surgical procedures and hospital stays.

The mid-19th century saw generally slow but steady development in the medical care system in the United States. Like all wars, the Civil War provided the dreadful conditions under which a generation of medical practitioners found invaluable clinical experience. A few decades later, aided by the work of germ theorists such as Louis Pasteur, they helped transform medical care and surgery in the United States to its modern form, and by the beginning of the 20th century, the U.S. medical EDUCATION system was standardized and professionalized, as was the hospital system.

Further reading: George Worthington Adams, *Doctors in Blue: The Medical History of the Union Army in the Civil War* (Baton Rouge: Louisiana State University Press, 1996); Horace H. Cunningham, *Doctors in Gray: The Confederate Medical Service* (Baton Rouge: Louisiana State University Press, 1993); Frank R. Freeman, *Gangrene and Glory: Medical Care during the Civil War* (Urbana: University of Illinois Press, 2001); Charles E. Rosenberg, *The Care of Strangers: The Rise of America's Hospital System* (Baltimore: Johns Hopkins University Press, 1995).

—Ruth A. Behling and Richard J. Roder

Memphis riot (May 1–2, 1866)

The Memphis riot grew out of the tensions that existed between the Irish-American and African-American workers just after the war. An economically vibrant port city, Memphis was also a rowdy, crime-ridden, corrupt place. From 1861 to 1866, Memphis experienced a tremendous rise in its black population, including African-American soldiers. The soldiers were stationed in Fort Pickering, alongside former CONTRABAND camps, which by 1866 were transformed into largely black neighborhoods. The influx of black people meant job competition with the large Irish immigrant population of Memphis, a source of steady and growing resentment for the latter group.

RECONSTRUCTION policy added to the uneasy atmosphere. Federal troops were still in the city. An unrepentant white citizenry despised FREEDMEN'S BUREAU agents and teachers. The prewar Memphis governing class was stripped of its power, and Confederate veterans were denied the vote. The Irish dominated the polls and controlled all city offices, including the mayorship, the board of aldermen, and the police and fire departments. There were frequent clashes between the Irish police and freedmen in south Memphis, where most of the African Americans lived in disease-ridden shanties. Newspapers played an important role in worsening an already bad situation by printing inflammatory and racist denunciations of the newly freed African Americans: "We are to have the black flesh of the Negro crammed down our throats," ran one such editorial.

On April 30, four policemen got into a fight with a group of recently discharged black soldiers. After a night of drinking, the soldiers roamed the streets shooting their guns, sparking fear and anger among white people. The next day, a collision between two delivery wagons attracted the attention of a large crowd of soldiers and other black men, who surged forth against the police. Soon, the situation spiraled out of control, and what little professional discipline the Memphis police previously exhibited was gone. The mayor was too drunk, and the sheriff too weak, to organize a restraining posse. Mobs of white people, including policemen and firemen, searched out and attacked helpless African Americans. What followed was a tragic race riot in which 46 black people and 2 white people were killed, 5 black women raped, and 80 people wounded. Property damage was estimated at $130,000, and black churches, schools, and homes were looted, destroyed, and burned. Order was restored when federal troops took control of the city.

The Memphis riot had national importance. It demonstrated to the North that the civil authorities in the South would not even minimally protect black freedom. This cast a bad light on President ANDREW JOHNSON's very lenient Reconstruction program and gave power to the RADICAL REPUBLICANS in Congress, who wanted a harsher policy toward the South.

See also NEW ORLEANS, LOUISIANA, RIOT.

Further reading: George C. Rable, *But There Was No Peace: The Role of Violence in the Politics of Reconstruction* (Athens: University of Georgia Press, 1984).

Milliken's Bend, Battle of (June 6–7, 1863)

The Battle of Milliken's Bend was a Confederate attempt to distract the Union's drive to take Vicksburg, Mississippi. The battle ended as a tactical stalemate: While the Confederates inflicted substantial casualties, they could not stop ULYSSES S. GRANT's siege. The battle's main significance is that African-American troops played an important role in fending off the Confederate assault, demonstrating to leaders on both sides that black soldiers could indeed fight.

The Union siege of Vicksburg began on May 19, 1863. The garrison's commander, John C. Pemberton, quickly pressed the Confederate government for assistance. President JEFFERSON DAVIS agreed with Pemberton's assessment that the situation was dire and ordered trans-Mississippi commander Edmund Kirby Smith to take immediate action. Smith decided to attack Union positions near Milliken's Bend. According to Confederate intelligence reports, Milliken's Bend was being used by the UNION ARMY as a supply depot. Smith believed that the position would be an easy target because it was being guarded by convalescents and African-American troops. He gave Gen. Richard Taylor responsibility for leading the assault. Taylor split his 4,500 troops into three groups. One brigade was sent to Milliken's Bend under the command of Gen. Henry McCulloch. Another was sent north to Lake Providence, and a third was sent south to Young's Point.

The Confederates got underway on June 6. Colonel Hermann Lieb, commander of Milliken's Bend, sensed that something was afoot and sent the 10th Illinois Cavalry and Ninth Louisiana Infantry to investigate. The men of the Ninth Louisiana were former slaves from Louisiana, Mississippi, and Arkansas and had been in the Union army for less than a month. Heavy skirmishing ensued when Lieb's soldiers encountered the Confederates, and the Federals were compelled to retreat. Lieb immediately requested support from Adm. DAVID DIXON PORTER, and two gunboats, the *Choctaw* and the *Lexington,* were dispatched.

Skirmishing continued through the night on June 6, and into the morning of June 7. When the sun rose at 5:30 A.M. the battle began in earnest. For more than an hour, the Confederates were able to push the Federals backward in bloody hand-to-hand combat. Then, at 7:00 A.M., the *Choctaw* and *Lexington* arrived, firing upon the Confederates with grape and canister shot. By 10:00 A.M. the rebels were in full retreat. This ended the Battle of Milliken's Bend, as the other prongs of the Confederate attack at Young's Point and Lake Providnet failed to engage the enemy.

Confederate losses at Milliken's Bend were 44 killed, 131 wounded, and 10 missing out of 1,500 engaged. Union losses were much more substantial, 101 killed, 285 wounded, and 266 missing out of 1,061 engaged. The three AFRICAN-AMERICAN REGIMENTS at Milliken's Bend—the Ninth Louisiana, the First Mississippi Infantry, and the 13th Louisiana Infantry—suffered a casualty rate of 35 percent. The Ninth Louisiana was hit particularly hard, and 45 percent of the regiment's members were lost.

The Battle of Milliken's Bend did a great deal to convince commanders on both sides that African-American troops were battle worthy. McCulloch, the Confederate commander, remarked that his troops' attack "was resisted by the negro portion of the enemy's force with considerable obstinacy, while the white or true Yankee position ran like whipped curs almost as soon as the charge was ordered." Ulysses S. Grant also noted his belief that African-American troops had passed an important test. A month and a half later, African-American troops would once again prove themselves, this time at Fort Wagner in South Carolina.

See also 54TH MASSACHUSETTS REGIMENT; VICKSBURG CAMPAIGN.

Further reading: Joseph T. Glatthaar, *Forged in Battle: The Civil War Alliance of Black Soldiers and White Officers* (Baton Rouge: Louisiana State University Press, 2000); Noah Andre Trudeau, *Like Men of War: Black Troops in the Civil War, 1862–1865* (Boston: Little, Brown, 1998).

—Christopher Bates

miscegenation

Miscegenation is a term invented in the 19th century to describe interracial sexual relations or marriage, usually between a black person and a white person. The practice first became a social and political issue in the early 17th century, two centuries before the CIVIL WAR, when Maryland and Virginia passed laws banning marriages between white people and people of other races. Many other states followed suit, although miscegenation laws were not always enforced.

Generally, those who opposed miscegenation, or race mixing, were most concerned with relations between white women and black men. In part, this was because a person's legal status derived from his or her mother. Thus, the child of a white woman and an enslaved African-American man was born free. Such children, free citizens despite having African blood, were perceived as a threat to the strict racial order of society. Children of enslaved African-American women and white men, on the other hand, were born slaves and thus posed no threat. Another reason that sexual contact between white men and black women was more tolerable was that it was much more common. Many of the men who owned slaves felt that it was perfectly acceptable for them to use slave women as concubines, even though it was almost invariably against the woman's will.

Prior to the 1860s, the term used to describe interracial relationships was *amalgamation*. The term *miscegenation* did not come into use until the election of 1864. David Croly and George Wakeman of the *New York World,* a Democratic newspaper, published a hoax pamphlet designed to convince people that Republicans favored interracial marriage. Their goal was to play on American fears that the Republicans were planning to overturn the racial status quo in the country. The ploy largely didn't work, although the fact that Croly and Wakeman thought it would is indicative of the state of race relations in mid-19th-century America.

After the war, miscegenation became largely a Southern issue. In the 1870s, most of the states in the North and West with remaining miscegenation laws repealed them, while most Southern states passed new laws with increasingly harsh penalties for interracial marriage. Republicans in Congress objected, and the laws were temporarily repealed before being put back on the books once RECONSTRUCTION was over. These laws were upheld in a series of

Supreme Court decisions in the 1880s, notably *Pace v. Alabama* (1883). Meanwhile, many Southerners dispensed with such legal niceties and simply hanged black men who were accused of sexual relations with a white woman. While the hangings eventually ceased, the attitudes behind them lasted well into the 20th century. When the Supreme Court reversed itself and declared miscegenation laws unconstitutional in *Loving v. Alabama* (1967), 16 Southern states still had such statutes on the books.

Further reading: David Henry Fowler, *Northern Attitudes towards Interracial Marriage: Legislation and Public Opinion in the Middle Atlantic States of the Old Northwest, 1780–1930* (New York: Garland, 1987); Martha Hodes, *White Women, Black Men: Illicit Sex in the Nineteenth-Century South* (New Haven, Conn.: Yale University Press, 1997); Joel Williamson, *New People: Miscegenation and Mulattoes in the United States* (Baton Rouge: Louisiana State University Press, 1980).

—Christopher Bates

Mississippi River

The Mississippi River, often called the "big muddy" or the "father of all waters," played a critical and, some historians argue, decisive role in the CIVIL WAR. After a stalemate settled on the eastern theater in the early part of the Civil War, Union forces turned to the West. In 1862 troops moved toward the Mississippi River in an attempt to control the important water TRANSPORTATION route and the influential port of New Orleans. If Union forces could control the lower Mississippi, they would divide the western from the eastern Confederacy. Control of New Orleans would also block an important Southern supply line while giving the North a direct transportation link into the heart of Confederate territory. In order to make headway in the western theater, Union troops employed a two-pronged plan of attack from the north and from the south.

Union success in the western theater rested largely on cooperation between the army and navy. Before the fall of 1862, the army controlled the operation of navy riverboats. The diverse naval gunboat crews that included volunteer riverboatmen, soldiers, steamboat pilots, and engineers, among others, did not come under complete U.S. Navy control until late 1862. This strange duality of command resulted from the War Department's belief that the inland waterways lay under the army's purview. Fortunately for the Union, the army and navy commanders in the theater worked well together, and their partnership ultimately propelled the Union to victory.

In April 1862 a squadron of Federal vessels, both IRONCLAD and wooden, gathered in the Gulf of Mexico near the mouth of the Mississippi River. Under the command of Flag Officer DAVID GLASGOW FARRAGUT, the Union forces easily took control of weakly guarded Confederate forts at the Mississippi's entrance. Because the South expected an attack from the North, their leaders left the Southern Mississippi, especially New Orleans, without adequate protection. A major Union naval victory occurred just days later on April 25, 1862, when the important Confederate port of New Orleans surrendered. The fall of this critical financial and transportation hub was a major blow to the South. After securing New Orleans, Farragut continued to move north up the river. En route, he accepted the surrender of two other port cities, Baton Rouge, Louisiana, and Natchez, Mississippi.

Just weeks before Farragut's campaign, Union naval forces attacked from the Mississippi Delta. The southward part of the attack began as Union troops advanced farther north on the Mississippi River headed toward Farragut's position. Two Confederate forts guarded the northern entrance to the interconnected western waterways, Fort Henry and Fort Donelson. General ULYSSES S. GRANT believed them to be vulnerable to attack. On February 6, 1862, Grant attacked Fort Henry on the Tennessee River, with land troops attacking from the rear and gunboats shelling from the river. The fort's defenders quickly surrendered and Grant proceeded to Fort Donelson on the Cumberland River. Confederate forces there put up a stronger defense, but superior Union naval and infantry forces controlled the fort by February 16. Thus, by the time of New Orleans's surrender in April 1862, the North had successfully blocked crucial Southern waterways, effectively halting Confederate commerce, transportation, and communication on those routes. Grant also succeeded in driving Confederate forces out of Kentucky and a large part of Tennessee.

After Grant's initial success in the western theater, he led approximately 40,000 troops south via land and water, aiming to cut off Southern railroad lines to destroy Confederate communication and supply lines. As the Union army marched through Tennessee, however, Confederate forces led by Gens. ALBERT SIDNEY JOHNSTON and P. G. T. BEAUREGARD surprised the Federals at Pittsburgh Landing on the Tennessee River. The BATTLE OF SHILOH, which ensued there on April 6–7, 1862, resulted in a very narrow but costly Union victory. The South lost 11,000 men and the North 13,000. Shiloh marked a crucial shift for both sides in the Civil War. The enormous losses were more than double the combined number killed and wounded at the FIRST BATTLE OF BULL RUN, Wilson's Ridge, Fort Donelson, and Pea Ridge. The battle destroyed the notion that the war would be won easily.

With Shiloh under Union control, Grant moved on to capture the central transportation hub of Corinth, Mississippi. Waterborne diseases such as typhoid and dysentery

U.S. gunboat *Fort Hindman,* part of the Mississippi River fleet *(Library of Congress)*

helped push Confederate troops out of the area and allowed Union forces to gain a hold. Rebel-held FORT PIL-LOW was all that stood in the way of the North controlling the Mississippi River as far south as Memphis, Tennessee. Confederates surprised Union forces with a new riverboat fleet. The steamboats, now set up as armed rams, attacked Northern vessels and achieved some initial success. The Union's river fleet adapted some of its own ships, manned them with riverboat rather than naval personnel, and quickly outmaneuvered the South, capturing Memphis.

In April 1862, the South held only two influential Mississippi River ports between Union-controlled New Orleans and Memphis. One of the strongholds, Vicksburg, Mississippi (called the "Gibraltar of the Mississippi"), had the benefit of natural protection. Located atop a sheer bluff overlooking the river, direct access to the city was treacherous from water due to well-placed artillery, and the natural inland topography itself—wild terrain to the north and very wet, marshy land to the west—made approach difficult.

Gen. Grant made an initial attempt to capture Vicksburg in late 1862 and early 1863. Joined by forces led upriver by Farragut, the Union troops tried to cut a channel to divert the Mississippi. They hoped to leave the city without a water source, but the arrival of an early summer stopped the North's attempts. Not only did the plan to cut

a new channel fail, but the river's water line surrounding the town lowered to dangerous levels for the boats. Many Northern sailors, essentially trapped on their vessels, fell ill and died of typhoid, dysentery, and malaria. Grant and Farragut temporarily abandoned their plans to take the city on the bluff.

In the spring of 1863, however, the North tried again. In May 1863, Grant began a drive toward Vicksburg. A combined mass of land troops and sailors moved to an area south of Vicksburg and attacked the city from the rear. Northern forces lay siege to the city and wore down local residents over a six-week period. Vicksburg's soldiers and civilians waited in vain for Confederate military help to arrive. Confederate general JOSEPH E. JOHNSTON's army was their only hope to save the city. However, he considered his position too weak to take on the powerful UNION ARMY. Outmanned and faced with starvation, Vicksburg commander Gen. John Pemberton surrendered to Grant on July 4, 1863.

The last Confederate stronghold fell just five days later on July 9, 1863. Under the command of Union general Nathaniel P. Banks, troops laid siege to Port Hudson, Louisiana. Starving after managing to subsist on a diet of mules and rats, the outnumbered rebels in the garrison gave up when they heard about the Union victory at Vicksburg. When Banks took Port Hudson, he gained control of the rich agricultural land along Bayou Teche for the North. With the entire length of the Mississippi River under the Union flag, the Federals split the Confederacy into east and west. The division left Louisiana, Texas, and Arkansas separated from their allies. Ultimately, Union control of the Mississippi proved to be a decisive turning point in the war.

Although Union victories on the Mississippi helped ensure the outcome of the Civil War, they also transformed local lives and customs. Before the Civil War, the lower Mississippi River Valley thrived on the connection between large plantation AGRICULTURE and commerce. Newly invented steamboats moved crops such as cotton and sugar grown by slaves. After the war, however, many of those steamboats were transformed into war ships, and the slaves became freedmen. The war on the river worked to liberate a population from chattel SLAVERY. It also dramatically changed the transportation system of the Old Southwest. Riverboats quickly lost their preeminence to the new steam-powered behemoth—the RAILROADS.

See also CORINTH, BATTLE OF; NEW ORLEANS, BATTLE OF; VICKSBURG CAMPAIGN.

Further reading: Bruce Catton, *Grant Moves South* (Boston: Little, Brown, 1960); James M. Merrill, *Battle Flags South; The Story of the Civil War Navies on Western Waters* (Rutherford, N.J.: Fairleigh Dickinson University Press, 1970); John D. Milligan, *Gunboats Down the Mississippi* (New York: Arno Press, 1980).

—Samantha Holtkamp Gervase

Mobile campaign (March 17–April 12, 1865)

The Mobile campaign brought the capital of Alabama under Union control. Although the city would have been an attractive prize early in the war, its capture in April 1865 had little significance because it came after the conflict was effectively over.

Before the CIVIL WAR, Mobile was one of the most prosperous cities in the South. The only major seaport in Alabama, it exported all of the state's cotton. Among the cities on the Gulf Coast, Mobile was second only to New Orleans in total value of exports. When the Civil War came, Mobile's cotton trade was largely cut off by the Union's naval blockade, but the city continued to serve a variety of other important roles. It housed a number of large hospitals, along with training camps for soldiers, and a shipyard used to construct IRONCLADS.

Although Union leaders had an eye on Mobile throughout the war, particularly after the fall of New Orleans and Vicksburg, it took until the summer of 1864 for Northern forces to move against the city. On August 5 a Union naval fleet led by Adm. DAVID GLASGOW FARRAGUT seized control of Mobile Bay. This brought an end to Confederate shipbuilding in the city and rendered the port unavailable to Southern ships trying to avoid the Union blockade. Farragut hoped that control of Mobile Bay would facilitate the quick capture of the entire city, but eight months of naval bombardment failed to drive the Confederates out of Mobile. Finally, on March 17, 1865, 20 ships and 45,000 men were ordered to undertake an offensive against the city. The Union force vastly outnumbered the 10,000 men and five boats left to guard Mobile under the command of Gen. Dabney Herndon Maury.

The Mobile campaign was a two-pronged offensive. To the south of Mobile, 32,000 troops under Gen. Edward Canby laid siege to the Spanish fort, beginning on March 27. The Confederates there, outnumbered by a margin of eight to one, held on for as long as they could but were compelled to surrender after an infantry assault on April 8. To the north of Mobile, 13,000 troops under Gen. Frederick Steele laid siege to Fort Blakely beginning on April 1. On April 9, Steele's troops were joined by most of the 32,000 men who had captured the Spanish fort, and an infantry assault was undertaken. After only 20 minutes, the Confederates holding Fort Blakely were compelled to surrender. This was the final infantry engagement of the Civil War, as Maury evacuated Mobile three days later.

Union losses for the Mobile campaign were 1,417 men killed, wounded, or missing, while Confederate losses exceeded 4,000 men. The majority of these losses occurred after the Confederate capital of RICHMOND had fallen and the Army of Northern Virginia had surrendered, events that essentially concluded the Civil War. Union general in chief ULYSSES S. GRANT later expressed his regrets that so much blood had been shed unnecessarily, writing:

> I had tried for more two years to have an expedition sent against Mobile when its possession by us would have been of great advantage. It finally cost lives to take it when its possession was of no importance, and when, if left alone, it would have within a few days fallen into our hands without any bloodshed whatever.

See also NEW ORLEANS, BATTLE OF; VICKSBURG CAMPAIGN.

Further reading: Sean Michael O'Brien, *Mobile, 1865: Last Stand of the Confederacy* (Westport, Conn.: Praeger, 2001).

—Christopher Bates

Monitor-Merrimack (Hampton Roads, Virginia)
(March 9, 1862)

The *Monitor* and *Merrimack* fought the first battle between ironclad vessels at Hampton Roads, Virginia, a battle that changed the nature of naval military strategy while inaugurating a new age of naval military technology.

The use of ironclad technology became widespread during the French-British-Russian conflict known as the Crimean War, in which vessels, made largely immobile by the weight of heavy iron plating, had been constructed for shore bombardments. Following the Crimean War (1853–56), improvements to the technology by the British and French navies produced superior models with better seafaring capabilities. Not until the onset of the CIVIL WAR, however, did the emergent technology, developed in two radically different forms by the Union and Confederate navies, encounter full combat testing.

The UNION NAVY had the advantage of greater numbers and an industrial ECONOMY. Seeking to negate these advantages, the CONFEDERATE NAVY, under the leadership of Secretary of the Navy STEPHEN R. MALLORY, turned to the ironclad. Working from plans drawn up by John Brooke, the Confederates began to build their first ironclad using the reclaimed wooden steam frigate *Merrimack* (the common spelling *Merrimac* is an oft-repeated misspelling of the name of the original vessel), which had been abandoned by the North at the Norfolk Navy Yard. The wooden upper hull was covered with iron plating and equipped with 10 heavy guns (including four rifled guns) and, borrowing from presail warships, a ram. Rechristened the CSS *Virginia,* the ship's appearance was described as "the roof of a sunken house with a smokestack protruding from the water."

The Union navy, faced with the threat posed by the ongoing construction of the *Merrimack,* responded with the construction of its own ironclad warship. The Union vessel, developed by Swedish-born marine engineer John Ericsson, featured a dual-hulled design with extensive armor plating. With its deck located at the waterline, limiting the exposed surface area, and a cylindrical turret rising prominently from the ship's center, the USS *Monitor* was said to look like a "cheesebox on a raft." Armed with only two cannons located in its slowly rotating turret, the design of the smaller ship, at 172 feet in length to the *Merrimack's* 275 feet, emphasized its maneuverability and defensive strengths.

In an effort to break the Union naval blockade and to reestablish strategic lines to RICHMOND, Confederate secretary Mallory sent the *Merrimack* to Hampton Roads, a harbor at the mouth of the James River. On March 8, 1862, the *Merrimack,* under the command of Capt. Franklin Buchanan, began an assault on the wooden ships of the Union naval blockade at Hampton Roads. First

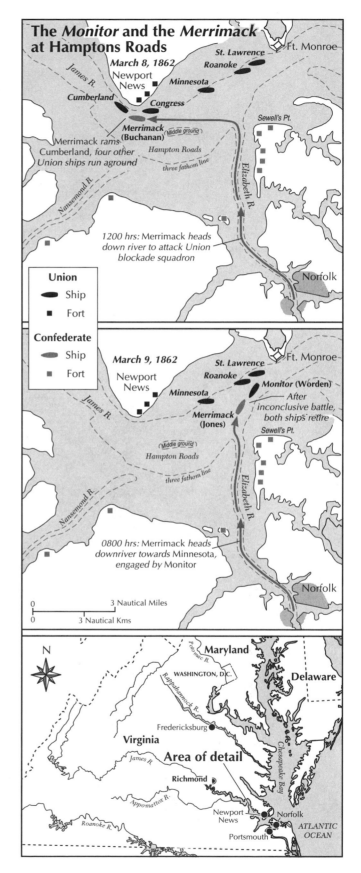

The *Monitor* and the *Merrimack* at Hamptons Roads

attacking the *Cumberland,* the *Merrimack* encountered substantial cannon fire but sustained little damage while firing upon, then ramming and sinking the Union sloop. Turning to the frigate *Congress,* the *Merrimack* unleashed a cannon barrage that forced the Union ship to run aground and surrender, while a third Northern warship, the *Minnesota,* also ran aground. When Union troops on shore fired on the Confederate vessels accepting the surrender of the *Congress,* injuring a number of Confederates including Captain Buchanan, the captain ordered the demolition of the Union frigate. By the time darkness and low tide forced the *Merrimack* back to Norfolk, the Union had lost more than 300 men, including acting captain of the *Congress* Joseph Smith, while those Union ships not already run aground or destroyed were forced to flee the area.

The following morning, the *Merrimack,* now under the command of Lt. Catesby Jones as a result of Buchanan's injury, set out to complete the destruction of the *Minnesota.* However, the *Monitor,* having completed a per-ilous journey from New York during which the ship nearly sank twice, reached Hampton Roads in time to prevent the destruction of the *Minnesota.* The Union ironclad, commanded by Lt. John Worden, engaged the *Merrimack* in a four-hour battle during which each ship landed a number of direct hits on the opposing vessel at short range with little effect. Though the *Merrimack* ran temporarily aground during the battle, the *Monitor,* with only two guns firing a light powder charge, was unable to take advantage of the vulnerability. Late in the conflict, the *Monitor*'s pilot-house was hit, temporarily blinding Worden and forcing the ship to disengage, once again exposing the *Minnesota.* The *Merrimack,* however, fearing the receding tide and in need of ammunition and mirror repairs, returned to the Norfolk Navy Yard, ending the battle.

Despite the prominent role of both warships in naval history as a result of their famous stalemate, neither was to enjoy a long life at sea. The *Merrimack,* forced to flee Norfolk, was unable to navigate safely up the James River and

Battle between the *Monitor* and the *Merrimack* in Hampton Roads, Virginia *(Library of Congress)*

was sunk on purpose on May 10, 1862. The *Monitor,* though nimble by ironclad standards, was barely seaworthy in rough conditions and sank during a storm off Cape Hatteras on December 31, 1862.

See also IRONCLADS.

Further reading: Jack Greene and Alessandro Massignani, *Ironclads at War: The Origin and Development of the Armored Warship, 1854–1891* (New York: Da Capo Press, 1998); David A. Mindell, *War, Technology, and Experience aboard the U.S.S. Monitor* (Baltimore, Md.: Johns Hopkins University Press, 2000); Arthur Mokin, *Ironclad: The Monitor and the Merrimack* (Novato, Calif.: Presidio, 1991).

—Adam Barnhart

monuments

Honoring people, places, or events of enduring importance, monuments have long served to memorialize various aspects of U.S. history. Throughout the United States there are approximately 10,000 CIVIL WAR monuments in national parks, large cities, and small town squares. Monuments for those who fought in the American Civil War are etched in stone, cast in marble, and molded in brass across the country. Monuments provide a continuing history of the Civil War for modern-day Americans. Fraught with political and social meaning, they reveal much about the culture they represent, as well as the culture the United States has developed.

Civil War monuments and memory sites are found in cemeteries, national parks, and buildings. The town of Blakely, Georgia, boasts the "Confederate Flag Pole," the last pole flying the Confederate flag at the end of the Civil War. Joliet, Illinois, is home to the "Civil War Bench," which was dedicated to the city's members of the Grand Army of the Republic. Shiloh, Tennessee, has Shiloh National Military Park, some 4,000 acres of land that attracts nearly 400,000 visitors per year. Within Shiloh Park are thousands of stone monuments marking the place where various regiments fought. WASHINGTON, D.C.'s Farragut Square provides a scenic backdrop for a statue of Adm. DAVID GLASGOW FARRAGUT made from the propeller of his flagship the *Hartford.* While Civil War monuments obviously vary widely in type as well as design, they usually contain dates, such as days in battle, as well as lists of casualties, deaths, and those who fought, in addition to the names of the commanding officers and the date the monument was dedicated.

The money for Civil War monuments was raised by public and private sources. Washington, D.C.'s first two Civil War monuments (to Maj. Gen. John A. Rawlins and Lt. Gen. Winfield Scott, both erected in 1874) were paid for entirely by the federal government. Individual states frequently funded monuments like the Tiffany windows in the beautiful chapel at Hollywood Cemetery in RICHMOND, Virginia. VETERANS groups or women's associations often held fund-raising events and donation drives to raise money for statues commemorating war-related activities.

Typically, monuments began to be funded and erected around the 25th anniversary of the Civil War. Commonly, elaborate ceremonies and speeches accompanied the unveiling of a monument. At the 1908 dedication of Washington, D.C.'s monument to Gen. PHILIP H. SHERIDAN, DANIEL E. SICKLES shared with the audience his hope that the statue would "recall to those who come after us the magnitude and glory of the struggle for the preservation of the Union."

The victorious North initially dominated the commemoration of the war, while the South lagged. As time progressed, however, monuments to Confederate soldiers and leaders were designed and placed in many Southern towns and cities. Indeed, at battlefields such as Gettysburg, veterans of the Southern forces were allowed to erect monuments as early as the 1890s. In 1909 the UNITED DAUGHTERS OF THE CONFEDERACY erected a monument to Henry Wirz, commander of ANDERSONVILLE PRISON. The National Park Service at Gettysburg preserves ROBERT E. LEE's headquarters. The R. E. Lee camp of the United Confederate Veterans erected the Alexandria Confederate Memorial (Alexandria, Virginia) to honor their community's Confederate veterans.

America's Civil War monuments memorialize the struggle for the preservation of the Union and the ABOLITION of SLAVERY, but they also honor the Confederacy's war effort. The Lincoln Memorial in Washington, D.C., and the huge General Grant National Memorial (Grant's Tomb) in NEW YORK CITY memorialize two of the Union's heroes. The cliff-sized, bas-relief equestrian figures of JEFFERSON DAVIS, THOMAS J. "STONEWALL" JACKSON, and Robert E. Lee at Stone Mountain, Georgia, do the same for Confederate heroes. Visitors can see the Confederate soldiers' monument on a stroll through the grounds of the Texas state capitol or pause at Augustus Saint-Gaudens's memorial sculpture of the 54TH MASSACHUSETTS REGIMENT on Boston Common.

Thus, the United States has preserved memories of the Civil War from both sides of the battle lines. This type of evenhanded commemoration reflects a general belief that both sides fought with equal valor during the war while it ignores the more divisive implications such as slavery and the legacy of racism. The verse by Reverend Randolph McKim, a Civil War veteran, on the Confederate monument in Arlington National Cemetery sums up best the ideology behind most Civil War monuments:

Not for fame or reward
Not for place or for rank
Not lured by ambition
Or goaded by necessity
But in simple
Obedience to duty
As they understood it
These men suffered all
Sacrificed all
Dared all
And died

In addition to the social and cultural implications tied to the meaning of these monuments, there is the question of preservation. From a simple brass statue to a sprawling national park, it is not always easy to determine how, why, and to what end a monument or memorial should be preserved. In addition, the guardians of such monuments—the federal government, and individual states—rely on the funds of taxpayers and are therefore subject to their thoughts and opinions as well. Knowing when to clean a cannon on a particular battlefield may not be such a difficult task, but deciding where to locate a visitors center and how to interpret the monuments and battlefield is much harder.

Further reading: David J. Eicher, *Mystic Chords of Memory: Civil War Battlefields and Historic Sites Recaptured* (Baton Rouge: Louisiana State University Press, 1998); Kathryn Allamong Jacob, *Testament to Union: Civil War Monuments in Washington, D.C.* (Baltimore, Md.: Johns Hopkins University Press, 1998); J. Michael Martinez, William D. Richardson, and Ron McNinch-Su, eds., *Confederate Symbols in the Contemporary South* (Gainesville: University Press of Florida, 2000).

—Lee Ashley Smith

Morgan, John Hunt (1825–1864)

John Hunt Morgan, known for his raids behind Union lines, was born on June 1, 1825, in Huntsville, Alabama, and raised in Lexington, Kentucky. As a young man, Morgan participated in the Mexican-American War and was promoted to first lieutenant in a cavalry regiment. After the war's conclusion he became a businessman in Kentucky. However, Morgan's interests remained in the military, and in 1857 he helped organize the Lexington Rifles, a local militia group. With the outbreak of the CIVIL WAR, he quickly joined the Confederate forces and was commissioned captain of a squadron of cavalry. At first, it was the squadron's main duty to scout. The following year, Morgan's focus shifted to raiding. At the BATTLE OF SHILOH in

April 1862, he was promoted to colonel as a result of his courageous actions.

Morgan became famous for his raids throughout Kentucky and Tennessee in 1862. His first engagement began on July 4, 1862, as Union forces moved toward Chattanooga. Their operation was thrown into confusion by Morgan when he led two regiments on an attack and captured a cavalry post. He went on to capture two depots and had several engagements with militia encountered along his path. Morgan then moved from town to town throughout Kentucky, all the while destroying Union supplies. He returned to Tennessee on July 22 after covering more than 1,000 miles, capturing 1,200 prisoners, and losing fewer than 100 men. Morgan's raids did much damage to Northern morale.

Morgan went on to lead many more raids throughout the war. His successes included the capture of numerous Union posts; the destruction of RAILROADS, bridges, and lines of communication; and the capture of many prisoners of war. These raids caused great damage behind Union lines and cost the Union dearly in terms of men and money. After demolishing a strong garrison at Hartsville, Tennessee, Morgan was promoted to brigadier general on December 11, 1862. Though victorious during 1862, he faced failure during the latter half of 1863. While on a raid through southern Indiana and Ohio, Morgan and most of his men were captured by Union cavalry and imprisoned for several months. General Morgan managed to escape and return to the Confederacy, but the Ohio raid was considered a reckless adventure by many Southerners and damaged Morgan's reputation.

Nevertheless, in the spring of 1864 he was placed in command of the Department of Southwestern Virginia. Six months later he received command of the forces stationed at Jonesboro, Georgia. However, when he and his men reached Greenville, Tennessee, he was surprised by the Union army and shot and killed on September 4, 1864.

Further reading: James D. Brewer, *The Raiders of 1862* (Westport, Conn.: Praeger, 1997); James Ramage, *Rebel Raider: The Life of General John Hunt Morgan* (Lexington: University Press of Kentucky, 1986).

—Emily E. Holst

Morrill Land-Grant Act (Agricultural and Mechanical Colleges Acts) (1862)

The Morrill Act—named for its sponsor, Vermont congressman Justin Morrill—established the land-grant college system, which widened the reach of higher EDUCATION while supporting agricultural, mechanical, and military education and research.

Morrill first introduced the bill in December 1857. A largely self-educated man, Morrill conceived of the legislation as a means of addressing the declining agricultural productivity of the 1850s. Taking inspiration from the agricultural schools and colleges of western Europe and observing the development of new technical and vocational colleges in the United States, Morrill proposed the sale of federal lands to fund the creation of colleges in each state. A founding member of the Vermont REPUBLICAN PARTY, Morrill's vision of an expanded role for the federal government in funding education met with strong opposition from legislators from the South and West, including JEFFERSON DAVIS and James Mason, who found the bill to be questionable. Mason called it "an unconstitutional robbing of the Treasury for the purpose of bribing the states." Despite the opposition, the efforts of Morrill and Ohio senator BENJAMIN WADE led to the passage of the bill in both houses. JAMES BUCHANAN, however, at the urging of Louisiana senator John Slidell and other Democrats, vetoed the bill, questioning its necessity and constitutionality.

Reintroducing the bill in December 1861, Morrill strengthened its provisions, allotting each state 30,000 acres of federal land to be sold for each member of its congressional delegation. The language of the bill continued to emphasize the development of technical and agricultural curricula, endowing in each state "at least one college where the leading object shall be, without excluding other scientific and classical studies, and including military tactics, to teach such branches of learning as are related to AGRICULTURE and mechanic arts." Motivated by the onset of war, the inclusion of military training in the provisions of the bill allowed for the development of the Reserve Officers Training Corps (ROTC), an educational program from which military officers could be drawn. Without the presence of the Southern Democratic delegation to fight the bill, it encountered comparatively little opposition and passed both houses easily, by a 32–7 vote in the Senate and a 90–25 vote in the House. President ABRAHAM LINCOLN signed the bill into law on July 2, 1862.

The parameters of the act allowed for the founding or expansion of a number of prominent American institutions of higher learning, including Ohio State University, Cornell University, Massachusetts Institute of Technology, Rutgers University, the University of Wisconsin at Madison, and the University of California system. Providing the backbone of the American state college system, the Morrill Act aided in bringing an expanded body of academic programs, including agricultural science, botany, veterinary medicine, and engineering, to a larger proportion of the American population. Offering higher education at a lower cost and employing more liberal admissions standards, the land-grant colleges improved educational access for women, the working class, and marginalized ethnic groups. The formation of Alcorn State University in Mississippi, Hampton University in Virginia, and Clafflin University in South Carolina after the CIVIL WAR gave America its first land-grant colleges for African Americans, though funding from the Morrill Act continued, in general, to serve predominantly white institutions during the remainder of the 19th century.

A second Morrill Act, passed in 1890 under President Benjamin Harrison, increased and solidified economic support for colleges founded under the 1862 legislation. Denying funding to states "where a distinction of race or color is made in the admission of students," the act encouraged the development of institutions of higher education for African Americans. In doing so, however, the act allowed for the construction of separate facilities for black and white students, declaring the legitimacy of a "separate but equal" doctrine affirmed six years later in *Plessy v. Ferguson.*

The land-grant college system created by both Morrill acts has continued to have a considerable influence on American education, now including more than 100 institutions that have granted more than 20 million degrees since 1862.

See also EDUCATION.

Further reading: Ralph D. Christy and Lionel Williamson, *A Century of Service: Land-Grant Colleges and Universities, 1890–1990* (New Brunswick, N.J.: Transaction Publishers, 1992); Coy Cross, *Justin Smith Morrill: Father of the Land-Grant Colleges* (East Lansing: Michigan State University Press, 1999).

—Adam Barnhart

Mosby, John Singleton (1833–1916)

Confederate colonel John Singleton Mosby was a leader of the Partisan Rangers in northern Virginia from 1863 to 1865. Originally a scout for Maj. Gen. J. E. B. STUART in the First Virginia Cavalry, Mosby successfully lobbied for his own company, which grew from nine men to as many as 1,900 before the war's end, with no less than 400 serving at one time. His guerrilla operations in Virginia were an interminable nuisance to the Union picket posts in the defensive parameters around WASHINGTON, D.C., as well as to UNION ARMY efforts in the Shenandoah Valley. He constantly diverted troops, supplies, and attention away from intended Union campaigns, often capturing forces several times larger than his own.

Born on December 6, 1833, in Powhatan County, Virginia, Mosby was a sickly child, though intelligent and well read. He attended college at the University of Virginia in

Charlottesville until he was expelled and imprisoned for shooting a fellow student. While in jail, he studied law, and upon his release he practiced law in Howardsville, Virginia. In 1857 he married Pauline Clarke of Frankfort, Kentucky, and they moved to Bristol, Virginia, a year later. In December 1860 he enrolled in the state militia and became a Confederate cavalryman when Virginia seceded in April 1861.

Mosby quickly became one of J. E. B. STUART's most trusted scouts, obtaining information that helped pave the way for Stuart's raid around the Union army during the PENINSULAR CAMPAIGN of 1862. Like Stuart, Mosby was flamboyant in dress. Sporting an ostrich plume in his hat, the slight, blonde cavalier wore a gray cape with bright red lining. In January 1863, Stuart permitted Mosby and a detail of nine men from the First Virginia Cavalry to begin partisan, or guerrilla, operations in Loudoun County, Virginia. The outfit officially became the 43rd Battalion of Virginia Cavalry in June 1863, and Mosby was promoted to colonel on December 7, 1864. The battalion's operations were based in Loudoun and Fauquier Counties in north-central Virginia, an area that became known as "Mosby's Confederacy."

One of the best-known exploits of Mosby's rangers was the capture of Union Brig. Gen. Edwin H. Stoughton, who was captured while sleeping in a house in Virginia, five miles inside the line of Union defense. Other successful raids include the "Great Wagon Raid" and the "Greenback Raid" in August and October 1864, respectively. The rangers also succeeded in cutting TELEGRAPH wires, halting traffic on the important B&O Railroad, and hampering Union Maj. Gen. PHILIP H. SHERIDAN's supply line during his SHENANDOAH VALLEY CAMPAIGN. Although determined and forceful in command, Mosby and his men never lapsed into the cruel and criminal behavior that characterized other Southern guerrilla units.

Rather than surrender his command, Mosby instead disbanded his battalion on April 21, 1865. After the war, he practiced law in Warrenton, Virginia, and outraged fellow Confederate VETERANS when he expressed Republican sympathies and actively supported President ULYSSES S. GRANT's 1872 reelection campaign. Grant admired his former foe and wrote, "Since the close of the war, I have come to know Colonel Mosby personally. . . . He is able and thoroughly honest and truthful."

Under President Rutherford B. Hayes, Mosby served as consul in Hong Kong and helped expose and correct the abuses of his corrupt predecessors in office. He also served in the land office in southern Nebraska and as assistant attorney in the Justice Department. In 1908 he published an impassioned defense of Stuart's actions during the Gettysburg campaign, a topic of hot debate in Confederate cir-

cles after the war. Mosby died on May 30, 1916, at the age of 82.

Further reading: John Singleton Mosby, *Memoirs*, ed. Charles Wells Russell (Bloomington: Indiana University Press, 1959); James A. Ramage, *Gray Ghost: The Life of Col. John Singleton Mosby* (Lexington: University Press of Kentucky, 1999); Jeffry D. Wert, *Mosby's Rangers* (New York: Simon & Schuster, 1990).

—Stacey Graham

Murfreesboro/Stones River, Battle of
(December 31, 1862–January 2, 1863)

The Battle of Murfreesboro (or Stones River, as it is also known) brought a much-needed victory for the North, but one that came at a high price. Following his failed invasion of Kentucky in mid-November 1862, Confederate general BRAXTON BRAGG moved his Army of Tennessee into central Tennessee, where he aimed to reclaim a large portion of that state and, in the words of President JEFFERSON DAVIS, help the Confederacy "recover from the depression produced by the failure in Kentucky." Union forces, under the command of Gen. WILLIAM S. ROSECRANS, countered this move by taking position around Nashville. Not an aggressive fighter, Rosecrans settled into resupplying and resting his Army of the Cumberland.

Rosecrans's inaction quickly ended under pressure from politicians claiming that the Union war effort was moving too slowly. The December disaster at the BATTLE OF FREDERICKSBURG and Gen. ULYSSES S. GRANT's stalled invasion of Mississippi further eroded public confidence. In response, President ABRAHAM LINCOLN and General in Chief HENRY W. HALLECK urged Rosecrans to move on the rebels. On December 26, 1862, he began a general advance on Murfreesboro. A cold rain fell on the Union soldiers as they marched south from Nashville. Sleet, fog, and icy roads continued to plague Rosecrans, but by December 29 and 30 his army began to move in on the rebel troops.

At 6:30 A.M. on December 31, Bragg launched a major attack, sending his left-most divisions forward with instructions to drive back enemy forces while turning to the right. The attack caught the Union troops off guard and overwhelmed them. Within half an hour, two Union divisions had been driven from the field, disorganized and demoralized. However, Bragg's overly complex plan caused severe confusion among his troops. Federal resistance also stiffened as Union soldiers took strong positions among the cedar glades and limestone outcroppings.

The Confederates continued to fight, however, and by noon Union forces had been pushed back into a line almost perpendicular to their original position just in front of the main line of retreat, the Nashville Pike. The line along the Nashville Pike was a strong one on a slight rise in front of largely cleared fields. Confederate attacks were thrown back by rifle and artillery fire, and the Confederate advance ground to a halt in a series of poorly coordinated assaults. After a day of resting and watching Union forces dig in, on January 2, rebel troops launched an attack on the Federals' left flank. The Confederates were beaten back, suffering heavy casualties, especially among the Kentucky units led by Gen. John C. Breckinridge. On January 3 Bragg retreated to a position near Shelbyville and Tullahoma, Tennessee.

The battle was costly. Both armies lost nearly one-third of their total forces in killed, wounded, and missing. Of the 41,400 Federal troops, 12,906 were casualties; the Rebels suffered 11,739 losses out of a total of 34,739. Union forces alone had a 31 percent casualty rate, which made Murfreesboro the war's most deadly battle when casualties were looked at in proportion to the number of troops fighting. The forced retreat of the Army of Tennessee brought a glimmer of hope to the North and diminished some of the COPPERHEAD sentiment, but it left Rosecrans's army badly crippled. For the Confederacy, Murfreesboro was terrible news. Bragg, never popular with other commanders, was even less so now. Bragg went so far as to offer to resign, but JEFFERSON DAVIS left him in control, thus setting the stage for continued divisiveness and infighting within the western CONFEDERATE ARMY.

Further reading: Peter Cozzens, *No Better Place to Die: The Battle of Stones River* (Urbana: University of Illinois Press, 1990); Earl J. Hess, *Banners to the Breeze: The Kentucky Campaign, Corinth, and Stones River* (Lincoln: University of Nebraska Press, 2000).

—James Daryl Black

music

"Without music, we would have no war." ROBERT E. LEE's famous remark accurately depicted the truth that music played an important role in the CIVIL WAR. Both armies drew upon a common musical heritage and common musical practices. Field music provided communication, and brass bands created some sense of home while the songs of the camp filled the empty hours and warmed hearts made cold by war. From early in the morning until late at night, music filled the air in both Northern and Southern camps.

All army units had field music: drummers and fifers for the infantry and drummers and buglers for cavalry and artillery. Under the guidance of a drum major, the field musicians learned to play and perform dozens of calls, tunes that regulated a soldier's day and allowed officers to communicate on the field. Drum majors carried heavy responsibility, since drummers were the youngest members of the armies. Johnny Clem of Ohio enlisted when he was only nine years old, and Johnny Walker from Wisconsin was 12 at the beginning of his service. These youngsters became heroes, and composers sentimentalized their exploits in songs like, "For the Dear Old Flag I Die," "The Drummer Boy of Shiloh," and "The Little Major" with its pathetic refrain, "can you friend refuse me water, can you when I die so soon?"

The young musicians controlled the movements of the army. Beginning with "The Long Roll" and ending with "Taps after Tattoo," field music not only signaled meals, visits to the doctor and church, and camp duties but also sent men charging into the enemy or racing away from it. "Taps," as modern listeners know it, was created as a method of ending confusion during battle. One general told his field musicians to play a melody based on his name, "Dan, Dan, Dan—Butterfield, Butterfield," before sounding the required call for his men. Played slowly and sweetly, the phrase became the melody most associated with military funerals.

Brass bands played a central part in community life throughout the 1850s. Because of technological advances in the 1840s, brass instruments could be played using a simpler set of fingerings, thus allowing people to learn to play with minimal training. Books of music containing parts for small bands became widely available, and musical organizations sprang up in settlements of all sizes. Local militia units hired town bands to perform during drill weekends, and they recruited the band members to join them as regimental bands following Lincoln's call for volunteers in 1861. It is estimated that the North paid as many as 10,000 musicians as much as $15,000,000 during the course of the war. To decrease the cost of supporting the musicians, regimental bands were discharged in July 1862, and only the best units were retained as brigade bands.

Bands varied in size and quality. The 26th North Carolina band, reputed to be the favorite of Robert E. Lee, had fewer than 10 players. Post bands, like the U.S. MARINE CORPS band, could have as many as three dozen players, but field bands averaged 12 to 18 players. Some, like the band of the First Brigade of Wisconsin Volunteer Infantry, contained excellent musicians. Others, like that of the Sixth Wisconsin Infantry, knew only one song and played that badly. One Northern band practicing near the cook tent was chased away so their music would not "spoil the meat."

Military band books contained a wide range of music. Musicians played patriotic airs such as "Columbia, the Gem of the Ocean," "Red, White and Blue," "Battle Cry of Freedom," and "The Star Spangled Banner" at recruiting events and for military parades. Hymns and dirges, including "Mother, I've Come Home to Die," were used for church services and funerals. Waltzes, polkas, schottisches, and other dances helped pass the long hours of inspection and calmed men waiting to go into battle. Most bands had a huge supply of quicksteps—marches employed when moving the army from place to place along long, dusty roads. They also had a good number of arrangements of opera songs—the musical THEATER of the day.

The most prized arrangements were those of pieces written during the Civil War. Most Northern groups had one or more versions of "JOHN BROWN's Body" about the famed ABOLITIONist who led the raid on HARPERS FERRY, Virginia, before the war. The song had a simple melody and the words were repetitive, so soldiers sang it endlessly. Following a long day of visiting army camps, the song stayed in the mind of JULIA WARD HOWE. In the middle of the night she awoke and wrote a new set of words for the tune and called it "The Battle Hymn of the Republic." Very lucky bands played "Hell on the Rappahannock," a song complete with the thunder of battle provided by drums. The piece was made famous by the 114th Pennsylvania ZOUAVES.

Other popular compositions were by Henry C. Work and George F. Root, who owned and operated publishing houses specializing in sheet music. Root's company published both "John Brown's Body" and "The Battle Hymn of the Republic," and Work composed equally popular tunes including "Marching Through Georgia," which memorialized the movement of Sherman's army across the South near the end of the war.

As the soldiers settled in for the night, officers frequently called for their band to come out to perform a serenade, a concert of sentimental and patriotic favorites. When a band was not present, the soldiers did the honors themselves, gathering around campfires to sing songs that reminded them of home. When feeling particularly patriotic, Southerners sang "The Bonny Blue Flag," a song that listed the names of the SECESSIONist states. Well aware of their precarious supply system, the Confederates marched along to the strains of "Goober Peas," a jaunty tune honoring the lowly peanut. Northerners countered with the rousing "Battle Cry of Freedom" and "We Are Coming Father Abra'm."

The music of the Civil War came from a shared heritage. Both sides claimed songs like "America," and both shared the beautiful hymns of the day, such as "Abide with Me," "Old Hundreth," and "Rock of Ages." The song most closely associated with the Confederacy, "Dixie," was written by a New Yorker, Daniel Decatur Emmett, and was one of ABRAHAM LINCOLN's favorite tunes. A minister from Elkhorn, Wisconsin, composed "Lorena," the favorite love song of Southerners. Men of one side borrowed the songs of the other side. Confederates sang, "Oh, I wish I was in the land of cotton. Old times there are not forgotten," while Northerners intoned, "A way down south in the land of traitors, rattlesnakes and alligators." This shared heritage caused one of the most poignant moments of the war. On one evening at the BATTLE OF MURFREESBORO, a Union band marched down to the river's edge and struck up a patriotic air. As they completed the tune, a Confederate band struck up a song of their own on the other side of the river. Turn after turn the two bands played through their music books. Finally, the Union band began the song "Home, Sweet Home." Softly the Confederates chimed in. As the two bands finished, the voices of the armies encamped on either side of the river took up the strain: "Be it ever so humble, there's no place like home."

Southerners worked to create music that was uniquely theirs. A new national anthem, "God Save the South," appeared in the songbooks of many Confederate units but never achieved the popularity of "Dixie." Writers composed new words for old, familiar songs, like the French anthem "Le Marseillaise." The old Irish tune "The Wearing of the Green" became "The Wearing of the Grey," and the German Christmas carol, "O, Tannenbaum" served as the basis for "Maryland, My Maryland."

"O, Tannenbaum" was not the only holiday song loved by soldiers and used by musicians. "Jingle Bells" had been written shortly before the Civil War and was sung in many winter camps. Since bands had to perform during funerals, they needed a supply of dirges. By changing just a few notes, one band used an old Latin hymn, "O Come, All Ye Faithful," to send the dead to their final resting place. One well-loved Christmas song had its origins in the Civil War. In 1863 Henry Wadsworth Longfellow composed a poem that was set to music in 1872. "I Heard the Bells on Christmas Day" reflected Longfellow's agony following the death of his son at Gettysburg in 1863. He began, "I heard the bells on Christmas day / Their old familiar carols play." Rather than a song of joy, the tune first became despairing but ultimately turned hopeful: "'There is no peace on earth,' I said, / 'For hate is strong and mocks the song / of peace on earth good will to men.' / Then pealed the bells more loud and deep: / 'God is not dead nor does he sleep; / The wrong shall fail, the right prevail / With peace on earth good will to men.'" The men of both sides embraced the ideas of that song.

The music of the Civil War clearly reflected the multiethnic nature of the United States. Many popular songs were written in dialect of one sort or another. While some used the speech patterns of slaves to add a touch of authenticity or comedy to their music, others bore witness to the hopes for a better future for African Americans found in songs like "Kingdom Coming." A few songs, such as the "Marching Song of the First Arkansas," recorded the entry of African Americans into the armed forces of the country and declared, "We have done with hoeing cotton, we have done with hoeing corn." Dialect songs also indicate the presence of other groups within the armies. "I Goes to Fight Mitt Sigel" recorded the experiences of one German volunteer who fought "To Save der Yankee Eagle." The tune was a popular humorous ditty, but band books indicate that ethnicity was treated with equal respect. Songs like "Russian Hymn" were a regular part of the Civil War repertoire.

The sentimental songs of home and of shared suffering brought the two sides together again after the war. "Tenting Tonight on the Old Campground," with the haunting refrain "many are the hearts looking for the right, to see the dawn of peace," became a kind of generational anthem.

Songs like "Tenting," which memorialized the Civil War efforts of both the North and South, had companion pieces particular to their region like "I'm a Good Ole Rebel" proclaiming the singer's stand on postwar politics with the line: "I won't be reconstructed and I don't give a damn!"

Further reading: Lawrence Abel, *Singing the Music of a New Nation: How Music Shaped the Confederacy, 1861–1865* (Mechanicsburg, Pa.: Stackpole Books, 2000); Kenneth E. Olson, *Music & Musket: Bands and Bandsmen of the American Civil War* (Westport, Conn.: Greenwood Press, 1981); Frank J. Rauscher, *Music on the March, 1862–65 with the Army of the Potomac: 114th regt. P.V., Collis' Zouaves* (Philadelphia: W. F. Fell, 1892); Irwin Silber, ed., *Songs of the Civil War* (New York: Columbia University Press, 1960).

—Karen Kehoe

N

Nast, Thomas (1840–1902)

Perhaps the best-known political cartoonist of the 19th century, Thomas Nast was born on September 30, 1840, in Landau, Germany. His family fled the coming revolution in Germany by immigrating to NEW YORK CITY in 1846. Although Nast demonstrated exceptional artistic talent as a very young child, he was never particularly successful academically. As a result, Nast left school and obtained a position as a student of Theodore Kaufman, a German artist working in New York.

Attracted to the new illustrated weeklies, in 1855 Nast was hired as a junior artist for *Frank Leslie's Illustrated Newspaper.* Beginning in 1858, Nast worked for *Leslie's* and other papers, producing illustrations for *Harper's Weekly* and the *New York Illustrated News.* In need of income so that he could marry, Nast accepted a position as a permanent staff illustrator with *Harper's* in 1862. Nast's first wartime assignment for *Harper's* was to draw illustrations of Union encampments. Nast surpassed his journalistic assignment, however, by illustrating not only the physical results of battle but the emotional toll of separation from loved ones and sacrifice for the nation. His illustrations prompted Union soldiers to write hundreds of LETTERS thanking him and elicited an equal number of outraged letters from Southern readers who felt Nast was unfair toward the South.

Some of Nast's most powerful cartoons of the war years were those that supported ABRAHAM LINCOLN's 1864 reelection campaign. Nast used his drawings to suggest that Lincoln's critics, who favored making peace with an undefeated South, were betraying the sacrifices of the Union dead. He also attacked the COPPERHEADS, portraying them as supporters of a country in which the Constitution was irrelevant and the immorality of SLAVERY was acceptable. Several of Nast's drawings were reprinted as campaign pamphlets by Lincoln's supporters. By the end of the war, both Lincoln and ULYSSES S. GRANT expressed their appreciation for Nast's work, which they agreed had been beneficial to both morale and recruitment.

After the war, Nast's reputation soared. His cartoons addressed every political issue of the Gilded Age, from RECONSTRUCTION through the presidential campaign of Theodore Roosevelt. Although his cartooning continued, Nast's relationship with *Harper's Weekly* did not. By 1872, his strained relationship with the influential editor George William Curtis had become so widely publicized that at least one rival cartoonist made it the subject of his own work. Nast left *Harper's* in 1886 and attempted, unsuccessfully, to launch his own magazine.

Nast is best known for several drawings that established two enduring images of American life. His CIVIL WAR–era drawings of a fat, jolly Santa Claus provided a face for the American vision of Santa as a benevolent emissary of consumerism, while his 1870 drawing of a Democratic donkey and 1874 creation of a Republican elephant established the political iconography of America's two major parties. Nast's two most important political goals were the reelection of Grant for a second term and the destruction of the Tammany Hall political machine in New York City. Both goals were met by 1872, when Nast drew a melancholy cartoon suggesting that his career was over because there was nothing left to attack. This proved premature, as Nast went on to address IMMIGRATION, the Catholic Church, the Irish, the presidential campaign of James G. Blaine, and the Progressives.

Nast's work provides an interesting window into the contradictions of Gilded Age politics. On the one hand, he championed Reconstruction, opposed Southern vigilante racism, and vilified the anti-Chinese violence of railroad workers. On the other hand, he drew vicious images of African-Americans, Irish immigrants, and Catholics, many of whom he portrayed as only barely human. He was capable of great compassion for suffering but could be petty and bigoted in his approach to the lives of the poor and oppressed. Although he abandoned the REPUBLICAN PARTY briefly over its selection of Blaine as a presidential candidate, for most of his life Nast was a committed supporter of the Republicans and of their presidents. His work on behalf of Theodore Roosevelt prompted the new president to offer Nast a consulship in Guayaquil, Ecuador, in 1902, which Nast accepted because virtually every investment he had ever made had failed. The consular position offered a guaranteed income that Nast hoped would help his family. Instead of a tranquil sinecure, however, Guayaquil proved deadly: Nast died from yellow fever within six months and was buried in Ecuador.

See also JOURNALISM.

Further reading: Morton Keller, *The Art and Politics of Thomas Nast* (New York: Oxford University Press, 1986); Stephen L. Nissenbaum, *The Battle for Christmas* (New York: Vintage Books, 1997); Albert Bigelow Paine, *Thomas Nast: His Period and His Pictures.* (Princeton, N.J.: Pyne Press, 1974).

—Fiona Galvin

National Labor Union (NLU)

Founded in Baltimore, Maryland in 1866, the National Labor Union (NLU) was the first nationwide association of trades unions in American history. Following the CIVIL WAR, unions made tremendous gains in terms of numbers and political strength. This upsurge led to the first "congress" of all labor organizations, held in Baltimore in August 1866. The result was the formation of the National Labor Union, which first consisted of 77 delegates representing some 60,000 workers. It established a program that called for all workers to join trade unions to have "an equal voice with the employer," the granting of public lands to settlers only (as opposed to business interests), the abolition of contract labor, the establishment of cooperative workplaces (as opposed to wage labor), and most importantly the establishment nationwide of the eight-hour day. Within a span of a few short years, the NLU represented 640,000 workers.

William Sylvis, the president of the Iron Molders' International Union, was elected president of the NLU in 1867 and helped shape it into an influential national organization. Sylvis was a hardworking leader who sought an end to the system of wage labor that was rapidly taking hold in the country. He also advocated increased involvement of people of color and women in the unionization process. Sadly, his early death at age 41 in 1869 left the labor movement bereft of one of its ablest leaders.

Because employers were largely successful in foiling the effort for a national eight-hour day, the NLU began to focus more on political reform and in 1872 formed the National Labor Reform Party. Unfortunately, the nominee Judge David Davis declined to run. The Panic of 1873 the following year plunged the United States into a depression, which put unions on the defensive. This depression sounded the death knell for the NLU, which soon collapsed.

See also COLORED NATIONAL LABOR UNION.

Further reading: Melvyn Dubofsky, *Industrialism and the American Worker, 1865–1920* (New York: Crowell, 1996).

—Troy Rondinone

National Woman Suffrage Association (NWSA)

To secure voting rights and fair treatment for women, ELIZABETH CADY STANTON, Susan B. Anthony, and others formed the National Woman Suffrage Association (NWSA) in 1869.

Women had gathered to secure the vote long before 1869 and the founding of the NWSA, most notably at the 1848 Women's Rights Convention at Seneca Falls, New York. During that time, women had gained the support of male advocates of temperance and ABOLITION. Nevertheless, after the CIVIL WAR, abolitionists—anxious to pass the FIFTEENTH AMENDMENT to the Constitution—excluded a woman's right to vote from consideration. This effectively forced the leaders of the woman suffrage movement to form their own organization, which soon split into two camps.

The National Woman Suffrage Association, headquartered in New York, represented the more radical branch, which rejected the Fifteenth Amendment because it granted voting only to freedmen. Besides working to secure voting rights through a new constitutional amendment, the NWSA fought to correct unfair practices used against women in the workplace and courtrooms. The NWSA sought reforms in divorce laws, child custody, property rights, college admissions, and wages for female workers. The NWSA published a newspaper, *Revolution*, outlining their positions.

Six months after the NWSA's founding, in November 1869, Lucy Stone and other former colleagues of Cady Stanton and Anthony formed the less radical American Woman Suffrage Association (AWSA). The founders of the AWSA supported the Fifteenth Amendment and concentrated their efforts on securing the vote for women, paying scant attention to other social issues. The division between these two branches of the women's rights movement would hamper feminist advances in law and society for decades.

In 1890, after much negotiation, both organizations merged to become the National American Woman Suffrage Association. Elizabeth Cady Stanton, who had been the first president of the NWSA, served as first president of the new organization.

Although the Civil War did not, in and of itself, delay the achievement of female suffrage or equal rights, the Fifteenth Amendment divided the women's rights movement so drastically that it remained at odds for almost 30 years.

See also WOMEN'S STATUS AND RIGHTS.

Further reading: Ellen Carol DuBois, *Feminism and Suffrage: The Emergence of an Independent Women's Movement in America, 1848–1869* (Ithaca, N.Y.: Cornell University Press, 1999); Marjorie Spruill Wheeler, ed., *One Woman One Vote: Rediscovering the Woman Suffrage Movement* (Troutdale, Oreg.: NewSage Press, 1995).

—Vickey Kalambakal

Native Americans

Despite nearly a century of negative experiences in dealing with American government institutions, Native Americans actively participated in the American CIVIL WAR. More than 20,000 Native Americans fought in the war within the Union and Confederate armies, their reservations were turned into battlefields, and their homes and property were often destroyed. In some nations, as many as one in four soldiers died from battle wounds. As soldiers, Native Americans fought in lesser known battles in the trans-Mississippi West as well as in the eastern theater at the BATTLES OF SECOND BULL RUN, ANTIETAM, and THE WILDERNESS, the PETERSBURG CAMPAIGN, and SHERMAN'S MARCH THROUGH GEORGIA. As nations, the conflict provided new opportunities to pursue long-standing goals, and it also reinvigorated long-standing political divisions. In the end, however, the Civil War resulted in the further dispossession of lands and the further deterioration of self-rule.

At the Civil War's outset, most Native Americans proclaimed their neutrality. Recognizing that the United States was preoccupied with the war, they took the opportunity to chase unwanted Christian missionaries and American agents out of their territories. Others hoped that the war would weaken the ability of the United States to further dispossess them of their lands. As the Civil War continued, at least for many Indians, neutrality became less possible and desirable. Rather than something to avoid, the Civil War became an opportunity to protect their self-interests.

When federal agents abandoned the Indian Territory in 1861, many Native Americans were receptive to Confederate agents and the alliances and offers of protection that they proposed. In the summer of 1861, the Confederacy had treaties with various Indian nations, including the Five Civilized Tribes (Choctaw, Chickasaw, Creek, Cherokee, and Seminole), as well as the Caddo, Osage, Quapaw, Seneca, Shawnee, and Wichita. The Confederacy also had alliances with some Indians who lived within the South. The Catawba nation in South Carolina, for example, enthu-

siastically supported the Confederacy, with nearly all of its eligible men enlisted.

The decision to support the Confederacy did not merely result from an attachment to SLAVERY. Although several Indian nations had sizable slave populations, their alliances with the Confederacy were also based on other needs. The Confederacy promised that it would assume all federal obligations to Native nations, guaranteed Indian self-determination, offered to protect the nations from invasion, allowed Indians to define citizenship for themselves, and asked for Indian representatives in the Confederate Congress. Such terms convinced Native Americans in the desirability of an alliance and the subsequent providing of troops for Confederate defenses. Other issues convinced individual Indians to participate. The CONFEDERATE ARMY offered EMPLOYMENT, often paid a bounty to those who enlisted, and provided an opportunity to prove in war one's manly virtue.

Other Native Americans pursued their self-interests by supporting the United States. By 1862, for example, 170 of the 201 men eligible for service in the Delaware Nation had enlisted in the UNION ARMY. Although the Delaware later signed a treaty of amity with the Confederacy, most Delaware Indians continued to support the Union war effort, especially as scouts. The Ottawa and Ojibwa Indians kept their distance from the war for its first two years. In 1863, however, they began to enlist in the "First Michigan Sharpshooters." Some Indians who remained in the Southeast, especially the Pamunkey in Virginia and the Lumbee in North Carolina, used the Civil War to further resist attempts by Southern states to limit tribal sovereignty. By joining the Union army, they sought to protect their communities and voice their opposition to the racist policies of their Southern neighbors. Throughout the war, Pamunkey men served as pilots on federal boats and Lumbee soldiers served as guerrilla warriors, especially as WILLIAM T. SHERMAN's men marched through the Carolinas. Other Union supporters left their nations and enlisted in the army as individuals. Seneca Indian ELY S. PARKER, for example, became adjutant general in the Union army and assistant to Gen. ULYSSES S. GRANT.

The alliances with the Confederacy resulted in the formation of four Native American regiments. The regiments, which originally comprised nearly 5,000 members of the Five Civilized Tribes, fell under the command of Col. Douglas Cooper. Later in the war, soldiers from the other Indian nations joined the regiments, and the number of Confederate Indians in the western theater alone surpassed 10,000. Even as the regiments were formed, however, dissent within the nations continued. Tribal leaders signed treaties but did not have the power to enforce compliance within the nations. As a result, the Confederate Indian regiments focused much of their efforts on the Civil

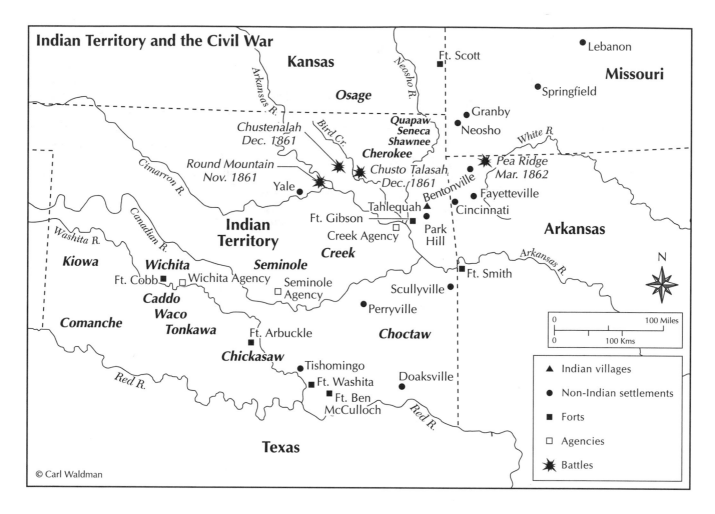

Indian Territory and the Civil War

© Carl Waldman

War atmosphere within Native communities, especially within the Cherokee Nation.

By late 1861 the Confederate Indians had forced most supporters of neutrality in the Indian Territory to flee to Kansas. With the supporters of neutrality temporarily out of the way, several regiments of Confederate Indians joined Union troops in a series of battles. Their participation, however, magnified the distrust between Indian and white soldiers in both Confederate and Union camps. In several instances, especially after the BATTLE OF PEA RIDGE, Native troops found themselves accused of scalping and committing other "savage" atrocities.

In June 1862, most of the Native American REFUGEES in Kansas abandoned their stance of neutrality. They formed two Union regiments, invaded the Cherokee Nation, and captured the capital of Tahlequah and Fort Gibson. As a result, the Union gained the allegiance of many former Confederate Cherokee. The Confederate Cherokee forced the Union supporters to withdraw back to Kansas, and the Civil War in the Indian Territory continued. The following year, at the Cowskin Prairie Council,

the pro-Union Cherokee denounced the Confederate Cherokee, invalidated their treaty with the Confederacy, abolished slavery, and elected a new chief, Thomas Pegg. That spring, with the support of federal troops, they went back on the offensive. They forced the Confederates out of the Cherokee Nation and recaptured Fort Gibson and Tahlequah. Later that summer, federal troops destroyed a munitions depot in the Choctaw Nation and then captured Fort Smith, Arkansas.

The final year of the Civil War was its most destructive for Native Americans in the western theater. Union and Confederate sympathizers burned homes, slaughtered and stole livestock, and destroyed other forms of property. Guerrilla-style raids destroyed supply lines, and members of both armies took vengeance on each other.

Although Ely Parker, the Seneca aide to Grant, drafted Confederate general ROBERT E. LEE's surrender on April 9, 1865, the Civil War did not immediately end for Native Americans. Three months later, on July 14, the Chickasaw and Caddo finally surrendered. In the months that followed, the United States punished the Native nations for their alliance with the Confederacy. The Five Civilized Tribes were forced to surrender much of their lands, grant a right-of-way through their territories to American RAIL-ROAD companies, accept U.S. territorial governments within their lands, and, of course, abolish slavery.

After the Civil War, even those Native Americans who supported the Union found themselves punished. In the early years of RECONSTRUCTION, Indian nations of the West were the focus of attention of the U.S. Army. As more settlers moved west to make homestead claims or mining strikes, Native Americans were pushed farther and farther to the fringes of the U.S. territory. American hunters tapped into a new FASHION craze, the buffalo robe, and slaughtered the majority of the herds on the American plains, thus decimating a crucial Native resource. The battles and relocations subsequent to the BATTLE OF LITTLE BIGHORN in 1876 and the Nez Perce War of 1877 set the standard of postwar Indian settler and government relations.

Further reading: Anne Heloise Abel, *The American Indian in the Civil War, 1862–1865* (Lincoln: University of Nebraska Press, 1992); Ralph K. Andrist, *The Long Death: The Last Days of the Plains Indian* (New York: Maxwell Macmillan International, 1993); Laurence Hauptman, *Between Two Fires: American Indians in the Civil War* (New York: Free Press, 1995).

—Andrew K. Frank

nativism

The flourishing of American nativism, or anti-immigrant sentiment, accompanied the great wave of Irish and German immigrants to American shores in the 1830s and 1840s. For the first time in the history of the nation, many of these newcomers were not middling- or upper-class Protestants but working-class Roman Catholics. Spawned in large part by the anti-Irish sentiments of English arrivals a generation earlier, nativist feeling in the United States took on a particularly anti-Catholic cast. As the church expanded both in number and in its acquisition of property, and as the new arrivals clustered together in crowded urban enclaves, anxious nativists blamed immigrants for the growing problems of the cities. In some quarters, it was even felt that Catholics posed a threat to America's sovereignty. Some nativists feared a Catholic conspiracy to establish a beachhead in the United States and deliver the country to papal rule.

As early as 1830, nativist publications such as *The Protestant* began to appear. These were followed by the formation of nativist societies, such as the New York Protestant Association. Encouraged by anti-Catholic speeches of famous ABOLITIONist minister Lyman Beecher

and tracts denouncing Catholicism written by Samuel F. B. Morse, nativism grew and occasionally erupted into violence. In the summer of 1834, for example, a nativist mob stormed and burned the Ursuline Convent in Charlestown, Massachusetts. By 1835 a nativist political party, the Native American Democratic Association, appeared in NEW YORK CITY. Although internal divisions caused the party to collapse, less than a decade later a more powerful nativist party, the American Party, appeared and permanently altered the existing political system. The American Party was more commonly known as the Know-Nothings because of party members' tendency to answer questions about the organization with the phrase, "I know nothing."

Coupled with an economic depression and increased competition for housing and jobs, the Know-Nothings appealed to artisans and merchants who hoped to stop the flow of immigrants. The party offered an alternative to what the public perceived as the Catholic-controlled DEMOCRATIC PARTY. Whigs, too, were seen as being too friendly to immigrants, and the Know-Nothings were particularly successful at converting Whigs to their cause. The primary agenda of the Know-Nothings consisted of diminishing or even eliminating the power of the immigrant voter by extending the naturalization period to 21 years.

The Know-Nothings only fielded a candidate in one presidential election. In 1856 they nominated former president Millard Fillmore to run against JAMES BUCHANAN, the Democratic nominee, and John C. Frémont, nominee of the newly formed REPUBLICAN PARTY. In losing to Buchanan, Fillmore attracted 22 percent of the vote and won eight electoral votes. Ultimately, however, the Know-Nothing agenda proved less compelling than Republican arguments about the spread of SLAVERY. Shortly after 1856, the Know-Nothing Party disbanded. Although the Know-Nothing movement did not achieve its goal, it did provide the final blow to the faltering WHIG PARTY and furthered the nation's growing sectional division.

Further reading: Ray Allen Billington, *The Protestant Crusade, 1800–1860: A Study of the Origins of American Nativism* (Chicago: Quadrangle Books, 1964); John Higham, *Strangers in the Land: Patterns of American Nativism, 1860–1925* (1955; reprint, New Brunswick, N.J.: Rutgers University Press, 1994); David Roediger, *The Wages of Whiteness: Race and the Making of the American Working Class* (New York: Verso, 1999).

—Rebecca Dresser

New Orleans, Battle of (April 18–25, 1862)

A great Union victory of the CIVIL WAR occurred with the surrender of New Orleans on April 25, 1862. Control of the MISSISSIPPI RIVER was a major Union objective, and the capture of New Orleans was a crucial part of that control. During the 1850s, New Orleans ranked as one of the Confederacy's most important cities. Not only did it lie at the mouth of a major supply and TRANSPORTATION route, it was also a major banking city. When New Orleans fell, the North gained more than just strategic geographic control.

As part of a two-pronged plan to gain control of the Mississippi River, Union Flag Officer DAVID GLASGOW FARRAGUT led a squadron of IRONCLADS and wooden vessels from the Gulf of Mexico to the mouth of the Mississippi. A veteran of the War of 1812 and the Mexican-American War, the 60-year-old Farragut drew upon extensive military experience. Confederate forces, who wrongly assumed that the attack on New Orleans would come from the area north of the city, inadequately defended the forts guarding the entrance to the Mississippi River.

Union ships, however, did not get through without a fight. Confederate garrisons opened fire with approximately 90 guns; the ships responded with twice as much firepower. Southern gunboats attempted to sink Union naval vessels but succeeded only in sinking the Union's *Varuna*. Confederates also tried to use fire as a weapon. Tugboats pushed flaming rafts toward Union ships and into the path of moving vessels.

In one and a half hours, all but four of the Union vessels managed to get past the one-mile area near the two forts and quickly traveled upriver to New Orleans. Thirty-seven Union men died in the initial battle and another 147 were wounded. Although they suffered fewer human losses, the Confederate garrisons ultimately mutinied and surrendered to Union forces.

As Farragut's men moved into New Orleans, an angry armed mob met them. Other rebel supporters burned bales of cotton. Despite this, the large guns of the Northern military easily subdued the largely civilian population of the Southern city. Union control was quickly established even though New Orleans' mayor refused to surrender. Federal leaders responded by raising the Union flag over city hall.

On May 1, 1862, Maj. Gen. BENJAMIN F. BUTLER led a fresh army of 15,000 troops to occupy New Orleans for the remainder of the war. The Union thus gained control of the Confederacy's largest and most international city. In coming months, Farragut used New Orleans as a base to launch successful campaigns against Baton Rouge, Louisiana, and Natchez, Mississippi, which further secured Union control of the Mississippi River.

The capture of New Orleans proved easier than maintaining peace. Many New Orleans citizens refused to recognize Butler and the UNION ARMY as their rulers. Upper-class women, in particular, went out of their way to be rude and disrespectful to the Federals. In retaliation, just two weeks after the city surrendered, Butler issued an order that equated these women with prostitutes. An uproar ensued, and for this and other reasons, the controversial Butler was reassigned. Nevertheless, Union control of New Orleans and large parts of Louisiana benefited the Union cause and made a war hero of David Farragut.

Further reading: Gerald Mortimer Capers, *Occupied City: New Orleans under the Federals, 1862–1865* (Lexington: University of Kentucky Press, 1965); Charles L. Dufour, *The Night the War Was Lost* (Lincoln: University of Nebraska Press, 1994).

—Samantha Holtkamp Gervase

New Orleans, Louisiana, riot (July 30, 1866)

The New Orleans riot in 1866 was one of several postwar civil disturbances that demonstrated to the North that white ex-Confederates were not accepting of Unionism and EMANCIPATION. Immediately after the CIVIL WAR ended, Northerners had turned their sights to governing the South. Angered by the refusal of the Louisiana legislature to grant African-American men the right to vote, and spurred by the enactment of BLACK CODES, RADICAL REPUBLICANS reconvened the Louisiana constitutional convention of 1864. Approximately 200 African-American Civil War VETERANS joined the 25 white delegates who arrived in New Orleans for the convention. This show of support by African Americans upset white former Confederates who felt that Louisiana would fall out of Southern white control and into the hands of freedmen and Northerners.

On July 30, 1866, the ex-Confederates and local residents along with New Orleans police attacked both the white delegates and African-American supporters. Although they raised white flags of surrender, delegates and supporters were shot as they fled the convention proceedings. In all, the fighting injured 100 persons. Rioters also killed 34 African Americans and three Northern white Radical Republicans. Witnesses remembered the riot being as violent as some of the Civil War battles in which they had participated. Although federal troops were called in to mediate the conflict, they arrived too late to help.

The New Orleans riot became an important benchmark for Northerners, illustrating the necessity of a firm RECONSTRUCTION policy. Along with the establishment of Black Codes, the disturbance helped Radical Republicans win a decisive victory in the November 1866 election.

See also MEMPHIS RIOTS.

Further reading: James G. Hollandsworth, *An Absolute Massacre: The New Orleans Race Riot of July 30, 1866* (Baton Rouge: Louisiana State University Press, 2001); Gilles Vandal, *The New Orleans Riot of 1866: Anatomy of* *a Tragedy* (Lafayette: Center for Louisiana Studies, University of Southwestern Louisiana, 1983).

—Samantha Holtkamp Gervase

New York City, New York

By the middle decades of the 19th century, New York had become the biggest, wealthiest, and noisiest city in the United States. One observer exclaimed after a visit to the city that it "always kills me—dazzles, dizzies, astonishes, confounds, and overpowers poor little me." New York City, then as now, was the financial capital of the country.

In 1850, a dozen years after the arrival of the first transatlantic steamer out of Great Britain, New York City was already handling half of U.S. imports and one-third of its exports. Railways developed extensively during the 1850s, so that the city was handling more rail tonnage than Philadelphia and Baltimore combined. The extensive trafficking of goods created an upsurge in the banking business; 600 of the nation's 700 commercial banks maintained permanent accounts in New York to facilitate international transactions. Attracted by investment capital, hundreds of brokerage houses opened in New York City in the 1850s, helping to pull the stock market out of a depression.

Other ventures, such as insurance, prospered as well. Seventy-one of the 95 New York City insurance companies existing in 1860 had been established in the previous decade. New York became the fastest growing manufacturing center in the world. In 1855 one of every 15 people employed in U.S. manufacturing worked on Manhattan Island.

Manhattan also became the nation's information center. As terminus of the first transatlantic TELEGRAPH transmission in 1858, New York City celebrated its position as a link between Old and New Worlds. The city's telegraph system was used to link police stations, to coordinate train schedules, and to set security prices for the nation via the Stock Exchange. New York's journalists became particularly dependent on the telegraph. They used it to collect news and other information, and in the process they transformed their newspapers.

The booming city was home to both major national political parties, who headquartered in New York City to have easy access to campaign contributors and organizational talent. Of course, local politics were also important in New York. William Tweed embarked on a fateful political career in 1851. By 1869 he had risen through New York City political channels to effectively control the city and the state. If corruption reigned with Tweed's "machine," so did reform movements flourish. Tweed's downfall in the early 1870s was accomplished with the help of reformers and crusading newspaper reporters.

Great wealth and great poverty dominated New York City's landscape. The lavish mansions of families like the Astors and the Vanderbilts were built on the most stylish street in America, Fifth Avenue. FASHION was set in New York, where fancy hotels boasted 500 rooms and restaurants hired French waiters. THEATERS flourished between Union and Madison Squares along Broadway. Department stores also graced Broadway Street, and middle- and upper-class women shopped on the so-called Ladies' Mile in the afternoons.

New York City was the place where the most influential newspapers were published; it was also the center of the book, journal, and magazine publishing industry. By 1860 New York dominated newspaper publishing, producing more than 37 percent of the nation's publishing revenue with only 2 percent of the population.

Monumental cultural institutions such as the Metropolitan Museum of ART and the American Natural History Museum were established in the late 1860s and 1870s to enlighten and bring pleasure to those so inclined. Beautiful Central Park, the largest open-space park in the country, assumed its modern form just after the CIVIL WAR.

New York's ECONOMY was tightly bound to Southern cotton. The Civil War interrupted this commerce, and in 1861 New York experienced a panic. Democratic mayor Fernando Wood, known as a champion of workingmen, advocated a neutral position for the city. Wood abandoned his suggestion in the wave of patriotic fervor after FORT SUMTER. In fact, the mayor authorized loans to equip Union recruits and to care for their dependents.

Many of the famed Union ethnic regiments originated in New York City. Later, the city was the site of the NEW YORK CITY DRAFT RIOTS that broke out in July 1863, the most deadly civil riot in the country's history. Overall, New York City quickly recovered from its loss of revenues from the South. The city's industrial output nearly outpaced that of the entire Confederacy. The exuberance continued after the war as New York City's growth and development exceeded every other city in the United States.

Alongside the power and the glory, however, was the reality of a teeming mass of immigrants whose lives were restricted to hard work and poverty. New York City was the entry to the vast majority of 19th-century immigrants; three of four European immigrants between 1840 and 1860 entered the country through Castle Island in the Port of New York. More than 3 million immigrants arrived in New York City over that period, but only one of every six remained in the metropolitan area. Still, that meant an increase of 750,000 inhabitants.

Out of sight and mind to comfortable New Yorkers, Irish Americans and members of other ethnic groups built the infrastructure—trains, subways, bridges, and skyscrapers—that sustained New York's remarkable economic growth to the end of the 19th century. The Irish settlements with long muddy streets and little wooden shacks offered a stark contrast to the ostentatious display of wealth in affluent neighborhoods. Homeless children lived in slums alongside the beggars, drifters, thieves, and prostitutes of the most notorious and crime-ridden wards (local government units) of New York.

Even for the wealthy, New York City streets had a distinctly unpleasant side, as manure from the endless parade of horse-drawn carriages, streetcars, and delivery wagons was deposited by the tons on the streets, the odor pervasive. Despite its drawbacks, New York City became the magnet for ambitious people from all over the country and, indeed, the world.

See also CITIES AND URBAN LIFE; IMMIGRATION.

Further reading: Edwin G. Burrows and Mike Wallace, *Gotham: A History of New York City to 1898* (New York: Oxford University Press, 1999); George J. Lankevich, *American Metropolis: A History of New York City* (New York: New York University Press, 1998); Ernest A. McKay, *The Civil War and New York City* (Syracuse, N.Y.: Syracuse University Press, 1990).

—Richard J. Roder

New York City draft riots (July 13–17, 1863)
Between July 13 and July 17, 1863, a massive social disturbance wracked NEW YORK CITY. The draft riots resulted in more than 100 deaths and the destruction of numerous city structures, making this event the most deadly urban revolt in American history up to that time. The riots also revealed social divisions within metropolitan society in the 19th century, as political and racial tensions exploded in a single week of mayhem.

In March 1863 the Republican-controlled government passed the CONSCRIPTION ACT, a piece of legislation that made all men aged 20 to 35 and all unmarried men between 35 and 45 eligible for the draft. By this time, the CIVIL WAR was not going well for the North. Tensions between Northern Democrats and Republicans over the conduct and continuance of the conflict were increasing throughout the Union. The TELEGRAPHic press reported horrific stories of gory violence daily. There was a sense of uncertainty over the aims and possible outcome of the Civil War.

The unpopularity of the conflict was compounded by the Conscription Act. Perhaps the most distressing aspect of the act was a commutation clause that allowed draftees to pay $300 to avoid service. This was seen by many poor white people as evidence of a common sentiment: that this was a rich man's war but a poor man's fight. Many poor Democrats felt that the wealthy Republican elite was

intent on carrying out a war while avoiding combat themselves.

A racial dimension exacerbated the tension. The Conscription Act was the latest in a series of Republican actions that were increasingly unpopular among many white Northerners. The EMANCIPATION PROCLAMATION, carried out several months earlier, was seen as threatening to working-class white people, who feared the competition of Southern black workers migrating into their cities. The Conscription Act itself declared that all "citizens" must register, and in 1863 this excluded African Americans, which contributed to the racist notion that white people were being unfairly sent to fight for a party that catered specifically to African Americans. Most white people at this time considered black people to be inferior to them, and lower-class white people felt threatened by the intrusion and social ascent (slight as it might have been) of African Americans. One distressed Anglo-American noted that "[they] say that [poor white people] are sold for $300 whilst they pay $1,000 for negroes."

The pressure created by racial hatred and working-class anxiety exploded in violence in New York City on Monday, July 13, 1863. Four hours before the draft was to begin there, hundreds of workers went on strike as a form of protest, meeting at Central Park for an antidraft rally. This was followed by a mass of people marching in a parade to the draft office carrying "No Draft" placards. Soon, things turned violent.

The first acts of violence were relatively minor. A few telegraph poles were cut down, and a hardware store was broken into and the axes inside stolen. Events quickly escalated, however, as Irish women used crowbars to uproot railroad tracks and small crowds of men attacked police officers. By noon, business had halted and the draft office had been burned to the ground.

The draft riots continued for the next four days, resulting in an unprecedented level of destruction and carnage. Police and firemen were violently attacked as symbols of hated authority. Because of this, they could not do their jobs as buildings burned and other people were assaulted. Rioters also focused their vengeance toward issues unrelated to the draft. Representatives of the Republican elite, symbols of pro-Union patriotism, and the city's population of African Americans were all targets. Pro-Republican and pro-ABOLITIONist newspaper buildings were burned down as well as those used as federal government offices. The homes of noted abolitionists were ransacked, forcing some to flee to the homes of sympathetic friends outside the city. American flags were even torn down, and some crowds shouted hurrahs for JEFFERSON DAVIS, the president of the Confederacy.

African Americans soon found themselves victims of the mobs. Blacks were harassed and assaulted by violent

Engraving depicting a scene from the New York draft riots
(Library of Congress)

groups of white people. Any African American caught in the streets by the mob quickly found his or her life in danger. Some African Americans were lynched, their bodies afterward mutilated. A black orphanage was even set aflame. In all, 11 African Americans perished during the riotous week.

The draft riots ended after Union troops, detached from nearby Gettysburg, Pennsylvania, were mobilized to stop the unrest. Once the soldiers arrived in New York, they met with the crowd head-on and occasionally exchanged fire with them. Eventually, some 6,000 soldiers occupied the city. By Friday, July 17, the riots were suppressed and order reigned once again.

In addition to the 11 African Americans killed, two police officers, eight soldiers, and 84 white rioters died during the draft riots. Countless others were wounded. The damage to property was about $1.5 million. The draft resumed again on August 19, but the New York City Council voted to hire substitutes for all those drafted in order to avoid another riot.

Historians have shown that the draft riots actually consisted of two phases. The first phase lasted from Monday morning through the early afternoon of the same day. This phase was marked by rioters who conceived of the violence as a demonstration of resistance against Republican leaders and what was seen as an unfair law. These rioters felt unjustly targeted by the Conscription Act and more specifically by the Republicans in power.

The second phase started Tuesday morning with the burning of Republican-related buildings. On this day, the most vicious assaults on African Americans began to occur, and the original leaders of the draft protest disappeared from the scene. Some of the people involved in the first day's protests even tried to stop the violence, though with little success. By mid-week the turmoil had reached its peak.

Largely carried out by working-class Americans (though not necessarily the poorest citizens) against those perceived to threaten their interests, the draft riots reveal much about racial, class, and political divisions in the North in the mid-19th century. The attacks on African Americans by large mobs of Irish-Catholic immigrants reflected older tensions resulting from the influx of black laborers into areas of unskilled labor that the marginalized Irish-American population struggled to control. Earlier in the same year, shipping companies had employed black laborers to break a longshoreman's strike of largely Irish workers in New York, causing uneasiness within the Irish-American community.

The draft riots can also be understood as a means of comprehending the impact of the Civil War on 19th-century urbanites. Different groups of poor immigrants competed for jobs and political power in New York City during this time, and the riots illustrate one of the ways that working people expressed their grievances over conditions that they felt were oppressive. The targets of worker grievances, namely buildings of the Republican-dominated government and local African Americans, were representative of perceived threats to the independence and livelihood of many poor white people.

After the riots, fears of social upheaval remained a constant threat for many years. A book on the subject referred to the "volcano under the city" that could erupt at any time.

See also IMMIGRATION; NATIVISM.

Further reading: Iver Bernstein, *The New York City Draft Riots: Their Significance for American Society and Politics in the Age of the Civil War* (New York: Oxford University Press, 1990).

—Troy Rondinone

nurses

The great medical demands of the CIVIL WAR accelerated the development of the nursing profession in America. While the first official nursing school was not opened until 1872, many on-the-job courses of training were available in medical relief and support during the war.

For the Union, Dr. Elizabeth Blackwell and Louisa Lee Schuyler helped form the Ladies (later "Women's") Central Relief Committee shortly after the war began. The committee's many duties included identifying the army's nursing needs, creating a bureau for examining and registering nurses, and coordinating medical relief efforts. The committee later participated in the successful petition sent to President Abraham LINCOLN for the UNITED STATES SANITARY COMMISSION. The earliest nurses training program in the country was begun in NEW YORK CITY under the auspices of the Women's Central Relief Committee. Also, early in the war the Union appointed Dorothea Dix, a mental-health activist, to supervise a federal office. Dix attempted to set qualifications for becoming a nurse (to discourage young glory seekers), but others like New Jersey's Cornelia Hancock and the famed CLARA BARTON saw the great need for volunteer care and bypassed official channels. Dix's power was diminished in 1863 when Surgeon General William Hammond authorized male surgeons to make staff assignments for nurses.

In the Confederacy, Juliet Opie Hopkins operated a makeshift hospital in RICHMOND from the outset of the war, and the government hired paid female nurses in 1862. Slaves also participated in menial nursing work, often assisting the volunteer white nurses who were their owners. The majority of the nurses (about 60 percent) during the Civil War were men. Injured and ill soldiers were detailed as nurses as soon as they were mobile, serving until they recovered sufficiently to return to their units. However, some civilian men volunteered as nurses, such as poet WALT WHITMAN, who worked in hospitals in WASHINGTON, D.C.

Women who served as nurses had to overcome many obstacles and performed hard work under horrendous conditions. One barrier was the overwhelming societal concern with modesty and virtue; for instance, one potential nurse from Alabama inquired whether "young ladies" would be expected to dress abdominal wounds or witness amputations. Mothers who wished to become nurses had to send their children to relatives, hire housekeepers, or bring their children along out of economic necessity. Many women were pressed into nursing duties in or near their homes at major battle sites. Such was the case for the Northern women of Sharpsburg, Maryland, and Gettysburg, Pennsylvania, and the Southern women of Vicksburg, Mississippi, Atlanta, Georgia, and countless other places.

Civil War nurses performed a wide range of tasks, many of them custodial. They constantly strove for cleanliness, tending hospital wards, washing ambulances, cleaning wounds, and bathing soldiers. They distributed food and medicine, and sometimes their duties extended to cooking and laundry. Women who were slaves, CONTRABAND, or working class were relegated exclusively to such menial tasks. A runaway from South Carolina, SUSIE KING TAYLOR, who became regimental laundress for the 33rd U.S. Colored Troops, exemplified how roles often expanded; she cleaned weapons, cared for horses and livestock, nursed soldiers with smallpox and typhoid, and taught them to read and write.

Nurses often were expected to help the wounded write home or to read LETTERS aloud when soldiers proved unable. In fact, nurses sometimes acted as unofficial religious counselors at the request of dying soldiers, administering last rites or accepting conversions. Some nurses claimed the role of recruiter, often convincing convalescent soldiers to switch allegiances. Women nurses added a degree of humanitarianism, refusing to give up on dying soldiers when doctors declared their injuries untreatable, standing in the way of amputations when they felt them unnecessary, or just by providing words and deeds of kindness and sympathy.

The typical female nurse in the Civil War was white, middle class, and single or widowed. Women hired as nurses in the North made $12 per month with a daily ration, and cooks and laundresses made $6 to $10 per month. Confederate nurses received better pay, as much as $40 per month, but they had less buying power due to inflation and shortages. In all, approximately 30,000 women performed nursing work during the Civil War. By the end of the war, many hundreds of women, having served four years or more, could claim to be war VETERANS. The U.S. government in 1892 finally granted a monthly pension to nurses (excluding cooks and laundresses) who could prove at least six months of service. In the postbellum period, some of the women with war experience continued their important nursing roles or entered nursing administration or related medical fields. Many others took their newfound confidence into EDUCATION, JOURNALISM, social activism, or governmental work.

See also LADIES AID SOCIETIES; MEDICINE AND HOSPITALS.

Further reading: Thomas J. Brown, *Dorothea Dix: New England Reformer* (Cambridge, Mass.: Harvard University Press, 1998); Mary Gardner Holland, *Our Army Nurses: Stories from Women in the Civil War* (Roseville, Minn., Edinborough Press, 1998); Stephen B. Oates, *A Woman of Valor: Clara Barton and the Civil War* (New York: Free Press, 1994); Walt Whitman, *Memoranda during the War & Death of Abraham Lincoln* (Westport, Conn.: Greenwood Press, 1972).

—Richard J. Roder

Oates, William C. (1833–1910)

Lawyer, Confederate officer, and politician, William Calvin Oates was born on November 30, 1833, in Pikes County, Alabama. His parents, William and Sarah Oates, were poor farmers in the southeastern Alabama frontier. The first of eight children, William had little EDUCATION and was reared in a strict environment that stressed RELIGION and hard work. After a period of youthful rebellion, William settled down in Abbeville in Henry County and worked as a teacher, lawyer, and political activist in the state's DEMOCRATIC PARTY. In 1860 Oates opposed SECESSION, but after FORT SUMTER, he volunteered enthusiastically and raised his own company, the Henry Pioneers.

Captain Oates's company joined the 15th Alabama Volunteer Regiment, which fought with the Army of Northern Virginia in most of the major battles of the eastern theater. Oates, a large, bearded man who took to military life easily, was considered a good officer by his men. By the time he arrived on the Gettysburg battlefield on the afternoon of July 2, 1863, he was the lieutenant colonel of the 15th Alabama, part of Evander Laws's brigade in JOHN BELL HOOD's division and attached to JAMES LONGSTREET's corps. Ordered with his brigade to attack the far left of the Union line at a small hill named Little Round Top, Oates shouted, "Forward, men, to the ledge!" The battle raged back and forth for more than an hour, with the 15th Alabama retreating after the famous bayonet charge of the 20th Maine. Oates fought in several other notable battles and lost his arm to an injury in Petersburg in August 1864.

After the war, Oates returned to Abbeville, determined to rebuild the South. Affectionately called "the one-armed hero of Henry County," Oates established a successful law practice and was elected to the state legislature. He worked hard to reestablish the Democratic Party in Alabama during RECONSTRUCTION. Not a racial progressive, he nevertheless detested the KU KLUX KLAN's methods, preferring nonviolent means of subverting the African-American vote.

In the 1880s and 1890s, Oates served in the U.S. Congress, where he developed a reputation as an excellent legislator, always supportive of Southern interests. In 1894 Oates was elected and served two years as governor of Alabama. He spent the last years of his life giving speeches at VETERANS' reunions and writing his memoirs. William C. Oates died in Montgomery, Alabama, in 1910.

See also GETTYSBURG, BATTLE OF; LOST CAUSE, THE.

Further reading: Mark Perry, *Conceived in Liberty: Joshua Chamberlain, William Oates, and the American Civil War* (New York: Viking Press, 1997).

Olmsted, Frederick Law (1822–1903)

Landscape architect and author Frederick Law Olmsted was born April 26, 1822, in Hartford, Connecticut. Olmsted rose to prominence with his designs for New York's Central Park, Boston's Emerald Necklace, and the 1893 World's Columbian Exposition. In addition to his landscape work, Olmsted was a journalist and an administrator.

After leaving home and school at the age of 18, Olmsted embarked on a varied career path. During the 1850s, at the urging of *New York Daily Times* editor Henry J. Raymond, Olmsted traveled the southern United States, gathering information and writing essays on SLAVERY and the South. These essays were later published in a series of volumes: *A Journey in the Seaboard Slave States* (1856), *A Journey through Texas* (1857), and *A Journey in the Back Country* (1860). The essays were highly critical of the slave South, and Olmsted made unflattering comparisons with the free-labor system in the North. Olmsted went on to pursue JOURNALISM as a career until 1857, when he was appointed as superintendent of NEW YORK CITY's Central Park, still in the planning process. While working as superintendent, Olmsted and architect Calvert Vaux submitted a design for Central Park. Their plan, called "Greensward," was selected as the park's ultimate plan.

257

Desiring to contribute to the Union war effort, Olmsted took a leave of absence in 1861 to serve as executive secretary of the UNITED STATES SANITARY COMMISSION (USSC). The commission acted as a citizen advisory and investigative board that supplemented the Army Medical Bureau. Eventually, the commission became a political power, advocating health-care reforms. As part of its services, the commission aided soldiers in various capacities, including providing medical supplies, inspecting and supplying military hospitals, and recruiting NURSES. Olmsted served for two years with the USSC and then moved to California.

In 1865 Olmsted returned to New York and his work with Vaux. As the champion of the "City Beautiful Movement," Olmsted aimed to create city parks as oases of calm and harmony for people of all classes. Olmsted, both in partnership with Vaux and on his own, designed city parks in Buffalo, New York; Chicago; and Boston. The 1893 World's Fair in Chicago showed off new industrial forms and included a "dream city" based on his architectural plans. In addition to city parks, Olmsted designed community developments, such as Riverside, Illinois (a Chicago suburb), some individual homes, and parts of Stanford University and the University of California, Berkeley.

Olmsted's own architectural landscaping philosophies and design ideas left marks not only in the cities in which he built parks but also in those where his followers worked. For example, an Olmsted disciple built San Francisco's Golden Gate Park. Olmsted changed the way Americans viewed architecture and the urban world. He died on August 28, 1903.

See also CITIES AND URBAN LIFE.

Further reading: Charles E. Beveridge, *Frederick Law Olmsted: Designing the American Landscape* (New York: Universe Publications, 1998); Frederick Law Olmsted, *Defending the Union: The Civil War and the U.S. Sanitary Commission, 1861–1863,* ed. Jane Turner Censer (Baltimore, Md.: Johns Hopkins University Press, 1986); Witold Rybczynski, *A Clearing in the Distance: Frederick Law Olmsted and America in the Nineteenth Century* (New York: Scribner, 1999).

—Samantha Holtkamp Gervase

Orphan Brigade

Orphan Brigade is one of several names, including Kentucky Brigade and First Kentucky Brigade, for the Kentucky infantry brigade that served primarily with the Confederate Army of Tennessee. The origin of the name *Orphan Brigade* is not certain. By one account, Gen. John C. Breckinridge (a division commander whose command included the Kentucky Brigade) coined the name after a disastrous attack at the BATTLE OF MURFREESBORO in which the brigade's commander Roger W. Hanson died. Riding among the survivors, he reportedly exclaimed, "My poor orphan brigade! They have cut it to pieces!" Most likely, however, the name emerged during the postwar period, reflecting the VETERANS' memories of being cut off from home throughout the war. The name was popularized after 1882 by *Southern Bivouac* magazine.

The brigade was created during the summer and fall of 1861 and consisted of pro-Confederate Kentuckians from no less than 32 counties. Prevented by their state's neutrality to organize within Kentucky, these units gathered in two camps of instruction (Boone and Burnett) near Clarkesville in northern Tennessee, where they were formed into four infantry regiments, three artillery batteries, and a squadron of cavalry. For most of its service, the brigade consisted of the Second, Fourth, Fifth, Sixth, and Ninth Kentucky infantry regiments and Robert Cobb's battery of artillery. Roughly in this form, the brigade fought at Fort Donelson; Shiloh; the summer 1862 defense of Vicksburg; Murfreesboro; Jackson, Mississippi; Chickamauga; Missionary Ridge; and the ATLANTA CAMPAIGN. Virtually destroyed during the summer 1864 campaign in Georgia, the Kentucky Brigade was reorganized as mounted infantry under Confederate cavalry commander JOSEPH WHEELER and helped resist SHERMAN'S MARCH THROUGH GEORGIA. During the last months of the war, the Kentuckians operated in west-central South Carolina and east Georgia. Five hundred men, of an original 4,500, officially surrendered at Washington, Georgia, on May 6–7, 1865.

Following the CIVIL WAR, former members of the brigade made significant contributions to Kentucky public life. A partial list of positions held by brigade veterans includes many state legislators, U.S. district attorneys, superintendents of public instruction, one GOVERNOR, three cabinet members, six militia leaders, two state supreme court justices, four congressmen, a mayor of Louisville, and one nominee for vice president of the United States.

See also CHATTANOOGA, BATTLE OF; CHICKAMAUGA, BATTLE OF; SHILOH, BATTLE OF; VICKSBURG CAMPAIGN.

Further reading: William C. Davis, *The Orphan Brigade: The Kentucky Confederates Who Couldn't Go Home* (Garden City, N.Y.: Doubleday, 1980); John S. Jackman, *Diary of a Confederate Soldier: John S. Jackman of the Orphan Brigade,* ed. William C. Davis (Columbia: University of South Carolina Press, 1990).

—James Daryl Black

Ostend Manifesto (1854)

The Ostend Manifesto was a statement prepared in 1854 by U.S. ministers to Great Britain, France, and Spain meeting in Ostend, Belgium. The statement recommended that the United States either buy the island of Cuba from Spain or, if Spain refused to sell, take the island by force.

While most of the rest of Latin America had gained its independence in the revolutions of the 1810s and 1820s, Cuba had remained a Spanish colony. The island's value to Spain was in its sugar PLANTATIONS. Worked by 400,000 African-Cuban slaves, the plantations produced one-third of the world's sugar, with considerable profit both for planters and the Spanish government.

Advocates of U.S. expansionism had set their sights on Cuba as early as the 1810s. For these Americans, Spanish control was an affront to the independence movements that had swept the Western Hemisphere between 1776 and 1830. Some also argued that Cuba, a mere 90 miles from Florida, might at some future date pose a threat to United States security. The greatest enthusiasm for Cuba came from pro-slave Southerners, who saw the island as a stepping stone toward U.S. control of a "golden circle" of SLAVERY extending around the entire Caribbean Sea and Gulf of Mexico. All these views were summed up by a contributor to *De Bow's Review*, who in 1850 declared, "[T]he possession of Cuba is indispensable. . . . Call it the lust of dominion, the relentlessness of democracy, the passion for land and gold, or the desire to render our interior impregnable by commanding the keys of the Gulf—the possession of Cuba is still an American sentiment."

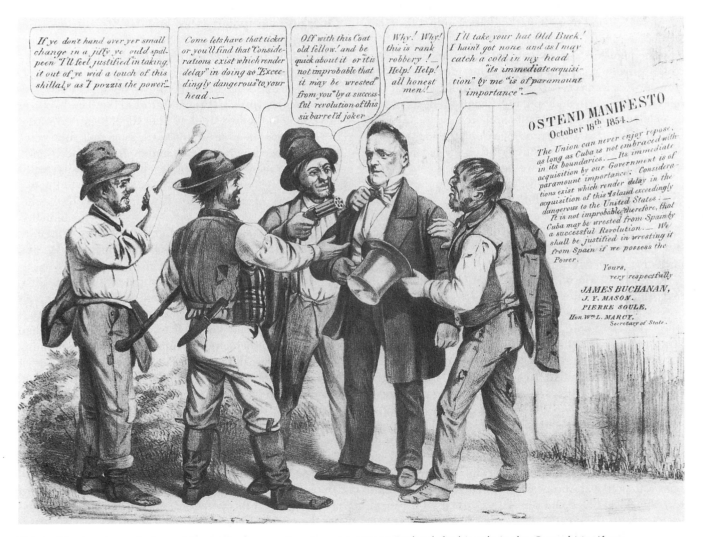

This political cartoon singles out James Buchanan, American minister to England, for his role in the Ostend Manifesto controversy. *(Library of Congress)*

With U.S. victory in the Mexican-American War, expansionists insisted that the United States annex Cuba. In 1848 President James K. Polk offered Spain $100 million for the island, earning an angry Spanish rejection. In 1849, 1850, and 1851, FILIBUSTERING expeditions were organized to drive the Spanish from Cuba. Some senators criticized Southern "marauding" from U.S. shores, but Southerners such as Louisiana senator Pierre Soule defended the expeditions.

When President FRANKLIN PIERCE appointed Senator Soule his minister to Spain, Soule immediately set out to negotiate Cuba's purchase on behalf of the United States. However, Soule's blusters, threats, and blunt diplomacy angered Spanish government officials. In the wake of Soule's failure, Pierce's secretary of state, William Marcy, instructed JAMES BUCHANAN, U.S. minister to Britain, and John Mason, U.S. minister to France, to discuss the matter with Soule. The three met in the Belgian city of Ostend in October 1854 and soon drafted a statement that they then sent home to the United States.

The ministers argued first that U.S. purchase of Cuba would prevent the island from failing into the hands of stronger European powers and more deadly potential enemies than Spain. In addition, they painted a bleak picture of a Cuba torn by slave revolts and creating an "Africanized" republic that would present a challenge to the United States. "We should . . . be unworthy of our gallant forefathers," they wrote, "should we permit Cuba to . . . become a second St. Domingo [Haiti], with all its attendant horrors to the white race, and suffer the flames to extend to our own neighboring shores, seriously to endanger or actually to consume the fair fabric of our Union." Outside U.S. control, Cuba represented an "unceasing danger, and a permanent cause of anxiety and alarm."

Buchanan, Mason, and Soule depicted Cuban white people as desperate for liberation from the "extreme oppression" of Spain's "corrupt, arbitrary, and unrelenting" colonial government. They also noted that Spain had proven too weak to halt the illegal importation of slaves from Africa. This, they claimed, was a job only the United States could accomplish. In seizing Cuba, the ministers argued, the United States would be advancing the cause of human rights.

Published throughout the United States and Europe, the Ostend message, called a "manifesto" by its detractors, failed to persuade Spain. The Spanish government, far from being intimidated into selling Cuba, opened discussions with potential European allies to defend Cuba against U.S. attack. At home, antislavery activists used the manifesto to justify the creation of the new REPUBLICAN PARTY and defeat Southern efforts to extend its "slaveocracy" into Latin America.

With the Ostend Manifesto shaping up as a disaster for U.S. foreign relations and for the DEMOCRATIC PARTY, Secretary of State William Marcy disavowed the entire statement, blamed Soule for the debacle, and forced his resignation as minister to Spain.

Though the United States made no further effort to acquire Cuba during the 1850s, the Democratic Party supported annexation of Cuba until the eve of the CIVIL WAR. In 1898 the United States went to war against Spain over Cuba. As a result of the Spanish-American War, Cuba won its independence. However, U.S. involvement in Cuban affairs continued well into the 20th century.

Further reading: David Potter, *The Impending Crisis, 1848–1861* (New York: Harper & Row, 1976).

—Tom Laichas

Overland campaign (May–June 1864)

The Overland campaign was part of the wide-ranging Union effort to win the war after the stunning victories of the summer and fall of 1863. When the approximately 120,000-strong Army of the Potomac (versus Lee's 65,000-man Army of Northern Virginia) crossed the Rapidan River in Virginia in the first week of May 1864, it carried with it the high hopes of a war-weary Northern people for a quick end to the seemingly endless conflict. A weakened South, low in both materiel and morale, could not possibly withstand the mighty numbers and logistical power of the two major Northern armies gathered in Virginia and Tennessee. They were poised to strike and destroy under the direction of Generals ULYSSES S. GRANT and WILLIAM T. SHERMAN, the victors of Shiloh, Vicksburg, and Chattanooga and heroes of the Union's western armies.

At least that was the common wisdom in early 1864. Despite the optimism, there was much reason to be suspicious of an easy victory, as President ABRAHAM LINCOLN and General Grant knew all too well. Experience had demonstrated that superior numbers and overwhelming industrial power did not translate into winning the war, at least not without the kind of military leadership that would bring decisive victory on the battlefield. Leadership was particularly deficient in the hard-luck Army of the Potomac, the Union's principal military unit in the eastern theater, despite its recent (and only) clear-cut victory at Gettysburg under the command of Gen. GEORGE GORDON MEADE. That is why Grant, by this time commander of all Union forces, chose to personally accompany the eastern army and direct its operations, even at the risk of confusing the chain of command. Gen. ROBERT E. LEE was a formidable foe, and his soldiers had bested their opponents in many battles fought in 1862 and 1863 on some of the same ground across which the Army of the Potomac was now marching. Grant's plan for victory was simple and straightforward: Force the Army of Northern Virginia out into the open and defeat them in battle, then "On to RICHMOND." With other Union armies also on the attack, the war could be over shortly, if all went well.

All did not go well, however. The movements of the Overland campaign brought with it the dramatic unraveling of the Union strategy against Lee. Grant's attempt to move swiftly through a thick patch of overgrown brush and trees known locally as the Wilderness (May 5–6) was foiled as Lee adeptly blocked his way and forced a battle, which resulted in a tactical victory for the rebel defenders. The two-day BATTLE OF THE WILDERNESS resulted in 18,000 Union and 11,000 Confederate casualties. A shock for General Lee came when Grant refused to pack up and go home, as so many Union commanders had done before him.

Grant moved south from the Wilderness and brought his army to Spotsylvania Court House, where Lee's men were waiting behind a line of strong earthworks. The BATTLES OF SPOTSYLVANIA raged back and forth for several days. The Confederates fought off repeated Union assaults behind a defensive position known as the "Mule Shoe." On May 12 the Federals broke through a part of Lee's formation, but the Southerners stood their ground for 22 hours of fighting in what came to be called the "Bloody Angle." On May 18, after many days of constant fighting, Grant turned southeast again, but Lee continued to thwart the UNION ARMY's thrusts toward RICHMOND at North Anna River (May 23–27), Totopotomoy Creek (May 26–30), and Bethesda Church (May 30).

The spring of 1864 was one of Lee's finest moments, when he switched from his favored aggressive style to a more defensive approach, thus prolonging the life of the Confederate nation. Weakened by illness, handicapped by the deaths and injuries of Gens. JAMES LONGSTREET, RICHARD S. EWELL, A. P. HILL, and J. E. B. STUART, and faced with a much larger opponent, Lee and his army adapted brilliantly. He knew that the Confederacy's best hopes rested on a failure of Northern will to carry on the war, once the high cost of these battles was widely known. Lee hoped Lincoln would lose the presidency and that a Democratic administration favorable to Southern independence would bring the participants to a conference table. The stakes were high, indeed.

Thus, decisions made by both Grant and Lee (and backed fully by their presidents) turned the war into a relentless, exhausting, horrific experience for the soldiers. Cold Harbor, the misnamed tiny crossroads town deep in rural Virginia, is a case study of the new style of warfare.

The BATTLE OF COLD HARBOR, the last fight of the Overland campaign, began on the morning of June 3, with 59,000 well-entrenched Confederates facing 109,000 Federals across a seven-mile front. The assault was a disaster, and before the end of the day, Grant stopped the fighting. The details of the carnage retain their power to shock and sadden. Grant's massive frontal assault on entrenched Confederate lines failed miserably. That terrible day saw some 7,000 Union casualties compared with less than 1,500 for the rebels, shattered three Union corps, and lent truth to the anguished memories of a Southern soldier who wrote, "It was not war, it was murder."

Grant and Lee's movements across the countryside of Virginia came to an end when Grant ordered the Army of the Potomac to cross the James River and head for Petersburg, the vital rail center of the Confederacy. There, he would stay for 10 months before the fall of Richmond.

The costs of the Overland campaign were huge. For 40 days, Grant had waged a war of attrition in a series of battles that resulted in 60,000 Union losses against approximately 35,000 Confederate. Both sides, however, were determined to prevail and, even in those dark months, found the will to continue fighting. Undeniably, the costs of the war escalated dramatically in 1864, and, undeniably, Ulysses S. Grant, called "the butcher" after Cold Harbor, played a large role in that escalation, as did Robert E. Lee. But the bigger picture must be kept in mind, and that bigger picture is neatly summed up by Gen. Horace Porter, of Grant's staff, who described his superiors' attitude after June 3: "General Grant, with his usual habit of mind, bent all his energies toward consummation of his plans for the future." The Overland campaign, though wasteful and bloody, brought Lee's army to a state of immobility, backed up against Petersburg and Richmond. In the end, Grant's plans, fully endorsed by Lincoln, were consummated, as the armies he commanded successfully defeated the Confederates, restored the Union, and brought (although imperfectly realized) freedom to 4 million slaves.

See also CHATTANOOGA, BATTLE OF; PETERSBURG CAMPAIGN; SHILOH, BATTLE OF; VICKSBURG CAMPAIGN.

Further reading: Gordon C. Rhea, *The Battle of the Wilderness: May 5–6, 1864* (Baton Rouge: Louisiana State University Press, 1994); Gordon C. Rhea, *The Battles for Spotsylvania Courthouse and the Road to Yellow Tavern, May 7–12, 1864* (Baton Rouge: Louisiana State University Press, 1997); David J. Eicher, *The Longest Night: A Military History of the Civil War* (New York: Simon & Schuster, 2001).

P

Pacific Railroad Act (July 1, 1862)

By the 1840s the United States had grown to be a bicoastal nation. Cheap land and gold fever had sparked a westward exodus of Americans that would continue through the end of the century. When traveling by horse or horse-drawn wagons, the trip was long and arduous, with harsh terrain, a punishing climate, and sometimes hostile NATIVE AMERICAN tribes. A better mode of TRANSPORTATION was needed, not only to facilitate migration but also to speed the exchange of manufactured goods and the movement of soldiers and military equipment.

The obvious solution to most Americans was a railroad that would connect the West to the East. RAILROADS had come to the United States in the early part of the 19th century, and by the late 1840s new track was being laid at a brisk pace in the eastern part of the country. On December 9, 1852, the Pacific Railroad of Missouri (or P.R.R.M) made its first trip, in the process becoming the first railroad to travel west of the MISSISSIPPI RIVER. At that point, many Americans sensed that the construction of a transcontinental railroad was imminent.

It was not to be, however. As early as 1832, Congress had begun considering the possibility of building a transcontinental railroad, and invariably plans were stalled by political bickering. Some congressmen were skeptical that a transcontinental railroad could even be built. Included among the naysayers was powerful Senator Daniel Webster, usually a firm advocate of internal improvements. There was also little agreement about how such a project would be paid for—with government money, private capital, or a combination of both. The primary issue of contention, however, was the route that the proposed railroad would follow. Southern leaders and congressmen, led by JEFFERSON DAVIS, argued that the railroad should travel through the South. Northern leaders and congressmen, led by STEPHEN A. DOUGLAS, argued that the railroad should travel through the North. Congress appropriated $150,000 for a survey of four possible routes

with hopes of resolving the problem, but the results of the survey indicated major problems with each of the possible routes, and so the stalemate remained.

The turmoil surrounding the plans for a transcontinental railroad would not be resolved for nearly a decade. Two key developments finally allowed Congress to agree on a plan for action. First, the Southern states left the Union. Second, two independent engineers named Theodore Judah and Grenville Dodge presented complete surveys of a Northern route for the railroad that was not nearly as problematic as other routes that had been considered. With a viable route all mapped out, and no substantial opposition, Congress passed the Pacific Railroad Act, signed into law by President ABRAHAM LINCOLN on July 1, 1862. The act granted two charters, one to Grenville Dodge's employers, who would take the name Union Pacific, and one to Theodore Judah's employers, who would be known as the Central Pacific. The roads' charters granted 10 miles of land for each mile of track laid, plus loans of $16,000 a mile for rail laid on plains, $32,000 a mile for land in the Great Basin, and $48,000 a mile for land in the mountains. The two roads were supposed to meet, though the location where they would do so was not specified.

Although everything was in place for work on the transcontinental railroad to begin, little progress was made over the course of the next four years, because the CIVIL WAR tied up most of the nation's available capital and manpower. In 1866, however, construction began in earnest. The Central Pacific, utilizing mostly Chinese labor, built eastward from Sacramento, California. The Union Pacific, utilizing mostly VETERANS and German and Irish immigrant labor, started in Omaha, Nebraska, and built westward. Constructing the railroad was difficult, dangerous work. In particular, laying tracks through the Rocky Mountains required dynamiting and removing countless tons of rock, all at the expense of dozens of workers' lives.

After three years, the railroads were nearly complete, and the government decreed that they should meet at

Promontory Point, Utah. On May 8, 1869, representatives of the Central Pacific and Union Pacific laid the last rails and hammered in the final spikes. The railroad was complete. Americans took pride in the accomplishment, many believing that the country had fulfilled its "Manifest Destiny" to conquer the North American continent. The Pacific Railroad Act also set a precedent for cooperation between government and private business. Over the course of the next three decades, the federal government would grant 116 million acres in land and would advance $64 million in loans to western railroads. With so much assistance from the government, trans-Mississippi railroad mileage grew from the five miles built in 1852 by the P.R.R.M. to 72,000 miles in 1890. By 1893 there were five different railroads stretching from the Atlantic to the Pacific.

Further reading: David Haward Bain, *Empire Express: Building the First Transcontinental Railroad* (New York: Viking, 1999); Dee Alexander Brown, *Hear That Lonesome Whistle Blow: The Epic Story of the Transcontinental Railroads* (New York: Owl Books, 2001); Alexander P. Saxton, *The Indispensable Enemy: Labor and the Anti-Chinese Movement in California* (1975; reprint, Berkeley: University of California Press, 1995).

—Christopher Bates

Panic of 1857

During the Kansas controversy of 1857, as the dispute over SLAVERY grew more tense, a financial crisis struck the United States. Many northern businessmen and workers blamed the economic slide on the Tariff Act of 1857, in which a Southern and Democratic controlled Congress had lowered duties on imported goods to their lowest rates in nearly 50 years. Before the panic struck in 1857, the United States had enjoyed more than a decade of general economic growth and prosperity. RAILROADS, textiles, AGRICULTURE, and manufacturing all flourished during these years. The number of banks in the country doubled within only a few years in the 1850s, and the prices of stocks and bonds also rose. Some of this expansion was a result of the Crimean War (1854–56), during which western European nations lost access to Russian agricultural products and turned to the United States to make up the difference.

As was the case with previous economic crises, the problems in 1857 were partially international in their origins. Much of America's economic growth was fueled by investment from Europe, especially Britain. The price of American stocks and bonds in 1856 and 1857 began to decline as European nations began to sell off their interests in the United States to pay for their involvement in the Crimean War and other international ventures.

As a result, American banks lost part of their assets, and some enterprises, especially in textiles, suspended operations. The economic good times of the previous decade had encouraged much speculation and borrowing, and much of the growth was fueled by paper money. A run on banks by nervous depositors resulted in the banks calling in loans to pay off their customers with specie. Before long a general panic began to sweep the nation, sped along by a relatively new communications system, the TELEGRAPH, which quickly relayed the increasingly grim financial news around the country.

As with previous panics in 1819 and 1837, the Panic of 1857 saw factory shutdowns, business failures, a steep decline in prices, and a rapid increase in unemployment. In 1857 many railroads, an increasingly important part of the national ECONOMY, went out of business. In several cities there were demonstrations and marches by the unemployed, and one crowd in New York City menaced a federal customshouse on Wall Street that had $20 million in its vaults. Fears of widespread unrest and disorder were unfounded, however. The panic was relatively short-lived and not as severe as it might have been. One thing that did result was a religious revival in which many people, especially in the North, gathered at prayer meetings to reflect on the immorality of extravagant living, believed by some to have contributed to the crisis.

Coming as it did during a tense moment in the growing sectional crisis over slavery, the Panic of 1857 had political implications as well. The new REPUBLICAN PARTY blamed the national's financial troubles on the Democrats, especially the Southerners who had been most responsible for lowering the TARIFFS. The Republicans pledged to work for higher tariff rates, which most Northern manufacturers and workers supported. They also bid for the support of farmers by proposing a HOMESTEAD ACT by which the federal government would give 160 acres of land free of charge to people who would settle on it. These appeals helped the Republicans in the ELECTIONS of 1858 as the nation moved closer to CIVIL WAR.

—Jason Duncan

Parker, Ely Samuel (1828–1895)

Seneca Indian chief, adjutant general in the U.S. Army, and commissioner of the Bureau of Indian Affairs, Ely Samuel Parker was born in 1828 just outside the Tonawanda Reservation in New York. Parker attended a Baptist mission school as a child and later the Yates Cayuga Academies. Parker studied law, but his lack of citizenship (due to his NATIVE AMERICAN heritage) prohibited him from being admitted to the New York bar.

In 1846 Parker lobbied in WASHINGTON, D.C., as a representative of the Tonawanda Reservation and in 1851 became a sachem of the Iroquois (Six Nations) Confederacy. Six years later, he negotiated a treaty that enabled the Tonawanda Seneca to purchase two-thirds of their reservation land back from the United States.

When the CIVIL WAR began, Parker proposed raising a New York regiment of Iroquois soldiers and offered his engineering services to the UNION ARMY. Both offers were refused. In 1863 he obtained an appointment as a captain in the U.S. Army and soon served with Gen. ULYSSES S. GRANT at the Battle of Vicksburg. Parker later served as Grant's aide-de-camp during the 1864–65 campaign against the Army of Northern Virginia. On April 7, 1865, Parker was present at the surrender at the APPOMATTOX COURT HOUSE.

After the war, Parker helped negotiate treaties with several Indian tribes, and in 1869 Grant appointed him commissioner of the Bureau of Indian Affairs. He was the first Native American to hold that office. Parker shaped the Grant administration's controversial "Peace Plan," which abolished the treaty system and advocated the assimilation and Christianization of Native peoples. In 1871 Parker resigned that commission after being accused of fraud by the U.S. Senate. He was later exonerated.

Parker moved to Fairfield, Connecticut, where he struggled as a businessman and investor. His fortune lost and political connections no longer in power, Parker finally took a position as a clerk for the NEW YORK CITY Police Board of Commissions. Parker died on August 30, 1895, of complications from diabetes.

Further reading: William Armstrong, *Warrior in Two Camps: Ely S. Parker, Union General and Seneca Chief* (Syracuse, N.Y.: Syracuse University Press, 1978).

—Andrew K. Frank

Pea Ridge/Elkhorn Tavern, Battle of

(March 7–8, 1862)
The Battle of Pea Ridge, Arkansas, was an important and clear-cut Union victory in which the usual numbers disparity was reversed, with 14,000 Confederates outnumbering the 11,250 Federals. Most important, the Northern victory secured the Union's hold on the border state of Missouri.

Early in 1862, Union major general Samuel R. Curtis, commander of the Army of the Southwest, was charged with driving the Confederate forces out of Missouri once and for all. The 8,000 Missourians under the command of Confederate brigadier general Sterling Price left Missouri for a safer position in northwestern Arkansas. There, Price combined his units with those of Brig. Gen. Ben McCulloch, just south of Fayetteville, Arkansas. At Fayetteville, the commander of the trans-Mississippi District, Maj. Gen. Earl Van Dorn, joined Price and McCul-

loch. Van Dorn was now in charge of the campaign. An aggressive general, Van Dorn wished to recapture the ground that the Confederates had lost in their hasty retreat from Missouri. He planned a surprise attack on the Federals, who had moved into Arkansas. In late February, the ration-starved rebels began their 55-mile advance toward the Union position in the middle of a winter snowstorm.

Curtis heard of Van Dorn's forward movement from his trusted scout "Wild Bill" Hickock. He immediately ordered his infantry units to concentrate on a high ground near Pea Ridge, Arkansas. Supported by artillery and cavalry, the outnumbered Union forces established a superior defensive position, and on March 6 there were a series of inconclusive skirmishes between Northern and Southern troops. Van Dorn, who was sick, directed the Confederate battle plan from an ambulance behind the lines. He wanted to destroy the enemy with a major movement against the left rear of Curtis's army, centered by Elkhorn Tavern.

The battle began in earnest on the morning of March 7. General Price attacked the Union position and was twice repulsed. The third time, he succeeded. At the other end of the line from Price, a Cherokee Indian unit under the command of Brig. Gen. STAND WATIE took on a Union division but failed to achieve any meaningful gains. The end of the first day of fighting brought a stalemate, as neither side retired from the field.

The next day's battle secured the Union victory. Curtis, confident that reports of the lack of Confederate ammunition were true, ordered Gen. Franz Sigel to attack Price's Missourians. Supported effectively by Union artillery, the Federals drove the Confederates from Pea Ridge. The rebels broke in confusion, and Gen. Van Dorn ordered a retreat to the Arkansas River. The causalities were high. The Federals lost 1,384, and the Confederates anywhere from 800 to 1,300, with 300 captured. Despite suffering greater losses, the battle was a Union victory because it achieved their desired objective. Missouri was secured for the Union until a brief, and ultimately futile, Confederate invasion was mounted in the fall of 1864.

See also JAYHAWKERS.

Further reading: William L. Shea and Earl J. Hess, *Pea Ridge: Civil War Campaign in the West* (Chapel Hill: University of North Carolina Press, 1992).

peace movements

Every American war has had its protesters, and the CIVIL WAR was no exception. There were a variety of reasons why people opposed the war. Some individuals rejected warfare as an immoral practice. Others were opposed to the policies being pursued by their government. Still others had simply grown tired of fighting.

There are several religious sects in the United States that object to war on moral grounds. These include the SOCIETY OF FRIENDS (Quakers), the Mennonites, and the Church of the Brethren. Members of these RELIGIONS, called conscientious objectors, have declined to participate in every American military conflict dating back to the Revolutionary War. Often, although not always, conscientious objectors were exempted from military service during the Civil War. Most of these individuals lived in the North and thus benefited from ABRAHAM LINCOLN's sympathy for pacifists. Ultimately, the loss of these conscientious objectors, who comprised a tiny minority of the population, had a very nominal impact on the Union and Confederate armies.

In addition to its pacifist religious sects, the Union had a number of prominent nonreligious pacifists. Noted orators Elihu Burritt and Joshua P. Blanchard objected to the war on moral grounds. Lindley Spring wrote a pamphlet entitled *Peace! Peace!* that urged all soldiers to lay down their arms. In 1863 prominent anarchist Joshua Warren published *True Civilization, an Immediate Necessity,* in which he condemned the war as a barbarian action undertaken only for the betterment of war profiteers. The voices of these men, however, were largely ignored. In part, this was because most Americans rejected the notion that war was inherently immoral, and, in part, it was because a large number of well-known pacifists actually endorsed the Civil War. For example, the American Peace Society issued a statement outlining their position that armed action was appropriate because the Confederacy was guilty of an unlawful rebellion against authority.

The North's largest and most influential peace movement was the peace wing of the DEMOCRATIC PARTY. The Peace Democrats, derisively called COPPERHEADS by their detractors, were in the minority in the North, even in their own party. Nonetheless, under the leadership of CLEMENT L. VALLANDIGHAM, they exerted a great deal of influence among the Northern voters, particularly in Ohio, Indiana, and Illinois. Their objection to the war was based on political rather than moral grounds. They argued that the Lincoln administration was undermining the Constitution and the North's social order through its actions, especially forced CONSCRIPTION, the suspension of HABEAS CORPUS, and EMANCIPATION. The Peace Democrats reached the high point of their influence in the summer of 1864, as the Union armies seemed to be stalemated in the field. At the Democratic convention, they were able to convince party members to include a plank in the party's platform calling for the immediate cessation of hostilities. Gen. GEORGE B. MCCLELLAN, chosen as the party's presidential nominee

shortly thereafter, quickly repudiated this part of the platform. Renewed Union military successes and the reelection of Abraham Lincoln put an end to the Copperheads once and for all.

The peace movements of the South were not as prominent as in the North. Almost invariably they arose from frustration with the war and its conduct rather than from a moral objection to warfare. The boldest move for peace in the South occurred in 1863, shortly after the fall of Vicksburg and the BATTLE OF GETTYSBURG. North Carolina governor Zebulon Vance, who was distraught over Confederate losses and weary of the sacrifices that Southerners were being forced to make, called for a convention to bring about peace and the reunification of the states. In North Carolina, more than 100 peace meetings were held, and throughout the South more than 100,000 people joined secret peace societies. Eventually, the CONFEDERATE ARMY regained some momentum, and sentiment for immediate reunification faded away.

On balance, movements for peace during the Civil War had only a small influence on the conflict. Certainly, there were flare-ups of peace sentiment in both North and South, but it would be difficult to identify any meaningful impact these episodes had on the ultimate outcome of the war. The Peace Democrats came close to achieving their goals, but Union victories in late 1864 ultimately dictated that Lincoln's vision of peace would carry the day.

Further reading: Arthur Alphonse Ekirch, *The Civilian and the Military: A History of the American Antimilitarist Tradition* (Colorado Springs: Ralph Myles Publishers, 1972); Frank L. Klement, *The Limits of Dissent: Clement L. Vallandigham & the Civil War* (New York: Fordham University Press, 1998); Georgia Lee Tatum, *Disloyalty in the Confederacy* (Chapel Hill: University of North Carolina Press, 1934).

—Christopher Bates

Pember, Phoebe Yates Levy (1823–1913)

Born August 18, 1823, in Charleston, South Carolina, Phoebe Yates Levy Pember became a CIVIL WAR hospital administrator and a writer.

Pember was the fourth of seven children to prosperous Jews Fanny Yates and Jacob Levy. In the 1850s the family moved from Charleston to Savannah, Georgia, where they stayed until 1862, when they moved to Marietta, Georgia, to escape the hardships of the war. Before the Civil War, Phoebe married Bostonian Thomas Pember. After he died (July 1861) in Aiken, South Carolina, Pember returned to her family.

Pember's connections to the Southern elite led to a November 1862 offer to become chief matron of a division of RICHMOND's Chimborazo Hospital. This position made Pember the first female administrator at Chimborazo. As head of the second division (Hospital No. 2) Pember oversaw patients' care as well as housekeeping, supplies, and staff issues. She did little medical work, although during emergencies she occasionally dressed wounds. Pember's sex made her job difficult. Male physicians often interfered with her and she endured insults. Pember also had to struggle effectively to manage the hospital with inadequate supplies.

Pember remained a matron of Chimborazo until after Union officials took charge. During this chaotic period, she did whatever she could to help her patients. She refused to leave the hospital until her remaining patients had died or recovered.

After the Civil War, Pember recorded her experiences at Chimborazo in her memoirs, *A Southern Woman's Story.* In this book, she recounted her difficulties as a hospital matron as well as harsh living conditions in Richmond, wartime inflation, and the dangers of wartime travel. She also painted a portrait of the soldiers who fought for the Confederacy.

Pember returned to Georgia after the Civil War. In later years she traveled throughout the United States and died in Pittsburgh on March 4, 1913. She was buried in Savannah.

See also HOMEFRONT; MEDICINE AND HOSPITALS; NURSES.

Further reading: Phoebe Yates Pember, *A Southern Woman's Story: Life in Confederate Richmond, Including Unpublished Letters Written from the Chimborazo Hospital,* ed. Bell Irvin Wiley (St. Simon's Island, Ga.: Mockingbird Books, 1988).

—Lisa Tendrich Frank

Peninsular campaign (March 17–July 1, 1862)
The winter of 1861–62 passed without significant action in Virginia. The principal Union and Confederate armies, commanded respectively by GEORGE B. MCCLELLAN and JOSEPH E. JOHNSTON, remained near Manassas Junction, where they had created extensive opposing lines. McClellan, who functioned as the Union general in chief as well as commander of the Army of the Potomac, devised a plan to turn Johnston's flank by moving troops to the Rappahannock River by ship and taking Fredericksburg. That would isolate Johnston in northern Virginia, forcing him to attack McClellan in order to reach RICHMOND. McClellan delayed his plans, however, until a frustrated ABRAHAM LINCOLN finally ordered him to commence his campaign

on February 22, 1862—George Washington's birthday. When that date came and went without a movement and the first days of March slipped by, Lincoln removed McClellan as general in chief.

Reduced to army command only, McClellan changed his plans when word arrived that Johnston had retreated to the Rappahannock line. On March 17 the Army of the Potomac began a larger turning movement toward Fort Monroe, situated at the tip of the finger of land between the York and James Rivers known as the "Peninsula." By the end of April, Confederate planners faced a range of threats in Virginia: The bulk of the Army of the Potomac lay on the lower Peninsula, with another 30,000 Federals under Irvin McDowell near Fredericksburg, 15,000 under Nathaniel P. Banks in the lower Shenandoah Valley, and nearly 10,000 under John C. Frémont in the Allegheny Mountains west of the valley. Initially, only 17,000 Southern troops under John Bankhead Magruder, positioned between Yorktown and the Warwick River, were available to resist McClellan's movements on the peninsula.

The Confederates soon concentrated more of their forces near Richmond, and they mounted a diversion in the Shenandoah Valley designed to prevent reinforcement of McClellan. Johnston shifted his army to the peninsula, where he contested a slow Union advance toward the capital. Confederates gave up Yorktown on May 3 after a virtually bloodless month-long siege. They continued their withdrawal after the Battle of Williamsburg on May 5, a hard-fought action that resulted in 2,200 Union and 1,750 Confederate casualties. The port of Norfolk, with its immense naval installations, capitulated on May 9.

As the forces under Johnston and McClellan moved slowly toward Richmond, each striving to gain advantage over the other, the IRONCLAD CSS *Virginia* (popularly called the *Merrimack*), which had fought the Union ironclad USS *Monitor* to a draw in their famous duel at Hampton Roads on March 9, was destroyed on May 11. "No one event of the war," remarked Confederate ordnance chief JOSIAH GORGAS from his post in Richmond, "created such a profound sensation as the destruction of this noble ship." Heavy rains drenched the peninsula during May, adding to Confederate gloom over the loss of the *Virginia* and affording McClellan a good excuse for making little headway. The end of the month found the two armies—more than 100,000 Federals and about 70,000 Confederates—arrayed opposite one another along the Chickahominy River just east of Richmond.

Many Confederates believed Johnston was giving up too much ground without a serious fight. A North Carolina diarist had a typical reaction, pointedly contrasting THOMAS J. "STONEWALL" JACKSON's accomplishments in the Shenandoah Valley with Johnston's performance: "Jack-

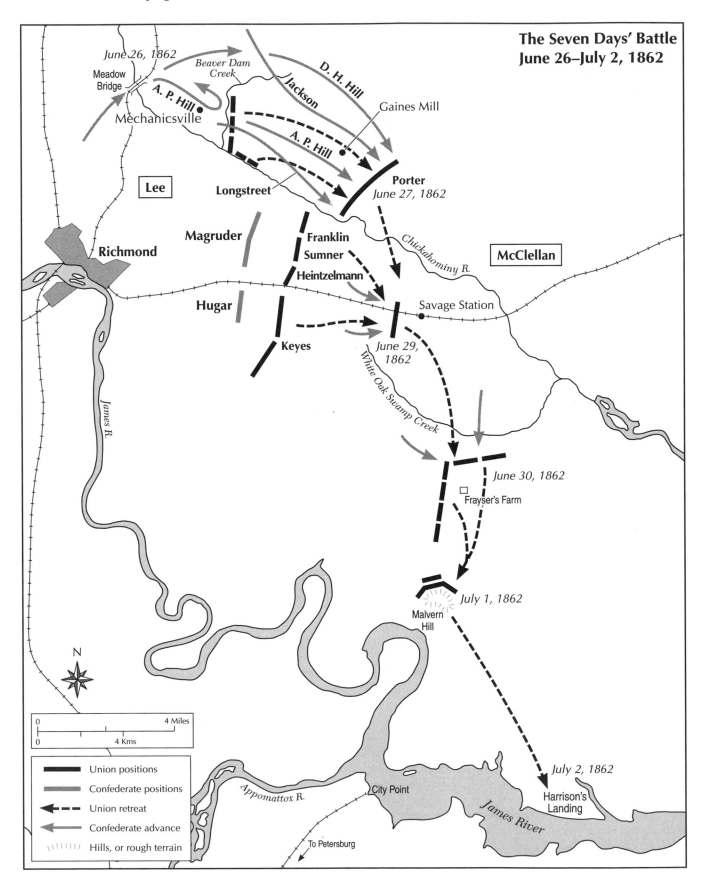

**The Seven Days' Battle
June 26–July 2, 1862**

June 26, 1862

Meadow
Bridge

Beaver Dam
Creek

D. H. Hill

Jackson

Gaines Mill

A. P. Hill
Mechanicsville

A. P. Hill

Lee

Longstreet

Porter
June 27, 1862

Chickahominy R.

Magruder

Franklin

McClellan

Sumner

Heintzelmann

Savage Station

Hugar

June 29,
1862

Keyes

White Oak Swamp Creek

James R.

June 30, 1862

Frayser's Farm

July 1, 1862

Malvern
Hill

0   4 Miles

0   4 Kms

Union positions

Confederate positions

Union retreat

Confederate advance

Hills, or rough terrain

July 2, 1862

Appomattox R.

City Point

Harrison's
Landing

James River

To Petersburg

son . . . is the only one of our generals who gives the enemy no rest, no time to entrench themselves. Matters before Richmond look gloomy to us out siders. McClellan advances, entrenching as he comes. Why do we allow it?"

The situation at Richmond looked grim for the Confederates by the end of May. Having retreated to within about five miles of the capital, Johnston understood that he must deliver a blow. He and McClellan had remained relatively inactive during much of Jackson's SHENANDOAH VALLEY CAMPAIGN, but the Confederates could retreat no further without reaching the defensive works of Richmond and engaging in a siege that inevitably would favor McClellan. At the end of May, Johnston detected an opening. McClellan's army was divided by the Chickahominy River, with two corps isolated south of its rain-swollen banks. Johnston attacked the exposed portion of the Union host on May 31 in the Battle of Seven Pines (also called Fair Oaks). The only full-scale engagement between McClellan and Johnston on the peninsula, Seven Pines lasted two days. Poor coordination, a confused grasp of local terrain, and other factors plagued the Southern army in a contest that ended in tactical stalemate. More than 6,000 Confederates and 5,000 Federals fell in the two days, and the Southern commander Johnston suffered a severe wound in the chest. On June 1 JEFFERSON DAVIS named ROBERT E. LEE to succeed Johnston. Thus did the man who would become the greatest Confederate general step into the limelight.

This change of leadership occurred as George B. McClellan and his Army of the Potomac, which numbered more than 100,000 men, approached the climax of their grand offensive against the southern capital. Although Lee later achieved a towering reputation, news of his appointment provoked widespread concern across the Confederacy. A North Carolina woman gave voice to a common evaluation of Lee: "I do not much like him, he 'falls back' too much. . . ."

The next five weeks proved Lee's doubters wrong. No general exhibited more daring than the new Southern commander, who believed the Confederacy could counteract Northern superiority in numbers by seizing and holding the initiative. He spent June preparing for a supreme effort against McClellan. When Stonewall Jackson's command from the Shenandoah Valley and other reinforcements arrived, Lee's army, at 90,000 strong, would be the largest ever gathered by the South. By the last week of June, the Army of the Potomac was divided by the Chickahominy River, two-thirds of its strength south of the river and one-third north of it. Lee hoped to crush the portion north of the river, then turn against the rest. Confederates repulsed a strong Union reconnaissance against their left on June 25, opening what became known as the Seven Days' Battle and setting the stage for Lee's offensive.

Heavy fighting began on June 26 at the Battle of Mechanicsville and continued for the next five days. Lee consistently acted as the aggressor but never managed to land a decisive blow. At Mechanicsville, he expected Jackson to strike Union general Fitz John Porter's right flank. The hero of the valley failed to appear in time, however, and A. P. HILL's Confederate division launched a useless frontal assault about mid-afternoon. Porter retreated to a strong position at Gaines's Mill, where Lee attacked again on June 27. Once again Jackson stumbled, as more than 50,000 Confederates mounted savage attacks along a wide front. Late in the day, Porter's lines gave way, and he withdrew across the Chickahominy to join the rest of McClellan's army.

Jackson's poor performance, usually attributed to exhaustion verging on numbness, joined poor staff work and other factors in allowing Porter's exposed portion of McClellan's army to escape. In the wake of Gaines's Mill, McClellan changed his base from the Pamunkey River to the James River, where Northern naval power could support the Army of the Potomac. Lee followed the retreating McClellan, seeking to inflict a crippling blow as the Federals retreated southward across the peninsula. After heavy skirmishing on June 28, the Confederates mounted light attacks on June 29 at Savage's Station and far heavier ones at Glendale (also known as Frayser's Farm) on June 30. Stonewall Jackson played virtually no role in these actions, as time and again the Confederates failed to act in concert.

By July 1 McClellan stood at Malvern Hill, a splendid defensive position overlooking the James. Lee resorted to unimaginative frontal assaults that afternoon. Whether irritated at lost opportunities or driven by his natural combativeness, he had made one of is poorest tactical decisions. As evening fell, more than 5,000 Confederate casualties littered the slopes of Malvern Hill. Some of McClellan's officers urged a counterattack against the obviously battered enemy; however, "Little Mac" retreated down the James to Harrison's Landing, where he awaited Lee's next move and issued endless requests for more men and supplies.

Casualties for the Seven Days were enormous. Lee's losses exceeded 20,000 killed, wounded, and missing, while McClellan's surpassed 16,000. Gaines's Mill, where combined losses exceeded 15,000, marked the point of greatest slaughter. Thousands of dead and maimed soldiers brought the reality of war to Richmond's residents. One woman wrote, "death held a carnival in our city. The weather was excessively hot. It was midsummer, gangrene and erysipelas attacked the wounded, and those who might have been cured of their wounds were cut down by these diseases."

The campaign's importance extended far beyond setting a new standard of carnage in Virginia. Lee had seized the initiative, dramatically altering the strategic picture by dictating the action to a passive McClellan. Lee's first effort in field command lacked tactical polish but nevertheless brought great rewards. The Seven Days saved Richmond and uplifted a Confederate people depressed by bad military news from other theaters. On the Union side, the campaign dashed expectations of victory that had mounted steadily as Northern armies in Tennessee and along the MISSISSIPPI RIVER won a string of successes. McClellan's failure also deepened Northern political divisions, clearing the way for Republicans to implement policies that would strike at SLAVERY and other rebel property. The end of the rebellion had seemed to be in sight when McClellan prepared to march up the peninsula; after Malvern Hill, few failed to see that the war would continue in a more all-encompassing manner. "We have been and are in a depressed, dismal, . . . state of anxiety and irritability," wrote a perceptive New Yorker after McClellan's retreat. "The cause of the country does not seem to be thriving just now."

The campaign also underscored the degree to which events in the Virginia theater dominated perceptions about the war's progress. Despite enormous Northern achievement in the western campaigns, most people North and South, as well as observers in Britain and France, interpreted the Seven Days as evidence that the Confederacy was winning the war. Lincoln wrote about this phenomenon in early August, complaining that "it seems unreasonable that a series of successes, extending through half-a-year, and clearing more than a hundred thousand square miles of country, should help us so little, while a single half-defeat should hurt us so much." Lincoln did not exaggerate the impact of McClellan's failure. Taken overall, the ramifications were such that the Richmond campaign must be reckoned one of the turning points of the war.

See also IRONCLADS; *MONITOR-MERRIMACK.*

Further reading: Stephen W. Sears, *To the Gates of Richmond: The Peninsula Campaign* (New York: Ticknor & Fields, 1992).

—Gary W. Gallagher

Pennington, James William Charles (1807–1870)
Noted ABOLITIONist James Pembroke was born into SLAVERY in Queen Anne's County, Maryland. As he grew up under the oversight of an especially harsh master, he became an expert blacksmith and taught himself to read, write, and calculate. In 1827 Pembroke escaped slavery via the UNDERGROUND RAILROAD and was taken in by a Quaker (SOCIETY OF FRIENDS) family in Pennsylvania. He spent nearly three years in their employ, all the while continuing his EDUCATION. In 1830 he traveled to King County, New York, where he took the name James W. C. Pennington.

Over the course of the next three decades, Pennington achieved success in three different careers. He was a minister, serving as pastor of several different churches. Pennington was also an educator. He worked as a teacher for several years, and in 1841 he wrote A *Textbook of the Origin and History of Colored People,* one of the earliest books written on African-American history. The book emphasized the importance of black Americans' African heritage and denounced the common stereotypes of the day.

Pennington's chief fame, however, came from his work as an abolitionist. As early as 1831, he became known for his outspoken criticism of the American Colonization Society. By the mid-1830s, Pennington was working with the nation's most well-known abolitionists. Among his close friends was FREDERICK DOUGLASS, at whose wedding Pennington officiated in 1838. Pennington attended several important gatherings of abolitionist leaders, including the Philadelphia Negro Convention in 1832 and the World Anti-Slavery Conference in 1843. In 1849 Pennington made his single most important contribution to the abolition movement, penning an autobiography entitled *The Fugitive Blacksmith.* The work was a powerful condemnation of slavery and quickly went through several printings. For most of the 1850s, Pennington traveled throughout the United States and Europe delivering antislavery speeches.

The publication of *The Fugitive Blacksmith* marked the high point of Pennington's career. Shortly before the CIVIL WAR started, Pennington's struggles with alcoholism were made public, and his reputation was destroyed. He struggled to support himself during the war, suffering a series of indignities that included being jailed for allegedly stealing a book. He died penniless in Jacksonville, Florida, a few years after the war ended.

Further reading: James W. C. Pennington, *The Fugitive Blacksmith, or, Events in the History of James W. C. Pennington* (1849; reprint, Westport, Conn.: Negro Universities Press, 1971); Herman Edward Thomas, *James W. C. Pennington: African American Churchman and Abolitionist* (New York: Garland, 1995).

—Christopher Bates

Petersburg campaign (June 1864–April 1865)
The ten-month Petersburg campaign was the longest military operation of the CIVIL WAR. From May to June 1864, Gen. ROBERT E. LEE had blocked successive attempts by Lt. Gen. ULYSSES S. GRANT to destroy the CONFEDERATE ARMY and capture RICHMOND in the OVERLAND CAMPAIGN. Frustrated at the stalemate after the BATTLE OF

COLD HARBOR in early June, Grant decided to cross the James River and seize Petersburg, Virginia, a vital communication and rail center 20 miles south of Richmond. If the UNION ARMY prevailed at Petersburg, the Confederate capital would likely fall shortly afterward.

On June 12 the Union's largest fighting force, the Army of the Potomac, left Cold Harbor and marched more than 50 miles to the James River. Waiting for them was a 2,100-foot-long pontoon bridge built by the Yankee soldiers, a triumph of engineering. By June 16 the entire UNION ARMY was on the south bank of the river. Moving swiftly, the Federals were closing in on Petersburg, a day's march away. Soldiers and officers alike wondered what they would find when they reached the city gates.

In 1860 Petersburg was Virginia's second largest city, with a population of 18,000, half of whom were black, and of these, one-third were free. Petersburg enjoyed a thriving ECONOMY. A city of cotton mills, tobacco factories, and RAILROADS, Petersburg was poised to play an important part in the war. From the beginning, Petersburg's streets and railroad stations were clogged with soldiers and sup-

plies. All but one of the railroads that tied Richmond with the rest of the southern and western Confederacy passed through its smaller neighbor to the south.

Not surprisingly, Petersburg, along with Richmond, was a desirable target of the Union army, and in the summer of 1862 slaves and soldiers began construction of a 10-mile line of fortifications around the city. Finished by 1863, the lines were held by a small force of 2,200 men under the command of Brig. Gen. Henry A. Wise as the First Federal Corps approached the city. Inside, the civilian population, mostly made up of women, children, and slaves, watched and worried. Already suffering from the effects of inflation, food shortages, and other inconveniences, women—black and white, upper and lower class—prepared their families for the worst.

From June 15 through June 18, the Union forces, numbering around 63,000, threatened to overwhelm the much smaller Confederate defenders. Gen. Ulysses S. Grant, the commander of all the Union armies, was supervising Maj. Gen. GEORGE GORDON MEADE's Army of the Potomac. His strategy was to take Petersburg by storm,

Engraving showing a regiment of the XVIII Corps carrying a portion of Beauregard's line in front of Petersburg, Virginia
(Library of Congress)

cut off all Confederate supply lines, and confront and defeat Lee's army on the way to Richmond. Unfortunately, due to a combination of long-standing command problems within the Army of the Potomac, confused and contradictory communications between units, and the extreme battle fatigue of the men after weeks of heavy fighting, Union assaults failed to capture the Petersburg works. The Confederates quickly brought in reinforcements that made their defensive position even more formidable. Four days of fighting left the Federals with losses of 10,586 compared with 4,000 for the rebels. On June 18, Lee arrived to direct operations. Grant realized that continued frontal attacks would be useless and ordered his men to "use the spade." The siege of Petersburg had begun.

Both Grant and Lee realized the disadvantages of a long siege. Under heavy pressure to win the war quickly, Grant was aware that the success of his military career was tied to the political fortunes of his commander in chief ABRAHAM LINCOLN. At this point, only victories in the field could sustain the Republicans in the fall ELECTIONS, and during the spring and summer of 1864 all of the Union armies, east and west, were stalemated. Large parts of the North were expressing dissatisfaction with the war's costs. Lee, on the other hand, would not win a war of attrition with the enemy. Time was not on his side. The Southern population could not endure much more privation than had already been inflicted. Confederates now hoped that the war-weary Northern nation would oust Lincoln and elect a Democrat who might stop the war and accept Southern independence. Despite their misgivings, Grant and Lee adjusted to a type of warfare that they neither anticipated nor desired.

Grant planned to encircle Petersburg and cut off all of Lee's supply lines. He ordered his soldiers to build a trench system around Lee's 26-mile line of defensive fortifications stretching from Petersburg to Richmond. By late June the Confederates had approximately 50,000 men to 112,000 for the Union. Grant established his military headquarters at City Point, Virginia, on the James River halfway between Petersburg and Richmond. From City Point, Grant presided over a vast logistical operation that kept the supplies flowing in to the troops in the field. Whereas Union soldiers were relatively well fed, clothed and armed, the Southern soldiers suffered from hunger and other privations. As the siege wore on, as the Union shelling pounded the Southern lines and the city behind day after day, DESERTION among the Confederates rose and civilian morale plunged. "The vandals are still throwing shell into the city, and it is very distressing to see the women and children leaving," wrote one diarist. Thousands of residents fled the city as REFUGEES, flooding the roads to Richmond.

As the summer wore on, Grant's army extended their lines around the city. In addition, he sent units out to cut the major railroad connections. Lee dispatched mobile forces to stop the Union's forays, and many battles took place away from the siege area. Lee also mounted another major campaign in the Shenandoah Valley under Gen. JUBAL A. EARLY to draw troops away from Petersburg and Richmond. This campaign resulted in the defeat of the Confederates in the valley, and the triumph of one of Grant's best generals, PHILIP H. SHERIDAN.

Grant periodically ordered big attacks, such as the famous and ill-starred "Battle of the Crater," which occurred on July 30, 1864, and involved a division of African-American soldiers who performed bravely in battle in spite of poor leadership from white officers and little support. On September 1, Atlanta fell, and Lincoln's reelection was assured. The hard winter of 1864–65 brought Lee's army to the breaking point. In March 1865, a desperate Lee launched the first big assault of the spring at Fort Stedman. Grant counterattacked with great effect. For all intents and purposes, the long siege of Petersburg was over, at the cost of 42,000 Union and 28,000 Confederate casualties.

On April 1 Union cavalry under Sheridan attacked the western end of Lee's defensive line. Lee decided to cut his losses and move southward. In doing so, he hoped to join another Confederate army in eastern North Carolina to prevent Maj. Gen. William T. Sherman's western army from combining with Grant's. On April 2 Grant ordered an assault on a weakened Petersburg line, winning the city before dawn on the next day. Richmond fell only hours later, on the morning of April 3. Shortly thereafter, Grant accepted the surrender of Lee's army at APPOMATTOX

Union Victory

Union Movements
← Grant

Confederate Movements
← Lee
〰 Confederate defense line

0 ___ 20 Miles
0 ___ 20 Kms
N

Virginia

Maryland
Potomac R.

The Wilderness
May 5–7, 1864
Chancellorsville
● Fredericksburg
Rappahannock R.

Spotsylvania
May 8–19, 1864

James R.

North Anna
May 23–26, 1864
Cold Harbor
June 1–3, 1864

Sayler's Creek
April 6, 1865
Appomattox R.   Richmond ◉

Appomattox Court House, Lee surrenders to Grant, April 9, 1865

Amelia Court House

Five Forks
April 1, 1865

Petersburg Campaign
June 1864–April 1865

COURT HOUSE, Virginia. Most of the remaining civilians of Petersburg had been evacuated to safety. The city was in ruins. One Yankee soldier remembered: "Petersburgh has been a pretty Place but it is a hard looking Place now."

Further reading: A. Wilson Greene, *Breaking the Backbone of the Rebellion: The Final Battles of the Petersburg Campaign* (Mason City, Iowa: Savas Publishing Co., 2000); Suzanne Lebsock, *The Free Women of Petersburg: Status and Culture in a Southern Town, 1784–1860* (New York: Norton, 1984); Noah Andre Trudeau, *The Last Citadel: Petersburg Virginia, June 1864–April 1865* (Boston: Little, Brown, 1991).

photography

Through portraits of participants and battlefields, photography dramatically influenced how Americans perceived the CIVIL WAR.

Photography democratized individual portraiture. Newly enlisted soldiers sat for inexpensive studio portraits, often purchasing 2- by 4-inch *cartes de visites* to distribute to family and friends. The portrait business thrived during the war as enterprising photographers set up studios near army camps. Photographs that captured the faces of men who might never return home became prized family possessions. Soldiers carried pictures of their loved ones with them to battle as well. Family portraits gave Civil War soldiers a visual link to home that had not been available to ordinary combatants in earlier wars.

Field photographs gave Americans additional visual information about the war. The fragility of photographic equipment and the need for long exposure times and immediate processing in portable darkrooms meant that photographers recorded the aftermath of battle rather than the fighting itself. These photographs departed from romantic depictions of the battlefield and unflinchingly documented the horrors of war. In 1862 Alexander Gardner recorded a sensational series of images from the BATTLE OF ANTIETAM that showed the mutilated bodies of anonymous soldiers. Displayed in the New York studios of Gardner's employer, MATHEW B. BRADY, and published as engravings by the *New York Times* and *Harper's Weekly,* the Antietam series shocked Americans with stark evidence of the terrible human costs of battle. The public erroneously credited this work to Brady, a misconception he did nothing to discourage. He remains the photographer most closely identified with well-known Civil War images, even though he actually took very few of them.

In 1863, hoping to duplicate the success he had enjoyed with the Antietam series, Gardner rushed to the battlefield at Gettysburg, Pennsylvania. Gardner, who had left Brady's employ, worked with Timothy H. O'Sullivan and James F. Gibson. Together, they produced a famous series of photographs that recorded dead bodies lying on the Gettysburg field. Gardner was not averse to manipulating photographs to serve his needs. His most famous image, a dead Confederate lying in the "Devil's Den," was staged—the man had died on another part of the battlefield. Although most of the dead men in his pictures were Confederates, Gardner and the newspaper editors who purchased his images identified some of the men as Union soldiers to better illustrate the Northern narrative of battle. As with the Antietam photos, the public was fascinated.

The photographs of Antietam and Gettysburg were different from most Civil War photography. Antietam and Gettysburg were both fought in Northern states, so it was possible to get the photographers and equipment necessary for battlefield photography in place fairly quickly, within two or three days of the fighting. In most other cases, it took a week or more to get men and equipment in place, by which time most battlefields had been cleared of bodies and other signs of carnage.

The logistical difficulties of battlefield photography meant that images of everyday military life far outnumbered photographs of war dead. Americans were educated about the war by pictures of breastworks and military fortifications, field hospitals and army camps, artillery placements and railway trestles, freedmen's shanties and Confederate ruins. Capt. Andrew J. Russell, attached to the U.S. Military Railroad, documented rail lines in Virginia and was present at the BATTLES OF FREDERICKSBURG and Petersburg and at the fall of RICHMOND. His photographs included noteworthy images of black laborers who contributed to the Union war effort. George N. Barnard, a former Gardner associate attached to the chief engineer's office of the Division of Mississippi, photographed Gen. WILLIAM T. SHERMAN's 1864 campaign in Tennessee, Georgia, and South Carolina. Gardner himself documented the ruins of Richmond in 1865. He also photographed the executions of the conspirators who plotted the ASSASSINATION OF ABRAHAM LINCOLN.

Field photographs were distributed widely during and after the war in the form of inexpensive mass-produced stereographs. These popular side-by-side exposures took on a three-dimensional appearance when viewed through a handheld stereograph. For the upscale market, Gardner and Barnard each published expensive collector's editions of their work in 1866. Gardner's *Photographic Sketchbook of the War* and Barnard's *Photographic Views of Sherman's Campaign* featured large prints accompanied by patriotic captions. Americans have continued to be fascinated by Civil War photography. In 1875 the government paid Mathew Brady $25,000 to gain exclusive title to his collection so that it could be preserved for future generations. In

1911 Francis Trevelyan Miller published his influential 10-volume *Photographic History of the Civil War.*

The proliferation of Civil War photographs was not the only story of the postwar era, however. Photographic equipment became more portable, enabling photographers to reach important locations more quickly. In the 1880s, halftone printing was developed, enabling newspapers to print actual photographs rather than engravings. By the 1890s Americans could open their morning paper and expect to read about *and* see what had happened the day before.

See also PETERSBURG CAMPAIGN; SHERMAN'S MARCH THROUGH GEORGIA.

Further reading: William A. Frassanito, *Gettysburg: A Journey in Time* (New York: Scribner, 1975); Web Garrison, ed., *Brady's Civil War* (New York: Lyons Press, 2000); Francis T. Miller, *The Photographic History of the Civil War: Complete and Unabridged* (1911; reprint, Secaucus, N.J.: Blue & Grey Press, 1987).

—Amy J. Kinsel

Pickett, George Edward (1825–1875)

Best known for his leadership of Confederate forces in a failed charge at Gettysburg, Gen. George E. Pickett was born into a wealthy PLANTATION family in RICHMOND, Virginia, on January 28, 1825. He studied law in Illinois with his uncle and was appointed to the UNITED STATES MILITARY ACADEMY AT WEST POINT by Congressman John Stuart. Pickett was not a success at West Point, where he was graduated last out of his class of 59 in 1846.

Although many West Pointers of the 1840s served only perfunctory military service before entering civilian life, Pickett remained with the army long after graduation. He served in the Mexican-American War, where he met and became friends with Lt. JAMES LONGSTREET. Afterward, he was assigned to Company K of the Eighth Infantry on a temporary basis, a command he relinquished to Longstreet in July 1854. Pickett served under Longstreet in Texas until 1855, when he was reassigned to the Washington Territory. It would be his last post in the U.S. Army. Pickett married twice during his time in the U.S. Army. Both marriages ended with the death of his wives, although his second marriage did produce a son, James Tilton Pickett.

With the outbreak of the CIVIL WAR, Pickett resigned his commission and returned to his home state of Virginia to enlist in the CONFEDERATE ARMY. Accepted into the Gamecock Brigade as a colonel, Pickett fought at Williamsburg and Fair Oaks. In May 1862 he was wounded in the shoulder at Gaines's Mill. The combination of his fighting record and his wound brought him to the attention of Confederate leaders, who were engaged in restructuring the Army of Northern Virginia. Pickett's old friend Longstreet, then a commanding general of ROBERT E. LEE's First Corps, recommended that Pickett be appointed major general of one of the divisions. The appointment was approved, and Pickett's division of Virginians saw their first action under his leadership when they defended Confederate lines at the BATTLE OF FREDERICKSBURG.

It would be Pickett's next major action that would forever ensure his place in history. In the summer of 1863, Lee ventured north and engaged Union general GEORGE GORDON MEADE at Gettysburg, Pennsylvania. On the third day of a three-day battle, Union lines were reinforced on the left and right flanks but not in the center. Lee determined that the center of the line was vulnerable, and he planned an attack there—a huge display of artillery power intended to deprive the Union forces of artillery support. Once the bombardment had silenced Union guns, a massive infantry assault would charge the line. Lee assigned this task to Longstreet, who in turn selected Pickett's Virginians and Gen. Johnston Pettigrew's North Carolinians, the most rested soldiers at that point in the battle, to make the charge.

On the afternoon of July 3, 1863, what would be known afterward as Pickett's Charge got under way. The Confederate artillery bombardment had begun early in the afternoon and destroyed a few Union batteries before ammunition began to run low. Shortly after Union artillery ceased firing, and at 3:15 P.M. 13,000 Confederate infantrymen were commanded to move forward across roughly one mile of open ground. Pickett organized the attack well, but it was unsuccessful. Confederate bombardment had not inflicted enough damage on the Union guns, and close-range artillery fire wiped out most of Pickett's men. A total of 10,000 were killed, wounded, or missing in action. Pickett withdrew with a casualty rate of more than 60 percent. When asked by Lee later that day to re-form his division, Pickett answered, "General Lee, I have no division." The failure of Pickett's charge on Union lines was an omen of other failures to come. After a modicum of success as the commander of the Department of North Carolina, Pickett returned to the Army of Northern Virginia. He bungled an engagement at the BATTLE OF FIVE FORKS during the Appomattox campaign and Lee removed him from his command the day before the surrender of the Army of Northern Virginia at APPOMATTOX COURT HOUSE.

After the war, Pickett fled to Canada with his third wife, LaSalle Corbett, whom he had married shortly after the BATTLE OF GETTYSBURG. Pickett left the United States because he was concerned that he might have to face charges in connection with his mistreatment of Union captives while in command in North Carolina. The khedive of Egypt offered Pickett a commission, but he refused. Shortly thereafter, President ULYSSES S. GRANT offered him a pardon and an appointment as marshal of Virginia. Pickett accepted the pardon but declined the appointment and instead worked as an agent of the Washington Life Insurance Company. Pickett strove to remedy his reputation by writing LETTERS and articles that eulogized his charge as evidence of the romantic vision and tragic dignity of the Southern cause. After his death on October 25, 1875, his wife LaSalle took up the cause of reinventing her husband's memory, producing even more written material than he had.

Further reading: Kathleen R. Georg and John W. Busey, *Nothing But Glory: Pickett's Divisions at Gettysburg* (Gettysburg, Pa.: Thomas Publications, 1993); Lesley J. Gordon, *General George E. Pickett in Life and Legend* (Chapel Hill: University of North Carolina Press, 1998).

—Arthur E. Amos

Pierce, Franklin (1804–1869)

Lawyer, soldier, and the 14th president of the United States, Franklin Pierce was born on November 23, 1804, in New Hampshire. Pierce graduated from Bowdoin College in Maine, and in 1827 he began practicing law in New Hampshire. Pierce was a staunch Democrat and a great admirer of President Andrew Jackson. His early political career was very successful. He served as a member of the New Hampshire state legislature and then in the U.S. Congress from 1833 to 1842, first as a representative and then a senator.

Pierce's political principles were those of the DEMOCRATIC PARTY he loved. He was a strong supporter of limited government, economy and efficiency in the federal budget, and STATES' RIGHTS. He was also a fierce patriot who detested the rising Northern ABOLITIONist movement as a threat to the sectional harmony he was determined to preserve. Married and with a growing family, Pierce resigned from the Senate in 1842. He returned to New Hampshire to a thriving legal practice but remained a major force in his state's Democratic Party.

In the Mexican-American War (1846–48), President James K. Polk appointed Pierce first as a colonel and then as a brigadier general. His military career was brief and undistinguished, and he happily left the army to return to New Hampshire. Pierce was prominent in supporting the Compromise of 1850 and especially the Fugitive Slave Law, the most controversial part of the compromise. Pierce became known as a "doughface," that is, a Northern man with Southern sympathies. His support did not go unnoticed in the South, and when the 1852 Democratic National Convention deadlocked, Southern politicians propelled Pierce's candidacy to a successful conclusion. Pierce won the presidency by a small margin.

Pierce assumed office in a period of great turmoil. His major goals were to continue the expansion of U.S. territory and to avoid sectional controversy. He achieved a limited measure of success in the former and failed miserably in the latter. Under his administration the Gadsden Purchase (1853) was negotiated, adding greatly to the nation's Southwest territory. The issue of SLAVERY, however, once again threatened the stability of the country when Senator STEPHEN A. DOUGLAS of Illinois pushed the KANSAS-NEBRASKA ACT of 1854 through Congress. The act superseded the Missouri Compromise and threw open all the territories to popular sovereignty. Soon, massive voting fraud and violent clashes between proslavery and free-labor factions demanded presidential intervention.

Pierce did not demonstrate strong leadership in handling the major crisis of his presidency. A weak, indecisive man, he favored the South over the North in Kansas and elsewhere, helping to set in motion a chain of events that led to the CIVIL WAR. By 1855 Pierce's many blunders had alienated Americans and made his renomination impossible. Pierce died in obscurity in Concord, New Hampshire, on October 8, 1869.

See also BLEEDING KANSAS; BUSHWACKERS; JAYHAWKERS.

Further reading: Larry Gara, *The Presidency of Franklin Pierce* (Lawrence: University Press of Kansas, 1991).

Pinchback, Pinckney B. S. (1837–1921)

An important African-American politician of the RECONSTRUCTION era, Pinckney Benton Stewart Pinchback was born in Macon, Georgia, to a white father and a free African-American mother. He grew up in Mississippi and Cincinnati, becoming the sole support of his mother and seven siblings after his father died in 1848. In 1862 Pinchback settled in New Orleans, where he raised a company of African-American soldiers for the UNION ARMY. Because Union policy did not allow Pinchback to command his company, he left New Orleans, returning in 1867 to participate in the reorganization of Louisiana politics. He started the Fourth Ward Republican Club and participated in the creation of the new Louisiana Constitution, championing the adoption of civil rights and EDUCATION provisions.

In 1868 Pinchback was elected state senator, and from that position he became lieutenant governor. When Governor Henry C. Warmouth was impeached in December 1872, Pinchback became acting GOVERNOR, the first black governor of any state in the United States. He held that post until November 1873, when the newly elected governor took office. By then Pinchback had been elected, simultaneously, to both a congressional and a senatorial seat in the national legislature. He chose to take his Senate seat, but the U.S. Senate refused to recognize his election, finally deciding in 1876, after almost three years of debate, not to seat him. After this defeat, Pinchback served as an internal revenue agent in 1879 and became surveyor of customs for the port of New Orleans in 1881. Pinchback entered and graduated from the Straight Law School in 1885. In 1890 he organized the American Citizens Equal Rights Association. In 1892 he was a delegate to the Republican National Convention, and in 1898 he helped to unveil the FREDERICK DOUGLASS monument in Rochester, New York. He moved to WASHINGTON, D.C., in the 1890s to raise his grandson, Jean Toomer, later a Harlem Renaissance poet. Pinchback died in Washington, D.C., in 1921.

See also SCALAWAGS.

Further reading: James Haskins, *The First Black Governor: Pinckney Benton Stewart Pinchback* (Trenton, N.J.: Africa World Press, 1996).

—Fiona Galvin

plantations

Plantations were agrarian enterprises that employed large numbers of workers who produced crops for domestic and foreign markets. Before the CIVIL WAR, plantations primarily relied on the labor of African-American slaves who tended to a wide range of crops, including cotton, rice, and tobacco. After EMANCIPATION, SHARECROPPING and other labor systems replaced slave labor in the South, but plantations remained a part of the region's agricultural system.

In the 19th century, plantations were not confined to the American South or to slaveholding societies. Spanish and Portuguese colonists ran sugar plantations in their South and Central American colonies, and English colonists used the system in Ireland and in many of their 17th- and 18th-century colonies. The ECONOMY of colonial Virginia relied heavily on tobacco plantations, while rice and indigo plantations were particularly widespread in South Carolina and the Georgia low country.

Southern plantations dramatically changed as a result of Eli Whitney's cotton gin. This machine, which appeared in 1793, drastically cut the costs of growing short-staple cotton, making it the most profitable crop available to planters. They subsequently turned to it in great numbers, and it became known as "King Cotton." The gin allowed planters, who originally grew cotton in the South Carolina and Georgia up-country, to move the crop south and west toward occupied NATIVE AMERICAN lands. The cotton kingdom further expanded after the forced removal of the southeastern Indians in the 1830s and the 1845 annexation of Texas. Cotton plantations were ultimately concentrated

in what became known as the "Cotton Belt," a stretch of fertile land in Alabama, Mississippi, and Louisiana, where more than half of the nation's cotton was grown by the 1830s. South Carolina, which grew 60 percent of the crop in 1800, had fallen to less than 10 percent on the eve of the Civil War. Although cotton was king at the start of the war, Southern planters also grew tobacco, rice, hemp, indigo, and wheat.

Not all Southern farms were plantations, and not all slave owners were planters. Plantations had large labor populations and usually specialized in one agricultural product. In order be considered a planter, one had to own at least 20 slaves and a significant piece of land. In 1860 only about 50,000 of the 400,000 Southern slave owners were classified as planters. Wade Hampton, the largest slaveholder in 1860, owned more than 3,000 slaves who worked his Mississippi and South Carolina plantations.

Throughout the year, male and female slaves performed an endless number of tasks on Southern plantations. Crop cultivation consumed most of their time, with the harvest generally demanding the longest and hardest hours of work. African-American slaves hoed, weeded, picked, watered, reaped, and planted, often from sunup to sundown. They sometimes oversaw the labor of their fellow slaves. In slower months, slaves mended fences, cleared lands, and performed other seasonal tasks. Large plantations contained house slaves who tended to various needs of the plantation's mansion, or the "big house." Although not all domestic tasks were reserved for females, slave women frequently served as nursemaids, mammies, seamstresses, laundresses, and cooks for their planter masters and mistresses. In addition to slave quarters, plantations also had smokehouses, stables, barns, sheds, a chapel, and an occasional schoolhouse for white children.

The Civil War physically devastated many Southern plantations. Early in the war, the Union blockade limited the South's ability to export its raw goods. In addition, the Confederate military enlisted many white planters and overseers, leaving white Southern women to run the plantations. Although planters could sometimes avoid military duty under the Twenty-Slave Law, which exempted any white man who had 20 or more slaves under his control, only 4,000–5,000 men claimed exemptions during the war. With most white men serving in the CONFEDERATE ARMY, slaves increasingly resisted their bondage, refusing to work, wandering the countryside, and when possible, running to the safety of Union lines. A more direct devastation of Southern plantations resulted from the various invasions visited upon the South by the UNION ARMY. In particular, Union soldiers on WILLIAM T. SHERMAN's 1864–65 march through Georgia and the Carolinas burned millions of acres of cotton and other crops, destroyed homes, broke fences

Two cotton pickers painted by William Walker *(Hulton/Archive)*

and farming implements, and otherwise razed plantations in their path.

When the war ended, Southern planters struggled to rebuild. Only 180 of the more than 1,200 sugar plantations in Louisiana, for example, sold any surplus in 1865. Many plantations were sold to pay off debts. By the end of RECONSTRUCTION in 1877, however, about half of Southern plantations were once again in the hands of the families who had owned them when the war began. To compensate for the labor lost from emancipation, many postwar planters turned to sharecropping. They contracted former slaves to live on portions of the plantation that had been subdivided into family lots. Owner and sharecropper would presumably share the harvests produced, but this system resulted in a cycle of debt and hard labor for the freedpeople.

See also SHERMAN'S MARCH THROUGH GEORGIA; SLAVERY.

Further reading: Andrew Frank, *Routledge Historical Atlas of the American South* (New York: Routledge, 1999); Eugene Genovese, *The Political Economy of Slavery: Studies in the Economy & Society of the Slave South* (Middletown, Conn.: Wesleyan University Press, 1989); Gavin

Wright, *The Political Economy of the Cotton South: Households, Markets, and Wealth in the Nineteenth Century* (New York: Norton, 1978).

—Lisa Tendrich Frank

population trends

The CIVIL WAR and RECONSTRUCTION era brought unprecedented transformation to the United States. Particularly striking was the growth of IMMIGRATION, the rise of cities, and a general population explosion.

National Trends

In the 30 years between 1850 and 1880, U.S. population more than doubled, from 23 million to 50 million. Births within the United States account for much of the increase; families averaged 3–4 children in 1850, a number that had declined from that of 1790 and would continue to decline through the 20th century.

An increasing number of Americans were foreign-born. Immigrants accounted for just under 10 percent of the country's population in 1850 but were more than 14 percent by 1880. Irish, Germans, and English accounted for most of these immigrants. While not comprising a large proportion of all immigrants, other groups were important in particular regions: Chinese in California and the Mountain West; Czechs and Slovaks (often called "Bohemians") in Texas and the lower Great Plains; and Scandinavians in Minnesota and Wisconsin. Together, these immigrants are sometimes classified as the "old immigration," contrasted with the "new immigration" of the 1890s through the 1920s, which included mostly Jews, Russians, Italians, Poles, Greeks, and other eastern and southern Europeans.

Immigration swelled the already growing American cities. The proportion of Americans living in urban areas almost doubled between 1850 and 1880, from 15 percent to 28 percent. This figure is a bit deceptive, however; "urban" at this time included any town with 2,500 persons or more. A better measure, perhaps, is cities containing more than 100,000 persons. There were six such cities when the Census Bureau took its 1850 census; their combined populations included just one of every 20 Americans—only 1.2 million persons. When the census takers returned in 1880, there were 20 such cities totaling 6.2

million Americans—about one in ten. The population of NEW YORK CITY alone in 1880 nearly equaled the total population of the six largest American cities in 1850.

There were two other notable characteristics about the people of the period: the large numbers of younger people and the lack of older ones. The average American was around 20 years old; fully a quarter of the nation's people were under 15. Average life expectancy was about 60 years.

Regional Issues

The urbanization, industrialization, and immigration of the mid-19th century were felt most dramatically in the Northeast and Midwest, which had a little less than 15 million people in 1850 but more than 32 million by 1880. While overshadowed by population growth in the North, shifts in the South and West would also have long-term consequences.

Southern leaders had long feared the increasing pace of Northern growth. While fully half of Americans had been Southerners in 1790, the proportion had dwindled to

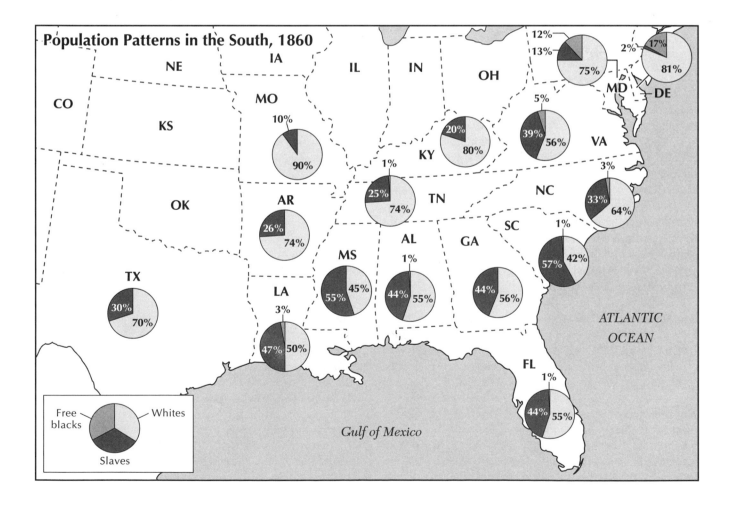

33 percent by 1850. Because northern and midwestern members constituted majorities in the Senate as well as the House, Northerners could set the conditions and the pace for admission of new states from the western territories. Southern leaders realized that unless they checked growing Northern power, there would come a time—1870? 1880? 1890?—when Northerners would control the two-thirds of the House, two-thirds of the Senate, and three-quarters of the state legislators necessary to amend the Constitution and force the end of SLAVERY. This possibility hardened Southern attitudes toward territorial compromise in the 1850s and contributed to the outbreak of the Civil War.

The South absorbed fewer immigrants than any other part of the country, a fact directly related to the region's reliance on slave labor before the Civil War, and after the war, the region's economic dislocation and growing reliance on SHARECROPPING and tenant farming. While immigration swelled the Northeast's labor pool, the postwar South relied on former slaves, with 90 percent of the nation's 6.5 million African Americans still living in the South in 1880. While African-American communities could be found in the North, these would not become large until the "great migration" of the 1940s.

The trans-Mississippi West faced different issues. The most obvious demographic fact about most western states was their skewed ratio of men to women. Mining and lumber camps disproportionately attracted young men. Indeed, 90 percent of California's 1850 population was male. While a few states, such as Oregon and Utah, attracted families, in most states, the number of women did not match the number of men until the early 20th century.

Between 1850 and 1880, migration from the eastern United States swamped indigenous NATIVE AMERICAN and Mexican populations. Native peoples were increasingly herded onto reservations or else killed in the wars that were waged against them. The Mexican population of southern California was numerous and powerful enough to require that the state's constitution establish both Spanish and English as official languages. With California's white population rising rapidly over the next 30 years, the 1879 state constitution removed this provision.

Further reading: Andrew Hacker, *U/S: A Statistical Portrait of the American People* (New York: Viking Press, 1983); Peter D. McClelland, *Demographic Dimensions of the New Republic: American Interregional Migration, Vital Statistics, and Manumissions, 1800–1860* (New York: Cambridge University Press, 1982); Riley Moore Moffat, *Population History of Eastern U.S. Cities and Towns, 1790–1870* (Metuchen, N.J.: Scarecrow Press, 1992); Riley Moore Moffat, *Population History of Western U.S. Cities and Towns, 1850–1990* (Lanham, Md.: Scarecrow Press, 1996).
—Tom Laichas

Port Royal, South Carolina, Experiment

The Port Royal experiment was an attempt by ABOLITIONISTs to test the transition from slave labor to a free-labor system on an isolated slave population beginning early in the CIVIL WAR. The issues that arose at Port Royal, South Carolina, included the future of cotton production, land redistribution, and the status of the freedmen. The Port Royal experiment also served as a dress rehearsal for RECONSTRUCTION.

Port Royal was part of a series of islands along the South Carolina coast known as the Sea Islands. Separated from the mainland by rivers, creeks, and swamps, the islands proved an easy target for the U.S. Navy. In November 1861, Union naval forces captured Port Royal and the Sea Islands and used them as a coaling station for the blockading fleet. Ahead of the invading army of federal troops, white planters fled inland to seek refuge behind Confederate defenses, leaving behind 10,000 slaves. An opportunity presented itself. Here, in one of the richest cotton regions of the South and in the absence of white owners, there was a possibility of transforming slaves from an unfree labor force into free workers. If the experiment were successful, Northern values of self-reliance and pride in labor would enhance the productivity of the workers and produce higher-quality cotton more efficiently.

Northern abolitionists jumped at this chance. At the request of Secretary of the Treasury SALMON P. CHASE, Edward Pierce, an abolitionist attorney experienced in working with CONTRABAND slaves, organized a contingent of teachers, missionaries, young college graduates, and other volunteers. This group, known as "Gideon's Band," took on the experiment in free labor, but they also sought to educate the slaves, provide moral uplift, aid physical needs, and generally to reform Southern society.

From the beginning, African Americans had little interest in growing cotton for their new bosses. Instead, they planted subsistence crops like corn and potatoes. Ex-slaves considered picking cotton too much like slave labor. Moreover, because of the wartime disruption of the cotton ECONOMY, grain production seemed a more plausible alternative for their families. Ex-slaves wanted to use their freedom and money gained from wage labor to purchase family amenities, like new clothes. They were showing an independence of mind that unpleasantly surprised the abolitionists on the island.

A skeptical labor force was not the only problem that the Northerners faced. They underestimated the extensive management system that white planters utilized to produce a profit and failed to account for the peculiarities of the physical environment, which were ill-suited for long-staple cotton. Ironically, in their quest to prove the superiority of free labor in cotton production, the white abolitionists found themselves in the same social position as the former masters—coercing black labor. "They force men to prove they are fit to be free by holding a tyrant's power over them," noted Laura Towne, a teacher in the Sea Islands, somewhat sardonically. It is little wonder that cotton production at the end of the first year was substantially lower than in the prewar years.

The question of landownership had wide-ranging implications for Reconstruction. Because the white planters had fled the Sea Island PLANTATIONS, most freedmen sought to claim the land as their own. Ex-slaves did what they could to settle the matter. Some pooled their meager resources and purchased 2,000 acres in a delinquent tax sale, but most leased the land from the federal government.

Gen. WILLIAM T. SHERMAN's famous SPECIAL FIELD ORDER NO. 15 offered the most far-reaching land redistribution plan during Reconstruction. It designated the entire Sea Island region for black settlement on 40-acre plots. However, within a year, President ANDREW JOHNSON, in his Proclamation of Amnesty, revoked Sherman's order and decided that all confiscated lands would be returned to their prewar owners (except those lands sold for taxes). What was most unjust for the freedpeople, besides losing land promised to them, was that they would have to work for their former masters. Many of the freedpeople just wanted to be left alone.

Notwithstanding the problems of growing long-staple cotton, naïve Northern abolitionists trying to run plantations, and the betrayal of the federal government, the Port Royal Experiment failed because African Americans in the Sea Islands considered independent production and individual choices to be the hallmarks of freedom. In other words, cotton production was less important than the goal of family self-sufficiency. Though few Southern black families were ever able to become sufficient in the post-Reconstruction South, some Port Royal families did prosper because they retained ownership of their own land.

Further reading: Willie Lee Rose, *Rehearsal for Reconstruction: The Port Royal Experiment* (1964; reprint, Athens: University of Georgia Press, 1999).

—Justin J. Behrend

Porter, David Dixon (1813–1891)

CIVIL WAR admiral David Dixon Porter was destined for naval service. As the son of Comdr. David Porter and Evelina Anderson Porter, he frequently joined his father on expeditions, including a mission against Caribbean pirates in 1824. In 1829 Porter joined the U.S. Navy and began his own distinguished naval career. He rose through the

ranks and was promoted to commander when war broke out in April 1861.

Throughout the Civil War, the U.S. Navy was given responsibility for cutting off Southern commerce, according to the "Anaconda Plan" of Gen. WINFIELD SCOTT. For the first several years of the war, Porter played an important role in making the Northern blockade a reality. Porter's most important contribution came in March 1862, when he joined his foster brother, Adm. DAVID GLASGOW FARRAGUT, in an attempt to capture the crucial Southern port of New Orleans, Louisiana. Porter commanded several mortar boats that were responsible for shelling Forts Jackson and St. Philip. When the forts fell, New Orleans was open to capture by the Northern military. The victory was a critical step in the Union's goal, ultimately successful, to control the MISSISSIPPI RIVER.

Porter's success led to his promotion in September 1862 to command of the Mississippi Squadron as acting rear admiral. In that capacity, Porter worked with Gen. ULYSSES S. GRANT and his troops to take the Confederate stronghold of Vicksburg, Mississippi, in 1862 and 1863. Porter took part in one of the first failed attempts to skirt the fortifications at Vicksburg. He led his boats on a treacherous attempt to navigate the lower Yazoo to Steele's Bayou, but the ships foundered in the narrow waters, which were filled with trees and debris. Porter's fleet was nearly destroyed by Confederate forces, and he had to call in ground help to rescue his naval force. Ultimately, Porter redeemed himself with a daring midnight run past blazing Confederate batteries on April 16, 1863. Porter's fleet of ships successfully delivered Grant's troops to a location past the city, allowing them to march on and seize the Mississippi capital of Jackson. This cut off Vicksburg's supply lines and made the fall of the city almost inevitable.

In October 1864 Porter was promoted to command of the North Atlantic Squadron. Shortly after assuming his new command, Porter again found himself in a tough spot, this time during Gen. Nathaniel P. Banks's RED RIVER CAMPAIGN. Porter's forces just barely escaped destruction by Confederates after becoming stranded by the low water level in the Red River. Quick action by Lt. Col. Joseph Bailey and his engineering brigade was all that saved Porter and his men. Bailey designed dams along the river so as to raise the water level enough to allow Porter's ships to run the treacherous Alexandria Rapids and escape.

In the fall of 1864, Porter led the war's largest fleet of ships against Fort Fisher, the garrison that guarded the entry to Wilmington, North Carolina. Porter's first shelling attempt did little damage, but a renewed attack allowed Gen. A. H. Terry's forces to storm and seize the fort on January 15, 1865.

After the Civil War, Porter remained in the navy and was named superintendent of the UNITED STATES NAVAL

ACADEMY AT ANNAPOLIS, a position he held from 1865 to 1869. While serving as superintendent, Porter helped to reform the curriculum and expand the facilities at the academy. Porter was promoted to the rank of vice admiral in 1866 and admiral of the navy in 1870. He died in WASHINGTON, D.C., on February 13, 1891.

See also NEW ORLEANS, BATTLE OF; VICKSBURG CAMPAIGN.

Further reading: Chester A. Hearn, *Admiral David Dixon Porter: The Civil War Years* (Annapolis: Naval Institute Press, 1996); David Dixon Porter, *The Naval History of the Civil War* (1886; reprint, Secaucus, N.J.: Castle, 1984).

—Ruth A. Behling

prisons

At the start of the CIVIL WAR, the U.S. Army totaled 16,000 men. Just over a year later, when troops under ULYSSES S. GRANT conquered Fort Donelson, they accepted the surrender of 15,000 prisoners in a single day. The capture of large numbers of prisoners became a common phenomenon during the Civil War, a by-product of the incredible growth in the scale of warfare at that time. Nothing in the experience of leaders on either side prepared them for the logistics of dealing with the 650,000 men that were taken captive during the Civil War. As the war dragged on, both sides struggled to develop workable solutions, with many soldiers suffering miserably or dying as a result.

In the early months of the war, prisoners were sometimes exchanged informally on the authority of field commanders, whose actions were governed by custom, their sense of chivalry, and logistical constraints. When an exchange could not be arranged, soldiers were paroled. A paroled soldier agreed to remain at home or at a specified location in enemy territory, staying out of the fight until an exchange had been arranged. While it was not technically within the power of field commanders to agree to exchanges and paroles, the practice was overlooked because of the widely held belief that the war would not last long.

By the end of 1861, however, it became clear that the war was not going to end quickly. The number of men being held prisoner increased dramatically, and Confederate authorities began to press for a formal agreement on the exchange of prisoners. President ABRAHAM LINCOLN hesitated, for to enter into such an agreement would be equal to recognizing the legitimacy of the Confederate government. Eventually, he was forced to bow to public pressure from the families of prisoners, and he appointed a negotiator to meet with Confederate authorities. After several rounds of negotiations, the Confederacy's D. H. Hill and the Union's John A. Dix reached agreement.

The Dix-Hill cartel, signed on July 22, 1862, was modeled after a similar agreement used during the War of 1812. By its terms, various ranks were assigned exchange "values." A noncommissioned officer was equal in value to two privates, a second lieutenant was worth three privates, and so forth all the way up to a commanding general, who could be exchanged for 60 privates or any combination of soldiers equal in value to 60 privates. Each side was to hold its own parolees until exchanges were arranged. Thus, Union authorities were responsible for holding paroled Union soldiers, while Confederate authorities were responsible for holding paroled Confederates. The Confederates were generally allowed to wait at their homes, but captured Union soldiers were held in one of three Union parole camps: Camp Chase in Ohio, Benton Barracks in Missouri, and Camp Parole in Maryland.

The Dix-Hill cartel quickly proved to be unworkable for a variety of reasons. First of all, there was constant conflict between Union and Confederate authorities. The most common debate was over the status of prisoners—whether they had been properly exchanged or not. Both sides invariably argued that the other was returning soldiers to duty too quickly. These disputes were complicated by personal animosities that existed between officials on both sides. The relationship between Confederate commissioner Robert Ould and the Union's BENJAMIN F. BUTLER, who temporarily oversaw prisoner exchanges for the Union before being reassigned, was particularly icy.

The Dix-Hill cartel was also problematic because its terms were highly unfavorable to the Union. In the early years of the war, there were invariably more Union prisoners than Confederate prisoners. For this reason, Union parolees were often detained for a long time while waiting for enough Confederate soldiers to be captured so that an exchange could be made. Union authorities had not planned for such long detentions, and their parole camps became dangerously overcrowded. Conditions were so bad that one superintendent of a Union parole facility noted that the soldiers would have been better off remaining in a Confederate prison.

Prison exchanges under the Dix-Hill cartel were unfavorable to the Northern war effort in another way. The Confederacy had a much smaller population than the Union. They could not replace captured soldiers. The Union, on the other hand, could replenish lost manpower. Therefore, the Union's bottom line dictated that it was better to keep captured Confederates imprisoned rather than try to exchange them. Of course, the implication of this was that many Union prisoners would be sacrificed by being allowed to remain in Confederate hands.

The Dix-Hill agreement ended with Lincoln's pledge to enlist African-American soldiers, contained within the provisions of the EMANCIPATION PROCLAMATION. The Confederacy refused to recognize black soldiers as legitimate prisoners, declaring that captured black soldiers would not be exchanged and, instead, would be enslaved. The Lincoln administration insisted on equal treatment for black soldiers and refused to continue exchanges under any other conditions. Confederate authorities would not back down. Union authorities were already unhappy with the terms of the Dix-Hill agreement, and this provided Lincoln with a compelling reason to abandon it. Thus, in mid-1863, prisoner exchanges were suspended.

The timing of the cartel's suspension proved to be catastrophic. Some of the largest battles of the war occurred in the summer of 1863, and many men were captured. Union and Confederate authorities, already having trouble caring for the prisoners they had, were now overwhelmed. The Confederates, under the direction of Gen. John Winder, responded by opening or expanding several prison facilities, the largest of which were Libby Prison in RICHMOND, Belle Isle just outside of Richmond, Salisbury Prison in North Carolina, and the notorious ANDERSONVILLE PRISON in Georgia. The Union, under the leadership of Col. William Hoffman, followed suit with Camp Douglas in Chicago, Camp Chase in Ohio, Johnson's Island in Ohio, Elmira in New York, Camp Morton in Indianapolis, and Rock Island in Illinois.

Life in these hastily created prison facilities was generally miserable for captives. This was especially true in the prisons of the resource-strapped Confederacy, but it was true in most Union prisons as well. Shelter was often inadequate, and many men had no shelter at all. Often prisoners were not issued replacements for items of clothing that wore out, and they were forced to brave the winter months with little protection from the elements. The amount of food that captives received tended to be insufficient. Prisoners were supposed to be issued the same rations active soldiers received, but this rarely was the case. Disease was rampant, due to the crowded accommodations and malnutrition.

Black prisoners, not surprisingly, had the worst situation of all. Often they were not afforded the opportunity to surrender but, rather, were slaughtered in cold blood. Those that did reach prisons tended to be mistreated and were generally compelled to perform menial labor. Although the Confederate government did not follow through on its threat to return them to SLAVERY, their situation was not much better than if they had been.

Prisoners did what they could to make their lives better. In officers' prisons, such as Libby Prison and Johnson's Island, men were permitted to purchase goods and receive packages from their families. Sometimes, inmates at enlisted men's prisons were afforded the same privileges. Generally, white prisoners were not expected to work, and so they had ample free time. The men read, participated in classes, played games, wrote LETTERS and diaries, made handicrafts, held religious meetings, staged plays, and did whatever else they could to relieve their boredom. Many inmates spent time making escape plans, which were occasionally successful. The largest escape occurred on February 9, 1864, when 109 Union officers traveled through an underground tunnel they had dug under Libby Prison.

Most prisoners, however, were unable to escape and were forced to endure prison life. By late 1863, the misery endured by captives on both sides became an important political issue, as both Confederate and Union authorities used stories of prisoner mistreatment as propaganda. Eventually, political pressure led to a compromise in April 1864, and the sickest prisoners on both sides were exchanged. The "living skeletons" returned by the Confederates seemed to confirm suspicions that they were deliberately mistreating prisoners. Some Northerners became determined to exact revenge on the South, and Secretary of War Edwin M. Stanton reduced Confederate prisoners' already inadequate rations. Many Northern citizens blamed the soldiers' suffering on President Lincoln because he had suspended prisoner exchanges, and for a time he believed the issue would have an impact on his reelection chances.

In January 1865 the desperate Confederates finally capitulated and agreed to exchange black soldiers. By this time, Northern authorities felt that the war was in hand and that nothing was to be gained by allowing imprisoned Union soldiers to suffer any further, so they agreed to resume the exchanges. By May 1865, all prisoners on both sides had been released. Of course, for many men it was too late. Of the estimated 462,634 Confederates taken prisoner, 25,976 died, a mortality rate of 12 percent. Of the estimated 211,411 Union soldiers captured, 30,218 died in captivity, a rate of 15.5 percent. Nearly 9 percent of the men who died during the war did so in prison.

After 1865, many Northerners pressed for the punishment of those responsible for the suffering of Union prisoners, and Judge Advocate General Joseph Holt was given the responsibility of investigating the matter. His efforts to identify and apprehend the presumed guilty parties were generally unsuccessful, although he was able to see to it that Andersonville superintendent Henry Wirz was tried and executed. Wirz, who was more incompetent than he was deliberately cruel, became the only person to be executed for war crimes during the Civil War. Meanwhile, Confederate authorities, including JEFFERSON DAVIS, argued in newspapers and books that Confederate prisons had done their best with the resources available to them. However, these apologists tended to be drowned out by the prisoners themselves, who also took pen in hand. Based on the available testimony, this was one area where the Confederacy proved unable to redeem itself after the war.

Further reading: Robert E. Denney, *Civil War Prisons and Escapes: A Day-by-Day Chronicle* (London: Sterling Publications, 1993); Michael P. Gray, *The Business of Captivity: Elmira and Its Civil War Prison* (Kent, Ohio: Kent State University Press, 2001); William B. Hesseltine, *Civil War Prisons: A Study in War Psychology* (Columbus: Ohio State University Press, 1998).

—Christopher Bates

prostitution

Women who engaged in sexual intercourse for money, or prostitutes, primarily worked in the urban areas during the 19th century. It is difficult to estimate with any reliability exactly how many prostitutes were working at any given time given the moral stigma associated with the profession. The best numbers available come from a study done by Dr. William Sanger, who was a well-known expert at the time. Studying prostitutes in NEW YORK CITY from 1850 to 1870, he found a steady rise in the number of women engaging in the trade, from 5,413 in 1850 to 8,750 in 1860 to 9,894 in 1870. By 1870, when he concluded his study, Sanger estimated that 2 percent of New York's women were working as prostitutes.

Prostitutes who worked in brothels, also known as "bawdy houses," "bordellos," or "bagnios," tended to be favored by the members of the upper class and by young, single, middle-class men living in the city on their own. These establishments were typically run by former prostitutes, called "madams," and were usually fairly discreet. Brothels often served liquor and food and would sometimes entertain men for an entire weekend. Less-affluent working-class men, such as sailors, could not afford such luxuries and were compelled to find prostitutes in the public places that they were known to frequent, particularly cigar stores, dance halls, and THEATERS.

The public presence of prostitutes in high-profile cities such as New York and Philadelphia called forth many moral reform or antivice movements, beginning early in the 19th century and gathering momentum in the 1830s and 1840s and lasting to the end of the century. Christian ministers and middle-class women agitated against prostitutes and their customers, calling for harsher laws on the one hand and positive programs to restore the "fallen angels" away from their degraded lives on the other. Victorian notions of Christian propriety elevated the status of women based on their domesticity, purity, and piety. Obviously, the idea of young women selling their bodies for the sexual pleasure of men was deeply disturbing to many citizens. Yet in an era of growing poverty, many prostitutes felt forced to enter the trade due to financial considerations. At a time when living expenses were about $1.50 per week for a single woman, factory and domestic jobs paid between 75¢ and $2.00 a week. A successful prostitute, on the other hand, could earn $50 to $100 a week.

Political authorities in cities, responding to public outrage, regularly took steps to curtail the spread of prostitution, passing vagrancy laws or arresting any woman suspected of being a prostitute. In 1873 New York's Committee for the Suppression of Legalized Vice was founded by prominent ABOLITIONists and feminists, including Susan B. Anthony and Elizabeth Blackwell. These female purity reformers demanded new and strictly enforced, laws against rape and prostitution.

There was opposition to these actions. Some doctors fought against antiprostitution laws, fearing they would lose business. Even some religious conservatives opposed steps taken to curtail prostitution, believing that God would punish prostitutes for their immorality by giving them sexually transmitted diseases. However, most Christian reformers believed in the redemption and reform of prostitutes and their clients.

Sexually transmitted diseases were indeed a major risk for prostitutes, particularly given the fact that some diseases, such as syphilis, could be fatal. Another problem was unwanted pregnancies. Although a number of methods of birth control, including condoms, were available, they were often unreliable or difficult to obtain. Rape was also a major concern of prostitutes, and although rape laws existed, convictions were rare. Most women worked as prostitutes for very short periods of their lives, and many came to tragic ends.

During the CIVIL WAR, prostitution increased. From 1861 to 1865, the majority of women worked as NURSES or in soldier's aid societies, fulfilling their traditional Victorian roles as domestic nurturers. Less motherly were the thousands of prostitutes who flocked to the cities from WASHINGTON, D.C., and RICHMOND to the lesser-known depots, such as Keokuk, Iowa, and Sewanee, Tennessee. Most notorious were Memphis and Nashville, where prostitution was placed under military licensing to control disease, an experiment that did not outlast the war years. One private described Nashville's red-light district: "There was an old saying that no man could be a soldier unless he had gone through Smokey Row. . . . Women had no thought of dress or decency. They said Smokey Row killed more soldiers than the war."

Many young volunteer soldiers, away from their families for the first time, took advantage of the opportunity to drink, gamble, and consort with the kind of women that were scorned back at home. Soldiers stationed in or near cities were particularly likely to solicit prostitutes, who often walked the streets quite openly. One reporter stationed in Washington, D.C., for example, complained that the city was "the most pestiferous hole since the days of Sodom and Gomorrah." Prostitutes sometimes traveled with the armies, as well.

Some commanders were unconcerned with the sexual behavior of their men. Generals DANIEL E. SICKLES and JOSEPH HOOKER were notoriously liberal in their attitudes about sex, although the story that the slang term *hooker* was adopted from the general's name is not true. Most generals and junior officers were less understanding than Sickles and Hooker, however, and did what they could to limit their men's access to prostitutes. This was due to a combination of moral concerns and practical matters—men inflicted with sexually transmitted diseases were made temporarily or permanently unavailable for duty. Despite the best efforts of Northern leadership, there were 182,482 diagnosed cases of syphilis and gonorrhea among Union soldiers during the Civil War. There is little statistical information available for Confederate soldiers, but it can be assumed that the rates of infection were similar.

Further reading: Lori D. Ginsburg, *Women and the Work of Benevolence: Morality, Politics and Class in the 19th-Century United States* (New Haven, Conn.: Yale University Press, 1990); Thomas P. Lowry, *The Story the Soldiers Wouldn't Tell: Sex in the Civil War* (Mechanicsburg, Pa.: Stackpole Books, 1994); David J. Pivar, *Purity Crusade: Sexual Morality and Social Control, 1868–1900* (Westport, Conn.: Greenwood Press, 1973); Luc Sante, *Low Life: Lures and Snares of Old New York* (New York: Farrar, Straus and Giroux, 1991).

—Christopher Bates

Q

Quantrill, William Clarke (1837–1865)

William Clarke Quantrill was a captain of the Confederate Partisan Rangers and the infamous leader of a guerrilla band known as "Quantrill's Raiders." Born in Canal Dover, Ohio, on July 31, 1837, he was a schoolteacher before moving to the Kansas Territory in 1857. Bitter antagonism between ABOLITIONists and proSLAVERY factions characterized the Kansas of the 1850s, and Quantrill joined the proslavery "border ruffians" after a series of odd jobs in Utah and Colorado. Operating under the alias Charley Hart, Quantrill switched loyalties to "jayhawking" abolitionists in Lawrence, Kansas, where he was wanted by authorities for kidnapping and theft. His ambush of his own JAYHAWKER band at Morgan Walker's farm in Jackson County, Missouri, however, established him firmly in the proslavery faction of the BUSHWHACKERS.

Quantrill's growing group of followers was loosely affiliated with the Missouri State Guard commanded by Confederate Maj. Gen. Sterling Price. Quantrill's cavalry company also participated in the Battle of Wilson's Creek on August 10, 1861, in which the CONFEDERATE ARMY, under Brig. Gen. Ben McCulloch, defeated the Union forces under Capt. Nathaniel Lyon. Quantrill's Raiders continued to aid the Confederate cause throughout the war, largely by keeping Union troops distracted and away from the larger Confederate armies.

Officially made a captain of the Partisan Rangers on August 15, 1862, Quantrill often referred to himself as a colonel, and his followers usually numbered from a dozen to a couple hundred. Some of the most prominent members of the band included George Todd and Cole Younger, and later William "Bloody Bill" Anderson and Frank and Jesse James. The raiders were successful in looting and burning several small towns and garrisons on the Kansas-Missouri border and in murdering Union sympathizers, military and civilian alike. They sacked the towns of Aubry, Olathe, and Shawneetown, Kansas, and were briefly assigned to Col. Joe Shelby's regiment in Arkansas.

The best-known exploit of Quantrill's Raiders was the destruction of Lawrence, the center of abolitionist activity in Kansas, on August 21, 1863. Quantrill gathered a force of about 450 men, the largest guerrilla force organized at one time in the CIVIL WAR, for what is now considered the most terrible massacre of the entire war. The raiders murdered 150 men and burned and looted almost all of the town, possibly in retaliation for the forced deportation of family members and other sympathizers in Missouri, or perhaps for the deaths of female relatives who were killed when the building in which they were forcibly held collapsed.

The Raiders headed south for winter quarters, routing a small federal force in Baxter Springs, Kansas, on their way to Texas. While encamped in Mineral Creek, Texas, during the winter of 1863–64, tensions among leaders led to a breakdown in group cohesion. After returning to Missouri in April 1864, a quarrel between Quantrill and Todd resulted in Quantrill's leaving the Partisan Rangers and Todd's taking over the leadership. However, Quantrill, Todd, and Anderson briefly reunited to support Sterling Price's invasion of northern and western Missouri in the summer of 1864, during which Todd and Anderson were killed in action. This last major Confederate assault in Missouri dissolved in failure, and the effectiveness of guerrilla activities decreased as well.

Quantrill led a small band into Kentucky, where Maj. Gen. John M. Palmer sent out a group of federal bushwhackers against him, led by Edwin Terrill. In an ambush at Wakefield's farm near Bloomfield on May 10, 1865, Quantrill was disabled by a shot to the spine and was later taken to a military hospital in Louisville. He died there on June 6, 1865, and was buried in an unmarked grave. A strange series of events, however, later brought his body to rest in Canal Dover (Dover), Ohio, while the disintegrated remains of his ribs and spine were left in Louisville and his arm and shinbone were eventually buried in Higginsville, Missouri.

William Clarke Quantrill was considered to have leadership abilities, a calm disposition under pressure, and a tendency toward ruthlessness. His activities are an example of guerrilla warfare during the Civil War and illustrate the scale and nature of hostilities between proslavery and abolitionist forces in Kansas and Missouri in the 1850s and 1860s.

See also BLEEDING KANSAS; KANSAS-NEBRASKA ACT.

Further reading: Carl W. Breihan, *Quantrill and His Civil War Guerrillas* (New York: Promontory Press, 1974); Albert E. Castel, *William Clarke Quantrill: His Life and Times* (Norman: University of Oklahoma Press, 1999); Michael Fellman, *Inside War: The Guerilla Conflict in Missouri during the American Civil War* (New York: Oxford University Press, 1989).

—Stacey Graham

R

race and racial conflict

Although race and SLAVERY were at the center of the long sectional conflict that led up to the CIVIL WAR, at the beginning of the war few Americans either Northern or Southern would admit that the war was about slavery. Leaders on both sides insisted that they were fighting to preserve the Constitution and to protect the rights of white citizens of the United States. Despite such statements, however, race was a central part of how Americans thought about the Civil War, and racial conflict was a key factor on the HOME-FRONT of both the Confederacy and the Union.

The Confederate Constitution guaranteed the rights of its citizens to own slaves and to take them into the western territories (the latter point was central to the debates and compromises of the antebellum period). It did not allow for the importation of slaves, and it held open the possibility that future states could choose not to allow slavery. There was little confusion in the South about the role of slavery in the Confederate war effort. For Southerners, the main concern was how to deal with the slaves they already had.

Most slave men and women knew that their futures depended on which side won the Civil War. Nearly 200,000 African Americans, mostly former slaves, were able to strike a blow against slavery by serving in the UNION ARMY. Those slaves who were unable to take refuge within Union lines sometimes broke the rules that had governed slavery for generations. They talked back to white folks, took liberties with their masters' property, and ignored restrictions on their movements. Kate Stone, a Southern plantation mistress, reported crowds of "strange Negro men" standing around Delhi, Louisiana, where her refugee family paused on their journey to Texas during the war. Although a mob of black men had reportedly robbed another party of REFUGEES, the men Kate saw simply stood and grinned, which "terrified us more and more." On another occasion, a company of black men actually threatened Kate and her mother with pistols. No harm came to them, but the incident was obviously frightening for a person raised around obedient slaves. Despite incidents like these, in which slaves took advantage of the confusion and of the absence of many white men to test the boundaries of slavery, there was surprisingly little serious resistance among Southern slaves during the Civil War. No slave rebellions were reported, although in 1861 a conspiracy among slaves living near Natchez was suspected; dozens of slaves were killed and beaten as a result. This was rare, however, and a majority of slaves remained on their masters' PLANTATIONS, doing their jobs and waiting for whatever the end of the war would bring.

One of the most difficult questions facing the United States was the issue of slavery. Congress passed several CONFISCATION ACTS during the first year of the war that allowed army commanders to confiscate the property, including slaves, of Southerners loyal to the Confederacy. President ABRAHAM LINCOLN refused to act. Northern ABOLITIONists wanted him to come out publicly against slavery and to make its destruction one of the official war aims of the federal government. HORACE GREELEY, the editor of the *New York Tribune*, urged the president to do just that in a letter published in his newspaper called "Prayer of Twenty Millions." Lincoln's famous reply was, "My paramount object *is* to save the Union, and *is not* either to save or to destroy slavery."

Lincoln's reluctance to come out against slavery was due to several factors. First of all, four slave states—Missouri, Kentucky, Maryland, and Delaware—had remained in the Union, and Lincoln did not want to anger them by taking steps against slavery. Secondly, Northern Democrats did not want to make the war to save the Union into a war to end slavery. Most soldiers in the UNION ARMY cared little about the issue of slavery, and most Northerners were not interested in the plight of slaves in the South. Finally, although Lincoln had hated the institution of slavery ever since witnessing it as a young man during a trip to New Orleans, the president did not believe that white people in the United States would ever allow African Americans to receive political or social equality. He even told a group of black leaders who visited him in 1862 that it would be better if the races were separated by sending black Americans to colonies in Africa.

Lincoln did, of course, make the elimination of slavery one of the war aims of the United States with the EMANCIPATION PROCLAMATION. He issued the preliminary version of the proclamation on September 22, 1862; the "final" version went into effect on January 1, 1863. The proclamation was undertaken, Lincoln said, as a military measure. It freed no slaves in the border states or in any areas occupied by U.S. forces. It applied only to slaves living in those parts of the Confederacy still "in rebellion" against the United States. His reasoning for the proclamation was that it would encourage slaves to run away, to resist their masters, and to undermine the Confederate war effort. He also believed that bringing the issue of slavery into the war would ward off any sort of intervention by European countries like Great Britain and France, who had considered helping the Confederacy but, because their governments were officially against slavery, could not very well support a country openly fighting to preserve it.

The Emancipation Proclamation was met with a storm of protest. Democrats hated it, and in the 1862 election a number of Democrats won races for state legislatures and Congress at least partly because of Lincoln's decision. Many white Americans opposed the recruiting of African Americans for the U.S. Army, which began late in 1862. And when New Yorkers rioted against being conscripted into the army in the summer of 1863, they made scapegoats out of African Americans, a number of whom were killed by mobs.

EMANCIPATION continued anyway, and most Northerners eventually got used to the idea. Union soldiers were even given pocket-sized versions of the Emancipation Proclamation to hand out to free African Americans and slaves. It is unknown how many read them, but wherever Union troops went in the South, slaves ran away from their masters and began their new lives as free people. When Congress passed the THIRTEENTH AMENDMENT late in the war and the states ratified it toward the end of 1865, the way was paved for all African Americans to begin the process of becoming full citizens, a result of the Civil War that few Americans would have predicted four years before. Unfortunately, the habits of the long span of U.S. history were hard to overcome, and despite the best efforts of Radical RECONSTRUCTION, racial assumptions and habits of the United States were not greatly changed by the victory of Union forces on the battlefield.

See also AFRICAN-AMERICAN REGIMENTS; BLACK CODES; NEW YORK CITY DRAFT RIOTS.

Further reading: Lawanda C. Fenlanson Cox, *Lincoln and Black Freedom: A Study in Presidential Leadership* (Columbia: University of South Carolina Press, 1994); James M. McPherson, *The Negro's Civil War: How American Blacks Felt and Acted during the War for the Union* (New York: Vintage Books, 1967).

—James Marten

Radical Republicans

A group of the REPUBLICAN PARTY that controlled Congress briefly in the post–CIVIL WAR period, the Radical Republicans sought a vastly changed Southern political, economic, and social world. They insisted on civil and voting rights for freedmen and opposed President ANDREW JOHNSON's efforts to reunite the sections without forcing major changes on the former Confederate states.

Throughout the Civil War, the Republican Party enjoyed a large majority of both houses of Congress. This majority was hardly unified, however, as ideological divisions between congressional Republicans became increasingly pronounced over the course of the war. Most Republicans were satisfied with the moderate approach to the war advocated by President ABRAHAM LINCOLN. Radicals, however, such as CHARLES SUMNER, BENJAMIN WADE, and THADDEUS STEVENS, were constantly at odds with the president over the timing and pace of EMANCIPATION, the enrollment of black soldiers, and the advancement of equal rights for the freedpeople. Already frustrated over Lincoln's slowness concerning racial progress, the Radical Republicans also clashed bitterly with the president over his lenient wartime RECONSTRUCTION policies.

As the war ended, Congress began to focus on plans for reconstructing the shattered nation. The Radicals believed that the end of the war represented an opportunity to remake Southern society into a free-labor, egalitarian, and racially just society. Senator Sumner of Massachusetts provided a clear justification for this position: He declared that the Southern states had committed "suicide" when they left the Union and thus had reverted to the status of territories. Conveniently, the control of territories fell to Congress.

Moderates such as James G. Blaine in the House and John Sherman in the Senate preferred a less revolutionary approach. They, like most Northerners, demanded that Southern citizens pledge loyalty to the Union, accept freedom for the African Americans, and provide basic protections to the freedpeople as they established their new lives.

Initially, these two views existed in a delicate balance. Congressional Republicans of all positions were willing to work with the new president, Andrew Johnson. They expected him to articulate his own reconstruction plan, and then compromise with Congress over points of disagreement. Unfortunately, Johnson believed that control of the reconstruction process should be exclusively in his hands. Radical Republicans took the lead in organizing the opposition to presidential Reconstruction, with serious consequences for Johnson.

Johnson, a clumsy politician, managed to offend his most sympathetic congressional constituents, the moderate Republicans. Now they totally supported the actions of Radical Republicans, who persuaded their colleagues to refuse to seat Southern congressmen elected under Johnson's reconstruction plan. Moreover, Radicals also established the Joint Committee on Reconstruction, a platform from which they led the anti-Johnson movement.

Johnson vetoed both the FREEDMEN'S BUREAU Bill and CIVIL RIGHTS ACT OF 1866. Congress passed both over his veto, signaling the final breakdown of relations between the Radicals and the president. All in the North seemed to support using the power of the federal government to ensure freedom and safety for the vulnerable population of ex-slaves. One Republican newspaper editorialized that civil rights for the freedpeople "follows from the suppression of the rebellion. . . . The party is nothing, if it does not do this the nation is dishonored . . ."

In 1867 Congress also overrode the president's veto of the RECONSTRUCTION ACTS, which divided the South into five military districts whose commanders were to exercise authority to oversee the steps of readmittance back into the Union. African Americans were to be registered to vote, while former Confederates were disqualified. Each state wishing to rejoin the Union had to ratify the FOURTEENTH AMENDMENT and to draft a new state constitution that guaranteed the citizenship rights of black people.

After the Tenure of Office Act was passed, forbidding Johnson to remove cabinet members without congressional approval, Johnson's only recourse was to remove the military commanders who did not support him. The former Confederates states were in near anarchy. This was particularly dangerous for African Americans, who were left unprotected from the fury of former Confederates.

By 1868 Congress and the president had become so estranged that the Radicals were able to bring articles of impeachment against the president. Johnson escaped conviction by one vote, and the failure of impeachment signaled the beginning of the end of the Radicals' hold on power.

The Radical Republicans lost their prominent position in the party by the election of 1868. The moderates, led by President ULYSSES S. GRANT, now had the responsibility of implementing congressional Reconstruction in the Southern states. The death of several of the Radicals' most powerful and famous leaders, especially Sumner and Stevens, contributed to the decline of the faction as well.

As the years wore on, white Southern resistance to efforts by Republicans to integrate freed people into Southern politics and society grew stronger, not weaker. The restructuring of Southern life from outside seemed useless, and the Northern public had lost its enthusiasm for it. Instead, Northerners wanted to forget the war and welcome Southerners back into the Union.

Although some historians have judged the Radical Republicans harshly for the failure or the inadequacy of their programs, other scholars argue that it is well worth recognizing the value of the goals for which the Radicals fought. Civil rights, suffrage, and the elimination of the racial hierarchy of the South seemed within their reach. After all, few could imagine in 1860 that 4 million African Americans would be free in just a few years. African Americans had achieved legal equality by the end of Reconstruction, although social and political equality would have to wait much longer. Perhaps the most important legislation in American history passed with the aid and guidance of the Radical Republicans and was the foundation for much of the racial progress in the 20th century.

See also BLACK CODES; IMPEACHMENT OF ANDREW JOHNSON.

Further reading: Michael Les Benedict, *A Compromise of Principle: Congressional Republicans and Reconstruction, 1863–1869* (New York: Norton, 1975); Allan Bogue, *The Earnest Men: Republicans of the Civil War Senate* (Ithaca, N.Y.: Cornell University Press, 1981); Hans L. Trefousse, *The Radical Republicans: Lincoln's Vanguard for Racial Justice* (New York: Knopf, 1968).

—Fiona Galvin

railroads

Inspired by success in Britain, American entrepreneurs lobbied for railroad construction in the late 1820s. By the end of the 1850s total rail mileage in the United States reached 30,000 miles. The initial boom of rail building was concentrated in the Northeast and Midwest. By 1860 one could reach almost anywhere east of the MISSISSIPPI RIVER from New York in a week or less. American lawmakers championed the railroad as a triumph over nature and claimed that its growth connected remote areas to a political and economic center.

When the CIVIL WAR broke out in 1860 railroad growth continued, but largely in the Northern states. Better TRANSPORTATION links ultimately helped Union troops by providing them quicker access to supplies and a means to move fresh troops. Confederate troops were hurt by a Southern railroad system geared toward the movement of cotton and reliant on Northern industries for repair

Photograph showing a construction train on the Union Pacific Railroad *(Library of Congress)*

materials. In the middle of the war, Congress created two federally chartered corporations to build a transcontinental railroad. The acts granted the Central Pacific Railroad the right to build eastward beginning in Sacramento, California, and the Union Pacific Railroad the right to build westward from Omaha, Nebraska. Each corporation was given land to lay rails as well as large parcels of land on either side of the line to develop as they saw fit. While the land grants created space for new towns, they bypassed other areas and upset already settled NATIVE AMERICAN lands.

Irish immigrants, African Americans, and Civil War VETERANS worked in gangs from Omaha to build 1,086 miles of the Union Pacific. From California, a largely Chinese labor force built 689 miles of the Central Pacific over the treacherous Sierra Nevada. On May 10, 1869, the two lines met at Promontory Point, Utah. The nation's first transcontinental railroad was completed.

Whereas before the Civil War rail lines followed the pattern of settlement, afterward the rapid expansion of the railroad usually preceded and encouraged settlement. The railroad acted as a major transportation system for western settlers. Railroads also shifted economic and political power westward.

Railroad enterprises became America's first major corporations. The amount of capital needed to build a road and maintain a line led to the increased economic power of banks and investment houses. After linking the West and East, railroads helped to focus attention on national issues, including the emerging connections between government and industry.

See also PACIFIC RAILROAD ACT.

Further reading: David Haward Bain, *Empire Express: Building the First Transcontinental Railroad* (New York: Viking, 1999); John E. Clark Jr., *Railroads in the Civil War: The Impact of Management on Victory and Defeat* (Baton Rouge: Louisiana State University Press, 2001); Mark W. Summers, *Railroads, Reconstruction, and the Gospel of Prosperity: Aid under the Radical Republicans, 1865–1877* (Princeton, N.J.: Princeton University Press, 1984).

—Samantha Holtkamp Gervase

Rainey, Joseph H. (1832–1887)

Four-term congressman and well-to-do barber, Joseph Hayne Rainey was born a slave in Georgetown, South Carolina. When he was a child, his family purchased its freedom and moved to Charleston.

Forced to labor on Confederate fortifications in Charleston at the beginning of the CIVIL WAR, Rainey fled to Bermuda with his wife, Susan, for the duration of the war. In 1865 he returned to South Carolina and involved himself in REPUBLICAN PARTY politics. He represented

Georgetown County at the state constitutional convention of 1868. A year later, he was appointed census taker and later served as county agent for the state land commission and brigadier general in the state militia. As a member of the state senate, Rainey had a generally conservative record. He rejected land confiscation for freedmen and endorsed a poll tax. In 1870 he was elected to Congress, the first black American to be seated in the U.S. House of Representatives.

Rainey was a member of the 41st–45th Congresses (1870–79). In the House, he was mostly known for his strident support of the ENFORCEMENT ACTS, legislation designed to protect African Americans from violent attacks by groups such as the KU KLUX KLAN. Speaking on the issue of whether the Civil War amendments necessitated the expansion of the powers of the federal government, Rainey said: "I desire that so broad and liberal a construction be placed upon its provisions as will insure the protection to the humblest citizen. Tell me nothing of a constitution which fails to shelter beneath its rightful power the people of a country."

Rainey was defeated for reelection in 1878. After leaving Congress, he was appointed a U.S. Internal Revenue agent, a position he held for two years. He then moved to WASHINGTON, D.C., where he was involved in the banking and brokerage business for several years. Rainey died in Georgetown, South Carolina in 1887.

See also KU KLUX KLAN ACT.

Further reading: Eric Foner, *Freedom's Lawmakers: A Directory of Black Officeholders during Reconstruction* (Baton Rouge: Louisiana State University Press, 1996); Cyril Outerbridge Packwood, *Detour—Bermuda: Destination—U.S. House of Representatives: The Life of Joseph Hayne Rainey* (Hamilton, Bermuda: Baxter's, 1977).

—Justin J. Behrend

Ray, Charlotte (1850–1911)

An activist for WOMEN'S RIGHTS and the first African-American woman admitted to the bar, Charlotte Ray was born in NEW YORK CITY to Reverend Charles Bennett Ray and his second wife, Charlotte Augusta Burroughs. Charles Ray, editor of the *Colored American,* was one of the most distinguished African Americans in New York. He also participated in the UNDERGROUND RAILROAD, assisting fugitives from SLAVERY. Charlotte, one of seven children, attended the Institution for the Education of Colored Youth in WASHINGTON, D.C.

After school, Ray obtained a position teaching in the normal and preparatory departments at Howard University. While at Howard, Ray attended law school, earning a Juris Doctoris in February 1872. In March of that year, Ray was admitted to the bar. She was the first African-American woman admitted to any bar and the first woman admitted to the bar in Washington, D.C.

Ray attempted to practice law in Washington but found that prejudice against her was too strong. In spite of Washington's long history as a haven for educated, affluent, and professional African-Americans, Ray was unable to sustain her practice and was forced to find other EMPLOYMENT. Her connection with the city of her birth had been renewed when she joined the NATIONAL WOMAN SUFFRAGE ASSOCIATION of New York, and in 1879 she returned to New York to live. Although she could not practice law, Ray used her extensive education by teaching in Brooklyn's public schools. In 1886 she met and married a man named Fraim, with whom she lived until her death from bronchitis in 1911.

Further reading: Darlene Clark Hine, *Black Women in America: An Historical Encyclopedia* (Brooklyn: Carlson Publishing, 1993); J. Clay Smith, *Emancipation: The Making of the Black Lawyer, 1844–1944* (Philadelphia: University of Pennsylvania Press, 1993).

—Megan Quinn

Reconstruction (1865–1877)

Reconstruction was the process of bringing the 11 seceded Southern states back into the Union. The goals of Reconstruction were twofold: to restore harmonious relations between the sections, and to define and secure freedom for the ex-slaves. The term also describes the period directly after the CIVIL WAR. Until fairly recently, Reconstruction was portrayed as an evil time when ignorant and base African Americans, corrupt and greedy CARPETBAGGERS, and treacherous SCALAWAGS ruled and ruined the helpless white Southern population. According to this interpretation, only when the Southern Democratic "redeemers" recaptured the state governments from the REPUBLICAN PARTY did sanity again prevail throughout the region. The current history books present a far more positive and more complex depiction of the era. Reconstruction was a huge task that not only involved readmitting the seceded states but also reinventing a South without SLAVERY and rebuilding the Southern infrastructure that had been destroyed by the war.

The South paid a very high price for SECESSION, war, and bitter defeat. One out of every 10 white men was killed; much of the rich agricultural land in Virginia and large parts of Tennessee, Mississippi, Georgia, and South Carolina lay in ruins. Most of the South's cities and towns were burned or destroyed, including RICHMOND, Atlanta, and Columbia, South Carolina. Thousands of black and white REFUGEES were homeless and in dire circumstances.

Slavery was destroyed, and millions of human beings that had been property and capital were now free. What would that freedom entail? Economic, political, and moral questions central to the conflict had to be addressed as early as 1863. Indeed, Reconstruction unfolded in several stages: wartime Reconstruction, presidential Reconstruction, and congressional Reconstruction. The last stage was the so-called REDEMPTION of the South.

Wartime Reconstruction

The necessity to plan for Reconstruction began well before the end of the war. When President ABRAHAM LINCOLN's EMANCIPATION PROCLAMATION of 1863 officially freed the slaves in the Confederate states, it set in motion a radical alteration of the American South, which would complicate the task of reuniting the nation should the North prevail. From 1861 to 1863, the major Northern goal in the war was restoration of the Union. Now, added to that was a second goal: freedom for the slaves. As is well known, every aspect of the Southern economy and society was connected with the institution of slavery. Even the majority of Southerners who did not own slaves had a deep stake in the system. They sold their crops to plantation owners and elected proslavery men to represent them in office. Ordinary white farmers also helped to enforce slave codes and aspired to own slaves themselves. Thus, Reconstruction would not only involve bringing white Confederates back to the national "family" table but also setting a place at that table for black people whose status beyond freedom was unclear.

The Emancipation Proclamation proved a powerful weapon for the Northern military cause as 180,000 black men, most of them ex-slaves, donned the Union blue. This struck a mighty blow against the Confederacy. Successful Union campaigns brought more and more Southern territory—in Louisiana, Mississippi, Tennessee, and Arkansas—under Northern military control. Lincoln wanted to reinstate loyal civilian governments as soon as possible and demonstrate to Southerners that the United States would be forgiving in welcoming back to the fold the "errant children."

On December 8, 1863, Lincoln unveiled his Proclamation of Amnesty and Reconstruction. Lincoln based his authority to control Reconstruction on the section of the U.S. Constitution that states "that the President shall have power to grant reprieves and pardons for offenses against the United States." The proclamation offered generous terms to individuals and a simple and easy method for citizens to reestablish local and state governments. Former Confederates who took an oath of loyalty to the Union were given amnesty. High-ranking Confederate governmental and military officials were exempted from the oath's provisions. Once 10 percent of a state's voting population in 1860 had sworn allegiance to the Union, they could write a new constitution and hold elections to establish the state government. Lincoln's one requirement was that all of the states accept emancipation.

Lincoln's "Ten Percent Plan" was based on his firm belief that, because the Southern states could not legally secede, they were never out of the Union. Lincoln, realizing that the RADICAL REPUBLICANS had a far harsher plan in mind, seized the initiative with his proclamation and proceeded to order it implemented in Louisiana. Radical Republicans in Congress, such as THADDEUS STEVENS and CHARLES SUMNER, attacked Lincoln's Ten Percent Plan. They were alarmed that the plan was too easy on the rebels and made no provision for incorporating civil-rights protections for African Americans. Indeed, Radicals attacked Lincoln for taking rightful power away from the legislative branch. Radicals put forward the idea that the Confederacy had committed "state suicide" and had reverted to the status of territories. Since Congress had control over the process of admitting new territories to the nation, it should also control the process of readmitting the former rebel states.

Congress formulated a reconstruction program of its own with the WADE-DAVIS BILL in July 1864. The bill set high standards for reunion. It required a majority of the white male population to swear allegiance to the Constitution before they could begin the process of electing delegates to a state convention. Suffrage would be restricted to only those who had signed an IRONCLAD OATH. Wade-Davis required that the new state constitutions guarantee black citizens of the state equality under the law.

Lincoln pocket-vetoed (he refused to sign the bill, and it failed to become law) the Wade-Davis Bill in the summer of 1864. Congress responded by refusing to seat congressional delegates from Ten Percent Plan states, which by the end of the war included Louisiana, Tennessee, Arkansas, and Virginia. A standoff between the president and Congress was avoided due to Lincoln's triumphant reelection and the feelings of harmony engendered by the Union victory in late 1864 and early 1865. At the time of his death, Lincoln anticipated working with Congress to forge a sensible compromise on Reconstruction. Doubtless, Lincoln's skills as a politician would have avoided the disastrous conflict between the two branches of government that characterized the administration of the new president, Tennessee Democrat and former slaveholder ANDREW JOHNSON.

Presidential Reconstruction, 1865–1867

President Johnson was determined to follow Lincoln's precedent and set the terms for Reconstruction from the White House. Congress was not in session when Johnson assumed the presidency, and he controlled Reconstruction for nearly eight months, creating a storm of protest with his actions. He granted liberal pardons to those former Confederates not covered by his amnesty proclamation of May 1865. He went on to appoint provisional GOVERNORS for any Confederate states that had not already been "reconstructed" by Lincoln. He charged those governors with convening state constitutional conventions that would adopt the THIRTEENTH AMENDMENT, nullify secession, and repudiate all Confederate war debts. Johnson did not demand that the former Confederate states accept black suffrage, and, in the end, his restored South looked very much like the antebellum South without the legal institution of slavery.

Radical Republicans were outraged, and moderate members of Congress were troubled by reports of violence against African Americans. Just as problematic was the fact that many of the former Confederates, acting defiantly, were in control of the governments of these reconstructed states. Congress pushed for guarantees of rights and freedoms for African Americans and for the imposition of harsh penalties for former Confederate officials and officers. They were also eager to oversee the establishment of a viable Republican Party in the South.

Although in late 1865 and early 1866 Radical leaders were convinced that Congress needed to take complete control of Reconstruction, the majority still hoped for a workable compromise with Johnson. The moderates were willing to keep the new governments as long as some crucial modifications were added to Johnson's requirements. They demanded the acceptance of the FOURTEENTH AMENDMENT, which granted citizenship to African Americans, and the CIVIL RIGHTS ACT OF 1866. Johnson refused to bend. He argued that the amendment and the bill represented an unconstitutional expansion of national power over state sovereignty. Johnson vetoed the Civil Rights Act, and his veto was promptly overridden.

The language of Johnson's veto was crude and insulting to the Republicans; clearly, he was not interested in compromise of any sort. His political incompetence pushed an increasing number of moderate Republicans into the Radical fold. The Radicals wanted to recast the South in the free-labor style and establish a Southern Republican Party with the support and the votes of the freedmen. The fall elections of 1866 had supplied the Radicals with a mandate to pursue their program. Presidential Reconstruction

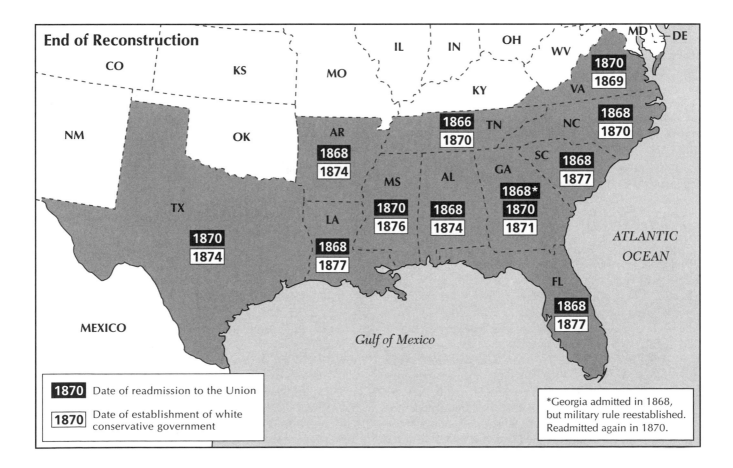

End of Reconstruction

| 1870 | Date of readmission to the Union |
| 1870 | Date of establishment of white conservative government |

*Georgia admitted in 1868, but military rule reestablished. Readmitted again in 1870.

was dead with the solid veto-proof Republican congressional majority.

Congressional Reconstruction 1867–1877

Congress passed the RECONSTRUCTION ACTS of 1867. The acts divided up the South into five military districts, each to be temporarily governed by an appointed U.S. army general who would oversee the transition of the new states back into the Union. The acts enfranchised freed people and disenfranchised many former officials of the Confederacy. The acts also made readmission to the Union contingent on granting suffrage to freedmen and ratifying the Fourteenth Amendment.

Johnson tried to block congressional Reconstruction, but his vetoes were overridden. The deeply hostile relationship between the president and Congress ultimately resulted in Johnson's impeachment trial. Despite avoiding conviction and removal from office by the Senate, Johnson was a lame-duck president. Congress controlled Reconstruction throughout the rest of his term in office and continued to hold the reins during the presidency of war-hero ULYSSES S. GRANT.

When Grant was elected in 1868, congressional Republicans believed they had a solid friend in the White House. Grant had previously sided against Johnson on matters pertaining to the reuniting of the Union, so Congress's plans for the Union seemed secure. Grant favored using the army and the federal Department of Justice to enforce Reconstruction in the South, and during his tenure in office the FIFTEENTH AMENDMENT granting suffrage to African-American men was passed.

The end of 1868 saw six former Confederate states—Alabama, Arkansas, Florida, Louisiana, North Carolina, and South Carolina—rejoin the nation under the Reconstruction Acts' requirements. In 1870, after ratifying the Fifteenth Amendment, Georgia, Mississippi, Texas, and Virginia were readmitted. Most of the above states were now under the control of the Republican Party, which governed with a biracial coalition. Southern Republicans were in power, but they faced momentous challenges in office. The Republicans needed the support of three major groups to establish a permanent presence in the Southern states. The first group comprised white Northerners that came South during the war and settled there after the war. These men were often former Union soldiers, Freedmen's Bureau agents, businesspeople, and teachers. Called carpetbaggers, they provided a solid core of leadership for the party. The second group was made of white Southerners sympathetic to the Union during the war. Scorned by many of their fellow Southerners, these "scalawags" desired a more economically progressive South that followed in the Northern footsteps. African Americans formed the third and largest group in the Republican coalition.

Under congressional Reconstruction and with the support of President Grant and the protection of the U.S. Army, freedmen joined UNION LEAGUES, voted enthusiastically, engaged in other political actions, and were elected to all levels of government throughout the South. South Carolina and Louisiana had a majority of African-American legislators, and there were 16 African Americans elected to the U.S. Congress. Most of the black officeholders were competent and intelligent men. The Republican state governments instituted positive changes during the 1870s, including introducing public school education, establishing welfare institutions, and encouraging business investment in the region. Unfortunately, corruption did taint many of the Republican administrations, an issue that the Southern Democrats used to great advantage.

Redemption

The depressed Southern economy could not be revived, and the region suffered from dire poverty throughout the Reconstruction period and well beyond 1877. The ex-slaves had hoped for land reform as well as the vote, but instead they settled for SHARECROPPING, a labor arrangement that favored the cotton planters. Meanwhile, the Republican coalition was coming apart under relentless pressure from white Democrats. Southerners railed against "Black Republicanism" and fought against "Negro rule." The KU KLUX KLAN and other terrorist organizations committed terrible acts of violence against African-American officeholders and Republican politicians and voters. The ENFORCEMENT ACTS stopped the Klan terror but could not stop the crumbling of the Republican Party and the reemergence of the Democrats. When white Southerners regained control of their state governments, they immediately removed African Americans from office and did whatever possible to deny black voters their voice in politics.

In the 1870s, both the federal government and the Northern people began to tire of the continual fight to reconstruct their former foes. Other issues, like the Indian Wars in the West and the CRÉDIT MOBILIER scandal, began to draw attention and energy away from Southern problems. The negative reactions to the Panic of 1873 brought the DEMOCRATIC PARTY back to power in the U.S. Congress for the first time since before the war. By 1876 only three Republican governments remained in the South: Florida, Louisiana, and South Carolina. After the close 1876 presidential election was marred by fraud, backroom deals allowed Republican Rutherford B. Hayes to take the White House over Democrat Samuel B. Tilden. Despite the fact that the Republican Party relied on African-American votes for their power in the South, Hayes ended Reconstruction when he pulled the army out of the South. By April 1877, "redemption" was complete and all of the states of the former Confederacy were again under Democratic rule.

Was Reconstruction a success or failure? If one of the goals of Reconstruction was to restore political, economic, and social relations between North and South, then it was a success. By 1876 the nation was stable and strong. If another goal was to bring justice to the freedpeople, then it was a failure. Four million Americans were free from the bonds of slavery, but poverty and racism severely limited their freedom.

Yet, the judgment of failure should be qualified. African Americans tested the limits of freedom and found pleasure in their new family and community lives. By late 1866, for example, Charleston's African-American community had built 11 churches in the city. By 1869 the FREEDMEN'S BUREAU, a federal welfare agency, was in charge of 3,000 schools that educated more than 150,000 black children throughout the South. Half of the teachers in those schools were African Americans. Finally, the Thirteenth, Fourteenth, and Fifteenth Amendments provided the foundation for the Civil Rights movement of the 1960s, when the promise of Reconstruction was fulfilled.

See also ASSASSINATION OF ABRAHAM LINCOLN; BLACK CODES; IMPEACHMENT OF ANDREW JOHNSON; KU KLUX KLAN ACT; LOYALTY OATHS.

Further reading: Eric Foner, *Reconstruction: America's Unfinished Revolution, 1863–1877* (New York: Harper & Row, 1988); John Hope Franklin, *Reconstruction after the Civil War* (Chicago: University of Chicago Press, 1994); Leon Litwack, *Been in the Storm So Long: The Aftermath of Slavery* (New York: Vintage Books, 1980).

—Ruth A. Behling

Reconstruction Acts (1867–1868)

The Reconstruction Acts were adopted by Congress in 1867 and 1868. These four bills laid out the terms for what would be known as congressional RECONSTRUCTION. The Reconstruction Acts were largely authored by the RADICAL REPUBLICANS and sought to remake Southern society.

When the CIVIL WAR ended, Congress was not in session. Responsibility for reconstructing the shattered nation fell upon President ABRAHAM LINCOLN and, after his death, President ANDREW JOHNSON. Johnson had used harsh rhetoric in condemning the actions of the Confederacy and its leaders, and it seemed that he might be prepared to take dramatic steps to fundamentally alter the social, political, and economic order of the South. Johnson's actions, however, revealed his conservatism. The terms of presidential Reconstruction were mild and did not force the South to change at all. Confederate leaders were promptly reelected to office, and the passage of BLACK CODES in every Southern state sought to restrict the new freedom of the ex-slaves.

When Congress met in December 1865, the Republicans had a large majority of the seats in both chambers. Initially most Congressional leaders appeared inclined to accept presidential Reconstruction, with some important modifications. The Joint Committee on Reconstruction was initially conciliatory, and its chair, William Pitt Fessenden, was in constant communication with the president. Most members of Congress ignored the Radical Republicans' plans for the South and instead passed two bills that were in harmony with the president's vision of Reconstruction. The more important of the two bills, which became known

This Thomas Nast cartoon from the September 5, 1868, issue of *Harper's Weekly* is criticizing the Democratic Party's opposition to Reconstruction legislation. Symbolizing the Democrats are caricatures of (from left) a stereotypical Irish American, former Confederate general Nathan Bedford Forest, and financier August Belmont. The three are shown trampling a black Union veteran. *(Library of Congress)*

as the CIVIL RIGHTS ACT OF 1866, extended civil rights and legal equality to African Americans but made their protection the responsibility of the states.

Johnson promptly vetoed the Civil Rights Act of 1866, declaring that Congress had no business involving itself in Reconstruction. Congressional Republicans, shocked by the president's actions, overrode his veto. The Radical Republicans gained support from their more moderate colleagues, and Congress considered the possibility of repudiating presidential Reconstruction. Nonetheless, the moderates still retained control, and they proposed the fairly conservative FOURTEENTH AMENDMENT. Like the Civil Rights Act of 1866, the Fourteenth Amendment was in essential harmony with presidential Reconstruction. Nonetheless, Johnson attacked Congress again. He traveled through the North, delivering a series of inflammatory speeches that came to be known as the "Swing Round the Circle." Meanwhile, all Southern legislatures voted overwhelmingly against accepting the Fourteenth Amendment.

The actions of President Johnson and the former states of the Confederacy played directly into the hands of the Radical Republicans. Between March 1867 and March 1868, enough moderates broke with the president to allow the Radicals to gain passage of a series of four Reconstruction Acts. The First Reconstruction Act divided the South into five military districts, with supreme authority vested in the military commanders of each district. African Americans were to be registered to vote, while leading Confederates were disqualified from holding office and disenfranchised. States desiring readmission the Union were required to ratify the Fourteenth Amendment and to write new constitutions that guaranteed black suffrage. The latter three Reconstruction Acts expanded and clarified the terms of the first, in particular eliminating the governments that had been elected under presidential Reconstruction and disqualifying former Confederates from holding office.

The Reconstruction Acts were far more sweeping than what the moderates had initially proposed. They incorporated almost all of the measures the Radicals deemed important, and the terms were mandatory rather than voluntary. The notion of STATES' RIGHTS was completely subverted, as state boundaries were effectively erased.

President Johnson vetoed each of the Reconstruction Acts and was overridden each time. He then tried to thwart the bills in a variety of ways—by removing military commanders who enforced the acts too strongly, by frequently challenging the authority of the law, and by trying to influence ULYSSES S. GRANT, who was in charge of all the U.S. armies. These actions increased Congress's fury. Shortly after his veto of the First Reconstruction Act was overridden, Johnson forced Secretary of War EDWIN M. STANTON from office and replaced him with Grant. This was a violation of the Tenure of Office Act, which Congress had passed in 1867. Congressional leaders used Johnson's violation of the law as an excuse to bring him up on articles of impeachment. He avoided conviction by one vote.

Johnson's impeachment was the high point of the Radicals' power. In 1868 a number of Radical leaders died or were defeated for reelection. Meanwhile, Ulysses S. Grant replaced Johnson in the White House. The impetus for action among congressional leaders had passed. By 1870 all of the former Confederate states had been readmitted to the Union under the terms of the Reconstruction Acts, and the task of making Reconstruction work would largely be left to the Republican governments in the states of the South.

See also ENFORCEMENT ACTS; IMPEACHMENT OF ANDREW JOHNSON.

Further reading: Michael Les Benedict, *A Compromise of Principle; Congressional Republicans and Reconstruction, 1863–1869* (New York: Norton, 1974); Eric Foner, *Reconstruction: America's Unfinished Revolution, 1863–1877* (New York: Harper & Row, 1988).

—Christopher Bates

redemption

"Redemption" refers to the 10-year period after congressional RECONSTRUCTION, in which conservative white Southern Democrats recaptured their states from Republican rule. White Southerners were determined to reduce the political power of African Americans and white Republicans. With the aid of such institutions and organizations as UNION LEAGUES and the FREEDMEN'S BUREAU, the South's former slaves were swiftly making inroads into American politics. Freedmen were winning elected offices on the REPUBLICAN PARTY ticket and filling government jobs on every level. The South's political practices were changing radically in the first few years after the CIVIL WAR, and in the view of the Democrats, for the worse.

In South Carolina, the birthplace of SECESSION, by 1872 African Americans held four of the state's five seats in Congress. The ENFORCEMENT ACTS and the KU KLUX KLAN ACT were passed by the federal government to sustain African-American political and civil rights in the South. In the early 1870s more and more Republican-dominated Southern legislatures were passing laws against discrimination in public facilities and on trains. While Reconstruction brought a capable political class of African Americans to power in the states of the old Confederacy, these successes were short-lived. White Southerners began moving to "redeem" their states by taking back control of the politics of their states and the region. The increasing state and federal push for civil and political rights stirred more vehement opposition on the part of white Southern Democrats.

Many Republican ballot-box successes were met with outright violence. Murders, beatings, lynchings, tar and featherings, and the like were potential outcomes of voting or in any way taking part in the political system for the freedmen and freedwomen as well as white Republicans in the South. The KU KLUX KLAN and other secret organizations of white Southerners dedicated themselves to ending what they called "black Republicanism" or "Negro rule" in the South through violence and economic intimidation.

While outright violence tended to bring federal reactions like the Ku Klux Klan Act, the Northern states were showing signs of fatigue with Reconstruction. President ULYSSES S. GRANT made it clear that he would tolerate no outright refusals of his orders by the former Confederates, but white Southerners believed that if the South refrained from gross violations of law and custom, Grant would allow them to take back a certain degree of control over their states. With this in mind, many Southern Democrats rejected violence in their attempt to redeem their states from Republican control. When running for governor of South Carolina in 1876, Wade Hampton declared that white Democratic candidates, like himself, wanted African-American votes and that his party was pledged to defending the "rights of the colored man."

Despite Hampton's moderate stance, South Carolina was a "redeemed" state in that the DEMOCRATIC PARTY had regained control of state politics. Republican Party election margins across the South began to slide by 1873. Some white Republicans in the South began to leave the party as African Americans became more and more prominent, despite the fact that white Republicans largely controlled the party in the South. Northern CARPETBAGGERS began to head home in the face of increasing violence. The Republican Party was disintegrating in the South, and that disintegration was allowing the Democratic Party to reassert control over the region.

Issues such as the economic crisis of 1873 and the Indian Wars of the Great Plains claimed Northern attention and diverted interest from "reconstructing" the former Confederacy. The "redeemers" took back power in Georgia, North Carolina, and Virginia relatively quickly. By the end of Grant's eight years in office, all of the Republican governments of the South had disappeared except for those in Louisiana and South Carolina. While African Americans continued to vote Republican in large numbers, voting became increasingly difficult for freedmen as newly elected Democratic officials instituted measures such as poll taxes, literacy tests, and grandfather clauses to reduce black voting.

Ultimately, the Compromise of 1876, which put Republican Rutherford B. Hayes in the White House in exchange for the removal of troops from the South, proved the success of redemption. Without U.S. Army troops to enforce federal voting legislation and stop violence, most African-American voters were disenfranchised. Redemption marked a return to "politics as usual" in the South, generally with the antebellum elite in control once again. Southern African Americans, who had made so many political strides during Reconstruction, would not regain the vote until the 1960s.

See also BLACK CODES; RECONSTRUCTION ACTS.

Further reading: Eric Foner, *Reconstruction: America's Unfinished Revolution, 1863–1877* (New York: Harper & Row, 1988); Michael Perman, *The Road to Redemption: Southern Politics, 1869–1879* (Chapel Hill: University of North Carolina Press, 1984).

—Ruth A. Behling

Red River campaign (1864)

A failed Union effort designed to capture Texas and the parts of Louisiana not under federal control, the Red River campaign sought to use the river as a conduit for troops and materiel, allowing easy access to key strategic targets. The campaign was widely criticized as an opportunity to plunder that was designed to enrich its commander, Nathaniel P. Banks, a political appointee and the former governor of Massachusetts. Opposing Banks, Kirby Smith commanded the Confederate forces of the trans-Mississippi region.

The campaign began on March 14, 1864, when Banks attacked a Confederate fort located approximately 30 miles west of the junction of the Red River and the Mississippi. Union forces succeeded in destroying the fort and proceeded along the farmland of the Red River, "liberating" cotton along the way. Banks hoped to make his expedition self-financing by selling the valuable cotton. When Confederate planters heard of the Union confiscations, however, they began to burn their fields. By the time Banks reached many PLANTATIONS, the cotton he had hoped to obtain was destroyed.

Operating under Smith was Maj. Gen. Richard Taylor, son of former President Zachary Taylor. Confederate troops led by Taylor met Banks's men on April 8 at Sabine Crossroads in the northwest corner of Louisiana, about 20 miles from the Texas border. Fighting through April 8–9, both sides suffered approximately 2,000 casualties, but the Southerners prevailed and Union forces retreated along the Red River. Federal engineers built a series of ingenious dams to transport gunboats across shallow spots. On May 13, having reached deeper waters, Union forces turned their attention to Alexandria, Louisiana, which they burned to the ground.

Confederates pursued Banks, and on May 18 Taylor attacked, pushing the Yankees to the banks of the Atchafalaya River. Taylor hoped to pin Banks against the river, forcing him to either fight or attempt to cross the dangerously swollen river. Union engineers, however, saved Banks' units, creating a makeshift pontoon bridge across the water. Once safely on the other side, Banks moved back up the Mississippi to Vicksburg. After a short rest, he and his men were transferred by ABRAHAM LINCOLN to WILLIAM T. SHERMAN's command in Georgia. The Red River campaign had failed to capture any significant territory and had cost many lives, needlessly.

Critics of Nathaniel Banks asserted that he had designed the entire campaign to acquire a fortune in stolen cotton. Because of these accusations, Banks never again held a battlefield command. On the Confederate side, Richard Taylor resigned his commission, accusing Kirby Smith of failing to supply enough men to destroy Banks's army. Texas remained Confederate until the end of the war.

Further reading: William R. Brooksher, *War along the Bayous: The 1864 Red River Campaign in Louisiana* (Washington, D.C.: Brasseys, 1998); Ludwell H. Johnson, *Red River Campaign: Politics and Cotton in the Civil War* (Kent, Ohio: Kent State University Press, 1993).

—Chad Vanderford

refugees

Tens of thousands of Southerners were forced from their homes during the CIVIL WAR, becoming refugees from encroaching battles or Union troops. Whenever Union troops appeared, Southerners took to the road. They did so for a wide variety of reasons: Some feared they would be arrested by Union troops for their political views (in fact, sometimes men, believing they would be treated more harshly, left their wives and children behind), while others simply could not bear the thought of living under Yankee rule and headed for unoccupied portions of the Confederacy. Many departed because their businesses, farms, and PLANTATIONS had been damaged or taken over by Yankees, and they had to move in order to find ways to support their families.

Although all refugees shared in the experience of abandoning their homes and most of their possessions and of having to get used to living in strange and potentially more difficult surroundings, there were big differences in the day-to-day lives of refugees. For example, wealthy Southerners who had relatives or friends living in safer places had a "home" to go to. Poor Southerners often lacked such comfortable options. One of the most common destinations for slave owners attempting to take their human property to a safer place was Texas, where as many as 50,000 slaves were taken during the war.

Despite the vast differences in the experiences of Southern refugees, there was one experience that they all shared: Their lives were turned upside down. Kate Stone, the oldest daughter of a wealthy plantation family who lived along the MISSISSIPPI RIVER near Vicksburg, escaped with her family from the Yankees in 1863. Kate, her mother, her many brothers, and a few slaves all rode, walked, and floated their way to Delhi, Louisiana, where hundreds of frightened and suddenly impoverished refugees crowded into this little town on the road to Texas. She described the scene in her journal: "Such crowds of Negroes of all ages and sizes, wagons, mules, horses, dogs, baggage, and furniture of every description, very little of it packed. It was thrown in promiscuous heaps . . . here and there, with soldiers, drunk and sober, combing over it all, shouting and laughing." The Stones, like most refugees of their class, endured scorching heat and bitter cold; dusty roads; sometimes-threatening groups of slaves; crowded, flea-bitten hotels; and crude food with, at best, only hunger to look forward to at the end of a hard day's journey.

Other parts of refugees' lives were disrupted. Leaving home made it harder to communicate with fathers, husbands, and sons in the army. Boys and girls had to grow up quickly, taking on more responsibility and doing more work for the family. The EDUCATION of refugee children was disrupted; few schools in the Confederacy stayed open throughout the war, and refugees rarely had the money to pay private tutors for lessons. Whenever refugees moved into a new area, local residents worried that the newcomers would make food and other resources scarce for everyone; in some places, refugees were suspected of being disloyal to the Confederacy. Many refugees could take only a few possessions—the clothes they wore, a doll or toy, a treasured pet—and some lost everything they owned. Regular meals were difficult to come by, and the health of refugees suffered. Finally, with so many people moving from the countryside into towns and cities, places like RICHMOND, Atlanta, and Charleston became extremely overcrowded, unhealthy, and expensive.

Similar problems faced refugee slaves. Since masters often chose to take only the most valuable slaves with them, African-American families were disrupted, and women and young children often were left to fend for themselves. The quality of the food and medical care provided for slaves became even worse than it had been before the war. Sometimes a slave who began the war in South Carolina would be "refugeed" several times until he or she was living in Texas by the end of the war.

Although most Civil War refugees lived in the South, upon occasion Northerners were also dislocated, especially when the CONFEDERATE ARMY invaded the North. During the weeks leading up to the BATTLE OF GETTYSBURG, for instance, many white farmers became temporary refugees when they transported their livestock out of reach of the Confederates. Hundreds of African Americans living in Maryland and southern Pennsylvania—some of them fugitive slaves—fled before the rebel army, fearing that they would be captured and sold into SLAVERY back in Virginia.

For the most part, refugees were overwhelmingly Southern, and the sight of displaced families, chiefly women and children, was common on the streets and roads of the Confederacy. The existence of larger and larger refugee "communities" had great negative impacts on Confederate morale and, ultimately, on the rebel war effort as HOMEFRONT support dwindled in the face of such harsh realities and soldiers deserted to look for or after their refugee families.

See also FORAGING.

Further reading: Mary Elizabeth Massey, *Refugee Life in the Confederacy* (Baton Rouge: Louisiana State University Press, 1964); Kate Stone, *Brokenburn: The Journal of Kate Stone, 1861–1868,* ed. John Q. Anderson (Baton Rouge: Louisiana State University Press, 1995).

—James Marten

religion

During the 19th century, Christian religious ideals were the center of American life and community. A period of intense commitment to religion began in the opening years of the century (called the Second Great Awakening) and continued with varying intensity until the CIVIL WAR began. Evangelical Protestant denominations gained the most during this period, and by the 1840s the Baptist, Methodist, and Presbyterian Churches, supported by a wide variety of religious newspapers and benevolent societies, played a major role in the cultural life of the nation.

The churches' influence was broad, and many important reform-movement leaders were religiously inspired. Women, in greater numbers than men, attended and supported churches and church-related reforms. At the same time, popular ideals such as Manifest Destiny rested on the assumption that God ordained national expansion, and political orators drew heavily on the image of the United States as a nation anointed by God.

Among most Protestants there existed a broad commonality in theology, and both Northern and Southern Protestants generally supported social reform movements such as temperance, Sunday school societies, and missionary efforts at home and abroad. However, differences over SLAVERY divided the churches. During the middle century, increasing number of Northern Protestants embraced ABOLITION. Southerners responded in part by increasing evangelical outreach to the slave population (referred to by historians as "the mission to the slaves") and simultaneously building a scripture-based defense of slavery (this was particularly true of rural PLANTATION-district congregations).

During the 1840s the sectional divisions over slavery created a dramatic rift within the major Protestant churches. The Baptist split that occurred in 1845 illustrates the general contours of the denominational divisions: After more than a decade of increasing conflict between Northern and Southern Baptist leaders, tensions mounted during the early 1840s following the formation of the American Baptist Anti-Slavery Convention. In its first public statement, the convention assailed slavery as "a violation of the instincts of nature,—a perversion of the first principles of justice,—and a positive transgression of the revealed will of God."

Throughout the North, associations and individual congregations began expressing support for the convention's principles. In response, Southerners took a defensive posture and condemned what they termed "harsh and abusive epithets heaped upon us." Some advocated a cessation of mutual cooperation in areas such as missions until the "fanatical course" of the North changed, while others demanded assurances from the Triennial Convention (the denomination's national body at the time) that it permitted slavery.

Despite their conviction that slavery was an appropriate civil institution and that the abolitionists were "exceedingly mistaken in the case they have undertaken," Southern Baptists despaired of the consequences of the increasingly contentious issue. As one Georgia congregation put it, "The threatened dissolution of the fellowship betwixt the North and South would be an event which we would deeply deplore and as an evil not only highly injurious to the cause of religion in general but calculated to bring other evils of great magnitude in its train." The preeminent Baptist leader in Georgia, Jesse Mercer, noted that the tendency of the conflict would be "to break up all our united operations [missionary societies, publishing efforts etc.], and I seriously fear our civil Union also."

Despite such concerns and the efforts of both Northern and Southern Baptists, the conflict over slavery and abolition grew and at times was aggravated by denominational newspapers. The conflict came to a head in late 1844 when the American Baptist Home Mission Society rejected the appointment of a Georgia minister who held slaves and the Triennial Convention stated that "we can never be a party to any arrangement which would imply approbation of slavery." By early spring 1845, Virginia and Georgia Baptists called for a meeting to create a new Baptist convention composed of Southern churches. The meeting convened May 8, 1845, and by Monday, May 12, had created a purely sectional denominational structure—the Southern Baptist Convention—based primarily on the support of slavery and its attendant cultural ideals.

That same year Southern Methodists, who had also engaged in a protracted debate with their Northern brethren over slaveholders' rights to hold national positions within the church, issued a statement that justified their split with the Northern churches. They claimed that "the opinions and purposes of the church in the north on the subject of slavery, are in direct conflict with those of the south, and unless the south will submit to the dictation and interference of the north there is no hope of anything like union or harmony."

By the late 1850s, the pro- and antislavery positions of the sectional churches had helped cement the idea that each side's "peculiar society best embodied republican, Christian virtue and that the other threatened both republican liberty and Christian order." In the South, preachers searched the Scripture to justify the institution of slavery and the hierarchical notions of society that came along with it. Northern preachers, meanwhile, penned abolitionist tracts and often celebrated the liberal culture that was emerging in the cities and towns of their section. Popularly, such images of a sanctified people helped both sides wrap themselves in the garb of holy righteousness and march to war carrying swords blessed by the cross.

While many preachers of both sections abhorred the onset of violence in 1861, their eventual support for their respective section served as a major element of national identity. Union pastors often preached political messages that overtly approved of the war effort and increasingly offered a message of "unconditional loyalty" to the state. Likewise in the South, ministers and editors blurred "the distinctions between secular and sacred" and promoted patriotism based in a close connection of civil and religious authority. Many rebel preachers argued that not only was the Confederacy the protector of civil liberty and constitutional rights but that it was also the defender of religious liberty.

At the everyday level, religion provided comfort and hope for soldiers and their families who prayed for divine favor and sought the comforts of spiritual assurance. At the same time, it served as a rallying point for "slaves reaching for freedom [who] praised God for their day of Jubilee." In both sections, religious promoters identified a remarkable opportunity to carry out missionary work within the armies. A burgeoning Southern military press played "a dynamic role in evangelizing soldiers, articulating war aims, and building morale." Religiously inspired agencies in the North such as the Christian Commission supported the war effort by providing both physical and spiritual comforts to the soldiers in the field. Within the armies, religion was ever present. Practiced in private by pious soldiers, promoted by regimental chaplains, and celebrated in large-scale revivals, religion provided both spiritual comfort and entertainment for soldiers looking for a change from the regular camp monotony.

Following the war in the South, the complexion of religion changed dramatically. African Americans, who had worshipped alongside white people in large biracial churches before the war, deserted en masse and created separate all-black Baptist and Methodist congregations. Defeated white Southerners created a civil religion that blended Protestant rhetoric and symbols with the rhetoric and imagery of an invented Confederate tradition. This form of LOST CAUSE mythology helped Southerners defend the "essentially religious and moral values" that had been defeated in war. Northern white Protestants, while faced with what they believed to be a decline in moral values, continued to play an important role in the social-political arena in the emerging Social Gospel movement.

See also UNITED STATES CHRISTIAN COMMISSION.

Further reading: C. C. Goen, *Broken Churches, Broken Nation: Denominational Schisms and the Coming of the American Civil War* (Macon, Ga.: Mercer University Press, 1985); Randall M. Miller, Harry S. Stout, and Charles Reagan Wilson, eds., *Religion and the American Civil War* (New York: Oxford University Press, 1998); Bell Irvin Wiley, *The Life of Johnny Reb: The Common Soldier of the Confederacy* (Baton Rouge: Louisiana State University Press, 1978); Steven E. Woodworth, *While God Is Marching On: The Religious World of Civil War Soldiers* (Lawrence: University of Kansas Press, 2001).

—James Daryl Black

Republican Party

The Republican Party was born in the middle of the national turmoil over the SLAVERY question in the 1850s. Within a few years of its establishment, the Republicans were one of the two major political organizations that governed the United States of America. From 1865 onward, Republicans proudly described themselves as the party that won the war, restored the Union, freed the slaves and guaranteed their civil rights, and brought unparalleled growth and prosperity to the country. Voters agreed, and by 1896 the Republican Party had fashioned an electoral dominance over the presidency that lasted, with only two exceptions, until 1930.

The immediate reason for the founding of the Republican Party was the controversy over the KANSAS-NEBRASKA ACT of 1854. The debate over STEPHEN A. DOUGLAS's bill set off a fierce protest over the "Nebraska Outrage" throughout the North in the spring and summer of 1854. Northern anger over slavery's possible extension into free territories sought a political outlet where none currently existed. The stability of the two-party system had been shaken with the demise of the WHIG PARTY by the mid-1850s. Some Whigs had joined the Free-Soil Party, which was dedicated to halting the spread of slavery. Meanwhile, the American or Know-Nothing Party, based on anti-

IMMIGRATION sentiment, had become a major force in politics, winning ELECTIONS in the North and even in the South.

Many former Whigs, anti-Nebraska Democrats, and Free Soilers, however, were uncomfortable with joining a political party based on an anti-immigrant platform, also known as NATIVISM. As the protests over the Kansas-Nebraska Act grew louder and larger, the disaffected groups determined to form a new political party. Most historians agree that the first official use of the term *Republican* came on February 28, 1854, at a meeting in Ripon, Wisconsin. The name, linking the new party with the legacy of 1776, quickly gained widespread acceptance. A great number of congressmen in WASHINGTON, D.C., formally adopted the name in time for the 1854 fall elections, in which the Democrats' fortunes fell and the Republicans' rose.

The Republican Party grew rapidly in the North, and the organization swelled with former Know-Nothings and Whigs. Indeed, the Whig Party provided most of the leaders and much of the economic program for the new political entity. The controversy over slavery in the territories continued unabated, and the Republican cause was helped by the uproar over the "little civil war" waged in BLEEDING KANSAS in 1855 and 1856. In 1856 the Republicans fielded their first presidential candidate, the western explorer John C. Frémont. "Free soil, free labor, free men, Frémont!" was the rallying cry. "Wide Awake Clubs" formed all across the Northern states, and huge rallies and parades spread the Republican message. The pro-Southern Democratic candidate JAMES BUCHANAN of Pennsylvania was the election's victor by a comfortable margin, but the Republicans did very well, particularly in New England and in Wisconsin, Michigan, and New York.

Republicans articulated and refined their platform in the four years between 1856 and 1860. Leaders such as WILLIAM H. SEWARD of New York, SALMON P. CHASE of Ohio, and ABRAHAM LINCOLN of Illinois broadened the appeal of the party. The Republican position on slavery was borrowed almost entirely from the Free-Soil Party: The national government should restrict the spread of slavery into the territories. Most Republicans pledged to protect slavery where it existed in the South but hoped that restriction would put it on the path to ultimate extinction. The opposition to slavery embodied in the Republican program did not stem primarily from moral concerns, however. Instead, the Free-Soil argument was focused on creating and maintaining opportunities for free white labor. There were some ABOLITIONists in the Republican ranks who saw slavery as an evil unto itself, but in general the party cared more about preserving and extending rights and opportunities for white people than it did about bringing freedom and justice to the nearly 4 million slaves living in the Southern states.

The anti-slavery message of the Republican Party was tied to a powerfully appealing program designed to ensure upward mobility for the ordinary men and women of the country. Free labor everywhere, according to party leaders, would guarantee the kind of dynamic capitalism that stimulated individual initiative and achievement. Republican rule meant government aid to the ECONOMY in the form of TARIFFS (a tax on imported goods), loans for transcontinental RAILROADS, a homestead act, a central bank, and funds for higher EDUCATION. This progressive vision would benefit farmers and urban dwellers alike. In 1862 due to the absence of Southern Democrats in the national legislature, the Republican Party enacted into law almost every single one of its economic proposals. The passage of the HOMESTEAD ACT, the PACIFIC RAILROAD ACT, and the MORRILL LAND-GRANT ACT, for example, laid the foundation for the surging postwar industrial economy.

The great enemy of economic, moral, and political progress, Republicans claimed, was the backward system of slavery and its protector, the "slave power," which controlled the DEMOCRATIC PARTY and, through it, the national government. Republicans pointed to the FUGITIVE SLAVE ACT, the repeal of the Missouri Compromise, the Kansas controversy, the caning of Senator CHARLES SUMNER of Massachusetts and the *DRED SCOTT* DECISION as proof for their contention that the liberties and freedom of white Americans were being seriously threatened.

The election of 1860 brought the presidency to the Republican Party. Abraham Lincoln, a moderate from Illinois, captured the nomination over more prominent and experienced, but also more controversial, leaders such as Seward, Chase, and Edward Bates of Missouri. During the summer of 1860, the Democratic Party split into Northern and Southern wings. Lincoln's main opponent was Democrat Stephen Douglas, but there were two other candidates who ran on a Southern-only ticket. The Republican platform reiterated their Free-Soil philosophy and accused Democrats of being the party of slavery, disunion, and corruption. When the votes were counted, Lincoln's substantial majority in the Northern states gave him the win over the other three candidates.

With Lincoln's victory, a party based wholly on sectional interest had captured the White House, and the cost was the Union. Seven Southern states seceded shortly thereafter, believing that their liberties were threatened. They quickly established the CONFEDERATE STATES OF AMERICA. During the tense months between the end of Buchanan's administration and Lincoln's March inauguration, the new president formed a cabinet, tried to reassure a nervous public, and made several attempts to bring back the seceded states. All efforts at compromise foundered on Lincoln's insistence that stopping slavery's advance into the territories was not an issue that could be compromised.

Election poster for the Republican Party presidential candidate in the election of 1860, Abraham Lincoln, and his running mate, Hannibal Hamlin *(Hulton/Archive)*

Between 1861 and 1865, the Republican Party was responsible for waging war against the seceded states, devising plans for RECONSTRUCTION, and attending to the normal chores of national governance. Led by Lincoln and pushed by a group of RADICAL REPUBLICANS led by Sumner and BENJAMIN WADE in the Senate and THADDEUS STEVENS in the House, the Republican Party passed the legislation that made the EMANCIPATION of the slaves a reality. Republicans soon divided into factions representing conservative, moderate, and radical positions over whether a harsh or lenient reconstruction policy should be implemented. President Lincoln provided a moderating voice and struggled to make the Republican Party into a truly national entity. In 1864 the Republicans were known briefly as the "National Union Party," and as a gesture to inclusion, the wartime governor of Tennessee, former Democrat ANDREW JOHNSON, was placed on the ticket with Lincoln.

After the defeat of the Confederacy and the ASSASSI-NATION OF ABRAHAM LINCOLN, congressional Republicans battled with Johnson over the right to control the process of Reconstruction in the South. The major achievements of the party include the THIRTEENTH, FOURTEENTH, and FIFTEENTH AMENDMENTs, the so-called Reconstruction amendments to the U.S. Constitution, which abolished slavery, established the criteria for federal and state citizenship and equal protection under the law, and ruled out race (but not gender) as a barrier to voting. In addition, Republicans passed other Reconstruction and civil rights acts that set up guidelines for readmitting the Southern states back into the Union.

Republicans narrowly missed removing Andrew Johnson from office in 1868, and in that same year their candidate for the presidency, ULYSSES S. GRANT, triumphed at the polls. President Grant and the Republican Party faced daunting challenges in putting a Reconstruction policy to work. They had two goals: The first was to remake the South from a slave society to a free-labor society, as close to the North as possible. The second was to protect the newly freed slaves' rights against a hostile white population. To do this, Republicans had to control the Southern state governments and to establish a viable two-party system in the South. The Republican coalition of CARPETBAGGERS, SCALAWAGS, and African-American voters could not withstand unrelenting and violent Southern white resistance. By the early 1870s "REDEMPTION" prevailed, and the South was once again becoming a solid Democratic Party stronghold controlled by white Southerners.

As the party was failing to establish a stronghold in the South, many Republicans were anxious to recast the message of the party for the future. Called Half Breeds, and led by the dynamic James G. Blaine of Maine, they looked to strengthen the economic nationalism of their party with policies furthering the development of an urban-industrial economy. Blaine and his supporters argued that most Americans were tired of hearing about the problems of the South and more interested in other issues like the TARIFF or monetary reform. Opposed to Blaine were the "stalwarts," like Roscoe Conkling of New York, who, while supporting economic advancement, wished to continue to try to make the South a good place for the Republican Party.

As Grant's administration became mired in scandals and charges of corruption, a group of disaffected "Liberal Republicans" called for civil service reform. Typical practice up to that time had been for presidents to appoint individuals to government jobs based on their party loyalty rather than their honesty or competence for the job. The Liberals wanted to end corruption in government, stop the "spoils men" from looting the treasury, and put the running of the government on an efficient and businesslike basis. This movement was led by the Missouri politician Carl Schurz, who formed an alliance with the Democratic Party in the election of 1872. Their candidate was the newspaper publisher HORACE GREELEY. Although Grant won handily, the threat to the Republican Party was clear. The chilling effects of the depression of 1873 led to a rise in support for the Democratic Party. Additionally, Northern voters turned a deaf ear to pleas from desperate Southern Republican governments fighting the KU KLUX KLAN. Northerners did not support Grant's use of federal troops to stop Klan violence, nor were they pleased with the passage of the CIVIL RIGHTS ACT OF 1875. The House fell to Democrats in 1875, the Senate in 1879, and the presidency in 1884.

The disputed presidential election of 1876, in which Ohio Republican Rutherford B. Hayes was awarded the election over the New York Democrat Samuel Tilden, is traditionally considered the end of Reconstruction. From that point on, the Republican Party would strive to maintain its majority status by stressing broad issues of economic advancement and culturally conservative issues like prohibition, appealing to its Protestant, native-born base. The freedmen would not again receive attention from a major party until the 1930s.

See also IMPEACHMENT OF ANDREW JOHNSON.

Further reading: Eric Foner, *Free Soil, Free Labor, Free Men: The Ideology of the Republican Party before the Civil War* (New York: Oxford University Press, 1995); William E. Gienapp, *The Origins of the Republican Party, 1852–1856* (New York: Oxford University Press, 1987); Phillip Shaw Paludan, *The Presidency of Abraham Lincoln* (Lawrence: University Press of Kansas, 1994); Mark W. Summers, *Railroads, Reconstruction, and the Gospel of Prosperity: Aid under the Radical Republicans, 1865–1877* (Princeton, N.J.: Princeton University Press, 1984).

Revels, Hiram R. (1827–1901)
Born free on September 27, 1827, in Fayetteville, North Carolina, Hiram Rhoades Revels became the first African American elected to the U.S. Senate. Revels was ordained a minister in 1845 and served at several AFRICAN METHODIST EPISCOPAL CHURCHES, traveling widely and often. In 1850 Revels married Phoebe A. Bass, and they had six children.

Before the CIVIL WAR, Revels did not join or publicly support the ABOLITIONist movement, although he later wrote that he had helped escaping slaves. Once the war started, however, Revels offered his support. He organized the first two black regiments in Maryland and a later one in Missouri. He served as a chaplain to African-American troops in the UNION ARMY, and he later worked with the FREEDMEN'S BUREAU, helping to establish schools in Mississippi. Revels's first position in government came when Mississippi governor Adelbert Ames appointed him alderman for Natchez, Mississippi, in 1868. He went on to be elected to the Mississippi State Senate.

In 1870 Revels moved onto the national political stage when the Mississippi legislature chose him to fill the remaining year of the state's Senate seat, previously held by JEFFERSON DAVIS. While in WASHINGTON, D.C., Revels championed EDUCATION issues, calling for an end to segregated schools. Revels's term ended on March 3, 1871, when he was appointed the first president of Alcorn University, the first black land-grant university in the United States. He served Alcorn from 1871 until 1874, when his support for Democrats in Mississippi resulted in his removal by the Republican governor. When the Democrats resumed control of Mississippi politics in 1875, Revels was restored to his position at Alcorn, which he held until 1882.

For the last 20 years of his life Revels served as assistant pastor of the Methodist Episcopal Church of Holly Springs, Mississippi, taught theology, and was a trustee at Rust College. He died at a church meeting on January 16, 1901.

Further reading: Elizabeth Lawson, *The Gentleman from Mississippi: Our First Negro Congressman, Hiram R. Revels* (New York: n.p., 1960).

Richmond, Virginia
In 1860 the city of Richmond, Virginia, had grown to become the 25th largest city in the United States with a population of nearly 38,000. Located at the falls of James River, Richmond was one of the South's most developed and bustling cities during the 19th century.

When the first shots were fired at FORT SUMTER on April 14, 1861, Virginia had not yet seceded from the nation. As a result, the Confederacy set up its government quarters in Montgomery, Alabama. However, due to Richmond's industry as well as its role as the capital of Virginia's state government, the Confederate leaders were hopeful that Richmond would soon become the permanent capital of the CONFEDERATE STATES OF AMERICA.

A few days following Virginia's SECESSION on April 17, 1861, the Virginia convention extended an invitation to the government officials to relocate the capital to Richmond, thus making it a target for Union attack. On May 20, the Confederate government voted to permanently move the capital from Montgomery to Richmond. This vote marked the beginning of four years of change and conflict for Richmond.

Many historians argue that the Confederates made a strategic error placing their capital in Richmond, thus making it a target for Union attakcs. Despite historians' views, however, the Confederates had substantial reason to place their capital in Richmond. Richmond's location, though only 106 miles from the Union's capitol in WASHINGTON, D.C., was an ideal site for the Confederate's capital. It was the home of important manufacturing concerns like the TREDEGAR IRON WORKS. Tredegar, which produced more than 50 locomotives for Southern RAILROADS between 1850 and 1855 alone, was not the only manufacturing establishment in the new capital city. Richmond had massive iron, flour, and tobacco mills in addition to its surrounding agricultural areas. Richmond was also the transportation hub of the South. Not only was it Virginia's largest port city via the James River and the Chesapeake Bay, but it was also very well connected to a number of the large cities on the Eastern seaboard due to its extensive railroads.

Richmond was the focus of the Union military strategy, characterized by the popular war cry "On to Richmond!" As a result, its citizens experienced a number of challenges. The first challenge was excessive inflation. The influx of the rebel government—officials, workers, and their families and slaves—as well as a considerable shortage of housing caused this rampant inflation. Richmond's population increased threefold to almost 100,000 by the war's end, which included a substantial number of REFUGEES. The city also held 13,000 prisoners in PRISONS such as Belle Isle, Libby Prison, and Castle Thunder. This dramatic increase put a considerable amount of strain on Richmond's municipal services such as the markets, the fire and police forces, and the public waterworks and gasworks.

The second immediate challenge faced by Richmond's inhabitants was a steep increase in crime. The significant rise in population, the instability of the Confederate currency, and the transformation of Richmond into a crowded military town caused an increase of muggings and PROSTITUTION. In order to prevent the further rise of crime in and around the city of Richmond, martial law within a 10-mile radius of the city was declared on March 1, 1862.

In spite of the conflict that raged around the city, the general mood of Richmond remained relatively high during the first two years of the war. The citizens of Richmond did their best to aid the wounded and the sick. Numerous hospitals were established throughout the city, including Chimborazo Hospital in the Church Hill section. There were also at least 60 smaller hospitals run by the government, the state, and private institutions that were located

The ruins of Richmond, Virginia, the Confederate capital, after it was burned down by its own residents to thwart the oncoming advance of Union general Ulysses S. Grant *(Hulton/Archive)*

throughout the city. At the same time, Confederate dead began filling Richmond's cemeteries: Oakwood, Shockoe, and Hollywood. Famous Confederate officers and officials such as J. E. B. STUART, GEORGE E. PICKETT, and JEFFERSON DAVIS and his family are all buried in Hollywood Cemetery.

Most importantly, Richmond was the strategic target of the Army of the Potomac, and its capture became a major aim of the Northern war effort. As a result, a series of forts and trenches surrounded the city to defend it from the campaigns of the Union forces. Despite numerous threats by Union troops during the first three years of the war, ROBERT E. LEE's army was successful in pushing back the Union attack. During the spring of 1864, the Union forces finally broke their defenses and cut the city's rail lines.

By cutting these lines, both the citizens and the military in Richmond found it difficult to remain adequately supplied. This feat isolated Richmond, and its inhabitants suffered greatly during the final year of the CIVIL WAR. When Lee's lines were finally cut at the BATTLE OF FIVE FORKS on April 1, 1865, Lee alerted Jefferson Davis that Richmond must be evacuated. In response to Lee's notice, the Confederate government abandoned the city on April 2, 1865. As the government, military, and citizens of Richmond fled the city, they destroyed not only the city's supplies of tobacco and cotton but they also set fire to bridges and railroads to make the city inaccessible. Due to the high winds, the fires spread throughout the city with unprecedented speed, a task that proved to be too large for Richmond's firemen to control. As a result, this evacuation fire consumed more than 800 buildings in the downtown area; Richmond literally lay in smoking ruins.

After the destruction of the Confederate capital, Lee's army did not last a week. On April 7, 1865, Gen. Lee surrendered to Gen. ULYSSES S. GRANT at the APPOMATTOX COURT HOUSE. The short amount of time it took for the CONFEDERATE ARMY to surrender demonstrates how vital Richmond had been as both a place and a symbol to Lee's army throughout the four years of the Civil War.

Though Richmond was no longer the industrial and transportation hub of Virginia, it did remain the capital following the war. Today it serves as a living museum of the LOST CAUSE. Monument Avenue, a street lined with MONUMENTS of notable Confederate leaders, the White House of the Confederacy, and the Lee House all serve as reminders of the history of Richmond during the four years of the Civil War.

See also HOMEFRONT; PETERSBURG CAMPAIGN.

Further reading: Ernest B. Furguson, *Ashes of Glory: Richmond at War* (New York: Knopf, 1996); Gregg D. Kimball, *American City, Southern Place: A Cultural His-*

tory of Antebellum Richmond (Athens: University of Georgia Press, 2000); Richard M. Lee, *General Lee's City: An Illustrated Guide to the Historic Sites of Confederate Richmond* (McLean, Va.: EPM Publications, 1987); Mike Wright, *City under Siege: Richmond in the Civil War* (Lanham, Md.: Madison Books, 1995).

—Megan Quinn

Rosecrans, William S. (1819–1898)

A Union general in the western theater of operations, William Starke Rosecrans was born on September 6, 1819, at his father's farm in Delaware County, Ohio.

Ranking fifth out of 51 cadets in the UNITED STATES MILITARY ACADEMY AT WEST POINT Class of 1842, he remained at the academy teaching engineering and performing various military duties after graduation. During the Mexican-American War of 1846–48, he saw no combat service but instead remained in the Northeast, supervising the construction of fortifications at Newport, Rhode Island. Rosecrans resigned from the service in 1854 to embark on a career as an engineer and businessman.

Following the Confederate shelling of FORT SUMTER, Rosecrans volunteered his services and was appointed colonel of the 23rd Ohio in June 1861. Rosecrans quickly advanced and succeeded Gen. GEORGE B. MCCLELLAN in command of the Department of Ohio. In November 1861, Brig. Gen. Rosecrans defeated ROBERT E. LEE's CONFEDERATE ARMY in the Allegheny Mountains, facilitating the creation of the state of West Virginia. Assigned to the western theater in May 1862, now Maj. Gen. Rosecrans led the Army of the Mississippi in the successful Battle at Iuka (September 1862) and the BATTLE OF CORINTH (October 3–4, 1862).

Rosecrans assumed command of the Army of the Cumberland in Nashville on October 27, 1862. Marching southeast on December 26th, he confronted Confederate general BRAXTON BRAGG's Army of Tennessee near Murfreesboro on December 31. After the bloody two-day BATTLE OF MURFREESBORO, the Confederates retreated. His June 1863 Tullahoma campaign successfully drove Bragg out of Tennessee but failed to destroy the Confederate army. Crossing the Tennessee River in the beginning of September, he captured Chattanooga. However, the Confederate commander, now reinforced by troops from Virginia and Mississippi, counterattacked on September 18 at Chickamauga Creek, southeast of the city. Although Rosecrans commanded ably on September 19, he made a tactical mistake the next day, leaving a gap in his line. Bragg exploited Rosecrans's error and drove the UNION ARMY from the battlefield. Fleeing to Chattanooga ahead of his troops, Rosecrans lost the moral authority to lead his army

and was relieved of his duty in October. His final active command was in the Department of Missouri in 1864.

Resigning from the service in 1867, he became minister to Mexico in 1868. Replaced by President ULYSSES S. GRANT, with whom he had a long-standing feud, Rosecrans became a resident of California. He served two terms in Congress (1880–1885) and remained active in VETERANS' affairs. He died at his Redondo ranch, near Los Angeles, on March 11, 1898. His remains were transferred with full military honors to Arlington National Cemetery in May 1902.

See also CHICKAMAUGA, BATTLE OF.

Further reading: William M. Lamers, *The Edge of Glory: A Biography of General William S. Rosecrans, U.S.A.* (New York: Harcourt, Brace, 1961); Steven E. Woodworth, *Six Armies in Tennessee: The Chickamauga and Chattanooga Campaigns* (Lincoln: University of Nebraska Press, 1998).

—Stephen A. Bourque

rules of war

Rules of war are designed to keep war "civilized." Generally these rules are concerned with two main issues. The first is how much force is appropriate. The second is what is a legitimate target for a warring army and what is not.

Before the CIVIL WAR, the rules of war generally were not formally recorded. Instead, combatants were expected to behave in accordance with established custom and their sense of fair play. During the Revolutionary War, for example, the UNIFORMS and tactics used by British redcoats left them highly exposed to gunfire. British commanders knew this, but they did not change their approach because they had been trained to believe that this was the polite way to fight a war. During the Civil War, many officers and soldiers continued to adhere to these unwritten rules. For example, when the Confederate ordnance department developed land mines, some Confederate commanders refused to use them because they thought them ungentlemanly.

Ultimately, however, the era of polite warfare and unwritten rules had come to an end. The Civil War was a time of transition between the limited warfare of the past and the "total war" that was to become the standard in the 20th century. Recognizing this new reality, Union leaders moved to formalize the rules of war, issuing the Lieber Code in May 1863. Prepared by legal expert and professor of political science at Columbia University Francis Lieber, the Lieber Code contained a list of 157 rules governing the conduct of Union armies and soldiers in the field. The code addressed a broad variety of topics: spies, prisoners, surrenders, noncombatants, and so forth.

The Lieber Code was not a treaty, and so Confederate soldiers were not subject to its conditions. It is perhaps worth asking, then, why Union leaders would willingly place such limits on their armies. In part, they were legitimately concerned with the actions of some Union soldiers and officers. Most of the men who fought in the Civil War were not professional soldiers and so had not spent their careers being taught to behave with restraint in a time of war. As the Civil War became increasingly brutal, and as participants on both sides grew increasingly desperate, there were numerous incidents of excessive violence or violence against inappropriate targets. Such incidents undermined support for the war among Northerners and among the international community, while often provoking violent retaliation from the Confederacy.

As the Lieber Code tried to limit the brutality of "total war" in some contexts, however, it also justified it in other contexts. Although the code placed "civilized" limits on what Union soldiers were allowed to do, it also provided broad discretionary powers for Union commanders to do what they deemed "necessary." For example, SHERMAN's 1864 MARCH THROUGH GEORGIA might have been unthinkable under the informal codes of conduct in place at the beginning of the war, but it was entirely justifiable under the terms of the Lieber Code.

Ultimately, the Civil War affected the rules of war in two important ways. The transition to total war continued unabated in the post–Civil War era. The Indian Wars of the 1870s were incredibly violent. The Spanish-American and Philippine Wars also had their share of brutality, and World War I may have set a standard that will never be matched in terms of the lack of restraint shown by combatants on both sides.

At the same time, while the Civil War helped to make war more violent, it also provided a precedent for trying to address that violence, as formal and comprehensive agreements about the conduct of war became an international standard. In 1864, for example, as the Civil War was still being waged, a consortium of European powers signed the Geneva Convention. The agreement, which governs the treatment of prisoners and other conduct in war, remains in effect to the present day and has been joined by a number of other international agreements about armed conflict.

See also FORAGING.

Further reading: Mark Grimsley, *The Hard Hand of War: Union Military Policy toward Southern Civilians, 1861–1865* (New York: Cambridge University Press, 1995).

—Christopher Bates

S

scalawags

From the Scottish word for "rascals," the term *scalawag* was applied to the white Southerners who cooperated with the REPUBLICAN PARTY during RECONSTRUCTION. Historians have overturned the common depiction of scalawags as no-good, poor white traitors. Indeed, the Republican Party had no chance at all to establish a presence in the South without the leadership and support of the large and diverse group of white men who allied themselves with the party of ABRAHAM LINCOLN during the years after the CIVIL WAR.

Although the scalawags ranged widely in terms of their social standing, economic background, and political loyalties, they did share common beliefs. First and foremost, they wanted the South to enjoy a progressive and prosperous ECONOMY based upon the benefits of free labor and industrialization. While the wealthier scalawags of New Orleans and Atlanta looked forward to government-sponsored subsidies and loans for RAILROAD construction and textile mills, the plain, hardworking farmers of North Carolina, Georgia, Virginia, and Texas hoped the Republicans would make good on their pledge for debt relief.

The Southern yeomanry, or small farmers, joined the Republican Party for their own reasons. Many of them had been Union supporters during the war and resented their harsh treatment by Confederate citizens and soldiers. Others wanted to help build a genuine two-party structure in the South and share in the benefits of healthy political competition. Most farmers never owned slaves and resented the prewar domination of the Southern slaveholding class. In every Southern state, they yearned to limit the power of the old guard with the help of the Republicans. The yeomanry wanted to put SLAVERY behind them and to look forward to the economic benefits of Unionism for themselves and their children. This sentiment did not mean, however, that they were in favor of social equality with the former slaves. Scalawags were not, like Northern CARPETBAGGERS, willing to make much room for the hopes and expectations of the much larger African-American base of voters for the Southern Republican Party. Ultimately, this racism, along with corruption within the party and violent attacks from white Southerners, undermined the Republican Party's future in the South.

At the beginning of Reconstruction, Republican leadership expected the party to be established with the help of a number of very fine scalawag leaders. One example is James L. Alcorn of Mississippi. A lawyer and Whig politician before the war, Alcorn served as a brigadier general in the CONFEDERATE ARMY. Returning to Mississippi in 1865, Alcorn became a spokesman for the moderates in his state, advocating racial cooperation and a willingness to forget the bitterness of the past. Alcorn, who served both as a U.S. senator and governor during Reconstruction, decided to tie his political fortunes to the Republican Party. He believed strongly that building up a party organization within Mississippi and in the other Southern states would bring stability and prosperity so desperately needed in the region.

Like other scalawag leaders, Alcorn had to contend with factions and divisions within his state's Republican Party. If African Americans were perceived as being given too much power and prestige, then white voters would leave the party in droves. On the other hand, the freedmen made up the majority of the Republican voters, and black Republicans demanded that they receive their fair share of rewards and patronage positions. Elected governor in 1869 when Mississippi adopted a new constitution, Alcorn made impressive gains in improving life for his constituents, including the establishment of a public school system. He urged fellow Mississippians to accept and support the freedom and political (but not social) rights of ex-slaves. Unfortunately for Alcorn, intraparty rivalries, intrigues, fights, and scandals dimmed the Republican light in Mississippi as in most other Southern states by the early 1870s.

Another prominent scalawag was former Confederate general JAMES LONGSTREET. One of Lee's top generals,

Longstreet joined the Republican Party immediately after he was pardoned in 1867. Related through marriage to President ULYSSES S. GRANT, Longstreet reforged a warm friendship with Grant that had been interrupted by the war. Throughout Reconstruction, Longstreet used his prestige and high profile to urge fellow Southerners to accept and even welcome reconciliation with the North. He served in a number of important positions, including surveyor of the port of New Orleans in 1869 and U.S. minister to Turkey in 1880. Instead of helping to achieve the sectional harmony he hoped for, Longstreet became a hated symbol of the white Southern traitor and the most notorious scalawag of all.

In the end, scalawag leaders of the Southern Republican Party were defeated by the legacy of slavery and racism in their region. They were simply unprepared for the extremely hateful and violent attacks upon their party from Democrats bent on "redeeming" their states from the clutches of Republicans, as well as from politically motivated terrorist groups like the KU KLUX KLAN. By 1876 most scalawags had returned to the DEMOCRATIC PARTY, and those who stayed with the Republicans did so only to receive the occasional patronage position offered by the national government.

See also RACE AND RACIAL CONFLICT; REDEMPTION.

Further reading: Richard H. Abbot, *The Republican Party and the South, 1855-1877: The First Southern Strategy* (Chapel Hill: University of North Carolina Press, 1986).

science and technology

In the 1840s and 1850s, industrialization in the United States accelerated. Rapid advances were made in the sciences and in technology. Americans found new and better ways to farm, to weave, to travel, and to communicate. Among the important inventions of the antebellum period were the steel plow (1837), TELEGRAPH (1837), PHOTOGRAPHY (1839), the rotary printing press (1844), and the sewing machine (1845).

A number of new technologies would be utilized during the CIVIL WAR, forever changing the nature of warfare. For example, combat on land had to be almost entirely reinvented during the war. In the Mexican-American War of 1846–48 and other conflicts before that, troops largely used smoothbore muskets. Smoothbores are not very accurate beyond 150 yards, and so opposing armies equipped with them had to be placed very close to one another. In the Civil War, smoothbores gave way to rifled muskets. Rifled muskets have grooves on the inside of their barrels that put spin on bullets, giving them a maximum range of about 500 yards. The rifled musket was actually invented

400 years before the Civil War, but the technology was not widely utilized because of a critical shortcoming: A bullet being fired from a rifled gun has to fit tightly within the barrel, or else the grooves will not put spin on it. Before the 1840s, the only solution to this problem was to use bullets that were exactly as large as the barrel of the gun. These bullets took a very long time to load, since they fit so snugly and they had to be forced down the barrel with a ramrod. A gun that can only be fired once every few minutes is not very useful in the heat of combat.

In 1843 a French soldier named Claude Minié finally found a way to make rifled muskets practical with the development of a bullet that he called the Minié ball. The Minié ball, which is actually conical in shape, is small enough that it can be dropped right down the barrel of a musket. Minié's key innovation was to make his bullet hollow at one end. The expanding gases released when a musket is fired cause the Minié ball to expand and touch the sides of a rifled musket. And so, the bullet fits loosely when it is being loaded, but tightly when it is being fired. This was the critical step in making rifled muskets viable for use in combat. With the introduction of the Minié ball, rifled muskets could be fired three times per minute, just as fast as smoothbore muskets.

Initially, the impact of the rifled musket on the Civil War was to inflict unheard of levels of carnage. Generals on both sides of the conflict had been trained in Napoleonic TACTICS AND STRATEGY, which emphasized frontal assaults and close proximity to the enemy. When the enemy has smoothbores and can only fire at a range of 150 yards, frontal assaults can be effective since there is only time for one volley of accurate shots. When the enemy has rifles and can begin firing at a range of 500 yards—time for two or three or four volleys—frontal assaults invite wholesale slaughter. The combination of rifled muskets and Napoleonic tactics is a primary reason, for example, that the BATTLE OF ANTIETAM remains the single bloodiest engagement in American history. Quickly, bloodbaths like this forced generals to rethink their tactics. By the end of the Civil War, turning maneuvers and trench warfare were much more common.

Although the Minié ball was the most important, other new technologies also became a part of ground warfare during the Civil War. In 1861 Richard Gatling developed the first reliable machine gun. Gatling guns were used in a few Civil War engagements, most notably the siege of Petersburg. Repeating rifles, which had been developed in the 1850s, were also issued to some soldiers during the Civil War. Union leaders hesitated to embrace them, however, because repeaters were unreliable and because of concerns that they would encourage soldiers to waste ammunition. Land mines were developed during the war by Confederate general Joseph Rains, although they were crude and some officers refused to use them because they felt they were a cowardly form of warfare. Hot-air balloons, invented in 1852 by Henri Giffard, were utilized to provide aerial reconnaissance. The most prominent example occurred during the Warwick-Yorktown siege in early 1862. Two balloons, commanded by Chief Aeronaut of the Army of the Potomac T.S.C. Lowe, were used for spying on Confederate fortifications and for making maps. Although these innovations did not influence the Civil War in a dramatic fashion, all would eventually become important tools for military leaders.

As war on land was evolving during the Civil War, so too was war at sea. In fact, the naval leaders during the Civil War moved very quickly to modernize their fleets. Both the Union and the Confederate navies began the war with vastly fewer boats than they needed, and both decided to build their navies around ironclad ships. IRONCLADS, which

had been used by European powers during the 1850s Crimean War, were wood vessels partially encased in iron plating. The plating made ironclads harder to maneuver but also much more difficult to sink. Ultimately, the Union was able to put 71 ironclads into service, and the Confederacy was able to commission 25. These ships played a role in many of the major naval engagements of the Civil War. Their most notable service occurred at Hampton Roads, Virginia, when the USS *Monitor* faced off against the CSS *Virginia*. Although the meeting of the *Monitor* and the *Virginia* was a draw and had little impact on the outcome of the war, it was important because it marked the first time that iron ships had faced one another in battle. The engagement of the *Monitor* and the *Virginia* made clear to both military leaders and civilians that the age of wooden ships was officially past.

Military maneuvers in the Civil War were helped tremendously by two recent technological advances, the railroad and the telegraph. In both areas, the North had a considerable advantage: It had many more miles of track than the South, plus a competent chief of military rail transport, General Herman Haupt (pictured here, top right, wearing a hat and coat, with a military track crew and a locomotive bearing his name). *(Library of Congress)*

Ironclads were not the only new technology utilized by the Civil War's naval leaders. Confederate leaders in particular were willing to be creative because of their lack of resources. For example, the Confederacy utilized both torpedoes and submarines at various points during the war. Although both technologies had been used for thousands of years in one form or another, the Confederate incarnations bear a much greater resemblance to the modern version. And when the *H.L. Hunley* sank the USS *Housatonic* on February 17, 1864, it became the first time in the history of the world that a submarine had successfully attacked and sunk an enemy vessel.

Military engagements on both land and sea, then, were influenced by new technologies. And at the same time, technology changed the way war was conducted on a broad scale. The telegraph was one critical new tool that Civil War commanders used for logistical purposes. The telegraph had actually been available during the Mexican-American War, but it was not until the Civil War that it became critical. With the spread of the telegraph, spies could gather intelligence and quickly transmit it back to their superiors. Generals could coordinate troop movements over large areas. Politicians could have more of a hand in running the war, albeit sometimes with detrimental effects.

Just as important as the telegraph in shaping logistical planning was the railroad. The railroad had first been developed in the early 19th century, and by the start of the Civil War the nation had 30,000 miles of track, more than any other nation in the world. RAILROADS provided critical logistical support for both the Confederate and the Union armies. Civil War armies were much larger than the armies that had fought in previous conflicts, and it would not have been possible to keep 50,000 men or more properly supplied if food and other necessities could not be brought to them, often from far away. Railroads were also used to move troops over long distances, which was absolutely critical to both sides. For the Confederates, railroads helped to mitigate their shortage of manpower by allowing soldiers to be moved around to the exact spots where they were most needed. For the Union, victory may not have been possible without the railroad. The Confederacy was a very large geographical area. It could not have been conquered, perhaps, if Union troops could not have been quickly and effectively deployed throughout the region.

Technology therefore influenced every aspect of the war front. Meanwhile, the HOMEFRONT was by no means immune to the influence of new inventions. For example, the clothing needs of the UNION ARMY caused the sewing machine to be implemented throughout Northern factories during the war. Although this was a fairly small change, the move toward mechanization would become a dominant theme of the postwar era. Another important change on the homefront during the war had to do with the role of JOUR-NALISM in American society and in warfare. The spread of the telegraph allowed news to be collected and reported much more quickly than it ever had before. And the rotary press made it possible for enough papers to be printed to meet the demand of a news-hungry American public. Henceforth, the American populace would not be kept in the dark about the operations of the country's armies.

As important as new technologies were to the Civil War, it bears noting that new scientific developments did not find their way into all aspects of the conflict, even when they easily could have. The most notable failures were in the area of MEDICINE. Anesthesia was developed by an American dentist more than a decade before the war started. In the 1850s, European doctors began to speak of germ theory, stressing the importance of using clean hands and instruments to perform medical procedures. Nonetheless, these ideas were not embraced by the Civil War medical establishment. As a result, countless thousands of soldiers suffered agonizing pain while undergoing amputations, and thousands of others died of unnecessary infections.

Ultimately, the Civil War had an important role in marrying new technologies with the conduct of warfare. Rifles, machine guns, aerial reconnaissance, iron and steel ships, and submarines would all be indispensable tools for military commanders in the late 19th and 20th centuries.

The Civil War also helped to spread technologies that would shape American life in peacetime. Mechanized factories, newspapers, railroads, and telegraphs would help to remake America's society and its ECONOMY in the postwar era. At the same time, a number of important new inventions and discoveries came about in the postbellum era, as INDUSTRIAL DEVELOPMENT gained momentum. The internal combustion engine (1875), the telephone (1876), refrigeration (1877), the phonograph (1877), and the incandescent light bulb (1879) were all invented in the two decades immediately following the Civil War.

See also BALLOON CORPS; *MONITOR-MERRIMACK*.

Further reading: Neil Baldwin, *Edison, Inventing the Century* (New York: Hyperion, 1995); David A. Mindell, *War, Technology, and Experience aboard the U.S.S Monitor* (Baltimore, Md.: Johns Hopkins University Press, 2000); Charles Ross, *Trial by Fire: Science, Technology and the Civil War* (Shippensburg, Pa.: White Mane Books, 2000).
—Christopher Bates

secession

Secession was the act by which the 11 Southern states that formed the CONFEDERATE STATES OF AMERICA withdrew from the Union. The secession crisis of 1860–61 led directly to the outbreak of CIVIL WAR. The North's victory in the war ensured that secession would no longer be a political issue of any relevance.

There is no provision for secession in the U.S. Constitution. Rather, secession was a concept that developed in response to a series of debates over the course of the antebellum era about the relationship between the states and the federal government. Which held the ultimate power? If the answer was the state, then that entity had the right to secede from the federal government if its liberties were endangered. Three events in particular from the late 18th to the mid-19th century would shape the secessionist position: the Virginia and Kentucky Resolutions of 1798; the War of 1812; and the Nullification Crisis of 1832–33.

America's first party system was founded in the 1790s under the leadership of Thomas Jefferson and Alexander Hamilton. Jefferson and Hamilton had radically different ideas on the nature of government. Hamilton, a Federalist, favored a strong national government, while Jefferson, the founder of the DEMOCRATIC PARTY, was committed to the supremacy of the states. He articulated his position in the Virginia and Kentucky Resolutions of 1798, in which he invented the term *nullification* to describe a state's right to overrule the federal government. The Constitution, argued Jefferson, was a "compact," or agreement, between the states and the national government. If the compact was seriously violated by the federal government, the states could legally withdraw, or secede, from the Union.

The first time states threatened to secede was during the War of 1812. Most New Englanders were opposed to the war, largely because Great Britain was the most important market for their manufactured goods. In 1814 representatives from the states of New England held a convention in Hartford, Connecticut, to discuss their grievances. Disunion was mentioned prominently on the convention floor. Ultimately, the issue was tabled after the war's end.

The question of secession again appeared in 1832 when the federal government adopted a tariff, or tax, on imported goods that Southerners felt was far too high. This was the third time in eight years the government had adopted a tariff that was contrary to Southern interests. In response, the South Carolina legislature passed an ordinance that nullified the federal tariff and stated that if the national government enforced the collection of the tariff, South Carolina would secede. The situation was resolved with a compromise tariff that South Carolina agreed to accept. Temporarily, the storm subsided, but the nullification crisis had major long-term implications for making the Palmetto State a leader of secessionist sentiment. Most importantly, South Carolinian John C. Calhoun emerged from the crisis a powerful voice for STATES' RIGHTS and the protection of SLAVERY. Calhoun was a former nationalist who served in the House, the Senate, in the cabinet as secretary of war and secretary of state, and as Andrew Jackson's vice president. In the 1830s, he turned his formidable intelligence to constructing a rationale for ensuring the perpetuation of slavery in a Union he perceived to be increasingly hostile to the minority slaveholders. Rejecting the current two-party system, Calhoun advocated a Southern sectional party based on states' rights that would be devoted to protecting that region's "peculiar institution." Failing to persuade his fellow Southerners to abandon the Democratic Party, Calhoun became increasingly pessimistic about the fate of the South within the Union. For him, secession was a logical and legal process should it become necessary.

By the 1840s, Southerners influenced by Calhoun had developed an intellectual justification for secession. The 1850s brought constant conflict over the future of slavery. Most Southerners felt that it was important that slavery expand to the territories to sustain the balance of power between slave and free states in the federal government. Many believed that slavery should be legal everywhere in the nation, even in Northern states that had banned the institution. The majority of Northerners felt very differently. They were willing to allow slavery to remain where it already was but wanted to reserve the territories for free labor only. In response to this attitude, a small group of rabid secessionists, called FIRE-EATERS, began to advocate loudly the dissolution of the Union in order to defend and preserve slavery and states' rights. In 1860 ABRAHAM LINCOLN was elected president on a Republican platform committed to stopping the spread of slavery in the territories. Prominent fire-eaters, such as WILLIAM LOWNDES YANCEY of Alabama, Edmund Ruffin of Virginia, and Robert Barnwell Rhett Sr. of South Carolina, saw Lincoln and the party he represented as deeply hostile to Southern slaveholding interests. Throughout the fall and winter of 1860 they worked hard to dissolve the Union. They had compelling arguments, all of which centered on the Republicans' desire to use the federal government's power to deny the property rights of Southerners.

The fire-eaters faced significant obstacles. The wealthy states of the Upper South like Virginia, Tennessee, and Kentucky were not interested in seceding. They wanted to watch and wait to see if they could forge a compromise that would be to their advantage. In the Lower South, it was not clear that the majority of nonslaveholding farmers were willing to support secession to save an institution they had no financial stake in preserving. There were also a substantial number of "cooperationists" in the lower South that favored continuing negotiations with the federal government. They argued that secession should be seen only as a last resort.

Southern radicals knew that they had to manage things very carefully or they would lose their momentum and

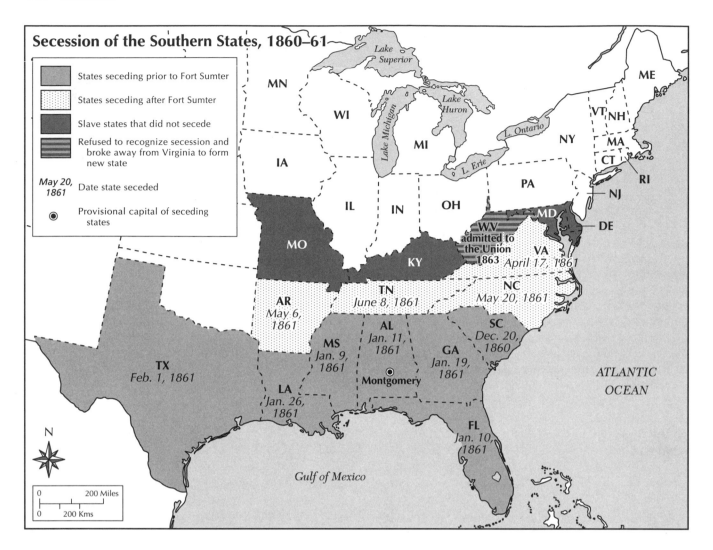

Secession of the Southern States, 1860–61

- States seceding prior to Fort Sumter
- States seceding after Fort Sumter
- Slave states that did not secede
- Refused to recognize secession and broke away from Virginia to form new state
- *May 20, 1861*   Date state seceded
- ◉   Provisional capital of seceding states

secession would fail. The fire-eaters chose to focus their attentions on South Carolina, in hopes that the state's leaders could be convinced to secede quickly and decisively. The Palmetto State was a natural choice to lead the secession movement. It had been the home of John C. Calhoun and a center of secessionist sentiment for more than three decades. Beyond that, South Carolina's constitution was unusual in that it required the state legislature to choose presidential electors. As such, when Abraham Lincoln won the election of 1860, most Southern legislatures had adjourned for winter, but the South Carolina legislature was still in session pending the results. They immediately approved Governor William Henry Gist's call for special ELECTIONS to choose representatives for a secession convention.

South Carolina's secession elections made the state's departure from the Union a certainty. Strong opponents of secession declined to run for seats at the convention,

knowing that they would be defeated. Cooperationists dismissed the convention as largely meaningless, believing that secession would only happen if a group of Southern states agreed to secede together. When the secession convention was seated on December 17, 1860, it was populated entirely by fire-eaters. A committee was appointed to draw up a secession resolution, and in short order they completed their work. The convention voted unanimously on December 20 to endorse the resolution that declared the union between the states to be "dissolved."

South Carolina's bold move gave a big boost to the efforts of fire-eaters in the other states of the Lower South. In each state, the same basic pattern had to be followed: elections, a secession convention, and the adoption of an ordinance of secession. In no state was secession as much of a certainty as in South Carolina, and in some states the issue was hotly contested. However, the inspiration provided by the Palmetto State, as well as skillful politicking by fire-eaters, eventually convinced the rest of the Lower South to join South Carolina in seceding. By February 1, 1861, Mississippi, Florida, Alabama, Georgia, Louisiana, and Texas had called secession conventions and voted to leave the Union. On February 4 delegates from the seceded states met to begin drawing up a constitution for the new nation.

The states of the Upper South hesitated much more than those in the Lower South. Pro-Unionist sentiment, Northern commercial ties, and a much lower number of slaves made secession more problematic. For the federal government, the key to retaining the loyalty of the Upper Southern states was a noncoercive policy. Compromise between North and South was discussed and rejected, and as time dragged on, hope faded. Supplies began to run out for the small Union garrison at FORT SUMTER located in Charleston Harbor in South Carolina. President Lincoln weighed his options, keenly aware that popular sentiment in the North heavily favored resupplying the fort and keeping it under the national flag.

On April 6 Lincoln went public with his decision to resupply Fort Sumter, but only with food and other necessities of survival. President JEFFERSON DAVIS could not abide by this decision, as he was well aware of the symbolic importance of allowing the North to keep possession of the fort. So, Davis decided to fire upon Sumter before the Northern ships arrived. On April 12, 1861, Confederate batteries attacked, and the garrison surrendered two days later.

Lincoln responded to the attack on Fort Sumter with a call for 75,000 troops to put down the insurrection. At this point, the states of the Upper South had a choice between taking arms against the South and taking arms against the North. This was an easy decision to make, and shortly thereafter Virginia left the Union. Over the course of the five weeks after Fort Sumter, Arkansas, Tennessee, and North Carolina followed suit. The secession crisis had ended and the Union was dissolved. The stage was set for the bloodiest conflict in American history.

Further reading: William L. Barney, *The Road to Secession: A New Perspective on the Old South* (New York: Praeger, 1972); William C. Davis, *Rhett: The Turbulent Life and Times of a Fire-Eater* (Columbia: University of South Carolina Press, 2001); William W. Freehling, *The Road to Disunion: Secessionists at Bay, 1776–1854* (New York: Oxford University Press, 1990); Kenneth M. Stampp, *And the War Came: The North and the Secession Crisis, 1860–1861* (Baton Rouge: Louisiana State University Press, 1970).

—Christopher Bates

Semmes, Raphael (1809–1877)

Rear admiral for the CONFEDERATE STATES OF AMERICA, lawyer, historian, and newspaper editor, Raphael Semmes is best known for his stewardship of the famed cruiser *Alabama.* Born on September 27, 1809, in Charles County, Maryland, Semmes attended the Charlotte Hall Military Academy. Appointed as a midshipman in the U.S. Navy in 1826, he found time between service in the Mediterranean and Caribbean Seas to study law and was admitted to the bar in 1834.

Semmes moved from Maryland to Cincinnati, where he married and began his family of six children. He served in the Mexican-American War of 1846 and later published a popular account of the event. Semmes and his family moved to Alabama, where he had bought property. When the war began, he resigned from the U.S. Navy and offered his services to President JEFFERSON DAVIS. His first assignment was to go north and buy supplies and ammunition from stores in New England and New York. Mission accomplished, he dropped in to view President ABRAHAM LINCOLN's inauguration in WASHINGTON, D.C.

Commissioned a commander in the CONFEDERATE NAVY, Semmes outfitted the cruiser *Sumter* in New Orleans and began an 18-month stint as a commerce raider running the Yankee blockade. After great success, Semmes traveled overseas to take command of the CSS *Alabama,* one of the rebel ships built in Liverpool, England. Sleek, fast, and powerful, the *Alabama* destroyed or captured 69 vessels before it was destroyed by the Union's *Kearsarge* off the coast of France in late spring of 1864. After a dramatic rescue at sea, Semmes returned home a hero and commanded the James River Squadron until the end of the war. Semmes applied for and received a presidential pardon in May 1865, but he was arrested on piracy charges upon his return to Mobile, Alabama. Cleared of all charges, Semmes worked as a judge, a teacher, a newspaper editor, and a lawyer. An accomplished writer, he published his story, *Memoirs of Service: Afloat during the War Between the States* in 1868. Raphael Semmes died on August 30, 1877, in Point Clear, Alabama.

Further reading: John M. Taylor, *Confederate Raider: Raphael Semmes of the "Alabama"* (Washington, D.C.: Brassey's, 1994).

Seward, William H. (1801–1872)

Lawyer, governor, senator, and secretary of state, William Henry Seward was one of the leading Republicans of his era. Seward was born in Florida, New York, on May 16, 1801. Graduating from Union College in 1820, he was admitted to the New York bar two years later. Son of a businessman and a county judge, Seward married a judge's daughter, Frances Miller. They settled in Auburn, New York, to raise a family. Their son, Frederick William Seward, served as his father's assistant secretary of state and close advisor during the most turbulent years of the elder Seward's career.

William H. Seward rose rapidly in New York State politics, advancing from WHIG PARTY leader in the state senate to the governor's office while still in his 30s. After his second gubernatorial term, Seward built his legal practice only to return to politics again in 1849, when he advanced to the U.S. Senate.

Seward quickly established himself as a powerful figure in Congress, one associated particularly closely with ABOLITIONism. He is known during the 1850s for two controversial remarks. During a debate over the Compromise of 1850, Seward urged senators to ban SLAVERY in the territories entirely. Replying to Southern attacks that such a ban was unconstitutional, Seward asserted that there was a "higher law" than the U.S. Constitution.

Echoing the rhetoric of abolitionists like WILLIAM LLOYD GARRISON, Seward earned a reputation in some circles as a radical abolitionist—a reputation that would prove both incorrect and damaging to his career. Again, in a speech at Rochester, New York, Seward denigrated compromise with slave owners, declaring that North and South

William H. Seward *(Library of Congress)*

were engaged in an "irrepressible conflict" between two fundamentally different views of America's future.

When the Whig Party collapsed following the KANSAS-NEBRASKA ACT, Seward joined the new REPUBLICAN PARTY, instantly becoming the leading candidate for the 1860 Republican presidential nomination. But Seward's flirtation with abolitionism, still largely unpopular in the North, alienated more moderate Republicans. During the 1860 Republican Convention, Seward watched his support ebb while ABRAHAM LINCOLN's swelled. Despite the disappointment, Seward actively campaigned for Lincoln throughout the fall and accepted Lincoln's invitation to serve as secretary of state.

By 1861 Seward had been in politics for nearly 30 years. Lincoln, in contrast, had served a single term as an Illinois congressman. Seward made the mistake of assuming that the inexperienced president would gratefully rely on his seasoned cabinet member to craft the new administration's key policies. Alarmed at what he took to be Lincoln's vacillation in the face of imminent Southern rebellion, Seward sent the president his recommendations for a more robust policy. The United States, Seward suggested, ought to abandon FORT SUMTER while arresting rebels throughout the United States. Meanwhile, Lincoln should rally the country around the Monroe Doctrine and challenge Spanish and French meddling in the Americas.

Once at war, the people would forget their regionalism and rally to the flag. Such a policy, Seward concluded, would need a strong hand to guide it—presumably, his own. Seward misread the depth of Southern commitment to SECESSION and seriously misjudged Lincoln himself. Lincoln's reply, while cordial, made it clear that Lincoln himself would be making the decisions.

Despite the awkward start, Seward proved himself to be an essential and loyal member of Lincoln's cabinet. He promptly dispatched Charles Francis Adams, son and grandson of presidents, to counter Confederate diplomacy in London, issuing veiled (and not so veiled) threats to go to war if the British recognized the Confederacy. In one sense, these threats were little more than bluff; the United States could not have simultaneously defeated the British and the Confederacy both. However, remarked Seward to French diplomats, though the United States might lose such a war, its enemies would know they had been in a fight. Strong words, combined with more tactful diplomacy, worked. Despite their economic interest in continued cotton exports, neither British nor French governments could afford to add a protracted conflict in North America to their obligations elsewhere in the world.

Seward handled three diplomatic crises with particular success. First, he persuaded French and British governments to withhold recognition from the Confederacy and to respect the Union blockade of Southern ports. Second, he forced the British to cease outfitting Southern privateers such as the *Alabama,* though the so-called *Alabama* claims were not settled until well after the war's end. Finally, Seward released two Confederate spies, captured from a British vessel in the *Trent* affair. Making this concession over the loud objections of congressional Republicans won Seward the respect of the British government officials, who came to see the American secretary of state as tough and shrewd—but a man with whom they could work.

At the end of the war, Seward was injured in a carriage accident and was bedridden when both he and his son, Frederick, became the victims of an assassination attempt by Lewis Paine, one of the coconspirators with JOHN WILKES BOOTH. On the evening of April 14, 1865, Paine's attempt on the lives of Seward father and son failed, while Booth's ASSASSINATION OF ABRAHAM LINCOLN succeeded.

Seward recovered and remained secretary of state after Lincoln's death, crafting an American FOREIGN POLICY whose expansionism and hemispheric ambitions prefigured those of Theodore Roosevelt half a century later. Citing the Monroe Doctrine, Seward pressured Napoleon III to withdraw French troops from Mexico, where they had established an "empire" at the start of the CIVIL WAR.

Seward urged Congress to authorize the building of a canal across Panama and to annex the Danish West Indies, Hawaii, Midway, and Santo Domingo. With the exception of Midway, Congress was unwilling. Many Northerners believed that the Civil War had erupted over the disposition of territories conquered from Mexico in 1848, and most wanted national resources devoted to RECONSTRUCTION. Even so, Seward's policies, while dormant in the 1870s, would catch fire again in the 1890s.

Congress did approve one of Seward's initiatives, however, authorizing $7 million to purchase Alaska from the Russian Empire. Seward's opponents derisively labeled the undeveloped Arctic wilderness "Seward's Folly" and "Seward's Icebox." Seward, however, correctly predicted that the region's value to the United States would not be apparent for another generation. It became so in 1898, when gold was found in the Klondike.

Seward remained loyal to ANDREW JOHNSON through the president's impeachment trial. Supporting Johnson's generous and gentle treatment of white ex-Confederates, Seward urged RADICAL REPUBLICANS to show the defeated opponents the mercy they now deserved. Seward displayed little interest in the problems faced by the freedpeople. Seward had believed slavery to be wrong, but he also believed Africans to be inferior to Europeans and their subordinate status to be inevitable and natural.

These views alienated Seward from the mainstream of Republican opinion; Republican president ULYSSES S. GRANT had little use for a Johnson administration loyalist. This time, Seward's retirement from public life proved permanent. Seward died at his home in Auburn, New York, on October 10, 1872.

See also FILIBUSTERING; IMPEACHMENT OF ANDREW JOHNSON.

Further reading: John M. Taylor, *William Seward: Lincoln's Right Hand* (New York: HarperCollins, 1991); Glyndon G. Van Deusen, *William Henry Seward* (New York: Oxford University Press, 1967).

—Tom Laichas

sharecropping

Sharecropping replaced slave gang labor after the CIVIL WAR. The cotton PLANTATIONS were cut up into small parcels, usually less than 40 acres, with the parcels farmed by free African-American families. The cotton grown by the former slaves was divided between the planter, the merchant, and the farmer. The conditions of sharecropping often brought black laborers into dependency and debt, making it difficult for them to improve their economic position in the New South.

After 1865 most freedmen worked for their former owners on a year-to-year contract. These contracts usually offered food and a small monthly stipend in exchange for working under gang labor, which was too much like SLAVERY for African Americans. They felt that freedom entitled them to break as far as possible from the world of prewar plantations. In great numbers, they broke their contracts and tried to lease small plots of land to live as independent farmers. One sympathetic observer wrote: "The sole ambition of the freedman at the present time appears to be to become the owner of a little piece of land, there to erect a humble home, and to dwell in peace and security at his own free will and pleasure."

Rejecting plantation labor, the freedpeople and the plantation owners came up with a compromise, which was sharecropping. Once they settled on a parcel of land, the ex-slaves entered into credit relationships with local merchants and landowners. Over time, a relatively predictable system was established. Landowners gave freedmen the bare necessities to farm the land: seeds, tools, fertilizer, clothing, and food. In return for the use of the land, sharecroppers paid plantation owners or landlords a share of the yearly harvest, usually about half. The freedmen retained their portion of the crop to feed their families and to pay merchants (owners could also be merchants) for goods purchased on credit during the year. However, these goods were often sold at inflated prices and with high interest rates. Thus, by the end of the year the tenant generally owed so much to the landowner that the debt could not be entirely repaid. Essentially, freedmen moved from lives of chattel slavery to lives of debt peonage.

Although sharecropping was especially common among African-American freedmen, it also affected white farmers. Yeomen who sought to participate in staple crop production were themselves caught in the web of debt that merchants could spin. This situation, which divided prosperous white landowners from indebted white and black people, created a potential racial problem for Southern leaders. The class divide between rich and poor white people held open a possibility that black and white farmers might unite politically.

Racism put an end to cross-color unity. Organizations such as the KU KLUX KLAN had formed as early as 1866, fostering white supremacy and solidarity. Because of this divide, sharecropping for white farmers proved a very different experience than for African Americans. Poverty was a serious problem, but white tenant farmers could count on the judicial system, community support, and family ties to help in their relationship with the owners.

While sharecropping prevented African Americans from enjoying the economic benefits of EMANCIPATION they had expected, it was not slave labor, and it allowed a limited amount of independence and power.

See also RACE AND RACIAL CONFLICT.

Further reading: Leon Litwack, *Been in the Storm So Long: The Aftermath of Slavery* (New York: Knopf, 1979); Edward Cary Royce, *The Origins of Southern Sharecropping* (Philadelphia: Temple University Press, 1993).

—Samantha Holtkamp Gervase

Shenandoah Valley: Jackson's campaign

(March 23–May 9, 1862)

The Shenandoah Valley held great logistical and strategic significance during the CIVIL WAR. With the Blue Ridge Mountains on the east and the more imposing Alleghenies to the west, the valley runs southwest to northeast and drops gently in its course to meet the Potomac River, which means that an individual traveling to the Potomac goes "down the valley"—an odd circumstance in a world where north is almost always "up." The premier grain-growing area in Virginia during much of the antebellum period, the valley produced a variety of agricultural products that helped sustain Confederate forces in Virginia. It also loomed large as a strategic avenue through which either side could mount a threat to the western parts of WASHINGTON D.C., and RICHMOND.

The 1862 Shenandoah Valley campaign of Gen. THOMAS J. "STONEWALL" JACKSON had its origins in Gen. ROBERT E. LEE's desire to limit the size of the Union threat against Richmond. In late April 1862, Gen. GEORGE B. MCCLELLAN's 100,000-man Army of the Potomac advanced toward the Confederate capital up the Virginia peninsula between the York and James Rivers. Fifty miles north of Richmond lay another major Union force commanded by Gen. Irvin McDowell. Smaller armies under Gen. Nathaniel P. Banks in the lower Shenandoah Valley and Gen. John C. Frémont in the Alleghenies farther west completed the roster of Union threats in Virginia. Lee functioned as JEFFERSON DAVIS's principal military adviser, and he wanted Stonewall Jackson, who commanded a modest force in the valley, to pin down all Federals west of the Blue Ridge; otherwise, Frémont and Banks could potentially join McDowell at Fredericksburg for an advance against Richmond in conjunction with McClellan. Jackson had taken an initial step toward this with an offensive movement that resulted in the Battle of First Kernstown, just south of Winchester, on March 23, 1862. A Confederate tactical defeat, First Kernstown nonetheless had persuaded the Federals to hold Banks and Frémont in the valley, which in turn set up subsequent Confederate success.

Jackson soon demonstrated how a resourceful commander of an inferior force could use speed and imagination to achieve great results. On May 8, 1862, he concentrated part of his troops at the village of McDowell, in the Alleghenies west of Staunton, Virginia, defeating the advance guard of Frémont's army and forcing its retreat into the wilds of western Virginia. Returning to the valley, Jackson marched northward and captured several hundred Federals in a minor battle at Front Royal on May 23. Two days later he won the Battle of First Winchester against Banks, driving the Federals toward the Potomac River and capturing a huge quantity of military supplies. By May 29, Jackson's troops skirmished with Federals near HARPERS FERRY, having cleared most of the lower valley of Union forces.

Near Harpers Ferry, Jackson's force occupied a vulnerable position. From Washington, ABRAHAM LINCOLN sensed an opportunity to deliver a decisive blow. He envisioned a three-pronged pincers movement to isolate Jackson in the lower valley. Frémont would march from the west, a division from McDowell's command under Gen. James Shields would move east from Front Royal, and Banks would apply pressure from the north. "I think the evidence now preponderates that Ewell and Jackson are still about Winchester," commented the president to General McDowell. "Assuming this, it is, for you a question of legs. Put in all the speed you can. I have told Frémont as much, and directed him to drive at them as fast as possible." But Jackson pushed his men to the limit and, aided by incredibly slow movements by all three Union commanders, escaped the trap and marched to the southern end of Massanutten Mountain near Harrisonburg. There, he defeated part of Frémont's force in the Battle of Cross Keys on June 8. The next day, he turned back Shields's command in the Battle of Port Republic. Frémont and Shields soon retreated northward on both sides of Massanutten Mountain, and Jackson moved to reinforce Lee's army outside Richmond.

Jackson had accomplished his strategic goals quite effectively. He pinned down Banks and Frémont and convinced the Federals to hold McDowell at Fredericksburg, thereby denying McClellan thousands of reinforcements. None of Jackson's battles had been a tactical masterpiece; indeed, he had struggled to win despite having superior numbers at McDowell and again at Port Republic, and Banks's soldiers had escaped from the battlefield at First Winchester with minimal damage. Still, these small victories reached a Confederate populace starved for good news from the military front and made Jackson a popular Southern hero.

Casualties in the 1862 Shenandoah Valley campaign were modest compared with the bloodier battles of the Civil War. They totaled just fewer than 5,500 Federals (more than half of whom were prisoners) and just more than 2,750 Confederates.

See also PENINSULAR CAMPAIGN.

Further reading: Robert G. Tanner, *Stonewall in the Valley: Thomas J. "Stonewall" Jackson's Shenandoah Valley Campaign, Spring 1862* (New York: Doubleday, 1976).
—Gary W. Gallagher

Shenandoah Valley: Sheridan's campaign
(August 1864–March 1865)
Early in the summer of 1864, with his army entrenched at Petersburg, Gen. ROBERT E. LEE ordered troops under the command of Gen. JUBAL A. EARLY into the Shenandoah Valley. The valley was of primary strategic value to both sides. Not only did it provide an avenue of attack into Maryland for the Confederates but it also provided necessary food supplies for Gen. Lee's Army of Northern Virginia. The Confederacy had attempted to maintain a presence there since the beginning of the war, and Union efforts to drive them from the valley had proven futile. Confederate Gen. THOMAS J. "STONEWALL" JACKSON's Shenandoah Valley campaign of 1862 helped to defeat Gen. GEORGE B. MCCLELLAN's attempts to take RICHMOND, and Lee hoped Early's operations there would have a similar effect on Grant.

With Early threatening WASHINGTON, D.C., Gen. ULYSSES S. GRANT united several commands into the Middle Military District under the direction of Gen. PHILIP HENRY SHERIDAN. Sheridan's command consisted of a newly created Army of the Shenandoah Valley, comprising the Sixth Corps, several brigades from the former Army of West Virginia, two divisions from Louisiana, and two divi-

sions of Sheridan's own cavalry. Sheridan was ordered to go after Jubal Early and "follow him to the death." If Early's army could not be destroyed, then Sheridan was to drive them up the valley and prevent the Confederates from returning to the lower valley again.

Sheridan had been made aware, by both Grant and Secretary of War EDWIN M. STANTON, of the importance of success in his campaign because of the impending presidential election. As a result, Sheridan initially displayed caution in assembling his command and sparred with Early for six weeks. However, on September 19, Sheridan's 37,000 men attacked the 15,000 rebels at Winchester. With his forces overrun and some 2,000 rebels captured, Early retreated to Fisher's Hill, just south of Strasburg. On September 22, Sheridan scored another victory and drove Early about 60 miles farther south to a pass in the Blue Ridge.

While attempting to destroy Early's army, Sheridan also followed the second part of Grant's instructions, which was to prevent any CONFEDERATE ARMY from returning to the valley. Grant ordered that "if the war was to last another year we want the Shenandoah Valley to remain a barren waste." Sheridan added, "The people must be left nothing, but their eyes to weep over the war." Sheridan followed Grant's instructions to the letter, destroying mills and barns filled with wheat, hay, and farming implements, taking whatever provisions and stock he needed, and ruining the rest. He promised that by the time he was through, "the Valley, from Winchester up to Stanton, ninety-two miles, will have little in it for man or beast." Sheridan was true to his word, destroying the farms of Confederate sympathizers.

Lee was determined not to lose the Shenandoah Valley without a fight, and he reinforced Early's depleted forces with an infantry division and a cavalry brigade. On October 16, Sheridan left his army near Cedar Creek, 15 miles south of Winchester, to go to Washington, D.C., for a war conference with Gen. HENRY W. HALLECK and Secretary Stanton.

On the night of October 18, Early ordered four Confederate divisions into a position for a dawn attack on Sheridan's unsuspecting forces. With the attack, the UNION ARMY was caught completely unaware and forced into retreat. Early's soldiers, hungry and poorly equipped, broke ranks to forage the Union camp. Sheridan, camped at Winchester on his way back from Washington at the time of the attack, arrived at the battlefield just in time. Coming across his retreating men, Sheridan quickly understood what had happened and realized that only he could restore confidence to his army. Riding among his men, hat waving, Sheridan was greeted with delight. He roused his men with such appeals as, "If I had been with you this morning this disaster would not have happened. We must face the other way; we will go back and recover our camp." On meeting a chaplain and asking him how things were at the front, the chaplain replied, "Everything is lost; but all will be right when you get there." Faced with a renewed attack by a revived Army of the Shenandoah Valley, Early's army disintegrated as it fled south ahead of the advancing Union forces. Sheridan's actions that day are generally recognized as one of the most inspired acts of personal battlefield leadership during the war. He turned a decisive defeat into a glorious victory.

Early's defeat at Cedar Creek destroyed the effectiveness of his army to operate in the Shenandoah Valley, though Sheridan's campaign continued there until March 1865. The Battle of Waynesboro marked the last encounter of the campaign, and with it Early's army was destroyed. Sheridan's success in the Shenandoah Valley meant that not only could Lee no longer threaten Washington through the valley but also that the Confederacy had lost a valuable source of food for the Army of Northern Virginia. Grant, thanks to the Sheridan campaign, could concentrate his entire force on the Richmond-Petersburg front and on bringing the war to an end without fearing a Confederate force in the Shenandoah Valley.

Further reading: Philip Sheridan, *The Personal Memoirs of P.H. Sheridan, General, United States Army* (New York: C.L. Webster, 1888); Edward J. Stackpole, *Sheridan in the Shenandoah: Jubal Early's Nemesis* (New York: Bonanza Books, 1961).

—Paul Manzor

Sheridan, Philip H. (1831–1888)

Union cavalry officer Philip Henry Sheridan ranked among the top three generals in the UNION ARMY along with ULYSSES S. GRANT and WILLIAM T. SHERMAN. Born in Albany, New York, to Irish immigrants, Sheridan's father was one of the workers on the National Road. His parents resettled in Ohio, where their son grew to his adult height of 5 feet 5 inches. In his youth, Sheridan was captivated by the news of soldiers and fighting in the Mexican-American War. His early fascination with all things military prepared him for his life's work.

Sheridan graduated from the UNITED STATES MILITARY ACADEMY AT WEST POINT in 1853, ranking 34th in a class of 51. He served in the West, including California, and the first year of the CIVIL WAR found him on duty as a quartermaster captain. In the spring of 1862, Sheridan was appointed colonel of the Second Regiment Michigan Cavalry. Acquitting himself honorably in the Corinth campaign, Sheridan was described to Gen. HENRY W. HALLECK as "worth his weight in gold." Shortly thereafter, he was appointed a brigadier general.

On December 31, 1862, Sheridan displayed his leadership abilities at the BATTLE OF MURFREESBORO, where his fast thinking and hard fighting helped to prevent the total destruction of the Union forces. As a result of his actions at Murfreesboro, Sheridan was appointed a major general, taking command of the Third Division, 20th Corps, Army of the Cumberland.

For the next year Sheridan and his division continued to fight hard through the Middle Tennessee campaign, June 24–July 5, 1863, and the BATTLE OF CHICKAMAUGA, September 19–20, 1863, displaying unusual dedication. By November and the Battle of Missionary Ridge, Sheridan was in command of the Second Division, Fourth Corps, Army of the Cumberland, in the Military Division of the Mississippi under the command of Gen. Ulysses S. Grant. The Battle of Missionary Ridge further polished Sheridan's growing reputation when his division played a major role in defeating Confederate troops. Importantly, the short, feisty Sheridan with his characteristic handlebar moustache became one of Grant's favorite generals.

After taking a brief leave of absence due to physical exhaustion, Sheridan returned to duty in March 1864, anticipating a resumption of the campaign in the west in April. Instead, he was ordered to move along with General Grant to the eastern theater. By the end of March 1864, Sheridan commanded the cavalry corps of the Army of the Potomac.

Sheridan's troops consisted of three cavalry divisions and 12 batteries of horse artillery. Included under his command were such notable officers as Brig. Gen. George A. Custer. Sheridan immediately invigorated the eastern infantry corps by advocating a change to an aggressive tactical force. Eagerly anticipating the opportunity to defeat the Confederate forces under the famed cavalry officer J. E. B. STUART, Sheridan was given the chance in May with the order to "go out and do it."

Taking 10,000 men, Sheridan rode out on a raid to cut Robert E. Lee's communications in the rear. Destroying some 20 miles of railroad and a large quantity of supplies, Sheridan reached Yellow Tavern on May 11, where Stuart waited. Outnumbering the Confederates two to one and with rapid-fire carbines, Sheridan's forces quickly defeated Stuart's men, took a large number of prisoners, and mortally wounded Stuart. Stuart's loss to the Confederates was comparable with the loss of Gen. THOMAS J. "STONEWALL" JACKSON.

In July Grant assigned Sheridan to the command of the Army of the Shenandoah Valley with orders to destroy the Confederate forces there and eliminate the valley as a supply base for the Confederates. Sheridan achieved lasting fame by rallying his troops from certain defeat at the Battle of Cedar Creek, and by early 1865, his job in the Shenandoah Valley had been completed successfully. Sheridan then rejoined Grant on the Petersburg-RICHMOND front.

At the beginning of March, Sheridan's men engaged at the BATTLE OF FIVE FORKS, which forced Lee to abandon Petersburg. Sheridan's cavalry and three infantry corps pursued Lee vigorously, constantly probing and attacking the retreating Confederates, wearing them down. At APPOMATTOX COURT HOUSE, with Sheridan on one side and the pursuing Grant on the other, outnumbered five or six to one, Lee had no alternative but to surrender.

As Grant's right arm of destruction in the eastern theater of the war, Sheridan became associated with devastation, particularly in the Shenandoah Valley campaign, as he carried out Grant's and Sherman's total war. No matter which position he held, Sheridan's concern was always for the well-being of his men and they, in return, repaid him with loyalty and affection.

Sheridan's postwar career was controversial, eventful, and distinguished. Sheridan was placed in charge of the Fifth Military District (encompassing Texas and Louisiana) under the congressional RECONSTRUCTION ACTS. A supporter of the RADICAL REPUBLICAN version of RECONSTRUCTION, Sheridan proceeded to remove uncooperative officials, including both state GOVERNORS, and enforce fair voting processes. In doing so, he created controversy, and ANDREW JOHNSON promptly removed him from the position.

In the late 1860s, Sheridan was transferred to the Department of the Missouri, where he turned his energies to defeating the NATIVE AMERICAN nations who refused to be resettled from their traditional lands to reservations. Headquartered in Chicago, Lieutenant General Sheridan was appointed by President Grant to the commander of the Division of the Missouri. Until 1870, he directed the U.S. military actions against such Indian nations as the Cheyenne, the Apache, and the Sioux. Sheridan's one notable failure, the BATTLE OF LITTLE BIGHORN, resulted in the death of his protégé, George Custer, as well as many U.S. soldiers.

Sheridan spent several years in Europe observing the Franco-Prussian War before returning at Grant's request in 1874. The president placed his trusted subordinate in charge of Louisiana, where terrorism and violence had left the state in turmoil. Calling the White Leagues "banditti," Sheridan crushed the resistance and brought some kind of order to bear on the volatile situation. Leaving Louisiana with charges that he overstepped his authority, Sheridan was returned to his earlier responsibilities in the West. In 1883 he was appointed general in chief of the U.S. Army and was promoted to general of the army: a four-star general, a rank previously held only by Grant and Sherman. Philip H. Sheridan died at the age of 57 in 1888 in Nonquitt, Massachusetts.

Further reading: Paul A. Hutton, *Phil Sheridan and His Army* (Lincoln: University of Nebraska Press, 1985); Roy Morris, *Sheridan: The Life and Wars of General Phil Sheridan* (New York: Crown, 1992); Philip H. Sheridan, *Personal Memoirs of P.H. Sheridan* (1888; reprint, Scituate, Mass.: Digital Scanning, 1998).

—Paul Manzor

Sherman, William T. (1820–1891)

Famed and feared Union CIVIL WAR general William Tecumseh Sherman is best known for his famous "March to the Sea," in which his western army invaded Georgia in the fall of 1864. A believer in a hard war but a soft peace, Sherman emerged from the Civil War an immensely popular and revered soldier among the former Union troops. Serving with distinction as general in chief of the U.S. Army until 1883, he declined the Republican presidential nomination twice, in 1872 and 1884, stating, "if nominated, I will not run; if elected, I will not serve."

Named after the warrior Indian chief of the Ohio Confederacy, Tecumseh was born on February 8, 1820, to Charles R. Sherman, a state judge, and Mary Hoyt Sherman in Lancaster, Ohio. Charles Sherman died suddenly in 1829, leaving his wife and 11 children in poverty. Thomas and Maria Ewing, a wealthy Catholic couple with six children, adopted Tecumseh. A long-time family friend, Thomas Ewing—prominent Whig, U.S. senator, and cabinet officer—exerted a significant influence on Sherman's life. The nine-year-old red-haired Tecumseh (called "Cump") was baptized in the Catholic faith and given the first name of William.

At the age of 16, William T. Sherman entered the UNITED STATES MILITARY ACADEMY AT WEST POINT. An excellent if troublesome student, Sherman graduated 6th in the class of 1840. From 1842 until 1846, Lieutenant Sherman served in the Seminole War in Florida and in South Carolina. To his disappointment, Sherman was sent to California during the Mexican-American War, missing the excitement and experience of the conflict. In California, he witnessed the transition to statehood and viewed firsthand the effects of the gold rush of 1849.

In 1850 Sherman left California and transferred to WASHINGTON, D.C. That same year, he married Ellen B. Ewing, his foster sister. The Ewings wished for Ellen and William to settle near them in Lancaster, Ohio. Ellen agreed with her parents and asked Sherman to leave the army, settle down, and take up a profession. This he refused to do for her, and it was the first of many bitter arguments between husband and wife. Stubborn and proud, Sherman was determined to prove to the powerful family who raised him, and who now welcomed him as a son-in-law, that he could be successful on his own terms.

By 1853, however, a discouraged Sherman resigned from the army to earn more money for himself and his growing family. Through personal connections, he accepted a position as a banker in San Francisco. At first, Sherman prospered and happily remained in San Francisco until 1857. Unfortunately, the ECONOMY crashed in that year, and Sherman's bank declared bankruptcy. Other business enterprises followed in short order and ended in failure as well.

Unfit for the world of finance, Sherman became the superintendent of the Louisiana Military Seminary in 1859. Leaving SECESSIONist Louisiana in 1861, Sherman returned to service in the UNION ARMY. His younger brother, John Sherman, had just been elected U.S. senator from Ohio and helped him obtain a commission as colonel in the regular army. He led his forces at the FIRST BATTLE OF BULL RUN in July 1861, where he was one of the few Union officers to distinguish themselves in that battle loss. Viewing the disorganized Federal retreat, he felt extremely pessimistic about the future of the Union and predicted that the war would take much longer than most people thought at the time.

In August 1861, Sherman was named brigadier general of volunteers and was sent to Kentucky as an aide to the commander of the Department of the Cumberland, Gen.

William Tecumseh Sherman *(Library of Congress)*

ROBERT ANDERSON. Kentucky was a key state for the Union to retain, and when Sherman declared that he would need 40,000 troops for its defense or 200,000 troops for an offensive attack against rebel forces, critics called him insane. Depressed, Sherman suffered a collapse and was relieved of his duties. Sherman served briefly as an aide to Western Division commander Gen. HENRY W. HALLECK in St. Louis and then was reassigned to a training post. His prominent family successfully defended Sherman against charges of instability during this difficult period. In February 1862, Halleck put Sherman in charge of the headquarters in Paducah, Kentucky, which was under the command of Gen. ULYSSES S. GRANT.

Sherman's military career took a sharply upward trajectory. Reassured by Grant's calm, steadfast demeanor and purposeful leadership style, the tall, slender Sherman had found a boss who appreciated his brilliant talents and protected him from his own worst traits. Never a modest man, Sherman admitted that he possessed more pure intellectual ability than his friend. But, he added of Grant: "He don't care a damn for what the enemy does out of his sight, but it scares the hell out of me." Truly, they were "partners in command," who would together bring the Union army its ultimate victory in the field. Sherman led a division at the BATTLE OF SHILOH in spring of 1862, and despite being surprised by the Confederate attack early on April 6, he rallied his men forcefully to win the next day.

Shiloh was a victory, but a costly and controversial one. Continued Southern resistance, even while under Northern occupation and after suffering terrible losses in battle, caused Grant and Sherman to have long conversations about the course of the war. Both decided that winning required not only the defeat of the Confederate armies but also the will of the Southern people. Sherman's experience as military governor of Memphis, Tennessee, drove home the hard lesson that Southern civilians were unrepentant. In an October 1862 letter to Grant, Sherman articulated his basic philosophy: "We cannot change the hearts of those people of the South, but we can make war so terrible that they will realize the fact that however brave and gallant and devoted to their country, still they are mortal and should exhaust all peaceful remedies before they fly to war."

Promoted to major general of volunteers and commander of the XV Corps, Sherman left Memphis for Grant's VICKSBURG CAMPAIGN during the winter of 1862. He and his troops suffered a terrible defeat at Chickasaw Bayou, Mississippi, on December 27, 1862. Sherman became convinced that Grant's plan was fatally flawed, but loyal to his friend and commander, he did everything he could to support the campaign's success. Against Sherman's advice, Grant decided to cut his supply lines and live off the land once his forces were across the MISSISSIPPI RIVER. The success of this strategy and the subsequent capture of

Vicksburg on July 4 provided him with a lesson that he put to use the following year in Georgia.

Famous and celebrated in the North, Sherman's pleasure in the victory was short-lived; his son, Willie, who had been visiting his father with Ellen, died from a fever contracted in camp. The pressures of war did not allow time for mourning, however. Grant was placed in charge of all the Union armies in the western theater. President Lincoln quickly approved his recommendation that Sherman succeed him as head of the Army of Tennessee. After the Union victory in the BATTLE OF CHATTANOOGA in the fall of 1863, Lincoln named Grant commander in chief of all the Union armies; Sherman again assumed Grant's former position. Grant's "total war" strategy for the spring and summer of 1864 included two vital tasks for Sherman's western campaign: to capture Atlanta and to destroy Gen. JOSEPH E. JOHNSTON's Army of Tennessee.

Marching east, Sherman's army fought Johnston's at several notable battles, including Kennesaw Mountain on June 27, 1864, where the Union's frontal assault failed at great cost to the men. Despite several drawbacks, Sherman besieged and then captured Atlanta on September 2, assuring Lincoln's victory in the 1864 presidential election. Leaving much of Atlanta in flames, Sherman moved eastward again, marching toward Savannah, Georgia. "War is cruelty, and you cannot refine it," Sherman warned. He targeted property and morale among Confederate citizens. By waging psychological warfare, Sherman believed that he made Union victories easier to obtain with fewer casualties among both soldiers and civilians. This idea was central to his "March to the Sea." With Savannah under Union control, Sherman and his army turned northward through the Carolinas, living off the land and terrorizing the inhabitants of PLANTATIONS. Historians have found that Sherman and his men, for the most part, acted with restraint until they entered South Carolina. "The whole army is burning with an insatiable desire to wreck vengeance upon South Carolina," Sherman wrote. "I almost tremble at her fate, but feel that she deserves all that seems in store for her." The destruction of Columbia, South Carolina, by the Union forces left the city a smoking ruin.

Sherman's strategy proved a military and political triumph for the Northern war effort. Throughout the Southern countryside, Sherman and his hardened, sunburned western soldiers burned designated property and destroyed homes and towns. Thousands of slaves followed in their wake. Sherman issued SPECIAL FIELD ORDER NO. 15, which set aside confiscated land for the freed people. He did so more out of a desire to rid his army of its African-American followers than from a genuine desire to bring revolution. Indeed, Sherman opposed the EMANCIPATION PROCLAMATION and the arming of black soldiers. He was mainly concerned with preserving the order and sanctity of the Union. Despite the

popular memory of Sherman's march, casualties were slight. With Union victory in hand, Sherman asserted that "the legitimate object of war is a more perfect peace."

Sherman accepted the surrender of his Confederate counterpart, Joseph E. Johnston, at Durham, North Carolina, on April 26, 1865. Sherman, acting on his understanding of Lincoln's desire to forge a generous peace, overstepped his military role in writing out the terms. The new president ANDREW JOHNSON and his secretary of war, EDWIN M. STANTON, rejected the agreement. Sherman renegotiated the surrender in a form similar to Grant's at Appomattox.

In 1869, with Grant as president, Sherman was the commanding general of the U.S. Army. He served for 14 years, presiding over the "pacification" of NATIVE AMERICAN tribes for the settlement and development of the western states and territories. Following his retirement on February 8, 1884, Sherman became one of the Gilded Age's most popular lecturers. When not speaking about his experiences, he wrote for national magazines, presenting his version of the history of the war. He published his *Memoirs* in 1875. Sherman was a passionate supporter of VETERANS' groups and often spoke at important anniversary celebrations. William T. Sherman died on February 14, 1891, in NEW YORK CITY, where he had lived since 1886. Sherman's legacy as one of the most important military leaders of the Civil War remains unchallenged.

See also ATLANTA CAMPAIGN; SHERMAN'S MARCH THROUGH GEORGIA.

Further reading: Michael Fellman, *Citizen Sherman: A Life of William Tecumseh Sherman* (New York: Random House, 1995); John F. Marszalek, *Sherman: A Soldier's Passion for Order* (New York: Free Press, 1993); William T. Sherman, *Memoirs of General W. T. Sherman* (1875; reprint, New York: Library of America, 1990).

Sherman's March through Georgia
(November 15–December 21, 1864)

Sherman's March through Georgia, commonly referred to as the "March to the Sea," began in Atlanta in November 1864 and culminated in the capture of Savannah on December 21 before the troops continued toward South Carolina. During this campaign, Union general WILLIAM T. SHERMAN and his force of 60,000 soldiers marched across Georgia, living off the land and terrorizing Southern civilians. The path taken by these men was scattered with evidence of their presence—railroad ties twisted around trees, burned houses and crops, and trampled countryside.

After a four-month-long campaign to capture Atlanta, Georgia, the city was evacuated by Confederate forces on

September 1, 1864. Sherman and his troops took control of the city on September 2. Sherman allowed the Southern troops to escape and focused his energy on the city. In establishing Atlanta as a command post for Union operations, Sherman issued Special Field Order No. 67 on September 8, 1864, calling for the evacuation of Atlanta's more than 1,500 civilians. Despite vehement protests from Southern officials and civilians, Sherman insisted that this evacuation was necessary for the Union's military operations. In addition, he did not want to be burdened with the protection and care of a hostile civilian population.

After several unsuccessful attempts to destroy Gen. JOHN BELL HOOD's Confederate forces, Sherman determined that the Union's best interests would be served by marching his troops across Georgia to demonstrate the power of the UNION ARMY. Sherman further proposed cutting off his own supply and communication lines and living off the countryside as he and his troops marched through Georgia. This would allow him to pursue the devastation of the Southern countryside without worrying about protecting RAILROADS and supply trains. Sherman wanted to "make Georgia howl" and to crush the Confederate civilian population's morale. Sherman received permission from General ULYSSES S. GRANT and President ABRAHAM LINCOLN to proceed.

Before departing from Atlanta on November 15, 1864, Sherman and his troops burned everything of military importance in the city—depots, shops, factories, and foundries. According to Union reports, only war-related businesses and factories were destroyed by fire. However, Southern reports blamed widespread destruction of homes and personal property on Sherman's troops. Such destruction, which likely occurred in Atlanta, would continue as Union troops made their way through Georgia. Leaving Generals GEORGE HENRY THOMAS and John M. Schofield with 60,000 Union soldiers to deal with Hood's troops in Tennessee, Sherman's troops began their March to the Sea to crush civilian and material support for the Confederacy.

To effectively forage, destroy, and demoralize the Georgia countryside, Sherman divided his troops into two wings, a left (northern) wing commanded by Gen. Henry W. Slocum and a right (southern) wing under Gen. O. O. HOWARD's command. Although the officers and soldiers began the 285-mile march toward Savannah with little knowledge of the plan, they confidently moved forward at Sherman's command. The route through a rich agricultural area of Georgia offered fertile opportunity for good eating and good spirits among the soldiers. In another tactical measure, Sherman spread his troops across a 60-mile path to give the Confederates the impression that they were heading for multiple places: Macon, Augusta, or Savannah. This allowed the Union forces to keep the Confederate troops spread thinly and prevented high casualties. Although there

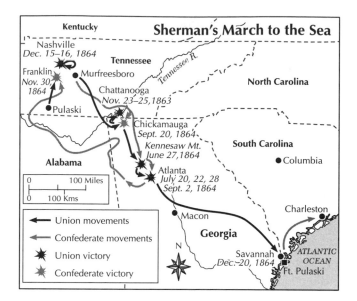

were several skirmishes as Sherman and his troops marched to the sea, Union casualties for the entire campaign numbered only 2,200. Union forces easily captured Milledgeville, Georgia's state capital, on November 23.

Sherman's troops marched from 10 to 15 miles each day, FORAGING and destroying Confederate property along the way. Reports describe a 60-mile wide swath of destruction. This, Union troops hoped, would destroy the material and moral support for the Southern war effort and bring the war to a close. Often, Union soldiers ate what they could and then destroyed whatever was left in order to keep excess supplies away from Confederate soldiers and civilians. In addition, they targeted and destroyed railroads, mills, and other places or items that supported the Confederate war effort. The Union troops became famous for their heating and twisting of railroad ties into "Sherman's neckties."

Although Sherman designated a specific group of men as foragers for the troops, the main columns and individual soldiers also searched for their own food and other spoils of war. "Sherman's Bummers," the official foragers, often seized personal property as souvenirs of their service. Women's clothes, LETTERS, linens, jewelry, silver, household furnishings, and dishes often became the spoils of war for Union soldiers. Some of these treasures were sent home to loved ones in the North, while others were dropped on the roadside as the march continued. Although Sherman officially opposed the wholesale plunder of Southern property, he rarely punished offenders and applauded the effects destruction had on the Southern civilian population.

Sherman's soldiers also freed the slaves that they encountered on Georgia PLANTATIONS and destroyed the trappings of SLAVERY, such as cotton gins, plantation houses, and agricultural equipment. Many Southern African Americans followed the Union troops, hoping to gain their freedom in the ranks of the Union army. Some served as spies for Sherman's army. Others cheered as the Union troops passed by. Although some officers were kind to the escaped slaves who followed the army, others allowed prejudiced attitudes to govern their actions. A tragic incident occurred on December 9, when Union Gen. Jeff C. Davis and his troops crossed Ebenezer Creek, closely followed by Confederate troops. Davis's 14th Corps, followed by black escapees, crossed the creek on a pontoon bridge and then quickly removed the bridge before the runaway slaves could do the same. Fearful of the repercussions they would face at the hands of Gen. JOSEPH WHEELER's Confederate cavalry for supporting the Union, the escaped slaves tried to cross the creek without a bridge. Many drowned or were captured by Southern troops. Neither Sherman nor Davis took responsibility for this tragedy.

The small opposition faced by the Union troops as they marched through Georgia consisted of approximately 8,000 Confederate soldiers in Gen. Joseph Wheeler's cavalry corps and Gen. Gustavus W. Smith's Georgia militia. Gen. William J. Hardee took control of Confederate troops in Georgia on November 17, 1864, but could not stop Sherman's progress through the state. Acknowledging this inability, Hardee focused his energy and forces on the protection of the shipping town of Savannah. Sherman and his troops cut through most of Georgia by December 10, and Sherman demanded the surrender of Savannah on December 17, 1864. When Hardee refused, the Union forces began a siege of the city while leaving Confederate troops free to evacuate it. Hardee and his force of approximately 10,000 men abandoned Savannah on December 21, escaping across the river to South Carolina. Sherman and his men took control of the city and its 200 artillery pieces, ammunition, and approximately 30,000 bales of cotton. On December 22, 1864, Sherman sent ABRAHAM LINCOLN a telegram, offering Savannah to the president as a Christmas present.

Once in control of Savannah, Sherman set about demonstrating to the city's residents that peaceful surrender and return to the Union would protect Southerners from Union wrath. To contrast his treatment of residents in Savannah to that of rebellious Atlantans, Sherman opened his headquarters to whomever wanted to visit. He also allowed the local government to continue functioning and made sure that food came in to the city to feed the residents. However, despite his attempts at reconciliation with those in occupied Savannah, Sherman noted that the Southern girls still "[talked] as defiant as ever" to their captors.

From Savannah, Sherman issued SPECIAL FIELD ORDER NO. 15 on January 16, 1865, granting freedpeople full control of the sea islands as well as coastal land 30 miles inland from Charleston to Jacksonville. Sherman and his troops left Savannah on February 1, 1865, and began marching toward Columbia and Charleston, South Carolina.

See also RULES OF WAR.

Further reading: Joseph T. Glatthaar, *The March to the Sea and Beyond: Sherman's Troops in the Savannah and Carolinas Campaigns* (Baton Rouge: Louisiana State University Press, 1995); Lee Kennett, *Marching through Georgia: The Story of Soldiers and Civilians during Sherman's Campaign* (New York: HarperCollins, 1995).

—Lisa Tendrich Frank

Shiloh, Battle of (April 6–7, 1862)

The Battle of Shiloh was a major Northern victory, although a costly one. It secured western Tennessee for the Union and set the stage for advances into Mississippi in 1862 and 1863.

The Battle of Shiloh was the culmination of a string of Union successes in Tennessee. The February 15, 1862, Union capture of Fort Donelson on the Tennessee River resulted in an important strategic shift in the western theater of the CIVIL WAR. As the greatest tactical victory in the war to that time, it marked the emergence of ULYSSES S. GRANT as a major military leader and opened the Tennessee River to Union naval traffic, allowing for a direct invasion of the Lower South. For the Confederates, the loss represented a significant disaster. With nearly 15,000 troops captured and the center of his defensive line in southern Kentucky pierced, Confederate department commander Gen. ALBERT SIDNEY JOHNSTON was forced to withdraw more than 100 miles into the Confederate interior. Nashville, a major site of war production, was captured by the Union, and the rich grain fields and pork-raising region of Middle Tennessee was overrun. The forts defending the MISSISSIPPI RIVER north of Memphis were threatened with being cut off from behind. Union forces stood poised to strike the Confederate RAILROAD centers at Jackson, Humbolt, and Corinth, Mississippi.

This threat to the rebel heartland forced the Confederate government to reconsider its previous policy of dispersing troops over a wide geographic area in an attempt to defend the entire perimeter of the Confederacy. Within a week of Donelson's fall, President JEFFERSON DAVIS wrote that he was determined to "assemble sufficient force to beat the enemy in Tennessee, and retrieve our waning fortunes in the west." At the end of February, the Confederate president ordered BRAXTON BRAGG, who commanded the Southern forces defending the Gulf Coast region around Pensacola, Florida, and Mobile, Alabama, to move his troops to Tennessee, where he would consolidate with

Johnston's force to counter the Union threat. While this concentration of military power was unprecedented, it was not as complete as possible. Bragg sent only 60 percent of his force to Tennessee, and several large contingents of Confederate troops remained idle in Texas and Arkansas. Nonetheless, the Confederate concentration at Corinth, Mississippi, drew together just over 40,000 troops.

As the Confederates consolidated their force, conflict among the Union high command in the west temporarily slowed the Union drive south. However, by early March a large expedition force had been organized at Fort Henry. Using the Tennessee River as an invasion route, Union troops under the overall direction of Gen. HENRY W. HALLECK and spearheaded by WILLIAM T. SHERMAN's Fifth Division quickly moved into southern Tennessee and established a base of operations around Savannah and Pittsburg Landing. By mid-March, five divisions of Union troops commanded by ULYSSES S. GRANT had concentrated there and threatened Corinth, the site of a major Southern rail connection. Throughout the last weeks of March and into early April, the area around Pittsburg Landing mushroomed into a vast army camp containing nearly 45,000 combat troops. While the army included several units that had seen combat at Fort Donelson and other smaller clashes, many of the Union troops had yet to engage the enemy. Still, confidence ran high among the rank and file who believed, as one soldier put it, "The rebellion is getting nearly played out, and I expect we will be home soon." Generals shared this confidence. One division commander wrote, "Sesech is about on its last legs in Tennessee." Grant himself wrote, "with one more success I do not see how rebellion is to be sustained."

Still, problems plagued the army. The arms carried by most Union soldiers were outdated flintlock muskets that had been converted to percussion locks. These muskets were accurate to about 100 yards. Beyond that, their accuracy diminished dramatically. Sickness also plagued the army, and doctors sent thousands of sick soldiers to large hospitals in the North, reducing the fighting capabilities of many regiments. Conflicts between top-level officers created more problems for Grant, who spent much of late March dealing with a variety of petty issues. Only one of the division commanders, WILLIAM T. SHERMAN, held a West Point degree. Most problematic was the choice of campsites. Located on the west side of the Tennessee River, the same side held by the Confederates, the Pittsburg Landing encampment lay open to attack. Union commanders could have moved to the other side of the Tennessee River or could have built defensive works, but they were convinced that the Southern army would never try to attack.

The Confederate leaders, meanwhile, prepared for an offensive that would drive the Union army back to Kentucky. However, they faced their own set of obstacles. The army that they assembled had never worked together, the staff were not coordinated, and many of the high-level officers had never commanded such large numbers of troops. Most of the regiments were undermanned, and the majority had never fired a shot in combat. Illness took a further toll on the army, and as much as 16 percent of the army was on the sick list on April 3. Arms consisted of a motley assortment of squirrel rifles, percussion muskets, flintlocks, and shotguns. Visual cues underscored the hodgepodge nature of the rebel force. Clothing bore no standard cut or fabric; as one soldier put it, "some wore uniforms, others half uniforms, some no uniforms at all." Despite these apparent weaknesses, the soldiers, citizens, and government called for quick and dramatic action to counter the Union success of the winter. Thus, Johnston prepared his army to strike what he hoped would be the decisive blow.

Faced with the knowledge that Don Carlos Buell's Army of the Ohio had departed Nashville and was moving to reinforce Union troops at Pittsburg Landing, Confederate commander Albert Sidney Johnston determined to attack Grant's force before a consolidation could be made. Johnston knew that if the two Northern forces combined, they would nearly outnumber his forces two-to-one. The rebels, faced with a rapidly closing window of opportunity, looked for any weaknesses in Grant's position. A March 31–April 1 reconnaissance led by Confederate Gen. Benjamin Cheatham suggested that Grant had divided his force. Johnston's second in command, P. G. T. BEAUREGARD, concluded that "now is the moment to advance and strike the enemy at Pittsburg Landing." On the morning of April 2, the Confederate leaders began drafting a plan to move forward. Primarily drafted by Beauregard, the plan proved disastrous. The scheme included a complicated advance along two roads and a confusing deployment that placed the army's three corps in successive lines of battle. Once in line, the inexperienced troops were to deliver an attack that would drive the Union left flank away from the Tennessee River into the bottoms of Owl Creek, where the Yankees would be compelled to surrender. Thus prepared, the Confederates marched out of Corinth on April 3, 1862.

The Confederate plan was ill suited to both the experience of the army and to the conditions in northern Mississippi and southern Tennessee. The first day's march proved a fiasco. Vague orders and mishandled communications led to clogged roads and much unnecessary marching and countermarching. Poor weather and the wretched condition of the two roads that led from Corinth to Pittsburg Landing resulted in delays and frustration. Once they neared the Union forces, chaos reigned. Johnston delayed the attack, planned for April 5, because several divisions had become entangled on the march and failed to arrive at their proper position. Furthermore, inexperienced soldiers

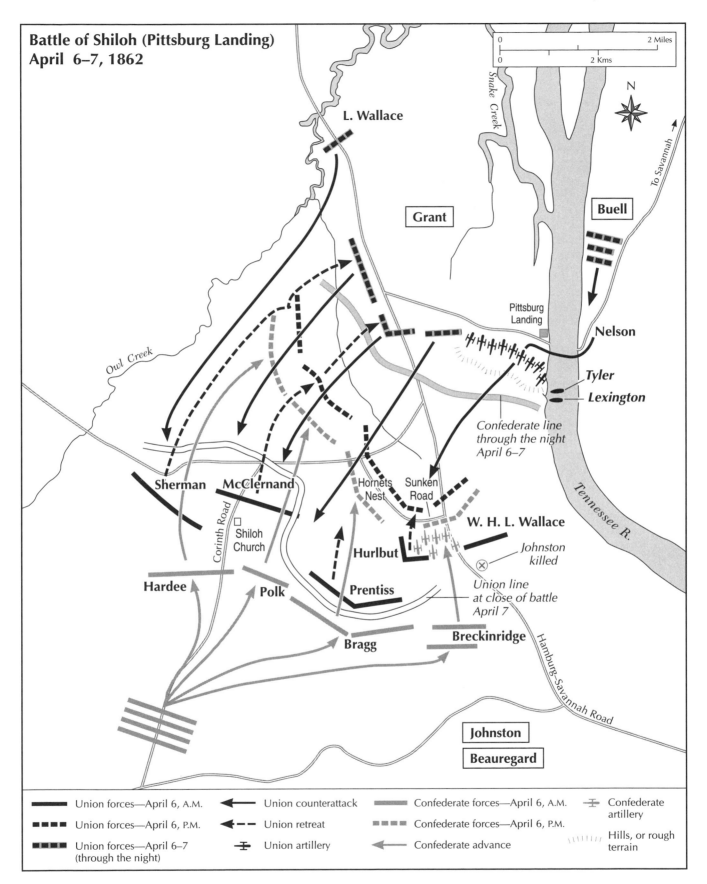

Battle of Shiloh (Pittsburg Landing)
April 6–7, 1862

L. Wallace

Grant

Buell

Pittsburg Landing

Nelson

Snake Creek

Tyler

Lexington

Owl Creek

Confederate line
through the night
April 6–7

Sherman

McClernand

Hornets
Nest

Sunken
Road

W. H. L. Wallace

Corinth Road

Shiloh Church

Hurlbut

Prentiss

⊗ *Johnston
killed*

*Union line
at close of battle
April 7*

Hardee

Polk

Bragg

Breckinridge

Tennessee R.

Hamburg-Savannah Road

To Savannah

Johnston

Beauregard

N

| | 0 | | 2 Miles |
| 0 | | 2 Kms | |

▬▬ Union forces—April 6, A.M.	◀▬ Union counterattack	▬▬ Confederate forces—April 6, A.M.	⟊ Confederate artillery
▬ ▬ Union forces—April 6, P.M.	◀- - Union retreat	▪ ▪ ▪ Confederate forces—April 6, P.M.	Hills, or rough terrain
▬▬ Union forces—April 6–7 (through the night)	⟊ Union artillery	◀▬ Confederate advance	

began firing their muskets to be certain they worked. Others cheered for their generals as they rode past, and throughout the army drums beat and bugles blared. Surely, several rebel leaders thought, the element of surprise had been lost. Johnston nonetheless decided to press forward with his attack on April 6.

Despite the Confederates' inefficient march, their initial attack against William T. Sherman's troops caught the Union forces entirely by surprise. Though warned by subordinates that a large SECESSIONist force lay within easy striking distance, Sherman scoffed at the idea and did little to prepare his men for a fight. His reassurances led Grant to write on the evening of April 5, "I have scarcely the faintest idea of an attack (general one) being made upon us." So unprepared were the Union troops that when the rebels poured out of the woods to their south, they were cooking breakfast and getting ready for their weekly inspection. The first Confederate attacks routed both Sherman's and Prentiss's divisions. Stout resistance, however, emerged in two sections: in the Union center and on the Union left, near a small chapel named Shiloh Church. The impact of the fierce fighting that raged all along the battle line threw the Southerners' cumbersome attack formation into confusion. Many of the brigades had lost all semblance of order as the lines piled upon each other, and officers were assigned command of portions of the line without regard to corps organization. To compound the command problems, at about 2:30 P.M., the rebel commander Johnston fell mortally wounded.

Meanwhile, as the fighting increased around Pittsburg Landing, Grant arrived to take charge of the action. He ordered reinforcements from Buell's army across the Tennessee River, gave orders to the troops in the center to hold on at all costs, and issued orders to create a final defensive line near Pittsburg Landing. Surviving nearly a dozen desperate attacks against the Union center, the line held until near dark. Centered on a large concentration of artillery and bolstered by the fire of Union gunboats on the river, Grant's line at the landing proved formidable, although its strength began to dwindle by the end of the day because the reinforcements Grant had ordered never arrived. Before the line could give way, nighttime came, and Beauregard, who had assumed command upon Johnston's death, ordered a halt to the rebel advance.

Beauregard felt confident that his troops would be able to break the Union line on April 7 and secure victory for the Confederacy. However, during the night, Buell's troops finally arrived. On the morning of April 7, Grant organized an attack led by three fresh divisions from Buell's army. At first successful in regaining the ground lost on April 6, the Union forces faltered as the Confederate defense stiffened, and the fight seesawed back and forth. The weight of Buell's reinforcements, however, proved overwhelming,

and at about 5:00 P.M. the Confederates retreated from the field. The day's heavy fighting discouraged a Union pursuit, and the Battle of Shiloh had come to an end.

Shiloh exacted a great toll on both armies. Confederate losses were 1,723 killed, 8,012 wounded, and 959 captured or missing out of 40,335 engaged. Union losses were 1,754 killed, 8,408 wounded, and 2,885 captured or missing out of 62,682 engaged. The battle enhanced Ulysses S. Grant's reputation as a general but also strengthened the perception of him as "Grant the butcher." After their victory at Shiloh, Grant and his troops would travel a difficult road. It would be more than a year before they would achieve their next major objective, the capture of Vicksburg, Mississippi.

See also VICKSBURG CAMPAIGN.

Further reading: James Lee McDonough, *Shiloh: In Hell before Night* (Knoxville: University of Tennessee Press, 1977); Wiley Sword, *Shiloh: Bloody April* (New York: Morrow, 1974).

—James Daryl Black

Sickles, Daniel E. (1819–1914)

Lawyer, politician, ambassador, and CIVIL WAR general, Daniel Edgar Sickles was born on December 20, 1819, in NEW YORK CITY to George Garrett Sickles and Susan Marsh Sickles. Sickles's father was a prominent lawyer and politician, and Daniel followed him into both careers. Sickles entered law school at New York University and was admitted to the bar in 1843.

Shortly thereafter, Sickles launched his political career, joining the New York Democratic political machine that operated out of Tammany Hall. In 1847 Sickles was elected to the New York Assembly, a position he left to serve as secretary to JAMES BUCHANAN, U.S. minister to England. After his return from England in 1855, Sickles won a seat in the New York State Senate and later in the U.S. House of Representatives, where he served from 1857 until 1861.

Sickles's political career was tarred by well-founded accusations of corruption. A national scandal erupted when the congressman shot and killed his wife's lover in cold blood on the streets of WASHINGTON, D.C. Sickles was acquitted when his legal team defended him on the grounds of "temporary insanity." In 1861 he abandoned politics for the UNION ARMY and raised the "Excelsior Brigade" in New York City. For that, he was made a brigadier general. Promotions followed when Sickles demonstrated some military ability in the PENINSULAR CAMPAIGN and at the BATTLE OF FREDERICKSBURG. In May 1863, Maj. Gen. Daniel E. Sickles commanded the III Corps at the BATTLE OF CHANCELLORSVILLE, where he ordered an attack that contributed to the Union's defeat.

Sickles is best known for his infamous decision on the second day of the BATTLE OF GETTYSBURG, when he joined the Union army on the field. Without informing his commander, Gen. GEORGE GORDON MEADE, Sickles moved his corps way out in front of the rest of the Union defensive line. This salient created a serious gap that allowed the Confederates under Gen. JAMES LONGSTREET to launch a devastating attack against the Federals. A last-minute save by Gen. Winfield Scott Hancock, commander of the II Corps, prevented a rout, and the Union line held. Sickles was badly injured in the leg by a cannon ball while he was commanding his troops, and later it was amputated. The injury removed Sickles from the battlefield for the rest of the war.

Undaunted, Sickles returned to public life after the war with the vigor of a man half his age. Active in RECONSTRUCTION politics, Sickles sided with the RADICAL REPUBLICANS against the administration of President ANDREW JOHNSON. An ardent supporter of ULYSSES S. GRANT for president in 1868, Sickles was appointed to the post of minister to Spain, 1868–74. Sickles was elected in 1892 to the House of Representatives, again as a Democrat. His major legislative achievement was in securing the passage of the act that enabled the federal government to acquire the Gettysburg battlefield.

Sickles was widely criticized after the war for his actions on July 2, 1863. Characteristically, he and his supporters attacked Meade and other top generals at Gettysburg for failing to recognize the superiority of Sickles's tactics. Although the criticism persisted, Sickles's crusade influenced interpretations of Gettysburg in much of the LITERATURE of his day. Sickles also participated widely in efforts to preserve the battlefield as a historical site.

Sickles died of a cerebral hemorrhage on May 3, 1914, at age 94. He is buried at Arlington National Cemetery.

Further reading: Thomas Keneally, *American Scoundrel: The Life of the Notorious Civil War General Daniel Sickles* (New York: Doubleday, 2002); Harry W. Pfanz, *Gettysburg: The Second Day* (Chapel Hill: University of North Carolina Press, 1987).

—Fiona Galvin

Singleton, Benjamin (Pap) (1809–1892)

Also known as "Pap" or "Pap Moses" for his role in the exodus of more than 25,000 freed people from the South to western Kansas in the 1870s, Benjamin Singleton was born a slave in Nashville, Tennessee. Little is known about the first 60 years of his life. Singleton evidently escaped from SLAVERY, going first to Canada and then to Detroit, Michigan, where he opened a boardinghouse for ex-slaves. Full of optimism for African Americans after the CIVIL WAR,

Singleton happily returned to Edgefield, Tennessee, in 1865 and supported his family by working as a carpenter. He quickly assumed a leadership role in the community and urged government support of black economic improvement through public schools and land reform. Singleton desired that African Americans enjoy the kind of independence that land ownership could bring—the same independence he felt was enjoyed by the white small farmers of the country. He supported President ULYSSES S. GRANT's efforts to establish the REPUBLICAN PARTY's Southern base with the help of African-American votes, because he reasoned that political power might speed up the growth of economic power. Singleton was bitterly disappointed as racism and violence gripped Tennessee and the South. "The whites had the land and the sense," he observed, "and the blacks had nothing but freedom."

Determined to make the most out of that freedom, Singleton became convinced that God had appointed him to lead his people out of the economic bondage of tenant farming and SHARECROPPING and the social bondage of discrimination in the postwar South. He wanted to establish autonomous all-black communities in the promised land of the West, where so many white migrants were heading in the 1860s and 1870s and where land was relatively cheap, or even free, thanks to the HOMESTEAD ACT of 1862. Kansas, the place where JOHN BROWN first came to the nation's attention in the 1850s, was Singleton's first choice for African-American migration. In 1873 Singleton took a preliminary trip to Kansas with several other interested people. Together, they formed the Edgefield Real Estate and Homestead Association. Flyers and other means of advertisement were distributed that exhorted African Americans to buy and settle on land outside the South. At first hundreds and then thousands of black people from Kentucky, Tennessee, Mississippi, and Louisiana moved west with hearts full of hope for a better future.

The most famous of the settlements was the town of Nicodemus, Kansas. Singleton himself moved west, and although he never made much money from the enterprise, he did begin a national controversy over the migration. White citizens of Kansas viewed the steady influx of African-American pioneers, named Exodusters, with alarm. So did white Southerners, who worried that the migration would drain their region of needed laborers and further depress their ECONOMY. Ultimately, there was little cause for concern because the exodus ended abruptly in the early 1880s when conditions in Kansas fell far short of expectations. Still, the African Americans who stuck it out in the West achieved a modest success. Singleton, called the "Moses of the Colored Exodus," became involved in black nationalist movements. He died in Topeka, Kansas, in 1892.

Further reading: Nell Irvin Painter, *Exodusters: Black Migration to Kansas after Reconstruction* (New York: Knopf, 1977).

slavery

Slavery is a system of labor where individuals are compelled to serve in perpetuity with little or no compensation. Slavery has existed, in one form or another, for thousands of years. The institution first came to the English colonies in North America in the early decades of the seventeenth century. It was quickly limited to African Americans and more gradually came to be restricted to the South.

Life under slavery was very harsh. Slaves were generally compelled to work long days doing backbreaking labor. As adequate clothing, food, and medical attention were generally not provided to slaves, death rates were very high. The laws of most states barely acknowledged slaves, and they were denied virtually every legal privilege, including the right to bring lawsuits or testify in court trials, the right to vote, and the right to marry. Masters' power over their slaves was almost unlimited. Slaves could be sold apart from their families, denied food, raped, or whipped mercilessly. Although the murder of a slave was supposed to be illegal, such crimes were rarely punished.

Slaves actively resisted the system whenever possible. Physical confrontations between slaves and their masters were not uncommon. Occasionally, full-blown slave revolts would develop, as groups of slaves banded together with the hope of escaping en masse or punishing cruel owners. The best-known revolts were led by Gabriel Prosser in 1800, Denmark Vessey in 1822, and Nat Turner in 1831, but there were a number of others. For some slaves, escape was a more feasible and more attractive option than revolt. The most widely repeated stories of escape involve the UNDERGROUND RAILROAD, which helped slaves travel to the states of the North or to Canada.

It was difficult and risky for slaves to revolt or for an individual slave to try and escape, however. As such, passive forms of resistance were much more common. Slaves might steal extra food, fake illness, deliberately break equipment, or subvert the will of their masters and overseers in any of a hundred other ways. At the same time, slaves resisted the slave system by developing a vibrant culture of their own. Slave RELIGION usually blended African and Christian beliefs, while teaching slaves that they would ultimately be delivered from bondage, if not in this life, then in the next. Slaves also had their own unique art, MUSIC, folklore, and medical practices. Like slave religion, these things typically blended African and American influences.

By the early part of the 1800s, slavery had all but disappeared from the states of the North, and some Northerners began to look southward in the hope of eliminating the institution there as well. A number of prominent Northerners came to believe that slaves should be purchased from their masters and returned to Africa. This plan came to be known as colonization, and it led to the formation of the American Colonization Society in 1816. Ultimately, however, the colonization movement was surpassed in size and importance by the ABOLITION movement, which advocated bringing slavery to an immediate end. By the end of the 1830s, the abolition movement was playing an important role in Northern politics, while at the same time increasing Southerners' sense of alienation from the North.

Although most abolitionist leaders were white, a number of ex-slaves played key roles in the movement. Slave narratives powerfully recounted the horrors of slavery for the Northern public. These included JAMES W. C. PENNINGTON's *The Fugitive Blacksmith*, WILLIAM WELLS BROWN's *Narrative of William W. Brown, an American Slave,* and FREDERICK DOUGLASS's *Narrative of the Life of Frederick Douglass, an American Slave.* In addition to penning books, Pennington, Brown, and Douglass also made tours throughout the North, delivering speeches to win converts to the abolition movement.

The antislavery arguments of abolitionists tended to focus on the immorality and inhumanity of slavery and on its negative effects on the slaves themselves. Meanwhile, a number of white Northern politicians began to develop an antislavery argument that emphasized the negative effects of slavery on white Northerners. The "Free-Soilers," as they came to be known, were focused on the vast territories that the United States had added via the Louisiana Purchase and the Mexican-American War. Free-Soilers were content to allow slavery to remain where it already was, but they believed that it was imperative that the institution be barred in the territories, so that free white labor could continue to spread and to flourish.

As Northern abolitionist and Free-Soil sentiment grew, white Southerners felt that their way of life was under attack. A number of Southern writers defended slavery and its superiority as a system of labor. The most prominent was GEORGE FITZHUGH, who wrote a pair of pro-Southern treatises, *Cannibals All!* and *Sociology for the South.* "We have no mobs, no trades unions, no strikes for higher wages, no armed resistance to the law," declared Fitzhugh. "We have but few in our jails, and fewer in our poor houses." Other Southern apologists echoed Fitzhugh's sentiments. While Southerners of Thomas Jefferson's generation had seen slavery as a "necessary evil," Southerners of Fitzhugh's generation came to see it as a "positive good."

By the 1850s, slavery was the dominant issue in the nation's political discourse, with the debate often erupting into violent confrontations. In 1854, proslavery BUSHWHACKERS and antislavery JAYHAWKERS began a series of

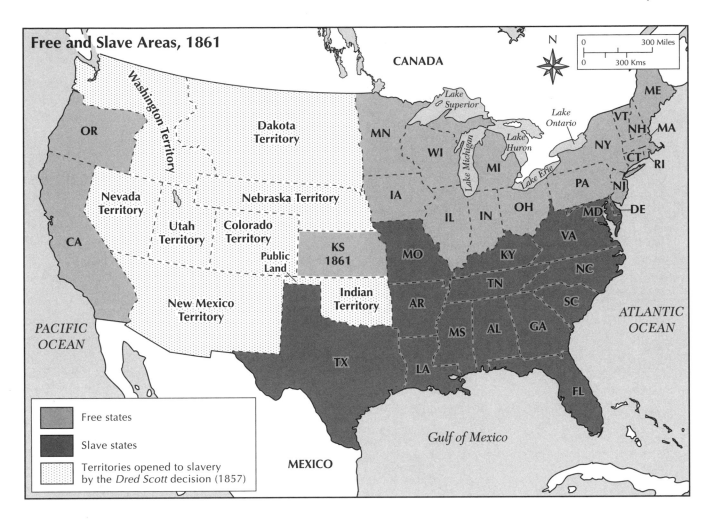

Free and Slave Areas, 1861

CANADA

OR

Washington Territory

Dakota Territory

MN

WI

Lake Superior

Lake Ontario

Lake Huron

Lake Michigan

Lake Erie

ME

VT

NH MA

NY

CT

RI

Nevada Territory

Nebraska Territory

IA

MI

PA

NJ

Utah Territory

Colorado Territory

IL

IN

OH

MD

DE

CA

Public Land

KS 1861

MO

KY

VA

ATLANTIC OCEAN

Indian Territory

AR

TN

NC

SC

PACIFIC OCEAN

New Mexico Territory

MS

AL

GA

TX

LA

FL

Gulf of Mexico

MEXICO

Free states

Slave states

Territories opened to slavery by the *Dred Scott* decision (1857)

armed clashes over whether the state of Kansas would have slavery or not. The fight in BLEEDING KANSAS would last through the end of the Civil War. In 1856 CHARLES SUMNER made an antislavery speech on the floor of the Senate that focused on the Kansas question and shortly thereafter was savagely beaten by Southern representative Preston Brooks. In 1857 the Supreme Court ruled in the DRED SCOTT DECISION that Congress could not restrict slavery anywhere in the United States. The ruling served to inflame Northern passions while resolving nothing. By the end of the 1850s, it was clear that slavery and free labor could not continue to coexist. In 1858 WILLIAM H. SEWARD described the tension between the two labor systems as an "irrepressible conflict," while ABRAHAM LINCOLN warned the nation that "A house divided against itself cannot stand." In 1859 JOHN BROWN's failed attempt to incite a slave revolt by capturing HARPERS FERRY brought the tensions between North and South to the breaking point.

As the political debate over slavery was heating up in the 1850s, the institution itself remained strong in the South. Post–Civil War Southern apologists would later claim that slavery would have died a quick natural death in the 1870s or 1880s even if the Civil War had never happened, but the evidence suggests that this was not the case. For PLANTATION owners, business was booming in the 1850s. Cotton-hungry manufacturers in the North and in Europe kept the cotton market strong, even through an 1857 recession. In the decade before the Civil War, "King Cotton" accounted for more than 50 percent of the United States's total exports and, in 1860 alone, the South produced 2 billion pounds of cotton, with a value of $250,000,000. Other slave-driven enterprises, including rice, tobacco, and indigo production, also did well. And although a majority of Southerners did not own slaves, they, too, continued to derive important benefits from the slave system. A strong economy made it possible for small farmers and manufacturers to sell their goods at a favorable price. Perhaps more important, all Southern whites benefited from the rigid racial hierarchy of the antebellum South that assigned a high

A slave family in South Carolina *(Hulton/Archive)*

Another problem posed by the slave system was that Confederate leaders were not comfortable using the South's 4 million slaves as soldiers. While Northern leaders depended upon the hundreds of thousands of free laborers who joined the Union ranks, the South's inability to draw on its labor force left Confederate armies constantly undermanned.

As the Confederacy's white population fought the CIVIL WAR, the South's slaves were impacted in a number of different ways. The CONFEDERATE ARMY regularly "impressed" slaves, compelling them to do whatever labor the military needed. The backbreaking work of digging trenches and graves, building fortifications, and hauling supplies was often even worse than plantation work. For those slaves fortunate enough to avoid IMPRESSMENT, however, the Civil War generally lightened their burdens. With the absence of so many Southern men, discipline became more lax and escape became much easier.

At the same time that masters' control of their slaves was weakening, Union armies were dismantling the slave system throughout the South. In 1862 the second CONFISCATION ACT defined slaves as enemy property and allowed Union commanders to free any slaves they captured. Huge CONTRABAND camps were set up and administered by the War Department. In 1863 the EMANCIPATION PROCLAMATION went even further, declaring all slaves in the Confederate states to be free and allowing for the enlistment of African-American soldiers. Most of the 180,000 black men who ultimately served in the UNION ARMY were escapees who wanted to have a hand in bringing an end to slavery. The THIRTEENTH AMENDMENT, adopted in December of 1865, made slavery's demise official.

For many Northerners, however, the end of slavery was not enough. The REPUBLICAN PARTY, particularly the RADICAL REPUBLICAN faction, took steps to ensure the political, social, and economic equality of the freedmen. For a period of time after the war, it seemed that meaningful progress was being made. Former slaves became loyal Republican voters, and a number of them were elected to political office. Families were reunited or established, and schools for freedmen were set up throughout the South. By 1900, literacy rates among African Americans were above 50 percent. This was quite an accomplishment for a population that had been legally barred from learning to read only 35 years previous.

Such progress proved to be short-lived, however. Throughout the era of RECONSTRUCTION, white Southerners were unwilling to accept African Americans as their equals. They pursued every possible means, both legal and extralegal, for returning freedmen to their former second-class status. Northerners eventually grew weary of the struggle, and by 1876 all of the former Confederate states were under the control of conservative white politicians.

social status to all white people and a low status to all black people.

In 1860 Republican Abraham Lincoln was elected the 16th president of the United States on a Free-Soil platform. Leaders in South Carolina decided they could not accept the results. Lincoln, they asserted, had been elected by Northern voters to bring an end to slavery. In December of 1860 South Carolina seceded from the Union. It was soon followed by 10 other states, and by April 1861 the CONFEDERATE STATES OF AMERICA had been established. Slavery was the backbone of the new Confederacy. Even if the majority of the South's white population did not own slaves, Southern economy, culture, and politics were all defined by the institution. Even the poorest of white Southerners was willing to volunteer to fight when the war started. Later in the war, however, many non-slaveholding Southerners came to resent the fact that they were being forced to fight to defend slavery, particularly while large plantation owners were exempt from the Confederate conscription, or draft.

The nature of the slave system also created other logistical problems for the Confederacy. The South's economy was entirely tied up in slaves and land. When war came, this meant that the South lacked the money and factories needed to purchase or create war matériel.

The freedmen were shut out of politics. Economically, the rise of the SHARECROPPING system denied African-Americans much hope of upward mobility.

Ultimately, the reliance of the South on African slave labor had a number of negative long-term consequences. The Southern economy failed to modernize in the antebellum era, and by the time the damage from the Civil War was repaired, the economies of the former states of the Confederacy lagged far behind the rest of the country. It would take many decades for meaningful economic progress to occur. For African Americans, both inside the South and out, the legacy of the slave system was a century of racism and other forms of economic, political, and social oppression. Although important laws were adopted during Reconstruction, their promise did not begin to be fulfilled until the latter part of the 20th century.

Further reading: Ira Berlin, ed., *Free at Last: A Documentary History of Slavery, Freedom, and the Civil War* (New York: The New Press, 1992); Frederick Douglass, *Narrative of the Life of Frederick Douglass, an American Slave,* ed. by Deborah E. McDowell (New York: Oxford University Press, 1999); Robert William Fogel, *Without Consent or Contract: The Rise and Fall of American Slavery* (New York: W. W. Norton, 1989); Eugene D. Genovese, *Roll, Jordan, Roll: The World the Slaves Made* (New York: Vintage Books, 1976).

—Christopher Bates

Society of Friends (Quakers)

The Civil War era was not only a political and social trial for the nation but a religious trial for the Society of Friends, or Quakers, in the United States. Several faiths, such as the Mennonites and Brethren, demanded pacifism of their members, but the most prominent pacifist sect in mid-19th-century America were the Friends. The Friends had come to America from England in the 17th century seeking to escape Crown persecution.

In the United States, though some Friends held slaves, most did not, and the meetings (congregations) soon came to hold that slavery was incompatible with the religion's emphasis on universal brotherhood. In 1754 the Friends became the first religious group to take a stand against SLAVERY by formally prohibiting their members from buying or selling slaves. Friends were instrumental in establishing many antislavery organizations, including the Philadelphia Anti-Slavery Society and the American Anti-Slavery Society. Friends were a majority in many abolitionist organizations by the 19th century. In particular, 40 percent of all female abolitionists were Friends, including Lucretia Mott and Angelina and Sarah Grimké. In addition to pressing for ABOLITION,

Friends promoted the UNDERGROUND RAILROAD and the names of Friends safe houses circulated amongst the slave community.

Despite their antislavery sentiments, the CIVIL WAR posed a dilemma to the Friends, who were caught between their antiviolence teachings and their stalwart support of antislavery. Even though the Union's war aims appealed to their idea of universal brotherhood, the decision to take up arms with the intent of committing violence upon fellow humans was more than most Friends could bear. For Friends, one evil could not be cured by another, and war, even in the service of a "just cause" went against the faith's fundamental tenets of nonviolence. Thus, during the Civil War, Friends became America's best-known conscientious objectors. In both the North and the South, Friends sought exemptions from military service when draft laws threatened to force them into uniform. Both Northern and Southern governments were fundamentally sympathetic to the conscientious objector's plight, but neither government would grant blanket exemptions from service for Friends. At various times, both the North and the South allowed conscientious objectors like the Friends, if drafted, to provide a substitute, pay a commutation fee, or volunteer for nonmilitary duty, such as hospital service (the Union offered the option of serving draft time in the South assisting and educating the newly freed slaves). Some Friends accepted these options as viable and provided essential services during the duration of the war.

Despite these allowances, many leaders of the Friends considered any connection with the war effort corrupt. There were, however, both regional and age splits over the war within the Society of Friends. Southern Friends (numbering roughly 10,000 at the outset of hostilities—most of whom lived in North Carolina), so long as they did not hinder the Southern war effort, found generally kindly disposed state and national officials willing to grant exemptions from service. Some Confederate leaders went so far as to concede that Friend farmers left to till their fields were as valuable to the Southern cause as any soldiers.

The Union was home to the majority of Friends, with 200,000 members in Pennsylvania, New York, New Jersey, Rhode Island, Massachusetts, Ohio, and Indiana. Of this Northern Friend population, relatively few broke with church doctrine and served in the war, but a significant number did. Generally, younger Friends volunteered or accepted military duty if drafted. Friends from the more western meetings were more likely to join the army than were their northeastern fellows. Only four of 105 Philadelphia Friends from Orthodox Meetings served in the army upon receiving draft notices, but Indiana sent approximately 1,200 Friends into military service during the course of the war.

There was considerable concern both among the soldiers and the Friends left at home about the impact that their wartime service would have on their character. It was generally expected that Friends who had supported the war would return to their meetings and formally acknowledge the error of the war, accept the responsibility for their incorrect actions, and seek forgiveness from their fellow Friends. But while refusing to acknowledge participation in the war as wrong could be grounds for a Friend to be disowned (excommunicated) by his meeting, not all returning Quaker VETERANS saw fit to apologize for their choices. Ultimately, in gestures that showed how great the faith's internal tension over the issue of fighting against something they abhorred was, few meetings disowned unapologetic members, and in subsequent years speakers found gatherings of Friends unwilling to tolerate criticism of veterans.

After the war ended, Friends continued their efforts on behalf of freed people during RECONSTRUCTION. Friends provided essential aid, especially in EDUCATION services to the FREEDMENS BUREAU. The rise of REDEMPTION governments in the South greatly troubled many meetings. But despite their long-standing stance of antislavery and their work on behalf of the freed people, Friends had views similar to those of many other white Americans. Their educational interests were predicated on the idea that African Americans were primitive and backward. Eventually, like other Americans', the Friends' interest in African-American rights and concerns waned. By the latter 19th century, Friends' financial and physical commitments to working with the freed men and women dwindled in the face of rising issues of Southern governmental corruption and political issues within the Friends' own Northern communities.

Further reading: Hugh Barbour and J. William Frost, *The Quakers* (NY: Greenwood Press, 1988); Philip S. Benjamin, *The Philadelphia Quakers in the Industrial Age, 1865–1920* (Philadelphia: Temple University Press, 1976); Thomas Edward Drake, *Quakers and Slavery in America* (Gloucester, Mass.: P. Smith, 1965); Jacquelyn S. Nelson, *Indiana's Quakers Confront the Civil War* (Indianapolis: Indiana Historical Society, 1991).

—Ruth A. Behling

Special Field Order No. 15 (January 16, 1865)

During the CIVIL WAR, a special order issued by a commanding general had the force of law behind it. Written by Union general WILLIAM T. SHERMAN, Special Field Order No. 15 granted Southern land seized by the Union in Georgia, South Carolina, and Florida to freed slaves. It also gave African Americans complete control over this land and government assistance to develop it. Special Field Order No. 15 was, however, only a short-lived boon for the freed men and women. Special Field Order No. 15 was rescinded in 1865 by President ANDREW JOHNSON.

Sherman issued Special Field Order No. 15 on January 16, 1865, while he and his troops occupied Savannah, Georgia. Special Field Order No. 15 was the result of a January 12 meeting that Sherman and Secretary of War EDWIN M. STANTON had with 20 leaders of the city's African-American community. The order granted freedpeople full control of the sea islands as well as of the coastal land 30 miles inland from Charleston, South Carolina, south to Jacksonville, Florida. This order helped the freed slaves who, as REFUGEES, had no place to go and no property. Specifically, Special Field Order No. 15 granted African-American heads of families 40 acres of land under "possessory title" and protection by the U.S. Congress. The purpose of Special Field Order No. 15 was to assist the freedpeople in creating self-governing and self-sustaining settlements free from the intrusion of white control.

In this revolutionary order, Sherman asserted that the African-American settlers had the opportunity to choose the land on which they would farm and to obtain government assistance in starting their agricultural settlements. To this end, Sherman promised to loan the freedpeople mules to help them work the land. Further, this order carefully laid out a description of the complete control freedpeople would have over their lives and livelihoods on the land formerly possessed by their masters. In Special Field Order No. 15, Sherman prohibited white people from any roles other than those regulated by the federal government, usually as military personnel placed on duty there. As a result, the freedpeople would have full control over their daily lives. Further, Sherman used these orders to stimulate enlistment in the UNION ARMY by guaranteeing land ownership to those freedmen who served, even if they could not immediately settle on the land.

To carry out this order, Sherman appointed Gen. Rufus Saxton as the inspector of settlements and PLANTATIONS. As such, Saxton took charge of settling the freedpeople on the land covered by Special Field Order No. 15, commonly referred to as "Sherman land." Saxton, like other ABOLITIONists, worried that Sherman's order isolated and colonized the freedpeople instead of helping them. African Americans eagerly tried to take Sherman up on his promise of land. Although thousands hurried to the sea islands to claim the land promised, many were turned away as ineligible. Only male heads of households had legal claim to the land under Sherman's orders, so freedwomen could not successfully petition for land. Even so, by June 1865, approximately 40,000 freedpeople inhabited 400,000 acres of land granted to them in Special Field Order No. 15. The U.S. government followed through with its promise of help by providing the settlers with farm tools, seeds, and advisors. On the urging of abolitionists, the government also sent missionaries and teachers to the area to help the freedpeople establish themselves.

General Field Order No. 15 helped instigate the congressional act that created a Bureau for the Relief of Freedmen and Refugees on March 3, 1865. However, postwar President Andrew Johnson rescinded Sherman's Special Field Order No. 15 on May 29, 1865, when he granted general amnesty to former Confederates and returned land to the former slaveholders. Those freedpeople settled on "Sherman land" lost their land ownership and returned to a life of working other people's land.

See also FREEDMEN'S BUREAU; PORT ROYAL, SOUTH CAROLINA, EXPERIMENT; SHARECROPPING.

Further reading: Willie Lee Rose, *Rehearsal for Reconstruction: The Port Royal Experiment* (Athens: University of Georgia Press, 1999); Leslie A. Schwalm, *A Hard Fight for We: Women's Transition from Slavery to Freedom in South Carolina* (Urbana: University of Illinois Press, 1997).

—Lisa Tendrich Frank

Spotsylvania, Battles of (May 7–21, 1864)

The Battles of Spotsylvania represented the second phase of the OVERLAND CAMPAIGN, which had commenced when ULYSSES S. GRANT and ROBERT E. LEE first took each other's measure in fighting at the BATTLE OF THE WILDERNESS on May 5–6, 1864. After combat ended on May 6, Grant made the crucial decision to press southward, seeking to reach Spotsylvania Court House ahead of Lee and thereby cut the Confederates off from the shortest route to RICHMOND. Hard marching on the night of May 7 allowed Richard H. Anderson's Confederate corps to reach Spotsylvania just ahead of Grant's leading units, which had wasted their advantage of marching on more direct roads.

Troops from both armies poured onto the field throughout May 8, and Union attacks failed to dislodge Confederate defenders. Lee's soldiers rapidly built a defensive line notable for its strong field entrenchments. The most memorable feature of the Confederate line was a large salient, called the "mule shoe," that emerged northward from near the center of the Southern position. Grant looked for weaknesses on May 9–11, starting heavy action in several places but gaining no decisive advantage.

At dawn on May 12, a massive Union assault commanded by WINFIELD SCOTT HANCOCK smashed through the northern arc of the mule shoe lines, threatening to cut Lee's army in half. The most desperate fighting of the entire war ensued, as the two armies struggled to control several hundred yards of Confederate earthworks, later labeled the "bloody angle," at the northwest corner of the salient. Action continued for nearly 20 hours and impressed even hardened VETERANS as uniquely hellish. "Nothing during the war has equaled the savage desperation of this struggle," reported one Northern newspaper correspondent, while a Confederate journalist wrote that fighting "roared and hissed and dashed over the bloody angle and along the bristling entrenchments like an angry sea beating and chafing against a rock bound coast."

As combat raged at the bloody angle, Lee's engineers constructed another line across the base of the mule shoe. By morning of May 13, Grant once again faced a strong Confederate position. Further Union attacks over the next five days failed to gain advantage. Repeated assaults at Spotsylvania taught Union infantrymen a bitter lesson about the power of defenders sheltered by field entrenchments, and soldiers on both sides realized that from now on the shovel would join the musket and the cannon as critical tools on all their battlefields.

Neither army could claim a clear-cut victory at Spotsylvania. More than 18,000 Federals and 12,000 Confederates had been killed, wounded, or captured in the course of reaching a tactical impasse. Grant resumed his southward movement on May 21, thereby maintaining strategic momentum and forcing Lee into the unaccustomed position of reacting to rather than dictating the action.

See also COLD HARBOR, BATTLE OF.

Further reading: Gordon C. Rhea, *The Battles for Spotsylvania Court House and the Road to Yellow Tavern, May 7–12, 1864* (Baton Rouge: Louisiana State University Press, 1997); Gordon C. Rhea, *To the North Anna River: Grant and Lee, May 13–25, 1864* (Baton Rouge: Louisiana State University Press, 2000).

—Gary W. Gallagher

Stanton, Edwin M. (1814–1869)

Edwin McMasters Stanton, a distinguished member of ABRAHAM LINCOLN's cabinet, was born on December 19, 1814, in Steubenville, Ohio. Stanton briefly attended Kenyon College in 1828 and then studied law. He began his career in Cadiz, Ohio. A Democrat, Stanton worked for Martin Van Buren in the presidential election of 1840. Known for his antiSLAVERY views, Stanton found it difficult but not impossible to support James Polk's expansionism in the Mexican-American War. Stanton's first wife died in 1844, leaving him a widower with two children. He later married Ellen Hutchinson, with whom he had four more children.

Stanton moved to Pittsburgh in the mid-1840s, where he developed a reputation as a dynamic and hard-hitting lawyer with an unerring instinct for his opponents' weaknesses. He often argued cases before the U.S. Supreme Court. President JAMES BUCHANAN appointed Stanton the U.S. attorney general in December 1860. After Southern SECESSION, Stanton labored long hours in his WASHINGTON, D.C., office to preserve the Union. He tried to convince the weak Buchanan to defend FORT SUMTER while secretly meeting with WILLIAM H. SEWARD, Abraham Lincoln's secretary of state, to forge a workable compromise. Stanton remained in Washington after Lincoln's inauguration as legal consultant to Simon Cameron, the secretary of war. Stanton also became very friendly with Gen. GEORGE B. McCLELLAN, soon to be commander of the UNION ARMY. Like many Democrats during this time, Stanton expressed contempt for President Lincoln.

That negative opinion of the president soon transformed into respect, and then a deep admiration. When Cameron resigned from the war department, Lincoln replaced him with Stanton. It proved to be a brilliant appointment. Stanton threw himself into organizing the massive war and stamped every area of military effort with his immense energy, impeccable honesty, and sincere belief in Unionism. He established a viable and respectful working relationship with Congress and modernized outmoded and corrupt War Department practices. Efficiency and fairness were the standards that he tried to bring to the military departments under his control. Stanton's ability to successfully coordinate complex logistical movements became legendary.

Along the way, Stanton made many enemies with his overbearing personality. He was impatient and rude, and former friends became opponents after feeling the sting of his sarcasm. As Lincoln and Stanton pushed for a harder, wider war, both became committed to EMANCIPATION and the enlistment of African-American soldiers. By mid-1863 Stanton had switched his allegiance to the REPUBLICAN PARTY. Indeed, it was Stanton who made sure that thousands of Union soldiers could receive special furloughs so they could return to their respective states and vote in the 1864 election. As he predicted, Lincoln won the soldier vote by a huge margin.

Stanton's position as the supervisor of internal security created controversy. From March 1862 Stanton was determined to crack down on all dissent and treason within the Northern HOMEFRONT, which was growing steadily. To ensure loyalty, Stanton expanded the suspension of the writ of HABEAS CORPUS, arrested Southern sympathizers, and created a special police force to enforce the draft laws. Late in the war Stanton pressed for the generous treatment of freed people and worked closely with Lincoln on RECONSTRUCTION policy. Shocked and grieving after the ASSASSINATION OF ABRAHAM LINCOLN, Stanton and the War Department took charge of the investigation. Stanton insisted that the conspirators be tried in military court and strongly favored the death penalty.

Stanton continued in his post during most of ANDREW JOHNSON's administration. His logistical skills were needed in the demobilization of the huge Union army, and his concern for the rights of freedmen and freedwomen was required to counter President Johnson's overly lenient plans for former Confederates. Increasingly, Stanton and Johnson were at odds over Reconstruction. Stanton advocated continued support for the FREEDMEN'S BUREAU and favored the FOURTEENTH AMENDMENT. He joined the RADICAL REPUBLICANS against the president. By the summer of 1867, Johnson, no longer confident of his secretary's loyalty, wished to remove him from the cabinet. Congress passed the Tenure of Office Act to stop Johnson from firing Stanton, but the president acted anyway, replacing him with Gen. ULYSSES S. GRANT. Johnson's violation of the Tenure of Office Act became the basis for his impeachment trial in 1868. After Johnson was acquitted, Stanton resigned from his position, confident that the fruits of the Union victory had not been wasted away and that the new nation would emerge under the control of the Republican-dominated Congress.

In 1869 President Grant appointed Stanton to the Supreme Court. He died in December of the same year, before he could take his seat.

See also IMPEACHMENT OF ANDREW JOHNSON.

Further reading: Benjamin D. Thomas and Harold H. Hyman, *Stanton: The Life and Times of Lincoln's Secretary of War* (New York: Knopf, 1962).

Stanton, Elizabeth Cady (1815–1902)

Born into a wealthy New York family, Elizabeth Cady Stanton became a leader of the women's movement through her involvement with ABOLITIONism. Unhappy with the limited role granted women by abolitionists, she played a central role in the Seneca Falls Women's Rights Convention of 1848. After the CIVIL WAR, Stanton and Susan B. Anthony led the faction of women's rights advocates that split from the abolitionists and Republicans, who placed a higher priority on the rights of freedmen than on those of women. Later, Stanton and Anthony created the first independent organization of women advocating women's suffrage.

A comfortable background did not provide full-time support for Stanton's activities on behalf of women's rights. The opposition of her father and husband and the demands of her seven children limited Stanton's role. She remained at home, writing many influential petitions and speeches while Anthony traveled to spread the message.

While advocating an expanded role for women, Stanton remained allied with the abolitionists through the Civil War. After the war, abolitionists joined with the REPUBLI-

Elizabeth Cady Stanton *(Library of Congress)*

CAN PARTY to protect the rights of freedmen, viewing the campaign for women's suffrage as a threat to the rights of ex-slaves. Rebuffed by their former allies, Stanton and Anthony hoped that the DEMOCRATIC PARTY would adopt their cause on the basis that educated women had a greater entitlement to the vote than did "illiterate" ex-slaves. A deep divide within the women's movement resulted, with those willing to postpone the vote for women until black suffrage was achieved remaining with their traditional abolitionist allies.

Stanton and Anthony became disillusioned when it became clear that Democrats were more interested in obstructing black rights than in establishing women's rights. Efforts to join with organized labor were unsatisfactory, as skilled workers did not welcome the competition of women in their fields, and class divisions separated the interests of Stanton and Anthony from those of working-class women. Unable to find a place for their movement in any established organization, they formed the NATIONAL WOMAN SUFFRAGE ASSOCIATION in 1869, which sought a constitutional amendment ensuring a woman's right to vote as the first step in establishing women's equal rights. Those who allied with the Republicans soon created the American Woman Suffrage Association, advocating only women's right to vote. The split between these two factions contin-

ued for more than 20 years. Blind and in ill health, Stanton died in New York in 1902.

Further reading: Ellen Carol DuBois, *Feminism and Suffrage: The Emergence of an Independent Women's Movement in America, 1848–1869* (Ithaca, N.Y.: Cornell University Press, 1999); Elisabeth Griffith, *In Her Own Right: The Life of Elizabeth Cady Stanton* (New York: Oxford University Press, 1984); Elizabeth Cady Stanton, *Eighty Years and More (1815–1897); Reminiscences of Elizabeth Cady Stanton* (1898: reprint, New York: Source Book Press, 1970).

—Martha Kadue

states' rights

The doctrine of states' rights was used to explain and defend the SECESSION of the Southern states during and after the CIVIL WAR. States' rights adherents put forth a strict interpretation of the U.S. Constitution of 1787. The Constitution, they argued, was nothing more than a compact between sovereign states that limited the federal government to specific powers such as the right to declare war and to conduct diplomacy. All powers and rights not expressly delegated to the national government were reserved for the states, including the right to leave the Union when one or more states determined that their liberties were threatened.

Southerners and Democrats favored a "strict" interpretation of the Constitution, allowing the federal government only the rights the Constitution set forth, therefore making all other rights the province of individual states. Whigs, later Republicans, and most Northerners favored a "loose" interpretation, providing the federal government with the additional power of those rights that were implied.

The authority of the national government was strongly contested in any number of areas, but the conflict was especially bitter and serious over the issue of SLAVERY in the territories. As the Northern ECONOMY flourished and its population skyrocketed, Southerners became worried that their influence in Congress would diminish. If the South as a region lost its political clout, then there was a danger that slavery could be outlawed, not only in the territories but in the region itself.

After the Mexican-American War, the United States added 1.25 million square miles of new territory. Southerners believed that only the expansion of slave owners and slavery into the territories could counter the growing power of the Northern states. A large number of Northerners, however, believed that the further expansion of slavery was unthinkable because it would hinder the spread of free labor. They advanced the argument that the national Congress had the constitutional authority to ban slavery from the territories. This argument was just as vigorously rejected by Southerners who claimed that only the states, which represented the true interests of the people, held that authority.

From 1846 through 1860, Southerners repeatedly threatened secession. With ABRAHAM LINCOLN's election, the South demonstrated its belief that the fundamental institution of its society, slavery, would not be protected under a Republican administration. Citing states' rights as a guiding philosophy, the South seceded and formed the CONFEDERATE STATES OF AMERICA, with a constitution that protected state sovereignty.

Ironically, the Confederacy's survival was threatened by its devotion to the states' rights philosophy. President JEFFERSON DAVIS determined that in order to wage an all-out war for Southern independence, he would need to nationalize the military and the economy. His moves in this direction included IMPRESSMENT, CONSCRIPTION, and TAXATION. Many in his own cabinet and government opposed these measures toward centralization, but none so bitterly or with more serious consequences than the state GOVERNORS. JOSEPH E. BROWN of Georgia and Zebulon B. Vance of North Carolina were two notable examples of this opposition. They refused to share their states' supplies, men, and labor with the rest of the Confederate nation. Citing a commitment to states' rights and individualism, Brown and Vance kept back militia units for local protection, refused to collect taxes, and balked at providing soldiers for the draft. Some historians have claimed that the Confederacy "died of states' rights."

After four years of hard fighting, Northern victory in 1865 ensured that the doctrine of states' rights would never again present a serious challenge to federal power and authority.

Further reading: Frederick D. Drake and Lynn R. Nelson, eds., *States' Rights and American Federalism: A Documentary History* (Westport, Conn.: Greenwood Press, 1999); Forrest McDonald, *States' Rights and the Union: Imperium in Imperio, 1776–1876* (Lawrence: University Press of Kansas, 2000).

—Lee Ashley Smith

Stephens, Alexander Hamilton (1812–1883)

Congressman, author, and Confederate vice president, Alexander H. Stephens was born into a prosperous Georgia farming family in 1812. Small and sickly as a child, he remained fragile throughout his life. Stephens never knew his mother, who died of pneumonia a few months after giving birth. His father remarried, but at the age of 14 Stephens was left an orphan when both his father and step-mother died within a few months of each other. After his parents' death, Stephens was adopted by his uncle, who saw to it that that the young man received an EDUCATION. He enrolled at Franklin College in 1828 and in 1832 graduated first in his class. After briefly working as a teacher, Stephens studied law, was admitted to the bar, and soon thereafter was elected to the Georgia state legislature. For the rest of his life, Stephens devoted himself entirely to politics. He maintained few close friendships, and he never married.

Stephens's time in the state legislature helped him develop the political philosophy that would guide him for the rest of his life. He came to identify with the Southern wing of the newly formed Whig Party, which meant that he favored federally sponsored internal improvements, government protection of SLAVERY, and compromise whenever necessary. Stephen served for six years in the legislature before deciding to run for Congress in 1843 as a Whig. He attracted national attention for his campaign speeches defending the Whig positions on the TARIFF and national bank, and he won election by a comfortable margin.

Although gravely ill for much of his first term, Stephens rapidly became an important leader of the Whig Party in Congress. In that capacity, he befriended fellow congressman ABRAHAM LINCOLN, with whom he carried on an active correspondence for two decades. Stephens worked hard for a variety of Whig causes, but he was most important in helping to secure passage of the Compromise of 1850 and the KANSAS-NEBRASKA ACT of 1854. In helping these bills to become law, however, Stephens found himself a man without a party. The Whigs collapsed in the 1850s as the Southern and Northern wings of the party became divided over the issue of slavery. Stephens operated as an independent for a short time before deciding to join the DEMOCRATIC PARTY. He did not strongly identify with the philosophy of the party, but he felt it was a more attractive option than the Know-Nothing Party or the newly formed REPUBLICAN PARTY.

Stephens served as a Democrat in Congress for a few years but became increasingly frustrated with the infighting between Southerners and Northerners in the Democratic Party. In 1859 he finally retired from Congress in disgust and returned home to Georgia. When Abraham Lincoln was elected the next year, Stephens urged his fellow Georgians to remain with the Union and to try to find a compromise. His cooperationist pleas fell on deaf ears, however, and Georgia left the Union. Once the issue was decided, Stephens bowed to his state's wishes and became a devoted Confederate. He helped draft Georgia's SECESSION ordinance, and he played an important role at the Confederate Constitutional Convention. When it came time for the convention to choose the leaders of the new government, they selected JEFFERSON DAVIS for the presidency and Stephens for the vice presidency. The convention's goal in making these choices was to unify different factions in the South. Stephens, as a prominent cooperationist and former Whig, was a natural complement to Davis, a prominent secessionist and former Democrat. Stephens accepted the assignment and was sworn in as provisional vice president on February 9, 1861. The pair was then elected officially on November 6, 1861.

The differences in philosophy that had made Davis and Stephens an attractive political pairing quickly proved disastrous for their working relationship. Problems began to appear as early as March of 1861, when Stephens gave an address in Savannah arguing that slavery was the "cornerstone" of the Confederacy and that the main reason the war was being fought was to protect the institution. The speech directly contradicted Davis's stated position that the war was about STATES' RIGHTS. Davis was furious that Stephens was so brazenly undermining his administration, and he began to exclude Stephens from day-to-day operations of the government. Stephens and Davis continued to disagree on government policies: Stephens was strongly opposed to CONSCRIPTION while Davis was strongly in favor; Stephens advocated peace overtures while Davis insisted on fighting until independence had been achieved; Stephens favored a stiff income tax while Davis preferred to finance the war by printing money. By the middle of 1862, Stephens was being almost completely ignored by Davis, and his only remaining responsibility was to preside over the senate, where he could neither speak nor vote. Disgusted by his irrelevance, Stephens returned to Georgia, where he remained for most of the war. He did accept several special assignments, including leading unsuccessful peace delegations in 1863 and 1865. In both cases, Stephens felt he had been set up to fail, and his dislike of Davis deepened.

At the war's conclusion, Stephens was arrested and briefly imprisoned. Shortly after his release, Stephens was elected to Congress but, along with other ex-Confederates, was barred from taking his seat. Temporarily unable to participate in public life, Stephens turned his attention to writing the two-volume *A Constitutional View of the Late War Between the States*, published between 1868 and 1870. The book provided a detailed legal justification of secession and the Southern states' prewar view of their place in the Union. Shortly after Stephens finished the book, he ran for office again. By this time the political climate of the nation had changed, and he was allowed to regain his seat as a representative from Georgia. Stephens remained in Congress from 1873 until 1882, when he was elected governor of Georgia. He only served

a short time before taking ill and dying in Savannah on March 4, 1883.

Further reading: Thomas E. Schott, *Alexander H. Stephens of Georgia: A Biography* (Baton Rouge: Louisiana State University Press, 1988); Alexander Hamilton Stephens, *A Constitutional View of the Late War between the States: Its Causes, Character, Conduct and Results, Presented in a Series of Colloquies at Liberty Hall* (1870; reprint, New York: Kraus Reprint Co., 1970).

—Christopher Bates

Stevens, Thaddeus (1792–1868)

Lawyer, congressman, and a leader of the RADICAL REPUBLICANS, Thaddeus Stevens was born in Danville, Vermont, on April 4, 1792. Son of a shoemaker who deserted his family in 1804, Stevens triumphed over the dual handicaps of poverty and a deformed foot, graduating from Dartmouth College in 1814. He immediately left New England for York, Pennsylvania, where he trained in law. First in York, then Gettysburg, and finally Lancaster, Stevens succeeded as a lawyer and as an admired state legislator in the 1820s, 1830s, and 1840s. Stevens's deserved reputation as an egalitarian began when he set aside time from his prosperous law practice to defend an increasing number of runaway slaves and to state on record his antiSLAVERY beliefs.

Stevens's political career in the Pennsylvania legislature's fractious and sometimes violent political scene paralleled the upward climb of his legal firm. He joined with the WHIG PARTY and the REPUBLICAN PARTY to advance his mixed agenda of humanitarian reform and capitalist economic development. Stevens virtually created the free public EDUCATION system in Pennsylvania, the crown jewel of his legacy to that state. A wealthy man by the time he was in his 40s, he was an enthusiastic supporter of favorable legislation for RAILROADS and banks and the owner of a number of iron mills.

Stevens also had a dark side to his personality. Sarcastic, witty, and possessing a boundless reservoir of vindictiveness toward his perceived enemies, the lifelong bachelor won the admiration but never the hearts of his loyal Pennsylvanian constituency, who sent him to Congress from the 1850s until his death. Scandals dogged Stevens from early on in his career: accusations of murder, womanizing, gambling, and other immoral acts found their way into unfriendly newspaper accounts. Many of these charges were false, and Stevens usually ignored them or challenged them in court. Stevens never refuted firmly the well-publicized accusation that Lydia H. Smith, his longtime African-American housekeeper, was also his mistress. Ultimately, Stevens's personal intrigues did not derail his political career, and few lawmakers have had such an impact on Congress as he did during the 1860s.

By 1861, Stevens in the House and CHARLES SUMNER in the Senate were leaders in advancing what would come to be called the "Radical Republican" agenda: abolish slavery, secure constitutionally guaranteed rights for ex-slaves, enroll black soldiers, and punish the Southerners harshly for their rebellion. "Free every slave," Stevens cried, "slay every traitor—burn every rebel mansion, if these things be necessary to preserve this temple of freedom to the world and to our posterity." For these sentiments, and for his harsh RECONSTRUCTION program that advanced the theory that the seceded states were conquered provinces, Stevens was singled out as the villain of Reconstruction by several generations of Southerners and by more than a few historians. In reality, Stevens was a practical politician as well as an ideologue. He made many compromises to get significant legislation such as the FOURTEENTH AMENDMENT passed by his more numerous moderate colleagues.

The "sparkplug" of the Republican Party, Stevens pushed and prodded ABRAHAM LINCOLN toward EMANCIPATION, and by 1865, the two men were working well together. It was a good thing that they did so, because Stevens occupied the chair of the all-important Ways and Means Committee. From this position, Stevens helped to finance the war. He supported strongly the Republican economic program of high TARIFFS, paper money, and railroad development. Because of his reputation as a fierce hater of slavery and slave owners (Stevens was known as "the scourge of the South"), Confederates took special pleasure in burning and destroying his property when marching through the Pennsylvania countryside on their way to Gettysburg in 1863.

With the ASSASSINATION OF ABRAHAM LINCOLN, responsibility for managing the transition to peace fell on his successor, ANDREW JOHNSON. Stevens and Johnson detested each other from the start, and the years from 1865 to 1868 were the most controversial of Stevens's very controversial career. The struggle between Johnson and Stevens was over the question of whether Congress or the executive was going to control the Reconstruction of the South. Stevens was a central figure in creating the famous Joint Committee on Reconstruction, which dominated all Southern issues. Johnson, a singularly inept politician, managed through his blunders to give the Radical Republicans the momentum they needed to impose military rule on the South and to bring impeachment proceedings against him. Stevens helped to write the articles of impeachment and was a powerful force behind the House vote to destroy Johnson.

Stevens, a passionate believer in congressional prerogative, pushed the envelope further when he unsuccessfully argued for the passage of a comprehensive land redistribution program. This example indicates that even at the height of Stevens's legislative power, he was never the "dictator" of Congress, as has been charged. Indeed, the moderate majority made it important for Stevens to compromise, and he did. In the end, however, Stevens did not reshape the South in the Northern mold, as he wished. Reflecting on his inability to impeach Johnson as well as to secure African-American economic justice, the ailing statesman declared, "My life is a failure." Stevens died in WASHINGTON, D.C., on August 11, 1868. In accordance with his will, he was buried in an African-American cemetery in Lancaster, Pennsylvania.

See also ABOLITION; BANKING AND CURRENCY; GREENBACKS.

Further reading: Hans L. Trefousse, *Thaddeus Stevens: Nineteenth-Century Egalitarian* (Chapel Hill: University of North Carolina Press, 1997).

Stowe, Harriet Beecher (1811–1896)

Writer and novelist Harriet Beecher Stowe was born in 1811 in Lichfield, Connecticut, the seventh of the nine children of Roxanna Foote and the Reverend Lyman Beecher. A bright child who listened eagerly to theological discussions, Harriet attended the Litchfield Academy. Between 1824 and 1827 she attended her sister Catharine's Hartford Female Seminary, where she became first an assistant and then a teacher (1828–32). She was an avid reader and showed considerable writing talent from early on, and with the help of Catharine Beecher she was able to develop it in a systematic way. In 1832 Lyman Beecher became president of Lane Theological Seminary in Cincinnati, Ohio; Catharine and Harriet moved to Cincinnati, too, with plans to establish a college, the Western Female Institute. A true intellectual, Harriet struggled to define her life constrained by "the constant habits of self-government which the rigid forms of our society demands," as she characterized it. She attended the Semi-Colon Club, a social and literary society, in order to stimulate her literary efforts. In Cincinnati she met and in 1836 married the Reverend Calvin Stowe, a recently widowed professor of biblical studies.

Stowe, who gave birth to seven children, began writing moral, temperance, and domestic tales for *Godey's Lady's Book* in 1839 to supplement her husband's income. Following the 1849 cholera epidemic, which claimed the life of the Stowes' infant son, the family left Cincinnati, first for Brunswick, Maine, then in 1851 for Andover, Massachusetts, where Calvin was offered the chair of Sacred Languages at the Andover Theological Seminary. Stowe published short pieces, including an outraged response to the Fugitive Slave Act. At the urging of friends and family, she resolved to use her literary talent to combat the evils of SLAVERY. She planned to write a series of sketches, published in installments in the *National Era.* "My vocation is simply that of a painter. . . . [T]here is no arguing with *pictures*," she wrote the editor. She drew from her personal experience with black servants, and the domestic nature of her experience sheds light on the blending of philanthropic and paternalistic attitudes toward African Americans. As a woman she identified with oppressed black women, but as a middle-class white woman she distanced herself from them, an attitude not inconsistent with antislavery sentiments in mid-19th-century America.

Stowe studied published accounts of slavery and slave escape narratives, as well as personal accounts of people who, unlike herself, knew the South. She strove to make her picture as true to life as possible while also combining her descriptive narrative with highly charged assaults on the proslavery clergy and on public indifference. In March 1852, *Uncle Tom's Cabin* was published to immediate success. In the following years, Stowe became a regular contributor of stories and sketches to the religious antislavery organ, the *Independent.* She also published *A Key to Uncle Tom's Cabin* (1853), a documentary evidence of slavery. *Uncle Tom* became the most read book after the Bible and propelled Stowe into antislavery politics.

In 1853 she sailed for England with her husband and brother Charles to receive the antislavery petition signed by half a million women. Mindful of her reputation as a modest and private woman, Stowe delegated all public speaking to the men. Both in England and in America, she was careful to avoid alienating her natural audience and original target—women. She repeatedly disclaimed public aspirations; "the nursery and the kitchen were my principal fields of labor," she wrote. Not having a clear and consistent stance within antislavery politics, Stowe urged cooperation between the various factions. She never allied herself with the ABOLITIONists, whom she considered extremists. *Dred* (1856), her second antislavery novel, reflected the shortcomings of her political thinking: She could neither embrace evolutionary reform nor advocate more radical solutions. She was interested in and wrote on the reform movements of her time, often in the Beecher sermonizing tradition.

The success of *Uncle Tom's Cabin* brought material comforts to the family as well as fame to Harriet. When she met President ABRAHAM LINCOLN for the first time, he reportedly exclaimed, "So you're the little woman who wrote the book that made this great war." Stowe's nostalgia for simpler times was consistent with mid-century ambivalence about materialism. *The Minister's Wooing* (1859) and *Old Town Folks* (1869) reflect the rural life of her childhood New England. As money disappeared fast in the Stowe household, she kept writing throughout the 1860s and 1870s, publishing more than 20 books. An intelligent

Harriet Beecher Stowe *(Library of Congress)*

and well-educated woman, Stowe's writings captured the sensibility of the native-born middle class. Harriet Beecher Stowe died on July 1, 1896, in Hartford, Connecticut.

See also LITERATURE.

Further reading: John R. Adams, *Harriet Beecher Stowe* (Boston: Twayne, 1989); Joan D. Hedrick, *Harriet Beecher Stowe: A Life* (New York: Oxford University Press, 1994).

—Zsuzsa Berend

strikes

Strikes—the stoppage of work by laborers in reaction to grievances—were a commonplace feature of working-class resistance. By the end of the CIVIL WAR era, American workers were calling more than 400 strikes a year. Among the more notable strikes in the Civil War era: (1) Lynn, Massachusetts, 1860: Shoemakers declare a strike, which quickly spreads throughout New England and involves 20,000 workers. Employers offer higher wages to strikers on the condition that they disband their union. Civil War army recruitment ultimately cripples labor organizing in

Lynn. (2) Cold Springs, New York, 1864: Employees at the town's gun works walk off the job, demanding better wages. Union troops forcibly break the strike. (3) Troy, New York, 1869: Collar laundresses strike for higher wages, drawing on the support of molders and other workers in the area. Employers lock out the strikers, who then organize independent cooperatives. Employers switch to paper collars, organize a business boycott of the women's co-ops, and defeat the strikers. (4) Pennsylvania, 1873: Anthracite coal miners begin a series of strikes. The dangers of mining had been dramatized by the Avondale mine disaster (1869), which left 179 miners dead. Violence, involving corporations, unions, and the state, is particularly sharp. (5) United States, 1877: Responding to wage cuts, the Great Railroad Strike idles more than 100,000 workers and sidelines half the freight cars in the United States. Open clashes pitting state militias and federal troops against striking workers leave more than 100 dead and considerable property destroyed before the strike is crushed.

What explains this labor unrest? Clearly, INDUSTRIAL DEVELOPMENT radically altered working conditions in the United States. At the beginning of the 19th century, workshops were small. A NEW YORK CITY tailor, for instance, would cut custom suits for the neighborhood's middle-class men, employing a few journeymen who looked forward, ultimately, to establishing their own shops. By the mid-19th century, some New York tailors had begun designing "ready-mades"—garments cut to standard sizes and sold for a national market accessible by canal and RAILROADS. Derided as "slop shops," these new firms hired low-wage, less skilled workers who could not hope to own such a business themselves.

Wages, meanwhile, rose and fell with the ECONOMY. While average earnings increased during the Civil War, so did prices. During the depression of 1873–78, daily wages sank by almost 20 percent, from $1.40 to $1.17. Even in good times, competition spurred employers to cut labor costs. Industrial development allowed employers to mechanize the workplace, replacing higher-wage workers with the unskilled or firing native-born workers in favor of rural migrants, foreign immigrants, or children.

Employers also imposed new work rules designed to increase the speed, uniformity, and efficiency of production. Some industries demanded that their employees work 12- or 14-hour shifts six days a week. Many workers found this new "labor discipline" dehumanizing and humiliating, reducing them to little more than gears in a larger machine. In response, their organizations defended the "dignity of labor": respect for worker humanity, skill, mature judgment, and familial obligations. As early as 1791, workers had demanded that work be limited to 10 hours a day. By 1860 unions were calling for an eight-hour day. In 1872, 100,000 New York City workers struck and

won an eight-hour day, though their victory was to be short-lived.

Strikers were building larger labor organizations, but they achieved few lasting gains during the Civil War era. While the NATIONAL LABOR UNION (NLU) won several strikes in the late 1860s, its leadership ultimately became more interested in currency reform and party politics than in workplace issues. The Chicago-based Workingman's Party supported labor actions in the Midwest during the 1870s. However, its affiliation with the Socialist International limited its appeal outside the industrial cities of the Northeast.

Other unions were hobbled by deep-seated ethnic and religious prejudices ingrained in their members. Employers could easily exploit the ethnic exclusivity of most unions, recruiting African Americans to break strikes called by all-white unions or importing Irish Catholics to take jobs from Anglo-American Protestants. While striking workers could draw on communal solidarity and aid, their resources were limited; those of the companies they resisted were, in the long run, far greater. A company that made a concession in one strike action could quietly build a war chest to see it through the next labor dispute, driving workers to the wall and breaking their union.

Violence played a role as well. State GOVERNORS frequently called out the National Guard to suppress larger strikes; the U.S. Army broke up strikes in 1864 and 1877. Companies hired their own security forces to intimidate and assault unions, but violence was not a monopoly of employers. Though some worker organizations insisted on nonviolence—the Troy laundresses and the Chicago Workingman's Party, for instance—others considered it an essential tactic.

The very size and diversity of the United States also complicated efforts to organize workers' parties. Those that did emerge, such as the Workingman's Parties in Chicago and San Francisco, were split by factional in-fighting and accused of communist sympathies or terrorist tactics.

Despite these problems, the Civil War-period labor organizers gained valuable experience that would lay the groundwork for the union activism of the 1880s and 1890s.

Further reading: Melvyn Dubofsky, *Industrialism and the American Worker, 1865–1920* (New York: Crowell, 1996); J. Matthew Gallman, *The North Fights the Civil War: The Home Front* (Chicago: I.R. Dee, 1994); David Montgomery, *Beyond Equality: Labor and The Radical Republicans, 1862–1872* (New York: Knopf, 1967).

—Tom Laichas

Stuart, J. E. B. (1833–1864)
Confederate cavalry officer James Ewell Brown Stuart was born in Patrick County, Virginia, on February 6, 1833, the

seventh of Archibald and Elizabeth Letcher Pannill Stuart's 10 children. Reared in a family with excellent political and social connections but relatively modest financial means, Stuart received schooling in southwest Virginia before attending Emory and Henry College in 1848–50. He entered the UNITED STATES MILITARY ACADEMY AT WEST POINT in 1850, graduating 13th of 46 members in the class of 1854.

Commissioned a second lieutenant in the Mounted Rifles in October 1854, he later was assigned to the First United States Cavalry at Fort Leavenworth. While serving with that unit on the Kansas frontier, Stuart was promoted to first lieutenant in December 1855. By that time he had married Flora Cooke, daughter of the post commandant at Leavenworth. The couple would have three children. As a U.S. officer, Stuart saw action against the Cheyenne at Solomon's Fork in 1857, where he received a severe wound. He also participated in peacekeeping duty in Kansas, where proSLAVERY forces contended with ABOLITIONists and Free Soilers, and he took part in the capture of JOHN BROWN at HARPERS FERRY in October 1859. Stuart was promoted to captain in April 1861, but he resigned his commission the next month, and he soon held the rank of colonel in the Confederate cavalry.

Stuart quickly made a name for himself as a flamboyant and effective cavalry officer. At the head of the First Virginia Cavalry, he led a dramatic charge at the FIRST BATTLE OF BULL RUN. Promoted to brigadier general on September 26, 1861, he performed mundane duties until mid-June 1862, when he earned renown with a daring reconnaissance that included a ride around GEORGE B. MCCLELLAN's entire Army of the Potomac. Typical of the Confederates who applauded Stuart's ride was a RICHMOND woman who wrote of "the brilliant, dashing exploits of General 'Jeb' Stuart and his gallant horsemen," who "became, from that time, famous in the annals of the war." Blessed with a famous nickname inspired by his initials and often described as a romantic cavalier, Stuart wore a scarlet-lined cape, boots that reached his thighs, a pair of golden spurs, a bright yellow sash, gauntlets of white buckskin, and a hat crowned with a long plume. He was promoted to major general on July 25, 1862, and given command of all cavalry in ROBERT E. LEE's Army of Northern Virginia, a post he held for the remainder of his Confederate career.

Stuart's colorful image sometimes overshadowed his mastery of cavalry operations. He played key roles in the SECOND BATTLE OF BULL RUN and the BATTLE OF ANTIETAM, screening Lee's movements, gathering intelligence about the Federals, and riding around McClellan's army again in October 1862. At the BATTLE OF CHANCELLORSVILLE, he temporarily replaced the wounded THOMAS J. "STONEWALL" JACKSON at the head of the Second Corps, acquitting himself well in the brutal offensive combat on May 3, 1863. His most controversial moments came in June and July 1863. Surprised at Brandy Station, Virginia, on June 9, he barely managed to hold off aggressive Union troopers. In the following Gettysburg campaign, he failed Lee badly, losing touch with the Army of Northern Virginia and leaving his commander to move blindly into Pennsylvania.

Stuart rebounded after the BATTLE OF GETTYSBURG, rendering solid work against a vastly improved Union cavalry during the autumn of 1863 and into the spring of 1864. His troopers fought well in the opening scenes of the OVERLAND CAMPAIGN of May 1864. As Lee and ULYSSES S. GRANT engaged at the BATTLES OF SPOTSYLVANIA, Stuart moved to block a Union cavalry raid against Richmond, and he received a mortal wound at the Battle of Yellow Tavern on May 11. As he was carried from the field, Stuart showed the spirit that had made him an effective soldier. "I had rather die," he said, "than be whipped!" He died in Richmond on the morning of May 12. When told of Stuart's fate, Lee remarked sadly, "He never brought me a piece of false information."

See also SHERIDAN, PHILIP HENRY.

Further reading: Emory M. Thomas, *Bold Dragoon: The Life of J. E. B. Stuart* (New York: Harper & Row, 1986).

—Gary W. Gallagher

Sumner, Charles (1811–1874)

Lawyer, reformer, and senator, Charles Sumner was a Massachusetts man by birth and a Puritan by ancestry. Sumner was born in Boston on January 6, 1811, the son of Charles Pinckney and Relief Jacobs Sumner. He received his early EDUCATION at the prestigious Boston Latin School. A brilliant student, Sumner graduated from Harvard College in 1830 and entered Harvard Law School in September 1831. He started practicing law in January 1834 and was admitted to the Massachusetts bar in September of that same year. From 1835 to 1837, he taught law at Harvard.

Sumner left Boston in 1837 to travel to Europe, where he intended to research the legal systems of England and France. His two and a half years abroad provided a foundation for his later contributions to FOREIGN POLICY while serving in the U.S. Senate. Sumner, a lifelong bachelor, except for a brief marriage in old age, was an admitted Anglophile and particularly enjoyed his time in London. He conquered the London social scene and gained access to the highest circles within a short period of time. While he also traveled to France, Italy, Germany, and Austria, the period in England reinforced his belief in the necessity of a strong alliance between the United States and Great Britain.

Charles Sumner *(Library of Congress)*

Upon his return to the United States in 1840, Sumner resumed his legal practice, albeit somewhat reluctantly. He preferred to pursue his growing interest in reform movements. The young lawyer had become very active in promoting the peace movement, penal reform, and ABOLITIONism. His reform fervor drove him to abandon the law. Conservative Bostonians were horrified by his radical positions, and as a result Sumner was not invited to rejoin the Harvard Law School faculty.

Sumner's public antiSLAVERY stance became well known in 1845 during the nationwide debate over the annexation of Texas. He spoke at a meeting in Boston's Faneuil Hall and stood with other prominent Massachusetts leaders in opposing the admission of another slave state to the Union. Over the next several years, Sumner became a voice of the "Conscience Whigs" in his home state and initiated a feud with his former Harvard classmate and current senator Robert C. Winthrop. Sumner denounced Winthrop's vote for the Mexican-American War bill in Congress, and in doing so he became even more involved in politics.

In 1848 Sumner supported the Free-Soil Party and ran on that party's ticket for Congress. Although he failed to win the seat, his tireless efforts to create a viable Free-Soil–Democratic coalition in the Massachusetts legislature did not go unappreciated. When Daniel Webster left his Senate seat to assume the position of secretary of state, that same coalition, after a fierce struggle with the Whigs, elected Sumner to the vacant post in April 1851.

Over the next two and a half decades, Sumner established himself as a recognizable force in the halls of Congress. Incorruptible, always outspoken, and often disagreeable, he prided himself on his lofty principles. Sumner was a tall and imposing person, with a handsome and distinguished profile. Notably lacking a sense of humor, his speeches were learned and sprinkled with many classical allusions. He deserved his reputation as a great if overbearing orator. Yet, Sumner possessed a moral passion that, for many, helped to define slavery's evil influence. Few of his Senate colleagues found fault with his steadfast commitment to his senatorial duties. Over the course of four terms he worked tirelessly for the causes of abolition and the equality and protection of freed people.

When he entered the Senate, Sumner found an assembly still recovering from the yearlong struggle over the Compromise of 1850. With emotions still raw, Sumner created a sensation with his first major speech, entitled "Freedom National, Slavery Sectional." Sumner argued against slavery in general and called for the repeal of the Fugitive Slave Act (part of the compromise). His four-hour effort described the FSA as being particularly offensive to Northern freedom-loving sensibilities. Sumner declared that because the Constitution did not recognize slavery, it could not exist where the national government maintained exclusive jurisdiction, as in the territories.

Sumner's speech raised him into the top ranks of antislavery politicians. Shortly thereafter, Sumner took another stand against slavery when STEPHEN A. DOUGLAS introduced the KANSAS-NEBRASKA ACT in 1854, which Sumner and many of his colleagues declared outrageous. The heated debates over the organization of the territories and the validity of popular sovereignty did not prevent the passage of the bill. Sectional tensions grew worse in the years that followed as Kansas turned into a battleground. Now a Republican, Sumner found the reports of fraudulent governments and vigilante violence alarming, and he prepared to deliver a speech denouncing what he referred to as "The Crime against Kansas." Over two days in May 1856, Sumner lashed out at the activities in Kansas, attacked the national government that allowed it to occur, and most important, castigated several of his Southern colleagues who supported this expansion of slavery.

All of his personal attacks were fierce, but his commentary directed at Andrew Butler, a senator from South Carolina, was particularly virulent. Preston Brooks, a congressman from that same state and a relative of Butler, felt it his duty to avenge this personal insult. On May 22 he entered the Senate and, finding Sumner at his desk, began hitting him repeatedly with a cane until it broke into pieces. Rendered defenseless by surprise and the confines of his desk, a weakened Sumner warded off the blows. Finally, he managed to wrench the desk from its moorings and staggered away. Although some of his colleagues rushed to his aid, many others, including Stephen Douglas, declined to enter the fray.

Brooks's caning made Sumner a martyr in the North but turned Brooks into a hero in the South. The shocking and violent act also became an electrifying issue in the political campaign in the fall of 1856. It was one more event that increased the hostility between North and South. Although reelected to the Senate in 1857, Sumner suffered severe physical and psychological wounds that affected him for the remainder of his life. His initial recovery proved fleeting, and Sumner was unable to resume his duties in the Senate until three years had passed. He spent much of this time in Europe, where he tried various remedies to recover his health.

Sumner returned to the Senate in December 1859, and by summer 1860 he was once again a fierce critic of the "slave power." In the months that followed SECESSION, Sumner did not favor any compromise measures. Sumner developed a close friendship with MARY TODD LINCOLN and ABRAHAM LINCOLN that allowed him unusual access to the White House, even when he opposed the president's policies. When the war began, Sumner and his fellow RADICAL REPUBLICANS strongly encouraged Lincoln to emancipate the slaves. Indeed, Sumner in the Senate and THADDEUS STEVENS in the House prodded and pushed President Lincoln toward enacting laws that would bring freedom and guarantee equal rights to all African Americans.

The Massachusetts senator also served the president in another important capacity. Sumner had been selected to chair the important Committee on Foreign Relations, a post he would hold for the next 12 years. In this capacity, he used his European contacts and command of international law to excellent effect. He was an invaluable asset as a FOREIGN-POLICY adviser to Lincoln, particularly in moderating the more strident rhetoric of Secretary of State WILLIAM H. SEWARD. For example, he played a large role in settling the *Trent* affair, which kept the peace with England. Sumner also worked hard and successfully to keep Great Britain neutral in the war. Afterward, Seward took a harder stance toward his beloved England. In 1869 he advocated that Britain should repay the United States for war-related costs having to do with the *Alabama* claims.

During and after the war, Sumner continued to press for the most advanced positions on race and the promotion of racial equality. In truth, Sumner was not the most effective leader for the cause of the freedpeople. Unwilling to compromise for the sake of principle, he often antagonized and offended his colleagues. He also became one of the strongest proponents of a hard RECONSTRUCTION policy. Sumner argued that the Southern states committed "suicide" and thus Congress, and not the president, should determine the process under which reconstruction should proceed.

Following the CIVIL WAR, Reconstruction and foreign affairs dominated Sumner's political career. He became a bitter enemy against ANDREW JOHNSON's lenient policies toward the South and fully supported the efforts to impeach Johnson in 1868. Unlike many other Radical Republicans, Sumner opposed the passage of the THIRTEENTH, FOURTEENTH, and FIFTEENTH AMENDMENTS, claiming that they did not go far enough to aid the ex-slave population. After his death, the CIVIL RIGHTS ACT OF 1875 provided his main legislative legacy to the country.

Reelected for a fourth term in 1869, Sumner found it hard to work with the sitting president, ULYSSES S. GRANT. Grant's failure to appoint him secretary of state infuriated Sumner and made him a thorn in the administration's side. Sumner retained his position as chairman of the Committee on Foreign Relations during Grant's first term, but his noisy opposition to the president's ill-fated plans to annex Santo Domingo sealed his fate. By 1872 Grant and Sumner were no longer on speaking terms, and Sumner supported the Liberal Republican candidate, HORACE GREELEY. Failing in health, Sumner spent his last days in Congress agitating for his civil rights bill. On his deathbed, Sumner spoke of the need to protect the rights of the freed people in the South. Charles Sumner died in WASHINGTON, D.C., on March 11, 1874.

See also BLEEDING KANSAS; IMPEACHMENT OF ANDREW JOHNSON; KANSAS-NEBRASKA ACT; WHIG PARTY.

Further reading: David Herbert Donald, *Charles Sumner* (New York: Da Capo Press, 1996).

—John P. Bowes

tactics and strategy

Tactics is concerned with deploying troops effectively at a local level, while strategy involves thinking more broadly. Military theorist Karl von Clausewitz provided a famous definition of the distinction between the two concerns: "Tactics is the art of using troops in battle; strategy is the art of using battles to win the war."

Tactics

The tactics used by both the Confederacy and the Union tended to be similar. Early in the CIVIL WAR, most generals' approach to battle mirrored that of the French general Napoleon Bonaparte. Napoleon did not invent this style of warfare; he was merely its most effective practitioner. Napoleonic tactics were oriented toward offense and dramatic victories. The hallmark of Napoleonic-era warfare was the massed infantry assault, where troops would advance within range of the enemy, fire a volley, and then charge forth with bayonets to finish the job.

Napoleonic tactics were effective in the time of Napoleon, as some Civil War generals had undoubtedly learned from reading the influential works of ANTOINE-HENRI DE JOMINI. The tactics had also worked during the Mexican-American War, where many of the army commanders of the Civil War saw their first military service. However, in the 1850s, most of the world's armies, including the army of the United States, began to use rifles. Rifles could fire bullets accurately at a range of 500 yards, compared with the 75-yard range of the smoothbore muskets used in Napoleon's time. For the military leaders of the United States, it was not immediately clear what the implications of longer-range weapons would be. In 1855 the army issued a new tactical manual, *Rifle and Light Infantry Tactics,* by William J. Hardee. Hardee's answer to the adoption of the rifle, in essence, was to keep using Napoleonic tactics but to go faster when doing so.

When the Civil War got underway, it was soon clear that the impact of rifles was going to be more substantial than anyone had anticipated. Over the first few years of the war, it became evident to commanders on both sides that the massed infantry assault was obsolete. When firing cannot begin until a range of 75 yards, only one volley can be gotten off before hand-to-hand combat begins. Charging infantry can reach their target with their ranks relatively intact. When firing begins at a range of 500 yards, on the other hand, three or four volleys can be fired before the infantry reaches its target. Under such circumstances, soldiers attempting a frontal assault are almost certain to be slaughtered.

The advent of the rifle had other implications as well. Cavalrymen and their horses presented easy targets for men armed with rifles. As such, cavalry was relegated to a largely supporting role during the Civil War—protecting the flanks of their armies, scouting out troop locations, pursuing defeated enemies, and sometimes dismounting to fight as infantry. Rifles also reduced the role of artillery. In Napoleon's era, cannons would have been located along the front lines of battles. During the Civil War, the ability to pick off artillerymen with rifles necessitated their removal to the rear of the battle. This relegated artillery to a largely defensive role in most engagements.

Despite the shortcomings of the massed infantry assault, Napoleonic tactics were not entirely discarded during the Civil War. Indeed, the most famous tactical maneuver of the war, Pickett's Charge at the BATTLE OF GETTYSBURG, was a massed infantry assault. However, commanders preferred to use infantry charges as a last resort. Their favored alternative was the turning maneuver. This tactic was taught at the UNITED STATES MILITARY ACADEMY AT WEST POINT and had been used to great effect during the Mexican-American War by Gen. Winfield Scott. In a turning maneuver, a commander tried to attack the enemy from the side or behind, so as to avoid the bloodshed inherent in a frontal assault. Turning movements could be difficult to achieve, however, and very dangerous if they failed.

Increased use of turning maneuvers was not the only development to come out of the Civil War. Most field commanders showed a willingness to embrace new technologies to gain a tactical advantage. The TELEGRAPH and RAILROADS became critical tools for generals during the Civil War. Commanders also experimented with hot-air balloons, land mines, and machine guns. An even more important change during the war was the increased use of defensive warfare. Commanders soon discovered that if their troops dug trenches and built fortifications, the number of enemy troops needed to take the position generally tripled.

Whether a commander was pursuing an offensive or defensive strategy, there were only a handful of ways in which troops were commonly deployed. A line was a group of soldiers standing next to one another, generally with three or four feet between each individual. Lines could fire thick volleys of bullets, but they were highly exposed to enemy fire. A column was a formation with many ranks standing one behind the other. A 100-man column, for example, might consist of 10 ranks, each made up of 10 men. Columns could not fire nearly as many bullets, but they were less likely to be destroyed by enemy fire. Mixed formations incorporated both columns and lines. For example, 100 men might be organized into an 80-man column, with its flanks guarded by two lines of 10 men.

During battles, a fairly common pattern of deployment emerged. Small groups of soldiers, called skirmishers, would move out in front of their armies to determine if enemy troops were present and in what numbers. During or after skirmishing, the armies themselves would march into battle in columns, often as much as four miles wide. Once soldiers reached the ground they were ordered to occupy, they would form into lines, usually in pairs. A company of 100 men, for example, would have a line of 50 kneeling men, and behind them 50 standing men. The two lines would alternate their volleys to provide a constant hail of bullets. If a charge was ordered, soldiers generally tried to maintain a two-line formation as much as was possible.

After the Civil War, American military commanders stopped using line and column formations, along with Napoleonic tactics. The Indian Wars of the 1870s and 1880s were largely based on defensive warfare, guerrilla tactics, and strategic raids. This trend continued into the 20th century.

Confederate Strategy

Strategically, the Confederacy had a much easier task than the Union. All the South wanted was to be allowed to secede, and so all the Confederates had to do was avoid being conquered. JEFFERSON DAVIS hoped to mirror the strategy of George Washington during the Revolutionary War, holding his ground when possible, retreating when

necessary. At the same time, Davis had to make some concession to political realities. A war following Washington's example may have been strategically advisable but not necessarily popular among the voters.

Early in the war, the Confederacy used what came to be called the "cordon strategy." No Southerners wanted their states to be invaded, and so Confederate leaders spread their troops throughout the Confederacy, particularly along the nation's borders. The disadvantage of this strategy soon became obvious—Union troops could concentrate on one position and break through with relative ease. After losses at Fort Donelson, Fort Henry, and Roanoke Island, it was clear that a new strategy was needed.

This new strategy evolved over the first few months of 1862, particularly after ROBERT E. LEE took command of the Army of Northern Virginia. Lee and Davis both favored an "offensive-defensive" strategy that had several components: First, Confederate generals would try to occupy strategically advantageous positions that the enemy would be compelled to attack, generally along the Union's lines of supply or communication. Second, key defensive points would be defended by concentrations of troops. These troops would be shifted around as needed, taking advantage of the Confederacy's shorter interior lines. Third, Confederate armies would go on the offensive whenever an opportunity presented itself. Sometimes these offensives took the form of small raids, sometimes large-scale attacks. Jefferson Davis particularly sought to make a move when he knew that it would hurt the political fortunes of the Lincoln administration and the REPUBLICAN PARTY.

The offensive-defensive strategy effectively blended the Davis administration's strategic concerns. It allowed the Confederacy to spend most of the time on the defensive and to keep important strategic points guarded. At the same time, it had enough of an offensive component that the Southern populace's thirst for dramatic victories could be satisfied. The offensive-defensive strategy governed Confederate thinking from 1862 through the end of the war.

Union Strategy

At the start of the Civil War, the Union faced a much more difficult task than the Confederacy. If they could not convince the South to return to the Union voluntarily, then the Northern armies would have to conquer an incredibly large area while destroying the populace's will to fight. In addition, like his Confederate counterpart, President ABRAHAM LINCOLN always had to keep political concerns in mind.

The Union pursued a number of strategies early in the war, all of them intended to compel the Confederacy to return to the Union rather than to conquer the South. The first strategic plan to be proposed to Lincoln came from Union general in chief Winfield Scott. Scott's proposal was almost entirely dependent on the UNION NAVY and the use of gunboats to gain control of Confederate ports and the MISSISSIPPI RIVER. This strategy would make it difficult for the Confederacy to get the materials needed to survive and wage war, ultimately forcing the South to give up on SECESSION. Scott favored this plan because it had the potential to bring the war to an end with minimal bloodshed.

The Northern public roundly ridiculed Scott's proposal. Newspapers derisively labeled it the "Anaconda Plan," after the snake that slowly squeezes its prey to death. Although Lincoln ordered the blockade that Scott suggested, he otherwise rejected the Anaconda Plan. Lincoln knew that the public wanted a dramatic victory and a quick end to the war, and the Anaconda Plan could provide neither. When Gen. Irvin McDowell suggested an offensive against Confederate forces at Manassas Junction, Lincoln was receptive, and he approved the plan. The result was a humiliating defeat in the FIRST BATTLE OF BULL RUN.

In November 1861, Winfield Scott was replaced as general in chief by GEORGE B. MCCLELLAN, who quickly went to work devising his own strategic plan. McClellan proposed to focus most of his attention on Virginia and on a campaign against the Confederate capital at RICHMOND. He felt that if the city could be captured, the South's will to fight would be broken. At the same time, McClellan sent a small group of troops under HENRY W. HALLECK to try and take the Mississippi River.

McClellan spent several months building the Army of the Potomac into a formidable fighting force, but he hesitated to actually move against Virginia. After many months of inaction, Lincoln grew exasperated with his general in chief and removed him from the post. McClellan was still allowed to lead the PENINSULAR CAMPAIGN, however, when it finally got underway in spring of 1862. Ultimately, it failed. Shortly thereafter, Henry W. Halleck took over as general in chief.

By the time that Halleck took responsibility for formulating Union strategy in the latter part of 1862, it was clear that the Civil War was not going to end quickly. At the same time, Lincoln had determined that EMANCIPATION would be added to the Union's war aims. From this point forward, Union strategy focused on conquering the Confederacy rather than convincing the South to return to the Union with minimal damage. Halleck, working with Lincoln, devised a plan that reversed the strategic priorities of McClellan. The Mississippi River and the liberation of eastern Tennessee became the Union's primary strategic objectives.

Halleck remained as general in chief for nearly two years. During his tenure, the Union's goals in the west were achieved, while a number of important victories were won in the east against the Army of Northern Virginia. By the end of 1863, however, the war had become stalemated and the Northern public was growing impatient. In March 1864, Halleck was replaced by ULYSSES S. GRANT.

Grant introduced wholesale changes in the UNION ARMY's approach to the war. Grant wanted to eliminate the Confederacy's ability to use interior lines to move troops to where they were needed. To accomplish this, he planned simultaneous advances on two fronts. General WILLIAM T. SHERMAN would lead the western armies through Georgia and the Carolinas, while Grant himself would lead the eastern armies through Virginia. At the same time, Grant realized that the Confederacy could not be conquered unless the populace's will to fight was drained. As such, he sought to make war on the citizens of the Confederacy, destroying crops, buildings, factories, railroads, and anything else important to the Confederate war effort. Grant's other western general, Philip Sheridan was ordered to destroy the rich resources of the Shenandoah Valley. Grant's notion of "total war" was one of the innovations to come out of the Civil War, and it would come to be a hallmark of warfare in the 20th century.

Grant's vision first came to fruition during SHERMAN'S MARCH THROUGH GEORGIA. Sherman vowed to "make Georgia howl," and he delivered on the promise. Sherman's armies cut a swath of destruction through the heart of Georgia. The campaign featured the capture of Atlanta, an event that secured Lincoln's reelection to the presidency. After completing his activities in Georgia, Sherman went on to conduct a similarly devastating campaign in the Carolinas.

The war that Grant waged in the east was not as destructive as Sherman's campaigns, but it was effective nonetheless. Grant repeatedly compelled the Army of Northern Virginia to retreat, usually after sustaining substantial losses. In April 1864, Lee was forced to abandon Richmond in hope of joining Confederate forces in North Carolina. Grant anticipated the maneuver and cut it off. With no other options, Lee was forced to surrender his army, effectively ending the Civil War.

Grant's strategy must be judged a success, not only for bringing an end to the war but also for bringing an end to the war when it did. The Confederacy still had troops in the field when Lee surrendered, and it could have continued to wage a conventional war or shifted to guerrilla warfare. This did not happen, however, because Grant had done more than checkmate the Confederate military. He had broken the Southern populace's will to fight, and that was the critical factor in bringing the Civil War to a close.

See also APPOMATTOX COURT HOUSE, VIRGINIA; ATLANTA CAMPAIGN; BALLOON CORPS; SCIENCE AND TECHNOLOGY.

Further reading: Paddy Griffith, *Battle Tactics of the Civil War* (New Haven, Conn.: Yale University Press, 2001); Henry W. Halleck, *Elements of Military Art and Science* (1846; reprint, Westport, Conn.: Greenwood Press, 1971); Joseph L. Harsh, *Confederate Tide Rising: Robert E. Lee and the Making of Southern Strategy, 1861–1862* (Kent, Ohio: Kent State University Press, 1998); Archer Jones, *Civil War Command and Strategy: The Process of Victory and Defeat* (New York: Free Press, 1992).

—Christopher Bates and Michael O'Connor

tariffs

A tariff is a tax levied on goods brought into or taken out of a country. Tariffs were the primary way in which the U.S. government raised money in the 19th century, and so the tariff received a great deal of attention from Americans in the antebellum era. Eventually, disagreements over tariff rates caused the country to become bitterly divided. Southerners came to believe that the tariff bills being passed by the government favored the North at the South's expense. At the same time, partisans on both sides of the question eventually came to equate the federal government's ability to impose a tariff with its ability to impose controls upon the institution of SLAVERY.

The tariff debate initially flared up in the 1780s. It immediately became apparent that while the government needed some revenue, each constituency wanted someone else to foot the bill. For example, New Englanders imported large quantities of molasses from the West Indies in order to make rum. They wanted the tariff on imported molasses to be as low as possible in order to keep their costs down. The Deep South, on the other hand, needed slave labor, and congressmen from those states pressed for a low tariff on slaves brought into the country. A compromise was called for, and on July 4, 1789, Congress passed a tariff bill that set fairly modest duties of 5 percent to 10 percent on most imported goods.

While this initial tariff had enough support for it to be adopted by Congress, some of the nation's leaders were dissatisfied. In 1791 Secretary of the Treasury Alexander Hamilton presented his *Report on Manufactures* to President George Washington and to Congress, in which he argued for a high tariff. Hamilton had several reasons for this position, called protectionism: First, he believed that the United States could become an industrial power, and he wanted American industrial interests to be able to develop without interference from goods made in Britain or France. A high tariff would accomplish this by driving up the price of foreign goods. Second, Hamilton favored a strong federal government that used its power to promote American development. He hoped the government could invest tariff revenue in EDUCATIONal institutions, roads, canals, and other sorts of internal improvements.

Hamilton's arguments were not immediately embraced by Congress, and for the rest of the 1790s, tariff rates remained low. However, the ideas presented in the *Report on Manufactures* found an audience in the next generation of congressional leaders. The most important was Whig leader Henry Clay, whose "American System" was largely a restatement of Hamilton's vision. In the first three decades of the 19th century, Clay and his allies persuaded Congress to adopt an increasingly protectionist stance, culminating in the Tariff of 1828, which set rates on some imports as high as 50 percent.

By the time the Tariff of 1828 was passed, Clay's successes with the tariff had inspired a great deal of animosity among Southern leaders, especially John C. Calhoun of South Carolina. Southerners objected to protective tariffs for a variety of reasons. They were opposed to a strong central government, which high tariff revenues helped to facilitate. Beyond that, because Southern products such as tobacco and cotton were not protected, it seemed that the North was building up its ECONOMY at the expense of the South. Most significantly, Calhoun believed that the North was using the tariff to become the dominant player in national politics, to the exclusion of the South.

For Calhoun and his supporters, the Tariff of 1828 was the final straw. Calling it the "Tariff of Abominations," Calhoun announced that South Carolina would not abide by its terms. To support his position, Calhoun borrowed the idea of "nullification" from the writings of Thomas Jefferson. This doctrine argued that states were the supreme authority in the United States and that they had the right to ignore the dictates of the federal government or even to secede from the Union if they wished to do so. Though it was left unstated, leaders on both sides of the conflict knew that the South was threatening not only to nullify future tariffs but also any future actions taken to curtail the institution of slavery.

Tensions remained high in the nation for several years, but eventually a compromise was reached. The Tariff of 1833 began a general reduction of rates that continued for the next 30 years. When the CIVIL WAR came, the South adopted a tariff that reflected its preference for low rates. The Northern Congress, meanwhile, passed the highly protectionist Morrill Act of 1861. After the war, tariff rates continued to be high as part of the Republican program of promoting the development of manufacturing. Although the tariff ceased to be a major point of political contention after 1833, the debate over the Tariff of Abominations had set a precedent that would eventually lead to the SECESSION of South Carolina and the start of the Civil War.

See also TAXATION.

Further reading: William W. Freehling, *Prelude to Civil War: The Nullification Controversy in South Carolina, 1816–1836* (New York: Oxford University Press, 1992); Jonathan J. Pincus, *Pressure Groups and Politics in Antebellum Tariffs* (New York: Columbia University Press, 1977); Sidney Ratner, *The Tariff in American History* (New York: Van Nostrand, 1972).

—Christopher Bates

taxation

Before the CIVIL WAR, the majority of Americans were not taxed directly. The budgets of both state and federal governments were small, and expenses were paid almost exclusively through duties on imported goods, sales of government-owned land, and property taxes on the wealthiest citizens. When the Civil War came, however, the financial needs of the Confederacy and Union grew to enormous dimensions, and both governments had to find ways to increase their revenues. Among these were several different taxes, the first that many Americans had ever paid.

TARIFFS are taxes on imported or exported goods. Tariffs are indirect taxes, because they are paid by the merchant who is selling the goods and then incorporated into the sale price of the goods. Tariff revenues were the single largest source of income for the federal government prior to the Civil War and were also a major source of controversy, as most Northerners favored higher rates while most Southerners favored lower rates. When the Civil War broke out, both governments quickly moved to adopt a tariff that reflected their prewar position. In March 1861, the Northern Congress adopted a high tariff, taxing imports at an average rate of 47 percent. Rates were increased several times over the course of the war, and by the end of the war the Union government had collected a total of $296 million in tariff revenue. In May 1861, the Confederate Congress adopted a tariff bill of its own, taxing imports at an average rate of 12 percent. Due to this modest rate, as well as poor enforcement and the small number of goods coming into the South, the Confederate tariff generated only $3.5 million over the course of the war.

When the Confederate tariff was adopted in 1861, it was immediately apparent that it would generate very little revenue and that the Confederate government would have to act quickly to find other ways to pay its bills. Some Confederate leaders favored taxation, but the general sentiment in the Confederate Congress was against such a step, fearing that it would undermine support for the war. As the Confederacy's situation became increasingly dire, however, advocates of taxation were able to persuade the Congress to adopt a tax of one-half of 1 percent of the value of all property, including slaves. This tax, adopted on August 19, 1861, ultimately had disappointing results. First, it raised only $17.4 million. Second, according to the bill's terms, states could pay the tax on a citizen's behalf at a discount rate. Most states did so, financing the payment through bond issues. This dried up much of the available capital in the South and undercut the bond sales of the Confederate government.

In the same month that the Confederacy adopted its property tax, the Union Congress adopted an income tax, the first in American history. The tax was fairly modest, requiring a payment of 3 percent on incomes more than $800. A year later, a much more comprehensive tax bill was passed. The Internal Revenue Act, adopted on July 1, 1862, levied a rate of 3 percent on incomes between $600 and $10,000 and a rate of 5 percent on incomes more than $10,000 (eventually increased to 5 percent and 10 percent, respectively, in 1864). It also established sales taxes on a broad variety of goods: yachts, newspaper advertisements, medicines, billiard tables, liquor, and tobacco, to name a few. In order to make certain that these sales and INCOME TAXES were properly collected, the Internal Revenue Act created a new government agency, the Bureau of Internal Revenue. The Union's income tax had two beneficial effects: It raised roughly $300 million for the Union war effort, and it helped to keep inflation in check.

Eventually, several financial difficulties in the South compelled the Confederate Congress to adopt an income tax of its own. The Confederate tax, adopted on April 24, 1863, established a graduated tax ranging from 1 percent on incomes between $1,000 and $1,500 up to 15 percent on incomes of $10,000 or more. The measure also included a sort of combination property/income tax for farmers called the "tax-in-kind." The tax-in-kind allowed farmers to set aside certain proscribed amounts of their crops for subsistence and then required them to give 10 percent of the remainder to the government. The Confederate income tax and tax-in-kind were almost unqualified failures. In 1863 inflation was wildly out of control, largely due to the Confederate government having printed too much paper money. By early 1864, it took $46 to buy what had cost $1 before the war. As such, the roughly $140 million collected in income tax and tax-in-kind between 1863 and 1865 had very little purchasing power. Meanwhile, the taxes generated all sorts of discontent on the HOMEFRONT. Farmers were especially angry about the tax-in-kind, because the system for collecting the crops owed to the government was filled with incompetence and corruption. Eventually, the Confederate Congress passed a series of bills modifying the income tax and tax-in-kind in order to make them more acceptable, but the changes came too late to be of much use.

Ultimately, taxation was much more effective in the wealthy North than in the cash-strapped South. The $600 million raised by the Union government covered more than 40 percent of the cost of the Union's war effort, while the $145 million gathered by the Confederate government paid less than 7 percent of its expenses. After the war, all of the national taxes except the tariff were repealed. However, a precedent had been set, and it would not be long before permanent income, sales, and property taxes would be established.

Further reading: Douglas D. Ball, *Financial Failure and Confederate Defeat* (Urbana: University of Illinois Press, 1991); J. Matthew Gallman, *The North Fights the Civil War: The Home Front* (Chicago: I.R. Dee, 1994); Heather Cox Richardson, *The Greatest Nation of the Earth: Republican Economic Policies during the Civil War* (Cambridge, Mass.: Harvard University Press, 1997).

—Christopher Bates

Taylor, Susie King (1848–1912)

Teacher, nurse, and author, Susie King Taylor was born a slave in Georgia on August 5, 1848. Her parents, Hagar Ann Reed and Raymond Baker, were both highly regarded by their owners and given privileges that benefited their daughter's future. At age seven, Susie was sent to live with her grandmother in Savannah, where she learned to sew and, more importantly, to read and write. An avid student, Taylor continued her studies up to the outbreak of the CIVIL WAR in 1861. Passionate in her conviction that SLAVERY was about to end, the 14-year-old fled Savannah for freedom with her uncle's family and found refuge on St. Simon's Island off the Georgia coast and under Union control.

Taylor joined the small but dedicated contingent of Northern missionaries, teachers, and ABOLITIONist soldiers who were part of an exciting experiment to educate and prepare the freedpeople for their expected transition to freedom. Located on several of the sea islands off the coast of South Carolina and Georgia, this "rehearsal for reconstruction" anticipated many of the challenges and disappointments that lay in store for ex-slaves. Taylor was quickly hired as a schoolteacher, and she taught during the day for children and at night for the adults. Exhausted but exhilarated by her work, Susie did not want to leave in the fall of 1862 when, for safety reasons, the Federals ordered that island civilians be removed to Camp Saxton in Beaufort, South Carolina.

In Beaufort, Taylor worked as a laundress for Company E of the famous First South Carolina Volunteers (later the 33rd U.S. Colored Infantry). The unit was the first authorized Union regiment of African-American soldiers. She met and married one of the regiment's soldiers, Sgt.

Edward King, sometime in 1862. Proud to be a part of an African-American unit fighting for freedom and equality, Taylor remained with the regiment throughout the war. She served as a laundress and cook, but her most important roles were those of nurse and teacher. The regiment's soldiers, which included a number of her uncles and cousins, cherished their teenaged "angel of mercy," and she returned their devotion in full. Taylor never received any wages for her work, nor was she eligible for a pension in later years. She did receive a widow's pension of $100 after her husband's death.

After the war Taylor and her husband settled in Savannah, where she opened a school for African-American children. Due to the extreme racial prejudice that existed in the country at this time, Edward King could not make a living as a carpenter, but he found a job as a longshoreman. In September 1866, he was killed in a work-related accident, leaving a pregnant wife. After the birth of their son, Taylor tried unsuccessfully to continue her work in EDUCATION. After a couple of failed attempts to run schools, she took a job as a laundress and cook for wealthy couple. In the early 1870s, Taylor determined that she wished to live in Boston, Massachusetts, where she moved to in 1874. A few years later she remarried to Russell B. Taylor.

Susie King Taylor spent the last two decades of her life working for VETERANS' rights and benefits. In the 1880s she helped to found the Corps 67 of the Boston branch of the Women's Relief Corps, the auxiliary to the Grand Army of the Republic. The GAR was a political and social organization for ex–Civil War soldiers and had many African-American units. Taylor, who worked as treasurer and in 1893 was president of the corps, agitated for the fair treatment of African-American veterans. Tragedy struck Taylor again in 1898 when her son died in Shreveport, Louisiana.

Disappointed by the lack of progress made by her people since the Civil War, Taylor blamed the racism of the white people in the United States. In 1902 Taylor published her autobiography, which focused on her war experiences. Susie King Taylor died in Boston on October 6, 1912.

Further reading: Gerda Lerner, ed., *Black Women in White America: A Documentary History* (New York: Vintage Books, 1992); Susie King Taylor, *Reminiscences of My Life in Camp* (1902; reprint, New York: Arno Press, 1968).

telegraph

The CIVIL WAR was the first military conflict in which long-range communications played a major role. The telegraph was developed and refined by a series of inventors during the first few decades of the 19th century. The most well known is Samuel F. B. Morse, whose main contribution was his development of Morse code in 1841. Morse code uses a series of long and short tones, called dots and dashes, to communicate messages one letter at a time. Morse also played an important role in arranging the financing to build a national telegraphic infrastructure. Thanks to his efforts, and to those of other businessmen, the United States had many thousands of miles of telegraph wire when the Civil War started, 90 percent of it in the North.

Given the Union's advantage, telegraphy played a critical role in its war effort. Before the technology could be fully utilized, however, a number of logistical issues had to be overcome. The most significant was the establishment of a bureaucracy to operate the North's telegraphs. Initially, the American Telegraph Company, a private business concern, was placed in charge of the Union's telegraphy operations. Many leaders on the Union side were uncomfortable with this arrangement, however, and in October 1861 the government stepped in and formed the U.S. Military Telegraph Service, under the command of Col. Anson Stager. Although Stager and a handful of his subordinates were commissioned officers, most of the Telegraphic Service's 1,300 employees were civilians, because Secretary of War EDWIN M. STANTON did not want them to be subject to the orders of field officers. The Telegraphic Service worked with the Army Signal Corps to maximize the value of the North's telegraphic system, and ultimately they enjoyed a great deal of success. More than 1,000 miles of telegraph lines were laid, and more than 6 million messages were transmitted over Union telegraphs during the course of the war.

Security was another concern with which Northern authorities had to contend. Telegraphs can be easily tapped by enemy spies or by enterprising reporters looking for items for the newspaper. One solution to this problem was censorship, and Telegraphic Service employees had the authority to censor anything they deemed problematic. Another, more effective solution was encoding messages, a technique utilized by both the Confederacy and the Union. By the middle of the war, virtually all messages dealing with military matters were encoded in one way or another.

Like the Union, the Confederacy depended on telegraphy during the Civil War. The Confederates were not able to use the technology as much as they would have liked, however, due to lack of materials. It proved difficult to keep all of the South's telegraph lines in working order, and it was almost an impossibility to provide telegraphic services at the actual sites of battles, a privilege enjoyed throughout the war by Union commanders. Dr. William S. Morris, placed in charge of the South's telegraph lines, did his best to be innovative despite short supplies and the fact that the Confederacy never established a bureaucratic counterpart to the Union's Military Telegraphic Service. Morris did an effective job, keeping information flowing at a high rate until the final months of the war.

In addition to the critical role telegraphy played in military operations, telegraphs were also important to newspapers. People on both the HOMEFRONT and the war front hungered for news of the war, and journalists were happy to comply. Before the Civil War, news stories would take a week to be printed. With the telegraph, the news could be communicated instantly and printed within a day or two. Civilians were well informed about war-related events. By the end of the Civil War, newspapers would have a permanent role in shaping public opinion.

Telegraphic communication would continue to be an important tool in the postwar era. Business leaders increasingly embraced the technology as a means of keeping up to date on the prices of stocks and commodities. By the 1870s more than 80 percent of telegrams dealt with business matters. Meanwhile, military leaders across the world took heed of the lessons taught by the U.S. experience in the Civil War. By 1875, every major European military power had established a telegraphic corps. The telegraph also became the basis for Alexander Graham Bell's telephone, which began to supplant the telegraph in the 1880s and 1890s.

See also JOURNALISM.

Further reading: David Homer Bates, *Lincoln in the Telegraph Office: Recollections of the United States Military Telegraphic Corps during the Civil War* (Lincoln: University of Nebraska, 1995); William R. Plum, *The Military Telegraph during the Civil War in the United States* (New York: Arno Press, 1974); Charles Ross, *Trial by Fire: Science, Technology and the Civil War* (Shippensburg, Pa.: White Mane Books, 2000).

—Christopher Bates

theater

The theater was an important cultural institution in cities, towns, and frontier settlements throughout the 19th century. Performances, plays, actors, and the theaters themselves were all elements of the vibrant public and participatory culture that existed in the United States. At a time when politics was overtly theatrical, the theater was often a venue for political acts. Nowhere was this fact demonstrated more dramatically than in the ASSASSINATION OF ABRAHAM LINCOLN in 1865. A lifelong fan of the theater, Lincoln was attending a play at Ford's Theatre in WASHINGTON, D.C., when he was shot and killed by the famously handsome and talented actor JOHN WILKES BOOTH of Maryland.

From the 1790s to the 1870s, the theater offered a fairly democratic setting for audiences of all classes and economic groups to enjoy plays, opera, dancing, minstrel shows, and magicians, sometimes all appearing together on the same stage. Whether attending a play in the impressive St. Charles Theater in New Orleans, NEW YORK CITY's vast Bowery Theater, or one of the many more modest establishments in Louisville, Cincinnati, Denver, Chicago, or Natchez, the American patron of the arts could generally expect performances of high quality received by an enthusiastic audience.

Most theaters were divided into separate sections to address the needs of different social classes. The boxes (in front) were reserved for the upper class, the pit for the middle class, the gallery for the working class, and sometimes, way in the back, special rows for African Americans. In some theaters, a section called "the third tier" was where prostitutes met their clients. American audiences were known for their boisterous behavior, often indicating displeasure with poor acting performances by shouting and booing, or even throwing eggs and vegetables at the stage. One newspaper review described the unlucky actor who drew an angry response from the audience: "Cabbages, carrots, pumpkins, potatoes, a wealth of vegetables, a sack of flour, and one of soot, and a dead goose, with other articles, simultaneously fell upon the stage."

Americans reserved their most passionate approval and disapproval for the plays of the English playwright William Shakespeare. Shakespeare was widely read in the United States, where his melodramatic tragedies and comedies seemed to strike a powerful chord with many citizens. *Hamlet* and *Macbeth* were two of the most popular of his plays and were performed in countless venues across the country. In part, Shakespeare's stage dominance can be attributed to the droves of English actors who came to the United States to make their fortunes. Edmund Kean, Charles and Fanny Kemble, William Charles Macready, and Ellen Tree all attracted great crowds to their performances.

One of the most brilliant and famous of English actors that came to America's shores was Junius Brutus Booth. Unlike most of his peers, Booth became a citizen. He married and raised his large family on a farm in Maryland. Three of his sons, Junius Jr., Edwin, and John Wilkes, followed in his footsteps. In stark contrast to his Confederate-loving brother, Edwin Booth was a staunch supporter of the Union and, after the war, the greatest actor of his generation. Booth and fellow Shakespearian actor Edwin Forrest also represented the emergence of an American style of acting that emphasized a vigorous style over the more genteel English approach. In a very real sense, actors were instrumental in creating an American identity based on a more informal, democratic, and personal method of stage performance.

The engine that drove the theater during the decades of the middle to late 19th century was commercialization. In an effort to expand the audience base, theater owners sought to appeal to the growing middle class, especially women and families. Laura Keene, an actress who became a stage manager in New York, was instrumental in bringing an influx of middle-class women theatergoers to view the sentimental plays that resonated with their lives. Increasingly, theaters presented different kinds of plays to different types of audiences: minstrel shows, vaudeville, opera, burlesque, ethnic and racial comedies, serious plays, and melodrama. Two of the most profitable and successful plays were about SLAVERY: HARRIET BEECHER STOWE's *Uncle Tom's Cabin* and Dion Boucicault's *The Octoroon*. Specialized touring companies spread out across the country, drawing huge crowds and filling the wallets of their producers. Touring was facilitated by urbanization and far-reaching and sophisticated TRANSPORTATION system. By the late 1870s the theater was flourishing as never before, with New York City's Broadway as the centerpiece of both highbrow and lowbrow American culture.

Further reading: Faye E. Dudden, *Women in the American Theatre: Actresses and Audiences, 1790–1870* (New Haven, Conn.: Yale University Press, 1994); Lawrence W. Levine, *Highbrow/Lowbrow: The Emergence of Cultural Hierarchy in America* (Cambridge, Mass.: Harvard University Press, 1990); Bruce A. McConachie, *Melodramatic Formations: American Theatre and Society, 1820–1870* (Iowa City: University of Iowa Press, 1992).

Thirteenth Amendment (December 18, 1865)

The Thirteenth Amendment officially ended SLAVERY in the United States, completing a revolution in America. The amendment to the U.S. Constitution was passed by Congress on January 31, 1865, and ratified on December 18, 1865. Its text reads:

SEC. 1. Neither slavery nor involuntary servitude, except as a punishment for crime whereof the party shall have been duly convicted, shall exist within the United States, or anyplace subject to their jurisdiction.

SEC. 2. Congress shall have power to enforce this article by appropriate legislation.

The march toward freedom that the Thirteenth Amendment capped began with runaway and CONTRABAND slaves that clogged Union lines. Their actions forced military and political leaders to confront the future of the institution of slavery. President ABRAHAM LINCOLN mortally wounded slavery in the United States with his EMANCIPATION PROCLAMATION and by prosecuting the CIVIL WAR until the Confederacy was destroyed. The course of the war evolved from an effort to preserve the Union to the radical undertaking of slave EMANCIPATION. As early as the 1864 election, Lincoln endorsed an amendment to abolish slavery.

Most Republicans assumed that with the ABOLITION of slavery, African Americans in the South would receive the same treatment as white people. This belief was due to an understanding that there was no middle ground between slave and free status. However, the BLACK CODES disabused congressional Republicans of the notion of equal treatment in the South. An incredulous Northern public felt that the sacrifices of the war did not warrant a return to slavery, as the Black Codes implied. Spurred on by white Southern intransigence, RADICAL REPUBLICANS pushed for a more specific and intensive federal effort to protect civil rights.

A key, and often overlooked, component of the Thirteenth Amendment is the enforcement clause, the first in the Constitution, which recognized Congress's power to define and protect freedom. Some Southern states, before Congressional RECONSTRUCTION, rejected the amendment, mainly because of the enforcement clause. It was viewed as an unwarranted expansion of federal power that nationalized racial problems.

Though the Thirteenth Amendment abolished slavery, it was unclear what freedom meant. In many ways, the ratification of the amendment marked the beginning of a long struggle over the implications of freedom. WILLIAM LLOYD GARRISON, the prominent abolitionist, considered his work complete after ratification. Others believed that formal, legal removal of slavery from the American system did not go far enough. "What is freedom?" argued Republican congressman James A. Garfield, "Is it bare privilege of not being chained? If this is all, then freedom is a bitter mockery, a cruel delusion." FREDERICK DOUGLASS, an articulate black abolitionist, challenged Republican leaders to go beyond a narrow conception of freedom. "Slavery is not abolished," said Douglass, "until the black man has the ballot."

The debate over freedom became a debate over the role of government in a democratic society. On the one hand, some Republicans and nearly all of the Democrats believed that it was up to the freedmen to make a life for themselves like white citizens. On the other side, Radical Republicans viewed emancipation as a unique event that required the federal government to take positive action to help the freedmen transition from slavery to freedom. The

Black Codes in no small way pushed the REPUBLICAN PARTY into embracing federal intervention to help exslaves. Congress passed the FREEDMEN'S BUREAU Bill, the CIVIL RIGHTS ACT OF 1866, and the FOURTEENTH AMENDMENT. The intent of the Civil Rights Act was to define what freedom meant for the former slaves. The bill was designed, said one congressman, "to secure to a poor weak class of laborers the right to make contracts for their labor, the power to enforce the payment of wages, and the means of holding and enjoying the proceeds of their toil."

Though one of the requirements under President ANDREW JOHNSON's plan for Reconstruction was the ratification of the Thirteenth Amendment, he took a narrow view of it, arguing that the amendment only ended formal slavery. President Johnson also vetoed both the Freedmen's Bureau Bill and the Civil Rights Act and condemned the proposed Fourteenth Amendment. Congress overrode the vetoes, a first for major pieces of legislation in U.S. history, and the Fourteenth Amendment was ratified two years later. The political battles over the meaning of freedom marked a major change in federal Reconstruction policy, with Radical Republicans assuming control over Southern Reconstruction. In the ensuing years, the FIFTEENTH AMENDMENT was ratified, and Congress passed the CIVIL RIGHTS ACT OF 1875, both efforts giving meaning to the Thirteenth Amendment.

Further reading: Harold M. Hyman and William M. Wiecek, *Equal Justice under Law: Constitutional Development, 1835–1875* (New York: Harper & Row, 1982); Michael Vorenberg, *Final Freedom: The Civil War, the Abolition of Slavery, and the Thirteenth Amendment* (New York: Cambridge University Press, 2001).

—Justin J. Behrend

Thomas, George H. (1816–1870)

A CIVIL WAR general nicknamed "the Rock of Chickamauga" for his valiant performance in that battle, George Henry Thomas was born on July 31, 1816, in Southampton County, Virginia. After graduating from the UNITED STATES MILITARY ACADEMY AT WEST POINT in 1840, Thomas served in the Mexican-American War of 1846 and later was appointed an artillery and cavalry instructor at his old school. When the war broke out Thomas was on military duty in Texas. Unlike most other Virginia-born West Pointers, Thomas remained with the Union. Throughout the war, however, questions of loyalty would cast a shadow on his career. Nonetheless, he was promoted to brigadier general of Volunteers in 1861. He saw early action in Virginia's Shenandoah Valley and in Kentucky, where he was made the commander of the First Division, Army of the Ohio.

Thomas led his division, and then corps, through several notable battles in the western theater in 1862 and 1863, including Shiloh, Corinth, Perryville, Murfreesboro, Tullahoma, Chickamauga, and Chattanooga. His leadership in battle was slow, careful, deliberate, and unusually effective. Thomas possessed a modest personality that made him one of the more underrated generals of the war. Maj. Gen. Thomas was offered, but refused, the command of the Army of the Ohio, believing that his friend Don Carlos Buell had more experience. After faithfully serving Buell, Thomas was transferred to the Army of the Cumberland under WILLIAM S. ROSECRANS. Thomas's outstanding defense in the BATTLE OF CHICKAMAUGA, Georgia, literally saved the UNION ARMY from certain destruction and allowed an orderly retreat back to Tennessee.

After Rosecrans was relieved of command, Thomas was appointed to head the Army of the Cumberland. He led his army to victory at Missionary Ridge at the BATTLE OF CHATTANOOGA in November 1863 and accompanied Gen. WILLIAM T. SHERMAN in the ATLANTA CAMPAIGN. In May 1864, Thomas's army fought at Kennesaw Mountain and Peachtree Creek. While Sherman marched through Georgia, Thomas was sent to defend Nashville, Tennessee, against the threat of JOHN BELL HOOD's army. In the two Battles of Franklin and Nashville in December 1864, Thomas smashed the Confederates, earning the grateful thanks of President ABRAHAM LINCOLN and the nation.

Thomas remained with the regular army after the war, and when he died in San Francisco on March 28, 1870, he was the commander of the Military Division of the Pacific.

See also CORINTH, BATTLE OF; MURFREESBORO, BATTLE OF; SHILOH, BATTLE OF.

Further reading: Francis F. McKinney, *Education and Violence: The Life of George H. Thomas and the History of the Army of the Cumberland* (Chicago: Abraham Lincoln Book Shop/American House, 1997).

Tourgée, Albion W. (1838–1905)

As a lawyer, a RECONSTRUCTION-era federal judge, a Republican activist, and a novelist, Albion Winegar Tourgée was one of the foremost champions of African-American civil rights in the 19th century. Tourgée was born in Williamsfield, Ohio, and was trained as a lawyer at the University of Rochester. During the CIVIL WAR he served as a Union officer, spending six months in a Confederate prison. Tourgée moved to Greensboro, North Carolina, following the war, and there he became active in REPUBLICAN PARTY politics and embarked on a career as a novelist.

As a judge of the North Carolina state superior court in the early 1870s, Tourgée became particularly outraged by the KU KLUX KLAN attacks against former slaves. In an 1870

letter to the *New York Times,* Tourgée described in detail Klan brutality over the previous 10 months: "four thousand or five thousand houses broken open. . . . Seven or eight hundred persons beaten or otherwise maltreated." The Republican Party, Tourgée concluded, was simply unwilling to act. "The government sleeps," Tourgée told the *Times;* "I am ashamed of a party which . . . has not the nerve or decision enough" to defend former slaves. Tourgée's novels written during this period reflected his disillusionment and bitterness. In *A Fool's Errand* (1879), Tourgée acidly recalled his own career as a North Carolina judge. In *Invisible Empire* (1880), Tourgée damned the "prejudice-blinded multitudes who made the Policy of Repression effectual."

During the 1890s Tourgée's activism intensified as Southern segregation hardened. In 1891 Tourgée helped establish the National Citizens Rights Association, devoted to securing civil rights and banning racially motivated lynchings. In 1896 he appeared before the Supreme Court on behalf of Homer J. Plessy in the landmark case *Plessy v. Ferguson.* Because the Constitution is color-blind, Tourgée argued, racial segregation is unconstitutional. The 8-1 majority rejected Tourgée's argument, although in 1954 a unanimous court would affirm it in *Brown v. Topeka Board of Education.*

In the years after the *Plessy* decision, Theodore Roosevelt appointed Tourgée to several European diplomatic posts. At the last of these postings, in France, Tourgée died in 1905.

Further reading: Otto H. Olsen, *Carpetbagger's Crusade: The Life of Albion Winegar Tourgée* (Baltimore, Md.: Johns Hopkins University Press, 1965); Albion Winegar Tourgée, *A Fool's Errand,* ed. John Hope Franklin (Cambridge, Mass.: Belknap Press of Harvard University Press, 1961).

—Tom Laichas

transportation

The 19th century saw a revolution in transportation. From road building to railroad building, from canal to steamboat construction, new thoroughfares and vehicle forms affected all Americans. The financing of roadways became one of the earliest issues of conflict between the federal and state governments. Sectional politics played a role in whether or not an area would have a federal or state built roadway. In most cases the federal government stepped in when a planned road crossed state lines. Such was the case of the National Road started in Virginia in 1808. When it was completed, this road, built through the Cumberland Gap in the Appalachian Mountains, eventually reached as far west as Illinois.

The National Road became a major route that settlers followed from the East Coast states to new western settlements. The solidity of the road, built from gravel on a stone base, allowed users a better chance at good road conditions. Other commonly used, but not constructed, roads were often muddy and impassable. Many states constructed roadways during the first half of the 19th century following older transportation routes and new paths leading from market to marketplace or from the site of raw materials to the site of production.

The booming ECONOMY of the United States also encouraged the building of canals. In 1816 President James Madison called for the federal government to sponsor a network of canals linked to a network of roads. He believed that economic growth would follow such a transportation web. New York governor DeWitt Clinton jumped on the idea when he proposed the construction of America's famous Erie Canal. In 1825, after years of backbreaking work, largely by Irish immigrants, New York's state-long canal opened. The waterway stretched 364 miles and connected NEW YORK CITY with the Great Lakes region. A technological masterpiece, the Erie Canal shifted the eyes of New York merchants away from European markets and toward the interior of the United States.

The ties created between the Northeast and Midwest also marked a shift in the focus of transportation routes. As did the National Road, the Erie Canal moved goods and people westward rather than to the south. This directional change differed from the previous North-South routes that had driven American communication and market patterns. This shift had lasting implications for national politics, local economies, and future settlement. The Southern areas of the United States became more isolated from the economically powerful Northern manufacturing centers. More importantly, the lack of transportation infrastructures hurt the Confederacy during the CIVIL WAR.

Especially used on the western rivers, steamboats revolutionized water transportation during the antebellum period. Robert Fulton first demonstrated the capabilities of steamboat travel in 1807. By the 1830s the city of Cincinnati, Ohio, had grown to be the leading builder of new steamboats, which enabled people and goods to be easily transported both up- and downriver. Prior to the invention of steam power, boats had traveled downriver with the current, but they did not return against it. Oftentimes sailors sold their boats for scrap at their final port and returned upriver on land. After 1807, though, transportation on the Ohio, Missouri, and MISSISSIPPI RIVERS became a two-way process. People moved goods north as well as south. River cities grew in economic and political importance as more and more money, goods, and people moved through them on a regular basis. Besides Cincinnati and already established New Orleans, St. Louis

became an influential and bustling hub in America's transportation system.

Steamboats drastically changed the landscape of the American river. Besides their use as vehicles, the boats shattered the quiet of the areas they passed and polluted the air of ports with their exhaust. Because of the unpredictable nature of steam and the relative youth of the technology, many deadly and expensive accidents regularly occurred. Such accidents, along with the widespread and dangerous practice of racing, moved the government to create some of its first federal transportation regulations. Congress passed the Steamboat Act in 1838 and strengthened it in 1852. The act established guidelines for the construction and maintenance of the riverboats in order to prevent accidents and the loss of life and property.

In response to the growth of water travel and encouraged by the successes they saw in Britain, American entrepreneurs began building RAILROADS during the first half of the 19th century. Cities such as Baltimore, Maryland, saw the possibility to compete with New York by constructing a railroad. Such a transportation system would not be affected by the same bad-weather problems as canals. Builders of the Baltimore and Ohio (B&O) railroad hoped that merchants would choose to move goods by rail, especially in the winter when alternative canals froze over. People also quickly realized the speed with which new railroads could transport passengers and goods to new markets. In spite of kinks in the system, such as nonmatching rail gauge, railroads quickly spread across the eastern (and especially northeastern) portion of the United States.

In 1862 Congress chartered a federal corporation to build a transcontinental railroad. The congressional act created the Union Pacific and Central Pacific Railways to begin construction of a railroad connecting the eastern portion of the United States with the Pacific coast. Both companies built their railroads on lands given to them by the federal government. On May 10, 1869, the two lines met at Promontory Point, Utah. Mostly Chinese immigrant men had labored from Sacramento, California, across the Sierra Nevada mountain range to build 689 miles of the Central Pacific Railroad. In Utah they met the end of 1,086 miles of the Union Pacific Railroad, which Irish immigrants, newly freed African Americans, and Civil War VETERANS had labored to build.

This new transportation route ushered in large-scale migration to the West. Whereas prior roads and routes had followed settlement, the shear magnitude and power of the railroad preceded and even predetermined settlement patterns. Because the federal government gave chartered railroad companies lands along their railways, those companies in turn sponsored migration to western lands. The enormous amount of capital needed to build and maintain a railroad also caused the political and economic growth of the West. As a form of transportation, railroads not only moved passengers and goods but also the power center of the United States. Along with shifting political power to the West, the railroad industry strengthened connections between industry and the federal government. Federal troops breaking up the Great Strike of 1877 highlighted this partnership.

Besides a revolution in national transportation patterns, the 19th century also saw a change in local transportation. Urban center such as San Francisco, Chicago, and New Orleans developed systems of cable and streetcars in the 1870s and 1880s. These urban transportation networks moved a growing number of people involved in emerging industrial and service jobs. In 1897 the nation's first subway system opened in Boston, a mere five years before New York's immense underground route started. Transportation in the 1900s followed, created, and spurred social, economic, and political changes.

See also PACIFIC RAILROAD ACT.

Further reading: David Haward Bain, *Empire Express: Building the First Transcontinental Railroad* (New York: Viking, 1999); George Rogers Taylor, *The Transportation Revolution, 1815–1860* (New York: Harper Torchbooks, 1968).

—Samantha Holtkamp Gervase

Tredegar Iron Works

Tredegar Iron Works, located in RICHMOND, Virginia, was the only first-class iron foundry and rolling mill in the Confederacy at the outbreak of the CIVIL WAR. The only manufacturing plant in the South capable of producing iron plating, heavy artillery, and major ordnance, it played a critical role in providing the materiel needed for the Confederate war effort, especially in the early years of the war.

Tredegar was founded in 1837 by Francis B. Deane, who was a poor administrator. Within a decade, ownership of the plant had passed to the hands of West Point graduate Joseph Reid Anderson, who proved to be a more able manager than Deane, and by 1850 Tredegar was thriving. When the Civil War broke out, Anderson immediately ceased doing business with his Northern customers, and he offered to lease the plant to the Confederate government. The Davis administration refused and instead signed several long-term contracts for Tredegar's services. For the first two years of the war, Tredegar supplied a substantial portion of the Confederacy's large guns and major ordnance. The iron plating used on the first of the Confederacy's IRONCLADS, the *Virginia*, was created at Tredegar. The plant also worked on experimental projects, including torpedoes and a submarine.

As the war went on, Tredegar was beset by a series of problems. The raw materials that the plant needed were in short supply, even at the outset of the war. The problem became much worse as the Confederate government opened its own iron foundries in other parts of the South. As a result, Tredegar rarely operated at anything more than one-third of its capacity after 1861. The plant also suffered from cash-flow problems, as payment for services was often late or not received at all. In fact, to keep afloat financially, Anderson was compelled to engage in blockade running. Labor shortages also had a negative impact on Tredegar's operations, as an increasingly large portion of the plant's labor force was compelled take up arms for the Confederacy. By the end of the war, Tredegar had lost its reputation for quality, and Confederate chief of ordnance JOSIAH GORGAS openly complained of his dissatisfaction with the work being done there.

Once the war was over, Anderson moved quickly to keep Tredegar in business. He reestablished his contacts in the North, and he met privately with President ANDREW JOHNSON to arrange a pardon for himself and his partners. Tredegar's time as a dominant player in Southern industry was over, however. Steel was becoming America's metal of choice, and Tredegar did not have the money to convert its equipment to steel production, particularly after taking a huge financial loss during the Panic of 1873. Tredegar scaled back its operations, finally closing its doors in 1958.

Further reading: Kathleen Bruce, *Virginia Iron Manufacture in the Slave Era* (New York: A. M. Kelley, 1968); Charles B. Dew, *Ironmaker to the Confederacy: Joseph R. Anderson and the Tredegar Iron Works* (New Haven, Conn.: Yale University Press, 1966).

—Christopher Bates

Truth, Sojourner (ca. 1797–1883)

Feminist, lecturer, and religious mystic Sojourner Truth was born a slave in Ulster County, New York, around 1797. Her birth name was Isabella Baumfree, and she was the 11th of her parents' 12 children. She never knew most of her siblings, who had been sold and scattered. As a young woman, Isabella entered into a respectful but not loving marriage with another slave, Thomas, and bore five children, two of whom were sold away from her.

In 1826, a year before the state of New York outlawed SLAVERY, Isabella fled her owner and lived as a domestic in the home of the devout Van Wegenen family, taking their name. Here, Isabella embarked on her own mystical and religious journey following an epiphany in which Jesus revealed himself to her. Shortly thereafter, she left for NEW YORK CITY, although her children remained behind, indentured by law. Isabella took up residence with Elijah Pierson and his wife Sarah, evangelists committed to saving prostitutes. Around 1833, Isabella and the Piersons joined a fringe religious group called Kingdom of Matthias, run by a fanatic named Robert Matthews. The sect lived communally near Ossining, New York, until it disbanded two or three years later following unfounded accusations of murder in the death of Pierson.

After the dissolution of the Matthias sect, Isabella returned to New York and worked as a domestic. In 1843, unable to ignore her religious calling, she traveled east on foot to Long Island and Connecticut. Renaming herself Sojourner Truth, she preached her own doctrine of love, brotherhood, and temperance to anyone who would listen. Isabella was a powerful and, at six feet tall, imposing speaker.

In the fall of 1843, Truth landed in Northampton, Massachusetts, and found a place in a utopian commune dedicated to ABOLITION and women's rights, causes she adopted as her life's work. While there she met abolitionists WILLIAM LLOYD GARRISON and FREDERICK DOUGLASS and became acquainted with feminist Olive Gilbert. Gilbert was inspired by Truth's story and was well aware of the passions it would generate among antislavery advocates. Because Truth was illiterate, Gilbert decided to write Truth's biography herself, and *The Narrative of Sojourner Truth* was published in 1850. The book covers Truth's early life in slavery and the triumph of her religious beliefs over her bondage. A publishing success, the book made Truth nationally famous.

In 1851 Sojourner Truth attended the Akron, Ohio, women's convention. In a powerful address to the convention, Truth argued that women were the equals of men. Baring her muscular shoulder for convention members to see, she said:

> I have ploughed, and planted, and gathered into barns, and no man could head me! And a'n't I a woman? I could work as much and eat as much as a man—when I could get it—and bear de lash as well! And a'n't I a woman? I have borne thirteen children, and seen 'em mos' all sold off to slavery, and when I cried out with my mother's grief, none but Jesus heard me! And a'n't I a woman?

Truth believed that her oppression stemmed as much from her gender as from her race. Thus, to her way of thinking, both obstacles had to be overcome in order for African-American women to achieve freedom.

Truth's speech was very well received in many circles, particularly among feminists. Her fame established, Truth traveled widely, astonishing and electrifying audiences,

Sojourner Truth *(Library of Congress)*

singing, preaching, and advocating equality: "We'll have our rights, see if we don't; and you can't stop us from them; see if you can." In 1863 a pair of highly flattering essays by Frances Dana Gage and HARRIET BEECHER STOWE were published, and they transformed Truth into a monumental, almost mythical persona.

During the CIVIL WAR, Truth raised money for volunteer AFRICAN-AMERICAN REGIMENTS. She frequently visited army camps in the North, earning money through lecturing and selling her autobiography. In 1864 ABRAHAM LINCOLN received Truth as a visitor at the White House. She remained in WASHINGTON, D.C., for a year, joining the National Freedmen's Relief Association to counsel newly freed people. She was also involved in a well-publicized lawsuit against a conductor who manhandled and injured her while throwing her off a streetcar.

After the war was over, Truth was active in finding jobs for individuals who had been displaced by the war. She advocated a plan of voluntary relocation of freedmen to Kansas to work their own farms on land provided by the government, but the plan came to nothing. She also opposed the FIFTEENTH AMENDMENT granting freedmen the vote on the grounds that it excluded women. In 1875 Truth moved to a commune among spiritualist Quakers (SOCIETY OF FRIENDS) outside of Battle Creek, Michigan. She remained there for the rest of her life, dying on November 26, 1883.

Further reading: Olive Gilbert, *Narrative of Sojourner Truth: A Bondswoman of Olden Time* (1850; reprint, Grand Rapids, Mich.: Candace Press, 1996); Nell Irvin Painter, *Sojourner Truth: A Life, A Symbol* (New York: Norton, 1996).

—Rebecca Dresser

Tubman, Harriet (ca. 1821–1913)

Liberator of slaves, spy, commando, nurse, and activist, Harriet Tubman was born a slave on a PLANTATION in Dorchester County, Maryland, around 1821. Tubman was one of Benjamin Ross and Harriet Greene's 11 children. Named Araminta at birth, Harriet worked as a domestic servant, but her housework did not satisfy her owners, who often complained about her. At the age of 13, Harriet was struck in the head with a heavy object by the plantation overseer and suffered a fractured skull. As a result of this injury, she suffered from periodic seizures for the rest of her life.

In 1844 Harriet married a free black man named John Tubman. Soon after, she learned that the financial troubles of her white owners might mean that members of her family would be forcibly separated. Tubman responded by fleeing bondage for Philadelphia, a Quaker (SOCIETY OF FRIENDS) stronghold where ABOLITIONists were often willing to help escaped slaves. John Tubman did not join Harriet in Philadelphia, nor did he help her to rescue her family, which she did in stages over the next few years. Within two years of her flight, Maryland plantation owners were offering $40,000 for her capture. In the next 10 years, Tubman helped almost 300 slaves reach freedom in the North, using the UNDERGROUND RAILROAD. John Tubman remarried and remained in Maryland.

When the CIVIL WAR began, Tubman committed herself to assist the Union effort. She believed strongly in both the value of a Union victory and the destruction of SLAVERY. Beginning in 1862, she traveled to various Southern states, including South Carolina, to spy and scout for the Union. Her work was made easier by a travel pass that Maj. Gen. David Hunter, commander of the Department of the South, provided for her. Harriet's experience with slavery and her efforts to free enslaved people during the prewar period made her an ideal envoy to plantation slaves, who welcomed her and gave her shelter and supplies. At times,

Harriet Tubman *(Hulton/Archive)*

Tubman served as a nurse for freedmen who had fled North.

Following the war, Tubman continued her activism for the freedpeople while caring for her elderly parents and a number of orphans. Her Harriet Tubman Home for Indigent Aged Negroes was founded in the postwar period and continued after her death. In spite of Tubman's ceaseless efforts for the Union, it took her nearly three decades of struggle to obtain a pension of $20 a month. This was the same amount given to most Civil War army NURSES, but it did nothing to recognize her many other wartime activities.

Tubman remained active in politics after the war as well. She was a dedicated supporter of African-American EDUCATION and suffrage, promoting the establishment of freedpeople's schools in the South and attending many suffrage and equal-rights meetings. In addition, she helped to establish the AFRICAN METHODIST EPISCOPAL CHURCH in upstate New York. It was not until 1869 that Tubman was recognized publicly for her work. In that year, Sarah Bradford published *Harriet Tubman, The Moses of Her People.* Also in that year, Tubman married Nelson Davis, a Civil War VETERAN.

In March 1913 Tubman contracted pneumonia, which eventually caused her death. A memorial plaque in her honor was dedicated by Booker T. Washington in the town of Auburn, New York.

Further reading: Sarah H. Bradford, *Harriet Tubman, The Moses of Her People* (1869; reprint, Bedford, Ind.: Applewood Books, 1993); Earl Conrad, *General Harriet Tubman* (Washington, D.C.: Associated Publishers, 1990).

—Megan Quinn

U

Underground Railroad

The Underground Railroad is the name that was given in the decades prior to the CIVIL WAR to a clandestine operation in which runaway slaves were aided in their flights to freedom in Canada or the far northern reaches of the United States by ABOLITIONISTs. The term *Underground Railroad* can be traced to about 1830, when a slaveholder traveling through Ohio with his slaves saw them all escape their bondage and complained that one of them had "gone off on an underground road." There had been efforts by the Quakers and others to help slaves escape as early as the 18th century. However, it was not until the 1830s, when abolitionism began to grow in strength, that the Underground Railroad, so named because it borrowed its operating terms, such as *lines, conductors, stations,* and *freight,* from RAILROADS, began to help fleeing slaves escape in growing numbers. Southern slaveholders became convinced that the Underground Railroad, which was also referred to as "the Liberty Line," was an elaborate and well-crafted system that robbed them of their property; they, in fact, may have exaggerated its size and sophistication out of fear and frustration at their slaves running away on their own with little or no aid from abolitionists.

The number of slaves who did find their freedom by heading north out of SLAVERY is impossible to determine with any real accuracy. Estimates range from about 40,000 to near 100,000. It is possible, however, that the actual figures are much lower. The legend of an Underground Railroad was established during the postwar years by those seeking to associate themselves with the heroic struggle against slavery. Some Northerners wrote and spoke of the Underground Railroad as if it were a highly organized system of aiding fugitive slaves. The reality was less impressive. The help that slaves did receive from well-meaning abolitionists and others often came near the end of the former's journey, when the greatest danger had already passed. The success of the Underground Railroad, such as it was, was often largely the result of the daring and bravery of individual slaves. A slave, or a small group of slaves (usually, but not always, men, for women often were responsible for small children with whom travel under the circumstances would have been extraordinarily difficult), would escape from the PLANTATION on which they lived and hide out in nearby woods or swamps until it was safe to proceed toward the North. Once they crossed the Ohio River or some other major divide between North and South and passed into a free state, members of the Underground Railroad would meet up with them. In the southern parts of Delaware, Pennsylvania, Ohio, and Indiana, there was an informal network that did help bring runaway slaves to freedom. Runaways would hide in the homes of the abolitionists, in attics, or in barns, and, on occasion, if they were men, dress as women to avoid detection. Many of the conductors on the railroad were free African Americans who often acted without much assistance from their white counterparts in the movement. Among the most prominent were Josiah Henson, Robert Purvis, William Still, and, the most well known of all, HARRIET TUBMAN. Some of these African Americans, including Tubman, had themselves escaped from slavery and willingly put themselves in harm's way in trying to free others. Many of the leading white abolitionists were members of the SOCIETY OF FRIENDS, or Quakers, who had a long history of being involved in antislavery causes. Most slaves who did escape their bondage were from the states of the Upper South; it was much more difficult for enslaved people living in the Deep South to make their way through slave states and get to freedom.

One reason for these elaborate efforts by abolitionists is that the Constitution and then the 1793 Fugitive Slave Law gave slaveholders the right to cross state lines in pursuit of their slaves, and once they had apprehended them, to bring them before either a local, state, or federal judge. During these proceedings, persons charged with being runaway slaves had no rights, as they were denied a jury trial and the chance to speak on their own behalf. To make matters worse for African Americans, slave catchers sometimes grabbed free blacks and dragged them into court as runaway slaves. In response to what many in the North considered outrageous abuses, several states passed personal liberty laws, which allowed those accused of being runaway or fugitive slaves their rights and also made it a crime to kidnap African Americans and try to force them into slavery. During the negotiations over what became the COMPROMISE OF 1850, Northern Senators unsuccessfully tried to get protection for the rights of runaway slaves written into the bill. One of the bills that comprised the omnibus measure of 1850 was a fugitive slave law, one which appeased southern interests. It did so by giving United States marshals the authority to deputize any citizen needed to capture a slave and mandating significant sentences for anyone found guilty of harboring a runaway slave, among other provisions. And since it did not contain a statute of limitations, African Americans who had been in some cases free for decades suddenly found themselves forced back into slavery. All of this political activity spurred on those who worked along the Underground Railroad.

It may be that the Underground Railroad's greatest legacy was in giving hope to enslaved persons who heard of its successes, as well as causing anxiety to slaveholders who feared that their property might escape via the Liberty Line. Although it may be that the Underground Railroad belongs to legend as well as to history, its existence in the decades prior to the Civil War demonstrates the rising determination of the enslaved to be free and the courage of those who helped them along the way.

Further reading: Henrietta Buckmaster, *Let Me People Go: The Story of the Underground Railroad and the Growth of the Abolition Movement* (New York: Harper & Bros., 1941); Larry Gara, *The Liberty Line: The Legend of the Underground Railroad* (Kingsport, Tenn.: Kingsport Press, 1961).

—Jason K. Duncan

uniforms

The purpose of uniforms is to be able to identify military personnel from civilians, to distinguish one army from another, and to promote group solidarity. In 1861 variety was the rule on both sides. By 1863 the Union and Confederate armies required a "standard" uniform for soldiers.

Their families, local communities, or states provided early Union and Confederate volunteer regiments with uniforms. This ensured that every unit had a slightly different look and quality of dress. Moreover, many regiments wore colorful costumes, following in the tradition of the "Zouave" French units who fought in Algeria. Some famous regiments who wore the outlandish uniforms were the

Portrait of a Confederate soldier *(Library of Congress)*

164th New York, the 114th Pennsylvania, and Coppen's Louisiana ZOUAVES. Although blue was the official color of the Union soldier, many units decided that they preferred the "cadet gray," the color of the student's uniform at the UNITED STATES ACADEMY AT WEST POINT, which was also adopted by the Confederate government for its armies. Similarly, many Southern soldiers took to wearing blue trousers. The FIRST BATTLE OF BULL RUN in July 1861 resulted in confusion, chaos, and tragedy when both Billy Yank and Johnny Reb wore blue *and* gray, and both had similarly outfitted Zouave units in the battle. Afterward, the respective governments struggled mightily to provide their soldiers with standardized uniforms that could be easily differentiated in battle. The Union succeeded in this task; the Confederacy failed miserably.

A top priority for the U.S. War Department was providing an efficient and cost-effective means of clothing the soldiers in the field. Overwhelmed by the demand at first, the War Department gave contracts to clothing suppliers who, seeking to make huge profits at the expense of the government, delivered uniforms of such poor quality that they fell apart almost immediately. *Shoddy*, was the name given to the clothes that were made out of scraps of shredded wool. One Northern reporter observed: "Soldiers, on the first day's march or in the earliest storm, found their clothes, overcoats, and blankets, scattering to the wind in rags, or dissolving into their primitive elements of dust under the pelting rain." Outraged parents demanded immediate reform. A change of leadership in the War Department and congressional oversight brought an end to most corrupt practices by regularizing the awarding of contracts. The Northern textile (especially wool) and shoe industry flourished during the wartime years, working at full capacity.

By 1863 all federal troops were adhering to the *Regulations for the Uniform and Dress of the Army of the United States*. The standard uniform for the infantry was a dark blue frock coat, a shorter "sack" coat, a muslin or wool shirt, wool socks, and light blue trousers. Soldiers were issued a tall black hat with a wide brim called a "Hardee hat" after Maj. William J. Hardee. Most, however, preferred the softer, smaller, forage cap (called the "kepi," a French word for cap) on the march. For their feet, Union men wore sturdy shoes called brogans (a Gaelic term for shoe). These simple clothes, together with the haversack, knapsack, canteen, blanket, tent, cartridge box, belt, bayonet, and musket made up the typical soldier's kit for war. Colored piping sewn on uniforms indicated branch of service: red for artillery, yellow for cavalry, and dark blue for infantry. Distinctions of rank were highly elaborated by decoration on coats and hats. Even after 1863 there was a wide variety in dress. Union soldiers in the western theater, for example, liked to wear informal slouch hats with wide brims to keep the sun out of their faces. To the end of the war, the Scottish-born men of the 79th New York Infantry, also known as the "Highlanders," insisted on wearing their kilts for formal marches!

Article 47 of the *Regulations for the Army of the Confederate States* listed the uniform of the Southern soldier: a gray double-breasted frock coat, a muslin or wool shirt, dark blue trousers, brogans, and a kepi cap or slouch hat. Like their Union counterparts, Confederates wore a more informal coat, called a "shell" jacket for its lightweight quality. Facing on coats and jackets indicated branch of service: red for artillery, yellow for cavalry, and light blue for infantry. Various buttons and insignia identified officers, noncommissioned officers, and enlisted men. For example, generals, lieutenant generals, major generals, and brigadier generals wore three gold stars on the collars of their frock coats. Although in theory the uniforms and equipment of the Confederate armed forces—army, navy, and marines— closely resembled those of the United States, in reality the difference was great because of the tremendous problem with supply in the Southern nation.

The Confederate national government strove to provide their armies with clothing, food, and arms. A largely rural and decentralized ECONOMY, however, could not be transformed overnight to meet the huge demands of wartime. Still, by 1863 factories in North Carolina, Tennessee, and Virginia were churning out clothes that were of varying quality or just downright inferior. Sometimes, the wrong dyes were used in the cloth, and the uniforms could be gray, blue, or brown. Many, if not most, COMMON SOLDIERS by the middle of the war depended on their families to send them HOMESPUN clothes, often with the distinctive butternut yellow-brown coloring—hence one of the nicknames for Confederates became "butternuts."

By 1863 Union control of huge amounts of Confederate territory created severe shortages of supplies and hampered distribution. Often, Confederates had no shoes, and their uniforms were in tatters. One soldier wrote: "I have no seat in my pants, the legs are worn out, have had but one pair of socks which are worn out completely, my shirt is literally rolled off me." By the end of the CIVIL WAR, Union soldiers were the best clothed, fed, and shod in the world.

Portrait of a Union soldier *(Library of Congress)*

Confederate soldiers, on the other hand, suffered from all kinds of privations, including the lack of a decent set of clothes.

Further reading: Ron Field and Robin Smith, *Uniforms of the Civil War: An Illustrated Guide for Historians, Collectors, and Reenactors* (Guilford, N.C.: The Lyons Press, 2001).

Union army

The Union army comprised the U.S. Army of full-time, "professional" soldiers and, quite literally, an army of volunteers. Through the course of the CIVIL WAR, those volunteers were largely CITIZEN-SOLDIERS who fought not only the most costly but the bloodiest war in U.S. history. The Civil War's victorious army, after a bumpy start, became the largest and best supplied military force the world had ever witnessed. By May 1865 the soldiers in the Union army numbered more than 1 million and the total count of men who served three-year enlistments was more than 2.3 million. Most importantly, the Union army was responsible for reuniting the nation and liberating 4 million slaves.

Creating and sustaining a formidable army to oppose Southern rebellion was initially very difficult. The North, like the South, was totally unprepared to train and supply the large number of men needed to fight what quickly became a total war. In early 1861, the regular army (the U.S. Army) consisted of only 15,259 enlisted men and 1,000 officers. After FORT SUMTER, President ABRAHAM LINCOLN called for 75,000 militia volunteers to serve for three months. Northern GOVERNORS offered 300,000 more troops and were responsible for providing equipment and UNIFORMS.

In May 1861, without explicit authority from Congress (which was not in session until July), Lincoln increased the size of the regular army to just over 22,000 soldiers. At the same time, Lincoln called for 42,000 three-year volunteers. Lincoln believed his position as commander in chief allowed for his actions without congressional approval. In July 1861, Congress affirmed Lincoln's extralegal decisions and authorized a VOLUNTEER ARMY of 500,000 men. Congress also called for 300,000 more men for three-year terms. As the war progressed, volunteering declined dramatically. Though the North had a large population advantage over the South (18,936,579 to 5,447,646, with 4,559,782 versus 1,064,193 of draft age), the terrible costs of the war made young men reluctant to join the army. Losses through battlefield casualties, DESERTION, illness, and expiration of enlistment made it imperative to continuously add more soldiers. Congress issued another call for 300,000 volunteers in July 1862. The low response led to the BOUNTY SYSTEM, which offered cash inducements to enlist.

By the spring of 1863, the Union army was in need of still more men. On March 3, Congress passed the Enrollment Act calling for the first forced CONSCRIPTION in U.S. history. By its terms, states were required to fill a certain quota of troops based on population and previous enlistment numbers. Any state failing to fill its quota would be subject to a draft. The Enrollment Act also contained a provision that allowed a person to hire a substitute or pay $300 to avoid service. More than 125,000 men took advantage of this. These exclusions reinforced the deep-rooted but erroneous notion among the immigrant working class that the Civil War was a "rich man's war and a poor man's fight." Resentment exploded into the NEW YORK CITY DRAFT RIOTS in 1863. After several days of rioting, Union combat troops were brought in from Gettysburg to put an end to the chaos.

Ultimately, draftees were not an especially important part of the Union army. Fewer than 1 man in 10 was a draftee, and beyond that, draftees tended to be poor soldiers. This is not to say that the draft was not important to the Union army, however. At the same time that Congress created the draft, it also established a series of incentives, mostly cash bonuses, in exchange for voluntary enlistment. Any soldier who was drafted forfeited these bonuses, while also carrying the stigma of being a draftee. It is impossible to say how many soldiers entered the ranks voluntarily in order to collect their enlistment bounty and avoid being drafted, but certainly their number was substantial.

The Union army, like its Southern counterpart, was divided into three parts: infantry, cavalry, and artillery, with by far the largest numbers in the infantry. In 1861 the cavalry and artillery forces were attached to infantry. By the end of the Civil War, in raw numbers, the North had raised 2,040 regiments, of which 1,696 were infantry, 272 cavalry, and 72 artillery. The Union army totaled more than 1 million men under arms, while the CONFEDERATE ARMY mustered out about 180,000 men in uniform. This overwhelming advantage of manpower played a role in helping the Union to win the war. However, the three-pronged structure with both the artillery and cavalry forces attached to infantry units did not allow for the most efficient use of the large number of federal recruits early in the war effort. Especially troublesome was the fact that this structure often did not allow concentration of cavalry and artillery where it was most needed. In 1862 the army converted a number of cavalry regiments into three formal mounted brigades. By 1863, a cavalry corps was finally formed, consisting of about 12,000 mounted men. The new arrangement helped the Union cavalry compete better in battle against their Confederate counterparts. In that same year, artillery batteries were placed under direct control of corps commanders. This change gave army commanders more flexibility and less administrative work in carrying out tactical plans.

At first, the federal government had difficulty finding competent officers. Of the officers trained at the UNITED STATES MILITARY ACADEMY AT WEST POINT, one-third resigned to fight for the Confederacy. In addition, seven of the nation's eight military colleges were located in the South, providing even more trained officers for the Confederate army. Also, political considerations were important in the appointment of officers. At the beginning of the war, Union soldiers, like their Confederate brethren, elected their officers. This disastrous practice was ended after 1862; nevertheless, politics continued to play an important role in appointment of generals, many with little military experience. By making these political appointments, Lincoln gained support for the war among key constituencies, particularly Democrats and certain ethnic groups.

Some political appointees did quite well. For instance, JOSHUA LAWRENCE CHAMBERLAIN of Maine and John Logan of Illinois built distinguished service records. The majority were not nearly as well regarded. Two generals from Massachusetts, BENJAMIN F. BUTLER and Nathaniel Banks, and California's John C. Frémont performed poorly in combat, costing many men their lives. Indeed, "political" generals performed so badly at the FIRST BATTLE OF BULL RUN in July 1861 that Congress was compelled to set up a watchdog group, the JOINT COMMITTEE ON THE CONDUCT OF THE WAR, which, among other things, established minimum qualifications for Union officers. Also, as the war went on, many of the Union's more incompetent officers were weeded out or resigned.

In the end, the formal structure of the Union command proved superior to that of the Confederacy and evolved into a modern, stafflike organization of hundreds of men, including a section of military intelligence operatives. Union officers took great risks during the Civil War. These men were 15 percent more likely to be killed in battle than an enlisted man. Generals had the highest risk for combat death; with a 50 percent greater chance of being killed than privates. Overall, Union soldiers were actually almost two and a half times more likely to die from disease than from combat during the war. Over the course of the war, the 2.5 million men who served in the Union army suffered 110,070 combat deaths and nearly 250,000 deaths due to DISEASE AND EPIDEMICS.

As Union leaders dealt with manpower issues, they also addressed the difficulties of supplying a force as large as the U.S. Army. At that time, an army of 100,000 men required 2,500 supply wagons, 35,000 animals, and an average of 120,000 pounds of supplies a day. The lack of army provisions early in the war forced states to make concerted efforts to provide troop provisions until the federal government could organize its Quartermaster Department and reimburse the states. This approach to provisioning the army led to a variety of problems in the first year. For example, Northern soldiers wore UNIFORMS of many different colors, which often made distinguishing friend from foe difficult. The resulting confusion ultimately led to the standardization of Union uniforms after the First Battle of Bull Run to light blue trousers and dark blue blouses.

There were many logistical issues to be resolved in order to keep Union troops provisioned. Secretary of War EDWIN M. STANTON did an excellent job of directing and planning the various elements of the conflict for the North. The Union Quartermaster Department, ably led by General Montgomery C. Meigs, worked with Stanton to supply the Federals in an effective and efficient fashion. Despite notable glitches, after 1863 the soldiers of the Union army enjoyed better food, TRANSPORTATION, clothing, arms, equipment, supplies, and health care than any other army up to that time.

Since volunteers formed the vast majority of the Union forces and came from local and state levels, regiments were named chronologically by state (for example, the First Pennsylvania Infantry Regiment was the first infantry regiment formed by the state of Pennsylvania). Some units were formed based on ethnicity; besides African-American troops, Scottish, Irish, and German units were also created. Training of these raw recruits first took place in designated camps in each state. The men were "mustered" into service with the U.S. volunteer army and began their lives as soldiers. Inexperienced officers, who often learned the elements of drilling by reading a military manual, emphasized regimental drill and moving from formation to fighting. Most volunteers, especially early in the war, hated the confines of camp life and were eager to get into the battle before the fighting was over. This anxiousness to get out of training camp and get into action before the "fun" was over was probably fostered by the training regime. Neither mock combat nor a meaningful amount of target practice took place. After the initial training period, the men would board trains or go on ships by regiments for transport to their assigned destinations. The Union army's basic organizational unit was the company (numbering 100 men), with 10 companies making up a regiment (1,000 men per regiment for infantry and 1,200 for cavalry), five regiments for a brigade, three brigades for a division, and three divisions for a corps. Several corps formed an army. The Union infantry (foot soldiers) forces consisted of 16 armies whose names were based on major rivers, such as the Army of the Potomac and the Army of the James in the eastern theater and the Army of the Tennessee, the Army of the Ohio, and the Army of the Cumberland in the western theater. Each army generally consisted of 35,000 to

Union troops about to fire a field gun during the Civil War *(Hulton/Archive)*

40,000 men, although the Army of the Potomac was much larger.

An army's numbers and organizational units fluctuated during the war. When a company became depleted due to illness, casualties, and desertions, new recruits were generally not brought in to fill spots beside veteran members, which ultimately diminished combat performance and increased casualties. Among the problems with adding new enlistees to battle-experienced units was the fact that existing regiments had built up through their service together an esprit de corps. Battle-hardened units frequently resented raw recruits, feeling that the "new guy" would threaten the efficiency of the unit. George Templeton Strong, in a LETTER home, went so far as to call new recruits "an undisciplined mob." There was always a question whether a new recruit could really be trusted in the heat of the fight to give his all—to die for his comrades. This was especially important late in the war, when the quality of enlistees was questionable, since bounties were

on the rise and "bounty jumping" (signing up, collecting the bounties, and then deserting only to sign up in another area to collect more bounties) became fairly common. On the political level, states preferred to build new companies and new regiments rather than fill gaps in existing units because there was more prestige in bringing more regiments to the Union effort, and each new regiment allowed the appointment of new officers, which was a convenient way to reward political colleagues. Generally then, new companies were formed with higher-ranking officers appointed by politicians. Thus, throughout the conflict, companies were usually at reduced strength. More companies were combined to make up regiments than army regulations specified. Therefore, some brigades consisted of up to 10 regiments, greatly complicating the logistics of army administration.

Because the government relied so heavily on civilian support (both in terms of political support and enlistments) for the war, public opinion and politics played a substantial role in determining Northern strategy. The key Union military strategy developed by Winfield Scott and refined and added to by GEORGE B. MCCLELLAN, ULYSSES S. GRANT, and others, can be summed up briefly in three slogans: the "Anaconda Plan," "On to RICHMOND," and "Total War." The first advocated encircling the Confederate coastline and rivers, thereby choking off its economic lifelines; the second called for moving quickly and decisively to defeat the Southern armies in the field and capture the Confederate capital; and the third employed the first two with the added goal of destroying the Confederate civilian will to fight.

McClellan's 1862 PENINSULAR CAMPAIGN, in part, was conceived of as a way to satisfy the Northern populace's demand for a strike against the heart of the Confederacy. When the Confederate army invaded Pennsylvania in 1863, Northern military leaders knew that fast action was necessary because Northern citizens would not abide by an invasion of their soil. The failure of the spring OVERLAND CAMPAIGN in Virginia drove Northern morale to new lows and placed Lincoln's reelection bid in jeopardy. In the fall of 1864, WILLIAM T. SHERMAN made haste to capture ATLANTA in time for the presidential ELECTIONS. Sherman's success undoubtedly clinched Lincoln's reelection.

Waging war in a democratic republic required the consent and support of the people through elections. Lincoln, as both president and commander in chief, had to lead the Union's war effort and explain and defend his policies to citizens. The political and military were thus closely connected in the Civil War. When the Union suffered severe battlefield losses, as it did during 1861 and 1862, drastic measures had to be taken to sustain the morale of the Northern people and achieve military aims.

One measure that heavily influenced the fate of the Union armies and the future of the United States was Lincoln's issuance of the EMANCIPATION PROCLAMATION on January 1, 1863. Although an earlier congressional act had allowed African Americans to join the Union army, the proclamation was Lincoln's first official endorsement of the idea and resulted in the formation of the United States Colored Troops (USCT). USCT forces totaled 178,975 by the end of the war and made up 12 percent of the U.S. Army. More than half of these soldiers were recruited in the South, so their addition to the Union army had the added benefit of draining the South of needed manpower. Indeed, in August 1863 Grant wrote Lincoln that the "freedom of Negroes is the largest blow to the Confederacy yet."

With the surrender of ROBERT E. LEE's Army of Northern Virginia in April 1865 at APPOMATTOX COURT HOUSE, the Civil War came to a close, but the Union still had a formidable army in the field. The peaceful demobilization of the Union army was accomplished in record time after Appomattox. Before the soldiers went home to their respective states, a huge celebration was held in WASHINGTON, D.C. For two days, May 23–24, 1865, the men of the Army of the Potomac and Sherman's western armies marched in the "Grand Review" down Pennsylvania Avenue to cheering crowds. Proud of their role in winning the war, freeing the slaves, and ensuring the continuance of the United States of America, Union army VETERANS after the war formed the Grand Army of the Republic, a powerful group that exerted considerable influence on the political and economic life of the reunited nation.

See also COMMON SOLDIER; HOMEFRONT; TACTICS AND STRATEGY.

Further reading: James W. Geary, *We Need Men: The Union Draft in the Civil War* (Dekalb: Northern Illinois University Press, 1991); Herman Hattaway and Archer Jones, *How the North Won: A Military History of the Civil War* (Urbana: University of Illinois Press, 1983); Fred A. Shannon, *The Organization and Administration of the Union Army, 1861–1865* (Cleveland: Arthur H. Clark Co., 1928); Bell Irvin Wiley, *The Life of Billy Yank: The Common Soldier of the Union* (Baton Rouge: Louisiana State University Press, 1978).

—Scott L. Stabler

Union League

The Union League was a REPUBLICAN PARTY membership organization that originated in the border states of the North in 1862 to promote patriotism in support of the Northern cause. Based on the model of fraternal organizations so common in 19th-century America, over the course of the war the league spread to many areas in the North and moved South with Northern soldiers and found support among freedmen, freedwomen, and white yeoman farmers who were dissatisfied with the Confederacy. Later in RECONSTRUCTION the League was significant for its part in organizing African-American political action.

In the North, the league bolstered sagging enthusiasm for the war effort. Many prominent citizens joined branches in cities like New York, Boston, and Philadelphia. In Midwestern states like Illinois the Union League movement stood strongly against rising COPPERHEAD sentiment in 1862 and 1863. For example, the St. Louis branch of the league resisted any attempts to bring Missouri into the Confederate column. Like one of its apolitical counterparts, the Free Masons, the league offered many social benefits. The men who belonged were known for their undying devotion to the Union cause. The Union League played an important role in mobilizing support for President ABRAHAM LINCOLN's reelection bid in 1864.

In the South, the league played an equally important role as it became a stronghold of the Southern Republican Party, while educating newly freed slaves about the democratic process and helping them to harness their newly acquired public power. The Southern branch was considered radical in its positive approach to African-American political participation in the South. There was strong resistance among white Southerners to any association enrolling freed slaves into an oath-bound association for the express purpose of making voting Americans of them. The National Council of the Union Leagues, headquartered in WASHINGTON, D.C., attempted to set a moderate tone for the Southern branch. The council, which funded the league, wished to establish a strong Republican Party in the South and to encourage political involvement for freedmen. At the same time, it wanted the Southern Union League to restrain its militancy, in order to avoid alienating white Southerners.

While the Union League functioned primarily as a political machine for the Republican Party, it provided education and social and economic support as well. The league hosted wide-ranging political discussions and debates and promoted schools and churches on the local level. It also petitioned against local officials hostile to freed members and supported African American claims for VETERANS' benefits. Finally, the Southern league offered African Americans advice in financial planning, EMPLOYMENT, legal issues, and politics.

Despite the enthusiastic participation of black Southerners in the Union League, the organization's existence was short-lived. Its obvious support of African-American political and social rights alienated interested white farmers. By 1869, membership numbers were in decline. The KU KLUX KLAN targeted league members and meetings as part of a campaign to disenfranchise freed people. That violence, in combination with the rise of REDEMPTION governments in the South, spelled the end of the Union League in the South. The failure of the Union League is reflective of the larger failure of Reconstruction to successfully establish a place for Southern African Americans and the Republican Party in the South's political landscape. The Union League clubs in the North continued to flourish, however, and remained stalwart in their support of the Republican Party to 1900.

Further reading: Michael W. Fitzgerald, *The Union League Movement in the Deep South: Politics and Agricultural Change during Reconstruction* (Baton Rogue: Louisiana State University Press, 1989); Frank L. Klement, *Dark Lanterns: Secret Political Societies, Conspiracies, and Treason Trials in the Civil War* (Baton Rouge: Louisiana State University Press, 1984).

—Ruth A. Behling

Union navy

The Union's strategy in the CIVIL WAR demanded a great deal of its navy. And despite starting the war with few ships of any value, the navy eventually proved up to the task, playing a critical role in helping the Union to achieve victory. "At all the watery margin, they have been present," noted President ABRAHAM LINCOLN toward the end of the war. "Not only on the deep sea, the broad bay, the rapid river, but also up the narrow muddy bayou, and wherever the ground was a little damp, they have made their tracks."

When Union secretary of the navy GIDEON WELLES took office, he found himself with a fleet that was entirely inadequate for the Union's needs. The navy had only 90 ships, and the vast majority were either unseaworthy, in faraway ports, or still under construction. Only 14 ships were actually in U.S. waters and ready for service, and the majority of these were not warships. So, like the Confederacy, the United States was largely forced to build its fleet from scratch. Ultimately, this proved a hidden blessing for the Union navy, because it benefited from a revolution in naval warfare begun in the two decades preceding the war. Steam engines replaced sails. Ships began to be plated with iron, which could withstand cannon fire much more effectively than wood. Powerful new guns and ordnance were developed. Welles was determined to piece together a large navy that utilized all of these new technologies, and backed by the economic power of the North, he was able to do so—building, purchasing, or leasing hundreds of vessels. Eight months after the war started, the Union navy had grown to 264 ships. A year later the number was at 427, and by the end of the war there were 671 ships on the Navy Department's register, making the Union navy the largest in the world.

Of course, so large a navy could not have been put out to sea without a substantial number of sailors. Unlike the Confederacy, the Union navy never had problems finding enough manpower. The officer corps, numbering 1,457 men at the start of 1861, did suffer some defections to the South. However, more than enough talented officers remained, among them DAVID GLASGOW FARRAGUT, Samuel F. Du Pont, DAVID DIXON PORTER, and JOHN A. B. DAHLGREN. The ranks of enlisted men grew rapidly throughout the war, from 7,600 in 1861 to 51,000 in 1865. Included in this number were African Americans, who were able to serve in the navy throughout the Civil War.

The Union navy had three main tactical objectives during the war. The first, and best known, was a blockade of Southern ports. The purpose of the blockade was to seal off Southern ports on the Atlantic coast, Gulf coast, and MISSISSIPPI RIVER so that the Confederacy would be unable to export cotton or import the goods that were needed to survive and to wage the war. This was not an easy job, for the

Sailors relaxing on the deck of the USS *Monitor* (Library of Congress)

Confederacy had more than 3,000 miles of coastline to be patrolled. In the early years of the war, when the Union navy lacked ships, the blockade was dismissed by critics as a "paper blockade." However, as the navy expanded and its officers grew more experienced over the course of the war, the blockade became fairly effective. In 1860, the last year before the Civil War began, the South exported 816 million pounds of cotton. In 1864 exports of cotton totaled less than 3 million pounds. The Confederacy kept no official records on how many ships trying to run the blockade were captured or destroyed, but Union officials placed the number at about 1,500.

The Union's navy's second goal was to protect Northern shipping routes from Confederate commerce raiders. The commerce raiders were generally operated by the CONFEDERATE NAVY and were responsible for capturing or destroying as many Northern merchant ships as possible. The fight against the commerce raiders was the most difficult of the Union navy's responsibilities during the Civil War. First, the open seas are almost impossible to patrol. Perhaps more importantly, the fight against the commerce raiders led to diplomatic conflicts. The most significant of these occurred in November 1861, when Capt. Charles Wilkes of the USS *San Jacinto* boarded the British steamer *Trent* and removed two Confederate agents on board. For a period of time, Britain threatened war over what came to be called the *Trent* affair. Eventually, the British were mollified, and war was averted. Union navy commanders learned their lesson, and though occasional missteps occurred throughout the war, none were as serious as the *Trent* affair. Meanwhile, the navy had a few notable successes in fending off the commerce raiders. The most prominent of these was the June 1864 sinking of the *Alabama,* the Confederacy's most successful raider.

The Union navy's final objective was to assist the army in its operations against the Confederacy. In some cases, the navy was able to capture key strategic locations largely on its own. Such was the case with New Orleans and Charleston. More often, the navy supported the UNION ARMY's forces on land. Naval bombardment played an important role in capturing Fort Donelson, Vicksburg, and Mobile Bay. Although regularly participating in engagements being fought on land, the Union navy rarely engaged in traditional warship-versus-warship naval warfare. This is because the Confederate navy would generally retreat from confrontations between warships, unable to afford the losses that such battles brought. The Union navy's most famous engagement did involve combat between warships, however. The Battle of Hampton Roads pitted the ironclad USS *Monitor* against the ironclad CSS *Virginia.* Although IRONCLADS had been in used in naval combat before the Civil War, Hampton Roads marked the first time that an ironclad faced off against another ironclad. The battle ended in a draw and had no impact on the overall course of the war. Nonetheless, Hampton Roads received a great deal attention in both North and South and throughout the world. This helped usher in an arms race among the naval powers of the world, as they scrambled to convert their fleets to ships made of iron and, eventually, steel.

Despite its humble beginnings, then, the Union navy came to play an important role during the Civil War. It helped disrupt the ECONOMY of the South, protected the economy of the North, and provided critical assistance for the Union army. The Union navy must be given a substantial portion of the credit for the defeat of the Confederacy.

See also *MONITOR-MERRIMACK*; VICKSBURG CAMPAIGN.

Further reading: William M. Fowler, *Under Two Flags: The American Navy in the Civil War* (New York: Norton, 1990); David Dixon Porter, *The Naval History of the Civil War* (Seacacus, N.J.: Castle, 1984); David G. Surdam, *Northern Naval Superiority and the Economics of the American Civil War* (Columbia: University of South Carolina Press, 2001).

—Christopher Bates

United Daughters of the Confederacy (1894–   )

The United Daughters of the Confederacy (UDC) was founded in 1894 in Nashville, Tennessee. Like so many women's organizations of the late 19th century, including the Daughters of the American Revolution and the Association for the Preservation of Virginia Antiquities, its purpose was primarily commemorative. Its membership was made up of the wives and daughters of the men who had fought for the Confederacy, and its mission was to perpetuate the memory of the Southern cause and to honor the soldiers who had defended it. Inevitably, of course, its membership was also entirely white and, unlike the troops who had actually fought the war, its ranks included a disproportionate number of the South's elite, patrician class who had a vested interest in maintaining the social and racial status quo.

The UDC was the driving force behind many of the South's most visible commemorative activities in the late 19th and early 20th century. It was also a key proponent of the "LOST CAUSE" ideology of the South. The UDC sponsored observances of Memorial Day, raised money for war memorials, and established museums and relic rooms throughout the South. Perhaps the organization had its most far-reaching influence, however, in its campaigns to censor Southern textbooks to ensure that only a pro-Confederacy view of the CIVIL WAR was taught in Southern schools. Due in large part to the United Daughters of the Confederacy, several generations of Southern white children were thus offered no alternatives to the view that SLAVERY was a benign institution, that SECESSION was a just and holy cause, and that RECONSTRUCTION had visited a great wrong and indignity upon an innocent South.

Further reading: Gaines M. Foster, *Ghosts of the Confederacy: Defeat, the Lost Cause, and the Emergence of the New South, 1865–1913* (New York: Oxford University Press, 1987); Mary B. Poppenheim, *The History of the United Daughters of the Confederacy* (Richmond: Garrett and Massie, 1938).

—Teresa Barnett

United States Army Corps of Engineers

The United States Army Corps of Engineers had its origins in the Revolutionary War and found a permanent home in 1802 when President Thomas Jefferson signed the bill founding the UNITED STATES MILITARY ACADEMY AT WEST POINT, New York. Jefferson believed strongly that the training of military officers in a democratic republic should take place within a curriculum that emphasized mathematics and engineering, after the French model. Until 1866 the Corps of Engineers ran West Point, and the top students of each class—such as ROBERT E. LEE and GEORGE B. MCCLELLAN—were always assigned to the Corps of Engineers.

From 1818 to 1863 there were actually two corps. The first, called the Topographic Engineering Corps, explored and mapped territory and rivers and designed and built harbors and other improvements. Robert E. Lee, who graduated second in his 1829 class, was assigned to oversee construction of the St. Louis, Missouri, harbor. The second part of the corps, named the Corps of Engineers, was concerned with building defensive fortifications. An excellent example of the latter was FORT SUMTER, South Carolina, begun in the late 1850s and still uncompleted when it was captured by Confederate forces in April 1861.

The fact that the graduates of the top military academy in the country were trained in engineering guaranteed that the corps would play an important role in the major wars of the 19th century, including the CIVIL WAR of 1861–65. The skills that corps members learned proved indispensable in wartime: mapping out the operational theaters, building and rebuilding bridges and rail tracks, assisting in the planning and preparation of sieges, and designing and building field fortifications. Thus, engineers were trained to be experts in both the offensive and defensive modes. As the first "modern war," the Civil War featured complex engineering feats such as General McClellan's and General ULYSSES S. GRANT's sieges at Yorktown and Vicksburg, respectively. Over the years, the two sections of the engineer corps were joined permanently, and its numbers expanded in 1863. After 1865, the U.S. Corps of Engineers helped to map and develop the western territories and assisted in building the transcontinental RAILROADS.

See also CARTOGRAPHY.

Further reading: Dale E. Floyd, ed., *"Dear Friends At Home:" The Letters and Diary of Thomas James Owen, Fiftieth New York Volunteer Engineer Regiment, during the Civil War* (Washington, D.C.: Historical Division, Office of Administrative Service, Office of the Chief of Engineers, 1985).

United States Christian Commission (1861–1866)

Reflecting both the deeply religious nature of 19th-century American life and a strong commitment to voluntarism, the United States Christian Commission (USCC) was formed to provide a variety of social services to the men who served the Union as soldiers. Like many other philanthropic organizations, the USCC mobilized civilian (and especially female) energies throughout the CIVIL WAR to ease the burdens of the troops in both material and spiritual ways.

When large numbers of volunteers began to leave for the war, many Northern Christian activists became convinced that soldiers' lives should be made easier. In November 1861, at a conference in Philadelphia, George H. Stuart, a wealthy merchant and staunch Presbyterian, was named the first president of the newly created United States Christian Commission. He remained president for the life of the Commission.

The USCC's original plan was to assist the chaplains of the armed services in their daily work. To do this, the USCC settled on eight unifying principles: compassion, voluntarism, benefits for the body and soul, personal distribution, personal ministrations, nationality (patriotism), cooperation, and respect for authority. Through adherence to these principles, the commission believed that it could assist in the war effort without interfering with military authorities.

An extensive administrative organization supported the USCC's work. There was an executive committee, station agents and field representatives served in the field, and the local organization was broken into branch commissions and ladies commissions. The executive committee oversaw the USCC's daily affairs. Initially, it was composed of only 12 members, but the number grew to 55 as the UNION ARMY grew and the extent of the need became apparent.

Station agents, often called ministers, oversaw the activities of the field representatives, volunteers who personally aided soldiers in the field. While field representatives worked directly with soldiers, station agents monitored USCC work for a particular army corps or a locale near the front line. Station agents also organized supplies, ensuring that each field representative had what he or she needed and directing aid first to those areas that needed it most.

The branch commissions and ladies commissions both served as fund-raising and public relations arms for the USCC. Although their ultimate goal was the same, they each used their own methods. Whereas the branch commissions primarily focused on raising cash for the war effort, the ladies commissions organized women to prepare food, clothing, and gifts for distribution to Union soldiers. According to the 1866 final report of the USCC, the ladies commissions consisted of 266 members in 17 states and had raised more than $200,000 during the course of the war. One of the most-notable members of the ladies commissions was Annie Wittenmeyer. Concerned about the diet of soldiers in Missouri, she established the first kitchen in the Cumberland Hospital in Nashville, Tennessee. Wittenmeyer's diet was a vast improvement in both health and satisfaction, providing nutritious, tasty foods.

The backbone of the USCC, however, was its delegates, or field representatives. These men and women went to the field equipped with a memo book, instructions, food, bedding, utensils, and publications of various kinds. Each delegate worked for an average of 38 days and was responsible for all the supplies sent to that particular spot, in addition to giving assistance to the surgeons and chaplains where necessary. Even though the delegates' primary responsibilities were to assist the chaplains in their pastoral and evangelical work, they often acted as lay ministers, librarians, NURSES, social workers, and worship leaders. By the end of the war, more than 5,000 people had served as delegates for the USCC.

President ABRAHAM LINCOLN's administration recognized the positive effect of the USCC on behalf of Union troops. Lincoln offered support to the commission wherever possible during the war. In addition, Gen. ULYSSES S. GRANT welcomed the commission and gave its members free access to his men.

The assistance provided by the USCC was invaluable. By the end of the war, the commission had raised more than $6 million to benefit the army. Delegates distributed 1.5 million Bibles and 1 million hymnals. In addition, they preached more than 58,000 sermons, held 77,000 prayer meetings, and assisted the soldiers in writing more than 92,000 LETTERS to their families and friends.

Further reading: Jeanie Attie, *Patriotic Toil: Northern Women and the American Civil War* (Ithaca, N.Y.: Cornell University Press, 1998); Lemuel Moss, *Annals of the United States Christian Commission* (Philadelphia: J. B. Lippincott, 1868).

—Megan Quinn and Fiona Galvin

United States Military Academy at West Point

The United States Military Academy at West Point, located about 40 miles north of NEW YORK CITY, provided the trained officer corps for the United States's small professional army in the 19th century. West Point occupied a location of key strategic interest during the Revolutionary War. George Washington made his headquarters there in 1779, and one year later Benedict Arnold, then in control of the encampment, tried to surrender the area to the British. Though soldiers have lived at West Point continuously since the Revolution, the founding fathers of the United States were initially apprehensive about establishing a military academy because they feared a standing army.

In 1776 George Washington, prodded on by General Henry Knox, undertook an early initiative on behalf of the academy. Washington believed that the United States must not become dependent on foreign officers for instruction. In 1790 the U.S. government purchased the land that would form the basis of the academy. Alexander Hamilton proposed that the academy be divided into four schools: a school for teaching military fundamentals, one school for teaching engineering and artillery techniques, another school for the techniques of cavalry and infantry, and finally a school for naval techniques. Yet at the end of President John Adams's administration, West Point had but 12 cadets and one teacher. Thomas Jefferson opposed the academy early on, but while he was president, his attitude softened, and West Point was officially founded under his administration in 1802. Jefferson realized that the academy was his best hope of a national university.

In 1815 James Madison stipulated that West Point should have an independent superintendent, a role previously fulfilled by the chief engineer. Indeed, the academy had long privileged its engineers (the UNITED STATES ARMY CORPS OF ENGINEERS was founded by the school), and this bias would continue under the direction of the new superintendents. In fact, it was not until 1866 that regulations permitted the superintendent to come from other branches of the army. In 1816 Madison's secretary of war introduced a four-year curriculum at West Point with general examinations held in July and September.

These examinations created West Point's famous ranking system. The ranking system determined the corps to which cadets went after graduation. Those who ranked highest went into the engineering corps; those who ranked lowest went into the infantry. All facets of cadet life contributed to the construction of these rankings. For instance, during the limited free time made available by the new curriculum, most cadets accumulated demerits for infractions of West Point's extremely strict regulations. However, one of the most notable alumni of the Academy, ROBERT E. LEE, never once collected a demerit. Most cadets found the spartan existence at West Point unpleasant. The artist James McNeill Whistler and the poet Edgar Allen Poe are two of West Point's most notable antebellum dropouts.

From 1817 to 1833, the most important man at "the Point" was Superintendent Sylvanus Thayer. Before becoming superintendent, Thayer went to France, where he purchased the books that became the building blocks of the academy library, the nation's first and, at the time, only military library. Thayer also abolished West Point's annual summer vacation in favor of "summer encampment." From then on, cadets would spend their summers living in tents and practicing unceasing drills. Only after the third year would cadets be able to enjoy a brief summer "furlough." In 1828 Thayer instituted the policy that a recommendation from a member of Congress be a prerequisite for gaining entry to the academy, a policy that continues today. Under Thayer's direction, the academy continued to emphasize the production of engineers, as the young nation still found itself very much in need of members of this profession.

One historian has labeled the years between 1840 and 1860 the "golden years" of West Point. It was during these years that a high percentage of the CIVIL WAR's best-known generals attended the academy. West Pointers dominated the United States's successful campaign in the Mexican-American War (1846–48) and continued to dominate the command of both armies during the Civil War. The most important battles of the Civil War featured West Point men commanding on *both* sides.

During the early years of the war, RADICAL REPUBLICANS attacked West Point for having produced a pro-

Southern army aristocracy. These Republicans had some telling evidence at their disposal: A majority of competent Confederate generals were West Point graduates, as was the president of the Confederacy himself. In addition, the West Point alumni who remained loyal to the Union tended to be conservative Democrats such as Gen. GEORGE MCCLELLAN. These Republican critics also asserted that the UNION ARMY showed too much favoritism to West Point graduates. It was true that some West Point alumni rose in rank in spite of their mediocre performance. Nevertheless, by 1863, Union armies commanded by West Point graduates had won enormous victories at Vicksburg and Gettysburg, and the anti–West Point mood quickly faded.

See also GETTYSBURG, BATTLE OF; VICKSBURG CAMPAIGN.

Further reading: Sidney Forman, *West Point: A History of the United States Military Academy* (New York: Columbia University Press, 1950); John C. Waugh, *The Class of 1846, from West Point to Appomattox: Stonewall Jackson, George McClellan and Their Brothers* (New York: Ballantine Books, 1999).

—Chad Vanderford

United States Naval Academy at Annapolis

The United States Naval Academy was established in 1845, nearly half a century after the founding of the UNITED STATES MILITARY ACADEMY AT WEST POINT in 1802. Originally known as the Naval School, it was located at Fort Severn in Annapolis, Maryland. Franklin Buchanan was appointed its first commandant, and in its first year the institution had seven faculty members and 200 students, most of whom had already served in the navy for five years or more. The original curriculum at the Naval School was modeled after that of West Point and included philosophy, mathematics, chemistry, ordnance, and navigation.

The school evolved a great deal in the 1850s when it was rechristened the U.S. Naval Academy and the curriculum was expanded. All students were required to wear UNIFORMS, and a system of demerits for midshipmen who misbehaved was established. The academy's campus was enlarged, and the faculty was expanded by adding both civilian and military instructors. By the late 1850s, the Naval Academy was one of the world's finest institutions for training naval officers.

When the CIVIL WAR broke out, the Naval Academy was only 15 years old, so it did not have nearly as much of an influence on the Civil War as its army counterpart at West Point. While most of the high-ranking Union and Confederate generals were trained at West Point, most of the war's prominent naval officers started their careers long

before the Naval Academy was established, and so they were not educated at the institution. The war did have a pronounced influence on the academy, however. With the outbreak of hostilities, a number of the academy's students and faculty, including its commandant Franklin Buchanan, resigned to join the CONFEDERATE NAVY. Shortly thereafter, fears that the Confederacy might attack the location at Annapolis prompted the academy to relocate to Newport, Rhode Island, for the duration of the war.

When the Civil War ended, the Naval Academy returned to Annapolis, and Rear Adm. DAVID DIXON PORTER was named commandant. Porter continued to expand and modernize the academy's facilities and curriculum. In the 1870s, the school experimented briefly with desegregation, but not one of the three African Americans admitted was able to graduate. By the 1890s, the Naval Academy had become the sole training ground for all of the United States's high-ranking naval officers.

Further reading: Jack Sweetman, *The U.S. Naval Academy: An Illustrated History* (Annapolis: Naval Institute Press, 1979).

—Christopher Bates

United States Sanitary Commission

Formed in response to the rapid growth of the U.S. Army during 1861, the U.S. Sanitary Commission (USSC) consisted of Northerners on the HOMEFRONT mobilized to provide medical care, supplies, and other necessities for the soldiers in the UNION ARMY. Inspired by the British Sanitary Commission that was active during the Crimean War (1853–56), this group hoped to improve the poor hygiene of the camps and the health of the soldiers while assisting the wounded and coordinating the distribution of food and supplies to the men in blue.

The Commission's network consisted of tens of thousands of mostly female volunteers in numerous soldiers aid and LADIES AID SOCIETIES. Many of the societies were affiliated with the Woman's Central Association for Relief, which provided the majority of the hands-on work at the local level. At the national level, the USSC was led by Henry W. Bellows, the president, along with George Templeton Strong, the treasurer, and FREDERICK LAW OLMSTED, the secretary. These men were dedicated to creating an organization that not only assisted the Northern soldiers but also educated people about the importance of discipline and sacrifice in society. While the hierarchy of the organization was male, the "foot soldiers" of the USSC's campaign were generally women. The women of the commission used grassroots, locally organized female activism to promote the USSC's goals. During the four years of the CIVIL WAR, the commission's men and women raised at least $7 million in cash and were responsible for distributing $15 million worth in supplies.

One of the commission's most reliable sources of income came from the numerous community fairs they held in the years during and after the war. These "sanitary fairs" were held in small and large cities throughout the North and usually lasted for 10 to 14 days. During this time, schools and businesses would close to allow the entire community to participate in the exhibits, shops, and entertainment presented at the fairs. The fairs raised money by charging admission, collecting donations, and selling toys, crafts, Civil War memorabilia, and food. The first large-scale sanitary fair, put on by the Northwestern Sanitary Commission in Chicago, raised more than $100,000 in October 1863. In April 1864 New York's "Metropolitan Fair" netted $1 million for the USSC. When all was said and done, the fairs

raised approximately $4 million, a significant portion of the U.S. Sanitary Commission's total budget.

The USSC served as an on-call support group for areas that suffered the most during the war. Following large battles where the military's medical staffs and the local citizens could not adequately provide for the sick and dying soldiers, the U.S. Sanitary Commission would be called upon to give them assistance.

Upon arrival at the scene, the U.S. Sanitary Commission helped set up temporary hospitals and provide medical assistance to the wounded. The commission's volunteers also wrote LETTERS for the soldiers to their loved ones at home, read the Bible to the soldiers, and provided moral support to the wounded. The volunteer work and assistance provided by the USSC enabled many of the wounded soldiers to recover and continue fighting with their regiments.

Men posing in front of the Sanitary Commission lodge, Washington, D.C. *(Library of Congress)*

Despite the philanthropic nature of the U.S. Sanitary Commission, there were many who disagreed with the management philosophies of the commission's administrators. Most of the complaints focused on excessive control by the administrators, who were accused of spending the organization's dollars frivolously.

It is important to note, however, that the vast majority of the men, women, and even children who volunteered for the commission did so out of the goodness of their hearts and for the benefit of their fellow compatriots. A number of smaller women's organizations and aid societies created to assist the soldiers were eager to help the USSC in every way possible.

The U.S. Sanitary Commission was the most recognizable philanthropic organization during the Civil War. Dedicated to improving the well-being of the Union soldiers, the commission provided invaluable medical assistance and moral support that enabled the soldiers to continue their fight to save the Union. The USSC also helped develop a nationally active women's community, elements of which went on after the Civil War to promote other agendas such as women's suffrage and temperance.

See also WOMEN'S STATUS AND RIGHTS.

Further reading: Jeanie Attie, *Patriotic Toil: Northern Women and the American Civil War* (Ithaca, N.Y.: Cornell University Press, 1998); Robert H. Bremner, *The Public Good: Philanthropy and Welfare in the Civil War Era* (New York: Knopf, 1980); Judith Ann Giesberg, *Civil War Sisterhood: The U.S. Sanitary Commission and Women's Politics in Transition* (Boston: Northeastern University Press, 2000); William Quentin Maxwell, *Lincoln's Fifth Wheel: The Political History of the United States Sanitary Commission* (New York: Longmans, Green, 1956).

—Megan Quinn

United States v. Cruikshank (1876)

The origins of *United States v. Cruikshank et al.* began on Easter Sunday 1873, when more than 100 African Americans were murdered in Grant Parish, Louisiana. The Supreme Court's ruling in the *Cruikshank* case curtailed federal powers of enforcement, set back the push for black suffrage in the South, and made it clear that voting, if you were African American, was a great risk.

In 1870 Republicans in Congress pressed for enforcement legislation for the FIFTEENTH AMENDMENT, which had guaranteed that the right to vote would not be denied because of "race, color, or previous condition of servitude." Pursuant to this, Congress passed the ENFORCEMENT ACTS. The first of these acts, passed in May 1870, outlined

federal voting protection policies. While Congress acted to shore up the voting rights of black Republicans in the South, REDEMPTION of Southern governments was beginning. Throughout the South, Democratic candidates were stepping forward to reclaim their local, state, and regional politics from the Republicans. The KU KLUX KLAN and other white supremacist groups gained members and were determined to keep African Americans from exercising their Fifteenth Amendment right to vote.

In this climate, the election of 1872 in Louisiana was a tense affair. Even in 1871, white Republicans in Grant Parish were harassed and attacked. In Grant Parish the local results of the election were hotly contested, and the issue of African Americans voting was certainly a concern because they voted for the Republican candidate. Both the Republican and the Democratic candidates claimed victory and established governments including a judge and a sheriff. Republican William P. Kellogg's appointees sealed off the town of Colfax to ward off the Democrats who claimed victory for their candidate John McHenry. While the political debates raged, rumors began flying of African Americans attacking white citizens on the outskirts of town, and then there were subsequent rumors of white peoples' plans to counterattack. For protection, African Americans began congregating at the Colfax Courthouse. By Easter Sunday of 1872, there were approximately 400 African Americans camped around the courthouse. The crowd of African Americans drew a crowd of some 300 armed white people to the courthouse. They were led by the local sheriff, C. C. Nash, a Democratic appointee who had earlier been charged with attacking white Republicans. Nash ordered the African Americans to disperse. When they refused, he gave the women and children 30 minutes to leave the area. When the time was up, the shooting commenced. The African Americans who tried to flee were chased down and killed if they were caught. The remainder barricaded themselves in the courthouse. They were eventually forced out and those that ran were also hunted down and killed if caught. By the late afternoon the battle was over, and 50 African Americans had been arrested. Nash promised that they would be released the next day. Instead of release, however, they were marched along isolated roads and executed in small groups. One man, Benjamin Brimm, survived his wounds and crawled away, and he became the chief witness in the government's case.

Upon news of these events, the U.S. attorney general ordered an investigation. Government investigators estimated that by the end of the day of fighting, at least 105 African Americans had been killed. There were 98 defendants charged in the case, but only nine were taken into custody to stand trial under the case name of *United States v. C. C. Nash and Others.* They were each charged with violating sections of the Enforcement Act. It took two trials to acquit one defendant completely, find five defendants not guilty of any charges, and convict three men of conspiring to block the "free exercise" of constitutional rights. No one was found guilty of any of the murder charges.

The case came to the Supreme Court as *United States v. Cruikshank et al.* (Cruikshank being one of the three convicted defendants) in 1874. In the decision of the Court in 1875, Chief Justice Morrison R. Waite declared the charges against the three men invalid because nowhere in the indictment did it specifically charge that the actions taken by the defendants were taken because the victims were African American. Waite stated that while one "may suspect that race was the cause of the hostility," it could not form the basis of a conviction since it was not in the indictment. Waite stated that since there was "no allegation" that the attacks were "done because of the race or color of the persons conspired against," then "[w]hen stripped of its verbiage the case as presented amounts to nothing more than that the defendants conspired to prevent certain citizens of the United States . . . from enjoying the equal protection of the laws of the state and of the United States. . . ." Waite also argued that the "fourteenth amendment prohibits a State from depriving any person of life, liberty, or property, without due process of law; but this adds nothing to the rights of one citizen as against another." Thus, since it was, according to the Court, merely a matter of individuals acting against other individuals and not the state of Louisiana acting against the individuals, the Enforcement Acts did not apply.

The Easter massacre at Colfax Courthouse in Grant Parish was the bloodiest of RECONSTRUCTION violence. When the Supreme Court was finished with the case, the practical enforcement of voting rights was left to local and state authorities. This meant that in the South, African Americans were essentially without recourse if any individual moved to keep them from voting. *Cruikshank* and what has come to be its companion case in legal history, *United States v. Reese* (which upheld poll taxes as legitimate voting requirements), sealed the fate of African Americans wishing to exercise their Fifteenth Amendment rights in the South. In keeping African Americans from the polls, these cases also doomed the REPUBLICAN PARTY in the South, because the party depended on the votes of the freedmen to stay in power. The decision in *Cruikshank*, though applauded by Southern and Democratic newspapers, did agree that the Fifteenth Amendment protected voters against discrimination based on race. Thus, it was a technical victory for those who wished to affirm that suffrage was a constitutional right that could not be abridged on the basis of race. But the message of the Court seemed clear to African Americans in the South: Voting is a risky business that may cost you your life.

Further reading: Robert M. Goldman, *Reconstruction and Black Suffrage: Losing the Vote in Reese and Cruikshank* (Lawrence: University Press of Kansas, 2001).

—Ruth A. Behling and Jennifer A. Berman

V

Vallandigham, Clement L. (1820–1872)

Lawyer and U.S. congressman, Clement Laird Vallandigham was the most prominent antiwar Democrat, or COPPERHEAD, during the CIVIL WAR. Vallandigham was born on July 29, 1820, in New Lisbon, Ohio, to Presbyterian minister Clement L. Vallandigham and Rebecca Laird. Young Clement was educated at New Lisbon Academy and at Jefferson College (now Washington and Jefferson College). After a brief stint as a teacher, he studied law and was admitted to the Ohio bar in 1842. Vallandigham quickly became a successful lawyer, ultimately forming a lucrative partnership with Thomas J. S. Smith in Dayton, Ohio. In 1845 he began his political career with his election to the Ohio legislature. He was reelected the following year and chosen as Speaker of the House. In 1847 Vallandigham married Louisa A. McMahon, with whom he had two sons.

During the 1850s, Vallandigham continued to practice law while also dabbling in a number of other professions. For two years, he was editor of the Dayton *Empire.* He served in the Ohio state militia, eventually rising to the rank of brigadier general. He also made a number of attempts to break into national politics. In 1852 and 1854 he was defeated as a candidate for the House of Representatives. Despite his losses, Vallandigham was able to make a name for himself as a Democrat in the Jeffersonian mold, who believed strongly in the strict construction of the Constitution and in STATES' RIGHTS. He expressed support for the Mexican-American War (1846–48) and the Compromise of 1850, and he condemned ABOLITIONists. Although Vallandigham was personally opposed to SLAVERY, he felt a special kinship with the South, which had been home to many of his ancestors. Finally, in 1858, Vallandigham was elected to the House. He was reelected in 1860, pledging that he would never "vote one dollar of money whereby one drop of American blood should be shed in a civil war."

When war finally came, Vallandigham continued to be vocal in his opposition, and he called for peace, even if it meant letting the Confederacy remain independent. He was roundly and bitterly denounced by Republican politicians and newspaper editors. For example, in June 1861, the editor of the *Louisville Journal* called Vallandigham "A Traitor, A Monster, A Disgrace to his Ancestry, A Shame to Posterity. . . ." The charge that Vallandigham had betrayed the Union effectively destroyed his chances for reelection in 1862, ending his tenure in Congress. In his final speech to the House, delivered on January 14, 1863, Vallandigham reiterated his call for peace and warned that the states of the Northwest might join the Confederacy in seceding if the war was allowed to continue.

Ousted from his seat in Congress, Vallandigham decided to run for the governorship of Ohio on an antiwar platform. In the spring 1863, Gen. AMBROSE E. BURNSIDE, commander of the Military District of Ohio, issued an order that said it would no longer be acceptable to criticize publicly the Northern war effort. Vallandigham defied the order and was arrested and charged with "expressing treasonable sympathy." Convicted by a military tribunal, he was sentenced to imprisonment at Fort Warren for the duration of the war. Shortly thereafter, ABRAHAM LINCOLN commuted the sentence and banished Vallandigham to the Confederacy. He remained there for a short time before relocating to Canada.

As a result of his conviction, Vallandigham became a powerful symbol for Northerners who opposed the war. The Sons of Liberty, a group of roughly 250,000 Confederate sympathizers in the North, rallied to Vallandigham's cause and named him supreme commander of their group. Meanwhile, angry Ohio Democrats gave Vallandigham their nomination for GOVERNOR. Ohio Republicans were incensed by the choice. A soldier in the 99th Ohio expressed the sentiments held by many of his comrades when he wrote, "Is the Democratic party so short of good men that they were compelled to take up a man justly banished for his treasonable practices?" In the election, Vallandigham was soundly defeated.

In 1864 Vallandigham appealed his conviction to the Supreme Court, which declined to hear the case, arguing that civilian courts have no jurisdiction over military tribunals. Despite losing his case, Vallandigham nonetheless returned to the states. Lincoln chose to ignore this, not wanting to draw any more attention to Vallandigham. At the Democratic convention in 1864, Vallandigham helped to write the DEMOCRATIC PARTY's platform. In it, he and his followers were able to include a plank calling for the immediate cessation of hostilities. GEORGE B. MCCLELLAN, the convention's choice as its presidential candidate, quickly repudiated the peace plank. That, along with renewed Union successes on the war front, effectively destroyed Vallandigham's power.

After the war, Vallandigham sought to rebuild his political career. He came to accept the end of slavery, and he said he hoped to work on bridging the gap between the Republican and Democratic Parties. In 1867 Ohio Democrats denied him an opportunity to run for the U.S. Senate, and Vallandigham returned to his law practice. In 1872 he was hired to defend a man accused of murder. While doing a demonstration of how the victim had been shot, Vallandigham inadvertently shot and killed himself. He won the case posthumously.

Further reading: Frank L. Klement, *The Limits of Dissent: Clement L. Vallandigham and the Civil War* (New York: Fordham University Press, 1998).

—Christopher Bates

Van Lew, Elizabeth (1818–1900)

Born to a wealthy and prominent family in RICHMOND, Virginia, Elizabeth Van Lew became one of the Union's most valuable spies, providing military and tactical information throughout the CIVIL WAR. Van Lew was born on October 17, 1818, to John and Elizabeth Van Lew. John Van Lew was an important Whig leader in Richmond, and his home was frequently full of local politicians whose presence certainly influenced the development of Elizabeth's own political philosophy. She was educated in Philadelphia, a city that was a center of antiSLAVERY rhetoric and activism in the antebellum period.

Returning to Richmond from Philadelphia, Elizabeth was committed to ABOLITION. When the war began, the unmarried 42-year-old Van Lew pleaded her loyalty to the Union, despite the obvious dangers of holding this view in wartime Richmond. Van Lew and her mother first helped the Union effort by assisting prisoners of war at Libby Prison, bringing them food, books, and clothing. Her family's prominence meant that Elizabeth was privy to a great deal of military information, and she devised a variety of ways to convey that information to Union leaders. When Richmond fell to the Union on April 2, 1865, Elizabeth recognized the value of the documentation left behind. Rushing to Confederate offices, she collected paperwork and records, conveying them to Union authorities.

After the war, President ULYSSES S. GRANT recognized Van Lew's contribution to the Union effort by appointing her postmistress for Richmond. Elizabeth lost her appointment in 1877 when Rutherford B. Hayes became president but regained it under Grover Cleveland. By the 1880s, however, Elizabeth's life in Richmond had become sad and lonely. Her mother dead, Elizabeth had few friends among the local population. Although her aid to the Union had been of great use, few citizens of Richmond approved of her activities. In addition, she had incurred large debts during and after the war and had no way to repay them or to support herself.

Elizabeth was rescued by the family of one of the Union soldiers she had assisted at Libby Prison. Relatives of Col. Paul Revere repaid her kindness and generosity by supporting her financially for the rest of her life. In the 1870s, Van Lew's activist nature found an outlet through her ardent support of the women's rights movement. She died in Richmond in 1900.

See also WOMEN'S STATUS AND RIGHTS.

Further reading: Penny Coleman, *Spies! Women in the Civil War* (Cincinnati, Ohio: Betterway Books, 1992).

—Megan Quinn and Fiona Galvin

veterans

At the end of the CIVIL WAR there were nearly 2.5 million men who had donned the blue or the gray. This was vastly more veterans than the combined total of all of the other American wars fought up to that time. These men had naturally formed bonds that they were reluctant to abandon, and the war had not been over for very long before groups of former soldiers began to seek out ways to come together at local, state, and national levels.

Former Union soldiers were the first to organize. Soon after the end of the war, several officers gathered in Philadelphia and founded the Military Order of the Loyal Legion of the United States, known also as MOLLUS. MOLLUS was never a particularly large organization because of its stringent membership requirements: only Union officers and their eldest male sons could join. However, MOLLUS inspired numerous imitators with more relaxed standards. Among them were the Society of the Army of the James, the United States Soldiers and Sailors Protective Society, the United States Service Society, and the Grand Army of the Republic (GAR). The GAR was the single most important Civil War veterans' organization, numbering 400,000 members at its peak in the 1890s. The GAR was able to enroll so many members because it allowed all Union veterans to join, including African Americans. Children and wives of veterans could also be a part of the organization.

Confederate soldiers soon followed the lead of their Union counterparts. In 1870 several former Confederate officers gathered in RICHMOND and founded the Association of the Army of Northern Virginia. Similar groups, mostly with limited memberships, were established in the other former Confederate states over the course of the next decade. The most prominent of these groups was the Association of the Army of Tennessee, the Grand Camp of Confederate Veterans of Virginia, and the North Carolina Society of Ex-Sailors and Soldiers. Finally, in February 1889, these groups came together to form the United Confederate Veterans, or UCV. The UCV founded two auxiliary organizations, the Sons of Confederate Veterans and the UNITED DAUGHTERS OF THE CONFEDERACY; both are still in existence. At its height in the early 1900s, the UCV counted 80,000 members among its ranks.

Both Confederate and Union veterans organizations served a variety of purposes in the lives of their members. Perhaps most obviously, they provided camaraderie. Most veterans posts held regular social meetings. They also organized regular reunions of regiments or brigades. Often, the UCV and GAR would coordinate on "campouts," where entire armies would reunite on the important battlefields on the anniversaries of the battles fought there. Campouts were held on the 25th and 50th anniversaries of Gettysburg, for instance.

In addition to their role as social organizations, veterans groups were also powerful political lobbies. The GAR was arguably the single most influential interest group in the United States in the years between Appomattox and the turn of the century. If a candidate for state or national office wished to be elected on the Republican ticket, the GAR's support was often critical. For example, of the men who won presidential ELECTIONS between 1868 and 1900, only Democrat Grover Cleveland was not a member of the GAR. Veterans expected concessions in exchange for their support. In the years immediately after the war, they pushed for harsh terms for the readmission of the South, and they were staunch supporters of Radical RECONSTRUCTION. Later, the GAR focused on securing federal funding for veterans' hospitals and pensions. A succession of pension bills was passed in the 1870s and 1880s, each increasing the amount being paid to former soldiers or relaxing the requirements for pension eligibility. By the mid-1890s, pension payments to Union veterans and their families accounted for 40 percent of the entire federal budget.

Confederate veterans did not have the political leverage that their Union counterparts enjoyed, but they nonetheless focused on the same issues. The FOURTEENTH AMENDMENT prohibited former Confederates from receiving federal benefits, so veterans groups in the South were compelled to turn to their state governments and private entities for support. Some Southern states, notably Louisiana, Georgia, and South Carolina, established relatively generous pensions for their veterans. Other states, including Texas and Louisiana, provided grants of land for former soldiers. In 1885 a combination of public and private funding allowed for the founding of Lee Camp, the first soldiers home for Confederate veterans. Ultimately, there were a total of 16 soldiers' homes that provided care for more than 20,000 indigent and disabled ex-Confederates.

As the GAR and UCV worked to provide health and pension benefits for veterans, they also strove to shape the memory of the war. Veterans were interested in placing the bravery and sacrifice of the COMMON SOLDIER at the heart of the narrative. To that end, the GAR, the UCV, and their auxiliary support groups undertook a variety of initiatives. Each organization commissioned history textbooks and lobbied for their use in schools so that children could be taught the "correct" version of what had happened during the war. Both organizations played a role in establishing Memorial Day as a national holiday, and both the GAR and the UCV erected countless MONUMENTS to soldiers and their leaders across the country, particularly at important battlefields and at cemeteries. Roughly 500 monuments were built by Southern veterans' groups, while approximately 5,000 were unveiled by the GAR and its allies. The majority of these monuments were built between 1880 and 1910.

In 1896 William McKinley became the last veteran of the Civil War to be elected to the presidency. By the start of the 1900s, the Civil War was beginning to seem distant in the minds of Americans, and a majority of veterans had already passed away. When the 50th anniversary campout at Gettysburg was held in 1913, it was widely understood that the event would be the final gathering for the men who had fought in the Civil War. By the time of World War I, the number of living veterans had been reduced to a few thousand, and by the time the GAR disbanded in 1949, it was down to less than a hundred. The last Civil War veteran, Albert Woolson, died in 1956, 95 years after the first shot was fired at FORT SUMTER.

See also LOST CAUSE, THE.

Further reading: Wallace Evan Davies, *Patriotism on Parade: The Story of Veterans' and Hereditary Organizations in America, 1783–1900* (Cambridge, Mass.: Harvard University Press, 1955); Patrick J. Kelly, *Creating a*

National Home: Building the Veterans' Welfare State, 1860–1900 (Cambridge, Mass.: Harvard University Press, 1997); Stuart McConnell, *Glorious Contentment: The Grand Army of the Republic, 1865–1900* (Chapel Hill: University of North Carolina Press, 1992); William White, *The Confederate Veteran* (Tuscaloosa, Ala.: Confederate Pub. Co., 1962).

—Christopher Bates

Vicksburg campaign (November 1862–July 1863)

ABRAHAM LINCOLN, hearing the news of the July 4, 1863, surrender of Vicksburg, Mississippi, to Union forces, exclaimed: "The father of waters again goes unvexed to the seas!" The loss of Vicksburg, and with it, the control of 250 miles of the MISSISSIPPI RIVER to Port Hudson, Louisiana, was a huge blow to the fledgling Southern nation. Vicksburg was a vital economic and military link between the Confederacy and its western states of Louisiana, Arkansas, and Texas. History records Maj. Gen. ULYSSES S. GRANT's strategy to capture the "Gibraltar of the West" as one of the greatest military campaigns of all time.

In 1861 Vicksburg had a population of 5,000, making it the second largest city in the state. Crisscrossed with narrow, twisting streets, Vicksburg was a bustling commercial center and TRANSPORTATION network for the planter class of Mississippi and Louisiana. Like Natchez, its downriver sister, Vicksburg's wharves teemed with riverboats loaded with cotton and passengers headed for New Orleans. Vicksburg was a railroad hub as well, with lines going east to the state capital, Jackson. "Vicksburg is the key," President Lincoln argued. "This war can never be brought to a close until the key is in our pocket." The president of the CONFEDERATE STATES OF AMERICA, JEFFERSON DAVIS, whose plantation was near Vicksburg, agreed that the citadel city was the "key," but he clearly wanted to keep it in the *Southern* pocket.

Vicksburg's role was defined early. A major strategic goal of the Union's war effort was to gain control of the Mississippi River from Illinois to the Gulf of Mexico. Necessarily, the Confederates' war aims were geared toward protecting the river and the surrounding Southern territory against Union invasion. Early on, Union armies in the west were successful in using a combination of naval and infantry forces to gain control of the upper part of the river from Illinois to just north of Vicksburg, and the lower Mississippi River, from New Orleans to just south of Port Hudson, Louisiana. Recognizing that the Confederacy must guarantee that the last large portion of the river remain open to traffic, Southerners poured their energies into making Vicksburg an "impregnable fortress."

In May 1862, Southern forces occupied Vicksburg and began a yearlong project of fortifying the city against Union invasion. In many ways, Vicksburg was naturally well protected due to its unique geographical position. Perched on bluffs more than 200 feet above the Mississippi River, Vicksburg was practically unassailable from the water. Defenders made sure of that when they placed 100 cannons along a nine-mile ridge. From that ridge, the Confederates controlled the river for more than 30 miles. Attack from land would be almost as difficult. Miles of swamps, thickets, bayous, and rivers bordered Vicksburg from both north and south. The only way to assault Vicksburg by land was from the east, and in 1862 middle Mississippi was firmly under Southern control. Taking no chances, however, rebels built strong defenses protecting their most vulnerable part. For nine miles east of the city, Confederate engineers constructed a series of watchtowers with walls up to 20 feet thick overlooking gullies and hollows. Along this line, 115 cannons were placed, and trenches and rifle pits were dug to protect both cannons and soldiers. Well before the final trench was dug, however, Vicksburg's position was challenged.

In late May and early June 1862 Union naval gunboats under the command of DAVID GLASGOW FARRAGUT began bombardment of the city. The cannons on the high bluffs overlooking the river fired on the Northern ships, and Farragut, realizing he was overmatched, withdrew. Throughout the summer other attempts were made to attack Vicksburg, all to no avail. Both sides realized that a massive show of force by the UNION ARMY was coming, and soon. In October, Confederate major general John C. Pemberton was appointed commander of Mississippi and eastern Louisiana. The Pennsylvania-born Pemberton, a West-Pointer and career military officer, married a Virginian and cast his lot with the Confederacy in 1861. Pemberton felt confident that his army of 30,000 would defend ably the fortress above the Mississippi.

On November 2, 1862, Maj. Gen. Ulysses S. Grant, victor of the Battles of Fort Henry and Donelson (which opened the South to invasion via the Tennessee River) and the BATTLE OF SHILOH, began a campaign to capture Vicksburg. He moved his army south from Grand Junction, Tennessee, along the lines of the Mississippi Central Railroad. His immediate destination for the 30,000-strong Army of the Tennessee was Holly Springs, Mississippi. Grant ordered Maj. Gen. WILLIAM T. SHERMAN to detach a part of his force and attack Vicksburg from the north. Both forces would converge on Vicksburg at the same time from different directions. It was a good idea that failed miserably. Confederate cavalry destroyed Grant's supply base at Holly Springs on December 20, and he lost contact with Sherman. A week later, Sherman's 32,000 men were decisively repulsed at the Battle of Chickasaw Bayou.

Grant retreated back to Memphis, Tennessee, in January 1863 to reconceptualize his campaign. He went down-

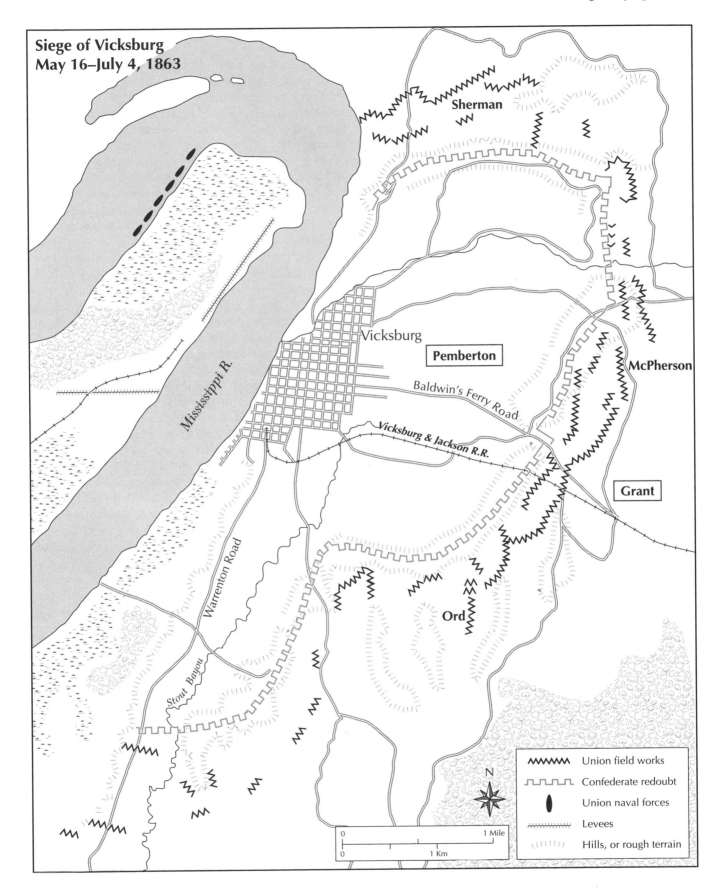

**Siege of Vicksburg
May 16–July 4, 1863**

Sherman

Vicksburg

Pemberton

Baldwin's Ferry Road

McPherson

Mississippi R.

Vicksburg & Jackson R.R.

Grant

Warrenton Road

Ord

Stout Bayou

N

0 ———————— 1 Mile

0 ———————— 1 Km

ᨑᨑᨑᨑ Union field works

ꖴꖴꖴꖴ Confederate redoubt

⬛ Union naval forces

⊥⊥⊥⊥ Levees

ꞁꞁꞁꞁ Hills, or rough terrain

river again and put his soldiers to work on building canals and other river projects. Hopefully, a water route could be opened that would allow his army to avoid the killing fire of the Vicksburg cannons and get on dry ground either south or east of the city. Months went by, and all the projects ended in frustration. "Grant has no plan for taking Vicksburg," one critic wrote from WASHINGTON, D.C. "He is frittering away time and strength to no purpose." Even his ablest generals agreed. Heavy criticism was leveled at Grant from many sides, but a worried Lincoln remained steadfast in his support.

Finally, Grant came up with a successful operation in March and April 1863. His plan was simple, bold, and ingenious. With the help of Adm. DAVID DIXON PORTER, commander of Union naval forces in the region, Grant marched his army down the west side of the Mississippi below Vicksburg. Porter's boats and transports, having earlier braved successfully the Vicksburg batteries, transported two of Grant's three corps safely across the river. Sherman was ordered to stay behind and make a false attack on Vicksburg to confuse Pemberton—and Pemberton's commanding general, JOSEPH E. JOHNSTON, headquartered in Jackson—as to Grant's real intentions. As soon as all of Grant's army was across the river, Sherman rejoined the main force.

Simultaneously, Grant ordered a young Union cavalry commander—Col. Benjamin H. Grierson, a former MUSIC teacher from Illinois—to take 1,700 horsemen on a diversionary raiding party across middle Mississippi. Grierson, riding hard from southwestern Tennessee, accomplished everything Grant asked for in his 16-day, 600-mile raid in April. Fifty miles of railroad track were destroyed, Confederate communications seriously disrupted, 500 rebel prisoners taken, Southern generals confused, and civilians up in arms.

On May 1, the main Union army was on the eastern side of the Mississippi. Grant was on the march and cut off from his supply base. Others fretted, but he decided to "carry what rations of hard bread, coffee, and salt we can and make the country furnish the balance." The next two and a half weeks saw Grant's army moving swiftly west and then east again, engaging and defeating two Confederate armies (Pemberton's and Johnston's) at Port Gibson, Raymond, Jackson (the state capital), Champion's Hill, and Big Black River. The Union soldiers' morale was high. In 17 days they had marched 180 miles and won five battles. The Union's casualty rate was costly at 4,300 but lower than the Confederates at 7,200. The defeat at Big Black sent Pemberton and his weary men scurrying back for the safety of the fortified city. By noon of May 19, the Federals had arrived at Vicksburg in force, and Grant, convinced that his men could take the city easily, ordered the first of two frontal assaults. Both were unsuc-

cessful, and Grant settled in for the long siege that he had hoped to avoid.

From the military point of view, a siege means the desire to capture a fortified position to gain territory. For Grant, this meant putting his men to work digging trenches until the nine miles of Confederate fortifications behind Vicksburg were encircled by 12 miles of Union earthworks. By June the Union army was not only well entrenched but enlarged greatly. Grant had roughly 75,000 men to deploy, with more arriving daily. Additionally, a steel wall of rifles and cannons ringed the increasingly beleaguered city, and the latter boomed all day and all night. General Pemberton, believing that help in the form of General Johnston and his troops would arrive at any time, vowed never to give up. Because all supply lines into Vicksburg were cut and communication difficult, Pemberton did not receive Johnston's message of June 15 in which he warned Pemberton to escape with his army intact, as saving Vicksburg was hopeless.

From the civilian point of view, a siege means possible starvation and certain disruption of life and destruction of property. At Vicksburg, 3,000 citizens and 30,000 soldiers were trapped and desperate. For almost six weeks, through the terrible heat of late May and June, the mostly women and children civilians of Vicksburg endured dwindling food and water supplies with great courage and spirit. Soon signs of malnutrition appeared in the population. Mule meat and a few handfuls of corn constituted a good day's diet for both soldiers and civilians. Moreover, the constant and deadly rain of Union artillery shells drove terrified families out of their homes and into caves dug out of the hillsides of Vicksburg. In the streets, the houses, fences, and trees that had not been obliterated by bombs were destroyed for firewood. On June 28, Pemberton received a letter, signed by "Many Soldiers," begging him to surrender if he would not see everyone die of starvation. The soldiers by now were too weak to even try to escape their prison. On July 3, Union soldiers near Confederate trenches claimed to see many white flags flying, the classic sign of surrender. On that day, General Pemberton met with Grant and agreed to surrender his army the next day.

The terms were generous. The Confederates—27,230 enlisted men and 2,166 officers—were given "paroles," pieces of paper signed by soldiers that allowed them to go home if they promised not to take up arms against the Union again, thus sparing them from incarceration in a Northern prison camp. Besides the surrender of the army, the Federals captured 200 cannons and 60,000 small arms, so badly needed by Southern armies. The most important outcome by far was that Vicksburg was captured, and on July 9 the Confederacy was split in two when Port Hudson fell to Union general Nathaniel P. Banks. Lincoln knew who deserved the credit for this great and decisive victory for the North. "Grant is my man," he said, "and I am his the rest of the war." Shortly afterward, Grant was promoted to head the Military Division of Mississippi, and Sherman, at Grant's request, assumed Grant's former position as commander of the Western Department and head of the Army of the Tennessee.

"This was the most Glorious Fourth I ever spent," remembered one Union soldier. Indeed, July 4, 1863, was widely celebrated in the North, and not just for the surrender of Vicksburg but also for the Union's win on the fields of Gettysburg, Pennsylvania, on July 3. Although almost two more years would pass before the war was finally over, it was clear, as Grant wrote in his memoirs, that "[t]he fate of the Confederacy was sealed when Vicksburg fell."

See also HOMEFRONT; REFUGEES.

Further reading: Bruce Catton, *Grant Moves South* (Boston: Little, Brown, 1960); A. A. Hoehling, *Vicksburg: 47 Days of Siege* (Mechanicsburg, Pa.: Stackpole Books, 1996); Mary Loughborough, *My Cave Life in Vicksburg, with Letters of Trial and Travel* (Vicksburg, Miss.: Vicksburg and Warren County Historical Society, 1990); Peter F. Walker, *Vicksburg: A People at War, 1860–1865* (Chapel Hill: University of North Carolina Press, 1960).

volunteer army

Roughly 90 percent of the men who made up the armies of the CIVIL WAR, a total of more than 2 million individuals, were volunteers. These amateur soldiers volunteered for a number of reasons, and while their service was invaluable, their approach to warfare often exasperated the professional generals who commanded them.

On the Union side, men were generally accepted into service through the U.S. volunteer system. The Confederates used a system that was identical in all but name. The U.S. volunteer system, used throughout the 19th century, placed the burden of responsibility for raising troops on the states. With congressional approval, GOVERNORS would nominate local notables as officers. These officers, in turn, would put together units by recruiting men from their community to serve terms ranging from three months to three years in length. Once a company or regiment had been formed, it would be accepted into federal service and henceforth commanded and paid for by the U.S. government. The only major exception to this pattern was AFRICAN-AMERICAN REGIMENTS, which, for the most part, were organized directly by the federal government.

In the first months of the war, there was no shortage of volunteers. Indeed, both governments were compelled to send men home because so many reported for duty. Ohio, for example, was asked to supply 13 regiments by

ABRAHAM LINCOLN, but Governor William Dennison wrote to explain to the president that "without seriously repressing the ardor of the people, I can hardly stop short of 20 regiments." After the patriotic furor of the first few months died down, however, volunteers were much harder to come by. Ultimately, both governments were compelled to resort to providing bounties, which were rewards of cash and/or land, for men who enlisted or reenlisted. Both governments also adopted a draft, although this only provided about 3–6 percent of the men who fought.

For the men who volunteered in the early months of the war, the experience could be quite exhilarating, as their communities rallied around them. Older men would regale the volunteers with tales of service in previous wars. Women would make UNIFORMS and other necessities and would smother the volunteers with attention. "If a fellow wants to go with a girl now," wrote one Indiana man in his journal, "he had better enlist. . . ." The new soldiers also had to take care of a number of formalities. Junior-grade officers, the captains and lieutenants, had to be chosen via popular vote. A physical exam had to be passed, although this exam was generally not very thorough, as evidenced by the fact that several hundred women managed to pass it. Once the volunteers had been supplied and all the formalities had been completed, there was usually a big send-off, perhaps with a picnic or a parade. Most units were presented with a flag made by the women of their community. At this point, the volunteers were ready to report for duty.

For many volunteers, perhaps even most, their service in the Civil War marked the first time they had ever left their homes. Why were men willing to abandon everything they had ever known in order to join the fight? There were a number of common reasons. Some men were motivated by the cause of their side or hatred for the other side. Others, particularly in the early months of the war, were attracted by the excitement that prevailed throughout the country and by a desire for new and different experiences. Still others felt pressure from the members of their community. A common attitude was that combat was a chance for a soldier to prove his manhood, and men of the proper age who chose not to enlist were often shunned. Economic motivations were also common. A soldier's pay represented a substantial increase in salary for some members of the working class. The generous bounties the Confederate and Union governments began to offer in 1862, often in excess of $1,000, made enlistment an even more attractive financial proposition.

For leaders on both sides of the Civil War, there were a number of benefits to having a volunteer army. "The patriot volunteer, fighting for his country and his rights," noted THOMAS J. "STONEWALL" JACKSON, "makes the most reliable soldier on earth." Jackson knew that many soldiers spent their terms of service surrounded by friends and relatives that they had known for years or decades. This situation reduced the chance that a soldier would "skeedaddle" during a battle or desert the army after a battle. Beyond that, soldiers maintained strong ties with people on the HOMEFRONT and could be valuable allies in sustaining the civilian population's support for the war. Northern soldiers, in particular, played a critical role in Lincoln's reelection in 1864, ensuring that the war would only end once reunion had been achieved. Finally, the enlistment of large numbers of volunteers added a number of talented soldiers to the ranks who otherwise would not have entered armed service. Widely respected Union generals Francis Channing Barlow and JOSHUA LAWRENCE CHAMBERLAIN were volunteers. On the Southern side, volunteering added Gens. PATRICK R. CLEBURNE and James J. Pettigrew to the ranks.

Although volunteers provided several useful advantages, they also had their shortcomings. A number of generals shared the sentiments of South Carolina governor James Henry Hammond, who wrote in 1861 that, "carrying on a war by volunteers is absolutely suicidal." Hammond's disdain was largely due to the poor soldiering he saw early in the war, when officers were being chosen by a vote of their fellow soldiers. These elections were popularity contests, and so the men chosen almost invariably had little military experience. They did a poor job of training the men under their command and an ineffective job of commanding them in battle. The situation demanded a solution, and by 1862 important changes had been put in place. Experienced military men from the U.S. Army and from Europe were brought in to properly train soldiers. Meanwhile, officers were no longer elected and, instead, were chosen based on merit.

Other problems with volunteers proved less easy to solve and were a constant headache for commanding generals. Volunteer soldiers were less disciplined than career men. Their beliefs about what kinds of behavior were appropriate during a war were not nearly as strongly held as among their professional counterparts. This tendency manifested itself in a variety of ways. The diversions that many volunteer soldiers pursued often shocked the Victorian sensibilities of people on the homefront: gambling, frequenting prostitutes, drinking, smoking, and so forth. Beyond that, Union and Confederate soldiers frequently had few doubts about associating with the enemy once battles were over, and the trading of such commodities as newspapers, tobacco, and coffee across the lines was common. Perhaps the greatest problem was the lack of restraint that many volunteer soldiers showed when interacting with civilians, regularly mistreating them and their property. These incidents undermined support for the war and sometimes provoked violent responses. Ultimately, repeated violations of the RULES OF WAR led the Northern government to issue the Lieber Code of 1863, a set of guidelines designed to control soldiers' behavior. The code was only partially successful.

Once the war was over, virtually all of the volunteers who remained in the armies of the United States and the Confederacy were quickly mustered out of service. After returning home, however, they continued to play an important role in national political life. The men who had served in the North became an important Republican voting bloc, while Southern VETERANS became a key Democratic constituency. Each of the presidents between 1876 and 1900, with the exception of Grover Cleveland, was a Civil War volunteer. The volunteers also worked to shape the memory of the war, writing memoirs of the war and erecting MONUMENTS on battlefields. They ensured that the COMMON SOLDIER would forever occupy a central place in the history of the Civil War.

See also BOUNTY SYSTEM; CONSCRIPTION.

Further reading: James M. McPherson, *For Cause and Comrades: Why Men Fought in the Civil War* (New York: Oxford University Press, 1997); Reid S. Mitchell, *The Vacant Chair: The Northern Soldier Leaves Home* (New York: Oxford University Press, 1993); Bell Irvin Wiley, *The Life of Johnny Reb: The Common Soldier of the Confederacy* (Baton Rouge: Louisiana State University Press, 1978).

—Christopher Bates

W

Wade, Benjamin Franklin (1800–1878)

Born in Fleeting Hills, Massachusetts, on October 27, 1800, Benjamin Wade moved with his family to Andover, Ohio, in 1821. He began practicing law in 1827, and over the next two decades served as a prosecuting attorney, a state senator, and a circuit judge. On March 15, 1851, he received the news of his election to the U.S. Senate.

Wade served his first term as a Whig, but in the two terms that followed he represented the REPUBLICAN PARTY. In his attacks on the KANSAS-NEBRASKA ACT and his defense of his colleague CHARLES SUMNER, Wade displayed both his principles and leadership ability. He earned the nickname of "Bluff" Ben Wade and the respect of his Northern colleagues for answering the challenge by a Southerner to duel with the reply that he favored squirrel guns at 20 paces. More important, within the Senate chambers during the war, the Ohio senator served as an outspoken voice of the RADICAL REPUBLICANS, pushing for a more aggressive military policy from ABRAHAM LINCOLN and his administration. Wade also utilized his chairmanship of the JOINT COMMITTEE ON THE CONDUCT OF THE WAR and the proposed WADE-DAVIS BILL to actively campaign for the ABOLITION of SLAVERY and a harsh RECONSTRUCTION.

In 1867 Wade became the president of the Senate. In this position he, along with Chief Justice SALMON P. CHASE, presided over the impeachment proceedings of President ANDREW JOHNSON. Following the unsuccessful attempt to remove Johnson from office, Wade retired from the Senate and returned to Ohio. In 1868 he failed to gain the vice presidential nomination on the Grant ticket, and in 1876 he served as a presidential elector, repudiating the compromise that gave Rutherford B. Hayes the presidency of the United States.

Benjamin Wade died in Jefferson, Ohio, on March 2, 1878.

See also IMPEACHMENT OF ANDREW JOHNSON.

Further reading: Allan Bogue, *The Earnest Men: Republicans of the Civil War Senate* (Ithaca, N.Y.: Cornell University Press, 1981); Hans L. Trefousse, *Benjamin Franklin Wade: Radical Republican from Ohio* (New York: Twayne, 1963).

—John P. Bowes

Wade-Davis Bill (1864)

In the winter of 1863–64, ABRAHAM LINCOLN set forth his vision for the policies regarding the readmission of Southern states to the Union. He proposed lenient regulations, and early in 1864 he went forward with his plans by initiating RECONSTRUCTION governments in both Louisiana and Arkansas. Upset with the fact that Lincoln appeared to be establishing the foundation of a Reconstruction policy without the consent of the legislative branch, the RADICAL REPUBLICANS passed a bill that presented their own version of Reconstruction on July 2, 1864. First initiated in the House of Representatives by Henry Winter Davis of Maryland, the measure gained approval in the Senate under the guidance of BENJAMIN WADE of Ohio.

The bill, known by the surnames of its sponsors, set out a stringent procedure for readmission. Most notably, it required a majority of white voters in the state under consideration to take the IRONCLAD OATH of allegiance to the United States, and it also demanded that the state's constitution include a clause abolishing SLAVERY. Although the bill did not include all of the points of the radical program, including African-American suffrage, it did give notice to the country and to Lincoln that congressional Radicals did not intend to allow the president solitary control of the Reconstruction of the South. The Senate approved the bill on the very last day of the summer session in a move designed to force Lincoln's approval. But rather than accede to the demands of the Radicals, the president pushed the bill aside and refused to sign it, taking advantage of his pocket-veto privilege. Lincoln's veto led Wade and Davis to issue a manifesto denouncing the president's action as an unconstitutional denial of legislative authority.

Further reading: Michael Les Benedict, *A Compromise of Principle: Congressional Republicans and Reconstruction, 1863–1869* (New York: Norton, 1975); T. Harry Williams, *Lincoln and the Radicals* (Madison: University of Wisconsin Press, 1960).

—John P. Bowes

Wakeman, Sarah Rosetta (1843–1864)

Female soldier Sarah Rosetta Wakeman was born in New York State to a farming family. In 1862 she left home because she "got tired of staying in [the] neighborhood." Dressed as a man, she signed on to be a boatman on the Chenango Canal in New York. A month later she went to the local army recruitment office and, giving her name as Lyons Wakeman, she enlisted in the 153rd New York Volunteer Infantry Regiment. Private Wakeman was mustered into service on October 17, 1862.

For the next 15 months, the 153rd was among the units responsible for defending WASHINGTON, D.C. Although Wakeman's regiment was regularly ordered to prepare for an enemy attack during that time, none came. Finally, in February 1864, the 153rd was transferred to the field to take part in Nathaniel Banks's RED RIVER CAMPAIGN in Louisiana. After an incredibly difficult 700-mile march, Wakeman and her unit participated in the second engagement of the campaign, at Pleasant Hill. They helped to turn back six Confederate charges before being forced to retreat. Shortly thereafter, Wakeman fell ill with dysentery. She reported to the regimental hospital on May 3 and was transferred to a general hospital in New Orleans in late May, where she died on June 19 without her secret being discovered. She was buried in New Orleans under a tombstone bearing her male enlisted name, Lyons Wakeman.

There were approximately 400 CIVIL WAR soldiers who are known to have been women disguised as men. We are left with very little information about most of them, but Wakeman is the exception to the rule. She wrote many LETTERS to her family, which were discovered and published in 1994. At present, this collection is arguably the best contemporary account of the experiences of a woman who donned a uniform during the Civil War.

See also WOMEN'S STATUS AND RIGHTS.

Further reading: Elizabeth D. Leonard, *All the Daring of the Soldier: Women of the Civil War Armies* (New York:

Norton, 1999); Sarah Rosetta Wakeman, *An Uncommon Soldier: The Civil War Letters of Sarah Rosetta Wakeman, Alias Private Lyons Wakeman, Co. H, 153rd New York State Volunteers, 1862–1864*, ed. Lauren Cook Burgess (New York: Oxford University Press, 1995).

—Christopher Bates

Walker, Mary Edwards (1832–1919)

CIVIL WAR doctor and MEDAL OF HONOR winner, Mary Edwards Walker was born on November 26, 1832, in Oswego, New York. She received an excellent EDUCATION as a young woman, eventually earning her medical degree in 1855 from Syracuse Medical College.

When the Civil War broke out in 1861, Walker immediately decided to get involved. She traveled to WASHINGTON, D.C., to offer her services as a surgeon to the U.S. Army's Medical Department. Walker was offered an appointment, but only as a NURSE, which she refused. She began a letter-writing campaign, and eventually a compromise was reached, with Walker agreeing to work as an unpaid volunteer surgeon in exchange for rations and housing.

Walker served in several locales throughout the war. Her main base of operations was the "Indiana Hospital," housed in the U.S. Patent Office in Washington, D.C. Walker also tended to wounded in the field at Warrenton, Virginia, and Fredericksburg, Maryland, as well as other locations. She earned the respect of each of the male surgeons she served under, all of whom urged the government to give her a formal appointment. In early 1864, after much lobbying on Walker's behalf, she was finally given a noncommissioned civilian surgeon's contract paying $80 a month. Walker's good fortune proved to be short-lived. She was captured a few weeks later by a Confederate sentry and spent the remainder of the war in PRISON.

Walker hoped that the government would recognize her contributions with a permanent position as an army medical inspector. After some deliberation, President ANDREW JOHNSON decided not to grant Walker's request. However, he did support her nomination for and eventual award of the Medal of Honor. Walker was the only woman to win the award for service during the Civil War. Later, Walker turned her attention to political issues, especially women's suffrage.

Throughout her life, she wore her Medal of Honor as a badge of the government's gratitude. In 1919 a review board revoked Walker's medal. She declined to surrender her medal and told the board "you can have it over my dead body." Six days later she died near Oswego, the place of her birth. In 1977 the medal was officially restored.

See also WOMEN'S STATUS AND RIGHTS.

Mary Edwards Walker *(Library of Congress)*

Further reading: Elizabeth D. Leonard, *Yankee Women: Gender Battles in the Civil War* (New York: Norton, 1994); Charles McCool Snyder, *Dr. Mary Walker: The Little Lady in Pants* (New York: Arno Press, 1974).

—Christopher Bates

war contracting

In the first months of the CIVIL WAR, thousands upon thousands of men rushed to join the ranks of both the Confederate and Union armies. These men had to be equipped with UNIFORMS, weapons, and other necessities. To do so was not an easy task, because the antebellum army was very small and therefore had only a very limited amount of modern military equipment. As such, both governments were forced to rely on private manufacturers to help provision their armies.

In the North, responsibility for supplying the military's needs initially fell on Secretary of War Simon Cameron.

Cameron was a political appointee, given a place in ABRAHAM LINCOLN's cabinet solely to satisfy Republican voters in Pennsylvania, and he was not capable of managing a large-scale mobilization. In the early months of the war, the process of awarding war contracts was rife with corruption. Manufacturers, with an eye toward maximizing profits, would overcharge the government or provide extremely inferior goods. Guns would misfire or jam, and food was often spoiled. Many uniforms were made of a material called "shoddy," a term that eventually came to describe anything of poor quality. Shoddy uniforms would generally disintegrate after a few months of use, leaving a soldier with no protection from the elements.

Eventually, the situation was so bad that a congressional investigation of the war-contracting process was launched. In the end, however, Congress took no action because President Lincoln acted first, sending Cameron to Russia to serve as the American foreign minister. EDWIN M. STANTON, Cameron's replacement, a no-nonsense lawyer from Ohio, quickly developed a reputation for efficiency and integrity. Stanton initiated a review process to make certain that contracts were only awarded to reliable manufacturers and that the prices the government paid were fair. By the end of 1862, Stanton had brought the situation under control, and for the rest of the war the Union forces were the best-supplied military in the world.

For the South, provisioning the army and navy was an even more difficult task. Food and cotton were abundant, but the Confederates had few other assets. The South had virtually no military equipment on hand at the beginning of the war, and almost all of what they did have was antiquated. Additionally, the South had little manufacturing capacity. At first, the Confederates relied on Europe for equipment, trading cotton for goods. However, this channel quickly dried up due to diplomatic pressure from the Lincoln administration as well as the Union blockade. And so, by the end of 1862, the Confederates largely had to rely upon themselves to equip the military.

Like the North, the South made as much use of private contractors as was possible. The privately owned TREDEGAR IRON WORKS in Virginia grew to be the single most important supplier of goods to the CONFEDERATE ARMY, and smaller firms such as Cook and Brother Armory in Georgia also made contributions. However, because there were so few manufacturing concerns in the South, the Confederate government also found it necessary to go into the manufacturing business for itself. By 1863, publicly owned firms were producing ships, guns, bullets, blankets, wagons, uniforms, and virtually every other manufactured good needed to wage war.

The Confederates had some notable successes in their manufacturing endeavors. In particular, the Confederate

Ordnance Department did a remarkable job of providing ammunition and gunpowder. Generally, however, the CONFEDERATE ARMY and NAVY were woefully undersupplied. Southern manufacturing capacity grew substantially during the war, but never to the point of being able to adequately equip the Confederate army. And even if Southern factories had the capacity to produce what was needed, they lacked the necessary raw materials and manpower. By the middle of the war, the disparities between the equipment of the Union military and the Confederate military were abundantly evident, and the gap continued to grow as the war dragged on. Necessarily, the Union government's success in war contracting must be counted among the reasons that the North was able to win the Civil War.

Further reading: Richard Goff, *Confederate Supply* (Durham, N.C.: Duke University Press, 1969); Herman Hattaway and Archer Jones, *How the North Won* (Urbana: University of Illinois Press, 1983); Frank E. Vandiver, *Ploughshares into Swords: Josiah Gorgas and Confederate Ordnance* (Austin: University of Texas Press, 1952).

—Christopher Bates

Warmoth, Henry Clay (1842–1931)

Born on May 9, 1842, in MacLeansboro, Illinois, Henry C. Warmoth became a lawyer, Union officer, and RECONSTRUCTION governor. As a young boy, he moved with his family to Fairfield, Illinois, where he received an EDUCATION in local schools. Warmoth studied the law in Fairfield, and when he moved to Lebanon, Missouri, in 1860 he received admittance to the bar, despite being only 18 years old. A bright and ambitious young man, Warmoth was appointed county attorney. During this period of increasing sectional tensions in a slave state, he joined the state militia. In 1861 Warmoth declared his loyalty to the Union and helped to raise an infantry regiment. In November 1862, he was rewarded with a lieutenant colonelcy in the 32nd Missouri Infantry Regiment. He served under Gen. John A. McClernand in the VICKSBURG CAMPAIGN of 1862–63 and was wounded in battle in May 1863.

Gen. ULYSSES S. GRANT relieved McClernand of command just at the time that Warmoth was injured. Warmoth was angry that his friend and mentor had been dismissed. Due to statements Warmoth made that expressed his displeasure, Warmoth was accused of maligning Grant's army and was promptly given a dishonorable discharge. He asked for, and received, reinstatement to his unit from President ABRAHAM LINCOLN. He then led the 32nd in the BATTLE OF LOOKOUT MOUNTAIN, near Chattanooga, Tennessee, in November 1863. Requesting a post in New Orleans, Warmoth moved to the Crescent City in 1864, and when the war ended, he was serving as a provost judge.

By 1865 Henry Warmoth had established a law practice in New Orleans and had helped the REPUBLICAN PARTY to organize in Louisiana. Popular and charming, Warmoth actively sought political office, and in April 1868 he was elected GOVERNOR of Louisiana. As governor, Warmoth was confronted immediately with organized white terrorist groups who stopped Republicans from voting for Grant in the 1868 election. Throughout his administration, Warmoth tried and failed to establish the legitimacy of his CARPETBAGGER Republican administration. Using fair as well as foul methods, Warmoth became mired in corruption and scandal. In the scandal-ridden Louisiana election of 1872, Warmoth became so embroiled in controversy that he was impeached, but he was never brought to trial. After 1872, Warmoth remained active in Republican politics, but he was more successful as a planter and businessman in his adopted city of New Orleans, where he died on September 30, 1931.

See also KU KLUX KLAN.

Further reading: Ted Tunnell, *Crucible of Reconstruction: War, Radicalism and Race in Louisiana, 1862–1877* (Baton Rouge: Louisiana State University Press, 1984); Henry Clay Warmoth, *War, Politics, and Reconstruction: Stormy Days in Louisiana* (New York: MacMillan, 1930).

Washington, D.C.

The CIVIL WAR drastically changed the capital city of the United States of America, Washington, District of Columbia. Often called Washington City in the 19th century, it was transformed from a small, provincial city of 63,000, in which the nation's Capitol was located, to the "Nation's Capital," of more than 200,000. In 1860 it was a sleepy Southern town, with muddy, dirty streets, an unhealthy, noxious environment, and many ramshackle buildings. By 1865 Washington, D.C., was the symbol of a newly reunited country, but more than that, it had become a distinctly cosmopolitan place. The former Southern population was enlarged and enlivened by a broad cross section of society—Southern, Northern, freed people, businesspeople, and a huge influx of middle-class women and men who came to work for expanded wartime government agencies and stayed to live. Between 1861 and 1865 the city's population nearly quadrupled.

Washington, D.C., during the Civil War stood for the heart and soul of the Union cause, a cherished symbol of the power of the United States of America. President ABRAHAM LINCOLN, the members of the cabinet, and members of Congress lived and worked in the city, carrying on the vision of the founding fathers. Washington, D.C., was also the most tempting target for Confederate armies. Its capture would be a brilliant prize for the Southern cause, and citizens learned to live with the threat of sudden invasion. The war's threat to D.C. was demonstrated graphically by the circle of forts guarding the city, the barracks crammed with soldiers, the shanty towns filled with ex-slaves bringing the revolution in freedom close to government scrutiny, and the hospitals teeming with wounded and dying soldiers.

Situated on the banks of the Potomac River, the District of Columbia at the start of the Civil War was composed of several small, distinctive communities in a rural setting. Much of the city was built on a swamp, and disease and illness were rampant, particularly in the hot, muggy summer months. The White House is a good example of the unhealthy conditions experienced by many Washingtonians: It was nearby the part of the Potomac River that met with the city canal (the sewer), the city dump, and a slum area called "Murder Bay." This unpleasant combination made life challenging and, occasionally, tragic for the chief executive and his family. The 1862 death of Abraham and Mary Todd Lincoln's son, Willie, was attributed to typhoid fever, a disease contracted through infected drinking water.

Washington City was in an unfinished state in 1860. The Capitol Building, where Congress holds session, was undergoing a major renovation, which included the addition of a huge dome. When criticized for spending money on this construction during wartime, Lincoln replied, "It is a sign we intend for the Union to go on." On December 2, 1863, the famous figure "Armed Freedom" was placed on top of the dome, and by Lincoln's second inaugural the Capitol was completed. Through the war years it also served as a fort, a barracks, a bakery, and a hospital. The Smithsonian Institute and the Treasury Building were also prominent structures; the latter also housed the State Department. The Navy and War Departments were located near the White House; Lincoln was usually able to walk there without fear of attack.

In the tense early days of the Civil War, Washington, D.C., was a city under siege. Though the district's responsibilities were national, its immediate safety was questionable. Roughly 100 miles from RICHMOND, the seat of the newly established CONFEDERATE STATES OF AMERICA, Washington was set amid the beautiful tree-lined hills of the Potomac River Valley; the 10-square-mile tract of the District of Columbia was bordered on three sides by Maryland, a slave state with divided allegiances. Virginia, the Confederate stronghold, bordered the fourth side.

At the outset of the Civil War, President Lincoln found himself and the Union government practically defenseless in the capital city. Dire as the situation was, it became even worse on April 19, 1861, when a confrontation threatened to speed Maryland toward SECESSION and isolate the capital city. The Sixth Massachusetts Regiment, the first fully armed unit to respond to Lincoln's call for troops, left home to defend Washington. Since no rail lines passed all the way through Baltimore, the unit had to detrain and march across the city to board another train. A mob formed in the path of the soldiers, and they were eventually surrounded. Citizens began pelting them with rocks, bricks, and pistol fire. A few men of the Sixth opened fire, and a nasty brawl ensued. By the time the regiment fought its way to the train and out of the city, four soldiers and 12 townspeople lay dead.

Because of the incident, Maryland governor Thomas Hicks, a Unionist, approved the destruction of RAILROAD bridges into the city. Secessionists tore down the TELEGRAPH lines that passed through Baltimore from Washington, and the Union capital was effectively cut off from the North. Fearing an attack, citizens and government clerks in Washington formed into volunteer companies. However, on the next day the New York Seventh Regiment arrived by train, having commandeered and repaired a dilapidated steam engine in Annapolis. Other units soon followed, and the imminent danger to the capital passed.

When Col. Charles P. Stone set about organizing the militias that would provide a permanent defense force for Washington, he faced a daunting task. The regiments that arrived in the early days of the war were impressive in number but questionable in quality. Most were untrained, and discipline was rarely enforced. Accommodations were insufficient; the Capitol housed the men of the Seventh New York who arrived in April 1861. Robert Gould Shaw, a private with the Seventh, addressed a letter to his parents in this way: "April 26, 1861, House of Representatives." He described his experience: "That evening we marched up to the Capitol, and were quartered in the House of Representatives, where we each have a desk, and easy-chair to sleep in, but generally prefer the floor and our blankets. . . . The Capitol is a magnificent building, and the men all take the greatest pains not to harm anything. Jeff Davis shan't get it without trouble." Many soldiers also encamped in the East Room of the White House.

The defense of Washington, D.C., proved a chronic problem for Lincoln and his generals. From the very steps of the White House, Lincoln could view Arlington, ROBERT E. LEE's former home, a constant reminder of the danger that surrounded the city. Even more problematic was the fact that the city was strategically exposed, situated at the point of the "V" formed by the Potomac and Anacostia Rivers. Approaches into the "V" from the north abounded; bridges provided access from the south.

Col. Joseph Mansfield, commander of the Department of Washington, was responsible for overseeing the construction of fortifications outside Washington. The projects were just underway when Union forces were defeated at the FIRST BATTLE OF BULL RUN in July 1861. Lincoln and other leaders, unsure of the CONFEDERATE ARMY's capability, feared invasion. Although it never came, Secretary of War EDWIN M. STANTON made it clear that Union campaigns in Virginia would always include provisions for the defense of Washington. GEORGE B. MCCLELLAN later claimed that the policy drastically hindered his PENINSULAR CAMPAIGN.

Batteries and forts eventually created a 37-mile circle around Washington. Including Alexandria, Arlington Heights, Chain Bridge, and Georgetown, there were 68 forts with more than 800 huge cannons, typically between 700 to 1,500 yards apart. Twenty-three miles of trenches and 93 manned artillery positions completed the ring of defense. Other important sites such as city reservoirs, major roads into the city from the southeast and the north, and the entrance from the Potomac River into the city were heavily protected. If the enemy got beyond the fort, preparations were made for the Treasury Building to be a barricade against attack and for the president and his cabinet to be hidden safely in its basement.

The strong fortifications were weakened from time to time by a chronic problem with understaffing. The men who stood behind the "ring of forts" numbered 30,000, sometimes more and sometimes far less. The latter was the case in July 1864. As ULYSSES S. GRANT directed the siege of Petersburg with an eye to capturing Richmond, Confederate Gen. JUBAL A. EARLY defeated Union forces on a march to Washington with 15,000 rebel soldiers. On July 11, Early appeared outside the Washington defense works, five miles north of the White House. In response to the frantic appeals of the War Department, Grant dispatched the Sixth Corps to Washington to bolster the convalescents, militia, and unit remnants on hand there. Early launched a tentative attack on July 12, the only combat personally witnessed by President Lincoln, who watched from Fort Stevens. Early was stopped from a full attack by the presence of the Sixth Corps, and he wisely withdrew.

Early's near-invasion was the closest the South ever came to attacking the Northern capital during four years of civil war. Other challenges were nearly as great. In May 1861 Washington had one hospital. Fourteen months later, 60 hospitals were built within the city. But it was impossible to build enough hospitals to house the thousands and thousands of sick, wounded, and dying soldiers from the nearby battlefields OF Bull Run, FREDERICKSBURG, and CHANCELLORSVILLE, to name a few.

The War Department had to take over hotels, churches, schools, colleges, and homes and turn them into hospitals. Living in Washington meant that locals were the first to know the terrible price of each battle, as the long line of horse-pulled ambulances deposited the bitter fruits of carnage. After 1863 specially designed "pavilion" style hospitals predominated. Cleaner and more efficient, the white shedlike structures could be expanded to meet the needs of the war.

Indeed, the whole city could be described as the major supply depot for the eastern UNION ARMY. Bakeries, butcheries (more than 10,000 head of cattle grazed on the grass near the unfinished Washington Monument), warehouses for food, clothes, and ammunition dotted the landscape.

Despite Washington, D.C.'s, vulnerable position during the Civil War, President Lincoln never seriously considered relocating further north. Overnight, the city stood as a proud symbol of the Union, the seat of governance, where politicians, wealthy businessmen, and senior military officials discussed and planned the unfolding war; a target for the Confederates and their spies and sympathizers to plot the Union's downfall; a safe haven for more than 40,000 escaped, and later freed, slaves; the destination for soldiers and many of their family members; a final stop for job seekers, women and men alike, to fill the thousands of new positions the expanded wartime administration required. The immense changes Washington, D.C., underwent during the war paralleled those of the larger nation.

See also BALTIMORE, MARYLAND, RIOTS; MEDICINES AND HOSPITALS.

Further reading: Kathryn Jacob, *Testament to Union* (Baltimore, Md.: Johns Hopkins University Press, 1998); Richard Lee, *Mr. Lincoln's City* (McLean, Va.: EPM Publications, 1981); Margaret Leech, *Reveille in Washington: 1860–1865* (New York: Carroll & Graf, 1986); William Osborn Stoddard, *Inside the White House in War Times: Memoirs and Reports of Lincoln's Secretary* (Lincoln: University of Nebraska Press, 2000).

—Richard J. Roder

Watie, Stand (1806–1871)

Cherokee political leader and Confederate brigadier general, Stand Watie was born on December 12, 1806, in the Cherokee town of Oothcaloga, near Rome, Georgia. His father was David Oowatie and his mother was Susannah Reese.

As a child, Watie attended the Morovian Mission School in Springplace, Georgia. He became a planter as well as a clerk in the Cherokee Supreme Court. In 1835, along with approximately 100 other Cherokee, he signed the controversial Treaty of New Echota. In the treaty, which Principal Chief John Ross and the majority of the Cherokee Nation opposed, the Cherokee agreed to cede their land to the United States and move to the territory now known as Oklahoma. Watie migrated in 1837, while most of the nation unsuccessfully tried to resist removal.

The tensions between Ross and Watie reemerged when the CIVIL WAR began. Ross led the Cherokee Nation to a stance of neutrality, but Watie immediately threw his support behind the Confederacy. Watie received a commission as a colonel, formed the Confederate Cherokee Regiment of Mounted Rifles, and arranged a Cherokee-Confederacy alliance. Ross reluctantly supported the alliance before fleeing the nation in 1862. With Ross gone, the Cherokee elected Watie principal chief. Watie participated in various cavalry engagements in Indian Territory, including battles at Wilson's Creek, Chustenahlah, Pea Ridge, Cowskin Prarie, Webbers Falls, and the First and Second Battles of Cabin Creek. In May 1864, the Confederacy rewarded Watie with a promotion to brigadier general, making him the only NATIVE AMERICAN to achieve this rank. Watie's military career ended when he surrendered on June 23, 1865.

When the war ended, Watie helped negotiate the Cherokee Reconstruction Treaty of 1866 and served as a delegate to the General Council for Indian Territory in 1870–71. Soon after, Watie returned to his Honey Creek farm, where he died on September 9, 1871.

See also PEA RIDGE, BATTLE OF.

Further reading: Frank Cunningham, *General Stand Watie's Confederate Indians* (Norman: University of Oklahoma Press, 1998); W. Craig Gaines, *The Confederate Cherokees: John Drew's Regiment of Mounted Rifles* (Baton Rouge: Louisiana State University Press, 1989); Laurence M. Hauptman, *Between Two Fires: American Indians in the Civil War* (New York: Free Press, 1995).

—Andrew K. Frank

Welles, Gideon (1802–1878)

Diarist and secretary of the UNION NAVY, Gideon Welles was born on July 1, 1802, in Glastonbury, Connecticut, to the merchant Samuel Welles and his wife Anne Hale. An excellent EDUCATION prepared Welles for a career as a newspaperman and politician. A staunch Democrat, Welles wrote for the *Hartford Times* while establishing a strong political base among Connecticut voters. In the 1820s and 1830s he was elected to the state legislature. Although ambitious for higher office, Welles was defeated in each of his attempts to become a congressman, a senator, and the GOVERNOR of his state. In 1846 Welles was appointed chief of the Bureau of Provisions and Clothing in the Navy Department. In this position he was responsible for supplying the U.S. Navy during the Mexican-American War (1846–48).

Married to his cousin Mary Jane Hale and the father of nine children, Welles spent the 1840s and 1850s actively opposing the extension of SLAVERY in the territories. He articulated his position in a series of editorials in the *New York Evening Post* denouncing the Compromise of 1850 and the Fugitive Slave Act. He broke with his party in supporting former Democrat Martin Van Buren on the Free-Soil ticket in the presidential election in 1848. In 1855 Welles joined the newly formed REPUBLICAN PARTY in protest over the Kansas-Nebraska "outrage." He established a Republican newspaper, the Hartford *Evening Press,* and was a force in mobilizing New England behind the young party. A member of the Republican National Committee, Welles was determined to elect a president in the election of 1860. Welles threw his support behind ABRAHAM LINCOLN of Illinois, and for that, he was given a position in Lincoln's cabinet. On March 4, 1861, Gideon Welles was appointed secretary of the U.S. Navy.

Secretary Welles faced formidable challenges at the beginning of the American CIVIL WAR. From a tiny, weak, and old-fashioned navy, Welles was expected to mount an effective blockade of Southern ports along the Atlantic coast, conquer Confederate forces protecting the vast interior water systems, and forge a smooth working relationship with the U.S. Army. From 1861, Welles expanded the fleet through buying, building, and leasing. For example, he leased 184 merchant ships from private companies and quickly converted them into IRONCLADS, ready for service. Realizing that a successful wartime navy demanded more than building gunboats, Welles assembled an impressive staff, including the brilliant assistant secretary of the Navy, Gustavus Vasa Fox. They worked together to make the navy contracting system efficient and relatively free of corruption. Just as important, Welles created a "Committee of Conference" to plan the overall strategy of the water war. Essentially a think tank, the committee also recommended specific tactical maneuvers and coordinated the movements of the various fleets in the eastern and western theaters.

Union naval victories achieved early in the war confirmed the correctness of Welles's program. PORT ROYAL in South Carolina fell in November 1861, soon to be followed by the fall of western Forts Henry and Donelson in early 1862, and New Orleans in the same year. Naval heroes such as DAVID DIXON PORTER and DAVID GLASGOW FARRAGUT drew attention to the fact that Union control of the Atlantic coast and the MISSISSIPPI RIVER would strangle and then stop the flow of goods and munitions to the Confederacy. Although the blockade was never totally effective, its success has to be counted as a major factor in the ultimate Union victory. In 1865 Welles could reflect with pride that the U.S. Navy was second in strength and numbers only to the British.

Welles was a loyal Lincoln man, but he engaged in bitter quarrels with the other cabinet members, most notably EDWIN M. STANTON and WILLIAM H. SEWARD, secretaries of war and state. He recorded the controversies and events of the Civil War in his remarkable and brilliant diary. Welles also recorded his growing dissatisfaction over the direction of RECONSTRUCTION policy. Although he supported EMANCIPATION, Welles opposed giving African Americans full civil rights. After the ASSASSINATION OF ABRAHAM LINCOLN, President ANDREW JOHNSON retained Welles in his cabinet, and the two men found they had much in common. Like Johnson, Welles favored STATES' RIGHTS and an easy reconstruction policy toward the former Confederacy. Eventually, Welles rejoined the DEMOCRATIC PARTY, and at the end of Johnson's administration returned to Hartford. He died on February 11, 1878.

See also KANSAS-NEBRASKA ACT; NEW ORLEANS, BATTLE OF.

Further reading: Gideon Welles, *The Diary of Gideon Welles, Secretary of the Navy under Lincoln and Johnson*, ed. Howard K. Beale (New York: Norton, 1960); John Niven, *Gideon Welles: Lincoln's Secretary of the Navy* (New York: Oxford University Press, 1973).

Wheeler, Joseph (1836–1906)

Joseph Wheeler is one of only two persons who achieved the rank of general in both the CONFEDERATE ARMY and the U.S. Army. Born in Augusta, Georgia, on September 10, 1836, he grew up in Connecticut and entered the UNITED STATES MILITARY ACADEMY AT WEST POINT in 1854. Upon graduation he served in the Regiment of Mounted Rifles at Fort Craig, New Mexico. In 1861 Wheeler returned to Georgia and was commissioned as a lieutenant, and soon after he became colonel of the 19th Alabama Infantry Regiment. Two years later, at the age of 26, he was promoted to major general of cavalry.

His skills as cavalry commander were most effective when he operated close to the army; he covered every retreat of the Army of Tennessee from Perryville, Kentucky, to Atlanta, Georgia. Instead of accompanying the army on its march toward Nashville in 1864, Wheeler's cavalry was assigned the difficult and mainly futile task of harassing the UNION ARMY of Maj. Gen. WILLIAM T. SHERMAN as it marched through Georgia and the Carolinas. Though many in the Army of Tennessee (as well as many historians) judged his offensive tactics and raids to be of little importance, Gen. ROBERT E. LEE considered him one of his two best cavalry officers.

After the end of the war, Wheeler married Daniella Jones Sherrod and settled in Lawrence County, Alabama, as a well-to-do lawyer, planter, and businessman. From 1884 to 1898, he served as a Democratic congressman from Alabama, in which capacity he actively opposed the tariff and supported Free Silver.

At the outbreak of the Spanish-American War in 1898, Wheeler offered his services to President McKinley and was commissioned major general of U.S. Volunteers. He participated in the capture of Santiago, where troops under

Joseph Wheeler *(Library of Congress)*

his command, the "Rough Riders," stormed San Juan Hill. He died on January 25, 1906, in Brooklyn, New York, and is one of a very few Confederate generals interred in Arlington National Cemetery.

See also SHERMAN'S MARCH THROUGH GEORGIA; STUART, J. E. B.

Further reading: John P. Dyer, *From Shiloh to San Juan: The Life of "Fightin' Joe" Wheeler* (Baton Rouge: Louisiana State University Press, 1992).

—Stacey Graham

Whig Party   See Volume IV

Whiskey Ring

The Whiskey Ring was a group of distillers who defrauded the government of millions of dollars in the 1870s. The national scandal stirred up by the exposure of the ring further tarnished the troubled presidency of ULYSSES S. GRANT and inspired a wave of reform.

In 1872 distillers in St. Louis, Missouri, devised a scheme to avoid the federal excise tax on whiskey. Paying off tax collectors to ignore the duty owed on their product, they began to earn tremendous profits. Working in collusion with a whole network of Treasury officials, the Whiskey Ring swindled the government of millions in tax revenues. The operation continued for several years, growing in size all the time. During this early period, special agents of the Treasury tried to stop the fraud but were always unsuccessful.

Eventually, news of the racket began to escape from the circle of distillers and the government agents that the Whiskey Ring was paying off. Newspaper reporters who checked out the story were given money in exchange for silence. Government officials who stumbled upon the ring were also paid to look the other way, and a fund was set up by the ring to distribute payoffs to a broad range of storekeepers, government employees, and collectors. It would not be long, however, before the secret became too large to easily manage. Far beyond the original city of St. Louis, there were now branches of the ring in Chicago, Cincinnati, Milwaukee, New Orleans, Peoria, and most ominously, in WASHINGTON, D.C., the nation's capital.

On May 1, 1875, newspapers in St. Louis reported that John D. McDonald, the city's supervisor of U.S. revenues, had conspired to defraud the government of more than $2 million worth of excise taxes. McDonald, a very highly positioned official, had accepted bribes from the distillers in exchange for ignoring their requirement to pay the federal tax on whiskey. McDonald also happened to be a close personal friend and appointee of President Grant. On May 10, Secretary of the Treasury Benjamin H. Bristow launched the investigation that would put an end to the ring. Bristow's agents seized 16 distilleries, and the indictments began.

The public uproar against the Whiskey Ring was deafening. As people learned just how far the corruption went, faith in the government and in their president declined sharply. After Bristow and the Treasury Department investigated the ring, 238 people were indicted, including President Grant's private secretary, Gen. Orville Babcock. President Grant himself was not involved in the scandal, but his proximity to it led to numerous accusations against his presidency.

Although most of the people who were indicted were not convicted, the scandal did a great deal of political damage to the Grant administration. Things were not helped any when President Grant personally intervened to ensure that Babcock was not convicted. Shortly thereafter, however, Babcock resigned his position.

The Whiskey Ring was the worst of the scandals that plagued Grant's presidency. The CRÉDIT MOBILIER scandal, the resignations of his attorney general and secretary of the interior under suspicion of corruption, and the impeachment of his secretary of war for selling military appointments—combined with the exposure of the Whiskey Ring—left many with the impression that Grant's

administration and the federal government itself were hives of corruption.

After the Whiskey Ring was exposed, the effort to "clean up" the government reached a new pitch. A reform GOVERNOR from Ohio, Rutherford B. Hayes, was nominated by the REPUBLICAN PARTY to be the next president. Due in part to the public anger over the Whiskey Ring, Hayes was elected on a platform of reform and honesty. Grant's image as a president who allowed corruption to run rampant permanently damaged his reputation.

Further reading: John McDonald, *Secrets of the Great Whiskey Ring; and Eighteen Months in the Penitentiary* (St. Louis: W.S. Bryan, 1885); William S. McFeely, *Grant: A Biography* (New York: W. W. Norton, 1982); Mark W. Summers, *The Era of Good Stealings* (New York: Oxford University Press, 1993).

—Troy Rondinone

Whitman, Walt (1819–1892)

Renowned American poet and CIVIL WAR nurse Walt Whitman was born on May 31, 1819, in Long Island, New York. He was the second child of Louisa van Velsor and Walter Whitman Sr., both of them poor farm folk with little formal EDUCATION and a diminishing tract of family land. In 1823 the Whitmans took advantage of an economic boom and moved to Brooklyn, New York.

There, Whitman attended public school, and at the age of 12 he entered the printing trade. Over the next several years, Whitman worked as a printer, teacher, and eventually he became a journalist, editing a daily newspaper in New York at the age of 23. In 1826 Whitman became editor of the Brooklyn *Daily Eagle*, but because of his Free-Soil politics, he was dismissed in 1848. After working two more years as a journalist in New Orleans and New York, Whitman built houses and sold real estate with his father from 1850 to 1855.

Throughout all of his years in New York, Whitman read voraciously and developed a love of THEATER and opera. Though he exhibited virtually no literary promise, Whitman published stories and poems in several newspapers and magazines. Eventually, he began experimenting with a new style of poetry, and in spring 1855, once he had composed several poems in this new style, Whitman published the first edition of *Leaves of Grass* at his own expense.

The text drew little attention, though Ralph Waldo Emerson praised it highly in a letter to Whitman. Another year went by before a revised second edition of *Leaves of Grass* was published. It too was a commercial failure. Following the release of the second edition, Whitman edited yet another daily newspaper, but he found himself once again unemployed by the summer of 1859. In 1860, however, a Boston publisher put out the rearranged and enlarged third edition of *Leaves of Grass*, which included Whitman's "Calamus" poems. In these poems Whitman wrote of an apparent homosexual love affair, though it is uncertain whether or not the affair ever actually happened. The publisher went broke with the onset of the Civil War.

With the start of the war, Whitman composed and published several poems for recruitment purposes, many of which were later printed in *Drum Taps* (1865). When Whitman's brother was wounded at the BATTLE OF FREDERICKSBURG in 1862, he went to WASHINGTON, D.C., staying a while in his brother's hospital camp and eventually taking a temporary post in the paymaster's office. Using his spare time to visit wounded and dying soldiers in the Washington hospitals, Whitman bought and delivered small gifts to both Confederate and Union soldiers in an attempt to alleviate their mental and physical suffering.

By mid-1865, the atrocities of the war and the ASSASSINATION OF ABRAHAM LINCOLN had left Whitman somewhat disillusioned with life. His changing attitude is reflected in *Drum Taps*, released in May 1865. Unlike Whitman's earlier oratorical recruitment pieces, this poetic collection showed a keen awareness of the realities of war and included his most well-known allegorical poem, "O Captain, My Cap-

tain." In the poem, Whitman eulogizes President ABRAHAM LINCOLN by using the metaphor of a ship's captain who has died at the end of a long voyage. The work concludes with one of Whitman's most famous verses:

> My Captain does not answer, his lips are pale
>   and still,
> My father does not feel my arm, he has no pulse
>   nor will,
> The ship is anchored safe and sound, its voyage
>   closed and done,
> From fearful trip the victor ship comes in with
>   object won;
> Exult, O shores, and ring O bells!
> But I, with mournful tread,
> Walk the deck my Captain lies,
> Fallen cold and dead.

In the fall of 1865, *Sequel to Drum Taps* was published; the collection contained "When Lilacs Last in the Dooryard Bloom'd," another well-known elegy for President Abraham Lincoln.

A reworked fourth edition of *Leaves of Grass* was issued in 1867. Whitman finally began garnering recognition, particularly in England, thanks to the writings of journalists William O'Connor and John Burroughs and the release of an English edition of his work edited by William Michael Rossetti.

Whitman fell ill in 1872, likely due to the emotional strain that resulted from his ambiguous sexuality. He was partially paralyzed by a stroke in January 1873, but in May he was healthy enough to journey to his brother's home in Camden, New Jersey, where his mother had died. Due to his uncertain EMPLOYMENT status and ill-health, Whitman decided to remain with his brother for several years, although by 1879 he was well enough to take an extended trip to the West.

In 1881 yet another edition of *Leaves of Grass* was published, and it was immediately denounced as immoral by the Society for the Suppression of Vice. Facing prosecution, the publisher gave the plates to Whitman, who printed an author's edition of the book. Thanks to the publicity generated by this controversy, the book sold much better than any of the preceding editions, and Whitman was able to buy a cottage in Camden, where he spent the rest of his life delivering lectures and receiving admirers. In April 1888 he suffered another stroke that left him almost completely incapacitated. Whitman died March 26, 1892, and was buried in a tomb he designed himself.

See also NURSES.

—Brian O'Camb

Walt Whitman *(Library of Congress)*

Further reading: Betsy Erkkila, *Whitman the Political Poet* (New York: Oxford University Press, 1989); James Edwin Miller Jr., *Walt Whitman* (Boston: Twayne, 1990); David R. Reynolds, *Walt Whitman's America* (New York: Knopf, 1995); Walt Whitman, *Leaves of Grass* (New York: Metro Books, 2001).

Wilderness, Battle of the (May 5–6, 1864)

The Battle of the Wilderness was fought on May 5 and 6, 1864, in a densely wooded area of the Virginia countryside. This first clash between the armies of ULYSSES S. GRANT and ROBERT E. LEE in the OVERLAND CAMPAIGN was a harbinger of the nonstop fighting and shockingly high casualty rates that stunned the American people in the last year of the war. The Battle of the Wilderness was a bloody stalemate, but Grant's decision afterward to fight it out until the end turned the tide toward Union victory.

The Battle of the Wilderness was waged at the same place that the BATTLE OF CHANCELLORSVILLE had been fought one year earlier. The conflict was Grant's first attack on Lee after having been named commander of all Union armies two months previously. As the Army of the Potomac approached the Rapidan River, Grant had four corps. There were three large infantry corps and also PHILIP H. SHERIDAN's cavalry corps for a total of 118,000 men. Lee had less than half the number of combat-ready soldiers as Grant, but he had the advantage of being familiar with the roads and rugged terrain.

On May 4, most of the Army of the Potomac crossed the Rapidan River without any resistance. Lee had settled on an attack of Grant's right flank, believing that the UNION ARMY was not prepared for an assault. The vicious fighting began along the Orange Plank Road on May 5 and proceeded in a "fog" as the dense forests made artillery useless and caused many soldiers to become disoriented.

By nightfall on May 5, the lines of battle stretched for 5 miles. Lee ordered Gen. JAMES LONGSTREET to make a night march to support Gen. AMBROSE P. HILL's men, who were confronted by a large Union force under the command of Gen. WINFIELD SCOTT HANCOCK. Longstreet's men arrived the next morning, just in time to avert Hancock's men from destroying both Confederate flanks. Longstreet prevented defeat and halted the Union onslaught, but at the cost of a large number of casualties. Longstreet was himself wounded by friendly fire as the Union forces retreated. This slowed the Confederate pursuit and allowed the UNION ARMY to reorganize. They quickly confronted CONFEDERATE ARMY under the command of Gen. Richard H. Anderson. The firefight that broke out was so intense that logs on Union breastworks actually caught fire, literally separating the two armies.

Attacks and counterattacks continued through the day on May 6 and made for a bloody field of battle. Near sundown, Confederate commander RICHARD S. EWELL attempted to restart the offensive by turning the Union right. Though his initial assault was partially successful, it was not completed due to nightfall. The battle had ended.

Grant had lost his first confrontation with Lee, suffering more than 17,000 casualties compared with the 8,000 inflicted on the Confederates, but he did not retreat. "At present we can claim no victory over the enemy," Grant wrote of the battle, but "neither have they gained a single advantage." Grant brought up reinforcements and continued to move the Army of the Potomac, much to their surprise and delight, in the direction of the Confederate capital. He told President Lincoln that, "whatever happens there will be no turning back." Grant had begun his plan of "total war." The next stop would be at the BATTLE OF SPOTSYLVANIA.

See also RICHMOND.

Further reading: Robert Scott Garth, *Into the Wilderness with the Army of the Potomac* (Bloomington: Indiana University Press, 1992); Grady McWhiney, *Battle in the Wilderness: Grant Meets Lee* (Abilene, Tex.: McWhiney Foundation Press, 1998); Gordon C. Rhea, *The Battle of the Wilderness: May 5–6, 1864* (Baton Rouge: Louisiana State University Press, 1994).

—Scott L. Stabler

Wilmot Proviso (1846)

The Wilmot Proviso was a bill proposed in the House of Representatives by Pennsylvania Democrat David Wilmot that would have prohibited SLAVERY in all territories added to the United States as a result of the Mexican-American War (1846–48).

In 1846, President James K. Polk told Congress that the war with Mexico was a legitimate defense of U.S. territory in newly annexed Texas. He expressed his belief that Mexican dictator Santa Anna had planned to reconquer the state, which had seceded from Mexico only a decade before. Northern ABOLITIONists were skeptical that the president was being forthright. They believed the war to be little more than a thinly disguised effort to expand Southern slavery at Mexico's expense.

Once the war was won, Polk requested a $2 million appropriation from Congress in order to negotiate a peace settlement with Mexico. Congressman David Wilmot decided it was time to act. He proposed an amendment to the "$2 million bill" which "provided . . . that neither slavery nor involuntary servitude shall ever exist in any part of said territory [acquired from Mexico], except for crime, whereof the party shall first be duly convicted."

Quickly called the "Wilmot Proviso," the proposed amendment touched off a storm of outrage throughout the South. Southerners saw the Wilmot Proviso as a cynical Northern effort to increase their political power. Responding to a New York congressman's support for Wilmot, Georgia congressman Seaborn Jones declared that Wilmot's real fear was not slavery at all but, rather, "the power of the South in Congress. . . . It was not . . . the damning sin of slavery that the gentleman could not tolerate . . . oh, no sir! It was the potential power thus acquired by another part of the Union that roused . . . holy indignation!"

While the House added Wilmot's proviso to the $2 million bill, the Senate adjourned before considering the legislation. In 1847 Polk increased his request to $3 million. Wilmot again added his proviso to the House version. This time, the Senate rejected the amendment outright.

The defeat of the Wilmot Proviso rallied antislavery forces, who abandoned the Democrat and Whig Parties in order to form organizations committed to keeping slavery out of the territories. The Liberty Party, the Free-Soil Party, and finally the REPUBLICAN PARTY all pledged themselves to passage of the proviso. David Wilmot himself was a part of this political transformation. Leaving the DEMOCRATIC PARTY, Wilmot first joined the Free-Soil Party and then, in the mid-1850s, became a Republican. During the CIVIL WAR, Wilmot served as a U.S. senator for Pennsylvania from 1861 to 1863 and then as a judge in the court of claims. By the end of the war, Wilmot's vision had become reality.

Further reading: Charles Buxton Going, *David Wilmot, Free-Soiler: A Biography of the Great Advocate of the Wilmot Proviso* (Gloucester, Mass.: P. Smith, 1966); Chaplain W. Morrison, *Democratic Politics and Sectionalism: The Wilmot Proviso Controversy* (Chapel Hill: University of North Carolina Press, 1967).

—Tom Laichas

Women's National Loyal League

The Women's National Loyal League was a political association of women in support of the Union war effort during the CIVIL WAR. Thousands of women worked to help Union troops by participating in the activities of the UNITED STATES SANITARY COMMISSION, UNITED STATES CHRISTIAN COMMISSION, and local soldiers' aid societies. The hospital clothes they made and the fruits and vegetables they packed for shipment to the front symbolized traditions of domesticity females usually assumed during the 19th century. However, a growing number of women tried to support the war effort by operating in the political sphere dominated by men.

Most Northerners understood that SLAVERY helped cause the Civil War and that resolution of the conflict depended on settling the questions about the position of African Americans. The debate on slavery allowed some women to assume purely political roles in their war work. They determined that the restoration of the Union depended on the EMANCIPATION of African Americans and began to plan a campaign in support of that end, calling upon women from all loyal states to join them at a convention to form the Women's National Loyal League. The meeting took place at New York's Church of the Puritans on May 14, 1863.

The drive toward emancipation for slaves undertaken that day built on earlier work done by women and on associations that men organized to support the ABRAHAM LINCOLN administration. Women had used the power of the petition to exert their influence in matters pertaining to ABOLITION as early as the 1830s. They collected signatures on documents supporting various resolutions and then sent the material to sponsoring congressmen. During the Civil War, men who supported the Republican administration formed UNION LEAGUE Clubs. These groups tried to convince citizens to support the war effort and to undercut the influence of Peace Democrats, or COPPERHEADS. At the same time, women founded their own Union League Clubs. Like soldiers' aid societies, these groups used traditional, domestic approaches to support the government. By reducing their consumption of food and textiles, needed commodities were made available for the military.

The Women's National Loyal League wanted to recognize and give moral support to the traditional work of aid societies while remaining focused on support of the government through political action. Women from more than a half-dozen states attended the first meeting. The most prominent members of the women's movement for full citizenship rights played important roles. Lucy Stone presided, and ELIZABETH CADY STANTON, Susan B. Anthony, Angelina Grimké Weld, Ernestine Rose, and Antoinette Brown Blackwell took part in the debates. The leaders announced the goal of collecting 1 million signatures on a petition calling for the emancipation of "all persons of African descent held in involuntary service in the United States."

Not all women favored the obvious political aims of the leaders, and many objected to the feminist nature of the gathering. They believed that Lincoln needed the support of women in order to restore the Union, but they felt it more appropriate to maintain a traditional role for women. They favored conservation of household goods, a focus on stimulating patriotism, and direct support of soldiers by writing LETTERS to the men and similar philanthropic activities. When the leaders of the convention refused to alter their plans, many of the conservative delegates withdrew.

Despite such objections, the organizers created a national association. Membership cost a one-dollar fee and allowed members to wear the league's pin, which had the figure of a slave whose chains had been broken and the words, "In Emancipation is national unity." The initial goal of mere emancipation for slaves changed as a result of violence against African Americans and others during the NEW YORK CITY DRAFT RIOTS in 1863. Following those events, the Loyal League petitioned for citizenship for all Africans Americans.

By 1864 the group had more than 5,000 members. Senator CHARLES SUMNER of Massachusetts presented their documents to the political leaders. Their work resulted in more than 20,000 petitions with more than 400,000 signatures. Although their labors did not lead directly to full citizenship for African Americans or women, the Women's National Loyal League, born in war and trained in the political battle of emancipation, gave women experience in the political world from which they would ultimately gain full citizenship rights.

See also LADIES AID SOCIETIES; WOMEN'S STATUS AND RIGHTS.

Further reading: Wendy Hamand Venet, *Neither Ballots nor Bullets: Women Abolitionists and the Civil War* (Charlottesville: University Press of Virginia, 1991).

—Karen Kehoe

women's status and rights

The mid-19th century proved a time of upheaval in women's lives. Women—black and white—organized, declared rights, and struggled to participate in the public (especially political) sphere. By the late-19th century, they had voiced revolutionary goals but had not achieved equality.

The demand for women's rights began before supporters organized any formal efforts. Initially, 19th-century white women achieved some success by taking their domestic responsibilities into the public sphere. They took active roles in voluntary and benevolent associations, including temperance, child labor, health reform, EDUCATION, and ABOLITIONism, that drew upon traditionally domestic chores such as child rearing, household tasks, and family management.

The links between women's rights and the abolition movement were drawn early. As abolitionists publicly demanded civil rights for African-American slaves, some women became aware of the similarities between their condition as women and that of slaves. They found it easy to draw parallels between their situation and that of African Americans: Neither group could vote, and the law deemed both inferior to white men. Women's commitment to anti-SLAVERY led some to form their own abolitionist organizations, including the WOMEN'S NATIONAL LOYAL LEAGUE. These female-run abolitionist groups eventually led to the founding of women's rights organizations, especially the American Equal Rights Association and the American Woman Suffrage Association.

The transition from reform movements to women's rights seemed a natural one. Women, frustrated with the restrictions placed on them in many organizations, gladly took up the fight to secure themselves a recognized place in society. They were aided by the ability to transfer the skills they had gained in the various associations to their campaigns for women's rights. In particular, women had learned the importance of organization, public speaking, persuasive writing, and argumentation. Many of the early leaders of the woman's rights campaign, including Lucretia Mott and ELIZABETH CADY STANTON, had been prominent and outspoken abolitionists. Susan B. Anthony had been both a temperance and an antislavery activist.

The first formal meeting in the fight for women's rights took place between July 19 and 21, 1848, in Seneca Falls, New York. At this convention a group of feminists, including Stanton, Mott, Jane Hunt, Mary McClintock, and Martha C. Wright, gathered together hundreds of supporters, male and female, and launched a national campaign for women's rights.

The activists at Seneca Falls presented a Declaration of Rights for Women, also known as the Declaration of Rights and Sentiments, which asserted a list of grievances and resolutions. Stanton, the declaration's author, modeled her document on the Declaration of Independence, but her rendition put American men in the role of oppressor. The declaration's list of grievances accused men of denying women the right to vote, to own property, and to access equal representation and education. It further berated men for taking away women's rights at marriage and highlighted the dangers of women's subordination to men, including their vulnerability to violence. It demanded the grievances be addressed and offered 12 resolutions. By the end of the convention, 100 people had signed the document, including 68 of the 300 women in attendance and 32 of the men. The Declaration of Rights became a rallying point for the women's rights movement. Stanton, much to the dismay of some of the people involved, also used the convention as an opportunity to demand women's suffrage.

Two weeks after the Seneca Falls Convention, an even larger women's rights meeting was held in Rochester, New York, and other women's rights conventions soon followed. The most well-known meetings took place in Salem, Ohio;

Worcester, Massachusetts; and Akron, Ohio. At the convention in Akron in 1851, runaway slave and women's rights activist SOJOURNER TRUTH addressed the audience. In response to ideas about the natural delicacy of white women, she recounted some aspects of her life as a slave. Although white women were seen as too feminine and delicate to do any hard labor or even get into a carriage themselves, Truth asserted herself as a woman despite her work as an enslaved field laborer and mother of 13. As she listed her hardships, Truth continued to ask her audience, "A'n't I a woman?" She and other free black women demonstrated that they, too, wanted equal rights.

Women continued to organize and lobby for their rights throughout the 1850s. In 1854 Stanton founded the New York Suffrage Society, which organized petition drives and gathered 10,000 signatures in favor of women's suffrage and property rights. That year, both Anthony and Ernestine Rose spoke to various legislative committees. In addition, Stanton became the first woman to speak in the New York Senate when she stood to present the society's petitions.

By 1860, women had gained access to public and private institutions that educated them for careers in teaching. Newly formed women's medical hospitals also trained them to work in the medical profession as physicians and medical missionaries. It was initially assumed that female doctors would care only for other women and children.

The CIVIL WAR brought women into the public sphere in even greater numbers—raising money for soldiers, nursing the wounded, and providing other valuable services. American women founded more than 20,000 aid societies to supply the troops with food, clothing, and medical supplies. In the North, women soon filled the ranks of the UNITED STATES SANITARY COMMISSION, a volunteer organization run by men but dependent on the efforts of women to get medical supplies and personnel to army hospitals. In addition, women also filled the jobs left empty by the soldiers on the battlefield, including those as PLANTATION mistresses, factory workers, NURSES, and treasury employees. Both the U.S. and Confederate governments, for example, employed several hundred women to work in the treasury and at other government posts during the war. Women's voluntary participation in various roles highlighted their desire to sustain the HOMEFRONT, even if it meant assuming traditionally male roles. Some women hoped that their successful performance during the Civil War would assist them in their fight for suffrage and other rights of citizenship.

Women in the North and South also asserted their rights as citizens through wartime protests. In 1863 angry women participated in FOOD RIOTS in the South and draft riots in the North. In separate but similar incidents, Southern women, especially in Virginia, Alabama, and North Carolina, took to the streets to demand fair food prices and government protection. Northern women similarly participated in antigovernment actions. Many lower-class women participated in the NEW YORK CITY DRAFT RIOTS in the summer of 1863 to protest the IMPRESSMENT of their husbands into military service and wartime policies designed to free slaves. During the lengthy and violent riots, several hundred women were arrested, convicted, and jailed.

As the Civil War came to a close and Congress discussed extending the vote to freed African Americans, feminists hoped that the expansion of the franchise would extend to female citizens. They were disappointed by the inclusion of the word *male* in the FOURTEENTH AMENDMENT, the first time gender-specific language had been used in the Constitution. Such wording made clear the idea that Congress intended to extend voting rights only to men. To protest the exclusion of women's suffrage in the Fourteenth Amendment, Stanton ran for Congress in August 1866. She gained only 24 votes.

After the passage of the Fourteenth Amendment, female activists regrouped. On May 10, 1866, the National Women's Rights Convention established the American Equal Rights Association to work for the rights of all women, regardless of race. The women involved hoped that a coordinated effort would ultimately result in woman suffrage. Republican men who felt threatened by the idea of woman suffrage often ridiculed the mostly Northern Republican women who were involved in this movement.

White feminists disagreed with the tactics of the American Equal Rights Association. Anthony and Stanton, for example, thought the biracial organization unfairly ranked African-American rights ahead of woman suffrage. Consequently, they formed the NATIONAL WOMAN SUFFRAGE ASSOCIATION (NWSA) in May 1869. Stanton became the NWSA's president and actively pursued a national campaign for white-woman suffrage. The NWSA attracted many working-class women and radicals and refused to support the FIFTEENTH AMENDMENT unless it enfranchised women as well as African Americans.

The NWSA had many opponents, even among those working for women's rights. Later that year, Lucy Stone, JULIA WARD HOWE, and other conservative feminists established the American Woman Suffrage Association (AWSA). In contrast to the NWSA, the AWSA invited male as well as female members and pursued a state-by-state, instead of a nationwide, strategy for woman suffrage. The AWSA supported the Fifteenth Amendment and lobbied at the Republican convention. The membership of the AWSA was largely middle class. Not wanting to detract from any effort for woman suffrage, many women joined both organizations.

Some of the efforts for woman suffrage proved successful. In Wyoming, women received the right to vote on

September 6, 1870. Few states followed suit, however, and it would be another 50 years before the right was given to women throughout the United States. The slow-moving results did not slow down radical feminists' attempts to gain rights. In an effort to gain the franchise, Victoria Woodhull presented a petition for woman suffrage to the House Judiciary Committee on January 11, 1871. Her address to the Judiciary Committee was the first one made directly by a woman.

Women continued to participate in reform movements in post–Civil War America. They primarily focused, as before, on issues seen as vital to the stability of the household. When the Women's Christian Temperance Union was established on November 18, 1874, Annie Wittenmyer became the organization's first president. The WCTU would play an integral part in the fight against alcohol's detrimental effects on fathers and families.

After EMANCIPATION, freedwomen worked to improve the legal and economic status of their families and communities. Like white women, they could not vote, but they participated in political activities. Black women attended rallies and parades and spoke at public meetings, encouraging their men to vote. They hoped that male African-American enfranchisement would give them a voice and the rights they had been denied as slaves. African-American leaders such as Ida B. Wells of Tennessee promoted education, civil rights, and campaigns against Southern violence. Black women also asserted themselves as women and mothers in the postwar years as they actively worked to reclaim their families and win legal recognition of their marriages. In addition, African-American women actively worked to gain voting rights as well as civil rights, even though they were often excluded from the larger, white-run women's organizations fighting for suffrage and other women's rights.

By the end of RECONSTRUCTION, the fight for women's rights remained close to where it was at the Seneca Falls Convention in 1848. For the U.S. Centennial Exposition of 1876, Stanton and Matilda Joslyn Gage prepared a document, the Declaration of Rights of Women, that they hoped would alert the public to the difficulties and inequalities that women continued to face in postwar America. This document, much like the Declaration of Rights and Sentiments in 1848, mirrored the rhetoric and ideas of the Declaration of Independence but highlighted the contradictions between the official ideals and the realities of women's lives. Members of the NWSA asked the centennial committee to allow them to present their document at the public celebration, but the committee denied this request. In protest, at the end of the official program, Anthony and Gage pushed their way to the speaker's platform and presented a copy of their Declaration of Rights. They demanded equal civil and political rights for American women, including the right to serve on juries, no TAXATION without representation, and the removal of the word *male* from state constitutions and judicial codes. Taking things further than did the 1848 declaration, the centennial document demanded equal political rights for American women.

See also LADIES AID SOCIETIES.

Further reading: Catherine Clinton, *The Other Civil War: American Women in the Nineteenth Century* (New York: Hill and Wang, 1999); Nancy F. Cott, ed., *No Small Courage: A History of Women in the United States* (New York: Oxford University Press, 2000); Linda K. Kerber, *No Constitutional Right to Be Ladies: Women and the Obligations of Citizenship* (New York: Hill and Wang, 1998).

—Lisa Tendrich Frank

Y

Yancey, William Lowndes (1814–1863)

Diplomat, politician, and orator, William Lowndes Yancey was born in Warren County, Virginia, in 1814 to Benjamin Cuworth Yancey and Caroline Bird. Yancey's father died when he was very young, and soon thereafter his mother married Presbyterian Reverend Nathan S. S. Beman. In 1823 Beman decided to move the family to New York, where he became involved in the ABOLITIONist movement. Beman's dignified public persona as a reverend and social reformer was in marked contrast to his conduct in private, where he verbally and physically abused his wife. Young William grew to hate his stepfather's hypocrisy, which he equated with his abolitionism.

In 1833 Yancey returned to the South. He dropped out of Williams College in Massachusetts and moved to Greenville, South Carolina. While in Greenville, Yancey tried his hand at a number of professions. He edited the Greenville *Mountaineer,* where he regularly attacked John C. Calhoun for his SECESSIONist rhetoric. He read law under Benjamin F. Perry and was admitted to the bar. He also became a PLANTATION owner after marrying Sarah Carolina Earle in 1835 and gaining control of her 35 slaves. The young couple settled in Alabama.

During the latter part of the 1830s, Yancey suffered a number of misfortunes. He lost a great deal of money in the Panic of 1837. In 1838 he was convicted of manslaughter after killing his wife's uncle during an argument. In 1839, shortly after his release from prison, most of Yancey's slaves died after an angry neighbor poisoned the well at his plantation. As a result, he was compelled to return to the practice of law to support himself and his wife.

In 1840 Yancey decided to become a candidate for political office. By this time, he had completely reversed his earlier position and was an ardent supporter of Calhoun and his STATES' RIGHTS philosophy. Yancey served in Alabama's legislature from 1841 to 1842 and in the state's senate from 1843 to 1844. He was then elected to two terms in the U.S. House of Representatives. Yancey's first speech as a congressman so enraged one of his colleagues that a duel was arranged, although no blood was shed. Yancey quickly grew weary of the need to constantly compromise his beliefs, and despite being reelected he resigned his seat in 1846.

Yancey did not return to politics before the CIVIL WAR started. Instead, he became a devoted and forceful speaker on behalf of secession. He wrote LETTERS and delivered hundreds of speeches on behalf of the cause, earning a name as the "prince of the FIRE-EATERS." In 1860 Yancey led the group of Southern delegates who abandoned the Democratic convention in Charleston. In 1861, he led the convention that took Alabama out of the Union.

Despite Yancey's prominence, he and other fire-eaters were not offered important positions in the Confederate government. JEFFERSON DAVIS needed to convince the states of the Upper South to join the Confederacy, and that goal was best served if moderates appeared to be in control. To keep Yancey quiet, Davis gave him responsibility for leading a delegation to England to try and secure recognition for the Confederacy. The mission failed, in part because the Confederacy had little leverage and in part because the hot-tempered Yancey was not a very good diplomat.

Yancey returned to the Confederacy in 1862 and was elected to a seat in the Confederate Congress. Convinced that Jefferson Davis had set him up to fail in England, he became one of the administration's harshest critics. Yancey attacked the president for seizing too much power and for failing to promote enough Alabamians to generalships. Yancey never received satisfaction on either of these issues, although he was able to help stop the Confederacy from establishing a supreme court in 1863. Shortly after this victory, Yancey was reduced to invalidism by the kidney disease he had suffered from for many years. He died in Montgomery in July 1863, just before his 49th birthday.

Further reading: John DuBose, *The Life and Times of William Lowndes Yancey* (New York: P. Smith, 1942); Eric H. Walther, *The Fire-Eaters* (Baton Rouge: Louisiana State University Press, 1992).

—Christopher Bates

Z

Zouaves

The word *Zouave* refers to a type of UNIFORM borrowed from French military FASHION by CIVIL WAR soldiers in both the North and South. The distinctive features of this style of uniform are baggy pants, frequently accompanied by a sleeveless vest, a collarless jacket, and a fez hat.

Some American Zouave units took their quest for authenticity to extremes. These soldiers might wear turbans instead of fezzes or even shave their heads in imitation of the original Zouave soldiers. Zouave UNIFORMS frequently came in high-visibility red, which apparently gave these 19th-century warriors little cause for concern. Whatever the style, all Civil War Zouaves went into the war clad in a similarly gaudy manner.

Zouave uniforms originated in Algeria, and Algerian men serving in the French Foreign legion introduced the uniform to Europe. These original Zouaves had a well-publicized reputation for military prowess, particularly for their ability to reload their rifles from the prone position. As Europeans adopted the uniforms, military units also took the name of "Zouave." Zouave fame spread worldwide in the wake of the Crimean War, where they performed valiantly. By this time, native-born Frenchman composed nearly all the Zouave units.

GEORGE B. MCCLELLAN served as the official U.S. observer of the Crimean War, and in this capacity he filed a report to the U.S. Congress. McClellan lavished praise on the Zouaves, claiming that they represented "the beau-ideal of a soldier." Although McClellan's report had some influence upon the Zouave craze in the United States, his influence was secondary to that of Elmer Ephraim Ellsworth.

In 1859 Ellsworth introduced the Zouave fashion to Chicago. Ellsworth was a charismatic militia leader, and he took a unit of the Chicago militia and transformed them into the "Zouave Cadets of Chicago." People paid to watch militia units drill, and Ellsworth's men became a crowd favorite throughout the Midwest and the East. In addition to the flashy uniform, Ellsworth's men appealed to the public with the gymnastic feats they incorporated into their drill routine.

When the Civil War began, Ellsworth became the colonel of the 11th New York Infantry, and he introduced the Zouave uniform to the New York soldiers under his command. Many of these soldiers had been members of the NEW YORK CITY Fire Department, so the 11th New York Infantry came to be called "Ellsworth's Fire Zouaves."

Ellsworth became one of the first casualties of the Civil War when an incensed innkeeper shot him for removing a Confederate flag from the roof of the Marshall House Tavern in Alexandria, Virginia, on May 24, 1861. Ellsworth's early martyrdom influenced many other Union units to adopt the Zouave uniform. By the end of 1861, New York City alone had four complete Zouave regiments. One of these regiments, the Ninth New York, commonly known as Hawkin's Zouaves, suffered 63 percent casualties at the BATTLE OF ANTIETAM. It is said that for a battle cry the Ninth chanted, "zoo! zoo! zoo!"

The South had very few Zouave soldiers except in Louisiana. During the course of the war, the Louisianians found it difficult to replace their distinctive uniforms. The Union blockade of the South made it nearly impossible to reacquire such fashions from abroad. However, the famed LOUISIANA TIGERS, who composed the 10th Louisiana infantry, maintained a ragged version of their uniform throughout the war.

Chatam Roberdau Wheat, a soldier of fortune who had fought with Garibaldi for the unification of Italy, created the 10th Louisiana, recruited from the roughest neighborhoods of New Orleans. Although the majority of the Louisiana Tigers were of Irish descent, the unit boasted soldiers of 15 different nationalities. The 10th Louisiana served throughout the war in ROBERT E. LEE's Army of Northern Virginia, and it is sometimes referred to today as "Lee's Foreign Legion."

A wounded Zouave being offered a drink by a companion after the Battle of Chancellorsville *(National Archives)*

Pennsylvania was the Northern state that boasted the most Zouave units. One Pennsylvania unit served as the personal bodyguard of Gen. Nathaniel P. Banks. This unit, which called itself the Zouaves d'Afrique, was chased from the field at FIRST BULL RUN by the 10th Louisiana Infantry. Later, at the BATTLE OF GETTYSBURG, the Zouaves d'Afrique played an essential role in turning back the Confederate assault on Cemetery Hill.

Northern Zouave units maintained their popularity with civilians throughout the war. Oftentimes, in the early years of the conflict, when patriotic sentiments still ran high, Zouaves participated in "musical entertainments." These entertainments involved brass band concerts interspersed with drill maneuvers, courtesy of the Zouaves.

Such concerts sometimes went on for two to three hours at a time. Even today, Zouave units are very popular among "living history" buffs who engage in Civil War reenactments. The gaudy Zouave uniform still appeals today, largely because it harks back to a moment outside of living memory: a time when leaders tried to make war into a chivalric spectacle.

Further reading: Michael J. McAfee, *Zouaves: The First and the Bravest* (Gettysburg, Pa.: Thomas Publications, 1991); William Wray, *Birney's Zouaves Civil War: Life of the 23rd Pennsylvania Volunteers* (New York: Bloch, 2000).

—Chad Vanderford

Chronology

★ ─────────────────────────────────────

1856

James Buchanan, a proslavery Democrat from Pennsylvania, defeats Republican candidate John C. Frémont in the presidential election.

Tensions between antislavery and proslavery settlers in Kansas erupt into a guerrilla war; the conflict is called "Bleeding Kansas."

Senator Charles Sumner's "Crime against Kansas Speech" vehemently denounces the Kansas-Nebraska Act of 1854 and its authors.

1857

In the *Dred Scott* decision, the U.S. Supreme Court rules that a slave is not a citizen; the ruling provokes criticism in the North.

Proslavery advocates draft the Lecompton Constitution of 1857 to organize the Kansas Territory as a slave state.

1858

The first transatlantic telegraph cable is completed; the project is backed by financier Cyrus Field.

U.S. consul general Townsend Harris negotiates the Harris Treaty of 1858 with Japan. The treaty opens Japanese ports to American trade, grants U.S. citizens resident rights in Japan, and establishes diplomatic missions in the capitals of both nations.

The U.S.-Chinese Treaty of 1858 allows U.S. ships increased access to Chinese ports and grants U.S. citizens in China exemption from local jurisdiction.

Albert Bierstadt begins painting his landscapes of the American West.

The Pike's Peak gold rush brings many settlers and miners into the Cheyenne and Arapaho hunting grounds in Colorado; when the Indians refuse to sell their land and move to reservations, Governor John Evans declares war on them, putting Col. John Chivington in charge of the operation.

Abraham Lincoln's senatorial nomination acceptance, the "House Divided" speech, declares that the Union could not continue as half slaveholding and half free.

U.S. senatorial candidates Abraham Lincoln and Stephen Douglas tour the state of Illinois debating the future of slavery and the Union.

1859

John Brown raids Harpers Ferry, Virginia (later, West Virginia), with a band of antislavery guerrillas and seizes a federal armory. He is captured by U.S. marines under Col. Robert E. Lee and is eventually hanged.

The U.S. Supreme Court decision *Ableman v. Booth; United States v. Booth* reverses a Wisconsin Supreme Court decision that freed an abolitionist who had defied the Fugitive Slave Act of 1850.

1860

Adventurer William Walker is executed in Honduras after a second attempt to conquer Nicaragua.

Abraham Lincoln's Cooper Union speech makes him a potential candidate for the Republican presidential nomination.

Members of the lapsed Whig and American Parties construct the Constitutional Union Party platform as an additional alternative to resolution of the slavery dilemma.

The Pony Express provides mail service from Missouri to California.

The Democratic Party's convention splits over slavery. Southerners nominate John C. Breckinridge of Kentucky. The Northern faction nominates Stephen A. Douglas, dividing the party's vote.

Republican Abraham Lincoln is elected as the 16th president of the United States, defeating John Bell, John C. Breckinridge, and Stephen A. Douglas.

South Carolina refuses to accept the results of the presidential election and secedes from the Union on December 20. Fort Sumter, a Union fort in the harbor at Charleston, South Carolina, is reinforced.

The Crittenden Compromise of 1860, which upheld the resolves of the Compromise of 1850, is a last-ditch effort to stave off civil war.

1861

Cochise leads the Chiricahua Apache in raids against white settlers and travelers in the Apache Pass in the Arizona Territory.

The Morrill Tariff Act of 1861 raises protective duties on such materials as iron and wool.

Over the objections of President Lincoln, U.S. Congress passes the Confiscation Act of 1861. The law allows the Union government to seize any property, including slaves, used to aid the Confederacy.

Gen. Frémont's Emancipation Order of 1861 declares martial law in Missouri and allows Union forces to confiscate the property and slaves of rebels.

U.S. Congress admits Kansas into the Union under its antislavery constitution.

Representatives from the secessionist states meet at Montgomery, Alabama, to draft their own constitution and establish themselves as the Confederate States of America. Jefferson Davis is chosen as the Confederacy's provisional president.

Abraham Lincoln is inaugurated as the 16th president of the (now divided) United States.

A memorandum to the president from his secretary of state, William Seward's "Plan to Avoid War," suggests how the president should bring the slavery conflict to a resolution without resorting to war.

Confederate shore batteries under the command of Gen. P. T. Beauregard begin firing on Fort Sumter, marking the start of the Civil War. The fort's commander, Maj. Howard Anderson, surrenders; he and his troops are allowed to return to the North.

Robert E. Lee resigns his commission in the Union army and becomes a Confederate commander.

President Lincoln calls for 75,000 Union volunteers to put down the Southern rebellion and forms the Army of the Potomac.

Confederates under Gens. Joseph E. Johnston and Thomas J. Jackson rout Union forces at the First Battle of Bull Run. Jackson earns the nickname "Stonewall."

1862

Union troops, after driving the Confederates out of New Mexico, begin a campaign, led by Gen. James Carleton and Col. Christopher "Kit" Carson, against the Mescalero Apache and the Navajo.

U.S. Congress passes the Legal Tender Act of 1862 to fund the Union war effort.

U.S. Congress issues the Ironclad Oath, which requires all federal, civil, and military officials—elected or appointed, honorary or paid—to swear allegiance to the U.S. Constitution.

The Morrill Land-Grant Act of 1862 gives states federal lands for the establishment of colleges.

The Homestead Act of 1862 is passed, providing for U.S. settlement of the West.

U.S. Congress passes the Pacific Railroad Act of 1862, which provides land grants and loans for the first transcontinental railroad.

U.S. Congress passes the Confiscation Act of 1862, providing for the seizure of property of rebel slaveholders and the emancipation of their slaves.

The Santee Sioux revolt in Minnesota after their government annuity is delayed; they are led by Little Crow. The uprising is put down by Gen. Henry H. Sibley.

The fight of the ironclads takes place between the *Monitor* and the *Virginia* at Hampton Roads, Virginia.

Jefferson Davis is inaugurated as the president of the Confederacy.

Union troops are ferried to the Virginia peninsula, beginning the Peninsular campaign.

The Confederates conduct a surprise attack on Gen. Ulysses S. Grant's forces in Shiloh, Tennessee. The Union suffers almost 25,000 casualties, but the army maintains its positions.

New Orleans falls to Union forces under Adm. David Farragut.

Confederate Gen. J. E. B. Stuart makes a daring cavalry foray against Union supply lines on the Virginia peninsula, bolstering Southern morale.

Gen. George McClellan repulses a Confederate attack at Malvern Hill in Virginia.

Union general John Pope's forces are dealt a severe blow at the Second Battle of Bull Run. Gens. Stonewall Jackson and James Longstreet command the victorious Confederates.

Confederate general Robert E. Lee's advance into Maryland is halted at the Battle of Antietam, the bloodiest one-day battle in U.S. history.

More than 100,000 Union troops led by Gen. Ambrose Burnside engage Robert E. Lee's Confederate forces at Fredericksburg, Virginia. After a bloody assault, the Union attack is repulsed.

The pro-Union western counties of Virginia form the state of West Virginia.

An entreaty to President Lincoln published in the *New York Tribune,* Horace Greeley's "Prayer of Twenty Millions," urges emancipation for the millions of enslaved blacks.

President Lincoln's reply to Greeley stresses his duty to preserve the Union by any means necessary—with or without emancipation.

1863

Abraham Lincoln issues the Emancipation Proclamation, which declares all slaves in Confederate-held territory free; in reality, the proclamation does not free any slaves, but it makes the destruction of slavery a Union goal.

Gen. Ulysses Grant's Order No. 11 expels all Jews from Union-controlled Tennessee. It is Grant's attempt to end war profiteering, which he attributed mainly to Jewish traders.

In an effort to halt hostility and insults directed toward Union troops by New Orleans residents, particularly women, Gen. Benjamin Franklin Butler's Order No. 28 declares that any female insulting or showing contempt for any U.S. officer or soldier should be treated as a prostitute.

The 54th Massachusetts Regiment, the first all-black regiment from the North, loses half of its men in a charge at Fort Wagner, South Carolina.

Gen. Joseph Hooker assumes command of the Army of the Potomac.

The Union suffers a setback in the Battle of Chancellorsville in Virginia. Confederate Gen. Stonewall Jackson is mortally wounded by one of his own men.

Vicksburg is under siege by the Union army.

The pivotal Battle of Gettysburg takes place as Confederate forces under Gen. Robert E. Lee advance into Pennsylvania. Union general George Meade defeats the Confederates in a battle that leaves 50,000 casualties on both sides.

The Union captures Vicksburg, Mississippi; Confederate forces are surrounded on land and on water and are running out of food. They surrender to Gen. Ulysses S. Grant, and Union forces take control of the Mississippi River.

The New York Draft Riots occur, leaving 1,000 people dead or wounded. Blacks are the principal targets of the violence.

Confederate leader William Quantrill raids the pro-Union town of Lawrence, Kansas, slaughtering more than 100 civilians.

Union forces at Chattanooga, Tennessee, are besieged by the Confederate army.

President Lincoln delivers his Gettysburg Address at the dedication of a military cemetery on the battlefield.

U.S. Congress passes the National Bank Act of 1863, which creates a national banking system.

Tennessee is conquered by Northern forces and prepared for its restoration to the Union.

President Lincoln's Proclamation of Amnesty and Reconstruction is an early attempt to create a coherent strategy for reincorporating rebel states into the Union.

In Frances Willard's "Women's Lesser Duties" speech, she stresses that women should learn the arts and domestic duties, as well as be pure, charming, and moral.

The Habeas Corpus Act of 1863 gives the government the power to imprison an individual indefinitely without being charged.

1864

Col. John Chivington leads the Colorado volunteers against the Cheyenne and Arapaho in the Sand Creek Massacre, despite the peace agreement at Camp Weld.

Confederate general Nathan Bedford Forrest captures Fort Pillow in Tennessee. Only 14 Confederates were killed and 86 wounded, while the Union forces had 231 killed and 1,000 wounded; many of the Union losses were black soldiers.

Gen. Ulysses S. Grant is given command of all Union forces.

The Spotsylvania campaign leads to a day of fighting at the "bloody angle."

With his direct assaults on Petersburg, Virginia, having failed, Union general Ulysses S. Grant prepares to besiege the city, whose defense is commanded by Confederate general Robert E. Lee.

A cavalry force under Confederate general Jubal Early reaches the outskirts of Washington, D.C., before deciding to withdraw.

The Confederate defenses at Petersburg, Virginia, are shattered by the huge explosion of a mine planted by Union engineers. Union assault troops fail to exploit the mine attack and are shot down mercilessly in the crater left by the explosion.

Adm. David Farragut leads a Union fleet to victory in the Battle of Mobile Bay and closes that port to the Confederacy.

Union troops begin their occupation of Atlanta after four weeks of siege.

Lincoln is reelected.

Union troops under Gen. William T. Sherman begin their destructive advance across Georgia, from Atlanta to the coast.

U.S. Congress passes the severe Reconstruction measure, the Wade-Davis Bill of 1864. It allows rebel states to return to the United States only after a majority of white male citizens take an oath of allegiance to the Union and after the adoption of a state constitution acceptable to the president and Congress.

1865

U.S. Congress passes the Thirteenth Amendment to the U.S. Constitution, which abolishes slavery throughout the nation.

Gen. Robert E. Lee surrenders to Ulysses S. Grant at the Appomattox Court House.

In his last speech, Lincoln advocates voting rights for black soldiers.

John Wilkes Booth assassinates President Lincoln; Andrew Johnson becomes president.

Mark Twain publishes *The Celebrated Jumping Frog of Calaveras County* to national acclaim.

Union Republican representative Henry J. Raymond's speech on Reconstruction proposes a moderate strategy for reincorporating rebel states into the Union.

Radical Republican representative Thaddeus Stevens's speech on Reconstruction advocates a harsh, punitive approach to the former Confederate states.

Confederate commander Gen. Robert E. Lee, in his farewell, praises his troops for their courage and devotion to their country.

U.S. Congress creates the Freedmen's Bureau to help educate freed slaves and integrate them into society.

President Johnson proclaims a general amnesty for all but the most prominent ex-Confederates.

A U.S. Congress dominated by Radical Republicans convenes in Washington; the Radicals advocate equal rights for blacks and a harsh Reconstruction program for the South.

The Black Codes (statutes that restrict the rights of African Americans) are passed in Mississippi and quickly spread throughout the South.

1866

Fisk University opens in Nashville, Tennessee.

Overriding President Johnson's veto, U.S. Congress passes the Civil Rights Act of 1866, which confers citizenship upon black people and grants the same rights and responsibilities to all persons born in the United States, except Native Americans.

Radical Republican Thaddeus Stevens proposes distributing 40-acre plots of land to freed blacks, but the plan is voted down in Congress.

The Ku Klux Klan, an organization of white Southerners, many of them ex-Confederates dedicated to white supremacy, holds its first meeting in Pulaski, Tennessee. The Klan spreads terror throughout the South for several years.

U.S. Congress adopts the Fourteenth Amendment, which grants full rights of citizenship to blacks.

The Grand Army of the Republic (GAR), an organization of Union veterans, is formed.

Jesse James and his brother Frank form a band of bank robbers.

1867

The Republican-dominated U.S. Congress passes two influential pieces of legislation: the Reconstruction Acts of 1867–68, which divide the South into five districts controlled completely by the military, and the Tenure of Office Act of 1867, which makes it impossible for the president to dismiss a cabinet member without Senate approval.

Secretary of State William Henry Seward negotiates the purchase of Alaska from Russia.

Jay Gould becomes director of the Erie Railroad; Gould oversees fraudulent stock sales to ward off a takeover attempt by Cornelius Vanderbilt.

The Peonage Abolition Act of 1867 outlaws involuntary servitude. It is designed to help support and amplify the Fourteenth Amendment to the U.S. Constitution.

Native American tribes in the southwestern Indian Territory cede lands in the Texas Panhandle to the U.S. government. This land was originally granted to the tribes in earlier treaties.

In *Mississippi v. Johnson,* the state of Mississippi seeks to prevent President Johnson from enforcing Reconstruction legislation.

1868

In the Treaty of Fort Laramie, the U.S. government guarantees the Sioux exclusive possession of the land in South Dakota west of the Missouri River.

The Fourteenth Amendment to the U.S. Constitution is ratified, granting citizenship to African Americans.

Sioux chief Red Cloud forces the U.S. Army to evacuate three western forts.

President Andrew Johnson, who advocates a lenient Reconstruction policy, fires Secretary of War Edwin M. Stanton. The Radical Republicans impeach Johnson for "high crimes and misdemeanors," and he is acquitted by a single vote.

Republican candidate and former Union general Ulysses S. Grant defeats Democrat Horatio Seymour in the presidential election.

Louisa May Alcott publishes her novel *Little Women.*

1869

U.S. Congress adopts the Fifteenth Amendment to the U.S. Constitution, which extends the right to vote to African Americans.

Inventor George Westinghouse applies for a patent on the air brake, which greatly improves railroad safety.

The Central Pacific Railroad, built east from California, connects with the Union Pacific Railroad at Promontory Point, Utah, completing the first transcontinental railroad.

Financier Jim Fisk tries to corner the gold market and causes a financial panic.

Susan B. Anthony and Elizabeth Cady Stanton found the National Woman Suffrage Association (NWSA).

Documents

★ ─────────────────────────────────

"House Divided" Speech (1858)
Abraham Lincoln

In Roy P. Basler, ed. *The Collected Works of Abraham Lincoln,* Vol. 2 (New Brunswick, N.J.: Rutgers University Press, 1953–55), pp. 461–469

June 16, 1858

Mr. President and Gentlemen of the Convention.

If we could first know where we are, and whither we are tending, we could then better judge what to do, and how to do it.

We are now far into the fifth year, since a policy was initiated, with the avowed object, and confident promise, of putting an end to slavery agitation.

Under the operation of that policy, that agitation has not only, not ceased, but has constantly augmented.

In my opinion, it will not cease, until a crisis shall have been reached, and passed.

"A house divided against itself cannot stand."

I believe this government cannot endure, permanently half slave and half free.

I do not expect the Union to be dissolved—I do not expect the house to fall—but I do expect it will cease to be divided. It will become all one thing, or all the other.

Either the opponents of slavery, will arrest the further spread of it, and place it where the public mind shall rest in the belief that it is in course of ultimate extinction; or its advocates will push it forward, till it shall become alike lawful in all the States, old as well as new—North as well as South.

Have we no tendency to the latter condition?

Let any one who doubts, carefully contemplate that now almost complete legal combination—piece of machinery so to speak—compounded of the Nebraska doctrine, and the Dred Scott decision. Let him consider not only what work the machinery is adapted to do, and how well adapted; but also, let him study the history of its construction, and trace, if he can, or rather fail, if he can, to trace the evidences of design, and concert of action, among its chief architects, from the beginning.

But, so far, Congress only, had acted; and an indorsement by the people, real or apparent, was indispensable, to save the point already gained, and give chance for more.

The new year of 1854, found slavery excluded from more than half the States by State Constitutions, and from most of the national territory by Congressional prohibition.

Four days later, commenced the struggle, which ended in repealing that Congressional prohibition.

This opened all the national territory to slavery; and was the first point gained.

But, so far, Congress only, had acted; and an indorsement by the people, real or apparent, was indispensable, to save the point already gained, and give chance for more.

This necessity had not been overlooked; but had been provided for, as well as might be, in the notable argument of "squatter sovereignty," otherwise called "sacred right of self government," which latter phrase, though expressive of the only rightful basis of any government, was so perverted in this attempted use of it as to amount to just this: That if any one man, choose to enslave another, no third man shall be allowed to object.

That argument was incorporated into the Nebraska bill itself, in the language which follows: "It being the true intent and meaning of this act not to legislate slavery into any Territory or state, not exclude it therefrom; but to leave the people thereof perfectly free to form and regulate their domestic institutions in their own way, subject only to the Constitution of the United States."

Then opened the roar of loose declamation in favor of "Squatter Sovereignty," and "Sacred right of self government."

"But," said opposition members, "let us be more specific—let us amend the bill so as to expressly declare that the people of the territory may exclude slavery." "Not we," said the friends of the measure; and down they voted the amendment.

While the Nebraska bill was passing through congress, a law case, involving the question of a negroe's freedom, by reason of his owner having voluntarily taken him first into a free state and then a territory covered by the congressional prohibition, and held him as a slave, for a long time in each, was passing through the U.S. Circuit Court for the District of Missouri; and both Nebraska bill and law suit were brought to a decision in the same month of May, 1854. The negroe's name was "Dred Scott," which name now designates the decision finally made in the case.

Before the then next Presidential election, the law case came to, and was argued in the Supreme Court of the United States; but the decision of it was deferred until after the election. Still, before the election, Senator Trumbull, on the floor of the Senate, requests the leading advocate of the Nebraska bill to state his opinion whether the people of a territory can constitutionally exclude slavery from their limits; and the latter answers, "That is a question for the Supreme Court."

The election came. Mr. Buchanan was elected, and the indorsement, such as it was, secured. That was the second point gained. The indorsement, however, fell short of a clear popular majority by nearly four hundred thousand votes, and so, perhaps, was not overwhelmingly reliable and satisfactory.

The outgoing President, in his last annual message, as impressively as possible echoed back upon the people the weight and authority of the indorsement.

The Supreme court met again; did not announce their decision, but ordered a re-argument.

The Presidential inauguration came, and still no decision of the court; but the incoming President, in his inaugural address, fervently exhorted the people to abide by the forthcoming decision, whatever it might be.

Then, in a few days, came the decision.

The reputed author of the Nebraska bill finds an early occasion to make a speech at this capitol indorsing the Dred Scott Decision, and vehemently denouncing all opposition to it.

The new President, too, seizes the early occasion of the Silliman letter to indorse and strongly construe that decision, and to express his astonishment that any different view had ever been entertained.

At length a squabble springs up between the President and the author of the Nebraska bill, on the mere question of fact, whether the Lecompton constitution was or was not, in any just sense, made by the people of Kansas; and in that squabble the latter declares that all he wants is a fair vote for the people, and that he cares not whether slavery be voted down or voted up. I do not understand his declaration that he cares not whether slavery be voted down or voted up, to be intended by him other than as an apt definition of the policy he would impress upon the public mind—the principle for which he declares he has suffered much, and is ready to suffer to the end.

And well may he cling to that principle. If he has any parental feeling, well may he cling to it. That principle, is the only shred left of his original Nebraska doctrine. Under the Dred Scott decision, "squatter sovereignty" squatted out of existence, tumbled down like temporary scaffolding—like the mould at the foundry served through one blast and fell back into loose sand—helped to carry an election, and then was kicked to the winds. His late joint struggle with the Republicans, against the Lecompton Constitution, involves nothing of the original Nebraska doctrine. That struggle was made on a point, the right of a people to make their own constitution, upon which he and the Republicans have never differed.

The several points of the Dred Scott decision, in connection with Senator Douglas' "care not" policy, constitute the piece of machinery, in its present state of advancement. This was the third point gained.

The working points of that machinery are:

First, that no negro slave, imported as such from Africa, and no descendant of such slave can ever be a citizen of any State, in the sense of that term as used in the Constitution of the United States.

This point is made in order to deprive the negro, in every possible event, of the benefit of this provision of the United States Constitution, which declares that—

"The citizens of each State shall be entitled to all privileges and immunities of citizens in the several States."

Secondly, that "subject to the Constitution of the United States," neither Congress nor a Territorial Legislature can exclude slavery from any United States territory.

This point is made in order that individual men may fill up the territories with slaves, without danger of losing them as property, and thus to enhance the chances of permanency to the institution through all the future.

Thirdly, that whether the holding a negro in actual slavery in a free State, makes him free, as against the holder, the United States courts will not decide, but will leave to be decided by the courts of any slave State the negro may be forced into by the master.

This point is made, not to be pressed immediately; but, if acquiesced in for a while, and apparently indorsed by the people at an election, then to sustain the logical conclusion that what Dred Scott's master might lawfully do with Dred Scott, in the free State of Illinois, every other master may lawfully do with any other one, or one thousand slaves, in Illinois, or in any other free State.

Auxiliary to all this, and working hand in hand with it, the Nebraska doctrine, or what is left of it, is to educate and mould public opinion, at least Northern public opinion, to not care whether slavery is voted down or voted up.

This shows exactly where we now are; and partially also, whither we are tending.

It will throw additional light on the latter, to go back, and run the mind over the string of historical facts already stated. Several things will now appear less dark and mysterious than they did when they were transpiring. The people were to be left "perfectly free" "subject only to the Constitution." What the Constitution had to do with it, outsiders could not then see. Plainly enough now, it was an exactly fitted niche, for the Dred Scott decision to afterwards come in, and declare the perfect freedom of the people, to be just no freedom at all.

Why was the amendment, expressly declaring the right of the people to exclude slavery, voted down? Plainly enough now, the adoption of it, would have spoiled the niche for the Dred Scott decision.

Why was the court decision held up? Whey, even a Senator's individual opinion withheld, till after the Presidential election? Plainly enough now, the speaking out then would have damaged the "perfectly free" argument upon which the election was to be carried.

Why the outgoing President's felicitation on the indorsement? Why the delay of a reargument? Why the incoming President's advance exhortation in favor of the decision?

These things look like the cautious patting and petting a spirited horse, preparatory to mounting him, when it is dreaded that he may give the rider a fall.

And why the hasty after indorsements of the decision by the President and others?

We can not absolute know that all these exact adaptations are the result of preconcert. But when we see a lot of framed timbers, different portions of which we know have been gotten out at different times and places and by different workmen—Stephen, Franklin, Roger and James, for instance—and when we see these timbers joined together, and see they exactly make the frame of a house or a mill, all the tenons and mortices exactly fitting, and all the lengths and proportions of the different pieces exactly adapted to their respective places, and not a piece too many or too few—not omitting even scaffolding—or, if a single piece be lacking, we can see the place in the frame exactly fitted and prepared to yet bring such piece in—in such a case, we find it impossible to not believe that Stephen and Franklin and Roger and James all understood one another from the beginning, and all worked upon a common plans or draft drawn up before the first lick was struck.

It should not be overlooked that, by the Nebraska bill, the people of a State as well as Territory, were to be left "perfectly free" "subject only to the Constitution."

Why mention a State ? They were legislating for territories, and not for or about States. Certainly the people of a State are and ought to be subject to the Constitution of the United States; but why is mention of this lugged into this merely territorial law? Why are the people of a territory and the people of a state therein lumped together, and their relation to the Constitution therein treated as being precisely the same?

While the opinion of the Court, by Chief Justice Taney, in the Dred Scott case, and the separate opinions of all the concurring Judges, expressly declare that the Constitution of the United States neither permits Congress nor a Territorial legislature to exclude slavery from any United States territory, they all omit to declare whether or not the same Constitution permits a state, or the people of a State, to exclude it.

Possibly, this was a mere omission; but who can be quite sure, if McLean or Curtis had sought to get into the opinion a declaration of unlimited power in the people of a state to exclude slavery from their limits, just as Chase and Macy sought to get such declaration, in behalf of the people of a territory, into the Nebraska bill—I ask, who can be quite sure that it would not have been voted down, in the one case, as it had been in the other.

The nearest approach to the point of declaring the power of a State over slavery, is made by Judge Nelson. He approaches it more than once, using the precise idea, and almost the language too, of the Nebraska act. On one occasion his exact language is, "except in cases where the power is restrained by the Constitution of the United States, the law of the State is supreme over the subject of slavery within its jurisdiction."

In what cases the power of the states is so restrained by the U.S. Constitution, is left an open question, precisely as the same question, as to the restraint on the power of the territories was left open in the Nebraska act. Put that and that together, and we have another nice little niche, which we may, ere long, see filled with another Supreme Court decision, declaring that the Constitution of the United States does not permit a state to exclude slavery from its limits.

And this may especially be expected if the doctrine of "care not whether slavery be voted down or voted up, " shall gain upon the public mind sufficiently to give promise that such a decision can be maintained when made.

Such a decision is all that slavery now lacks of being alike lawful in all the States.

Welcome or unwelcome, such decision is probably coming, and will soon be upon us, unless the power of the present political dynasty shall be met and overthrown.

We shall lie down pleasantly dreaming that the people of Missouri are on the verge of making their State free; and we shall awake to the reality, instead, that the Supreme Court has made Illinois a slave State.

To meet and overthrow the power of that dynasty, is the work now before all those who would prevent that consummation.

That is what we have to do.

But how can we best do it?

There are those who denounce us openly to their own friends, and yet whisper us softly, that Senator Douglas is the aptest instrument there is, with which to effect that object. They do not tell us, nor has he told us, that he wishes any such object to be effected. They wish us to infer all, from the facts, that he now has a little quarrel with the present head of the dynasty; and that he has regularly voted with us, on a single point, upon which, he and we, have never differed.

They remind us that he is a very great man, and that the largest of us are very small ones. Let this be granted. But "a living dog is better than a dead lion. " Judge Douglas, if not a dead lion for this work, is at least a caged and toothless one. How can he oppose the advances of slavery? He don't care anything about it. His avowed mission is impressing the "public heart" to care nothing about it.

A leading Douglas Democratic newspaper thinks Douglas' superior talent will be needed to resist the revival of the African slave trade.

Does Douglas believe an effort to revive that trade is approaching? He has not said so. Does he really think so? But if it is, how can he resist it? For years he has labored to prove it a sacred right of white men to take negro slaves into the new territories. Can he possibly show that it is less a sacred right to buy them where they can be bought cheapest? And, unquestionably they can be bought cheaper in Africa than in Virginia.

He has done all in his power to reduce the whole question of slavery to one of a mere right of property; and as such, how can he oppose the foreign slave trade—how can he refuse that trade in that "property" shall be "perfectly free"—unless he does it as a protection to the home production? And as the home producers will probably not ask the protection, he will be wholly without a ground of opposition.

Senator Douglas holds, we know, that a man may rightfully be wiser to-day than he was yesterday —that he may rightfully change when he finds himself wrong.

But, can we for that reason, run ahead, and infer that he will make any particular change, of which he, himself, has given no intimation? Can we safely base our action upon any such vague inference?

Now, as ever, I wish to not misrepresent Judge Douglas' position, question his motives, or do ought that can be personally offensive to him.

Whenever, if ever, he and we can come together on principle so that our great cause may have assistance from his great ability, I hope to have interposed no adventitious obstacle.

But clearly, he is not now with us—he does not pretend to be—he does not promise to ever be.

Our cause, then, must be intrusted to, and conducted by its own undoubted friends—those whose hands are free, whose hearts are in the work—who do care for the result.

Two years ago the Republicans of the nation mustered over thirteen hundred thousand strong.

We did this under the single impulse of resistance to a common danger, with every external circumstance against us.

Of strange, discordant, and even, hostile elements, we gathered from the four winds, and formed and fought the battle through, under the constant hot fire of a disciplined, proud, and pampered enemy.

Did we brave all then, to falter now?—now—when that same enemy is wavering, dissevered and belligerent?

The result is not doubtful. We shall not fail—if we stand firm, we shall not fail.

Wise councils may accelerate or mistakes delay it, but, sooner or later the victory is sure to come.

First Inaugural Address (1861)
Abraham Lincoln

Landmark Documents in American History. CD-ROM
(New York: Facts On File, 1998)

March 4, 1861

Fellow-Citizens of the United States:

In compliance with a custom as old as the Government itself, I appear before you to address you briefly and to take in your presence the oath prescribed by the Constitution of the United States to be taken by the President "before he enters on the execution of this office."

I do not consider it necessary at present for me to discuss those matters of administration about which there is no special anxiety or excitement.

Apprehension seems to exist among the people of the Southern States that by the accession of a Republican Administration their property and their peace and personal security are to be endangered. There has never been any reasonable cause for such apprehension. Indeed, the most ample evidence to the contrary has all the while existed and been open to their inspection. It is found in nearly all the published speeches of him who now addresses you. I do but quote from one of those speeches when I declare that—

I have no purpose, directly or indirectly, to interfere with the institution of slavery in the States where it exists. I believe I have no lawful right to do so, and I have no inclination to do so.

Those who nominated and elected me did so with full knowledge that I had made this and many similar declarations and had never recanted them; and more than this, they placed in the platform for my acceptance, and as a law to themselves and to me, the clear and emphatic resolution which I now read:

Resolved, That the maintenance inviolate of the rights of the States, and especially the right of each State to order and control its own domestic institutions according to its own judgment exclusively, is essential to that balance of power on which the perfection and endurance of our political fabric depend; and we denounce the lawless invasion by armed force of the soil of any State or Territory, no matter what pretext, as among the gravest of crimes.

I now reiterate these sentiments, and in doing so I only press upon the public attention the most conclusive evidence of which the case is susceptible that the property, peace, and security of no section are to be in any wise endangered by the now incoming Administration. I add, too, that all the protection which, consistently with the Constitution and the laws, can be given will be cheerfully given to all the States when lawfully demanded, for whatever cause—as cheerfully to one section as to another.

There is much controversy about the delivering up of fugitives from service or labor. The clause I now read is as plainly written in the Constitution as any other of its provisions:

No person held to service or labor in one State, under the laws thereof, escaping into another, shall in consequence of any law or regulation therein be discharged from such service or labor, but shall be delivered up on claim of the party to whom such service or labor may be due.

It is scarcely questioned that this provision was intended by those who made it for the reclaiming of what we call fugitive slaves; and the intention of the lawgiver is the law. All members of Congress swear their support to the whole Constitution—to this provision as much as to any other. To the proposition, then, that slaves whose cases come within the terms of this clause "shall be delivered up" their oaths are unanimous. Now, if they would make the effort in good temper, could they not with nearly equal unanimity frame and pass a law by means of which to keep good that unanimous oath?

There is some difference of opinion whether this clause should be enforced by national or by State authority, but surely that difference is not a very material one. If the slave is to be surrendered, it can be of but little consequence to him or to others by which authority it is done. And should anyone in any case be content that his oath shall go unkept on a merely unsubstantial controversy as to *how* it shall be kept?

Again: In any law upon this subject ought not all the safeguards of liberty known in civilized and humane jurisprudence to be introduced, so that a free man be not in any case surrendered as a slave? And might it not be well at the same time to provide by law for the enforcement of that clause in the Constitution which guarantees that "the citizens of each State shall be entitled to all privileges and immunities of citizens in the several States"?

I take the official oath to-day with no mental reservations and with no purpose to construe the Constitution or laws by any hypercritical rules; and while I do not choose now to specify particular acts of Congress as proper to be enforced, I do suggest that it will be much safer for all, both in official and private stations, to conform to and abide by all those acts which stand unrepealed than to violate any of them trusting to find impunity in having them held to be unconstitutional.

It is seventy-two years since the first inauguration of a President under our National Constitution. During that period fifteen different and greatly distinguished citizens have in succession administered the executive branch of the Government. They have conducted it through many perils, and generally with great success. Yet, with all this scope of precedent, I now enter upon the same task for the brief constitutional term of four years under great and peculiar difficulty. A disruption of the Federal Union, heretofore only menaced, is now formidably attempted.

I hold that in contemplation of universal law and of the Constitution the Union of these States is perpetual. Perpetuity is implied, if not expressed, in the fundamental law of all national governments. It is safe to assert that no government proper ever had a provision in its organic law for its own termination. Continue to execute all the express provisions of our National Constitution, and the Union will endure forever, it being impossible to destroy it except by some action not provided for in the instrument itself.

Again: If the United States be not a government proper, but an association of States in the nature of contract merely, can it, as a contract, be peaceably unmade by less than all the parties who made it? One party to a contract may violate it—break it, so to speak—but does it not require all to lawfully rescind it?

Descending from these general principles, we find the proposition that in legal contemplation the Union is perpetual confirmed by the history of the Union itself. The Union is much older than the Constitution. It was formed, in fact, by the Articles of Association in 1774. It was matured and continued by the Declaration of Independence in 1776. It was further matured, and the faith of all the then thirteen States expressly plighted and engaged that it should be perpetual, by the Articles of Confederation in 1778. And finally, in 1787, one of the declared objects for ordaining and establishing the Constitution was *"to form a more perfect Union."*

But if destruction of the Union by one or by a part only of the States be lawfully possible, the Union is *less* perfect than before the Constitution, having lost the vital element of perpetuity.

It follows from these views that no State upon its own mere motion can lawfully get out of the Union; that *resolves* and *ordinances* to that effect are legally void, and that acts of violence within any State or States against the authority of the United States are insurrectionary or revolutionary, according to circumstances.

I therefore consider that in view of the Constitution and the laws the Union is unbroken, and to the extent of my ability, I shall take care, as the Constitution itself expressly enjoins upon me, that the laws of the Union be faithfully executed in all the States. Doing this I deem to be only a simple duty on my part, and I shall perform it so far as practicable unless my rightful masters, the American people, shall withhold the requisite means or in some authoritative manner direct the contrary. I trust this will not be regarded as a menace, but only as the declared purpose of the Union that it *will* constitutionally defend and maintain itself.

In doing this there needs to be no bloodshed or violence, and there shall be none unless it be forced upon the national authority. The power confided to me will be used to hold, occupy, and possess the property and places belonging to the Government and to collect the duties and imposts; but beyond what may be necessary for these objects, there will be no invasion, no using of force against or among the people anywhere. Where hostility to the United States in any interior locality shall be so great and universal as to prevent competent resident citizens from holding the Federal offices, there will be no attempt to force obnoxious strangers among the people for that object. While the strict legal right may exist in the Government to enforce the exercise of these offices, the attempt to do so would be so irritating and so nearly impracticable withal that I deem it better to forego for the time the uses of such offices.

The mails, unless repelled, will continue to be furnished in all parts of the Union. So far as possible the people everywhere shall have that sense of perfect security which is most favorable to calm thought and reflection. The course here indicated will be followed unless current events and experience shall show a modification or change to be proper, and in every case and exigency my best discretion will be exercised, according to circumstances actually existing and with a view and a hope of a peaceful solution of the national troubles and the restoration of fraternal sympathies and affections.

That there are persons in one section or another who seek to destroy the Union at all events and are glad of any pretext to do it I will neither affirm nor deny; but if there be such, I need address no word to them. To those, however, who really love the Union may I not speak?

Before entering upon so grave a matter as the destruction of our national fabric, with all its benefits, its memories, and its hopes, would it not be wise to ascertain precisely why we do it? Will you hazard so desperate a step while there is any possibility that any portion of the ills you fly from have no real existence? Will you, while the certain ills you fly to are greater than all the real ones you fly from, will you risk the commission of so fearful a mistake?

All profess to be content in the Union if all constitutional rights can be maintained. Is it true, then, that any right plainly written in the Constitution has been denied? I think not. Happily, the human mind is so constituted that no party can reach to the audacity of doing this. Think, if you can, of a single instance in which a plainly written provision of the Constitution has ever been denied. If by the mere force of numbers a majority should deprive a minority of any clearly written constitutional right, it might in a moral point of view justify revolution; certainly would if such right were a vital one. But such is not our case. All the vital rights of minorities and of individuals are so plainly assured to them by affirmations and negations, guaranties and prohibitions, in the Constitution that controversies never arise concerning them. But no organic law can ever be framed with a provision specifically applicable to every question which may occur in practical administration. No foresight can anticipate nor any document of reasonable length contain express provisions for all possible questions. Shall fugitives from labor be surrendered by national or by State authority? The Constitution does not expressly say. *May* Congress prohibit slavery in the Territories? The Constitution does not expressly say. *Must* Congress protect slavery in the Territories? The Constitution does not expressly say.

From questions of this class spring all our constitutional controversies, and we divide upon them into majorities and minorities. If the minority will not acquiesce, the majority must, or the Government must cease. There is no other alternative, for continuing the Government is acquiescence on one side or the other. If a minority in such case will secede rather than acquiesce, they make a precedent which in turn will divide and ruin them, for a minority of their own will secede from them whenever a majority refuses to be controlled by such minority. For instance, why may not any portion of a new confederacy a year or two hence arbitrarily secede again, precisely as portions of the present Union now claim to secede from it? All who cherish disunion sentiments are now being educated to the exact temper of doing this.

Is there such perfect identity of interests among the States to compose a new union as to produce harmony only and prevent renewed secession?

Plainly the central idea of secession is the essence of anarchy. A majority held in restraint by constitutional checks and limitations, and always changing easily with deliberate changes of popular opinions and sentiments, is the only true sovereign of a free people. Whoever rejects it does of necessity fly to anarchy or to despotism. Unanimity is impossible. The rule of a minority, as a permanent arrangement, is wholly inadmissible; so that, rejecting the majority principle, anarchy or despotism in some form is all that is left.

I do not forget the position assumed by some that constitutional questions are to be decided by the Supreme Court, nor do I deny that such decisions must be binding in any case upon the parties to a suit as to the object of that suit, while they are also entitled to very high respect and consideration in all parallel cases by all other departments of the Government. And while it is obviously possible that such decision may be erroneous in any given case, still the evil effect following it, being limited to that particular case, with the chance that it may be overruled and never become a precedent for other cases, can better be borne than could the evils of a different practice. At the same time, the candid citizen must confess that if the policy of the Government upon vital questions affecting the whole people is to be irrevocably fixed by decisions of the Supreme Court, the instant they are made in ordinary litigation between parties in personal actions the people will have ceased to be their own rulers, having to that extent practically resigned their Government into the hands of that eminent tribunal. Nor is there in this view any assault upon the court or the judges. It is a duty from which they may not shrink to decide cases properly brought before them, and it is no fault of theirs if others seek to turn their decisions to political purposes.

One section of our country believes slavery is *right* and ought to be extended, while the other believes it is *wrong* and ought not to be extended. This is the only substantial dispute. The fugitive-slave clause of the Constitution and the law for the suppression of the foreign slave trade are each as well enforced, perhaps, as any law can ever be in a community where the moral sense of the people imperfectly supports the law itself. The great body of the people abide by the dry legal obligation in both cases, and a few break over in each. This, I think, can not be perfectly cured, and it would be worse in both cases *after* the separation of the sections than before. The foreign slave trade, now imperfectly suppressed, would be ultimately revived without restriction in one section, while fugitive slaves, now only partially surrendered, would not be surrendered at all by the other.

Physically speaking, we can not separate. We can not remove our respective sections from each other nor build an impassable wall between them. A husband and wife may be divorced and go out of the presence and beyond the reach of each other, but the different parts of our country can not do this. They can not but remain face to face, and intercourse, either amicable or hostile, must continue between them. Is it possible, then, to make that intercourse more advantageous or more satisfactory *after* separation than *before*? Can aliens make treaties easier than friends can make laws? Can treaties be more faithfully enforced between aliens than laws can among friends? Suppose you go to war, you can not fight always; and when, after much loss on both sides and no gain on either, you cease fighting, the identical old questions, as to terms of intercourse, are again upon you.

This country, with its institutions, belongs to the people who inhabit it. Whenever they shall grow weary of the existing Government, they can exercise their *constitutional* right of amending it or their *revolutionary* right to dismember or overthrow it. I can not be ignorant of the fact that many worthy and patriotic citizens are desirous of having the National Constitution amended. While I make no recommendation of amendments, I fully recognize the rightful authority of the people over the whole subject, to be exercised in either of the modes prescribed in the instrument itself; and I should, under existing circumstances, favor rather than oppose a fair opportunity being afforded the people to act upon it. I will venture to add that to me the convention mode seems preferable, in that it allows amendments to originate with the people themselves, instead of only permitting them to take or reject propositions originated by others, not especially chosen for the purpose, and which might not be precisely such as they would wish to either accept or refuse. I understand a proposed amendment to the Constitution—which amendment, however, I have not seen—has passed Congress, to the effect that the Federal Government shall never interfere with the domestic institutions of the States, including that of persons held to service. To avoid misconstruction of what I have said, I depart from my purpose not to speak of particular amendments so far as to say that, holding such a provision to now be implied constitutional law, I have no objection to its being made express and irrevocable.

The Chief Magistrate derives all his authority from the people, and they have referred none upon him to fix terms for the separation of the States. The people themselves can do this if also they choose, but the Executive as such has nothing to do with it. His duty is to administer the present Government as it came to his hands and to transmit it unimpaired by him to his successor.

Why should there not be a patient confidence in the ultimate justice of the people? Is there any better or equal hope in the world? In our present differences, is either party without faith of being in the right? If the Almighty Ruler of Nations, with His eternal truth and justice, be on your side of the North, or on yours of the South, that truth and that justice will surely prevail by the judgment of this great tribunal of the American people.

By the frame of the Government under which we live this same people have wisely given their public servants but little power for mischief, and have with equal wisdom provided for the return of that little to their own hands at very short intervals. While the people retain their virtue and vigilance no Administration by any extreme of wickedness or folly can very seriously injure the Government in the short space of four years.

My countrymen, one and all, think calmly and *well* upon this whole subject. Nothing valuable can be lost by taking time. If there be an object to *hurry* any of you in hot haste to a step which you would never take *deliberately*, that object will be frustrated by taking time; but no good object can be frustrated by it. Such of you as are now dissatisfied still have the old Constitution unimpaired, and, on the sensitive point, the laws of your own framing under it; while the new Administration will have no immediate power, if it would, to change either. If it were admitted that you who are dissatisfied hold the right side in the dispute, there still is no single good reason for precipitate action. Intelligence, patriotism, Christianity, and a firm reliance on Him who has never yet forsaken this favored land are still competent to adjust in the best way all our present difficulty.

In *your* hands, my dissatisfied fellow-countrymen, and not in *mine*, is the momentous issue of civil war. The Government will not assail *you*. You can have no conflict without being yourselves the aggressors. *You* have no oath registered in heaven to destroy the Government, while *I* shall have the most solemn one to "preserve, protect, and defend it."

I am loath to close. We are not enemies, but friends. We must not be enemies. Though passion may have strained it must not break our bonds of affection. The mystic chords of memory, stretching from every battlefield and patriot grave to every living heart and hearthstone all over this broad land, will yet swell the chorus of the Union, when again touched, as surely they will be, by the better angels of our nature.

Inaugural Address (1861)
Jefferson Davis

In James Andrews et al., eds. *American Voices, Significant Speeches in American History, 1640–1945* (New York: Longman, 1989), pp. 280–282

February 18, 1861

Gentlemen of the Congress of the Confederate States of America, Friends and Fellow-Citizens:
Called to the difficult and responsible station of Chief Executive of the Provisional Government which you have instituted, I approach the discharge of the duties assigned to me with an humble distrust of my abilities, but with a sustaining confidence in the wisdom of those who are to guide and aid me in the administration of public affairs, and an abiding faith in the virtue and patriotism of the people.

Looking forward to the speedy establishment of a permanent government to take the place of this, and which, by its greater moral and physical power, will be better able to combat with the many difficulties which arise from the conflicting interests of separate nations, I enter upon the duties of the office, to which I have been chosen, with the hope that the beginning of our career, as a Confederacy, may not be obstructed by hostile opposition to our enjoyment of the separate existence and independence which we have asserted, and, with the blessing of Providence, intend to maintain. Our present condition, achieved in a manner unprecedented in the history of nations, illustrates the American idea that governments rest upon the consent of the governed, and that it is the right of the people to alter or abolish governments whenever they become destructive of the ends for which they were established.

The declared purpose of the compact of union from which we have withdrawn, was "to establish justice, insure domestic tranquility, provide for the common defense, promote the general welfare;" and when in the judgment of the sovereign States now composing this Confederacy, it had been perverted from the purposes for which it was ordained, and had ceased to answer the ends for which it was established, a peaceful appeal to the ballot-box, declared that so far as they were concerned, the government created by that compact should cease to exist. In this they merely asserted a right which the Declaration of Independence of 1776 had defined to be inalienable. Of the time and occasion for its exercise, they as sovereigns, were the final judges, each for itself. The impartial and enlightened verdict of mankind will vindicate the rectitude of our conduct, and he, who knows the hearts of men, will judge of the sincerity with which we labored to preserve the government of our fathers in its spirit. The right solemnly proclaimed at the birth of the States and which has been affirmed and re-affirmed in the bills of rights of States subsequently admitted into the Union of 1789, undeniably recognizes in the people the power to resume the authority delegated for the purposes of government. Thus the sovereign States, here represented, proceeded to form this Confederacy, and it is by abuse of language that their act has been denominated a revolution. They formed a new alliance, but within each State its government has remained, and the rights of person and property have not been disturbed. The agent, through whom they communicated with foreign nations, is changed; but this does not necessarily interrupt their international relations.

Sustained by the consciousness that the transition from the former Union to the present Confederacy has not proceeded from a disregard on our part of just obligations, or any failure to perform any constitutional duty; moved by no interest or passion to invade the rights of others; anxious to cultivate peace and commerce with all nations, if we may not hope to avoid war, we may at least expect that posterity will acquit us of having needlessly engaged in it. Doubly justified by the absence of wrong on our part, and by wanton aggression on the part of others, there can be no cause to doubt that the courage and patriotism of the people of the Confederate States will be found equal to any measures of defense which honor and security may require.

An agricultural people, whose chief interest is the export of a commodity required in every manufacturing country, our true policy is peace and the freest trade which our necessities will permit. It is alike our interest, and that of all those to whom we would sell and from whom we would buy, that there should be fewest practicable restrictions upon the interchange of commodities. There can be but little rivalry between ours and any manufacturing or navigating community, such as the northeastern States of the American Union. It must follow, therefore, that a mutual interest would invite good will and kind offices. If, however, passion or the lust of dominion should cloud the judgment or inflame the ambition of those States, we must prepare to meet the emergency, and to maintain, by the final arbitrament of the sword, the position which we have assumed among the nations of the earth. We have entered upon the career of independence, and it must be inflexibly pursued. Through many years of controversy with our late associates, the Northern States, we have vainly endeavored to secure tranquility, and to obtain respect for the rights to which we are entitled. As a necessity, not a choice, we have resorted to the remedy of separation; and henceforth our energies must be directed to the conduct of our own affairs, and the perpetuity of the Confederacy which we have formed. If a just perception of mutual interest shall permit us peaceably to pursue our separate political career, my most earnest desire will have been fulfilled; but if this be denied to us, and the integrity of our territory and jurisdiction be assailed it, it will but remain for us, with firm resolve, to appeal to arms and invoke the blessings of Providence on a just cause.

As a consequence of our new condition, and with a view to meet anticipated wants, it will be necessary to provide for the speedy and efficient organization of branches of the Executive Department, having special charge of foreign intercourse, finance, military affairs, and the postal service.

For purposes of defense, the Confederate States may, under ordinary circumstances, rely mainly upon the militia; but it is deemed advisable, in the present condition of affairs, that there should be a well-instructed and disciplined army, more numerous than would usually be required on a peace establishment. I also suggest that, for the protection of our harbors and commerce on the high seas, a navy adapted to those objects will be required. These necessities have doubtless engaged the attention of Congress.

With a constitution differing only from that of our fathers, in so far as it is explanatory of their well-known intent, freed from the sectional conflicts which have interfered with the pursuit of the general welfare, it is not unreasonable to expect that States from which we have recently parted, may seek to unite their fortunes with ours under the government which we have instituted. For this your constitution makes adequate provision; but beyond this, if I mistake not, the judgment and will of the people, a re-union with the States from which we have separated is neither practicable nor desirable. To increase the power, develop the resources, and promote the happiness of the Confederacy, it is requisite that there should be so much homogeneity that the welfare of every portion shall be the aim of the whole. Where this does not exist, antagonisms are engendered which must and should result in separation.

Actuated solely by the desire to preserve our own rights and promote our own welfare, the separation of the Confederate States has been marked by no aggression upon others, and followed by no domestic convulsion. Our industrial pursuits have received no check; the cultivation of our fields has progressed as heretofore; and even should we be involved in war, there would be no considerable diminution in the production of the staples which have constituted our exports, and in which the commercial world has an interest scarcely less than our own. This common interest of the producer and consumer can only be interrupted by an exterior force, which should obstruct its transmission to foreign markets—a course of conduct which would be as unjust towards us as it would be detrimental to manufacturing and commercial interests abroad. Should reason guide the action of the government from which we have separated, a policy so detrimental to the civilized world, the Northern States included, could not be dictated by even the strongest desire to inflict injury upon us; but if otherwise, a terrible responsibility will rest upon it, and the suffering of millions will bear testimony to the folly and wickedness of our aggressors. In the meantime, there will remain to us, besides the ordinary means before suggested, the well-known resources for retaliation upon the commerce of the enemy.

Experience in public stations, of subordinate grades to this which your kindness has conferred, has taught me that care, and toil, and disappointment, are the price of official elevation. You will see many errors to forgive, many deficiencies to tolerate, but you shall not find in me either a want of zeal or fidelity to the cause that is to me highest in hope and of most enduring affection. Your generosity has bestowed upon me an undeserved distinction—one which I never sought nor desired. Upon the continuance of that sentiment, and upon your wisdom and patriotism, I rely to direct and support me in the performance of the duty required at my hands.

We have changed the constituent parts but not the system of our government. The constitution formed by our fathers is that of these Confederates States, in their exposition of it; and, in the judicial construction it has received, we have a light that reveals its true meaning.

Thus instructed as to the just interpretation of the instrument, and ever remembering that all offices are but trusts held for the people, and that delegated powers are to be strictly construed, I will hope by due diligence in the performance of my duties, though I may disappoint your expectations, yet to retain, when retiring, something of the good will and confidence which welcomed my entrance into office.

It is joyous, in the midst of perilous times, to look around upon a people united in heart, where one purpose of high resolve animates and actuates the whole—where the sacrifices to be made are not weighed in the balance against honor, and right, and liberty, and equality. Obstacles may retard—they cannot long prevent—the progress of a movement sanctified by its justice, and sustained by a virtuous people. Reverently let us invoke the God of our fathers to guide and protect us in our efforts to perpetuate the principles which, by his blessing, they were able to vindicate, establish, and transmit to their posterity, and with a continuance of his favor, ever gratefully acknowledged, we may hopefully look forward to success, to peace, and to prosperity.

Constitution of the Confederate States of America (1861)

Erik Bruun and Jay Crosby, eds. *Our Nation's Archive: The History of the United States in Documents* (New York: Black Dog & Leventhal Publishers) pp. 342–343.

March 11, 1861

We, the people of the Confederate States, each State acting in its sovereign and independent character, in order to form a permanent federal government, establish justice, insure domestic tranquillity, and secure the blessings of liberty to ourselves and our posterity—invoking the favor and guidance of Almighty God—do ordain and establish this Constitution for the Confederate States of America.

Art. I

Sec. 1.—All legislative powers herein delegated shall be vested in a Congress of the Confederate States, which shall consist of a Senate and House of Representatives.

Sec. 2. (1) The House of Representatives shall be chosen every second year by the people of the several States; and the electors in each State shall be citizens of the Confederate States, and have the qualifications requisite for electors of the most numerous branch of the State Legislature; but no person of foreign birth, not a citizen of the Confederate States, shall be allowed to vote for any officer, civil or political, State or Federal . . .

(3) Representatives and direct taxes shall be apportioned among the several States which may be included within this Confederacy, according to their respective numbers, which shall be determined by adding to the whole number of free persons, including those bound to service for a term of years, and excluding Indians not taxed, three-fifths of all slaves. The actual enumeration shall be made within three years after the first meeting of the Congress of the Confederate States, and within every subsequent term of ten years, in such manner as they shall by law direct. The number of Representatives shall not exceed one for every fifty thousand, but each State shall have at least one Representative; and until such enumeration shall be made, the State of South Carolina shall be entitled to choose six; the State of Georgia ten; the State of Alabama nine; the State of Florida two; the State of Mississippi seven; the State of Louisiana six; and the State of Texas six . . .

Sec. 9. (1) The importation of negroes of the African race, from any foreign country, other than the slaveholding States or Territories of the United States of America, is hereby forbidden; and Congress is required to pass such laws as shall effectually prevent the same.

(2) Congress shall also have power to prohibit the introduction of slaves from any State not a member of, or Territory not belonging to, this Confederacy . . .

Art. IV

Sec. 2. (1) The citizens of each State shall be entitled to all the privileges and immunities of citizens of the several States, and shall have the right of transit and sojourn in any State of this Confederacy, with their slaves and other property; and the right of property in said slaves shall not be thereby impaired . . .

(3) No slave or other person held to service or labor in any State or Territory of the Confederate States, under the laws thereof, escaping or unlawfully carried into another, shall, in consequence of any law or regulation therein, be discharged from such service or labor; but shall be delivered up on claim of the party to whom such slave belongs, or to whom such service or labor may be due . . .

Sec. 3. (3) The Confederate States may acquire new territory; and Congress shall have power to legislate and provide governments for the inhabitants of all territory belonging to the Confederate States, lying without the limits of the several States, and may permit them, at such times, and in such manner as it may by law provide, to form States to be admitted into the Confederacy. In all such territory, the institution of negro slavery, as it now exists in the Confederate States, shall be recognized and protected by Congress and by the territorial government; and the inhabitants of the several Confederate States and Territories shall have the right to take to such territory any slaves lawfully held by them in any of the States or Territories of the Confederate States . . .

Art. V

Sec. 1. (1) Upon the demand of any three States, legally assembled in their several Conventions, the Congress shall summon a Convention of all the States, to take into consideration such amendments to the Constitution as the said States shall concur in suggesting at the time when the said demand is made; and should any of the proposed amendments to the Constitution be agreed on by the said Convention—voting by States—and the same be ratified by the Legislatures of two-thirds of the several States, or by conventions in two-thirds thereof—as the one or the other mode of ratification may be proposed by the general convention—they shall thenceforward form a part of this Constitution. But no State shall, without its consent, be deprived of its equal representation in the Senate . . .

Art. VII.

1.—The ratification of the conventions of five States shall be sufficient for the establishment of this Constitution between the States so ratifying the same.

2. When five States shall have ratified this Constitution in the manner before specified, the Congress, under the provisional Constitution, shall prescribe the time for holding the election of President and Vice-President, and for the meeting of the electoral college, and for counting the votes and inaugurating the President. They shall also prescribe the time for holding the first election of members of Congress under this Constitution, and the time for assembling the same. Until the assembling of such Congress, the Congress under the provisional Constitution shall continue to exercise the legislative powers granted them; not extending beyond the time limited by the Constitution of the Provisional Government.

Adopted unanimously by the Congress of the Confederate States of South Carolina, Georgia, Florida, Alabama, Mississippi, Louisiana, and Texas, sitting in convention at the capitol, in the city of Montgomery, Ala., on the eleventh day of March, in the year eighteen hundred and sixty-one.

Homestead Act (1862)

United States Statutes at Large (37th Cong., 2d sess., chap. 75), pp. 392–393

May 20, 1862

An Act

to Secure Homesteads to actual Settlers on the Public Domain.

Be it enacted by the Senate and House of Representatives of the United States of America in Congress assembled, That any person who is the head of a family, or who has arrived at the age of twenty-one years, and is a citizen of the United States, or who shall have filed his declaration of intention to become such, as required by the naturalization laws of the United States, and who has never borne arms against the United States Government or given aid and comfort to its enemies, shall, from and after the first January, eighteen hundred and sixty-three, be entitled to enter one quarter section or a less quantity of unappropriated public lands, upon which said person may have filed a preemption claim, or which may, at the time the application is made, be subject to preemption at one dollar and twenty-five cents, or less, per acre; or eighty acres or less of such unappropriated lands, at two dollars and fifty cents per acre, to be located in a body, in conformity to the legal subdivisions of the public lands, and after the same shall have been surveyed: *Provided,* That any person owning and residing on land may, under the provisions of this act, enter other land lying contiguous to his or her said land, which shall not, with the land so already owned and occupied, exceed in the aggregate one hundred and sixty acres.

Sec. 2. *And be it further enacted,* That the person applying for the benefit of this act shall, upon application to the register of the land office in which he or she is about to make such entry, make affidavit before the said register or receiver that he or she is the head of a family, or is twenty-one years or more of age, or shall have performed service in the army or navy of the United States, and that he has never borne arms against the Government of the United States or given aid and comfort to its enemies, and that such application is made for his or her exclusive use and benefit, and that said entry is made for the purpose of actual settlement and cultivation, and not either directly or indirectly for the use or benefit of any other person or persons whomsoever; and upon filing the said affidavit with the register or receiver, and on payment of ten dollars, he or she shall thereupon be permitted to enter the quantity of land specified: *Provided, however,* That no certificate shall be given or patent issued therefor, until the expiration of five years from the date of such entry; and if, at the expiration of such time, or at any time within two years thereafter, the person making such entry; or, if he be dead, his widow; or in case of her death, his heirs or devisee; or in case of a widow making such entry, her heirs or devisee, in case of her death; shall prove by two credible witnesses that he, she, or they have resided upon or cultivated the same for the term of five years immediately succeeding the time of filing the affidavit aforesaid, and shall make affidavit that no part of said land has been alienated, and that he has borne true allegiance to the Government of the United States; then, in such case, he, she, or they, if at that time a citizen of the United States, shall be entitled to a patent, as in other cases provided for by law: *And provided, further,* That in case of the death of both father and mother, leaving an infant child, or children, under twenty-one years of age, the right and fee shall enure to the benefit of said infant child or children; and the executor, administrator, or guardian may, at any time within two years after the death of the surviving parent, and in accordance with the laws of the State in which such children for the time being have their domicil, sell said land for the benefit of said infants, but for no other purpose; and the purchaser shall acquire the absolute title by the purchase, and be entitled to a patent from the United States, on payment of the office fees and sum of money herein specified.

Sec. 3. *And be it further enacted,* That the register of the land office shall note all such applications on the tract books and plats of his office, and keep a register of all such entries, and make return thereof to the General Land Office, together with the proof upon which they have been founded.

Sec. 4. *And be it further enacted,* That no lands acquired under the provisions of this act shall in any event become liable to the satisfaction of any debt or debts contracted prior to the issuing of the patent therefor.

Sec. 5. *And be it further enacted,* That if, at any time after the filing of the affidavit, as required in the second section of this act, and before the expiration of the five years aforesaid, it shall be proven, after due notice to the settler, to the satisfaction of the register of the land office, that the person having filed such affidavit shall have actually changed his or her residence, or abandoned the said land for more than six months at any time, then and in that event the land so entered shall revert to the government.

Sec. 6. *And be it further enacted,* That no individual shall be permitted to acquire title to more than one quarter section under the provisions of this act; and that the Commissioner of the General Land Office is hereby required to prepare and issue such rules and regulations, consistent with this act, as shall be necessary and proper to carry its provisions into effect; and that the registers and receivers of the several land offices shall be entitled to receive the same compensation for any lands entered under the provisions of this act that they are now entitled to receive when the same quantity of land is entered with money, one half to be paid by the person making the application at the time of so doing, and the other half on the issue of the certificate by the person to whom it may be issued; but this shall not be construed to enlarge the maximum of compensation now prescribed by law for any register or receiver: *Provided,* That nothing contained in this act shall be so construed as to impair or interfere in any manner whatever with existing preemption rights: *And provided, further,* That all persons who may have filed their applications for a preemption right prior to the passage of this act, shall be entitled to all privileges of this act: *Provided, further,* That no person who has served, or may hereafter serve, for a period of not less than fourteen days in the army or navy of the United States, either regular or volunteer, under the laws thereof, during the existence of an actual war, domestic or foreign, shall be deprived of the benefits of this act on account of not having attained the age of twenty-one years.

Sec. 7. *And be it further enacted,* That the fifth section of the act entitled "An act in addition to an act more effectually to provide for the punishment of certain crimes against the United States, and for other purposes," approved the third of March, in the year eighteen hundred and fifty-seven, shall extend to all oaths, affirmations, and affidavits, required or authorized by this act.

Sec. 8. *And be it further enacted,* That nothing in this act shall be so construed as to prevent any person who has availed him or herself of the benefits of the first section of this act, from paying the minimum price, or the price to which the same may have graduated, for the quantity of land so entered at any time before the expiration of the five years, and obtaining a patent thereto from the government, as in other cases provided by law, on making proof of settlement and cultivation as provided by existing laws granting preemption rights.

Approved, May 20, 1862.

Pacific Railroad Act (1862)

United States Statutes at Large (37th Cong.,
2d sess., chap. 120), pp. 489–498

July 1, 1862

An Act

To aid in the construction of a railroad and telegraph line from the Missouri river to the Pacific ocean, and to secure to the government the use of the same for postal, military, and other purposes.

Be it Enacted by the Senate and House of Representatives of the United States of America in Congress assembled, That Walter S. Burgess, . . . together with five commissioners to be appointed by the Secretary of the Interior, and all persons who shall or may be associated with them, and their successors, are hereby created and erected into a body corporate and politic in deed and in law, by the name, style, and title of "The Union Pacific Railroad Company;" and by that name shall have perpetual succession, and shall be able to sue and to be sued, plead and be impleaded, defend and be defended, in all courts of law and equity within the United States, and may make and have a common seal; and the said corporation is hereby authorized and empowered to lay out, locate, construct, furnish, maintain, and enjoy a continuous railroad and telegraph, with the appurtenances, from a point on the one hundredth meridian of longitude west from Greenwich, between the south margin of the valley of the Republican River and the north margin of the valley of the Platte River, in the Territory of Nebraska, to the western boundary of Nevada Territory, upon the route and terms hereinafter provided . . .

Sec. 2. *And be it further enacted,* That the right of way through the public lands be, and the same is hereby, granted to said company for the construction of said railroad and telegraph line; and the right, power, and authority is hereby given to said company to take from the public lands adjacent to the line of said road, earth, stone, timber, and other materials for the construction thereof; said right of way is granted to said railroad, to the extent of two hundred feet in width on each side of said railroad, where it may pass over the public lands, including all necessary grounds for stations, buildings, workshops, and depots, machine shops, switches, side tracks, turn-tables, and water stations. The United States shall extinguish as rapidly as may be, the Indian titles to all lands falling under the operation of this act, and required for the said right of way and grants hereinafter made.

Sec. 3. *And be it further enacted,* That there be, and is hereby, granted to the said company, for the purpose of aiding in the construction of said railroad and telegraph line, and to secure the safe and speedy transportation of the mails, troops, munitions of war, and public stores thereon, every alternate section of public land, designated by odd numbers, to the amount of five alternate sections per mile on each side of said railroad, on the line thereof, and within the limits of ten miles on each side of said road, not sold, reserved, or otherwise disposed of by the United States, and to which a preemption or homestead claim may not have attached, at the time the line of said road is definitely fixed: *Provided,* That all mineral lands shall be excepted from the operation of this act; but where the same shall contain timber, the timber thereon is hereby granted to said company. And all such lands, so granted by this section, which shall not be sold or disposed of by said company within three years after the entire road shall have been completed, shall be subject to settlement and pre-emption, like other lands, at a price not exceeding one dollar and twenty-five cents per acre, to be paid to said company . . .

Sec. 5. *And be it further enacted,* That for the purposes herein mentioned, the Secretary of the Treasury shall, upon the certificate in writing of said commissioners of the com-

pletion and equipment of forty consecutive miles of said railroad and telegraph, in accordance with the provisions of this act, issue to said company bonds of the United States of one thousand dollars each, payable in thirty years after date, bearing six per centum per annum interest, (said interest payable semi-annually), which interest may be paid in United States treasury notes or any other money or currency which the United States have or shall declare lawful money and a legal-tender, to the amount of sixteen of said bonds per mile for such section of forty miles; and to secure the repayment to the United States, as hereinafter provided, of the amount of said bonds so issued and delivered to said company, together with all interest thereon which shall have been paid by the United States, the issue of said bonds and delivery to the company shall ipso facto constitute a first mortgage on the whole line of the railroad and telegraph . . .

Sec. 9. *And be it further enacted,* That the Leavenworth, Pawnee, and Western Railroad Company of Kansas are hereby authorized to construct a railroad and telegraph line from the Missouri river, at the mouth of the Kansas River, on the south side thereof, so as to connect with the Pacific Railroad of Missouri . . . upon the same terms and conditions in all respects as are provided in this act for the construction of the railroad and telegraph line first mentioned. . . The Central Pacific Railroad Company of California, a corporation existing under the laws of the State of California, are hereby authorized to construct a railroad and telegraph line from the Pacific coast, at or near San Francisco, or the navigable waters of the Sacramento River, to the eastern boundary of California, upon the same terms and conditions, in all respects, as are contained in this act for the construction of said railroad and telegraph line first-mentioned, and to meet and connect with the first mentioned railroad and telegraph line on the eastern boundary of California . . .

Sec. 10. . . . the Central Pacific Railroad Company of California, after completing its road across said state, is authorized to continue the construction of said railroad and telegraph through the territories of the United States to the Missouri river, including the branch roads specified in this act, upon the routes hereinbefore and hereinafter indicated, on the terms and conditions provided in this act in relation to the said Union Pacific Railroad Company, until said roads shall meet and connect, and the whole line of said railroad and branches and telegraph is completed.

Sec. 11. *And be it further enacted,* That for three hundred miles of said road, most mountainous and difficult of construction, to wit: one hundred and fifty miles westwardly from the eastern base of the Rocky mountains, and one hundred and fifty miles eastwardly from the western base of the Sierra Nevada mountains, said points to be fixed by the President of the United States, the bonds to be issued to aid in the construction thereof shall be treble the number per mile hereinbefore provided, and the same shall be issued, and the lands herein granted be set apart, upon the construction of every twenty miles thereof, upon the certificate of the commissioners as aforesaid that twenty consecutive miles of the same are completed; and between the sections last named of one hundred and fifty miles each, the bonds to be issued to aid in the construction thereof shall be double the number per mile first mentioned, and the same shall be issued, and the lands herein granted be set apart, upon the construction of every twenty miles thereof, upon the certificate of the commissioners as aforesaid that twenty consecutive miles of the same are completed: *Provided,* That no more than fifty thousand of said bonds shall be issued under this act to aid in constructing the main line of said railroad and telegraph.

Emancipation Proclamation (1863)
Abraham Lincoln

In John A. Scott, ed., *Living Documents in American History from Earliest Colonial Times to the Civil War,* Vol. 2 (New York: Trident Press, 1963), pp. 644–645

January 1, 1863

Whereas, on the twenty-second day of September, in the year of our Lord one thousand eight hundred and sixty-two, a proclamation was issued by the President of the United States, containing, among other things, the following, to wit:

"That on the first day of January, in the year of our Lord one thousand eight hundred and sixty-three, all persons held as slaves within any State or designated part of a State, the people whereof shall then be in rebellion against the United States, shall be then, thenceforward, and forever free; and the Executive Government of the United States, including the military and naval authority thereof, will recognize and maintain the freedom of such persons, and will do no act or acts to repress such persons, or any of them, in any efforts they may make for their actual freedom."

"That the Executive will, on the first day of January aforesaid, by proclamation, designate the States and parts of States, if any, in which the people thereof, respectively, shall then be in rebellion against the United States; and the fact that any State, or the people thereof, shall on that day be, in good faith, represented in the Congress of the United States by members chosen thereto at elections wherein a majority of the qualified voters of such State shall have participated, shall, in the absence of strong countervailing testimony be deemed conclusive evidence that such State and the people thereof, are not then in rebellion against the United States."

Now, therefore, I, Abraham Lincoln, President of the United States, by virtue of the power in me vested as Commander-in-chief of the Army and Navy of the United States, in time of actual armed rebellion against the authority and government of the United States, and as a fit and necessary war measure for suppressing said rebellion, do, on this first day of January, in the year of our Lord one thousand eight hundred and sixty-three, and in accordance with my purpose so to do publicly proclaimed for the full period of one hundred days from the day first above mentioned, order and designate as the States and parts of States wherein the people thereof respectively, are this day in rebellion against the United States, the following, to wit:

Arkansas, Texas, Louisiana (except the Parishes of St. Bernard, Plaquemines, Jefferson, St. John, St. Charles, St. James, Ascension, Assumption, Terrebonne, Lafourche, St. Mary, St. Martin, and Orleans, including the City of New Orleans) Mississippi, Alabama, Florida, Georgia, South Carolina, North Carolina, and Virginia (except the forty-eight counties designated as West Virginia, and also the counties of Berkeley, Accomac, Northampton, Elizabeth City, York, Princess Ann, and Norfolk, including the cities of Norfolk and Portsmouth) and which excepted parts are, for the present, left precisely as if this proclamation were not issued.

And by virtue of the power, and for the purpose aforesaid, I do order and declare that all persons held as slaves within said designated States, and parts of States, are, and henceforward shall be free; and that the Executive government of the United States, including the military and naval authorities thereof, will recognize and maintain the freedom of said persons.

And I hereby enjoin upon the people so declared to be free to abstain from all violence, unless in necessary self-defence; and I recommend to them that, in all cases when allowed, they labor faithfully for reasonable wages.

And I further declare and make known, that such persons of suitable condition, will be received into the armed service of the United States to garrison forts, positions, stations, and other places, and to man vessels of all sorts in said service.

And upon this act, sincerely believed to be an act of justice, warranted by the Constitution, upon military necessity, I invoke the considerate judgment of mankind and the gracious favor of Almighty God.

Gettysburg Address (1863)
President Abraham Lincoln

In John A. Scott, ed., *Living Documents in American History from Earliest Colonial Times to the Civil War,* Vol. 2 (New York: Trident Press, 1963), p. 646)

November 19, 1863

Four score and seven years ago our fathers brought forth on this continent, a new nation, conceived in Liberty, and dedicated to the proposition that all men are created equal.

Now we are engaged in a great civil war, testing whether that nation or any nation so conceived and so dedicated, can long endure. We are met on a great battlefield of that war. We have come to dedicate a portion of that field, as a final resting place for those who here gave their lives that that nation might live. It is altogether fitting and proper that we should do this.

But, in a larger sense, we can not dedicate—we can not consecrate—we can not hallow—this ground. The brave men, living and dead, who struggled here, have consecrated it, far above our poor power to add or detract. The world will little note, nor long remember what we say here, but it can never forget what they did here. It is for us the living, rather, to be dedicated here to the unfinished work which they who fought here have thus far so nobly advanced. It is rather for us to be here dedicated to the great task remaining before us—that from these honored dead we take increased devotion to that cause for they which gave the last full measure of devotion—that we here highly resolve that these dead shall not have died in vain—that this nation, under God, shall have a new birth of freedom—and that government of the people, by the people, for the people, shall not perish from the earth.

Proclamation of Amnesty and Reconstruction (1863)
Abraham Lincoln

Henry Steele Commager, ed. *Documents of American History,* 5th ed. Vol. 1 (Englewood Cliffs, N.J.: Prentice Hall, 1949), pp. 429–431

December 8, 1863

Whereas, in and by the Constitution of the United States, it is provide that the President "shall have power to grant reprieves and pardons for offenses against the United States, except in cases of impeachment;" and

Whereas a rebellion now exists whereby the loyal State governments of several States have for a long time been subverted, and many persons have committed and are now guilty of treason against the United States; and

Whereas, with reference to said rebellion and treason, laws have been enacted by Congress declaring forfeitures and confiscation of property and liberation of slaves, all upon terms and conditions therein stated, and also declaring that the President was thereby authorized at any time thereafter, by proclamation, to extend to persons who may have participated in the existing rebellion in any State or part thereof, pardon and amnesty, with such exceptions and at such times and on such conditions as he may deem expedient for the public welfare; and

Whereas, the Congressional declaration for limited and conditional pardon accords with well-established judicial exposition of the pardoning power; and

Whereas, with reference to said rebellion, the President of the United States has issued several proclamations, with provisions in regard to the liberation of slaves; and

Whereas, it is now desired by some persons heretofore engaged in said rebellion to resume their allegiance to the United States, and to reinaugurate loyal State governments within and for their respective States:

Therefore, I, Abraham Lincoln, President of the United States, do proclaim, declare, and make known to all persons who have, directly or by implication, participated in the existing rebellion, except as hereinafter excepted, that a full pardon is hereby granted to them and each of them, with restoration of all rights of property, except as to slaves, and in property cases where rights of third parties shall have intervened, and upon the condition that every such person shall take and subscribe an oath, and thenceforward keep and maintain said oath inviolate; and which oath shall be registered for permanent preservation, and shall be of the tenor and effect following, to wit:

"I, _____, do solemnly swear, in presence of Almighty God, that I will henceforth faithfully support, protect, and defend the Constitution of the United States and the Union of the States thereunder; and that I will, in like manner, abide by and faithfully support all acts of Congress passed during the existing rebellion with reference to slaves, so long and so far as not repealed, modified, or held void by Congress, or by decision of the Supreme Court; and that I will, in like manner, abide by and faithfully support all proclamations of the President made during the existing rebellion having reference to slaves, so long and so far as not modified or declared void by decision of the Supreme Court. So help me God."

The persons excepted from the benefits of the foregoing provisions are all who are, or shall have been, civil or diplomatic officers or agents of the so-called Confederate Government; all who have left judicial stations under the United States to aid the rebellion; all who are, or shall have been, military or naval officers of said so-called Confederate Government above the rank of colonel in the army or of lieutenant in the navy; all who left seats in the United States Congress to aid the rebellion; all who resigned commissions in the Army or Navy of the United States and afterwards aided the rebellion; and all who have engaged in any way in treating colored persons, or white persons in charge of such, otherwise than lawfully as prisoners of war, and which persons may have been found in the United States service as soldiers, seamen, or in any other capacity.

And I do further proclaim, declare, and make known that whenever, in any of the States of Arkansas, Texas, Louisiana, Mississippi, Tennessee, Alabama, Georgia, Florida, South Carolina, and North Carolina, a number of persons, not less than one-tenth in number of the votes cast in such State at the Presidential election of the year of our Lord one thousand eight hundred and sixty, each having taken the oath aforesaid, and not having since violated it, and being a qualified voter by the election law of the State existing immediately before the so-called act of secession, and excluding all others, shall re-establish a State government which shall be republican, and in nowise contravening said oath, such shall be recognized as the true government of the State, and the State shall receive thereunder the benefits of the constitutional provision which declares that "the United States shall guaranty to every State in this Union a republican form of government, and shall protect each of them against invasion; and, on application of the legislature, or the executive (when the legislature can not be convened), against domestic violence."

And I do further proclaim, declare, and make known that any provision which may be adopted by such State government in relation to the freed people of such State, which shall recognize and declare their permanent freedom, provide for their education, and which may yet be consistent as a temporary arrangement with their present condition as a laboring, landless, and homeless class, will not be objected to by the National Executive.

And it is suggested as not improper that, in constructing a loyal State government in any State, the name of the State, the boundary, the subdivisions, the constitution, and the general code of laws, as before the rebellion, be maintained, subject only to the modifications made necessary by the conditions hereinbefore stated, and such others, if any, not contravening said conditions and which may be deemed expedient by those framing the new State government.

To avoid misunderstanding, it may be proper to say that this proclamation, so far as it relates to State governments, has no reference to States wherein loyal State governments have all the while been maintained. And for the same reason, it may be proper to further say that whether members sent to Congress from any State shall be admitted to seats constitutionally rests exclusively with the respective Houses, and not to any extent with the Executive. And still further, that this proclamation is intended to present the people of the States wherein the national authority has been suspended, and loyal State governments have been subverted, a mode in and by which the national authority and loyal State governments may be re-established within said States, or in any of them; and

while the mode presented is the best the Executive can suggest, with his present impressions, it must not be understood that no other possible mode would be acceptable.

Second Inaugural Address (1865)
President Abraham Lincoln

Landmark Documents in American History. CD-ROM (New York: Facts On File, 1998)

March 4, 1865

Fellow-Countrymen:

At this second appearing to take the oath of the Presidential office there is less occasion for an extended address than there was at the first. Then a statement somewhat in detail of a course to be pursued seemed fitting and proper. Now, at the expiration of four years, during which public declarations have been constantly called forth on every point and phase of the great contest which still absorbs the attention and engrosses the energies of the nation, little that is new could be presented. The progress of our arms, upon which all else chiefly depends, is as well known to the public as to myself, and it is, I trust, reasonably satisfactory and encouraging to all. With high hope for the future, no prediction in regard to it is ventured.

On the occasion corresponding to this four years ago all thoughts were anxiously directed to an impending civil war. All dreaded it, all sought to avert it. While the inaugural address was being delivered from this place, devoted altogether to *saving* the Union without war, insurgent agents were in the city seeking to *destroy* it without war—seeking to dissolve the Union and divide effects by negotiation. Both parties depreciated war, but one of them would *make* war rather than let the nation survive, and the other would *accept* war rather than let it perish, and the war came.

One-eighth of the whole population were colored slaves, not distributed generally over the Union, but localized in the southern part of it. These slaves constituted a peculiar and powerful interest. All knew that this interest was somehow the cause of the war. To strengthen, perpetuate, and extend this interest was the object for which the insurgents would rend the Union even by war, while the Government claimed no right to do more than to restrict the territorial enlargement of it. Neither party expected for the war the magnitude or the duration which it has already attained. Neither anticipated that the *cause* of the conflict might cease with or even before the conflict itself should cease. Each looked for an easier triumph, and a result less fundamental and astounding. Both read the same Bible and pray to the same God, and each invokes His aid against the other. It may seem strange that any men should dare to ask a just God's assistance in wringing their bread from the sweat of other men's faces, but let us judge not, that we be not judged. The prayers of both could not be answered. That of neither has been answered fully. The Almighty has His own purposes. "Woe unto the world because of offenses; for it must needs be that offenses come, but woe to that man by whom the offense cometh." If we shall suppose that American slavery is one of those offenses which, in the providence of God, must needs come, but which, having continued through His appointed time, He now wills to remove, and that He gives to both North and South this terrible war as the woe due to those by whom the offense came, shall we discern therein any departure from those divine attributes which the believers in a living God always ascribe to Him? Fondly do we hope, fervently do we pray, that this mighty scourge of war may speedily pass away. Yet, if God wills that it continue until all the wealth piled by the bondsman's two hundred and fifty years of unrequited toil shall be sunk, and until every drop of blood drawn with the lash shall be paid by another drawn with the sword, as was said three thousand years ago, so still it must be said "the judgments of the Lord are true and righteous altogether."

With malice toward none, with charity for all, with firmness in the right as God gives us to see the right, let us strive on to finish the work we are in, to bind up the nation's wounds, to care for him who shall have borne the battle and for his widow and his orphan, to do all which may achieve and cherish a just and lasting peace among ourselves and with all nations.

Farewell to His Troops (1865)
General Robert E. Lee

> Henry Steele Commager, ed. *Documents of American History*, 5th ed., Vol. 1 (Englewood Cliffs, N.J.: Prentice Hall, 1949), p. 447

Headquarters, Army of No. Virginia
10th April 1865

General Order No. 9

After four years of arduous service marked by unsurpassed courage and fortitude the Army of Northern Virginia has been compelled to yield to overwhelming numbers and resources.

I need not tell the brave survivors of so many hard-fought battles, who have remained steadfast to the last, that I have consented to this result from no distrust of them.

But feeling that valor and devotion could accomplish nothing that could compensate for the loss that would have attended the continuance of the contest I have determined

to avoid the useless sacrifice of those whose past services have endeared them to their countrymen.

By the terms of the agreement Officers and men can return to their homes and remain there until exchanged. You will take with you the satisfaction that proceeds from the consciousness of duty faithfully performed, and I earnestly pray that a merciful God will extend to you His blessing and protection.

With an increasing admiration of your constancy and devotion to your country, and a grateful remembrance of your kind and generous consideration for myself, I bid you all an affectionate farewell.
R. E. Lee
Gen'l

Fourteenth Amendment to the U.S. Constitution (1868)

> Lewis Paul Todd and Merle Curti, eds. *Triumph of the American Nation*, (New York: Harcourt Brace Jovanovich, 1986), pp. 211–212

Amendment 14
Rights of Citizens (1868)

Section 1. All persons born or naturalized in the United States, and subject to the jurisdiction thereof, are citizens of the United States and of the state wherein they reside. No state shall make or enforce any law which shall abridge the privileges or immunities of citizens of the United States; nor shall any state deprive any person of life, liberty, or property, without due process of law; nor deny to any person within its jurisdiction the equal protection of the laws.

Section 2. Representatives shall be apportioned among the several states according to their respective numbers, counting the whole number of persons in each state [excluding Indians not taxed]. But when the right to vote at any election for the choice of electors for President and Vice President of the United States, Representatives in Congress, the executive and judicial officer of a state, or the members of the legislature thereof, is denied to any of the [male] inhabitants of such state, [being twenty-one years of age] and citizens of the United States, or in any way abridged, except for participation in rebellion, or other crime, the basis of representation therein shall be reduced in the proportion which the number of such [male] citizens shall bear to the whole number of male citizens [twenty-one years of age] in such state.

Section 3. No person shall be a Senator or Representative in Congress, or elector of President and Vice President, or hold any office, civil or military, under the United States, or under any state, who, having previously taken an oath, as a member of Congress, or as an officer of the

United States, or as a member of any state legislature, or as an executive or judicial officer of any state, to support the Constitution of the United States, shall have engaged in insurrection or rebellion against the same, or given aid or comfort to the enemies thereof. But Congress may by vote of two thirds of each house, remove such disability.

Section 4. The validity of the public debt of the United States, authorized by law, including debts incurred for payment of pensions and bounties for services in suppressing insurrection or rebellion, shall not be questioned. But neither the United States nor any state shall assume or pay any debt or obligation incurred in aid of insurrection or rebellion against the United States, [or any claim for the loss or emancipation of any slave]; but all such debts, obligations and claims shall be held illegal and void.

Section 5. The Congress shall have power to enforce, by appropriate legislation, the provisions of this article.

Fifteenth Amendment to the U.S. Constitution (1870)

Lewis Paul Todd and Merle Curti, eds. *Triumph of the American Nation* (New York: Harcourt Brace Jovanovich, 1986), p. 213

Amendment 15
Right of Suffrage (1870)

Section 1. The right of citizens of the United States to vote shall not be denied or abridged by the United States or by any state on account of race, color, or previous condition of servitude.

Section 2. The Congress shall have power to enforce this article by appropriate legislation.

Bibliography

Anderson, Bern. *By Sea and by River: The Naval History of the Civil War*. New York: Da Capo Press, 1989.

Andrist, Ralph K. *The Long Death: The Last Days of the Plains Indians*. Lawrence: University of Kansas Press, 2001.

Ash, Stephen V. *When the Yankees Came: Conflict and Chaos in the Occupied South, 1861–1865*. Chapel Hill: University of North Carolina Press, 1995.

Bain, David H. *Empire Express: Building the First Transcontinental Railroad*. New York: Viking, 1999.

Belz, Herman. *A New Birth of Freedom: The Republican Party and Freedman's Rights, 1861–1866*. New York: Fordham University Press, 2000.

Benedict, Michael Les. *The Impeachment Trial of Andrew Johnson*. New York: W. W. Norton, 1999.

Berlin, Ira, et al., eds. *Free at Last: A Documentary History of Slavery, Freedom, and the Civil War*. New York: New Press, 1993.

Blight, David. *Race and Reunion: The Civil War in American Memory*. New York: Belknap, 2001.

Boritt, Gabor S. *Lincoln and the Economics of the American Dream*. Memphis, Tenn.: Memphis State University Press, 1978.

———, ed. *Lincoln's Generals*. New York: Oxford University Press, 1995.

———, ed. *Why the Confederacy Lost*. New York: Oxford University Press, 1993.

Browning, Robert M., Jr. *From Cape Charles to Cape Fear: The North Atlantic Blockading Squadron during the Civil War*. Tuscaloosa: University of Alabama Press, 1993.

Brownlee, Richard. *Gray Ghosts of the Confederacy: Guerrilla Warfare in the West, 1861–1865*. Baton Rouge: Louisiana State University Press, 1958.

Burton, William L. *Melting Pot Soldiers: The Union's Ethnic Regiments*. New York: Fordham University Press, 1998.

Butchart, Ronald E. *Northern Schools, Southern Blacks and Reconstruction*. Westport, Conn.: Greenwood Publishing Group, 1980.

Calloway, Colin, ed. *Our Hearts Fell to the Ground: Plains Indian Views of How the West Was Lost*. New York: St. Martin's Press, 1997.

Carter, Dan T. *When the War Was Over: The Failure of Self-Reconstruction in the South, 1865–1867*. Baton Rouge: Louisiana State University Press, 1985.

Catton, Bruce. *The Army of the Potomac Trilogy*. New York: Doubleday, 1951–53.

———. *Grant Moves South*. New York: Book Sales, 2000.

———. *Grant Takes Command*. New York: Book Sales, 2000.

Clinton, Catherine, and Nina Silber, eds. *Divided Houses: Gender and the Civil War*. New York: Oxford University Press, 1992.

Connelly, Thomas Lawrence, and Barbara L. Bellows. *God and General Longstreet: The Lost Cause and the Southern Mind*. Baton Rouge: Louisiana State University Press, 1995.

Copper, William J., Jr. *Jefferson Davis, American*. New York: Vintage, 2001.

Crofts, Daniel. *Reluctant Confederates: Upper South Unionists in the Secession Crisis*. Chapel Hill: University of North Carolina Press, 1993.

Culpepper, Marilyn Mayer. *Trials and Triumphs: Women of the American Civil War*. East Lansing: Michigan State University Press, 1995.

Current, Richard N. *Lincoln's Loyalists: Union Soldiers from the Confederacy*. New York: Oxford University Press, 1994.

Daniel, Larry J. *Soldiering in the Army of the Tennessee: A Portrait of Life in a Confederate Army.* Chapel Hill: University of North Carolina Press, 1991.

Davis, William C. *An Honorable Defeat: The Last Days of the Confederate Government.* New York: Harvest, 2002.

Dew, Charles B. *Apostles of Disunion: Southern Secession Commissions and the Causes of the Civil War.* Charlottesville: University Press of Virginia, 2002.

Donald, David Herbert. *Lincoln.* New York: Touchstone, 1996.

———. *The Politics of Reconstruction.* Baton Rouge: Louisiana State University Press, 1965.

Douglass, Frederick. *Narrative of the Life of Frederick Douglass, an American Slave: Written By Himself.* Edited by John W. Blassingame. New Haven, Conn.: Yale University Press, 2001.

Durwood, Ball. *Army Regulars on the Western Frontier, 1848–1861.* Norman: University of Oklahoma Press, 2000.

Emilio, Louis F. *A Brave Black Regiment: The History of the 54th Massachusetts, 1863–1865.* New York: DaCapo, 1995.

Faust, Drew Gilpin. *Mothers of Invention: Women of the Slaveholding South in the American Civil War.* New York: Knopf, 1997.

Fehrenbacher, Don E. *The Dred Scott Case: Its Significance in American Law and Politics.* New York: Oxford University Press, 2001.

Foner, Eric. *Free Soil, Free Labor, Free Men: The Ideology of the Republican Party before the Civil War.* New York: Oxford University Press, 1995.

———. *Reconstruction: America's Unfinished Revolution, 1863–1877.* New York: HarperTrade, 2002.

Fox-Genovese, Elizabeth. *Within the Plantation Household: Black and White Women of the Old South.* Chapel Hill: University of North Carolina Press, 1988.

Frank, Joseph Allan. *The Political Socialization of American Civil War Soldiers.* Athens: University of Georgia Press, 1998.

Gallagher, Gary W. *The Confederate War: How Popular Will, Nationalism, and Military Strategy Could Stave Off Defeat.* Cambridge, Mass.: Harvard University Press, 1997.

———. *Lee and His Generals and War and Memory.* Baton Rouge: Louisiana State University Press, 1998.

Gillette, William. *Retreat from Reconstruction, 1869–1879.* Baton Rouge: Louisiana State University Press, 1982.

Glatthaar, Joseph. *Forged in Battle: The Civil War Alliance of Black Soldiers and White Officers.* Baton Rouge: Louisiana State University Press, 2000.

———. *The March to the Sea and Beyond: Sherman's Troops in the Savannah and Carolina Campaigns.* Baton Rouge: Louisiana State University Press, 1995.

Grant, Ulysses S. *Person Memoirs of U.S. Grant.* 1885. Reprint, New York: Tom Doherty Associates, 2002.

Grimsley, Mark. *The Hard Hand of War: Union Military Policy toward Southern Civilians, 1861–1865.* New York: Cambridge University Press, 1997.

Hattaway, Herman, and Archer Jones. *How the North Won: A Military History of the Civil War.* Urbana: University of Illinois Press, 1991.

Hattaway, Herman, et al. *Why the South Lost the Civil War.* Athens: University of Georgia Press, 1986.

Harsh, Joseph E. *Confederate Tide Rising: Robert E. Lee and the Making of Southern Strategy, 1861–1862.* Kent, Ohio: Kent State University Press, 1997.

Hauptman, Laurence M. *Between Two Fires: American Indians and the Civil War.* New York: Simon & Schuster, 1996.

Hess, Earl J. *Pickett's Charge: The Last Attack at Gettysburg.* Chapel Hill: University of North Carolina Press, 2001.

Jaynes, Gerald D. *Branches without Roots: Genesis of the Black Working Class in the American South, 1862–1882.* New York: Oxford University Press, 1989.

Jones, Archer. *Civil War Command and Strategy: The Process of Victory and Defeat.* New York: Free Press, 1992.

Jordan, Ervin L. *Black Confederates and Afro-Yankees in Civil War Virginia.* Charlottesville: University Press of Virginia, 1995.

Kenneth, Lee. *Sherman: A Soldier's Life.* New York: HarperCollins, 2001.

Leonard, Elizabeth. *All the Daring of the Soldier: Women of the Civil War Armies.* New York: Penguin Putnam, 2001.

———. *Yankee Women: Gender Battles in the Civil War.* New York: W. W. Norton, 1995.

Linden, Glenn M., and Thomas J. Pressly, eds. *Voices from the House Divided: The United States Civil War as Personal Experience.* New York: McGraw-Hill, 1994.

Linderman, Gerald F. *Embattled Courage: The Experience of Combat in the American Civil War.* New York: Free Press, 1989.

Litwack, Leon F. *Been in the Storm So Long: The Aftermath of Slavery.* New York: Vintage, 1980.

Massey, Mary Elizabeth. *Bonnet Brigades.* Reprinted as *Women in the Civil War.* Lincoln: University of Nebraska Press, 1994.

———. *Ersatz in the Confederacy: Shortages and Substitutes on the Confederate Homefront.* Columbia: University of South Carolina Press, 1993.

McFeely, William S. *Yankee Stepfather: General O. O. Howard and the Freedmen.* New York: W. W. Norton, 1994.

McPherson, James M. *Battle Cry of Freedom: The Civil War Era.* New York: Ballentine, 1989.

———. *For Cause and Comrades: Why Men Fought the Civil War.* New York: Oxford University Press, 1998.

———. ed. *The American Heritage New History of the Civil War.* Narrative by Bruce Catton. New York: Penguin Books, 1996.

———. ed. *The Atlas of the Civil War.* New York: Macmillan, 1994.

Mitchell, Reid. *The Vacant Chair: The Northern Soldier Leaves Home.* New York: Oxford University Press, 1995.

Montgomery, David. *Beyond Equality: Labor and the Radical Republicans, 1862–1872.* Champaign: University of Illinois Press, 1981.

Neely, Mark. *The Fate of Liberty: Abraham Lincoln and Civil Liberties.* New York: Oxford University Press, 1992.

Nieman, Donald J. *Promises to Keep: African Americans and the Constitutional Order, 1776 to the Present.* New York: Oxford University Press, 1991.

Nolan, Alan T. *Lee Considered: General Robert E. Lee and Civil War History.* Chapel Hill: University of North Carolina Press, 1991.

Oates, Stephen B. *The Approaching Fury: Voices of the Storm, 1820–1861.* New York: HarperCollins, 1997.

Paludan, Phillip S. *A People's Contest: The Union and Civil War, 1861–1865.* New York: Harper & Row, 1988.

Perman, Michael. *Reunion without Compromise: The South and Reconstruction, 1865–1868.* New York: Cambridge University Press, 1973.

Pfanz, Harry W. *Gettysburg: The First Day.* Chapel Hill: University of North Carolina Press, 2001.

Porter, Glenn. *The Rise of Big Business, 1860–1920.* Arlington Heights, Ill.: Harlan Davidson, 1992.

Potter, David M. *The Impending Crisis, 1848–1861.* New York: HarperCollins, 1991.

Rable, George C. *Civil Wars: Women and the Crisis of Southern Nationalism.* Urbana: University of Illinois Press, 1989.

Ransom, Roger. *Conflict and Compromise: The Political Economy of Slavery, Emancipation, and the American Civil War.* New York: Cambridge University Press, 1989.

Restad, Penne L. *Christmas in America: A History.* New York: Oxford University Press, 1995.

Rhea, Gordon C. *The Battle of the Wilderness, May 5–6, 1864.* Baton Rouge: Louisiana State University Press, 1994.

Rhodes, Elisha Hunt. *All for the Union: The Civil War Diary & Letters of Elisha Hunt Rhodes.* New York: Vintage Books, 1992.

Richardson, Heather Cox. *The Greatest Nation of the Earth: Republican Economic Policies during the Civil War.* Cambridge, Mass.: Harvard University Press, 1997.

Richardson, Joe M. *Christian Reconstruction: The American Missionary Association and Southern Blacks, 1861–1890.* Athens: University of Georgia Press, 1986.

Roark, James L. *Masters without Slaves: Southern Planters in the Civil War and Reconstruction.* New York: W. W. Norton, 1997.

Rose, Willie Lee. *Rehearsal for Reconstruction: The Port Royal Experiment.* Athens: University of Georgia Press, 1967.

Royster, Charles. *The Destructive War: William Tecumseh Sherman, Stonewall Jackson, and the Americans.* New York: Knopf, 1991.

Sears, Stephen W. *Chancellorsville.* Boston: Houghton Mifflin, 1996.

Silber, Nina. *The Romance of Reunion: Northerners and the South, 1865–1990.* Chapel Hill: University of North Carolina Press, 1993.

Silbey, Joel H. *A Respectable Minority: The Democratic Party in the Civil War Era.* New York: W. W. Norton, 1977.

Stampp, Kenneth M. *America in 1857: A Nation on the Brink.* New York: Oxford University Press, 1992.

———. *The Era of Reconstruction, 1865–1877.* New York: Vintage Books, 1967.

Stone, Kate. *Brokenburn: The Journal of Kate Stone, 1861–1868.* Edited by John Q. Anderson. Baton Rouge: Louisiana State University Press, 1995.

Stover, John F., and Mark C. Carnes. *The Routledge Historical Atlas of the American Railroads.* New York: Routledge, 1999.

Summers, Mark W. *The Era of Good Stealings.* New York: Oxford University Press, 1993.

———. *Railroads, Reconstruction, and the Gospel of Prosperity: Aid under the Radical Republicans.* Princeton, N.J.: Princeton University Press, 1984.

Thomas, Emory M. *The Confederacy as a Revolutionary Experience.* Columbia: University of South Carolina Press, 1991.

———. *The Confederate Nation, 1861–1865.* New York: HarperCollins, 1981.

Trachtenberg, Alan. *The Incorporation of America: Culture and Society in the Gilded Age.* New York: Hill and Wang, 1982.

Trefousse, Hans L. *Impeachment of a President: Andrew Johnson, the Blacks, and Reconstruction.* New York: Fordham University Press, 1999.

Trelease, Allen. *White Terror: The Ku Klux Klan Conspiracy and Southern Reconstruction.* Baton Rouge: Louisiana State University Press, 1995.

Venet, Wendy Hamand. *Neither Ballots nor Bullets: Women Abolitionists and the Civil War.* Charlottesville: University Press of Virginia, 1991.

Vinovskia, Maris, ed. *Toward a Social History of the American Civil War.* New York: Cambridge University Press, 1990.

Watkins, Sam. *Co Aytch.* New York: Dutton 1999.

Waugh, Joan. "A Sacrifice We Owed: The Shaw Family and the Fifty-fourth Massachusetts," in *Hope and Glory: Essays on the Legacy of the 54th Massachusetts Regiment.* Edited by Martin H. Blatt, Thomas Brown, and Donald Yacovone. Amherst: University of Massachusetts Press, 2000.

———. *Unsentimental Reformer: The Life of Josephine Shaw Lowell.* Cambridge, Mass.: Harvard University Press, 1998.

Weigley, Russell F. *A Great Civil War: A Military and Political History, 1861–1865.* Bloomington: Indiana University Press, 2000.

Wiley, Bell Irvin. *The Life of Johnny Reb: The Common Soldier in the Confederacy.* Baton Rouge: Louisiana State University Press, 1971.

———. *The Life of Billy Yank: The Common Soldier of the Union.* Baton Rouge: Louisiana State University Press, 1971.

Williams, T. Harry. *Lincoln and His Generals.* New York: Random House, 2001.

Wills, Garry. *Lincoln at Gettysburg: The Words That Remade America.* New York: Simon & Schuster, 1993.

Woodword, C. Vann. *Reunion and Reaction: The Compromise of 1877 and the End of Reconstruction.* New York: Oxford University Press, 1991.

Woodworth, Steven E. *Davis and Lee at War.* Lawrence: University Press of Kansas, 1995.

———. *While God Is Marching On: The Religious World of Civil War Soldiers.* Lawrence: University Press of Kansas, 2001.

Index

Boldface page numbers denote extensive treatment of a topic. *Italic* page numbers refer to illustrations; *c* refers to the Chronology; and *m* indicates a map.